W9-CFB-029

GunDigest 2012

Edited by
DAN SHIDELER

Copyright ©2011 F+W Media, Inc.

All rights reserved. No portion of this publication may be reproduced or transmitted in any form or by any means, electronic or mechanical, including photocopy, recording, or any information storage and retrieval system, without permission in writing from the publisher, except by a reviewer who may quote brief passages in a critical article or review to be printed in a magazine or newspaper, or electronically transmitted on radio, television, or the Internet.

Published by

Gun Digest® Books, an imprint of F+W Media, Inc.
Krause Publications · 700 East State Street · Iola, WI 54990-0001
715-445-2214 · 888-457-2873
www.krausebooks.com

To order books or other products call toll-free 1-800-258-0929
or visit us online at **www.gundigeststore.com**

CAUTION: Technical data presented here, particularly technical data on handloading and on firearms adjustment and alteration, inevitably reflects individual experience with particular equipment and components under specific circumstances the reader cannot duplicate exactly. Such data presentations therefore should be used for guidance only and with caution. Gun Digest Books accepts no responsibility for results obtained using these data.

ISSN 0072-9043

ISBN 13: 978-1-4402-1447-9
ISBN 10: 1-4402-1447-6

Designed by Paul Birling
Cover design by Tom Nelsen

Edited by Dan Shideler

Printed in the United States of America

John T. Amber
LITERARY AWARD

We at *Gun Digest* are delighted to announce that John Malloy has been selected as the recipient of the thirtieth annual John T. Amber Literary Award in recognition of his outstanding essay "The Colt 1911: The First Century," which appeared in the 65th (2011) edition of *Gun Digest*.

Few writers indeed have John's depth of experience with all types of firearms but with semi-automatic pistols in particular. And with 2011 being the centennial of this outstanding design, it was only natural that we should ask John to grace our pages with his perspective on J. M. Browning's most famous creation. In our opinion, John's piece on the 1911 is perhaps the best short introduction to the 1911 pistol ever written.

As its name implies, the John T. Amber Literary Award recognizes not only a writer's knowledge but his ability to express it with style and clarity. In this age of the self-appointed expert, it is the ability to write well that distinguishes the true gunwriter from the mere opinion peddler. Gunwriting has been referred to as a dying art, but it will live as long as there are those such as John Malloy to show how it should be done.

John has always been modest about his writing, although he has attracted quite a following through his writing for *Gun Digest*. I know from personal experience that he has many fans – because I am one of them.

John's shooting career and his involvement with *Gun Digest* coincide almost exactly. As he tells it,

The post-war years were a wonderful time to be a boy interested in guns and shooting.

We shot as Boy Scouts, and shot any WWII war souvenir firearms available. We studied guns of all types. We joined the NRA and read American Rifleman. Soon, we needed more reference material.

Gun Digest had appeared once during the war, reappearing afterward as an annual publication. A friend and I pooled the necessary two dollars from our lawn-mowing money to buy the 5th (1951) edition.

I was hooked! I began to acquire Gun Digest whenever I could.

By the early 1960s, I had become a rifle, pistol and shotgun competitor and an ardent hunter. By the late 1960s, I was an NRA Instructor working with youth programs and had become a gun-rights activist.

In hindsight, I waited a long time to begin writing. However by 1980, I had had firearms articles published. Gun Digest accepted an early effort that appeared in the 1984 edition. More followed as the years went on.

All writers published in Gun Digest have to be good. Those writers who win the John T. Amber Award are acknowledged to be the very best.

I am proud to be included in that group.

John, on behalf of *Gun Digest* and its readers, we offer a sincere thank-you for all the enjoyment you've brought us through your writing over the years. You're one of a kind.

Dan Shideler
Editor
Gun Digest

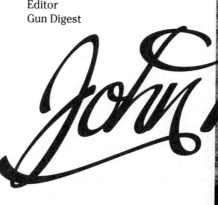

WELCOME
to the 2012 Edition of *Gun Digest*!

Dan Shideler
1960 - 2011

As excited as we are to bring you the 66th edition of *Gun Digest*, at the same time we are saddened to announce that the force behind the industry's No.1 firearms annual, Dan Shideler, passed away Sunday, April 3, 2011.

Though in poor health, Dan made it is his mission to round up and deliver the material for the 2012 edition, guaranteeing that the gun world would once again get to enjoy a fascinating collection of firearms literature.

Dan joined the Company in 2004, splitting his time between our offices here in Iola, Wisconsin, and his home in Indiana. He quickly gained respect throughout the company and the industry as an expert in firearms history, trends and pricing. Within a few years Dan took over as editor of *Standard Catalog of Firearms*. In 2010 he realized his childhood dream of becoming the editor of *Gun Digest*. It was the pinnacle of Dan's career. In the introduction to the 64th edition, he wrote:

"I was raised on Gun Digest. Once a year, in the long-gone Indiana of the 1960s and 1970s, my father brought home the new edition, which my brother Dave and I eagerly devoured. I mean we read it literally from cover to cover, absorbing whatever wisdom and insight that could be found in its pages. I still have some of those 40-year-old volumes, nearly all of them showing pencil marks in their catalog sections where we, with boyish enthusiasm, checked guns that we would surely buy someday …

"And now, forty-some years later, I am the editor of that same book. Karma? The inscrutable workings of Fate? Call it what you will, I will say simply that it is an honor — for me, it's the stuff that dreams are made of."

Dan never called himself an expert, preferring to be known as "just an old-fashioned gun guy." By the time he came to work at F+W, Dan had compiled a collection of every *Gun Digest* annual, starting with the inaugural 1944 edition. in 2008 Dan hauled his entire collection from his home to our office so it could be digitized and made available to everyone who shared his appreciation for firearms history.

I met Dan in 1997 while interviewing him for the position of "technical copywriter" at a previous company. Five minutes into our discussion, his gift for communication was obvious. He was wildly overqualified, but we hired him on the spot. To no one's surprise, within months Dan was running an entire division of our marketing department.

We soon became fast friends, and Dan made it his mission to further my education on firearms of all types. I confess that Dan and I spent too much time discussing guns and hunting, both on the job and off, so it seemed only natural that years later we ended up right where we both wanted to be – working for *Gun Digest*. Partnering with Dan to produce some of the greatest titles in the industry has been an honor, and I'm better for having known him.

While I could probably fill a *Gun Digest*-sized volume with fascinating, humorous and near-unbelievable stories about Dan (and perhaps someday I will), it's better for now that I let a few of his colleagues pay their respects …

Kevin Michalowski, Senior Editor, *Gun Digest the Magazine*

Dan was particularly fond of obscure pieces. I remember well the day he posed for a photo with an anti-garroting contraption. It was basically a cap-lock blackpowder barrel mounted to a metal plate, worn on your back and fired by pulling a string to drop the hammer. Apparently the idea was to blast anyone who would sneak up behind you intent on doing harm. You wouldn't have gotten me to wear it on a bet, but Dan loaded it up, strapped it on and, on the photographer's cue, yanked the cord. The flame and smoke emanating from his backside gave us a good laugh and unforgettable photo. We all miss Dan's vibrant mirth and sarcastic sense of humor. We also miss being able to pick up the phone and ask him about guns we've never heard of … And get a history lesson from his seemingly limitless knowledge.

Corrina Peterson, Gun Digest Books Editor

Watching Dan in action was awe-inspiring. He knew everything there was to know about firearms and their history. People call our office all the time with questions about guns they found in their father's attic or behind the bathtub in the cabin they just bought. No matter how sketchy the description, Dan could always ask a few pointed questions and identify the gun. The real kicker is that the information was all in his head – he never had to look up anything.

Dan was one of a kind – a genius, a gentleman and a true friend. It has been a blessing and an honor to know him, and I miss him terribly.

Patrick Sweeney, Gun Digest Books Author

I only knew Dan for a few years, but we quickly became co-conspirators. Together we schemed to find the best possible titles and content, for the benefit of ourselves, the publisher and the readers. He never complained about my complaining, and the only time he was upset was when I mis-remembered the details of a manuscript, and sent in twice as much text as needed. "I was crying as I was cutting stuff" he said.

He always had an idea, a plan, a funny line, and encouragement for the next project. Wise to the world, and the ways of publishing, he didn't let that knowledge discourage him. He always had fun. I'm going to miss him.

Massad Ayoob, Gun Digest Books Author

Dan Shideler was taken from us far too soon. He was a joy to work with, an advocate for the authors he brought into the fold, and likewise to those he inherited from his predecessors. His deep understanding of the book business would have earned him big bucks as an executive on Publisher's Row in New York City, but he chose instead to apply his talents to his avocation.

Dan understood the "art of the gun" — the form-follows-function sculpture of the things, and the way in which the sight of certain iconic firearms trip the pleasure centers in the enthusiast reader's brain, the way a '57 Chevy does for someone who grew up during the Eisenhower years, the way a distinctive Ansel Adams image does for a connoisseur of fine photography.

With his encyclopedic knowledge of firearms, Dan blended scholarship into art. Working with the author on one end and the art director on the other, he shaped books that will be on the shelves of gun collectors and shooters for many decades to come. The world of the gun is diminished by his loss.

Phillip Peterson, Editor, *Standard Catalog of Military Firearms*

Dan was the one who suggested I submit columns about collectible guns to *Gun Digest the Magazine,* back when it was called *Gun List* — when that publication expanded to include magazine content. And as his career with Krause expanded he was the one who suggested my name to the pub board to do the 4th edition of *Standard Catalog of Military Firearms.*

As I look at images of Dan that appear throughout the Gun Digest web site, I realize that I sold or traded from Dan every single firearm he is shown with. I happen to still have one firearm that came from Dan: A Winchester M1911 self-loading shotgun known as the infamous "Widowmaker." He gave it to me in February as part of a multi-gun swap. I had intended to sell it but I think I will now keep it.

Dan Shideler Memorial Fund

Another, lesser-known aspect of Dan's persona was his gift for music, both performing and composing. Dan was active in numerous community bands and composed several marches over the years. With that in mind, his family has established a memorial fund in his name:

Daniel Shideler Memorial Fund
John Philip Sousa Foundation Project
c/o Indiana Members Credit Union
7110 West 10th Street
Indianapolis, IN 46214

Acknowledgments

Many thanks to Dan's family, particularly Dave and Karen, for securing and organizing the contents of *Gun Digest 2012,* ensuring that our staff could produce this edition in a timely manner. I'm further indebted to Tom Nelsen and Paul Birling, who worked tirelessly to lay out and design the book you hold here. Without their dedication you might still be waiting to read this edition. And thanks also to Andy Belmas, Jake Edson and Dan Schmidt for pitching in with editing duties. For everyone who had a hand in this edition, you can rest assured that Dan is proud of you!

Cordially,
Jim Schlender
Publisher, *GUN DIGEST*

About the covers

FRONT COVER:

The **Taurus Circuit Judge** revolver carbine, manufactured for and sold through **Rossi**, builds on the huge success of Taurus's Judge .410/.45 Colt revolver series. Load it up with 2-1/2- or 3-inch .410 shells and/or .45 Colt ammunition in any combination. This lightweight (only 4-1/2 pounds) with 18-1/2-inch barrel is a dandy firearm for home defense, small-game hunting or simply a fun afternoon at the range. Learn more at www.rossisusa.com.

Springfield Armory continues to serve the concealed carry market well with the recent introduction of its **XD(M) 3.8 Compact** in 9mm and .40-caliber. It's built on the same-size frame as the wildly popular Sub-Compact XD and uses the same slide as the original XD(M) 3.8. Shown here is the 9mm with its 13+1 round magazine. Springfield's X-Tension magazine provides 19+1 round capacity. Get the whole story at www.the-m-factor.com.

BACK COVER:

It's important and appropriate, as Model 1911 enthusiasts continue to revel in the joy and wonder of passing the 100th anniversary of this iconic pistol, that we make note of **Kimber's 1911 Custom II Desert Warrior.** Built for use by our U.S. Marines, from the integral tactical rail to the Tactical Wedge tritium night sights to the G-10 grips, it's professional-grade at its finest. See the whole Kimber line at www.kimberamerica.com.

Beretta shotguns, about which you'll read much inside these pages, has long been a master of combining fit, function and beauty. The aluminum-framed **687 Ultralight Deluxe** 12 gauge is no exception, featuring a highly figured walnut stock and full floral engraving with gold-filled gamebirds, and weighing in at a wispy 6.4 pounds. See more at www.berettausa.com.

Gun Digest Staff

EDITOR
Dan Shideler

CONTRIBUTING EDITORS

Holt Bodinson: Ammunition, Ballistics & Components; Web Directory
Wm. Hovey Smith: Black Powder
John Haviland: Shotguns
John Malloy: Handguns/Autoloaders
Tom Tabor: Rifles
Jeff Quinn: Handguns/Revolvers

Tom Turpin: Custom and Engraved Guns
Wayne van Zwoll: Optics
Gila Hayes: Women's Perspective
Kevin Muramatsu: Gunsmithing
Tom Caceci: Airguns
Larry Sterett: Reloading

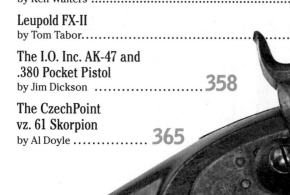

GunDigest 2012

TABLE OF CONTENTS

ITALY'S DOUBLE-BARREL BARGAINS

English shotguns set high standards.
Italy's best doubles match them – for a lot less!

BY **WAYNE VAN ZWOLL**

Stop reading here if you grew up in tweeds, shooting pairs of guns at driven grouse without once loading the barrels yourself. If there's a Jaguar in your garage and Eton graduates in your family tree, you might in fact find this treatise troubling.

But as a purveyor of truth (well, mostly), I just can't tender Bond Street any more plaudits. Land sakes, it's had plenty. This hallowed center of British gunmaking deserves most of them. It gave us names we've come to associate with the best hinged-breech guns:

Purdey, Greener, Westley-Richards, Holland & Holland and many others. It gave us the Anson & Deeley mechanism, patented in 1875. From this tight quarter of London came the form and function that defined double-barrel rifles and shotguns, fitted to the shooter. Elegance

A lightweight, fast-handling gun is a prerequisite for hunting chukar in Idaho's hill country.

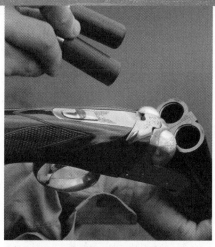

This hunter found his Fausti quick on target and smooth on the follow-through. There was also plenty of evidence of fine balance.

While Fausti Stephano specializes in small-gauge guns, it sells many 12-bores to hunters.

The author readies a Fausti-built Weatherby for another target. These guns endure extended shooting.

From left: Sisters Elena, Giovanna and Barbara Fausti run this Italian shotgun firm.

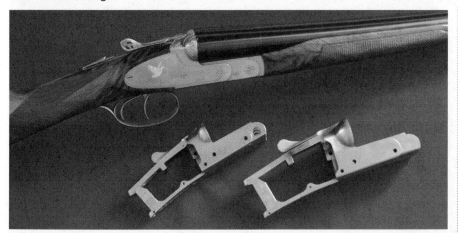

Most Faustis are small-bores, elegant in profile, and have frame sizes to match the barrels.

of profile and seamless marriage of parts set high bars for the competition. At the same time, legendary demands of each apprentice – hand-filing a two-inch steel cube to a one-inch cube perfect on all 12 edges – must have discouraged many aspiring gunmakers. Those who stuck it out endured long days in cramped, dimly-lit shops. One I visited years ago was little bigger than a storage unit, and hardly any brighter. The name above the door would have made anyone's Top 10 list of British gun firms.

That landmark work would come from such caverns is as remarkable as the sums charged for it. But while the venerable London names remain untarnished by time, they're not unchallenged. Italian shotguns have even upstaged them. Among competitive clay-bird shooters, Italy dominates. Perazzi guns account for more than half those used in target games there, and almost all the rest are Berettas. The same preferences show up in other Old World countries – and stateside. Hunters who follow suit aren't chasing a new trend; Brits may have developed the most celebrated game guns, but Italian makers served hunters first. In fact, Beretta is the world's oldest gunmaker. It was turning out barrels as early as 1526, predating by nearly three centuries the first barrel from Remington, America's oldest gunmaker.

Beretta

Beretta established itself in the Gardone region of northern Italy. "Beretta 1" (the main factory) now straddles the Mella River, which in the early days served as a source of power, people and iron. Most of Beretta's shotguns

A CNC machine operator at the Fausti plant needs digital as well as gunmaking savvy.

Fausti doubles incorporate forged monoblocks that are carefully machined and held to tight tolerances.

A Fausti worker files a grip tang. These Italian guns exhibit fine fit and finish.

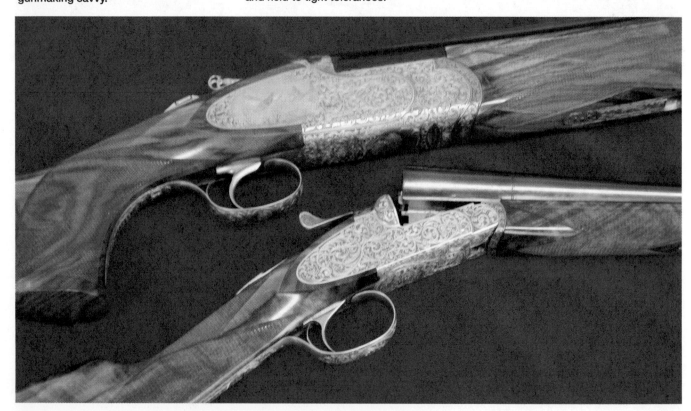

Fausti shotguns include side-by-side and over/under models in several frame sizes.

(and rifles and handguns) are built here. Shifts comprising about 900 workers keep this facility buzzing around the clock, except on Sundays. High-grade shotguns are assembled at "Beretta 2," a smaller facility, within walking distance. Most raw materials come from France and Italy, including "Steelium," an alloy formulated by and produced exclusively for Beretta. This steep-sided valley has long attracted skilled tradespeople and artisans, many of whom now provide Beretta with specialized parts, and services like engraving. "We're fortunate to have many able sub-contractors nearby," says the firm's Luisa Achino. "In the valley, there are 160 small shops, 40 within bicycling distance!"

While Beretta manufactures repeating shotguns, it is best known for its exquisite side-by-side and over/under models. The SO series offers several grades of embellishment on a true sidelock action. You can choose straight or pistol grip, fixed or interchangeable "Optimachokes." Heck, you can specify almost anything on the SO, from stock dimensions to engraving. By the way, the "EL" after a model designation stands for "extra lusso" or extra luxury. Double E double L shotguns are super-duper fancy. The sidelock Imperiale Montecarlo is the side-by-side counterpart to the SO series, which includes target, sporting and field sub-models in 12, 20 and 28 gauge. This top-end double shotgun has all the refinements you'd find on an English game gun. Choose Italian or rose-and-scroll engraving. Like the SO over/under shotguns, the Imperiale Montecarlo is part of Beretta's "1526 collection."

Sportsmen with mortgages might instead drift to the 680 series of stack-barrel Berettas: the 682 Gold competition guns (including a Trap bottom single version) with adjustable combs and the 687 and 686 over/unders. All feature a low-profile improved-boxlock mechanism. The 687 Silver Pigeon comes in several grades for upland hunters. The 687 Ultralight gives you 12-bore payloads in a 6.4-pound gun. The 686, in field and sporting form, is now Beretta's entry-level over-under. Want a side-by-side but can't dig the coin for a high-grade sidelock? The 471 Silver Hawk is still available. Beretta's boxlock double, in 12 and 20 gauge, features the single selective trigger, automatic safety and oil-finished checkered walnut that comes standard on all hinged-breech Beretta field guns. The EL version sports case-colored sideplates.

Each Fausti shotgun is hand-assembled and fitted. Manufactured parts show exceptional care.

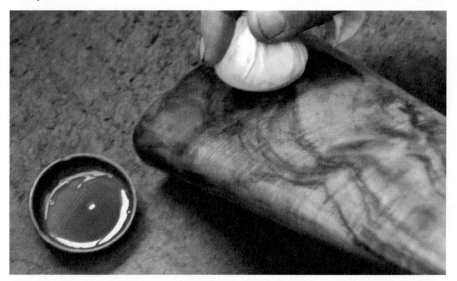

Hand-rubbed stock finish on figured walnut make Fausti guns as fetching as they are functional.

Colored, lifelike images and delicate scroll engraving mark Fausti guns. This one remains unfinished.

Select walnut goes on high-grade Fausti shotguns, some of which wear the Weatherby logo.

Headspacing a Fausti double is one of many traditional hand operations at the Gardone factory.

An engraver chases expertly cut scroll on a Fausti receiver. Such artistry is rare and costly.

A worker checks chamber length to ready a gun for mandatory federal (and C.I.P.) inspection.

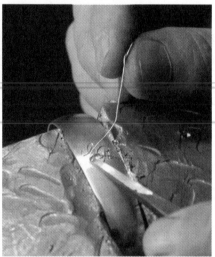

The Gardone region has long attracted artisans. Here one inlays gold wire on a Fausti shotgun.

Competitive shooters are familiar with the DT10 stable of trap, skeet and sporting over/unders. In 12 gauge only, they have manual safeties and detachable (DT) triggers. But on a recent visit, I direct my time at Beretta to the company's new SV10 Perennia O/U. The SV10 is a boxlock with traditional low-profile breeching, trapezoidal monoblock shoulders and double locking lugs. An oversize hinge pin with a new reinforcing shoulder holds up under extended use. "Extractors run the length of the monoblock, so they operate very smoothly," Luisa points out. "You can choose ejection or extraction." Machined from a steel billet, the nickel-finished receiver features an arrowhead motif in relief.

Like all Beretta shotgun barrels, those

Melding modern machines with Old World craftsmanship, Fausti builds fine but affordable guns.

Deft hands moving too fast to follow, a worker at Fausti Stefano assembles a boxlock shotgun.

Massive lugs and triangular, full-length ejector rods give Fausti guns exceptional longevity.

From forging to finished part, Fausti steel undergoes many inspections. Final fitting is by hand.

Giovanna (left) and Barbara take a break at an Italian skeet field, reserved for company guests.

The Beretta family has run the renowned Italian gun firm, the world's oldest, since 1526.

of the SV10 are cold hammer-forged. A thick steel tube is kneaded into a long, slim barrel around a mandrel, by hammers that deliver terrific pressure, 1,800 strikes per minute. They're joined near the muzzle with silver solder, which also secures the quarter-inch matted rib. Special welds mate the rear of the barrels at the monoblock. Five Optimachoke tubes come with every SV10. They're steel shot-friendly, as is the chrome-lined bore.

The SV10's trigger has titanium components for fast lock speed. The guard, an elegant steel loop, properly matches the curve of the trigger. The break is clean, consistent and manageable. A transverse button in the safety pad selects the barrel of your choice. It is snappy and refuses to hang up in the middle. The automatic safety works well

too – although I prefer a manual switch.

My first shots with the SV10 Perennia come on an Italian skeet field modified to give shooters of modest ability the illusion that they're competent. I'm duly grateful.

Shooting the SV10 proves a pleasure – in no small part because I'm having a good day, and the clay targets are not. Then too, the shotgun babies my clavicle. Its walnut buttstock features an optional "Kick-Off" mechanism, a pair of hydraulic pistons inside that absorb much of the jolt of firing. There's noticeably less muzzle climb too. Because claims of "less recoil" abound, I test the Kick-Off device by following target loads in the 7-pound gun with the potent 2.75- and 3-inch magnums you might choose for a goose hunt or turkeys. No pain! And

Beretta's SV10 Perennia is the company's most recent over/under, a low-profile boxlock.

Known for high-end guns, Beretta also offers more affordable O/Us, like this SV10 Perennia.

The internal Kick-Off recoil reduction system incorporates this buttpad on Beretta shotguns.

The author cheeks a new SV10. Kick-Off recoil damping tames even stiff goose and turkey loads.

Kick-Off doesn't compromise the SV10's sleek profile. The black butt assembly blends with the stock (length of pull: 14.7 inches) and doesn't impair handling in the least. In my hand, the SV10 Perennia has perfect balance with Kick-Off installed. Combined with a slim, open grip and slender forend, that balance puts the barrel instantly on the leading edge of the targets.

Among Italian gunmakers, Beretta is a giant firm, building rifles and pistols as well as shotguns, marketing both to sportsmen and military and police units worldwide. It has not, however, neglected its roots. The tall stone mansion marking Beretta headquarters has been a landmark for generations. It's also a museum. "We have 3,500 firearms on display," says Luisa, as we pass through a security check and a guard unlocks a heavy door. "The vault below holds another 4,000." We enter a long room with soaring ceilings. Dark wood on floor and walls give it a cavernous feel. The glow of bulbs glitters on the glass fronts of display cases wrapping the room. Glass cases cap a massive island of drawers commanding its middle. Everywhere there are guns – laddered on horizontal wall racks, stacked in vertical columns on the island, arrayed like silverware in the drawers. Pistols, rifles and shotguns.

Matchlocks, wheel-locks and flintlocks. Embellished percussion mechanisms and stamped-metal submachine guns. If there's any more complete firearms history in steel and walnut, I can't imagine where it might be.

Patiently Luisa endures. At last I blurt: "It'll take me another hour."

She must be tired of waiting. "Take your time," she says, and leaves.

I could, in fact, have stayed all afternoon. She retrieves me to visit another room, where we see punt guns Beretta built for 19th-century waterfowlers, and Beretta motorcycles and automobiles.

Few Italian gun firms have such a heritage. Still, you can find Old World quality from smaller and more recent operations. Unlike the American firearms industry, Italy's makers have hewed

Beretta's main factory employs 900 workers on the Mella River in Italy's Gardone district.

A spacious factory with robots and CNC machines produces Beretta guns on ancient grounds.

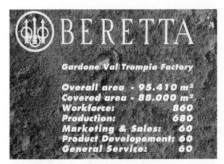

Beretta is a major employer in a string of villages with more than 160 small-gun shops.

closely to tradition in both the design and manufacture of shotguns. While new mechanisms, better steels and more efficient production are in style now, Italian companies take care not to compromise fit and finish, form and balance. The emphasis remains on quality. Production quotas grow with demand; demand depends on the appeal of the product. European shotgunners, it seems to me, spend more for fewer shotguns than do shooters Stateside. Hunting and even clay-bird shooting haven't been as available in the Old World. Use and ownership of sporting guns was established as a prerogative of the landed class, and remains so. The success of Winchester's 1897 pump gun – or, later, the Remington 870 – would have been hard to match in Europe. There, shotguns evolved as art forms, not reapers of meat. To be sure,

faultless function was and is expected. But so is close mating of parts, and a lively feel in the hand. Europeans in the market for new shotguns typically lean to the double gun for those reasons, and as a nod to tradition. Most have the wherewithal to buy them.

Fausti

Naturally, gunmakers who want to grow look offshore. Beretta has successfully expanded its line to include autoloaders that appeal to American shotgunners, while maintaining its classy side-by-side and over/under lines. Just up the valley from Beretta, another Italian firm has gone international with a similar strategy. Fausti Stefano has been around only since 1948 – it is a young company by local standards. But Fausti

hinged-breech guns have the feel of more expensive doubles. And the repeaters are extraordinarily agile. "High quality and traditional styling, but with modern innovation." Giovanna Fausti sums up what sounds like a winning combination. I've come to see it from the factory floor.

Giovanna is the most visible executive in the company. She guides the Fausti marketing effort in the U.S. Her younger sister, Barbara, takes care of accounts in eastern Europe. Third sister Elena keeps the factory on track at home. "That's right," laughs Barbara. "We control everything. We three sisters." There's a lot of truth in that claim. But it's not the whole story. Giovanna's husband also works in the business. And Barbara's husband came from the accomplished gunmaking house of Rizzini.

"We merged the Rizzini shop with our father's Fausti enterprise in 1991," says Giovanna as she ushers me into her office. "Five years later we dispensed with the Rizzini name because it remained an active brand within that family. We had to ensure that shooters wanting a Fausti came to us."

And they have. Shooters like Ed Weatherby, who has imported Fausti-made shotguns under the Weatherby label. In fact, I got my introduction to Fausti when shooting with Ed. I was mightily impressed with the fit of both over/under and autoloading shotguns. Never particularly skilled with a side-by-side (OK, I'm downright inept), I couldn't assess that shotgun with a sporting clays score. But the gun felt as if it should hit birds. The open Prince-of-Wales grip gives my big paws plenty of sliding room but is slim enough for smaller shooters. Lightweight at just under 7 pounds, it balances dreamily, with the weight between my hands and a slight tilt to the muzzle. It jumps to my cheek, swings smoothly. The Anson & Deely action

Receivers machined from lightweight alloy give Beretta autoloaders a lively feel and fast swing.

Barrels joined to monoblocks await finishing in a rack at Beretta 1, the main production plant.

features Purdey-style double lockup to ensure that barrels maintain precise alignment over an extended firing life. Like its Fausti over/unders, Weatherby's SBS features chrome-lined barrels and lengthened forcing cones for more uniform patterns, and automatic ejectors for fast reloading (fired shells get kicked out; unfired rounds are lifted for easy extraction). Single triggers on all three of these Faustis are recoil operated. O/U safeties incorporate barrel selectors; on the SBS, the right-hand barrel fires first.

"Take it afield," urged Ed, handing me a 20-bore over/under.

I did, on the bluffs above the Flying B, a bird-hunting mecca on Lawyer Creek south of Kamiah, Idaho. Shooting pheasants in the crop fields lining the canyon would have been easier, but trying to tag chukars in the steeps would test both the Weatherby and my legs. This particular gun was fancier than it needed to be for rough duty. An Athena D'Italia, it wore first-cabin engraving and classy Turkish walnut. You get the same mechanism with less embellishment but still attractive walnut in the Orion D'Italia. It retails for just $1,699 – not much more than a top-end synthetic-stocked autoloader!

"Point!" Phil Bourjaily was above me, the stylish English pointer between us. She was indeed locked up. "I'll back you," he grinned. Hoo boy.

Walking up on chukars is like stepping onto fresh ice. You hear it crack, see the fault lines, know that if you continue there's only a slim chance you'll reach the far bank with your dignity intact. When chuckars erupt, you have a short second to react. If there's no bird to retrieve, you must then explain to both the dog

(first) and your partner why no one could possibly have made that shot. I'm getting pretty good at this. So when the covey rocketed into the blue Idaho sky, banked sharply like a squadron of Red Arrows and plunged at Mach I toward the canyon floor, I expected to miss. Imagine my surprise when a puff of feathers blew from the rearmost bird and it cartwheeled through the October morning to bounce hard on the basalt far below.

"That shotgun must fit you!" Phil was more gracious than he needed to be. I would miss many more birds that day. To limit that tally, I prevailed upon him to join me later in the sorghum. Clobbering ringnecks with the lively 20-gauge felt like test-driving a Maserati in a parking lot.

"We build shotguns carefully, to look good, point quickly and endure a lot of shooting." There's no hedging; I can tell Giovanna believes in Fausti's shotguns. It's equally clear she's fiercely committed to the brand. "We're selling more guns in more places now. We expect good results in America, with our office there now, and aggressive marketing."

Italian shotguns aren't new to U.S. shooters, but they've not been marketed aggressively. "What can you offer that other makers don't?" I ask. Popular Berettas and Browning's Citori came to mind – and less successful hinged-breech imports. Not all Japanese-built guns have the lines or feel that appeal to hunters choosing doubles over repeaters. Maintaining quality in Turkish guns has become problematic. The Spanish AYA is pricey for weekend bird hunters. High-quality American-made doubles – the Fox, the Parker, Winchester's 21 – succumbed long ago to rising production costs. The A-10 American O/U introduced recently by

Connecticut Shotgun seems a bargain. But many hunters who recognize value in a shallow-frame sidelock with hand-detachable plates for less than $4,000 still blanch. "Surely, Giovanna, you can't avoid that cost-price squeeze!"

She assures me Fausti has met that challenge. A growing customer base confirms it, with orders for both types of doubles. "In Italy, we sell about 60 percent side-by-sides, 40 percent over/unders. But we export many more over/unders: roughly 65 percent." She adds that 20-bore guns account for half of Fausti sales, and that 28-gauge and .410 bores are as popular as the 12. Then Giovanna introduces me to Claudio, who will lead me through the factory.

As we walk across the drive, above a small garden plot that fronts the Mella, Claudio describes the guns and their manufacture. He tells me in near-perfect English what I learned from Barbara earlier: that frames are sized to the chambering, "so you get a gun that's perfectly proportioned." There are five actions for side-by-side Faustis, four for over/unders (the 28 and .410 stack-barrels use the same frame).

The factory comprises two buildings – each bigger than the London shops I remember. They're a curious mixture of CNC machines, traditional floor tooling and craftsmen wielding files and gauges. It is not, I think, a company in transition. Rather, Fausti seems a place where Old World priorities meet the efficiencies of mass production. What's best done by hand here is still done by hand; "but you can make more shotguns by harnessing machines for the drilling and rough contouring." Claudio has worked with both hand tools and sophisticated equipment. He shows me how hinges are fitted and triggers adjusted, by a fellow whose movements are so quick, the gun seems fluid in his hands. At another bench an artisan with a small file marries an inletted piece of flame-grain Turkish with a tang still in the white. We watch another Fausti worker slip headspace gauges into chambers, and another install choke tubes.

"Here's one reason Fausti guns last a long time." Claudio picks up an Anson & Deely side-by-side action. "The ejectors are in the forend iron. We use ejector stems that are triangular in cross-section. They're superior to round stems, especially in the smaller gauges." He inserts them, back to back, into a machined, box-shaped channel. They move as skates on ice, though this gun is far from finished. "There's no wobble as the gun wears in," says Claudio.

To make their guns distinctive, the Fausti sisters tap the talent of local engravers. In a room lined with high-grade Faustis, I watch one of these engravers. Light blows from a small hammer chase a chisel deftly over a game scene stunning in its realism. There's little room for error. And he makes none. Like many Gardone engravers, he is well past his 50th birthday. He cannot speak English, and my Italian is no better than my Mandarin. But he sees I appreciate his work, and he smiles.

"We'll go shoot this evening." Fabio, Barbara's husband, is at my shoulder. It is late afternoon now. I'm driven to my hotel, a modest but comfortable old building shadowing a quiet side-street. Fabio and Claudio pick me up at six. We drive north toward the Dolomites, downshifting on a steep climb up a long, serpentine canyon that joins the Mella. The shooting facility perches on a bench. It is well equipped, with several clay-target ranges that march in steps toward ridgetop. We trudge up the steep grade. All shooting lines are covered; we choose one with a half-dozen stations. Fabio unzips the two cases we've carried up. The guns are both exquisite. They're also .410s. I grimace.

"Pull!" My companion goes first. One of the targets, we're convinced, cannot be reached by our smallbore gun. Even shooters with 12s have trouble. "That's OK," grins Fabio after his third miss. "If you get all the close ones, you'll soon have an audience."

I don't, of course. But the Fausti over/under is a delight – unbelievably quick. I discover it wants my help on follow-through, and at last a couple of birds come apart. Duly humbled by the score, I watch other shooters arrive. Men and women, young and old, they slip well-made, well-used Italian guns from their sleeves. No novices, these. I can tell by their stance and swing. They laugh and joke until they step to a station. Then, leaning into the gun with practiced ease, they call for a bird and fire fast. They're smart to shoot quickly; these disks rocket away as if launched to destroy enemy clays.

"Just recreational shooters," smiles Claudio. No wonder the Italians fare so well in international shotgun competition! We three end the day over sandwiches, chips and wine at the gun club café.

If you've read this far, you're not a Bond Street blue-blood. Surely, if you want value and grace in a shotgun, the smoothbores of Fausti and Beretta warrant a look … after the prices on Bond Street send you south.

The Beretta mansion has been a landmark in the Gardone region for generations. It includes a museum inside.

GUNS FOR THE GREAT NORTH

An Alaskan hunt requires a specialized rifle.
The good news is that you have several options.

BY BRAD FITZPATRICK

It is often difficult for hunters to appreciate just how enormous Alaska is. This grandest of all North American sporting destinations is one-fifth of the size of the continental United States with more than twice the size of Texas with over 130 million acres of forest and even more tundra. The terrain varies widely, from Kodiak Island with its maritime climate to the highest mountain ranges in North America. There are alder thickets that are almost impenetrable and treeless tundras that stretch from one horizon to the next. But all of these varied habitats have one thing in common — they will test the hunter and his equipment to the limit.

In today's market of specialized rifles designed for specific purposes and hunting destinations, the "Alaskan" gun has become synonymous with guns that are built to be weatherproof, utterly reliable and as light as possible without produc-ing punishing recoil. Often these rifles are also chambered for rounds that can take down a wide range of game and, if necessary, stop a bear in its tracks.

Several companies have offered up their own versions of rifles designed specifically with the Last Frontier in mind. They vary in size, style and finish but they all represent their parent company's take on tough rifles. Here's a quick survey of what's available for America's greatest hunting destination.

Sako Kodiak

Finnish gunmaker Sako has a long-standing tradition for building precision rifles capable of incredible accuracy. The Kodiak shares the same engineering as the company's other 85-series guns, the heart of which is the company's outstanding action that features controlled-round feeding for positive extraction and ejection. The bolt throw is silky smooth and lockup feels tight and extremely solid. All metal parts are stainless steel.

The Kodiak's stock is weatherproof laminate and is reinforced with twin crossbolts to withstand punishing recoil, which is good because the Kodiak is available only in .338 Winchester Magnum and .375 H&H Magnum, two proven cartridges with an impressive record on game and the muscle to dump a bear should the need suddenly arise. The free-floated barrel is just over 21 inches long and comes complete with high-quality iron sights and a barrel-band front sling stud designed to prevent your fingers from colliding with the swivel stud during recoil. The 85-style receiver has integrated scope mount rails for increased stability and the trigger, like all Sako 85s, is adjustable between 2 and 4 pounds and breaks as cleanly as those on target rifles. With an MSRP of around $2000, it ain't cheap, but it's a unique

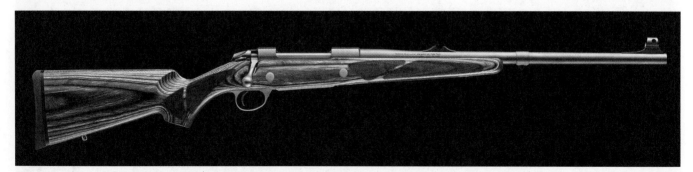

Sako took their venerable Model 85 action and built it into a rifle that is weatherproof and deadly accurate. Integral rails in the receiver lock the scope rings in place and the trigger is among the finest to be found in a production rifle.

Ruger's Alaskan is chambered in .375 and .416 Ruger, cartridges the company designed in conjunction with Hornady. The Alaskan comes with a short 20-inch barrel that makes it ideal in close cover.

blend of bench rifle and bear gun that performs flawlessly. Sako claims that custom is their standard and the Kodiak backs up that claim.

Ruger Alaskan

Ruger has been a friend to the Alaskan hunter. First, they coordinated with Hornady on the development of the .375 Ruger cartridge, which is an ideal Alaskan round. It is capable of producing energy levels greater than those produced by the .375 H&H Magnum without a significant increase in recoil. In addition, the .375 Ruger can be chambered in standard (.30-06) length actions, reducing rifle weight and cost. The round is flat-shooting enough to reach out and

powerful enough to settle things with an irate bear. In addition, the .375 Ruger performs very well in short barrels and is a natural chambering for stubby rifles designed for close-range work.

Ruger developed this great round and chambered it in their then-new Hawkeye African rifle. Shortly afterwards came the Alaskan version, with its short barrel and stainless finish designed to withstand the harshest conditions. The trucated barrel comes from the factory with a set of iron sights as well as rings that lock into integral scope rails built into the receiver. The Hawkeye's action features a full-length claw extractor that assures reliability in the field, which is a good thing when you are slipping through alder thickets that may or may not bring you nose to nose with a big bruin.

Ruger designed their Alaskan to be tough and accurate. As a bonus it is also one of the least expensive rifles on this list (MSRP $1079). But don't let the gun's bargain price fool you. The Hawkeye Alaskan is as tough as the landscape that inspired it.

Kimber Talkeetna

The Talkeetna is one of Kimber's specialty rifles based on the Model 8400 action that gets its own geographic call name (the others being the Caprivi, which is named after the great dangerous game hunting region of Northern Namibia, and the Sonora). The Talkeetna would serve a hunter well while hunting in the mountain range it was so named for. As a matter of fact, the Talkeetna will perform dutifully just about anywhere on the planet thanks to a rugged stock and all stainless construction.

But Kimber's take on the Alaskan rifle is much more than just a brawny bolt action that was built to shrug off the elements. Despite its tough guy exterior the Talkeetna is essentially a match-grade rifle at heart with many accuracy improving features that most companies wouldn't bother engineering into a dangerous game gun. Kimber builds each Talkeetna with a match grade barrel and action and includes a trigger that breaks sharply between three and a half and four pounds. The Talkeetna, like most Kimber rifles, comes glass and pillar bedded. The action is a Mauser-type with claw extractor and the safety is a three-position wing type similar to that found on the Winchester Model 70 that allows hunters to lock the action and to load and unload the rifle with the safety engaged. The stock is a nearly indestructible Kevlar-carbon fiber blend.

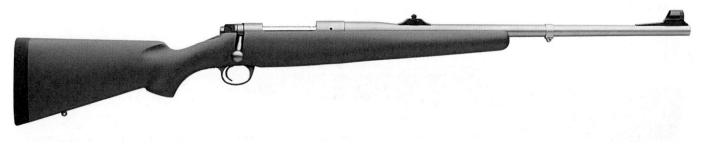

The Talkeetna and its siblings the Sonora and Caprivi are all rifles designed with a specific function and destination in mind. For the Kimber Talkeetna, that meant it had to be able to buck the elements while producing outstanding accuracy. Mission accomplished.

Remington's Alaskan Wilderness Rifle II is a custom shop gun available in a variety of calibers from .25-06 to .375 Remington Ultra Magnum. Accuracy is guaranteed to be sub-MOA in all rifles up to .30 caliber and is often even better than this.

The Talkeetna is available only in .375 H&H Magnum, but if you had to choose one all-around rifle capable of taking a variety of game and putting the brakes on a bear charge, the old H&H isn't too bad a choice. Unlike many safari rifles weighing close to 10 pounds, the Talkeetna weighs only eight, which is great for a big bore that will be carried on long walks up and down mountains. To mitigate the formidable recoil produced by the big .375 cartridge, Kimber uses a Pachmayr Decelerator recoil pad to cushion the rifle's thump. With a steady rest and a shooter experienced with large magnums the Kimber is capable of printing groups that will beat many high-end production deer rifles. The Kimber, like the Sako, offers many of the features normally reserved for custom dangerous game rifles at a price point that is still in the range for a production gun (MSRP $2108).

Remington Alaskan Wilderness Rifle II (AWR)

There are several reasons why the Model 700 is one of America's favorite bolt guns. It is well built and highly accurate, so much so that it is a favorite of military and police sharpshooters. But the Model 700 will always be best known as a hunter's gun, a rifle that has taken countless heads of game around the world and has served generations of sportsmen. It is available in a numbing variety of configurations and styles, from youth guns to safari rifles, mountain rifles and long range "beanfield" guns.

As good as production Remington

rifles are, those produced by the company's Custom Shop are truly outstanding, equal in finish and quality of materials to the finest handcrafted rifles available. Many custom builders use the trusted Model 700 action as the basis for their custom rifles so why shouldn't the parent company design their own upper level, hand assembled rifles?

The Model 700 Alaskan Wilderness Rifle II has all the trappings of a custom gun with the familiar ergonomics Remington aficionados will immediately recognize. The stainless steel action has been "Blue Printed" to insure exact fit with extremely tight tolerances. The trigger is borrowed from the company's 40-X target rifles and is pre-set by the factory to break cleanly at 3 pounds. The metal on the barrel and other exposed metal surfaces (except the bolt) receive the company's patented TriNyte exterior, a weatherproof coating that protects the rifle from the elements while it's protecting you from the bears. The Bell and Carlson stock includes a full length aluminum bedding block to improve accuracy. The barrel is one of the finest on the market: a hammer forged, custom turned pipe that measures 24 inches in standard calibers and 26 inches in magnums.

The AWR II is available in calibers ranging from .25-06 all the way up to the fire-breathing .375 Remington Ultra Magnum, so unlike many of the other guns here the Remington offers a wide array of available calibers to suit your personal needs and preferences. Remington guarantees sub-MOA accuracy in AWRII rifles in .30 caliber and smaller

but chances are that your rifle will be capable of nice little cloverleafs in just about any caliber if you feed it a load that it likes. Think of it as the Model 700 after basic training and finishing school, a level of sophistication that's reflectd in its MSRP ($4139).

Montana Rifle Company Summit Alaskan

Most custom rifle makers build their guns with actions borrowed from existing rifles. Not Kalispel-based Montana Rifle Company, who took two of the most respected actions of all time (Winchester Model 70 and the Mauser 98), combined the best elements from each and engineered their own action that they dubbed the 1999 Action. It is a controlled-round feed action with a full-length claw extractor that guarantees reliable extraction, ejection and chambering and includes a three-position wing safety. Mate this superb action with a precision #5 contour barrel, a crisp trigger that breaks at exactly three pounds and a carbon fiber Lone Wolf stock reinforced with Kevlar and you have the basic blueprint for Montana Rifle Company's Summit Alaskan Rifle.

The Summit Alaskan includes blued iron sights with three express leaves and a barrel band swivel stud. The gun weighs only 8 pounds with a 24-inch barrel (length varies depending upon customer preference) and is ideal for the hunter who wishes to hike far and wide in search of game. Available calibers include the .375 Ruger and .375 H&H

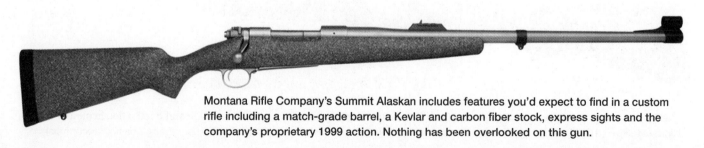

Montana Rifle Company's Summit Alaskan includes features you'd expect to find in a custom rifle including a match-grade barrel, a Kevlar and carbon fiber stock, express sights and the company's proprietary 1999 action. Nothing has been overlooked on this gun.

In today's market of specialized rifles designed for specific purposes and hunting destinations, the "Alaskan" gun has become synonymous with guns that are built to be weatherproof, utterly reliable and as light as possible without producing punishing recoil.

Magnum as well as true heavyweights like the .404 Jeffery, .416 Remington Magnum, .416 Ruger and .458 Lott. The Summit Alaskan is not cheap ($3599), but then again it is a true custom rifle built to customer specs with the best materials available. It is superbly accurate, utterly reliable and engineered to withstand the worst conditions.

Howa 1500 .375 Ruger

Unlike the other rifles mentioned here, the Howa 1500 in .375 Ruger does not carry a moniker that immediately ties it to the Great North. But with the features that Howa built into the rifle it is impossible to imagine that the company envisioned this as anything other than an Alaska gun. Howa started with their proven action, the same one that Weatherby uses in their reliable, accurate Vanguard line, and mated it to a Hogue stock. The barrel is free-floated for accuracy and comes standard with a good trigger, which makes the Howa in .375 Ruger one of the most accurate out-of-the-box guns on the market. It is available in barrel lengths of 20 and 24 inches. The longer barrel is a standard length for most .375 guns, but the 20-inch option indicates that Howa envisioned the 1500 .375 Ruger as a close-range, thick-cover big bore

that will work as well in an alder thicket as it will on the tundra. It is available with either a blued or stainless finish and with an OD green, Sand or black stock. In addition, the Howa is the least expensive Alaska gun listed here and can often be found at a street price of less than $800.

Alaska is a dream destination for many hunters. But nothing can turn your adventure into a nightmare faster than equipment that fails in the brutal conditions encountered in the Far North. Alaska requires a special breed of rifle to withstand the elements and provide protection from the big bears found throughout the state. The good news is that there has never been a better selection of rifles available to the hunter who longs for adventure in the Last Frontier.

Howa's 1500 is perfect for Alaska – it's weatherproof, reliable and chambered for the mighty .375 Ruger. This one is topped with a Hawke Endurance 1.25-4.25x illuminated 30mm scope.

SMITH & WESSON:
American Pioneer

BY STEVE GASH

American gun makers have played an indispensable role in the development of the country. Of course, war and conflict come to mind, but many have made tremendous contributions economically and in the development of new technologies that helped shape a nation.

One such industrial icon is Smith & Wesson. Based in Springfield, Massachusetts, the firm has a fascinating history that dates to its founding in 1852 by Horace Smith and Daniel Baird Wesson.

The start was not easy for the two entrepreneurs. Their dream was to produce a repeating firearm, and they did, in 1857: the Model 1 22 rimfire revolver. Concurrent with the Model 1 was a new self-contained cartridge, one still with us today: the .22 Short. The Model 1 was indeed unique, and offered truly revolutionary new features, most notably a bored-through cylinder (which had been previously patented by Rollin White in 1855).

A most interesting development occurred in 1870-1871. Like most arms manufacturers, S&W courted government contracts and in 1870 forwarded a Model 3 to General Alexander Gorloff, the Russian military attaché residing in Hartford, Connecticut, for testing. In various increments, Russia ultimately ordered a total of about 150,000 guns. The Russian Model 3 was similar to the American Model 3, except for the car-

Smith & Wesson's Springfield, Massachusetts, factory has been the company's headquarters for more than 150 years. It houses a treasure trove of history and innovation in gun making.

The portraits of Founders Horace Smith and Daniel Baird Wesson stand watch in the main lobby, a fitting testament to two great pioneers.

Security at the S&W plant was airtight. Everyone entering or leaving the facility went through a thorough yet speedy and friendly security system that was state of the art.

A brown bear taken, appropriately enough, with a new Smith & Wesson "X-Frame" revolver in the ponderous .500 S&W Magnum that launches bullets as heavy as 500 grains at velocities of 1,350 fps. Serious power for serious game. One shot was all it took.

These tables hold some the numerous awards received by Smith & Wesson for its products from various industry groups, along with representatives of some of the winning handguns under glass below.

tridge. Based on changes requested by the Russian government, the .44 Russian cartridge was born.

Here's the interesting part: Legend has it that S&W at the time did not have the capital for the required addition of machinery. But Russian Grand Duke Alexis wanted his pistols, so he forwarded an "advance" in the form of a chest of gold! And he got his pistols.

On December 6, 1871, Alexis visited the S&W factory and was presented with a fully engraved, pearl-grip Model 3 in a presentation case. The Grand Duke later toured the American frontier and carried this Model 3 on a buffalo hunt with "Buffalo Bill" Cody.

The Russian contract was an important milestone for S&W. It reestablished S&W financially, cemented its reputation as a first-rate firearm manufacturer, and led to other government contracts from other nations.

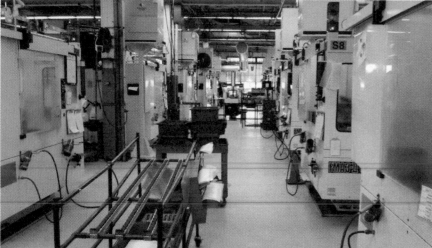

Director of Marketing Services Paul Pluff gave us a grand tour of the factory, and a fascinating review of company history. Here he describes the progression of machining steps in the production of a finished pistol slide.

Rows and rows of sophisticated, computer-controlled machines hummed a tune as they churned out precision parts for a variety of firearms.

During World War II, S&W was essential to the U.S. war effort, and its facilities were pretty much self-sufficient; it even had its own power plant. Most production operations were in the lower reaches of the plant as much as possible, and it is said that S&W was a prime target should the enemy ever attack the mainland.

It's not often that one gets to experience such a slice of firearms history, but I recently did. On a brisk November day,

I was invited to tour the Springfield, Massachusetts, factory. It was a fascinating glimpse back into history and a titillating view into the future. Our tour guide was the affable Paul Pluff, whose official title is "Director of Marketing Services," but that is so inadequate. He knows S&W inside and out, and it is rumored that Paul has worked every job in the factory. I can believe it, because as I walked and gawked, not only did everyone we met know Paul, he knew them, by name!

The modern-day S&W plant as we know it today was in large part the result of then-president Carl R. Hellstrom, who in 1946 convinced the Smith and Wesson families to expand. Smith & Wesson has expanded and modernized the Springfield facility several times in its 159-year history, and the scope and breadth of the Smith & Wesson factory is simply mind-boggling. The plant has more CNC machines than any other American company. Note that I did not say "any other American firearms company." In fact, as we toured the facilities, I saw a huge addition being readied for the installation of more CNC machines.

Today, S&W has over 1,500 employees at three facilities. In addition to the main plant and Shooting Sports Center in Springfield, they have a factory in Houlton, Maine. In a March 18, 2009, press release, S&W proudly reported that S&W had made its 6 millionth pair

The numerous computer keyboards showed the high-tech nature of gunmaking today. S&W craftsmen can input an established series of pre-programmed commands, and switch the tool from making one part to another in a matter of minutes.

Here are some of the many highly specialized cutting tools used by S&W that are made in-house.

This display case contains examples of the myriad small parts fabricated as part of the manufacturing process.

CNC machines are the wave of the future, and here a large section of the plant is readied to make way for more of these high-tech devices.

Examples of the progression from round bar stock to formed frame, plus samples of various small forged parts.

of handcuffs at Houlton. This plant also makes the Walther PPK of James Bond fame. The recently acquired Thompson-Center Arms plant in Rochester, New Hampshire, has about 350 employees and concentrates on rifle barrels, especially for S&W's new line of ARs. During 2011, T/C's production will be moved to S&W's main plant in Springfield. Regarding the move, Paul Puff stated that it is "designed to streamline our firearms manufacturing processes and improve our margins."

Most S&W employees have long histories with the company. The average tenure in 2009 was 28 years. Paul Pluff, for example, has been with the company 27 years.

Before we get to details of the tour, I must tell you about plant security. Like everything else at S&W, it was top drawer and airtight. Everyone entering or leaving the plant goes through a

metal detector, even if you left for lunch. Sharp-eyed armed guards carefully scrutinized everyone and everything, and key cards were required to move from one secure area to another. You couldn't boost so much as a side-plate screw out of that place. But due to their efficiency, this took only a couple of minutes. (TSA should take lessons from them.)

After we cleared security, we wound our way to the main lobby of the beauti-

ful edifice, where a huge brown bear (appropriately) stands guard. It was taken with a .500 S&W Magnum handgun; with one shot, of course. In a tastefully appointed conference room, Paul gave an overview of the company's history and the overall-manufacturing layout. Many impressive innovations stood out, and the triadic goals of modernization, efficiency, and innovation were paramount. Paul summed it up this way: "At Smith &

This monstrous Ajax forge was recently installed. This behemoth exerts 1,600 tons of force with each whack in the forging of revolver frames.

A forged revolver frame, ready for machining.

This computer-controlled instrument performs a variety of QA checks on barrels as they pass through the manufacturing process.

Parts polishing. Little ceramic cones, bathed with a special polishing compound, vibrate incessantly as small parts turn over and over.

This precision piece of automated hardware is doing multiple checks on pistol barrels.

Polished cylinders, ready for final fitting of the extractor star, and various other parts. These 7-shot cylinders are destined for the Model 686 Plus L-Frame .357 Magnum revolver.

Wesson, New World technology meets Old World craftsmanship."

One of the more impressive production goals was S&W's focus on eliminating what is called "tolerance stacking" in parts manufacturing. In the early days, a revolver cylinder, for example, might be tooled on as many as 12 different machines in its construction. Let's say that each machine may have a very acceptable tolerance of ±.0005 inch. But what if each machine had that same tolerance? By the time it exits the last tool, the total variance could be clearly excessive, and that part would have to be rejected.

Today, in S&W's modern CNC facility, cylinders are made on two robotic machines that produce a level of precision much higher than in the "good old days." This results in a much more uniform part that needs very little fitting. This makes for a much more better gun, and there are fewer rejected parts.

Revolvers, semi-automatic pistols, and AR-style rifles are made in the plant, and each has its own path to excellence. Most production progresses in three-stages: forging, machining, and

For all the sophisticated tools in the S&W plant, there is still no way to replace the experienced hands of skilled craftsmen. This gentleman is fitting a rear sight.

S&W's Master Engraver painstakingly embellishes a revolver. To the novice, cutting these tiny, precise lines by hand appears terrifying, but this artisan makes it look easy.

The Model 38 "Bodyguard" was introduced in 1955, and was the first aluminum-frame "Airweight" developed by S&W. These Model 638 revolvers were introduced in 2010, and represent the latest in the series. The one of the left sports a 2½-inch barrel, a first for the .38 Special for S&W. Both are rated for modern-day +P .38 Special ammunition.

A revolver frame in waiting, with gold wire ready for inlaying.

heat-treating. Machining itself is subdivided into what S&W calls the "A," "B," and "C" cuts to produce a finished frame, and this varies by frame size.

Revolver frames are forged – not cast – on a huge machine that looks like a gigantic reloading press that exerts 1,600 tons of pressure at temperatures of about 640° to 720° F, and two blows from the forge take only about 11 or 12 seconds. The parts are then heat-treated, which hardens the metal from the inside out, and some are annealed so that they're easier to machine. The semi-finished pieces go to various precise multi-head CNC lathes that zip the part from rough chunk of metal to a precise part, in just a few minutes. The robotic movements are eerily otherworldly to watch.

The heat-treating operation is very impressive. Parts on special racks progress through a long vat of a "salt bath" that must be maintained at a constant temperature of 1000° to 1600° F, so it's not practical to just shut this operation down when it's not in use. The reagents would set up like concrete, clog the system beyond usefulness, and they'd literally have to start over, so they keep it going 24/7. Here's an interesting sidelight: S&W is so adept at heat-treating that they custom treat parts for many other companies.

Slides and frames for semi-auto pistols go through several initial-machining

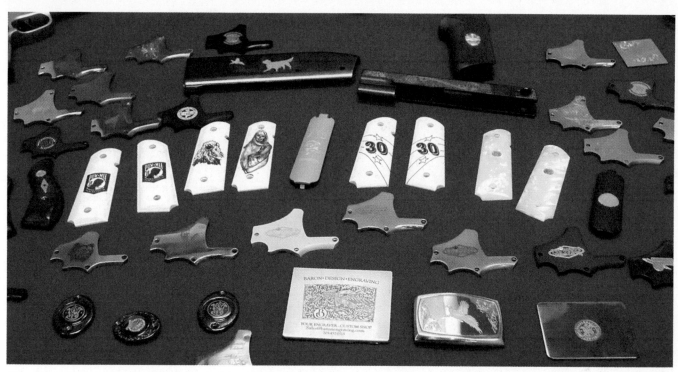

Examples of the engraving, inlaying, and scrimshaw work done at the custom shop. If you want it, and can pay for it, it shall be yours.

steps to emerge looking a lot like a part, but with blobs of metal sticking out here and there. One is reminded that John M. Browning saw a gun part "inside" a lump of steel. Just "file away everything that isn't part," he said. S&W's modern processes essentially do just that, but at a very rapid pace and at an extremely high level of precision. Whereas in the past, a side may have progressed to six or seven machines, now it's finished on just one; that tolerance stacking thing again. The cutters even have computer chips in them that "tell" the next station what has been done.

S&W is very environmentally conscious, and just invested an obscene amount of money on a state-of-the-art environmental control system. Everything reusable – metal cuttings, oils, cardboard, etc. – is recycled.

At work stations all over the plant, skilled craftsmen and women sat at their tidy stations, patiently doing the hand fitting for which S&W firearms are famous. Computer screen and keyboards grace most areas and show in real time what is about to happen to a part. There appears to be no rush, just an efficient progression from sub-assemblies to finished products. Here are a couple of examples. I watched as a worker cut the forcing cones on 2-inch barrels destined for .38 revolvers on what looked like a

The best of the best: An elaborately engraved and gold-filled N-Frame Model 29 .44 Magnum, behind glass, of course. Elmer Keith would approve.

high-tech, precision drill press, but it was guided by skilled and experienced hands. Before a barrel left his tutelage, a gauge was placed in the cone to ensure that it met specs. At another post, sights were being carefully hand-fitted on a series of N-frames. The fellow doing this was having fun, and it showed.

A test range is close at hand, and every gun gets its turn, and must muster out with flying colors. (Yes, some S&W folks get paid to shoot!)

S&W never rests on its laurels, it seems. The burgeoning demand for AR-style guns led S&W into that market, and was the prime reason for the acquisition of Thompson-Center Arms. It was simple synergism: S&W needed a supply of precision rifle barrels, and T/C already had the expertise and equipment and was well known for superb barrels on its own rifle line. Back in the day, the production of a rifle barrel might require as many as 85 operations. Today, it's all

A short distance from the factory is the Smith & Wesson retail store and shooting center. Here the shooter can pick from an impressive inventory of S&W products, as well as many accessories and other merchandise to enhance their shooting.

done on one machine, except for rifling, and Electric Discharge Machines (EDM) subsequently do this. This results in rifle barrels of extreme uniformity and great accuracy.

The upper and lower AR receivers are forged by S&W in Springfield, where final assembly and testing occurs. All S&W centerfire ARs are currently chambered to 5.56mm, but other calibers, such as 6.8mm SPC, may be added as soon as S&W can catch up with orders. S&W ARs have been torture-tested in excess of 17,000 rounds with no problems.

A hot new item in the S&W's line is the new AR in .22 Long Rifle. All controls are in the same place and operate just like those on centerfire ARs, so it's perfect for plinking or training purposes. We saw rack after rack of the .22s boxed up and ready to go. At a MSRP of under $500, it's been a huge hit. The uppers and lowers of the .22 ARs are polymer, however, and the pin placements are intentionally different, so you can't swap out with a centerfire upper.

S&W is well known for its beautiful custom guns, and it was a real treat as we were ushered into the enclave of the custom shop. Several customer guns were in various states of engraving and inlaying. Gold wire dangled from a gun barrel waiting to be carefully inlaid into grooves and markings. S&W's Master

S&W's X-Frame revolver in .500 S&W Magnum has recently been offered in a "bear stopper" model with a short barrel. While light and handy to carry, with factory loads, it was a handful, but it shot very well. Bears beware!

Engraver graciously interrupted his tedious work to give us the lowdown on the process. It takes about three weeks to complete an engraving project, and he often uses a signature, pattern or logo supplied by the customer, so that result is truly the reflection of the owner's taste and desire. It is reflective of this delicate job to note that he makes all of his own tooling.

It is easy to get lost in the glitz and hoopla of the of the here and now, but as we enter the 21st century, the fundamental legacy of Horace Smith and Daniel B. Wesson seems as strong now as ever. Smith & Wesson continues to introduce new and innovative products that entice the gun-buying public, as it has for over a century and a half.

THE KAUTZKY DYNASTY

Five generations of this gunsmithing and trapshooting family have left their mark on the shotgunning community.

BY JOHN E. KAUTZKY

I t was in the year 1908, the year Henry Ford's historic Model T Ford was introduced to the American public, that a single trigger system for double barrel shotguns became available to trapshooters around the world. It was invented by my grandfather, Joseph Kautzky.

The Kautzky Single Trigger was much more simple and satisfactory than its one and only competitor, a design manufactured by the Hunter Arms Company that was at that time available only on L.C. Smith shotguns. Joseph Kautzky, Sr., built his single trigger into more than 600 shotguns that were shipped to him from as far away as Australia and the Philippines.

In its day, the Kautzky Single Trigger was sought out by prominent sportsmen throughout the United States. One of his best customers was the world-famous bandmaster leader and march composer, John Philip Sousa. Sousa, head of the American Amateur Trapshooting Association and a top-rated shooter, had Joseph Kautzky repair and customize his own personal collection of shotguns, and many were fitted with the Kautzky Single Trigger.

In the year 1914, Joseph Kautzky's single trigger patent was sold to the Ansley H. Fox Gun Company of Germantown, Pennsylvania. The sale was signed and completed after grandfather Kautzky Sr. spent several months at the Ansley H. Fox Gun Factory supervising and training gun makers on how to build his single trigger device.

A Kautzky family photograph showing Joseph Kautzky, Sr.'s solid gold watch fob bars and numerous trophies that he won during his participation in trapshooting competition throughout the United States during the 1920s and 1930s.

The Kautzky Ancestry

According to our earliest family records, our traditional line of family history takes place in Bohemia (now part of the Czech Republic), near the village of Ritschka, around the year 1800. A young peasant by the name of Adalbert Kautzky was employed as a *Leibjager*, or hunting companion, to the Count and Countess Kilowrat of Reichenau. Hunting rights in those days were reserved of only those of the nobility, the royalty, and the rich.

As Adalbert Kautzky's position as a hunting companion to the famous Count required expert marksmanship, his duties kept him at the side of he Count during his hunting days, protecting the Count from danger in the event that the Count's own bullet failed to hit the mark. Adalbert was not only an expert marksman but also a skilled mechanic in the manufacture of shotguns and rifles. Consequently he was able to keep the Count's personal hunting equipment in perfect shooting condition for his hunting trips over his vast estate consisting of thousands of acres of rich farmland surrounded by countless square miles of towering pine forests.

Adalbert became the father of four sons who mastered their father's gunsmithing skills. Our family records show that Adalbert Kautzky was the great-grandfather of Joseph Kautzky, Sr., a fourth-generation gunsmith who was born in Rokitnitz, Austria, in 1862. Joseph, Sr., received from his father special tutelage in this most difficult art of engraving and other advanced skills of the gun maker's art. At the age of thirteen, Joseph Sr.'s father placed him in a large gunmaking establishment in Vienna, where he mastered his craft. Before completing his apprenticeship at the Vienna school, each student was required to build a "gun masterpiece." The masterful firearms that Joseph Sr. designed became the property of the school as payment for his tuition. Many of these firearms made by students were sold to Emperor Franz Joseph of Austria.

After completing his apprenticeship, Joseph Kautzky, Sr., returned to his home in Rokitnitz and there he assumed the responsibility of the operation of his father's gun shop, and later married. In Rokitnitz, three of his five children were born: my two aunts, Anna and Pauline Kautzky, and my father's brother Joseph Kautzky Jr. (my uncle), also known as Joe Jr.

Joseph Kautzky's workmanship is apparent in this 16-gauge hammer gun. The shotgun was built in 1897 using hand tools only. Note the graceful sideplate and tapered action. A 12-gauge hammerless double was also made during this period but has never been located.

The Kautzky Family Moves to America

It was now the year 1893. Joe Sr.' s two sisters and three brothers had already moved to America and settled in Des Moines, Iowa. The vision of hunting in the young America of the late nineteenth century with complete freedom and without the need for securing permission from the local duke, baron, or *Burgomeister* played an important part in the 31-year-old Kautzky, Sr.'s decision to emigrate from his native Austria. After arriving in America, Joe Sr. was united with his relatives in the modest town of Perry, Iowa, located a few miles outside Des Moines. With the help of his close friends, relatives, and family, Joseph began to establish himself in a small storefront gun repair shop and began to acquire a modest but promising gunsmithing trade.

One day Joseph selected one of his Damascus steel barrel blanks, originally brought across from the Atlantic Ocean, and began drawing plans for his first American gunmaking effort. His first 16-gauge hammer double shotgun was completed in 1895 and marked with the engraved letters "J KAUTZKY" and "PERRY IA" on the lockplates.

It was during the year 1897 when a group of professional businessmen from Fort Dodge, Iowa (about 100 miles north of Perry) came to Grandfather Kautzky's gun shop and persuaded him to move to Fort Dodge as this location would offer him and his two sons, Rudy and Joe, Jr.,

a greater opportunity to practice their gunsmith profession.

My Uncle Joe, Jr., started to learn gun repair work from his father at about 14 years of age. In 1912 my father, Rudy,

Joseph Kautzky Sr. is pictured here with one of his 16-gauge handmade shotguns with the famous 1910 Kautzky Single Trigger. Marie Kautzky Grant holds her Parker 12 gauge shotgun used in trapshooting competition.

THE KAUTZKY DYNASTY: FIVE GENERATIONS OF GUNSMITHING AND TRAPSHOOTING

continued to study and also mastered the gunsmith profession by age 17. Gradually, through the years, our Kautzky family gun shop became equipped with the very latest up-to-date electrical equipment, replacing the handmade tools that were brought across the Atlantic Ocean by grandfather Kautzky, Sr. Both Rudy and Joe, Jr., could repair shotguns and rifles along with other small firearms using an electric lathe, electric drill press, and with modem arc welding, brazing and grinding equipment.

Our Kautzky family sporting goods store now became known throughout the Fort Dodge, Iowa, community. The shop's motto stated: KAUTZKY SPORT-ING GOODS STORE – WHERE SPORTS-MEN SERVE SPORTSMEN and carried all state-of-the-art firearms, fishing tackle and name-brand athletic goods. In the 1930s, the Kautzky shop gained im-mortality of a quite different sort when Joseph, Sr., hired a Kansan named Newel Daniels to produce a wooden fishing lure that Daniels had designed. Known as the Kautzky Lazy Ike, it became one of the most well-known lures in the world. It's still being made today, in an updated plastic version.

In 1937 hundreds of spectators began arriving, crowding into our Fort Dodge gun club grounds, from all comers of he state and surrounding Great Plains, to witness a celebration birthday trapshoot honoring Joseph Kautzky Sr. Among the positioned trapshooters, lined up at their respective firing post in five-man squads were Joseph Kautzky, Sr.'s two sons, Rudy and Joe Jr. Standing alongside her father, waiting to give the command, "Pull!" was Marie Kautzky Grant (my aunt), Joseph Kautzky's famous trapshooting daughter, who had already achieved State and National trapshooting honors.

Joe, Sr. that day out-shot his two younger sons and 96 other trapshooters. The 75- year-old Austrian-born gun-smith-trapshooter stood near the top among 100 contestants, bringing down 147 targets out of 150, a truly remarkable score for a man of his years. Marie Kautzky had done even better, breaking 148 targets out of a possible 150.

It was soon after that memorable 1937 birthday-trapshoot given in his honor that Joseph Sr.'s health forced him to give up his gun bench. On August 21, 1938, he died of cancer at the age of 76.

Shrouded in an age-old coating of rust, or resting under a sheet of decades of dirt and debris, perhaps in your own

This photograph of Joseph Kautzky's famous trapshooting daughter Marie was taken in the family's shop in Fort Dodge, Iowa, during the late 1900s. Marie was 27 years old at the time.

This photograph was taken during the early 1950's inside our Kautzky family sporting goods store. The motto WHERE SPORTSMEN SERVE SPORTSMEN became somewhat of a tradition among the farmers and sportsmen of Fort Dodge and surrounding towns, who would bring their firearms to Rudy and Joe Jr. for professional alteration and repair during the deer, duck, and pheasant seasons.

attic, there, even today, may reside an old 16-gauge shotgun marked "J. KAUTZKY" and "PERRY IA" – a hallmark signifying one of American gunmaking's brightest lights. Should you discover that old double, study it as you ever-so-carefully cradle it in your hands. You'll be holding a masterpiece.

66TH EDITION, 2012 ◆ **33**

ME & MY DAD & GUN DIGEST

*We've traveled a long way together over the last half century.
It's been a great journey.*

BY ANDY EWERT

Since I was a little boy, my father and I shared a love of firearms. Fifty years have passed. In that time, we've journeyed through shooting, reloading, hunting, attending gun shows, perusing gun shops, and home gunsmithing, all the while buying, trading, and (very rarely) selling firearms. In addition, we spent thousands of hours reading about guns and engaging in serious – occasionally heated – dialog on the merits of a particular handgun, rifle, or shotgun over another.

Over that half century, one publication faithfully served as our compass to the firearms world. Through *Gun Digest*, we learned about firearms and the joys of owning and shooting them. While illness and age have taken away dad's ability to actively participate, we still share our passion through thoughtful discussions at his Milwaukee, Wisconsin, home. A copy of *Gun Digest* is always within arm's reach of his easy chair. We never lack for meaningful conversation.

The first *Gun Digest* I remember was the1963 issue. Every Christmas season, dad and I would compete to determine who would give the year's issue to the other. As we shared the same home, it really didn't matter. Regardless of who the recipient was, I selfishly snatched the gift and retreated to a quiet place to began reading. My parents had to pull me away so we could complete our holiday gift-giving ritual. Always, the bulk of my Christmas day was spent in deep study, taking in the wisdom of legendary Elmer Keith, Jack O'Connor, Charles Askins, and the immortal *Gun Digest* Editor John Amber, among many other fine authors.

Though I was too young to own a firearm, dad took me along to his range sessions and gradually introduced me to the art of informal pistol shooting. He was a patient and thorough teacher. Under his tutelage, I mastered firearms safety, the two-handed hold, sighting, breath control, and trigger release with a Smith & Wesson K-38. Back then, my father was a diehard revolver man. In time, I could reliably hit a quart-size tomato can at 25 paces with that classic wheelgun, stoked with full-wadcutter target loads. The K-38's moderate weight, superb balance, and light recoil were well suited to my physical capabilities. How I would love to have that sixgun today.

One day, a long box unexpectedly arrived at the house. It was a gift to me on my 12th birthday from my uncle Dick who, at the time, was working in Europe for the U.S. government. The box contained my first firearm, a Marlin 39A .22 caliber lever action rifle, purchased new from a military PX somewhere in the former West Germany. I still have it. Dad enhanced my prized possession with a low-power Leupold scope. No X-ring or tin can within 75 yards was safe from that tack driver. Accuracy was routine to the point of monotony.

In addition to shooting, I began accompanying my father on periodic visits to gun shops and gun shows. What a treat they were. Firearms of every conceivable kind. Derringers, pocket autos, snubnose revolvers, hand cannons, machine guns, double barrel shotguns and rifles, and antique specimens of every configuration.

I watched and listened, soaking up knowledge like a sponge. There were experts, professed experts, pontificators, and the occasional con man, all of whom

Author Ewert and his father examine one of their favorite 20th-century military bolt-action rifles: the Springfield 1903-A1 .30-06. Their half century firearms journey, guided in no small part by *Gun Digest*, included shooting, reloading, hunting, attending gun shows, haunting gun shops, and home gunsmithing, all the while buying, trading, and *(very rarely)* selling firearms.

who loved an attentive audience. Dad cautioned me not to believe everything I heard or saw. How right he was. I discovered there was often a self-serving motive behind glowing endorsements; that some "experts" really didn't know what they were talking about; and that a gun could be faked with replacement parts, fraudulent markings, and false claims. Dad was a former car salesman and knew the disreputable tricks employed by a few to separate folks from their money. And how he could wheel-and-deal for a gun! I gained an education right quick.

Also during those visits, I met some of the most knowledgeable, kind, and patient firearms authorities on this earth. I can't say enough good things about those men who took the time to share their wisdom and time with a youngster eager to learn. Several lifelong friendships were established. One of my fondest memories is of a gentleman at a show who, when seeing me admire his German P08 9 mm Luger, took the pistol from its display case and placed it smack

in my hand. "What do you think of that, son?" I remember the distinctive feel of that Teutonic masterpiece to this day.

When I reached my early teens, dad determined that I was old enough to hunt. Armed with my mother's svelte 16-gauge Winchester Model 12 pump shotgun, dad with its 12-gauge counterpart, we bagged our share of ducks, Canadian geese, pheasants, and the occasional unlucky woodcock. I liked that Model 12 but longed for a shotgun of my own.

Gun Digest was there to guide me to my first firearm purchase. An article by Francis Sell extolling the virtues of the 20-gauge magnum caught my eye. I frugally saved money from my first summer job and, with horse-trading assistance from dad, purchased a new FN Belgium Browning Auto-5 semi-automatic shotgun in, yes, the 20-gauge magnum – at a discount off list price to boot. With its slender, 28-inch ribbed barrel, precise handling and handsome French walnut stock, that fine scattergun harvested waterfowl and upland game aplenty,

mostly with a 1-1/4 oz. load of #6 lead shot. It held its own on the trap range, too. Today, the Auto-5 bears scars from four decades of field use, but its pedigree still shines bright, as it did the first day out of the box.

By my 16th birthday, my father had enough faith to let me purchase my first handgun: a 6-1/2-inch Smith & Wesson Highway Patrolman .357 Magnum. We quickly discovered factory .357 ammunition was the wealthy man's fodder. To conserve our limited finances, dad invested in a Lyman 310 "nutcracker" handheld reloading tool. In no time, we were burning through Hercules 2400 powder to our heart's content, leading the barrel of that .357 something fierce with economical cast lead bullets.

As our finances improved, we pooled our cash and bought an RCBS A3 reloading press along with suitable .38 Special/.357 Magnum dies. We still have that stalwart A3, along with more than 20 sets of reloading dies, ranging from .223 Remington to .458 Winchester Mag-

Gun Digest played a significant role in defining the author and his father's somewhat eclectic taste in long guns. A small cross section of their 50-year accumulation includes (top to bottom) the author's first firearm, a Marlin 39A .22 Long Rifle; German manufacture Model 1909 Argentine Mauser 7.65mm Mauser; CZ 550 Safari Magnum in .458 Winchester Magnum; and Colt HBAR .223 Remington.

Gun Digest was with us throughout this heyday. Every Christmas, it was still a test of wills to determine who was going to give "the book" to whom. My grandmother entered the fray, complicating matters no end. But every Christmas day, no matter the intended recipient, I ended up with the *Gun Digest*, in a quiet corner, deep in study, oblivious to the surrounding holiday festivities. Dad never voiced a word of complaint.

The next phase of our firearms odyssey brought us to the heart of Mother Nature. Father and I took up deer hunting, albeit late in life: he at age 51 and I 25 years behind. Our venture into big game hunting began the year Remington introduced its 700 Classic bolt-action rifle series. I snagged a very early issue .30-06 and swapped it a few years later to dad for his 7mm Mauser Classic. In an annual ritual that's holy in Wisconsin (and other states), every November we took to the North Woods to harvest a respectable number of Wisconsin whitetails with those magnificent rifles. We still have our 700 Classics, along with some impressive antler sets and a lifetime's worth of priceless memories.

Our subsequent firearms foray took a wholly unexpected turn. Under the influence of *Gun Digest*, over the next decade we plunged into military surplus small arms in a big way. Sparked by an article on the Mauser Model 1898 by Jim Thompson, we acquired German-made 98s in 8mm, 7mm, and 7.65mm caliber; .303 British Enfields; U.S. 1903-A1 and -A3 .30-06 Springfields; a remarkably advanced, high-quality, and accurate 7.7 mm Japanese Type 99 Arisaka; and an equally impressive .6.5 mm Model 1938 Swedish Mauser, along with the appropriate reloading dies and supplies to keep us in the ammo until our obsession ran its course. Eventually it did, after a lot of fun. In a final flourish, we added a Colt HBAR .223 and Springfield Armory M14 to our trove.

During our military surplus binge, dad and I didn't forsake handguns. We snapped up martial-issue Colt 1911-A1s and their Argentine offspring and clones; a .45 ACP-converted English Webley No. 1 Mark VI; a 9mm Parabellum Spanish Astra 600; a handy East German 1960s-vintage 9X18 mm Makarov; and a prime World War II issue German Walther P-38 9mm. What a wonderful, eclectic crop of handguns they are.

With the new millennium, father and I navigated our hobby through the digital age, seeking out guns, ammo, accesso-

num. Lord knows how many thousands of rounds passed through that press.

Always thinking ahead, dad built a king-sized, rock-solid reloading bench, designed to accommodate the A3, a top-grade reloading scale, a couple of powder throwers, a lead pot, a cast-bullet sizer, and other cost- and time-saving accessories acquired over the years. I can't begin to count the hours we spent together in the basement loading cases, casting bullets, solving problems, and talking guns.

Before our reloading "den" was complete, dad wisely added two sizeable bookshelves to safeguard an ever-growing reference library of *Gun Digests* and assorted firearms books and magazines. It was a good thing he did. A basement

flood during the 1980s took its toll on the low-lying contents. Fortunately, our prized possessions were spared.

Handguns were our first love and, over the decades, we bought and traded dozens of revolvers and later semi-autos at a rate of at least one a year. There were classic Colts, Smith & Wessons, and Rugers, along with a smattering of European makes. Exceptional specimens that stand out in my mind were a slick 4-inch S&W Model 19 Combat Magnum .357 Magnum (sadly traded away), a nickeled 70 Series Colt .45 auto, and dad's beloved .44 Special Colt New Service revolver that took almost three decades to secure. An ivory-stocked .45 Colt Single Action Army "Peacemaker" was the icing on our cake.

Early in their handgunning experience, the author and his father discovered that reloading saved money and boosted accuracy. Like many shooters before them, they began humbly with a Lyman 310 reloading tool, later graduating to more sophisticated gear. Home-rolled .44 loads served this 5-inch Smith & Wesson Model 29 very well.

Whetted by articles in *Gun Digest*, author and his father developed an appreciation of vintage Colt handguns produced during the first half of the 20th Century. Their thoroughbreds include (top to bottom): .44 Special New Service; pre-WWII Argentine military-contract 1911-A1 .45 ACP; and a 1933-vintage Colt Woodsman .22 Long Rifle. Fit and finish of this trio are superb, as is their performance on the range.

ries, literature, reloading supplies, and all sorts of useful information on the Internet. Utilizing *Gun Digest's* Web Directory *[Editor's note: Compiled by our esteemed friend Holt Bodinson – DMS]*, we saved time, money, and gasoline, not to mention

wear and tear on our automobiles, by conducting many of our transactions behind a computer screen. A good chunk of the time saved was spent at the range or in the field, a very satisfactory return on our online investment.

Then, in a symbolic return-to-the-roots of handgunning twist, dad and I took up cap and ball shooting with a pair of "second-generation" Colt percussion revolvers: a .36 caliber 1851 Navy and a .44 caliber 1860 Army. There were adventures and misadventures, probably more of the latter. Yes, *Gun Digest* was there too. Articles by Rick Hacker, R.C. House, and Phil Spangenberger, along with the publication's black powder section, provided badly needed guidance as we struggled to master the most difficult phase of our firearms experience. Eventually we did, but it was a long, trying journey. That proved to be our last hurrah.

This story wouldn't be complete without a mention of my father's remarkable gunsmithing, woodworking, and leather-crafting skills that added a special dimension to our hobby. Whether it was crafting a replacement firing pin "from the file" for a 70-year-old Colt sixgun, mounting rifle scopes properly the first time, building a beautiful cherry wood stock from scratch for a Stevens Favorite .22 rife, or carving, stitching, and finishing a handsome, historically correct replica of an 19th-Century British revolver holster, dad could do it all. His talents were truly remarkable.

As the cliché goes, all good things come to an end. Dad became ill and we became estranged from the new-age firearms world awash in synthetic materials, exotic metals, high-capacity firepower, and ballistics that defy reason. Admittedly, father and I are throwbacks, defenders of the proven and past, bearers of knowledge gained by doing in a society that increasingly values the new and novelty. Give us richly blued steel, fine wood, and one well-placed shot. Regretfully, we neglected an issue or two of *Gun Digest* in silent protest. *[Shame on you! –DMS]* But as lifelong friends, we resolved our differences and are together again.

No matter what the future holds, dad and I agree that ours was a wonderful half-century, father-and-son experience. It was capped off with my first published article in *Gun Digest*, the 2010 edition, on oddball military-surplus handguns. I remember with pride personally delivering dad's complimentary copy as he rested in his chair. His eyes lit up when I placed it in his hands, opened to the appropriate page. This was one time he wouldn't have to wait for Christmas day or for me to surrender "The World's Greatest Gun Book" to its rightful owner.

CUSTOM & ENGRAVED GUNS

A close-up look at the guns we never tire of dreaming about.

BY **THOMAS TURPIN**

A lovely matched set of Browning Citori O/U shotguns custom stocked for the client by **Al Lind.** They are a matched set rather than a matched pair as one gun is a 12 bore, and the other a 20 bore. The client provided the beautiful wood, two sticks of Iranian grown thin-shelled walnut. Al told me that the biggest challenge was doing the skeleton butt-plates on these through-bolt stoked guns. The matching skeleton grip caps were not nearly as difficult.

Photo by Tom Alexander

Al Lind

Each year, members of the American Custom Gunmakers Guild (ACGG) and the Firearms Engravers Guild of America (FEGA) build a special firearm that serves as the Raffle Rifle for the year. The team chosen to craft the project for a given year begins several years prior to the year it is offered as the raffle prize. This exquisite double rifle is #26 in the series and will be presented to the holder of the winning raffle ticket in June 2011. Each ticket costs $20 and a maximum of 4000 tickets will be sold.

For this project, the team of **Tony Fleming**, **Glenn Morovits**, and **Larry Peters** comprised the project team. They decided to craft a working .470 Nitro Express double rifle that would be right at home on an African safari. The metal components were procured from

Butch Searcy, raw from the factory. Metalsmith Tony Fleming converted this raw metal into a fine action, modeled after an early 20th century boxlock express rifle. Peters regulated the twin barrels and the gun delivers 2-3/4-inch groups at 100 yards – superb accuracy for a double rifle.

Stockmaker Glenn Morovits crafted the stock from a super stick of Turkish walnut, chosen for its dark color and tight, dense grain. Finally, Larry Peters added the exquisite English style scroll engraving in keeping with the tradition of double rifles. Gold inlay was added only at the safety. He modeled the engraving after a Joseph Lang & Son .577 BPE rifle, a gift to an Indian Prince in 1898.

Photos by Tom Alexander

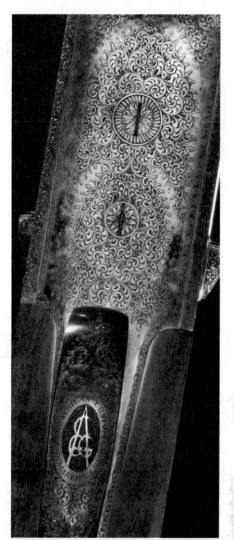

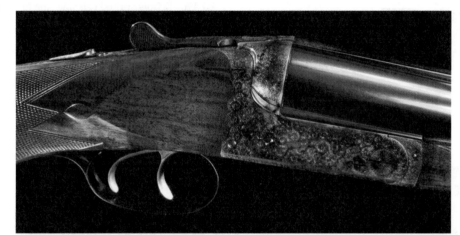

Glenn Morovits • Larry Peters • Tony Fleming

D'Arcy Echols

This .264 Winchester Magnum rifle features the only Monte Carlo styled stock that gunmaker **D'Arcy Echols** has ever built. All the other stocks that he has crafted have been straight combed and purely classic in design. The client for this rifle is rather small in stature and the Monte Carlo comb was necessary for him to properly use the scope. The rifle features a Model 70 action, Krieger barrel, Echols custom mounts and scope rings, and one of the last sets of bottom metal that Tom Burgess turned out before he passed. All other work on this rifle was accomplished in the Echols shop. Photo courtesy of D'Arcy Echols

D'Arcy Echols crafted this fine rifle in 1987. He started with a Sako L-79 action that was made for Browning Safari rifles. As such, it does not have the normal Sako dovetail scope-mounting system on the bridges of the action. Echols fitted a Steve Wikert barrel (Fred Wells was barrelmaker at the time) and chambered it for the 308 cartridge. He fitted Blackburn bottom metal to the action. He crafted the stock from a genuine stick of Thessier French walnut and fitted a Biesen trap buttplate to hold all the sight hardware. Photo courtesy of D'Arcy Echols

D'Arcy Echols

Steve Hughes began this project with a **Martin Hagn** single shot action and an octagon barrel with full integral rib. **Ralph Martini** did the barrel work. Hughes reshaped the action and lever to contours he preferred. He then milled bases for Talley rings into the quarter-rib on the barrel. The rifle is chambered for the .280 Remington cartridge. Steven stocked the rifle with an excellent stick of English walnut. He checkered the stock in a point pattern, 25 LPI, with a mullered border and fitted a steel buttplate. The rifle remains in the white awaiting the client's decision on engraving.

Photo by Steven Dodd Hughes

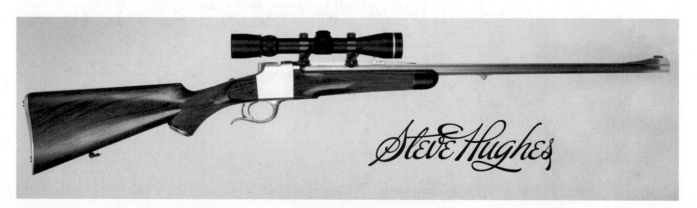

Steve Hughes

Starting with an original 1885 Winchester Low Wall action, Gunmaker **John Mercer** fitted a Green Mountain barrel and chambered it for the .22 Long Rifle rimfire cartridge. Mercer then designed a stock for scope use and crafted the stock in a stick of Circassian walnut from **Cecil Fredi**. He checkered it in a point pattern with mullered border, 24 LPI. He also fitted a Lyman tang peep sight; along with the Lyman Small Game 6X period styled scope.

Photo courtesy of John Mercer

This Model 42 Winchester skeet gun has been completely restored to new condition, mostly following the original Winchester styling. **Paul Lindke** stocked the little pump in a super stick of American black walnut. He shaped the stock following the lines of the original deluxe style grip, and fitted a steel grip cap. He checkered the stock, using the original Winchester Pattern "A" carving, at 24 lines per inch. **Franz Marktl** engraved the gun using a lovely scroll pattern.

Photo by Tom Alexander

The Winchester Model 21 double shown here was commissioned as a presentation gun for a retiring US Navy Seal. **Paul Lindke** was selected to do the stockwork on the project. He started with a very nice stick of Bastogne walnut. He shaped the stock following the lines of original Winchester stocks. To provide for the proper balance, he had to drill three 3/4-inch holes in the buttstock to reduce the weight of the wood. From the wood he cut from the buttstock to obtain the proper length of pull, he fashioned three plugs to fill and conceal the holes. The checkering of the butt makes the seams of the plugs totally invisible. **Franz Marktl** engraved the gun, to include a gold inlaid US Navy Seal emblem. Photo by Tom Alexander

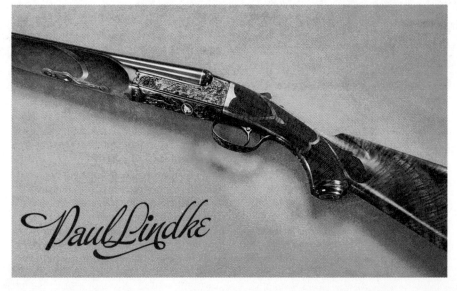

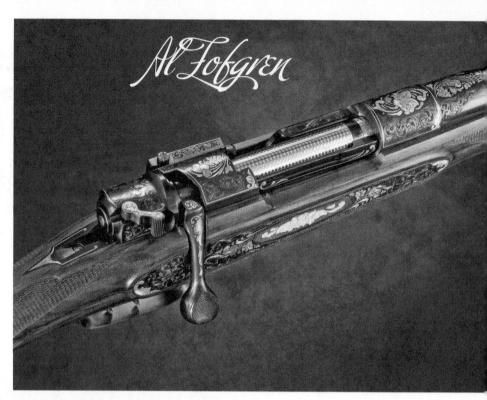

Al Lofgren

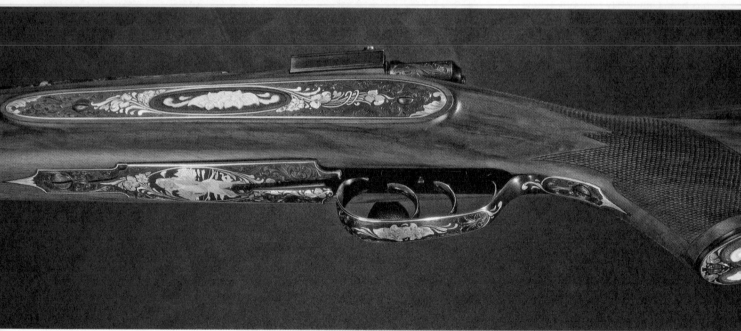

Gunmaker **Al Lofgren** began this project rifle with a small-ring Mauser '98 action and a blank of excellent California English walnut from the stash of **Steve Heilmann**. He cleaned up the action, truing all the surfaces, including modifying the rear action tang. He also modified the bottom metal. He then crafted the stock in an early 20th century styling. He added steel side-plates to the reinforcing

areas on either side of the stock. He added a skeleton buttplate crafted by **Glen Fewless**.

When the stock was finished, he turned the metalwork over to engraver **Brian Hochstradt**. Brian then designed and executed the superb engraving, featuring a scene of Diana, Goddess of the Hunt, on the floorplate. **Joe Coggin**'s work inspired his design for the pattern.

Brian also designed the ivory inlays in the stock, which were then carved by **Al Lofgren**. At the annual American Custom Gunmakers Guild/Firearms Engravers Guild of America combined Exhibition in Reno in January 2011, this rifle won the Best Carving Award, Best Engraved Rifle Award, and the Engravers Choice Award.

Photos by Tom Alexander

In addition to private clients, **Mike Dubber** is also a designated Colt Master Engraver, doing work directly for the Colt custom shop. This magnificent Colt SAA is such a project.

The Colt Collectors Association holds its annual meetings in a different state each year. That state determines the motif for the Grand Auction Gun for that year. In 2009, the state hosting the annual get-together was North Carolina.

Most notable of the state's recommendations are the two scrimshaw depictions on the ivory grips of the Wright Brothers airplane and the Cape Hatteras Lighthouse, both executed by **Catherine Plumer.** Behind the cylinder on the left side of the revolver is a gold inlaid depiction of the battleship *USS North Carolina*. As an interesting aside, after many years of honorable service, the powers that be scheduled the

dismantling of the battleship for scrap in 1960. The schoolchildren in the North Carolina school system volunteered to donate their lunch money once each week to preserve the state treasure. In the end the ship was spared, renovated, and now rests in North Carolina waters as a visitor's attraction. Mike did all the engraving and gold inlay work on the "Peacemaker."

Photo by Tom Alexander

Peter Ewalt is a German Master Engraver who studied under my old friend and fantastic engraver, the late Erich Boessler. Peter has been out on his own for many years and is turning out some superb engraving jobs. He did the pre-64 Model 70 floor plate shown here for a good friend (and excellent engraver in his own right) Terry Wilcox.

Photo courtesy of Peter Ewalt

Paula Biesen Malicki

This Kolar 12-bore trap gun was commissioned by a firefighter to honor the actions of the NYC police and fire departments on 9/11. The client chose engraver **Paula Biesen Malicki** to execute the engraving. Paula is the daughter of gunmaker Roger Biesen, and the granddaughter of the icon in the custom gun trade, Al Biesen. This fine competition gun was custom stocked by **Dennis DeVault**.

Photos by Tom Alexander

A magnificent 20 bore Parker double, restored to pristine condition and re-stocked in a lovely stick of thin-shelled walnut by **Roger Biesen**. Roger tapped his daughter, Paula Biesen Malicki, to cut the wonderful engraving pattern on the gun.

Photos by Tom Alexander

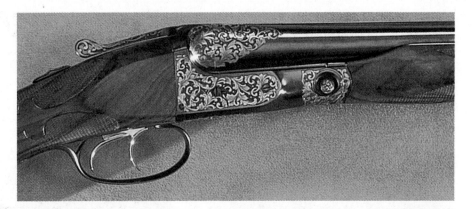

RetoBuehler

This superb double-square bridge Mauser express rifle is from the Oregon shop of **Reto Buehler**. The client that commissioned its crafting already had a very similar rifle chambered for the .500 Jeffery and wanted a matching rifle chambered for a smaller cartridge. He started with a Brno ZG 47 action. He did the normal blueprinting and slicking up the action, including installing a Wisner 3-position safety and Blackburn bottom metal. Buehler then installed a Pac-Nor 30-caliber barrel and chambered it for the ,30-06 cartridge. He installed a quarter rib with custom sights, a ramp front sight base, and banded front sling swivel base, re-milled the integral scope mount bases on the action, and extended the tangs on the action and bottom metal.

Next Reto stocked the rifle in the English style using a fine piece of Turkish walnut. When finished, he checkered the rifle using flat-topped diamonds and an H&H style pattern. The rifle is finished with the exception of the final metal finishing and bluing.

Photo by Tom Alexander

Roger Sampson

Engraver **Roger Sampson** did the exquisite scroll engraving and bulino scenes on this Ruger O/U 28 bore quail gun. Built for a lady, the gun is scaled in the proper proportions to fit the southern belle on her bobwhite quail forays. Al Linde stocked the shotgun. Sampson's work is superb.

Photo by Tom Alexander

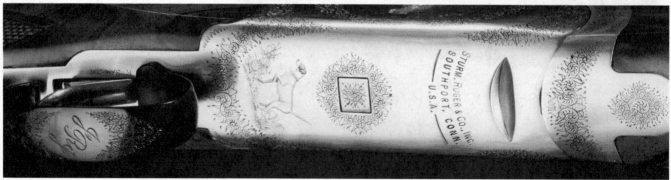

Gene Simillion

Gunmaker **Gene Simillion** began this project with a GMA Kurz action. GMA fabricated a special magazine box for their action to fit the .223 cartridge. According to Gene, the GMA response when delivering the box was "never again." Simillion fitted a Krieger barrel to the action and installed a quarter-rib with one standing leaf rear sight. He machined the action for Smithson quick detachable rings, fitted a barrel band front, and color casehardened the safety shroud, grip cap and rear sling swivel stud. He stocked the rifle with a superb stick of Turkish walnut and checkered it in a point pattern 26 LPI with mullered borders. There are no flies on this rifle.

Photo courtesy of Gene Simillion

Joe Smithson

Here is Joe Smithson's left-hand .416 Rigby on a GMA action and Krieger over-size barrel blank. He recontoured the factory GMA action and bottom metal to be more to his liking. He then machined the Krieger barrel blank to provide for an integral quarter-rib, front sight base, and front sling swivel stud. He fashioned the stock from a piece of Circassian walnut, fitting a Jerry Fisher grip cap and checkering it in a point pattern, 24 LPI, with mullered borders. This rifle also features **Joe Smithson** quick detachable scope mounts.

Photo by Steven Dodd Hughes

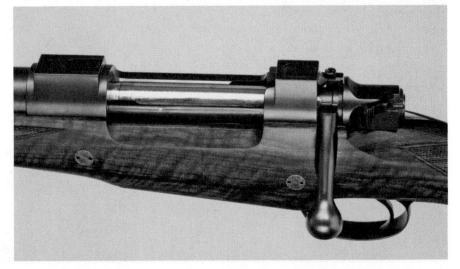

Steve Nelson

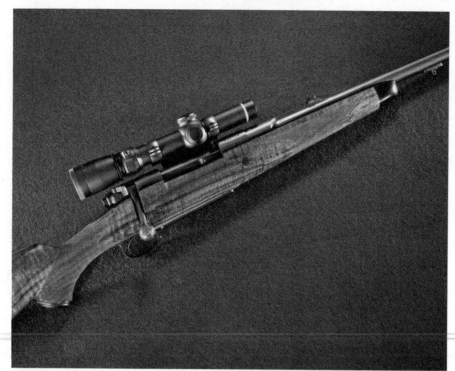

Steve Nelson's client wanted a rifle chambered for the .375 Ruger, built on his pre-'64 Winchester Model 70 action. He also wanted the rifle to be takedown capable. He additionally specified that Steve make a barrel featuring an integral quarter-rib done in Nelson's unique style.

Nelson started with a Pac-Nor blank that was 1.300" in diameter and machined the rib with a radius where it meets the round barrel. Due to time constraints, he chose to add the front sling swivel stud rather than machining it integrally. The client chose a Griffin & Howe side mount to permit a very low scope mounting as well as allowing him to easily mount one of two scopes, a VX-3 1.5x5X or a VX-7 30mm scope. Nelson chose a 20-plus-year-old Bastogne walnut blank for the stock. As stable as wood can be, he turned it into a magnificent stock featuring a tung oil, hand rubbed finish, checkered in a point pattern 24 lines per inch. No closet queen, this rifle has already been on a six-week safari to Tanzania and will be off to the elk woods this fall.

Photo by Tom Alexander

PCSACs:
Pistol-Cartridge Semi-auto Carbines

BY **J.B. WOOD**

I have always called them "PCSACs" – pronounced pick-sacks – because that's a lot easier to say or write than "Pistol-cartridge Semi-Auto Carbines." Either way, the description is accurate. Some of them are simply semi-auto versions of submachineguns, and others were separately designed. In handling, at least, they offer a hint of the full-auto experience for those who find the real thing too expensive.

The semi-auto versions are sometimes dismissed as just "fun guns," but they actually have practical applications. One of these is that they can be chambered to match the cartridge for a given sidearm. Another, of course, is their appearance – they look like submachineguns.

More than two dozen of these carbines have been made, and several are still in production. Predictably, most of the chamberings are 9x19mm or .45 Auto, but there are a few odd variations, such as .32 Auto and .30 Mauser. Let's take a look at some of my favorites, in no particular order,

The AWI Feather RAV9

The original Feather company, located in Boulder, Colorado, from 1986 to 1995 made this neat carbine as the AT22 (.22LR) and AT9 (9 X 19mm). Later, a new company, AWI LLC, acquired the tooling, and returned to production in 2007 under the name Feather USA.

The new Feather PCSAC is offered in .22 LR, 9x19, .357SIG, .40S&W, .45ACP, 10MM and .460 Rowland. AWI's version, while mechanically the same as the original, adds a generous set of rails on the receiver for accessories – a red-dot sight, flashlight, and laser. The RAV9 that I have has always performed nicely – in fact, I have never had a malfunction with it. As with most of these carbines, two-inch groups at 25 yards are not unusual.

The firing system is closed breech, striker-type. The manual safety is a little lever just forward of the trigger on the right side, inside the guard. It is very convenient.

The aperture-type rear sight is fully adjustable, and the front post has a protective ring that is also a sighting aid. The 25-round magazine is an Uzi-type, slightly altered to work with the Feather's push-button release. If you wanted more or less capacity, any Uzi magazine could be easily changed to function. .

Because of U.S. law, barrels of all PC-SAC carbines, the Feather included, must be at least 16 inches in length. In most cases, this results in eight or 10 inches of bare barrel sticking out, spoiling the true SMG look. As several others have done, Feather improves the carbine's profile by enclosing the barrel in a perforated sleeve. Finally, there is a sliding buttstock that is easily stowed. In some models, it can become a front handgrip.

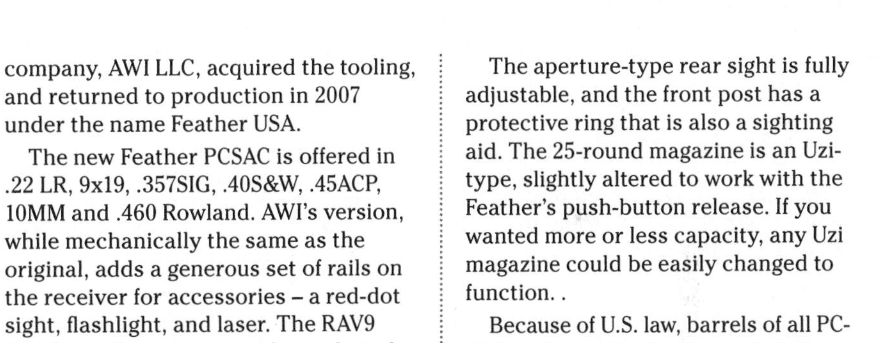

Feather RAV-9

Action Arms Uzi with stock deployed

The Inimitable Uzi

The semi-auto versions of the Uzi SMG that were made by IMI in Israel were marketed in the U.S. by Action Arms, Ltd. between 1983 and 1994. I don't have the total importation figure, but whatever it was, demand has caused the value of these guns to drastically escalate. Its fame has, of course, been enhanced by numerous film appearances, and by exploits in the real world.

The semi-auto version of the Uzi is striker-fired and closed breech, and its 25-round through-the-grip magazine is familiar to most gun people. It is notable for its "telescoping" breech-bolt that surrounds the barrel ahead of the chamber. This feature was borrowed by Major Uziel Gal from the Czech Model 23 and 25 submachineguns. With around 7 inches of barrel inside the receiver, this allows minimal protrusion at the front.

A top-mounted bolt handle keeps it flat, and a grip safety prevents jarring-off if you drop it. The manual safety is conveniently located at the top of the left grip panel, and slides back for safe, forward to fire. On my early gun, there is a small receiver mark at the "A" – full-auto – position. Alas, it won't go there.

The rear aperture-type sight is a flip-type, marked for 100 and 200 meters. The post front sight is adjustable. Both sights are well-protected by rounded ears. Unfolding the buttstock and re-folding it requires some practice, but once you have learned it, it's easy. There are good sling loops on the left side. My gun has always worked perfectly.

The Chopper: The Thompson

What can one say about this classic that hasn't already been said many times? Okay, for those who may have joined us recently, the original Thompson SMG was first made in 1921, and modified in 1928, by the Auto-Ordnance firm. Most of the actual production was by Colt and Savage, especially in the World War II era. The original design concept is attributed to Brigadier General John Taliaferro Thompson, but the actual nuts-and-bolts stuff was done by Auto-Ordnance Chief Engineer Theodore Eikoff and Engineer Oscar V. Payne.

In 1943, production ended at Colt and Savage, as the Thompson began to be replaced in service by the cheaper and easier-to-make M3 "Grease Gun" SMG. Much later, Auto-Ordnance became a subsidiary of Numrich Gun Parts Corporation, and they produced several nice semi-auto versions of the Thompson. Finally, in 1999, Auto-Ordnance was purchased by Kahr Arms, and the semi-auto Thompson is still being made.

I have visited the Kahr factory in Worcester, Massachusetts, and these guys are nuts about precision. My Kahr-Thompson is beautifully made. It is the full-sized version and accepts both the box magazines and the larger-capacity drum types. The firing system is closed-breech, striker-fired. The manual safety is on the left side, rotating rearward for safe, forward to fire.

The rear sight is a copy of the original Thompson SMG sight. It is adjustable for elevation only but offers a choice of aperture or notch. With the two hand-grips, the handling qualities are marvelous. However, I will note that this is no lightweight carbine. Empty, it weighs around 13 pounds. Imagine its heft with a loaded 50-round drum magazine! Anyway, it's beautiful.

The Revolutionary Kel-Tec SUB-2000

In firearms design, I don't use, the term "genius" loosely. It applies, of course, to the Grand Old Men of the past, such as John Moses Browning. In more recent times, I have used it to describe the late Harry Sanford and John Raymond Wilkinson. And, among the living, Justin Moon of Kahr and George Kellgren of Kel-tec merit "genius" status.

In 1997, Kel-Tec introduced the SUB-9, an entirely new 9mm carbine not related to any previous SMG. It had several excellent features, one of them being alternate grip-frame assemblies that would accept pistol magazines from Beretta, Glock, and others. Its only negative point was a receiver of alloy that was costly to produce, pushing the price to around $700.

Re-designed in 2000 with a receiver of high-tech polymer, it emerged in 2001 as the SUB-2000, and the retail price was around $300 less. It retained all of the desirable features of the SUB-9, and weighed about a half-pound less. One of those features was a hinged barrel unit that allowed it to fold, going from around 30 inches to 16 inches in length.

Aside from the storage and carrying convenience, the fold-up feature has other advantages. The chamber and bore are totally accessible for cleaning. When folded, the base of the front sight latches at the buttplate, and the latch is lockable. The front sight, translucent orange polymer, is vertically and horizontally adjustable. The fixed rear aperture sight magically emerges during the unfolding.

Kel-Tec SUB-2000

The cross-bolt push-button manual safety is located on the grip frame at upper rear, and has a raised fence to prevent inadvertent depression. The off-safe movement is toward the right. The magazine release is in the usual location, on the left side, just to the rear of the trigger. The bolt handle is on the stock-tube, underneath, behind the grip frame. Thus nothing sticks out on either side.

With an unloaded weight of only four pounds and having good balance, the SUB-2000 handles extremely well. There is one thing, though – don't ever fire it tucked under your arm at waist-level, in classic SMG style. Remember, that bolt handle moves. It will give you a good pinch. I learned this by the empirical method the very first time I fired it. I still shoot it, often.

The Beretta CX4 Storm

As the writer of two books on Beretta pistols, I was very interested when the CX4 Storm carbine appeared in 2003. Its thumb-hole stock and racy, sweeping lines are the result of a collaboration with Giugiaro Design. The internal mechanism is all Beretta, so of course it works, every time. In addition to the 9mm version, it has since been offered also in .40 S&W and .45 Auto.

My CX4 is 9mm, so the remarks that follow will apply to that caliber. It can be used with regular M92 pistol magazines, but nice 20-round types are available. The front sight is adjustable vertically and horizontally. The rear sight is a flip-over aperture, is two lobes marked "SR" (short-range) and "LR" (long-range).

The left-handers out there will be pleased to know that all of the controls on the CX4 are easily reversible. This feature includes the manual safety, magazine release, and bolt handle. There's even a little plate you can switch to close the ejection port on the opposite side. The bolt stays open after the last round, and the release lever is within easy thumb-reach.

The cross-bolt manual safety, located just above the trigger, is designed to be operated with the trigger finger. Thus, in right-handed mode, the off-safe movement is toward the left side. The magazine release is in the traditional location, at the rear terminus of the trigger guard. It is low-profile, to guard against inadvertent depression.

The butt-stock has soft rubber in the cheek-piece area and butt-plate. With

Beretta CX4 Storm Carbine

Iver Johnson 9mm

this moderate recoil you don't need the one at the back, but the cheek-piece is nice, especially in very cold weather. There are sling attachment posts at front and rear. The unloaded weight of the CX4 is 5-3/4 pounds. For quality, handling, and over-all performance, I would rate it excellent. With the Beretta name on it, it's what you would expect.

The Iver Johnson M1 Carbine – in 9mm!

Back in 1958, Universal Firearms of Hialeah, Florida, began making commercial versions of the classic U.S. M1 Carbine. The earliest ones used G.I. surplus parts, and receivers made for them by Repp Steel of Buffalo, New York. The great majority of these were chambered for the .30 M1 cartridge.

In 1983, the Universal firm was purchased by the Iver Johnson company of Jacksonville, Arkansas, and IJ continued production of the Carbine. Along the way they made a few, very few, in 9x19mm. It had the same gas-actuated bolt system as the .30 version, and to my knowledge it is the only 9mm carbine with this feature.

Its controls and operation are familiar to anyone who knows the old .30 U.S. Carbine. It uses a 20-round FN/Browning Hi-Power pistol magazine, altered to

work with the carbine magazine catch. They did make one little mistake here – a lower magazine guide made of brittle plastic. I simply removed the shattered remains and installed a steel cross-pin of the right diameter, and the problem was solved.

For those who are fond of the venerable Carbine but find the .30 cartridge to be a little too zippy, this 9mm would be a fine alternative. That is, if you are able to find one. After obtaining mine in 1994, I have checked a great many sales lists and gun show tables, and so far I have not seen another one.

The Tommygun That Wasn't: the Commando

Designed to look like the classic Thompson, the Commando carbine was in the same chambering, .45 Auto. From 1969 to 1976 it was made in Knoxville, Tennessee by Volunteer Enterprises, Inc., and called the "Commando Mark 45". It returned, briefly, in 1978, still in Knoxville, with a company name-change to Commando Arms.

Later, in the 1980s, it resurfaced in Lenoir City, Tennessee, a short distance southwest of Knoxville. The maker was Manchester Arms, Inc., and, still later, the Storm Lake Machine company. Using formed sheet steel and polymer,

Volunteer Arms Commando

D-Max (PGW) Carbine

Demro Wasp

"PGW" marking on the guns, which can mean "Powers Gun Works" or, possibly, "Pacific Gun Works." The designer was obviously influenced by the British Sterling SMG, as the D-Max has a side-entering magazine and a perforated barrel sleeve.

A handgun version was also made. The carbine has the buttstock, fore-arm and pistol-grip in nice walnut. The over-all phosphate finish is perfectly done. It fires from a closed-breech, and has an internal pivoting hammer, which gives it a better trigger-feel than the striker types. The lever manual safety is just above the hand-grip on the left side, turning rearward for on-safe, downward to fire.

The magazine release is a lever on the left-side housing. The bolt handle is also on the left side. The rear sight is an excellent Williams, fully adjustable. The extractor is a heavy T-slot type, and looks as if it will last forever. As mentioned earlier, production-time was brief, and these guns are not often seen. If you find one, it is definitely worth having.

The Open-Bolt Demro

When this gun was first made, the designer gave it his own last name, and called it the "Fox." Alas, the owners of the trademark for the venerable A. H. Fox shotgun took offense at this. Their attorneys rattled their sabers, and Mr. Fox quietly changed the name to "Demro." The guns were made by Demro Products, Inc., of Manchester, Connecticut, around 1980-1984.

They were offered in .45 Auto and 9mm versions, and there were two models. The TAC-1 was larger, had a fixed buttstock, and was notable for having a combination lock built into the receiver. The handier XF-7 Wasp, the one shown here in 9mm, had a folding stock of particularly neat design. The barrel had an integral muzzle-brake/flash-hider. The stock extension was fully adjustable.

The takedown for cleaning is a masterpiece of simplicity. With the stock unit removed, you just push a latch at the rear of the receiver, tip the barrel and upper receiver over forward, and lift out the bolt and recoil spring unit. In the firing sequence, the front tip of the recoil spring guide emerges to become the ejector a neat engineering touch.

The magazine catch is a lever-type, centrally located at the lower front of the trigger guard. The 32-round magazine is the British Sten, altered to

the Commando avoided the high cost of machining, and the retail price was moderate. This has led some to dismiss it as a "cheapo," and this is a mistake. It works fine.

The buttstock of my Commando is a nice piece of walnut, but the handgrip and foregrip are polymer. It has a finned barrel, and at the muzzle is a Cutts Compensator replica that is purely cosmetic. The rear sight is a simple aperture that can be bent upward or downward for adjustment. The nicely-knurled bolt handle is on the left side of the receiver.

The lever-type magazine catch is centrally located, thus ambidextrous. The 20-round Thompson magazine in my gun is unaltered. The cross-bolt manual safety is within easy thumb-reach, and the off-safe movement is toward the

right. The Commando handles like a Thompson, but weighs far less – about 8.5 pounds, unloaded. I have fired this one on numerous occasions, and it has never failed to work.

The Scarce D-Max (PGW)

Beautifully made and totally reliable, this one had a very brief production time, around 1990-1991. Working from old article notes, I find the name of D. M. "Doc" Dugger, and I believe he was the D-Max's talented designer. The original company was located in Auburn, Washington, a Tacoma suburb, and was called D-Max Industries.

Most of the actual production, though, was in Powers, a very small town in southwest Oregon. Hence, the

function. So far, its functioning has been flawless. There was a grip-type safety, but I cancelled its operation long ago. The manual safety is in exactly the right place on the left side, up for safe, down to fire.

The left-side bolt handle is large and nicely knurled. Sights are non-adjustable, but the rear one gives you a choice of notch or aperture. The Wasp fires from open-bolt position, and this may have contributed to its early exit. Our friends at the BATFE frown on such guns that can be easily converted to full-auto. Even so, as originally made, it is legal to own. And it's one of the best.

The Elusive Jäger

This is a nicely-done copy of the Colt AR-15, made in Italy by a company with a German name, Jäger, located in Turin. The E.M.F. company of Santa Ana, California, sold them from 1974 to 1989, in .22L R and .32 Auto versions.

For some readers, making a carbine of this type in .32 Auto may seem like a goofy endeavor. Remember, though, that for many years in Europe this was an accepted police round. As for me, it's one of my favorite cartridges. In fact, I carry a Kel-Tec P-32. With Cor-Bon loads, it will be quite adequate if it is ever needed.

The E.M.F. company marketed this AR-15 copy as the AP-74, presumably for the year it was introduced. The manufacturer marked them "Model AP 15." If you are familiar with the .223 version, everything is exactly the same, except the magazine catch. There is a cosmetic full-sized "magazine" that is part of the lower receiver, with a smaller entry for the nine-round .32 magazine. The push-button release is at the lower rear edge on the right side.

Everything else is just as you expect it to be – the little door that flips open at the ejection port, the sights, the "carrying handle" at the top, and so on. The takedown is even the same. The manual safety lever goes upward to off-safe, down to on-safe, exposing red and white dots. As an overall copy of the AR-15, it's perfect. I even like the cartridge!

The Humble Hi-Point

Made in Mansfield, Ohio by the Beemiller company, the Hi-Point carbine was introduced in 1996. It is marketed by MKS Supply of Dayton, and the Model 995 shown here is in 9mm chambering. A later offering, the

Jäger Carbine

Hi-Point Model 995

Model 4095, is in .40 S&W. The use of formed steel, alloy, and polymer keeps the price at just a little over $200. Those who sneer at it because of this are making a big mistake.

A good design, and well-made, it is absolutely reliable. A good number of them are actually in law enforcement use. One example of good engineering is the double extractor – in the unlikely even that one breaks, there's still one there. Also, an internal automatic "drop safety" keeps it from firing if you lose your grip on it during a serious social encounter.

Its single-row 10-round magazine is of very good design, and the release button is at the rear terminus of the trigger guard. The manual safety is on the left side at the top of the hand-grip. Turned upward, the lever covers a red dot for on-safe. The bolt handle is also on the left, conveniently located toward the rear.

The sights are excellent. The ring-protected front is vertically adjustable, and the aperture-type rear is fully adjustable. It is protected by sturdy side-ears. Among several neat accessories offered is an elastic slip-on magazine pouch by Allen that retains two spare magazines, giving you a total carry of 30 rounds. I like the Hi-Point Model 995. It's not fancy, but it's very good.

The Wilkinson Terry

When John Raymond Wilkinson designed the Terry carbine, he first licensed manufacture to a California firm, and they did it badly. One example of this was a plastic cartridge guide, which didn't last long. At that time, the gun was not called the "Terry." Later, Ray moved to Parma, Idaho, opened his own factory, and began to make it right.

The Terry uses the "telescopic" bolt design of the Uzi, with around seven inches of barrel being inside the receiver for a more compact package. At the ejection port, there's a little flip-open cover, like an AR-15, to keep dirt out of the action. It's hammer-fired from a closed breech, and its trigger system has a good feel.

The manual safety is a cross-bolt push-button type, located just to the rear of the trigger pivot. It is designed to be operated with the trigger finger, hence the off-safe movement is toward the left. The 31-round magazine enters through the grip, and the release button is in the usual guard-terminus location. The bolt handle is on the left side.

The buttstock and the little fore-end piece on my Terry are maple, but black polymer was also used. The barrel has a conical flash-hider at the muzzle, and a large knurled ring at the front of the receiver makes it easy to remove the barrel for cleaning. The sights are well-protected, non-adjustable, and the rear one is an aperture-type.

The original Terry was made for a relatively brief time, 1996 to 1998. After the death of Ray Wilkinson, a new company, Northwest Arms, produced it between 2000 and 2005. For some unknown reason, they called it the "Linda" carbine. This has caused some confusion, as this was actually Ray's name for the handgun version. Anyway, by whatever name, this carbine is a beautiful piece of work.

A MAC by Any Other Name: The Cobray Cobray

Gordon Ingram's original MAC-10 design has been made in many varia-

tions, handgun and carbine, mostly in 9mm and .45 Auto chambering. There have been several makers in the Atlanta, Georgia, area: RPB Industries (1979-1982), and SWD, Inc. (1986-1994). The Cobray name was owned until recently by Harvey Demars of Westhope, North Dakota, who passed away in 2009. It is my impression that the Cobray is not currently in production.

The earlier Cobrays fired from open-bolt position, earning them a frown from the BATFE. Even so, if they are unaltered, they are legal to won. The gun shown here is in an unusual chambering, .380 Auto. Made by the RPB firm, it is marked as model "SM11-A1". It has a fixed wood buttstock, and the barrel has a perforated sleeve. Sights are non-adjustable, the rear one an aperture.

The 17-round double-row magazine has a lever-type latch at lower rear that is pulled downward to release. The other operational features are in standard MAC-10 style. The bolt handle is on top, and the manual safety is on the right side, just forward of the trigger. It aligns with "SAFE" (back) and "FIRE" (forward) when slid by the trigger-finger.

In regard to the government concern about selective-fire conversion, this is downright silly. The trigger mechanism, in a sub-frame in the lower receiver, is welded in place. Any attempt to get it out and alter it would result in a gun that couldn't be fired at all. It's a handsome little carbine in an odd .380 Auto chambering, and I'd bet that not many were made.

The Marlin Camp Carbine

When the Marlin company introduced the 9mm version in 1985, they called it the "Model 9 Camp Carbine," and this was in keeping with its sporting-rifle appearance. There was no para-military look there at all. In the following year, a .45 Auto version was made. The 9mm gun, shown here, was supplied with magazines in 12-round and 20-round capacities originally. Production ended in 1999.

The Model 9 had numerous nice features, including a rifle-type wood stock and hot-blue on the barrel and receiver. The receiver top is drilled and tapped for scope mounts. The rear open sight is vertically adjustable, and the front has a hood. There's a half-inch rubber buttplate with the Marlin horseman logo.

The 12-round magazine is completely enclosed by a housing in the trigger assembly, and the release button is on the left side, forward edge. When the magazine is removed, there is an automatic internal safety. The bolt stays open after the last shot. The manual safety is Garand-style, inside the front of the trigger guard, alternately exposing a big "S" and "F".

Firing is closed-breech with a pivoting internal hammer. The trigger-pull of my gun is particularly nice. This is a handsome little carbine, and for those who like the pistol-cartridge concept but don't want an SMG look-alike, it would be a perfect choice. Also, they were made for more than 10 years, and are not that difficult to find, though values are escalating steadily, especially for the .45 version. Keep an eye peeled for the nickel-plated 9mm version – it's especially scarce and quite an eyeful.

Wilkinson Terry

RPB Cobray M-11

Marlin 9mm Camp Carbine

The Black Forest C96

Val Forgett (the elder) of Navy Arms is, alas, no longer with us. About 25 years ago, he had a marvelous idea. Quantities of old C96 ("broomhandle") Mauser pistols were showing up overseas, and he had a factory in Europe add stock units, fore-end pieces, and carbine-length barrels. He called it the "Black Forest Carbine," and I've been told that only around 500 of them were made.

To avoid any possible feeding difficulties, Forgett retained the original chambering, .30 Mauser (7.63 Mauser). As those familiar with the C96 know, the magazine is part of the lower receiver, and loads from the top with stripper-clips. The capacity is 10 rounds. Note that the 7.62x25 Tokarev cartridge will interchange with the Mauser, but beware of Balkan-area 7.63 SMG loads that might put a strain on the old Mauser action.

When the stock is detached, a regular Mauser pistol can still be used as a handgun. This is not the case with the Black Forest Carbine, as the handgrip comes off as part of the buttstock, just as on the original Mauser factory gun. All of the other mechanical features are of regular C96 pattern. The open rear sight is adjustable for elevation and is optimistically numbered to a thousand meters.

The lever-type manual safety, located at left rear, directly blocks the hammer. The bolt stays open after the last shot, and is released when the empty stripper-clip is pulled out. An original Mauser Carbine of this type can easily cost around $15,000. The Navy Arms Black Forest is hard to find, but will cost considerably less. Mine is not for sale!

The Calico

The original Calico company was located in Bakersfield, California, and the trade name stood for California Instrument Company, later changed to California Light Weapons Systems. The company started production around 1986. From 1995 to 2001, the location was Sparks, Nevada. More recently, in 2007, they were located in Hillsboro, Oregon.

The Calico carbine is notable for its top-mounted rotary magazine, offered in 50-round and 100-round capacitates. After loading, the crank at the rear is given 10 turns for the 50-round, 23 turns for the 100-round, and you are ready. The ejection port is at the bottom, just forward of the trigger guard.

Black Forest Carbine

Calico Carbine

Author J.B. Wood with the Kel-Tec SUB-2000

Author J.B. Wood with the Thompson

The good open sights have three white dots, and the front post is fully adjustable. The rear sight is fixed, on the top rear of the magazine. The bolt handle, on the left side, does not reciprocate with the action. There is a manual hold-open, useful for cleaning, on the right side. The ambidextrous manual safety is a lever-type, located just forward of the trigger. Forward is the off-safe movement.

The slide-out buttstock is easily deployed. On top of the magazine, there are little "windows" with numbers, so you can watch the count when loading or shooting. The Calico has also been made in a handgun version, and in .22 LR. In terms of capacity, its only rival would be the Thompson with a drum magazine. It's a marvelous little gun.

Final Notes

There are at least eight or 10 more guns that qualify as PCSACs. The EMF company recently introduced one, and Century Arms is currently offering semi-auto versions of the British Sterling. Going further back, there was the US-issue Reising, made in semi-auto. Others have been done by Heckler & Koch, Federal Engineering, Action Arms, York, and Enfield America.

As I said back at the start, yes, these are fun guns, but they can have some serious applications. They can be matched to your pistol cartridge, they are large capacity, and they are very accurate. Then, there's their "look." If you ever have to confront an unruly mob, someone will say: "Look out! He's got a machinegun!"

HK
A History of Innovation

BY **MASSAD AYOOB**

Through the latter half of the 20th century and thus far into the 21st, the firm of Heckler and Koch, GmbH, has been providing sophisticated small arms to armies, law enforcement agencies, and discriminating private sector shooters all over the world. There have been a few glitches, a few less than shining stars in the firmament of HK weaponry, but remarkably few. In a real world where consistent absence of failure is often more important than occasional flashes of spectacular success, that counts for a lot.

A Brief History

The HK marque has a unique background. Born in the rubble of post-WWII West Germany, with little more than a national heritage of engineer-

> Quietly favored by a surprisingly large percentage of the professionally armed, Heckler and Koch products are mission-designed and built on a baseline of reliability.

HK's current P2000 with LEM trigger: an excellent service pistol.

Left: Modern HK pistols are very southpaw-friendly. This P7M8 rides in the off-duty holster of left-handed police chief and pistol champion Bob Houzenga.

Tip of Spyderco knife points to essential P7 cleaning area. Barrel affixed permanently to frame helped the P7 establish its excellent reputation for accuracy.

ing excellence and understanding of weapons design and realization of the importance of product quality to sustain it, HK developed with the same determined and plodding steps of the nation that gave it birth.

Above, the HK P7M13; below, the P7M8.

There is no better concise history of the firm than that written by Ned Schwing, for many years the author of the annual small arms encyclopedia *Standard Catalog of Firearms*. Writes Ned, "At the end of WWII, the French dismantled the Mauser factory as a part of their reparations; and the buildings remained idle until 1949, when firearms production was again allowed in Germany. Heckler & Koch was formed as a machine tool enterprise and occupied the vacant Mauser plant. In the early 1950s Edmund Heckler and Theodor Koch began to produce the G3 automatic rifle based on the Spanish CETME design and progressed to machine guns and submachine guns and eventually to the production of commercial civilian rifles and pistols. In 1990 the company got into financial difficulties because of a failed contract bid. In December 1990 the French state consortium GIAT announced the

purchase of Heckler and Koch, but a little more than a year later the contract was cancelled. Later in 1991 the company was purchased by Royal Ordnance of Britain. In 2002 the company was sold to a combined group of European investors and long-time company managers."

In a sad footnote, HK rifle design has tenuous roots in the darkest portion of German history, the Nazi years. Shortly before the end of WWII, small arms engineers of Oberndorf am Neckar came up with a "roller lock" mechanism that would theoretically provide a more controllable fully automatic assault rifle. Ludwig Vorgrimmler, late of Mauser, continued work on that design in France after WWII. He was recruited by Spain's Centro de Estudios Tecnicos de Materiales Especiales (CETME), leading the team that finalized the CETME automatic rifle in 1952. Perceiving a need for German technology, the Spaniards invited H&K to take a piece of the action, and in 1956, the Heckler and Koch selective-fire 7.62mm NATO battle rifle was born. Christened the G3, it would later be dubbed the HK91 in its semi-automatic version. Heckler and Koch had begun its forward roll into arms-making history.

HK Pistols

Most folks think Glock innovated plastic-framed pistols. Not so. Heckler and Koch did.

In the late 1960s, Heckler and Koch introduced their P9 with plastic frame. A single action semi-auto, it was made primarily in 9mm though 7.65mm (.30 Luger) barrels were also produced for it in small numbers. It was the time of double action automatic pistols, though, and the P9 quickly gave way to the P9S.

The P7M10. Note disproportionately high slide, needed for enough mass to reduce slide velocity from the high-pressure .40 S&W cartridge.

The rare P7M10, caliber .40 S&W. From the Penny Dean collection.

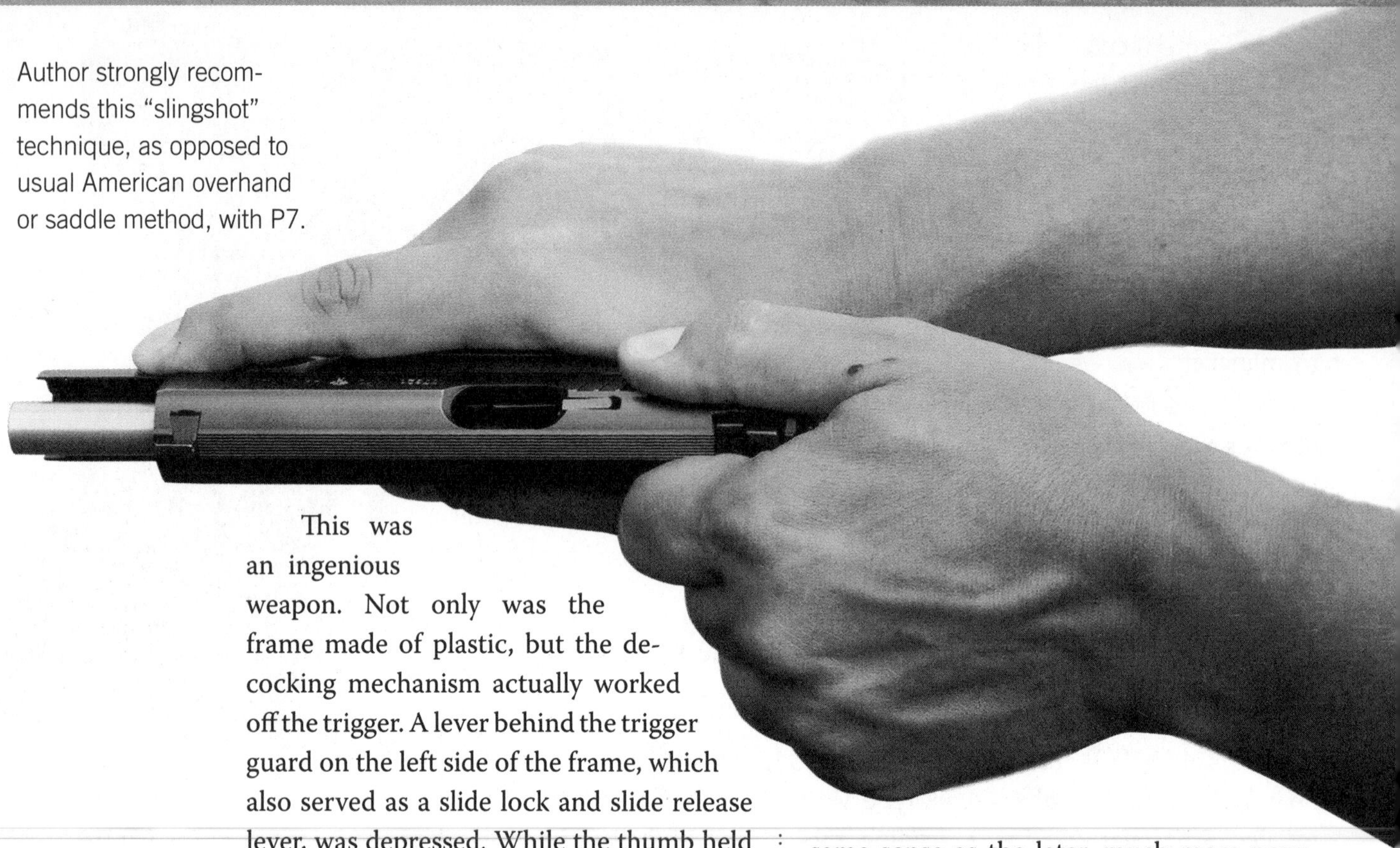

Author strongly recom-
mends this "slingshot"
technique, as opposed to
usual American overhand
or saddle method, with P7.

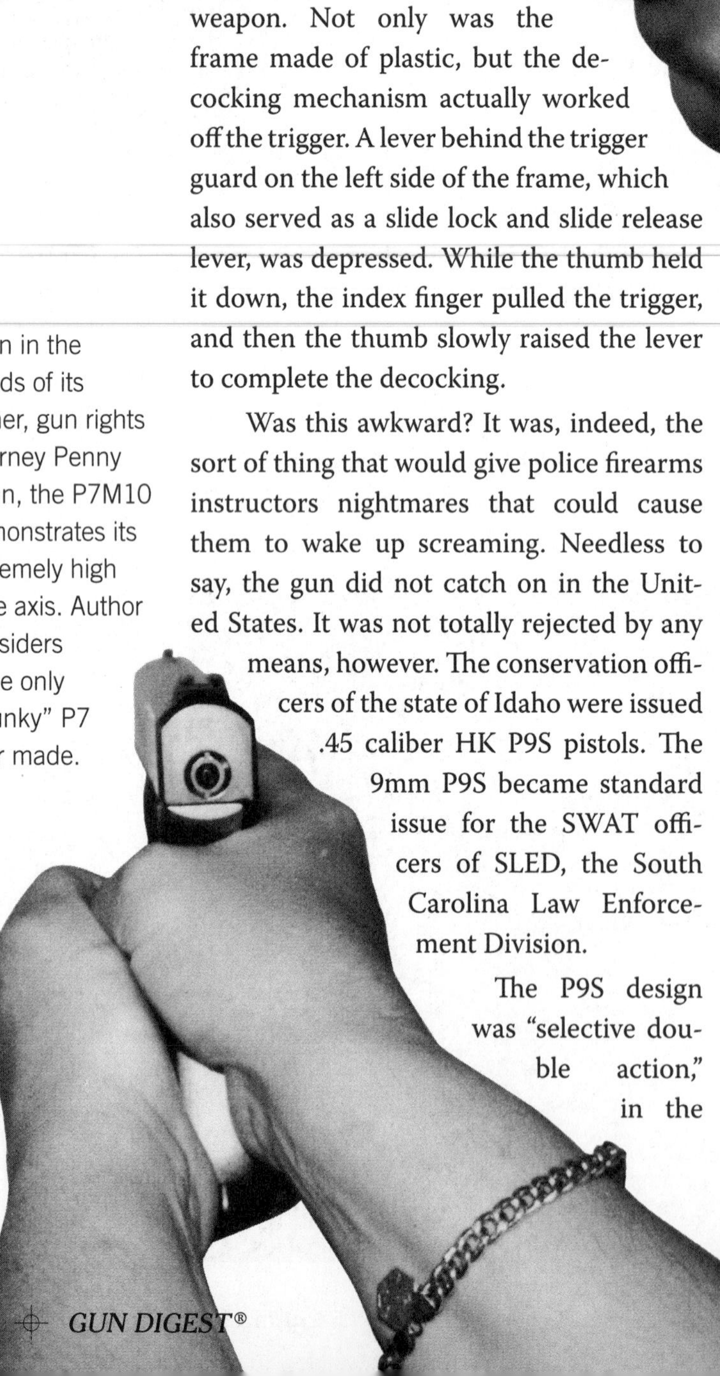

This was
an ingenious
weapon. Not only was the
frame made of plastic, but the decocking mechanism actually worked
off the trigger. A lever behind the trigger
guard on the left side of the frame, which
also served as a slide lock and slide release
lever, was depressed. While the thumb held
it down, the index finger pulled the trigger,
and then the thumb slowly raised the lever
to complete the decocking.

Was this awkward? It was, indeed, the
sort of thing that would give police firearms
instructors nightmares that could cause
them to wake up screaming. Needless to
say, the gun did not catch on in the United States. It was not totally rejected by any
means, however. The conservation officers of the state of Idaho were issued
.45 caliber HK P9S pistols. The
9mm P9S became standard
issue for the SWAT offi-
cers of SLED, the South
Carolina Law Enforce-
ment Division.

The P9S design
was "selective dou-
ble action,"
in the

Seen in the
hands of its
owner, gun rights
attorney Penny
Dean, the P7M10
demonstrates its
extremely high
bore axis. Author
considers
it the only
"clunky" P7
ever made.

same sense as the later, much more popular CZ75. In other words, while the first
shot could be set to require a long, heavy
double-action trigger pull, all subsequent
shots would be self-cocked to fire single action – but, instead of using the scary P9S
decocking mechanism, you could just leave
it cocked and engage the manual safety.
This was the pattern that most professionals seemed to choose once they got to know
their P9S pistols.

One could write a full-length disserta-
tion on "ergonomics and the HK P9S pistol." Yes, decocking it would make your
skin crawl. Yes, the slide-mounted safety
catch was "backwards" in the American
judgment of the time: up for fire and down
for safe, instead of vice versa as on a "real
American's 1911 pistol." What made that
worse was that the safety lever was a vestigial little nub that could not be activated by
the normal human hand under stress. Virtually ALL of us who used these guns and
carried them cocked and locked, had them
fitted with oversize safety levers by custom

pistolsmiths. (Nolan Santy did mine.) The magazine used a butt-heel release in the traditional European style, much slower than the push button release an American named Georg Luger had popularized three quarters of a century before, and which another American named John Browning had made his nation's standard.

However, the accuracy was phenomenal. The .45 ACP version, developed exclusively for the American market, could put five out of five in an inch at 25 yards with Match hardball. The 9mm could do the same with Federal's 115-grain JHP load. It has been postulated, though never really proven, that one reason for this superior accuracy was the fact that the P9S used a roller-lock mechanism that brought the barrel/slide assembly back into a constant relationship with the frame after every shot.

The trigger pulls were an interesting mix. If you go on the Internet, you'll find people saying the P9S had a horrible trigger, and people saying it had a great one. Neither are lying. You just have to know which trigger system they had.

The Service models of the P9S had atrocious double action trigger pulls – heavy, draggy, and lo-o-ong. Their single action pulls weren't particularly light and had so much backlash that when the sear released, the now un-resisted trigger finger would slam back against the inside of its guard on the plastic grip frame so hard that it could literally move the gun before the bullet left the barrel.

However, the Target and Sport/Target versions had single action trigger pulls that were as good as the service models were bad. A lever built into the back of the trigger guard on the polymer frame, adjustable and lockable by a set-screw, acted as a trigger stop. With it set to do its job, the double action function of the pistol was locked out

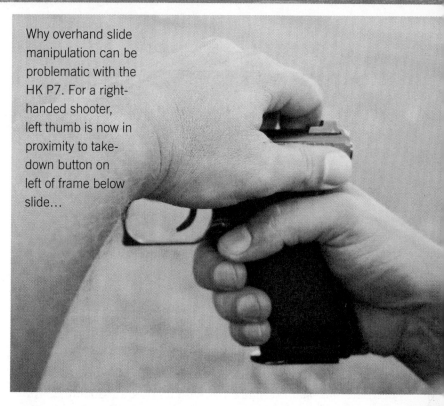

Why overhand slide manipulation can be problematic with the HK P7. For a right-handed shooter, left thumb is now in proximity to take-down button on left of frame below slide…

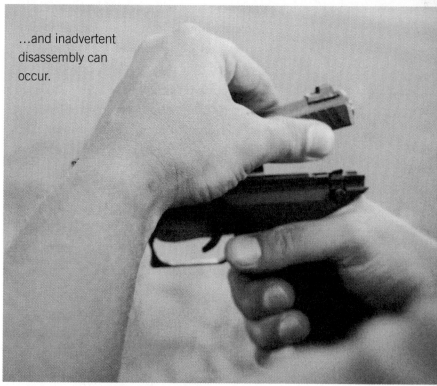

…and inadvertent disassembly can occur.

and the P9S became single action only. The backlash was completely eliminated.

That was only part of the trigger package in the Target and Sport/Target models. The other element was a trigger adjustable in pull weight that was simply the best of

Fat magazine plus squeeze-cock lever means the P7M13 has a lot of grip girth for fingers to get around, as seen here. Author finds the slimmer P7M8 far more ergonomic. HK sales figures showed that most other shooters felt the same.

its time, and one of the best ever. You could get the pull down into the high two pounds weight range without the gun "doubling." The adjustment was a simple slot-head screw in the trigger mechanism, readily accessible as soon as you field-stripped the barrel/slide assembly off the polymer frame.

Another polymer framed HK pistol that predated the Glock and all the rest of today's crop was the VP70Z. HK definitely made the first polymer framed pistol: whether that HK was the P9 or the VP70 may depend on which was on the drawing board first *vis-à-vis* which left the factory first. It is possible that the VP70 was indeed the first polymer handgun, though by this writer's lights the P9 would have been the first successful polymer frame pistol.

While all P9-series HKs had single stack magazines, the VP70 had a fat double stack magazine that let the gun hold 18 rounds. Originally designed as a machine pistol, it would only fire full auto when attached to its shoulder-stock. The rate of fire on full auto was stated by some experts to be over 2000 rounds per second, generally deemed too fast to control with a machine pistol. With the stock removed, and the pistol sold by itself, it became the HK VP70Z. "VP" pur-

portedly stood for *volkspistole*, or "people's pistol"; the "Z" suffix meant "zivil," a civilian model.

Having shot the VP70 both as a machine pistol and a semiautomatic handgun, this writer remains unimpressed. If it worked as a buzz gun, it would have stayed in the HK catalog. It did indeed function with ball ammo, but I found that with any hollow point except Remington, it was likely to choke. The gun had odd sights, a front that completely filled the rear notch, with the designers counting on a "shadow" concept to make the front sight visible to the shooter under stress. It didn't work well. An early striker-fired design, the VP had a horrendously heavy and difficult-to-control trigger pull. Introduced in 1970, the VP70 went under in 1989.

Every gun company that has been around a while has had a model that was to its brand what the Edsel was to Ford. For HK, I submit, that model was the VP70Z. This may be unfair to the Edsel. At least the Edsel actually worked. I've seen more than one jam-a-matic VP70Z pistol.

Perhaps the iconic HK pistol is the P7. Known to the public as the "squeeze cocker," to its advertising agency as "continuous action," and to Jeff Cooper and his acolytes as the "squirt gun" because you had to squeeze it to shoot it, the HK P7 occupies a unique place in handgun history. The lever at the front of its grip-frame had to be firmly depressed for it to work.

Originally designated PSP, supposedly for Police Self-loading Pistol, it was soon renamed the P7. These original P7s had slim, smooth grip-frames containing slim, smooth eight-shot magazines. The sights were big and blocky, much more so than most pistols of circa 1980. This contributed to a "shootability" that took advantage of their inherent accuracy, which was enhanced by a barrel solidly fixed to the frame.

A fountain of brass is airborne as Bob Houzenga fires a "Bill Drill" with HK P7M8. Named for pistol champ Bill Wilson, that means...

(Inset): ...that Houzenga has reacted to a start signal, drawn, and fired six hits all in the center of this IDPA target from seven yards – all in under two seconds. P7s help the best shooters shoot their best.

Tip of Spyderco knife points to the inconspicuous lever which must be pressed rearward to manually lock back the slide of a P7 pistol.

With a very low bore axis, the P7 was also gas operated, which bled off some of the recoil impulse. With these two factors in play, the P7 had extraordinarily mild recoil. That was another big plus for the serious shooter. Soon, the P7 fan club had spread, gaining almost cult status.

The first PSPs had a butt heel magazine release. This was typical of European auto pistols, but the P7's differed in that instead of the usual set-up where the catch was pressed toward the rear of the pistol to release the mag, the P7's catch was pressed forward. This turned out to be much faster than the typical butt-catch. On most such guns, including HK's own P9S, the thumb pushed the latch to the rear and the middle and/or index finger caught the lip of the floorplate and pulled the magazine out. On the P7, a simple forward pressure caused the mag to fall free. Not so fast as the Luger/Colt/Browning push button style, it was distinctly faster than others of its kind. HK followed with a more streamlined version of the butt catch that was shielded by newly-designed grip panels so it did not protrude, thus protecting it from inadvertent dropping of the magazine when the gun butt brushed against seat cushions while sitting,

or against the ground while shooting from prone.

As butt catches go, the P7/PSP's was fast, but not fast enough for the American market. In the early 1980s, as momentum was building up for what would be a massive nationwide switch from service revolver to semiautomatic pistol in American police service, the New Jersey State Police approached H&K with a request for modification. They loved the P7, they said, but rapid reloads were seen as essential to their mission. Could they put a thumb-activated release on the gun?

Since the squeeze-cocker mechanism would have gotten in the way of a conventional magazine release button on the side of the grip-frame, HK engineers came up with an ingenious ambidextrous lever located at the rear of the trigger guard. A press downward instead of inward would dump the magazine. As an added bonus, this allowed the shooter to do so with his thumb on one side or his index finger on the other. For many, the latter was faster since the trigger finger could snap back to do the job without shifting the hand, as was often necessary to get a thumb in position to activate a side-mounted magazine release.

Because of the gas operation, it was noted that the P7 heated up quickly in the frame area during long strings of fire, as in training or competition. The updated design, called the P7M8, included a "heat shield" in this area, which also required a re-shaping of the trigger guard. NJSP adopted the P7M8, with each trooper carrying four spare eight-shot magazines. To work with the new design release, the P7M8 magazine had a sharp little projection on either side. P7 purists felt this interfered with the smooth lines of their icon, and within the P7 cult traditionalists would always favor the original style. While the P7 was officially discontinued circa 1984 in favor of the P7M8, it would occasionally be run in small lots by the factory to satisfy insistent demand from aficionadoes.

The early '80s were also the time of the JSSAP (Joint Services Small Arms Project) tests to select a 9mm service pistol to replace the 1911A1 .45 with the US Armed Forces. HK widened the grip frame and came up with a 13-shot magazine, and the result was the P7M13, following the tradition the company had established when it named the P7M8 after the magazine capacity. While it did not find favor in JSSAP circles, the P7M13 was adopted by a number of American police departments, becoming for instance standard issue for Utah's state troopers.

When Smith & Wesson and Winchester jointly announced the .40 S&W cartridge in 1990, it was accepted more quickly than any new service round since the .38 Special. Splitting the difference between 9mm Parabellums such as the P7 series and the .45 ACP of the classic Colt and some others, the .40 was recognized as a compromise that could solve debate and get past controversy so trainers could concentrate on the tactics and marksmanship under stress that would really decide whether their officers lived or died. Demand for .40s was so great that every mainstream maker jumped on the bandwagon, and HK was no exception. The firm went in two directions: one was the USP, which we'll discuss shortly. The other was the P7M10.

This was the only "clunky" P7 to ever make it out of the factory. Since brutal slide velocity was beating up most makers' "9mms suddenly rechambered for .40," Heckler and Koch went for a massive slide that brought weight up to about two and two-thirds pounds and felt heavier than that in the hand. In the P7M10, the slimness and lithe, fast

Below: Activating the P7. Front lever is at rest, trigger finger in register unseen on opposite side of the frame. Now…

Left: …shooter's grasp tightens, squeeze cocking the pistol. Note that cocking indicator at rear of slide is now protruding. Lever must be held in (minimum pressure is required) to keep the gun firing. P7s demand firm grasp…a good thing.

handling of the original P7 was simply gone. The gun was a massive sales failure, soon discontinued, and today is a rare oddity that seems to be loved only by P7 collectors.

P7s were produced in small quantities in other calibers. A scaled down version, the P7K3, was manufactured in .380 ACP and .22 Long Rifle. It was the only true in-house HK pocket pistol design. For years the company offered the HK4 in .22 LR, .25 auto, .32 ACP, and .380, but that gun was little more than an updated Mauser HSc, another thread of the Mauser karma that runs through the history of Heckler and Koch. The rarest of P7 pistols is the P7M7, a seven-shot .45 ACP produced experimentally circa 1983. It is believed that no more than six were ever made, none leaving the possession of HK. One is occasionally displayed in the expansive HK booth at SHOT and AWA trade shows.

Today, the P7 is available only in the M8 configuration. Its high price drove it out of market competition with armies, with police departments, and with American consumers.

The mainstay of the HK pistol line today is the USP and its derivatives. Greeted by a collective yawn when they pioneered plastic pistol frames with the P9 and VP70Z, HK put all its money on the all-steel P7 to win the pistol races, only to see it eclipsed by less expensive polymer frame guns after Glock ran with the plastic ball and changed the face of the market. Priced out of the market

with the P7, HK went back to the drawing board and came up with the Universal Service Pistol in 1993.

A modular fire control system created a "Burger King" gun in the USP: you could "Have it your way." Ned Schwing lists the variants of the USP fire control system as follows:

1. DA/SA with safe position and control lever on left side of frame.
2. DA/SA with safe position and control lever on right side of frame.
3. DA/SA without safe position and decocking lever on left side of frame.
4. DA/SA without safe position and decocking lever on right side of frame.
5. DA only with safe position and safety lever on left side of frame.
6. DA only with safe position and safety lever on right side of frame.
7. DA only without control lever.
8.
9. DA/SA with safe position and safety lever on left side of frame.
10. DA/SA with safety lever on the right side of frame.

The empty spot I've left by Variant 8 is not a misprint. For some reason, HK set aside one number for a fire control system not yet planned. Just what Variant 8 was or would have been remains an unsolved mystery among HK fans.

Variant I, for most of the USP's epoch, was the most popular format. It gave the shooter choices of double action first shot, carried on safe or off, or the option of single action cocked and locked carry. A press downward on the lever brought it from "safe" to "fire," and pressing still further down decocked the pistol.

Early versions were marked "PSP," lacked the longer trigger guard/"heat shield" treatment, and had magazine release catches mounted at the butt.

Today, there is great demand for a variant not anticipated in 1993: the LEM. The Law Enforcement Module or Law Enforcement Modification came out of HK's recognition that the police market was going double action only for reasons of perceived safety. HK's own DAO variant of the USP had a trigger pull that could most charitably be described as mediocre. The ingenious LEM changed that.

In the May-June 2003 issue of *American Handgunner* magazine, Dave Anderson described the new mechanism succinctly: "Compared to the original double-action only trigger, the LEM provides a pull that is lighter, smoother, with shorter trigger travel and much quicker trigger reset. Currently it's available for law enforcement personnel only with a pull of 7.5-8.5 pounds. A variation with a 4.5-5.5 pound pull is planned which should have considerable potential for production-class competition."

Dave continued, "The LEM hammer is actually a two-piece unit with an internal cocking piece separate from the external hammer. When the shooter inserts a loaded magazine and racks the slide to chamber a cartridge, the mainspring is fully compressed. The external hammer then extends slightly from the slide, serving as a visual and tactile indicator the gun is cocked. When the trigger is pulled, instead of having to overcome the resistance of the powerful mainspring, the shooter is pulling only against the lighter resistance of the trigger return spring for the initial take-up. During this take-up the external hammer is rocked back to its full rearward position. With the test gun it took a pressure of 3.5 pounds to move the trigger through a travel of 7/16 inch. From there, pressure built smoothly and predictably to 8.5 pounds over an additional 5/16 inch of travel, at which point the sear released to fire the gun. After firing, a forward movement of the trigger of just 5/16 inch was required to reset the trig-

ger for the next shot. There is no need to let the trigger move all the way forward for follow-up shots, although the gun will function just fine if you do. Quick trigger reset is a feature competitive shooters value, as it's one of the keys to fast and accurate shooting."

The LEM vaulted into the forefront of police auto sales by HK, and became the heart of the company's superb follow-up to the USP, the P2000 series. Very accurate, and with light recoil, the P2000 guns ushered in a new feature: ambidextrous slide stop/slide release levers.

Top: This hard-chromed HK P7M8 makes an excellent carry pistol, in properly trained hands.

Bottom: Author's favorite P7 is this early generation 9mm.

The USP is available today in 9mm, .40 S&W, .357 SIG, and .45 ACP, while the P2000 and the compact P2000K are made primarily in 9mm and .40. When virtually all serious service pistols were put through the grueling ICE tests for adoption by Homeland Security a few years ago, only these HKs and the SIG made it through. No one seriously questions the endurance of today's "plastic" HK pistols.

A pioneering feature on the first USP was an integral accessory rail molded into the frame. Designed to take HK's proprietary UTL (Universal Tactical Light), it was an instant success and quickly copied by almost every other maker. Others went to the universal rail configuration to allow lights such as the superb SureFire X-series. HK followed in turn, incorporating a universal rail in the P2000 series.

Today, you'll literally find polymer frame HK pistols in police holsters in the four corners of the continental United States. Maine State Troopers have USP .45s at their hips, and the Washington State Patrol issues the USP in .40 S&W. San Bernardino, California, once the murder capitol of the nation, selected the HK USP .40 for its city police. In humid Florida, deputy sheriffs from St. John's County on the Atlantic Coast to Leon County, surrounding the state capitol of Tallahassee on the Gulf, are issued the HK USP pistol in .45 ACP. Feds from the Border Patrol to the US Park Police now also issue modern polymer HK pistols.

The HK Legacy

Fine German workmanship has come to be so expected that it's something of a stereotype. Mercedes and Volkswagen. Leica. Zeiss and Schmidt & Bender.

And, of course, Heckler and Koch.

Machines. Machines designed precisely to do a certain job. Machines designed to work without fail with minimal maintenance. Machines designed with little subtleties of ergonomics that make them easier to use.

Call it a stereotype if you want, but HK "fits the profile."

HK Weaponry: A Personal Perspective

Every reader has a right to know where the writer of an article is coming from. "In the interest of full disclosure," as journalists are supposed to say. Fair enough.

I started working seriously with H&K firearms in the late 1970s. I was invited down to South Carolina for a bash hosted by H&K with SLED SWAT, the South Carolina Law Enforcement Division's elite Special Weapons and Tactics Team. The several days included an introduction to the then-new PSP pistol, later dubbed the PSP – I believe my article on it tied for the first published in this country, or came out a day or two ahead of the nearest competition – and a blend of Southern deer hunt and scheutzenfest. We chopped down trees with G3 .308s on full

Second generation of P7 butt-heel magazine release, prior to HK going to the M-series system.

auto. We hunted deer with the G3 and its sporterized cousin, the sleek Model 770. I hunted the small South Carolina white-tails with an HK P9S .45 auto with extended barrel, though I never got close enough to take a shot. We ran the G3 full auto next to the FN FAL, and the HK33 full auto next to the M16. We shot their sniper rifles, and we shot about every pistol they had.

I left impressed. A couple of years later, when John Bressem took over marketing for HK in the USA and decided to put together an official HK pistol team, I found myself on board. My choice was the phenomenally accurate P9S Sport .45 and Sport/Target 9mm. The latter came in a kit with wooden flat grips, wooden International-style thumbrest target stocks, barrel weight, and the whole nine yards including a short Service barrel/slide assembly that I rarely used. It sold for over $1,000 in the early 1980s. I just saw one on the Internet selling for $6000. Didn't even feel tempted. Mine is not for sale. I won High HK Shooter one year at Bianchi Cup with the 9mm Sport/Target, shooting it with the 1200-foot-second, 112-grain "saw tooth hollow point" 9mm rounds of my ammo sponsor at the time, Super Vel. I was told by the range staff who chronographed our ammo that I was shooting the single hottest load of the hundreds of competitors that year. It was no handicap in the easy-kicking, factory muzzle-weighted P9S Sport/Target, and indeed an advantage: it shot so flat I didn't have to change either sights or hold all the way out to 50 yards on Match One, the Practical, and I didn't have to lead as much as everybody else on Match Three, the Mover.

John Lawson and I were both writing for *American Handgunner* magazine back then, I as law enforcement editor and John as gunsmithing editor. John put a humongous barrel weight onto my HK .45, and Larry Kelly gave it the first trapezoidal version of MagnaPorting. John was kind enough to etch "Ayoob Special" onto the compensator, and I won a few guns with it at the Second Chance Shoot, with the 190-grain Super Vel .45 hollow points easily reefing the heavy pins back three feet off the table. I don't remember either gun ever jamming, though in fairness John had to "throat" the .45 for hollow points and Nolan Santy did the same for my 9mm.

The years went on. Briefly, I carried the P9S and the P7 on uniformed police patrol, in Gordon Davis and Safariland thumb-break duty holsters, respectively. Off duty, the P7 went many a mile with me in a variety of hideout holsters, most commonly Ted Blocker's LFI Concealment Rig. The only dedicated concealment holster I had for the P9S was a Summer Special-like IWB produced for the late, great Austin Behlert, but the 4-inch Target versions spent their time on my hip, especially in winter in the '80s because the big, Alpine-influenced Teutonic trigger guard made these guns friendly to the gloved hand.

The years went on. I had the chance one day at an IDPA match to stay late and re-enter with each of the four gun categories then in effect (the organization had not yet separated revolvers into two distinct categories). I managed to win three out of four and shot the

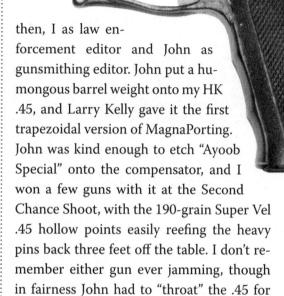
Author set a short-lived national record with this HK P9S Sport/Target 9mm. Note long barrel with removable weight, integral adjustable trigger stop at lower rear of trigger guard, excellent sights, and oversize Nolan Santy thumb safety. Pistol is shown cocked and locked.

Heckler and Koch has produced some superbly accurate pistols. Top: target grade Tactical USP .45. Below: 9mm P9S Sport/Target.

Below: The ergonomic, ingenious ambidextrous magazine release of the M-series HK P7. A similar design followed in USP and P2000.

best overall score of the match with a P7M8 HK 9mm.

Nowadays, I still have several HKs in my gun safes. I don't shoot Bianchi Cup anymore, but if I did, I wouldn't hesitate to bring that grand old belt-carried small caliber rifle, the P9S Sport/Target, back out of retirement. Bowling pin shooting has become moribund, but if it catches back on, I'll consider one of my HK .45s. I change guns every teaching cycle and usually have my HK USP Compact Variant One .40 on for a week of the year, and still feel totally confident with it. I don't remember it ever shooting less than a perfect 300 score when I had to demonstrate the course of fire for the students. And the .45 USP is never gonna leave 'til I'm dead; it's just too big for a little guy like me to carry concealed for a week on the road.

It has been a long time since my department issue HK MP5-A3 has gone to work with me in its inconspicuous little gym bag on the floor of my patrol car. For my needs, "a bigger gun gives you more/of what you carry a big gun for." But once a year or so I teach the submachine gun, and the old MP5 comes out, and still struts its stuff with a few thousand rounds downrange with zero malfunctions and total control, so long as it's in hands that know what to do with it.

The HK remains a favorite of professionals. I personally understand, and appreciate, why.

This article is an excerpt from Massad Ayoob's *Greatest Handguns of the World,* published by Gun Digest Books. For more information or to purchase, please visit www.gundigeststore.com.

My 33 Years with the .338 Magnum

A Schmidt & Bender 4X was one of at least a half-dozen scopes I used on the .338 at different times. All worked well.

BY **BOB BELL**

I don't know how many guns I've had altogether. Dad gave me my first, a Daisy, for my fourth birthday, and that's more then 80 years ago. It was a single-shot BB gun that I couldn't even cock then, but he did that for me countless times.

Two years later my birthday present was a Crosman .22 pellet gun. I couldn't pump that up either, so he did that too, until a few years later when I was able to do it myself. My primary targets for both were sparrows and starlings, though once I hit a crow with a pellet when it flew overhead.

Both of those guns have been gone for many decades now, as have other rifles and shotguns that Dad gave me for subsequent birthdays, until I was old enough to buy my own. Like every other shooter who's ever parted with a gun, I often wish I had them back. But the time always comes when it's more sensible to part with guns than to get more, and that's what I've done in recent years. Of a fairly large accumulation – not a true "collection" in any sense of the word – I have only a few left, five rifles and four handguns, and one of these is actually my wife's, a .257 I gave her when we got married. (Not being from a shooting/hunting family, she was doubtless confused by such a gift, but what did I

know, I'd never been married before.) The other rifles are a Hart-barreled .22-250, a custom Mauser .338 Magnum, a .348 Winchester, and a Ruger No. 1 .45-70 Lyman Centennial Model. The handguns are a Colt Woodsman Sport Model .22 rimfire and three Ruger Blackhawks in magnum calibers.

They're all favorites but it's the .338 I want to tell you about. Winchester brought out the .338 in 1958, and by 1960 I had one. For years I'd been using the .348 for elk and deer, and, actually, I'd done well with it. But I wasn't happy with metallic sights in the black timber of the Rocky Mountain states, so I wanted a scope. I'd gone so far as to have Stith mount a 2X Alaskan on the top-ejecting

M71, but the wide cartridge case necessitated offsetting the scope so much that I had to add a cheekpiece to the stock to get proper eye alignment. Ultimately, these changes spoiled the smooth, fast-handling characteristics that the 71 was noted for, and it became obvious that the only way I was going to get a scoped elk rifle was to go to a bolt action.

No problem. I'd used bolt guns for years, a Springfield '03-A4 in the mid-1940s, a couple of 8x57 Mausers, a M30 Remington .30-'06 and others. So I went to a longtime friend, the late gunsmith Al Wardrop, and told him I wanted a .338 Magnum.

"That's a good idea," he said. "Everybody oughta have a .338. And if you don't want to just buy a Model 70, I happen to have a new FN Mauser action with adjustable trigger that you can have. I'll have to open up the bolt face, though."

"Okay," I said. "Get me a Buhmiller barrel with a 10-inch twist, 'cause I'll be using heavy bullets, mostly 250s with a few 275s thrown in, probably. That twist will work okay with 200s too, if I want to use them for deer. You always said it's better for a bullet to be a bit overstabilized than under."

"That's how I've always found it," Al replied. "What about a stock?"

I thought for a moment. "Bump has some good dry wood. I'm sure he'll whittle me one – guess I better have a recoil pad too. That way I can get the cheekpiece that the 70 doesn't have."

Al chuckled. "Bump" referred to another good friend, Harold "Bump" Lynn, a patternmaker by trade who occasionally made gunstocks in his spare time. He'd previously made several for me, and his inletting was airtight, the way I wanted it. I know many prefer floating barrels nowadays, and doubtless that's easier to do, but as long as the wood is dry, I want 'em tight.

Eventually both Al and Bump finished their work. It didn't take long, it just seemed that way. The barrel finished up at 22 inches from the front of the action. Al had also installed and bore-sighted a 2-7X Redfield scope in Redfield Jr. mount, a design I'd been using since the mid-1940s; it's never failed me, even on a hard-kickin' cartridge such as the .458 Magnum.

While waiting, I'd bought a hundred new Winchester cases and an assortment of bullets of all common weights from 200 to 275 grains. Most were spitzer boattails, but some had flat bases and some had flat points. Most came from Hornady, Nosler, Sierra, Bitterroot and Speer. For the lighter weights, powder was usually 4895 or 4064, for the heavier ones 4350 or 4831. At one time or another, primers included the Winchester 120, Federal 215, and Remington 9-1/2. All loads were tested for accuracy off a sandbagged bench, most giving 1-moa groups or a bit less. One five-shot group went well under an inch at 100 yards. That of course doesn't mean much; it's the sort of thing that happens sooner or later if you shoot enough groups. Still, it's nice to know.

One group I like to think about even more than that occurred when I was getting ready for a hunt, using the 250-gr. Nosler Partition and a max load of 4831. After zeroing +3 inches at 100 yards, I was also up 3 at 200 and down 4 at 300. I had seven cartridges left then, so I shot them all at 300. They made a 4-inch group. Three hundred yards is about the maximum range I want to shoot at any big game animal, so it was satisfying to know that a hunting-weight rifle that churned up almost 4000 ft.-lbs. of energy was grouping well enough to hit a woodchuck at that distance. Still later, I tried the same load again. This time I fired only five shots, and the group was a bit larger, 5 inches. But four of those

My biggest whitetail also was taken with the .338. Its size is obvious when compared with this Ontario moose outfitter, who was 6 foot 3 inches and weighed 240 lbs.

Nice Idaho mule deer taken with the .338 using a 275-gr. Speer and a heavy load of 4831, when I was elk hunting. Worked okay there, too.

went into 3 inches, so maybe I jerked one of the shots, huh? Well, mebbe not. Nevertheless, I was happy with it.

Velocities were essentially as advertised for factory loads. These were taken on Herter and Avtron chronographs at first, on an Oehler 35P later. I spent so much time testing for wear accuracy, chronographing, etc., that a friend said I'd wear out the barrel before I ever got to shoot a critter with my .338. I doubted that, but I wasn't really sure. I'd never before done so much shooting with loads that often used 75 grains or more of powder.

I didn't get to try the .338 on game until 1961. The previous season I got to hunt only whitetails, and it seemed ridiculous to carry such a powerful

outfit to shoot a 140-lb. deer. So I used my .284 Mauser. But in October of 1961, several of us were camped outside of Elk City in western Idaho. (I'm not sure how "City" became part of the name. Populationwise, it didn't qualify then – maybe it does now.) On the second day, a couple of us were hunting in parallel, about a hundred yards apart, and one of them unknowingly kicked out a small mule deer which came angling in my direction.

I happened to see it coming. It had a small rack and I decided not to shoot, but when it broke through a patch of mountain mahogany a short distance ahead of me, my rifle just raised itself and the 275-gr. Speer drove through right behind the shoulders and my .338 had its

first kill. "At least he'll be good eating," I remember muttering as I knelt down with my knife. I began to think that the .338 was a lucky gun when two days later I came out of the timber at the top edge of a steep ravine, and on the facing slope perhaps 40 yards away a bull elk plowed his way upward. I don't know whether he had heard or scented me, but he sure was anxious to leave the area!

Again my rifle came up, seemingly of its own volition. I was actually looking downward at the surging animal, and when the Redfield's reticle centered itself, my trigger finger contracted and the 5x4 bull collapsed. Again, the big Speer bullet penetrated completely, smashing the spine from above and exiting low in the brisket to bury itself in the ground. It was an instant kill and not an ounce of meat was spoiled. The rack wouldn't go in any record book, but I was glad to get it. It was the only one we had to show for our 5600-mile drive from and back to Pennsylvania that year.

The following year our tent was pitched not far from Lucille (which doesn't exactly qualify as a metropolis, either), not far from Hell's Canyon, and we were hunting with an old friend, Harry Stubblefield, who lived in an isolated log cabin the rear corner of which literally overhung Cow Creek. Years earlier Harry had been a scriptwriter for MGM in Hollywood; I have no idea how he ended up in backwoods Idaho, married to a local woman. Maybe he just preferred hunting and fishing and loafing to stressful city life.

We'd been there three days and only Andy Hufnagle had fired a shot. But one shot with his wildcat 8mm-06 was enough, for its 196-gr. Hornady went through the shoulders of a wide-spreading 3x3 mule deer. The next day, as Al and Harry sat watching a high-country meadow (probably telling themselves they were hunting but more likely swapping lies about past hunts and hoping they wouldn't see anything they'd feel obligated to shoot), Andy and I worked up the opposite sides of a densely wooded, brushy ravine. Andy was doubtless hoping to see an elk; I was hoping to see anything legal.

We hadn't gone 200 yards before I was beginning to wonder what we were doing in a place so thick it was impossible to move quietly. Then in a shaft of sunlight 75 yards ahead, I saw a foot-long forked-branch section of antler shining. I stopped, breath held, and eased my rifle up. Through the scope I could see a hand-size spot of grayish-white that I knew was a deer's neck. A buck. I knew if I took another step he'd be gone. But could I hit a spot that small, offhand? There was no choice except to try. When the rifle cracked, the spot disappeared, and I didn't hear an animal running.

He hadn't moved a step. The heavy Speer bullet had centered the neck, smashing the spinal column. No eyeguards, but it was a 4x4 and I learned later it had better than a 26-inch spread. It was the biggest rack and biggest-bodied deer I'd ever killed. Al had to help Andy and me drag it out, even though it was downhill all the way.

A few years later Andy and Earl Hock and I were south of Eagle in Colorado's high country. (Is there any other kind in Colorado?) One day I was sitting on a small log at one end of a mile-long, 50-yard-wide stretch of quaking aspen. It seemed just the sort of place an old elk would lie up in, and Andy and Earl had started at the far end to shove it my way. On the quakies' lower side scattered trees and rough spots marked a long, narrow field. On the upper side was a slightly rolling, hip-high weedfield that extended to a line of trees marking the steep dropoff of the ridge. I happened to be looking that way when a mule deer walked out of the aspens and started across the weedfield.

It was a long distance away, maybe half the length of the aspen stand, which meant it was a half-mile or so, some 800 to 1000 yards. In the woods I usually carry the Redfield set at 2X, but at that power I couldn't even tell if it was a buck or doe. Cranked to 7X I could see a large, high rack. It was undoubtedly the largest I'd ever seen on a live deer. Just to see it was a thrill. But I'm a hunter and a thrill wasn't what I was after. What could I do? There was no chance of hitting that deer, and in seconds it would be gone forever.

I did the only thing I could think of. Maybe I could startle or confuse it, I thought, make it change direction, come toward me. So I slid down behind the log, used it as a rest for my left hand, held I'm not sure how far above and ahead of the buck and shot, and shot, and shot again. He didn't react in any way. Didn't speed up, didn't alter his course in the slightest, just walked out of sight in that treeline.

So why do I tell about an animal that I missed? Because, with a rifle that I used for 32 consecutive seasons, every fall from 1961 through 1992, hunting in many states and Canadian provinces, that was

The author got his .338 because he wanted an elk rifle. For 33 years it was all that, and much more.

the only critter I ever shot at that I didn't kill. I don't remember how many deer – whitetails and mulies – it accounted for while I was hunting larger critters, plus bear, caribou, pronghorns, elk and even one woodchuck! Probably there were other species I can't think of at the moment.

No moose, though. Seven times I've hunted moose, once in Alaska, even fired at one – but never connected! Everybody else makes camp, just wanders up alongside a creek and pops one. Not I – I'm forever mooseless. Maybe this ol' .338 of mine, so lucky on so many critters, just ain't a moose gun. That's OK. Everyone and everything should be allowed one weak spot. So I just don't hunt moose anymore.

In the beginning, I got my .338 because I wanted an elk rifle. It's been that, in Idaho, Montana, Wyoming, Colorado and New Mexico. I've shot 'em broadside through the shoulders, coming straight at me, even going straight away (what some guys call a "Texas heart shot") but a good bullet placed just below the tip of the spine discombulates the rear legs and makes a finishing shot easy. I've always used good bullets on elk, either the 275-gr. Speer or the 250-gr. Nosler Partition. There are many other good ones now, of course, and many other

good elk cartridges. But I've never seen any reason to change. I don't know how any other could be significantly better than a .338.

I haven't used it since 1992, though. I had a physical problem that year, and when I got out of the hospital the doctor, who was a friend and knew I was a shooter, told me I couldn't use a heavy-recoiling rifle anymore. I thought he meant something like a .505 Gibbs, but he said, "No, I mean your .338." So I haven't shot it since. But I take it out of the cabinet now and then and wipe it with an oily rag and remember past days. It's been a good gun.

PS: Remember that big mulie I didn't get? I suppose I could claim that I didn't actually miss him, that I hadn't been trying for a hit but simply tried to make him come closer to me so I could get a reasonable shot. Then I could say that I never missed an animal with this gun. But that doesn't seem copasetic. If by some fluke I had actually hit that deer I doubtless would have have been talking about it ever since, maybe sorta bragging, maybe admitting the shot was 99+ percent luck but it was still a hit. But since I did shoot three times and didn't hit, it obviously was a miss – so if I'm gonna be honest I have to admit that too!

THE EXPRESS BULLET IN AMERICA

BY JIM FORAL

From acceptance to indifference, this British idea literally shaped projectiles forever.

1873 was a milestone year in American firearms history. The antiquated percussion ignition system was finally laid to rest when Army Ordnance adopted the breechloading Trapdoor Springfield together with its ammunition, the .45-70 central-primed metallic cartridge. Another combination paramount in significance was the Colt Single Action revolver and its companion .45 Colt cartridge, also introduced in 1873.

Success and survival of the newly organized National Rifle Association was dependant on the existence of a range suitable for national and international competition. On June 21, 1873, the first meet was held and the dedicatory matches fired at the newly-opened NRA Creedmoor facility on Long Island.

And on Aug. 14, 1873, Charles Hallock released the inaugural bi-weekly issue of *Forest and Stream*, a paper its founder was pleased to subtitle "the recognized medium of entertainment, instruction, and information between American sportsmen."

Forest and Stream included sections devoted to gunning for birds and waterfowl, fishing, boating, travel, natural history, and the other outdoor pursuits popular at the time. Matters important to the rifleman were not overlooked. Long-range marksmanship had developed into a national preoccupation, and readers were presented reportage of the thousand-yard competitions from the new Creedmoor range. Match coverage was thorough to a fault, and the consistently high scorers were celebrated and idolized to the point of glorification. Also, the minutiae of the fledgling NRA's official and administrative goings-one were the basis of the journal's review and editorializing. Staff writers assembled much of the content and relied heavily on reader's letters for the rest.

Forest and Stream's circulation grew as English-speaking foreigners became aware of the publication's existence. When their letters arrived on Hallock's desk, they received the customary editorial consideration. Many were subsequently published. Most bore United Kingdom postmarks, penned by prosperous English adventurers just back from one of the far-flung British Empire outposts in India or Africa, where they had a wildly successfully go at the region's dangerous beasts.

Their batteries followed a common thread: the rifles were side-by-side doubles of large bore, chambered for massive cartridges holding an eighth of a cup of black powder. The bullets had a visible hole at the front end. These correspondents told tales of sinfully huge bags of lions and tigers cleanly and crushingly slain with a novel and "most fatal type of projectile" known in their circle as the Express bullet.

This series of broadcastings was the first exposure to the Express bullet for most Americans, and they demanded elaboration. In the forum that *Forest and Stream* afforded, this awakening led to curiosity and then to suspicion and doubt. Further enlightenment resulted in conviction, and the desire and determination to emulate naturally followed. The spark which had been struck by a few letters was fanned into a flame by other writers.

An Alexander Henry damascus barreled double rifle, chambered for the .450-400-2-5/8" case. It was made in 1879 and typical of the type used by the Brits in their globetrotting glory days of slaying the world's dangerous game with Express bullets.

Photo provided by Mike Harell.

The Express principle was nothing more or less than high velocity applied to a comparatively light bullet. High velocity was attained by burying a large amount of gunpowder behind a bullet lightened by both a reduction in length and the forming of a cylindrical cavity in the point. Flattening the high arcing trajectories of the era's big-bore cartridges reduced both holdover and the need for precise range estimation. Hits at ordinary game shooting ranges could then be accomplished more easily, and by less skilled riflemen. This was the primary objective – and practical consequence – in increasing the velocity, as gravity had less time to act on the bullet. In 1878, one correspondent expressed this distinct advantage quite simply, if a bit optimistically: "It makes no difference whether you shoot at ten yards or 150 yards, aim just the same."

The Express style was intended exclusively as a mid-range game bullet. The hollow cavity served to initate an immediate and unfailing action upon animal flesh, unfolding itself as it plowed through the tissue, and imparting its full measure of striking energy without exiting. The greater rotational speed of the bullet was also found to aid its "tearing" effect.

The Express bullet was intended for use at ranges not greater than 150 to 200 yards where its ballistic and trajectory straightening advantages were optimal. "Stonehenge," the *nom-de-plume* of the editor of *The Field*, England's period counterpart of *Forest and Stream*, once defined the Express rifle as one "with a velocity of 1,750 feet per second and thus taking a 'fine' or 'full' sight 'Kentucky' style would ensure hitting a vital part at 150 yards." Holding the bead suitably on the target's shoulder out to this distance greatly simplified sighting and eliminated altogether the frenzied fumbling with the rear sight's elevating mechanism.

Factoring in too was the German strict *Jaeger* code barring shooting at game past 150 meters, a practice considered unsportsmanlike and in opposition to the debt owed the animal. This ingrained Teutonic cultural discipline was not forsaken when the emigrants streamed out of the Motherland, but migrated along with the bulk of the Europeans.

In 1878, John Rigby was a distinguished international long range rifle competitor who also superintended the British Government Small Arms factory. He was a gun maker and a recognized authority from the "other side of the water." In *Forest and Stream* of Jan. 29, 1878, Mr. Rigby published his numerical prescription for developing the Express effect when he wrote that the proportion of powder to ball needed to be one to three, and he was totally uncompromising with this stance. The British Express cartridges of 45 caliber had ratios of 1:2.92 to 1:3.18, and the 500 calibers 1:2.92 to 1:3.20. Velocities were in the 1,800 to 2,000 fps range. The solid bulleted American cartridges, in contrast, had a proportion of 1:5 and higher. Many had case capacities to accommodate lighter bullets and more powder, and thereby the potential to approach Rigby's numbers.

English letter writers cautioned their American counterparts that their vaunted Express principle was unworkable in the ordinary U.S. sporting rifles. This alleged unsuitability rested upon a pair of restrictive factors. First, a bullet introduced to the shallow square-cut form of rifling at 1,600 fps or thereabouts was simply unable to withstand the violent wrench of engagement without stripping the rifling. To contain the tremendous torque and take the rifling reliably, only the Henry rifling served. This was the British rifleman's dogmatic assertion.

The Henry rifling style, better known as "Express rifling," was invented in 1859

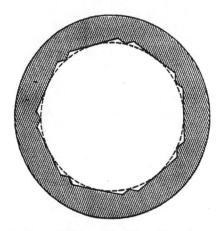

Similar to Whitworth's rifling, Henry's rifling added a land in place of the Whitworth style's corners.

and adopted by the British government in 1871. Henry rifling was developed by Scottish gun maker Alexander Henry. Essentially the Henry scheme was a polygonal form of rifling, guiding the projectile with seven wide grooves each .007 to .009" in depth.

Initially, the rifling's incompatibility with American cartridges was accepted by most. For a time, the American opinion of the Express system was wholly based upon the foreign experience with it, as it was conveyed in the sporting journals. Some Americans perceived an advantage with the Express plan, but weren't flush enough to spring for a costly but properly Henry rifled double. They already had a perfectly good, conventionally grooved Sharps or Remington rifle that they weren't about to discard.

Over the course of a few weeks in *Forest and Stream*, the actuality of this stumbling block was under question, which mutated into doubt, and transformed into challenge before finally being put to the test. In 1878, a point was reached when American rifleman endeavored to lay a foundation of Express bullet experience of their own, using domestically produced rifles.

To a greater or lesser extent, a gaggle of individuals dabbled with adapting the Express bullet to perform in American sporting arms. One man's efforts exemplified this investigative spirit and resulted in its most significant contribution.

A Montana rifle crank who signed his *Forest and Stream* submissions simply with the letter "P" put on the record his interesting experiments with a long

range Sharps .44-100 Creedmoor, set up and sighted to punch holes in the thousand-yard target. "P" set out to prove that the Express principle could be successfully applied to rifles of this class and engrossed himself in the project. At the cost of $12, not an insignificant investment in 1878, he had the Sharps Rifle Co. make for him a special mold to cast a 44-caliber paper patched bullet, 7/8 inch long with a 3/16-inch hole in its nose extending three-quarters of the length of the 270-grain bullet. (We nowadays routinely shoot 44-caliber *pistol* bullets that approach these dimensions.) In contrast, the contemporary 44-caliber solid rifle bullet of the day weighed 450 to 520 grains.

Results with a 96-grain black powder charge at the 200-yard range showed the same 7/8-inch groups seen previously with 450-grain slugs, but with dramatic changes in elevation. Using a three-foot drop tube, it was possible to compact 105 grains of Curtis and Harvey's finest #6 black powder into the case, with no deterioration in accuracy and fewer "unaccountables" (i.e., flyers) than with the heavier bullets. A consequent trajectory flattening allowed "P" to set aside his towering heel-mounted vernier sight and replace it with an accurate hunting sight.

After a winter, seven pounds of powder and several more of lead "P" was able to conclude that the Sharps would do "as accurate and uniform shooting up to 200 yards as with a 450-520 grain solid bullet."

Earlier that year, George W. Davison, superintendent of sporting rilfes at Providence Tool Co., the Peabody-Martini manufactory, had contacted A.C. Hobbs, who worked at a similar capacity for Union Metallic Cartridge Co. Mr. Davison appealed to the ammunition maker for some bullets of the Express type for trial in his company's mid- and long-range rifles. Obligingly, Hobbs designed a 44-caliber projectile that was dimensionally a duplicate of the one designed by "P." So as to keep air out of the hollow cavity, a thin copper tube lined the hole and capped the bullet's flat nose.

Noted especially eagerly were the 200-yard trajectories against the 100 yard impacts. With loads comparable to those that "P" had put up, the .44 bullet only dropped nine inches at 200 yards and a foot at 250. A group fired using 44-caliber 540-grain pointed bullets, shot to compare drop between the two styles, landed an eye-opening 33 inches beneath the 250 yard Express bullet

cluster. Accuracy with the hollow points was all that could be hoped for.

Proven beyond contention in 1878 was that the Express principle's fundamental advantage of flattening the trajectory of the bullet's flight could be realized in an American production rifle. Also laid to rest that year was the soundness of the British belief that no other than the deeply grooved Henry rifling could withstand the unsettling torque to clench and properly spin a soft lead bullet at Express rifle speeds. The contention that a patched bullet had not escaped the grip of shallow groove rifling had been publicly and persuasively demonstrated. Just as importantly, the powder to bullet ratio formulated by "P," which he had calculated to be 1: 2-5/8, was in conformity with the Rigby edict and actually bettered by an appreciable degree Rigby's 1:3 directive.

"Bear Paw," another Montanan who also contributed significantly in this direction, eyewitnessed the shooting of a 40-caliber American rifle using a homemade 102-grain Express bullet with enough powder behind it to give a 1:2.38 proportion. On the 200-yard target, 13 shots grouped into an 8-inch circle. The conclusions of these men proved beyond contention that whatever merit found in the Express system could indeed be successfully utilized by most domestic rifles in regard to accuracy and trajectory.

High velocity coupled with flat trajectory were all for naught, however, if the Express bullet were not proven inherently accurate. Francis J. Rabbeth was a master rest shooter, prominent member of the august Walnut Hill coterie, and oft-cited *Forest and Stream* contributor. He owned an imported rifle grooved on the Henry system and chambered for a 45-caliber shell of undisclosed identity. Backed by 110 grains of powder, it would put 10 550-grain solid lead bullets into a three-inch group at 200 yards. Substituting a 275-grain Express bullet over the same charge, 10 shots required a 28-inch circle to hold them all. Curious about the results of his F&S Ltd. fellows, Rabbeth, in January of '79, issued a call for their 200-yard groups.

Response to the appeal was immediate. A citizen shooting an Alexander Henry rifle almost identical to Mr. Rabbeth's duplicated his outcome on the target. Bullets recovered from a snow bank had turned almost inside out. Regarding accuracy, though, "G.J.R" had this to say: "I had rather estimate elevation for the long range bullet than take the chances of the Express bullet going where it is aimed." A Pennsylvanian firing an English-made double rifle of 500 caliber, charged with 164 grains of black powder and 340 grains of lead, put his 10 shots in 7 inches. Over the course of the winter, several other correspondents mailed in their results. Compared to Rabbeth's, some were much better and some worse, with no clearcut standard emerging.

Every indicator suggests that the great majority of this generation's hunters were of the "a bullet is a bullet" school and were thus hopelessly uninterested in the purported advantages of Express loadings. In the main, these men hunted their deer with whatever gun was available to them, "held for hair," and hopeful of a happy result pulled their triggers. More than occasionally, the half-hearted follow-up of a cripple was just part of the hunt.

Early on, people speculated as to the action of Express bullets on animal flesh but left it to the more analytically inclined to arrive at the facts. Across America, inquisitive men straddled carcasses and waded through gore. Pushing aside organs, they probed and explored wound channels, studied the anatomic course the bullet took through the vitals and measured its track. They picked out the splintered bone shards, fingered the ruined bloodshot meat and noted generally the fullness of destruction. During these post-mortems, many bullets lacking the steam to exit were recovered. Dissectors pored earnestly over the mushroomed shapes and marveled at the particularly striking telescoping stretching back upon the base. Automatically contrasted were the bent and minimally expanded remains of the familiar solid bullet, the relatively unchanged round ball, as well as the dramatic differences in the frontal areas of the types.

Tissue damage seemed not to be the only, or even the primary, function in the actual mechanics of the Express killing. The Express penetrated generally less than any other similarly profiled projectile, but the key to the violent working associated with it seemed to center on its internal hollow. Intelligent deducers and educated guessers gathered and surmised what was happening. Meeting the resistance of blood and semi-fluid flesh, the air in the cavity compacted on impact, forcing the ductile nose

section apart, initiating its stretching and peeling rearward. At the same time, this compressive motion imparted an indefinable life-snuffing effect that the 1870s amateur ballisticians awkwardly tried to describe but fell short of fully conveying. This abstract phenomenon is well known to 21st-century fans of fast, light bullets as hydrostatic shock. The intangibility that came to be known as "Express Shock" was an unanticipated side-effect that was universal in its observance. No one pooh-poohed its reality. To the extent that this range of investigators were afforded magazine space, their discoveries were shared with *Forest and Stream* subscribers and shined a beacon's light to illuminate the Express bullet system.

Historically, penetration in wood has been thought to be the acid test of ballistic potency, and how far an Express bullet would pass through cellulose became an issue in 1879. A few of that era's well-intentioned experimenters, eager to serve, lined up the winter's cordwood, pointed their muzzles, and let fly. These penetration tests were individually conducted, and thus lacked regulation. The unstandardized wood medium varied according to locality from the softest pine to flinty black walnut and burly oak. Many bullet paths were carefully measured but some were

not. A common observation was that the Express bullet, shot into timber, did not expand to any great extent. Generally, they could be counted on to perforate 9 to 12 inches of "wood."

Some Americans questioned the need for the gaping opening found on the foreign Express bullets, and there was a measure of stateside experimentation to establish the optimum depth and shape of the hollow. The determination was left to the small handful of theorists with the willingness to delve into it. Reports from these scattered analysts agreed that overly long cavities produced uniformly poor results at the target – if the bullet made it that far. The deepest were proven to fail when a lead base plug was blown through the hole, leaving a shell of the metal lodged in the bore. A short hollow resulted in a heavy bullet that in all regards behaved like a solid one. Learning from failure, a happy medium was the committee's conclusion. The most favorable point to terminate the orifice was at the internal juncture of the bullet's nose and its bore riding body. The "more is better" sentiment didn't apply to the width of the hole either. Tests suggested that there was little to be gained from an opening wider than between 1/16 and 1/8 of an inch. There seemed to be no universal preference for either a cylindrical or tapered hole,

Winchester provided its answer to the European Express system in its line of repeating and single shot arms. This advertisement appeared in the Feb. 7, 1889, issue of *Shooting and Fishing*.

In wide use for more than a century, the Gould 330-grain Express (aka Ideal/Lyman 457122) has been touted as the perfect .45-70 cast bullet for deer.

though the latter had the advantage of being easier to cast.

Since the 1884 founding of the Ideal Manufacturing Co, it behooved John Barlow as a businessman to keep abreast of the American rifleman's trends and fancies. Indeed, his firm's success was dependent upon ministering to the era's hand loaders and furnishing the molds and tools to assemble ammunition for the latest cartridges together with the bullets currently fashionable. Toward this end, Express-style bullets were added to his ever-increasing line. In the main, these were worked up by very capable personalities who had achieved notoriety or a following via journal contributions. Few were in-house designs. Col. W.D. Pickett, a well-known killer of Wyoming grizzlies, designed 205-grain paper-patched .32-40 and 325-grain 45-caliber Express bullets, both featuring inordinately deep burrows. Shown in the earliest Ideal Handbooks was the Gay '90s state-of-the-art 45-caliber Express bullet. The 45-330 Express, drawn up by Barlow himself for A.C. Gould, the editor of *Shooting and Fishing* magazine, became instantly and enduringly popular. Recently resurrected as #457122, the timeless Gould's Hollow point is once again available from Lyman. Winchester also supplied molds for the fashionable Express bullets, as did Providence Tool Co.

Some of the non-handloading American hunters felt that factory solid bulleted cartridges kept them out of the Express race. These malcontents agitated for a low cost American Express

rifle, and there was enough disturbance to convey a demand. Winchester, always ready to meet a demand, responded with their Model of 1876, chambered in .50-95 Express, at the height of the mania.

The February 8, 1883, number of *Forest and Stream* carried an Englishman's challenge of Winchester's "misleading" attachment of the Express designation to the cartridge. Since the Winchester round's underachieving 95-grain charge was little more than half of the 165 grains William A. Baillie-Graham burned in his 50-caliber double rifle chambered for a real Express, he'd determined the American lever action was "decidedly not an Express rifle." Though the 50-95's 1:3 ratio harmonized with John Rigby's gospel, contemporary British wisdom now dictated that a cartridge case holding less than 110 grains of powder failed to qualify as a proper Express cartridge. Baillie-Graham had hunted the U.S. western wilderness considerably. He signed his essays "Stalker" and was the author of the 1882 work *Camps in the Rockies,* in which an admission is found wherein a Wyoming elk having absorbed 14 of Stalker's celebrated 50-caliber Express balls, and was finally reduced to possession on the fifteenth. He routinely hunted with an Express load in the left barrel and a solid in the right, and laid claim to popularizing the practice among his fellow British globetrotters.

The ammunition plant of the Winchester Repeating Arms Co. began loading Express bullets late in 1879 after being granted a patent in September of that year. The hollow of the Winchester bullet was lined with a drawn copper tube,

The .50-95-300 Express as loaded by Winchester. This cartridge was Winchester's answer to the European big-bore Express cartridges, and several fit into the tubular magazine of their Model 1876 lever action rifle.

closed at the exposed end, and imprinted with their distinguishing raised "X." Some loadings of the various 45- and 50-caliber cartridges adapted to the Winchester Models 1876 and 1886 were available with the special bullet. A .45-90 Express load bore the WRA headstamp by 1887, and the .45-125-300 and .40-110-260 special chamberings for the Model 1885 Single Shot were unveiled the following year. Union Metallic Cartridge Co. also loaded several cartridges and calibers with their own Express bullets.

The shorter Express bullets required a slower twist to properly stabilize. Winchester cut their rifling for the .45-70, which commonly held bullets of 405 to 500 grains at 1:22. The pitch was slowed to 1:36 in the Single Shot High Walls chambered for the .45-125 Express and loaded with a stubby 300-grain projectile. In like manner, their 50-110-450 used a 1:54 twist, while the .50 Express shells, the .50-95 and .50-100 Express, were rifled at 1:60.

As defined by the British, the genus of Express bullets included several species of "expansive bullets." Detonation, rather than expansion, was the reason why our 1870's forebearers developed types of fragmenting projectiles collectively known as exploding bullets. Early in the 1860s, the English tried exploding bullets as range finders in their 577 Enfields. The strikes could be seen in the tell-tale puffs of smoke on rocky ground and answered well for the purpose. Later they were barred by the Geneva Convention. All was fair in shooting dumb animals, of course, and the sportsman's effort at development was exerted in this direction. It was their intention that an explosive bullet would penetrate to the vitals of the largest or most dangerous game, destroying tissue along the way, and detonating on contact with heavy bone, instantly immobilizing the animal. At the same time, explosive bullets were hoped to instantly anchor deer and elk.

The preparation of an explosive bullet began with placing a hollow in a standard solid bullet, either by casting it in an Express mold or more popularly by boring with a common drill. Fulminations were initiated most often with an ordinary primed rimfire case pressed tightly into the hole. Sam H. Mead staked a claim to the idea of using a rimfire to spark the explosion, and filed a patent on it in 1872. Proving that great minds think alike, Army officer Gen. M. G. Meigs envisioned the same possibly independently and concurrently and publicized the notion in *Forest and Stream* early the next year.

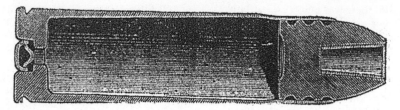

The .50-115-300 Bullard Express was the most powerful chambering in the Bullard line of lever actions competing with the Winchester. This cut of a sectioned cartridge, and its Express bullet, was published in *Forest and Stream* on March 20, 1884.

An entire .22 rimfire cartridge, with the bullet nipped flush with the case mouth, was sometimes substituted. The lowly percussion cap was also contrived to work effectively. The handloaders doctored their bullets prior to loading, but the multitudes performed their applications on live black powder cartridges.

Before being topped with the priming mechanisms, cavities were sometimes filled with a sundry assortment of detonating agents or explosive mixtures. Black powder, dynamite, and nitroglycerine were among the first tried. Later, various "ate"-suffixed chemical compounds (e.g., lead styphnate) were put to use. To these, ground glass was sometimes added to increase the blend's sensitivity. During this course of refinement, many promising combinations were found to be about as explosive as baking powder. Some unlucky or careless experimenters lost beards and eyebrows to certain concoctions being touched off while being ground in a porcelain mortar.

The accounts of modest successes notwithstanding, *Forest and Stream* contributors made known the unimaginary dangers associated with the explosive bullet. In 1877, "Mountaineer" recorded an episode involving a bullet containing 5 grains of dynamite (!) in its cavity. He pulled the trigger on his Remington .44 and the heavy barrel burst into a thousand pieces. The ground was sprinkled with globules of melted lead. "The concussion of the powder charge was too quick for it," he tried to explain. For those reckless enough to monkey with the mini-grenades, "Mountaineer" advanced a stern admonition: "Don't try it! Emphatically, don't do it!" Some years later, another contributor who tried the same stunt and reported a similar outcome was charmingly expressive with his advice to emulators: "I would not fool with no dynamite bullet!" At least one account exists of an explosive bullet of some description spontaneously igniting while innocently stored in the breast

pocket of a user. Serious burns resulted. For those lacking the sense to realize that these things had no place in tubular magazines, the warning was repeatedly broadcast. There is no record of anyone having learned the hard way.

Danger apart, the most serious drawback to the explosive bullet was lack of penetration, the first requisite of a killing bullet. From the sum of readers who chimed in with their first-hand experiences, the most important and authoritative data on this area of study was mailed from Miner's Ranch, San Diego, California. T. S. Van Dyke hunted the deer inhabiting the thick chaparral ranch country, and shot them with a 44-70 Maynard rifle. By January of 1879, he'd struck 42 deer, 11 of which escaped entirely. Twenty-four dropped in their tracks or nearly so. The balance required some trailing. A studious carcass analysis proved the action of the homemade explosive bullet. Typically, the ball penetrated about an inch before bursting and making a wedge-shaped two- to four-inch hole. The sides adjoining the cavity blew away, and the butt of the projectile passed on as an independent bullet. For the masses he summarized: "That these balls are a great improvement over solid balls of the same caliber (except where great penetration is needed, when they are decidedly inferior)." By the time he sat down to write *The Still Hunter* in 1882, the deer tally taken by explosive bullets had risen to over 300 and his mind had evidently changed. Van Dyke then regarded that form of hunting bullet to be "absurdly overrated." In the main, the collective experiences of other *Forest and Stream* writers coincided.

Still, this type of bullet continued to be reasonably popular for almost 30 years. User accounts were sporadically written up but petered out entirely about 1900.

Lord Keene's unique split point bullet of the mid-1880s combined the instant expansion of the Express bullet with the uncropped length and beneficial weight

of the conventional solid lead projectile. The Keene was cast in an ordinary bullet mold and was somewhat labor intensive to fabricate. Prior to ladling the molten metal, a thin strip of paper was placed at the point between the mold halves, microscopically separating them. After the bullets dropped from the mold, the narrow division was closed in a swage. Essentially the same end could be achieved with a fine-bladed jeweler's saw, and the Keene principle was safely applied to the bullets of factory cartridges this way. Correspondents of the era recorded procuring ready-made Keenes of various diameters directly from Winchester.

When striking flesh, the soft bisected nose peeled back to the base of the split, ideally remaining intact. Too long of a slit, or one not sufficiently closed, weakened the bullet and increased the likelihood that the bullet would open in flight, a fairly common complaint. Narrowing the paper used or locating the division just below the point of the bullet were adjustments that solved the problem. Testing one's molded Keene bullets on a series of pine boards was the precautionary recommendation. A clean entry proved the bullet didn't widen before striking, while a larger hole in board No. 2 indicated the desired result.

Fully as accurate as any other bullet, the Keene design had every potential to be a good killer and the many favorable testimonials finding their way onto the printed page proved it to be. Opinions didn't vary much.

Divided somewhat over his keenness for the Keene was a New York sportsman who'd given them a fair trial. With his .45-90 Winchester, he'd taken bear, caribou,

The Keene bullet could either be purchased from Winchester and other vendors, or cast in a mold with a strip of paper (represented by the rectangular outline) separating the mold halves. Ideally, the bullet unfolded on impact as the illustration on the left suggests it should. Cut taken from the 1898 *Ideal Handbook*.

and several deer during the extended hunting season of 1887. During the next fall's outing, he'd determined the bullets opened "all right" on a mountain ram and antelope, but "acted like solid balls" on a bear and a caribou. "I suppose there is not enough powder back of them" he offered as a possible explanation. These were the observations of a hunter 10 years away from the "crowded hour" in Cuba that would catapult him to national prominence and whose missive was published in the December 6, 1888, number of *Forest and Stream*, over his signature, which was "Theodore Roosevelt."

The Keene pattern of expansive bullet achieved a level of popularity and body of admirers surpassed only by the Express bullet. Well into the 20th century, John Barlow's *Ideal Handbook*, the *vade mecum* of the rifleman, carried instructions for molding the Keene bullet.

An inspiration, particularly within the sphere of ordnance, is likely to occur to any number of individuals, often separated by years and miles. Periodically, someone stumbles onto the scene who proves the accuracy of the adage "there is nothing new under the sun."

Captain John Forsyth, in his seminal 1867 treatise *The Sporting Rifle and its Projectiles*, described a tubular bullet, one having a longitudinal hole through its axis. Great ballistic advantages were claimed for the concept, and theoretically it seemed workable. Forsyth semi-successfully tested his bored end-to-end bullets and broadcast his findings where few would have noticed. Teeming with possibilities though they might have been, the entire unsophisticated world still clung to the spherical lead ball and wasn't ready for the captain's potentially two-steps-forward notion.

Inevitably imitators or the likewise inspired surfaced. None could overcome the common obstacle of boring a hole perfectly centrally through a lead bullet with available tooling. What bullets were produced were unbalanced; it varied only in degree. A generation passed before one A. Weed envisioned the ultimate Express bullet, one minimally affected by air resistance. In 1889, Mr. Weed was convinced that his hollow bullet brainstorm was an idea whose time had come. The Weed bullet was a three-piece assembly. A felt base wad sealed propellant gases and protected the bullet base. Sandwiched between base wad and projectile was a sheet copper disc. The wad was unattached and dropped back after exiting the muzzle.

A fair number of whitetails died during field testing of Weed's bullet. Results ran the gamut from lengthwise penetration and total evisceration to glancing off a buck's shoulder blade. Weed's friend, using .40-60 Marlin handloads topped with the Forsyth re-invention, pronounced the bullet to be a "most destructive missile."

There was a more than modest regional interest and an effort to market these bullets commercially, but the idea shriveled up until it's next incarnation, which happened at least twice in the ensuing black powder years.

The preponderance of Express bullet discussion sparked not only experimentation, but an insightfulness beyond the craze. A New York reader known only as "Hawkeye" had been paying attention and noted the bountiful reportage of the Express bullet's failure to penetrate and became convinced that a bear skin should show two holes. He then tendered a projectile combining the qualities of both the hollow pointed and solid bullets with a description and sketch of an "express envelope bullet."

The mantle was of unspecified composition, which brings to mind the old gag about how to become a millionaire: first, acquire a million dollars. The pure lead core was poured through the jacket's point, and was secured by flanges formed at the base. On impact, the envelope was to open and the intact bullet proper penetrated and expanded. Rife with flaws, the thing had some merit on paper. "Hawkeye's" pipedream made it into print in the April 10, 1884 number of *Forest and Stream*, but progressed no further.

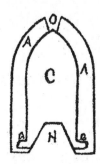

Hawkeye's 1884 visionary and totally theoretical solution to the Express bullet's lack of penetration. This bore-diameter projectile incorporated futuristic notions such as a lead core that was surrounded by and physically secured to a jacket, and a deep concavity at the base that ensured a perfect gas seal.

By the early 1890s the Express bullet phase had run its couse and most of the era's hunters went back to the proven lead solids to humanely dispatch the annual venison. Thereafter, keeping apace with ballistic advancement, the expanding game bullet has been in a state of continuous evolution. Presently, the earliest smokeless powders were pushing metal cased 30 calibers to over 2,000 fps. For a few years the generic "soft point" was all the rage before being supplanted by the speedy jacketed spitzer capped, wedged, dimpled, or tubed, depending on the expansion initiation principle involved. Stripped of the gimmickry, the simple cup jacket and lead core was refined into the reliable killing bullet that three generations found satisfactory.

Period acceptance of the Express, explosive and expansive bullets ranged from genuine exuberance to utter indifference, and impressions with it varied according to the user's own experience. Many, it seems, felt that their personal trials with the hollow point had been a waste of powder, lead, and unrecovered game. In the end, it was learned that nothing killed North American herbivores quite so dependably as did the standby solid lead bullet.

An early 1890's show of hands in the magazines implies that the Express system had had its day and was found wanting, and all indicators suggest that one reflective sportsman was not alone in his sentiments when he lamented in the December of 1898 issue of *Recreation*: "I was foolish enough to try the Express."

In the end, the Express bullet in all its forms was just another of the finicky rifleman's fads. *Forest and Stream,* on the other hand, was not a flash in the pan. It lead the way in the earliest conservation efforts, initiated legislation outlawing market hunting and campaigned for more restrictive game laws. After 57 continuous years of serving and informing the American outdoorsman, it was absorbed by *Field and Stream* in 1930.

[Editor's Note: The now-forgotten Hoxie Bullet Company of Chicago also offered a proprietary version of an Express bullet. The Hoxie bullet contained a deep hollow-point partially filled with a steel pellet that supposedly aided expansion. Customers could send their bullets to the company to have them "Hoxieized" – at least they could before the company failed altogether around WWI. –DMS]

In Search of the Perfect Upland Autoloader

BY NICK HAHN

I f an average shotgunner were asked to conjure up in his mind's eye a scene depicting an upland hunter, no doubt that hunter would be armed with either a side-by-side or an over/under shotgun. For the past half-century or so, we have been conditioned to think that an upland gunner should be armed with a two-barreled gun. Repeaters are permissible in the wetlands when shooting waterfowl, but for upland game, double guns are what we believe are best suited. But despite all the articles and advertising about double guns, if an accurate survey were conducted, the results would show that more upland game is shot with repeaters than with doubles.

It used to be that the vast majority of repeaters found in the field were pump guns. However, in the last couple of decades, the autoloader has gained considerably on the pump gun in popularity. Today it is possible to find an autoloader that is priced a few bucks less than

Browning A-5 Sweet Sixteen, a popular upland autoloader from its first appearance in 1936 through the 1960s.

some of the pump guns. Although the most popular and best-selling shotgun in North America is still the pump gun, the autoloader is not far behind, certainly ahead of the over-under and the side-by-side. Interestingly, shortly after the introduction of the first successful autoloading shotguns in America, the Belgian Browning and the similar Remington Model 11, the autoloader outsold all other shotguns six to one in

the northeast and about four to one in the rest of the country. However, with the appearance of increasing number of less-expensive pump guns, the pump gained on the autoloader, while the double continued to slide.

There is no denying that a good double gun is truly a delight in the field. In the uplands where hunters log more miles than shots, a light, fast handling shotgun is what is needed. A quality side-by-side or an over/under, especially one that is made in the smaller gauges, tends to be light, fast-handling, and easy to carry. But please note that the key is a *quality* double, which translates to more money! A cheap, poorly constructed double gun is just that: a cheap, poorly constructed gun. It is far better to get a quality autoloader than to settle for a cheap double. But "just any autoloader" will not necessarily be a better choice. Most autoloaders, especially those made in this country, are better suited for ducks than upland gunning.

A typical 12-gauge 7-1/2-pound muzzle-heavy autoloader does not make for an ideal upland gun. Probably more upland game has been shot in the last 40 years in America with a 12-gauge Remington Model 1100 than with any other autoloader. Prior to that, it was the Browning A-5 and Remington 11 and 11-48. However, they were used in the uplands more often than not, because they were the only shotguns available to the hunter, not because the gun was selected specifically for upland gunning. If any of these guns was selected for upland gunning, it was usually chambered in one of the smaller bore sizes.

Ideally, for upland gunning an autoloader (or any other gun for that matter!) should be fairly light and have a balance that tends to be light up front. The arbitrary weight limit should be no more than 7-1/4 pounds, preferably closer to 7 or under, regardless of gauge. This eliminates some autoloaders, but at the same time, still provides adequate choice to upland hunters. Among modern gas operated autoloaders, the Beretta comes to mind in its various models. Going back to the earlier Models 302 and 303 to current models, Berettas always tend to be light, averaging around 7 pounds with a 26-inch barrel in 12 gauge. They are not exactly barrel light, but they are light overall and handle very well in the uplands. The latest Beretta, A400 XPLOR, is about as light a 12 gauge autoloader you will find today. It is listed at 6.6 pounds!

Benelli, of course, leads the field in light autoloaders. Whether it is the Montefeltro, the M1 or M2, they are all not just light, but balance right with muzzle lightness. The Benelli Montefeltro, M1 and M2 weigh 7 pounds or less and the Ultra Light model weighs closer to 6 pounds. There are other makes that you might find, but the bottom line is to find one that is not just light, but is barrel light. Browning's Maxus, although

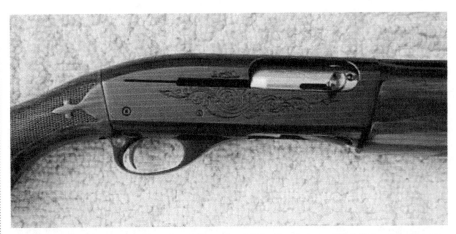
Remington Model 1100 12 gauge. Although a bit hefty at around 7-1/2 pounds, it was still very popular with upland gunners through the 1960s and 1970s. In the lighter 20 gauge at 6-1/2 pounds, it continues to be a popular upland gun.

A Browning Gold Evolve in 12 gauge weighs around 6-3/4 pounds and should make a good upland gun.

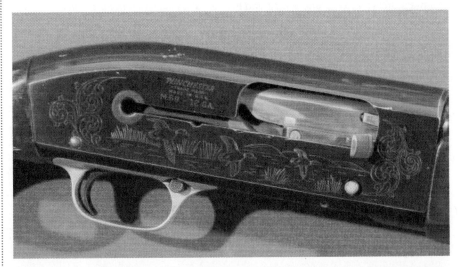
The Winchester Model 59 was especially designed for the uplands at 6-1/2 pounds in 12 gauge but never really caught on with hunters. The gun was revolutionary in that it used a lightweight barrel that was a steel liner wrapped in fiberglass, and it was the first American-made gun to use screw-in choke tubes, later known as "Winchokes."

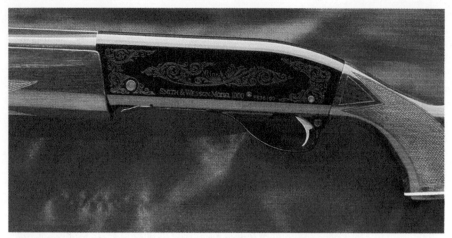

Smith & Wesson's Model 1000 looks a lot like the Remington 1100 but is considerably lighter. At around 7 pounds in 12 gauge, it made for an excellent upland autoloader. The 20 gauge model weighed around 6-1/4 pounds. It is discontinued.

Beretta's Urika 2 in 20 gauge is light and makes for an excellent upland gun.

built for waterfowling with its 3-1/2 inch chamber and camouflage finish, can still be a very effective upland gun. It is surprisingly light and handles very well.

Among older autoloaders, there were quite a few that were very good if not superb for upland gunning. The old Browning Double Auto was originally designed for boxed pigeon shooting and balances like a double gun. The "Twentyweight" model weighs around 6-1/2 pounds and the "Twelvette" closer to 7 pounds. Both are superb upland guns. There is also the old Winchester Model 59 with its revolutionary fiberglass-wrapped barrel that weighed 6-1/2 pounds in 12 gauge. The Winchester was revolutionary not only because of its unusual barrel, but also because it was the first American made shotgun with screw-in choke tubes. The Franchi 48AL could weigh as little as 6-1/4 pounds in 12 gauge with a plain, short barrel. Perhaps the lightest of all was the futuristic Armalite AR-17 or the "Golden Gun" as it was called. The Armalite was made in 12 gauge only, and like the Browning Double Auto, it was a two-shooter and operated on the short recoil system. The Armalite tipped the scale at a wispy 5-1/2 pounds in 12 gauge! There were other imported autoloaders that were pretty light in 12 gauge. In the 1950s and 60s there was the Breda, a unique, exceptionally well-made long recoil-operated autoloader. The Breda normally weighed around 7 pounds in 12 gauge but could be had in the Superlight model that weighed 6-3/4 pounds. So there has never been a shortage of light, properly balanced autoloaders for the uplands.

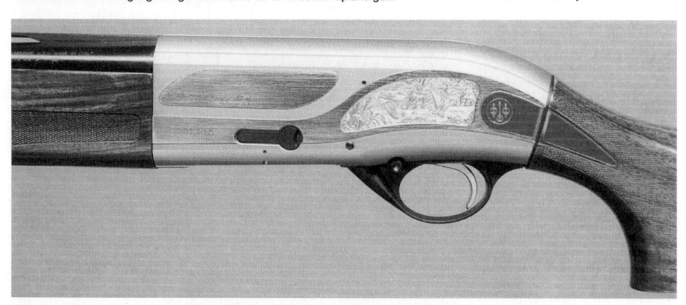

Beretta AL391 Tekny's Gold. Like all Berettas, it is fairly light at 7 pounds in 12 gauge.

In 16 gauge, the Browning Sweet Sixteen in the old A-5 configuration – and its licensed Remington and Savage humpback knockoffs – is just about all that was and is available. However, it is possible to locate an old Remington 11-48 16 with a receiver that was "shaved" to better suit the smaller gauge. Savage did make a rather bulbous-looking Model 775, a lightened version of the odel 755 that weighed around 7 pounds, but it was an ugly gun and did not sell well. Whatever the case may be, in the older models it is best to avoid ventilated ribbed barrels for upland gunning. Not only does the ventilated rib contribute significantly to overall gun weight (about a quarter of a pound) but it adds weight in a crucial area, up front. A Browning Sweet Sixteen with a plain 26-inch barrel averages 6-3/4 pounds and handles beautifully. With a ventilated rib, the weight can increase to over 7 pounds. A 7 pound gun should be a 12, not a 16, if it is to be used in the uplands.

The same thing can be said about the Remington 11-48. With a short plain barrel, the Remington could weigh as little as 6-1/2 pounds, while with a ventilated rib it tends to be closer to 7. The legendary Remington 1100 did come in 16, but as good as the 1100 is for a variety of shotgunning, it is not the best gun for the uplands in 12 or 16 gauges. Besides being somewhat heavy, it was always a bit nose-heavy, not the best thing for an upland gun. Yet, because it points so well, it has served as an upland gun for many a successful upland hunter.

In the 1980s Remington attempted to correct the nose-heavy tendency of the 1100 for the uplands and came out with their Special Field models with 21-inch barrels. But these guns, although lighter with their short barrels and shortened magazines, did not have a very good balance. Merely chopping the barrel shorter, as most manufacturers are prone to do, does not make an "upland" gun, it just makes it a shorter gun! Although there are upland gunners who swear by the Remington Special Field"models with their stubby barrels, they are not ideally suited and tend to have poor balance. The current Remington "contour" barrels are a much better solution, and the new Model 105 CTI made of lightweight materials makes for a dandy upland autoloader at around 7 pounds in 12 gauge.

In 20 gauge, the picture changes somewhat and even the nose-heavy Remington 1100 Lightweight 20 can

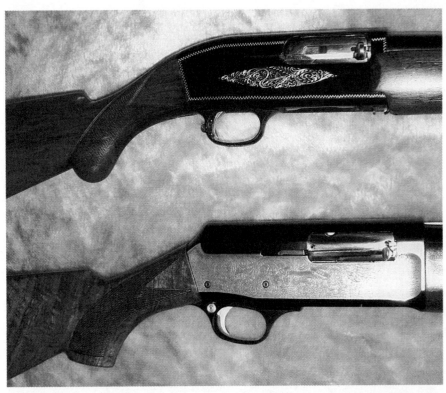

Two of the best 12 gauge upland autoloaders ever made in the past, the Browning Double Auto in "Twelvette" at 6-3/4 pounds and the Franchi 48 AL "Eldorado" grade at 6-1/2 pounds. Both guns could be had lighter if equipped with shorter, ribless barrels.

make a good upland gun. Just about all the 20 gauge autoloaders are suitable for upland gunning provided that they are properly choked. Some are, of course, better suited for upland gunning than others. Perhaps the best way to separate the 20 gauges is by using three categories. The first category is "standard models" and includes those weighing between 6-1/2 and 7 pounds such as the Remington 1100 LT 20, Browning Gold, etc. These guns make good upland guns if they are choked properly.

The second category, the "light-weights" includes 2- gauge autoloaders such as the Berettas and Benellis, and even the old Browning A-5 "Twenty" (commonly referred to as "Light Twenty") and the earlier-mentioned Breda. These are 20 gauges that all weigh somewhere between a few ounces under 6 pounds and 6-1/2 pounds. They are all balanced right for the uplands and their light overall weight makes them ideal for carrying over hill and dale.

The third category is what can be termed as "ultralight" autoloaders. Currently there are only two that qualify as ultralights. Although there are Benelli M-1s, M-2s and Montefeltros that dip under 6 pounds, to qualify as an ultralight the

gun has to weigh closer to 5-1/2 pounds in 20 gauge.

The Benelli Ultra Light model in 20 gauge is claimed to weigh 5 pounds, 2 ounces. It is indeed a feathery, delightful autoloader, but not quite as light as claimed. Benelli achieved lighter weight by using a shorter magazine tube, shorter barrel, and a carbon fiber ventilated rib. But despite its shorter barrel, it balances very well because its receiver is longer by about an inch than the average autoloader's, and the barrel is not seated as deeply, giving it another inch of length. Therefore, the Benelli with a 24-inch barrel is of same overall length as a Browning A-5 with a 26-inch barrel.

A sleeper in this group of ultralight autoloaders is the Franchi 48AL. The Franchi was always considered to be the lightest autoloader one could get. It used to be advertised as the world's lightest autoloader and I suppose that is still true today. The Benelli Ultra Light is indeed very light, but it is a few ounces heavier than the Franchi. The Franchi has excellent balance combined with feathery weight. A typical Franchi 48AL 20-gauge (the earlier model without screw-in chokes) with 26-inch ventilated rib barrel weighs 5 pounds, 4 ounces. With shorter barrel (Franchi made 24-inch barrels) it would weigh-in at the advertised 5 pounds 2 ounces. Today's guns, because of the screw-in chokes, tend to weigh a few ounces more, although they are still feathery. The Benelli Ultra Light 20 gauge with 24-inch barrel averages around 5 pounds, 6 ounces, which is 4 ounces more than the advertised 5 pounds, 2 ounces. Perhaps Benelli's advertising claims are a bit overly optimistic. Still, at less than 5-1/2 pounds, it is plenty light!

In 28 gauge, there is the Remington 1100 and the Franchi 48AL. The Remington tends to be heavier, but it still makes for an excellent upland gun, as does the discontinued Remington, 11-48 which is lighter than the 1100. The Franchi is one of the lightest 28 gauge autoloaders on the market today. It is built on the 20 gauge receiver and weighs about the same as the 20. It make for a wonderful upland gun with an average weight of around 5-1/2 pounds. There's also the now-defunct Charles Daly import, a gas-operated gun that appears to be pretty good, but the gun has not been around long enough to provide adequate assessment.

A pair of vintage Franchi 48 AL "Eldorado" grade. A 12 gauge (1986; top) at 6 1/2 pounds and a 20 gauge (1968) at 5 1/2 pounds. Both excellent upland autoloaders.

Browning Double Auto "Twelvette." One of the finest upland autoloaders ever made. Initially designed for the European market, the Double Auto could be had in the "Twentyweight" model, which weighed one-quarter to one-half pound less than the "Twelvette."

The latest addition in 28 gauge comes from Benelli. It is a scaled-receiver Legacy Model that weighs 5 pounds. There haven't been enough of these Benellis in the field yet for them to have built a reputation. They seem to be great little autoloaders, but they are pricey. Benelli would have been better served putting out a Montefeltro or M2 model in 28 gauge rather than the more expensive, engraved Legacy model.

There are those who use the .410 on upland game. However, it should be confined to use on the smaller game birds such as quail and dove and not the larger birds. I know, many a game farm pheasant has been shot with a .410, but a game farm bird is a totally different animal from the tough wild ringneck. Also, shots should be kept to closer distances. For most gunners, 30 yards would be about the maximum distance that they should attempt to use the .410. There just aren't enough shot pellets in the skinny little hull.

When it comes to the .410 autoloader, there is currently only the Remington 1100. It makes for a fine skeet gun as well as small bird shotgun, although it is a bit hefty at over 6-1/2 pounds. The older Model 11-48 is about a half a pound lighter but is extremely scarce on the used-gun market.

There are a number of inexpensive double guns on the market today that cost less than the pricier autoloaders. But as the old saying goes, "you get what you pay for." The inexpensive doubles may very well be durable, but you can rest assured that they will more than likely be crudely finished or with a lot of glitz to cover up poor workmanship. Balance and handling qualities will not be something you will find in these cheaper doubles. It is far better to spend your money on a quality autoloader than on an inexpensive double gun.

ADDICTED TO MILITARY IRON

A recovered military bolt-action-rifle addict tells all.

BY **ANDY EWERT**

I plead guilty to behavioral addiction to 20th-century military bolt-action rifles. The good news is today I'm clean. The bad news is that relapse is always a possibility.

My "illness" began innocently enough in 1991 with an article in this very publication extolling the virtues of the Mauser 1898 military rifle. In that piece, one Jim Thompson shared his wisdom regarding what arguably is the world's greatest military bolt-action rifle. If memory serves me right, Mr. Thompson earned the Gun Digest John T. Amber Literary Award for his handicraft. It was a great read and, for me, the beginning of an extraordinary adventure.

Suitably enlightened, I promptly purchased not one but two military Mausers: a fine German DWM Model 1909 Argentine-contract 7.65X53mm

With proper modification, all the military surplus bolt action rifles featured in this article would make excellent hunting rifles. The author's sporterized specimens include (top to bottom) No. 4 Mk II Lee Enfield, featuring a Canadian Long Branch action, great sights, five-shot magazine, and the best-fitting stock he's ever shouldered, purchased ready-to-go for $150; a handy Czech CZ24 Mauser scout rifle, crafted specially for harvesting deep-woods whitetails; and a silky 6 lb. DWM 1908 Brazilian Mauser, fashioned by the author's father with a replacement barrel and aftermarket sights and trigger. The original military stock was retained, though shaped to a pleasing fit.

The stampings on the barrel of the author's 03-A3 Springfield indicate it was manufactured by Remington Arms, on or around September 1943, and that the completed rifle was successfully proof fired, as indicated by the prick punch inside the ordnance bomb insignia. Appropriate literature solves the mystery of proof marks, but sometimes you have to dig the information out. The internet sometimes can be a quick fix, but it's wise to double check online claims.

Long Rifle and an 8mm 1945-vintage Czech "mongrel" 98k, both sight unseen, from Samco Global Arms, Inc., for about $200 apiece. To feed my acquisitions, I stocked up on economical military surplus ball ammo, conveniently packed in five-round stripper clips for fast loading. I spent that summer learning the joys of open-sight riflery.

Fast-forward two decades. Today, I manage more than a dozen well-traveled bolt-action Mausers, Enfields, Arisakas, and Springfields. Most remain in their original military configuration. A select few found a new life as sporterized hunting rifles. While my 20-year itch is over, at least from the acquisition standpoint, many fond memories are rekindled every time I shoulder one of these venerable old battle rifles and sight down its barrel. To me, they're treasures of world history, firearms design, and manufacturing excellence. Each has its own story to tell.

The Brothers Mauser and My 98s

Whether or not the Mauser 98 is the greatest military bolt-action rifle is irrelevant to me. The fact is the 98 is the innovative design on which most bolt action rifles – military and commercial – are based. More so than other designs, the 98 transcended its military roots and, due to its renowned strength, reliability, and quality, is the standard for

custom hunting-rifle actions.

Introduced 113 years ago, the Mauser 98 served the Fatherland with distinction during its almost half century run that ended, for the most part, in 1945 with Germany's defeat in World War ll. Construction of military rifles based on the 98 outside of Germany continued into the 1950s. To this day, manufacturers craft expensive 98-based actions to meet the unceasing demand.

A culmination of their earlier designs, Peter and Paul Mauser's Model 98 spawned an extensive family of long-, medium-, and short-barreled military rifles, produced at factories in Germany for its military and export around the globe. The world's armies couldn't get enough of them. Under license and technology-transfer agreements, 98s were produced in Argentina, Austria, Belgium, China, the former Czechoslovakia, Iran, Mexico, Poland, Spain, and Yugoslavia, among others. America's Springfield 1903 rifle is an inexact 98 clone that earned the Mauser company royalty payments until our entry into World War I.

This prolific manufacturing base produced a lot of 98s, by some estimates over 100 million. A good number of them are still with us today, thanks to their longevity and persistent importers who seek them out. Remarkably, Mausers are still seeing combat in remote corners of Asia, Africa, Latin America, and the Middle East, usually in the hands of under-funded local insurgents.

The author and his father longed for a 1903 Springfield. Their choices, purchased from the U.S. Department of Civilian Marksmanship, were (top to bottom) a 1943-vintage Remington '03-A3 and late-1930s '03 Springfield arsenal rework, along with a 1,000 round crate of U.S. 30-06 military surplus ball ammo. In the author's view, the 03-A3's superior aperture sight makes it a better choice of the two. The author's father favors the 03's milled construction. Both old veterans function reliably, very smoothly, and are more accurate than most folks can see or hold "out yonder" with GI-issue sights.

Model 1909 Argentine

My 1909 Argentine is a superb example of German design and craftsmanship. Many of the German-produced rifles (some were also built in Argentina) have been used as the basis for fine sporting arms. Custom gun makers cherish the 1909's exquisitely milled construction, particularly its trigger guard/magazine assembly with a clever floor-plate-release lever in the guard that alone, when fabricated today, costs more than twice the $200 I paid for the entire rifle. The quality of the '09's dark-grained walnut stock is better than many of those on today's commercial rifles.

With its ladder-style military sight, rough trigger pull, 29-inch barrel, and my bifocaled eyes, off the bench it will put five rounds of surplus Argentine non-corrosive ball ammo into about 2-3/4 minutes of angle at 100 yards. (On average, with issue iron sights, all the surplus military bolt-action rifles mentioned here group about the same, some significantly less so on a good day. With a scope and match-grade handloads, however, accuracy can be astounding.)

Because of its value as an action of choice for custom rifle making, stock DWM 1909s are becoming scarce. This shortage will only become acute over time. Hopefully, a few originals will be preserved for posterity and those incurably obsessed collectors.

[Editor's note: We agree that the Argentine is one of the more attractive Mausers. However, the newbie should be aware that 7.65mm Argentine ammunition is occasionally difficult to obtain. Reloading is one obvious solution. –DMS]

Czech Mongrel 98k

Clearly 1945 was not a good year for German military rifle production. Hampered by Allied aerial bombardment, a shortage of skilled labor and raw materials, and the need for faster output, manufacturing standards slipped. One way Germany coped was by building 98k rifles at captured arms factories they controlled in Czechoslovakia.

Markings on my Czech 98k's receiver ring indicate that its receiver was produced in 1945 at the Waffenwerke Bruenn, A.-G. Werk Bystrica, in what is now in the Slovak Republic. Markings elsewhere on the rifle suggest it was assembled at the CZ factory in Brno, in the Czech Republic. Whatever this arrangement lacked in material-handling efficiency, it worked. Judging by its unmarred condition, my rifle was never issued.

Germany also dealt with production shortfalls by instituting certain manu-

facturing shortcuts. On my rifle, these included a curious-looking (though practical) oversized stamped steel trigger guard assembly that accommodates a gloved finger, and a stamped, non-detachable magazine floor plate. Eliminated were the bolt guide and cleaning rod. Gone too were milled barrel bands, replaced by stampings. The Czech 98k's firing-mechanism-disassembly washer tube on the stock was supplanted by a hole in the side of the stamped butt plate.

On the plus side, the rifle sports quality machining, fit, finish, and a handsome composite stock. To 98k purists, this dumbed-down plowhorse is downright crude. Aesthetics aside, its performance is quite another story.

One gray, snowy winter afternoon, suffering from acute cabin fever, I packed my humble 98k and a cigar box full of mixed, weatherworn military 8X57 mm and drove 60 miles to my favorite shooting ground. Wind gusts whistled across the deserted firing line. The lone range officer, ensconced in a toasty clubhouse, eyeballed me quickly, decided I wasn't a threat to anything, collected the fee, and returned to his perch by the fireplace, Sunday newspaper in one hand, mug of steaming coffee in the other, Green Bay Packer game on the radio.

Bundled up against the cold, I trudged through knee-deep snow, stapled up my target, and settled onto the bench for some introspective research. Blowing ice crystals filled the rifle's bolt raceway, my eyes watered, and fingers went numb. The oversize trigger guard came in handy that day. Fifty rounds later, I marveled with delight not only at the target's ragged, apple-size hole, but also at the rifle's flawless feeding and ejection. What it lacked in pedigree, my lowly warrior made up for in harsh weather performance. Moral of story: Never judge a Mauser 98 by its cover.

Czech VZ 24/Yugoslav 24/47

My next venture into military bolt guns brought me a pedestrian, standard-length, 8X57mm Czech VZ 24 Mauser, refurbished by the Yugoslav military following World War ll, and christened the Model 24/47. A print ad claimed that the rifle was among a cache captured from the Wehrmacht by Yugoslav partisans. Right. Sure it was. Habitually cynical of advertising spiel,

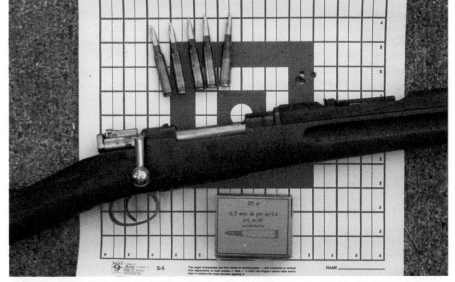

The Swedish Model 1938 short rifle is known for fine workmanship and equally fine accuracy. The author's example didn't disappoint. With a long-eye-relief scope, secured on the rifle's rear-sight mounting platform, and Swedish 6.5X55mm military surplus ammo, it posted impressive groups off a sandbag rest at 100 yards. With a prime-condition rifle and good ammunition, eyesight and trigger control are the limiting factors in shot placement, author believes. He prefers to leave his battle rifles stock and master the as-issued iron sights.

I nevertheless plunked down a money order for two C-notes and began the process of collecting my prize.

Doubts about the 24/47's alleged heritage softened while stripping its thick, very old Cosmoline coating. Across its receiver and barrel were Czech, German, and Yugoslav proof marks. Undeniably, this three-lives long arm had some interesting history.

On the bench, with affordable Belgium-manufacture machine gun fodder, my multinational distinguished itself in smooth functioning, accuracy, dramatic muzzle flash, and apocalyptic muzzle blast. To some, its horizontal bolt handle is unseemly, but it worked fine for me. With practice, one can "flick" the bolt and fire with remarkable speed, much more so than with bent-down geometry. This could come in handy when armed hordes are advancing. Respectful of range etiquette, I refrained from rapid-fire exhibitions.

The Yugoslav arsenal that refurbished my rifle did an admirable job. A dark ring of fine pitting on the bolt face indicated heavy use with corrosive-primed ammunition. The refurbished 24/47 featured a pristine replacement barrel, a butter-smooth, predictable two-stage trigger, and the Yugoslavian Communist Party crest thoughtfully stamped on the receiver ring. The stock, most likely a surrogate, is of Spartan-grade walnut, with an unsightly but practical varnish finish. However, the combination of Cosmoline, varnish, and warehouse "aging" culminated in a sticky, oily wood surface. What the heck, it's military surplus, right?

Model 1908 Brazilian

By now, I was fully infected with Mauser fever. My next acquisition was a well-preserved DWM Model 1908 7X57mm Brazilian-contract Long Rifle. It set me back $125 plus shipping. With the exception of its caliber and lack of the aforementioned hinged-magazine floor plate and lever, it is virtually identical to the Model 1909 Argentine. Accordingly, it too is high on the list of actions used in custom rifles.

By this time, I owned a fine Remington 700 Classic deer rifle in 7X57 and was reloading the caliber. A good thing, too. The only surplus 7X57 ammo available to me at the time was corrosive-primed, 1937 Kynoch full-metal jacket. Despite a gritty trigger, the Brazilian grouped well and functioned with traditional Mauser reliability and smoothness.

1941 Oberndorf Portuguese-Contract 98k

Despite a chronic shortage of infantry rifles during World War II, Germany for some reason exported a small quantity of 8X57 98ks from Mauser's famed Oberndorf plant to Portugal. The quality of this lot was exceptional. By luck, I latched onto one for $350, courtesy of a one-time trade-press listing. The rifle is adorned with Portuguese coat of arms stampings on the receiver ring and stock, and a multitude of proof marks, illustrating Germanic attention to detail.

From its commercial-grade bluing to handsome walnut stock, my '41

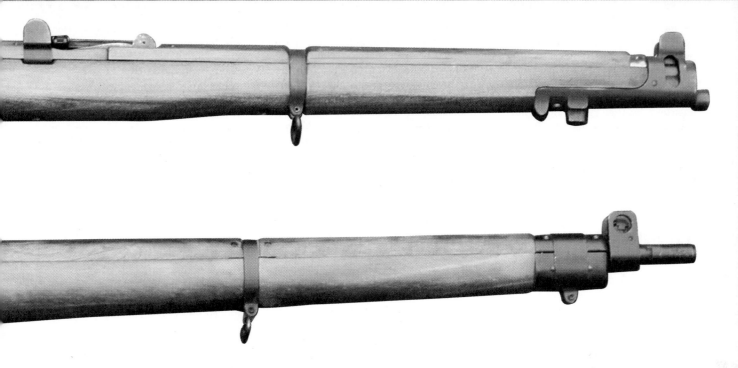

The author thinks this 1915-vintage Australian Lee-Enfield No. 1 Mark III (top) and No. 4 Mk II produced in England during 1954 are the world's greatest bolt-action battle rifles due to their well-proven durability, reliability, accuracy, rapid rate of fire, and 10-round magazine capacity. The Lee-Enfield family has a remarkable worldwide service record that stretches over 115 years. They're still fighting today, in obscure parts of Africa and the Middle East where shooting distances are long and the ubiquitous Kalashnikov comes up short.

Oberndorfer is prime. Its bright bore and absence of dings and gouges reflect a pampered existence. The only signs of use are a pleasing patina to the metal surfaces and a severely dented butt plate. It appears the rifle's military tour was spent on a parade ground, not the battlefield. Neutrality served Portugal and my Mauser rifle well. Like all 98s I've encountered, performance was top shelf.

From the pages of *Gun Digest*, competing publications *[as though there were such a thing. –DMS]*, and pilgrimages to shops and shows, I learned a military bolt-action world exists outside the Mauser universe. Although this piece may sound like MauserMania Smackdown 2011, other nations produced very good military bolt rifles, too. The more I learned, the more I yearned to explore them.

Lee-Enfield Rifles

While Germans unquestionably were the leaders in producing military and commercial bolt-action rifles, their English cousins were worthy competitors.

Over their history, the Lee-Enfield family of combat long arms, consisting of 24 rifles and two carbines, stood toe-to-toe against their Teutonic counterparts across many a bloody battlefield and, some might argue, even surpassed them. Sporterized versions served sportsmen in game fields worldwide.

Lee-Enfield .303 caliber rifles are durable, reliable, accurate, smooth cycling, and capable of extremely rapid fire. Significantly, these Brits hold 10 rounds, their German counterparts but five. Like the Mauser, Lee-Enfields enjoyed production longevity, from 1895 to at least 1954. They served the Crown with distinction in conflicts far and wide, ranging from trenches of France, the boulevards of Singapore, dusty plains of El Alamain, to the beaches of Normandy and points beyond. They're still fighting today, in obscure parts of Africa and the Middle East, in remote outbacks where shooting distances are long and the ubiquitous Kalashnikov comes up short.

Of the extended Lee-Enfield family, two models are the most distinguished.

The No. 1 Mark lll, also known as the SMLE (Short Magazine Lee-Enfield) was introduced in 1903, with production in England and later Australia and India. Known for its ruggedness, reliability, and legendary speed of fire, the SMLE served admirably in World War l.

One world war later, the SMLE was supplanted In 1939 by the Lee-Enfield No. 4 Mk series, an upgraded, easier-to-manufacture design that sported a heavier barrel and receiver, better sights, and simplified barrel bedding. To meet the Commonwealth's wartime demands, No. 4s were built in England, Canada, and by Savage Arms in the U.S. After the war, they were military issue not only in Great Britain but also Italy, Greece, and some Arab countries. No. 4s later served with distinction in the Korean War (interestingly, Mauser 98s were employed by the other side in that action) and in regional donnybrooks across the former British Empire.

For brevity, I'll merely say that my 1915 No. 1 Mk lll Australian (Lithgow arsenal) and 1954 English No. 4 Mk ll (Fazakerly) are indeed very fast to fire and easy cycling, and they place .303 British bullets with lethal consistency. I acquired the pair separately at gun shows for about $150 and $350 respectively. The No. 4 was fresh from armory storage, unissued, swathed in cosmoline, and wrapped in waxed paper. The Enfields' rimmed cartridge feeds reliably and yes, 10 rounds are superior to five when the lead is flying in your direction. Due to these attributes, the Lee-Enfield gets my vote as the best bolt-action combat battle rifle.

Swedish Model 1938 Short Rifle

Borrowing design elements from the 1893 Spanish Mauser, Sweden in 1894 developed the first in its family of three bolt-action military rifles, the Models 1894, 1896, and 1938 respectively. Their cartridge, the 6.5X55mm Swedish Mauser was, as its name implies, formulated jointly by Mauser and Swedish ballisticians. The Swedish clan is of very high quality and was snapped up eagerly by the American arms-buying public. Military surplus Swedish Mauser ammunition proved equally high in quality and plentiful, to the delight of rifle owners.

I acquired my Swedish Model 38

(manufactured by Husqvarna in 1941) Short Rifle at a Milwaukee gun show for $350. Perhaps I overpaid a bit, but print advertisements for the turned-down-bolt version had ceased and I wanted one badly. My initial range session with the M38 didn't disappoint. With stock iron sights at 100 yards, it would group well under 2 inches with Swedish military ball. One day, my father installed a long-eye relief scope that mounted on the rear sight platform, without having to alter the original equipment. To my surprise, the Swede started dropping slugs into one-inch clusters.

At that point, Dad stepped in and decided that the M38 was going to be his go-to military rifle. I couldn't refuse. Besides, by then my hands were full with seven other vets. Father remains devoted to that Swede today.

Japanese Type 99 Arisaka

Americans have often been accused of a dangerous naiveté regarding foreign affairs. Time and again history proved this out, costing us dearly in blood, treasure, and prestige. At the outbreak of World War II, many in this country held the Japanese and their weaponry in low esteem. Fighting them would teach us many painful lessons.

One example of this ignorance is the

Type 99 Arisaka rifle. To this day, the uneducated view the Arisaka as crude, cheap, and ineffective. Those of us who shoot them know better.

I became acquainted with these rifles through references in the firearms press and by an article in *Gun Digest* many moons ago by the estimable John Malloy. In that piece, Mr. Malloy shared his experiences using an Arisaka in a target shoot. While the author didn't win a prize for marksmanship, he placed respectfully and doled out a compliment or two to his Nipponese partner.

Like most of my other military bolt-action rifles, the Type 99 descends from a family dating back to 1897, based on a modified Mauser design. Refinements in design and caliber were incorporated over time. Introduced in 1939 in long- and short-rifle versions, the 99 is remarkably advanced for its day, initially featuring a chrome-plated bore and bolt face, stock drain holes (both very useful in jungle fighting), and an effective but noisy dust cover. While not quite as smooth cycling as other bolt guns, it's well suited for warfare. The rifle also fielded a monopod for steady hold and a special rear sight with fold-down "wings" to obtain proper lead when potting low-flying aircraft. These features illustrate

Beauty and the beast. Inspired by an article in Gun Digest, the author began his 20-year military surplus bolt action rifle "adventure" with two very different Mausers: (top) a fine 1909 DWM Argentine-contract long rifle and a Czech late-war "mongrel" 98k with a stamped, oversize triggerguard (handy for a gloved finger) and other manufacturing shortcuts. Beauty is as beauty does. Despite its mixed lineage and lack of refinements, the humble warrior proved itself to the author in harsh winter performance. Moral of story: Never judge a Mauser 98 by its cover.

Markings on surplus military bolt action rifles often tell a story, if you make the effort to decipher them. The receiver ring is a starting point. The author's examples include (left to right, top) DWM Mauser 1909 with the Argentine crest; 1941 German Oberndorf contract 98k Mauser with the Portuguese crest; Czech "mongrel" 98k with "dou" code, indicating manufacture at the Waffenwerke Bruenn, A.-G., Werk Bystrica, in what is now the Slovak Republic, model designation, and 1945 production; (left to right, bottom) Japanese Arisaka featuring the royal chrysanthemum, symbol of the Japanese Emperor, and characters indicating 99 Type; Remington 03-A3 Springfield (prick punch at the bottom indicates the rifle passed proof testing); and Swedish Model 1938 short rifle displaying its production site (Husqvarna) and date. Proper literature aids in clarifying these markings.

the creative thinking of Japanese arms designers. Evidently, some of that creativity wasn't appreciated by the Emperor's boots on the ground. Japanese soldiers quickly discarded the rattle-prone dust cover that compromised stealthy approach and the cumbersome, brush-collecting bipod, and Arisakas retaining these features fetch a premium.

Like Germany's, the quality of Japan's small arms declined precipitously with the fortunes of war. The chromed bore and bolt face vanished, as did the anti-aircraft sights, milled parts, and other discretionary upgrades adopted over the previous 40-plus years. "Last ditch" Type 99s are rough, unsafe, barely recognizable shells of a very sound weapon. It seems many armchair experts base their opinions of Arisakas on late-war specimens, which is as ignorant as it is inaccurate.

With typical addict compulsion, I scored my Type 99 7.7mm Short Rifle at a gun show for $250. At the time, I didn't know what model it was, but the rifle was quite exotic with its eye-catching tropical wood stock and intact royal chrysanthemum (the Emperor's symbol;

most Arisaka' had their mums ground off after the war at the direction of Gen. Douglas MacArthur) adorning the receiver ring. Not entirely of unsound mind, I also picked up a copy of Duncan McCollum's *Japanese Rifles of World War II* that taught me everything I needed to know and a lot more about this gem.

Its distinctive markings indicate that my 99 was manufactured at the Toyo Kogyo factory around 1939, the zenith of Japan's military rifle-making prowess. Other than minor stock dents, it's in excellent condition. While it lacks a dust cover and monopod, I could have picked up replica replacements at modest cost. No need to repeat the mistakes of the past, I reasoned, so I restrained myself.

My first surprise came in stripping down the Arisaka. From the start, the high quality of early war Japanese manufacturing and attention to detail became apparent. Fit and finish of the components is comparable to that of their German ally's and military rifles produced elsewhere. With a bit of oil, the bolt slid effortlessly down its rails and locked solidly into place.

The second surprise was painful. There was (and is) no military surplus 7.7

Japanese Arisaka ammunition to be had. The only alternative was commercial Norma loads at nearly two bucks every pull of the trigger, not including tax. Ouch. With fanatical devotion, I chased down every ejected empty. My final surprise was very pleasant. Shooting offhand, the rifle balances the best of my entire military entourage and is accurate to boot.

Model 1903 Springfields

My military bolt-action rifle addiction eventually ran its course, but not before a grand finale that was long in the making. Twenty years previous, Dad and I said it would be nice to own a 1903 Springfield rifle. Gun mongers were charging outrageous prices for '03s back then, so we held off. After a little research, we each bought a rifle from the U.S. Department of Civilian Marksmanship: Dad's a late 1930s '03 Springfield arsenal rework and mine an original 1943 vintage '03-A3 Remington, for $500 apiece. We added a 1,000-round case of 1954 Rock Island 30-06 military ball for good measure.

Dad and I are more than satisfied with

our Springfields. While his '03 displays beautiful milled parts, my 03-A3's ungainly-looking-but-vastly-superior aperture sight is a fair trade-off for its wartime stamped trigger guard/magazine assembly and barrel bands.

Both rifles, while clearly used, are in very good condition, function smoothly, and are far more accurate than we can see or hold "out yonder" with GI-issue sights.

Military Surplus Rifles – Where to Find 'Em

The 1960s-era "golden age" of military surplus firearms is water long gone under the bridge, but there's no need for despair. Plenty of fine vintage military bolt guns can still to be found at reasonable prices with a little effort. Start with the Web Directory section of *Gun Digest* (under the Firearms Manufacturers and Importers listing), then *Shotgun News* and *Gun Digest Magazine*. If you're a dedicated surfer, some of my favorite surplus rifle sites are Samco Global Arms, Inc, J&G Sales, Century International Arms Inc., and InterOrdnance of America, LP. Google "military surplus rifles" and you'll find plenty more.

Gun shows, gun shops, small-town sporting goods stores, and rural garage sales are all potential sources of military surplus rifles. It takes time and gasoline, but one never knows what surprises – and bargains – await you on the road. Surplus firearms can also be had from online dealers like AuctionArms.com, Gunbroker.com, and GunsAmerica.com. Also check out Firearms Auction Sites in the Web Directory section of this book.

To purchase most surplus firearms direct from importers or dealers by mail, you'll need a Federal Firearms License, a Curio & Relics (C&R) license, or someone who does to conduct your transaction (for a fee), in accordance with federal, state, and any local firearms laws.

A cautionary note,:when buying a military surplus rifle: pay the extra tab for higher quality. There are plenty of worn-out, corroded, and damaged rifles on the market today and scoundrels trying to peddle them. Steer clear of rusty or excessively pitted bores and actions that don't lock up solidly. Avoid scrap iron if you value your hide and pocket book. While replacement parts are often available, they may require professional installation (particularly barrels) at further cost.

For peace of mind, whenever purchasing a surplus firearm, know and fully understand the conditions of sale, particularly the seller's return policy and costs thereof.

You've Snagged Your Prize. What Now?

Savor that moment when you have your newly purchased rifle in the security of the hearth. After all, you paid for it. The first thing to do is obtain literature detailing your rifle's history, its operation, and take-down instructions. I found most of my books and booklets through browsing at gun shows. I also know several firearms book dealers and either visit their website or contact them by e-mail when in need.

The *Gun Digest Book of Firearms Assembly/Disassembly* (separate volumes for various types) by J.B. Wood (www.gundigeststore.com) is a priceless resource. So is the *NRA Guide to Firearms Assembly* (separate volumes for rifles, shotguns, and handguns).

Armed with support literature, you're ready to disassemble your rifle for inspection and cleaning. By the nature of their design simplicity, most bolt-action rifles are easy to dismantle and reassemble, stripping the bolt perhaps a bit less so. Watch for damaged, badly worn, or corroded components. Warehouses of replacement parts abound. My favorites are Numrich Gun Parts Corp., Springfield Sporters, Inc., and Sarco, Inc., listed in the Web Directory section at the back

Markings on the receiver of the author's Type 99 Arisaka indicate (left to right) Series 31, the rifle's serial number within that series, and that it was manufactured at Toyo Kogyo (Oriental Manufacturing Company) in Honshu, Japan's main island. Using the arsenal mark, series number, serial number, and the rifle's features, the author determined that his Type 99 was produced early in the type's 1939-1945 manufacturing run.

Markings on the receiver of the author's Type 99 Arisaka indicate (left to right) Series 31, the rifle's serial number within that series, and that it was manufactured at Toyo Kogyo (Oriental Manufacturing Company) in Honshu, Japan's main island. Using the arsenal mark, series number, serial number, and the rifle's features, the author determined that his Type 99 was produced early in the type's 1939-1945 manufacturing run.

of this book under Gun Parts, Barrels, Aftermarket Accessories.

A special surprise awaits many owners of military surplus rifles during strip down. Examine the rifle's components carefully and note their markings. These tell a story, for those who make the effort to decipher them. Most of the world's arms makers coded their hardware to indicate country, production site, year of manufacture, proof testing, and arsenal refurbishing, among other vital factoids. Some countries intentionally coded their weapons to conceal production information. Even a rifle's serial number can have special significance.

On most military rifles, the receiver ring is the starting point in determining its heritage. It helps to have authoritative literature detailing the meanings of these marks. Ludwig Olson's comprehensive book *Mauser Bolt Action Rifles* details markings on Mauser 98s. Gerhard Wirnsberger's *The Standard Directory of Proof Marks* is helpful for many European and Scandinavian arms. There is a seemingly endless supply of information on military weapons. The specifics you seek are out there somewhere, but sometimes you have to dig for them. The internet is a good starting point, but cross-check for accuracy through authoritative literature.

Why bother, you ask? In a nutshell, many military bolt action rifles played a decisive role in shaping today's world. By learning where and when your rifle was manufactured and gleaning other information provided by its markings, you develop a fuller knowledge and appreciation of that hunk of steel and wood resting in your hands, along with its role in world affairs. You're holding a piece of history, you know. Either you understand its significance or you don't. Knowledge is always better than ignorance.

Once your rifle is cleaned, inspected, and reassembled, it's time to score some ammo. First and foremost, always make sure the ammunition you purchase is correct for your firearm. Mistakes can occur, particularly with Mauser metric-denominated cartridges.

Sadly, the days of cheap, non-corrosive, military-surplus ammo for many 20th-century military bolt-action rifles are over. Happily, not so for our beloved .30-06, .308 Winchester (for rechambered Mausers and No. 1 Mk lll Lee Enfields), Swedish 6.5X55, and 7.62X54R Russian for you Mosin Nagant fans out there. Corrosive-primed .303 British, 8X57, and 7X57 can still be had. If you choose this route (make no mistake, semi-corrosive is corrosive),

be prepared to thoroughly clean and dry your rifle's bore, bolt, and surrounding metalwork promptly after shooting. Either hot detergent water or U.S. GI bore cleaner Mil Spec C372 will do the trick. A thorough inspection of surrounding metal work the following day is advised.

Military surplus and competitively priced foreign commercial ammunition is available from arms importers and dealers. New shipments arrive periodically so it pays to watch the trade press and web sites every so often. For starters, check out the Ammunition and Components section of this book's Web Directory. If you want more, Google "military surplus ammunition. "

After firing those first shots, inspect your rifle's empties for signs of trouble, i.e. cartridge splitting, separation, or punctured/blown/flattened primers.

If you plan more than occasional shooting, over the long run reloading will strengthen your finances and resolve problems. Yes, there is a dark side to some military bolt-action rifles: chamber dimension. Understand that military firearms are designed to go bang with every pull of the trigger, not produce reloadable brass. To function when stuffed with battlefield debris and fed corroded ammunition, many surplus rifles came from the factory with generous chamber dimensions. This is good for combat soldiers for whom reliability means survival, but bad for reloaders seeking to extend the life of their empties.

Split or separated cases are the warning signs of either an oversize chamber (from your resizing die's perspective, not the rifle's) or excessive headspace (common with improperly installed replacement barrels). I've never had a case split or separate from first-time-fired military surplus or commercial ammunition. I've had some with reloaded ammunition, however.

Reloading for a rifle with an oversize chamber can usually be solved by ordering a custom resizing die manufactured to its chamber's dimensions. I provided RCBS with one factory loaded round and three fired cases from my Arisaka. Their die saved me a bundle by extending the life of precious Norma 7.7 brass. Unless you're a knowledgeable do-it-yourselfer with the right tools, an improperly headspaced rifle is best left to a professional gunsmith.

Flattened/punctured/blown primers may be an indication of excessive pressure. I wouldn't expect these maladies with military surplus or commercial ammo, but they occur with handloads. While bolt-action rifles are very strong, don't tempt fate by OD-ing on gunpowder. Follow your reloading manual and back off the charge if necessary. Some of these rifles are approaching 100 years old, and there's no reason to run them at red-line.

If you decide to reload military brass (as I did for my 7.65mm Argentine for significant cost savings), stick with boxer-primed, non-corrosive cases. For reliability, some military primers were crimped in place. This may cause primer seating problems when reloading. If you own a quantity of brass with crimped primers, it's economical to invest in a primer-pocket-swaging die. I did for the 7.65 and was very satisfied with the outcome. A lower-price option is to purchase a hand primer-pocket reamer but go very easy on shaving brass. Too much and you have enlarged primer pockets.

There are a handful of military surplus rifles chambered for obscure calibers. Finding ammunition or brass can be a problem. If this is the case, contact The Old Western Scrounger at (304) 262-9870 or on the web. OWS's Dangerous Dave Cumberland should be able to help you out.

To Sporterize or Not to Sporterize?

The allure of the sporterized rifle, built to your specifications, is a powerful narcotic, particularly when you own the primary ingredient. In the right hands, all the military rifles listed here would make excellent sporters. Every single one of them.

The Czech/Yugoslav CZ24 24/47 is today a handy scout rifle with several whitetails to its credit. My father commandeered the 1908 Brazilian and, with a sweet 18-inch 7X57 replacement barrel acquired at a gun show for $25, aftermarket sights, an adjustable, single-stage, trigger, and his handiwork (with a gunsmith's assistance with rebarreling and bending the bolt), crafted a silky 6 lb. sporter.

I surprised myself by purchasing an equally sharp, No. 4 Mk ll Lee Enfield sporter, fabricated with a Canadian Long Branch action, great sights, five-shot magazine, and the best-fitting stock I've ever shouldered, for $150. With Sierra MatchKing slugs and a 4X scope, off the sandbags it will on occasion group three shots into less than half a minute of angle. That's outrageous, fantastic, and totally superfluous. Who hunts deer with Match King bullets? I would really like to shake hands with whoever put that fine Enfield hunting rifle together.

If the bug bites and you have the time and funds, go ahead and pay a master gunmaker big bucks for one of the greatest gifts a rifleman can dream up. Why not? Just don't expect it to outperform your out-of-the-box hunting rifle. If I had the financial wherewithal and patience (I don't), I'd send my 1909 Argentine to Darcy Echols tomorrow and order up the best grade .375 H&H African safari rifle money can buy.

An economical alternative is to do most or all of the sporterizing yourself, using off-the-shelf or custom components. All the pieces are out there. There are books telling you how to do it. Just know your limitations and don't imagine that your handiwork will out shoot or cost less than name-brand commercial rifles. If it does, well, you've got another reason to smile. But please, if you can help it, don't cut up a pristine, scarce example of military firearms history.

Why I Have No Regrets

I'm through acquiring military surplus 20th-century bolt-action rifles. I have almost everything I want and enjoy them all as time permits. My heart still skips a beat at the sight of a military classic tucked away in an obscure corner or display table, but that's OK.

Not too long ago, in a small northern Wisconsin gun shop/repair store, I spied a stack of Czech Brazilian-contract Model 1908/34 7X57 Short Rifles. My eyes roamed hungrily up and down their ranks, seeking the prime specimen. "Uh uh, those aren't for sale," the owner cut in, before I could get the words out. "I'm saving them for customers who order a custom job." "Right," I smiled, realizing that, despite momentary weakness, I had finally conquered my addiction.

I'll close out by putting my "adventure" in perspective. I spent plenty of time and a smart amount of hard-earned cash on my hobby. I have no regrets. I had a lot of fun and learned a great deal along the way. When one specializes in acquiring, shooting, and researching period firearms, he becomes a student of world history, geopolitics, economics, industrial science, and human behavior. It's a comprehensive education that brings fulfillment to the hobby and to life.

Bibliography

Barnes, Frank, *Cartridges of the World*, DBI Books, Inc., Northfield, IL, 1980.

Hogg, Ian V., *The New Illustrated Encyclopedia of Firearms*, Secaucus, New Jersey, Wellfleet Press, 1993.

Kuhnhausen, Jerry, *The Mauser Bolt Actions, M91 Through M98 A Shop Manual*, VSP Publishers, 1991.

McCollum, Duncan O., *Japanese Rifles of World War ll*, Excalibur Publications, Latham, NY, 1996.

Mott, Dr. Thomas, Karns, John, Brophy, Lt. Col. (Ret) William, Whelen, Lt. Col. Townsend, Waite, M.D., and Hoffschmidt, E.J., *Model 1903 Springfield Rifles*, National Rifle Association of America, Washington D.C. 1992.

NRA Technical Staff, Yust Jr., Charles, *Military Rifles*, National Rifle Association of America, Washington D.C. 1991.

Numerous authors, *The Big Book of Surplus Firearms, the Best of Volumes 1, 11, and lll*, Petersen Publishing Company, Los Angeles, CA 1998.

Numerous authors, *Mausers – The World's Greatest Bolt Rifles*, Primedia Inc., 2007.

Olson, Ludwig, M. D. Waite, Dennis Riordan, Thomas E. Wessel, E.J. Hoffschmidt, and the NRA Technical Staff, *Mauser Rifles*, National Rifle Association of America, Washington D.C. 1992.

Olson, Ludwig, *Mauser Bolt Rifles*, Third Edition, F. Brownell & Son, Publishers, Inc., Montezuma, Iowa, 1976.

Reynolds, E.G.B. and Hoffschmidt, E.J., *British Enfield Rifles*, National Rifle Association of America, Washington D.C. 1992.

Wirnsberger, Gerhard, *The Standard Directory of Proof Marks*, Blacksmith Corporation, Chino Valley, AZ (undated).

IN THE SERVICE OF THE CROWN

THE WEBLEY-GREEN "ALTERNATIVE" ARMY REVOLVER

BY **TOM CACECI**

Accurate, strong and masterfully made, the Webley-Green revolver was Webley's crowning achievement.

The origins of the famous gunmaking firm of Webley date to 1827, when 14-year-old Philip Webley was apprenticed to the Birmingham gunmaker William Davis. Davis died in 1831 and his daughter Caroline and her mother carried on the firm's business. Upon completing his apprenticeship in 1834, Philip went into partnership with his brother James as a "percussioner and gun lock maker," and in what was probably an inevitable development, in 1838 he followed the time-honored tradition: he married his former boss's daughter. The Webley brothers had prospered and by 1840 they making (among other things) gun implements for the Crown and for the East India Company. They had done so well, in fact, that by 1845 Philip was able to buy out the assets of the Davis firm run by his wife and his mother-in-law, and take his late father-in-law's place in the Birmingham gun trade as an independent maker.

In the 1850's Britain was a big market for firearms and Birmingham was the center of production. Strong-jawed Builders of the Empire bringing the Queen's Rule to India, Africa, and the wilds of Canada needed guns; so did explorers and even missionaries risking life and limb in the fetid jungles of the Dark Continent. So too did the considerable numbers of domestic

Lest there be any doubt, the model designation is clearly marked on the topstrap.

customers who lived in a society plagued by crime but lacking an effective police force. Philip Webley did business at the upper end of the market, producing high-quality firearms that quickly cemented his reputation as one of Birmingham's best gunsmiths.

In 1857, Sam Colt made a business decision that transformed the British market: he closed his factory in England, creating an opening for domestic firms to serve the growing domestic market with less expensive mass-produced guns. Webley was well positioned to seize this opportunity. He had been working steadily to adapt the "American method" of standardized production using interchangeable parts and was ahead of many of his competitors. The years after 1860 saw the expansion of his trade to include more civilian sales and the development of popular new product lines. Many of Webley's most famous solid-frame revolver designs were introduced from 1860 onward, including

The Army-Navy Cooperative Society Ltd. was the premiere provisioner of Britain's officer corps in the colonial era. Many sporting arms dating from the period bore the "Army & Navy CSL" legend.

the Royal Irish Constabulary series, the widely-imitated "British Bulldog," and the Metropolitan Police series adopted by Scotland Yard. Webley's leadership of the field was undisputed.

Then as now the Holy Grail of any arms-making firm was getting the Army to adopt its products. A lucrative military contract eluded Webley for years, and despite his success with police and civilian sales it would not be until 1887 that Webley won a contract to provide a revolver for general Army service: the Mark I, first of the long series of military top-breaks that would serve the Crown until well after World War II.

But Webley had forged ahead with refinement of the top-break concept, gradually perfecting it. The firm held numerous patents on ejector designs, breech-closing devices, and internal lockwork mechanisms, all of which steadily improved performance and reliability. Simultaneously Webley developed methods to reduce unit cost with improved methods of manufacture. He was very savvy about customer service as well, happily providing small shops with "private label" guns marked to order. All of these production and marketing innovations kept the company's name at the front of the pack and solidified its reputation for solid, utterly reliable, and very accurate weapons. Among the technical innovations was one of importance that would be used in all the firm's subsequent top-break designs: the stirrup breech catch, covered by British patent #4070 of 1885. It provided a locking system that made the top-break as strong as any solid frame design. It was one of the features that convinced the Army to adopt the Mark I.

The officers of Her Majesty's forces in those days were drawn from the upper crust of British society. As befitted an institution that was part of a culture resting on class distinctions, the Army drew a well-defined line between the enlisted "rankers" drawn from the lower orders and the gentlemen who commanded them. It was standard practice among the gentry and the nobility to send off at least one of their sons into a military or naval career. An officer's pay was nowhere near enough to meet the financial demands placed on a gentleman, who after all had a place in society to uphold; but most if not all of them had private means (in the form of an allowance from the family or income from estates) that was adequate for the expenses of military service. Upon graduation from the military academy at Sandhurst, a newly commissioned subaltern "kitted out" for active service at his own expense. Among the items he was required to buy was his sidearm.

With the adoption of the Mark I as official issue in 1887, Webley gained a reputation among the officers of the Queen's Army as the "official" gun maker. This gave the firm an "in" to the niche market of privately-purchased officer's sidearms. In the early 1880s, Webley had brought out a new series of target revolvers incorporating simultaneous ejection of spent cartridges and the strong stirrup breech lock initially developed by Edwinson C. Green. The "Webley-Green"

Lt. Gen. Robert Baden-Powell, hero of Mafeking and founder of the Boy Scouts, in a formal portrait complete with his Webley-Green.

Webley's "winged bullet" logo was as iconic in its day as Colt's rearing stallion.

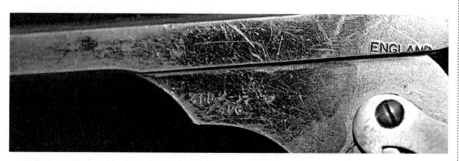

The ".455/.476" caliber marking, denoting that either cartridge could be used in the Webley-Green.

a rather long travel back and a solid impact when it falls, the pull is clean and even throughout its length. In single action the trigger is crisp, and if not especially light, is very consistent from shot to shot. The target published in *The Field* is one that an expert marksman today could still – perhaps – duplicate using one of these beautifully fitted and polished guns.

Many retailers sold W-G Armies, but the most prominent of these, certainly the most important one for Army officers, was the Army & Navy Cooperative Society, Ltd. Founded in 1871 by a group of military and naval officers, its mission was to supply "articles of domestic consumption and general use to its members at the lowest remunerative rates." The "Army & Navy Store" sold, among many other things, all the items an officer needed, including household goods, fishing tackle, and guns for service and sport. The CSL was a major outlet for Webley's production. W-G Armies sold through them are marked as such on the barrel rib.

The "W-G Army" went through several minor variations, all of which were popular with officers, and deservedly so. They were powerful, accurate, and durable. They fit perfectly in the holsters issued for use with the Marks I though VI. The Army Models had 6-inch barrels and fixed sights, could be had with either birds-head grips or flared "target" style ones, and would fire the standard military issue round. With the adoption of the Mark I, the Army switched over to the first of several variations of what is now called the ".455 Webley" round. The W-G would of course shoot this caliber as well, so that an officer who'd equipped himself with an earlier W-G Army had no problems and didn't have to buy another gun. Many post-1891 W-G Armies are stamped ".455/.476" to indicate the fact that whatever ammunition was on hand in the remote outposts to which an officer might be sent could be used.

Though not so well-known as the "issue" Webley top-breaks, especially the Mark VI used in both World Wars, the W-G Army provided sterling service to the Crown throughout its production life, and for long afterwards. And not only to the Army: The Bank of England and the Union Steamship Company are two commercial firms known to have purchased W-Gs in quantity for use by their staffs. The target versions won many medals at the annual Bisley

or "W-G" target guns were perhaps not only the most finely crafted revolvers ever made, representing Victorian-era workmanship at its absolute zenith; they were exceptionally accurate and found great favor with target shooters.

The Field reproduced a target fired by a Mr C. Dixon in October of 1889, showing one ragged 6-shot hole in a 20-yard bullseye, a level of performance that would be competitive even today. To increase their appeal to Army marksmen, the early W-Gs were chambered for the then-standard .476 round used in the ungainly Enfield Mark I and Mark II revolvers that were still official issue. Webley's status as an official supplier, coupled with the W-G's reputation for ruggedness and accuracy, led the firm to develop a version for use on "active service" in 1892. This was the first of the "W-G Army" models, released in the official caliber of .476. This "Army

Model" was produced concurrently with the target versions and in due time was approved by the Army as a type suitable for officers' use and private purchase.

Unlike the military top-breaks (Marks I through VI) the "W-G Army" was never official issue, but those who were authorized to carry sidearms and who could afford the best could choose to substitute the W-G Army for the issue weapon of the day. Many officers did, because the W-G was not only sturdy and accurate, it had exceptionally good lockwork in both double and single action modes. Shooting one of these big guns is a revelation as to just how good a revolver can be, and to the kind of craftsmanship in which Webley's firm took justifiable pride. The action is as slick and smooth as could be desired. Even though the huge hammer (with an integral firing pin that looks as if it could punch holes in an oil drum) has

This label denoted the finest in British arms craftsmanship.

Still admirable even by today's standards, this target was shot by Mr. C. Dixon – offhand – around 1889 with a Webley-Green at 20 yards. Those are six shots in the bull. Group size is approximately two inches. As published in *The Field,* 1889.

competition and were highly favored by the "name" shooters of the day such as the American Olympic medalist, Walter Winans (1852-1920), author of *The Art of Revolver Shooting.*

Never "official," but always faithful and reliable, the W-G Army soldiered on for many years after production ceased. The total number of each variation made and the exact date when the line was discontinued aren't easy to determine, but W-G Armies were certainly made at least as late as 1897: many specimens are marked "W. & S. Ltd" and the firm name "Webley & Scott" came into existence in that year. Some references imply without so stating that W-Gs in various configurations were made at least as late as 1904, carrying produc-

tion through the Boer War. This seems highly likely. This conflict was Britain's largest up to that time and the Army greatly increased in size.

The W-G was highly popular with officers in the Boer War: many of them can still be found in South African gun shops. Even so august a personage as Lord Baden-Powell, the heroic general who relieved the Siege of Mafeking, preferred to wear a W-G Army at his side. It also seems likely that production of the W-Gs ceased no later than 1914, with Britain's entry into World War I and the need to ramp up production of the Mark V and later the Mark VI standard issue revolvers.

Since Webley's pre-1945 production and sales records have been badly frag-

mented (and mostly destroyed) by two wars, a major fire, and the Blitz, it's not really possible to reconstruct the history of any specific W-G Army with any accuracy. But given the small size of the British Army in the late 19th century and its involvement in several small and large wars after 1887, the likelihood that any officer's sidearm was carried into combat and probably "fired in anger" is very high. A W-G Army manufactured in 1892 that belonged to a career officer could very easily have ascended the Nile in the River War against the Mahdi in 1896 and would almost certainly have been used in the Anglo-Boer War of 1899-1902. I once owned such a CSL-marked gun that had come to me from a South African shop: one of those "I wish it could talk!" guns that you know had a tale or two to tell.

Depending on the age of its original purchaser, a W-G could well have seen trench service in the First World War as well. Given that these finely crafted weapons were valued possessions, a retired officer might even have passed on his trusty old "defender" to a son serving in World War II. In the years before 1968 a fair number were imported to the USA and sold here on the surplus market. Some unfortunately were mutilated by having the cylinder turned to shoot .45 ACP in half-moon clips (a very bad idea for a gun proofed with black powder!) but most have not. If one is marked ".455/.476" it will accept the .45 Colt Long and shoot "Cowboy Action" loads safely, so there is no need for this to be done if you are lucky enough to come across one of these beautiful relics of a bygone age.

America's Forgotten Big Game Rifle:

The 1886 Winchester .33WCF

BY **CHRIS LIBBY**

Photographs by Beth Libby and Chris Libby

On October 28, 1955, as Leonard Stevens lit his pipe with his Zippo lighter, he thought to himself how perfect the morning was for opening day of the deer hunting season. He stood near a large oak tree on a knoll, over-looking a small pond near Millinocket, Maine. He pulled his wool hat down over his ears and fastened the top button of his red and black plaid Woolrich hunting jacket around his neck to shield himself from the cold, crisp autumn morning, as the sun struggled to make its way through the dark forest. The thermometer at camp had read in the low 30s, but he could have sworn it was colder, perhaps in the low 20s.

The pipe smoke drifted south in the cold morning air, reminding him of his home and family. He ran his fingers over the bowl of the hand-carved pipe, which was in the shape of an Indian head. Although cold, the forest was quiet and peaceful this morning, giving him time to relax and contemplate his life, as he was now in his early 40s. As much as he loved hunting and being away from his job for a week at the Central Maine Power company, the big rawboned Yankee missed his wife and three daughters,

Leonard Stevens in 1955, with his Winchester Model 1886 .33 Winchester rifle and the eight-point, 228-pound (field-dressed weight) whitetail buck he shot in northern Maine.

who were at their small farm in southern Maine, several hundred miles away. He guessed that his wife was awake by now and most likely had the wood stove going to warm the house up before she and her daughters ventured outside to the barn in order to tend to the farm animals.

As he drew in a puff of hot, sweet tobacco smoke, he wondered if the other members of his hunting party, miles away, were seeing any game. The big breakfast that the crew had consumed earlier, consisting of eggs, pancakes and thick slabs of bacon, did little to fend off the cold. He smiled as he thought of the lone man who stayed behind at camp, probably still in his bunk in a deep sleep from an excess of Kentucky bourbon during last night's card game.

That fellow, the sole member of the hunting party who stayed in camp this morning, had obnoxiously made fun of Leonard's hunting rifle, an old 1886 .33-caliber Winchester lever action, during the euchre game last night: "It's 1955, Leonard, and that damn gun of yours is obsolete. They don't even make bullets for it anymore. You should trade it in on a new pump in .35 Remington with a scope, like I have. Now *that's* a gun!"

Most sporting equipment, if well cared for, will last for several generations even if used hard. Leonard's rifle, now owned by the author, is still in use today.

Leonard attempted to explain that although his gun and cartridge were indeed old, the gun was well-made and accurate and that the .33 Winchester cartridge had a slight edge in both velocity and muzzle energy over the .35 Remington. But the "expert" was too stubborn and intoxicated to listen and proceeded to instruct the rest of the hunting party on proper hunting strategies for the next morning. Leonard let the issue drop. He recalled being taught as a child not to cast pearls before swine.

Suddenly, Leonard saw movement in the distance, along the shore line of the pond. Well over a hundred yards away, a massive whitetail buck was making his way through the brush. Luckily, the buck was traveling to Leonard's north, and the pipe smoke was drifting to the south, so he knew he was downwind and undetected and would remain so if he remained unseen.

Partially hidden from the buck's view by the oak tree, Leonard clenched his pipe between his teeth on the left side of his face and slowly raised the Winchester. The deer was big, really big. As the thick-bodied buck slowly made its way towards a clearing, Leonard could see its breath every time it exhaled in the cold morning air. Being a meat hunter with a family to feed, he usually shot the first deer to come along, be it a spike or a doe. But his heart started pounding as this was a trophy buck, the kind most hunters only dream about seeing, much less getting a shot at. He struggled to control his breathing and his racing pulse.

He carefully removed his right glove, cocked the ice-cold steel hammer back, squeezing the trigger before the hammer came to its highest notch, then releasing the trigger, bypassing the loud metallic "click" that can often spook game. He

leaned against the oak tree for additional stability, pressed his cheek into the stock, drew a careful bead behind the big buck's shoulder and slowly squeezed the trigger. As the hammer dropped on the Winchester Staynless cartridge and the 200-grain soft point bullet exploded from the muzzle, thunder boomed across the cold Maine woods. And then all was silent.

Much later, at dusk, the hunting party gathered back at camp around the massive buck, now dressed out and back from the tagging station. The eight-point buck dressed out at 228 pounds, and the live weight was estimated by officials to be around 270 or better. Certainly not the largest deer to ever be shot in the state of Maine, but huge nonetheless, and quite impressive hung up on the seasoned game pole that bent sharply under its weight. The gang stood around outside of the cabin in the bitter cold

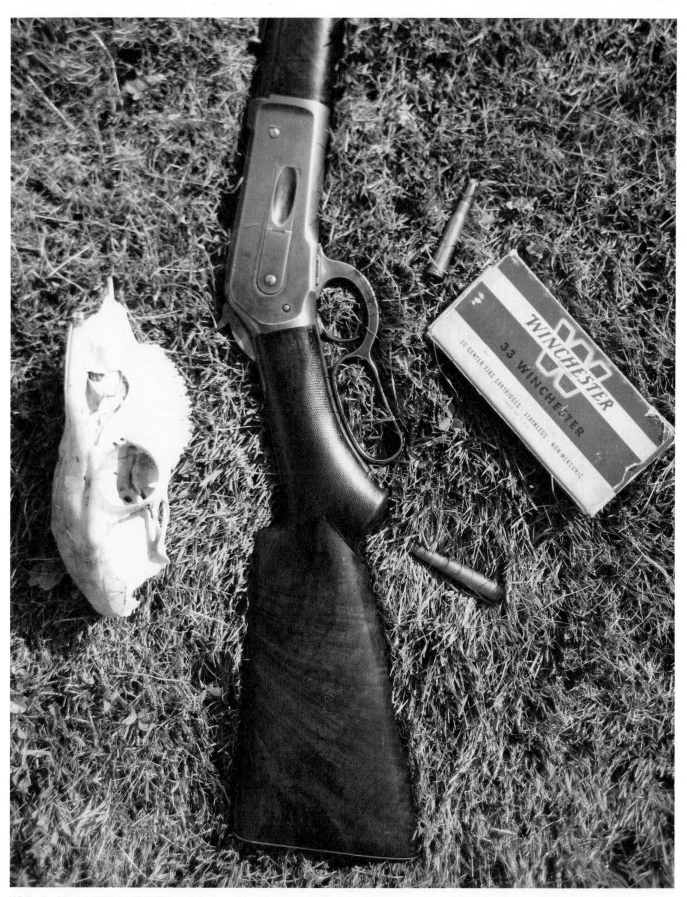

While the Model 1886 in .33 WCF was designed for big game such as moose, bear and elk, it is the perfect combination for whitetail deer.

Clint Libby holds his greatgrandfather's hunting rifle (empty), and marvels at the fancy grade stock.

Leonard Stevens' trophy deer mount sporting an eight-point rack. The deer was accepted into "The Biggest Bucks of Maine Club."

admiring the deer, congratulating and asking Leonard the details of his success, wanting to hear the story again and again, as if he was holding back a secret, some piece of arcane wisdom or woodcraft that would guarantee their own success.

At that point the "expert," now apparently recovered from his hangover after a full day of rest in camp by the woodstove, stepped forward to examine the buck. As he examined the bullet wound behind the foreleg, he said, "Lucky shot. You know Leonard, this deer might just qualify if you entered into the biggest bucks of Maine club," he stated with a tone of pompous authority.

Leonard, exhausted from dragging the monster deer out of the woods by himself earlier that day, took a long draw on his pipe and looked deep into the man's eyes before replying, "Do you think that they will accept my entry when they hear that I used an obsolete rifle?" The rest of the group erupted in laughter, as pompous nimrod stood there, red-faced and, for the first time during that trip, speechless.

That hunt occurred over 55 years ago, and Leonard Stevens, my maternal grandfather, and the other members of that party have all passed on to the happy hunting grounds. Leonard gave me his beloved 1886 Winchester a few

years before his death in 1990. The rifle has been used to take countless deer and other game over the years, and has even on occasion clipped the heads off a few ruffed grouse and rabbits for camp meat. My father, Stan Libby, often borrowed it back in the 1960s and used it to shoot several deer. It's as fine a hunting rifle as there's ever been.

The 1886 is justly revered for having one of the smoothest actions of any lever action ever to leave Winchester's New Haven, Connecticut, plant, noticeably easier to operate than the Models 1873, 1892 or 1894. The 1886 in its Takedown and Carbine versions is light and comes up to the shoulder quickly, a necessity in a hunting rifle designed to be used in forests and thick brush. The buckhorn sights are accurate and can be brought on target fairly quickly, ideal for brush hunting.

With a 24-inch barrel, the Model 1886 chambered for .33 Winchester Center Fire (WCF) has a 1:12 twist and is a very accurate hunting rifle up to 150 yards. My rifle has the fancy wood, checkered stock and forend, and metal butt plate. According to available dates of manufacture, my rifle's five-digit serial number indicates that it was made in 1890. As the .33 WCF chambering wasn't introduced until 1903, this rifle was re-barreled and upgraded by Winchester Repeating Arms Company for the .33 caliber smokeless round sometime after 1903. The barrel reads "NICKEL STEEL

The author takes aim with the "obsolete" rifle, using vintage Winchester ammunition for target practice, prior to the hunting season.

The author enjoys a fine cigar after sighting in his .33 W.C.F.

BARREL ESPECIALY FOR SMOKELESS POWDER" and "33 W.C.F." What was the original chambering? I don't know, but it may have been .45-70 Government, the most common choice.

President Roosevelt, a great hunter, writer and conservationist, loved Winchester lever action rifles with a passion. They were rugged, reliable and powerful enough for hunting large, dangerous game. Although perhaps better known for his affinity for the 1895 .405 lever action Winchester that he referred to as "Big Medicine" that he used with great success in Africa, Roosevelt also owned and used a model 1886 for big game hunting. President Roosevelt thought so much of the Model 1886 that he even gave several of them to friends as gifts. The John M. Browning-designed 1886 Winchester was originally intended to utilize the heavy and powerful black powder cartridges of the day. The 1886 in all its various calibers and variations were used as hunting rifles across the entire North American continent, and it's a safe bet that Presidential approval helped to spread its popularity.

Pre-1964 Winchester rifles and shotguns, of course, are synonymous with quality and durability and have a higher collector value than those manufactured after 1964. Collectors and shooters can expect to find a wide range of prices for the various styles and grades of

1886 models, depending on caliber and condition. Winchester Repeating Arms produced around 160,000 Model 1886s between 1886 and 1935. Fancy grades of wood stocks were available (for a premium price of course), as well as various barrel lengths and styles. Sporting, Takedown, Carbine and Musket versions of the rifle were all offered during the 49 years of the original Model 1886's production.

According to the *Standard Catalog of Winchester* (Krause Publications, 2000), the Model 1886 was "based on a John Browning patent, the Model 1886, [and] had one of the finest and strongest lever-actions ever utilized in a Winchester rifle." "Winchester introduced the Model 1886 in order to take advantage of the more powerful centerfire cartridges of the time." It was originally offered in .40-65 W.C.F., a powerful black powder round. As stated previously, the .45-70 is by far the most common caliber in which the Model 1886 was offered, but Winchester also chambered the model for the .45-90 W.C.F., .50-110 Express, .40-82 W.C.F., .38-56 W.C.F., .38-70 W.C.F., .40-70 W.C.F. and the .50-100-450 – and of course the .33 WCF. All of these calibers were a huge step up in knockdown power from the 1886's predecessor, the Model 1873, and offered hunters and ranchers big-bore bullets and velocities that had previously only been available

in single-shot rifles. This upgrade in design and caliber from Winchester Repeating Arms offered hunters state-of-the-art design and firepower for dangerous game such as grizzly bears, which had on more than one occasion killed hunters desperately trying to reload their single shot rifles.

Winchester Repeating Arms Company first offered the smokeless high-velocity (for its day) .33 WCF round in the Model 1886 in 1903 as a more powerful alternative for big game hunters seeking more power, range and penetration. Until then, Winchester's smokeless lever-action champion had been the Model 1894 in .30-30. *[Editor's note: And, no, we haven't forgotten the Model 1895 lever gun in .30 Government. –DMS]* The .30-30, although a potent big game round itself, fired a .308" 170-grain bullet with a muzzle velocity of 2200 feet per second for a muzzle energy of 1830 ft-lbs. The new .33 WCF cartridge featured a .338" 200-grain soft-point flat-point bullet that traveled at sizzling 2180 feet per second and had muzzle energy of 2110 ft.-lbs., very respectable ballistics in 1903!

The new .33 WCF round even offered hunters a more potent lever gun round than the .303 as offered by Winchester's competitor, Savage. The Model 99 in .303 Savage fired a 190-grain bullet at 1960 feet per second for a muzzle energy of 1620 ft-lbs., far below that of the .33.

The ancient Winchester cartridges worked fine, producing this excellent two-shot group in the center of the target, offhand at 65 yards. Forget the flyer below; the author called it. *[Editor's note: Sure he did. –DMS]*

Stan Libby, the author's father, prior to buying a new Winchester Model 100 in .308, borrowed the 1886 from Leonard in the 1960s and used it for a few hunting seasons and shot several whitetail deer with it. Stan says the .33 WCF 1886 is "a damm good gun."

Winchester also offered the .33 in its Model 85 single-shot rifle. Winchester's other competitor, Marlin, began chambering the .33 WCF round in its model 1895 lever action rifle, due to its widespread popularity. From 1903 until 1935, when Winchester ceased production of the 1886 and replaced it with the similar Model 71 lever action in .348 Winchester, countless hunters seeking big game such as moose, elk and bear wisely chose the powerful .33 WCF to get the job done.

In the 1946 Second Annual Edition of *Gun Digest*, noted big game hunter, guide and arms expert Elmer Keith wrote an article titled "The Proper Big Game Rifle." In the section on lever action timber rifles, he wrote, "In the older Winchesters, we have the excellent Model 86 in both .33 WCF as well as the .45-70-405 caliber." (Keith was referring to the .45-70 cartridge with a 405-grain bullet). "These heavier calibers are preferred by many experienced hunters, particularly where a little more actual knockdown power is needed for large eastern whitetails and the big mule deer of the Northwest timber lands.

"Heavier calibers than the .30-30," Keith continues, "are also advisable for all large black bear shooting as that

animal can carry off a lot of lead unless hit properly. . . . High velocity is neither necessary nor desirable in brush and timber shooting where the ranges are short. . . . What is needed is a heavy bullet that will, at moderate velocities of 1800 to 2300 feet, buck a lot of brush without disintegration and reach game. Both black bear and deer require a bullet with plenty of lead exposed to surely expand on impact with the game and give uniformly good wound channels."

With an endorsement like that in 1946 from a world renowned hunter and gun expert like Elmer Keith, it is understandable why the 1886 in .33 WCF, despite its production having been halted a decade before, still had a loyal following. It worked well for its manufacturer's adver-

tised intended purpose, big game hunting, at the beginning of the century and onward. The 200-grain .33 Winchester cartridge was designed specifically for hunters. In fact, with Elmer Keith touting the gun's and cartridge's effectiveness to tens of thousands of victorious returning WWII veterans, I'm surprised that Winchester Repeating Arms Company didn't resume production of the model and chambering. After all, it was common knowledge in that post war era that, as my step-father, Ray Robey, a WWII Pacific Naval Veteran himself once said, "Returning to the States, we had two things on our mind, and the second one was hunting!"

Although ammunition for the .33 WCF was still available in 1955 (Winchester

Although officially designated as an "obsolete" cartridge, the .33 WCF has a strong cult following, and ammunition can be located and or reloaded.

Staynless .33 WCF had a listed suggested retail price $3.70 for a 20-round box at the time), within a few years it would be designated as obsolete and quietly dropped from production by both Winchester and Remington. Over the years I have met other .33 shooters and found them to be as fond of the round as I am. Obtaining ammunition can be difficult, but it's well worth the trouble and effort.

.33 WCF shooters can scrounge for vintage Winchester or Remington ammunition, or limited contemporary production runs of ammunition from gun shops and at gun shows, but be forewarned that you will most likely end up paying a premium price. I have an ample supply of original Winchester cartridges purchased by my grandfather and modern manufactured .33 caliber cartridges (circa late 1980s, produced

by Midway Arms). Buffalo Arms of Ponderay, ID (phone 208-263-6953; website www.buffaloarms.com) offers brand-new .33 WCF ammunition in 20-round boxes at competitive prices.

Perhaps a much more sensible and cost effective alternative to buying vintage or modern manufactured ammunition is to reload. I purchased a vintage Lyman 200-grain flat point .338" bullet mould at a gun show, and .45-70 brass can be cut and re-necked to proper size (.365" neck) if original or modern .33 WCF brass is unavailable. If using older, original brass, reloaders of the .33 and other obsolete calibers should always use caution and check every case carefully for signs of stress, cracks and wear, and stay well within safe recommendations pertaining to powder charges. Of course, reloaders should use common sense and follow

established component guidelines, and work up to desired loads slowly.

New 200-grain flatnosed .338" bullets can be used without undue concern, but DO NOT use pointed bullets in lever action rifles, as the points could possibly ignite a primer in the tubular magazine under heavy recoil. In a pinch, pointed bullets can be used by cautious shooters in tubular magazine lever action rifles, provided that the rifle is used as a single shot, or as a two-shot repeater, if only one single round is placed in the tube and one in the chamber.

The *Hornady Handbook of Cartrige Reloading*, Vol. II (1973) states, "While cases for this obsolete cartridge can be formed from .45-70 brass, reloaders who've wanted to shoot the .33 Winchester have been hampered by the lack of suitable bullets for it. While there are many popular 338-caliber bullets on the market, they have been designed for the much more popular .338 Winchester Magnum and either their weight or their pointed shape makes them inappropriate for use in the tubular magazine of the Model 1886 or Marlin's Model 95 lever action. In 1973 Hornady introduced a 338-caliber 200-grain flat point designed expressly for the .33 Winchester. The old 33 probably never had it so good; our new flat point is made to accuracy standards unattainable 50 years ago, and its jacket design features the Hornady Inner Groove to facilitate deadly and dependable expansion at 33 Winchester velocities." Today, almost four decades since that those words were written, Hornady has not forgotten .33 WCF aficionados and offers several different reloading dies for the .33, while RCBS offers a .338" 200-grain flat nose bullet mold.

Despite being first offered in 1903, the .33 WCF Model 1886 Winchester rifle is still a grand old American hunting arm, just as effective and deadly as when it was first offered for sale. It was, and still is, a fast-handling, powerful brush gun for heavy timber country.

And if by chance you have one of these old lever actions and decide to take it to hunting camp and a self-proclaimed "expert" chastises you or tells you that your rifle is obsolete and that you need a new gun and caliber to be successful, just ignore him. However "obsolete" the .33 WCF Model 1886 may be, you and the big game that you are pursuing with it will never know the difference!

Protecting Your Collection Investment

Popular television programs such as "Pawn Stars" and "American Pickers" show what can happen when unsuspecting surviving family members suddenly have to dispose of a loved one's collection. Here is a practical approach to protecting your estate and your family's financial security.

BY JACK MYERS

Increasing numbers of older gun collectors are becoming aware of a huge problem their heirs will face in the future: the (usually) ever-rising value of their collectible firearms. And as we all know, there are many unscrupulous folks out there ready and willing to "assist" your family in disposing of these valuable items. So how can you protect your loved ones from falling victim to these predators? Using the following record-keeping method, you can make sure your heirs get full value from your collection after your demise.

Collectible guns have become much more than just a relaxing hobby. They're now considered by most collectors and their families as a valuable part of their estates. Because your collection is a major asset that you might plan to pass on, it should be fully described and recorded in a manner in which you and your family members can find it quickly. Also, In case of loss due to burglary, fire or flood, this information can help you establish ownership and value of each item in your collection.

With a reasonable amount of luck, you'll never experience a loss of your collection through theft or mishap. However, it's a sure bet that some day, hopefully well in the future, the gaunt hooded gentleman carrying the scythe will come a-knocking at your door. In the unhappy event of your passing, your knowledge of each piece in your collection is suddenly lost. However, the procedure I'm outlining here will help those loved ones who will inherit your collection to obtain the highest possible value when they have to liquidate your collection. Your knowledge and help today can prevent a financial disaster tomorrow.

I began documenting my collection in earnest about five years ago. After a lot of thought and experimentation I came up with a solution for my personal concerns. Yours may differ. If this method does not fit you completely, you can easily tailor it to accomplish the same results. Use what is best for you and yours.

Before you begin, it's a good idea to keep handy the latest edition available of *Standard Catalog of Firearms* (www.gundigeststore.com) or other reputable firearms value guide to give you, and your heirs, an up-to-date, current evaluation of most firearms. I might also point out that the approach I describe below works not only for gun collections but for those of virtually any type: ammunition boxes, fishing lures, you name it.

Essential Data

At a minimm, your records should consist of the following data:

1) *Complete, detailed descriptions of each piece, including photographic proof of ownership and relevant information.* This also greatly simplifies the chore of an heir having to identify each piece. NOTE: Should your collection be placed into the hands of an auction house for disposal, it is a great help to them if you have already composed a history of each piece which explains why it may be of more than ordinary interest to their bidders. This may also help boost the price that particular piece may bring.

Most auction houses appeciate it when a seller can furnish good, clear, detailed photos of the guns being offered. When photographing your guns, make sure to take close-ups of smaller details such as scratches, dents, cracks, repairs and other small flaws which might aid in

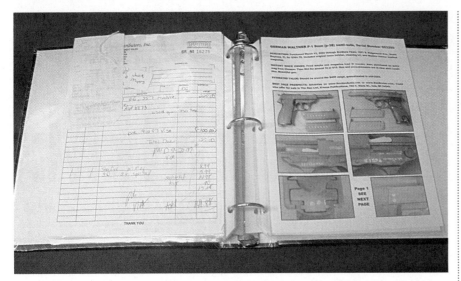

Open loose-leaf binder with sheet protectors on right show the illustrated record of the firearm or item, and the backside of the previous record (at left) shows receipts, bills of sale, and other documentation stored behind each firearm or item in its sheet protector.

CIL Long Shot - Full (Top Flap Box)

FULL original rounds. Brass case, D headstamp. Paper overwad.

Purchased 11/11/08 from Glenn Rossong, 3796 Main St., W. St. Paul, Manitoba, R4A 1A4, via eBay. COST: $25 with conversion.

Box in good condition. Some wear evident.

Best sales prospects: at auction on www.Gunbroker.com or www.AuctionArms.com. Or list in Gun Digest The Magazine, 700 E. State St., Iola, WI 54990-0001 or www.gundigestmagazine.com Phone: (715) 445-2214.

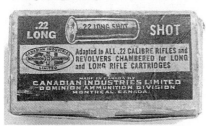

BOTTOM of box is blank and solid yellow.

This scan illustrates how the record keeping idea can be as easily applied to collectible ammo boxes or any other collectible items. Taking detailed photos from all angles provides more identifying data, which helps pinpoint the value of a specific item.

identifying a piece which may not have serial numbers stamped on it. Federal law did not mandate serial numbers until after 1968, so a lot very valuable older pieces are NOT numbered; thus detailed photos would be even more important in identifying them in case of theft.

2) *Details of WHEN obtained; FROM WHOM obtained; WHERE obtained; and at WHAT COST.* I also record how much I believe the piece should sell for when it is offered for sale. What may appear as a beat-up old junker to others could be one of the most valuable pieces in your collection due to its provenance – which only you know and can furnish.

3) *EVERY receipt, invoice, bill of sale, ad, owner's manual, or any other items connected to your acquisition of EVERY piece.* Photocopies of various historical magazine articles can be slipped into a sheet protector, to add credence to your claims about any particular piece. Exploded views of guns with parts lists, are some of the items you may wish to include in those pockets. I preserve as much info as possible on each piece, info which will come in handy whether your heirs decide to keep the piece or sell it.

How To File Your Data

I use a loose-leaf, three-ring binder containing clear plastic page protectors. Each individual piece is filed in the binder in alphabetical order according to maker name or description (if no maker name is known). I have separate binders for each category in my collection: HANDGUNS, LONG GUNS, AMMO BOXES, and ACCESSORIES.

All of this information is then copied onto an inexpensive 4GB Flash Drive that is well labeled and kept in a bank safety deposit box with other important items I wish to protect. Depending upon how often you add to your collection, you can add the new piece to your computer files and at-home three-ring binders, then do a new, updated Flash Drive and take it to the deposit box, regain your previously recorded flash drive, and erase it for use at a later time when updating your files.

You must be sure to fully instruct your heirs as to where this valuable information is located, and especially to instruct them on how to use it.

Remember that in some states, your heirs might not have immediate access to the contents of your safety deposit box, so it behooves you to leave your hard-copy bound records where they can be found quickly.

THE GARIN SURESTRIKE SYSTEM:

A New Family of Wildcat Cartridges

BY **THOMAS C. TABOR**

Most of the time when the topic of wildcat cartridges is brought up, someone points out that everything has already been done; that the cartridge frontiers are long gone; and that if a cartridge were meant to be, one of the big ammunition or firearms manufacturers would already offer it.

During the wildcat heyday of the 1960s, it sometimes seemed as though every aspiring gunsmith had dreams of developing a revolutionary new cartridge. Some of those individuals hoped that once Federal, Remington or Winchester got a glimpse of their ingenious new design, it would immediately be snatched up for production, which of course would elevate the designer into legendary status. But as history shows, few wildcats ever reach that pinnacle of success.

Maybe I'm a bit of a dreamer when it comes to shooting, but I believe there are still a few inroads to be explored in cartridge designs and I believe that I have recently unearthed such an example. No, it doesn't carry my name, nor can I lay claim to any of the creative designs within this project. All that credit must go to its developer, Paul Garin. I only had a small part in the testing phase of the project, but it quickly became apparent to me that this venture

Shown here are the five Garin SureStrike Cartridges and for comparison purposes a normal .30 Carbine case loaded with a spitzer style bullet (L-R): .17 Garin, .20 Garin, .22 Garin, 6mm Garin, .25 Garin and the .30 Carbine, all based on the .30 Carbine case.

The three Garin cartridges the author agreed to test and perform the initial load development for (L-R): .17 Garin, .20 Garin and .22 Garin.

All Garin cartridges possess a 40-degree shoulder angle that has shown to be effective in Weatherby cartridges. On the left is the .20 Garin as opposed to the .30-378 Weatherby Magnum.

had far-reaching possibilities. Unlike most wildcat endeavors, this project isn't limited to a single cartridge. It includes a whole series of new cartridges, which carry the names of .17, .20, .22, 6mm and .25 Garin. All utilize the .30 Carbine as their parent case and each possesses an identical Weatherby-like shoulder angle of 40 degrees. In order to accommodate the different bullet diameters and still maintain that same shoulder angle, the length of the shoulders and necks had to be varied, but other than those dimensional variations all five cartridges are for the most part identical except for caliber.

The claimed benefit of the Garin wildcats is their extreme efficiency as compared to their larger-case counterparts. As you'll see, there's more than a little merit to the claim.

I got involved with the Garin SureStrike System cartridges when Mr. Garin asked if I would be interested in doing the load development work and the initial testing of the first rifles to be chambered in the cartridges. Being limited, however, on the amount of the time I could devote to such a project, I decided that I could only do the work on the the smallest cartridges of the series, the .17 Garin, .20 Garin and .22 Garin. The remaining two cartridges, the 6mm and .25 Garin, would have to be wrung out by someone else.

After the initial design concepts had been completely worked out, a set of Hor-

nady reloading dies for each cartridge was procured. Chamber reamers were built by Pacific Tool & Gauge. Once the very first newly-formed brass had been formed, Mr. Garin further got the ball rolling by commissioning Cooper Firearms of Montana to build him five rifles, one chambered for each of the Garin SureStrike System cartridges and built on Cooper's well-established and reliable

Model 38 action. Each rifle would come with two stocks: a synthetic "Phoenix" style and a broad forearm laminated stock designed for competitive shooting.

Because I had no way to actual measure chamber pressure I felt it best to set some guidelines for my involvement early on. I would have to rely on what I frequently call the ol' seat-of-the-pants method of examining the spent primers, being alert for any signs of action stickiness and using a micrometer to check for any case head expansion. Paul had provided me with some speculative data he had generated through a computer program called "Quick Load," which helped me greatly in getting started.

Nevertheless, I did not feel comfortable pushing the cartridges to their full potential when the rifles did not belong to me. I agreed only to work up what I believed to be moderate pressure loads for each cartridge and made it clear that I would make no effort to develop maximum loads. Once we were in agreement on that issue, we began to move forward. But while this approach would generate some rudimentary loading data, it would fail to show the full potential of the cartridges. Nevertheless, even working with such limited parameters, the velocities far exceeded my expectations and the accuracy seemed in all cases to be extremely good.

[Editor's note: The following load data is not warranted to be safe in any particular rifle and is presented here purely for illustrative purposes. Neither the editor nor the author assumes any responsibility for its use. Always follow the manufacturer's published data when reloading any cartridge.]

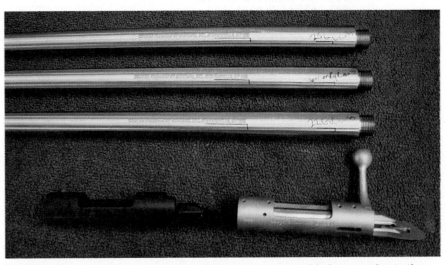

Once the Garin barrels were chambered they went to assembly for mounting to the actions.

.20 Garin

The first rifle to come out of the Cooper factory was the .20 Garin. Because of the recent popularity of this bore diameter, I was particularly anxious to see how it would perform. I had always held a special fondness for Berger bullets, particularly when loading small cartridges, so I decided to use Bergers exclusively for all three cartridges. For the .20 Garin I picked the 30-grain Match/Varmint. For powders I selected three types produced by three different manufacturers: Accurate's 1680, Alliant's 2400 and Hodgdon's new 8208 XBR. While the 8208 XBR produced excellent accuracy results, I found the case capacity of the .20 to be the major limiting factor. Seventeen grains completely filled the .20 Garin case and produced only what I would call a moderate velocity of 3,064 fps. On the other hand, 15.0 grains of Accurate 1680 produced a little tighter groups and generated a better velocity of 3,286 fps.

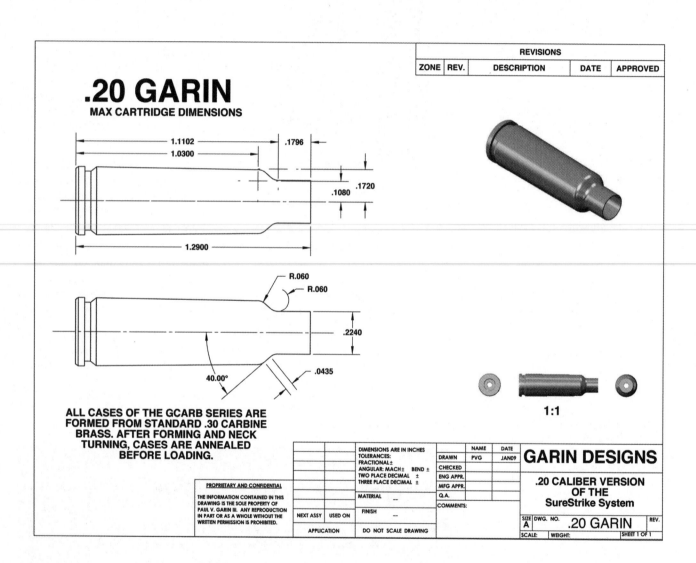

.20 Garin Ballistics

Powder	Charge Wt.	Bullet Mfr.	Bullet Wt.	Primer	O/A Length (inches)	Group (3-shots)	Average Velocity (fps)
1680	15.0	Berger	30-grain	CCI BR-4	1.770	1/4-inch	3,286
2400	9.5	Berger	30-grain	CCI BR-4	1.770	5/16-inch	2,839
8208 XBR	17.0	Berger	30-grain	CCI BR-4	1.770	3/16-inch	3,064

.22 Garin

The next rifle to move from the Cooper factory to my hands was the .22 Garin. I had high hopes for this particular cartridge for a couple of reasons. I felt it would likely outperform both the .22 Hornet and the .221 Fireball and could even become a better overall choice than its only real competition, the .222 and .223. Rocky Dubuis of Cooper Firearms seemed to agree as he handed me the completed rifle, saying that he felt there was just something special about this particular cartridge.

I felt the best approach for the .22 Garin would be to stay a bit on the light side in regard to bullets and so chose the Berger 30-grain Match/Varmint and the 40-grain Varmint. For powders I selected Alliant's 2400, Hodgdon's 'Lil Gun and Hodgdon's H110. In the area of accuracy all three powders produced excellent results. I used the slightly slower-burning powders of 'Lil Gun and H110 to back the 30-grain Bergers and the 2400 for the 40-grainers. The differences in accuracy between the three loads varied only by 1/8-inch, but the heavier 40-grain bullet backed by the 2400 powder experienced a consider reduction in velocity. I am quite sure that higher velocities could be achieved with a 40-grain bullet through the use of elevated powder charges and the loading of different types of powders.

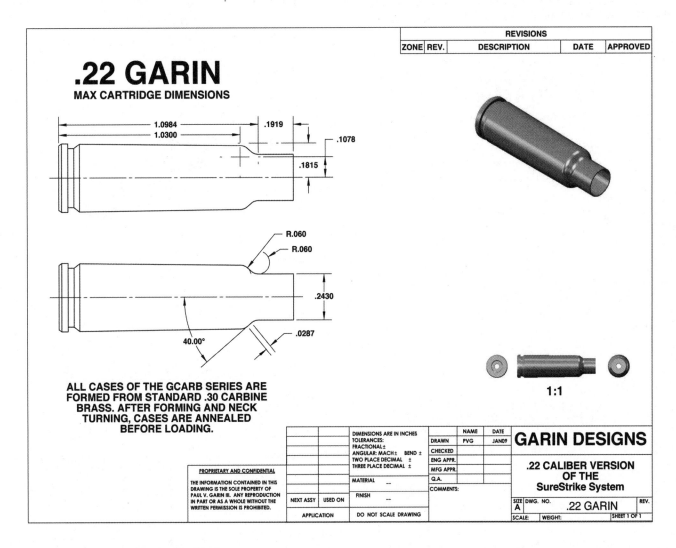

.22 Garin Ballistics

Powder	Charge Wt.	Bullet Mfr.	Bullet Wt.	Primer	O/A Length (inches)	Group (3-shots)	Average Velocity (fps)
'Lil Gun	14.0-grains	Berger	30-grain	CCI BR-4	1.792	1/2-inch	3,783
H110	15.5-grains	Berger	30-grain	CCI BR-4	1.792	5/8-inch	3,870
2400	12.0-grains	Berger	40-grain	CCI BR-4	1.792	1/2-inch	3,127

.17 Garin

As with the other Garin/Cooper rifles I began my testing and load development work on the range. I selected my favorite .17 caliber bullet – the 20-grain Match/Varmint Berger – and backed it with a diverse selection of four powders: Hodgon's 'Lil Gun, Alliant's 2400, Hodgon's H110 and Accurate's 1680. Looking back now I sincerely regret not trying Hodgon's Benchmark. Benchmark has always worked exceptionally well in my .17 Mach IV. But nevertheless, all of the .17 Garin test loads produced what I

would call good velocities and accuracy. Even though this particular Garin didn't seem to be quite as accurate on the range as either the .20 or .22 Garin, it nevertheless was pretty darn good. On the other hand, as I will get into a little later on, I found its performance poking holes in ground squirrel to be quite exceptional.

When the little 20-grain Berger was backed with 12.0-grains of 'Lil Gun powder it sent the tiny bullet on its way at the phenomenal average speed

of 4,150 fps. That is pretty close to the performance of the much larger .17 Remington. Because of the Remington's larger case capacity, it generally takes a slower burning powder than the Garin, but if we look strictly at the weight of the powder charge we find that the Garin uses only about half the charge that the Remington requires. This certainly equates to a higher level of efficiency in the case of the .17 Garin and could result in extending the life of the barrel as well.

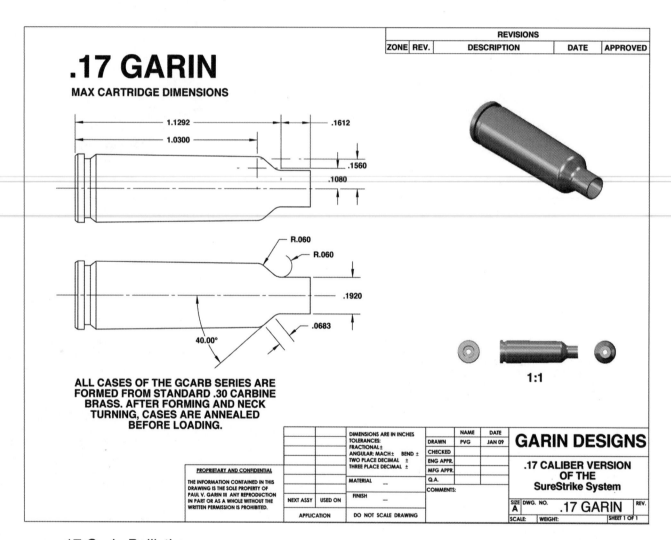

.17 Garin Ballistics

Powder	Charge Wt.	Bullet Mfr.	Bullet Wt.	Primer	O/A Length (inches)	Group (3-shots)	Avg. Velocity (fps)
Lil'Gun	12.0-grians	Berger	20-grain	CCI BR-4	1.642	5/8-inch	4,150
2400	9.5-grains	Berger	20-grian	CCI BR-4	1.642	1/2-inch	3,430
H110	12.2-grains	Berger	20-grain	CCI BR-4	1.642	1/2-inch	3,844
1680	14.0-grains	Berger	20-grain	CCI BR-4	1.642	3/4-inch	3,822

6mm Garin and .25 Garin

While I didn't have an opportunity to personally test the two remaining Garin cartridges, Paul Garin has taken that on himself and the first of the preliminary results are now in hand. Paul likes the .25 Garin very much and thinks of it as "a 21st century 25-20." The very first of that data shows the cartridge producing only about 25,000 psi and pushing a 60-grain bullet out the muzzle at 2,600 fps muzzle velocities (24-inch barrel). Those results were achieved with a loading of Accurate 1680 powder. Producing this high of velocities and generating such a moderate level of chamber pressure would certainly lead me to believe that the real potential of the .25 Garin has not yet been tapped.

Like the .25 Garin, the first data is only now starting to roll in on the 6mm version. This cartridge also shows a great deal of potential with an average velocity of 3,055 fps and a pressure of less than 40,000 psi. Those results were generated when loading a 55-grain Comtech spitzer boattail backed with a charge of Hodgdon Lil' Gun powder. Once again, this data is only the very first data for the cartridge and it is likely that other powders and components will show even better performance.

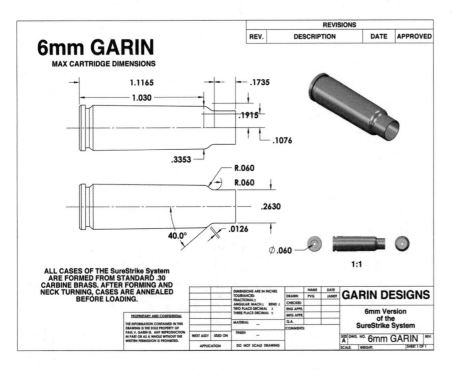

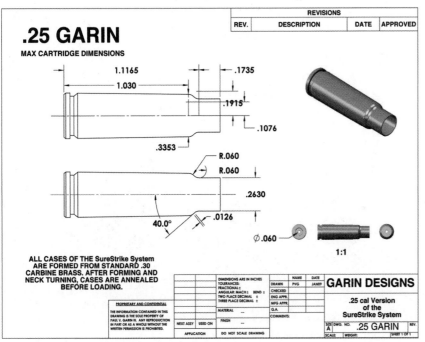

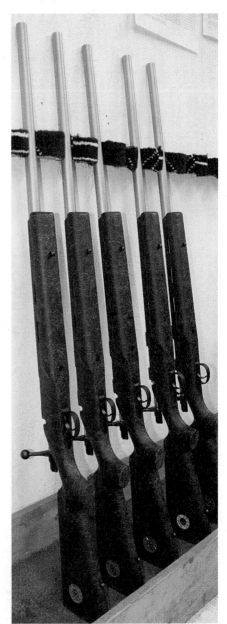

Nearing completion, the five rifles equipped with their Phoenix stocks await final performance checks before being released to author and eventually to Paul Garin.

Paul Garin was quite pleased to finally be able to hold one of his five rifles at the Cooper plant.

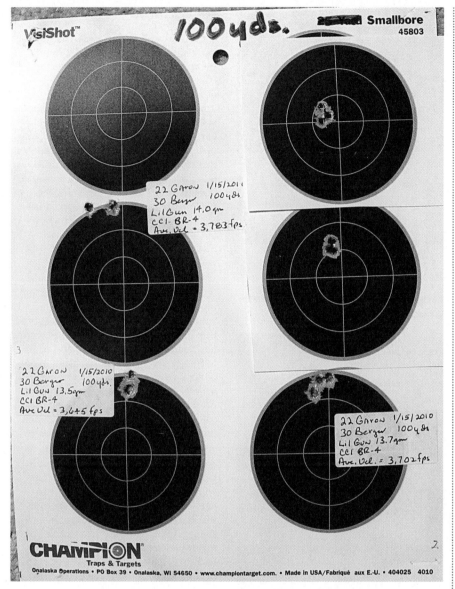

VisiShot™ · 100 yds. · 25-Yard Smallbore 45803

22 Garon 1/15/2010
30 Berger 100 yds.
Lil Gun 14.0 gr
CCI-BR-4
Ave. Vel. = 3,783 fps

22 Garon 1/15/2010
30 Berger 100 yds.
Lil Gun 13.5 gr
CCI BR-4
Ave. Vel. = 3,645 fps

22 Garon 1/15/2010
30 Berger 100 yds.
Lil Gun 13.7 gr
CCI BR-4
Ave. Vel. = 3,702 fps

CHAMPION®
Traps & Targets
Onalaska Operations • PO Box 39 • Onalaska, WI 54650 • www.championtarget.com. • Made in USA/Fabriqué aux E.-U. • 404025   4010

This is just a sampling of the phenomenal 3-shot 100-yard groups produced by some of the Garin cartridges.

The Garins in the Field and a 542-Yard Kill

Punching holes in paper provides a great deal of information and allows a person to accomplish a baseline of data and information, but sometimes the real test comes when you move from the range to the field. So, after I had completed the "paperwork" on the three test rifles, Paul Garin and I met up in a remote outback farmer's field in an effort to use them to help reduce the population of some problematic ground squirrels (a.k.a. sage rats).

Paul had loaded a significant pile of ammunition for the work and soon we were making the farmer happy by picking off the little pests one by one. This type of shooting provided a great way to evaluate how the various rifles would do from the close quarters of 30 or 40 yards all the way out to beyond 500 yards. All three rifles performed in exemplary, first-class fashion. The little bullets of the Garin SureStrike System provided devastating results on everything they touched, but what surprised me most was the .17 Garin. By most shooters' standards its accuracy was pretty darn good on the range, but when I switched from poking holes in paper targets to poking holes in the local pests my opinion of its performance improved greatly.

I know there is little logic behind this, but it almost seemed as though I couldn't miss those pesky little rodents and on one occasion I was even able to stop the reproduction capabilities of a sage rat at the phenomenal (measured) range of 542 yards. Certainly no one should reach the erroneous conclusion that these cartridges are best suited for long-range

Paul Garin was eager to see how his new cartridges and rifles would do on some of the ground squirrel population.

Paul Garin designed a color-coded medallion designating the cartridge caliber for each of his rifles. These emblems were inlaid into the buttstock of the rifles by Cooper.

Field testing the .17 Garin on a farm population of ground squirrels, author was able to make a phenomenal 542-yard shot on one of the pesky rodents. Photo courtesy Will Garin.

A Last Word

Certainly the Garin SureStrike System cartridges are not your normal run-of-the-mill, backyard-gunsmith wildcats. Paul Garin is moving forward in a determined, commercial manner with this project. Cooper Firearms of Montana is now chambering for all five of these cartridges, but if you prefer to build your own rifle, chamber reamers are available through Pacific Tool & Gauge; Hornady reloading dies are in stock and available directly from Paul Garin by going through the SureStrike website; and if you don't like the idea of reforming your own .30 Carbine cases, the formed cases are also available through Paul's SureStrike website (surestrikesystem.com).

By the time this article is published there should also be reloading data and pressure testing data on the website. Walt Berger of Berger Bullets has agreed that once the formulized pressure testing has been completed he will add the data to Berger's website and publish it in one of his upcoming manuals. As I write this article, Paul is well underway with his pressure testing and it is believed that Alliant Powders will also be doing some testing of their own in the near future.

The ball is rolling on the Garin SureStrike System of wildcats and it is gaining momentum very quickly. Time will only tell in how important these cartridges will become in the shooting world, but it appears to me that everything is in place for them to become major players both as varmint and small game rounds as well as in competitive shooting events.

shooting and capable of producing consistent performance at a range of 500+ yards. In reality I would rate all three as essentially in the 250 to 300 yards category of cartridges. Nevertheless, as the ol' saying goes: "even a blind hog finds a root sometimes" and likely that is what my phenomenal 542-yard shot was. But such as it was, I am still proud of it. I'm not sure how many pests fell that weekend to the Garin SureStrike System of cartridges, but the count was well in the hundreds.

I've struggled over and questioned the data provided in trajectory tables over my entire shooting life and having done so I have come to the conclusion that the only reliable way to determine actual bullet drop is to do so on the range under live fire. But having said that, I would venture to say that in the case of the .17, .20 and .22 Garin cartridges, it would be reasonable to expect, with a 100-yard 0.0-inch point of hold, that at 300-yards the bullets would likely be down about 10 or 15 inches. Of course the actual results will depend upon the ballistic coefficient of the bullets, starting velocity and, to a lesser degree, elevation.

Resources

Garin Designs SureStrike Systems
Website: http://www.surestrikesystem.com/
Email: Info@SureStrikeSystem.com
Telephone: 1-800-232-8205

Berger Bullets
Address: 4375 N. Palm St., Fullerton, CA 92835
Website: http://www.bergerbullets.com
Email: sales@bergerbullets.com
Telephone: (714) 447-5456

Pacific Tool & Gauge
Address: PO BOX 2549, 598 Ave C, White City, Oregon 97503
Website: http://www.pacifictoolandgauge.com
Phone: (541) 826-5808

FIT FOR A LADY:

The Mauser of Osa Johnson

Osa Johnson and her well-traveled Mauser.

BY **THOMAS TURPIN**

Color photos by Terry Wieland.

Back in the innocent days before television, films provided visual entertainment. In the early 20th century, even films were in their infancy. Global travel was restricted to a precious few, and the public visually experienced most of what went on in the rest of the world through the magic of the cinema. Those of you who are old enough might remember the newsreels that were often shown in theaters before the start of the feature film, along with the previews of coming attractions and a cartoon or two.

One of the pioneer duos making adventure films for the cinema market was the team of Martin and Osa Johnson. Back in those days when there were no 24/7 cable channels or constantly-updated websites, all that many Americans knew of the world that surrounded them was gleaned from the pages of *National Geographic* or the cinematic travelogues of Martin and Osa Johnson.

Both of the Johnsons hailed from Kansas: Martin from Lincoln and Osa from Chanute. Martin began his thrill-seeking career as a part of author Jack London's crew in the 1907-1909 voyage across the Pacific Ocean aboard London's boat, *Snark*.

After that adventure, Johnson started a touring road show, traveling the USA displaying various photos and relics amassed during the *Snark* voyage. During a visit by his road show to Chanute, Kansas, Martin met Osa Leighty. At the time, he was 26 years old, and she was but 16. Martin swept the young Miss Leighty off her teen-aged feet,

Closeup of receiver.

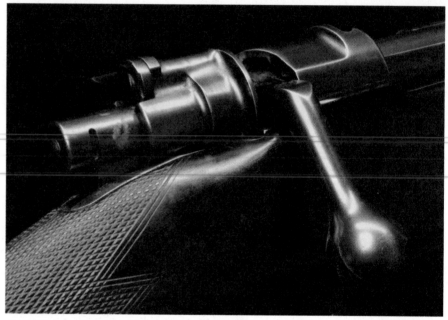

Osa's Mauser has undoubtedly seen use, but they just don't make them like this anymore.

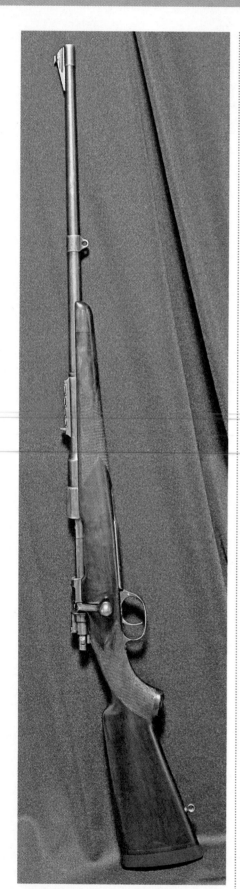

Osa Johnson's Type A/"Type E""
commercial Mauser sporter in 9.3x62.

and they eloped in 1910. It seems that Father Leighty was none too keen on the marriage or with his new son-in-law, at least initially. Osa's mother Belle, on the other hand, was more accepting of the situation as she had married at a very young age herself.

The Johnson team began their life of adventure together with a nine-month long trip to the New Hebrides and Solomon Islands in 1917. During this trip, they had a particularly frightful experience when visiting a wild tribe called the Big Nambas. Nihapat, the chief, decided that he wasn't going to permit the Johnson's to leave, and it took the assistance of a British gunboat to allow them to escape. The footage from that trip resulted in a feature film, *Among the*

Cannibal Isles of the South Seas, which debuted in 1918.

They returned for another visit with the Big Nambas in 1919 but this time took the precaution of traveling with an armed escort. They completed that trip in 1920 with a visit to British North Borneo, and a sailing trip up the coast of East Africa. This trip resulted in the release of two films, *Jungle Adventures* in 1921, and *Headhunters of the South Seas* in 1922.

Other films followed. *Trailing Wild African Animals* resulted from their first African expedition in 1921-1922. From 1924 until 1927, they took their second and longest trip to Africa, spending much of their time in Kenya living on a lake they called Paradise, near Mount Mars-

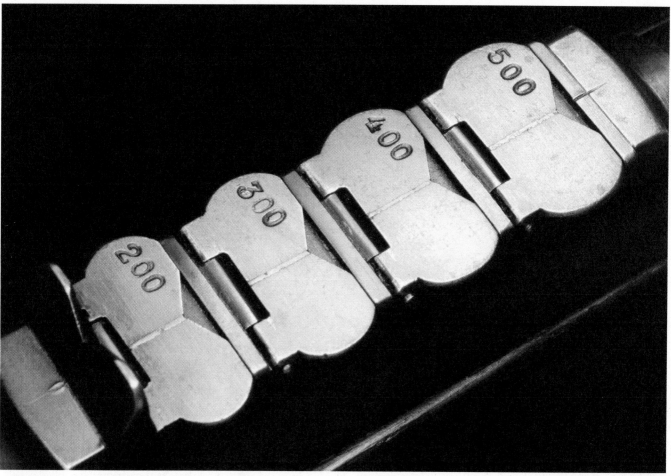

Even the Mauser's folding leaf sight is a work of art.

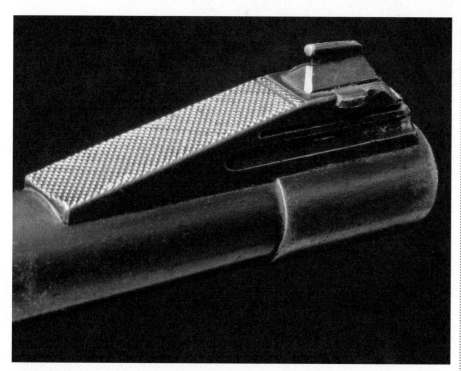

A crosshatched front ramp topped with a brass bead made sense in 1931 – and still does today.

abit. Martin's *Safari* (1928), Osa's *Four Years in Paradise* (1941), and *Simba: King of the Beasts* (1928) all resulted from the footage collected during that long trip.

George Eastman of Eastman-Kodak joined the Johnsons on their third African trip during 1927 and 1928 for a tour of the Nile. Eastman was both a good friend and a financial supporter of the Johnsons' efforts. *Across the World with Mr. and Mrs. Johnson* resulted from this trip. Coming out in 1930, it was one of the first films with sound from the Johnsons.

A trip to the Belgian Congo was next for the pair, beginning in 1929 and lasting into 1931. The feature movie *Congorilla*, released in 1932, partly resulted from this trip. It was the first film featuring a sound track that was recorded in Africa.

The Johnsons both learned to fly in 1932 and purchased two airplanes, both Sikorsky amphibs. They took these planes to Africa in 1934, where they flew all over the continent, collecting aerial footage of wildlife and scenery. They were the first pilots to fly over Mt. Kilimanjaro and Mt.

The rifle's provenance in unquestioned.

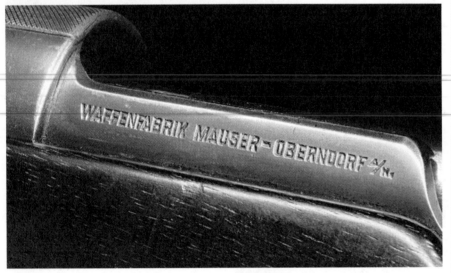

Words to quicken the heartbeat of any rifle connoisseur.

Osa is known to have owned several firearms in her life. However, at the time of her death, she had but two, a rifle and a shotgun. At least those are all that were listed in her personal effects. On October 17, 1953, the Plaza Art Galleries, Inc., auctioneers and appraisers of New York City, sold the two guns from the estate. One was a 20-gauge Ithaca #4 Grade shotgun, and the second was a Commercial Mauser 9.3x62 magazine rifle, made by Mauser and inscribed on the barrel "Made for Chas. A. Heyer & Co. Nairobi." Though it is not listed as such, the rifle is clearly a Type A Model commercial sporter, referred to in the Mauser catalog as the Type E (for English) model.

This well-traveled rifle recently surfaced and was purchased by a Texas collector, Bob Faucett. I learned of its existence when Faucett published some photos of the rifle on an internet forum for hunters and shooters that I occasionally visit. I was vaguely familiar with the names Martin and Osa Johnson, knowing only that they had been in the business of producing films on nature and the peoples of foreign lands.

The rifle was very intriguing to me, and for several reasons. First, a commercial Mauser is a very desirable collector's item. Secondly, I happen to be a big fan of the 9.3x62 cartridge; and, finally, the historical significance of the find was appealing.

Though I did not know Mr. Faucett, I contacted him via e-mail and asked if he might be amenable to my doing a story on the rifle. He responded right away and sent me his phone number. I called and we had a delightful conversation about the Johnsons and Osa's rifle. Not only was he receptive to my doing the story, but he also was most helpful in assisting me in every way.

The rifle was physically located in the Houston, Texas, area. Faucett had the rifle shipped to his gunsmith to give it a thorough cleaning and to check for any minor restoration that might be needed, as long as it didn't depart from the rifle's original specifications. He offered to make the rifle available to me for photography. I could even shoot it if I wished.

Alas, the rifle was in Houston and I live in Arizona, not exactly right next door. As it turned out however, my friend and colleague, Terry Wieland, also a lover of fine old vintage guns, had a trip planned to Houston. He agreed to perform the photography for me, for which I am most grateful.

Kenya. *Baboona*, a feature film released in 1935, resulted from this trip.

The Johnsons took their final trip together in 1935 to 1936, when they visited British North Borneo again. They took one of the planes with them on that trip. Film shot during that trek resulted in *Borneo*, released in 1937.

Their adventuresome relationship together ended in 1937, when Martin died from injuries he received in the crash of a commercial flight. Osa was seriously injured but later recovered.

Osa made at least one more African trip after Martin's death, writing dispatches for the *New York Times* on the subject of lifestyles and practices of the Masai and other tribes in the area. One would think that with all her experiences

in life that her demise would result on the tusks of an elephant, on the horns of a Cape buffalo, or in the jaws of a crocodile. Such was not to be. Osa Johnson died of a heart attack at the age of 58 in New York City on January 7, 1953.

Osa was a crack shot, having learned how to shoot on the Kansas prairies. She was actively involved in all aspects of their production of films and books, including manning a camera or piloting a plane. One of her jobs was using a rifle to feed the numerous hands required for their trips to Africa. When their assignments included the filming of wild and dangerous animals, she also had the task of protecting the crew. Some of the animals being filmed did not take too kindly to the interference in their activities.

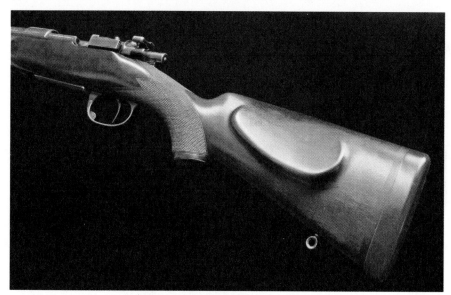

Stock has graceful lines despite the red rubber pad, not original and probably added to accommodate Osa Johnson's small frame.

The photos of the rifle that Terry provided me were taken in the Pearland, Texas, shop of gunsmith Todd Johnson. It was exactly as it had been received from the seller; no cleaning and no restorative work had yet begun. There is little doubt that Osa Johnson used this rifle in Africa. I suspect that she acquired it there, since it was originally made for the Heyer Company in Nairobi. As best I can tell, the rifle was produced around 1930 or 1931 and therefore could not have been purchased during the Johnson's extended stay in Kenya from 1924 - 1927.

What happened to the rifle during the period from its sale for $65.00 at the estate auction in October, 1953, until it was acquired by Bob Faucett a year or so ago is anyone's guess. Considering the rifle is now some 80 years old, it is in surprisingly good condition. It desperately needs a little TLC, mostly a thorough cleaning, but functionally, it is fine. I wouldn't hesitate to take it hunting.

It seems to be totally original, complete with horn forend tip and grip cap. I believe that it probably originally came with a horn buttplate as well but now has a rubber recoil pad fitted. Original photos of Osa holding the rifle show that it had the pad when she owned the rifle. Osa was a small lady, barely 5' 2" tall, and I suspect that when she purchased the rifle, she had the stock cut and shortened and the pad fitted. That is pure conjecture on my part, but it makes perfect sense.

Perhaps Bob will take the rifle back to Africa one day and shoot a buffalo with it. I can't imagine a more fitting tribute to the rifle, and to the adventurous Osa Johnson, its former owner.

A Mauserless Osa Johnson, looking quite fashionable in *haute couture* civvies.

The French Service Revolver Model of 1892

BY **RAYMOND CARANTA,** European Editor

Left side view.

The French service revolver Model 1892, right side view.

About 10 years after the adoption by the French services of the Cha-melot-Delvigne rod ejector revolvers Models 1873 and 1874, the Technical Division of the War Department, in charge of new armaments development, was entrusted with the task of designing a new model incorporating the most advanced features possible while using existing materials. The goal was to improve the handling characteristics of the M1873/1874 and to strengthen the design as much as possible.

The Experimental Models of 1885 and 1887

The French didn't start with a blank slate; they look to the new Swiss service Model of 1882 designed by the famous manager of the Bern Federal arsenal Rudolf Schmidt. The Swiss M1882 featured, among other niceties, a simplified action with a "V" mainspring that eliminated trigger return spring failures. In 1885 the French Technical Division developed a first prototype

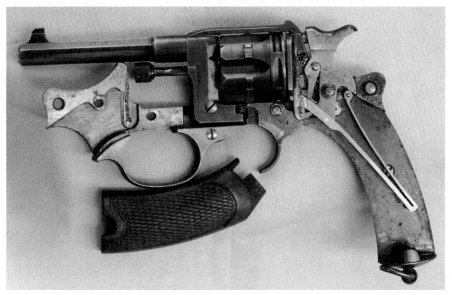

The 1892 revolver opened, with the left grip panel removed, showing the action at rest.

The loading door closed, in shooting configuration.

However, not everyone was enthusiastic about the proposed new design. The production of the Model of 1887 was delayed by that of the Lebel rifle Model of 1886. The Versailles Experimentation Commission, who was in charge of evaluating the new improved revolver, stated notably:

Both the loading and unloading procedures adopted may be a source of accidents in such a double action arm intended for general use among troopers.

As a matter of fact, some foreign competitive designs seem to offer, in this connection, more attractive features, particularly as far as swiftness and ease of operation are concerned.

The Emergence of the 1892 Service Revolver

Meanwhile, aross the Atlantic in America, Colt introduced its M1889 "Navy" .38 Long Colt swing-out cylinder revolver, of which 5,000 units were ordered by the US Government [2]. This cylinder on this new American design swung out to the left, which has since become the universal standard for double-action revolvers, but in those days it had not become gospel. Accordingly, in 1891, the French M1887 revolver was once more changed and fitted with a cylinder swinging out to the right. It also featured an original and sturdier locking device. In this form it became known as the final Model of 1892, the first specimen of which was delivered to the Saint-Etienne arsenal on June 3, 1892.

The new revolver cost the Government 56,30 Francs (around $11.00 US) compared to 62,96 Francs ($12.59 US for the former 1873 model revolvers as made in 1886, and it was 32 per cent lighter. When it was introduced, this new model – extremely sturdy, reliable, light and easy to load and unload thanks to its swing-out cylinder – was perfectly adapted to the requirements of the colonial wars of the time. Therefore, it was highly appreciated by its military users.

However, during World War I began some 22 years after the M1892's adoption, the revolver began to be transcended by the fire-power of the automatic pistols used most notably by the Germans. Accordingly, in 1921, the French Government launched a call for bids concerning a 15-shot 9 mm automatic pistol featuring a long barrel and a shoulder stock, which gave birth later to the famous Browning "Hi-Power" P35 – but that's another story!

chambered – as were its predecessors – in 11mm (.44 caliber) but featuring a pivoting ejection rod fitted to a collar encircling the barrel. Then, with consideration to the concomitant development of the military Lebel repeating rifle chambered in 8mm Lebel and to the recent invention of the smokeless powder, the French engineers decided to match the service caliber of their revolver, as the Swiss had done with their 7.5mm 1882 model.

Such a caliber reduction had the primary effect of significantly lightening the new design: it was 11 ounces lighter than the 1873 model and six ounces lighter than the 1874.

According to a ballistic report dated February of 1887, "Moreover, the development of the new 8mm revolver round with its jacketed bullet. . .resolved a great worry of our cavalrymen[:] how to immediately stop a horse in motion. . . ." [1] The new 32-caliber round pierced 3.7 inches of dry fir, instead of the two inches achieved by the earlier M1873's 11mm lead bullet. Furthermore, the new bullet was much steadier and better directed in the barrel, which significantly improved its accuracy potential.

These technical and ballistical improvements were the first steps toward what would become the new French service model of 1887.

The loading gate opened, enabling the cylinder to swing out.

The 1892 revolver with the cylinder opened. Note the dual clinder locking lugs, two per chamber.

ejector rod for ejecting the empties and close both the cylinder and the loading gate.

Handling Characteristics

The M1892's European style grip is very similar to those of the previous 1873 and 1874 revolvers. The revolver balances at approximately 39 per cent of its length overall, on the rear section of the cylinder, behind the trigger location with the hammer lowered.

In double action, the distance between the hollow section of the trigger and the backstrap is 2.6 inches, which is rather short for a military revolver but very convenient for small or average hands. In single action, the distance is 2.16-inch.

The height of the rear sight above the hand is 1.4-inch, identical to that of my modern Smith & Wesson Model 66. Both the front and rear sights are precisely shaped and much superior to those of the previous 1873 and 1874 models.

Finally, the hump at the rear of the frame is very efficient for preventing the gun from pivoting upward or rolling back in the hand on shooting. This makes reacquiring the target easy and rapid.

As previously stated, the trigger pull on the basic military model is quite stiff, as intended for use by horsemen. However, on the commercial market, up to World War I, when a civilian revolver Model 1892 was available at the price of 45,00 Francs ($9.00 US), target shooters

M1892 Technical Description

More than a century after its aoption, the French revolver Model 1892 is still quite a modern double action design, featuring a solid frame with a swinging cylinder, an articulated side-plate including an elegant elongated trigger guard, a rebounding external hammer and an oscillating firing pin. The cylinder is locked in firing configuration by a pivoting loading gate and the ejection rod terminates in a large checkered fitting enabling easy extraction.

Among the M1892's excellent characteristics are the following:

• *The action consists only of four main components consecutively numbered in the field stripping sequence.*

• *The mainspring is a particularly sturdy design.*

• *For field stripping this revolver, one only needs to release the large slotted screw located at the rear end of the frame right side ("Q" in the list of parts).*

• *The curved cylindrical grip features two checkered walnut panels and a circular bottom plate supporting a swivel ring.*

• *The fixed sights were neat and sturdy.*

• *This service revolver, like its predecessors, can be entirely disassembled without tools, contrary to its American competitors, and all components are interchangeable.*

Loading, Firing and Unloading

To load the M1892 revolver, rock back the loading gate, swing out the cylinder, load the six chambers and close the action.

For double action shooting, aim and squeeze the trigger for every shot. The cocking stroke is quite stiff at approximately 15 pounds and requires approximately a .6-inch trigger travel.

In single action, when the hammer is cocked, the direct letoff is quite instantaneous at 7.7 pounds pull on average. Such letoff pressures may seem quite high to modern target shooters, but one must keep in mind that these guns were intended for use mostly by horsemen for whom a very light letoff would be a real disadvantage.

For unloading, the procedure is reversed: rock back the loading gate, swing out the cylinder, push back the

Military proof nomenclature for the left side of the barrel; also appears on the right side.

On the top barrel flat, the military model nomenclature.

Military proof nomenclature for the left side of the barrel; also appears on the right side.

Ammunition

With standard military loadings, the flat-point 7.85-gram jacketed bullet (121 grains) had a modest 220 m/s (720 fps) muzzle velocity for a muzzle energy of 139.6 foot-pounds. This produced a recoil velocity of 6.22 fps (for a 32.6-ounce loaded gun) to 6.55 fps recoil velocity (for a 30-ounce unloaded gun).

If loaded with black powder, the standard charge was 75 centigrams (11.53 grains). For smokeless powders, the charge depends on the nature of the product involved. Such loads normally pierced 3.5 inches of dry fir, this being the standard test medium of the day.

Notes

[1] *L'Aristocratie du Pistolet*, Raymond Caranta and Pierre Cantegrit, Crépin-Leblond, Paris, 1997 (in French).

[2] *Règlement sur l'instruction du tir des troupes de cavalerie*, page 159, dated September 16, 1894.

Specifications: French Service Revolver, Model of 1892

Manufacturer: Manufacture d'Armes de Saint-Etienne

Years of manufacture: 1892-1927

Caliber: 8mm Model 1892 (also called "8mm Lebel" for export)

Cylinder capacity: 6 shots

Length overall: .52 inches

Total height: 5.47 inches (from lanyard ring axis)

Thickness: 1.53 inches (at cylinder)

Empty weight: 29.6 ounces

Loaded weight: 32.3 ounces

Barrel length: 4.6 inches

Rear sight: Fixed "U" notch .078" wide and .086" deep

Front sight: Fixed bead type .082" wide

Trigger pull: Single action 7.7 pounds
Double action 5.3 pounds

Safety: Safety notch on hammer

Frame material: Carbon steel

Finish: Blued with trigger and hammer light yellow heat treated ("straw")

Action type: Single action or Double action with V-type mainspring fitted with roller, rebounding hammer and oscilating firing pin.

---

could obtain, for 10,00 more Francs ($2.00 US), a "Concours" version with special finishing, selected components and improved trigger pull.

This writer has seen such a specimen in Italy during the 1960s. It belonged to a former international champion who had won it before the war and still used it with commercial Fiocchi ammunition.

Accuracy

If we refer to military regulations of the time, the accuracy standards were the same, for competition, for those already mentioned in our previous article covering the 1873 and 1874 service revolvers.

According to the "Shooting Regulations for Cavalry" of 1894 ("*Règlement sur l'instruction du tir des troupes de cavalerie*," dated september 15, 1894), the shooting distances were 15 and 30 meters (49 and 98 feet) at circular targets of respectively 20 and 40 centimeters in diameter (8 and 16 inches). The larger target featured an internal 8-inch-diameter ring counting for two points and an outer one for one point.

At 30 meters, shooting was performed single action only (12 rounds) and, at 15 meters, both in single and double action (12 rounds each) for a total of 36 rounds. The larger targets were used at 30 meters only and the smaller ones, at 15 meters.

With scores reaching or exceeding 24/36, shooters were rated first class; at 12/36, they rated second class; and, under 12/36, third class. (Now, 115 years later, we shoot at 25 meters single action only, at the ISU international circular target featuring a 2-inch ten ring.)

BOLT-ACTION BALONEY

BY **BERNARD H. DIGIACOBBE**, M.D.

To hear some people talk, you'd think that the bolt action rifle is the greatest innovation ever to grace the American shooting scene. Its virtues are so obvious that no other action even approaches it in terms of safety or utility.

Baloney.

Over the past century or so, the bolt action has acquired a rather thick protective patina of myths and outright mistruths. The truth is that after a hundred years of refinement, the modern bolt action is a good, serviceable design. However, to appreciate the bolt action purely on its merits, we must first clear up some misconceptions about its virtues.

Gas-proof?

One of the primary attributes of the bolt action, according to its proponents, is its gas-proof design. It's said to be the best action for handling cartridge gas leaks.

In reality, nothing could be further from the truth. Obviously, the best way to contain gas leaks is by placing a solid steel wall between the bolt and the shooter's face. The modern Remington pump actions and the (unfortunately) obsolete Winchester 88 lever action and even the venerable old M1 Garand are good examples of this. Guns such as the Marlin 336 lever action, with its tight fit between the bolt and receiver, are almost as good. However, conventional bolt guns need rather large horizontal passageways to accommodate the bolt's front lugs when retracting the bolt.

No, this picture isn't upside down and the glass of soda proves it. A push-round feed gun like this Model 700 will reliably feed even if held upside down.

These passageways are unfortunately equally adept at sending the gases straight back toward the shooter's face if the cartridge head leaks gas around the lugs. Worse yet, the large circular recess in a bolt action's receiver ring (which is necessary to accommodate the rotation of the lugs) readily communicates these gases to the aforementioned horizontal passageways.

The much-lauded shroud on the cocking piece is merely a last-ditch

effort to spare the shooter from the hellacious experience of taking a blast of superheated gas right in the puss. Oh, but what about those small transverse gas vents in the receiver ring and the corresponding side of the bolt? If you take a look at these small, transversely oriented holes and compare them to the size of the passageway for the bolt lugs, you will soon figure out where the bulk of the gas flow will go. The large oblong vents on the left side of some bolts will do what they were designed to do: dump the gas from a ruptured primer into the left raceway!

Alternately, some bolts have large vents located above the magazine, virtually assuring a blown floor plate if a case fails. If you are still in doubt just consider the (again, unfortunately) out of production Remington 788. This innovative action had its locking lugs in the rear of the bolt, allowing for a snug fit between the round bolt and its corresponding round passageway in the receiver. What it didn't have is any gas vents! Why? Because it didn't need any! In this action, the small diameter of the firing pin and the tight fit of the bolt in the receiver sealed off the action.

The reason why lever actions and pump actions don't have elaborate gas venting systems is because they simply don't need them. In fact, some knowledgeable authorities maintain that the the small transverse gas vents in a bolt action exist mostly to give the advertising department something to work with rather than being a fully effective way to handle gas leaks.

Push Feeding

Undoubtedly, one of the biggest myths concerning bolt actions deals with push-round feeding. With push-round feeding, the extractor doesn't slip over the rim of the cartridge until the cartridge is completely chambered. Alternately, with controlled-round feeding, the cartridge rim slips under the extractor during the initial forward movement of the bolt. According to universally accepted dogma, controlled-round feeding is 101% reliable while push-round feeding is positional or gravity dependent, and therefore somewhat unreliable.

With either system, the bullet will be in the chamber portion of the barrel and the forward portion of the cartridge case will be well into the receiver ring before the magazine lips release the cartridge. Thus, the cartridge has no place to go but in the chamber. Yes, both controlled-round feeding and push-round feeding will function even if the gun is upside down or on its side when reloading. Don't believe me? Just try it for yourself. For safety's sake, be sure and use a dummy round. And, as always, the case needs to have been full-length resized or previously fired in the same chamber.

Actually, push-round feed may be the more reliable system. With this system, the magazine lips need only direct the

The 700-type extractor and plunger ejector are among the most reviled innovations on bolt actions. Yet they are very reliable, even when subjected to the rigorous extraction and ejection of an autoloading rifle.

Some optimists actually believe that this extra safety lug will restrain the bolt against any force that was powerful enough to sheer the bigger front lugs. I doubt it!

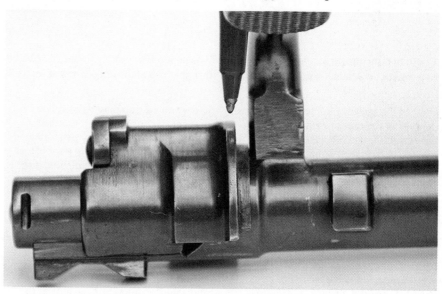

Rather than being a superior design feature, the gas shroud at the back of the bolt is a last-ditch effort to protect the shooter.

The best way to deal with the gas of a ruptured case head is to place a solid wall of steel between the case and the shooter as in this Remington 760.

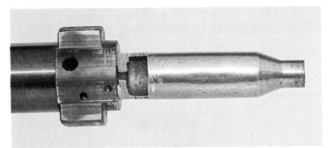 

Photo at right shows a cutaway case in a fully-recessed Remington Model 700 bolt head while photo at left shows a cutaway case in a traditional Mauser type bolt head. Note the thickness of the case webs at the unsupported area.

point of the bullet at the large opening at the rear of the receiver ring. By the time the extractor overrides the cartridge rim, the cartridge is firmly entrapped within the chamber. However, with controlled-round feed, things are a lot more complicated. For the cartridge rim to slide under the extractor, the magazine follower and magazine lips need to be precisely shaped. Worse yet, these configurations need to be changed for each differently shaped cartridge/degree of tapering of the cartridge case. In addition, if the magazine spring is too weak or too strong, the system may not function perfectly.

Controlled-round feed does, however, prevent the possibility of "double loading." This explains why it was preferred for military applications. In double loading, the bolt of a push-round feed gun is pushed forward to strip a cartridge from the magazine. However, before the bolt is pushed fully forward (which snaps the extractor over the rim in push round feed) the bolt can be unintentionally fully retracted, leaving the cartridge in the chamber. The retracted bolt can then be pushed forward to try and chamber another cartridge in the already-loaded chamber, thus causing a sort of ammunition traffic jam that ties

up the rifle. While it sounds a bit complicated, it is easy to do if you are looking through the ejection port while slowly operating the bolt. I suspect that it is nearly impossible to do if rapidly operating the gun from a shooting position.

Controlled-round feed requires that the bottom of the bolt face be flat to allow the cartridge rim to slide under the extractor. So with controlled-round feed, a portion of the circumference of the cartridge head is unsupported or "bare." This weak area, however, occurs at the base of the case web, where the case is the thickest. Actually the case was designed accommodate this potential

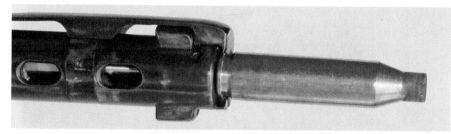

Ithough the claw extractor is frequently lauded for its strength, few shooters appreciate that the non-rotating claw extractor also allows the case head to be seated several thousands of an inch deeper into the chamber for maximal support of the cartridge. However, both the Winchester 94 and Marlin 336 lever actions provide for deeper seating and support of the base of the case than any rotating bolt head can!

Although this bolt head has nine small lugs it still has the same bearing area as a conventional two-lug bolt.

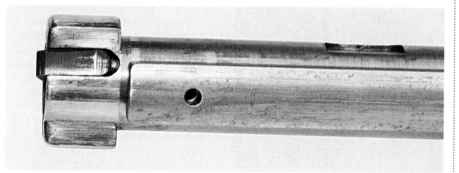

Although this bolt head has nine small lugs it still has the same bearing area as a conventional two-lug bolt.

weakness in the design of the gun. With push-round feeding, the bolt head can be fully recessed to better support the case head. This does transfer the gap between the bolt and barrel up along the side of the base of the case. This part of the case is slightly thinner, so some consider this a design flaw. However, modern cases extend the case web up to this area to avert this potential weakness.

The protruding, non-rotating Mauser-type claw extractor allows the cartridge to be seated several thousandths of an inch deeper into the chamber (for better support of the base of the case) than

is possible with the extractors used in push-round feeding. To compensate for this, the ubiquitous Remington 700 has its recessed bolt head telescoped into the back of the barrel. While Remington is generally given credit for this innovation, the Japanese Type 38 military rifle (introduced in 1905) also had its non-recess bolt head recessed into the back of the barrel. On the Remington design, however, the recessed bolt head is designed to fully obdurate if it is over-stressed, thus securely sealing the bolt face into the back of the chamber. So, if you ever see an expanded or "blown out" bolt head on a 700 you can appreci-

ate the ingenuity of the design rather than fault its strength. Incidentally, both the Winchester 94 and Marlin 336 provide for deeper seating and better support of the cartridge than any turn bolt can!

To maintain a fully shrouded bolt face, the Remington 700 needs an especially small extractor fitted into the shallow recess of the bolt face. Remington's solution was a small, C-shaped extractor. As flimsy as it appears, it works. In fact, it even works well with the forceful extraction of their auto-loading rifles, the Remington Models 7400 and 750. Incidentally, some gunsmiths used to custom-fit Mauser type claw extractors in place of the thin sheet metal extractors on the Remington 700s. It turned out that the flimsy-looking sheet metal extractor often functioned better than the conversions!

Cock-On-Closing? Not Really

On some older bolt actions, the main spring is cocked on the final closing of the bolt. This is commonly referred to as cock-on-closing. With this system, the effort of extraction occurs on the initial opening of the bolt and the effort of cocking is confined to the final closing of the bolt, dividing the effort. The extra effort to close the bolt is easily adapted to; however most American shooters object to the final extra effort required at the end of the closing of the bolt. On the 98 Mauser, and virtually all modern B.A.'s, the cocking occurs on the opening of the bolt combined with the extra effort of extraction. This is commonly referred to as cock-on-opening. While Mauser is usually credited with this innovation, it was introduced on earlier bolt guns like the 88 Commission Rifle. In actual fact, the compression of the main spring on modern cock-on-opening bolt actions (including 98 Mausers) actually occurs on both the opening and closing of the bolt, distributing the effort. However, the bulk of the effort does occur on the initial opening of the bolt.

The Third Safety Lug

Another "advantage" of the bolt action that's more apparent than real is its all-important third safety lug. On the 98 Mauser actions, there is an extra lug projecting from the sides of the mid-back portion of the bolt. This lug fits into, but does not bear against, an additional

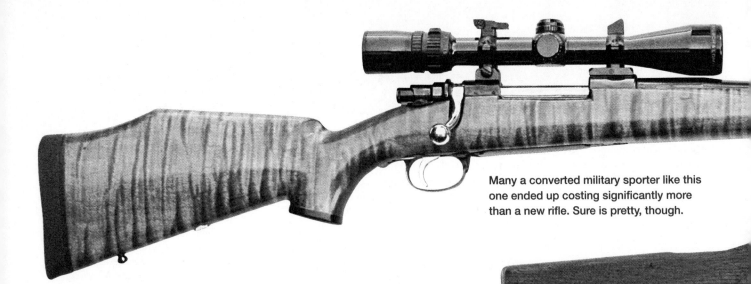

Many a converted military sporter like this one ended up costing significantly more than a new rifle. Sure is pretty, though.

locking recess in the receiver. In fact, it only makes contact and comes into service in the event of a catastrophic failure/sheering of the front lugs. The thinking goes like this: if an overloaded cartridge or barrel obstruction causes the front lugs to be sheared off and allows the bolt to acquire subsequently undesirable momentum, this extra safety lug will accomplish what the front lugs couldn't.

Oh, really? That dinky third lug is somehow going to provide more strength than the front lugs? It just doesn't add up. On some modernized versions of the 98 Mauser, the root of the bolt handle is allowed to fit into a small appropriately recess in the receiver to accomplish the same function as the third safety lug. Either way, you've got to be skeptical. Perhaps a quick "Hail Mary" would offer more protection. But then again, did you ever even hear of the lugs being sheared off a properly manufactured bolt in the first place ?

The third safety lug does, however, protect the shooter from a "slam fire" if the gun malfunctions or possibly in the event of a high primer. This explains the coincidence of the third safety lock being introduced on the 98 Mauser when Mauser converted from cock-on-closing to the cock-on-opening feature. Remember at this point that on the initial closing rotation of the bolt, the bolt is being "cammed" forward before the locking lugs are seated. Incidentally, sometime around 1911, abutments were placed on the firing pin itself which served to prevent a "slam fire" from occurring when the bolt is forcefully pushed forward.

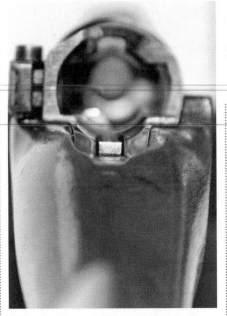

This view through the receiver of a 98 Mauser should bust the myth of a bolt action's superior gas handling.

When Weatherby introduced the full-diameter bolt with recessed lugs it was a design breakthrough. It not only resulted in smoother retraction of the bolt but also eliminated the expense of broaching the passageway for the lugs the length of the receiver. The recessed multiple lugs were spaced in sets of three, not two. Most shooters falsely assumed that nine is always more than two. Not always: because of the need to reduce the diameter of the lugs those nine small lugs actually have the same bearing area of conventional two-lug designs!

"Short" Bolt Lift

Similarly, many falsely assume that 60 is always less than 90. Supposedly, the 60-degree bolt lift on a three-lug bolt is faster to operate than a two-lug bolt requiring a 90-degree lift. However, the laws of physics decree that you can't get something for nothing. Since the total effort to compress the firing pin spring is the same, the bolt lift is significantly stiffer on a three lug bolt, nullifying the advantage. Think of it as the difference between starting off your car in third gear as opposed to starting off in first gear even though, theoretically, third gear may be faster.

Bolt and Lug Strength

Bolt actions are renowned for their strength, an attribute that is usually attributed to their large front rotating locking lugs. The same front rotating locking lugs are also used in modern lever action and pump action rifles. However, upon close inspection, it will be noted that not all of these large front lugs of a bolt action bear evenly or completely with the locking recesses! Inaccurate machining is usually blamed. Actually, the subtle warping that occurs during heat treatment is more likely the cause. Either way, if the lack of contact is severe, bolt setback will occur until

Despite their superior metallurgy and array of design features, these Japanese Type 38 Arisakas remain the most maligned bolt action rifles. Their looks may explain why.

sufficient contact is achieved. So, the process is self-limiting, provided excessive head space doesn't develop in the meantime. According to rumor, one large American manufacturer of multi-lug bolt rifles actually used proof loads to fully seat the lugs.

The original Mauser 98 and later Sakos and Weatherbys had their bolt handles forged integral with the bolt. This eliminates the possibility of separation. However, to reduce manufacturing cost, most manufacturers have the bolt handle made as a separate component to be later brazed onto the bolt. According to one knowledgeable source, these built-up bolts allow for greater accuracy in manufacturing after the heat treatment than the original one-piece bolts. If you doubt this last claim, just remember that Remington "built-up" bolts were used in custom bench rest actions until 1975 when Remington discontinued the sale of separate bolts. Obviously the people making and buying custom bench rest actions are more interested in extreme accuracy rather than cost.

Older bolt action designs had their recoil lugs formed integral with the receiver ring. Later designs with tubular receivers utilized a thin recoil lug between the barrel and the front of the receiver. This allowed for a simple tubular-shaped receiver. The simple tubular shape, in theory, minimizes head distortion of the lug recesses during heat treatment. Placing the recoil lug ahead of the receiver also maximizes

the thickness/strength of the wood of the stock between the recoil lug and the magazine well, a previously weak area in a bolt action rifle stock. And you thought that those added-on recoil lugs just saved money.

As an extension of this philosophy, some bolt guns like the Voere of the 1970s and the later Browning BAR had a separate locking seat ring threaded to the back to the barrel and then later press-fitted into the receiver. In addition to being cheaper, it eliminated the need to heat treat and potentially warp the tubular receiver.

When Ruger first introduced its Model 77 bolt rifle, it featured an investment-cast bolt with the lugs and bolt handle manufactured as one single unit. Ruger pointed out that these lugs offered approximately twice the sheer strength as the older Mauser lugs. True enough; however they weren't significantly stronger than the lugs on contemporary bolt actions. This is in no way meant to impugn the Model 77. It just demonstrates that those connoisseurs who build custom bolt rifles on remodeled old actions are purchasing old, potentially inferior metallurgy!

Reliability

According to myth, bolt actions are 101% reliable. In reality, like other guns, bolt guns also jam and malfunction. If you don't believe me, just ask a professional gunsmith. Before going on any

hunt with any new gun, you need to try it out, not just at the loading bench but also shooting rapid fire off-hand. When a bolt action malfunctions, it is written off as an aberration. If a lever or pump gun jams, it is taken as an indictment against the whole type. The same bias occurs regarding accuracy. You've heard the story many times before. Someone's lever or pump will only group approximately three inches at 100 yards. However, with select loads, and perhaps after a bit of tuning, their BA will print approximately 1.5-inch at the same distance. Unfortunately, no one bothers to work up loads or tune up a pump or lever action. I sometimes wonder if manufacturers incorporate the same bias and save their best barrels and trigger tuning for BAs only. Once exception to rule is the Browning L.A. They generally shoot better than you can hold them, right out of the box! Perhaps, they should have sued for slander on the rumor of L.A. inaccuracy.

Previously, the best trigger mechanisms/pulls were found on BA's. More recently, legal constraints have crept in, overriding quality concerns and now weigh heavily on current B. A. triggers, nullifying their previous advantage.

Most readers think of B.A's as repeaters. For sure, shooters that practice enough will eventually become proficient enough to operate a BA with great rapidity. However, many if not most casual shooters cannot get off a second shot at a bounding deer. For them, the

BA is just a cumbersome single shot. Yes you can adapt to the deficiencies of any machinery, but somehow those of us who embrace technology believe that the machine should adapt to our limitations not require that we adapt to their deficiencies. Obviously autoloaders, levers, and pump actions have the advantage on this point.

Those Sporterized Military Guns

Certainly the most expensive myth deals with the converting of old military BA into sporters. During the post-WWII years many believed that they could save a few bucks by remolding a surplus military BA into a sporter. By the time they paid a gunsmith to re-barrel, restock, refinish the gun then replace the two-stage military trigger and then drill and tap for scope mounts, it would have been significantly cheaper to buy a top-grade commercial rifle. The better refinishing efforts improved the contact of the locking lugs and polished the extractor cam, sear and passage ways for the bolt's lugs. On some actions, particularly Mauser actions, the metal was only surface hardened. Excessive "polishing" would expose the softer metal, leading to rapid wear. As always, changing the angle/contour of the sear/trigger can adversely affect the trigger pull and lead to a dangerous situation. Excessive polishing of the passage ways for the lugs can induce an undesirable wobble when cycling the bolt. The quality of such conversions was no better than the skill of the converter, a fact to remember when considering the purchase of one of these guns.

A Few Comments on Specific Designs

Remington Model 788

The unfortunately out of production Remington Model 788 was one of the most innovative bolt actions of of the 20th century. With its simple cylindrical receiver, equally simple rear lockup and bolt fabricated from three pieces, the gun could handle both rimmed and rimless cases. However, this utilitarian economy gun established a reputation for outstanding accuracy right out of the box. Readers may be surprised to learn that the 788's receiver and bolt required more machining cuts, and hence expense, than the Remington Model 700's.

Many believe that Remington

stopped production of the 788 because it was detracting from the sales of the 700. However, after talking to several people in the know at Remington and getting the same answer, I believe the 788 was dropped simply because of declining sales. It had a reputation as an "economy-grade" gun, in the same league as the nearly-forgotten Winchester Models 670 and 770, none of which were barnburners in terms of sales.

Remington Model 40 YBR

Remington 40 YBR rifles are recognized for their quality and accuracy. Yet you may occasionally encounter one with the top of the receiver appearing unfinished/ unpolished. After heat treatment, the receivers were "true ground" on the bottom of the receiver (the bedding surface), occasionally sparing the top. To continue grinding down until the top was included would have required removing extra metal, thus compromising the all-important rigidity of the receiver. Only after this grinding/finishing was the Remington logo and model number etched into the top of the receiver.

The Sainted Pre-'64 Winchester Model 70

For those gun fans who worship BA rifles, and many do, none is more sacred than the pre-1964 Model 70 Winchester. It represented the ideal combination of form and function of components

which were painstakingly "machined from forgings." While other side rail receivers were prone to flexing, limiting their accuracy, the pre-1964 Model 70 had unusually stiff receivers accounting for their legendary accuracy. Winchester accomplished this through the judicious retention of extra metal along the bottom of the receiver. However, with the rifle's coned breech configuration, the cartridge head was poorly supported by the bolt head. This, combined with a dubious gas handling system, unfortunately ducted gas back through the left bolt lug passageway. Worse yet, on the short stroke versions (which had modified bolt stops and magazine) the gas ports on the underside of the bolt were covered by the bolt stop extension.

A somewhat controversial two-piece floor plate and difficult-to-operate quick-release floor plate plunger, topped (or bottomed) out the package. The gun ultimately proved too expensive to manufacture. Its replacement, the much-reviled post-1964 Model 70, actually tried to address many of these shortcomings. It's worth noting that the post-1964 Model 70 was actually machined from forgings while the pre-1964 version was machined from bar stock, not forgings. Will any of the pre-1964 devotees acknowledge this as a feature in favor of the post-1964 version? I doubt it!

Weatherby Mark V

Over the years, Weatherby Mark V ac-

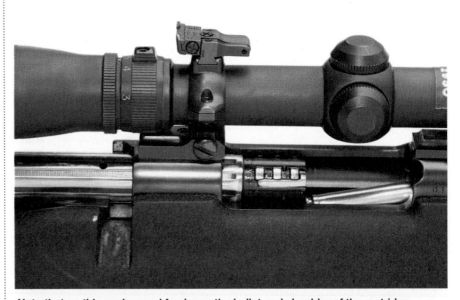

Note that on this push-round feed gun, the bullet and shoulder of the cartridge are already entrapped within the receiver ring before the magazine lips release the cartridge. This explains why push-round guns can feed reliably, even if upside down, just like controlled round feed guns.

tions have been manufactured here there and everywere, including California, Germany, Japan and most recently back here again in the U.S. No matter where they were made, these forged actions are justifiably renowned for their quality and strength. Yet few people are aware that the early "Southgate" actions utilized investment castings.

Ruger Model 77

Most people assume that the original version of the Ruger Model 77 was the 77th design project of the company. It wasn't. Since it was envisioned to compete against the Remington 700 and the Winchester Model 70, Ruger chose to retain the numbering tradition, and called their version the model 77. With its non-rotating Mauser claw extractor, most people assumed that it was a controlled-round feed design. As such, they presumed that it would seat the cartridge deep into the chamber like the Model 98 Mauser. In actual fact, neither is true. The gun functions as a push-round feed with a shallow-recess bolt head and plunger ejector. To further complicate the issue, when the Mark II version was phased in circa 1993, it was a true controlled-round feed with a Mauser blade type ejector.

When the Magnum version of the M-77 was introduced, it was generally assumed to be a scaled up version of the original model. However, there are some subtle proportional changes for optimal functioning and aesthetics. Either way, both versions have three large gas ports along the bottom surface of the bolt. While they could function as gas ports in the event of a leaky cartridge head, they primarily function to stabilize the casting core when the molten metal is investment-cast.

Pre-98 Mausers

Because of their questionable metallurgy and design deficiencies, most shooters view the pre-98 Mausers with disdain. While these criticisms are generally true, it besmirches the 96 Mauser. Not only are these actions smaller and lighter than the 98's, they demonstrate a level of fit and finish that rival the best commercial actions. While their cock-on-closing can be converted to cock-on-opening, it need not be considered an undesirable feature. It's worth noting that while some of the 96 Mausers were made in Germany those made in Sweden were made of Swedish steel, which is generally regarded as superior. It also bears remembering that

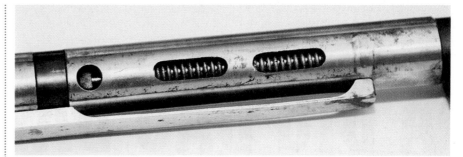

These large gas vents on the underside of the bolt allows gas from a ruptured cartridge case to convert a quick release floor plate into a self-opening floor plate.

these actions were made as late as the 1940s, hence with modern steels. The year of manufacture was boldly stamped on the top of the receiver ring, a marking that is often misinterpreted as the model number.

Japanese Arisaka Type 38

Certainly the most misunderstood and maligned bolt action rifle of all time was the Japanese 6.5 caliber Type 38 deployed in 1905. Though generally regarded as junk, they demonstrated metallurgy superior to the 98 Mausers, 1917 Enfields, or even the 1903 Springfields. In addition to a Mauser-type extractor, it had the bolt handle forced integral with the bolt. The front of the bolt telescoped into a special recess counter bored into the breach of the barrel.

A large cap at the back of the bolt forms an excellent gas shroud and also serves as a safety, locking the firing pin and locking the bolt. Admittedly, the addition of a built-up projection would have made this safety easier to manipulate. As an added feature, if you push the shroud in and rotate it clockwise one-quarter turn, it can be removed and dropped out the back of the bolt along with the firing pin and its spring. Ingeniously simple and effective – but, sadly, never copied. Unfortunately, this action cocked on the closing stroke of the bolt. While this is a deal-breaker for most Americans, it is easily adapted. to In addition, a few people maintain that the cock-on-closing feature makes it faster to operate than conventional cock-on-opening BA rifles.

The Type 38 rifle also had, as an innovation for its time, a small diameter firing pin, to mitigate gas entering the bolt in the event of a cartridge head failure. As another practical feature, the bolt stop came to rest against the guide lug along the side of the bolt rather than potentially battering the main left lug. It's really quite a rifle, though clearly not much in the looks department.

1917 Enfield

The 1917 Enfield action was considerably bigger than it needed to be for the .30-06 cartridge. As such, they were coveted for their strength and many were converted to handle magnum cartridges. A number of them were subjected to the questionable practice of "relieving" the front part of the magazine/ rear locking seat of the receiver ring to accommodate the .300 H & H and .375 H & H Magnum cartridges. However, in actual fact, the action wasn't always as strong as its design. Because of faulty heat treatment, some of the earlier receivers, most noticeably those produced at Eddystone, were prone to developing hairline cracks, usually around the receiver ring. Incidentally, many pre-1918 '03 Springfields were also the victim of faulty heat treatment. In addition to the fault treatment of the 1917 Enfield's receiver, the ejector spring was made integral with the ejector and prone to breakage. Fortunately many of those ejectors were later retrofitted by gunsmiths to utilize coil springs.

What If. . .

At this point, the pragmatists will begin to say "So what?" Because of the intensive developments supplied initially by the military and later by numerous civilian manufacturers, the bolt action has outgrown many of the problems of its youth. It is now thoroughly sorted out and utterly reliable and accurate. However, you must forgive some of us for wondering, "What if the lever action or pump action had received even a fraction of this level of development?" Would they, and not the bolt action, have ultimately proved to be the superior design?

A BIG BAD BALL GUN:

The 6-Bore Isaac Hollis & Sons Smoothbore

BY **NICK STROEBEL**

The late Jeffrey Boothroyds' *Revised Directory of British Gunmakers* tells us that Issac Hollis & Sons was in business starting in 1861 and operated until 1900 in Birmingham, England. Prior to 1861 they operated as Hollis & Sheath at 5-11 Weaman Row. In 1861 they reorganized as Issac Hollis & Sons, first at 83 Cheapside Street and later, 1884

until 1900, at Great Winchester Street. To quote Boothroyd, "They were large scale manufacturers of sporting arms for the South African market and of cheap trade guns."

It was common practice at the time for many Birmingham makers to have show-rooms in fashionable sections of London to show off their guns. Many Birmingham

makers felt their guns were the equal of the best London-based makers, and many decidedly were. Isaac Hollis & Sons was one of these and had retail offices at 9 New Bread Street in London as well as in Birmingham. This London address is the origin of the barrel address given on this six-bore gun. "I. Hollis & Sons, London" is prominently engraved on

Issac Hollis & Sons 6 Bore accompanied by a contemporary powder flask and shooting bag. The custom sheath knife is made by Jim Lofgreen.

the barrel. However the gun was made in Birmingham and carries the correct Birmingham Proof House markings.

Between 1850 and 1875, and probably later, merchants bought these heavy big-bore percussion trade guns in large quantities from the Birmingham makers. These trade guns, as well as other western-manufactured goods, were in great demand by African tribal leaders as a means of enforcing their leadership and trading positions. These big-bore Ball Guns, as they were termed, were prized by native hunters. They were used to hunt big game using a heavily charged, patched round ball, or thin-skinned game with "buck and ball" loads (i.e., a load consisting of a single round ball loaded on top of a number of buckshot). They could also be employed to shoot large flocks of sitting wildfowl as punt guns, firing a single heavy charge of shot.

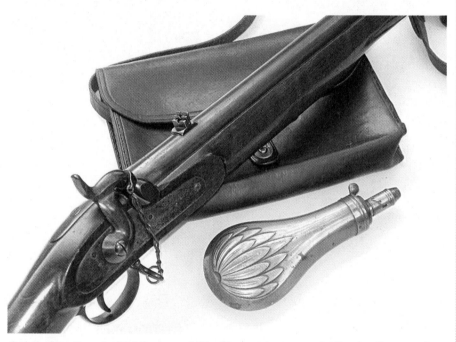

Detail of the three leaf folding rear sight with a contemporary leather hunting pouch and flask.

Chained, leather-lined nipple protectors were in common use on these guns.

The Gun

The Hollis 6-bore gun is in exceptional condition considering its more than 140 years of service. Belying its original £6 cost (about $30US at the time), it is nicely finished with a piece of uncheckered tiger-stripe grain English walnut. The gun measures 45 inches in overall length. The 28-inch, smoothbore unchoked barrel is rust browned. It appears to be forged or welded steel rather than skelp or damascus. The massive musket lock retains traces of its original case coloring and is marked "I. Hollis & Sons" with a roundel announcing "Makers to Her Majesties War Department." The chained, leather-faced nipple protector is still attached to the steel sling loop of the cast brass trigger guard, and all other mountings are cast brass. The bore remains in excellent condition. Most African-used guns I have inspected, while looking as if they had been dragged behind a wagon for 20 miles, all had excellent bores. One might speculate that the anecdotal evidence that African big game guns were washed through using water (or human urine if water was scarce), dried, and oiled every night, whether having been fired or not, just might be true.

The three-leaf rear sight is graduated in wildly optimistic 100-, 200-, and 300-yard ranges. The front sight is a traditional barleycorn. The original steel ramrod is missing, as is a large sling loop near the muzzle, its pin hole plugged by a wooden dowel.

The gun weighs 9-1/2 pounds, which considering the size of hole in the muzzle may prove to be on the light side. The bore measures 0.919 inches. According to the Birmingham Proof House Rules of 1887, the service charge for this 6-bore gun is a little over 6-1/2 drams of black powder (to be exact, 6-17/32 dram or 179 grains), firing either a 1090-grain round ball (over 2-1/2 ounces of lead) or 2-3/8 ounces of shot. Definitive Birmingham proof for this same 6-bore gun is 13-1/6 drams (357 grains) of black powder and a 1090 grain ball or 3-1/8 ounce of shot.

We are lucky to have the writings of the contemporary hunters who used these big, smoothbore muzzleloaders in Africa and India. They all universally report that in use, their own guns spent all their lives digesting the equivalent of very heavy definitive proof loads without a whimper. (Whether the shooter could make the same claim is another matter.)

The I. Hollis on Richard Akehurst's classic book *Sporting Guns*, showing some of the wonderful 19th century prints used in his book. A highly recommended read!

To demonstrate just how these guns were able to repeatedly withstand these massive overloaded charges, a few words about English gun proof may be in order. In 1672 an act was passed in London stipulating that "all arms whether made in London or within ten miles of thereof, imported from foreign parts or otherwise brought thither for sale" were subject to compulsory testing for proof. This and several subsequent acts in the ensuing years proved ineffective as they were easily evaded. Eventually, in 1868, an Act was passed that had real teeth. It made it illegal to sell "any gun the barrel of which has not been proved" and "that any person or persons forging the stamps or marks of either of the two proof-houses should be liable to a penalty of twenty pounds, and in default of payment, to a certain term of imprisonment." That worked.

Birmingham had installed its own proof house by act of parliament in 1813, but it suffered the same growing pains,

finally effectively operating in 1815.

There were three stages of proof in effect in 1868; Provisional, Definitive, and Supplemental and also an approved service charge. There were myriad variations for special applications, and classification of weapons, but these three were, and still are, basic to the system.

Provisional Proof is the first proof applied to "barrels of plain metal that shall be fine bored and turned or ground and those of twisted metal shall be struck up in addition. They shall have plugs attached with touchholes drilled in the plugs not exceeding one-sixteenth of an inch." In other words, barrels "in the rough" are fired with a charge approximately three times the service charge. After firing, the muzzle is plugged with a lead plug, the barrel is filled with boiling water and the breech is fitted with a similar lead plug. The breech plug is struck with a hammer so that the water being compressed exerts

internal pressure on the barrel and any flaw or minute hole created by the firing will leak water. The barrel is then left standing upright for 24 hours, during which the acid residue produced by the firing and water eats into the metal and make flaws more apparent. If the barrel survives, it is cleaned and stamped with the Provisional "View" mark, a "V" with either a crown or crossed scepters.

Definitive Proof is "applied to barrels that shall be struck up and smoothed, insides shall be clean, the ribs fairly struck up and such as are muzzle loading shall have breeches properly percussioned, huts filed up, and proper nipples and breeches attached, with the thread of the screw sound and full. Barrels for rifled arms shall be rifled." These are fired on an individual basis, with a charge approximately twice the service charge. If they pass, they are stamped with a Definitive "Gunmakers Proof" mark, a "GP" with crown or crossed scepters.

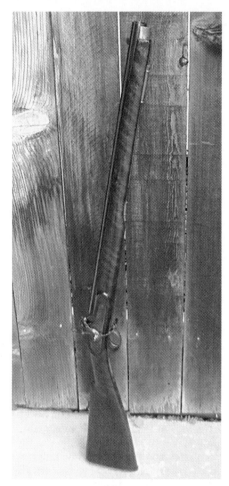

This Hollis is a real brute, similar in shape to a colonial-era Dutch Fowler but much bulkier.

Supplemental Proof is applied to barrels with the action attached in the finish filed state. In 1893 it was called to attention that Supplemental Proof was rarely employed, and in 1896 new rules were substituted by which testing of all guns intended to be used with nitro powder "are ordered to be made [proofed] with treble-strong fine grain sporting powder, specifically Curtis & Harvey No. TS2 powder or any powder the sender specifies, in addition to the ordinary test with the regulation black powder. On passing these are to be marked 'Nitro Proof' in bold capital letters."

Hunting

When Englishmen were first able to hunt in India and Africa they quickly discovered that the more or less standard rifled 16-bore percussion rifle firing a one-ounce ball that they were using for deer stalking in Scotland did not do the required work on the beasts they were now facing in the jungles or veldt.

But a dilemma was at hand. In order to get the required shocking power needed to stop large and determined game, both the powder charge and weight of the ball had to be dramatically increased. The heavy powder charges caused the heavy ball to strip through rifling, causing a dramatic decrease in accuracy. The only answer was to use a quickly-reloaded smoothbore with a heavy powder charge and massive ball and keep the range of the game to within 50 yards to ensure an accurate hit. Most dangerous game shooting prior to 1860 was done at ranges of 10 to 25 yards. The shooting was done on foot, from an elephant howdah or on horseback.

A vivid description of the use of these brutish Ball Guns comes from Samuel White Baker's book, *Albert Nyanza, the Great Basin of the Nile*, written in 1866. To quote Baker:

> Among other weapons I had an extraordinary rifle that carried a half pound shell (this calculates to a 2 Bore). This instrument of torture to the hunter was not sufficiently heavy for the weight of the projectile, it weighed only twenty pounds, and with a charge of ten drams of powder behind the half pound shell, the recoil was so terrific, that I was spun around like a weathercock in a hurricane. I really dreaded my own rifle, although I had been used to heavy charges and severe recoil for many years. None of my men would fire it, and it was looked upon with a specie of awe, and was named "Jenna el Mootfah", (Child of a Cannon) by the Arabs, which being far too long a name for practice, I christened the "Baby"; the scream of "Baby" loaded with its half pound shell was always fatal, but it was far too severe, and I was afraid to use it, firing only twenty shots over a period of many years.

It should be noted that 10 drams is actually the service charge for a 4-bore, so it would actually be a light charge in a 2-bore! One can only cringe at what carnage a full charge of fifteen drams or so would have inflicted on the shooter.

In the same text Baker speaks of using a 20-pound 4-bore made by Gibbs of Bristol in which he routinely charged 16 to 18 drams of powder behind a 4-ounce ball. Here again we see the somewhat caviler attitude toward proof rules, an 18-dram charge being almost twice the service charge and nearly equivalent to a Definitive Proof charge.

Baker did use 10- and 12-bore Ball Guns, but he urged that the ball be hardened for use against big game. To do this he recommended the lead pot be brought to a red heat, at which point mercury would be quickly stirred in with an iron bar at the ratio of nine parts lead to one part mercury. Obviously, concerns about inhaling the poisonous mercury vapor created by such chemistry was not considered!

Baker claimed these hardened round balls combined with heavy charges of fine-grained, strong powders were real "Devil Stoppers." Cringe!

Fredrick Courtney Selous (pronounced sel-oo) was one of the last, and greatest, of the Ball Gun hunters. Hunting in Africa between 1871 and 1913, he killed 78 elephants with a pair of cheap Birmingham-made 4-bore duck guns (trade guns) after his double 12-bore Reilly rifle was stolen from his wagon on his first trip. These English 4-bores sold for £6 in Africa and weighed around 15 pounds each. Each fired a "handful" (about 16 to 18 drams) of black powder behind a four-ounce ball. Selous would keep up a running battle with the elephants, pursuing them on foot, and shooting and reloading as he ran. When charged he would run for it until able to reload and return to do battle again. I have read that he employed a small folding ladder while hunting elephant in tall grass. He would work his way downwind onto the edge of the herd. He would then climb the ladder, pick the closest bull and fire. The massive recoil would knock him off the ladder, causing him to disappear from the view of the surrounding herd. As soon as they calmed down he would repeat the procedure. I read this tale about Selous many years ago, and have been unable to relocate the source of the story, but considering everything I know about him, it certainly is believable.

Selous, writing in later years, said this of his Ball Gun shooting experience: "They kicked most frightfully and in my case the punishment I received from these guns has affected my nerves to such an extent as to have materially influenced my shooting ever since, and I am heartily sorry I ever had anything to do with them."

These big, smoothbore guns were absolutely deadly at close range. They were relatively fast to reload: the shooter scooped a palmful of black powder from a leather pouch, dumped it down the muzzle, and rammed home a huge round ball that already had a muslin patch pre-waxed in place. There

A massive 1090-grain lead ball fired with 6-1/2 drams of FG powder is the standard service load in a 6-bore gun.

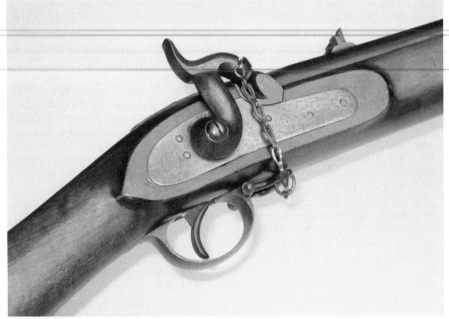

This beautiful condition Hollis & Sons gun was collected at a small Texas gun show! How did it get to Texas? Who knows?

was no rifling to grip the patched ball, which could be seated without much resistance. But they were not accurate, and close-in shooting was a dangerous business. If the gun misfired or the animal did not go down with the shot, the odds quickly shifted in the prey's favor. An enraged and wounded elephant, rhino, or tiger can cover 50 yards faster than the telling, and certainly faster than one can reload even a smoothbore muzzleloader.

As game became more wary and harder to approach, gun makers and experimenters worked to devise a method that would allow the use of the heavy ball at higher velocities and with better accuracy so the shot could be taken at farther and safer ranges. By employing two to eight coarse grooves in the bore with matching male grooves on the ball, the heavy ball could be fired at high velocity without the ball stripping the rifling. Accuracy was good enough that shots could now be made up to 150 yards. These 10- and 12-bore "Belted Bullet" guns quickly became the weapon of choice in Africa and India.

William Cotton Oswell, hunting Africa from 1837 to 1852, often accompanied David Livingston on his expeditions. He regularly used a 10-bore Belted Ball gun loaded to Definitive Proof levels with six drams of fine grain black powder. Oswell hunted on horseback, running his quarry to exhaustion and then bringing the game to bay. The gun he used was accurate enough at short range and the overloaded, belted 10-bore had the velocity to dispatch the animal humanely.

Indigenous Africans continued to use these big smoothbores well into the 20th century because they were cheap, simple, and effective. In fact, I'd be willing to bet that in some parts of remotest Africa there are some of these guns still belching acrid black powder smoke and filling the family larder. Long Live The King!

MY PISTOLAS OF THE CONTRA WAR

BY **CARLOS SCHMIDT**

Nicaragua in the 1980s was awash in guns of all sorts. It was at the height of the Contra War, and both superpowers – the USA and the Soviet Union –were dumping in a cornucopia of weaponry from all over the globe. Nicaragua had an added advantage in that its army and police force had received American surplus military arms since the 1920s. In the 1980s there were still reasonable numbers of Krags, Model 1903 Springfields, Model 1917 Springfields and a lot of Garands alongside AK-47s, Moisin Nagants, Tokarevs, and Model 1928 Thompsons. During the decades before the Sandinista Revolution of 1979, Nicaragua's president, Anastasio Somoza, allowed the relatively painless private ownership of small arms. Colts and Smith & Wessons sold well there, and even the 1920s revolutionary leader Augusto Sandino carried a .44 Smith & Wesson revolver. For an old pistolero like me, it was heaven.

I worked part time as a journalist and made good money taking foreign journalists, mostly from the Eastern bloc, to some of the areas in the northern mountains where the Contra War was hotly contested by both sides. (You may recall that the conflict pitted various U.S.-backed insurgent groups against Nicaragua's Sandinista gover-

ment.) In those halcyon days, there was little paperwork involved in purchasing firearms, and an exchange of money – in U.S. dollars, please – was all that was needed to obtain a piece, including

fully automatic weaponry of all sorts. The most expensive was a Model 1928A1 Thompson, and in good shape, some with the original Colt royal bluing, which might fetch $100. The U.S. Marines had

Author, trying to figure out how that 8 got there.

The author's pistol team, from Ave Maria University Latin American Campus, with trophy for winning first place civilian in the 2010 Nicaraguan Army National Shooting Matches. Major General Oscar Balladares congratulates the team, made up of Costa Rican Eloy Leon; Taiwanese Alec Chow; gringo businessman Scot Vaughan, the youngster of the group; and the author.

used these in the civil wars of the 1920s and had also used the 50-round drum magazines. No one liked them, however, as most of their winding keys had been lost, so the drum magazines cost only about a buck each. Somoza's warehouses were also full of ammo, in .45acp, all WCC 71, very fine ammo indeed, and so shooting was cheap.

I also worked a bit as a gunsmith, reconditioning old American military arms and getting paid in guns. One day, old Colonel Roberto Calderon of the Nicaraguan Army asked me if I would like to assemble a bunch of Smith & Wesson model 1917s. The colonel had 50 revolvers in the form of parts that some idiot had disassembled for some unknown reason, but no one knew how to put them back together. He told me he could not pay me but that I could have some of the revolvers as payment. He also told me that he had a 55-gallon barrel full of old junker pistols that had been confiscated at the beginning of the revolution in 1979, and that I could help myself to some of them, even though some lacked parts and all were really rusty. This all sounded good to me, and so I got to work.

I soon found out that the Smith & Wesson model 1917 revolvers, all made during the First World War, were blued

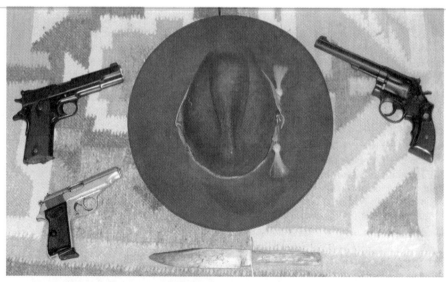

Montage of the author's saddle blanket, from Suchitepec, Guatemala. Hat is from Pinedale, Wyoming; Colt military model 1911 .45 semi-automatic; Walther Manhurin .380 semi-auto; Smith & Wesson K22; dagger carried by Dagoberto zeledón, soldier, in the Constitutionalist Civil War in Nicaragua, 1925-27.

and did not have U.S. government property stamps and so were all commercial models. They had all their parts packed separately. The serial number range of all the frames was all under 19,000. At first glance, I thought this would be a cakewalk, as the basic Smith & Wesson N frame revolver is pretty easy to assemble. But I soon learned that life was not that simple: all of these revolvers had been hand fitted and had the really smooth old long action, but there was surprisingly little parts interchangeability, especially in the lockwork. The guns would go together all right, but they would not cycle at all.

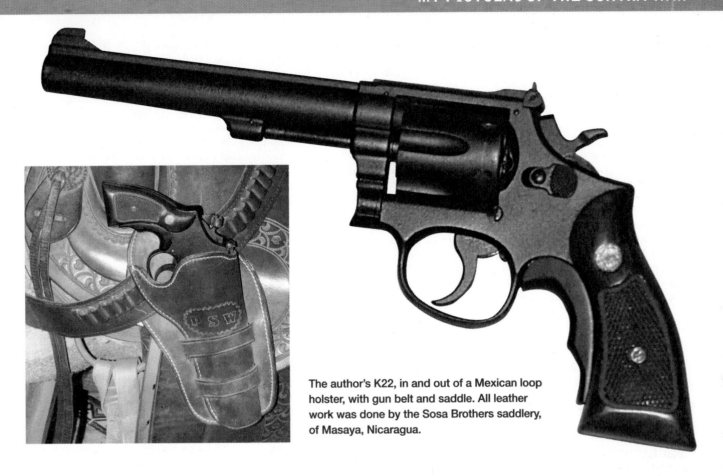

The author's K22, in and out of a Mexican loop holster, with gun belt and saddle. All leather work was done by the Sosa Brothers saddlery, of Masaya, Nicaragua.

That made life interesting, as the number of possible permutations of parts in those 50 revolvers was astronomical. Regardless, I somehow got about 30 revolvers cycling and working smoothly. I took some of the best with me, and gave the very best example, which had the very fine commercial blue and was essentially new, to Colonel Calderon. The colonel had also promised me my pick of junkers in that 55-gallon barrel, so I started pawing through the big rust bucket.

Nicaragua has a climate nearly identical to that of Viet Nam, as it shares the same latitude and very similar landscape, temperature, and monsoon rains. Things rust quickly in Managua. I had many hard choices to make, and I passed up some nice pieces, like a Walther PPK in .32 ACP, a caliber I never liked; a Browning Medalist target pistol; and a mint condition MAB 9mm, I think the largest 9mm ever made. But I did find some things that reminded me of growing up in Michigan, and so I made my choices. In many ways, a specific caliber and model carries with it memories of good times past and family and friends who used them, and so I let my memories guide my choices.

Smith & Wesson K22

In the barrel, for example, was a Smith & Wesson K22 in really rusty condition. In the summer of 1961 my brother Mike and I decided to become pistoleros in Bay City, Michigan. We saved money from cutting all the neighbor's lawns and car washing and made a trip to the closest gun store, Breen's Bicycle and Gun Store. Old Pete Moreau sold us, collectively, a spanking new Smith & Wesson K22 with a 6-inch barrel. That revolver could really shoot. We killed many rabbits with it, and Mike successfully shot a clay pigeon thrown from a trap with it and carried it on his many hunting trips. I used it to begin shooting NRA bullseye competition. I shot my first score of 270 in gallery practice with it and learned to cock the hammer for rapid fire. Mike carried it as a sidearm on hunting trips for the rest of his life and shot at least one rattlesnake with it in the Wind River mountains of Wyoming.

From that barrel I chose first a K22 that was a sorry sight. It had been confiscated sometime during the revolution and had been brought back to an army base and thrown on the floor, smashing the rear sight. It lay on the concrete floor, perhaps for years, and

the wooden magna grips partially rotted away. The bluing was gone and rust had eaten deep pits in the grip frame. Worst of all was that the mechanism had rusted together so the cylinder would not revolve. That gun was a challenge. A combination of kerosene and brake fluid got the parts loosened up, and, in those good old days, I could order a new Smith & Wesson sight and magna grips by mail. One saving grace was that the previous owner had probably shot some .22 rounds through the barrel which left some wax that protected the rifling, which was perfect. Biggest problem was the complete lack of bluing on the outside. I fixed that with Brownell's oven cure Teflon spray. Now, 20 years later, the finish is perfect.

I had the chance to try out my sort-of-new, tefloned K22 at the local shooting range located on the slopes of the active Masaya Volcano. Proprietor Salvador Luna had just opened the range to the public, which has shooting bays for IPSC and is the only 1,000-meter range in Central America. He had already built the first of many buildings, mainly shaded firing spots. Some really nasty tropical wasps quickly built their nest in the corner of that first building and regularly stung anyone who ventured into the shelter. Olod Salvador and I dreamed up the perfect way to exterminate those wasps: death by firing squad by means of .22 shot cartridges. Salvador used a rifle but I used my K22, and Salvador called off the classic firing squad commands: Preparen, Apunten, Fuego! (or, "ready, aim, fire!"). Several of the wasps tried to escape, but we were too fast for them, and I put two cylinders full of shot cartridges into the nest while Salvador shot more rounds from his .22 rifle. It was a massacre, and the wasps lay dead and dying on the ground, a fitting end to usurpers of the finest shooting range in Central America.

All through high school, my son Stuart carried that K22 revolver on hunting expeditions in an original 1920s Mexican double loop holster. The rig was hell on the tropical version of cottontail rabbits. I still use the K22 for bullseye and steel challenge competition. It groups around 1-1/2 inches at 25 meters with Russian and Mexican Aguila ammo, and it is a keeper. No finer .22 revolver has ever been contemplated by the mind of man.

Manhurin Walther PP .380

When I was picking through the barrel, I did not choose the Walther PPK because I did not like the .32 ACP caliber, and the grip of the PPK is really quite short for my hand, all romance notwithstanding. However, I found a slightly rusty, nickeled Manurin Walther PP in .380 caliber with a bunch of parts missing, and I grabbed it up right quick. I had some experience with the PP and always liked it. During the 1970s, I worked as a judicial officer, enforcing court orders and arresting recalcitrant evildoers. The warrants were civil warrants, and so I did not have to go through the Miranda warning mumbo-jumbo when I arrested someone. I just jugged them, read them no rights, and politely told them that if they wanted to walk all they had to do was pay their back child support. Not many of them thought this was funny, but it was amazingly effective. Accompanying me on my usually nocturnal jaunts was a Colt Model 1911. I had a really nifty Jackass holster and wore it under a suit jacket. I soon learned that this sort of hardware had its drawbacks: it pulled my pants down, and the hammer wore a hole in every suit jacket I owned. Since I never had to use the Colt and was always accompanied by some really tough street fighters, I decided to find a lighter pistol. The PP fit my bill. It fit my hand, let me keep my pants at a decent level, and left my suit jackets alone. I had a wartime PP with the waffenamt stamp on it. It was built like a Swiss watch and shot any sort of reload or factory ammo. Never had to use it, and I ended up finishing off several whitetails with it.

The nickeled PP .380 that the Colonel gave me lacked several parts in the slide, the grips, and a magazine. I sent the slide to old Bill Laughridge with a note to put in the parts, and I would pay him in part with Nicaraguan cigars, which may be the best in the world, like its rum. He liked the cigars, and he did a first rate job of refitting the safety hammer drop system and put in a firing pin. When I put everything back on the frame, like all PP .380s, it shot high at 25 meters but was very accurate. I had a special holster made by the saddle makers of Masaya, and even today it goes along with me when I venture into Managua at night. I never feel alone.

Colt Model 1911, .45 ACP

This one had me drooling. I saw in the bottom of the barrel a model 1911 frame, with the original long trigger, a 1911 slide, and some parts including a hammer and a really rusty barrel and bushing. I scooped them up with a cackle and a smile and put them together.

I have a long and happy relationship with the old Army .45 semi-auto. In 1962, after shooting the K22 for a year, I decided I needed to graduate to a .45 auto for outdoor NRA bullseye shooting at the Saginaw Valley Pistol Club. I talked my father, who really did not like guns that much, into buying from the DCM a 1962 version of the .45 National Match pistol, produced by, I believe, Springfield Armory. It cost Pop $82, including shipping by railway express. That was the finest-fitted .45 that I ever saw, and one that I used in competition for years. It had the coveted NM stamp on the side of the trigger guard. It was a killer-diller at the 50 yards slowfire stage.

I liked it so much I talked the Old Man into buying another .45 auto, this one a reconditioned Model 1911 sold by the DCM for a whopping $23, including shipping. It had been rebuilt at Atlanta Arsenal and had the AA stamp on the trigger guard. It was a bit loose. I did the mandatory trigger job and got it where it should be, and decided to do something creative with the sights. I found an old tobacco-chewing machinist in Lansing, Michigan, who put on a set of Smith & Wesson revolver sights by machining them into the slide. He did a fine job, and they looked like they were the original sights. That old M1911 was loose, and the slide rattled a bit, but it shot decently, and I really liked carrying it. So it went along with me for years until it wore holes in all my suit jackets and got retired.

Walther Manhurin PP .380, scrounged from a rusty barrel.

I carried it hunting, but never shot anything with it. One fall day, when I was hunting woodcock and ruffed grouse in Gladwin County, Michigan, with old Greg Kershul, then a judge and now retired in Emmett, Idaho, we decided to grill some woodcock breasts, have a few beers, and tell tall tales. We got around to shooting, and I told him my M1911 was the best thing since sliced bread for killing trees and such. He made a gentlemanly challenge to see who could hit the farthest. He had

a cut-down .44 Magnum single action. We paced off 50 paces, and I noted there was a tree with a broken limb on it. I put an empty beer can on a branch next to the tree about four feet to the side. Greg took the first shot and missed. I took the second shot, aimed at the branch, and hit the beer can square. Old Greg could not believe I hit the beer can at that range with one shot. I told him he owed me dinner at a restaurant in town. He agreed. But what I never did say is that I was aiming at the tree, not the beer can.

I never used that pistol again to shoot anything long distance.

In Nicaragua I acquired my rusty old M1911 from Colonel Calderon at a good time, as I was contemplating going into the fish export business on the Nicaraguan Miskito Coast. There was no official trade between the Caribbean Coast of Nicaragua and Costa Rica as the Contra War was on and travel around the coastal lagoons and San Juan River was a bit dicey, with shipments being a duke's mixture of fish and freight,

The author's Colt military model 1911 .45 auto. It has the Smith & Wesson sights and Brownell's overcure teflon. The author has carried it for almost 20 years with the teflon coating and it does not rust. If anyone is interested, the author's target load consisted of 4.9 grains of Titegroup and a cast 230-grain bullet lubricated by hand with pure beeswax. No leading.

The author's Model 1911 in a holster made by the Sosa Brothers Saddlery of Masaya, Nicaragua. The holster is inspired by holsters of El Paso Saddlery of El Paso, Texas. The Sosa boys can make about anything in leather, with a little guidance. I left my pistola with them for one day and they turned out the holster in a week. Cost was $20 and I complained to them that they were getting too pricey. I have now carried that holster for years, and am satisfied with it. They have made me several other holsters, of various designs.

Salvador Luna, owner and operator of the largest organized shooting range in Central America, takes careful aim with author's Colt Model 1911.

contraband guns, and the beginning of the Caribbean dope trade. The attraction was that I could buy all the snook I could transport from native fishermen in Nicaragua for about 50 cents a pound, including transportation, and sell it to fish buyers in Puerto Limon, Costa Rica, for about a dollar a pound, sometimes more. Transportation from Bluefields, or Corn Island, took about six hours to cross the 120 nautical miles of the Caribbean to Limon, so I could double my money in a day, if everything went as planned, and if everything went as planned.

I usually made that journey in the middle of the night, and after getting kicked out of the port of Puerto Limon for lack of paperwork for a load of dried shrimp, I ended up selling my catch a few miles north of Limon at a smaller international port called Moín, which was a stone dock 30 feet long. And on those trips I took along my beloved M1911.

I had many fine adventures, and a few scary ones, and eventually made it back to Managua in search of slightly tamer endeavors. I got hired by an Eastern bloc news agency to take journalists into the northern mountains to find wild and woolly stories of the Contra War that was beginning to wind down, and the pay was pretty good. The downside was that I had to drive a Russian WAS jeep, the most ergonomically painful vehicle ever designed. I made many trips close to the Honduran border, and on those trips my M1911 accompanied me. The barrel was corroded and the outside rusty from the salt air of the Caribbean, but it always went bang when I pulled the trigger and never let me down. Never. It is close to a perfect pistola.

With the end of the war, I went back to more peaceful activities, did some teaching, did some writing, did some placer gold mining, and eventually

wrote a book about the early gold mining in Nicaragua. And I decided to slick up my 1911. I got a Storm Lake stainless steel barrel and bushing, which helped accuracy immensely, and I got out more Teflon oven finish and baked my pistol like a big cookie, 350 degrees for 20 minutes. For the sights, I sent the slide to old Bill Laughridge, and this time asked him to mount Smith & Wesson revolver sights on the slide, as I had 25 years earlier in Lansing, Michigan. When I got the slide back and mounted it on the frame, I had a right smart-looking and smart-shooting weapon. It gobbled up the remaining stocks of WCC 71 ammo and every kind of reload I could invent. I found that even though the slide was a loose fit to the frame, the unit of the barrel, bushing, sights and slide fit tightly together as a unit, and the pistola would group around two inches at 25 meters from a benchrest. I carried that pistola for years in the mountains when I was placer mining and always felt secure. It always hit where I aimed it and never jammed, and so I got the idea to do a little competition shooting with it.

In 2010 I put together a geriatric pistol team including some old friends – and friends who were old – and started practicing. I talked to old Major General Oscar Balladares, second in command of the Nicaraguan army, and asked him to let my really old Pistol Team compete in the Nicaraguan Army National Shooting Matches. He agreed, and in August, 2010, my boys and I (with my Colt Model 1911) stood shoulder to shoulder with 350 of the finest shots in Nicaragua and competed in the civilian National Pistol Matches. Our team, made up of two *gringos*, a Costa Rican, and a Taiwanese, shot well. Individually, Costa Rican Eloy Leon took second place overall, and I took fourth place, using my old Colt 1911. I was the oldest shooter, and my Colt Model 1911, made in 1913, was the oldest pistol. It was also the only 45-caliber pistol in the competition. We both functioned well and we both won.

What this all means I do not know, as I am beginning to feel the twinges of aging and I know less now than ever before. Except maybe that old pistolas, cared for with affection, always shoot well, and life is *tranquilo* here in the tropics. And some things never change. Which is good.

WARTHOG RIFLES AND CARTRIDGES

There's more than one way to tackle Old Ugly…

BY **WILLIAM V. WOODWARD**

That first warthog is etched in my memory. He trotted out of the Kalahari at sunset, his tusks white against the gathering darkness. Behind him a blood-red sun hung on the horizon. The picture is as clear as yesterday: the Bushman tracker at my side, the chill of an African evening and the perfect balance of the short, heavy-barreled Sako. The boar grunted as he came in to feed, like an old man muttering to himself. Then he stopped, sensing danger. I raised the .243, placed the post reticle between his tusks and gently squeezed the trigger.

Since that evening 30 years ago, I've been hooked on warthogs. Along the way, I've had a great deal of fun experimenting with different rifles and cartridges.

Warthogs are found throughout Sub-Saharan Africa, except in heavily forested areas near the equator. In fact, it's tough to find a safari destination

On his first African hunt in 1981, Woodward and partner, Windy Gale, killed these three warthogs in a single evening on swampy ground. The author's rifle was a Sako in .243 Win.

This is the author's best warthog yet, with tusks just at 12 1/2- inches long. This boar was dropped with a Remington CDL in .30-06, shooting a 200-grain Nosler Partition.

The author's wife used his Sako, rebarreled to 7mm-08, to take these two excellent boars an hour apart. Each was taken with a single 160-grain Speer Hot Cor spire point at a modest 2,500 fps.

where warthogs are not available. Warthogs should be tops on the list of anyone making a first trip to the Dark Continent. They are plentiful, make dramatic mounts and are affordable. Trophy fees are less than $400. They're often taken as targets of opportunity during the search for larger plains game, so few hunters devote time to warthog. That's a shame, because, to bag a boar with really good tusks, you have to spend time hunting the swampy ground and waterholes where warthog feed and drink. Hogs can be taken with any rifle or cartridge suitable for plains game, like kudu, zebra, wildebeest and impala. But some rifles work better than others.

In 1981, a Boer farmer showed me an elegant Walther bolt action in .22 Hornet. He and his family enjoyed roasted warthog loin served with sauerkraut. So, as a boy, he would sit high in a windmill overlooking swampy ground, waiting for a tender young hog. When everything was just right, he'd place the tiny 40-grain bullet just behind the pig's ear and head home with dinner. Old African hands know that warthogs can be killed with light rifles like the Hornet if great care is taking in selecting shots. But, again, that takes time — a commodity in short supply on the average 10-day plains game hunt. On such a hunt you may not have time to wait for the perfect shot.

When everything is just right, I prefer a high heart shot. That means — with a boar fully broadside — coming straight up the front leg and placing the bullet slightly lower than halfway up the body.

Killing big boars consistently from less-than-ideal angles requires a tough bullet that penetrates, and a rifle that balances and handles well. Since that first boar 30 years ago, I've enjoyed experimenting with different rifles. I've used everything from the .243 Win. to a .400 caliber Cape buffalo rifle. I've found that, pound for pound, no African game animals shrug off a "near perfect" shot like the zebra, the wildebeest — and the warthog. Average warthog boars weigh in at 200 pounds, with the rare animal hitting the 300-pound mark. Even at 200 pounds, a heavily muscled boar requires perfect shot placement.

In 1981, on my first safari in Southwest Africa, I met a Dutch hunter with a Holland and Holland .375 on a '98 Mauser action. He'd shot a boar "a little far back," following up with a raking shot as the animal headed for cover. The pig absorbed nearly 8,000 pounds of energy — and was never recovered!

Professional hunter Gary Baldwin's head tracker, James, stands behind the author's .400 Brown Whelen. Woodward used this rifle to take Cape buffalo on the Chiredzi River in Zimbabwe and warthog in Namibia.

On my second safari, in Zimbabwe, I again carried my .243 Sako as a light rifle. One evening, at dusk, we jumped a herd of hogs in a maize field. Resting against a tree, I shot a large boar. The pig flinched, raised his tail, and trotted into the high grass. The Shona tracker followed. Fifteen long minutes later, we heard a triumphant whoop. The tracker had found the animal, dead from a high heart shot. The boar had run 200 yards. The experience left me wondering if the .243 was enough gun. I decided it was time to move up to a heavier caliber.

Returning home, I had my Sako re-barreled to 7mm-08. The gunsmith improved the rifle's balance by turning the new barrel to a slightly smaller diameter, retaining the large shank section near the receiver ring. The result was a rifle that handled like a fine British shotgun, with the weight nicely distributed "between the hands." The short 20-inch barrel moved the balance point back toward the shooter, making the rifle a dream to shoot off-hand. The broad forearm and slender pistol grip contributed to a gun that maneuvered effortlessly in thick cover or in a blind.

I load the Sako with a conventional bullet pushed at a moderate velocity: the 160-grain Speer spire point at 2,500 fps. At this velocity, the Speer bullet shoots minute-of-angle groups, penetrates deeply, and produces perfect mushrooms — and dead warthog. Like other African hunters, I've discovered that, at moderate velocities, conventional bullets often perform like premiums.

At the other end of the spectrum is a heavy express rifle: a .400 Brown Whelen built on an FN Mauser action. The .400 is comparable in power to Jeffrey's 450-400 Nitro Express (3-inch)—a double-rifle cartridge used in the British Empire for everything from Indian tiger to African elephant. (Both cartridges propel a 400-grain bullet at 2,100 fps.)

The .400 Whelen was created by three gunsmiths: one welded a new bolt handle; another chambered and fitted the barrel; a third inletted and glassed the stock. I shaped the stock myself, crafting a slender pistol grip with a palm swell and a straight comb designed to minimize recoil. The finished rifle is heavy enough to absorb recoil and displays the classic lines of a London-made express rifle. It carries a Leupold 2.5X scope in Talley mounts and is quite accurate. This gun has become an old friend. It's killed Cape buffalo, several zebra, a wildebeest and numerous impala. I hunted plains game with Hornady's 300-grain .411 softnose, intended for the .405 Win. I loaded this bullet to 2,200 fps.

Jim Ferries took this excellent boar while hunting near the Zambezi River in Zimbabwe. The rifle is a Lancaster double rifle in 450-400 (a 400-grain bullet at 2,150 fps).

The .400 produced one of my most exciting and memorable warthog hunts. One morning in Namibia, I tried my Boer friend's windmill trick. Sitting on a rickety platform 20 feet in the air, I rested the .400 across my knees. In five hours, 74 warthog approached the wallow below me. Only two mature hogs appeared, both with tusks barely eight inches long. Near noon, a lone boar with good tusks circled my stand and stopped below me. Only then did I realize my dilemma. Where do you hold on a boar from above?

I finally figured it out, sighting so the 300-grain Hornady would enter on one side of the spine and angle forward to the heart. The shot slammed the boar to the ground. One leg twitched and he lay still, a potent testimony to the effectiveness of large calibers. While the 300-grain Hornady performed well on impala and warthog, it wasn't tough enough for heavier game. So, I've switched to the 400-grain Woodleigh softnose, an excellent bullet for most everything Africa offers.

Between the .243 and the .400 Whelen I've romanced other warthog rifles. One I remember with great fondness was a 6.5x55 Swede on a Mauser '98 action. I fashioned the stock myself from a Fajen blank. This was early in my checkered stock-making career and I failed to craft an adequate palm swell. So I created a substitute with a glob of stained epoxy. The rifle handled and shot well, but the stock looked like it had been shaped by a hungry beaver. The gun shot pencil-like 160-grain Hornady roundnoses, right at 2,500 fps, with great accuracy. It killed smaller plains game well, but was a little light for zebra and kudu.

I regret that I no longer own that rifle. The 6.5 Swede cartridge, with that long, elegant 160-grain roundnose, evoked memories of the golden age of safari hunting in the 1920s and '30s. I eventually parted with the Swede because the ammunition is virtually unavailable in Africa. That dilemma led me to my fourth rifle, a .30-200.

What, you may ask, is a .30-200?

The .30-200 is nothing more than the .30-06 loaded with 200-grain bullets. In a pinch, if your rifle arrives but your luggage doesn't, you want a cartridge that is in the ammo locker of most camps. Two cartridges fill that bill — the .375 H&H and the .30-06.

The .30-200 is a great combination overlooked for many years. Most hunters favor the 180-grain spire point in the

From left: The author has had good luck with these cartridges on warthogs: 6.5x55 Swedish Mauser with 160-grain Hornady round nose; 7mm-08 with 160-grain Speer Hot Cor; .30-06 with 200-grain Speer; .400 Brown Whelen with 400-grain Woodleigh softnose. All these combinations feature a bullet that is "heavy for caliber." The k nife is a hunter/Bowie by Terry Davis of Sumpter, Oregon.

'06, but if you read between the lines in books and articles on the Springfield, you'll discover some thought-provoking comments on the 200-grain bullet. Words like "devastating" and "impressive" keep cropping up. Why?

The sheer sectional density (SD) of the 200-grain bullet (in excess of the mythical .300 SD figure) makes it a great penetrator on tough game like zebra and oryx. Surprisingly, the 200-grainer gives up little to a 180-grain bullet in terms of trajectory at ranges up to 200 yards. When 200-grain bullets (at 2,500 fps) are sighted dead-on at 200 yards, they're 2.81 inches high at 100 yards. The 180-grain bullet (at 2,800 fps) is only slightly flatter at 1.78 inches high. In the bushveld, 200 yards is a long shot and the difference in trajectory is insignificant. I've had excellent results on mountain zebra and warthog with the 200-grain bullet and I believe it moves the .30-06 up one notch on the caliber scale.

I had never owned a .30-06 rifle before but decided the cartridge's popularity, and the wide availability of '06 ammo in Africa, made it a likely choice. I was taken by the classic lines of the then-new Remington 700 CDL. It was such a good-looking, easy-handling rifle it was hard to believe that it was a production

model! Especially intriguing was the slim, brilliantly shaped pistol grip and the excellent checkering on the grip and forearm. The rifle featured a slender, elegant 24-inch barrel. Initial groups confirmed the need to rest the rifle between shots, allowing time for the barrel to cool. With that precaution, the gun turned in consistent 1.1-inch groups with 200-grain Speers and Nosler Partitions. Pushing 200-grainers at 2,500 fps, this rifle is remarkably comfortable to shoot, largely a result of Remington's high-tech recoil pad.

The rifle is topped with a durable, dependable Leupold 6X scope. In its sturdy Leupold mounts, the scope seldom changes zero from my home in Wyoming to the green hills of Africa.

Only one cosmetic problem arose with this rifle: the absence of a front sight. I believe a bare-barrel African rifle looks like a Jeep with whitewalls. So my Remington 700 — as do all my African rifles — features a gunsmith-installed barrel band front sight. They also have after-market triggers set to three pounds' pull.

Warthog rifles that work well tend to shoot bullets that are "heavy for caliber." This is a concept pioneered by such stalwarts as Karamojo Bell,

Three warthog rifles. Top: a custom FN Mauser in .400 Brown Whelen, with a 2.5X Leupold scope; middle: a 700 Remington CDL in .30-06, with a 6X Leupold scop;.bottom: a 1960s-era Sako in 7mm-08, with a Weaver K-3 scope. These rifles combine balance, accuracy and a classic African profile.

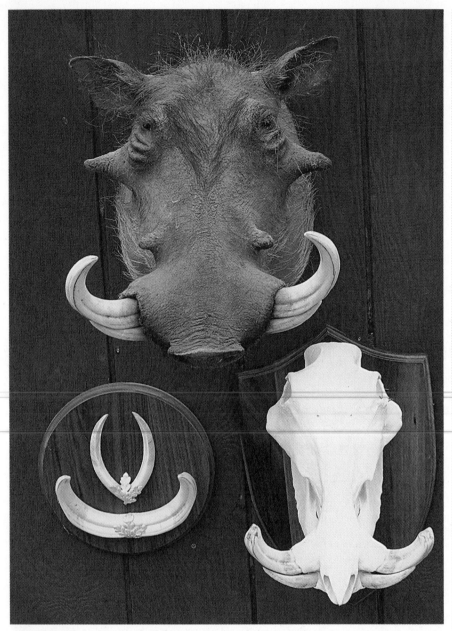

The warthog is unique in that it offers several options for mounting. Top: good warthog boar conventionally mounted; bottom left: German mount with fighting tusks inside rooting tusks, each pair joined by a silver oak leaf; bottom right: European mount featuring bleached skull.

He recommends choices for everything from dik-dik to elephant. Both volumes are available from Safari Press.)

"Heavy for caliber" translates into bullets with good sectional density. Those I've used include the 6.5x55 with 160-grain Hornadys (SD .328) and the .400 Brown Whelen with .411-diameter 400-grain Woodleigh softnoses (SD .338). My 7mm's 160-grain Speers (SD .286) are quite effective, as are 200-grain Nosler Partitions (SD .301) in the .30-06. Each of these bullets penetrates very well and seems to offer more knock-down power than lighter bullets in the same caliber.

Warthogs are like whitetail deer: you get a good trophy by passing up a lot of mediocre ones. Of course, that takes time. One hunt aptly illustrates that fact. For two days my wife and I sat up over swampy ground and counted 143 pigs — boars, sows and piglets. No long-tusked boars appeared during the long hours. Finally, on the third day, I lost interest and went off to hunt kudu. When I returned, my wife proudly displayed two exceptional hogs, both in the 12-inch category, taken with my Sako 7mm-08. She'd shot them an hour apart. The Holy Grail for warthogs (and the minimum for Rowland Ward's Records of Big Game) is 13 inches — the hog of a lifetime. I've never been that lucky!

Warthogs make dramatic trophy displays and offer lots of options. German mounts display the tusks on round plaques, the upper and lower tusks overlapping and accented with silver oak leaves. European mounts are classic bleached skulls. Perhaps the most impressive is the familiar shoulder mount.

Warthog tusks are considered ivory. Unlike other forms, however, warthog ivory does not yellow with age, which is why it is used for beads on the front sights of express rifles. It also makes great knife handles.

If you plan to hunt Africa, don't overlook the warthog. Warthog hunting offers genuine excitement, great satisfaction and impressive trophies. And because there is a great safari tradition associated with any hunt, take care selecting a rifle. Carrying an accurate, classically designed, well-balanced gun will insure clean kills and magnify your entire experience. Later, leaning in the corner under your mounted boar, the rifle will call to mind one of Africa's most memorable hunting adventures.

a student of elephant anatomy. At the dawn of the 20th century, Bell used 160-grain solids in a .256 Mannlicher to brain-shoot elephant.

Dr. Kevin Robertson, a veterinarian and professional hunter who lives in Africa, writes on practical ballistics. Robertson also favors bullets that are long for caliber. He recently wrote advocating 350-grain bullets in the .375 H & H for dangerous game! Moreover, Gregor Woods is another African writer who lives on the continent and

champions bullets that are heavy for caliber. He has broad experience hunting with everything from wildcats such as the 6x45 to old standbys such as the 9.3x6262 Mauser. (Robertson and Woods are the authors of two books essential for anyone planning a trip to Africa. Roberton's *The Perfect Shot* offers an excellent mix of practical ballistics paired with anatomical diagrams of game. Woods' *Rifles for Africa* covers the whole spectrum of African cartridges and their history.

THAT CUSTOM TOUCH

BY **TOM TABOR**

Many shooters find that simply plucking a rifle off the shelves of their local sporting goods store is a fast and easy way to satisfy their shooting desires. Doing so allows the shooter without hesitation to jump right into burning powder. But if you are looking to distinguish yourself from the masses and at the same time achieve a higher degree of performance and accuracy than the typical mass-produced rifle is usually capable of, maybe you need to join the growing number of shooters who are looking elsewhere for their firearms.

Having a rifle custom built specifically around your likes, desires and needs has many benefits. A competent and capable gunsmith can focus his work specifically in the areas that produce the best results and match more closely your specific hunting or shooting needs. And certainly for those shooters who are seeking to break away from the crowd, the individuality and pride of owning and shooting a rifle that was specially built for them is a commodity on which it's hard to put a price.

But with every choice in life, there are both positive as well as negative points to be considered – and having a custom rifle built is no exception. First, good things seldom occur overnight. It takes time to handcraft a firearm, so a procurer of a fine custom-built rifle has to learn a bit of patience. And then of course there's the cost. With few exceptions, having a rifle built for you will generally cost more than simply buying something off the shelf. Nevertheless, by picking your component parts wisely and not having unrealistic priorities and objectives, you might be surprised at just how inexpensively you can accomplish the goal of deviating from the mainstream.

I was recently faced with the decision of whether to buy or build. It had come

In general appearance the Husqvarna rifle looked okay, but its 20-inch barrel was certainly not capable of completely burning the heavy powder charge of a belted magnum cartridge. Aside from the fact that the accuracy was far from being acceptable, the iron sights mounted on the Husky's skinny barrel certainly weren't what author was looking for in a hunting rifle. Nevertheless, the action was sound and in great condition, making it a fine platform to build on.

time to replace an ol' *compadre* of many adventures, a rifle chambered in .300 Winchester Magnum that had become a mainstay for my big game hunting for decades. Even though it was a production-built firearm I considered it better than most. and over all those years I had developed a great deal of confidence in its abilities. It had traveled with me to many exotic and challenging locales and no matter what conditions we faced, it had always performed its duties exceptionally well. But in the last couple of years, it had begun to show its age.

For months I considered all the options available to me. I could have my ol' friend professionally rebuilt; I could purchase something off-the-shelf; or I could commission a gunsmith to build a replacement rifle for me. After several months of mulling over my situation I finally chose the latter and decided to replace my .300 with a custom built rifle of the same caliber.

Selecting the Action

The decision to go custom creates more decisions. Possibly the first of those is which action to use. There are basically two broad options available to you: you can cannibalize an action from another rifle, or you can buy a new action.

In my particular case I was in the happy position of owning another rifle that would be a good candidate for action salvage. A few years earlier I'd

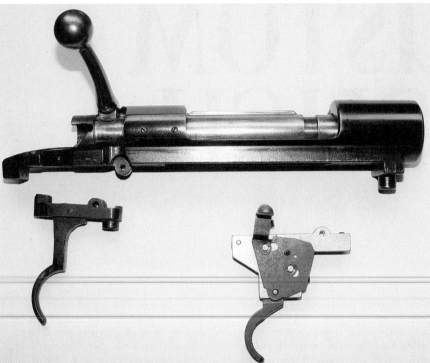

Like many shooters today, the author found that replacing the original trigger with a better aftermarket trigger made good sense and was well worth the money. In this case the Husky factory trigger was replaced with a new trigger from Timney Manufacturing (shown on the right). Timney triggers are fully adjustable and moderately priced, and this one made a huge improvement to the performance of the rifle. Once installed it was adjusted to a little under two pounds pull.

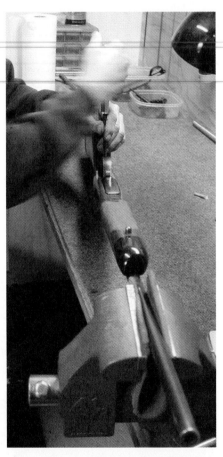

The only part of the Husqvarna rifle that the author would be using for his new rifle would be the receiver and bolt. Dan Coffin made quick work of first removing the stock, followed by the removal of the barrel.

Properly designed muzzle brakes have the ability to reduce the felt recoil of a rifle by approximately 50% over that generated from a non-ported barrel. Author decided to take advantage of this benefit by having Dan Coffin install a muzzle brake made by Pacific Tool & Gauge. In order for it to be installed it became necessary to ream the throat of the brake to the proper bore diameter, cut the barrel threads, index and position the brake so that the gases would vent in the proper direction, and blend or taper the unit to match the contour of the barrel. Author also asked Dan Coffin to also provide a removable screw-in replacement cap to protect the barrel threads when the brake is removed.

Most replacement barrels are available in a selection of barrel contours and in blank form. This permits the purchaser to select whatever weight barrel he or she prefers, but a gunsmith can also turn the outside diameter of the barrel down.

Chambering the barrel is accomplished on a metal lathe. Author chose a barrel made by Wilson Arms because Wilson has an established reputation for the high quality barrels used by Cooper Firearms of Montana. Like many barrels, this one came unchambered making it necessary for Dan to cut the chamber to the desired .300 Win. Mag. specs. Author also requested a short-throated chmber, which required a custom-built reamer.

Once the threads have been cut and the barrel has been screwed into the receiver, a chisel is used to place a witness mark across the union point between the barrel and receiver. This ensures that the barrel can always be screwed in precisely to the same point no matter how many times it is removed.

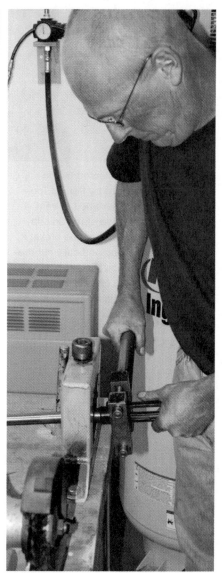

In the rifle building process the barrel has to be removed from the receiver several times. In order to assist in this process Dan Coffin uses a vise specially designed for this operation.

purchased an old and somewhat abused Husqvarna rifle simply because the price was right. It certainly wasn't much to look at, but it did have potential as a basis to build from. I'd played around with the rifle, hoping to better its performance, but its pencil-thin short barrel certainly wasn't something I was fond of. The bluing was worn with some pits in the barrel; the stock needed attention; and I found the accuracy to be less than acceptable. For all practical purposes it had become a collector of dust in my gunroom, but its small ring Swedish Mauser action was strong, tight and still in great condition.

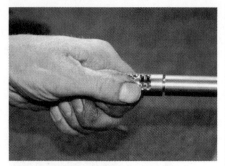

The muzzle brake selected by the author was produced by Pacific Tool & Gauge and was designed to vent the gases out the side of the unit. In order to properly position the brake, it was necessary to methodically cut the barrel threads in slow incremental steps until the vents were exactly positioned horizontally when the muzzle was snugged down tight.

There are several names associated with this fine tool. Some call it a "short chamber seating tool" and others call it a "neck-leade tool," but whatever you call it, having your gunsmith make you one of these is a great benefit to handloaders. Essentially all it takes is an inch of barrel. The gunsmith then uses the same chamber reamer that is used to chamber the rifle barrel in order to cut a shortened version of the chamber in the piece of barrel. Once this has been done, it can be used to check your handloads for the maximum cartridge length. If the shoulder of the cartridge does not properly seat against the gauge it means that the bullet is seated too far out of the cartridge case to fit in the chamber. By incrementally seating the bullet a little deeper, followed by rechecking it with the gauge, will permit you to better seat your bullets.

At some point it had been converted from .30-06 to .308 Norma Magnum, a popular conversion back in the early 1960s. For a competent gunsmith, this was a fairly easy conversion to make and involved opening up the bolt face and sometimes a slight opening of the rails to allow the cartridges to feed properly. I decided the Husky action represented a super platform for my new custom rifle.

There are other options, of course. Using an action from another rifle is a good way to go in some cases, but if that isn't practical you can easily have your gunsmith purchase a new action. There are a few production rifle manufacturers that offer their actions for sale to the public, CZ-USA being one of the more popular, but most sell only completed rifles because of liability concerns. Yet another option is to purchase a new action from one of the many custom rifle manufacturers.

Selecting a Gunsmith

Selecting a gunsmith to do your work is possibly the most important decision that you will make in any rifle-building project. If you aren't thoroughly familiar with the gunsmith's qualifications, be sure to check references thoroughly and review some of his or her work before committing. For my project, that decision was an easy one. Without hesitation I choose Dan Coffin of the Victor, Montana-based Coffin Gunsmithing. Dan was a close friend and one of those rare craftsmen in whom you can place your

total confidence and be assured he will make the right decisions. For more than a decade Dan is the personal gunsmith of country/western singer Hank Williams, Jr., but aside from maintaining Mr. Williams' vast firearms collection he has recently been undertaking rifle-building projects for others, too. This would be the fourth firearm Dan had built for me, which also included two big-bore dangerous game rifles and one wildcat varmint rifle.

Selecting the Barrel

Sometimes choosing the barrel supplier can seem to be a daunting experience but, like the previous decision, it is a crucial one when it comes to accuracy. I don't believe there are

any truly bad barrels out there, but clearly some are better than others. For my rifle I choose a barrel made by Wilson Arms. This decision was largely based on the fact that Wilson is the sole supplier of the barrels used by Cooper Firearms of Montana. I have a high regard for the rifles produced by Cooper and have always found them to possess a superb level of accuracy. I chose a medium-weight, stainless steel barrel and, because I strongly believe the best-performing bullet for a .300 Win. Mag. is one weighing 180 grains, I picked what many consider to be the standard twist rate for a .300 of 1:10. Generally a faster twist rate will do a better job at stabilizing the heavier, longer bullets, while a slower rate will do better on the lighter, shorter projectiles.

When selecting a piece of wood to be used for a gunstock it is best that the wood grain follows the contour of the pistol grip. This is the weakest and most vulnerable area of a stock, and if the grain is not properly flowing through this point it could result in the stock cracking or breaking. Note how the grain essentially follows the lines of the forearm, but as it moves toward the butt area it "flows" perfectly with the lines of the pistol grip.

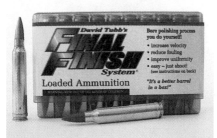

Author decided to use a box of David Tubb's Final Finish System cartridges in the barrel break-in process. The bullets in these cartridges are impregnated with two different polishing compounds. When fired in a new barrel it is said that they will produce a more uniform and polished finish inside the bore. Final Finish System bullets are available as a handloading component in boxes of 50 or in loaded cartridges (as shown here) in boxes of 20.

In order to obtain a matte finish it is necessary to glass bead-blast the metal. The coarseness of the blasting media determines the final appearance. For author's new rifle he chose to install a Wilson Arms stainless steel barrel, but the action would be blued in matte finish. In order to accomplish this, the barrel was screwed into place and the entire barreled action was then bead-blasted. From there the barreled action went directly to the bluing baths. Because stainless steel does not accept bluing, at least in the normal hot bluing manner, the action came out blued and the barrel retained its matte stainless appearance.

A custom rifle stock begins as a rough-cut blank as shown here on the left. From there it gets roughed into the general shape and configuration of the stock. Once this has been accomplished the gunsmith/stockmaker fits the barreled action to the stock and does the final shaping and sanding, followed eventually by the application of the finish. Once the stock has been finished it is then sent to checkering. Dan Coffin likes to apply one last thin coat of stock finish after the checkering work has been completed.

Many barrel manufacturers, including Wilson Arms, hand-lap their barrels at the factory. This is crucial in the search for a high degree of accuracy. Essentially it consists of polishing the bore to remove any slight imperfections that may

have occurred when the rifling was cut. But the chambering process can also account for additional burrs and imperfections located deep inside the throat of the chamber. This area is almost impossible to polish-out using traditional methods. Because of this I decided to include the firing of a box of David Tubb's Final Finish System cartridges as part of my barrel break-in process. The bullets used in these cartridges are impregnated with polishing compounds. I hoped this would eliminate any imperfections that may have occurred inside the chamber throat.

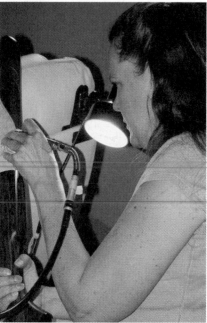

Gun bluing is a multi-stage process in which cleanliness is truly next to godliness. The metal must be absolutely free of any oil or other contamination in order for the bluing to come out properly. The temperature is carefully regulated and monitored throughout the process. Once the bluing process is complete the parts must cure for several hours before becoming durable enough to handle.

Dan Coffin uses the services of Pam Wheeler to do the vast majority of his stock checkering work. Pam has worked for a number of top-notch firearms manufacturers including Weatherby, Cooper Arms, Kimber, Ljutic, and the late custom shotgun manufacturer Tommy Seitz. She does excellent work and is flexible enough to provide the customer with virtually any pattern, from a standard no-frills pattern, like the one author chose for this rifle, all the way up to the most delicate and elaborate.

Triggers

In many cases I hold the triggers used on most production-made firearms in very low regard. They are often set to a pull weight or six or even sometimes eight pounds and worse yet, they are often plagued with what I would characterize simply as "slop" in their movements. So I decided to switch out the stock Husqvarna trigger with a quality trigger made by Timney. I asked Dan to adjust it to have a trigger pull weight of around two pounds, which is light for a rifle intended for field use, but this was a level that I had over the years become accustomed to.

Muzzle Brakes

Whether to muzzle brake or not to muzzle brake is a decision that every shooter must make for himself. The obvious advantage is less abuse to a shooter's shoulder, but reducing a hunting rifle's felt recoil can have the added benefit of allowing the shooter to get back on the target a bit quicker in the event that a follow-up shot is needed. The downside is increased noise. Many guides and professional hunters hate muzzle brakes for that very reason.

There is, however, a way to achieve the best of both worlds. For my new rifle I decided to have Dan install a muzzle

brake produced by Pacific Tool & Gauge, but I also asked that a cap be supplied in the event I decided to remove the brake. This would provide me a little more flexibility, but if you choose to go that route there is something that you must keep in mind. A barrel's harmonics can

The final rifle turned out to be a work of gunsmithing art that any rifle hunter would be proud to carry to the field.

A couple of months after author picked up the new rifle from Coffin Gunsmithing, deer season opened in Montana. This fine 4x4 muley fell to the author's handloads of with 180-grain Barnes Tipped Triple Shock X bullets. The bullet entered just behind the front shoulder, traveling diagonally and exiting in front of the opposite hindquarter for a clean, quick kill.

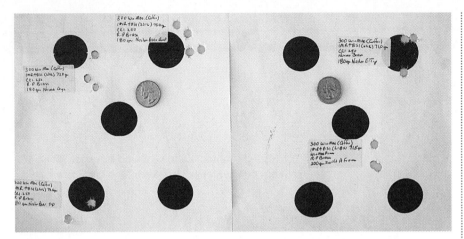

The finished rifle turned out to be very accurate and one of the most consistent-performing rifles author has owned. Virtually all of his handloads shot right around 1-inch groups at 100-yards no matter which bullet or components were loaded. Shown here are a few of those groups from the initial load development work. In time the size of the groups will likely shrink in size as more component combinations are tried.

change depending upon whether or not the muzzle brake is in place. The result is that your bullet impact point could change depending on whether the brake is in place.

Selecting a Stock

Type of stock is a matter of personal preference. Possibly the easiest way to go and sometimes the least costly is to use a drop-in style of synthetic or composite. There are some really great stocks available today to select from and they come with the advantage of being nearly impervious to the affects of the changes in the weather. For me, however, I have a passion for real wood that I simply can't deny and decided to instead utilize a piece of semi-figured black walnut for my stock.

Dan and I discussed the subtleties that I wanted in the stock including a slight palm swell; a fairly heavy butt to absorb a little more of the recoil of the .300; a slightly longer than normal pull length to accommodate my long reach; and a bit of a teardrop shape for the forearm. One of the distinct advantages that comes with building a custom rifle is the fact that you can incorporate things into the rifle that hold a special meaning to you. In my case this took the form of a piece of Australian water buffalo horn that came from a Down Under culling operation I participated in the year before. It became a bit of a tricky maneuver to incorporate the horn, but eventually persistence won out and I wound up with a personal keepsake in

the form of an end cap and pistol grip cap formed from the buff's horn.

Once Dan's stock work had been completed he sent the stock off to Pam Wheeler for the final act of checkering. Pam has the ability of producing virtually any checkering design you can specify, but because this was going to be a rifle simply dedicated to heavy use hunting I asked that only a basic pattern design be used.

Finally with Rifle in Hand

After several months of anxious anticipation, finally I received the long awaited call from Dan that my new rifle was completed and ready to be picked up. After making a quick stop at the teller's window at our local bank, I made my way to his shop and soon was admiring my new hunting rifle. It was without a doubt a real work of gunsmithing art and a rifle I was sure would provide me many years of faithful service. Returning home I quickly mounted one of Weaver's new Super Slam 2-10x42mm scopes using Warne quick detachable scope bases and rings. This would permit me to remove the scope while traveling in order to protect it from being damaged or knocked out of alignment. When traveling by airlines I frequently remove my scopes and pack them in my carry-on luggage separate from the rifle. Thus far the airlines have not had a problem with this approach and it helps to ensure that when I arrive the scope will be in good shape.

As with any new rifle I always have a twinge of fear that it will not perform up to my expectations, but Dan Coffin had never let me down and he didn't in this case either. From the onset virtually every cartridge I put through the new rifle produced close to 1-inch groups at 100-yards off the bench. I'm sure in time, through a more careful selection of components, those groups will be squeezed down even further, but 1-inch is close to the potential for my somewhat aging eyes.

Resources

General Gunsmith
Dan Coffin
Coffin Gunsmithing, LLC
375 Sweathouse Creek Rd.
Victor, Montana 59875
E-Mail: coffingunsmithing@msn.com

Checkering
Pam Wheeler
P.O. Box 827
Stevensville, Montana 59870
Telephone: (406) 381-1484

Muzzle Brake
Pacific Tool & Gauge, Inc.
P.O. Box 2549
598 Ave. C
White City, Oregon 97503
Telephone: (541) 826-5808
Website: http://old.pacifictoolandgauge.com/index.htm

Barrel Supplier
Wilson Arms
97-101 Leetes Island Road
Branford, Connecticut 06405
Telephone: (203) 488-7297
Website: http://www.wilsonarms.com

Trigger Supplier
Timney Manufacturing, Inc.
3940 West Clarendon Ave.
Phoenix, AZ 85019
Telephone: (866) 4TIMNEY
Website: http://www.timneytriggers.com

Barrel Prep
David Tubb's Final Finish System
DTAC, LLP
800 North Second Street
Canadian, Texas 79014
Telephone: 1-806-323-9488
Website: www.DavidTubb.com

Scope Mounts
Warne Manufacturing Company
9057 Southeast Jannsen Rd.
Clackamas, Oregon 97015
Telephone: (503) 657-5590
Website: www.warnescopemounts.com

A LABOR OF LOVE OR A LOVE OF LABOR?

Cap and ball sixgunning can be fun, but it's not for everyone

BY ANDY EWERT

As a pistolero with more than 40 years experience under my belt, I've owned and fired many fine handguns. My current inventory includes vintage Colts, Smith & Wessons, and Rugers, plus select specimens from Europe, England, and South America.

Despite my interest, prudence kept me away from cap and ball revolvers.

My enthusiasm for labor-intensive recreation, after decades of reloading, casting bullets, trimming cases, and cleaning primer pockets, has worn thin. It seemed shooting charcoal burners, particularly six shooters, involved a lot of work. This perception was reaffirmed by none other than the late Col. Jeff Cooper. He states, in *The Complete Book*

of Shooting, "Actually a cap and ball revolver is a dreadful nuisance to load and clean." That was all I needed to know.

Maybe it was a midlife crisis or a softening of the brain, but now I know firsthand how much of a dreadful nuisance loading and cleaning cap and ball handguns is. Not only did I succumb to temptation, but I did so twice. If

Author fires a chamber from his Colt 1860 revolver. He learned fast that there's a steep learning curve in cap and ball sixgunning. One must be patient and persistent to master it.

that wasn't bad enough, I've become hopelessly hooked on this fascinating, sometimes frustrating, and yes, labor-intensive pastime. Hopefully, my tale will serve as either a guide or warning shot for those interested in giving cap and ball revolvers a try.

My cap and ball experience began one sunny winter weekend five years ago while browsing a rural Wisconsin gun shop. Tucked in a corner display case

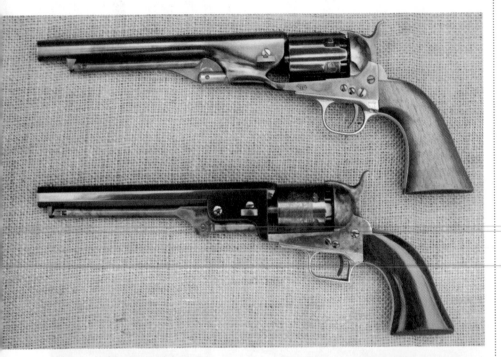

was a "second-generation" Colt 1851 Navy, complete with original wooden box, powder flask, bullet mold, bullets, a combination nipple wrench/screwdriver, and modest price tag. Once it was in my hand I had to have it. My discounted offer was readily accepted. I smiled all the way home, clueless to what lay ahead.

This second-generation Navy is among a family of percussion wheelguns marketed by Colt during the 1970s

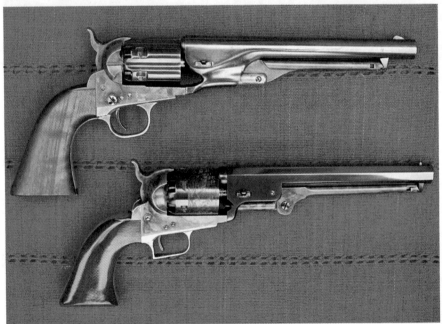

Seond-generation Colt 1860 Army (top) and Colt 1851 Navy revolvers, left and right views. The first generation of these iconic revolvers forged a colorful history during the Civil War, the taming of the Western frontier, and many points in between.

and 1980s. Using castings from Italy along with subcontracted machining, finishing, and assembly courtesy of Iver Johnson in the U.S., Colt reentered the market founder Samuel Colt created in 1836 – with the Paterson revolver – and departed after the introduction of its legendary Single Action Army cartridge revolver in 1873.

Firearms enthusiasts had kind words for these second-generation Colt frontstuffers. So do I. Fit and finish of my Navy are first rate. Thumbing back the hammer to full cock, one is treated to the sweet, precise clicks of finely-tuned indexing that are music to revolver aficionados' ears.

The first step after acquiring my prize was to scour a four-decades accumulation of gun books and magazines to bone up on cap and ball shooting. Writings by Rick Hacker, R.C. House, Phil Spangenberger, Jerry Burke, Elmer Keith, and Col. Cooper – many from the pages of *Gun Digest* – whetted my appetite. Subsequently, I invested in Sam Fadala's *Blackpowder Handbook* and Mike Venturino's *Shooting Colt Single Action Handguns*.

In my research, I learned that all sorts of mischief lurks in cap and ball shooting. Fortunately, there are ways to avoid much of it. After acquiring basic knowledge, I gathered my remaining cash and headed out to the nearest full-service gun store. Alas, no appropriate black powder, properly sized lead balls, or lubricating wads were in stock. The sympathetic proprietor astutely steered me to Hodgdon's easy-to-clean Triple Seven FFFG black powder substitute and its handy brochure.

Before assembling the basics to launch my cap and ball odyssey, I succumbed to temptation again. At some point during my readings, I begin to covet the .44 caliber Colt 1860 Army percussion revolver. Instead of letting the urge pass, I detoured to GunsAmerica.com on the web and traded a good chunk of my federal tax refund for a second-generation Colt 1860 fluted cylinder "Cavalry Model," unfired in its original cardboard box, price tag hanging on the triggerguard, along with a fistful of 25-year-old+ Colt cap and ball literature. Maybe I paid a fair price.

On advice from a friend, I ordered a Dixie Gun Works catalog. For anyone serious about percussion firearms, Civil War reenactment, cowboy shooting or American firearms history, this remarkable volume is the closest you'll come to

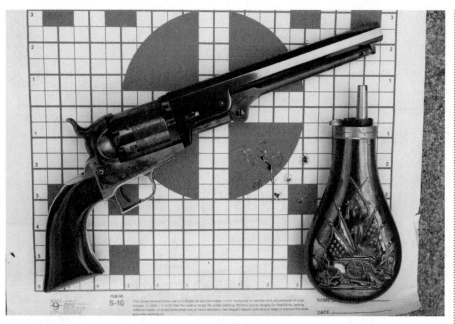

As Wild Bill Hickok and others proved, the Colt 1851 Navy is capable of fine accuracy, despite its rudimentary sights. Moderate weight, superb balance, and light recoil contribute to its performance.

a one-stop shop. The polite, savvy, and efficient folks in Union City, Tennessee, met all my needs in one succinct 800-number telephone call. You can also go to Dixiegunworks.com. and order right off their easy-to-navigate website.

First to the range was the1860. My percussion debut had its setbacks but was encouraging. From the start, I discovered my name brand cappers and powder flask left something to be desired. Burrs in the cappers and variances in cap size caused feeding delays. One capper self destructed during loading. Then the flat spring on my shiny new flask lost its temper, causing the sliding cover to stick open. I persevered.

As the acrid plume of burned powder wafted downrange, it was embarrassingly clear my first shot didn't even hit the paper 25 yards distant. It occurred to me, as I had read, that cap and ball sixguns tend to shoot high at normal handgun ranges. Elmer Keith claimed this was intentional to increase maximum point blank range in man shooting, the primary purpose of handguns a century and one-half ago. Okay, Elmer. Whatever.

My third shot, aimed a foot low, cut the center of the black. Glory be. All my accumulated doubts, frustrations, and disappointments vanished like a wisp of gun smoke in the wind.

After tacking up a second "aiming" target below my original, I fired four cylinders of the manufacturer's recom-mended charge of Triple Seven, an Ox Yoke Wonder Wad, topped off with a 138-grain, .457" swaged lead ball, into a group you could cover with your hand, fingers extended. Now I was having fun. Velocity was approximately 600 fps. Recoil was negligible. There was a flyer or two, understandable in offhand shooting.

The Colt's rudimentary hammer-notch-and-front-blade sights proved surprisingly adequate for my bifocaled eyes. With its eight-inch barrel, slim profile, and smooth trigger pull, my 1860 is a force to be reckoned with, just as it was for Wild Bill Hickcock, John Wesley Hardin and Jesse James, among other notables who purportedly employed this model at some point in their careers.

Despite initial success, there were amateur missteps. Among them was a failure to ram the ball down into the cylinder with sufficient force to keep it there. One worked forward in recoil, locking up the cylinder when it met the barrel in rotation. A painful bit of hammering on a wooden dowel with the palm of my hand was required to drive that ball down to where the cylinder would rotate, permitting the rammer to engage for reseating. At the time, I didn't realize how lucky I was. Air space between powder and ball during ignition raises chamber pressure to dangerous levels and should always be avoided.

Once I was distracted while load-ing and failed to pour powder into a chamber. Unfortunately, I didn't neglect to load the wad and ball and cap the nipple. Lacking an extraction tool, I had to remove the unfired caps, disassemble the sixgun, unscrew the nipple, and pound the ball out from the back end of the cylinder with a thin brass rod.

Safety is always job one in any type of shooting. Loading a cap and ball handgun involves multiple operations. They require time, patience, and a degree of manual dexterity. Always devote every ounce of concentration to the loading process. A lapse can impair your enjoy-ment, possibly your handgun and, in the worse case, your health. Develop a rou-tine that's safe and reliable and stick to it. A tip for beginners – I found a loading stand invaluable throughout the charging process. This "third hand" is truly the novice's best friend. (See photo.)

My cap and ball loading routine is as follows:

1. Cap the nipples of the unloaded revolver with a capper (moisture from your hands can render caps inert) and fire the caps to clear any oil or debris from inside the nipples. Then remove the spent caps.

2. Thumb the hammer to half-cock so the cylinder rotates and place the handgun in its loading stand, barrel pointing skyward.

3. After pouring powder in each chamber from a flask or other measuring device, inspect the chambers to guard against overloads or empty chambers. Note: Black power and black-powder substitute loads are measured by volume, not by weight.

4. Place a lubricating wad over each chamber and, using the rammer, seat it on top of the powder with the rammer. *[Editor's note: This wad, or a thick plug of grease smeared over the end of the chamber after the ball has been seated, is absolutely critical. It reduces the chance of a chainfire, an unpleasant expe-rience that occurs when hot gas or debris from one chamber ignites the charges in adjoining chambers. This occurred to your editor once with a LeMat reproduction revolver when three of the nine chambers fired simultaneously. –DMS]*

5. Place a ball over the chamber mouth and seat it down on top of the wad and powder with the rammer using a firm, continuous stroke. Repeat this process until all chambers are charged. Note: Correct ball diameter is crucial to accuracy, reliability, and safety. A tight chamber fit holds the ball in place dur-ing recoil. Correct diameter is indicated

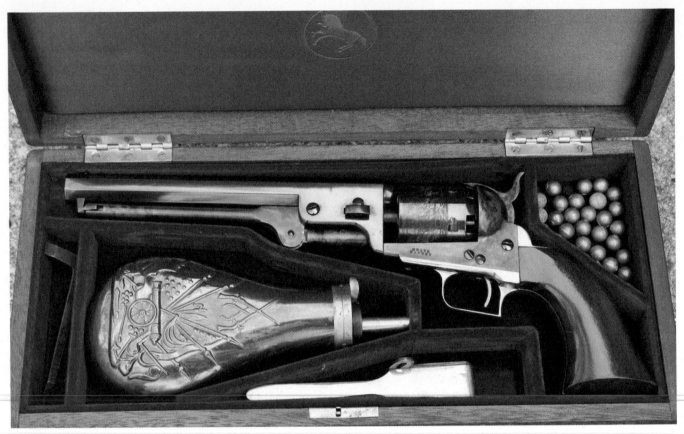

The author was seduced by this "second-generation" Colt 1851 Navy, complete with original wooden box, powder flask, bullet mold, bullets, a combination nipple wrench/screwdriver, and modest price tag.

by a thin ring of lead that peels off as the ball is pushed into the chamber. The ball should never drop down into the chamber.

6. Manually rotate the cylinder, inspecting each chamber again to ensure proper, uniform seating depth.

7. When all six chambers pass inspection, remove the handgun from the stand, point the muzzle towards the ground and cap the nipples, completing the loading process.

There are other loading formulas that incorporate chamber fillers such as corn meal and over-the-ball grease in place of lubricated wads. My goal is keep the loading process as simple as possible. The powder/wad/ball combination works well for me.

Not everyone is up to the cap and ball challenge. During one range session, a well-wisher asked for a loading demonstration. Afterwards he shook his head. "I guess I'll just leave mine on the wall." Another time I commiserated with a gentleman and his wife struggling to load their Remington percussion replica. During my time on the firing line, they managed but two shots.

With each outing, my knowledge and skill increased. As anticipated, burned-powder residue caused the 1860's cylinder to bind after about 18 shots. I found this could be negated somewhat – more wisdom from Elmer – by blowing down the barrel after every six shots to soften the build-up.

Cylinder and hammer jams from spent caps were further obstacles. At first, I experienced one or two jams every six shots. Caps vary by size and brand. So do the nipples that hold them. Finding the right cap for your handgun is a trial and error process. Even when correctly sized, spent caps frequently fall off the nipples and can affect functioning. The old timers' practice of flipping the shooting wrist briskly to the right after each shot while cocking the hammer sometimes expelled the fired cap. Often it didn't. A long, narrow tweezers helps in plucking troublemakers from your handgun's innards.

Ignition problems were another headache. Misfires occurred with residue build-up on the hammer and inside the hammer recess. Scrubbing both vigorously with a wire brush can prolong

your shooting session. Misfires also resulted when residue build-up on the nipples prevented proper cap seating. I countered this by brushing the nipples and picking their vents clean with pin. During one particularly exasperating range session, I suffered a plague of misfires early on. That day more expletives than shots were fired off. Investigation revealed the misfiring caps were only slightly dented. After trying everything I could think of, I backed out the nipples a couple of threads. Volla. No more misfires that day. Backing the nipples out of the chambers just a tad brought them closer to the hammer and provided a more effective "whack" on the caps.

Hangfires are potentially lethal hazard. I've experienced only one to date, but it scared the devil out of me. If you pull the trigger and the cap ignites but the powder doesn't, keep the muzzle pointed in a safe direction for a slow count of ten. My hangfire occurred a full two seconds after the hammer dropped. Minimize this risk by keeping your powder dry, storing it properly in a cool, dry environment, and ensuring that your handgun's chambers are moisture-free.

This brings us to another valuable piece of advice for cap and ball beginners: Come equipped with the right tools. I learned quickly that proper implements are vital in keeping your handgun booming.

Over the weeks, the contents of my shooting box grew steadily. The basics included safety glasses, hearing protection, homemade loading stand, powder, balls, caps, wads, cappers, nipple wrench, pin, tweezers, a wood dowel and rubber hammer (to remove the barrel wedge key for disassembly and dislodge migrating balls), and a thin metal rod that fit inside the threaded nipple portals (to remove balls from the chambers). Now I also pack a wire brush for dry scrubbing the nipples and hammer, a dental pick to clean crevices, a clean rag, screwdriver, and pocketknife. A few packaged, moist towelettes come in handy for cleaning the inevitable lubricant and power residue from the hands once the fun is over.

After satisfactory progress with the 1860, I switched to the Navy. My first surprise was an unpleasant one. Neither of my size 10 and 11 caps fit the nipples right. Soon after purchasing my Colt, I noticed several of the original conical slugs were missing from the box's compartment. A closer examination revealed a fine ring of shallow pitting in the barrel breech. Someone had fired the 1851 and neglected to clean it properly – a mortal sin with black powder. I suspect the original nipples were corroded and had been replaced with off-size aftermarket substitutes. Once again, the fine folks in Union City bailed me out and in short order the Navy was back in action.

As Elmer Keith noted in *Sixguns* – later reaffirmed by other writers – the Colt 1851 Navy is an accurate weapon. The combination of grip profile (wisely retained on the Single Action Army), seven-inch barrel, and medium weight add up to superb balance. To me, no handgun, percussion or cartridge, points as natural as this six-shooter.

With the manufacturer's suggested charge of Triple Seven, wad, and an 80-grain .375" swaged lead ball, six-shot, two-inch+ groups were achieved firing offhand at 25 yards. Listed velocity was 830 fps. Recoil was light. Not only is my Navy sweet shooting, it behaves. Cap jams are rare. I can fire 30 loads before fouling becomes an issue.

It's no surprise to me that Wild Bill earned the nickname "Prince of the Pistoleers" with his brace of ivory-

stocked 1851s. Seventy-some years after Bill met his demise at a poker table, Col. Cooper and a crew from the Eaton Canyon Muzzle Loaders' Association of Pasadena, California, equipped with Navies, 1860s, and a New Model Army Remington 44, proved some of Wild Bill's alleged shooting exploits were indeed possible. (To learn more about this fascinating historical side note, see Chapter 17 of *They Called Him Wild Bill* by Joseph G. Rosa.)

This treatise wouldn't be complete without stressing the importance of properly cleaning cap and ball handguns. I value the function and finish of my Colts, so I'm prompt and thorough. All firearms using black powder or its substitutes must be cleaned right and right fast. Be prepared to work after your fun.

My routine with the Colts is to first disassemble them into barrel assembly, grip frame, wood grips, and cylinder;

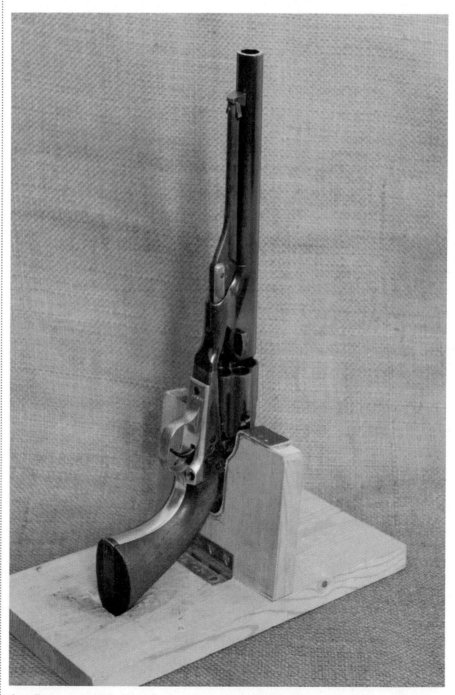

Loading a cap and ball revolver requires concentration and patience. The author's found homemade loading stand is a valuable "third hand" in the charging process.

remove the nipples; and wipe away as much built-up fouling as possible with a stout rag. This is followed by thoroughly scrubbing all exterior and interior surfaces (excluding the wood grips) and the nipples with a bristle brush in hot detergent water.

I employ oversize wire brushes to thoroughly scour the inside of the barrel, chambers, and cylinder-pin and rammer recesses. A special, snug-fitting brush cleanses the threaded nipple portals. The frame and every crevice and cranny within are brushed clean. After the scrubdown, I rinse everything in boiling water and hand dry each component with a thick, clean towel. Then I run dry patches through the barrel, chambers, and all recesses until they come out spotless. I finish up with Q-tips in the tight spots.

When the handgun is completely dry, I coat the cylinder pin grooves with gun grease, lightly oil all moving parts, and run an oiled patch through the bore and chambers. I make especially sure that the bottoms of the chambers are clean, water free, and oiled. In my experience, this is the first place rust occurs. Untreated, even a light coating of rust can advance to pitting in short order. Use a flashlight to inspect the chamber bottoms if necessary.

The nipple vents are picked clean with a pin before being screwed back into place, and the wood grips are wiped clean. Then I reassemble everything and thoroughly wipe all exterior surfaces with a clean, dry rag. I let my prizes rest overnight on newspaper, allowing excess oil to run off.

When the day's "dreadful nuisance" is complete, I cleanse the powder residue from my throat with a cold brew and celebrate the day's cap and ball adventure in an easy chair. By then, I've earned it. Every session is a learning experience, worthy of reflection.

The following day, I again wipe all exterior metal surfaces with a rag. To some, this protracted process may be overdoing it. Not to me. The day before the next range outing, I disassemble the revolver, run clean patches through the bore and chambers until they're absolutely oil free to prevent misfires from oil-contaminated powder.

Because of all the effort devoted to loading, overcoming adversity and cleaning, I've developed a special attachment to my Colts. I believe this is the crux of my cap and ball enjoyment. It's hard to explain, but I just don't feel the same connection with my cartridge handguns.

My cap and ball journey is now at a crossroad. A host of interesting options await, should I choose. I could test conical bullets and paper cartridges, give point shooting a try, or maybe loosen the purse strings for a top quality replica holster and belt. If a financial windfall comes my way, genuine ivory grips might be a possibility. Eventually, I could take the plunge and indulge in real black powder. That would be the pinnacle of my percussion adventure.

If you're thinking of following in my footsteps, think twice and again. As my experiences demonstrate, cap and ball shooting is a labor of love and certainly not for everyone. For those who appreciate these historic handguns, are patient, thorough, careful, and dedicated problem solvers, this may be a hobby for you. Then again, it may not.

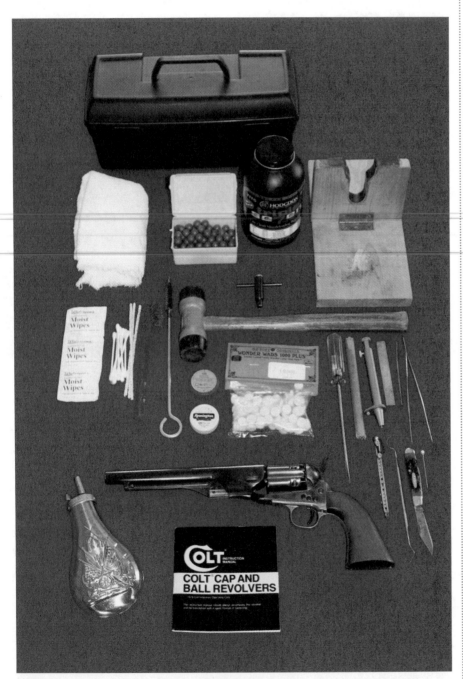

Don't expect to travel light when beginning cap and ball handgunning. This cache of supplies and tools proved necessary for extended shooting sessions. Did pistoleros 150 years ago pack this much gear?

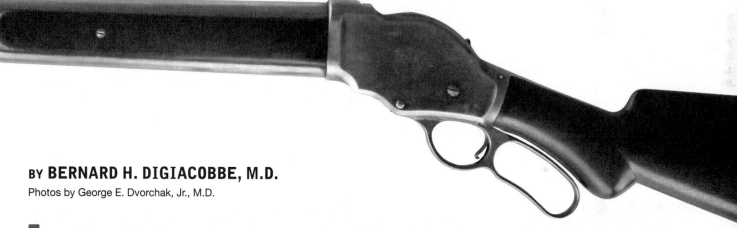

THE WINCHESTER MODEL 1887 LEVER ACTION SHOTGUN:
THE BEST LEVER ACTION RIFLE THAT NEVER WAS

BY **BERNARD H. DIGIACOBBE, M.D.**

Photos by George E. Dvorchak, Jr., M.D.

I suspect that most readers are already vaguely familiar with the Winchester Model 1887 Lever Action Shotgun. Its distinctive buffalo-humped receiver appeared in the movies in the hands of characters as diverse as Judge Roy Bean and the Terminator. The original guns, as well as modern reproductions, have also become quite popular in cowboy action shooting events.

However, few if any readers realize that the Model 1887 was probably the best lever action rifle that never was. To fully understand why, you'll need to take a long look inside the story of the Model 1887.

It all began sometime around 1884. Winchester was well on their way to dominating the lever action rifle market. In addition to the success of their Model 73, Winchester had very recently acquired the patent rights to manufacture the soon-to-become-popular Model 1886, which would handle powerful cartridges like the

.45-70 Government cartridge. To extend their domination, Winchester asked the legendary John Moses Browning if he would design a lever action shotgun. Browning explained that a pump action would be a better choice for a shotgun. While Winchester agreed, they indicated that lever actions had sort of become a Winchester trademark. The conversation took place in October of 1884 and the initial provisional patent for what would become the Model 1887 shotgun was applied for in the following June.

While there is no proof of it, I strongly suspect that the Spencer lever action rifle of Civil War fame was the inspiration for the Model 1887. Both use a breechbolt that pivots from below and are probably the only two lever action arms to do so. The Spencer lever action was well known during the Civil War and later out west. Since John Browning and his family were gunsmiths in Utah, he would have been familiar with the

Spencer. Now, designing a repeating shotgun is considerably more difficult than designing a repeating rifle. Not only are shotgun shells larger, but there is considerably more difficulty in creating a mechanism to reliably feed shotgun shells with their blunt noses.

The Spencer utilized a half circle shaped "carrier" with a separate under-lever and a separate vertically-rising breechbolt and springs and a few other small components. In a stroke of genius, Browning integrated all of these parts into a single component. While the large size of this component made it and the receiver difficult to forge, it greatly simplified production of the gun. By elongating the pivot hole of the bolt, the Model 1887 utilized the initial opening of the lever to lower the bolt down and out of its locking engagement within the top back of the frame. Further rotation of the lever/bolt extracted the shell from the chamber. Similarly, the end of the closing

This right-sided view of the gun shows the unique buffalo hump configuration of the gun in addition to its overall massive proportions. The single screw on the forend indicates that this is an early production version of the gun. Later, production versions had two screws securing the forend.

stroke of the lever raised the back of the bolt up against the locking abutments in the back of the frame.

The design is elegant in its simplicity if not its actual execution. Early catalogs boasted that the entire mechanism had only 16 parts! An additional extractor was added to later models. While the Spencer lever action had its magazine located within the buttstock, the 1887's magazine was located below the barrel in conventional fashion. With the lever is in its full forward position, the 1887's magazine is loaded through the rear of the frame; eliminating the need for a separate loading gate. The Spencer's hammer was located externally along the right side of the frame, as was typical of muzzleloaders, while the hammer of the 1887 was located in the bolt and its spur protruded through the top.

As with other lever actions, the Model 1887 cannot be fired until the lever is completely closed. However, the Model 87 accomplishes this with fewer parts than other lever actions. Despite its minimal number of parts, the 1887 offered a range of advantages not found in other lever action rifles, then or now. On other lever actions the hammer spring is compressed on the initial retraction of the bolt. However, on the Model 1887 the hammer spring is compressed on the closing stroke of the lever. This divides the effort required to operate the gun.

As with other lever action guns, the effort required to extract the shell occurs on the opening stroke of the lever. The extra effort to compress the hammer spring then occurs on the closing stroke. This added resistance is more comfortably placed against a more padded palmar aspect of the shooter's fingers *[Editor's note: That's doctor's talk – he means the fleshy palm side of the fingers – DMS]* rather than the bony back of the shooter's fingers. The relative great distances of the restraining surfaces of the hammer and trigger from their pivot points allow for a relatively light trigger pull. During the closing of the lever, the trigger lies against the back of the trigger guard until the lever is almost fully closed. This subtle feature virtually excludes the unpleasant possibility of the shooter "spearing" his finger when closing the lever. In addition, with the lever in the open position, the barrel can be cleaned from the rear. This is of course of greater significance on a rifle than a shotgun but a handy feature nevertheless.

The gun demonstrated Browning's genius as a gun designer, both in terms

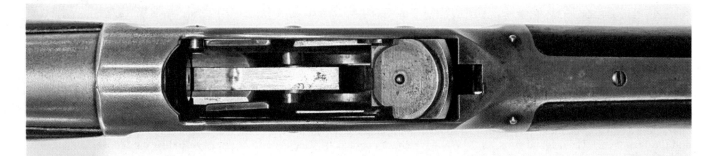

The lifter mechanism and extractor.

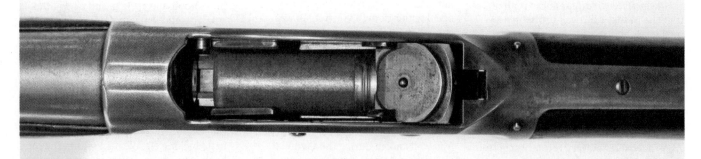

A view through the breech with the lever down and the breech block rotated backward shows how the magazine can be loaded through the receiver.

This top view shows the location of the firing pin retaining screw, visible from the top of the bolt as found on the earliest production versions of the gun. Later, firing pin screws were inserted from the underside of the breechbolt.

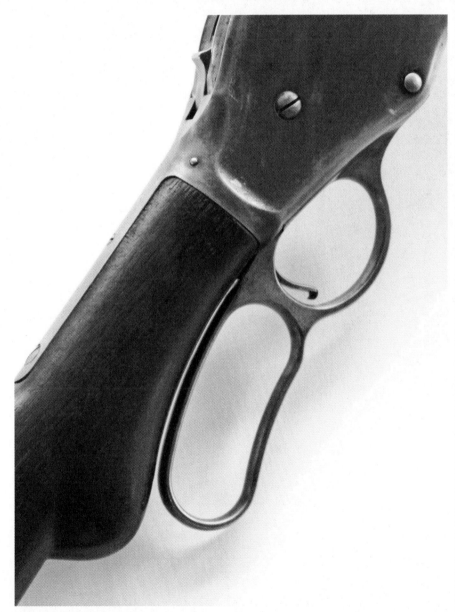

This close up shows the hook on the back of the trigger used to retain the trigger guard in the up position after the gun has been fired.

of the innovative features of the gun as well as his prediction that a pump-action would have been a better choice for a shotgun. The Model 1887 is a big and rather clumsy gun. Now, any 10 or 12 gauge repeater is a big gun. Placing a lever on its underside only makes it bigger. The appearance is further exaggerated by the short, thick shape of the buttstock and the long barrels (which were typical of all black powder shotguns at the time). This clumsy appearance would have been especially apparent to the shooters of the time who were accustomed only to single-shot or side-by-side shotguns rather than the later-to-be-developed repeaters. The 1887 is hardly the gun you would take to the thickets for hunting grouse or woodcock. However, the 1887 had four big advantages over contemporary side-by-sides: the four extra shells in the magazine. It's worth remembering at this point that the side-by-sides of the time were external hammer guns that had to be manually cocked, and were not fitted with ejectors. The extra capacity was greatly appreciated by market hunters of the era. Expectedly, the same extra capacity was also greatly valued by those who hunted for animals that wore boots and carried guns. The 1887 soon became a favorite with guards including the Denver and Rio Grande railroad as well as the American Express.

The chief disadvantage of the 1887, its large size, would certainly have been eliminated if it had been manufactured as a rifle, preferably a rifle chambered for a small cartridge such as the popular .44-40. Manufacturing the gun as a rifle would also have highlighted its previously-mentioned technical advantages. Since the 1887 loads from the rear, the same components could also have been used to make a single-shot rifle. This would have been especially applicable in a scaled-down version. While the rear lockup would not have been as strong as the Winchester Model 1885 High Wall single-shot, it would certainly have been amply strong for the black powder cartridges of that era.

Unfortunately for the concept, Winchester already had a lever action rifle, the renowned Model 1873, that was chambered for the .44-40 cartridge, as well as a single-shot rifle and the soon-to-be-introduced Model 1886 lever action rifle for more powerful cartridges. Thus Winchester had no incentive to offer a rifle version of the 1887, which would have competed against their other products. However, Winchester

This photograph from the breech shows the lever down and the breechblock rotated backward, allowing loading of the barrel from the rear of the receiver.

did make some standard-size 12 gauge 1887s for use with solid bullets. These rare guns had smoothbore barrels with a very short length of rifling near the muzzle. The system was very similar to the system used by contemporary English side-by-side shotguns such as the H&H "Paradox" gun for firing rifle shells. For use in these Winchester rifled-bore shotguns, 12-gauge brass shotgun shells were loaded with 150 grains of black powder behind a 70-caliber bullet weighing between 700 and 900 grains. Such a cartridge would have been a real "kicker" and would have probably limited the popularity of the gun.

The gun was introduced as a 12 gauge in the 1887 catalog with the 10 gauge version added in 1888. Consistent with that era, the 12-gauge guns were chambered for the 2-5/8-inch 12 gauge shell and weighed approximately 8 pounds The 10-gauge guns were chambered for the 2-7/8-inch shell and weighed approximately 9 lbs. *As modern shotgun shells are 2-3/4 inches in length and use smokeless powder, they should definitely not be used in these short-chambered guns, which were intended for black powder shells.* Fortunately, modern

reproductions of the Model 1887 are chambered for 2-3/4-inch shells.

On the originals, the standard barrels were full choked and made of rolled steel and were generally 30 inches in length. A 32-inch length was specified on special request. A 20-inch barrel was offered for both models in 1898. A three-blade damascus barrel was available for an additional $15. In addition, a four-blade damascus barrel was available for an extra $20, almost doubling the original price of the gun! Other options were available. It is worth noting that at this time Winchester made a significant effort to accommodate individual customer's requests. So, if you're contemplating buying a "standard" Model 1887, it pays to check it closely, as it might be worth more money.

The pistol grip buttstock was uncheckered with a 2-3/4-inch length of pull and a 2-5/8-inch drop. Although almost all of the frames were case-hardened, the colors vary considerably, from almost black to gray. These later frames are sometimes mistaken for nickel-plated receivers. Although plated receivers were available, they are readily identifiable as their plated finish

inevitably flaked. Reportedly, some frames were blued.

There were several subtle variations. The earliest guns had a cartridge guide on the right side and a single extractor on the left side of the bolt. However, later guns had duel extractors, one on the right as well as the left side of the bolt. Presumably, there must have been some extractor difficulty early on, perhaps resulting from aligning the curve travel of the extractor/bolt with the horizontal retraction of the shell. On the earliest guns, the firing pin retaining screw was located on the top front of the bolt. Early on, the forends were retained by only one screw. Later ones had two screws. The method of supporting the magazine tube varied throughout production.

While the Model 1887 was generally considered a financial success for Winchester, by the mid-1890s sales started to slip. Much of the competition came from Winchester's own Models 1893 and 1897 pump action shotguns also designed by Browning. Production was halted in 1901 after manufacturing of about 64,855 model 1887s. According to one source, the last batch of Model 1887s were sold in Mexico.

While the Model 1887 had the firepower of a repeater, it certainly lacked the elegance of a double.

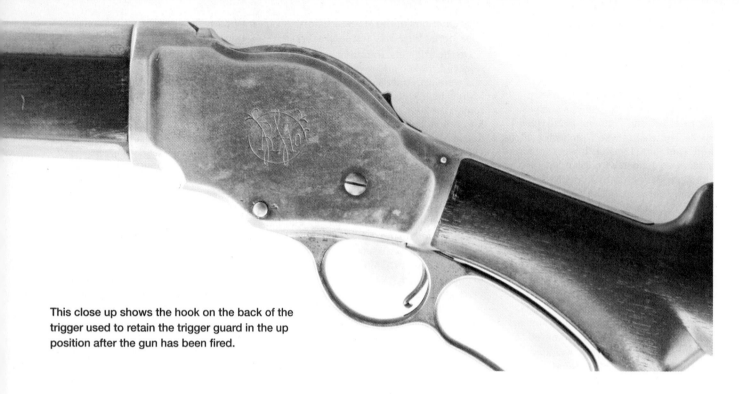

This close up shows the hook on the back of the trigger used to retain the trigger guard in the up position after the gun has been fired.

To boost their sales, Winchester then introduced a near-identical version known as the Model 1901. It was available in 10 gauge only. The 1901 was designed for smokeless powder and featured a "tighter breech joint" and a more completely supported breech and cartridge head.

The most obvious difference between the two can be seen in the lever. On the 1901 the lever is a separate component from the breechblock. While they look nearly the same, a hook on the back of the 1887 was used to retain the lever in the closed position when the gun had been fired. The 1901 had a small pivot point located between the trigger guard and the lever. The lever locked the gun against opening; however, downward pressure on the separate finger lever on the 1901 released the action for opening. A less obvious difference was the provision for positive retraction of the firing pin on the 1901. The frames on the 1901 were hardened and browned and damascus barrels were available as an extra-cost option. The Model 1901 was discontinued in 1920 after approximately 13,500 had been produced. With the rising popularity of cowboy action shooting, the models suddenly were in short supply and several manufacturers commenced reproduction of the Model 1887. Fortunately these guns are chambered for 2-3/4-inch shells and designed for smokeless powder.

Many consider the Model 1887 the first successful repeating shotgun. Although Spencer made a pump action shotgun that was introduced earlier sometime around 1883 or 1884 and may have been more practical, it was not a financial success. The Model 1887, however, was a financial success for Winchester. Although rendered obsolete by Winchester's pump action shotguns, the 1887 filled a definite market need at the time. Somehow, though, I cannot help but feel that the Model 1887 would have been better off as the best lever action rifle that never was.

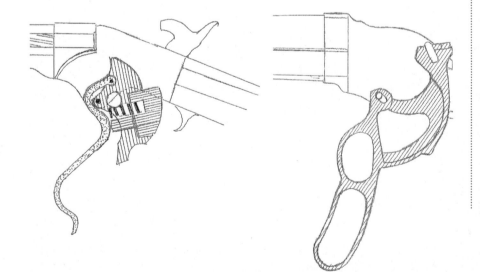

Compare the diagram of the older Spencer rifle on the left to that of the later-designed Model 1887 shotgun on the right. The one-piece pivoting bolt of the Model 1887 is dramatically similar. Did the Spencer inspire the Model 1887? Who knows?

THE HUSQVARNA AND THE ZEBRA

BY TOM CACECI

The mountains east of Windhoek in Namibia are part of the native range of the Hartmann's Mountain Zebra (*Equus zebrae hartmanni*), a species slightly smaller than the common Burchell's Zebra. The mountain zebra is also found in Angola and some parts of South Africa. These animals live in rocky, dry habitat and prefer slopes and plateaus as high as 3000 feet or more above sea level. They aren't called "Mountain" zebra for nothing: the area in which we hunted them may not have been the Rockies, but they were sure-enough mountains whose steep slopes go up, down, and back up again.

It's challenging terrain in which to hunt a skittish and elusive herd animal with a reputation as one of the toughest non-dangerous game animals to kill. The hide, which lacks stripes on the belly and the "shadow stripes" of the Burchell's, makes a spectacular trophy for display as a wall hanging or rug.

Since I was hunting in a former German colony, I used a rifle chambered for the 8x57JS Mauser, one of the first — and one of the greatest — smokeless powder rifle rounds ever developed. Originally used in the revolutionary Gewehr 1888 "Commission" rifle, the 8x57 is still popular in Europe although it has faded away for sporting use in the USA and in Africa. This is unfortunate, because it's as effective and efficient a medium-bore hunting caliber as could be found, the equal of the .30-06 in the field. American ammunition companies deliberately underload it (out of fear that it may be used in weak Gew88 rifles); the best American factory load is a 170-grain bullet at 2360 fps generating only 2102 fpe. Norma loads it to its full potential: 196-grain bullets with a muzzle velocity of 2526 fps and 2776 fpe.

My rifle for this hunt was a Husqvarna sporter built in 1944, one of the last true purpose-built sporters on the Mauser 1896 action (Husqvarna resumed sporting rifle production in 1948 using FN-made M98 actions). It's not an ex-military weapon: it lacks the "thumb cut" in the left receiver rail, the barrel is not stepped, and the rear sight is a single fixed open leaf. The stock is a Schnabel-tipped piece of European beechwood with modest checkering but no other ornamentation beyond a plastic grip cap. All in all, a plain-vanilla working rifle, intended for the domestic market — the European export market was pretty dismal in 1944! My only changes were addition of a recoil pad and a Burris Timberline 4x20 scope in a detachable mount.

The pre-1898 Mauser actions aren't as highly regarded (or as widely used) as the Model 98s, for reasons that, frankly, escape me. While the M98 is the most successful Mauser for both sporting and military use, but I've always felt it was a little too porky for a light hunting rifle. The M96 is sleek and graceful, trimmer and better balanced, producing a wonderful lightweight sporter. Commercially made examples of sporting 1896s aren't often seen, more's the pity.

They call it the "mountain zebra" for a good reason!

Made in 1944, the Husqvarna sporter packs a wallop with Norma 196-grain Oryx ammunition.

One reason the M96 is disliked by American shooters is the cock-on-closing bolt. But the truth is that this allows a simpler, lighter, and slimmer bolt design. Another is the lack of the M98's so-called "safety lug." This doesn't bother me. Any cartridge that produces enough pressure to require a safety lug is too hot for my taste! The M96 is amply strong for the calibers it was intended to use.

We were hunting on a huge property about 60km east of Windhoek, and the zebra were leading us a merry chase up and down the hills. Rarely did we get within 200 yards of a herd before being spotted by a pair of sharp eyes — and off they would go again. At best we were offered a couple of Hail-Mary op-

portunities at ranges too far for me to be comfortable with. I'm not built for rapid up-and-down movements over uneven ground. Once or twice I actually got the shooting sticks up, but the pounding of my heart and the heaving of my chest from exertion precluded any possibility of a hit. Nor am I at my best shooting from sticks when standing: I never use them hunting in North America and though I'd practiced a bit before the trip, I never really got comfortable using them.

But in the afternoon everything came together. After another couple of hours spotting and stalking, running while trying simultaneously to be quiet and yet get close enough, I was more than a little winded by the time we encountered

a small group on the other side of a deep valley. They were perhaps 180 yards away. I was puffing pretty hard when my PH urged me to take a shot. I was willing but I insisted it be done from a sitting position.

"Brace my back," I asked. This elicited a quizzical look, and I further explained, "I shoot best from a sitting position: I always have. Sit down and I'll lean against you." He seemed a bit puzzled by this request and by my refusal to use his sticks, but complied. I dropped to the ground, waited a few seconds to catch my breath again, braced my elbows on my knees, and put the crosshairs on the shoulder of the biggest animal in the group.

A zebra has a "triangle" of stripes on the shoulder, and this is, I had been told, the best aiming point, as the heart lies right behind it. I could see the triangle quite clearly, and miraculously I was pretty steady and confident. The shot rang out: the zebra stood stock still momentarily, then began to trot slowly away. Before I had time to work the bolt for a second shot, it dropped. The little Husky had shot straight and true: when we crossed the valley to the site of the kill, the zebra was stone dead, the bullet having gone exactly where I wanted it to, dead smack in the middle of the triangle. The Norma "Oryx" bullet had punched through the bone to shred the heart.

The Husky has proven to be one of those "lucky" rifles. Bought on a whim and selected for a possibly frivolous reason, it proved to have been a fine choice for a plains game hunt. On this trip it took several other trophies, including a huge eland. I know nothing of its history before it came into my hands, but I believe that in its 66 years it probably served its previous owners as well as it has served me.

Hartmann's Mountain Zebra (Equus zebrae hartmanni) and author's M96 Mauser-actioned Husqvarna.

A Mysterious Stranger from Canada:

The Tobin $5.00 Boy Scout Rifle

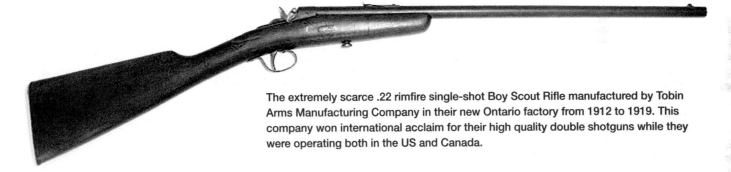

The extremely scarce .22 rimfire single-shot Boy Scout Rifle manufactured by Tobin Arms Manufacturing Company in their new Ontario factory from 1912 to 1919. This company won international acclaim for their high quality double shotguns while they were operating both in the US and Canada.

BY JACK A. MYERS

In the Fall of 2008 I ran across a little single-shot .22 rimfire rifle I had never heard of. Offered in an online auction in Georgia, the rifle was listed as a Canadian Tobin .22 rimfire single-shot rifle. Because I specifically collect .22 rimfire single-shot firearms made in the USA or Canada, I felt that I had to own this strange little oddball. My bid was the winner and within a week or so it arrived at my door. I was surprised how closely it resembles the Winchester Model 1902 rifle.

The old boy had obviously seen some rough times. It reminded me of our many "Little Boys' Rifles" which usually have undergone decades of tender ministrations from an army of boisterously active youngsters handling these new toys. These boys and girls seemed to have never heard of oil or proper tools. Or perhaps they just couldn't afford such luxuries during the hard times prior to and during WWI. Usually their only tools

available for any needed repairs were a screwdriver or two; a hammer; a pair of pliers; a handful of nails, screws and bolts; plus a lot of energy and a creative imagination.

This welcome addition to my collection had suffered the usual neglect but its only "big" problem was that it suffered a cracked wrist. Luckily, previous

owners had not tried nailing or taping it together. They had taken the time to glue it, and considering the situation of the times, they did a pretty fair job. Though its original bluing was now an even gray patina overall, all its metal parts were mercifully free of rust, quite unlike the condition of most old boys' rifles, many of which spent their later

This is the only stamping on the rifle, except for a small numeral 1 on the bottom of the barrel, under the forestock. Of the five existing rifles thus far observed, three of them had the numeral 1 there. Its meaning or use remains unknown.

days sitting in the corner of some leaky old barn or corn crib as a quick cure for rodents.

The only identifying markings on the gun, appearing on the top of the barrel, read "TOBIN ARMS MFG, CO. WOODSTOCK. ONT., CANAD". I have no idea why "Canada" was truncated in this manner – perhaps the result of a faulty rollmark die. This is the only stamping on the rifle, except for a small numeral 1 on the bottom of the barrel, under the forestock. Of the five existing rifles thus far observed, three of them had the numeral 1 there. Its meaning or use remains unknown.

Through a web search for Tobin Arms Mfg. Co., I learned from Wikipedia, a usually reliable source, that a 33-year-old Canadian immigrant to the U.S., named Frank Major Tobin, started up a company in 1903 in Norwich, Connecticut, with a group of businessmen for manufacturing high grade double barrel shotguns. Just six years later in 1909 he had obtained enough Canadian investors to buy out his U.S. partners and move his gun company to Woodstock, Ontario, where his group built Canada's very first shotgun factory.

Some of Tobin's very first advertisements were placed in a locally published outdoorsman's magazine, *Rod And Gun in Canada*. This was the only such magazine in Canada at the time and that's where Frank introduced his company with a full-page ad in their December 1909 issue. Note that at this time no mention was made of a .22 rimfire rifle.

Their next full-page ad, the one which would make the first and only mention of their rifle, was one that appeared three years later in the July 1912 issue, where they named their new product the "Tobin Boy Scout Rifle." For some unknown reason, this little rifle does not appear in any known later Tobin catalog observed to this date.

Eventually, due to poor economic times across the globe, by 1916 the Tobin Arms Manufacturing Co., Ltd. was coming to an end and other companies had begun to take over parts of Frank's new factory. Tobin's company surrendered its charter in 1921. Another Canadian entrepreneur named G.B. Crandall took up the manufacture of Tobin shotguns about 1930 and it's thought that he continued making them until at least 1951. However, if for no other reason, Frank Tobin will always be remembered as the first person to build a shotgun factory in Canada.

Nowhere in any of Tobin's known company literature does the little .22 rimfire rifle appear. I've had an opportunity to look at several of the early Tobin catalogs and it is not even mentioned. Through asking questions on a Canadian gun collector website I learned that the monthly outdoor magazine *Rod and Gun in Canada* had once offered a Tobin rifle to youngsters willing to sell five annual subscriptions to the magazine.

It's interesting to note that shortly after the turn of the century, another gun manufacturer, the Hamilton Rifle Company of Plymouth, Michigan, was becoming well-known throughout the firearms industry for their small, inexpensive and unusually made, single-shot rifles which began

50 ROD AND GUN IN CANADA

Canada's First Gun Factory
READY FOR INSPECTION

Canadian sportsmen are invited to visit one of the most modern and complete plants for manufacturing HIGH GRADE FIREARMS, now nearing completion at

Woodstock, Ontario, Canada

Believing that the business warranted it, and in order to furnish the Canadian Sportsman with an

All Canadian Made Shotgun
Superior to any other made

we have moved our entire plant from Norwich, Conn., to Woodstock, Canada, where the

Tobin Simplex Guns

will be made. We invite comparison with the best guns on the market, and can show the following superior features:

Lightest Weight
Greatest Strength
Fewest Parts
Simplest Construction
Finest Balance
Strongest Penetration

Mr. Frank M. Tobin, with an experience of over a quarter of a century, among the Trade and Sportsmen of the United States, will continue in charge of the business.

Our Export Trade with Australasia and the Orient will continue to have our special attention.

Your dealer will have these guns: ASK HIM.
Our new catalogue is in press: SEND FOR IT.

Tobin Arms Manufacturing Co., Limited
Woodstock, Ontario, Canada

When writing Advertisers kindly mention ROD AND GUN IN CANADA.

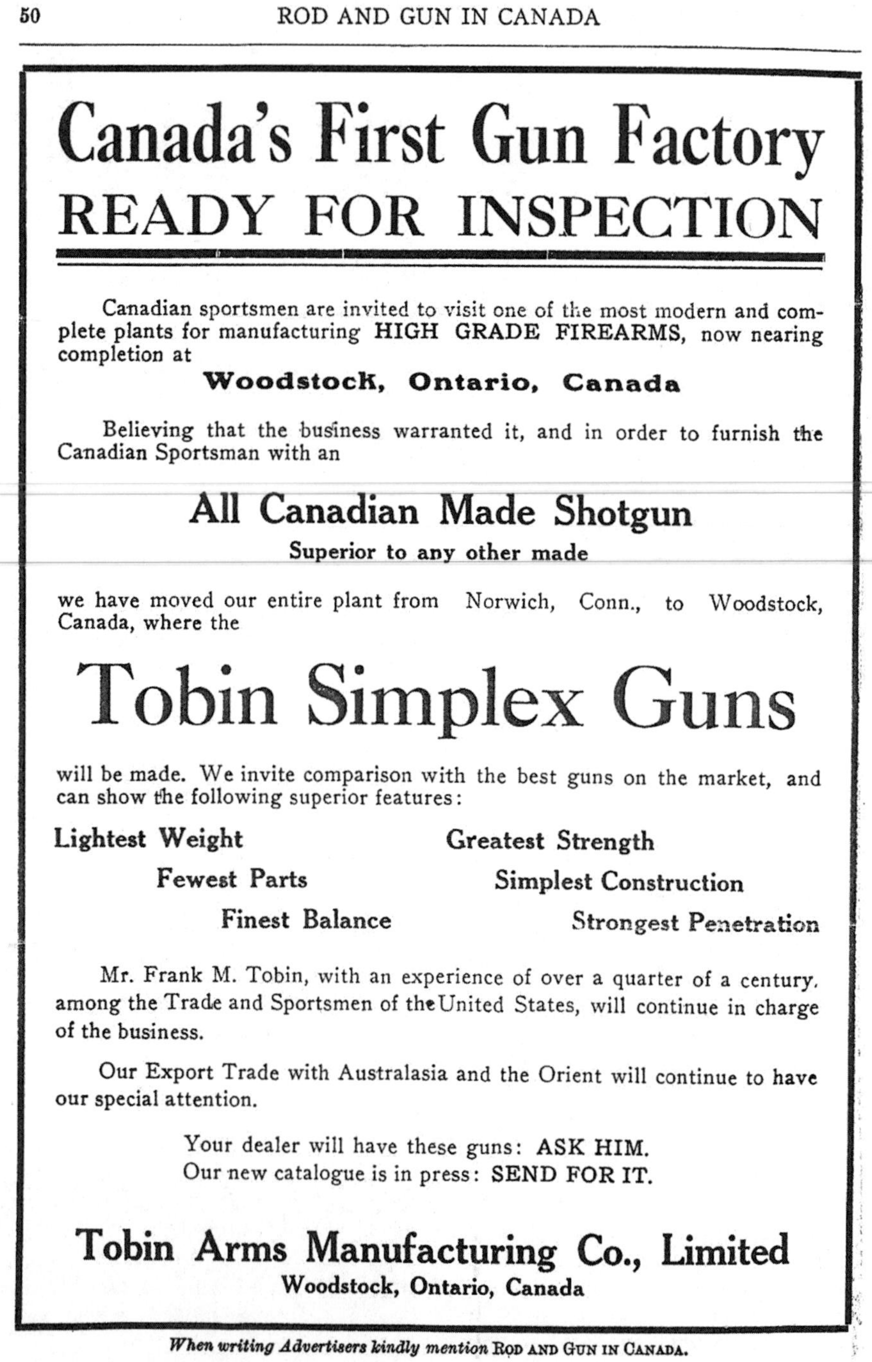

Earliest known advertisement to announce the opening of Canada's first shotgun factory, where the Tobin Boy Scout Rifle was produced from inception until the company shut down (c. 1906 - 1916). This full-page ad appeared in the December 1909 issue of *Rod And Gun In Canada*.

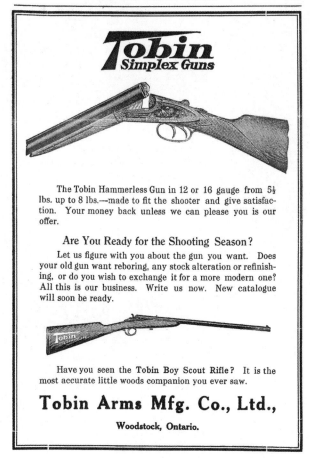

ROD AND GUN IN CANADA   273

Tobin
Simplex Guns

The Tobin Hammerless Gun in 12 or 16 gauge from 5¼ lbs. up to 8 lbs.—made to fit the shooter and give satisfaction. Your money back unless we can please you is our offer.

Are You Ready for the Shooting Season?

Let us figure with you about the gun you want. Does your old gun want reboring, any stock alteration or refinishing, or do you wish to exchange it for a more modern one? All this is our business. Write us now. New catalogue will soon be ready.

Have you seen the Tobin Boy Scout Rifle? It is the most accurate little woods companion you ever saw.

Tobin Arms Mfg. Co., Ltd.,

Woodstock, Ontario.

This July 1912 full-page *Rod And Gun in Canada* advertisement is the first known mention of a rifle being made by a company internationally known as a scattergun maker. No price is mentioned and no description whatsoever is given! Very unusual advertising technique.

Model 1913 improved 'Boy Scout' with detachable stock for convenience in packing, made for either short, long or long rifle 22 calibre, rim fire cartridges— Fitted with miniature Rocky mountain rear sight, Self ejecting Extractor—guaranteed for either black or smokeless powder. Accurately sighted for target shooting---Barrel, 22 inches long with increased twist rifling---few parts, very simple, strong and durable.

The Most Complete $5 Rifle on the Market

NOTICE---If your dealer does not handle this rifle, send to us and we will deliver same prepaid to any express office in Canada on receipt of price.

Tobin Arms Mfg. Co., Ltd.

WOODSTOCK, ONTARIO.

Though badly fragmented, this page from the June 1913 issue of *Rod And Gun In Canada* is our only documentation that the company actually first offered the little rifle to the general public, and not just as a selling premium to the magazine's army of young salespeople.

production in 1899. It's estimated that approximately half a million were sold or given away as premiums to children who went door to door, selling just about everything you can think of. Cloverleaf Salve was one of the best known major promoters of these popular sales prizes. Corn seed companies offered discount coupons for a Hamilton rifle in their bags of seed. Hamilton ended manufacturing in 1945 after producing more than 1,000,000 various "little boys' rifles."

Even with today's increasing popularity of collecting these "little boys' rifles," both here and abroad, it surprised me to learn the little Tobin "$5.00 Boy Scout Rifle" is a very similar rifle to the ultra-popular Hamiltons, but has remained virtually unknown for almost 100 years, even though it was made and offered throughout North America just after the turn of the century.

Another info source dealing with a huge amount of archived info on early Canadian gun collecting led me to an Ontario resident, a Mr. Blyth, who was said to own a Tobin rifle. In a phone conversation he told me he had owned four of these rifles over six decades, but had never seen or even heard of another in 60 years of collecting – until I contacted him. He said he later lost interest in guns and started selling off his collection. He then told me that his last Tobin rifle was at an Ontario auction house and would be sold that coming weekend.

I got the name of the auction house and phoned the owner. He told me they had the rifle but they would not even consider trying to export it to me if I should win it. I contacted Mr. Blyth, the consigning owner, after the weekend sale and learned from him that a collector had paid the equivalent of $750 for his rifle.

That rifle had been offered in the Ontario auction as being in 90+ percent condition, and still had a tag attached that indicated it had once been the property of the Winchester Museum. Mr. Blyth said he had bought it decades earlier from the Flayderman company here in the United States. The rifle sold with the Flayderman tag still on it.

We discussed the unusual firing pin system I had discovered in my rifle. Mr. Blyth said all of his rifles had round firing pins rather than the thin block of machined steel used in mine, which is pinned on a slot through the block so it may rebound once the primer is struck. The little handle on the breech block is screwed through the steel "firing pin" block.

Like the Hamilton rifles, the Tobin has a quick takedown bolt in the bottom of the gun which enabled its owner to break it down to a much handier 22-inch

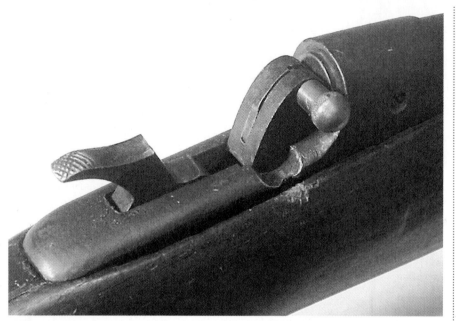

Pictured is a type of "firing pin" I've never observed in any other firearm. Instead of being round, it is a shaped bar which is loosely mounted so that it rebounds after firing. Mr. Don Blyth of Ontario, a gentleman who has previously owned four of these little rifles, has said that all of his rifles had a normal, round firing pin. He was not aware of this variation.

The unusual takedown bolt on the Tobin rifle has no screwdriver slot, but its sides are fully knurled to ease one's grip on it. This indicates that the gun's makers figured "finger tight" was adequate.

The rifle's unusual rear sight has an unusual near full-width V notch and no slot to accommodate a small, stepped elevator, nor does it have a screw-type elevation adjustment. It would appear the only elevation possible is by actually bending the metal up or down.

length for camping, fishing or hiking. Interesting to note is that unlike most of our takedown-type guns, the Tobin's takedown bolt has no slot in the head for a screwdriver. However, the large, thick head is completely knurled to aid in grasping it when your hands might be wet. I guess the makers felt "finger tight" was more than adequate to hold the stock onto the barreled action.

Another unusual feature of this rifle is the fact that it s rear sight has no slot in it to accomodate a stepped elevator as most of our similar rifles have. One would have to assume the elevation was accomplished simply by bending the sight to desired height.

Here are the stats on this "little rifle that never was."

The Tobin Boys' Rifle

Manufacturer: Tobin Arms Mfg. Co., Ltd., Woodstock, Ontario, Canada

Overall length: ....37 inches

Barrel length: ....22 inches muzzle to breech

Caliber: ....22 rimfire (Short, Long, and Long Rifle)

Weight: ....3-3/4 lbs.

The rifle's years of production and quantity manufactured remain unknown. From these few vintage advertisements I've obtained we learn only that they could not have been produced until after Tobin had moved his business to Woodstock in 1906 and gone into production some time after that. It's also known that even though he was enjoying worldwide sales of his high quality scatterguns, by 1916 he was in the process of shutting down his factory and business. (Frank Tobin passed away in 1939.) Therefore, we can state with some confidence that the little Tobin rifle was manufactured between 1906 and 1916. However, given the nature of things, some Tobin rifles may have trickled out of the factory a bit later than that.

Anyone with any information on Frank Tobin or his boys' rifle may contact me care of *Gun Digest*. Together, we may yet piece together the entire story of the elusive Tobin Boys' Rifle!

Note: My thanks to Mr. Don Blyth, who furnished the copies of the old advertisements. Mr. Blyth, along with the well-known Tony Dunn, is a published co-author on Canadian .22 rimfire ammo boxes. He has also spent decades asking Canadian gun shops for info on the Tobin rifle and reports only one man even knew such a rifle existed – but had never seen one!

While most similar, inexpensive rifles might have no buttplate of any kind, the Tobin has a surprisingly well-fitted and formed steel buttplate, quite similar to the kind found on top quality shotguns, anchored solidly with large wood screws.

The Beretta S680 Series Over/Under

BY **NICK HAHN**

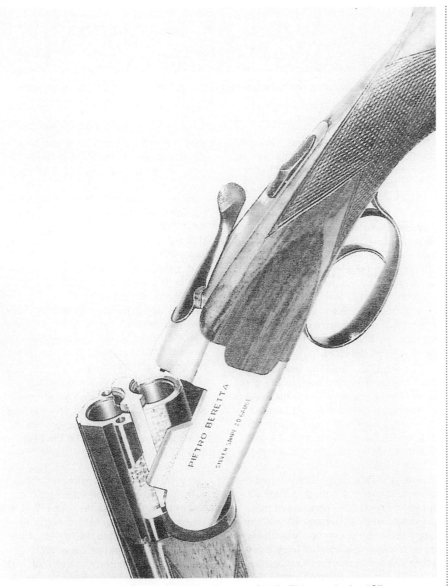

The forerunner of today's Beretta S680 series, the S55B. This one is the "Silver Snipe" made for the American market with a single trigger. The early Beretta's were powered by "V" springs.

he Beretta boxlock S series over/under has not had as long a history as some of the others that are on the market today. The Browning, in its original form as the Superposed, has been around since 1926, and some of the British and European over/under action designs go back to even earlier dates.

The low-profiled Beretta boxlock, the one with the unique lock-up using two conical rods that engage the two holes located in the stubs that are on the sides of the top barrel, made its first appearance in 1956 in the form of the S series beginning with the Model S55B (the numerical designation indicating the year of its design). Some will argue that the higher-quality Model ASE is the progenitor of all Beretta boxlock over/under shotguns. But aside from the fact that both models are boxlock actions with monobloc barrels (Beretta first started using monobloc in 1913 and since have used this system almost exclusively), they are very different in their lock-up mechanism. While the S series uses the conical rods which secure the barrels to the frame, the ASE locks up with a modified (simplified) Kersten type system that is also used in the more expensive sidelock SO series. The ASE, which was introduced in 1946 and dropped in 1964, was resurrected in the 1990s and still survives today with a detachable trigger group as the DT 10. The S series were built on the assembly line with complete parts interchangeability, something that the ASE and the SO series did not have. Prior to the appearance of the S series,

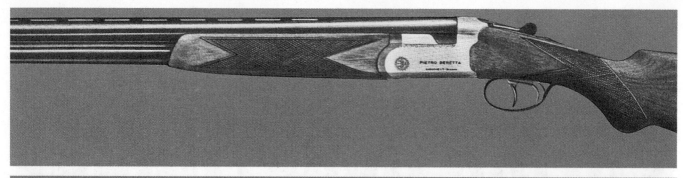

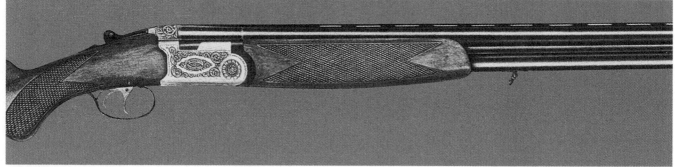

These are the European-market Beretta S55B (top) and S56E (bottom), with double triggers, mid 1970s. By this time, all Berettas had coil springs.

all Beretta shotguns had to be hand fitted. In short, the S series modernized over/under shotgun making for Beretta.

The S series has been tweaked and modified here and there and has continued on uninterrupted for nearly 40 years. The S55B was a severely plain model with no engraving and no ejectors. It could be had with a ventilated rib and a single non-selective trigger in the U.S. market, but that was about it. The next one was S56E, which was followed by the S57EL, which was lavishly hand engraved with sideplates. The same year that S series was introduced, two versions, the Silver Snipe and Golden Snipe, were introduced for the U.S. market and distributed by J. L. Galef & Sons of New York. The Silver Snipe was basically the S55B, except that whereas the S55B had double triggers, the Silver Snipe came standard with a single non-selective trigger. But otherwise it was plain. A ventilated rib was avaible at extra cost and ejectors were not available. To get ejectors, one had to move up to the Golden Snipe, which came standard with ventilated rib and ejectors. In 1963 when the Browning Superposed ruled the over/under market in the U.S. and cost $315 and the newly introduced Winchester Model 101 was $249.00, the Beretta Golden Snipe listed at $263.75. It was certainly competitively priced, but the Browning Superposed was the top

choice in America so the newly introduced Browning lookalikes such as the Winchester Model 101 and the Charles Daly-Miroku outsold the Beretta.

The S series used flat "V" springs whereas the Browning and the Japanese-made guns all used coil springs, although some very early Mirokus were made with flat springs. Some American shotgunners believe that the coil springs are superior to the flat springs, so naturally the Beretta Silver Snipe suffered on that account. However, not everyone believed in the inferiority of the flat springs and happily used their Silver and Golden Snipe Berettas.

Around 1965, Galef representatives began to mention that there was a new Beretta over/under model in the making. However, by 1966 Beretta terminated its arrangement with Galef and struck a deal with Garcia Corporation, known mostly for fishing tackle, and started to market a new line of Beretta over/under boxlocks in 1968. These were called the BL series for the U.S. market. Basically they were "updated" versions of the previous S series. The new BL and the new S series were outwardly unchanged from the older models, but they now all employed coil springs and, except for the basic BL-1 model, all came with a single selective trigger.

The BL-1/S55B was unengraved and ribless and had double triggers while

the BL-2 had an odd contraption that Beretta called "selective speed-trigger" but was still unengraved and without a rib or ejectors. The BL-3 had a modest amount of hand engraving, a ventilated rib and a selective single trigger but still lacked the ejectors. It was the BL-4/S56E that had the whole works as well as some 75 percent coverage of receiver with very nice hand engraving. The BL-4 was called the Windsor Grade. In 1970 the Beretta BL-4 sold for $325, compared to Browning Superposed's price of $420. The Winchester Model 101 was $325 and the Charles Daly Field Grade a few bucks more at $329. So the Beretta was very competitively priced.

The BL-4 was a very good gun. It had everything that most Americans wanted: the ventilated rib, the ejectors, and the single selective trigger. Some consider the old BL-4 to be the best assembly-line Beretta over/under ever made. Yet it was obvious that the American gun buying public was enamored with the Browning and opted for it or one of its many lookalikes. The BL-4 was an excellent gun but just did not sell well. There were also the higher grade BL-5/S57E with deeper cut engraving and the top-of-the-line BL-6/S57EL with heavily engraved sideplates.

By 1976 the BL series disappeared, mainly because Garcia Sporting Arms Corporation, as it called itself during

BERETTA BL: 12s that handle like 20s ... and 20s that handle like lightning!

The BL-4 was one of the nicest models that Beretta produced. It had very nice hand engraving and everything American shooters wanted: single selective trigger, ventilated rib and automatic ejectors.

the period it handled Beretta, was no more. However, in 1977 Beretta Arms Company established itself in the U.S. and started to market the S55B, S56E and S58. Essentially these were "Americanized" versions of the existing S55B, S56E and the S58 (a trap and skeet gun). The new American version, the S55B, had a ventilated rib and a single selective trigger, but lacked the ejectors. For the European market, the S55B still came with double triggers, although now it too had a ventilated rib just like the U.S. version. It was still minimally engraved. The new S56E like the BL-4 had the whole works. However, unlike the 75 percent coverage of hand engraving of the BL-4 and the older S56E, the new S56E had about 50 percent coverage of rolled engraving. It was mechanically identical to the BL-4/S56E and was a light, wonderfully-handling gun.

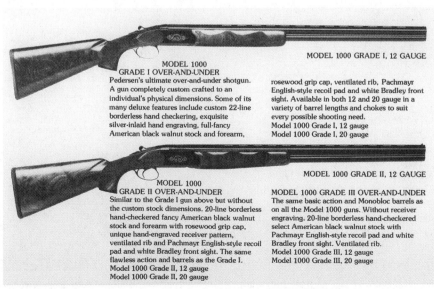

MODEL 1000 GRADE I OVER-AND-UNDER
Pedersen's ultimate over-and-under shotgun. A gun completely custom crafted to an individual's physical dimensions. Some of its many deluxe features include custom 22-line borderless hand checkering, exquisite silver-inlaid hand engraving, full-fancy American black walnut stock and forearm, rosewood grip cap, ventilated rib, Pachmayr English-style recoil pad and white Bradley front sight. Available in both 12 and 20 gauge in a variety of barrel lengths and chokes to suit every possible shooting need.
Model 1000 Grade I, 12 gauge
Model 1000 Grade I, 20 gauge

MODEL 1000 GRADE II OVER-AND-UNDER
Similar to the Grade I gun above but without the custom stock dimensions. 20-line borderless hand-checkered fancy American black walnut stock and forearm with rosewood grip cap, unique hand-engraved receiver pattern, ventilated rib and Pachmayr English-style recoil pad and white Bradley front sight. The same flawless action and barrels as the Grade I.
Model 1000 Grade II, 12 gauge
Model 1000 Grade II, 20 gauge

MODEL 1000 GRADE III OVER-AND-UNDER
The same basic action and Monobloc barrels as on all the Model 1000 guns. Without receiver engraving. 20-line borderless hand-checkered select American black walnut stock with Pachmayr English-style recoil pad and white Bradley front sight. Ventilated rib.
Model 1000 Grade III, 12 gauge
Model 1000 Grade III, 20 gauge

Mossberg-Pedersen's custom stocked and engraved Beretta S56E barreled actions.

Jagd- und Sport-Bockdopp

Sauer Beretta

ORIGINAL SAUER & SOHN

Programm der 80er Jahre

Neue Erkenntnisse im Waffenbau
veranlaßten Sauer,
die Beretta-Bockdoppelflinten
diesem Stand der Waffentechnik
anzupassen.
Das Ergebnis ist überzeugend.

**Neuartige, solide Konstruktion,
auswechselbare Scharnierzapfen,
automatischer Schlagbolzen-Rücksprung!**

Kaliber und Läufe:
Kaliber 12/70. Lauflänge 71 cm, ¼–¾-
oder ½–¹/₁-choke. Sportflinten mit ande-
rer Lauflänge und Chokebohrung. Mit
Ejektor und innen hartverchromten Läufen, daher korrosionssicher. Monobloc-
Laufverbindung, spannungsfrei durch
weichgelötete Schienenverbindung.
7 mm breite, ventilierte Laufschiene, fein
guillochiert. Mit Neusilber-Perlkorn oder
rotem Leuchtkorn – je nach Modell.

Selbstspannersystem:
Hakenloser Flankenverschluß. Verschluß-
keile und Scharnierzapfen austauschbar.
Geschlossenes Verschlußstück, deshalb
keine Verschmutzungsmöglichkeit. Ser-
vicefreundlich. Hartverchromt, daher rost-
sicher und verschleißfest. Traditionelle
Muschelform. Mit Seitenspiegel. Bruch-
freie Schraubenfedern als Schlagfedern.

Abzug:
Umschaltbarer Einabzug oder Doppelabzug. Der Abzug ist wahlweise auf Ein-
oder Doppelabzug umrüstbar. Rückstoß-
umschaltung.

Modell Sporting mit Ejektor
(ohne Abb.)
Mit feiner Arabeskengravur, Einabzug,
71 cm langen Läufen, 10 mm breiter, ventilierter Schiene, ½–¹/₁-Chokebohrung.
Nr. 71151 **2215,–**

Modell Regent (ohne Abb.)
Mit kleiner Randstichgravur.
Ohne Ejektor.
Mit Einabzug	Nr. 71138	**1586,–**
Mit Doppelabzug	Nr. 71147	**1515,–**
Mehrpreis Linksschaft		**372,–**

Modell Favorit mit Ejektor
Mit feiner englischer Gravur mit Rosetten.
Mit Einabzug	Nr. 71139	**1890,–**
Mit Doppelabzug	Nr. 71148	**1824,–**
Mehrpreis Linksschaft		**372,–**

Modell Diplomat mit Ejektor
Mit reichhaltiger feiner englischer Gravur
mit Bouquets und ventilierter Schiene.
Mit Einabzug	Nr. 71146	**2125,–**
Mit Doppelabzug	Nr. 71145	**2053,–**
Mehrpreis Linksschaft		**372,–**

Beretta Favorit ab 1824,–

Beretta Diplomat ab 2053,–

Beretta Club-Trap **3010,–**

Sauer-Beretta shotguns from the pages of German catalog, Waffen-Franconia, late 1970s. They are the early S680 series made to Germanic taste. The Sauer-Beretta partnership lasted more than 25 years and helped establish the Beretta over/under in Europe.

Despite Beretta's inability to overtake Browning in America, elsewhere in the world the Beretta boxlock over/under enjoyed great success. The highly-respected German gun maker J. P. Sauer & Sohn had Beretta make over/under shotguns for them and sold for many years as Sauer-Beretta (the guns were so marked on the receiver). Something that not all gun enthusiasts are aware of is that in the 1970s, the venerable old British gun maker Holland & Holland imported Beretta S56E barreled actions and stocked, engraved, and finished them in London. To this day Holland & Holland maintains a connection with Beretta; at H&H's London Shooting Grounds, Beretta S686s are being used routinely. In the U.S., there was the Mossberg-Pedersen, a custom gun branch of Mossberg that imported Beretta barreled actions and finished them locally. So it wasn't just the Europeans who recognized the fact that the Beretta boxlock over/unders were of excellent design. The Mossberg-Pedersen Berettas were designated as Model 1000 in three grades. All grades were equipped with single selective trigger, automatic ejectors, and ventilated rib. Grade III was unengraved; Grade II had some engraving; and Grade I was most heavily engraved. All three grades had fancy American walnut stocks with Grade I having the fanciest.

In 1979 Beretta introduced the new 680 series with the S685, S686 and S680. They were beefed-up from the previous S55B series, the ejectors were modified and the hinge pins or stubs were made thicker. Cosmetically the receiver sides were given bosses and the tops of the shoulders were sculpted to give a nice custom touch. Essentially, today the Beretta boxlock over/under is the same as the original S680 series of 1979. But Beretta continually tweaks the design here and there, updating it constantly. In 1980 Beretta redesignated the series as S686 and S687 series, although the competition model S682 was retained.

Perhaps the most significant date for Beretta, when it comes to the U.S. market, was Jan. 14, 1985. On that

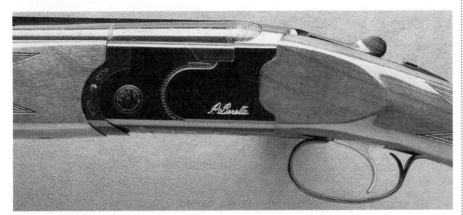

The basic S680 Onyx, a popular platform for restocking by some stateside retailers such as Orvis and Kevin's.

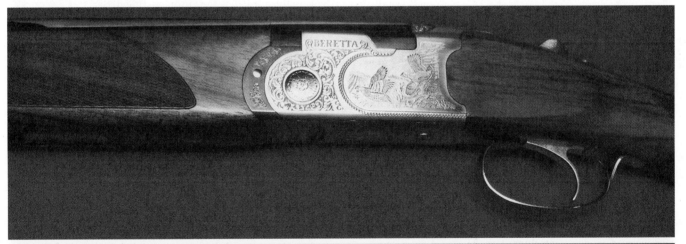

Current production S687 Silver Pigeon III (top) and Silver Pigeon V (bottom).

date the Pentagon announced that the Beretta 92F pistol was the new official U.S. military sidearm, replacing the old Colt 1911A1. The popularity of Beretta guns skyrocketed. After all, if Uncle Sam thought that the Beretta firearm was good enough, surely it was good enough for the average Joe! Even car makers got into the act and Chevrolet came out with a model called Beretta, which I believe resulted in a lawsuit.

In concert with their new status in America as the supplier of the Army's official sidearm, Beretta launched a very aggressive campaign advertising and promoting their line of shotguns. Many champion trap and skeet shooters were recruited to represent Beretta, and naturally, gun writers began to pay notice and write more and more about Beretta shotguns. Although the Beretta boxlock over/under shotguns were always considered to be excellent products, they lacked the kind of exposure and cache that other big name gun companies enjoyed in the U.S. But now, suddenly Beretta began to surge in popularity among shooters in the U.S. across the board; in trap, skeet, sporting clays, and the field.

In the past, whether under J.L. Galef or Garcia Corporation, advertising was not as aggressive as it could have been. Garcia's advertising was a bit more aggressive than Galef's, but still it was not anywhere like that of Browning and Winchester. Even Charles Daly had a stronger advertising campaign promoting their line of Miroku over/unders. But now, operating under its banner, Beretta had a very aggressive campaign. To top it off, now they could claim to be the suppliers of the official U.S. sidearm.

By the 1990s, the Beretta over/under S680 series was solidly established. It was no longer a question of whether they were as good as Brownings, it was now simply a choice based on style and personal preference

If you take the stock off the S680 series Beretta over/under, you will find that the mechanism is very simple and uncomplicated. The machining, inside and out, is beautifully done, much better than on some guns costing twice as much. The selective trigger mechanism – indeed, the entire fire control system – is simplicity itself. This is in stark contrast to some other Beretta guns that seem to have countless little springs and pins. It is no wonder that these barreled actions are a favorite with some custom gun makers. Some of the better-known

S687 EELL "Extra" Model with fine bulino style engraving, which was first rolled-on, then "hand chased."

gun retail sales outfits used to, or still buy, plain Beretta S686 barreled actions, the Onyx model, and restock them in fancy wood. These "semi-custom" guns are somewhat pricey. But then, good wood is awfully expensive and the guns are stocked to custom dimensions.

The Beretta box lock action is an extremely successful design. It is ironic that it took so many years for it to finally be appreciated for what it is: an excellent, simple, yet strong action that is quite simply unique. There is no other over/under boxlock design quite like the Beretta S680 series.

It took some time, but in the last couple of decades, Beretta has finally emerged as a leader in over/under sales in the world. In the U.S. the Browning Citori still appears to have an edge, but in the rest of the world, it is the Beretta S680 series that outsells all others. All one has to do is look at the sporting press from other countries to see that Berettas are by far the most dominant over/under shotguns in the world. Aside from the U.S., Japan might be the only exception to that rule. Although Berettas are popular in Japan, the Japanese have their guns and their own version of the Beretta in the form of the SKB, a Merkel/Beretta hybrid. When you consider the fact that in Japan a Beretta will cost several times more than a similarly-equipped SKB, it is not surprising that most Japanese shooters opt for home-grown shotguns. But in Europe, even in Germany – a country that produces the Krieghoff, Blaser, Merkel, and several

other famous brands – Beretta still gets a big chunk of the market, partly thanks to Sauer who sold the Sauer-Beretta for many years. With favorable trade agreement between countries belonging to the European Union, Berettas are priced competitively with domestic products, so they sell very well. In the United Kingdom, a long-time stronghold of both Winchester Model 101 and Miroku shotguns for Sporting Clays, now more and more shooters are seen with Berettas both for game and clay.

What started as a somewhat unique over/under in 1955 has now literally taken over the over/under shotgun world. According to Beretta USA's Jim Gerondakis, Beretta's shotguns outsell all others by a three to one margin. Of course that includes their very popular semi-automatic shotguns. But according to some sources, Beretta sells more boxlock over/under shotguns world wide than any other maker.

Through the years Beretta has changed the various model designations from time to time and made minor changes. But basically they have remained the same, all with ventilated ribs, single selective trigger and ejectors, for the U.S. market. Currently the basic models start with the unengraved White Onyx (there were Black Onyx and Onyx Pro as well) on up to the side-plated, hand-engraved Diamond Pigeon, with the Silver Pigeon through Silver Pigeon V grades in between. Then there is the S682 Gold E, strictly a competition model, and the new SV 10, which is available in field model only. The SV 10 differs from the S680 series in that aside from the style of sculpting of receiver, it has a quick detachable stock and other changes that Beretta says are improvements. Beretta claims that the SV 10 owes its lineage to the sidelock SO-10, but, at least superficially, it resembles more the boxlock series than the sidelock gun.

There are also the special, very expensive Gallery Models and the top-of-the-heap Giubileo (Jubilee) Models as well as the S687EELL Extra Models. There have also been even less expensive models than the unadorned Onyx. The economy models that resemble the old S55B in appearance were the so-called "Essential," the "White Wing," and its counterpart the "Black Wing," with plain flat-sided receiver lacking the bosses, and the unsculpted shoulder tops. Also, the wood is about as plain as you can get and the middle rib is missing on these models. More recently a similar gun was marketed as the "Silver Perdiz."

There are also the "Ultralight" models with a lightweight alloy receiver that is flat-sided and not sculpted at the fences. They range from plain to fancy versions with gold game scenes. It is hard to keep up with model designation changes. There are numerous special and commemorative models such as the "Ringneck," "Quail," "Ducks Unlimited," and the "King Ranch," just to name a few. Aside from all these different shotgun models, Beretta makes high powered rifles on the same action, a testament to its strength. These are numbered as S689 and vary in grades from S689 Silver all the way to S689EELL. Beretta seems to change things, including model names, every couple of years. Suffice it to say that Beretta appears to have filled every niche for the over/under shotgun.

Recently there has been some talk that the S680 series will be replaced by the so-called "third generation" of Beretta boxlock over/under, the new SV 10. If indeed that is the case, I believe it would be mistake. The new gun supposedly has a host of improvements, but I thought

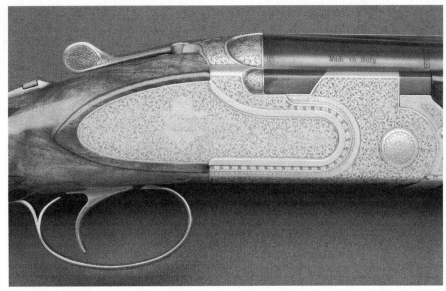

Guibileo ("Jubilee") Model with fine hand engraved scroll. This engraving is not rolled-on!

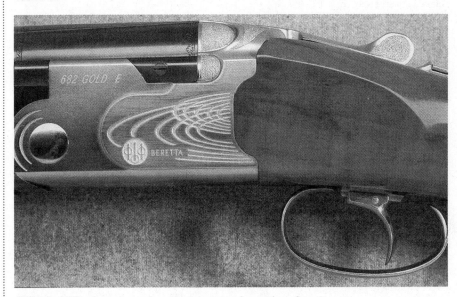

S682 Gold E, a target gun for skeet, trap, and sporting clays.

the S680 series were an improvement over the earlier S55B series. Aside from looking somewhat rakish, I can't see what other changes could have been made to cause a major improvement over the S680 series. But then again, I used to think that the Beretta A303 autoloader would not be replaced for many years. There have

been at least three or four subsequent models, and three or four before! Beretta is constantly changing its line-up, so it is possible that the S680 series will fade away, like the S55B series before.

If that happens, hang on to your old S680 series, if you have one. It is a keeper!

WHAT'S UP DOWN UNDER

Some of the world's greatest hunting can be found in Australia

BY L.P. BREZNY

Australia is to the rifleman what Argentina is to the wingshooter. With its limitless miles of outback hunting and a list of possible game and varmints that goes on almost forever, it is inconceivable that a hunter would ever run out of targets. Game animals ranging from fallow deer to water buffalo abound in selected regions of the country, but it is in the area of specialized goat, hog, dingo, and – yes – kangaroo hunting, where to my way of thinking the best and most flexible field experiences are found.

Late in 2009 I was approached by an outfit dubbed Big Shooter Products

Emu on open flatlands. These large birds are huntable with the proper tags. They're also very good camp meat (referred to by the locals as "tucker food").

out of Blaine, Minnesota (phone 612-386-5771; website www.thebigshooter.com) regarding a possible hunting trip to Queensland, a northeastern state in Australia, the Land Down Under. As a ballistics writer and hunter, I was interested to say the least. These folks were not talking about just flying all the way down there to drop a cap on, say, a buffalo or deer, then heading back across the big pond for home. This hunt would consist of a varied combination of both game and the local varmint-class animals, and it didn't take very long to fully understand that this last category would be just about limitless in scope. With the exception of various types of

Marc was setting up on the gun truck with my .22-250 as we used camo brush cuttings and parked against a billabong steep bank for cover.

Rusa Stag. Big game do exist here, but all have been imported into the country in years back. Photo by Scott Withey, Queensland, Australia.

kangaroos, just about everything else out in the bush country is feral and in effect not an original resident of the country. This non-resident alien animal element, and the fact that many of the animals don't have to face much in the way of natural enemies, makes for population explosions beyond belief at various times. While a kangaroo for example is protected in one district or part of the country, it is open season in another due to overpopulation, and as the Aussies say, "we are at times being overrun with mice," one of their terms for kangaroos.

Hunting Australia can be a real challenge if you don't have the paperwork skids greased in advance. With gun laws that are overly strict and massive regulations and paperwork required when bringing in guns and taking to the field, it is critical to have a very good guide service or booking agent watching your back. As previously indicated, I used Big Shooter Products, with my in-country contact being Marc McDonnell, a local Brisbane area guide. Marc is an expert at getting everything in the government paperwork department done correctly.

In terms of guns, you can't bring any

handguns of any type into Australia. Also, rifles must be confined to single shots, double rifles (English style) or bolt guns. Allowable shotguns include doubles, either side-by-side or over/under, but not standard pump-action shotguns and semi-autos. Bolt- or break-action firearms are accepted as hunting class weapons. In my case I used my guide's stack-barrel Winchester 101 in the scattergun department, and my own custom-built .22-250 crafted by Rhys Precision Gunworks of Wheatland, Wyoming (phone 307-322-1725; email rpg@rhysprecision.net). Coated in a flat shadow-laced gray paint as a camouflage pattern, the rifle fit right into Queensland's Australian outback bush country. The paint pattern was so good, in fact, that I was sure the rifle would be lost if I set it down while in the bush without marking its location. Everything on the rifle was specially glass bead-blasted and then covered with a baked camouflage coating over all metal receiver parts, sights, and mounts.

The Rhys rifle mounts a 21-inch barrel in the R-5 class, a five-groove design that had been exclusive to sniper service in our military for a very long period of time. I would be shooting a medley of different bullets in some hands-on field testing, and the R-5 barrel – which is known for accommodating a wide range of bullet types and weights – was able to group all of them rather well.

With the rifle mounting a Leupold VX 3 at 4.5x14 and a 30mm side-focus tube, the scope quality was not even remotely a question. Good glass sights are mandatory and you want enough quality

The author and blond trophy goat. This 34-inch spread is a good goat by local standards. However, some grow to over 40-inch spreads. That's next time's event for this hunter.

Rabbits are a real threat and not to be kept in this land of massive overpopulation.

in that system to feel confident that it will not fail you in the field. Bouncing over rough ground in a 4x4, or busting through bush country on foot, can have a wearing effect on a sight system, so quality counts in this area of firearms field preparation. My Leupold featured a Boone and Crocket reticule and Jef Rice, the gunsmith rifle builder at Rhys Precision Gunworks, had sent along detailed data covering a 62-grain Berger bullet with 37 grains of Big Game pushing the projectile for starters. After correcting my field zero for Norma 55-grain Oryx factory cartridges at targets out to 400 yards, then adding several other cartridges in the 50- through 55-grain V-Max brand to my list of loads, I felt very confident that this combination of varied loads and the custom Rhys rifle would work out well.

Even the act of transporting a rifle and ammunition into Australia has some very strict requirements attached. Rifles need to be in locked cases that are airline-approved, and the bolt must be removed during transit. A copy of your transport paperwork is best left in the gun case with a second set of papers carried by the traveler. The original paperwork, except for my passport, was being held by my guide just outside Customs in the Brisbane airport.

Your guns also need to be cased with bolts removed when you're transporting them on the road. Also, the rifle or shotgun needs to be housed in a locked container separate from the ammunition. While your guide should know all of this information, it is best to have a working knowledge of the laws yourself, just as an added element of safeguarding your property while in-country. The bottom line here is yes, you can own or travel with a firearm in Australia, contrary to some reports here in America. While the country did confiscate many fine guns in years past, there is a standard that is still adhered to regarding the use of a working field rifle or shotgun Down Under.

Australia has some of the most liberal shooting regulations I have ever encountered in spite of the ridiculous gun ownership laws. The simple fact is that both game and varmints are always on the verge of overrunning the environment out beyond the big cities. Rabbits at one time almost destroyed the sheep and cattle industry, and today if you trap or possess a common live rabbit, you'll be fined a cool $30,000 US dollars and face possible jail time as well. It is hard to even imagine the massive

Billabong (water hole) in the outback. This is the kill zone for taking all sorts of game and varmints. The .22-250 got a workout to be sure near these hot holes.

King Brown snake. One of the most deadly snakes in the world, it'll kill you in minutes if it can. Australia has nine of the top 10 deadliest snakes on the planet. Keeping your eyes open is required when in the bush.

A nice example of a trophy dark phase goat. The .22-250 and Norma 55-grain did a good job on three of these critters during my 11-day hunt.

Kangaroo is some of the best leather in the world. This hide will be a rug in the office upon getting it back home.

population explosion problems these folks in the outback areas of the county face from year to year. One answer is the rifle. It's a good start against this major problem.

As you can clearly see, rifles are tools of the outback trade, and as such commercial market hunting is a major part of the rural economy. Commercial "roo" hunters take on kangaroo and shoot for both the local market and the international export market in meat and hides. I was able to interview professional kangaroo hunters who can make up to $900.00 per night hunting population-dense areas. With specialized off-road Toyota diesel trucks mounting armored front ends and rows of powerful spot lights, the commercial hunters start work at dusk and hunt until dawn.

Australian laws regulate the shooting of kangaroo to the point that head shots must be attempted on standing targets. This is because many hunters will shoot economy types of ammunition in the .222 Remington or .223 class. Also, the animal has most of its vitals well up and above the front legs, thus leaving most of the body as a non-lethal target area and one to be avoided. Because the .222 has always been associated with deadly accuracy, it has been and still is a popular cartridge Down Under. As for the .223, its being based on a military gives it a major following due to the availability of ammunition and its ability to do clean work at medium ranges when head or neck shots are taken.

In general, if you're going to hunt Australia for general game or varmints it is best to stay with one of the more common centerfire cartridges. When reviewing the ammunition selection available in local gun shops, I found that not only were the .222 and .223 very popular among both novice and professional hunters, but the old .303 British, .308 Winchester, .243 Winchester and .30-06 Springfield, as well as my own

Believe it or not, camels abound Down Under. They are often hunted as they infest some areas.

The author with a red roo of a good size for eating.

Marc with a nice white goat that he shot with his custom Magnum Research 6XC Tubbs 6mm and 107-grain Sierra softpoint.

Gun truck set up like most used down under. Small Toyotas with great diesel engines and off-road abilities.

.22-250 Remington, were easy to obtain. Move into the wildcat realm, however, and good luck finding anything to shoot if you run out of cartridges.

When I asked where were the new short magnums being so touted in America, the answer was simple: there was no need to change what was already working just fine. If there is an exception to this direction in cartridge selection, it would be in regard to water buffalo. Here the heavyweights in big-bore calibers are required, or at least suggested, by Australian guides. I was not hunting massively large game save for a few big kangaroo, goats, and fallow deer, and as such my choice in the use of the .22-250 Remington worked out just fine. In fact I believe it is the best of the lot when taking on game from 70-pound young bush hogs to 155-pound trophy-class angora goats and kangaroo.

When shooting my .22-250 rounds for zero and an accuracy check prior to leaving for Australia, I found that in almost every case my groups held at sub-MOA, and with the exception of some small corrections in elevation regarding impact, the R-5 barrel put everything from 50-grain to 60-grain bullets into the vital kill area well out to 300 yards or more.

Norma 55-grain Oryx shot to an average of .540" for three rounds on target, Federal 60-grain Nosler Partition shot to .556", and Black Hills V-Max 50-grain shot to .448" on average. In the field I only sent one bad round at an adult kangaroo, which resulted in a lost animal. In every case there was a slight time delay between bullet impact and the animal going down. I attributed this effect to the fact that while the bullets were deadly choices, they all were somewhat light in weight, and lacked that knockdown power, or whatever it is, we associate with larger-caliber rounds. Over the course of six days shooting my rifle, I accumulated a total of 64 harvested animals ranging from four types of kangaroo to many large hogs and goats. At no time did I feel the effects of any possible bullet failure or a general ability of the .22-250 cartridge being unable to do its job. As is stated by some in this business, the rifle and cartridge were closely matched to the task at hand.

To be sure, Australia's outback is no place to do a great deal of walking and expect to see game. Also with their snake population – home to nine of the 10 deadliest snakes in the world – I was not interested in walking long grass or brush much of the time. This gets back to the

The author with red roo. This was a solid 300-yard poke with Norma fodder. One-shot kill.

4x4 vehicle, and again by way of the tough compact Toyota that is a major part of the field-gunning approach to both game and varmints. Most trucks in the outback carry extra tanks of fresh water, fuel, and enough supplies to camp for several days if required. Leaving a stock station you always have a radio, cell phone, and ground directional plan that is left with someone at the station. The outback is unforgiving, and here is where your guide is very important for both bringing together a successful hunt and keeping you in one piece during the event.

Our HiLux Toyota hunting truck ran on a small four-cylinder diesel engine and mounted extra tires and wheels. We did indeed need two of these tires over the course of our 2,300 kilometer hunt. Because the power plants are small and very efficient, mileage is quite good, as is required of a far-ranging machine that takes on some of the most desolate but grandest country I have ever experienced.

Mounted on the truck's box are a set of elevated shooting chairs and a large flat steel bench setup. Protective piping is installed all around the gun positions for the shooter's safety, protecting him or her from tree branches that frequently hit the rig when the truck is moving. Hunters make use of short bipod rests that are easily moveable over the surface of the wide and deep flat steel surfaces above the trucks' cab. This system is well thought-out for long-range shooting and is one major reason the hit-per-rounds fired average turned out to be very

The author's walla roo. These shaggy critters are big and make outstanding rugs.

Hogs were abundant down under. Wild and made for some fast-action shooting.

The author's sweet custom .22-250 from Rhys Precision. This rifle has it all and did it all. Never a glitch.

good on my hunt. A good solid shooting position is everything when kangaroo are bouncing ahead of the vehicle down a deep draw, and a single shot is all you might get when they hit an obstruction that slows them a bit.

Hunting Australia is very much like hunting Africa or any other very different foreign country. Even though the people in general are very nice and helpful to Americans, the use of a quality guide service and booking agency is still mandatory. This is not a place to be a do-it-yourself hunter, as that approach will just not work out at all.

In terms of cost, I hunted for a total of six days in the field on an 11-day trip for just over $3000 US. This included my airfare from central South Dakota to my boots on the ground in Brisbane. I estimate that a major Northern Territory hunt for water buffalo and crocodile would run about $18,000 and change. It's a big difference in price, but it involves more flying, more game fees, and more time in-country, and that adds up quickly. What you won't find is added fees tacked on because you want to shoot goats or hogs when encountered during, say, a kangaroo hunt. Kangaroo tags are bought in a block of more than a hundred for under $75.00 US, and that's about it for license fees as I experienced the hunt.

Because Australia is a very unique country – clean and friendly – I believe it has the makings of the hunt of a lifetime. Now eight months after my first hunt I'm on my way back Down Under because I miss the place already. For the most part I can't commercial-hunt elk or even deer in the American west for what an Australian varmint/deer hunt costs me – and for that I get to visit one of the most unique sporting locations on the planet!

CAPE BUFFALO REALLY ARE TOUGH!

BY BILL PACE

As Jack O'Connor once said,
"There is little argument about buffalo being a hard animal to stop
and a hard animal to kill. You almost have to shoot it to pieces!"
You'll get no argument from the author.

My Jeffrey .500 double rifle with all its goodies. Note the size of the cartridges.

"Bill, those bullets will let you down; they're too soft. Cape buffalo have tough skin and muscles and their ribs overlap. You need a hard cast bullet!" The speaker was Ross Seyfried, well known guru on old double rifles. The bullet in question was Woodleigh's 440-gr. 50-caliber softpoint. Further input from Dave Scovill also confirmed the need for a "hard cast bullet." So some of Finn Aagaard's old cast bullet linotype quickly turned into "hard cast" .50 calibers weighing 435 grains as I prepared for my first African hunt with HHK Safaris.

My rifle was a Jeffery .500 BPE shown in Jeffery's records as sold in 1893; alas, no original buyer's name was found. This rifle was regulated for the normal .500x3" BPE load of 136 grains of Curtis & Harvey # 6 Diamond grade powder and either an expanding 340-gr. lead "tubed" bullet at 1,950 feet per second, or a 380-gr. lead solid at 1,850 fps. (Kynoch later loaded a 440-gr. jacketed soft point in a "Nitro for Black" cartridge at 1,900 fps). It took some fancy stepping on my part to work up loads for the heavier bullets necessary for buffalo that would regulate well enough for "minute of buffalo heart." I ended up loading three different bullets for my adventure with old *Syncerus caffer caffer* and a 350-gr. Hawk JSP for lesser game.

Loads finally developed and African dirt under my feet, I got my opportunity to test the buffalo's fabled toughness. In an exciting shoot-out that started with a running bull at 9 yards and ended 10 shots later at 12-15 yards, all the warnings and admonishments I had heard were confirmed! My front-and-back sketches at the time shows the placement of the bullet holes – the impact

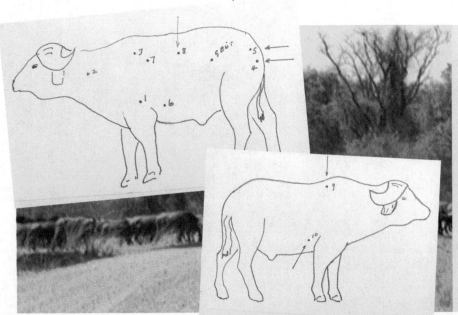

Probable Shot Placement Effects:

1. Obviously fatal; it hit the top of the heart and both lungs. It really shows their indomitable life force.
2. May have gone over spine, but did not exit the heavy neck muscle.
3. Probably nicked the scapula; may have gotten top of lung.
4. Fractures left femur.
5. May also have hit the femur or joint. A fragment of jacket exited the flank.
6. Just missed heart; may have gotten edge of lungs.
7. Into top of lungs.
8. Possibly top of spleen; missed the spine.
9. Missed spine; into lungs.
10. Into edge of liver and lung.

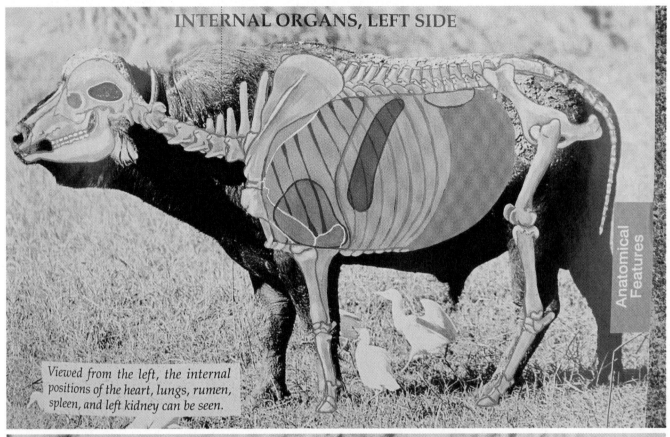

INTERNAL ORGANS, LEFT SIDE

Viewed from the left, the internal positions of the heart, lungs, rumen, spleen, and left kidney can be seen.

Anatomical Features

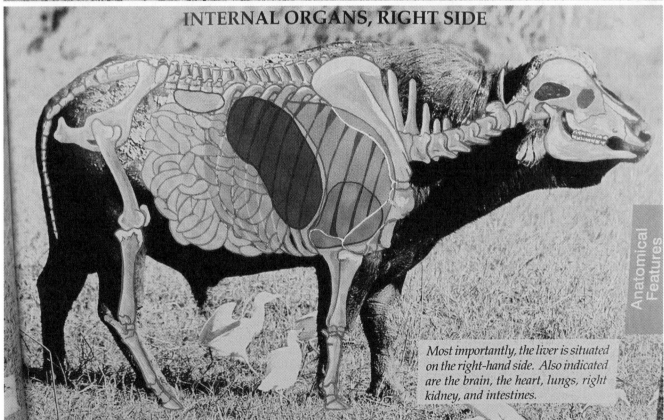

INTERNAL ORGANS, RIGHT SIDE

Most importantly, the liver is situated on the right-hand side. Also indicated are the brain, the heart, lungs, right kidney, and intestines.

Anatomical Features

Knowing the location of internal organs of the game species you are hunting is invaluable. These excellent anatomical pictures are courtesy of Dr. Kevin Robertson, better known as "Doctari," from his recent book *Buffalo Shot Placement and Trophy Evaluation*, published by Safari Press. His intimate knowledge of game animal anatomy has been a boon to the hunting world.

Mopani thicket. If you look carefully, you can just make out the hunter in the bush.

locations on the old fellow tell how hectic the action was. As you can see, I used the whole animal!!

Except for shots one, four, five and 10, I shot at and hit what little I could see in the thick Mopani bush. Shot number one was at the running bull's shoulder at about 9 yards; numbers two and three at a "black spot" in the brush at about 12 yards with the bull facing towards 7 o'clock, apparently looking through the brush at us; shots four and five were into the buff's hindquarters as he was running away at about 15-18 yards. One or both of these shattered his left femur.

Then came the wonderful "death bellow" from further in the bush. "He's down, let's go!" our professional hunter Lou Hallamore exclaimed. But oddly, despite the death bellow, he was *not* down! We found him standing in some very thick stuff, well screened at 15 yards. Lou was excitedly telling me, "Shoot – shoot! He's still on his feet!" I fired the sixth and seventh shots as fast as the front sight found black in the

bush, shot number 7 while I was still in recoil. The bull went down, but at that moment neither of us was very "cool," as the death bellow is usually considered a conclusive sign of death and this bull had already proven itself a notable exception to that rule. Lou's "better hit him some more" didn't get any argument from me! Shots number eight and nine went into his shoulder as "finishers" as he lay on his left side.

Shot number 10 provided yet more excitement. The bull down, we approached him carefully from the rear, rifles at the ready. It was completely unmoving; no labored breathing, no anything. Before Lou could complete the usual "eye touch," I took a step too near, just inside the outstretched front legs. I was shocked when his head lifted and then swung up!

Lou barked, "Hit him in that white spot!" and I hastened to comply, as you might imagine. (There is an area behind the foreleg where little hair grows, thus the white spot.) The *coup de gras* came at less than 30 inches.

After the excitement had faded, I made a somewhat sober evaluation of hit locations and animal stance at each shot. Remembering Seyfried's and Scoville's remarks, I realized how true they were. Despite all shots being under 20 yards, none of the 10 rounds exited the animal (though a fragment of number five tore a small hole in the side). Several bullets were found under the offside skin. Even the last round, a 350-grain Hawk softpoint at 1,950 fps fired at such close range, did not exit, and expanded to more than an inch!

I was quite amazed: nine rounds consisting of 440-gr. Woodleighs, 400-gr. thick jacketed Hawks, and 435-gr. hard-cast bullets, fired at a minimal velocity of 1860 fps at close range with none getting through that leathery, elastic skin on the far side. Unfortunately, none of the recovered bullets were Woodleigh softpoints, which were designed for behind the shoulder heart and lung shots; not penetrators. I would like to have examined them, but they were probably lost during the field butchery

Good old dagga-boy.

Old bull; old rifle; old hunter!

required to load the bull and transport him to the skinning shed. (An important comment: Nothing was wasted. The hide went for leather; all the meat was used for food. This is typical in Africa; people are protein-poor and game meat is a real boon for them. All the body cavity contents were used for lion bait.)

After 10 hits, a very obvious question arises from my experience: is the .500 BPE an adequate caliber for buffalo? I will say yes, with the usual caveat, only as long as you have a well-armed experienced P.H. as back-up whose rifle is a stopper. With a "marginal" rifle, the first shot placement is even more paramount; thankfully my first shot was a heart shot and, as Berit said, my "first shot killed him…he just didn't know it!" Mr. Bull would have died shortly, but unusual circumstances allowed me to pour in more lead, all in two to three minutes.

But is the old .500 a "stopper"? My experience indicates that it isn't, if we define "stopper" to mean a cartridge that can be relied on to drop a Cape Buffalo in its tracks – though a brain or spine shot with any reasonable caliber "stops 'em." (I discovered how effective the .500 BPE could be when I spined a huge 2,500+-lb. Asian bull with this same rifle in the Northern Territory of Australia. The result was incredibly dramatic as he literally crashed to the ground, dust and gravel flying.) Would I hunt buffalo with it again? In fact I did, a few years later, and made a one-shot kill.

Like most hunters, I have read for years about the buffalo's incredibly dense bones, hard muscle, puncture-proof hide and fierce nature. Until I experienced this hunt, however, I didn't grasp – really could not conceive of – such vitality. Now I better understand how that formidable tenacity for life, coupled with wariness and an aggressive nature have combined to make them one of the world's most truly dangerous animals. The potential for disaster is always very real when you trespass into a Cape buff's territory.

Today all my doubts and questions about the toughness of Cape buffalo have been answered. Despite their threatening stare, so well described by Ruark, it's their innate vitality and unpredictable violent nature that makes our adrenaline rush so when we face a big, old dagga boy. They truly deserve their reputation and our respect.

Yes, they really are tough!

REPORT FROM THE FIELD:
NEW RIFLES

BY **TOM TABOR**

I am always amazed at the creativity and innovation displayed by the world's firearms manufacturers. No matter which area of shooting discipline you enjoy, the inventiveness these companies bring to the table each year is truly something to be admired.

This year, has brought significant expansion in the area of scaled-down rifles specifically dedicated to the younger and/or lighter-framed shooter; significant improvements in trigger and stock designs; emphasis on lighter-weight hunting rifles; and within your favorite models it is likely that you will find a larger selection of cartridge chamberings.

There continues to be a growing interest in tactical and AR style firearms, not only for the traditional police and military usage but also for hunting purposes. And in order to meet those new challenges, a higher degree of emphasis has been placed on accuracy and better performing cartridges within that so called "black rifle" category.

With that said, the following are a few specific examples of the improvements you can expect to see on your dealer's shelves.

Browning

Browning has capitalized on the growing interest in shooting sports by the ladies and younger shooters with the introduction of the company's new Micro Midas X-Bolt bolt-action rifle. This rifle features a 20-inch barrel and a shorter 12-1/2-inch LOP black walnut stock topped off with an Inflex Technology recoil pad. The wood/metal surfaces are nicely matched with a satin finish on the stock and a low-luster bluing of the metal parts. Currently the Browning Micro Midas X-Bolt is available chambered in .22-250 Remington, .243 Winchester, 7mm-08 Remington and the .308 Winchester. It comes with a suggested retail price of $799.99.

Browning is also now offering their X-Bolt Medallion, X-Bolt Hunter and the X-Bolt Micro Hunter model rifles in left-hand versions. This expansion within their current lines allows the lefties to take full advantage of all the innovative features currently available in the newest of Browning's bolt-action rifles. Those features include the Feather Trigger, X-Lock scope mounting system, detachable rotary magazine and Inflex Technology recoil pads. Suggested retail prices for the left hand versions range from $869.99 to $1,039.99.

Bushmaster

Not too long ago Bushmaster released their innovated new Adaptive Combat Rifle (ACR), which has redefined the term "modular" when it comes to rifles. The ACR was the product of a joint collaboration between Bushmaster, Magpul and Remington Arms, culminating in a design that allows the user to quickly and easily change calibers, barrel lengths and stock configurations without the need of a single tool. It includes an AD flash hider, adjustable 2-position gas piston system and full ambidextrous controls. It is available in three different designs, each built with a specific purpose in mind. Recently

Browning Micro Midas X-Bolt rifle

Bushmaster Adaptive Combat Rifle
(ACR) Basic Folder (right hand)

Bushmaster .308 AR Hunter Rifle

the company further expanded their ACR line to include the new ACR Optics Ready Carbine (ORC), ACR Basic Folder and ACR State Compliant versions.

Bushmaster has also focused on the growing interest in the use of the ARs for hunting purposes with their new Bushmaster 308 Hunter Rifle. Combining the benefits inherent in the AR platform with the recognized big game killing capabilities of the .308 Winchester cartridges is sure to appeal to a great many sportsmen. In my personal opinion this rifle is a pleasant blend of features. Not only does it have all the necessary capabilities to make it a fine hunting rifle, Bushmaster has seen fit to deviate from the usual blasé military AR styling in order to make it much more pleasing to the eye.

Citadel

The M-1 Carbine played a significant and important role for our U.S. troops during World War II and the Korean conflict. Being scaled back in both size and weight from the 30-06 M-1 Garrand rifle, the M-1 Carbine became the preferred weapon for many artillery crew officers, tankers, drivers, mortar crews and other infantrymen during these conflicts. Unfortunately, today it is difficult to find one of the original military rifles on the open market, but the good news is that Citadel is now producing a reproduction rifle that is built to the exacting specifications of the G.I. model. The one major difference is that rather than firing the expensive .30 Carbine cartridges the Citadel rifle is chambered for the fun and economical-to-shoot .22 long rifle ammo. The Citadel M-1 .22 Carbine is available

equipped with either a synthetic, or the more traditional black walnut stock. They come with a 6-groove, 1:16 twist, 18-inch barrel, adjustable rear sight and a 10-round magazine. Overall length is 35 inches and the weight is a very modest 4.5 to 4.75-pounds. Suggested retail price is $331.

Cooper Firearms of Montana

In recent years Cooper Firearms of Montana has substantially expanded their family of rifles to include a much more diverse selection of calibers. The most recent of those new offerings is a magnum length bolt-action rifle the company has dubbed their Model 56. This latest addition is specifically intended for the 7mm Remington Magnum/300 Winchester Magnum family of belted

Citadel M-1 .22 Carbine

Cooper Firearms of Montana Model 56
Magnum Length Rifle

CZ-USA Model 455 American Switch Barrel Combo
Rifle available in .22 LR and .17 HMR

CZ-USA Model 512 Semi-automatic rifle available in
.22 LR or .22 WMR calibers

magnum cartridges, ranging from the .257 Weatherby Mag. up to and including the big .340 Weatherby Magnum. Like all Cooper Firearms the new 56 is a work of gunsmithing art and is available in a wide variety of options. Currently it can be ordered in the Cooper styles of: Classic, Custom Classic, Western Classic, Jackson Game, Jackson Hunter, or the Excalibur. Depending upon the styling, the weight runs from 8 up to 8.5-pounds. MSRP begins at $2,795.for either the Classic or Jackson Hunter (synthetic) up to the Western Classic priced at $4,395. Left hand versions are also available, but incur an additional charge of $250. And, as usual with Cooper's rifles there are various optional upgrades available on a special-order basis.

CZ-USA

Today there is growing interest in the advantages inherent with switch-barrel rifles and that fascination by shooters has not gone unnoticed by CZ-USA. The company's new CZ 455 American Switch Barrel Combo Package permits the user to easily switch barrels back and forth as needed to shoot either .22 LR or .17 HMR. This combination package comes inherent with a barrel chambered and designed for each cartridge and everything you need for switching. The Model 455 will eventually consolidate all of the receivers currently used in the company's Model 452 line of rifles into one single common platform. This will allow the CZ 455 shooter to not only switch calibers, but also change stock configuration quickly and easily. The new CZ 455 rifle has retained the same adjustable trigger, hammer-forged barrel and billet-machined receiver as used on the CZ 452s. Improvements that the 455 bring to the table include new manufacturing technology and closer tolerances for improved accuracy and smoother opera-

tions. The CZ 455 American Switch Barrel Package includes one 5-round magazine for each of the two calibers and the wrenches needed for the barrel switch for a suggested retail price of $531.

Also entirely new this year at CZ is the Model 512 Semi-automatic rifle, which comes in the choice of .22 LR or .22 WMR calibers. The action of the 512 is composed of an aluminum alloy upper receiver that secures the barrel and bolt assembly and a fiberglass-reinforced polymer lower that houses the trigger assembly and detachable magazine. The magazine and scope rings of the CZ 512 are interchangeable with the bolt-action CZ 455 rifles, making them perfect companion rifles. The features of the CZ 512 include dual guide rods for smooth operation and reliability, an accurate hammer forged barrel, adjustable sights and an integral 11mm dovetail for easy scope mounting. Suggested retail price is $449. for the .22 LR and $479.for the .22 WMR.

Heckler & Koch Model MR556A1 Rifle

Howa Talon Fluted Black Rifle

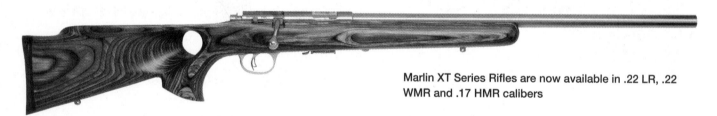

Marlin XT Series Rifles are now available in .22 LR, .22 WMR and .17 HMR calibers

Heckler & Koch

HK continues to expand their line of semi-automatic AR-type carbines and rifles with their new Model MR556A1. This rifle is a direct descendent of the HK416 and like that rifle, the MR556A1 does not introduce propellant gases and carbon fouling back into the rifle's interior, thereby providing a higher degree of functional reliability. Many of the same assemblies and accessories originally developed for the HK416 can be utilized on the MR556A1, including the free-floating four-quadrant rail system (FFRS). This hand-guard system accepts all the current accessories, sights, lights, and aimers, which are commonly used on M4/M16-type firearms. The HK rail system comes with the added benefit of being able to be installed and removed without the use of tools and with no fear of changing the bullet impact point. Both U.S. and German-made component parts are used in the construction. Suggested retail price is $2,995.

Howa

Howa is offering a number of advancements and improvements in their firearms this year, including optional fluted barrels for select models within their M-1500 line of rifles. This translates into reduced weight and better heat dissipation. These new barrels are available within the Howa Talon, Howa Heavy Barrel Varminter and Howa/Hogue series rifles. A few of the other cool features within Howa are some great looking laminated thumbhole stocks, a new rwo-stage trigger for improved accuracy, a Howa logo-etched floor plate and the blued Howa M-1500 rifles will now feature a blued bolt. In addition, the company is also offering new detachable magazines for Howa and Weatherby Vanguard rifles from Adaptive Technologies, Inc. These are available in either 5 or 10-round capacity for rifles in .223 or .308 and similar styled optional magazines will soon be available for .22-250.

Marlin

For the past 120 years Marlin has been instrumental in producing a broad array of rimfire firearms. The most recent of those is the company's new Marlin XT Series rifles, which include a wide variety of choices and many inherent favorable features. In all there are 28 different rifles within this series,

Marlin XT-Youth Model Rifle

including several youth models. All of these rifles are equipped with the newly designed XT Pro-Fire® trigger, developed to provide ease of adjustability, crispness, accuracy and safety. The XT Pro-Fire triggers are user adjustable from 3 to 6 pounds pull and for an added degree of security, a new trigger safety has been added prohibiting the rifle from firing until the safety has been fully depressed. These new rimfire rifles come in a wide variety of stock configurations, including those made of wood, laminates and synthetics. Within the wood category there is a Monte Carlo walnut-finished hardwood stock, a hardwood laminate, and an American black walnut stock, all coming with a finish of Mar-Shield clear-coat. The calibers available within the XT Series are .22 LR, .22 WMR and .17 HMR.

For the first time, Marlin is offering several rifles specifically dedicated to young shooters. Appropriately called the XT-Youth Models, these rifles feature a shorter length of pull, shorter trigger reach, smaller pistol grip and a raised

comb. And if that isn't enough, the company has also designed the actions to require less force to open the bolt, making ejection and chambering faster and easier for those young muscles.

Suggested retail price for the adult sized XT Series rifles is from $213.26 up to $450.63. The XT-Youth Models carry a suggested retail price starting at $219.31 up to $247.31.

Nosler

In 1948 John Nosler began marketing his legendary Nosler Partition bullets. In an effort to keep that milestone date alive and as a tribute to the man who built the company, Nosler dubbed their rifles the Model 48. Over the years the 48 has grown to include a couple of different submodels, including the Hunter, Varmint and even a limited edition offering. Recently in order to fully compliment Nosler's Varmint Rifle Series, two new chamberings has been added: the .223 Remington and the ever-growing popular .204 Ruger. The

Model 48 Varmint features a matte black Cerakote finish on all exterior metals. A coating of MicroSlick is also applied to the interior metals, which provide maximum corrosion protection and wear-resistance. To encourage the highest degree of accuracy, these rifles come with a crisp 3-lb. trigger, a hand-lapped 24-inch free-floated match-grade stainless heavy-contour barrel, hand-laid, desert sand colored Kevlar stock and a glass-bedded action. All this combines to allow the company to provide a phenomenal performance guarantee of half-inch 3-shot groups at 100-yards (when Nosler ammunition is used). MSRP for the Model 48 Varmint is $2,995.

Remington

The Remington Model 700 has been a favorite of shooters ever since its introduction a half a century ago in 1962. During that long reign the 700 has become the preferred choice by hunters worldwide; it has frequently dominated a diverse variety of shooting competitions;

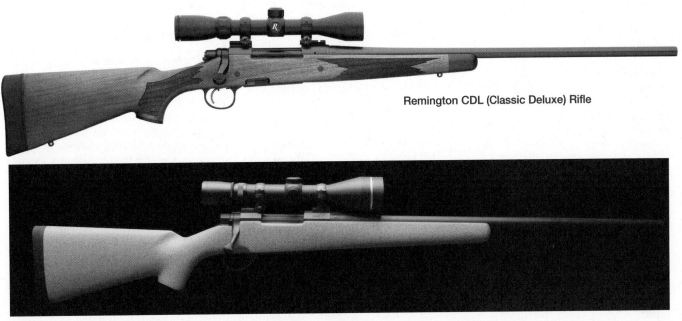

Remington CDL (Classic Deluxe) Rifle

Nosler Model 48 Varmint Rifle available in .223 and .204 Ruger calibers

and it has been used and embraced by the U.S. military and many policing agencies. Remington continues to expand and make improvements to this showcase of models with one of the company's best selling choices: the Model 700 CDL (Classic Deluxe).

Some of the noteworthy features included within the CDL subset of rifles include: a receiver machined from solid-steel bar stock; a recessed bolt face that locks up inside the counter-bored breech of the barrel while surrounded by the receiver, forming three rings of steel around the cartridge case head; integral extractors set in a groove inside the rim of the bolt face; and a new trigger design called the X-Mark Pro Trigger. Unlike most adjustable rifle triggers, the X-Mark Pro permits the shooter to adjust the pull weight without the necessity of removing the stock. Some more of the favorable and noteworthy features include a choice of either left- or right-hand models, fluted or non-fluted barrels and a limited edition stainless steel model chambered in 6mm Remington. The company has recently added a detachable box magazine model. Suggested retail price for the Model 700 CDL begins at $959.

Ruger

Through a joint effort with Gunsite instructor Ed Head, Ruger has added a new platform within their M77 family of rifles they call their Gunsite Scout Rifle. Believed to be the ideal "fighting carbine," this new addition is a credible rendition of Col. Jeff Cooper's Scout Rifle concept. It comes chambered for the well-respected .308 Winchester cartridge and is relatively lightweight and hard-hitting. It's essentially a do-all rifle that in the right hands has the ability to place accurate, sustained firepower at long range, yet is quick-handling and light enough to be carried all day in the field. The rifle comes with a 16.5-inch long, medium contour, cold hammer-forged, alloy steel barrel, which is equipped with

Ruger's Gunsite Scout Rifle

a Mini-14 protected non-glare post front sight and a receiver mounted adjustable ghost ring rear sight. A forward mounted Picatinny rail allows the mounting of a wide variety of optical products. Seemingly, the perfect add-on for this rifle would be a scope like Leupold's FX-II 2.5x28mm IER Scope, or one of the Burris extended eye relief models. By mounting the scope farther away from the shooter's eye it encourages shooting with both eyes open for a faster sighting and target acquisition and there is never a chance of getting hit in the eye with the rim of the scope.

The Ruger Gunsite Scout Rifle features a matte black oxide alloy steel barrel and receiver and a black laminate weather resistant stock, which comes with sling swivel studs installed and a checkered grip and forearm. Three half-inch spacers have been provided between the rubber recoil pad and the stock, permitting the length of pull to be varied from 12.75 to 14.25 inches. The trigger guard and magazine are formed from glass-reinforced nylon and a 10-round magazine comes with each rifle. The suggested retail price for the Ruger Gunsite Scout Rifle is $995.

Sako

The popularity of big-bore rifles has never been greater than they are today and if you're like me, the sight of a rifle barrel that could double as a stovepipe is certain to get your blood pumping. That being the case, I'm pretty sure you will like what Sako is offering in their

new limited edition Model 85 Safari Rifles, or what I would prefer to call, "rifles that are dedicated to those critters than have a tendency to stomp, gore, claw or bite you to death." These rifles are built around the Sako 85 size L and XL actions designed with Sako's Round Control System and integral dovetail rails for scope mounting. Their presentation-grade stocks come with hand-cut checkering and are accented with an ebony fore-end tip and pistol grip cap of the same material. Four calibers are available including the .375 H&H (built on the L action), the .416 Rigby, the .450 Rigby, and my personal favorite, the .500 Jeffrey (built on the Sako XL 85 action). And, when it comes to the best-of-the-best, Sako is offering a very limited run of 90th Anniversary Safari Grade Rifles, all chambered in .450 Rigby. Only 10 of these rifles will be built and each will feature individually engraved actions. Three will be sold at various tradeshow auctions, the Beretta Galleries will sell six, and the remaining one will permanently reside in Sako's Riihimaki, Finland showroom.

Savage Arms

The firearms produced by Savage Arms are no longer the guns of your grandfather. In recent years, under the specific direction of Ron Coburn, Owner/CEO of Savage, the company has moved into the role as a major and well-respected player within the firearms manufacturing community. In my opinion the rifles built by Savage are some of the best and most accurate of any found

Savage Light Weight Hunter Model 11/111 Rifle

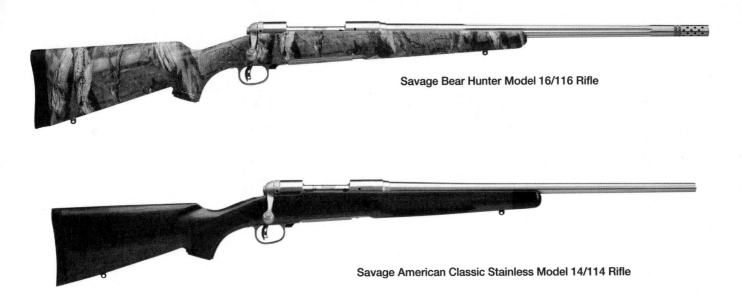

Savage Bear Hunter Model 16/116 Rifle

Savage American Classic Stainless Model 14/114 Rifle

today. And possibly best of all, you won't have to mortgage the homestead to pay for them. One of the many new choices within the Savage line today is the Light Weight Hunter 11/111. This lightweight, walk-about style rifle has a starting weight of only 5.5-pounds for the short actions and 6 pounds in the long action rifles. They feature a slimmed down oil-finished American Walnut stock, AccuTrigger, hinged floorplate and a light-taper 20-inch barrel. Suggested retail is $875.

Also new is the company's Bear Hunter 16/116 Model, which is elegantly equipped with a polymer Mossy Oak Infinity AccuStock, an AccuTrigger, and a hinged floorplate featuring an attractive bear paw logo. It is available in a range

of both long and short action calibers, including the popular .325 WSM. Suggested retail price starts at $939.00 and runs to $973. There is also a Model 25 Walking Varminter, which features a synthetic stock and weighs in at less than 7 pounds in .223 Rem., .204 Ruger, .22 Hornet, .222 Rem. and 5.7x28 calibers for a suggested retail price of $551.

In addition, Savage has expanded the available features and choices for many of their other rifles including: the Model 12 Long Range Precision, AXIS Stainless, 14/114 American Classic Stainless and the Model 110 Predator Hunter Max I and enhanced several other models with threaded muzzles to accommodate aftermarket suppressors or muzzle brakes.

Stag Arms

Owners of the new Stag Arms Model 3 can say hello to the company's new and improved Diamondhead V-RS. This is the only modular mil-spec drop-in handguard platform that can be used with or without accessory rails and is said to be the most adaptable drop-in handguard currently offered for the M4/AR15s. The V-RS can be accessorized with short and/or full length Picatinny rail tracks, or fitted with full length smooth "bumpers" that provide an ergonomically contoured handguard. The new Stag Model 3 ships complete with the versa rail base at no extra charge. Suggested retail price for the Model 3 is $895.

Stag Arms Model 3 with the new and improved Diamondhead V-RS

Steyr Arms Model SSG 08 Long Range Tactical Rifle now available in .338 Lapua Magnum caliber

Steyr Arms

The first Steyr SSG 08 long range tactical rifle made its debut back in 2009 but recently the company has upped the ante with a brand new adaptation chambered in what many believe to be the ultimate long-range tactical cartridge, the .338 Lapua Magnum. This new version was released only after the prototype rifle underwent a grueling 10,000-round endurance and reliability testing at Steyr's Austrian factory. The SSG 08 is based on Steyr's unique Safe Bolt System (SBS) action, which is bedded in a skeletonized aluminum stock. The stock is equipped with an UIT rail (running the length of the forend), an adjustment cheek piece and buttplate, an integrated, finely adjustable rear-elevation pod and a butt capable of being folded forward for transport. For further versatility there are also multiple mounting points for attaching a wide variety of Picatinny rail-mounted accessories. The enclosed detachable box magazine holds

six of the big .338 Lapua Mag. rounds and the rifle comes with a Versa-pod, or heavy-duty bi-pod, and a hard travel case. Recommended retail price for .338 Lapua Mag. chambered Steyr SSG 08 is $6,795.

Weatherby

Weatherby is now offering a combo package, including everything needed to get you shooting as quickly as possible. It includes their famous Vanguard Synthetic rifle, known for its guaranteed accuracy, and a versatile Simmons 3.5-10x40mm scope equipped with the company's TrueZero technology. The Vanguard Synthetic includes a factory-tuned fully adjustable trigger, 24-inch hammer-forged barrel, a black injection-molded composite Monte Carlo style stock and a low-density recoil pad. All of the Vanguard series rifles are based on the company's legendary Mark V action and come with a one-piece machined bolt, fully enclosed bolt sleeve and

three rings of steel surrounding the case head for an extra measure of strength and structural integrity. This combo set comes guaranteed to be capable of placing three shots within an inch and a half at 100 yards when premium factory ammo is fired from a cold barrel. It is currently available only in a right-hand version and comes in the calibers of .243 Winchester, .270 Winchester, .308 Winchester, .30-06 Springfield, .257 Weatherby Mag. and .300 Weatherby Mag. The manufacturer's suggested retail price, including the rifle, scope, Leupold Rifleman rings and bases, is a modest $629.

Weatherby takes accuracy even further in the company's new Vanguard Series 2 (S2) rifles, guaranteeing accuracy down to under sub-MOA (3-shot group of .99-inch or under at 100 yards) when firing factory or premium grade ammunition. To be released in Spring 2011, this new rifle series will be offered in either blued or stainless and will feature a new two-stage match quality target trigger

Weatherby Vanguard Synthetic Combo Rifle Package including the Vanguard rifle, Simmons 3.5-10x40mm scope, Leupold Rifleman rings and bases.

Weatherby Vanguard S2 Blued Rifle equipped with the Griptonite stock

Winchester Model 94 Sporter available in either .30-30 Winchester
or .38-55 Winchester calibers

Winchester Featherweight Compact Model

and a 24-inch barrel. The trigger is adjustable down to 2.5 pounds pull weight and has an auxiliary sear pre-set with a sear engagement of .008"-.012". The non-slip panels and a right-side palm swell of the Griptonite stock make the S2 stock functionally efficient and give it a slightly contemporary look. Both the blued and stainless versions come with the metal matte bead-blasted, producing a non-glare finish. Total rifle weight is approximately 7.25 pounds. The blued version is available in 15 calibers from .22-250 up to .300 Win. Mag. and the stainless rifles come in a choice of eight calibers from .223 up to 7mm Rem. Mag. The blued S2 rifles carry a MSRP of $450. and the stainless comes in at $600.

Winchester Repeating Arms

Winchester continues to expand their rifle choices this year to include a new Model 94 Sporter that is elegantly equipped with a 24-inch half-round/half-octagon blued barrel, a straight traditional grip and a classic crescent-shaped blued steel buttplate. The stock is finely checkered and finished in a satin oil finish with the receiver drilled and tapped for scope mounts. Currently this rifle is offered in the traditional .30-30 Winchester, or the historic .38-55 Winchester. Suggested retail price is $1,129.99.

The Model 70 Winchester continues to be one of the most popular rifles available and this year the company has added a new Featherweight Compact Model to its line. This rifle's light 6-1/2 lb. weight makes it near perfect for smaller-framed shooters, ladies, young people, or for those of us who spend long and hard days afield in the high country. It comes with the Pre-64 controlled round feeding design, a three-position safety, jeweled bolt body, knurled bolt handle, adjustable M.O.A. Trigger System and a 20-inch barrel. The walnut stock is satin finished, checkered, and equipped with a Pachmayr Decelerator Pad. Available cartridge choices include .22-250 Remington, .243 Winchester, 7mm-08 Remington and .308 Winchester calibers. Suggested retail price is $899.99.

NEW SHOTGUNS

BY JOHN HAVILAND

Firearm sales set a brisk pace the last few years due mainly to fears of gun control from the current administration in Washington. Those worries have eased with a resulting turn down of guns sales, particularly handguns. Shotgun sales, though, have declined the least and companies continue to introduce new shotguns, especially for the tactical and turkey hunting markets. Let's see what is new for this year for shotgun shooters.

Benelli

In keeping with the premise of bigger is better, Benelli has chambered its Vinci 12-gauge shotgun for 3 1/2-inch shells and called it the Super Vinci. The Super weighs 7 pounds, which is only a couple ounces heavier than the 3-inch Vinci. In comparison, Benelli's Super Black Eagle II weighs 7.3 pounds. A 3-inch 12 gauge shell should accomplish any shotgun killing required by hunters, but many hunters like having the option

of shooting the 3 1/2-inch shells loaded with steel shot for goose hunting.

The standard Super Vinci comes with a black synthetic stock and forearm with a matching matte finish on the metal. Realtree MAX-4 or APG camo patterns that completely cover the gun are optional. Barrel lengths are 26 or 28 inches with screw-in chokes of cylinder (C), improved cylinder (IC), modified (M), improved modified (IM) and full (F). The stock detaches from the receiver with a simple turn of a lock

Joe Arterburn is shooting Browning's new Maxus Hunter 12-gauge at fast flying clay targets. Even the recoil from 1 1/8 oz. target loads barely raised the muzzle of the Hunter.

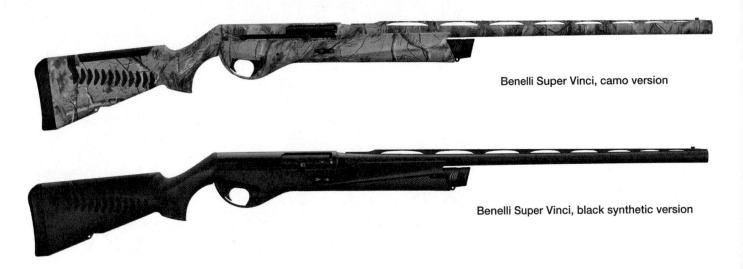

Benelli Super Vinci, camo version

Benelli Super Vinci, black synthetic version

to allow installing an optional tactical grip or a turkey/slug hunting Steadygrip stock. With the stock removed, it's easy to adjust drop and cast with the standard shim kit. When you just know another rooster is going to tear out of the corn stubble the Super Vinci is quick to reload by dropping a shell in the open ejection port and hitting the release lever to chamber the shell. An oversized and beveled loading port helps guide shells into the magazine, allowing you to keep your eyes peeled for the anticipated flush.

Beretta

Beretta has slimmed down last year's Xplor Unico 3 1/2-inch 12-gauge into the A400 Xplor Light with a 3-inch chamber that weighs 6.28 pounds. The Light has many of the features of its big brother with the Blink operating system that incorporates a rotating bolt head lock-up and feeding system that increases cycle rate. The gas system contains a piston with an elastic scraper band to remove carbon build up. The Light's walnut stock is capped with a black Micro-Core

recoil pad that contrasts nicely with the silver receiver.

The A400 Xcell is similar to the Xplor Light, but also has the Gun Pod and Balance Cap System competition features. The Gun Pod is a computerized display inlayed in the grip that shows air temperature, cartridge pressure of the round fired and the number of rounds fired in series or the total number shot fired through the Xcell. Lea Ramthun of Beretta says the Xcell comes with a Gun Pod installed or the grip inletted and ready to install a Gun Pod at a later time.

Beretta Xplor Light

The Balance Cap System includes three interchangeable weights to alter gun balance.

At a price of $2,075, the Silver Pigeon I 12-gauge costs a third less than the Silver Pigeon II. That lower cost, though, still buys the same 3-inch receiver as the more expensive gun with top mounted, dual conical locking lugs and chrome-lined hammer forged barrels. The Silver Pigeon I also has a nickel-plated receiver with English-style scroll and floral engravings, gold colored trigger and walnut stock and Schnabel forearm.

Browning

Browning offers six new variations of its Maxus 12-gauge autoloader.

The Maxus Hunter is a traditional looking gun with gloss-finish walnut stock and forearm with 22 lines-per-inch checkering. The stock has a tightly curved grip, and after shooting a box of shells through the Hunter at clay targets I liked how it held my wrist straight. The Hunter is available with a 3- or 3 1/2-inch chamber in a 26-, 28- or 30-inch barrel with screw in Invector-Plus IC, M and F choke tubes. Guns weigh the same for both chambering, 7 pounds for 28-inch barrel guns.

I appreciated the Hunter's Inflex Technology recoil pad while shooting 1 3/8 oz. magnum loads on a bird hunt at Castle Valley wingshooting lodge (castlevalleyoutdoors.com; 800-586-6503) in Utah last December. Over several days of hunting I shot about a hundred of the magnum loads. The recoil accumulated a bit, but not near enough to stop me from blasting away at clay targets during the slack time of midday. On the target line friends and I shot several hundred target loads through the Hunter without a single hiccup.

Kristin Lauver holds up a rooster she shot with her Browning Citori over/under Micro Midas 20-gauge.

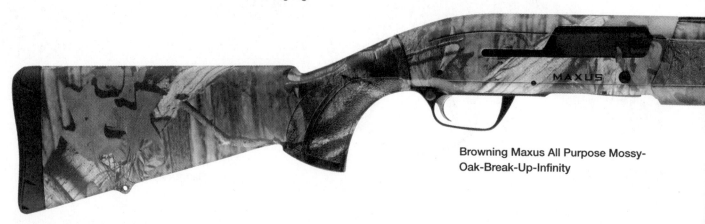

Browning Maxus All Purpose Mossy-Oak-Break-Up-Infinity

The Maxus Sporting is the same gun with a 3-inch chamber and has some added refinements for bird hunting and target shooting. The Sporting stock is adjustable for length of pull, cast and drop for an exact fit. Invector-Plus skeet (SK), cylinder (C), IC, IM, M and F choke tubes allow tailoring pattern size to the shooting situation and a HiViz Tri-Comp fiber-optic front sight helps keep track of the muzzle. The Sporting Carbon Fiber has a composite stock and forearm with a textured gripping surface.

The Maxus All-Purpose is covered with Mossy Oak Break-Up Infinity camouflage over the Dura-Touch Armor Coating synthetic stock and forearm. Its 26-inch barrel is chambered for 3 1/2-inch and shorter 12-gauge shells

and comes with Invector-Plus extra full (XF), F, M and IC choke tubes and a HiViz 4-in-1 fiber-optic sight set with eight light pipes.

The Maxus Rifled Deer, Mossy Oak Break-Up Infinity and Rifled Deer Stalker are for slug gun hunters. The guns have thick-walled 22-inch fully rifled barrels and composite stocks and forearms. Length of pull, cast and drop can also be adjusted. Both guns have a Weaver-style scope base mounted on the barrel that extends back over the receiver for mounting a scope or other sights.

For smaller stature hunters, the Citori over/under Micro Midas and Micro Midas Satin Hunter have a 13-inch length of pull. The guns are chambered in 12- or 20-gauge with 3-inch chambers, but

the 20-gauge is the one to pick because, at two ounces over 6 pounds it weighs a half pound less than the 12-gauge. The guns have either 24- or 26-inch barrels with F, M and IC choke tubes.

Another trim and lightweight gun is the Silver Hunter Micro Midas gas-operated autoloader. The Silver's 13-inch length of pull, thin grip and 24 or 26-inch slim barrels make a gun easier to handle for smaller stature folks. The 12-gauge Micro weighs 7.3 lbs. with a 26-inch barrel or 6 lbs. in 20-gauge with a 24-inch barrel.

On to an even smaller gauge, the Citori Heritage 28-gauge weighs 6.56 lbs. with 28-inch barrels. At a price of nearly six grand, the heritage is evident with high-relief gold engraving depicting

It's back: the resurrected Browning A-Bolt Shotgun Hunter

Browning Citori Heritage

Browning Citori Satin Hunter

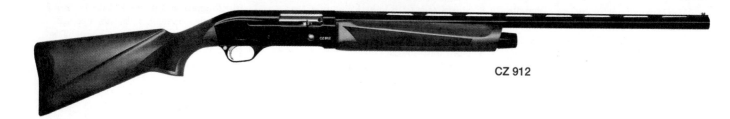

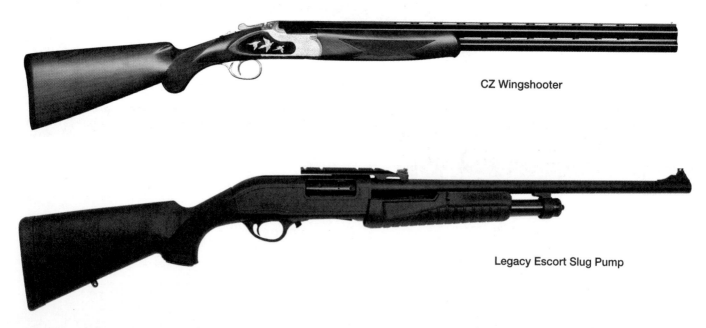

CZ 912

grouse on the right and quail on the left side plate. Grade V or VI walnut completes the gun.

On the larger side, the 8-lb. Citori White Satin Hunter and Satin Hunter are chambered in 3 1/2-inch 12-gauge with 26- or 28-inch barrels. The White Satin has a silver nitride finish on its receiver, while the Satin Hunter has a matte blue finish. At about the same 8 lbs., the Citori 625 Sporting Left-Hand has 30- or 32-inch barrels and a left-hand palm swell on the grip and Schnabel forearm. Adding half a pound gets the Citori Trap XT Left-Hand with a gloss finish to the walnut stock with a palm swell on the left side of the grip and a semi-beavertail forearm with finger grooves.

The Cynergy over/under has three new finishes in 12-gauge guns with 3 1/2-inch chambers. The Cynergy Satin Composite wears a nitride finish on its metal and a black composite stock with rubber grips. The two camo models are covered in Mossy Oak Break-Up Infinity or Mossy Oak Duck Blind. All three have F, M and IC choke tubes, a medium thickness Inflex recoil pad and one .25-inch length of pull spacer.

Today's sabot-encased shotgun slugs

are incredibly accurate fired from a shotgun with a tightly fixed breech. Years ago Browning's A-Bolt bolt-action was one of the most accurate of such slug guns. Now the A-Bolt slug gun is back in 12-gauge models: the Hunter with a one-piece walnut stock and the Stalker with either a black composite stock with Dura-Touch coating or Mossy Oak Break-Up Infinity camo finish. The guns' 22-inch rifled barrel wears a TRUGLO/Marble's fiber-optic front sight and rear sight adjustable for windage and elevation. Of course the receiver is ready to accept bases for scope rings. A detachable two-round magazine is standard.

The Browning Pump Shotgun has two new High Capacity models. The BPS All Weather High Capacity 12-gauge has a black composite stock and forearm that contrasts with the matte nickel-finish on its metal. The 20-inch barrel has a cylinder bore and a HiViz Tactical fiber-optic front sight. The tube magazine holds five 3-inch shells. The BPS Wood High Capacity holds five 3-inch .410s. It has a silver front bead on the 20-inch cylinder bore barrel. A matte blue finish on the steel gun nicely compliments the satin finish walnut stock and forearm.

There's some heft to the BPS's steel receiver, which puts the weight of the .410 at 6.6 lbs.

CZ

An upgraded autoloader and two over/unders are CZ's new guns for the year.

The CZ 912 12-gauge recoil-operated autoloader features a long recoil spring located in the buttstock that requires infrequent cleaning to cycle a variety of 2 3/4- and 3-inch loads. Removal of the installed magazine plug requires only unscrewing the magazine cap. With the plug out, the magazine holds four 3-inch shells. The chrome-lined bore is threaded to accept five supplied screw-in choke tubes. The gun weighs 7.4 lbs with its 28-inch barrel.

The fancy CZ Wingshooter has Turkish walnut with 18 lines-per-inch checkering and a Schnabel forearm. The boxlock frame contains selective mechanical triggers and coil spring operated- hammers. The Wingshooter is chambered in 12, 20 and 28-gauges and .410-bore.

Only 50 of the Limited Edition over/

CZ Wingshooter

Legacy Escort Slug Pump

unders will be made this year. It has a Circassian walnut wood and a silver-engraved receiver. It will be chambered in 12, 20 and 28-gauges and .410-bore.

Legacy

The Escort EXTREME gas-operated 12-gauge is designed for the muck and mud of pheasant thickets and duck swamps. It has a synthetic stock with raised and textured grip pads on the grip and forearm. The Waterfowl version of the EXTREME is covered with Avery Outdoors' KW1 or Buck Brush camo. The EXTREME is built with the SMART Valve gas pistons that regulate gas blowback to cycle all 2 3/4- to 3 1/2-inch 12-gauge shells. A magazine cut-off button allows you to remove a chambered round

without another round feeding from the magazine. HiVis MagniSight fiber optic sight and Hevi Shot mid-range choke tubes are standard.

The Escort Slug Gun is available in either a pump or autoloader. The 22-inch barrel on both guns are made by Badger Defense and have cut 1-26-inch twist rifling for shooting sabot slugs. A cantilever sight base includes a fiber optic rear sight to go with the front fiber optic bead. Scope package models are also available. The guns are chambered in 12 or 20 gauge with a 22-inch barrel.

Mossberg

Mossberg is offering a variety of tactical and turkey shotguns on its 50th anniversary.

In my lazier moments while camping I've always thought about using a shotgun to chop some kindling. Now that's something of a legitimate idea with the new 500 Chainsaw shotgun with a unique chainsaw handle attached to its forearm. According to Mossberg, the unusual grip provides the shooter with added muzzle control. This grip is easily removable for conversion to a standard forearm. The Chainsaw also features a tri-rail forearm with an integral full-length bottom rail and two removable side rails for mounting tactical lights and sights. If nothing else, the chainsaw grip makes the gun look tough.

The Blackwater Series of shotguns are based on three of Mossberg's most popular models the 590A1, 500 Cruiser and the 930SPX. The Blackwater 590A1

It's got a handle on the situation: the Mossberg 500 Chainsaw.

Mossberg 590A1 Blackwater SPX

Mossberg Maverick HS12 Over-Under

Mossberg Turkey THUG Pistol Grip

Remington 1100 Competition Synthetic

Remington VersaMax Black Synthetic

and 930 SPX models feature XS sights with a ghost ring rear sight and AR-style white stripe front post on a receiver-mounted rail.

It was only a matter of time before an over/under received a tactical makeover. The Maverick HS12 over/under features 18.5-inch barrels and receiver and under-barrel rails for attaching sights and accessories. The HS12 is offered with either interchangeable IC and M tubes or fixed cylinder bores.

Mossberg's 20-gauge autoloaders have expanded to include two SA-20 Tactical guns equipped with a magazine tube tri-rail for mounting lights and a top rail mounted with a ghost ring rear sight and AR-style winged front sight. The guns have cylinder bores with a choice of full-length stocks with a vertical or standard grip.

The Turkey THUG Series pump-action shotguns are equipped with a TRUGLO Red Dot sight, vertical or standard grip synthetic stocks of either black matte or Mossy Oak Break-Up Infinity and a receiver-mounted rail for optics installation. All the Turkey THUG guns feature a LPA adjustable trigger and adjustable fiber optic sights.

Remington

Perhaps every conceivable variation of the Model 870 pump gun has been made because Remington has no new 870s this year. It only took 60 years and over ten million 870s to get the job done.

Nearly as old and enduring is the Model 1100 that started production in 1962. This year's new 1100 is the Competition Synthetic. The Competition Synthetic is tuned for the competitive scene with an overbored 30-inch barrel and a lengthened forcing cone. The receiver and internal parts are nickel-Teflon coated. The synthetic stock has an adjustable comb and the barrel has a 10 mm target-style rib.

The problem with gas-operated autoloading shotguns is to controlling gas pressure so the gun readily cycles with the heaviest and lightest loads. In its new VERSA MAX gas-operated autoloader, Remington has created a seemingly simple solution to reliably cycle 12-gauge 2 3/4-inch light target loads to 3 1/2-inch magnum turkey shells. The VERSA MAX's VersaPort Gas Piston System has seven holes drilled through the barrel in front of the chamber. Powder gases from a firing shell funnel through these holes into two piston chambers brazed onto each side of the barrel chamber. A rod in each piston has five steel rings and gas entering the pistons pushes the rods about a half an inch to the rear to open the bolt and eject the empty shell and the returning bolt picks up a fresh shell and chambers it.

When the crimp on a 2 3/4-inch shell opens on firing all seven ports remain exposed to funnel a maximum amount

Remington VersaMax Mossy Oak Duck Blind Camo

.45 Colt/.410 Rossi Circuit Judge Tuffy

of gas into the pistons to cycle the gun. The mouth of a 3-inch shell seals three of the ports to reduce gas pressure fed into the piston chambers. A 3 1/2-inch shell seals four holes, leaving only three to direct gas into the pistons. The result is consistent pressure and bolt speed.

The VERSA MAX is designed for the rough conditions of duck blinds and goose pits with an anodized aluminum receiver; TriNyte-coated barrel and nickel-plated bore; nickel-Teflon plated internal gas system components; stainless steel magazine tube; and nickel-plated springs. A wide trigger guard and large button on the cross-bolt safety enable working the gun while wearing gloves.

The stock wears a SuperCell recoil pad

and comes with a Spacer Kit that can adjust stock length up to one inch. Stock drop and cast can also be fine tuned with a shim system and included wrench. An interchangeable, padded cheek comb insert allows for better sight alignment and comfort when shooting.

The 12-gauge VERSA MAX models include a 26- or 28-inch barrel with a black or Mossy Oak Duck Blind or Realtree AP synthetic stock and forearm with grey overmolded grips. The black synthetic guns come with Flush Pro Bore F, M, LM and IC choke tubes. The camo versions come with four Pro Bore Extended choke tubes designated Flooded Timber, Over Decoys, Pass Shooting and Turkey/Predator.

Rossi

The amazing success of Taurus's Judge revolver that fires .410 shells or .45 Colt cartridges has spawned several new long guns based on the revolver from Taurus's sister company Rossi. The Taurus/Rossi Circuit Judge Tuffy has an open grip synthetic buttstock that stores five shells. The muzzle of the 18.5-inch barrel is threaded for a straight-rifled choke tube and sights include a fiber optic front sight and base for mounting optics. The Tuffy weighs just 4.6 pounds. The 28-gauge is now chambered in the regular Circuit Judge. It also has a straight rifled choke tube in its 18.5 inch barrel and weighs 5.6 lbs.

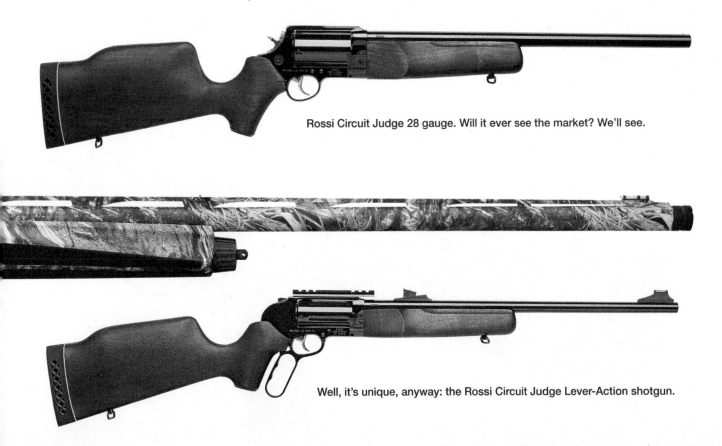

Rossi Circuit Judge 28 gauge. Will it ever see the market? We'll see.

Well, it's unique, anyway: the Rossi Circuit Judge Lever-Action shotgun.

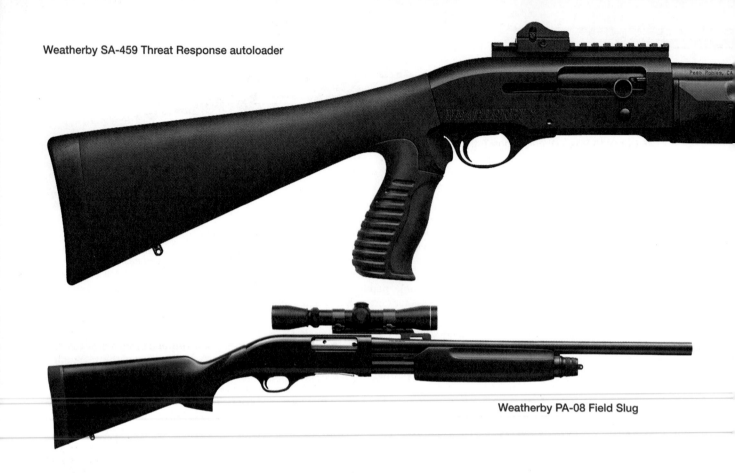

Weatherby SA-459 Threat Response autoloader

Weatherby PA-08 Field Slug

The Circuit Judge Lever Action is offered in a blue finish with a Monte Carlo stock. Chambered in .410/.45 Colt, the rifle weighs 5.3 pounds with a 18.5 inch barrel with a straight rifled choke tube. The Trail Judge Lever Action .410 has a 12-inch barrel and stock bobbed off right behind the grip. Its overall length is 24.3 inches and weight is 4 pounds.

Weatherby

Weatherby has new variations of their shotguns for hunting big game, upland birds and turkeys and defending the homestead.

The PA-08 Field/Slug Combo 12-gauge pump comes with 24-inch rifled barrel for hunting big game and a 28-inch barrel for hunting birds. The eight-groove rifled barrel has a 1:28 twist with a bore diam-

Weatherby SA-08 Entre Rios 28 gauge

eter of .718 inch and groove diameter of .728 inch. A Weaver-style cantilever base is attached for mounting sights. The smoothbore barrel is chrome-lined with lengthened forcing cone. To add more versatility, Full, M and IC choke tubes come with the barrel.

The PA-459 Turkey model is covered with Mothwing Camo's Spring Mimicry pattern on the stock and forearm. The Turkey's barrel is 19 inches long and chambered in 12 gauge. The stock's length of pull is a bit short at 13 1/2 inches and has a rubber-textured grip. A low-density recoil pad maximizes recoil absorption, making the PA-459 Turkey model easy on the shoulder. A rail is installed on the action with a clamp on ghost ring rear sight adjustable for wind-

age and elevation. Magazine capacity is four 3-inch rounds or five 2 3/4-inch rounds.

The SA-08 Entré Rios features a scaled-down frame to fit the 28 gauge and weighs only 5 1/4 pounds. A checkered walnut stock and forearm is finished with a high-gloss that matches the metal. The gun comes with SK, IC and M choke tubes.

The Threat Response (TR) line has two new shotgun models: the SA-459 TR autoloader and PA-08 TR pump. The SA-459 TR 12 or 20-gauge wears a trim forearm and has an hourglass-shaped oversized bolt handle that makes the bolt easy to locate and operate. The SA-459 TR has a chrome-lined 18.5-inch barrel and a rail on the receiver with an

adjustable ghost ring rear sight to go with a red fiber optic front bead. The PA-08 TR 12-gauge has a black synthetic stock and forearm and an 18.5-inch barrel with a blade white dot front sight.

Winchester

The 20-gauge versions of the Winchester Super X3 autoloader have arrived. The Super X3 All-Purpose Field 20-gauge is concealed with Mossy Oak Break-Up Infinity camo and then coated with Dura-Touch Armor Coating. Barrel lengths are 26 or 28 inches. The longer-barreled gun weighs 6.62 lbs. Choke tubes include F, M and IC. Two length of pull stock spacers and drop and cast adjustment shims are included. The Su-

Weatherby PA-459 Turkey

Winchester Super X3 Waterfowl

per X3 Compact Field 20-gauge is pared down to 6.37 lbs. with an aluminum receiver, light magazine tube, thin 26 or 28-inch barrel and walnut stock cut with a relatively short 13-inch length of pull. The Super X3 Cantilever Deer 20-gauge has a rifled 22-inch barrel that shoots 2 3/4- or 3-inch slugs. A Weaver-style sight mount base extends back over the receiver for mounting a scope or other sights. The black composite stock and forearm are coated with Dura-Touch Armor Coating and the stock can be altered for fit with two LOP spacers and drop and cast spacers. The gun weighs 7.5 lbs. The Super X3 Composite 20-gauge joins its big brother 12-gauge with a Dura-Touch Armor Coating on the composite stock and forearm Perma-Cote metal coating. An aluminum magazine tube and slim 26- or 28-inch barrel trim the gun weight to 7 lbs. The same gun in Mossy Oak Duck Blind camo is called the Super X3 Waterfowl. The Black Field wears walnut and a black anodized metal finish.

Of course there are a couple new 12-gauge Super X3s. The Black Field has the same features as the 20-gauge Black Field but is chambered for the 3-inch 12-gauge. The Sporting Adjustable is intended for competition shooting with a thin profile barrel with gas ports to reduce muzzle jump. The gun is

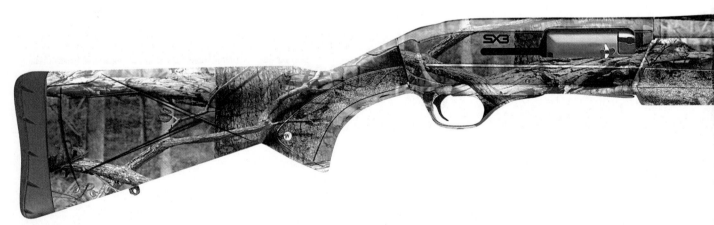

Winchester 20-gauge SuperX3
All-Purpose Field

Winchester Super X3 Cantilever Deer

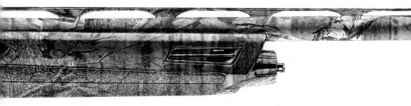

chambered for 2 3/4-inch shells, and Winchester states a new gas piston reliably cycles all those 12-gauge loads. An adjustable comb and Decelerator recoil pad help absorb recoil. Five choke tubes come with the gun from SK to F.

The Super X3 NWTF Extreme Turkey shotgun comes in both 12- and 20-gauge models. The 12 gauge has a 3 1/2-inch chamber and the 20 gauge a 3-inch chamber. Both guns feature a 24-inch back-bored barrel and an Invector-Plus Extra-Full Extended Turkey choke tube. The guns are camouflaged in Mossy Oak Break-Up Infinity and the stock and forearm are covered with Dura-Touch Armor Coating. Sights include an adjustable rear sight and a TRUGLO fiber-optic front sight. An Inflex Technology recoil pad helps reduce felt recoil.

A new version of the Super X pump-action includes the 12-gauge Waterfowl SXP in Mossy Oak Duck Blind with a chrome-lined chamber and bore. The Back-Bored barrel is oversized at .742-inch diameter and F, M and IC Invector-Plus choke tubes. The SXP Camp/Field Combo has one 12-gauge barrel 18 inches in length and a more regular length 26- or 28-inch barrel that accept supplied F, M and IC choke tubes. The Combo has a black synthetic stock and anodized finished metal.

SEMI-AUTOMATIC PISTOLS

BY **JOHN MALLOY**

Has anyone missed the fact that the 1911 pistol design reached its 100-year anniversary in 2011?

With good reason, 2011 has been called the year of the 1911. Now, as we move into the future, we have new companies just beginning to offer 1911s, and "old" companies making many different variants. Just collecting 1911 Centennial commemorative pistols should keep collectors busy for some time. (Collectors, use this report as a guide.) New 22-caliber versions of the 1911 are being offered by a number of companies. Historic versions of the 1911, built to old original specifications, have appeared. The 1911 is coming into Cowboy Action Shooting, and "Wild Bunch" versions are offered by some companies that have never marketed a semiautomatic pistol before. At the time of this writing, the state of Utah is considering making the 1911 the state firearm!

But even during its 100th anniversary, the news was not all 1911. Semiautomatic pistols for personal protection come in many sizes, shapes and calibers. Increase in concealed carry has created great interest in smaller, easier-to-carry pistols. The recent trend of downsized 380-caliber pistols continues. Related to this trend is the fact that the .32 ACP chambering (considered a dead duck some years ago) still has small .32s appearing on the market. New calibers are being introduced.

If it had not been for the 1911, the year 2011 might well have been called the year of the downsized 9mm pistol. A number of subcompact 9s have been introduced. Here we might pause to ask: What, exactly, is a "subcompact?" Well, there is no standard convention, but I use a system of common rectangles. A pistol that can fit on an 8x10 photograph is a full-size pistol. A 5x7 photo covers a compact. Thus, a pistol that can hide under a 4x6 index card is a subcompact. (Some very small pistols can be covered by a 3x5 index card—I'm not sure what to call them…little, perhaps?) Because this system is arbitrary, we won't quibble if a little sticks out here or there.

Some unconventional pistols are much larger than an 8x10 picture. These long-range pistols are generally based on rifle actions, and are specifically made as pistols. Also, pistol-caliber carbines have had a hard time being included in reports on rifles, so we'll continue to cover them for the time being.

The recent activity in the world of semiautomatic pistols has been nothing short of breathtaking. Let's take a look at what the companies are doing:

Akdal

The Turkish-made Akdal pistols, mentioned last year, have had two variants (TR 01 and TR 02) approved for importation by American Tactical Importers (ATI). The polymer-frame pistols, designed for the 9mm Parabellum cartridge, had not made it into the United States in quantity by the time of the January 2011 SHOT Show, but were expected later in 2011.

Both variants are tilting-barrel-locking pistols with "Glock-type" trigger mechanisms and have 15-round magazines. The fancier TR 02 has interchangeable grip back straps, a sculptured slide, and front and rear slide grasping grooves.

American Classic

The American Classic line of Philippine-made 1911 pistols now has a down-sized variant. The new 45-caliber Amigo has a 3.5-inch barrel. It is 7.25 inches long and 5 inches high, and weighs a bit over 32 ounces. The Amigo has a 4140 steel frame and slide, and can be had in deep blue or hard chrome finishes.

The company also catalogs the American Classic 22, a 33-ounce 1911-style pistol chambered for 22 Long Rifle. The pistol is offered with a matte blue finish, and has a 10-round magazine.

American Classic pistols are imported by Eagle Imports of Wannamassa, NJ.

Armalite

The Armalite pistol line has new adjustable-sight variants. The 15-shot AR-24 and the 13-shot AR-24K now are available with precision adjustable sights. The new variants are cataloged as the AR-24-15C Combat Custom and the AR-24K-13C Combat Custom Compact.

All the AR-24 pistols are chambered for the 9mm cartridge, and are based largely on the CZ 75 design. They are made with close tolerances. Weights are about 35 ounces for the full-size and 33 ounces for the compact. The new adjustable-sight variants also have nicely-checkered grip front and back straps. I had the chance to shoot both of the adjustable-sight variants, and was impressed with the triggers while firing single-action.

Armscor

Armscor president Martin Tuason points out that according to industry production records, the Philippine manufacturer is the largest maker of 1911 pistols in the entire world. Pretty nice to be able to say that, on the 1911's 100th anniversary. In the United States, Armscor pistols are generally marketed under the Rock Island Armory name.

Several new Armscor variants were produced during 2011.

The 1911 – Tactical 2011 features a frame with the forward portion, called by some the dust cover, extended forward to the end of the slide. The extended frame is equipped with a longer Picatinny rail. The new pistol is available with Meprolite night sights.

An interesting new pistol is the 1911–Micromag. The full-size gun comes with two barrels: 9mm and .22 TCM.

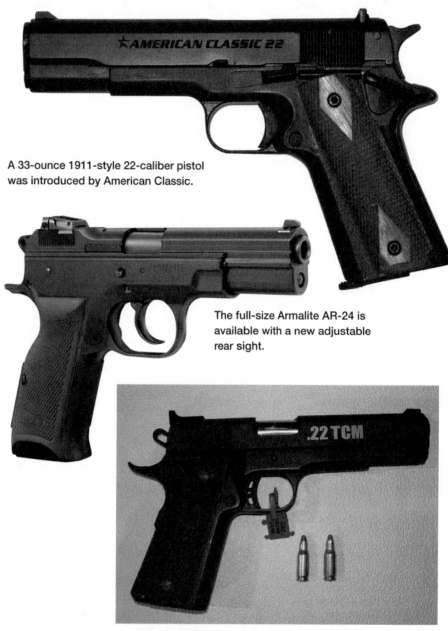

A 33-ounce 1911-style 22-caliber pistol was introduced by American Classic.

The full-size Armalite AR-24 is available with a new adjustable rear sight.

Armscor pistols will be available in .22 TCM chambering. The bottleneck high-velocity 22-caliber cartridges are shown with a prototype pistol.

The Armscor 22 TCM, left, is the latest high-velocity 22-caliber pistol cartridge offered. Others are the 22 WMR and the FN 5.7x28mm. A 9mm cartridge is on the right for comparison.

The .22 TCM (.22 Tuason Craig Magnum) cartridge is an Armscor development. It uses a 22-caliber jacketed bullet in a shortened .223 Remington case. The overall length of the 22 TCM is a bit longer than that of the 9mm, but is close enough to work in their 9mm magazine. The case base diameters are close, and the pressure levels are similar. Thus, the gun can be switched from one caliber to another with just a barrel change. The double-column magazine holds 18 rounds of either cartridge.

The new XT22 offered this year is the final development of the prototype 1911 .22 LR target pistol pictured on these pages last year. Like the prototype, the final design has an open-top slide. The blowback XT22 weighs 38 ounces and comes with a 15-round magazine. Trigger pull is set at a light 3.5 pounds.

To celebrate the 100th year of the 1911, Armscor has issued a very limited edition, the Centennial Elite. The engraved gun has both frame and slide fully gold-plated.

ATI

American Tactical Imports continues to become a bigger player in the world of semiautomatic pistols. A number of imported and domestic handguns were offered.

The .22 LR pistol, the GSG-1911, made by German Sporting Guns, was introduced last year too late to get into the 2010 catalog. It is now in good production, with shipping well under way by early 2011. It is offered with variations in grips, and with an optional Picatinny rail on the frame. All GSG-1911 pistols have threaded barrels. In keeping with the interest in the centennial of the 1911 design, a commemorative GSG-1911 was introduced. The gloss-blue commemorative guns come with a matching knife. An appropriate legend (wording not available at press time) appears on the slide. Only 1,911 were scheduled for production.

A line of FX 1911 pistols are offered in traditional .45 ACP chambering. Prototypes were displayed last year, and now eight production variants exist. The Military is a full-size basic "wartime" pistol with updated specifications. The Thunderbolt is an enhanced full-size variant with adjustable sights and a rail. The (oddly named) GI model is a 4.25-inch commander-size pistol with burr hammer and beavertail tang. The GI Enhanced has Novak sights. The Titan is a short gun with a barrel about 3.4 inches long (company literature lists several conflicting lengths and I didn't get a chance to measure it) and shorter grip frame. The Titan SS is a similar pistol in stainless steel. The Fat Boy is a further shortened double-column pistol with a 3.2-inch barrel. It is offered in two versions—10-round and 12-round. By January 2011, the Fat Boy pistols had been BATF approved, but were not ready for shipping at that time. ATI plans to come out with additional ported and stainless FX variants. The ATI FX 1911 pistols are made in the Philippines by Shooters Arms Manufacturers (SAM).

The US-made FMK 9mm double-action pistol was introduced two years ago by EMF. Now, a new Generation 2-inch version is offered by ATI. Recall that the Bill of Rights was engraved on each pistol. Now, it is also available without the inscriptions, if an owner so desires. The new FMK Model 9C1B has a 4-inch barrel and comes with two 10-round magazines.

Auto-Ordnance

The 100th anniversary of the 1911 was commemorated by Auto-Ordnance. The A-O Anniversary Edition 1911 is a .45 ACP, made in the style of the World War II 1911A1. The 5-inch special pistol is blued and has checkered wood grips. In keeping with its GI heritage, it is made with vertical slide serrations and has a lanyard loop. Engraving on the right slide flat reads, in three lines: *1911 45 ACP / 1911 – 2011 / 100 Years.*

Auto-Ordnance is part of Kahr Arms. (See Kahr)

Beretta

The Beretta Px4 Storm Compact, introduced on these pages last year, filled the gap between the full-size 4-inch-barrel Storm and the 3-inch Sub-compact. As of early 2011, the Compact was in full production.

Beretta has developed a new 17-round 9mm magazine that will fit all the existing Model 92 pistols, giving extra capacity. Still not enough? The company also offers an extended 20-round magazine. It protrudes below the bottom of the grip but works with all the 92-series guns.

The little .32 ACP Tomcat now has an optional new sighting system. A large round-bead front sight and a shallow V rear sight is now available. This is sometimes called the "Express" sighting system. The new Tomcat variant using it is called the Alley Cat.

Bersa

The Argentine Bersa company is finally getting its first polymer-frame pistol into its line. The slim new BP CC 9, a thin 9mm for concealed carry, was announced two years ago and has now made it into the catalog. Availability was scheduled for April 2011. With a tilting-barrel locking system and short-reset DAO trigger mechanism, the new pistol is less than an inch wide. Weight is 21.5 ounces, with a 3.3-inch barrel. Size is 6.3 inches long by 4.8 inches high, so a bit sticks out from under a 4x6 index card. The extra length is put to good use: Capacity of the BP CC 9 is 8+1.

Browning

John M. Browning designed the Colt pistol that was finalized as the 1911 US service pistol. So, the Browning company certainly could have been expected to bring out their own commemorative 1911 during the year of 2011. And so they did – in a way.

Instead of producing a full-size .45, Browning decided to scale the design down 15% and make it into a .22. Looking almost exactly like a tiny 1911A1, the new Browning 1911-22 is an attention-getter because it is a cute little thing.

All the controls work exactly as they do on the full-size 1911. The 15-ounce pistol is a blowback, as would be expected, but Browning avoided the temptation to use an external extractor. The grip safety, manual safety, slide release and magazine release all work as do the original. Although I did not get to disassemble one, I was told that the take-down procedure is the same as the original.

Slide and frame are of aluminum alloy, with a matte blue finish. The slide has the original vertical grasping grooves. Grips are checkered brown composite. The A1 model has a 4.25-inch barrel (about the same scale as a 5-inch original) and a Compact 3.63-inch version was also offered. Each pistol made during the first year of production includes a certificate of authenticity and a special commemorative zippered pistol rug.

The little Browning 1911 feels good in the hand, a bit like the old Llama pocket pistols of decades ago. Those small Llama pistols were popular, in part, because they looked and worked like "little 45s." The little Browning 1911-22 may well achieve its own popularity.

ATI's GSG1911 is a full-size German-made 22-caliber 1911.

The FX Titan is a short variant of the FX 1911 line that ATI carries.

A special Auto-Ordnance pistol, with high-polish blue, wood grips and engraving on the right slide flat recognized the 100-year anniversary of the 1911.

Bersa's first polymer-frame pistol, the BP9CC, is a bit larger than other subcompact 9mm pistols, but offers 8+1 capacity.

The Browning 1911-22 is an 85% scale 1911 version in 22 LR caliber.

The Century International C93 Sport Pistol is based on the HK33 action, chambered for .223 Rem.

Century International's US-made Centurian 7.62x39 long-range pistol is based on the AK action.

Century International Arms

Century International Arms has celebrated its 50th anniversary! The company's Colefire semiautomatic pistol, based on the Sterling submachinegun, was introduced last year in 7.62x25mm chambering. Now, it is also available in 9mm. Although surplus 7.62x25 is currently the least expensive pistol ammunition on the market, many shooters prefer the 9mm. Now they have a choice.

Century, in January 2011, also introduced two large unconventional pistols. These long-range pistols are chambered for intermediate rifle cartridges.

The Centurion 39 (C39) is based on the AK action, and is chambered for the 7.62x39mm cartridge. It has a polymer stock and magazine and has accessory rails and a flash hider. Although the AK system was developed elsewhere, the C39 is 100% American-made, manufactured in Fridley, MN.

The C93 Sport Pistol is another large pistol based on a rifle action, this time the HK33, but is chambered for the 223 (5.56mm) cartridge. Century feels this is a nice alternative to long-range 223-caliber pistols based on the AR platform. Two 40-round magazines come with each pistol.

These two long-range pistols were added to the line too late to appear in the Century catalog, but were displayed at the January 2011 SHOT Show.

Chiappa

Introduced here two years ago, Chiappa's Model 1911-22 pistols, in several variants, have been well-received.

For this year, Chiappa's offering is another 22-caliber pistol. However, this one is an unconventional pistol based on the US M4 Carbine. The Chiappa M four-22 has familiar AR-15 style controls and comes with a 6-inch barrel. Two 28-round magazines are furnished with each pistol, which should keep a shooter plinking for some time. It has a "quad-rail" forearm that allows mounting of a number of accessories.

Displayed at the January 2011 SHOT Show was a prototype M9-22 pistol. The 22-caliber pistol is a visual replica of the M9 9mm US service pistol. When it becomes available, the M9-22 is planned to come with a 5-inch barrel and a 10-round magazine, with either wood or black plastic grips.

Chiappa pistols are marketed by MKS Supply of Dayton, Ohio.

Christensen

A brand-new 1911 maker! Christensen Arms, a rifle maker since the mid-1990s, introduced a line of 1911 pistols during the design's 100th anniversary. Offered in four variants, the Christensen 1911s were displayed for the first time at the January 2011 SHOT Show.

All the Christensen pistols have titanium frames, stainless-steel slides and carbon-fiber grips. They all are equipped with beavertail tangs, ambidextrous thumb safeties and Tijicon/Novak sights.

The Classic pistol has a 5-inch barrel. The Tactical 5-inch also has a rail on the front of the frame. The Commander has a full-size frame and shorter 4.29-inch barrel. The Officer has a shortened frame (and a shorter magazine that holds one round less) and a short slide to match its 3.65-inch barrel. All variants were to be offered in 9mm, .40 S&W and .45 ACP.

Cimarron

The Cimarron 1911 did not make it into the company's 2011 catalog, but it is in production! Designed for the "Wild Bunch" competition coming into Cowboy Action Shooting, the Cimarron 1911 features a true 1911 frame (no recess cuts behind the trigger). The pistols come in three variants: high-polish blue, nickel, and parkerized.

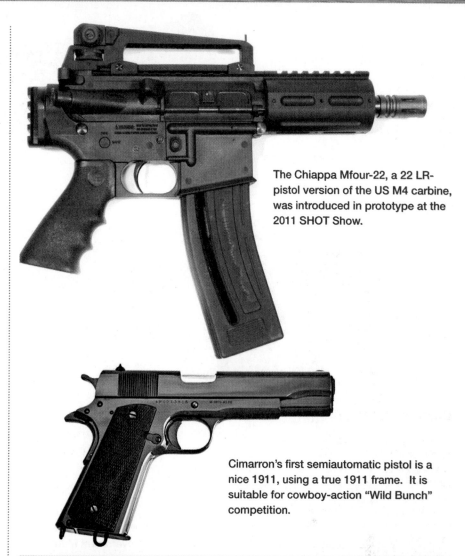

The Chiappa Mfour-22, a 22 LR-pistol version of the US M4 carbine, was introduced in prototype at the 2011 SHOT Show.

Cimarron's first semiautomatic pistol is a nice 1911, using a true 1911 frame. It is suitable for cowboy-action "Wild Bunch" competition.

A new entry into the 1911 world is the Christensen 1911. Displayed for the first time at the 2011 SHOT Show, this is serial number 32, a commander version.

Colt

Not only was 2011 the 100th anniversary of the 1911, but it is the 175th anniversary of the founding of the Colt company in 1836. Is it any wonder that Colt put substantial emphasis on guns that would commemorate these anniversaries?

There is the "Anniversary I," a single special 1911 specimen, a one-of-a-kind commemorative. It is a true 1911 — made to 1918 specifications, with extensively

Of course Colt made 100th Anniversary commemoratives. This is the one-of-a-kind "Anniversary I" that was donated to the National Rifle Association.

Colt is back in the Double-Action business with a lightweight Government Model DAO pistol.

engraved frame and slide, with gold inlays. Ivory grips have scrimshaw pictures, with Samuel Colt on the left grip. John M. Browning appears in gold on the right slide flat. Colt donated the unique gun to the National Rifle Association to be auctioned off at the 2011 NRA annual meetings.

A short New Agent DAO pistol with a "trench sight" aiming system gave acceptable results.

The "Anniversary II" is limited to 750 commemorative 1918-specification pistols, featuring high-polish blue with engraving and gold on the slide flats. These guns have Cocobolo grips with gold-plated medallions.

The "Anniversary III" guns are also of 1918 configuration, with special commemorative rollmarks on the slide flats, and "big diamond" grips. No specific number was set; plans were that orders taken before November 30, 2011 would be filled.

As if that were not enough to commemorate the 1911, Colt planned that, during the year of 2011, all the Series '70, 1991, XSE, New Agent, Rail Gun and Defender pistols – an estimated 75% of the modern 1911 lines – have a special rollmark ("100 Years of Service") on the right slide flat.

Colt didn't just sit back and make commemoratives. The double-action-only variants quietly announced last year are now production items. Colt's previous foray into double action, the Double Eagle, did not meet great success for several reasons. Among them, they really didn't look like 1911s, and would not fit into most holsters designed for 1911s. The new double-actions proudly display their 1911 heritage. I got a chance to shoot the two variations now offered: the full-size lightweight Government Model 45, and the trench-sight New Agent DAO 45. I was impressed, positively, with the way they handled and shot. Even the 3-inch trench-sight variant (with only a sighting groove on the slide) demonstrated better accuracy than I had expected.

There is a new family of 22-caliber Colt 1911 pistols, provided by Umarex USA. The variants include a 22 Government Model, and adjustable-sight Gold Cup Trophy and a Rail Gun version. They are made under license in Germany.

Before concealed-carry became widespread, Colt was ahead of the times in the small .380 field. Many were sorry to see the nice little Colt Mustang .380 go out of production. They will be glad that one variant is back in the line. The aluminum-frame Mustang Pocketlite 380 has a stainless-steel slide, a 2.75-inch barrel and 6+1 capacity. Too late to get into the 2011 catalog, the little Mustang was scheduled for summer 2011 production.

Oh, yes, there are also 175th Anniversary guns. However, they are revolvers, so you'll have to read about them elsewhere.

The Colt "Anniversary II" is limited to 750 pistols.

Cylinder & Slide

Pistolsmith Bill Laughridge of Cylinder & Slide is building true 1911 pistols representative of the first 500 ever made. In an amazing job of research, the dimensions of verified original parts and old blueprints have been documented. The research extended to the tools and procedures used to make the parts. The final pistol is as close to an "original" 1911 of the 1911-1912 period as can be made. Polishing and bluing methods match the originals as closely as possible.

Laughridge planned for 115 commemorative reproduction 1911 pistols to be made during 2011. The schedule of production: 100 pistols marked MODEL 1911 US ARMY; 10 marked MODEL 1911 US NAVY; and FIVE marked MODEL 1911 USMC. Laughridge noted with a smile that there never were any original pistols marked for the Marine Corps, but reckoned rightly that some Marines would want one with that legend!

Cylinder & Slide's authentic recreation of an early (1911-1912) production 1911.

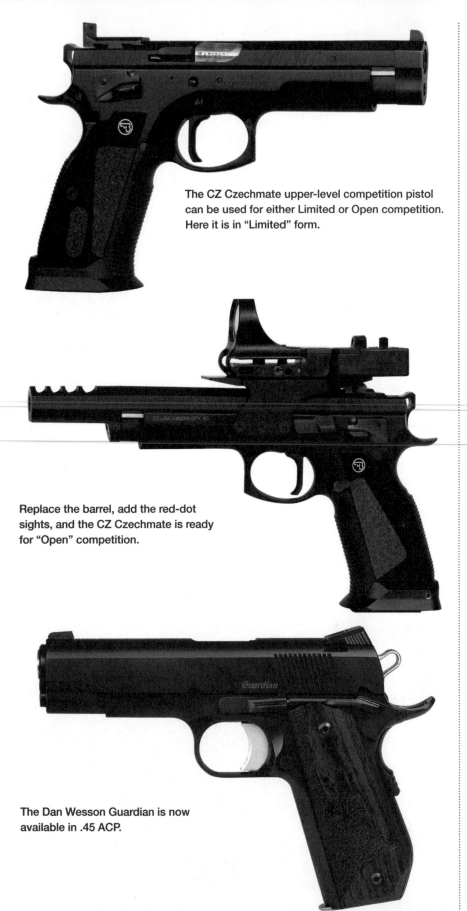

The CZ Czechmate upper-level competition pistol can be used for either Limited or Open competition. Here it is in "Limited" form.

Replace the barrel, add the red-dot sights, and the CZ Czechmate is ready for "Open" competition.

The Dan Wesson Guardian is now available in .45 ACP.

CZ

CZ's 9mm pistol line, based largely on the famous Czech CZ 75, has two new additions.

The CZ single-action Czechmate is an upper-level competition pistol. It comes configured for IPSC/USPSA Open division competition, with a compensator and C-More red dot sight installed. However, it also has an extra fitted barrel and metallic sights that allow it to be switched to Limited division configuration. A "big stick" 26-round magazine and three 20-round magazines are included. The undercut trigger guard and high-mounted beavertail allow a high grip.

The CZ 75 SP-01 Shadow Custom is built by the CZ Custom Shop. Similar to the existing Shadow Target, the new SP-01 Shadow Custom has a fixed competition rear sight, slim aluminum grips, and comes with a two-tone (blue slide/nickel frame) finish. 19-round magazines are furnished.

CZ also markets pistols under the Dan Wesson name.

Dan Wesson

The Dan Wesson Guardian pistol, introduced here last year, is now a production item. A light Commander-size 1911 pistol, it has a bobtail grip frame treatment. Introduced in 2010 as a 9mm, the Guardian is now available in 45 ACP chambering.

Dan Wesson's new upper-end 1911 Elite Series comprises four different pistols. They offer an interesting choice for competition and combat shooters. The Titan is a 10mm, holding an 18- or 21-round magazine, and using a 4.25-inch barrel. The Mayhem is a long 6-inch-barrel 40 S&W with an 18-round magazine. The Havoc in 9mm has a 4.25-inch barrel and holds a 21-round magazine. A similar Havoc model is also available as a 38 Super. The two Havoc variants can also use available 24-, 27- or 29-round magazines.

Diamondback

The 8.8-ounce Diamondback 380, introduced on these pages in the last edition, now has been joined by other models. Diamondback, a relatively new Florida company, has joined other makers offering a subcompact 9mm pistol.

The new 9mm, the DB9, is slightly larger than the 380, but only slightly. With its 3-inch barrel, the new 9mm

The Dan Wesson Mayhem, in the upper-end Elite series, is a .40-caliber 1911 with a 6-inch barrel and 18-round magazine.

The Diamondback DB9 weighs 11 ounces and has 6+1 capacity. (right view)

The new DoubleStar Combat Pistol is the company's first 1911 without a frame rail.

New Diamondback pistols are now offered in 9mm (left) and .32 NAA (center). The original 380 is on the right for comparison.

weighs just 11 ounces. Width is just over three-quarters of an inch, at .080". The small locked-breech 9mm DB9 has 6+1 capacity.

The subcompact 9 is not the only new item from Diamondback. Another new model, the DB320 was announced in the rip-snorting .32 NAA caliber, which drives a 32-caliber bullet out of a short barrel at around 1200 feet per second. Regular readers may remember that the 32 NAA cartridge was introduced in the 2003 edition by North American Arms for its Guardian pistol. NAA essentially necked down a .380 case to put a larger powder charge behind a 32-caliber JHP bullet. It is good to have another factory pistol for this interesting cartridge, which is loaded by Cor-Bon. The locked-breech DB320 weighs only 8.8 ounces and has a 2.8-inch barrel. Like the 380 and 9mm pistols, it has 6+1 capacity.

DoubleStar

Recall that DoubleStar began its 1911 program by making rail-equipped frames. Then, three years ago, they introduced a complete 45-caliber pistol built on that frame. They eventually realized that not everyone needs or wants an accessory rail, so in early 2011, the company offered its Combat Pistol either with or without a rail frame. Equipped with Novak sights and a Novak 8-round magazine, the new rail-less DoubleStar pistol has 25 lpi checkering on the frame.

Ed Brown

Two Ed Brown 1911 Centennials were to be made only during 2011. The Classic Custom Centennial is blued, with engraved slide and frame, jeweled barrel and Trulvory grips. The Executive Centennial is a similar gun without the

engraving. On the left slide flat appeared the legend, "Centennial Edition 1911-2011."

Among the new offerings in the regular line is a Lightweight Kobra Carry, an aluminum-frame pistol with thin wood grips.

EMF

Recall that, two years ago, EMF added semiautomatic pistol to their line. The Hartford 1911 pistol line was American-made, in Tennessee. This has changed. The 1911 guns are still made in America, but are now made by JPS Manufacturing in Scottsdale, AZ. As the new guns are phased in, EMF will start with one variation, a simple basic model 1911. It will have a dovetailed front sight.

The JR Carbine, an innovative pistol-caliber carbine, was introduced last year and is in full production. The JR Carbine is available in 9mm, .40 S&W and .45 ACP. The guns can be adapted to use different pistol magazines.

FNH-USA's new polymer-frame FNP-45 Competition pistol has a fiber-optic front sight and frame rail.

The Turkish Girsan firm is providing their MC1911 for US sales.

FNH USA

The FNP-45 Competition pistol is a new addition to FN's 45-caliber pistol line. The new gun is designed for major-caliber action pistol shooting. It comes with a fiber-optic front sight and an accessory rail. The slide has a removable top plate so that optical sights can be mounted.

The FNP-45 Competition is a conventional-double-action pistol. It is offered with a black finish and weighs 33 ounces. Magazine capacity is 15 rounds. Each pistol comes with three 15-round magazines and a black nylon case.

Girsan

Last year, this report made the first introduction of the Turkish Girsan 1911 pistols. Now, SAMCO has been named as the importer, and plans were for the first guns to be imported into the United States during 2011.

The Girsan MC 1911 is a nicely made full-size 1911. Caliber is, of course, .45 ACP, and specifications are traditional for this gun. Magazine capacity is extended to eight rounds. A variant with an accessory rail will be offered as the Model MC 1911 S.

Glock

Glock pistols have been available in the United States for 25 years. To commemorate this achievement, the company offered a special 25th anniversary Limited Edition Glock 17 pistol. Recall that the Model 17 was the first Glock pistol imported into America, and this special gun is the latest "Gen4" variant. The top of the slide bears the legend, "25 Years of Glock Perfection in USA." Special "25 Years" medallions are inset into the grip frame. Plans were to make only 2500 of this particular variation.

Shooter Karen Curry tries out the full-size Gen4 Glock 34.

The special 25th Anniversary Glock is a Gen4 Model 17 with a special insert in the grip. Gen4 pistols have interchangeable grip straps.

The 9mm Goncz Hi-Tech Pistol, unavailable for some years, may be handled by the new TWA company.

The High Standard Duramatic Plinker, long unavailable, has returned to production, in improved form.

The commemorative Glock 17 is a Generation 4 (Gen4) pistol. Recall that Gen4 treatment was introduced last year, available on the 40-caliber Glock 22. Now, ten Gen4 pistols are available, including 8 variants of 9mm and 40 S&W pistols, and one each of 357 SIG and 45 GAP. The new Generation 4 modifications include three inter-changeable backstraps, a reversible magazine release (about 30% larger), a dual recoil spring assembly, and an improved gripping surface, referred to as tactile squares, forming a Rough Textured Frame (RTF). Because of the reversible magazine catch feature, Gen4 magazines have two notches on the opposite sides of the magazine body, so they will work both ways. A small "Gen4" notation follows the model number on the left slide flat of the new pistols.

High Standard

The High Standard Duramatic "Plinker" is back. High Standard is back in the moderately-priced 22-caliber auto-loader field with the renewed production of the innovative little pistol.

The pistol is not a new design. It was produced by High Standard as one of the inexpensive utilitarian .22 semiautos introduced during the years following World War II. (The others were the Ruger and Whitney designs.) The High Standard Duramatic (later called the Plinker) was also sold by Sears (mail-order, in those innocent days) as the J.C. Higgins model 88.

The design was innovative. The barrel was attached to the upper front part of the frame, forward of the trigger guard, by a screw with a large head. The entire grip frame assembly also was attached by a long screw to the lower rear part of the frame. This system was later used by Beretta for its 22-caliber NEOS pistol.

Because the original High Standard pistol had originally gone by two different names, the rejuvenated company decided to cover all bases and use both names. The new gun is referred to as the High Standard Duramatic "Plinker." A few improvements have been made: the barrel screw, for instance, now tightens with an allen wrench instead of finger pressure.

The Duramatic Plinker has a 4.5-inch barrel and weighs 34 ounces. It is 8.5 inches long and 4.75 inches high. The magazine holds 10 rounds.

The Hi-Point .45 ACP carbine is finally a reality. Here is a shot of one of the first ones, gussied up with front grip, scope and holder for extra magazines.

Glock-styled ISSC 22-caliber pistols are now available with colored frames. This one has a Desert Camo (tan) frame.

This is one of the first 100 new Ithaca 1911 production pistols, displayed at the 2011 SHOT Show.

Hi-Point

The 45-caliber Hi-Point Carbine is finally available! After being promised for some time, the new 45 was displayed at the January 2011 SHOT Show.

Hi-Point Carbines began with the 9mm version. Then a .40 S&W carbine was added. Now, the family is complete with the .45 ACP variant. The 45 carbine uses the same magazine as the Hi-Point 45-caliber pistol, so will also have 9+1 capacity. The Model number is 4595TS. The TS stands for "target stock," and the carbine features Hi-Point's new stock with recoil-absorbing buttpad and plenty of rails.

A conversion stock to update previous 9mm and 40-caliber carbines is also available.

HK

Heckler & Koch is offering two new variants of their P30 pistol. The P30S has an external thumb safety. The pistol is fitted with right and left ambidextrous safety levers.

The P30L, which has a barrel and slide that are 1/2-inch longer than those of the standard P30, was previously available only in 9mm chambering. It now is offered in .40 S&W also.

I O, Inc.

The IO Hellcat, a small 380 with a polymer frame and milled slide, was introduced here last year. By early 2011, it had achieved full production and widespread distribution. A few variations have appeared along the way. A stainless-steel slide is an option, and a finger-rest magazine is now available. Besides basic black, frames are now also offered in olive drab and in pink (a kinder, gentler Hellcat?).

IO also offers large unconventional long-range pistols based on the AK design. One is in 7.62x39mm. Another is in 223, and a clever magazine release allows use of AK- or AR-type magazines.

ISSC

The Austrian ISSC 22-caliber pistol looks quite a bit like a Glock with a hammer. It went into production last year and now has several modifications.

Shallow cuts were made on the slide to reduce reciprocating slide weight. Also, subtle differences were made on the frame. These make the pistol feel a bit more like a Glock. Cosmetic options are now offered. Previously offered only with black frames, now they are available in Blush (pink) and Desert Camo (tan) colors.

ITHACA

Last year, Ithaca displayed prototypes of a 1911 pistol. By January 2011, the pistol was going into production, and Ithaca was taking orders. Some of the first 100 manufactured were on display at the 2011 SHOT Show. Full production was anticipated during the first quarter of the year.

Recall that Ithaca was one of the three major producers of 1911A1 pistols during WWII. Ithaca pistol production was third, only behind Remington-Rand and Colt. My first .45 was an Ithaca 1911A1 purchased through the Director of Civilian Marksmanship, so I must admit I have a soft spot in my heart for Ithaca-made 1911 handguns. It is good to have the company back in the pistol business.

Iver Johnson

Rails are in, and Iver Johnson has introduced a new 45-caliber 1911, the Eagle LR (for "Light Rail"), with a Picatinny rail on the forward part of the frame. Iver Johnson 1911 pistols have forged slides and CNC-machined cast frames. They are assembled in the Philippines by SAM, then sent to the United States for enhancements and finishing by IJ. All guns come with Big Diamond wood grips that also have the old Iver Johnson Owl Head logo in the middle.

An interesting concept from IJ is furnishing completely-assembled upper assemblies (slide, barrel and all contained parts) and lower assemblies (frame and all contained parts) as separate units for shooters who want to create something special. Iver Johnson also offers .22 LR conversion kits for 1911 pistols, with either fixed or adjustable sights. Complete IJ 22-caliber 1911 pistols were anticipated to be in the line by mid-2011.

Kahr

Kahr Arms now offers 1911-type pistols under the Auto-Ordnance, Thompson and Magnum Research names (See Magnum Research). The 100th anniversary of the 1911 was commemorated by a special Auto-Ordnance pistol. (See Auto-Ordnance),

Under the Kahr name, several new pistols were introduced in early 2011. Laser sights are becoming more popular as more people avail themselves of the option of concealed carry. Now, two Kahr models, the P380 (.380 ACP) and PM45 (.45 ACP) are available with Crimson Trace Laserguard laser devices. The lasers are adjustable for windage and elevation.

The P380 has a 2.5-inch barrel, a black polymer frame and matte stainless-steel slide. The PM45 is a larger gun with a 3-inch barrel, made of similar materials. The lasers mount forward of the trigger guard, and Kahr offers holsters designed to fit the new guns.

The Kahr P380 now has a new California-legal variant. The gun has a loaded-chamber indicator and a magazine disconnector to comply with California regulations.

Kahr also introduced a new line of CM series pistols, designed as value-priced carry guns. They started with the CM9, a true subcompact 9mm. With a polymer frame and stainless slide, the CM9 can be thought of as a less-expensive PM9. The differences found in the CM9 include conventional rifled barrels, fewer machining operations on the slide, simpler markings, a pinned front sight, and only one magazine furnished. These features allow a lower price range. The subcompact CM9 is 6+1, weighs less than 16 ounces, and measures 4x5.3 inches.

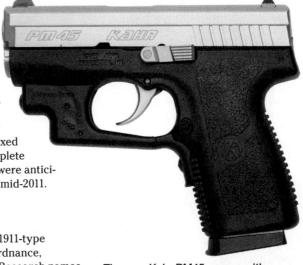

The new Kahr PM45 comes with a Crimson Trace Laserguard laser sight.

The Kel-Tec PMR30 (left view), introduced in the last edition, is in full production. The 30-shot .22 Magnum is large but weighs less than 14 ounces.

Kel-Tec

Kel-Tec's light 30-shot .22 Magnum pistol, the PMR-30, was introduced last year. It seems to have been well-received. The 13.6-ounce large-capacity pistol rapidly achieved full production. By the January 2011 SHOT Show, the PMR-30 was joined by a rifle version, the RMR-30. The 3.8-pound carbine uses many of the same internal parts as the pistol and uses the same 30-round magazine. The RMR-30 has a collapsible shoulder stock, and the 16-inch barrel is threaded to accept various muzzle attachments.

Recall that Kel-Tec was an early manufacturer in the true subcompact 9mm niche. Its P-11 (10+1) and PF-9 (7+1)

pistols have remained in continuous production since their introduction.

Kimber

Kimber decided to make only 250 cased sets of special pistols to commemorate the 100th anniversary of the 1911. The commemoratives sold out so fast that the company turned its attention to the design of a new subcompact 9mm pistol.

That pistol went quickly into production. It was introduced as the "Solo," an entrant into the new breed of small subcompact pistols for the 9mm cartridge. The Solo, with its 2.7-inch barrel, measures just 3.9x5.5 inches, small enough to hide completely under a 4x6 index card.

The new little pistol doesn't look much like a 1911. However, with Kimber's 1911 experience, it is no surprise that it incorporates a number of 1911 charac-

teristics. The controls – manual safety, slide release and magazine release – are in the same locations as on the 1911. The grip angle is close to the 74-degree angle of the 1911. There are, of course, differences. The safety and magazine release are ambidextrous. The single-action trigger is pivoted in the frame (and actually looks like a double-action trigger). The all-metal pistol weighs 17 ounces. The frame is aluminum, and the slide stainless steel. Two variants were offered—the Solo Carry, with a black frame, and the Solo Carry Stainless, with a silver frame. A neat little pistol.

Kimber also introduced several new variants in its 1911 line. The Ultra + CDP II combines a 3-inch barrel and a full-length grip. The Super Carry pistol line (which features a nicely-rounded rear grip) now has HD (heavy-duty) variants with stainless-steel frames. With all the commemoratives gone, the upgraded Royal II is about as close as one can get. A classic full-size 1911, it has a splendid charcoal blue finish and bone grip panels.

The Kimber Solo 9mm (beauty shot)

In the two years since its introduction, the Legacy Citadel has grown into a full line of 1911 variants.

Kriss

Rails are "in" and the Kriss line of carbines, short-barrel rifles and pistols have added accessory rails.

TDI, the parent company of the Kriss guns, will be importing the nicely-made Swiss Sphinx pistols. Availability of the Sphinx in the United States was scheduled for early 2011.

Legacy

New in Legacy Sports International's Citadel line of 1911 pistols is their 22-caliber Target pistol. So new that it did not make it into the 2011 catalog, the new .22 wears Hogue grips and has fiber-optic sights. Previous Legacy 22-caliber 1911s were Chiappa-design pistols marketed under the Puma name. The new pistols will be marketed under the Citadel brand name.

Les Baer

Les Baer Custom did pay homage to 100 years of firearms history. Appropriately named the Centennial, their full-size commemorative gun had "Centennial 1911" engraved on the right slide flat. Charcoal blue finish and real ivory grips made the pistol stand out, and a special presentation box came with each pistol.

To acknowledge the importance of the

television series, Shooting USA, a Baer custom 1911 pistol was made with the "Shooting USA" logo engraved on the right side of the slide.

The new Ultimate Tactical Carry is considered a serious self-defense pistol. Carefully fitted with rounded edges, the gun has slim grips, tritium sights, extended controls and a 4-pound trigger. It is a full-size 5-inch pistol.

Magnum Research

Recall that last year, Magnum Research made news by entering the 1911 field, and by introducing an innovative small .380.

Since last year, the company has been acquired by Kahr Arms. (See Kahr.)

The Magnum Research line of handguns, including the big Desert Eagle .357, .44 and .50 AE pistols, continues under Kahr ownership.

And – a new addition (well, actually a reintroduction) – the "Baby" Desert Eagle is back in the Magnum Research line. The present catalog description is "Baby" Desert Eagle II. These highly-regarded Israeli-designed pistols, based in part on the CZ 75 design, were introduced several decades ago as the Jericho. Imported by different companies at different times, it is the "baby" of the Desert Eagle line. This accounts for the unusual designation for pistols that can weigh up to 40 ounces.

They are offered with either polymer or steel frames, and in full-size (4.5-inch barrel), "semi-compact" (3.9-inch) and compact (3.6-inch) variants. Full-size and semi-compact pistols come standard with accessory rails. Calibers are 9mm, .40 S&W and .45 ACP. The .45 chambering is only available in a steel-frame 3.9-inch version.

Dedicated readers may remember that last year the "Baby Desert Eagle" name was used to introduce a new polymer-frame "fast-action" pistol. The pistol is now in production as the MR Eagle. It is available in 9mm and 40 calibers. With 4-inch barrels, the guns weigh about 25 to 26 ounces. The innovative pistols are made with German and American parts, assembled in Minnesota.

Masterpiece Arms

Masterpiece Arms, maker of "MAC-10" type pistols and carbines, now offers very small personal protection pistols.

The new little pistols are offered in .32 Auto and .380 calibers. With a 2-1/4-inch barrel, the MPA Protector measures just 3.2x4.3 inches. Thus, the little pistol can just about hide completely under a 3x5 index card. Weight for the all-steel, machined pistol is about 11.8 ounces. For such a small pistol, the grip is especially good. On a small scale, it reminds me a bit of the WWII Polish Radom 9mm pistol—the straight front strap and slanty rear strap give a grip that allows good control of the pistol.

Sharp-eyed regular readers of this publication may see something familiar about the MPA Protector. In the 1997 edition, a pistol of similar appearance was introduced by Autauga Arms as the Welsch 32 (named for designer Manford Welsch). In the following 1998 edition, the pistol was reported in production as the Autauga .32. MPA, then a young company, did the CNC production for Autauga. About 5000 32-caliber pistols were made under the Autauga name before the gun was discontinued.

In 2008, MPA changed ownership. The new owners considered the growing interest in personal protection arms and reevaluated the pistol. The old guns were made from castings; the new MPA pistols are machined from steel billets. Thus, the design is strong enough to handle .380 as well as .32 ammunition.

Updated Masterpiece Arms Protector pistols, since February 2011, come with mechanical improvements and a magazine grip extension as well as the flat floorplate. The pistols have a lifetime warranty.

Nighthawk

Nighthawk Custom has offered two 100-Year Anniversary 1911 commemoratives. The Standard Grade was built to resemble the original issue, but with custom fitting. Engraved on both sides of the slide, it has a black Melonite finish. On the right is the Seal of the United States. On the left is engraved, "We the People." On the right frame appears "100 Years Serving America."

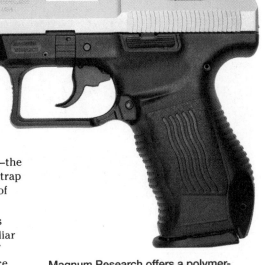

Magnum Research offers a polymer-frame "fast-action" pistol as the MR Eagle.

The "Baby" Desert Eagle is back. The Israeli pistol is once again offered by Magnum Research.

The new little MPA Protector pistol is offered in both .32 and .380 ACP.

The Nighthawk 1911 Centennial High Grade pistol has a stainless-steel slide with engraving and gold inlays.

For the growing "Wild Bunch" segment of Cowboy Action Shooting, PARA has introduced – what else? – its Wild Bunch pistol.

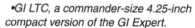

Grips are traditional "big diamond" walnut panels, but Nighthawk's special G10 Centennial grips are optional. Plans were to offer these guns until December 31st, 2011.

The High Grade guns were made to the same specifications, but were built with stainless-steel frames and slides. The engraving is cut after the Melonite finish is applied, so that the stainless steel shows through. Gold inlays include the seal on the right slide, and "We the People" on the left. High Grade guns were limited to a total production of 100.

Will anyone actually shoot such commemoratives? If so, Nighthawk has fitted them with subtly-modified hammers to prevent "hammer bite."

Olympic Arms

Olympic Arms realized that a polymer frame can be made in just about any color. New variants of the company's polymer-frame Whitney Wolverine pistol are now available in three different colors. The full-size but lightweight 22-caliber pistols can be had in Coyote Brown, Desert Tan and, to appeal to the ladies, in pink.

PARA USA

Yes, PARA offered a 100th year 1911 commemorative in 2011. In fact, two separate guns were offered. The first is the 1911 100th Anniversary pistol, a fairly traditional pistol with a few modern touches and Cocobolo grips. The second is the 14-45 100th Anniversary gun, more or less commemorating PARA's first 1911 brought up to 2011 with modern embellishments. It has a double-column light-rail frame, and is gussied up with beavertail tang, fiber-optic sights and extended controls. Both the 1911 and 2011 pistols are engraved "100th Anniversary" on the right slide flat. Cased sets containing both of the two pistols were in limited production, with only 100 sets being made.

As part of a perhaps unintentional tribute to its first 14-shot pistol, the two PARA Anniversary pistols were just the first two of 14 new 1911 variations offered in 2011. Here are the other 12:

•GI LTC, a commander-size 4.25-inch compact version of the GI Expert.

•1911 Wild Bunch pistol, a retro sidearm for SASS "Wild Bunch"competition.

•P14-45, a recreation of PARA's first large-capacity .45 pistol, back in the line.

•All-black Warthog, a stubby 10-shot with fiber-optic front sight.

•Hawg 7, a slim 3.5-inch variant with a 7-round magazine.

•Companion, a 3.5-inch LDA (Light Double Action) .45.

•Companion II, a 4.25-inch LDA .45.

•1911 Limited, full-size 5-inch .45 with modern enhancements.

•14-45 Limited, double-column version of the Limited.

•18-9 Limited, a 9mm Limited with 18-round magazine capacity.

•LTC Tactical, a 4.25-inch .45 variant with a rail.

•14-45 Tactical, a 5-inch double-column .45 with a rail.

Ruger's new LC9 pistol is a 17-ounce subcompact 9mm with a polymer frame.

Remington

Remington is back in the pistol business!

In the Civil War era, Remington percussion revolvers challenged Colt revolvers. The Old West saw Remington revolvers and derringers. In the 1900s, Remington pocket pistols were highly regarded. Remington (Remington-UMC after 1912) even submitted a prototype 45-caliber pistol for government tests in 1917. After America entered WWI, Remington-UMC manufactured 1911 pistols in 1918, delivering 21,677 before the Armistice cancelled the contract. (Note that a name-related business-machine company, Remington-Rand, also made 1911A1 pistols during WWII). However, Remington-UMC dropped pocket pistol production in 1934, and never made another pistol—until now.

Now, 1911 pistols with the Remington name are in production again. Named the 1911R1, the new Remington was a mixture of 1911 and 1911A1 and modern features. The standard 1911R1 came with flat mainspring housing and big-diamond grips (1911), a narrow hammer and short trigger (1911A1) and flared, lowered ejection port and high 3-dot sights (modern). The company also offered an Enhanced version with beavertail tang, adjustable fiber-optic sights and other niceties.

And, of course, there were not one, but two, commemorative versions. The 1911R1 Centennial was scheduled to be offered only during 2011. It featured special engraving on the slide and special grips with a Remington medallion. The 1911R1 Centennial Limited Edition (only 300 of these to be made) was highly polished, charcoal blued, and with an engraved and gold-inlaid slide. The Limited Edition had smooth walnut grips, and was offered in a walnut presentation case.

Remington has been a major supplier of rifles and shotguns. It is good to have them back in the pistol business.

Rohrbaugh

Rohrbaugh's line of light subcompact 9mm and 380-caliber pistols continues to be popular. However, the company has something else in the works: a .45 ACP of entirely new design. I don't have any details now. Watch this space.

Ruger

The downsized 380-caliber Ruger LCP proved to be popular, so why not a downsized 9mm? The LC9 (Light Compact 9) was thus formally introduced in January 2011. Ruger's new subcompact 9 has a 3.12-inch barrel and weighs 17 ounces. Height and length are 4.5x6 inches. Thus, the LC9 can almost hide under a 4x6 index card. (All right, the grip sticks out a little.) Flat and extended floorplates are furnished for the LC9 magazine, which holds 7 rounds.

The little .380 LCP, by the way, is now also available with a Crimson Trace Laserguard. Weight goes up from 9.4 ounces to only 10 ounces.

The full-size 9mm polymer pistol, the SR9, has been joined by a .40 S&W, variant, logically called the SR40. Barrel length is 4.14 inches, and the pistol measures about 5.5x7.5 inches. The SR40 comes with either 15+1 or 10+1 capacity. The original SR9 is now available in an all-black version.

In the 22-caliber pistol line, the polymer-frame 22/45 pistols were available with nice-looking thin checkered Cocobolo grips. Threaded barrels (1/2x28 thread) are available on some models, with the threads protected with a removable cap. These threaded barrels can accept a number of muzzle accessories.

SIG-Sauer

SIG-Sauer introduced a number of new models and variants of existing models at the 2011 SHOT Show.

Let's start with their brand-new subcompact 9mm, the P290. Weighing in at about 20 ounces with its 2.9-inch barrel, the P290 measures 3.9x5.5 inches, easily hiding under a 4x6 index card. Capacity is 6+1. The new subcompact is a polymer-frame, double-action-only, hammer-fired pistol with a tilting-barrel locking system. Siglite night sights are standard. A number of options are also available. An integrated laser module fits right in front of the trigger guard. Replacement grip inserts of wood, aluminum or polymer can slide right into frame slots. An extended 8-round magazine is also offered. The P290 is available in black Nitron or two-tone finishes.

SIG-Sauer recognized the 100th anniversary of the 1911 by introducing new "Traditional" 1911 models. Recall that when the company introduced its 1911 line in 2004, the pistols were basic modern 1911s. The slides, however, were modified to give the 1911 a more Teutonic look, resembling the slides of other SIG-Sauer pistols. Now, the Traditional series looks more, well… traditional, with round-top, flat-sided slides. "SIG SAUER 1911" appears on the left forward portion of the slide.

A new 1911-22 was also introduced. The new 22 LR pistol uses the "Traditional" slide form.

A number of modifications were offered in the popular, long-running P226 / P229 series pistols. Introduced as Extreme and Enhanced Elite guns, they offer new niceties. Some have strangely added an unneeded, but trendy, beavertail tang.

Old-timers may rejoice! The beautiful single-action Model P210 has quietly returned to the SIG-Sauer lineup. It has been slightly modified with some modern features. The big 37-ounce 9mm carries 8 rounds in its single-column magazine.

The SIG-Sauer 1911-22 is built with the new "traditional" slide.

SIG-Sauer recognized the 100th Anniversary of the 1911 with its "traditional" pistols.

Smith & Wesson

Introduced last year, several of S&W's semiauto pistol offerings are in full production now. Among these are the little Bodyguard 380 and the M&P Pro Series guns. Smith & Wesson considered the Pro Series to be intermediate between the regular line and the Custom Shop pistols.

Newly-introduced at the 2011 SHOT Show were several new items:

The M&P 22, a polymer-frame .22 LR lookalike for the centerfire M&P pistols. Made by Walther in Germany for S&W, the M&P 22 comes with either a 10-round or 12-round magazine.

The S&W M&P 22 allows 22 LR practice with an M&P-frame pistol.

S&W offers a Carry and Range Kit, which has an M&P pistol, extra magazines, pouch, loader, holster and carry case.

For the S&W SD pistols, a Home Defense Kit is available, with a pistol, two magazines, a pistol light and a nano-vault.

Some shooters want a light attached to their pistols, and Smith & Wesson now offers an S&W-brand pistol light.

The S&W M&P Pro Series pistols are in production, featuring improved sights and triggers

The SD (Self Defense) polymer-frame pistols. Available in 9mm or .40 S&W, they have Tritium front sights and Picatinny rails. The guns are also available in a special SD Home Defense Kit. The kit includes a 9mm or 40-caliber pistol with two magazines, a small Nano-Vault with cable and keys, and an S&W pistol light to fit the rail.

The M&P pistol is also available in a Carry & Range Kit. This kit has a carry case, a 9 or .40 M&P pistol, three magazines, a holster, magazine pouch, magazine loader and ear plugs.

The SW1911 pistols are available now in a new Enhanced "E" Series. They have "fish-scale" front and rear slide grasping areas, frame checkering and titanium firing pins. A number of "E" variants are offered. Depending on model, the enhanced pistols may have Tritium sights, square or round butt, or an accessory rail. Barrel lengths available are 5 or 4.25 inches.

Springfield

Springfield Armory has two new pistols, a new 1911 variant and a new polymer-frame XD variant.

The 1911 is the Range Officer 45. The concept seems to have been to provide a basic gun, without a lot of frills, built to the same standards as Springfield's top competition pistols. A shooter could

The S&W SW1911 E-series guns (think "enhanced") have a number of embellishments. Look for the "E" on the grips.

leave it as is, or modify it to his liking as his skill improved. The Range Officer is a full-size 5-inch 45, with a forged steel frame and slide. The 40-ounce pistol has an adjustable long trigger, with a 5- to 6-pound pull. A very nice adjustable rear sight, a beavertail tang, match barrel and a beveled magazine well complete the package. Finish is parkerized, and there are no ambidextrous controls. The Range Officer comes with gear: a plastic carry box, holster and magazine pouch, a cleaning rod and two 7-round magazines.

The XD(M) Compact was added to the polymer-frame XD line. Recall that the XD(M)3.8 was added to Springfield's polymer lineup last year. The new Compact is essentially the 3.8 with a shorter grip to make it a smaller package for concealed carry. But wouldn't it be nice to have the magazine capacity of the larger grip? Ah, Springfield has solved that problem. The 9mm XD(M) Compact comes with a 13-round magazine that fills the grip. It also comes with a 19-round magazine that has a grip extension attached. The gun weighs an ounce more (from 26 to 27 ounces) with the "MagX-Tension." It is also offered in .40 S&W.

Firearms writer Magali Compagnon shoots the Springfield XD(M) Compact. The "MagX-Tension" offers a full-size grip.

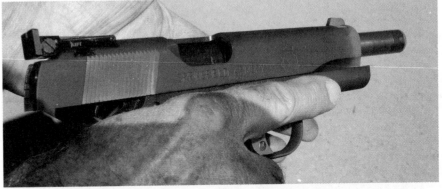

Malloy liked the rear sight on Springfield's Range Officer 45, and the gun performed well on the firing line.

The Steyr "S" series pistols feature shorter barrels and grip frames.

The Taurus 1911 Anniversary pistol is a basic .45 with an engraved slide.

Steyr

The modern Steyr pistols are back. The Steyr guns have received acclaim for their natural pointing characteristics. Now, the trigger systems have been improved to a new reset action system. A roller mechanism makes for a better pull and a shorter reset. The loaded chamber indicator is now on the extractor.

Offered in 9mm and .40 S&W, the pistols were offered as the M-A1 (think M for "medium") with a 4-inch barrel, and S-A1 (think "smaller") with a 3.6-inch barrel. Weight runs about 26-27 ounces, depending on model.

STI

STI International went into the 1911-2011 Commemorative project in a big way. The theme was "The Continuing Evolution of the 1911." Two types of guns were made. A basic "Government" version was made to represent 1911. An "Enhanced" modern variant, to represent 2011, was made with wide double-column frame, fiber-optic and adjustable sights, beavertail tang, ventilated hammer and trigger and other modern niceties.

Slides are engraved and inlaid with three banners reading "1911–100th Anniversary–2011." The two guns will be made in 500 cased sets, offered in

special wood boxes. Serial numbers will be the same for both models of guns in a set. Pistols with serial numbers 001 of both types were on display at the 2011 SHOT Show.

Stoeger

With the growing interest in concealed carry, Stoeger has downsized its rotating-barrel Cougar pistol. The new 9mm pistol, the Cougar Compact, is now available. With a 3.7-inch barrel, the new Compact weighs 30 ounces. The shorter grip frame still holds a double-column magazine, offering 13+1 capacity. In matte black finish, the pistol carries black synthetic grips.

An accessory rail is now offered on the .45 ACP full-size Cougar, which was introduced last year.

Taurus

Taurus, billing itself as the "World's Foremost Pistol Maker," introduced its first 1911 back in 2005. In the intervening years, the Taurus 1911 line grew to well over a dozen variants. To commemorate the 100th anniversary of the 1911, the company introduced several different limited-edition models. All these pistols had special engraving on the slide. The Model 1911 Anniversary is a "basic" 1911, the 1911 Anniversary Match is a modernized handgun with "match" features such as beavertail tang and Novak adjustable sights. The Anniversary Duo-Tone has a two-tone finish. A 1911-22 conversion kit with adjustable sights was also offered.

There were other offerings. The DT Hybrid pistols have a steel frame with

500 cased sets of STI's 100th Anniversary pistols were offered.

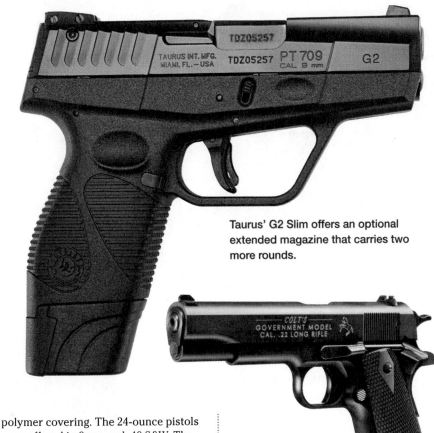

Taurus' G2 Slim offers an optional extended magazine that carries two more rounds.

The Umarex/Colt Government Model 22 is made in Germany.

polymer covering. The 24-ounce pistols were offered in 9mm and .40 S&W. The DT Integral pistols have an aluminum frame and polymer grip panels. Calibers are .380, 9mm and .40, all weighing in at 21 ounces. As an aside, it is always interesting to speculate about Taurus abbreviations. My guess is that DT stands for "duo-tone," as the materials used form color contrasts.

The G2 Slim is a thin 19-ounce carry pistol offered in 9 and .40. Capacity is 7+1 for the 9mm, and 6+1 for the .40. However, an available extended magazine boosts capacity by two extra rounds for each caliber.

With all the recent emphasis on downsized .380s, we must remember that moderately-large, higher-capacity .380 pistols are still in demand. Taurus' new 638 ProCompact weighs 28 ounces and boasts 15+1 capacity.

Taylor's

Taylor's & Co., importers and distributors of replicas of historic firearms, has moved into the 20th Century for its latest offerings. The Taylor's 1911 is a close reproduction of the 1911 as made in years past. The pistol can be had with straight or arched mainspring housings, or a straight housing with a lanyard loop. A competitor can thus order his pistol suitable for the time period in which he is shooting. A modern shooter can opt for Taylor's Combat Model, with fiber-optic adjustable sights, beavertail tang and skeletonized hammer and trigger. The 1911 pistols are made for Taylor's by Armscor.

Well into the modern age, Taylor's also offers the Chiappa Model 1911-22, and the M4 22 pistol, a .22 LR handgun version of an M4 carbine.

Turnbull

Turnbull Manufacturing Co. of Bloomfield, NY, is a major restorer of 1911 pistols. To celebrate the 1911 centennial, Turnbull decided to make exactly 100 true 1911 pistols. The guns were made to approximately 1913 specifications, with a true 1911 frame, hammer, and the appropriate rounded rear sight. The magazines are the old-style two-tone type, with a lanyard loop at the bottom and the "keyhole" at the upper rear portion. Correct polishing and blueing methods were used.

Markings are correct for an early 1913 gun. Some guns were planned to be marked U. S. Army or U. S. Navy. Like Cylinder & Slide (*q.v.*) Turnbull planned to mark, at a customer's request, some guns "U. S. Marine Corps" although no originals were ever made that way.

TWA

Trans World Arms is a new company in the pistol field, but it has a familiar name involved. Recall that the KBI company, which marketed handguns bearing the names Charles Daly and Jericho (among others) went out of business in January 2010.

No one in the industry expected KBI president Michael Kassnar to just sit around twiddling his thumbs. Kassnar has started TWA to import and distribute a single product: a traditional 9mm Hi-Power pistol as made by FEG in Hungary. Importation was scheduled to begin by Spring 2011.

TWA might be the vehicle of the return for another pistol. At Kassnar's booth at the 2011 SHOT Show, a specimen of a Goncz 9mm pistol was displayed. Long-time readers of this publication may remember the Goncz Hi-Tech handgun from the 1980s. It is just possible it may come back as a TWA item.

Umarex

Umarex USA describes itself as "one of the fastest-growing sporting gun companies in the United States." Starting a while back with tear-gas and signal pistols, then moving into airguns, then "replica" firearms, the company offers new pistols based on the 1911 design.

The dedicated .22 LR pistols made for Colt are manufactured under license by Carl Walther in Germany. About the same size and weight as the original 1911, the new Umarex/Colt .22 pistols are made in three versions. The Government Model is visually similar to 1911A1/pre-'70 big-caliber Colts. The Gold Cup Trophy has adjustable sights and other embellishments. The Rail Gun has a frame-mounted accessory rail. Controls work in the same manner as those on the original 1911, and field-stripping is the same. The .22 can use 12-round or 10-round magazines. All variants have 5-inch barrels.

Umarex makes the 22-caliber Colt Rail Gun.

The Walther PPQ features a quick-reset trigger.

Umarex is now the marketer of the Turkish-made 45-caliber Regent pistol. Recall that the nicely-made Regent was introduced last year by Interstate Arms Corp. (IAC). Made by Tisas in Turkey, the Regent is a full-size 1911A1-style 40-ounce pistol with a 5-inch barrel. The Regent R100 is offered by Umarex as an affordable 1911 "with the quality to customize." Hogue grips are installed.

Uselton

Uselton's 100-year 1911 commemorative was made in matched pairs of "government" and "officers" pistols. The guns had casehardened frames, stainless-steel slides with Gold inlays, and straw-blue parts.

Something new is an aluminum frame with 330 stainless steel bonded to the frame to provide the slide rails. Uselton believes this will provide an aluminum-frame gun "that will last."

A new specialty of the company is grips made of mammoth ivory. How much of that is still around?

Volquartsen

Volquartsen made its reputation building excellent 22-caliber pistols and rifles, most based on Ruger designs. Now, for the first time, they are working on a centerfire pistol. No details were available. Watch this space.

Walther

Walther's latest offering is the Model PPQ, with a redesigned "quick defense trigger." The trigger travel is a modest 4/10 of an inch, and the pull weight is about 5.5 pounds. What is most noticeable, though, is the reset distance of only 1/10 of an inch. Reset is audible.

Similar in size and construction to the P99 (Walther's first polymer pistol), the new PPQ has a 4-inch barrel and measures 5.3x7.1 inches, putting the pistol almost into the "compact" category. Weight is in the 24/25 ounce range. Available in 9mm or .40S&W, the magazine capacity is 15 rounds in 9mm, 12 in 40. An extended 17-round magazine is also available for the 9mm. 10-round magazines in both calibers are also available for jurisdictions that don't trust their citizens. Three backstraps are furnished to fit the pistol to the shooter's hand, and an accessory rail is moulded into the front of the polymer frame.

REPORT FROM THE FIELD:
REVOLVERS
(AND A FEW OTHERS)

BY JEFF QUINN

Here we are, heading into the second decade of the twenty-first century, and I sit here hammering away on the keyboard, writing about handgun designs that have been given their last rites several times over the past few generations. Various revolver designs, and even more so the single and two-shot pistols which also bear the scars of age, have been declared obsolete by many experts who are surely much more knowledgeable than I. Yet shooters and hunters and those who just desire to level the playing field against the criminals in our society still purchase these antiquated designs, relying upon them daily to do that upon which a handgun is called to do.

While the semi-automatic pistol far outsells the revolver in the US today, enough of us are still buying the revolvers, single shots, and derringers to keep many manufacturers cranking them out. New revolver designs and variations upon existing revolver and derringer designs are being introduced every year, and high-quality single-shot hunting pistols like the Freedom Arms and Thompson-Center are produced for hunters and target shooters who want to squeeze the most accuracy and distance possible from a handgun. These precision hand-rifles rival the accuracy of many modern bolt-action rifles, yet retain their relatively light weight and handy size.

Modern revolvers designed for concealed carry abound, with some made largely of modern polymers and lightweight metals. Areas in which the revolver still shines are as a tool for the outdoorsman and in the hunting fields. While some excellent auto pistols are produced that do well for hunting large game, the revolver is still king, loved for its accuracy, reliability, power, and simplicity. A good 10mm auto will do just about anything that a .357 or .41 Magnum revolver will do, but most will not do it as accurately. In the hunting field, one or two shots is usually enough, and the revolver provides that, with more to spare. When it comes to rimfires, a .22 auto-pistol is a delight, but a good .22 revolver will handle anything from lowly .22 Short CB caps to hyper-velocity Long Rifle ammunition, and with the simple switch to a Magnum cylinder, the same sixgun can fire the dandy little .22 Rimfire Magnum cartridge as well.

No handgun is quite as versatile as a trail gun as is a good .22 revolver. I can do probably ninety percent of what I need to do with a handgun using a good .22 revolver. They are reliable, accurate, and easy to shoot well. The whole family can enjoy a good afternoon shooting a .22 for less than the price of a couple of tickets to a movie at the local theater.

Jeff Quinn with customized Ruger .357 Maximum

Uberti El Patron revolver

North American Arms .22 Magnum break-top Ranger

A trim, lightweight double action .22 revolver, such as a Smith & Wesson Kit Gun, carries afield without bother at all in a slim little holster, yet is ready to go to work to put meat in the pot or to just provide entertainment around the camp, and is a good choice for a trail gun in areas where large carnivores are not a problem. In bear country, the revolver can be found riding the holster of many fishermen and outdoorsmen who need reliable, powerful protection while in the wild. Chambered for cartridges such as the .44 and .454 Magnums, or even the even more powerful .475 and .500 class cartridges, the revolver can deliver bone-crushing power in a relatively compact package, while not being a hindrance to going about one's daily life.

Cowboy Action Shooting competition continues to enjoy great popularity, and there, the single action revolver dominates, being the sole handgun choice of most competitors. Over the past couple of years, we have seen a resurgence in the popularity of the .44 Special cartridge in the single action revolver. This cartridge has lived in the shadow of the .44 Magnum for over 50 years now, but is being discovered for its own virtues by shooters who really never considered the fine cartridge before. Another great advantage of a good revolver is that the beautiful design lends itself well to customization. Exotic grips and beautiful finishes, along with artful engraving for the well-heeled, are easy ways to make a mass-produced sixgun your own. Many

Freedom Arms is now offering real Micarta grips for their revolvers.

Poly Taurus Model 85 Polymer 38 Special revolver

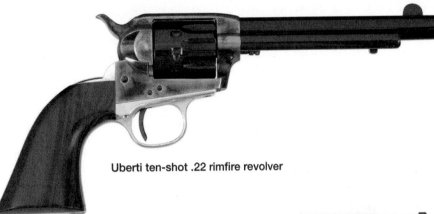

Uberti ten-shot .22 rimfire revolver

Smith & Wesson's new six-shot Governor .45 Colt/.45 ACP/.410 Shotshell revolver

talented gunsmiths make a good living reworking single-action revolvers to suit their customer's needs, but changing grips is something that is easily done, and really adds a touch of class to an otherwise ordinary revolver.

Here we will alphabetically take a look at some of the revolver, single shot, and derringer offerings out there today, from some of the current manufacturers and importers of the most versatile of handgun designs.

American Western Arms

The Mateba is a very unusual-looking revolver, and its uniqueness is not just limited to its appearance. The Mateba turns upside-down the sixgun as we know it. These futuristic-looking revolvers feature interchangeable barrels and are chambered for the .357 and .44 Magnum cartridges, as well as the .454 Casull. The Mateba fires from the bottom chamber in the cylinder, lowering the center of the recoil in relation to the shooter's hand, for a more straight-back recoil impulse, lessening muzzle jump and making target acquisition between shots faster. (In this regard it resembles the new Chiappa Rhino but is an older, separate revolver.) AWA also has a line of lever and pump-action pistols, as well as their well-known stable of Single Action Army replica sixguns which feature some of the slickest actions available on a revolver today.

Beretta

Beretta is best known for producing quality shotguns and auto-pistols, but since their acquisition of Uberti, they are marketing some Beretta-quality replica sixguns as well. Building upon the classic firearms produced by Uberti, Beretta markets their Single Action

Army replicas with some high-grade finishes like a brilliant carbona-type blue, along with authentic-looking case coloring and a high polish. Beretta adds a transfer bar safety system to their revolvers that allows the firearm to be carried fully loaded, with a live cartridge under the hammer, unlike the original style 1873 single action, which should be safely carried with an empty chamber under the hammer. Beretta offers not only the 1873 Single Action Army style Stampede, but a modified Bisley style sixgun as well. There is also the Stampede Marshall, which has a Thunderer-style birdshead grip frame, which makes for a relatively handy packing or hideout gun. Beretta revolvers are chambered for either the .357 Magnum or .45 Colt cartridges, with various finishes offered, including an antiqued finish that makes the sixguns appear to be original nineteenth century sixguns.

Bond Arms

The more I carry my Bond Arms two-shot Snake Slayer derringer, the better I like it. It is a relatively light, handy, and easily-concealed pistol that is ideal for carry in the deep woods in the summertime South, where venomous snakes are encountered on a regular basis. Bond derringers are often regarded as the best that money can buy, top-of-the-line quality in the derringer market, and Bond offers an extensive variety of chamberings, from .22 Long Rifle up through .45 Colt/.410 Shotshell, covering many popular chamberings in between. Bond derringers are built primarily of stainless steel, and they exhibit first class craftsmanship and are built with quality materials. Bond offers a variety of barrel lengths, and derringers with or without trigger guards are available to suit the buyer's preference. Besides being ideal

to use for protection from venomous reptiles, the .410 derringers are also a fine personal defense arm for use against carjackers and other two-legged predators. Loaded with 000 buckshot or Winchester's new PDX-1 load, that compact two-pipe would be a very effective close-range defensive weapon.

The Bond Arms derringers offer a lot of versatility, with the barrels being interchangeable, so one can switch calibers as needed. Bond Arms also offers some high quality leather holsters in which to carry your derringer. I particularly like the horizontal driving holster. It is ideal to wear while riding in a vehicle or on an ATV or motorcycle, placing the handgun within reach for a fast and comfortable draw. Bond Arms leads the market in the extensive variety of chamberings offered, but their .45 Colt/.410 Shotshell versions are very popular these days, not just as a backup to a larger handgun, but for primary carry as well.

Charter Arms

Charter Arms has been producing affordable and reliable revolvers for decades now. I have owned many throughout the years, and probably still have all of them but one, which I sold to a good friend that needed it worse than

I. It was a 44 Bulldog, which epitomizes the big-bore belly gun. The Bulldogs are the workhorse of the Charter line. While the .38 caliber revolvers are a dandy choice for personal protection, some knowledgeable folks prefer a bigger bullet, and the Charter 44 Bulldog is in a class of its own. It is a lightweight, reliable five-shot .44 Special and is relied upon by many for daily carry. The Charter revolvers are available in blued steel or stainless, and recently they have added alloy frames to the lineup for those who want to carry the lightest possible package.

The latest innovation from Charter is the finishes that they apply to their alloy-frame guns. Made in a variety of colors, their pink finish has proven to be extremely popular with women, in Charter's Pink Lady variation of their five-shot .38. In addition to the Pink Lady, Charter now has their "Chic Lady," which comes packaged in a good-looking alligator-textured pink hard carry case. They also have their line of revolvers with a mottled finish. I refer to them unofficially as their "Cat" revolvers. The Cougar has a pink mottled finish, and the Panther a medium-dark bronze mottled finish. I have handled and shot both of these, and they are indeed good-shooting lightweight revolvers. Both have exposed hammers and black synthetic grips, they still draw a crowd when brought out in public, and they still evoke a "love it or hate it" reaction. There seems to be no middle ground. However, the choice is there.

Charter offers more unique finishes than anyone else, but for the traditional among us, the company offers plenty of standard blued or stainless models as well. In addition to their popular .38 Special and .44 Special revolvers, Charter still has their rimfire Pathfinder line in .22 Long Rifle and .22 Magnum, along with revolvers chambered for the .32 H&R Magnum, .327 Federal Magnum, and the highly-respected .357 Magnum cartridge. Charter also makes a true left-handed snubnose revolver called the Southpaw. The Southpaw is a mirror image of their standard revolver design, but the cylinder latch is on the right side, and the cylinder swings out to the right as well.

Charter is still producing the dandy little Charter Dixie Derringer. The Dixie is a five-shot .22 Long Rifle or .22 magnum mini-revolver with a crossbolt safety, built of stainless steel. Weighing in at just six ounces, the Dixie Derringer can hide just about anywhere, and is pretty effective at close range, especially the .22 magnum version. Charter is now also offering a combo Dixie, which comes with both .22 Long Rifle and .22 magnum cylinders.

Chiappa

Chiappa is getting closer all the time to begin shipping out their Rhino revolvers in quantity. This unique "upside-down" sixgun has the barrel located to fire from the chamber which is lowest in the frame, instead of firing from the top chamber in the cylinder as do most other revolvers. This unique feature makes for an odd-looking revolver that is a delight to shoot. Anxious to send a few rounds down the bore of a Rhino revolver, I finally got to do so earlier this year, and the experience was everything which I had hoped it to be. Firing full-power 357 magnum ammunition, the felt recoil was straight back, helping to keep the sights on target for fast repeat shots. I got to shoot only a few cylinders of ammo, perhaps close to 50 rounds, but I anxiously await the arrival of a Rhino of my own to shoot extensively. Chiappa has several

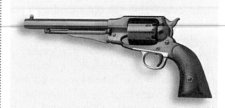

Cimarron 1858 Army cap-and-ball percussion revolver

Cimarron Holy Smoker sixgun replicates the the gun from the movie *3:10 To Yuma.*

Thompson/Center G-2 Contender single-shot pistol

variations of the Rhino in the works, featuring various barrel lengths, and even a model with an accessory rail.

Cimarron

Cimarron Firearms of Fredericksburg, Texas, continues, as they have for many years, marketing some of the best-quality replicas of sixguns of nineteenth century design. Featuring a wide assortment of Colt and Remington pattern cap-and-ball and cartridge revolvers, Cimarron also has designs of some of the transitional cartridge conversion sixguns which bridged the gap from the weapons which were stuffed with loose powder and ball, to the introduction of the self-contained brass cartridge as we know it today. Cimarron also does not ignore some of the lesser-known revolvers from the nineteenth century, keeping alive the look and feel of those old revolvers that were around at the time that the Confederate States were invaded by aggressors from the north *(who, it should be remembered, unlawfully fired on Federal property on April 12, 1861 – DMS).* Without Cimarron's replica of the Leech

& Rigdon, such historical firearms would have fallen into obscurity, as most of us will never see an original. Cimarron still has their derringer line as well, and though I have yet to see one, was told at the 2011 SHOT Show that Cimarron will be introducing a .45 Colt/.410 Shotshell derringer this year. Cimarron replicas have a fit and finish that is a cut above many of the other imported historical sixgun replicas, and they are a lot of fun to admire and to shoot.

Cobra

Cobra Firearms is relatively new to revolver manufacture, but they produce some good-looking pocket revolvers on the five-shot pattern that are similar in size and design to the Smith & Wesson J-frame revolvers. The Shadow is a Plus P rated five-shot 38 Special revolver has a concealed hammer, and looks very much like a Smith & Wesson model 642. These revolvers have stainless cylinders

Engraved Smith & Wesson Schofield from the S&W Performance Center.

Rossi Ranch Hand lever-action pistol

Them's the Breaks:
NAA's Ranger Break-Top
.22 Magnum Mini-Revolver

The Ranger's automatic extractor.

By Jeff Quinn

I have always had a love for break-top revolvers, especially break-top single actions. I think that the most beautiful handgun that I own is my Navy Schofield Founder's Model 45 Colt. Maybe it's because I am left-handed, and am fond of ambidextrous designs. The break-top is absolutely ambidextrous. It allows fast unloading and reloading like a modern double-action revolver with a swing-out cylinder, but is just as easy for a left-hander to operate as it is for the other 90% of the shooting population.

A couple of months ago, when I heard that North American Arms was making a mini-revolver as a break-top, I knew that I just had to have one, before ever even seeing a picture of the little jewel. NAA makes some dandy little revolvers, as they have for many years. Lots of folks depend upon the miniature revolvers for close range personal protection. They are simple, reliable, and well made. I especially like the .22 Magnum version

Break-tops come in all sizes. Here, the NAA Ranger poses with a Navy Schofield.

and barrels and an aluminum frame for a weight of fifteen ounces. They also produce some small and reliable two-shot single action derringers, marketed under the Cobra name, as well as making those derringers for other firearms brands. These compact derringers are made in .22 Long Rifle, .22 magnum, .38 Special, 9mm Luger, .25 Auto, .32 Auto, .380 Auto, and .32 H&R magnum. Their Titan model is built of stainless steel, and is offered in 9mm Luger or .45 Colt/.410 shotshell. These derringers are available in a variety of colors, and each sells at an affordable price.

Colt

This year marks the 175th Anniversary of Sam Colt's first successful revolver, the Paterson, set the stage for all revolvers that have followed. Colt still offers the venerable Single Action Army. The SAA is probably the most recognized handgun in the world, and is certainly the most copied revolver design ever produced. While Colt still produces the SAA, and the latest sixguns that they have been shipping for the past few years are as good as any that Colt has ever produced, there are other Colt re-introductions this year that will surely stir your soul, if you have one.

The wonderful SAA is available in three barrel lengths; 4.75, 5.5, and 7.5 inches, and the Single Action Army is chambered in a choice of .357 Magnum, .44 WCF, .45 Colt, .38 Special, .32 WCF, and .38 WCF. The SAA is available in blued/case-hardened or nickel finishes. Through the Colt Custom Shop, many options are available such as non-standard barrel lengths and hand engraving. New for this year, Colt is reviving the New Frontier. The New Frontier was one of the best-looking firearms to ever leave the Colt factory. For some reason, the originals were shipped with some of the plainest, ugliest wood that Colt ever slapped on the grip frame of a revolver, and I don't know why. The rest of that sixgun was pure class, and hopefully, Colt will outfit the resurrected New Frontier with some nice walnut that looks better than as if it was carved from a Chinese shipping crate, or maybe they will just ship the New Frontier with the hard plastic checkered SAA grips. Anything would be better than the grips that were placed upon the originals, but no matter. I can always change the grips, if necessary, and hope to get my hands around the grip of the latest New Frontier soon.

Handcarved rig to hold two Schofield replica revolvers built by Richard Gittlein of Alaska; stag grips by Eagle Grips.

It is also rumored, and I have it from a good source within the factory, that Colt is bringing back the double-action Colt Trooper .357 Magnum this year as well. I hope so.

European American Armory

EAA Corp still has their line of imported Single Action Army replica revolvers called the Bounty Hunter. These sixguns are available chambered for the .22 Long Rifle and Magnum cartridges, with an alloy frame and a choice of six or eight-shot cylinders. They're also available chambered for the .357 and .44 Magnums, and the .45 Colt. These centerfire sixguns are built with all-steel frames in a choice of nickeled, blued, or case-hardened finishes. These sixguns have the traditional half-cock loading feature, but have a modern transfer bar safety action that permits carrying fully loaded, with a live round under the hammer without fear of firing if accidentally dropped.

The double-action Windicator revolvers are chambered for the .38 Special cartridge with an alloy frame, or the all-steel .357 Magnum version. Both revolvers have a synthetic rubber grip and a business-like matte blue finish, with a choice of two- or four-inch barrels.

Freedom Arms

Now on the market for a couple of years, the Freedom Arms Model 2008 Single Shot pistol is a high-quality single shot handgun that is made for hunting and long-range target shooting. Current chamberings offered are the .223 Remington, 6.5 Swede, 7mm BR, 7mm-08, .308 Winchester, .357 Magnum, .357 Maximum, .338 Federal, and .375 Winchester. Standard barrel length options are 10,15 or 16 inches, depending upon the caliber chosen, but non-standard lengths are available as well for a nominal extra cost. What makes this single shot so comfortable to shoot is the single action revolver

grip style. Shooting the pistol allows the gun to recoil comfortably, with no pain at all to the hands as is encountered with some single shot pistols. The barrels are interchangeable, with extra fitted barrels available from Freedom Arms, allowing the shooter to switch among any of the available barrel and caliber options all on one frame.

The Model 2008 weighs in around four pounds, depending upon barrel and caliber chosen. The barrel is drilled for a Freedom Arms scope mount, and the scope stays with the barrel, allowing the interchange of the barrels without affecting the sight adjustment. The Model 2008 wears beautiful, expertly-fitted laminated wood grips and forends that are the best-feeling, most comfortable single shot handgun grips that I have ever handled.

Heading up the Freedom Arms revolver line is the large-frame Model 83. The Model 83 is chambered for the .454 Casull and .475 Linebaugh cartridges,

of the NAA Mini Gun. The .22 Magnum is a very underrated cartridge that as a defensive round offers good penetration in flesh.

These smallest examples of the revolver maker's art have long been relied upon as a last-ditch weapon for uniformed law enforcement officers, hidden away in a pocket or boot, used as an up close and personal defensive weapon in the event that the officer lost the use of his primary duty gun. These compact five-shot rimfires are also carried daily by thousands of people who cannot, for whatever reason, conceal a larger weapon, or carried in addition to a larger handgun as a back-up gun.

Some sneer at the diminutive power of these 22-caliber revolvers, and while they do not possess the force of a big-bore handgun, one of these tiny revolvers in the pocket is much better than a .45 that is left at home. The basic premise of carrying a handgun for protection is that it is ALWAYS within reach. Always. The need for a defensive firearm is, by definition, a response to an imminent or in-progress attack. When you need your defense handgun, you need it immediately. There is no time to go get it. It needs to be within reach. If you can't reach it, it is of no use to you. As law-abiding citizens, we carry a defensive handgun as we go about our daily lives, doing the things that we do routinely every day. If we were expecting trouble, we would choose to be in another place, or would be armed with a fighting shotgun or rifle. If I were certain that trouble was coming, a .22-caliber rimfire revolver that is no bigger than a pack of smokes would be way down on my list of preferred weapons.

Somewhat higher on the list, but still not near the top, would be a larger handgun. However, the handgun is a compromise as a fighting weapon. We carry them because they are so handy. We can do the things that we must do everyday with a handgun hidden somewhere within reach because the handgun is easier to carry and conceal than a 12-gauge pump. If we ever need our handgun for defense, it will be in response to an attack, and will, as stated above, have to be within reach. That is where the compromise comes in. We must choose a balance between portability, concealability, and firepower.

The NAA Ranger with frame in the open or "broken" position.

While way down on the firepower chart, the mini revolver is at the top of the easy-to-carry, easy-to-hide list. Also, especially in .22 Magnum caliber, these little guns can do quite well in a pinch, and I would much rather have one of these in my pocket than a knife as a defensive tool. In my experience, a .22 Magnum penetrates flesh better than a .38 Special, and with any small caliber handgun projectile, penetration is paramount.

in addition to the .357 Magnum and .500 Wyoming Express cartridges, as well as the .41 and .44 Magnum cartridges. They are available with fixed sights, or rugged adjustable sights. The adjustable-sight guns will also accept a variety of scope mounts. The fixed sight models have an available dove-tailed front sight, to easily regulate bullet impact, while retaining a low profile and rugged durability.

The Model 97 is Freedom's compact frame single action revolver. Built to the same tight tolerances as the Model 83 revolvers, the Model 97 is a bit handier to carry all day and is chambered for the .17 HMR and .22 Long Rifle/Magnum rimfire cartridges, as well as the .327 Federal, .357 Magnum, .41 Magnum, .44 Special, and .45 Colt centerfire cartridges. In addition to these standard handgun cartridges, the Model 97 is also available in Freedom Arms' own .224-32 cartridge, which is a fast-stepping .22 centerfire based on the .327 Federal cartridge case.

The Freedom Arms revolvers are widely known as premium revolvers, built for those who appreciate high quality and hand-fitted workmanship. You never regret buying the best.

Legacy Sports

Legacy Sports has their 1873 Colt replica sixgun called the Puma Westerner. The Westerner is a reliable and well-built sixgun, chambered for the .357 Magnum, .44 WCF, and .45 Colt cartridges, with 4.75-, 5.5-, or 7.5-inch barrels. These replica sixguns are offered with a blued and case-hardened finish with walnut grips, nickel finish with walnut grips, or with a stainless finish and white synthetic ivory grips. The Puma line also includes a very affordable single action replica chambered for the .22 Long Rifle or .22 Magnum cartridge that would make a good trainer for the larger bores, but will be a lot less costly to shoot, using low-cost 22 rimfire ammo.

The Puma Lever action pistol has been a big success, replicating the sawed-off lever gun made famous by the old television Western *Wanted: Dead or Alive*. Nostalgia aside, the Puma Bounty Hunter is a fun, handy lever gun that scratches the itch of those who have always longed for a mare's leg rifle, without the legal hassle of cutting down a lever-action carbine. The Bounty Hunter is legally a pistol, and can be purchased just as easily as any other handgun in most of the US.

The author's custom Ruger .357 Maximum with Eagle Stag grips and shortened barrel.

Magnum Research

Magnum Research of Minneapolis, Minnesota, is now part of the Kahr family of firearms. These robust single action revolvers are built for hunting the largest, most dangerous game on the planet, as well as for recreational shooting fun. The BFR is available in high performance calibers like the .460 and .500 Smith & Wesson Magnums, the .44 Magnum, the .454 Casull, the .50 Action Express, the .475 Linebaugh, and .480 Ruger revolver cartridges, as well as the .30-30 Winchester, .444 Marlin, and .45-70 rifle cartridges. The BFR is also available chambered for the ever-popular .45 Colt/.410 Shotshell combination, which offers a lot of versatility in a handgun.

North American Arms

North American Arms still offers their excellent line of high quality mini-revolvers, but new from NAA is the dandy little break-top NAA Ranger. The Ranger is chambered for the .22 Rimfire Magnum cartridge, and looks very much like a miniature Schofield. Of course, it is not. It does not have the Schofield latch design, and is made of modern stainless steel on CNC machinery, but I have a weakness for break-top revolvers, and the little NAA Ranger is one of my favorite new guns to hit the market. Besides its novelty as a modern break-top, the Ranger is much faster to reload than

any other NAA revolver, and makes for a dandy little pocket gun that can always be within reach.

The North American Arms lineup of mini revolvers have been in production for a long time now, and seem more popular than ever. These little five-shot miniature revolvers are more often than not bought as deep-concealment handguns. These lightweight firearms are small enough to fit into most any pocket, and are handy enough to always be with you, no matter what the attire or climate. Chambered for the .22 Short, .22 Long Rifle, or .22 Magnum cartridges, these little jewels are easy to carry, and surprisingly accurate within their intended range.

Rossi

Rossi USA has introduced their version of the popular Mare's Leg lever-action pistol, called the Ranch Hand. The Ranch Hand is a six-shot lever gun that is built for pure fun, but also has the power for more serious purposes as well. The Ranch Hand is quality-built but priced well under its competition. I have one that is chambered for the .45 Colt cartridge, but the Ranch Hand is also available chambered for the popular .357 and .44 Magnum cartridges.

Rossi has been producing reliable and affordable revolvers for decades. These double-action sixguns are available chambered for the .38 Special and .357

magnum cartridges, in either blued steel or stainless finishes. Rossi was acquired by Taurus a couple of years ago, and all of the Rossi revolvers are now produced by Taurus in Brazil. They are quality, reliable revolvers built for concealed carry or as a duty/hunting gun. Available with short barrels and fixed sights for concealment, or longer barrels and adjustable sights for precision shooting, the Rossi line still means a quality product at an affordable price.

Ruger

Since 1953 Ruger has been producing rugged, reliable, and accurate revolvers. Starting with their Single-Six rimfire revolvers, they built upon that single action rimfire design to introduce their Blackhawk and Super Blackhawk center-fire sixguns as time went by. The Ruger Single-Six and Blackhawk revolvers are still in production today, and have expanded to include the very popular New Vaquero line of fixed sight revolvers. Ruger now has as a regular catalog item the Flattop .44 Special, which has proven to be a very good seller among revolvers. This is the long-awaited .44 Special built on the frame that is sized like the original .357 Blackhawk. The .44 Special Flattop is also available in a Bisley model, with a blued finish, and also as a regular Flattop made of stainless steel.

Ruger has also taken the .327 Federal cartridge that they introduced a few years ago in the SP-101 compact revolver and chambered it into the Blackhawk. This stainless Blackhawk has an eight-shot cylinder, and is strong enough to use the full potential of the .327 Federal cartridge. This little cartridge really performs, offering high velocities and deep penetration. The Ruger's cylinder is long enough to handle the long 120- and 135-grain bullets, which actually measure from .312 to .313 inch in diameter.

While it looks as if the big-bore Super Redhawk chambered for the .480 Ruger cartridge is on the way out, there are still new ones available in the distribution pipeline as of this writing. The .44 Magnum and .454 Casull Super Redhawks are still in production, and hopefully we will see a resurgence in interest in the .480 Ruger cartridge. Also in their double action revolver line, Ruger is chambering the relatively new .327 Federal in their GP-100 revolver. This revolver is also built from stainless steel, wears a four-inch barrel, and has a seven-shot cylinder. Of course, Ruger still offers the GP-100 in .357 Magnum. This is one of

That's some close fitting, an NAA hallmark.

Another use for which these little revolvers really shine is as a snake gun. Every time I write about killing snakes, I get several emails from those who proclaim that we should never kill a poisonous snake and condemning me for promoting such practices. I get the feeling that these folks most likely live in the city somewhere and never encounter a poisonous snake outside the confines of the local zoo. They certainly do not live out in the woods of the South or the deserts of the Southwest. I never kill a harmless snake, but around here, cottonmouths and copperheads are shot on sight. Tree-huggers tell us that a cottonmouth will not attack a human unless cornered, but they have failed to inform the cottonmouth population in the Tennessee Valley of this rule. I have first-hand experience that they will absolutely pursue a human being. Rattlers are not nearly as aggressive in my experience, but if found around my house, they get the same treatment, and that treatment is usually a dose of lead shot. The CCI shotshells pattern very well from these little revolvers, and especially in .22 Magnum caliber, dispatch a viper handily.

When I first opened the box containing the NAA Ranger, I said; "Now this is cool!" And I was right. It is a really cool little revolver. However, after shooting the Ranger, I soon realized that aside from the uniqueness of the design in a mini-revolver, it is very practical as well. Like its larger brethren – the big Scho-field, American, and Russian S&W revolvers of many years ago – the Ranger design has tactical advantages over conventional mini-revolver designs as well. Just as with the large guns, the Ranger can be unloaded and reloAaded many times faster than can the mini-revolvers that require removal of the base pin, followed by poking out the empty cases one at a time, reloading the cylinder, inserting it into the frame, and reinstalling the base pin. With the NAA Ranger, one fires the weapon, opens the break top, dumps the empties, reloads, and closes the action.

Shooting the Ranger is very easy and simple to do. After loading, simply cock the hammer, point the weapon, and press the trigger. Shooting every brand and type of .22 Magnum ammo that I have on hand, I prefer hollow points for most uses. From the short barrels of the mini-revolvers, they do lose a lot of velocity compared to a longer-barreled handgun, but some of the .22 Magnum loads still manage to exceed one thousand fps from the one and five-eighths inch barrel of the Ranger. For defensive purposes, I like the PMC Predator, Armscor, or Winchester Dynapoint hollow point cartridges. I fired several types of ammunition for velocity readings at a distance of ten feet, with the results listed in the chart below. Velocities are listed in feet per second (fps). Bullet weights are listed in grains. JHP means jacketed hollowpoint. Velocity readings were taken at an elevation of approximately 541 feet above sea level, with an air temperature of 34° F.

the strongest, most reliable, and most durable double action .357 Magnum sixguns ever built. Moving up in size a bit is the Ruger Redhawk, chambered for the .44 Magnum and .45 Colt cartridges. The Redhawk is bull-strong and as reliable as any revolver can be.

Ruger introduced their polymer-framed LCR five-shot .38 Special revolver a couple of years ago, and it has been a runaway success. Ruger has sold many thousands of these little pocket revolvers, and now Ruger has added a .357 Magnum version of the LCR to the catalog. It is a powerful pocket gun, but is not at all painful to shoot, despite its light weight and small size. Mine has proven to be strong, reliable, and accurate. As always, Ruger has other interesting revolver designs in the works. I am really excited about one in particular, but cannot disclose any details as of the date of this writing. Hopefully soon.

Smith & Wesson

The big revolver news from Smith & Wesson this year is their Governor, built on the new Z frame. The Governor is a six-shot .45 Colt/.410 Shotshell revolver that also fires .45 ACP ammunition using moon clips. I had the opportunity to fire a few rounds through the Governor, and was well-pleased with the handling and shooting qualities of this new sixgun. The Gov weighs in at slightly under two pounds with a 2-3/4-inch barrel. It also wears a tritium front sight for use in low light conditions, and would be an excellent revolver for self defense while traveling in a vehicle. Even with its large-sized frame, it conceals pretty well under a jacket properly holstered in something like a Sourdough Pancake from Simply Rugged Holsters. S&W offers the Governor initially with either a synthetic rubber grip that is very comfortable, or with an equally-comfortable grip that houses the excellent Crimson Trace laser. Especially with the Lasergrip, the Governor makes an excellent piece for social work, and also as a trail gun to carry in areas where both predators and venomous snakes might be a problem. The Governor has a scandium frame with a stainless steel cylinder and wears a matte black finish overall.

Smith & Wesson also offers an extensive line of high quality engraved handguns for the well-heeled among us. They do a really nice job of making a beautiful revolver a real classy-looking showpiece. Engraved firearms were once offered by almost every American and

Ruger limited production .32 Magnum John Wayne Commemorative

Smith & Wesson .44 Magnum Model 629 Deluxe

Beretta Stampede SAA replica with antiqued Old West finish

European gun company, but these days, engraving is usually a cheap imitation of the true engraver's art. I am glad to see that S&W still offers quality engraving, straight from the factory.

Smith & Wesson has an extensive line of revolvers available, from the .22 rimfires up through the .500 S&W Magnum, and almost every sixgun cartridge in between. The small J-frame five-shot .38 Special revolvers are some of the most popular self defense guns ever produced, and remain so today. The Model 642 is probably still the best-selling revolver in the S&W line, as it is very popular for concealed carry. Lightweight and simple to operate, the J-frame Smiths ride easily in the pocket and can always be within reach if needed. The J-frame Smiths are compact, reliable five-shot revolvers with concealed hammers and lightweight frames. Even the all-steel models carry well. They are easily slipped into the pocket, where they ride comfortably, day in and day out, ready for action when needed. Also falling squarely into the carry gun category is the relatively new polymer-framed Bodyguard.\ .38 Special revolver. This weapon is lightweight, compact, and comes with a built-in laser sight, ready-made for concealed carry.

Moving up in size, the S&W K&L frame revolvers are the mainstay of the Smith & Wesson duty line. Not many law enforcement agencies issue S&W revolvers as they did for many decades, but the traditional double-action revolver is as good now as it ever was. These revolvers have served well many generations of sixgun users, both for defense and for hunting. Moving up to the N-frame, the classic Models 27 and 29 are back in the lineup, and are beautiful and functional examples of the timeless double action

revolver. Large but well-balanced, these .357 and .44 Magnum sixguns define the double action revolver to many shooters. With their crisp single action trigger pulls and butter-smooth double action trigger pulls, they are reliable and accurate.

Next up in size, strength, and power we have the big S&W X-frame guns. The .460 and .500 S&W Magnums are at the upper limits of what most would ever consider possible in a hand-held revolver, and many shooters are intimidated by the power of these weapons, but the large frames and ported barrels handle the recoil well, and they are really not painful to shoot, at least with most loads.

Taurus

Taurus USA has continued to introduce new revolvers every year. They make quality revolvers that are suitable for concealed carry, hunting, or target shooting. From their small lightweight pocket revolvers up through their 454 Raging Bull, Taurus has a wide selection of revolvers from which to choose. Their small-frame snubnose revolvers are available chambered for the .22 Long Rifle, .22 Magnum, .32 H&R, .327 Federal, .38 Special, and .357 Magnum calibers. They are available in blued, nickel, or stainless finishes, mostly with fixed sights, but a couple of models have fully adjustable rear sights. Their duty-size four- and six-inch .357 Magnum revolvers are still in production, with a wide variety of models available. The Raging series of hunting handguns chamber powerful cartridges like the .44 Magnum and .454 Casull and are good choices for hunting dangerous game.

Adding to their extremely popular line of Judge .45 Colt/.410 Shotshell revolvers, Taurus has now introduced a Judge chambered for the 28-gauge shotshell. Throwing a bigger payload of shot than the .410 bore, the 28-gauge Judge qualifies for close-range bird hunting, if the shooter is up to the challenge. I also

have been shooting the new Polymer Judge a bit, and really like it. The Judge Poly is the lightest Judge yet, and is the best suited for concealed carry of the Judge series.

Taylor's & Company

Taylor's imports some great-looking and useful replica sixguns, some of which have unique features to make the weapons better-handling and easier to shoot well, such as their new Smoke Wagon. This SAA replica offers a lower hammer spur and larger fixed sights for easier and faster action, and should prove popular with Cowboy Action competitors. Taylor's also has Remington and Mason design conversion revolvers, as well as other unique sixgun replicas.

Thompson/Center

Thompson/Center keeps plugging along with their tried and proven single shot pistol design. Starting with their Contender model decades ago, the T/C pistols have evolved into the Encore and Contender G2 designs, but both are just improvements and refinements of the original Contender pistol. Offered in just about any chambering that one would want from .22 Long Rifle up through powerful rifle cartridges such as the .45-70 Government, and all the magnum handgun cartridges, including the .460 and .500 S&W Magnums. Thompson/Center offers both wooden and synthetic stocks, and a variety of barrel lengths. The barrels are interchangeable within the same frame group, and these hand-rifles come pre-drilled for scope mounts to take full advantage of their power and accuracy potential. Thompson/Center will be moving all production to the home of the parent company, Smith & Wesson, this year. After four decades, the T/C plant will be closed, and all production will take place in the S&W factory in Springfield, Massachusetts.

NAA Ranger .22 Magnum Ballistics

Ammunition	Bullet	Weight	Velocity
PMC	JHP	40	938.4
Winchester	Dynapoint	45	847.5
CCI TNT	JHP	30	1129
Winchester Supreme	JHP	30	1118
Winchester Supreme	JHP	34	1096
CCI +V	JHP	30	1100
Federal	JHP	50	722.3
Armscor	JHP	40	1088

Recoil is mild, but the small grip on the 7.1 ounce Ranger does not allow for much of a hold, so the revolver does move a bit upon firing, but there is no recoil pain at all. The little Ranger is a delight to shoot. The trigger pull measured slightly under six pounds, and was very crisp and consistent. The Ranger holds five rounds in the cylinder. Up close and personal, it is easy to hit the target with the Ranger, but due to its short sight radius and diminutive size, no attempt was made to shoot for groups on paper at 25 yards. On a human paper silhouette, hits in the vital zone were easy at three, five, seven, and 15 yards.

Like other NAA minis, the Ranger is very well-made. It worked perfectly as designed. Extraction of empty cases was easy, with none sticking in the chambers. The NAA Ranger is unique among handguns, and is even in its own class as a mini-revolver. It is the only small-frame top-break revolver currently made, and the only top-break of any size being made in the US. That is a shame, as the top-break is a good design, and was once a unique American icon among revolvers.

I would love to see the top-break revolver make a comeback in the United States, and perhaps this smallest of all top breaks will lead the way. The NAA Ranger is a limited-production revolver, chambered for the 22 magnum cartridge only, so if you want one, now is the time. NAA also offers a variety of accessory holsters and grips for the Ranger.

[Editor's note: Sandy Chisholm, president of NAA, tells me that the initial 5,000-piece run of Rangers might be the last one, too, depending on public demand. The Ranger retails for considerably more than a basic NAA mini-revolver but in our opinion, it's worth it. If you agree, visit NAA's website at naaminis.com and drop Sandy a line. –DMS]

The Ranger isn't a six-shooter but a five-shooter.

Uberti

Uberti Firearms is the premier Italian producer of quality replica revolver designs, marketing handguns under their own banner, as well as for several other replica importers. Uberti offers many different caliber options and finishes, and replicates some of the less popular, but historically accurate designs such as the cartridge conversions, transition model Colts, and the Remington 1875 and 1890 cartridge revolvers.

U S Firearms

USFA of Hartford, Connecticut builds some of the best 1873 style Single Action Army revolvers that money can buy, crafted to precisely replicate one of the finest sixguns ever designed, but built on modern CNC machinery and hand-fitted by American craftsmen." That was my opening sentence for the U S Firearms section of this piece last year, and it holds more true today than then. US continues to introduce new variations on the thirteen-decades-old Single Action Army design. Newest from US is their Double Eagle. This short-barreled single action has a birdshead grip, lowered hammer spur, and a slightly enlarged trigger guard for easier, faster shooting. The sights are also improved with a larger, easier-to-see configuration, all while retaining the classic look of the old Colt design. In addition to this newest creation from US Firearms, they also have a whole raft of other traditional single action revolvers, some exactly replicating the looks and feel of nineteenth century state-of-the-art fighting handguns.

While the semi-auto pistol is still the darling of the handgun industry and the world is celebrating the centennial of the Colt 1911 auto, Colt's classic 1873 revolver design is still as popular today as ever among Cowboy Action Competitors and those who just love the looks and feel of the classic sixgun. For the more modern among us, revolvers are still being introduced that push the limits of the concept, while others hearken to a more simple time, when if a man went heeled, he usually had a sixgun on his hip. Today, more pocket revolvers are being sold. While the pocket auto is still wildly popular for concealed carry, many choose to rely upon that antiquated design that was inspired by the paddle wheel on a river boat, as it is still one of the best designs ever produced for a handgun upon which one could bet his life, whether it be while facing human vermin or the largest of carnivores. The revolver still gets the job done.

REPORT FROM THE FIELD:
NEW GUNSMITHING PRODUCTS

BY **KEVIN MURAMATSU**

We are still awaiting the ultimate gunsmithing tool to appear. Someday, some enterprising hyper-genius will have a mind-blowing epiphany, virtually audible as the loudest crack of thunder. It will do anything, from hammering its own pins, to holding like a vise, to drilling, reaming, turning, machining, and even glass bedding.

Likewise, we have yet to see the ultimate rifle or accessory which would begin a whole new generation of gunnery – nay, might even skip an entire generation and go one beyond. But of course we're not there yet.

This is not for lack of trying, though. Plenty of small entrepreneurs (and as we all know, the vast majority of these little innovations originate from the little guys) continue to make the attempt to create something new. Perhaps not at this author's desired pace, yet at least it proceeds.

The 2011 SHOT show, like all those previous, was an excellent venue to discover if any of those little tidbits of human inventiveness would appear for the coming year. Of course, many of these discoveries are permutations of current products, and they deserve notice, surely. One astonishing example of this trend is the regular appearance of new grip patterns and designs. As young as I am, I still remember the day when pistol grip stocks came in any material you wanted, as long as it was wood, to paraphrase Henry Ford. Nowadays, wood is almost passé. At least, normal wood is anyway, since some of these beautiful exotic woods on the market can mess you up quickly if you inhale the dust from their manufacture. We have progressed beyond exotic wood to plastic, rubber, steel, aluminum, carbon fiber, and so many kinds of fiberglass-based products that it is mindboggling – mindboggling in a good way, that is. In fact, I'll bet a dude could even find a set of grips that incorporates all the above.

Of course grips are hardly the only thing out there. The really mind-blowing stuff tends to be the forehead-slapping type of thing that, when you look at it, makes you wonder in exasperation why no one came up with that simple idea before.

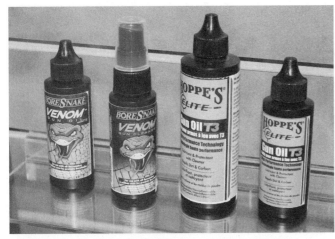

Hoppe's reformulated Elite oil now has T3 for maximum lubricity and corrosion protection.

Iosso's new AR-15 cleaning kit includes a special brush for cleaning the gas tube.

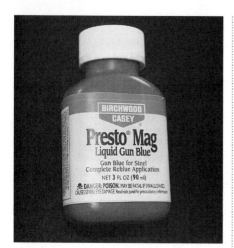

Birchwood Casey's new Presto Mag gives a much richer blue color than most cold blueing solutions.

Birchwood Casey's new RIG 2 formula, which includes PTFE to make things smooooooth.

The Du-Lite all in one cleaning kit, including Kwikseal.

Cleaning Stuff

Cleaning materials continue to be refined as the years pass. Not so long ago, **Hoppe's** No. 9 was the solvent for cleaning carbon fouling from firearms. That product is still going strong, despite the ridiculous amount of newer chemicals designed for the same purpose. Then came the BoreSnake, a pull-through brush/fabric cord. Now the **BoreSnake** line has been expanded with the addition of Venom gun cleaner and Venom gun oil with T3, which are especially formulated for use with the BoreSnake. The addition of T3, a blend of liquid molybdenum and liquid polytetraflouroethylene (PTFE) gives it an extremely high coefficient of friction and extensive corrosion protection.

By the way, Hoppe's Elite Gun Oil has also been upgraded with T3 and should improve this venerable product even further.

Iosso Products has added to their line with the Eliminator AR-15 cleaning kit. Having received customer requests for a tool to clean their gas tubes, Iosso responded, in this kit, with a long skinny brush with a stiff wire core that can be pushed town the gas tube. It is guided by a small bore guide that is inserted into the charging handle slot. Also in the kit are five other brushes for cleaning the upper receiver, chamber, bore, bolt carrier gas key, and bolt carrier bore. These brushes are utilized with a handle compatible with civilian and military cleaning tool threads and can be used with the extension also included. A cord was also thoughtfully put into the kit for drawing the bore brush down the barrel.

All of this stuff fits into an accessory bag which comes with the kit.

Birchwood Casey has expanded their offers with a new cold bluing solution called Presto Mag. This solution is designed to give a finish more like a classic dark blue. Previous types of cold bluing solution rendered a finish that looks more like black oxide (black rather than blue). Birchwood Casey has also formulated RIG 2 Gun Oil and Rust Inhibitor, which is safe for use with all materials currently used in firearms.

Du-Lite, the company whose Kwikseal oil is used by many manufacturers for protection while shipping and sitting on shelves (the stuff you get on your fingers when you open your gun box), is now making this oil available in a handgun cleaning kit, with other associated equipment such as brushes,

solvent and rod.

A neat new cleaning product from **Shooter's Choice** is called the Barrel Wizard. It is a telescoping shotgun cleaning rod with several unique features. First of course, is that it is adjustable in length from 27 to 40 inches. It terminates in a large 12 gauge snap cap which includes an oil reservoir. A section is also textured to allow the rod to use paper towels wrapped around it, to make a tight fit in the bore for swabbing. It is threaded for standard shotgun brushes, jags, and loops. Finally, because of the snap cap, the rod can be stored in the chamber and bore, taken to the range, removed for shooting, then used and replaced in the bore for the trip home. It is an amalgamation of aircraft grade aluminum, Delrin, and brass.

Boyds' now makes gunstocks for the Dakota Arms selection of rifles like this Hunter model, top, and the Remington 597 TactiCool model below it.

These stylish leather-skinned grips from Hogue are just the thing for spiffing up your pistol.

Alumagrips now has these stylish models for the Sig-Sauer P238.

Grips and Stocks

Boyds' has expanded their selections of gun stocks. Most notable this year is the inclusion of units designed to accept the Remington 597 rifle and also stocks for Dakota Arms rifles.

Hogue continues its introduction of pistol grip stocks. With numerous 1911 types already in stock they have now added a leather-skinned grip to the lineup. These grips are really neat. Only the outer surface is leather, and that outer surface is detailed extravagantly. They come in numerous pigmentations, and are often labeled for matching purposes with a manufacture's name, such as "Colt."

In a similar, yet different vein, **Alumagrips** expands their selection by crafting very eye-catching grips for one of the hottest .380s on the market, the SIG-Sauer P238. Several patterns are available, very durable, and still thin enough to enhance the concealment qualities of that skinny little gun.

On to the Tools

Dave at **Manson Precision Reamers** is now marketing a new type of torque wrench. It is the Multi Torque Driver, and rather than using a more traditional adjustable handle which uses variable spring tension to determine the torque setting, it uses a leverage type of action. There are six holes in the bar, and depending on which hole you use, you get a different torque setting. Flipping it over gives you another six: twelve settings for twelve commonly used torque settings, and it is factory calibrated to break within 4% of the listed rating. It all fits into a nice nylon roll-up case with a number of hex bits, sockets and a ratchet. Designed as a field tool for snipers and armorers, it is also useful in the shop and at the range.

Hyskore's bench vise selection has expanded to include a clamp-on unit that attaches to your bench top edge, shooting range bench, or whatever. It has a locking clutch which allows the vise to rotate 360 degrees yet lock up solidly. This Portable Armorer's Vise could fit in any gunsmith's tool selection, or any shooter's.

Berry's has a wonderful selection of tools in their Versacradle sets. Everything from vises to shooting rests can be found and the coolest one has just been introduced. Now the gunsmith has a top-rate checkering cradle that is solid and adjustable and rotates along the long axis (like a checkering cradle should) and can be used with a floor stand, if so desired. The best part is the trademark Versacradle, which is basically a ball joint with a very tight lock. Essentially it has a joint like a human shoulder but it only locks up when you want it to. It rotates, tips, and rocks for your checkering pleasure. Furthermore, retention on the stock can be adjusted with the thumbwheels on either end. I want two.

Some Really Cool Parts

XS Sight Systems has a nifty new piece of hardware designed to complement Ruger's new Gunsite Scout rifle. This rifle, a bolt gun in .308 Win., is built on the scout concept: a lightweight, bolt action carbine with a low power extended eye relief scope mounted over the barrel. For whatever silly reason(s),

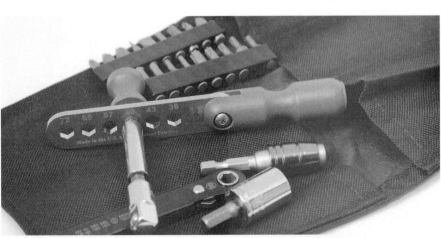

This oddly effective and precise little torque wrench kit was designed for field use, but Manson Precision Reamers would agree that it has a home in the shop as well.

The table edge armorer's vise from Hyskore is a great addition to the gunsmith's range equipment.

The Volquartsen V-Comp, made for the tapered barrels of Ruger Mark III pistols.

This Volquartsen Bolt Assist fits right onto a Ruger Mark III pistol's bolt to make it easy as pie to draw the bolt back, and with no more complaining because the grippy spots are too small.

XS Sight Systems made this rail for the Ruger Gunsite Scout rifle to allow mounting a traditional optic instead of a scout scope.

this concept has yet to catch on with the American public, so XS has built an extended Picatinny style scope mount that reaches from the rear receiver bridge to well over the barrel. This will allow the owner to use both scout type scope mountings or standard higher power scope setups on the same rifle. For that matter, an optic plus night vision gear would work too.

Volquartsen has expanded their offerings with many items but the two that caught my attention were designed for the Ruger Mark III handgun. Many owners have lamented the reduction in bolt handle size in the newest offerings of the Ruger .22 auto. Ostensibly, these bolts are significantly more difficult to grasp;

not impossible, mind you, but much more difficult than the older Mark IIs and Standards. So Volquartsen went crazy and made a toggle like Bolt Assist that completely eliminates that problem. The second item was a muzzle compensator called the V-Comp that fits right around the front sight on the tapered Ruger barrels. It is not gaudy and should make a nice addition to the plinking pistol.

The trigger masters at Timney are working on an AK drop-in trigger group that will be available later this year. While not considered a precision rifle, the AK triggers are usually so unrefined that they defy definition. For a match trigger snob like me, a nice crisp, take-up free trigger unit is like a gift from God, because regardless of the accuracy of the firearm it's put in, it will be much more fun to shoot. Last year's 10/22 drop-in trigger was a hit, but then Timney figured: Why not just make an entire fire control module to drop right into the 10/22 receiver? So they did, and it has a long magazine release lever that conforms to the underside of the trigger guard, kind of reminiscent of

some of the old lever action rifles from the 19th century. It looks good and works just as well.

Cylinder and Slide just introduced a retro 1911 pistol that is an exact duplicate for the original from so long ago. All the internals are made from forgings rather than castings, like the originals, and are to the same dimensions. For example, the trigger is a one-to paraphrase Henry Ford piece machined unit, unlike modern triggers where the bow is a separate piece attached to the trigger piece. Anyway, all of these parts are now available for custom building purposes (or quality replacements), not just as assembled components in the retro gun. These parts can also be purchased in alternative finishes, including the totally awesome nitre blueing. Finally, they also indicate that the forged slides and frames will also be available for your custom building pleasure.

Timney has added an entire fire control group to their lineup which includes their previously available modular trigger. They've also added a long magazine release lever.

Timney has also developed a really nice feeling trigger for AKs.

A small selection of new forged retro 1911 parts available from Cylinder & Slide.

Score High Gunsmithing's new cheek adjuster hardware allows you to remove your cheekpiece for bolt removal without losing your cheek rest setting.

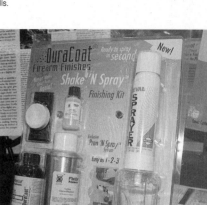

This new AR charging handle from Brownells promises to offer the best of all possible worlds, having a lower profile when folded, yet larger grip surface when open than a standard charging handle. Photo courtesy of Brownells.

Brownells new Heavy Duty Rem 700 rail is sturdy and attaches with larger than normal screws for maximum retention under recoil. Photo courtesy of Brownells.

The Shake and Spray Duracoat kit from Lauer Custom Weaponry makes it easy to Duracoat your gun without having to buy any expensive equipment.

Score High Gunsmithing just released an adjustable cheek piece hardware set. Very similar to the set in the stocks manufactured by McMillan, it one-ups the older set. If one wants to remove the bolt from the gun, the raised cheek piece on the older unit must be removed by literally screwing it out. This is slow and makes it necessary to re-zero the rifle, not for accuracy, but for fit (fit can have a great effect on the shots). Score High's unit allows the shooter to remove the cheek piece and replace it without changing the setting, by the use of two heavy duty thumbscrews. This will seriously minimize the frustration level for those folks using this type of firearm.

Of course **Brownells** is ever in the game, not just distributing all these other fine products but also developing their own. The first item is a set of pillar bedding sleeves that are made from G-10 synthetic. Completely impervious to solvents, temperature, and bad tempers, and practically weightless, custom rifle builders now have another option for the accurization of their products.

On that same rifle might be installed Brownells new Remington 700 Heavy Duty Picatinny Scope Base. It is a sturdy, one piece aluminum Picatinny rail that is fastened to the receiver with four 8-40 screws. Standard 700 rail screws are 6-48, so a little bit of drilling and re-tapping is necessary, but for good reason. 8-40 screws are significantly stronger than 6-48 screws (duh, they're bigger) and those with high recoil rifles can feel safer about their optic retention when using the larger rail, with larger screws. This rail comes either in standard, or 20 MOA elevation, and of course in short and in

long action lengths. The Picatinny aspect of the rail being the most useful part, as rings can be placed in two of any thirteen spots on the rail, allowing the user to mount the optic in the most practical, useful, or fashionable manner needed.

The neatest addition from Brownells is the AR-15/M-16 Paratrooper Charging Handle. You don't need to be a paratrooper, or any kind of trooper, to see the utility in this charging handle. The latch itself is two pieces, the hook and the folding handle. This folding handle opens out to about two inches then collapses to a width thinner than the original standard handle. The usefulness here is three-fold: A much larger grasping area allows more leverage to be exerted to retract the bolt; its length while open allows easy manipulation when an optic is mounted; and while folded in to a low profile it stays out of the way, and out of your gut. Brownells will sell a lot of these.

Lauer Custom Weaponry, the manufacturer of the hugely popular Duracoat products, has identified a trend. There are lots of folks who don't engage in the very easy means to corrosion-proof and prettify their firearms for the simple and understandable reason that they don't want to buy a lot of equipment to coat one or two guns. So LCW has packaged up a 4 oz. bottle of Duracoat with a Preval sprayer kit in one little plastic blister pack. Now you need no airbrush or HVLP gun to coat your firearm. You simply mix everything together and spray it on. No

measuring, adjusting, or cleaning necessary. That 4 oz. bottle is also enough for two to four guns depending on how thick you spray it on and what kind of gun you finish. This package is also extremely reasonably priced, so much so that even the least expensive gun you may purchase on the modern or surplus markets can be affordably finished with Duracoat.

In Conclusion

I was well pleased with this year's SHOT offerings. All those wonderful little guys, the small businesses, are doing their jobs for America by creating innovative, useful, and fun products for their industry. The sheer amount of selection blows the mind and may be another indicator that despite the really stupid gun laws that abound in some areas in the country, we are in the middle of a Golden Age of gun ownership. At no other time in history could you walk into a gun store in America and paw through such a wide selection of guns for every purpose imaginable. Nor could you access the enormous supporting industry involved in parts, accessories, ammo, and custom equipment, either at the retail counter or via the internet. All in all, we've never had it so good!

REPORT FROM THE FIELD:

THE FEMININE PERSPECTIVE

BY **GILA HAYES**

Not too many years ago, men were the primary participants at gun shows, shooting ranges, and in the firearms industry. Not anymore! If ever you wanted to see how things have changed, four days viewing the exhibits at the gun industry's premier trade show, the Shooting, Hunting and Outdoor Trade Show (SHOT Show) should underscore the shift. Nowadays, nearly as many women as men walk from booth to booth, contacting the manufacturers of guns and accessories, placing inventory orders, and getting an idea what is new and improved in the world of the firearms. Many are industry representatives, business-women from gun stores, distributors' representatives, firearms instructors and gun writers.

Tasked with identifying some of the industry's best products for women, I queried the women I saw at SHOT Show to learn what caught their eye. I've been in the industry for so many years that I find it hard to get excited about yet another pink gun. These ladies, on the other hand, find the trade show a fascinating opportunity to identify new products for their students, their readers and their customers. What innovations did they find most noteworthy in 2011?

"This is good," Kathy Jackson's expression seems to say, as she shows the author the .22 LR caliber M&P from Smith & Wesson.

Gunstore owner Jennie Van Tuyl shows how well the ATI Atika Adjustable Stock fits short shooters.

Smith & Wesson's "System"

Kathy Jackson, a firearms instructor and editor of *Concealed Carry Magazine*, was delighted to find Smith & Wesson's .22 LR variant of the popular M&P semi-automatic pistol. Already a fan of the centerfire M&P with its backstrap sizing options, reliable function and caliber choices, Jackson enthused that adding a .22 LR option to the M&P line creates a tremendous training system for anyone wishing to introduce women to the fun of shooting. "This is a system that will

encourage women to learn to shoot well on a small-caliber model, and then they can take the same manual of arms and apply it to a handgun that is big enough for self defense when they are ready to begin shooting a 9mm, .40 or .45," she enthused.

Learning to shoot on a centerfire-caliber pistol is inefficient in terms of effort required to master trigger control and is financially wasteful now that ammunition prices are so inflated, Jackson pointed out. A beginner who is encouraged to shoot thousands and thousands of

rounds of .22 LR ammunition enjoys the considerable benefit of many successful repetitions of trigger control, use of the sights, and going through the steps to safely load, unload, and operate the handgun. With the .22 LR caliber option, none of those skill repetitions requires the new shooter to put much effort into counteracting the jolt of recoil and they are less likely to begin to flinch away from it as is so frequently the case when learners start with a centerfire pistol.

Of course, as the new shooter's skills grow, it is entirely appropriate to ask how the techniques and shooting methods they've been practicing apply to self defense. With a .22 caliber handgun, the answer is "not so well." This is the time when the woman who is learning about self-defense guns must face the question of whether the handgun she has learned on is adequate for self-defense concerns. At this point in the experience, it's easy to upgrade to a 9mm Smith & Wesson M&P since with the small backstrap option installed it feels essentially the same in her hands as the .22 caliber M&P used in initial training and familiarization.

While developing confidence and comfort with a larger caliber handgun calls for training and practice, that doesn't mean that the .22 must go into mothballs! It still offers the economic advantage of cheap ammunition for some of the practice and a lot of the just-plain-fun shooting we all love to do.

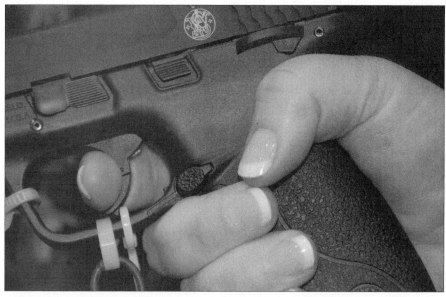

Jackson demonstrates how well the .22 caliber M&P fits a woman's small hands.

Stock Options

Kent, WA, gun store owner, firearms instructor and competitive shooter Jennie Van Tuyl has such energy and enthusiasm that it is easy to forget that at about five feet tall, she finds it even more difficult than most women to find equipment that fits. When Van Tuyl shoulders a shotgun it is painfully apparent that gear that fits that mythical "standard-sized shooter" will never work for her – or for most other women who are often a full 8-12 inches shorter than the men with whom they shoot on the range during firearms classes and in competition.

Although Van Tuyl enthusiastically enjoys shotgun and rifle shooting, she has also spent considerable time finding short rifle and shotgun stocks, not only for herself but also for customers at her gun store, Rivendell Consulting. She had a big grin on her face when she took me over to the Advanced Technology International booth at the 2011 SHOT Show so I could see the very sophisticated shotgun stock replacement system this company sells.

Until now, adjustable stocks for shotguns have pretty much followed the pattern of adjustable AR-15 stocks and

Van Tuyl lowers the demo shotgun with the ATI adjustable stock set at its shortest dimension.

Turquoise-colored fabric and sensible construction makes this bag from Gun Tote'n Mamas not only very serviceable but not likely to be identified as a holster bag when carried in public. The nylon shoulder bag hides a holster in a rear pouch with an easy-open zipper, while looking for all the world like a traveler's shoulder bag.

while they reduce stock length, some have been incredibly uncomfortable to shoot, seemingly increasing the recoil's impact on face and shoulder owing to poor ergonomics in how the stock was shaped. ATI's Akita Adjustable Stock has a four-position butt stock, recoil reducing butt pad and a neoprene cheek rest that is height-adjustable. The high tech material of the butt pad offers incredible impact absorbing qualities.

Now the short-statured shotgunner can custom fit the stock not only for length, but so they can attain a solid cheek weld where they can look through the sights or straight down the rail to the bead. The adjustability becomes even more valuable when couples outfit a shotgun for home defense, as well as in other multi-user situations, including law enforcement and security personnel who share one shotgun, with four positions changing length of pull from 12-3/8 to 14-3/8 inches to fit shooters of a variety of sizes.

I was still studying the adjustments when long-time friend and firearms instructor Vicki Farnam walked by. I jumped at the opportunity to ask what she thought of ATI's adjustable shotgun stocks. As a police firearms trainer, Farnam knows that a shotgun must be set up so the shooter can put a considerable number of rounds downrange in training and practice before it is fair to expect them to use it competently on duty. Equipment that hurts or does not fit makes it nearly impossible to master the shotgun.

As another shooter of quite short stature, Farnam was quick to slip the ATI Stock to its shortest setting and bring the shotgun to her shoulder. The design of ATI's adjustable cheek piece is very welcome, she enthused, because the cheek piece protects from pinches and abrasion commonly inflicted by adjustable stocks on which the shooter is expected to maintain a cheek weld atop the seam of two telescoping parts.

It was hard to tell whether Farnam or Van Tuyl was more enthusiastic about the ATI adjustable shotgun stock! The gun store owner, however, was also interested in the colored and patterned stocks – including a beautiful muted purple and blue camouflage print dubbed Twilight DyeHard Camo. Farnam, on the other hand, saw the value of the black replacement stocks for law enforcement agencies. Both women emphasized that setting the adjustable stock at its shortest length would give them the ability to shoot without sacrificing proper technique to accommodate an overly long stock.

Price options include single-color stocks at just under $90, packages with a matching forend for $129 and stock and forend sets in beautiful colored and camouflage patterned variations at $159. Each stock package includes mounting hardware to make it fit 12 gauge Mossberg, Winchester and Remington shotguns.

In the Bag

While visiting with Farnam, I was delighted to make the face-to-face acquaintance with Dianne Nicholl, co-author of *Teaching Women to Shoot and Women Learning to Shoot*, who also works with Farnam in teaching firearms to police personnel. Asked what had caught her attention, Nicholl smiled and pointed at the small nylon shoulder bag she was carrying. A test sample of Gun Tote'n Mamas Concealed Carry Shoulder Pouch, the dark turquoise Cordura bag looked for all the world like a small travel purse from Orvis or TravelSmith. The rearward pouch contained a holster, but the forward compartments were put to good use holding notebook, cell phone, pen, and business cards – all the necessaries for a day at a trade show. In a different environment, the shoulder bag would never have been identifiable as a holster bag!

Both Nicholl and Farnam enthusiastically endorsed Gun Tote'n Mamas, saying that rarely have they encountered a manufacturer so eager to integrate user suggestions into their product. The result is a collection of holster handbags and carry cases that have features like slash-proof straps and hidden holsters inside secure but easy-to-open compartments, in a wide variety of fashionable sizes, shapes, materials and colors.

Guns, Guns, Guns

Diane Walls writes about guns – about rifles, about shotguns and about pistols for both men and women. The 2011 SHOT Show found her expressing considerable interest in the super compact 9mm handgun Kimber introduced. With lines that bring to mind the Colt 1903, Kimber's Solo is a 7-shot (6 in the magazine, one in the chamber) 9mm semi-automatic operating on the locked-breech principle.

Kimber's new Solo has nary a sharp

edge and, as it is striker fired, there is no hammer to catch on jacket linings when carried concealed. Its 4"x5.5"x1.2" dimensions bode well for easy concealment, and a mere 17 ounces of unloaded weight will also carry easily. The 4-inch height doesn't leave a lot of grip area, but women's hands tend to be small and fine-boned, and when Diane handed me the display Solo at the Kimber booth, I was surprised at how well it fit.

With the Kimber reputation behind it, this new mini-9 is an excellent option for the woman shooter of intermediate skill level. Walls suggested that it might not be the best choice for beginners who are still learning to operate semi-automatic pistols, owing to a fairly stiff recoil spring that may really challenge shooters who do not have a considerable amount of hand strength.

Walls makes an excellent point. In addition to the heavy recoil spring, the Solo is right on the edge of being too small for the dedicated training and practice required to develop skill with equipment we obtain and carry for defense of life. The Solo is a good choice for shooters who already possess a good degree of shooting skill.

Writer Diane Walls shares some of her enthusiasm for the Kimber Solo.

So Many Small Guns

I saw a lot of ultra-tiny handguns at the 2011 SHOT Show. As with the Solo, I was reminded that for many shooters, especially those of modest experience levels, a mid-sized handgun usually serves far better than one that is so light-weight that the felt recoil and torque of shooting it feels like firing a much larger caliber. Super compact handguns frequently lack good sights or shallow sights may be machined into the slide itself and thus are not even windage adjustable. Sometimes the safety or decocking lever is vestigial, the slide stop is either missing or too small to engage reliably every time you need to manually lock the action open, and those deficits are just the tip of the iceberg!

As we see more and more ultra-miniature handguns in calibers .380 and 9mm we are also forced to consider how much grip length and circumference is necessary to assure the shooter of a firm hold that does not require regripping between each shot. The smaller and lighter the gun is, the more even 9mm recoil is going to move the gun in the shooter's hand. An extremely abbreviated grip can render the possibility of rapid multiple shots entirely unrealistic owing to the gun's tendency to twist in the hand during recoil.

Small guns for concealed carry comprise a big part of new products introduced in recent years. While we recognize these as guns so small that they are "carried often, shot rarely," we must remember that concealed carry practitioners DO need to shoot what they carry with sufficient frequency that if the worst thing happens and that gun must be fired in self defense, that the gun's operation is habitual, requiring little or no conscious thought about which steps are needed to get it into operation.

Shootable Subcompacts

I was very pleased to see that Glock, one of our biggest gun manufacturers, now makes the adjustable grip sizing options available for their Models 19, 26 and 27. The Model 26, in particular, is a handgun that is used and carried by many, many women. Unfortunately, the thick double-column grip has made it necessary for a lot of the women who shoot Glocks to make compromises in their shooting grip. The streamlined proportions of the Fourth Generation

The perfect compromise: Para Ordnance's Carry 9 is small enough for concealed carry but large enough to shoot well.

One-stop-shopping puts holster, magazine pouch, pistol and other accessories in the Springfield XD-M hard-sided case.

Glock design are a very welcome improvement! The advantages of the Glock pistol are considerable. First, the operation is extremely user-intuitive, with a large enough grip for a solid hold and a reasonable sight radius. Few pistols boast such a wide variety of aftermarket accessories.

Another user-friendly small handgun is Para Ordnance's downsized 9mm PDA. The frame is small, but the PDA has enough grip that even a hotly-loaded 9mm cartridge remains manageable. Springfield Armory's EMP is another such pistol. Women buyers often want one gun that will do it all. Instead of wanting one pistol for plinking, a second, full sized gun for competition, a different gun for training and a super-miniaturized pistol for carry, women tend to think that buying one gun should do the trick. That is why buying an 8-ounce .380 with 1½ inches of grip length is disastrous. While it may be easy to forget you are carrying such a small gun, it has virtually no other merits! Para Ordnance understands the importance of shootability, and this sensible principle is evident in all of their sub-compact pistols.

The new shooter equipped with a light-weight miniaturized pistol is unlikely to get through a two-day, 500-round defensive handgun class, let alone something like a weeklong Gunsite 250 or other classes of sufficient length to really habituate the elements of defensive handgun use. A subcompact like a Springfield XD or an EMP, Glock 26 or Para Ordnance PDA gives the weight, frame size, and user features, as well as durability, to carry the shooter through the training and practice to attain competency.

One-stop Shopping

Pulling together all the accessories that go with a good handgun in preparation to take training and to carry a self-defense pistol is challenging. I like the approach Springfield Armory takes in packaging their XD-M handguns. A hard-sided carrying case fits pistol, magazines, backstrap options, a holster, magazine carrier and other accessories in a foam-cushioned interior. The result is one-stop-shopping for the shooter who wants the equipment needed to go to the range, to take a defensive handgun class, and to get off to a good start.

Will the holster and magazine pouches probably be replaced eventually? Sure. But by that time, the XD owner has had the chance to attend several classes, interact with a number of other shooters, learn what works and what doesn't work well for concealed carry and now, using that experience and knowledge, can more confidently invest the kind of money needed for a well-made holster that fits their own individual needs. I love it that Springfield helps the shooter get through their first-steps all in one package!

Different Needs, Different Viewpoints

Looking for women's products at SHOT Show reminded me of the parable of the blind men and the elephant. "Feels like a rope," reports the guy who encounters the tail. "I think it is a hose," says the one at the front end. "No, you fools, it is definitely a wall," says the fellow running his hands along the beast's side. Women looking for the guns and shooting accessories that make a difference for themselves, their students and their customers, all found different manufacturers, guns and accessories that they recommended. All found products that they believed would make learning to shoot and remaining in practice easier.

An industry that sells a product purchased for such a serious purpose – nothing less than defending life and limb – has to offer a tremendous variety of options and accessories since the needs of the end users are so diverse. Some guns and accessories are better quality than others, some appeal to sportsmen more than self-defense practitioners, some leave you scratching your head and saying, "what is that for?" Still, there are a lot of good products being made for female shooters, though not necessarily among the items marketed as being "specially for women." A solid variety of gun sizes, and accessories like stocks and grips, offer good choices for women shooters from beginner to pro.

Resources

Smith & Wesson
2100 Roosevelt Avenue
Springfield, MA 01104
800-331-0852
http://www.smith-wesson.com

Glock
6000 Highlands Parkway
Smyrna, GA 30082
770-432-1202
http://www.glock.com

Para Ordnance
Para USA, Inc.
10620 Southern Loop Blvd.
Pineville, NC 28134
704-930-7600
http://www.paraord.com

Kimber Mfg., Inc.
1 Lawton Street
Yonkers, NY 10705
914-964-0771 x 267
http://www.kimberamerica.com

Springfield Armory
420 West Main Street
Geneseo, IL 61254
800-680-6866
http://www.springfield-armory.com/

Advanced Technology International
2733 West Carmen Ave
Milwaukee, WI 53209
800-925-2522
http://www.atigunstocks.com

Gun Tote'n Mamas
Northbrook, IL 60062
http://www.guntotenmamas.com/

REPORT FROM THE FIELD:
AIRGUNS

BY **TOM CACECI**

The 2011 SHOT Show introduced several new and exciting developments in airguns; and reflected the growing trend in airsoft products toward extraordinarily realistic replicas of true firearms for training and simulation purposes.

Airgun manufacturers have recognized the demand for larger calibers (up to .357), driven largely by the growth of airgun hunting. After a long-term decline in hunting license sales, states updating their regulations to permit airgun hunting have seen increases, especially among very young people. Figures from the U.S. Fish & Wildlife Service show an uptick of 3.6% in license sales in the past year, thanks to recruitment campaigns and new products that are effective and humane for use on small game and pests. Airguns are good choices for very young hunters and for use in densely-populated areas, but give up nothing in terms of effectiveness. Increased demand has also spurred ongoing efforts to bring better products to the market at reasonable prices.

Airsoft guns shooting small (6mm) low-velocity plastic pellets were originally regarded as little more than backyard toys, but today's airsoft products are line-for-line copies of conventional firearms, so realistic as to be indistinguishable from a few feet away. Since they're not firearms these guns can legally be set up for full-automatic shooting. The amazingly realistic appearance, freedom from legal issues, safety, and low cost all have great appeal to police and military agencies for simulated combat training as well as to re-enactment and theatrical groups. To protect "trade dress," the appearance and styling of a product, manufacturers of iconic weapons have negotiated licensing agreements with airsoft manufacturers permitting accurate imitation not only of the exterior appearance but even the logos and trademarks found on real guns.

Air Arms

Air Arms has announced the new "Twice," a PCP rifle that, as the name implies, has not one but two air chambers, for greater power and a higher shot count. It's a 10-shot repeater with a side cocking lever and a barrel by Lothar Walther. This UK-made product is distributed by Air Venturi. They have also introduced the "2i" PCP rifle, available in .177, .22, and .25 calibers.

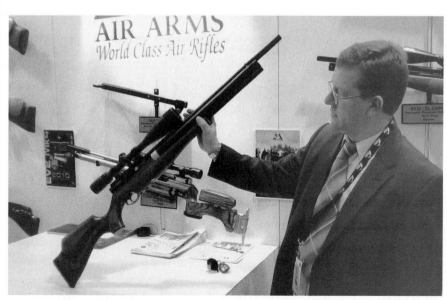

Air Arms "Twice," a PCP rifle that has not one but two air chambers for greater power and a higher shot count.

Air Force

Air Force has added .25 caliber barrels to their product line in the form of accessory barrels for existing rifles. The Talon and Condor rifles are now also made in .25, a bore size which is growing in popularity among airgun hunters. Air Force also is making a pistol version of the Talon, also in .25. Complementing their line of guns, they have available a set of scope mounts, sold under the BKL name, which include bubble levels to prevent canting. The levels fold during transport to prevent breakage. Also sold under the BKL trademark is a self-centering accessory rail base to accept the scope rings.

Cometa

Cometa, one of Spain's oldest airgun makers, have put their "Lynx" rifle into production. Designed as an economical entry-level gun for target work and hunting, the Lynx uses standardized components including a paintball-type regulator and tank, but also features an adjustable trigger. The Lynx is made in .177 and .22 caliber and is equipped with a threaded muzzle brake. The Lynx V10 has an integral barrel shroud that acts as a noise suppressor. Both are available with blue or natural wood finish stock.

Crosman

Crosman Corporation has introduced a new large-bore air rifle, the Benjamin-branded "Rogue," scheduled for the Spring of 2011. The Rogue is a .357-caliber repeating PCP rifle with fully electric

Cometa Lynx was designed as an economical entry-level PCP gun for target work and hunting.

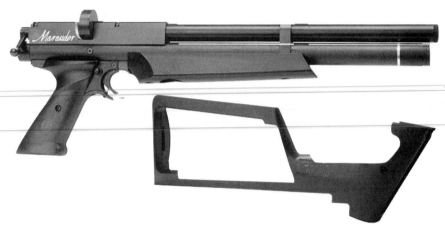

The .22 pistol version of the Benjamin Marauder has a detachable shoulder stock that enables it to be used as a light carbine.

Crosman optimus entry-level springers are available in .177 and .22 versions.

Benjamin .357 Rogue can generate up to an astonishing 300 foot-pounds of energy using the proprietary "Pursuit" bullets.

Prototype of Crosman National Match Air Rifle, built on an AR-15 upper.

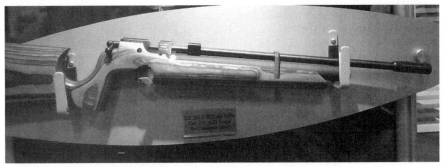

CZ's .17-caliber PCP Model 200.

Airguns of Arizona, importer of the ultra-high end FX Airguns.

Gamo is a major player on the world airgun scene.

valving that Crosman calls the "EPIC" (Electro-Pneumatic Intelligent Control) system. The Rogue can generate up to an astonishing 300 foot-pounds of energy using the proprietary "Pursuit" bullets (a 90-grain hollow point and a 175-grain round nose in lead alloy) and the "eXTREME" Ballistic Tip 145-grain bullet developed for this rifle by Nosler.

Also new for this year is a .22 pistol version of the Benjamin "Marauder." It has a detachable shoulder stock that enables it to be used as a light carbine. The Benjamin "Trail" series is well established, but now Crosman has a larger caliber version: the .25 "Trail NPXL" break barrel with Nitro Piston technology and a bull barrel, sold with a 3-9X CenterPoint scope in place. It is rated for 900 FPS and 30 foot-pounds of energy. Still in development and not yet on the market,

Crosman displayed the prototype of what they call the "National Match Air Rifle," a complete upper receiver assembly for the AR-15 platform, in .177 caliber. It is intended to afford service rifle competitors low-cost (and indoor) practice while retaining the balance, feel, and trigger of their match weapon. It has a variable-orifice technology to maintain consistent velocities and performance.

Crosman has introduced under its own brand name the "Optimus" line of

Available in .17 or .22 caliber, the Gamo Varmint Stalker is capble of velocities well in excess of 1000 fps.

break-barrel guns, which come with scopes, at a very affordable price for new shooters. They are available in .177 and .22 caliber. The company has also brought out the repeating "Silhouette" PCP pistol for match competition and has entered the airsoft field with its "Mayhem" and "Elite" pistols, realistic enough for combat training and with the blowback feature for even greater verisimilitude; and the "Predator," an AR-15 style replica.

CZ

CZ, the Czech manufacture of high-quality firearms, has entered the airgun market with a .17 caliber PCP rifle, the "CZ 200S," sporting a red-colored laminated wood stock.

FX

FX Airguns, made in Switzerland, are top-of-the-line products imported by Airguns of Arizona. The FX offerings include the "Royale" and the "Independence" series. The "Royale" rifles are PCP powered, come in .177 and .22, and feature side cocking, an adjustable two-stage trigger, and walnut or synthetic stocks. The Royale 200 is a smaller version. The FX "Independence" package is interesting in that it has a built-in pump to pressurize its tank up to 230 Bar, eliminating the need for a separate hand pump.

FX has an exclusive license for a new, patented form of "smooth twist" rifling, used in their top-end guns. At first glance the bore appears to be smooth: but the last few inches have been swaged in a die around the exterior of the barrel. "Lands" and "grooves" impressed on the barrel are twisted, so that the "smooth" bore is as well. This is reminiscent of the "Lancaster Oval Bore" system of the 19th Century. As used in the FX guns it lowers internal friction, spins the pellet uniformly, decreases pressure needed for a given velocity, and increases efficiency. It eliminates the notorious problem of "pellet sensitivity" that many air rifles have.

Gamo

Gamo has announced the "Varmint Hunter HP" rifles, break-barrel guns with gas piston technology and all-weather stocks. They boast a 4x32 scope and laser on an olive drab stock. Also new is the "Varmint Stalker," also made in .177 and .22, which has a bull barrel and sound dampener, at a slightly lower price point than the Varmint Hunter. These guns are available in .177 (rated at a blistering 1300-1400 FPS) and .22 (at 975 FPS). The "Whisper CFR" is an underlever .177 with something new for Gamo: a fixed barrel. It features ND52 noise suppression technology, an integral non-removable dampener. With Gamo's PBA (Platinum Ballistic Alloy) non-lead pellets it will produce 1100 FPS. The "SOCOM Extreme" rifles are powerful break-barrel guns in .177, .22, and .25 with very high velocities using the PBA pellets: 1650, 1300, and 1000 FPS respectively.

Gamo offers pistol shooters their "P-25 Blowback" and "P-25 Blowback Tactical" series. The P-25 Blowback is a semi-automatic CO_2 powered pistol with reciprocating slide for extra realism. It is in .177 caliber. The Tactical version has a longer barrel resembling a silencer, as well as a quad rail mount for a light and a RGB sight. Both are designed for the PBA pellets, producing 450 and 560 FPS respectively.

Daystate

Daystate guns, imported and distributed by Airguns of Arizona, include the Daystate "Mark IV" with a computer-metered valving system. This constantly monitors internal pressure and shots fired to maintain consistent performance by controlling the valve timing. Daystate calls this "MCT Technology" and says it's far more efficient than other systems in that it wastes no air. The Daystate "Air Ranger" in .25 caliber, which generates up to 80 foot-pounds of energy, is similar to the Mark IV but has a mechanical valving system. Daystate guns have barrels made by Lothar Walther.

Stoeger

Stoeger continues to import air rifles from China, and now markets what it says is the "quietest air rifle made," the

Ruger "LGR" is a bolt-action CO_2 powered rifle with a two-stage trigger and the capability of using either a refillable tank or CO_2 cylinders.

The quietest air rifle made? Stoeger says its Suppressor is just that. This 1200-fps gun (in .177 and also available in .22) has a synthetic stock and very low price point.

Gamo P-25 Blowback is a semi-automatic CO_2 powered pistol with reciprocating slide for extra realism.

"Suppressor." This 1200-FPS gun (in .177 and also available in .22) has a synthetic stock and is placed at a very low price point, sure to appeal to someone thinking about hunting with an airgun but hesitant to spend a lot of money.

Umarex

Umarex has signed an agreement to import airguns to be sold under famous firearm names: the Ruger "LGR" is a bolt-action CO_2 powered rifle with a two-stage trigger and the capability of using either a refillable tank or CO_2 cylinders. The Ruger "Air Magnum" is a .177 break-barrel type developing 1200 FPS. It comes equipped with a 4x32 scope. Another new line for Umarex is the fixed-barrel, under-lever "Leverage" air rifle carrying the famous Browning name. The Browning Leverage comes in .177 and .22.

Umarex hasn't forgotten pistol shooters. They are now importing a Walther "PPQ" repeating pistol that uses an eight-shot magazine and closely resembles the real firearm it imitates. It has a polymer frame and an integral quad rail: it will shoot either BB's or .177 pellets. Umarex is also importing two products licensed by S&W: the "M&P 45" and the "M&P R8," both powered by CO_2 and in .177 (BB) caliber. These are accurate replicas of two famous handguns, suited to indoor training and general shooting. Umarex has license agreements with major firearms brands not only for BB and pellet guns, but airsoft replicas of Beretta, Walther, and H&K weapons.

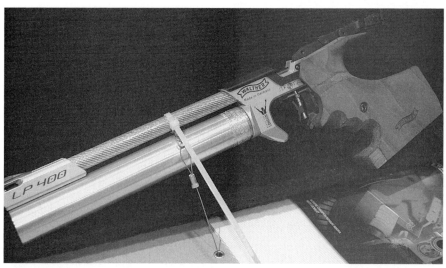

Walther LP400 air pistol is a high-level competition target product with custom-tailored grips, carbon-fiber barrel jacket, and a compensation system that dissipates gas around the barrel, inside the jacket, for uniform velocity.

Aftermath's display for full-auto and selec-fire replicas.

Walther

Walther has a line of target guns that are "Ready For London" in 2012's Games. The LG400 air rifle and LP400 air pistol are high-level competition target products with custom-tailored grips, carbon-fiber barrel jackets, and a compensation system that dissipates gas around the barrel, inside the jacket, for uniform velocity. Sliding weights permit customization of the balance point. A newly-designed valve operates at minimal pulse, to decrease shake on firing, and both front and rear sights are completely adjustable. The rifle version of the LG 400 has a completely adjustable stock and ambidextrous diopter sights.

The amazing realism of airsoft guns was evident in the products displayed by several companies. The hot items in the current market are replicas of various combat weapons, especially "assault rifles," but also many classic "fighting irons" of the past, including the M-1 Garand and the M-3 Grease Gun. Apart from the blaze orange muzzle paint required by U.S. law, these cannot be told from the real thing from a few feet away, and they duplicate the weight, balance, and heft of the guns they imitate.

Aftermath

Aftermath in Miami, Florida, is a subsidiary of Gamo Outdoors. Working with and through Action Sport Games, Inc., who negotiate license agreements with major firearms manufacturers and arrange for the production of replicas in Asia, Aftermath offers accurate renditions of rifles, pistols, and even shotguns. These copies include airsoft twins of the Armalite AR series, Franchi's shotguns, the Steyr-Mannlicher AUG, and such iconic firearms as the Soviet-era Dragunov LMG, the Czech-made "Skorpion" machine pistol, and of course the AK-47.

Blackwater

Blackwater has exact copies of the SIG-Sauer X-5 pistol, and the M1911 pistol, both equipped with recoil simulation and powered by CO_2. They also produce a line of tactical style AR-type rifles.

KWA

Operating out of Taiwan, KWA is one of the leading companies in airsoft, serving the need for safe and realistic

Airsoft M3 "Grease Gun" and M60 machinegun from ICS.

tactical training equipment. Their replicas feature rugged internals and the exact appearance of firearms by H&K, including several submachine guns that operate on full auto, just as the originals do. Duplicates of the H&K Compact and USP pistols, the H&K US SOCOM pistol, the MP7A1 subgun, and the G36C assault rifle are available, as well as near-identical copies of the M-16, the US issue M-4A1 Carbine, and the MAC-10 submachine gun. A licensed airsoft ver-

Echo USA airsoft minigun.

sion of the Magpul PTS is offered as well. KWA's products sold to law-enforcement agencies and the military do not have the orange muzzle paint, but they also sell to the consumer market. To enhance the realism of their products, KWA has developed a "Kinetic Feedback System" in some of their products. This simulates

actual recoil, and in most cases, the movement of the bolt that would be experienced in firing a real weapon.

ICS Limited

ICS Limited, another Taiwanese company, also makes incredibly lifelike copies of classic weapons, including one of the WWII vintage M-3 "Grease Gun," and the equally nostalgic British Sten. These have found special favor with re-enactment and theatrical groups. They are, like the originals, capable of full-automatic fire. ICS is producing replicas of virtually every famous assault rifle, including the M4, the M16-A3, the AK-47 and AK-74, and a grenade launcher. Nor are bolt action rifles ignored: in the works is a replica of the SMLE!

Echo USA

Echo USA is making what could be considered the "ultimate airsoft" products. Among them are the Model 240, a multibarreled affair resembling the 7.62 Mini-Gun used by the US forces. This company also has licensed and will shortly introduce an airsoft version of the Barrett .50-caliber sniper rifle.

AMMUNITION, BALLISTICS and COMPONENTS

BY **HOLT BODINSON**

Once again, new ammunition offerings continue to drive the firearms market faster than any other factor. Some of the interesting trends in 2012 are the appearance of low-cost, steel-case loads in the Black Hills and Hornady lines; the release by Hodgdon of the LEVERevolution and Superformance powders that Hornady has been using to great effect; an emphasis on short-barrel revolver and pistol ammunition for self-defense; the modern reintroduction of the historical buck-and-ball load by Winchester; lots of new "green" ammunition; the reintroduction by CCI and Winchester of segmented .22 LR rounds that fragment upon impact; and the development of hexahedron-shaped shot. Those are just a few of the surprises and highlights in our "Ammunition, Ballistics and Components" chapter this year.

Advanced Armament Corporation

Looking for a larger caliber cartridge with more punch and versatility than the 5.56 NATO while fitting the magazine and bolt face of the standard M15/16 platform, AAC has developed the 7.62x35, naming it the .300 AAC Blackout, or simply, the .300 BLK. The .300 BLK is based on a shortened 5.56mm case necked to .30-caliber. The ballistics of the .300 BLK match those of the 7.62x39 while avoiding the steeply tapered case, larger head size and .311" bullet diameter of the Russian round. From a 16-inch barrel, the .300 BLK with a 123-gr. FMJ produces 2315 fps and 1462 ft-lb, which exceeds the energy of the 5.56mm M855 round by 23%. Another key advantage the .300 BLK offers over the 5.56 round is its versatility as a

lethal, suppressed round featuring a 220-gr. Sierra HP at 1010 fps. Get the complete story at www.300aacblackout.com.

Aguila

Is their continued promotion of the 5mm Remington Rimfire Magnum just a tease? Once again at the 2011 Shot Show, we were told by Aguila that there will be new firearm offerings in this hot little rimfire cartridge. We're waiting. www.aguilaammo.com.

Ballistic Products

The one-stop shopping spot for shotgun reloading components, manuals and tools, Ballistic Products is the exclusive source for lead-free, ITX Shot that is 10% denser than steel and more importantly, safe to shoot in all shotgun barrels. The

ITX line has been expanded this year with the addition of #00 buckshot and surprisingly, .50-caliber, muzzleloading round balls in .487" and .490" diameters. Additional new offerings include the RSS-12 sabot that accepts a .50-caliber pistol bullet, a swaged .660" diameter, 450-gr. "shuttlecock" shaped slug, and a .729" diameter, 375-gr./12 ga. non-toxic slug featuring a copper jacket and aluminum core. This store has the widest and most complete shotgun components catalog out there. See them at www.ballistic-products.com.

Barnes Bullets

The company seems to be thriving as part of the Freedom Group. Barnes just got into the match bullet business with a major introduction of eight, new competition bullets made with lead cores ranging from classics like the .224"/69-gr. to the .264"/140-gr. and .308"/175-gr. It's been long in coming, but Barnes is also now in the ammunition business. Big game hunters will be pleased with the VOR-TX Safari TSX and the VOR-TX Safari Banded Solid lines. Both the Triple-Shock X bullet and the Banded Solid will be loaded to the same grain weight in seven classic safari cartridges ranging from the .375 H&H to the .500 Nitro, giving the hunter the ability to switch back-and-forth between a fast expending soft tissue bullet and penetrating solid. And there's new pistol hunting ammunition this year as well carrying the name VOR-TX Handgun Hunting ammunition. Initially offerings in the line will include a 140-gr. XPB bullet in the .357 Mag., a 225-gr. XPB in the .44 Mag. and a 200-gr. XPB in the .45 Colt. Barnes offers a very informative web site at www.barnesbullets.com.

Berger Bullets

Berger's remarkable VLD bullets have always been sensitive to seating depth so Chief Ballistician Bryan Litz sat down and designed a "Hybrid" bullet to address the problem. The new Hybrid features a tangent ogive that begins at the end of the bearing surface which has the effect of reducing seating depth sensitivity. Progressing down the nose of the bullet, the tangent ogive gives way to a secant ogive which has been the secret to the VLD's wind-bucking ability. The first Hybrid will be a 7mm/180-gr. bullet offered in the Match Target line. There's also an exciting new VLD hunting bullet this year, an 87-gr./.243". Don't miss their complete catalog at www.bergerbullets.com.

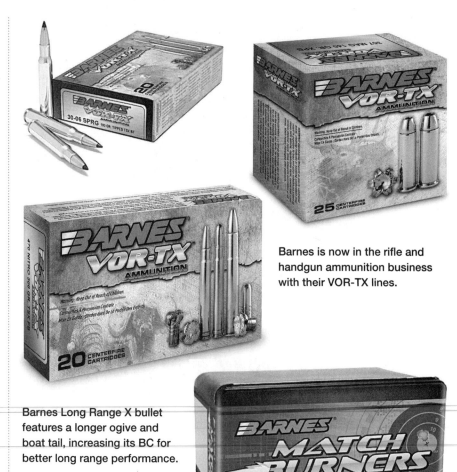

Barnes is now in the rifle and handgun ammunition business with their VOR-TX lines.

Barnes Long Range X bullet features a longer ogive and boat tail, increasing its BC for better long range performance.

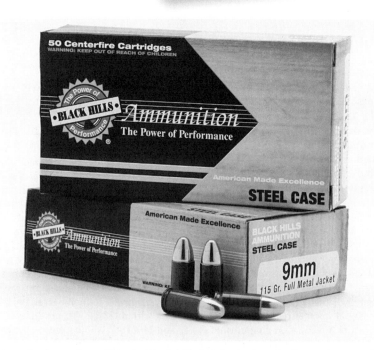

Due to a shortage of used brass, Black Hills is introducing steel-cased ammunition to keep costs down for the consumer.

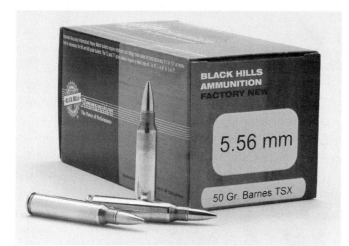

Black Hills special 50-gr. .223/5.56 TSX loading is designed to engage targets behind slight barriers.

Black Hills milspec 77-gr. MatchKing .223/5.56 loading achieves optimum long range accuracy from the M15/16 platform.

Berry's

Known for the quality of their copper plated lead bullets, Berry's is expanding its handgun offerings this year with a 9mm/124-gr. HP and a .45/185-gr. HP and is considering offering a .40/165-gr. HP. Having a full machine shop at their disposal and looking for a new product to make, Berry's has designed and is manufacturing a full line of firearm cradles that can be rotated 360° and rigidly locked at any adjustment point. It's a unique tool that can be seen along with their extensive offering of bullets at www.berrysmfg.com.

Black Hills Ammunition

From tactical to practical, Black Hills Ammunition is bringing to the consumer market two 5.56mm loads that have found great acceptance in the military and law enforcement markets.

Using a specially-made solid copper Barnes 50-gr. TSX bullet, Black Hills has developed a 5.56mm load that is effective against open targets as well as targets behind barriers such as automobile glass. The bullet is designed to expand immediately to .50-caliber and penetrate 14 inches in soft tissue. The other 5.56mm loading features a specially produced Sierra 77-gr. Match-King at 2750 fps from a 20-inch barrel. It's a full milspec load with crimped-in and lacquered primers, flash-suppressed, temperature-stable powder and certified military brass. It is designed for optimum long range accuracy from a M15/16 platform. In the popular Gold line, Hornady's lead-free Gilding Metal eXpanding (GMX) bullets have been added to eight popular hunting rounds ranging

from the .243 Win. to the .300 Win. Mag. With a shortage of available fired brass in 9mm, .40 S&W and .45 ACP for their traditional "remanufactured" ammunition line, Black Hills has turned to steel cases to provide a quality product at an affordable price. See the full range of great products at www.black-hills.com.

Brenneke

You have to get Brenneke's new catalog. In it are pages of colored photographs showing comparative shotgun slug results conducted by Tom Burczynski, the ballistics genius who has given the shooting world a variety of effective bullets like the Hydra-Shok. Looking at the data, don't ever underestimate the performance of Brenneke slug loads compared to all their competitors. Exciting and different this year are two slug loads that are compatible with the .410 revolvers by Taurus and Smith & Wesson and the 28 ga. "Raging Judge" revolver from Taurus. There's a 1/4 oz./.410 slug with a muzzle velocity of 1500

fps and a 5/8 oz. slug for the 28 ga. with a MV of 1459 fps. There's also a 2-3/4"/12 ga. reduced recoil, Tactical Home Defense loading featuring a full diameter 438-gr.slug with a MV of 1256 fps. It's designed for maximum impact while minimizing over-penetration to protect innocent bystanders. Take a look at some of the finest slugs ever designed at www.brennekeusa.com.

CCI

With the widest selection of rimfire ammunition in the industry, CCI is the world's rimfire specialist. Remember the Quik-Shok .22 LR? The bullet was designed to fragment into three parts upon impact. In concept, it's back. CCI calls it their "Segmented HP Sub-Sonic" featuring a 40-gr. bullet at 1050 fps. Going "Green," CCI has developed two new offerings: a .22 LR cartridge with a 21-gr. bonded copper powder bullet at 1650 fps called "Short Range Green" and a .17 HMR load labeled "TNT Green" with a 16-gr. HP at 2500 fps. With all the new AR-type

Brenneke's Special Forces slug is designed to penetrate windshields, tires and engines.

Brenneke's Tactical Home Defense slug offers maximum stopping power while lowering the risk of injuries to bystanders.

CCI's Sub-Sonic Segmented HP fractures into three separate missiles upon impact.

tactical platforms coming on-line chambered for the .22 LR, CCI has added a new "22 AR Tactical" round to its line. It's optimized for reliable function in AR-22s and features a 40-gr. copper plated target bullet at 1200 fps. See the Good Old Boys at www.cci-ammunition.com.

Century International Arms

CIA has a reputation for turning up some of the most exotic ammunition from some of the most obscure parts of the world. This year CIA is a gold mine for original Kynoch .577/.450 ammunition loaded with smokeless powder and a 480-gr. patched lead bullet. The boxes carry a June, 1952, production date and they're in beautiful shape. Get those Martini-Henrys shooting. Lots of great ammo, firearms and parts at www.centuryarms.com.

CorBon

Expanding the existing CorBon hunting ammunition line, President Peter Pi is rolling out an extensive line of big bore, big game ammunition under the "Expedition Hunter" label. Loaded with either copper DPX or solid brass bullets, the new line includes 12 classic calibers from the .375 flanged to the .577 Nitro Express. CorBon has also signed an exclusive arrangement with Dynamic Research Technologies to introduce their controlled frangible bullet across the whole CorBon ammunition line. Keep up-to-date at www.corbon.com.

D Dupleks

Here are some wicked, high tech, shotgun slugs from the Latvian firm of

D Dupleks' steel slug becomes an enlarged cutting machine on impact.

DRT's powdered core, frangible bullets are proving lethal on large and small game.

D Dupleks. The body of the slug is steel encased in a polymer, bore-riding jacket. Upon impact, the slug is designed either to peel out six cutting blades and turn itself into an enlarged cutting machine or to fragment, creating seven separate wound channels. Optimized for the Taurus and S&W .410 revolvers, their DUPO 7 Short Magnum 2-1/2"/.410 features a 110-gr. slug at 1670 fps.

See their innovative shotgun slug line at www.ddupleks.com and www.dkgtrading.com.

Dynamic Research Technologies

DRT has developed a new self-defense and hunting bullet that defies traditional logic. The bullet looks very traditional, being a copper jacketed HP. What's inside is different. The core is made from compressed, powdered titanium. The resulting bullet is totally frangible and because of its uniform core, highly accurate. On soft tissue, it is designed to penetrate 1-1/2 to 2 inches and then disintegrate, creating a wound cavity 6 to 8 inches in diameter for a distance of at least 10 inches. Last fall, I used 60-gr. DRT bullets in a .223 for hunting whitetail deer and wild hogs. The bullets performed as advertised and now that CorBon will be loading them across their entire ammunition line, we'll be hearing a lot more about DRT's unusual design and performance. See them at www.drtammo.com.

Extreme Shock Ammunition

Aimed directly at the expanding concealed carry market, Extreme Shock has designed the ideal "Snubby .38" cartridge. Their .38 Special Snub Nose round features a 50-gr., copper-core, jacketed bullet with a MV of 1220 fps from a 2-inch barrel. Designed to fragment violently upon impact, the round also minimizes recoil in the ever popular

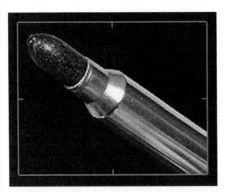
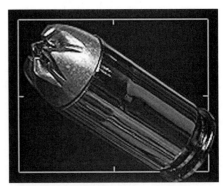

Extreme Shock's ammunition is designed to fragment immediately.

snubnose revolver. At the other end of the performance scale, there's a new .32 H&R 60-gr. "Enhanced Penetration Round" designed to penetrate automobile glass, light sheet metal and wood, yet expand violently in soft tissue. We've needed a frangible, sub-sonic round for the .223 and Extreme Shock has it, the .223 ASP.

The old .30-30 gets a boost with a new 160-gr. "Trophy Game Hunting" round, designed to give 3 to 4 inches of penetration before fragmenting, releasing 100% of its energy into the soft tissue. There are a lot more exotic rounds that can be seen at www.extremeshockusa.com.\

Federal Premium

"Guard Dog" is no longer a pooch's name. It's the label Federal is giving its new home defense round that features a copper alloy jacket and a rubber core backed by a lead core. Upon impact the FMJ fractures allowing the rubber core to extrude slightly. The Guard Dog projectile in 9mm, .40 S&W and .45 ACP is light, fast and while it expands quickly, it will not over-penetrate. Fusion technology that electrochemically plates the jacket to the bullet core has been applied

Federal's rubber core Guard Dog ammunition expands immediately but will not over-penetrate.

Federal's Fusion line now includes the classic big bore cartridges under the Fusion Safari label.

to a new line of big bore ammunition with the moniker, Fusion Safari. Initially, the Fusion Safari line will be offered in .375 H&H, .416 Rem., .416 Rigby, .458 Win. and .458 Lott. Waterfowl, look out. There's a new Black Cloud High Velocity FS Steel loading for the 3"/12 ga. pushing 1-1/8 oz. of #3 and #4 steel at 1635 fps! The 20 ga. got a bit of attention this year with a 1 oz./2-3/4" Prairie Storm FS Lead load featuring a mix of #4, #5 and #6 copper-plated lead and nickel-plated Flightstopper lead at 1350 fps and in the 3" hull, 7/8 oz. of FS steel at 1500 fps. Lots of new and inexpensive steel shells under their Speed.Shok Waterfowl brand for 2012 including BBB and T shot loads for the 16 and 10 gauges. Responding to the needs of AR-15 handloaders, there's a new small rifle primer with a heavier cup to avoid slam-fires in this popular platform. It's being sold under the Small Rifle AR Match label. Speaking of new primers, Federal has developed an in-line muzzleloader 209 primer that they guarantee will fire soaking wet or freezing cold.

Federal Premium full range of ammunition and components can be found at www.federalpremium.com.

Federal's Prairie Storm FS features a mixture of #4, #5 and #6 plated lead shot.

Fiocchi of America

At last, a shotgun tracer shell that uses a non-pyrotechnic, non-toxic, biodegradable tracer element that is safe for any gun or choke restriction. In fact, the tracer element is a small, cold light stick made by Cyalume. As loaded, the light capsule is seated on top of the shot charge and is activated by setback when the shell is fired. In flight, the light capsule tracks the trajectory of the shot column out to 50-60 yards. It's visible in daylight and especially when shot against dark backgrounds or during early morning or evening hours. Bringing over a concept from their military lines, Fiocchi is introducing new waterproof and long storage packaging to its ammunition lines. Calling the packaging "Canned Heat," Fiocchi's centerfire and rimfire ammunition will come sealed in enamel coated cans to prevent electrolysis and corrosion. Sporting shotgun ammunition will be available packaged in 100-round, rigid, plastic buckets that can serve as a seat, a game carrier or whatever around the homestead. New also this year is a complete line of Cowboy Action cartridges including hard-to-find calibers like the .380 Long, .38 S&W Short and .44 S&W Russian. Great stuff at www.fiocchiusa.com.

Hevi-Shot by Environ Metal

Hevi-Shot has developed some innovative ways of mixing shot and shot sizes to maximize pattern density. In their Heavy Metal lines of waterfowl and upland game loads, steel shot is loaded first, followed by Hevi-Metal and then a layer of flax seed as a final crimp spacer. The layers are stacked and not mixed

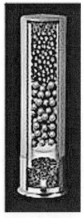

Hevi-Shot is improving pattern density by stacking Hevi-Metal shot above steel shot.

Hevi-Shot's Magnum Blend is a turkey killer with a mixture of #5, #6 and #7 Hevi-Shot.

and according to Hevi-Shot the system delivers 20% more pellets on target than a plain steel load. In their Hevi-13 Magnum Blend, designed specifically for turkey hunting, #5, #6 and #7 Hevi-Shot are blended together to provide a denser pattern with up to 40% more pellets on target. These and more great ideas for better hunting can be found at www.hevishot.com.

Hodgdon

In a move that surprised us all, Hodgdon is offering the handloader the two powders that Hornady used to create the LEVERevolution and Superperformance lines of high velocity cartridges. The powders are being produced by General Dynamic's St. Marks Powder Co., which is a major supplier of ball powders to ammunition manufacturers throughout the world. Loading data for the new powders is covered extensively in Hodgdon's "2011 Annual Reloading Manual" that contains over 5,000 handloading recipes. There's also a new, less expensive, black powder in the Hodgdon line called "Reenactor." "Reenactor" by GOEX is designed specifically for shooting blanks in muzzleloading muskets, carbines, pistols and cannons, although it is also suitable for low-cost plinking with round ball muzzleloaders. Hodgdon offers a great web site at www.hodgdon.com.

Hornady

Varmint hunters take note. Hornady has just expanded its "Superperformance" line to put some octane into the cases of four of the most popular varminting cartridges around: the .222 Rem., .223 Rem., .22-250 Rem. and the .243 Win. The new velocities Hornady is achieving are phenomenal. Take for example the .222 Rem. Historically, with a 50-gr. bullet, the cartridge would produce 3110 fps at acceptable pressure

Hornady's high velocity secrets are out with Hodgdon's release of LEVERevolution and Superformance powders.

Hornady's LEVERevolution ammunition provides up to 40% more energy than traditional flat point loads.

Hornady's economical Steel Match line combines less expensive steel cases with match quality bullets.

Hornady's high velocity Superformance hunting ammunition now features their bonded core InterBond bullet.

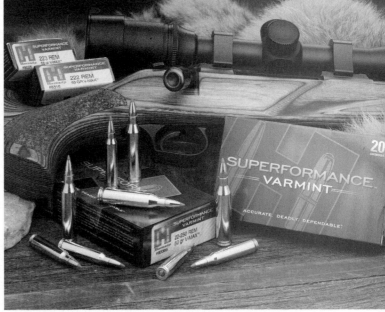

Hornady has boosted the velocities of popular varmint cartridges by 100-200 fps in its Superformance Varmint line.

levels. Hornady has just pumped up the velocity to 3345 fps. The complete Superformance Varmint line is impressive if you're looking for the utmost level of performance in the field. A similar tack has been taken in Hornady's match cartridge line for the .223, 5.56 NATO and .308 Win. The new line is called "Superformance Match" and again, historical velocities have been increased by 100-200 fps. To lower the price of match ammunition, Hornady has developed the "Steel Match" line of competitive rifle and handgun ammunition. The new line is loaded using imported steel cases and match bullets, and the cost reduction at the consumer level approaches 40%. There are two new interesting additions to the Critical Defense handgun line: a 45-gr. FTX bullet in the .22 WMR and a 90-gr. FTX bullet in the 9x18 Makarov. Lots of neat stuff at www.hornady.com.

Hornady's new .444 Marlin load gives their 265-gr. bullet a sensational velocity of 2400 fps.

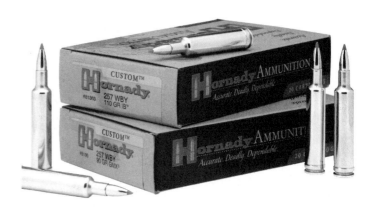

The .257 Weatherby cartridge is now being loaded by Hornady with either 90-gr. monolithic GMX or 110-gr. InterBond bullets.

With its hollow point filled with a polymer post, Hornady's Critical Defense ammunition expands without failure.

Huntington

Huntington is once again able to supply the consumer with the complete line of RWS ammunition, cases and projectiles. It's great news for metric caliber shooters. Visit www.huntingtons.com.

Lapua

With a well-deserved reputation for producing some of the most uniform brass in the world, Lapua has tightened its already tight specifications for their Scenar line of match bullets. Lapua continues to promote

Lightfield's less-lethal .410 cartridges carry four, .41-caliber rubber buckshot at a velocity of 1400 fps.

Lightfield's 20 ga., less-lethal loads deliver two .60-caliber rubber balls at 900 fps.

Lightfield offers two, less-lethal options in the 12 ga. — a rubber sponge or a hard .73-caliber rubber slug

its unique 6.5x47 match cartridge with a reference in the current catalog to necking that case down to 6mm. It's a fascinating company. See them at www.lapua.com.

Lightfield

Less-lethal shotgun projectiles are a specialty at Lightfield. Their less-lethal shotgun loads offer homeowners an attractive alternative for self-defense or critter control. This year there's a .410/2-1/2" loading featuring four .41-caliber rubber buckshot with a total weight of 42 grains. Muzzle velocity from a 4" revolver such as the Taurus Judge or the S&W Governor is 1150 fps. A 20 ga./2-3/4" loading features two .60-caliber rubber balls at 900 fps from an 18-inch barrel while the 12 ga./2-3/4" gets either a rubber sponge at 850 fps or a hard, .73-caliber rubber slug weighing 130-grs. at 600 fps. Great website at www.lightfieldlesslethal.com.

Magtech

Magtech is fielding the second generation of their "First Defense Justice" lead-free handgun ammunition in 9mm + P, .40 S&W and .45 ACP+P. The new generation adds a thin tin coating over their proven solid copper HP. Magtech claims the plated bullet increases velocity and reduces barrel wear. Visit www.magtechammunition.com.

Norma

Norma is introducing a new line of lead-free hunting ammunition named the "Kalahari."

The calibers included in the Kalahari line are the .270 Win., .270 WSM, .280 Rem., 7mm Rem. Mag., .308 Win. .30-'06, .300 Win. Mag. and .300 WSM. The very successful bonded core Oryx line gets some new combinations including a 156-gr./6.5x284, 165-gr./.270 Win. and a 250-gr./.35 Whelen. Great website at www.norma.cc.

Nosler

While handloaders are familiar with Nosler bullets, they're probably less so with Nosler brass. Well, Nosler Custom brass is a handloader's dream. Available in calibers ranging from the .204 Ruger to the .375 H&H, the cases are actually weight-sorted to +-1/2 grain into 25 or 50 count boxes and are fully prepped with deburred flash holes and deburred and chamfered necks.

Just open up the box and load 'em up. The AccuBond line has been expanded to include a 6mm/90-gr. There's a new .277/85-gr. E-Tip while the Custom Competition line sees the addition of a 6mm/107-gr. and an 8mm/200-gr. The Sporting Handgun Pistol offerings are expanded with the addition of a 9mm/124-gr. HP, 10mm/200-gr. HP and a .45/230-gr. FMJ.

See their components, loaded ammunition and custom rifles lines at www.nosler.com.

Quality Cartridge

Quality Cartridge is one of the field's most unique companies, drawing

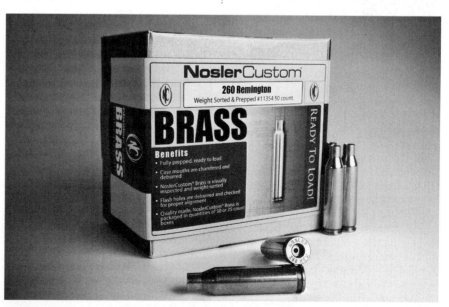

Nosler's Custom Brass is weight sorted to +/-1/2-gr., deburred and ready to load out of the box.

Loaded to 1700 fps, Remington's HyperSonic Steel ammunition can cut lead by 11%.

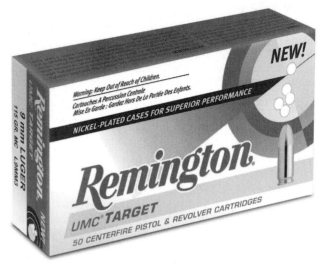

Remington's UMC economy target ammunition now features nickel-plated cases.

brass for custom, obsolete and wildcat cartridge cases for everything from the .17 Shrew to the .550 Magnum plus a complete line of metric calibers. One of their new services is to provide modified cases for use with the Hornady or Stoney Point OAL tools. How about a modified case for the .250 JAWS Micro Mag. or the .500 Mbogo? Quality Cartridge has them. See them at www.qual-cart.com.

Rainier Ballistics

Known for the exceptional quality of their copper-plated lead bullets, Rainier Ballistics came up with a new idea for the cowboy action shooter. Under their Red River brand, Rainier took the most popular cowboy action bullets in their product line and plated the copper coating to look like lead. Cowboys and cowgirls can now obtain the full benefits of copper-plated bullets without looking too modern and garish. Great website at www.rainierballistics.com.

Remington

Big Green has broken new ground with the release of their super-charged "HyperSonic Steel" shotgun ammunition. Available in 3" or 3-1/2" 20, 12 and 10 ga., HyperSonic Steel ammunition is loaded to a standard velocity of 1700 fps which Remington claims shortens leads on crossing targets up to 11%. New, too, is a complete line of UMC Target handgun ammunition that is designed to be sold through authorized shooting ranges. Available in calibers from .380 to .45 ACP, the new UMC economy brand features

nickel-plated cases for smooth and reliable functioning in handguns. The UMC centerfire rifle line is upgraded with a 115-gr. MC loading for the 6.8 Rem. SPC. The traditional Core-Lokt ammunition line has been expanded with the addition of the popular 7x64 Brenneke and 9.3x62mm cartridges while the big game Premier A-Frame line sees the addition of a 180-gr. A-Frame pill to the .30-'06 and the .300 Rem. Ultra Mag. cartridges. Big Green is always adding new products at www.remington.com.

Sellier & Bellot

Concerned that the EU would begin limiting the use of leaded projectiles, S&B has developed and will be loading

its own monolithic, copper alloy bullet under the "eXergy" label. The bullet features a hollow cavity capped by an aluminum nose while the body is grooved to reduce fouling and pressure. It will initially be loaded in the 7x57, 7x57R, 7x64, 7x65R, 7mm Rem. Mag., .308 Win., .30-'06, .300 Win. Mag., 8x57JS and 8x57JRS. Get the full details at www.sellier-bellot.cz.

Sierra

The Bulletsmiths are introducing four new bullets this year. In the Pro-Hunter line, there's a 225-gr./.338 SPT. In the varmint or BlitzKing line, the .25-caliber offerings have been expanded to include a 70-gr. flat base and a 90-gr. boattail.

The newest member of Sierra's Pro-Hunter line is a 225-gr./.338 SP bullet.

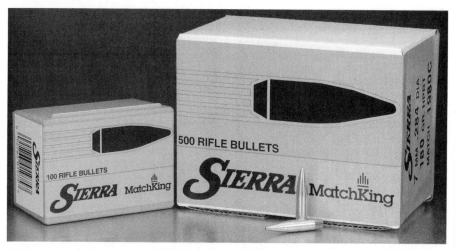

Sierra's snaky, 180-gr./.284 HPBT MatchKing is designed for the discerning long range marksman.

Responding to requests from .25-caliber shooters, Sierra has added 70-gr. and 90-gr. BlitzKing bullets to their varminting line.

For the .500 Nitro, .500 Jeffery and .505 Gibbs, Swift is making 535-gr. and 570-gr. A-Frames.

With a large HP and thin jacket, Speer's Short Barrel Protection loads are designed to expand reliably at lower velocities.

Both bullets will be available in 100- and 500-round boxes, and factory moly-coating is an option. Over in the MatchKing line, there's a 180-gr./7mm HPBT that provides a higher weight/higher ballistic coefficient option for long range shooters. See Sierra's complete line-up at www.sierrabullets.com.

Speer

Building on the excellent reputation their Gold Dot bullet enjoys, Speer is expanding its Gold Dot Short Barrel Personal Protection offerings with a new .22 WRM load featuring a 40-gr. bullet at 1150 fps. Speer's Short Barrel Personal Protection loads are designed with a large cavity and thinned jacket to insure consistent bullet performance in snubnose and compact semi-auto handguns. These specialized bullets are also offered as reloading components in calibers ranging from the .25 ACP to the .45 ACP. See Speer's terrific lines at www.speer-ammo.com and www.speer-bullets.com.

Silver State Armory

Silver State Armory is an integrated ammunition company that draws its own brass and makes its own AP bullets. Their specialty is the 6.8 SPC for which they offer 15 different loadings. The other two calibers they offer with a variety of loads are the 5.56mm and .308 Win.

See them at www.ssarmory.com

Winchester's .410 Personal Defense load consists of 16 BBs and four 70-gr. disk projectiles.

Winchester is loading "hexahedron" shaped shot in its latest waterfowl load, Blind Side.

Winchester's M-22 ammunition is designed to function perfectly in the increasingly popular .22 LR AR platforms.

Swift

With the increasing popularity of the big bores for dangerous African game, Swift is adding four new .50-caliber bullets to its A-Frame family. In both .505" and .510" diameters, Swift is offering 535-gr. and a 570-gr. A-Frames. Great performing bullets for the .500 Nitro, .500 Jeffery and .505 Gibbs cartridges. See their complete lines of Scirocco and A-Frame bullets at www.swiftbullets.com.

Winchester

"They'll never see it coming!" That's what Winchester says about its new cubical-shaped shot, called "Hex," being introduced under the "Blind Side" label. With rounded corners and edges, Hex shot stacks perfectly in a shot cup, providing up to 15% more non-toxic shot in each shell. The 12 ga. Blind Side loads will be available in 3" and 3-1/2" with 1-3/8- and 1-5/8-oz. payloads of BB's or #2s at 1400 fps. Winchester's rimfire lines have really been given a facelift with the

addition of the Varmint HE .22 LR featuring a segmented 37-gr. bullet at 1435 fps that fragments into four parts upon impact; the M-22 LR, a new round with a 40-gr. bullet at 1255 fps designed specifically for reliable functioning in the numerous .22 LR AR platforms coming on the market; a .17 HMR lead-free loading

featuring a 15.5-gr. bullet at 2550 fps and a new, conventional plastic tipped 30-gr. bullet at 2550 fps in the .22 Win. Mag. In the centerfire lines, there's a new E-Tip .308 Win. loading with a 168-gr. bullet at 2675 fps; five new lead-free additions to the Super X Power Core 95/5 line ranging from a 64-gr. Power Core 95/5 bullet in

Winchester's "Power Max Bonded" ammunition is designed specifically for whitetail deer hunting.

the .223 at 3020 fps to a 150-gr./.30-30 loading at 2380 fps; finally, in the Winchester Power Max line, offering bonded bullets designed specifically for whitetail deer hunting, there's a 64-gr./.223 at 3020 fps, a 220-gr./.325 WSM at 2840 fps and a 200-gr./.338 Win. Mag. at 2960 fps.

If you own a 3" chambered Taurus Judge or Circuit Judge, you'll love Winchester's new .410 Personal Defense load consisting of 16 BBs stacked under 4 copper-plated, 70-gr., flying saucer-looking slugs. If that won't get the job done, there's a new Winchester Supreme Elite PDX1 2-3/4" buck-and-ball load consisting of three copper-plated #00 buckshot layered in Grex buffering media over a 1 oz. Foster-type, Power Point slug with a payload velocity of 1150 fps.

Big Red has been busy this year. See all of these and more at www. winchester.com.

Wolf Performance

Wolf has gained an excellent reputation with its polymer coated, steel cased ammunition and is introducing a new line of economical priced loads for volume shooters under the "Military Classic" label. The Military Classic line features some interesting loads including the 6.5 Grendel, 7.62x54R Extra Match and the Russian .50-caliber machinegun round, the 12.7x108mm. See the complete Wolf line of rimfire, centerfire and shotshell ammunition at www.wolfammo.com.

The new SuperX "Power-Core " ammunition features a monolithic, copper alloy HP bullet.

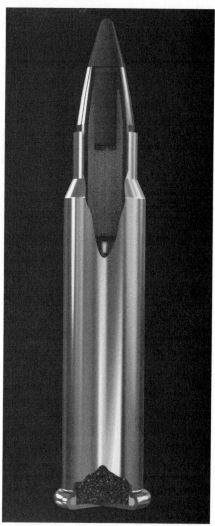

Winchester's latest .17 HMR load, the Varmint LF, is lead-free.

REPORT FROM THE FIELD:
BLACKPOWDER UPDATE

BY **WM. HOVEY SMITH**

As reflected in the economic times of "The Great Recession," the 2011 SHOT Show brought sighs of retrenchment, relocation, reorganization and reductions, with companies that offered replica cartridge guns along with muzzleloaders generally faring better than those who did not.

One maker, **Millennium Design Muzzleloaders** (MDM), had a powder mill explosion which set back production, caused financial distress and is causing the company's owners to reconsider its market position.

Makers and dealers of traditional arms apparently took the hardest hits, but there is a promise that the 150th Anniversary celebrations of Civil War events will revive that portion of the market, and several new, or ratherreintroduced, guns were offered to reenactors and shooters.

Making muzzleloaders easier to use and rust-free was the objective of new coating technologies by **Thompson/Center Arms** and **Traditions**. **Connecticut Valley Arms** (CVA) sought to add value to their products by shipping all of their guns with scope mounts and equipping even their lowest-cost Wolf with an easily-detachable breech plug.

The most excitement in the market, however, revolves around some hunter-friendly versions of the Winchester lever guns, including versions of the 1886 Winchester by **Davide Pedersoli**

and **Chiappa** as well as a .38-55 Model 94 Winchester that will be sold through **Cabela's** and **Browning-Winchester**. The .38-55 got another boost with a **Lyman**-branded reduced-scale version of the Sharps 1874 single-shot made by Chiappa. Coming next year will be a half-magazine version of the 1876 Winchester chambered for the .45-60 from **Uberti** that will be marketed by **Cimarron Firearms**.

Hodgdon Reenactor Powder

The **Hodgdon-GOEX** brands of powders introduced a new black powder line, Reenactor, which will be a less expensive variety of the traditional GOEX. **Western Powders**, Inc. has their Blackhorn 209 black powder substitute powders for modern muzzleloaders and cartridges like the .45-70 and .35-55 as well as a new KIK Black Powder in FFFFG, FFFG and FFG granulations imported from Slovenia. I tried some of the new powder in FFG granulation in a variety of rifles, shotguns and revolvers. The only difference that I could tell between it and GOEX was that the KIK powder tended to clog measuring tubes and flasks.

A new PowerBelt bullet was announced by **Black Powder Industries**, Inc. (BPI, Inc.) with the AeroLite bullet which features the lead body and plastic skirt of the PowerBelt, but has a plastic tip and stem that extends deeper into the bullet. This modification results in a lighter .50-caliber projectile. This better ballistic shape provides flatter trajectories with 100-grain charges for reduced recoil from 5-1/2- to 6-1/2-pound guns while retaining good killing characteristics on deer-sized game. With more makers producing lighter guns that are uncomfortable to shoot with magnum loads, these reduced-weight .50-caliber bullets and 100-grain charges are reasonable alternatives.

In black-powder revolvers, **North American Arms**' .22-caliber Companion

Western Powder's Blackhorn and KIK Black Powder

Christian Cranmer published a book, *Treasure is Where You Find It,* about his 30-year quest to obtain and export these guns from Nepal. It contains many photos of the guns, cannon, knives and swords as they were being moved and packed at the Royal Arsenal, which was located in the old Lagan Silekhana palace in Katmandu.

For prices and availabilities on these guns, check with Atlanta Cutlery Co., at www.atlantacutlery.com. Prices and availabilities may change.

1842 Percussion
.75-caliber musket with
East India Co. Markings made by
Wilkinson Sword in England.
(Not presently catalogued.)

This gun is the percussion version of the flintlock Brown Bess .75-caliber musket, but was a new design, rather than a conversion. My gun had external rust pits on the barrel, but was sound. I re-proofed this gun and subsequently used it with loads of non-toxic HeviShot and 12-gauge plastic wads in its 11-gauge barrel to take ducks, geese and swan. I have also taken a deer with this gun using patched round-ball loads.

revolvers have been the smallest of the small. Past Companions suffered from not having long-enough barrels to allow for more precise shot placement. The Earl Companion has a 4-inch barrel and a loading lever that retains the cylinder pin. This 5-shot revolver uses black powder, no. 11 percussion caps and elongated .22 caliber bullets.

Companies that have withdrawn from the black-powder market this year include **Navy Arms Co**. (Although they may restock some replica muzzleloaders next year.), Savage no longer offers muzzleloading rifles. Knight Rifles ceased production last year and was purchased by a North Carolina company who announced they were moving production from Ohio to North Carolina. Thompson/Center is also to leave New Hampshire and go to Springfield, Massachusetts, the home of Smith & Wesson, their parent company.

Getting and Shooting Original Guns

The opportunity to refurbish and perhaps hunt with some original muzzle-loading guns has been available in recent years through the efforts of International Military Antiques, Inc. (IMA) and Atlanta Cutlery Co. who are selling the contents of the Royal Arsenal of Nepal. These

companies make no warranty as to the safety of these arms and take no responsibility if they are shot.

Arms at the arsenal included Brown Bess flintlocks through the entire range of British arms used during World War II. These guns range from rusted, broken, worm-eaten relics that are beyond further use to those that may be cautiously returned to limited service. There is a mix of guns that were made by British makers, those apparently made elsewhere in India and those made in the Nepalese Arsenal.

These Nepalese guns were produced with available technologies. Early guns have poor inletting and metal work. Progressively better skills and equipment were incorporated to make reasonable copies of British-pattern arms even though the barrels were still hand-forged through the time that the Snyder .577 breech loaders were in service.

These barrels were not as strong as those made in England, and the Nepalese ammo, from period reports, used a weaker home-produced black powder. Consequently, modern loadings should be kept at moderate levels. The observations given below were made on guns that I purchased from Atlanta Cutlery and you may, or may not, have similar results.

Wilkinson Sword 1842 .75 caliber musket with non-toxic shot was used to take this NC swan.

.75-caliber Brunswick Rifle (Uncleaned ($494.95) – Cleaned and complete ($895.00) – Parts gun usually with missing buttstocks and some broken fittings, ($129.95).

Bowing to pressures to adopt many improvements that been developed for civilian arms into an improved military rifle, the British Brunswick rifle utilized many then-modern muzzleloading innovations. Most significantly it had a rifled 2-groove barrel fitted to a false breech and a central sub-chamber to provide more efficient combustion. The most instantly recognizable thing about the Brunswick rifle is its robust bayonet lug mounted on the side of the barrel, allowing for the firm attachment of a sword bayonet.

From the two Indian-made guns that I have worked with, it appears that this was the makers' first attempts to produce rifled guns. On one gun, sharp ridges of metal stood above the guns' grooves. Although the guns could be shot with patched round balls they were very poor shooters, even at 20 yards. I had a custom mold made for my rifle by Jeff Tanner in England. Ultimately I took a deer with this gun on a hunt at Hard Labor Creek State Park in Georgia.

I have five videos on my YouTube channel wmhoveysmith about this gun including "Brunswick Rifle at Hard Labor," as well as blog entries at www.hoveysmith.wordpress.com describing in details my efforts to "make a hunter" out of this old relic. After lapping rough ridges of metal on either sides of the grooves out of the barrel, I managed to get it to shoot with sufficient accuracy to take on both deer and elk hunts. I did get my Georgia deer, but no Idaho elk appeared before the gun.

Both the Russians and Confederate forces that used the Brunswick made .75-caliber hollow-based bullets for this rifle. Although they differed in shape, they did allow more rapid loading. I expanded the base of a .69-caliber Minie Ball bullet intended for the Springfield rifled musket, and tried it. The general concept worked, but recoil was very tough. A lighter weight hollow-based Buffalo Bullets' Ball-ET style projectile in .75 caliber might offer possibilities for these guns, although demand would be very limited.

Brunswick Rifle prior to cleaning.

.69-caliber smoothbore version of the Brunswick Rifle (Uncleaned, $375.00)

According to Atlanta Cutlery Co., the smoothbore versions of the Brunswick rifle were issued to NCOs so that they could load their guns as fast as the troops they supervised. My gun was .69-caliber and was not inlet for a patch box. This gun had a broken mainspring. After fitting a replacement, I developed a load that enabled this 14-gauge gun to take a wild turkey. I used 85 grains of FFG black powder, a 14-gauge over-powder wad (Dixie Gun Works), 20-grains of Cream of Wheat filler, a 16-gauge plastic shot cup from Remington and 1-1/8 ounces of no. 6 lead shot for my turkey load. Sixteen-gauge plastic wads will work in 14-gauge muzzleloaders just as 12-gauge plastic wads work in 11-gauge (.75-caliber) muzzleloaders.

The wood on this gun had deteriorated to the extent that I returned the broken spring to the lock and gave it to a friend as a wall hanger. Some guns of this type were also made by private makers in England for export to India, and those I have seen are much better crafted than the Nepalese guns.

The cleaned Brunswick rifle with mold and cast balls.

*1853 .58-caliber
smoothbore 3-band Enfield
pattern musket Battlefield Pick-up
uncleaned ($350.00)*

These smoothbore muskets are externally identical to the 3-band Endfield percussion rifle used worldwide in the British serviced and in large numbers by both sides during the American Civil War. Although cosmetically similar to British issue rifles, these guns' lock parts were poorly hardened and many were bent or chipped. It is likely that these smoothbore guns were made somewhere else in India and awarded to the Nepalese. The guns are useful to someone who wants experience in cleaning antique firearms. Even with functional parts (only the lockplate, hammer and some screws were salvageable on my gun), I would be dubious about shooting these guns.

*1864 .577 Snyder
(Uncleaned, $349.95)*

My example is of a later pattern that was made originally as a cartridge gun and includes a sliding locking rod at the rear of the horizontal-swinging breechblock. Because of this gun's historic connection with the British Empire, shooters in England's former colonies have made manful efforts to work up loads for these relics. I obtained some custom-loaded rounds and experimented with them. The gun shot better after I had cleaned the barrel, fired 20-rounds and re-cleaned the bore.

I have had it out hunting, but have not found a cooperative animal.

This rifle showed signs of lots of use, but its parts were intact and functional. The barrel's bore cleaned up surprisingly well. Apparently Gurkha units were well drilled in keeping their guns cleaned. Although gunmakers in Nepal were now adept in making properly hardened lock and action components at this time, they still produced barrels by lap-welding strips of metal on a mandrel. According to Atlanta Cutlery even the Snyder had such barrels and some of them were "sprung." Caution should be utilized in shooting these guns.

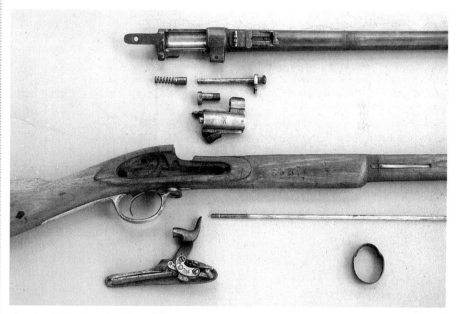

Snyder Rifle after cleaning.

*.577/450 Gahendra
(Uncleaned $189.95)*

This was a Nepalese variation of the usual Martini-Henry .577/450s. This gun is unusual in that removing one pin allows the action to drop as a unit from the receiver for easier cleaning. Almost all of these guns have loose buttstocks. I found that the buttstock could be tightened with a screwdriver after the buttplate had been removed. Many of these guns have broken mainsprings.

Although all of the older guns suffered from poor storage conditions, the interiors of the rifled barrels of the

Snider rifle with .577 Snider cartridge.

few cartridge guns that I have cleaned were remarkably good. I have not located suitable .577/.450 ammo for the Gahendra. With British service loads the Martini-Henry was a hard-kicking gun, and there is no reason to suspect that the Gahendra would be any different.

Black Powder Industries, Inc. (CVA and PowerBelt Bullets)

CVA has continued a general upgrade of their muzzleloaders for 2011. These includes shipping scope mounts and Quick-Release Breech Plugs for their all-stainless Apex rifles ($600-$740; these have interchangeable muzzleloading and centerfire barrels) as well as their budget-priced Wolf ($230) drop-barreled gun. The Wolf is the lightest of the CVA Muzzleloaders with a weight of 6.25 pounds and even less in its compact stock which has a 13-inch pull.

Note to readers: If you feel like you might want one of these shorter stocks for your child, order it now. These are low-demand items and may be available only for a year or two.

For an adult shooter, the Wolf is best paired with a 100-grain (2-pellet) load and PowerBelt Bullet's new .50-caliber AeroLite bullets that are available in 250- ($30 for 15) and 300- ($32 for 15) grain weights. To reduce recoil for the youngest shooters, the lowest charge that I suspect would give good accuracy with the new PowerBelt bullet would be 85 grains of FFg. These guns will shoot

patched .490" round balls with good accuracy if the charge is reduced to 55 grains (or lower) of FFG to prevent tearing up the patches. The same can be said for any of the modern .50-caliber fast-twist modern muzzleloaders.

Chiappa Firearms

Chiappa was among several companies to introduce commemorative guns honoring the 150th anniversaries of the American Civil War. This year's gun is the 1842 Springfield which is an "armory bright" finished .69-caliber smoothbore musket. Compared to others of its day,

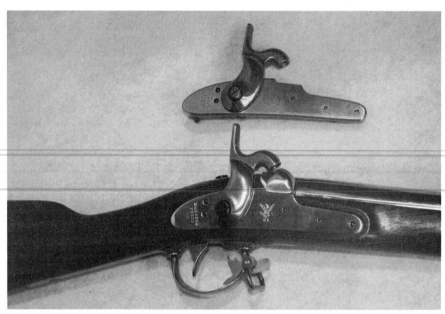
Chiappa Springfield musket with extra lock.

this is not a "sexy" gun, but a practical military arm.

I do not know why this gun was issued in "armory bright" finish this late in the history of muzzleloading arms. Although a few dollars were saved on each gun, troops in the field had to spend endless hours attempting to keep their black-powder-using guns from rusting when exposed to rain, snow and salt water. Rusting was particularly rapid if they had been shot and the corrosive residues of combustion had a chance to work on the gun's steel components.

The 1842 Springfield was typically used with paper cartridges loaded with "buck

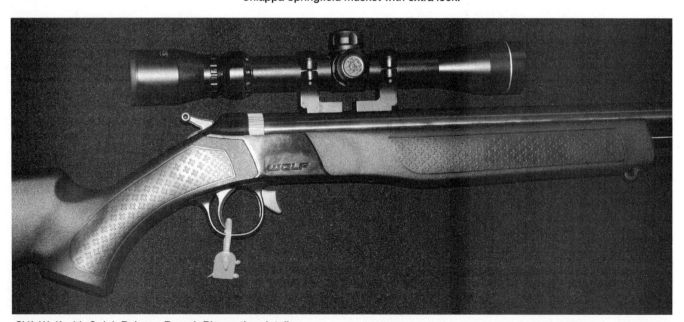
CVA Wolf with Quick Release Breech Plug action detail.

Pedersoli's four replica guns from the American Civil War.

Davide Pedersoli and Co.

Newly announced muzzleloaders from Pedersoli include a 1861 Springfield ($940), Richmond Model ($1,135), Mississippi Rifle ($1,411) and Cook & Brothers carbine ($1,100). All of these guns are rifled .58-caliber guns. Both the Richmond rifle and the Cook & Brothers (Athens, Georgia) carbine will be welcomed by Confederate reenactors who have not had many replicas of rifles and carbines produced by Confederate manufacturers during the Civil War. The Springfield and Richmond rifles are full length at 56 inches long, the Mississippi rifle with its distinctive patch box slightly shorter at 49 inches and the carbine shortest of all at 40-1/2 inches.

Dixie Gun Works

This long time importer of Pedersoli and other replica muzzleloading and cartridge guns is featuring a CS Richmond Musket. The rifle is a .58-caliber gun with a 40-inch tapered round barrel, three barrel bands, a brass forend cap and buttplate and a weight of 10.5 pounds. The gun is made by Euro Arms in Italy and has a suggested retail price of $1,050.

For Sportsmen, Dixie now markets Davide Pedersoli's Old English Shotgun which is a cylinder and cylinder double with a round patch box, browned barrels, case hardened lock and straight English grip weighing 7-1/4 pounds. This gun has a suggested retail of $1,500.

Although introduced in Europe last year, Dixie now has in stock the Davide Pedersoli An IX Gendarmerie (police) pistol. This flintlock pistol has a robust lock that takes a 3/4–inch flint and is offered in a smoothbore .595-caliber and 5-inch tapered round barrel. The gun weighs 1-3/4 pounds with an overall length of 9-3 /4 inches. The price of this pistol is currently $550. This handgun was designed to perform under field conditions, and its reliability was so impressive that it was also used by French military units.

In Europe indoor "Parlor Shooting" was popular, and some very expensive guns were made featuring all of the refinements of off-hand target rifles. These guns were powered by percussion caps and shot a round ball. A less expensive version is the White Hawk 209 rifle from Pedersoli that uses 209 percussion caps to propel .177 lead BBs. The gun weighs 3-1/2 pounds and retails for $325.

and ball." This consisted of one .69-caliber round ball and three buckshot. This was a devastating charge at close range. Adjacent to the "Stone Wall" on the Gettysburg battlefield there is a monument to the 12th New Jersey. This is a stone sphere surmounted by a pyramid of three smaller spheres. This monument represents the "buck and ball" loads fired to repel Picket's Charge. Many of the originals were used as shotguns in following decades and literally shot to pieces.

To keep Chiappa's replica guns as close to the originals as possible, two locks are issued with each gun. One is marked "Springfield" and the other "Harpers Ferry." These guns also have acceptance stamps. A bayonet and sling is also supplied with the gun. The completed package has a suggested retail of under $900.

Made by Chiappa and offered exclusively by Lyman, the Ideal Model Sharps ($1,500) is a 20% scale model of the Sharps 1874 with special finish and engravings. The plain-Jane version of this gun is marketed by Chiappa as The Little Sharps. The Little Sharps is chambered for 10 rifle and pistol cartridges ranging from the .22 L.R. to the .38-55 Winchester. The Lyman Ideal Model is chambered for the .38-55 and .22 Hornet.

The .38-55 has an outstanding reputation as an accurate black-powder cartridge and a deer killer. I have little doubt that this new Sharps variant will do very well as a handy hunting gun.

Chiappa is also among the suppliers of replica 1886 Winchester rifles ($1,400 and up) in both rifle (26-inch barrels at 9 pounds) and carbines (22-inch barrels at 8 pounds). Both are chambered for the .45-70 and .444 Marlin, and both have full-length magazines.

Navy Arms Company

If you have ever had a "hanker" to own your own Gatling gun, have room for it and about $35,500 to spend, Navy Arms company has an exacting replica of the 1877 Colt Bulldog .45-70 five-barrel Gatling gun for you. This gun is mounted on a stout tripod with swivel head allowing 360 degrees of movement. Most of the exterior of the gun is brass as are most of the fittings. Always a crew-served weapon, this gun comes with single-column magazines and a steel hand crank to fire the gun.

Although among the shortest of the commercial Gatlin guns, it is only light weight compared to the 20mm models intended for use aboard ships. Also shown at the Shot Show was the steel twin-barreled full-sized version of the 1879 Gardner crank-operated rapid-fire gun in .45-70 ($26,000) that uses twin single-column magazines to feed its two operating mechanisms. This is a lighter-weight unit than the Gatling Gun with a more compact profile.

These guns are made by U.S. Armament Co. of Ephrata, Pennsylvania, who also builds Navy Arms' Springfield bolt-action rifles.

North American Arms

Some guns are just fun to shoot and North American Arms' Earl Companion percussion revolver ($300) is one of these. The little five-shot revolver has a length of 7-3/4 inches, a 4-inch barrel and weight of 8.6 ounces. I fired the gun and then reloaded it with the recommended scoop (4-grains) of FFFFg black powder and 30-grain lead bullet ($4.00 per 100). This load produced 623 fps, generated 25.9 fpe of muzzle energy, and penetrated 40 sheets of cardboard plus 1/2 inch of pine. This compares to 344 fps and 7.88 fpe of muzzle energy from the 1-5/8-inch barrel version. For comparision, .22 shorts often have velocities of about 1,000 fps. and energies of 80 fpe from 22-inch barrels.

I outfitted the Earl with a larger pair of finger-groove grips and managed to shoot a 2 1/2-inch group at 10 yards with the little gun. I found the trigger pull a long and grating for such a light-weight pistol, but for finishing off squirrels and similar game at point-blank range it will serve. The longer barrel increases the possibility of making reasonable hits at longer ranges.

Muzzle End of Colt 1877 Bulldog Gatling Gun.

North American Arms new Earl percussion revolver a longer barreled version of the Companion.

Taylor's & Co.

While it cannot be said that every gun that was available in 1880s-1890s can now be purchased as new guns from Taylor and Co., a remarkable number can be. Taylor imports from several companies and offers percussion and cartridge revolvers, many varieties of lever-action rifles, Sharps and Winchester single shots and even the Winchester 1887 Lever-action shotgun.

Not only are these guns often made of better steels and materials than were available when the guns were new, they are also chambered for modern-day cartridges. For example, the 1887 Lever shotgun has been redesigned to take the standard 2-3/4-inch 12-gauge hull and the S&W Schofield comes in .45 Long Colt. Similarly, replica 1873 Winchesters are being sold in .45 Long Colt and .357 Magnum chamberings. Even the venerable Spencer can be had in .45 Long Colt.

The majority of these guns are being purchased by Cowboy Action Shooters, but increasing numbers of the Sharps and Winchester single shots and 1886 Winchesters are finding their way into the deer woods – particularly, in shortened and lighter-weight versions. If tempted to hunt with any of these guns use modern jacketed expanding bullets, rather than the much less effective Cowboy Action Loads.

Taylor also has cartridge-conversion cylinders that allow shooting the 38 Long Colt and .45 Long Colts through some makers of .32, .38 and .44 percussion revolvers, including the Colt Walker. These have detachable backs with centerfire firing pins and operate with the original percussion hammers. Only low pressure loadings should be used in these guns.

Thompson/Center Arms

The adoption of a new Weather Shield technology for its value priced Impact muzzleloader ($249), mid-ranged priced Triumph Bone Collector ($650) and upper end Pro Hunter muzzleloaders ($970 vs. $835) provides not only better corrosion resistance, but also savings of up to $200 compared to the previous all-stainless Pro Hunter.

Applied on the exterior metallic components, the Weather Shield technology is a ceramic coating that is bonded to the underlying metal – something similar to enameling on a cooking pot. Unfortunately, this treatment is not suitable for the inside of the bore, so even the Weather Shield protected guns need to be cleaned with soap and water and black-powder solvents.

The three guns mentioned above differ in that the Impact uses a manually operated shroud similar to that used on some Remington shotguns and the Valmet shotguns to lock the barrel in the closed position. Pulling the aluminum shrouding back allows the barrel to fall as in a break-open shotgun exposing the chamber for reloading. The Triumph has an aluminum frame and an underlever attached to the bottom of the trigger guard

to drop the break-open barrel. With the Encore family of pistols and rifles, this all steel falling-block action is locked by the trigger guard. When the trigger guard is pushed forward the barrel falls for reloading. All of these muzzleloaders take 209 primers.

For the states of Washington, Oregon and Idaho that require exposed ignition, the Omega NorthWest Explorer ($325-$400) (also available in Weather Shield) uses a pivoting block action with choices of no. 11 or musket cap ignition. On my Idaho elk hunt I experienced the trials of using an open-ignition gun under snowy conditions. I either carried my guns in a sheath or used a leather mule's knee to protect the action. These are sold by Dixie Gun Works and called a "Lock Boot" in their catalogue.

Thompson/Center Arms now only has two "traditional" muzzleloaders. These are the company's flagship muzzleloader the T/C Hawken and the flintlock Firestorm. Both are only available as .50-caliber rifles. It will be interesting to see if these guns survive the company's

move from New Hampshire to Springfield, Massachusetts. I tried hard with the Firestorm, but could never get its lock to function well enough even after buttressing its spring with washers. Only with absolutely sharp flints could I achieve reliable ignition with the issued T/C flintlocks in either the Firestorm or T/C Hawken rifle. In contrast, the percussion version of the lock worked well.

One way to get a better lock is to install one of the L&R RLP replacement locks for the T/C Hawken and similar Lyman flintlocks for $135. These will require a small amount of inletting, finishing and bluing. There are two shapes for variants of the Lyman locks. Call (803) 775-6127 for details and pricing or Google L&R Lock Company to bring up an on-line catalog.

Traditions Performance Firearms

Lighter guns, CeraKote Finishes and quick clean up using their Accelerator Breech Plug were Traditions' chief

Action detail of Thompson Center Arms Impact Rifle with sliding hood lock.

Thompson Center Pro Hunter XT Weather Shield Camo

Traditions Vortek with CeraKote finish

Traditions Pursuit Ultralight XLT

advances in muzzleloading technology for 2011. The new 6-1/2 pound Vortek UltraLight ($420-$590), has all of these features plus a drop-out trigger assembly with a 4-pound trigger pull for improved shooting characteristics.

The lightest Traditions in-line is the Pursuit Ultra Light XTL ($290-$440) which weighs in at 5.1 pounds without a scope. Recoil increases with reduced weight. A 100-grain charge and Traditions Smackdown 250-grain saboted bullet would appear to be optimum for this gun for deer-sized game.

Unlike CVA and Thomson/Center Arms, Traditions continues to carry an extensive line of traditionally designed muzzleloaders. Among these are the budget-priced Deerhunter Flintlock and Percussion rifles ($249-$369) in both .50 and .32 calibers. About five years ago, Traditions redesigned their flintlocks with the result that they are much improved. These new locks are in the Pennsylvania ($790), Shenandoah ($660) and Tennessee ($520) as well as in the modernized PA Pellet Flintlock ($440) which now also has the Accelerator Breech Plug.

Rather than using expensive bullets for the entire sighting-in process, Traditions offers a Sight-In-Pack Combination with both 240-grain Saboted pure lead Plinkers and the jacketed polymer-pointed Smackdowns with 15 of each bullets for $19.99. The pure lead, hollow-pointed plinkers costs $10.95 for a pack of 20 and will kill deer and at ranges of under 100 yards. This is an excellent bullet for a younger shooter using light-weight .50-caliber muzzleloaders and loads of 85-100 grains of powder.

The late Ian McMurchy killed scores of deer with similar pure lead "Plinker" saboted bullets and they were among his favorite projectiles for the variety of in-line muzzleloaders that he used.

New to Traditions, Hornady's hollow based, copper jacketed and polymer pointed bullets in 300 and 350 grain weights are now offered in a pack of 15 for $20. They are designed to be loaded directly over the powder. With pellets, I usually load a felt wad over the pellets and 25-grains of Cream of Wheat to expand the base and keep the wad from being stuck in the bullet cavity.

REPORT FROM THE FIELD:
HANDLOADING

BY **LARRY STERETT**

The economy, as this is written, may not be in the best shape, but with the inflated prices of many items used by shooters, handloading could see an increase in growth. New products for handloaders, including equipment, components, and reloading and instruction manuals keep being introduced, and that's good news.

Forster Products, home of the lathe-type case trimmer invented and popularized by in 1946 by the Forster brother, Bob and Henry, is still in production, and in three versions, Original, Classic, and .50 BMG. (There is even a non-lathe type Power Case Trimmer for use with standard drill presses.) A host of accessories are available for the Trimmers, including pilots and collets capable of fitting almost every case type ever produced, including the big English calibers, plus neck reamers, outside neck turners, primer pocket cleaners and chamfering tools, hollow pointers for bullets, and more. There is even a 3-in-1 case mouth cutter that trims and chamfers the case mouth inside and out.

The latest addition to the Forster line is the introduction of loading dies for the .300 AAC Blackout (.300 BLK) cartridge developed by the Advanced Armament Corporation. (This cartridge was designed for use in AR rifles, and with a 123-grain bullet generates more energy than the 6.8mm SPC or 5.56mm M855 rounds. It is with the standard AR bolt and there is no reduction in the magazine capacity.) The new dies are available as a standard BenchRest set, as single full length sizing die, or the full length sizing die with an Ultra Micrometer Seating Die. (Forster currently has loading dies to handle cartridges from the .17 Remington to the .375 Remington Ultra Magnum.)

The 8th edition of the *Hornady Handbook of Cartridge Reloading* features the latest reloading data on the newest cartridges, using the newest components, along with data on popular cartridges and components previously available.

The new Hornady Lock-n-Load Case Prep Assistant ready to deburr case mouths. Space along the sides is provided for storage of other tools.

Lee Precision introduced many handloaders to the reloading game with their hand-operated Lee Loader. The Loader is still being produced for the most popular metallic cartridges, but is no longer catalogued for shotshells, having been replaced by the Lee Load-All II press, available for 12, 16, and 20 gauge shells. New to the Lee line is a steel Reloading Stand, an 18 Cavity 00 Buckshot Bullet Mold, a hand-held Auto-Prime XR for handloaders who like to feel the primers being set, and a Lock-Ring Eliminator. (The popular Lee Hand Press is now equipped with a Breech Lock System.)

The Lee Loader is available for 14 rifle cartridges and six handgun cartridges, while the regular 7/8x14 tpi dies, including those with carbide sizers, are available for over 40 handgun cartridges from the .25 ACP to the .500 S&W Magnum, and 80 rifle cartridges from the .17 Remington to the .458 Winchester Magnum, plus the .50 BMG. (Lee has a Classic 50 Caliber BMG Press Kit containing everything necessary to reload the .50 BMG cartridge, except the components. There's even a tube of case sizing lube.)

The new Lee Precision 00 Buckshot Mold produces enough 00 buck in one casting to load two 12 gauge shotshells with a charge of nine 00 buck each. There's a complete line of Lee bullet molds available to cast a 93-grain design for the .32 S&W Long to a 500-grain for the .50-70 Government cartridge, Minie, R-E-A-L, and round balls for muzzleloaders, conical for black powder revolvers, and slugs for 12 gauge shotguns.

The new Lee Reloading Stand comes with a patented Quick-Change Plate System, pre-drilled to permit rapid switching of Lee reloading presses, even from the Lee Classic Turret to the Lee Challenger to the 50 Caliber BMG Presss, if so desired. There's a shelve for storage of extras presses, etc., and the legs each have eight holes drilled to accommodate the mounting of bins, racks, and other accessories.

Handloaders reloading once-fired surplus military or commercial cases need boxes or cartons to store their cartridges. **MTM Molded Products Company** has hinged lid and slip-top cases in varying capacities, from 10 rounds to 100 rounds to fit cartridges from the .25 ACP to the .50 BMG. (There are also boxes for rimfire cartridges, for those shooters liking a bit more protection for their ammunition than the factory chipboard boxes provide.) MTM also has Universal Loading Trays for rifle, handgun, and shotgun cartridges. Open cell foam pads can be obtained, and cut to size to line the bottom of shells boxes, for those shooters desiring less rattle and more bullet tip protection.

Powder funnels, die storage boxes, load labels – metallic cartridges and shotshells – and a primer flipper are featured in the MTM line, as is a Mini Digital Reloading Scale with a 750-grain capacity. The labels provide plenty of room for recording load data, number of times the cases has been loaded, and other useful information. Another useful item is the Handloaders Log, consisting of a three-ring binder with five sets of

data sheets for recording reloading data and four sets of targets.

Handloaders in need of once-fired brass might find it at **TopBrass** (www.SCHARCH.COM). This firm has once-fired Lake City .50 BMG brass, which has been full-length sized without the mount being expanded, deprimed, and cleaned. (This .50 BMG brass will require mouth trimming and primer pocket reaming.) Deprimed, cleaned, sized, trimmed and reamed, once-fired military brass in .223 and 7.62x51mm cases is available unprimed or primed, and so is processed, unprimed handgun caliber brass in five popular calibers, from the .38 Special to the .45 ACP. TopBrass even has new brass and card and/or plastic 20-round or 50-round storage boxes or trays for the reloaded ammunition.

Mayville Engineering Company (MEC) has shotshell reloading presses to handle every gauge from the 10 to the 28, plus the .410. Not every press will handle every gauge, but most will. The SteelMaster is available only in 12 or 10 gauge, while the 650N, 8567N Grabber, and 9000 Series (GN, HN, and E) presses will not accommodate the 10 gauge shells. The 8447-600 Jr. Mark V, 8120 Sizemaster, and 8119 Super-Sizer presses are available in the entire range. Most of the presses come with a primer feed, charge bar, and three powder bushings, and some of the presses, but not all, can be converted to handle another gauge using he appropriate die die. (Collet and pad to switch

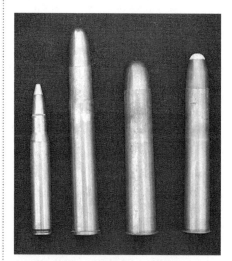

Some of the cartridges for which Huntington Die Specialities, Hornady, and others can supply reloading dies. Left to right: .30-06 Springfield, .475 No. 2 Nitro Express, .577 Nitro Express, and .500 Nitro Express. (Not all firms stock the .475 No. 2 or the .577 N.E. dies.)

The Lyman Reloading Handbook, 49th edition contains up-to-data reloading data for current and some obsolete rifle and handgun cartridges using both jacketed and cast bullets. The much smaller *Ideal Hand Book No. 34* from 1942 contains data on some cartridges seldom seen, or even heard of today.

The RCBS Accessory Handle-2 with a deburring tool attached, with Powder Trickler-2 behind.

gauges are also available for the 8119 Super-Sizer, and steel shot kits for most of the presses are obtainable.)

Lyman Products Corporation has been providing service to handloaders for more than a century. During that time span the firm occasionally issued reloading manual/handbooks. The latest is the *Lyman Reloading Handbook*, 49th edition, available in either soft or hardbound versions. This 464-page gem, which tips the scales at 2 lbs., 12-1/2 oz. in the softbound version, compared to the 6-ounce, 160-page *Ideal Hand Book No. 34,* published by the Lyman Gun Sight Corporation back in 1942, is worthy of space on any handloader's reference shelf. The first four chapters in this volume, which was edited by Thomas J. Griffin, consist of articles devoted to handloading, including four specialty articles covering such subjects as "Handloading the 1876 Replicas" and "Handloading Winchester's Stubby Cartridges." The balance of this tome consists of loading data for rifle and handgun cartridges, plus a special section on loads for the Thompson/Center Contender and Encore pistols, followed by a reference chapter containing four appendices, a reloader's log and some note pages. (Shotshell reloading data

is featured in a separate handbook, unlike the hand books and manuals of yesteryear in which shotshell reloading data was included.)

Each cartridge featured in the rifle and handgun data sections is introduced with a brief history, plus a dimensioned drawing, accompanied by a list of the test components and specifications. There's a black-and-white photo of each of the bullet types – cast or jacketed – and tested and starting and maximum loads are listed with a variety of powders per bullet. Muzzle velocity and pressures are provided, along with the overall loaded cartridge length, bullet sectional density and ballistic coefficient. The rifle cartridges range from the .17 Remington Fireball to the .50-70 Government and include some older cartridges, such as the .22 K-Hornet, .348 Winchester, .40-65 Winchester, and .45-70 Sharps Straight, and many of the more recent, such as the .375 Ruger and .450 Marlin. Handgun cartridges, such as the 9mm Luger and .357 S&W Magnum, which are used in carbines, are also featured in this rifle data section.

Cartridges in the handgun data section range from the 5.7x28mm FN to the .500 S&W Magnum, and in the T/C section from the .22 Hornet to the

.500 Smith & Wesson, including the .460 Smith & Wesson. Loads for those cartridges generally considered rifle calibers should be observed carefully when loaded for use in handguns. Information in the reference section consists of abbreviations, formulas, an extensive listing of shellholders for the four major firms and a table of power burning rates.

New products from Lyman include a Master Reloading Kit in T-Mag and Crusher press versions. Everything necessary to start reloading is included, including a 49th edition *Handbook*, except components and the reloading dies for a specific cartridge. (The Ideal 310 Tool introduced more than century ago is still available, but only for three handgun and four rifle cartridges, although the .44/40 Winchester could be a crossover, as could all the 310 rifle calibers, if used in the T/C Encore pistols.

Another new Lyman tool is the Deluxe Carbide Expander/Decap Die Rod. Available in six calibers from 22 to 30, the carbide button floats free on the rod and helps reduce case neck stretching. The rod will fit all Lyman sizing dies.

More emphasis is being placed on case preparation and Lyman has a new Case Prep Xpress tool and a Turbo Sonic Cleaner. The Xpress, available for 115 or

The RCBS Accessory Handle-2, Powder Trickler-2 and the ChargeMaster Combo at rear center.

Looking for loaded cartridges from which you can reload later? These five cartridges, by DoubleTap Ammunition are, left to right: .45 Auto Rim, .44 Special, .50 BMG, 6.8mm SPC, and the 9x25mm Dillon.

230 volt operation, features inside and outside deburring tool, larger and small primer pocket reamers and cleaners, neck brushes in four calibers, Mica case neck lube, and more. The Turbo Sonic Cleaner can be used to process up to 900 9mm cases or a smaller number of larger cases. Solutions are available for cleaning brass cases and for cleaning steel and stainless steel small parts: loading dies, revolver cylinders, shellholders, etc.

For handloaders having less need to process large number of cases, Lyman has a new two-piece Case Prep Multi-Tool, the handle of which unscrews in the middle to store the parts. Both ends of the handle are threaded to accept the individual tools, one on each end. Each tool comes with inside and outside deburring tools, small and large primer pocket reamers, and small and large primer pocket cleaners. The same six tools, each with separate handles, plus two rifle primer pocket uniformers can be purchased in an Universal Case Prep Accessory Kit.

Lyman Products has one of the largest selections of rifle and handgun bullet casting molds, plus molds for shotgun slugs. New is the 4th edition of their

Cast Bullet Handbook. This 320-page softbound volume, edited Thomas J. Griffin, contains 18 informative chapters, 15 of which were written by Mike Venturino on such subjects as Why Cast Bullets, Casting Trouble Shooting, Gas Checks, and Sizing and Shooting. The 18th chapter, The Metallurgy of Cast Bullets, features six different topics, and was written by Robert J. Block, Ph.D. Among the topics covered are The Mechanical & Thermal Properties of Metals, and The Microstructure of Bullet Alloys.

The remaining two-thirds of this volume is devoted to rifle and handgun loading data for use with cast lead bullets. Each cartridge for which data is presented features a dimensioned drawing, an informative paragraph or two, test components, and specifications, and suggested loading data. A photograph of each type cast bullet, along with the mould number (Lyman, Saeco (Redding), Lee, and RCBS. (There is even some data for a few of the swaged Hornady lead bullets.) Rifle cartridges for which loading data, starting and maximum, is provided range from the .22 Hornet to the .50-70 Government, and included are some of the newer calibers, such as the .300 and .338 RCM and the .375 and .416 Ruger, in addition to some of the older ones as the .40-65 Winchester, .40-70 Sharps Straight, and .45-120 Sharps.

The same method of presentation is used for the handgun cartridge reloading data. The cartridges covered range from the .30 Luger to the .500 Smith & Wesson, and include such cartridges as the .44 Russian, .45 Auto Rim, .460 Smith & Wesson Magnum, and .50 Action Express

The final section is the Reference section, which contain five appendices, among which is a listing of all Lyman bullet molds, including those for black powder guns and shotguns, plus a listing of shellholders, top punches, and a six-page reloaders log. It's a very thorough volume on the subject, and worthy of shelf space for any shooter who casts bullets or is even considering doing so.

Another useful item for handloaders is the **Hodgdon Annual Reloading Manual** containing data for reloading handgun and rifle cartridges using Hodgdon, IMR, and Winchester powders. The latest magazine-style manual contains 170 pages, and contains eight handloading related articles prior to the loading data sections. The articles are illustrated and range from "The Accuracy Fair" by Jim Carmichael, to "Slow Burners for the Big Boys" by Layne Simpson.

The 9th edition of the *VihtaVuori Reloading Guide for Centerfire Cartridges* contains data for reloading with VihtaVuori powders, and includes some cartridges not found in other handbook or manuals.

In the loading data section starting and maximum loads are provided for more than 125 different rifle cartridges from the .17 Ackley Bee to the .50 BMG. Both new cartridges, such as the .30 AR Remington, .300 RCM, and .338 Marlin Express are featured, along with some of the older calibers, such as the .30-40 Krag, .40-65 Winchester, .45-120 Sharps, .470 Nitro Express, and .50-140 Sharps. No dimensioned cartridge drawings appear in this reloading manual, but the case brand used, trim length, primer type and brand, barrel length, and rate of rifling twist are listed For each bullet, the weight, type, diameter, and brand are listed along with a variety of loads with different powders for each bullet, and the overall loaded cartridge length.

The introduction to the Reloading Data section features useful material in the form of a Powder Usage chart, a table of Relative Burn Rates for 144 powders from fastest to slowest: NORMA R1 to VihtaVuori 20N29. There's also a paragraph description for each of the Hodgdon, IMR, and Winchester, a listing of abbreviations relating to handloading, such as LFN=Lead Flat Nose, ST= Silver Tip, and TMJ=Total Metal Jacket. A shaded sidebar of warnings is provided just prior to the actual data section.

The Chamberlain Cartridge Comparison Guide is not a reloading manual, but it does contain a tremendous amount of information useful to handloaders. Spiral bound, the pages lie flat.

Starting and maximum loads are listed for over 70 handgun cartridges, from the .22 Remington Jet to the 500 S&W Magnum. Data presentation is the same as for the loading data in the rifle cartridge section. Some of the cartridges, such as the Jet, the 6.5mm JDJ, .30 Herrett, .357 Herrett, .375 JDJ, .45 S&W Schofield, and .50 Action Express, covered in this handgun section are not listed in every handloading manual, so the data becomes even more useful.

If a handloader were to purchase a single reloading manual each year, without making a large investment, this Hodgdon Annual Manual would be good place to start. If dimensioned case drawings are needed, than a larger manual would be a wise investment.

It's not a reloading manual, but the **Chamberlain Development Cartridge Comparison Guide** is loaded with useful tables and charts. This 226-page softside, spiral-bound volume features four chapters with all four devoted to use of the manual, extensive rifle cartridge and handgun cartridge data tables, and a "baker's dozen" appendices. The chapters have a few illustrations, but the introduction contains a fold-out page spread which amounts to five regular pages of full-color, near full-size photographs of 150 cartridges from the .17 Mach 2 to the 50 .BMG. Among the cartridges are such calibers as the

.224 Weatherby, .338-06 A-Square, .358 Norma Magnum, .404 Jeffery, .450 Bushmaster, .470 Nitro Express, .50 Beowolf, .505 Gibbs, and .577 Nitro Express.

Featured in the Rifle Data Tables are such topics as Base-Total Cartridge Information, Bullet Weight Sorted by Muzzle Velocity, Recoil (Sorted by Bullet Weight) and Recoil (Calculated for 5.5, 8, 11 & 14-lb rifles). The tables are arranged according to caliber from .172 through .585, and include data relative to cartridge, bullet brand, type, weight, and sectional density, muzzle velocity, efficiency, momentum, and recoil energy when fired in a specific weight rifles. (Similar information is provided for handgun cartridges, from .172 to .500. The recoil is grouped by bullet energy from low to high, and there is a table for the recoil generated for handgun weights of 1.5, 2.5 and 5 pounds.)

The 13 appendices are devoted to specific topics, including Identifying Game Animal's Physical Structures, Cartridge Selection for Game Animals, Bullet Expansion, Purpose Built Bullets, Felt Recoil, What a Cartridge Name Tells You, and Terminal Ballistics. (There are some black-n-white photo illustrations in the appendices, but none in the tables preceding them.) Checking the appendices prior to loading a particular cartridge for hunting use, might alter the thinking on a specific load. The final appendix is divided into five parts, from Equations, Terms, and Source Information to Ballistic Comparison Graphs. Most of these graphs are double-page fold-outs, and the last page in the book is a double-page fold-out of Barnes bullets in full-color.

The Cartridge Comparison Guide is not a "reloading manual." It does contain a great amount of information useful to handloaders. You can find this great reference book at www.gundigeststore.com.

Helvetica Trading USA (www.SmartReloader-USA.com) is a new kid on the block in the field of reloading equipment. Italian designed and Swiss engineered, according to their advertisements) the **SmartReloader** line almost everything needed to hacndloader rifle and handgun cartridges but reloading (sizing and seating) dies and the components. The loading presces include the originally introduced SBP (Smallest Biggest Press), a C-frame single stage tool, the Omega 800 and the Mark XVI, both O-frame tools. (The Mark XVI is massive and will accept 1-1/4 x 12 thread dies (.50 BMG), and with an adapter regular 7/8x14 thread dies for most cartridges.

There are two SmartReloader Powder Measures, the SR400 and the more expensive SR800. The SR400 is constructed of anti-static plastic and aluminum, while the SR800 features a machined cast iron frame, steel stand, and a micrometer metering chamber. Both measures have anti-static powder hoppers.

There are six SR powder scales, all digital. These include the iScale Digital Touch Screen Powder Scale, which operates on four AAA batteries, and the iSO Reloading Powder Scale Dispenser, which operates on 110 or 220-volts. The iSO has a 50 memory storage capacity and a scale capacity of 1,500 grains with +/- .1 grain accuracy. The iScale has a 1,000 grain capacity with +/- .1 grain accuracy, and both come with calibration weights. (The iScale has no button, but functions by screen touch only.) The SR750 model scale operates on two AA batteries, has a weighing capacity of 750 grains, an accuracy of +/- .01 grain at 50 grains and comes with a 50-grain calibration weight and two powder measures. (The SR750 is also available as an Extreme Powder Package, which includes the SR750 scale package, a powder funnel, a Baby Powder Trickler, and a 10-grain testing weight along with the 50-grain calibration weight.) The SR1000 Bench Rest Grade Digital Scale operates on three 1.5-volt LR44 lithium batteries, or the included AC adapter, has a capacity of 1,000 grains. It will weigh in grains, grams, ounces or pennyweights, and comes with powder pan and calibration weight. (All the SR scales include a powder pan.) The largest of the SR powder scales is the SR2500, which operates on six AAA batteries or with a provided 100-240VAC adapter. It features four adjustable feet for leveling, a built-in bubble level, and weighs in grains, grams, pounds, ounces, and Troy ounces.

The SR777 Bench Rest Case Trimmer is a lathe-type trimmer which comes with a dozen pilots, two primer pocket cleaners (small and large) and two case neck brushes. (Spare cutter heads are available, if needed.) A powered Extreme Case Preparation Kit features a complete set of tools—three neck brushes, two primer pocket reamers, two primer pocket uniformers, a deburring tool for inside and outside deburring of case mouth, a case cutter (trimmer), and two Lock Studs, one for the various tools, and the second for use with Lee Precision case length gages. (The various tools can also be obtained separately with a handle — one handle with three brushes, one handle with two primer pocket uniformers, etc. — or as a Complete Case Care Kit with handle — all the tools with one handle — for manual operation. (SmartReloader has available an Electronic Digital Caliper accurate to the .001" to insure those trimmed cases are correct.)

Other items in the SmartReloader line include a plastic SRSS Universal Powder Funnel, a steel MPT (Monster Powder Trickler) which weighs over two pound and features the largest powder capacity reservoir in the industry, a Universal Reloading Tray capable of holding rifle cartridges from the .17 Remington through the .458 Winchester Magnum, including most WSM, WSSM, and RUM cases, and handgun cartridges up through the .500 S&W Magnum. The tray has a combination of 50 large holes and 36 small holes.

Good handloads require clean cases and SR has a number of case thumblers, plus two Ultrasonic Cleaners, the SR4235 and the SR4270. The SR4235 has a capacity of 1.5 quarts and will hold approximately 100 5.56x51mm (.308) or 200 5.56x45mm (.223) cases, or a number of small parts. The SR4270 has a capacity of 2.6 quarts and can hold about 360 5.56mm cases or half that number of .308 cases. (The SR4270 is large enough to hold some handgun frames for cleaning, if so needed.)

The SR Tumbler line includes the SR787 Dream, which has a capacity of 3.7 quarts capable of holding about 600 9mm Luger cases or a smaller number of rifle cases. (Spare bowls are available to house different media if desired, and this tumbler is included as a part of the Omega 800 Pro Kit for handloaders.) This Pro Kit is the ideal way for beginners to get started handloading. It has about everything, except components and loading dies, including the Omega 800 press, SR750 scale, powder funnel, Baby Powder Trickler, etc.) The big boy is the SR747 Jumbo, which has a capacity of 14.3 quarts, providing room to hold up to 2,000 9mm cases. There is also the SR737 Nano with a capacity about half that of the SR787 at a bit more than half the price. (This Nano tumbler is included as part of the SBP Reloading Kit, which features a SR750 scale and a SBP reloading press.)

For separating the cases from the polishing media in the tumblers, there's the SR405 Media Separator, which will hold nearly 200 medium caliber rifle

The massive TX-40 arbor press by Ten-X Tactical is used to reload non-lethal 40mm training rounds, thereby reducing the cost per round from about $25 to $1 apiece. An expanding die can be used to reform the mouth of dented aluminum 40mm cases.

cases, or double that number of handgun cartridge cases, depending on the caliber. Just dump the Tumbler contents into the basket, close the SR405 lid and crank the handle a few times. The media drops into the bucket portion of the Separator, leaving clean cases in the basket.

Other reloading items in the SR line include the SR1750 Bullet Puller, the SR916 Hand Priming Tool for those handloaders with a preference for feeling the primer set, a SR104 Case Lube Pad – a necessity to insure proper case sizing, unless carbide sizing dies are being use, and even then the lube helps – and the SR plastic cartridge boxes. The cartridge boxes come in two types, hinged lid and slip lid, and 16 sizes, and will hold from 10 to 100 cartridges, depending on the model; box #7 will hold 50 cartridges having a .223 or 5.56x45mm head size.

Considering bullet swaging? **Corbin** (www.Corbins.com) has two H-frame presses for manual bullet swaging and the Hydro-Press to take the effort out of the process. The S-Press uses S-type 5/8x24 tpi dies to swage bullets from .10" to .458" size, and with and adapter bushing it can be used to load cartridges using regular 7/8x14 tpi reloading dies. The CSP-2 press uses H-type dies, and can swage bullets from .17 to 25mm sizes, or with

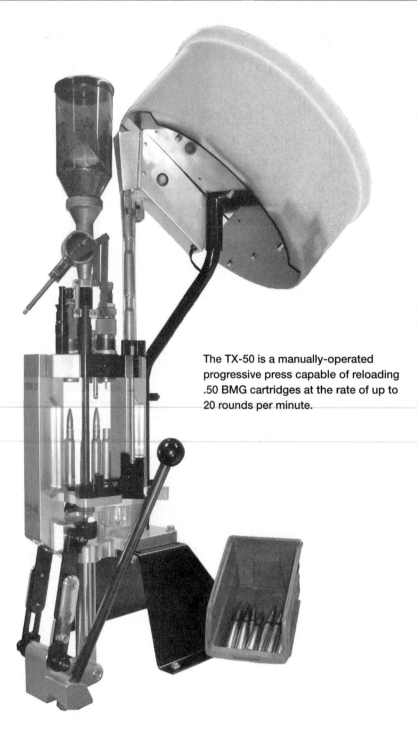

The TX-50 is a manually-operated progressive press capable of reloading .50 BMG cartridges at the rate of up to 20 rounds per minute.

Nitro Express, and sizing and seating dies for loading 25mm cartridges are availabcle. However, **Ten-X Tactical** (www.TenXAmmo.com) has a massive arbor-type C-frame press, the TX-40, for reloading 40mm training rounds. With commercial 40mm ammunition costing up to $25.00 per round, the training of law enforcement, etc., is often limited due to budget priorities. Using the TX-40, and a TX-40 Expander Die to reform dented aluminum case mouths, less-lethal 40mm rounds can be reloaded for approximately $1.00 per shot. The TX-40 press is capable of loading most 40mm brands – CTS, ALS, Defense Tech, etc. – and has a lifetime warranty.

Ten-X Tactical has a TX-50 reloading press designed to load up to twenty .50 BMG shells per minute, or an equal number of small cartridges, such as the .510 DTC, .460 Steyr or 416 Barrett. There's a LRP (Large Rifle Primer) system conversion available to load such cartridges as the .338 Lapua Magnum. The TX-50 accepts up to 1-1/2" loading dies, and the case-activated powder measure is capable of dropping up to 250 grain powder charges. (Reducer bushings for dies measuring less than 1-1/2" are not available from Ten-X, but are normally available from firms such as RCBS.

Readers may recall the **Woodleigh** homogenous copper alloy Hydrostatically Stabilised Bullets introduced a couple of years back. These bullets, which feature full bore diameter bodies with shallow driving bands and a depressed nose to produce deep penetration with a large wound channel, are now available in 15 calibers from .308" to .585" allowing use in most .30 caliber cartridges up to those in the .577 Nitro Express class. (Weights of these HS bullets range from 180 grains to 750 grains, and in length from 1.250" to 1.424".) Woodleigh currently has five VLD solid brass bullets from .338" to .564" for use in loading the tactical cartridges as the 338 Lapua to the 55 Boys. These bullets range in weight from 250 grains to 700 grains, with the 700 bullet for the 50 BMG cartridge measuring 2.475" in length.) Regular copper jacketed Woodleigh bullets are available in more than forty calibers from 6.5mm (.264") to 700 Nitro Express (.700").

Redding Reloading Equipment has new Instant Indicator Headspace and Bullet Comparators for the .204 Ruger and .338 Lapua Magnum cartridges, D Series loading die sets for the .260 Remington Improved, 6.5mm Creedmoor, .370 SAKO Magnum, and .458 SOCOM

adapters can be used to handload regular cartridges or .50 BMG cartridges.

Bullet types which can be swaged are almost unlimited in design. Wadcutter, solids, hollow points, boattails, ULD, truncated, rebated heel, cup heel, and more are possible, including a wide variety of shotgun slugs up to at least 12 gauge. Using scrap lead, or more expensive lead wire and fired .22 Long Rifle or WRM cases, new .224 bullets can easily be produced, as can .243 caliber, using Corbin's 7/8x14 swaging dies. If a can-

nelure is needed on the bullets, there's a PCM-2 Cannelure Machine which can do up to 50 bullets per minutes, or a more economical HCT hand tool in three versions for manual operation at a more leisurely pace. (Bullets from .22 to .72 can be given a cannelure.) Corbin also has swaging supplies, and books on swaging available.

Many reloaders may be under the impression that handloading the .50 BMG is the top of the hill, but the .577 Nitro Express is larger, as is the .700

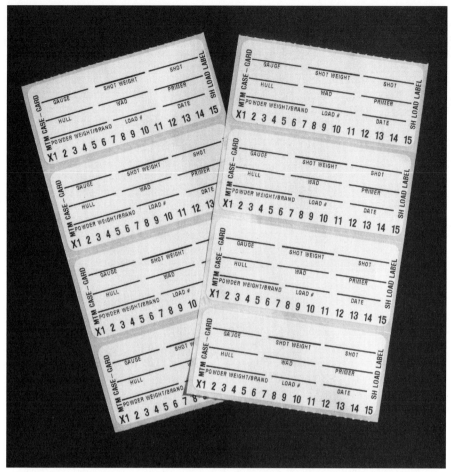

MTM shotshell reloading data labels provide all the information needed on a box of reloaded shotshells: gauge, shot weight and size, brand of hull, wad column, primer, powder charge and brand, date loaded, etc. At the bottom, the label provides a space to circle the number of times the hulls have been reloaded.

cartridges. There's a new National Match Die Set for military match shooters. These die sets feature a full-length sizing die, a Competition Bullet Seating Die, and a Taper Crimp Die and are available for the .223 Remington, .308 Winchester, and .30-06 Springfield cartridges.

Other new products from Redding include Bullet Seating Micrometers to accommodate standard (STD) and the new VLD bullet shapes. They will fit all seating die bodies having internal 1/2x20 threads. The micrometer heads replace the original seating plugs and can be changed from one seating die to another.

Handloaders reloading large quantities of popular straight wall handgun cases (e.g., .357 Magnum, .40 S&W, .44 Magnum, .45 ACP and .45 Colt) might consider the new Redding Dual Ring Carbide Sizing Dies. Incorporating two carbide within one die body, sizing the case body and the case mouth separately without overworking the brass. The process is

said to increase the case life and also give the case a better appearance.

Long range shooters, such as those shooting at 1,000 yards using such cartridges as the .338 Lapua, .416 Barrett, and .50 BMG should appreciate the new Redding Competition LR-1000 Long Range Powder Measure. This new measure has all the features of the Match-Grade and Competition powder measures, including the hemispherical metering chamber of the BR-30, but with the cavity enlarged to drop charges of up to 140 grains.

Comp reloading manuals from the powder companies provide reloading data of the most up-to-date variety and sometimes on cartridges not found in regular loading manuals. The 70-page *Reloading Guide for Centerfire Cartridges,* Edition 9, from **VihtaVuori** (www.lapua.com) provides loading data for more than 55 cartridges from the .204 Ruger to the .50 BMG, and more than two dozen

handgun cartridges from the 7mm TCU to the .500 S&W Magnum, using Vihta-Vuori powders and a wide range of bullet types. Starting loads and maximum loads are listed, along with the test barrel length, muzzle velocity, trimmed case length and brand, and primer. (Loading data is also given for five popular Cowboy Action handgun cartridges.) Among the rifle cartridges for which data is provided are the 6mm PPC-USA and 6mm BR Norma, 6.5mm Grendel, 6.5-284 Norma, .300 and .338 Lapua Magnums, 9.3x66mm SAKO, and .416 Rigby. Among the handgun cartridges are the 7mm TCU, 7mm GJW, 9x23mm Winchester, .357 Remington Maximum, .38 Super Lapua, and .50 AE. (This manual features an excellent Burning Rate Chart for eleven different brands of powders used for handloading, from VihtaVuori to Ramshot. Descriptions of the various VihtaVuori powders is provided, along with storage suggestions, reloading safety, and other useful information.)

RCBS, one of the leaders in handloading equipment for several decades, has many new items, starting with their AR Series of loading die sets. These dies, designed for use AR-type semi-automatic rifles, feature a Small Base sizing die and a Taper Crimp seating die to insure the reloaded round will chamber, plus the Taper Crimp allows a bit more tolerance in the case neck lengths if different brand cases are used. Currently, the new AR dies are available for 13 cartridges, from the .204 Ruger to the .338 Federal, including the 264 LBC-AR, 6.5 Creedmoor, 6.8mm SPC, and .30 Remington AR.

For handgun cartridge handloaders there is a new Pistol Bullet Feed Die for progressive loader and new Pro 2000 Pistol Powder Expanders. Use of the Feed die shorten reloading time by using another Feed die in place of changing die plates, adjusting bullet fingers and guides. This new Die comes with a Feed Die body, a set of Bullet Fingers, and a retaining clip. The Pistol Powder Expanders are currently available for eight popular calibers from .38 to .500, and is used on the progressive loading presses and is used in connection with the Case Activated Uniflow Powder Measure.

With a trend from the balance-type powder scale to a digital model, powder tricklers are sometime not able to reach the scale pan. The new RCBS Powder Trickler-2 features a non-skid, height adjustable base and a powder tube extension. There's also a Trickler-2 Upgrade Kit which can be used convert your existing 09094 Powder Trickler to equal the new Trickler-2 design.

Handloaders using non-conditioned surplus military 5.56mm and 7.62mm cases will find the new RCBS TM Military Crimp Removers handy. Available for small and large sizes, and designed to speed up case processing, the TM also reduces the amount of primer pocket being removed. There's also a new Primer Pocket Swager Tool-2, redesigned to fit a larger group of cases, and with swaging rod made from stronger high tensile strength steel.

RCBS has one of the largest inventories of loading die sets of any firm – approximately 650 special order die sets, 1,000 plus other calibers and 350 case forming die sets – other than Huntington Die Specialities, and has added two more – the 6mmx45-AR, and the .264 LBC-AR – to their D Series die sets. (RCBS no longer will produce custom, one-of-a-kind die sets or bullet molds.) The 1-1/2x12 tpi dies are now available for the .416 Barrett and .40 Steyr, in addition to the .50 BMG, while the Safari Dies are available for seven big bore cartridges from the .404 Jeffery to the .505 Gibbs. (The .505 and the .500 Jeffery are made on 1" die bodies and require a special press adapter bushing.)

Other new RCBS products for reloaders include a .50R Pilot/50-caliber Cutter for rotary or Trim Pro case trimmer, for trimming .50-90 Government, .500 Smith & Wesson, or similar cases, a larger, ergonomical handle for use with RCBS accessories, and new Carbide deburring, chamfering and cutter heads for the Case Trimmer.

For shooters reloading the .50 BMG cartridge, RCBS has a AmmoMaster .50 BMG Pack which includes everything necessary to start reloading the "Big Fifty" except the components. Available extras include a high capacity Case Trimmer Kit, a 1-1/2-12 Bullet Puller to salvage components, if necessary, a Carbide Primer Pocket Uniformer to square the bottom of the primer pocket, Military Crimp Remover to permit easier primer seating, and a Priming System with tube to hold twenty .50 BMG primers.

Hornady Mfg. Company continues to expand their line of reloading products, along with components and loaded ammunition. The 8th edition of the *Hornady Handbook of Cartridge Reloading* is now available. Hardbound and containing over 1,000 pages, the new Handbook provides reloading data for the new Hornady bullets – FTX, GMX,

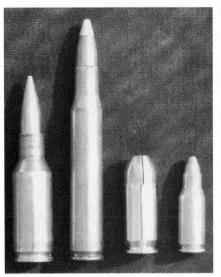

A couple of new cartridges for which loading dies should be available by the time you read this: the .300 Olympian, left, with a .30-06 cartridge for comparison; and a .22 CTM on the right, shown with a .45 ACP to its left. The Olympian is for use on an AR-style rifle and the CTM with a 1911 pistol from Rock Island Armory.

DGS, DGX – along with the SST, V-MAX, XTP, and other favorites, the new Superformance and LEVERevolution powders, as well as other Hodgdon powders. Data for the newer cartridges is extensive, and new additions include the 6.5mm Creedmoor, 6.5mm Grendel, .300 and .338 RCM, .30 TC, .308 and .338 Marlin Express, .375 and .416 Ruger, .450, .470, and .500 Nitro Express cartridges and more. It's a great reference volume for handloaders. It's the most comprehensive handbook the Hornady has ever published. (Another handy item for the bench is the new non-skid bullet mat featuring the entire line of Hornady bullets listing caliber, diameter, weight, ballistic coefficient, sectional density and item number.)

The Hornady Lock-n-Load Power Case Prep Center introduced a couple of years back represents the ultimate in cartridge case preparation – trimming, reaming, chamfering, deburring, primer pocket reaming and uniforming, etc. Reloaders using lathe-type case trimmer, but wanting to speed up deburring, chamfering, and related steps, will find the new Hornady Lock-n-Load Case Prep Assistant useful. Powered by 110/220 volts, the Assistant any 8-32 tpi tools, buts comes with deburring and chamfer tools.

Fired cartridge cases have been cleaned and polished in tumblers in the past, and many handloaders still use such accessories. However, sonic case cleaning is becoming more popular, and the new Hornady Lock-n-Load Magnum Sonic Cleaner with a 3.2 quart capacity, more than twice that of the original Lock-n-Load Sonic Cleaner previously available, can be used not only to clean cartridge cases, but small gun parts as well. Constructed of stainless steel with a tight wire mesh basket, the Cleaner is available in two models, 110VAC or 220VAC, depending on the power source available. Featuring two transducers and an adjustable heating element, the new Magnum may be the "Big It" of sonic cartridge case cleaners.

With a weighing capacity of 1,500 grains, accurate to +/- 0.1 grain, Hornady's new Lock-n-Load digital Bench Scale comes with regular 110/220 VAC power adapters, two calibration weights, and a metal powder pan. The large LCD display is easy to read, especially useful for older eyes, making it ideal for checking the accuracy of powder measure charges. (Hornady has three Lock-n-Load powder measures, including a Bench Rest model, and a Blackpowder model which features a non-static aluminum hopper tube and cap, and a brass metering unit.)

Handloaders using a Hornady Lock-n-Load AP press may want to check out the new Lock-n-Load Bullet Feeder for handgun cartridges. The hopper holds up to 200 handgun caliber bullets and features an adjustable centr plate and bullet feed wiper to ensure smooth feeding. (Bullet Feeder Dies in five calibers from .380/9mm to .451/.452, are sold separately.) The Bullet Feeder was designed for the AP press, but can be used with any press having regular 7/8-14 threads.

Hornady has introduced four new Series II three-die Cowboy Action sets, plus three (9mm, 10mm and 45 ACP) Series II Custom Grade Taper Crimp die sets into their line. They are available as sets, or as individual dies (sizer, seater, and expander). Not new, but Hornady has Series IV Speciality Die Sets for the .404 Jeffery, plus the .450, .470, and .500 Nitro Express cartridges.

There are no doubt other new products for handloaders available today, but those I've mentioned here will keep you busy. Others will no doubt make an appearance by the time you read this, and that's good. Handloading is alive and well!

REPORT FROM THE FIELD:
NEW OPTICS

BY **WAYNE VAN ZWOLL**

Rifle-scopes, spotting scopes and binoculars not only magnify. They help you find and assess targets, determine range, dope wind. And aim. They even add shooting light. Here's the best of the new.

The first Shooting, Hunting and Outdoor Trade Show happened 32 years ago in St. Louis. Credit the National Shooting Sports Foundation for organizing the event and for conducting every SHOT Show since. Ted Rowe, president of Harrington & Richardson in the late 1970s, came up with the acronym. The 290 exhibitors in that first SHOT Show occupied 52,153 square feet of the convention center. SHOT has grown considerably since. In 2010 it was the 11th-largest trade show in the country. Though it is not open to the public, 58,400 people attended in 2010. I expect the 2011 event, also held in Las Vegas, drew as many. The crowds represent manufacturers and sales agents, distributors and retailers and scribes such as I who report on new merchandise. SHOT has become so big that just eight cities have hosted it. Few now offer the necessary exhibit space and hotel accommodations.

A week long if you include Media Day at the Range – when the press gets brief trigger time with new hardware – SHOT comes early. The mid-January slot this year made it the ideal venue for official unveilings. Consumers have come to depend on SHOT for first peeks of products. Subsequent magazine coverage, though, may reflect less the merits of

A high-quality binocular shows you details that become animals. Buy the best you can't afford!

items than the ad budgets of manufacturers. Advertising revenues fuel magazines; free-spending advertisers expect editorial support. Gear from smaller firms can thus get short-changed.

In *Gun Digest,* there's no such pressure on journalists, so a synopsis of new offerings can give worthy products their due. While we try to divide column inches equitably among manufacturers, there's room to praise innovation and dote on favorites. Ideally readers get distilled reports, with enough detail to inspire trips to websites. Still, after 30 years of reporting on SHOT introductions, I've learned that quality and value don't necessarily drive sales. Political events can influence buying, as happened after the 2008 presidential election, when pistols and AR-15 rifles set sales records. And recession can pull in the reins.

Market trends affect R&D, especially when companies feel their budgets squeezed. The current interest in long-range shooting, and in so-called tactical firearms, has hiked the number of new products in these categories. Ditto demand for electronic and laser-assisted instruments. As iron sights gave way to scopes in my youth, so traditional optics are yielding to those that with illumination, laser-ranging options and bullet-drop-compensating capability. Better stuff? That depends on your point of view. Here, without further analysis, are the optics that got my attention at SHOT 2011.

NightForce high-power scopes are a top pick of marksmen firing super-accurate long-range rifles.

Aimpoint

With Gunnar Sandberg's first "single-point sight" you looked into the tube with one eye while your other saw a dot on the target. That was in 1974. Sandberg refined the device and founded Aimpoint to produce it. The brand is still considered the leader in red dot sights. Front lenses of current Aimpoints are achromats (doublets) that correct for parallax – unlike most such sights, whose reflective paths move with eye position. The Aimpoint's dot comes to your eye in a line parallel with the sight's optical axis, so you hit where you see the dot, even if your eye is off-axis. A 1x Aimpoint gives you unlimited eye relief. Aimpoint's 9000 series sights weigh as little as 6.5 ounces. W/E adjustments move point of impact 13mm at 100 meters. The four 1x Hunter models, with long and short tubes, 34mm and 30mm in diameter, have 2-minute dots. A 12-position dial lets you tune dot intensity: low for dim light, high in sunlight. One CR-2032 battery lasts 50,000 hours with a mid-level setting. Aimpoints have been adopted by armed forces and by sportsmen in 40 countries. I've killed moose with these sights in timber – and printed plum-size groups on paper at 100 yards. They're perfect for shotguns and handguns in deer cover. Aimpoint.com

Alpen

The highly rated optics from this importer include two new rifle-scope series. Apex XPs feature 1-inch tubes, fast-focus eyepieces, turret-mounted parallax dials. I favor the 3-9x40 for hunting, but you can also get a 1.5-6x42,

Trijicon earned its stellar reputation with the illuminated ACOG sight, here on an AR rifle.

You don't need high magnification for hunting, even on the plains. This buck dropped at 40 steps.

a 2-10x44, a 4-16x44 and a 6-24x50. The IR line boasts 30mm tubes and illuminated reticles. Choose a 1.5-6x42, 2.5-10x50 or 4-16x56. If you haven't peered through a Wings ED binocular, introduced last year, you should! At just 21 ounces, the 8x42 and 10x42 are lighter than standard Wings. Expect sharper images too. Consider Alpen's Apex 12x50 binocular a double-barrel spotting scope. Using both eyes, you'll look longer and more comfortably than if you were squinting

through a spotting scope. The more time you spend looking, the more you see, whether you're looking for elk on the hill or reading mirage at the range. Alpen has won many awards for its optics, delivering exceptional value in mid-priced products. Alpenoptics.com

Brunton

Once noted mostly for compasses, Brunton has expanded its market base

to include high-quality camping gear and binoculars. Brunton now catalogs dozens of binoculars in four main lines. The $2,600 Epoch tops that chart. The Eterna offers more selection at more modest prices. My time afield with Eterna glasses confirms what local birders tell me: these binoculars are good buys! The Echo fills a lower price niche in Brunton's stable. The Lite-Tech includes compact and Porro prism models that list for as little as $40. Oddly enough, there's scant news in Brunton optics for 2011. Changes at the company's helm may have something to do with that. I expect a raft of new products next year. Brunton.com

Burris

The 4-12x42 Eliminator is a programmable rifle-scope with laser-ranging capability. It not only tells you the distance to your target; it provides a lighted aiming point for a dead-on hold. Of course, you must first feed it trajectory data for your load (bullet drop at 500 yards). After that, forget about holdover. The bottom segment of the plex reticle contains a tightly packed column of dots. Ranging the target, you activate the Eliminator's memory. The dot that lights up is the one to place in the middle of your target; drop is already figured in. Not long ago I used an Eliminator to print a 3-inch group at 400 yards, aiming dead-on! At 26 ounces, and with a bit more bulk than most scopes, this new Burris

Wayne used a Leupold VX-3 on a Ruger No. 1 in 7mm WSM to take this fine Idaho elk.

Zeiss lists some of its superb rifle-scopes with rail mounts, as on this lovely Mauser rifle, a .404.

is ill suited to petite rifles. But it's selling well to shooters wanting to hit far away. For hunters of traditional bent, there's a new Fullfield E series. These scopes (2-7x35, 3-9x40, 3-9x50 or 4.5-14x42) feature the original Fullfield 1-inch tube with upgraded W/E adjustments. They're sleeker in profile, with one-piece power ring and eyepiece. The etched Ballistic Plex E reticle helps you compensate for bullet drop and drift. Fullfield's TAC30 line includes a new 1-4x24 with Ballistic CQ 5.56 reticle. Ideal for tactical carbines. The Burris catalog has 55 pages of rifle-scopes (and mounts), binoculars and spotting scopes. Burrisoptics.com

Bushnell

Shooters hewing to tight budgets should appreciate the new Trophy XLT spotting scopes: a 15-45x50 and a 20-60x65. Designed for hunting, with convenient front-facing focus knob, the scopes weigh 32 and 42 ounces and wear weather-proof rubber armor.

A hunter takes aim with an AR rifle equipped with Trijicon AccuPoint. The BogPod tripod helps!

The Weaver K6 on this Ruger is lightweight, handsome, economical. And optically excellent.

Trophy XLT binoculars have a new housing this year. The 8x32 and 8x42 are most useful, but there's a 10x28 and a 12x50 too. The Elite 6500 rifle-scopes now include a 1.25-8x32, a 2.5-16x42, a 4.5-30x50. Their 30mm tubes and 6 ½ times magnification range are shared by a line of seven new tactical sights (two with 1-inch tubes). Target knobs permit quick, easy adjustments. Mil

dots are standard, illuminated mil dots available on a 3-12x44 and a 6-24x50. Six new Elite 1-inch hunting scopes, 1.25-4x24 to 8-32x40, include upgrades of mid-range variables. Bushnell's Fusion 1600 ARC (Angle Range Compensating) laser-ranging binocular gives sportsmen an affordable option to the few other instruments in this category. Pick a 10x42 or a 12x50. The new Elite 1600 ARC

laser range-finder has 7x magnification and just about every feature you could dream up for range-finders. The 4-12x42 laser-ranging rifle-scope weighs a modest 24 ounces and incorporates a mil dot reticle. Add a Bullet Drop Compensating turret programmed to your load, and you can dial up for a dead-on hold at any range. Bushnell's popular Backtrack, a handy, easy-to-use GPS device, has been improved for 2011 – but still won't intimidate you! Bushnell.com

Cabela's

Cabela's, now 50 years old, began on a kitchen table, with the packaging of fishing lures. Now this outdoors mega-store markets a huge variety of hunting and shooting items, many under its own label. I'm keen on the Alaskan Guide scopes. They're affordable ($200 to $320) but reliable. A 4x44 on a hard-kicking 9.3x62 gave me a moose and a goat in British Columbia's back country. I took another Alaskan Guide sight on a wilderness elk hunt. All models have 1-inch tubes and 3 ½ inches of eye relief, with fast-focus eyepieces. They're lightweight too. The 3-9x40 scales 13 ounces, the 4-12x40AO and 6-20x40AO a couple of ounces more. There's plenty of free tube for spacing the rings to your liking. The modest 40mm objective affords a low

Trijicon's AccuPoint, here on an AR, has dual reticle illumination, with tritium and fiber optics.

Scopes specially built (or marketed!) for AR rifles proliferate. Standard scopes work on ARs too.

Bushnell's long-eye-relief scopes serve handgunners. Here: a variable on a Smith & Wesson 460.

New at Zeiss this year: a Dialyte 18-45x65 spotting scope with fixed eyepiece. Focus is up front.

The straight, sleek profile of Zeiss's new Dialyte makes it easy to pack. Power range is practical.

fit to the rifle. Cabela's Pine Ridge Lever Action line is unique. All seven versions are 15-ounce 3-9x40s. Each has a reticle specific to a single Hornady LeverEvolution load. Reticle hash marks correspond to specific points of impact for each load. The generous 5 ½-inch eye relief enables you to mount these scopes well forward, to clear exposed hammers. Pine Ridge scopes cost less even than the Alaskan Guide series. Cabela's.com

Leica

Leica's first rifle-scopes sold under its own name appeared last year, but many shooters don't yet know about them. The 2.5-10x42 and 3.5-14x42 have 30mm tubes and rear-plane reticles, 4 inches of eye relief and quarter-minute

Weaver's SuperSlam series includes 1-inch and 30mm models, some with target-style W/E dials.

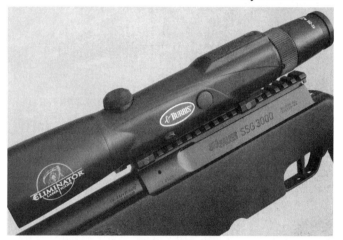
With laser-ranging and electronic drop-compensating features, the Burris Eliminator extends your reach.

Leupold resurrected the Redfield brand. Three models include this handsome, economical 3-9x.

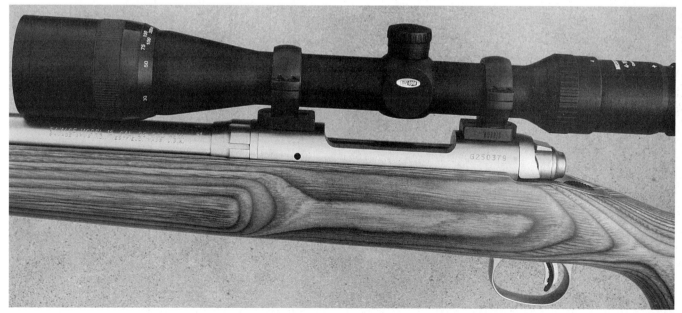
Czech-made Meopta scopes include the excellent high-power target model on Wayne's .22-250.

click W/E adjustments. They scale either side of 16 ounces. A large selection of reticles includes fast-adjust versions. These scopes are cosmetically attractive and have lots of free tube for easy mounting. AquaDura external lens coatings protect the glass and let water skitter off. There's not much new in Leica's binocular lines for 2011 – it's hard to improve on the superb! Leica Ultravid and the range-finding Geovid glasses already top the heap, in my view. There is a new CRF laser range-finder, and it costs less than its parent. Accurately ranging reflective objects to 1,000 yards, the CRF 1000 delivers a lightning-fast read. Its 7x magnification allows for precise targeting. The clean LED display adjusts for brightness. The CRF's strong, waterproof, carbon-reinforced body (with AquaDura-coated lenses) weighs just 8 ounces and fits in a shirt pocket. Leicasportsoptics.com

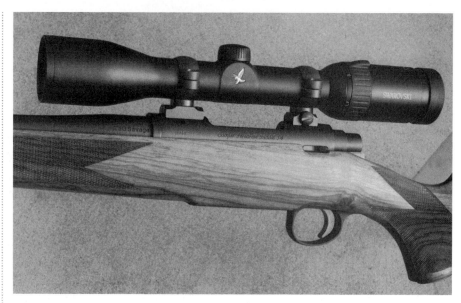

Swarovski's Z6, here a 1.7-10x42 on a Cooper 54 in .250, has 30mm tube, six-times power range.

Sightron's bright, sharp SIII 6-24x50 has lots of free tube, offers a fine dot as a reticle option.

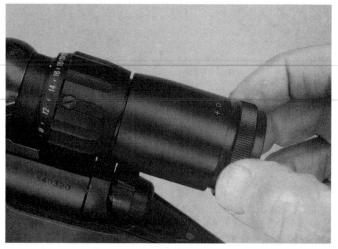

Many shooters fail to adjust the eyepiece to their vision. It focuses the reticle, not the target!

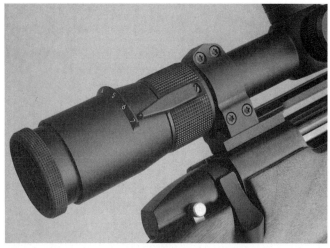

This Vortex 2-7x Viper has a distinctive eyepiece. Vortex has several new scopes and binoculars.

Schmidt & Bender's 2.5-10x40 Summit is a 1-inch scope for American hunters. A superb sight!

Leupold

In what at first glance seems a backward move, the VX-7 scope is being replaced by the VX-6. But truly, the VX-6 is state-of-the-art. It's named for its six-times power range, while the VX-7's moniker derives from its year of introduction: 2007 (also Leupold's centennial). The VX-6 debuts as a 1-6x24 and a 2-12x42. Now Leupold's top-rung big game scope, it features a 30mm tube and three reticle options, plus the best lens coatings available. The VX-3 still has the most configurations in a 30mm, three-times-magnification scope. A new VX-R, with 10 models, bridges the VX-3/VX-II gap. From 1.25-4x to 4-12x, these 30mm scopes feature illuminated FireDot reticles. Like the VX-6 and VX-3, it has DiamondCoat lens coatings to prevent scratching. There's a new Mark 8 scope this year, a 1.1-8x24 listed as a tactical sight but useful too on hunting rifles. Its 34mm tube looks obese on svelte sporters, but the eight-times magnification range gives it great versatility. An illuminated reticle is standard. Auto-locking Pinch & Turn dials make W/E adjustments easy. Also for the tactical shooter: Leupold's Mark 4 HAMR (High Accuracy Multi-Range) 4x24 red dot sight. Its etched-glass reticle is visible with or without illumination. Leupold has dropped Golden Ring binoculars but catalogs several new mid-priced models and three new spotting scopes (including a 15-45x60 that weighs just 30 ounces). In Leupold's 2011 catalog you'll find more than 100 pages of optics for shooters, including my favorite fixed-power hunting scopes and the Rifleman, a value-priced variable that performs above its pay grade. Leupold.com

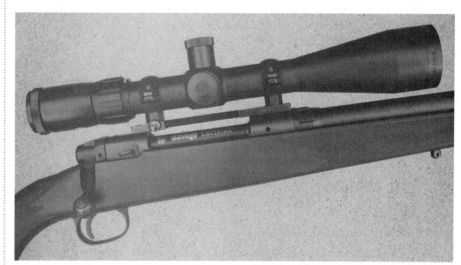

A Leupold variable with GreyBull reticle and turret help Wayne shoot with precision at distance.

This Savage wears a Sightron SIII scope, as appropriate on "tactical" bolt rifles as on varminters.

High-quality binoculars make glassing comfortable. You look longer, see better, find more game.

Meopta

This European firm has it figured out: you don't need huge objective glass to deliver bright sight pictures. Its MeoStar R1 4-12x40 sucks in more light than your eye can use at 6x, even in timber at dusk. Seldom do I shoot big game at higher magnification. When I need it, there's usually plenty of light for a bright image even at the top of the power dial. Many scopes with 12x magnification wear big objectives that put the scope high over the bore, making the rifle top-heavy and slow to aim. I prefer the R1's sleek form and tight fit to the rifle. You can also get MeoStar scopes in other sizes: 1-4x22, 3-10x50, 3-12x56, 4-14x44, even 7x56 (for

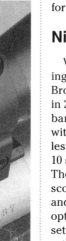

shooting the European boar raiding your melons at night). All have satin finish and etched reticles. This year a 6-18x50 joins the 3-9x42 and 4-12x50 MeoPro line. Like its stable-mates and the MeoStars, it has a quick-focus eyepiece and MeoShield exterior lens coating over MeoBrite 550 anti-refractive treatments. Meopta binoculars are equally well made. They come in four sizes, 7x to 12x; the 8x32 is my pick for hunting. Meopticsportsoptics.com

Nightforce

Want to drill a 10-shot group measuring 4.22 inches – at 1,000 yards? Kyle Brown did that with a NightForce scope in 2003. Matthew Kline broke the 3-inch barrier in the heavy-gun class last year, with a 2.815-inch group at 1,000. That's less than a third of a minute of angle for 10 shots – again, with a Nightforce scope. The firm's NXS line of high-power target scopes with clever reticles (illuminated and not) now has a Hi-Speed Adjustment option. ZeroStop lets you adjust W/E settings, then return quickly to zero settings by feel. On the 8-32x56, choose graduations of 1/4-minute, 1/8-minute or .1 mil (10 mils per revolution). ZeroStop is standard on five new F1 (first focal plane) reticles for the 3.5-15x50 sight. All 12 Nightforce scopes, 1-4x24 to 12-42x56,

The Schmidt & Bender Summit has Posicon resettable dials that show remaining adjustment.

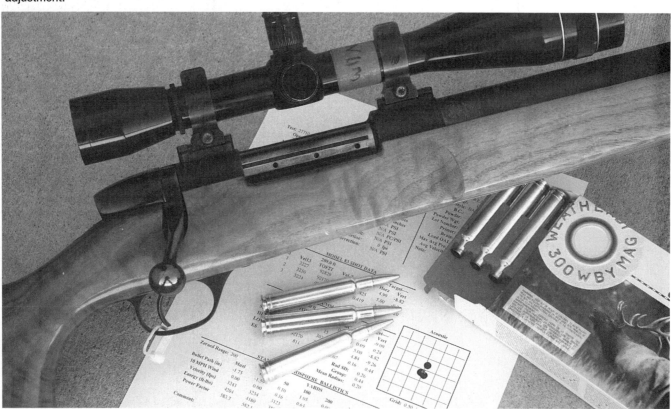

Wayne used a Leupold target scope to drill this group recently, with a 1950s-era Weatherby rifle.

Quick offhand shooting with a Bushnell Elite 6500 brought this eland to bag after much tracking.

have 30mm tubes. While most are meant for long shooting, the 1-4x and 2.5-10x32 excel on the hunt. They weigh less than 20 ounces but feature the precise adjustments and brilliant glass of NSX target scopes. NightForce scopes are built in Idaho. Nightforceoptics.com

Nikon

Hunters covet high-quality binoculars – not just for long viewing, but to catch small swatches of animal hide or the glint of an eye through small windows in cover. Most binos are 8x or 10x, but the new EDG line from Nikon includes a 7x42. The modest magnification delivers a 6mm exit pupil, for brighter images in dark places. It also has a wider field, and one with more depth, so you can distinguish detail in more than one plane. Nikon's new ProStaff rifle-scopes offer traditional form, modest prices. Optically, they're a fine value. I like the 2-7x32 on my .30 TC. You'll also find a 3-9x40, a 3-9x50 and a 4-12x40, plus a 2-7x32 Shotgun version with 75-yard parallax zero. If you're scoping a .22, try a Prostaff 4x32 or 3-9x40 with BDC 150 reticle. For AR shooters, the M-223 Laser IRT scope lets you range a target and aim without lifting your cheek from the comb. There's a 3x32 scope for crossbows too. Nikon's best 2011 product, however, may be on line. The Spot On ballistics program introduced last year is improved, with more loads and more options. Spot On can help you shoot better. Now there's also a DVD and an iPhone app. Entertainment or information? It's both! Get Spot On! NikonHunting.com

Schmidt & Bender

Known for its trend-setting tactical scopes with superb glass and innovative features, S&B has introduced a new 3-20x50 PM (Police/Marksma) II. The near-seven-times magnification range gives you nearly every power setting you could want. W/E adjustments lock in place and can be quickly returned to zero. The illuminated reticle has an 11-position rheostat and an automatic shut-off. A 34mm tube and turret-mounted parallax dial boost weight; but sophistication trumps portability when you must make a shot. Among the best hunting scopes I found at SHOT was S&B's new 1-8x24 Zenith. Its 30mm tube has no front bell – very sleek! Still, the huge magnification range affords precision for long shots. A black reticle and FlashDot illumination lie in

the second focal plane. Turn power to its bottom setting, and your sight picture is parallax-free at 75 yards. Combining the advantages of a red-dot sight and a variable scope with eight-times magnification, S&B's 1-8x24 Zenith may well be

the most versatile sight ever for hunters. It follows the company's 1-inch 2.5-10x40 Summit scope, introduced last year. The lightweight and optically brilliant Summit was designed for North American hunters. Schmidtbender.com

Swarovski makes some of the best binoculars. Many guides and hunters world-wide prefer them.

This professional hunter is using his binocular to locate game, the spotting scope to examine it.

Sightron

Minding trends in rifle-scopes, Sightron is adding long-range and tactical sights. New for 2011: SIII series (30mm) side-focus Tactical models, 3.5-10x44 to 10-50x60. Illuminated reticles are an option. ExacTrack W/E adjustments and oversize finger-friendly knobs make these scopes perfect for target and varmint shooting at distance. Choose from five range-finding reticles. A fast-focus eyepiece is standard. Sightron has also unveiled an 8-32x56 Long Range rifle-scope with dot reticle. I adore dots, especially in high-power scopes, and have used several of Sightron's dot-equipped scopes. While not new this spring, SIII fixed-magnification Tactical scopes deserve a word. In 10x, 16x and 20x with 42mm front glass, they have mil dot reticles and clean profiles, with W/E dials that make zero change easy from behind the rifle. Sightron SII and SI rifle-scopes have 1-inch tubes and come in a dizzying number of configurations. The SII Blue Sky binocular line, has doubled in size, with 8x32 and 10x32 open-hinge models to complement 8x42 and 10x42 closed-hinge versions. The 32s weigh just under 20 ounces – ideal for hunting with the binocular on a single neck strap. Sightron delivers fine value in mid-priced shooting optics. Sightron.com

Simmons

Dating to 1983, the Simmons brand wedged itself into the optics market between too cheap and too expensive. Several lines evolved; changes in ownership have consolidated the Simmons stable. The Predator Quest, 4.5-18x44

and 6-24x50, tops the current selection of Simmons rifle-scopes. Both versions have 30mm tubes, side-mounted parallax dials. Six models appear under the .44 Mag banner, though they have nothing to do with handguns or .44 Magnum cartridges. From the 3-10x to the 6-24x, all feature 1-inch tubes and 44mm objectives. Only the 3.5-10x lacks a parallax dial. As lightweight as any scopes in their class, they weigh between 11 and 13 ounces. Prohunter-series scopes are of modest magnification. It seems all eight were designed for deer hunters. I'm pleased 4x32 fixed-power models remain. ProSport scopes – 3-9x40, 3-9x50, 4-12x40 and 6-18x50 – give some relief to tight budgets. Simmons also offers red dot sights, rimfire scopes, binoculars and spotting scopes. Trail cameras too. Simmonsoptics.com

Steiner

Biggest news at Steiner is its Military Riflescope line, with five models. The 1-4x24, 3-12x50, 3-12x56, 4-16x50 and 5-25x56 all feature 34mm tubes, .1-mil W/E clicks, turret-mounted parallax dials and illuminated reticles with 11 brightness settings. For those very long shots, you get 19.5 mils of elevation gain. The dial brings you to extreme range with two revolutions. An indicator deploys with the second rotation, so you won't make a full-rotation error. Also on tap: a laser range-finding binocular, the 10x50 LRF. It ranges to 1,600 yards on reflective targets, with 1-yard accuracy to 500. This 46-ounce LRF has HD glass. Steiner's bright C5 8x56 and 10x56 Predator binoculars have been joined by a Predator Xtreme se-

Fully multi-coated optics reduce light loss in your binocular and rifle-scope, so you can see more clearly in the dim light of dawn and dusk.

ries. It includes an 8x42 and a 10x42 with polycarbonate chassis. There's a Nighthunter XP line too, 8x and 10x with both 42- and 56mm objectives. Steiner has moved its marketing headquarters Stateside to Greeley, Colorado. But Burris insists the two brands will not merge. Steiner-binoculars.com

Swarovski

Austria's premier optics firm has adopted a "Z" designation for its rifle-scopes. The attached number refers to magnification range. Z3 scopes – the

Illuminated reticles are finding their way onto more hunting scopes, like this low-power Zeiss.

The Zeiss Victory series includes the versatile 2.5-10x42, one of Wayne's favorite hunting sights.

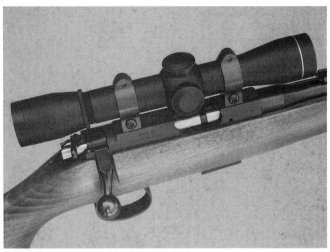

A .22 rimfire, this CZ 452 is well equipped with a Compact Leupold 4x, 75-yard parallax zero.

Cabela's sells many brands of optics but also markets its own value-priced Alaskan Guide series.

3-9x36, 3-10x42 and 4-12x50 – have three-times magnification (the top power three times the bottom). The Z5 packs greater range into 1-inch tubes. The 5-25x52 has more magnification than big game hunters need, but the 3.5-18x could serve on a long-range rifle used in summer for prairie dogs. The Swarovski flagship is the Z6. All seven models (more, if you count lighted reticles) have 30mm tubes. I've hunted with the 1.7-10x42 – a superb sight! It and the 2.5-15x44 work exceedingly well in country that can yield shots in thickets or across canyons. Now you can get, at no charge, two ballistics programs from Swarovski. Distance Reticle and Ballistic Turret software helps you get the most from your scope. Swarovski's binocular line has a new entry for 2011: a full-size version of the 32- and 42mm open-frame binoculars many hunters favor. The 10x50 and 12x50 have HD Swarovision glass. Fast-pitch focusing goes from close to far with two spins. Swarovskioptik.com

Tasco

Like Simmons, Tasco now resides in Overland Park, Kansas – home, of course, to Bushnell. The optics giant has kept the brands separate. All have earned their followings. Tasco's reputation: importer of low-priced optics. While that's true enough, I'll add that some of these are very good optics. A 6x Tasco I picked up at a gun show years ago became a go-to scope for rifle tests, because I didn't get heartburn over its accumulation of scope ring marks. To my surprise, target images were almost as bright and sharp as those from much more costly sights. It stood up just

fine under the battering of .375s. I still use it. Tasco's 2011 line features target scopes up to a power range of 10-40x. More practical is the 6-24x42. A plethora of hunting scopes, 1.5-4.5x32 to 4-16x40, includes rimfire versions. There are red dot sights, binoculars and spotting scopes in the Tasco catalog, all at low prices. Tasco.com

Trijicon

ACOG sights made Trijicon a name to remember. But the Advanced Combat Optical Gunsight was battle-rifle specific and seemed out of place on sporting rifles – if only cosmetically. Enter AccuPoint scopes. These variables feature traditional lines and power ranges but also the lighted reticles that endear ACOGs to soldiers. Tritium and a fiber-optic coil in an adjustable window provide a dual

Josh Cluff fires an H-S Precision rifle with Leupold Long Range scope. The LR series is growing.

John Burns reads the range and mirage with a Zeiss 20x60 binocular. The tripod is a huge help.

lighting source. AccuPoint's lighted delta on a post is a company favorite, but you can also pick a plex, mil dot or German #4 reticle. Trijicon glass and coatings, incidentally, are first-cabin. Last year an AccuPoint helped me take a fine whitetail. In a Colorado thicket some seasons back, I swung on an elk with a 1.25-4x24 AccuPoint on a Marlin 1895 in .45-70. The lighted reticle speeded my shot, which killed the bull. New 30mm scopes have four-times magnification (up to a 5-20x50 with turret parallax dial). There's an AccuPin bow sight now too, with a tritium-phosphor lamp plus fiber optics. The illuminated rim of this sight incorporates a level under a clear sight stem with that triangular illuminated tip. Another worthy item: Trijicon's RMR red dot sight. It's one of the lightest and smallest – and strongest – available. Trijicon.com

TruGlo

Adding to its lines of illuminated open sights, bow-sights and shotgun beads, TruGlo has beefed up its market muscle with rifle-scopes and binoculars. Also fresh in the catalog is the Tru-Brite open red dot sight. It has a generous 24x34mm window that delivers parallax-free sighting at 30 yards. Choose in the field from four reticle styles in two colors. The Tru-Brite red dot sight has click-stop W/E adjustments and a Weaver-style base. New Tru-Brite open-bridge binoculars feature 8x42 and 10x42 optics, twist-up eyecups and locking diopters. Like all TruGlo products, they're modestly priced. Truglo.com

Weaver

An expanded line of Buck Commander binoculars and rifle-scopes highlights Weaver's brand for 2011. They're value-priced scopes (the 2-8x36 and 2.5-10x42 list for under $290); but they deliver sharp sight pictures. The 4-16x42 wears a turret-mounted parallax dial. The Command-X reticle (a plex is listed too) wears tics on its lower stem to help you aim high at distance. Cosmetically, Buck Commander sights are quite appealing. ATK has decided to shelve the Nitrex label, promoting instead Weaver Super-Slam and Grand Slam optics. SuperSlam scopes give you five-times magnification ranges in 1-inch tubes (1-5x24 to 4-20x50). The Euro versions feature 30mm tubes. Tactical scopes with five-times power ranges now offer illuminated reticles. Budget-friendly Weavers include a new 2-7x32 sight in the 40/44 group. Yes, the Classic T-,V- and K-series remain – all great values, in my opinion. There's a new Classic 15-45x65 spotting scope in the stable too, with straight or angled eyepiece, Weaveroptics.com

Vortex

You'll find four fresh scopes in the Viper line: HS models with 30mm tubes and ED (extra-low-dispersion) lenses. This quartet – 1-4x24, 2.5-10x44, 4-16x44 and 4-16x50 – should woo hunters. Long-range versions of the 4-16s include target elevation dials with 1/2-minute clicks, so you can move point of impact fast. Most Vortex binoculars are new this year too. The flagship Razor full-size models (42- and 50mm objectives) feature HD (high-density or high-defini-

The popularity of AR rifles has spawned AR-specific scopes. Ordinary scopes work fine on ARs.

A GreyBull-modified Leupold scope helped Wayne get five consecutive hits on this steel rodent from prone with a Remington 700 in .22-250. Range: 500 yards.

tion) glass. Their magnesium frame has an open hinge, now in style if not functionally superior to the traditional bridge. Full- and mid-size Viper HD and Talon HD binoculars have the same high-performance lenses but differ in hinge design. In a concession to codgers like me, Vortex catalogs a Porro prism binocular, the Raptor. In 6.5x32 and 8.5x32, it weighs a tad over 17 ounces and reminds me of the B&L 7x35 Zephyr I once carried. In spotting scopes, the firm has announced straight 65- and 80mm Vipers with HD glass, both with rotating tripod mounts. Vortex has also entered the software wars with Long Range Ballistics Calculator. Use it to determine bullet drop and install Trajectory Matched Turrets on your scope. So equipped, you can dial up the scope for a center aim at distance. The Vortex catalog has enough glass to be required reading for riflemen. Vortexoptics.com

Zeiss

When you already produce some of the finest optics in the world, coming up with new products can be tough. Zeiss, once so conservative that American shooters rarely saw its wares, has made long strides of late. It now lists scopes and binoculars that marry legendary Zeiss quality with features proven popular Stateside. The Conquest line of rifle-scopes became a hit because the company delivered top performance at modest prices. Innovation, evident in its laser range-finding binocular and rifle-scope, has hiked Zeiss fortunes in the U.S. For 2011, Zeiss has recently announced an 18-45x65 Dialyt spotting scope. Focusing down to 33 feet, this Dialyt's useful power range delivers a field of view 70 to 120 feet wide. A straight 16-inch tube with integral eyepiece packs easily. Rubber armor cushions and quiets the 42-ounce scope. It is tripod-friendly and optically superb. I've found that at bottom power I can hand-hold it against a rest to good effect – one of those imperatives that arises from time to time on big game hunts. The new Dialyt is quite affordable. Pair it with a Zeiss ball-head tripod, another 2011 item. A footnote: If you have a 65mm or 85mm DiaScope, consider Zeiss's new Vario eyepiece. Power range is 15-56x in the 65 and 20-75x in the 85. At 18 ounces, it's a third heavier than a15-45x (20-60x) eyepiece. But oh, so versatile! Zeiss.com

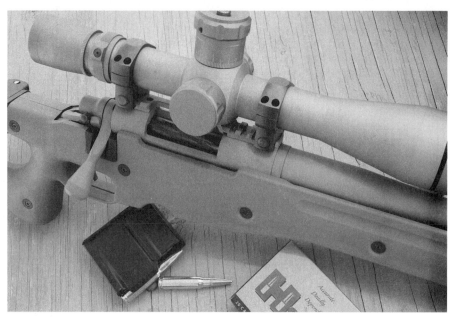

Color-coordination is an option in Leupold's custom shop. Here: an H-S Precision tactical rifle.

Conclusion

The optics field has more players than ever – more than we can cover in detail here. Some merit your attention. BSA for example. Beyond motorcycles and bolt-action rifles, BSA catalogs an affordable line of scopes. Some are cosmetically challenged, with paddle-steamer wheels where a dial should be; but I'm told an overhaul is coming. Recently a BSA variable on a Kimber 84L in .30-06 gave me half-minute groups and a fine buck. Pentax (which last year introduced a 3-9x40 scope for $99) delivers great value in both rifle-scopes and binoculars. A 9x28 Pentax bino, thrown into my kit as a backup, became my go-to glass for a couple of seasons. It is wonderfully lightweight, with images bright and sharp beyond its price.

Then there's Redfield. After Leupold re-introduced the label last year with three models, hunters flocked to buy them. My 3-9x40 Redfield is not only a handsome sight, but optically excellent – a must-see if you want an all-around big game sight at a reasonable price. Another new old name in the news is Premier, a firm long known for custom reticles. It now sells a 3-15x50 Hunter scope, with 30mm tube and side parallax dial. This scope has a near-perfect five-times magnification range and a flat, high-resolution field that impresses me. Of course, you can pick from several unique reticles, illuminated and not.

Horus appeared some years back with range-compensating reticles (which even those of us who think they clutter the field admit are effective). It now markets scopes. All feature 30mm tubes; most have four-times magnification. But there's a Horus 1.5-8x24 and, for varminters, an 8-26x50. Illumination is an option. I must also mention Nikko-Stirling, a Japanese brand imported by Legacy Sports International. A target model, 8-32x44 with 1/8-minute clicks, introduced me to the N-S line. Last fall I used a hunting-class variable on a deer hunt. Both sights impress me as fine values.

Rifle-scopes now complement the long-respected Minox binoculars. My ZA3, a 3-9x, features a clean BDC reticle with two intelligently placed hash marks. One of the brightest new scopes I've carried, this Minox has finger-friendly W/E dials and a fast-focus eyepiece. Like most sporting optics these days, it features fully multi-coated lenses. That is, all lens elements, inside and out, wear multiple coatings of rare earths that reduce light loss, enhancing brightness. Every scope and binocular you consider should be clearly marked as fully multi-coated. It's the first step to clear images of what's downrange.

A CENTURY OLD HAMMER GUN

Suddenly, it struck me: Grandpa's massive turn-of-the-century side-by-side hammer-gun needed to go turkey hunting.

BY **JIM SCHLENDER**

The hammers on the old gun work just as well now as they did 110 years ago when the author's grandfather acquired the 12-gauge side-by-side, manufactured by the American Gun Co. of New York.

Grandpa never hunted turkeys, mostly because he lived in southern Wisconsin in the early 1900s when there were no turkeys to hunt. But he put food on the table — rabbits, squirrels and pheasants — before and during the Great Depression with the help of a massive 12-gauge side-by-side shotgun made by the American Gun Co. of New York.

His gun was one of countless thousands of "hardware store" guns manufactured to provide function first and form second — a real working man's tool.

Grandpa turned the treasure over to me sometime about 1980. The hammer gun has hung on various walls the past 30 years. Recently, it occupied a space high above the computer desk in my home office.

Thinking about turkeys late one night this past winter, I glanced up at the family heirloom like I'd done thousands of times. Suddenly, I was struck by the obvious: Grandpa's gun needed to go hunting.

The Big Question

Why it took me so long to make that decision, I'll never know. I guess I'd always considered the old gun nothing more than an antique. But if Grandpa used it with smokeless powder shells, so could I — couldn't I?

I wasn't sure, so I proposed my idea to Dan Shideler, editor of the *Gun Digest Annual* and *Standard Catalog of Firearms,* and the most knowledgeable firearms historian I've ever met.

"So, can I shoot this thing or not? Is it safe?" I asked.

Shideler, not wanting to imply permission for me to risk any of my appendages, first went lawyer-like.

"It's wise to be prudent in firing any old shotgun," he said. "Old in this sense means pre-World War II. If you're intent on shooting that gun, the good news is that most shotguns made in the 20th century had barrels of nitro, or modern, steel."

Damascus barrels, the precursor to modern steel barrels, definitely would not be suitable for firing modern ammo, he explained.

How do you know the difference?

"Not all barrels are marked as to the type of steel used in their construction," Shideler said. "Nitro steel barrels may be marked as 'nickel steel' or, especially in the case of Winchester, 'Krupp steel,' 'fluid steel' or perhaps a half-dozen other names, and Damascus barrels might be marked as 'twist,' 'stub twist,' 'laminated' or 'ribbon' steel, to name just a few."

My American Gun Co. shotgun is

The author answered all the questions he needed to know about his grandfather's gun. Along the way, he made a long overdue connection with his family's past and gave the old gun another story to tell.

marked "Armory Steel," which sounds pretty darn tough to someone like me who's relatively uneducated in barrel steel. But I don't have to be a gun expert to see that the barrels are super-thick and fashioned from one hunk of iron, as opposed to the wavy lines that indicate Damascus-style manufacturing, which was the standard before the turn of the century.

First Shot

Dropping a light trap load into the right barrel of Grandpa's gun during a chilly April morning, I was still wondering why I'd never shot the gun before. Just a bit nervous about firing

the 110-year-old relic, I strapped it to a Caldwell Lead Sled and then fastened a string to the trigger. I cocked the hammer and backed up until I was around the corner of the shooting house. A jerk of the string produced a bang that sounded no different in 2010 than it did in 1900.

I jokingly referred to my testing method as "redneck" proofing, and then found out I hadn't coined that phrase. When I related my experiment to Shideler, he told me Turner Kirkland, founder of Dixie Gun Works, had always advocated the "tire-and-string test" — securing the butt of the gun in an old tire and pointing it downrange before firing it via a string.

The author (right) and his friend, Rick White, show off a very wet Michigan turkey. Grandpa's hammer gun had spoken after a long hiatus on the wall.

He then reminded me that the opinion of an experienced gunsmith was probably a better option. I'm sure he's right, but the gun and I survived just fine. But was it turkey-worthy?

I shot a few more trap loads from each barrel and found that the words "choke bore" stamped on the barrel might have made a great selling point back in the day, but the gun would probably be a 30-yard shooter at best with the right barrel and maybe a 25-yard shooter with the left. Just as importantly, or maybe remarkably, both barrels delivered the shot to the same point. It was nice to know I wouldn't have to introduce any Kentucky windage if I was lucky enough to put the bead on a tom's neck. Both barrels also shot a bit low, but with a little practice, I knew I could deal with that shortcoming.

Not wanting to push the pressure limits of the old gun, I decided a Kent 1¼-ounce load of No. 5s in a 2¾-inch shell (remember, there were no 3-inch "magnums" at the turn of the century) would be about right. Patterns to 30 yards were roughly equivalent to what you'd get out of a modern improved-cylinder barrel. I'd limit any shot to 25 yards or less, I decided.

Off to Michigan

I hauled Grandpa's gun along this past May on a hunt in Michigan's Upper Peninsula with Pat Muffler and Rick White from Hunter's Specialties. At the end of the third day, one hunter out of six — guess who — was still turkey-less.

With one morning left before heading home for Memorial Day, I asked (OK, I kind of begged) for White to take me to the roost area of the "beardless tom." This was a turkey the guys had hunted for two mornings before I arrived, trying to shoot it on camera for an H.S. video. The bird cooperated on the second morning, but Muffler had passed on it because its beard was nothing more

than a little jake-like stub. Whether it was beard rot, genetics or something else, they didn't know, but such turkeys don't make for great video, so Muffler let him walk. I, however, don't discriminate against beard-challenged birds.

White consented to dragging himself out of bed in the dark one more time to show me the way to the stubby-bearded tom. Mindful of the limits of my shotgun, we staked out a lone hen at 20 yards and set up. As the first streaks of light appeared, the tom began hammering from the same roost tree he'd been in the previous time they'd tried him. It was barely cracking light when he pitched down, popped into strut and moved in on our decoy.

I'd already drawn back the tighter barrel's hammer during the bird's fly-down, and I just needed him to pop his head up.

"Cluck!" went White's mouth call, and right on cue, the tom stretched his neck out.

The load of 5s rushed down the 30-inch barrel no differently than if the pellets had been launched from one of Grandpa's old paper shells. And the turkey … didn't drop. He sort of stumbled for a second, and then rolled to the ground before flopping violently in the wet grass. He was down for good, but I knew I'd delivered a few too many pellets to the body and not enough where they mattered.

It felt like an ugly win, or maybe I was just too used to pounding gobblers with 2-plus ounces of 21st century metal composites driven through ultra-tight chokes. Either way, I'd answered all the questions I needed to know about Grandpa's gun. I'd made a long overdue connection with my family's past, and now the old hammer gun has another story to tell.

It's back on the wall above me as I write this, and I think that's where it will stay.

ONE GOOD GUN:
REMINGTON MODEL 11-48 28 GAUGE

BY **STEVE GASH**

The tentacles of John M. Browning's genius for gun design extend far and wide, not only to Browning firearms, but to many other brands, as well. While he is probably most remembered for various lever-action rifles, a good case can be made that Browning contributed more to the development of the shotgun than any other individual.

The Model 1887 and Model 1892 lever-actions were unique scatterguns, and the iconic Model 1897 pump-action is legendary. But his most seminal shotgun design is most certainly the Auto 5.

Browning's first patent for a "recoil operated firearm" was filed in 1899, and after a circuitous sequence of corporate events, the "Auto-5" saw production in

1903 by Frabrique Nationale of Belgium.

Although Remington had missed out on this design, the success of the new-fangled semi-auto was not lost on Big Green's brass, so the first new shotguns they introduced after World War II were autoloaders. It is interesting to note that the Model 11 Remington (which actually debuted in 1906) was an almost exact

The Remington Model 11-48 debuted in 1949 in 12, 16, and 20 gauges, followed by the 28 gauge in 1952, and a .410-bore in 1954. It was the company's first shotgun after WWII, and was the first autoloading shotgun offered in 28 gauge. It became a hit with hunters and target shooters alike.

The Model 11-48's long-recoil action is very similar to the older Browning Auto-5 and Remington Model 11. The receiver is milled from a solid billet of steel.

The Model 11-48's ordnance-steel barrel was topped with a neat little ramp and a prominent bead. (Yes, that's a small streak of leading.)

Almost all Model 11-48 28-gauge barrels were 25 inches in length and furnished without ribs, although both solid and ventilated ribs were available.
The most popular choke was modified, although full, improved cylinder, and skeet were also offered. The date code of "AP" translates to manufacturer in March 1967.

duplicate of the Auto-5 in appearance and operation.

Occasionally, fate smiles on the firearm enthusiast, and a prize specimen becomes available for less than various body parts. So it was with this Model 11-48 28 gauge. An older gentleman had left the range, and his son, having little interest in things that go "boom," contacted a co-worker, my good friend Bob French, to take a look at the items. In the mix was the Model 11-48. Bob, knowing I'm a certified 28-gauge addict, asked the price. It was very reasonable, and he called me post haste. He described the neat little gun as "as-NIB;" the only thing missing was the box. I pounced on it like a ravished hyena.

The Remington Model 11-48 has an intriguing path in the evolution of recoil-operated shotguns. It was based on the Model 11, and was designed in 1948 by L. Ray Critendon, Ellis Hailston, and C. R. Johnson. The Model 11-48 was introduced in 1949 in 12, 16, and 20 gauges, and a 28-gauge version followed in 1952. It is of historical significance that the Model 11-48 was the first production of an autoloader in this gauge. A version for the 3-inch .410-bore followed in 1954, and its barrel was marked "FOR PLASTIC SHELLS ONLY." Production of

the Model 11-48 lasted until 1968, with approximately 455,535 being made. A three-shot version called the Sportsman 48 was also produced.

The development of auto-loading firearms in this period coincided with the development of smokeless powder, and ammo manufacturers had not yet solved the problem of gun operation with various loads. For the A-5, Browning

had designed a friction ring that could be adjusted, depending on the power level of the load. It worked, but was a bit cumbersome if you changed loads a lot. This was carried over in the Model 11.

The new Remington Model 11-48 addressed that problem, and added some spiffy cosmetic touches, as well. It retained the same bolt-barrel, long-recoil system as the A-5, but had a sleek and rounded receiver at its back, rather than the Browning's "hump." The A-5's recoil system consisted of a recoil spring, and a ring and "friction piece" that bore on the magazine tube to regulate action cycling. It was adjustable for different loads, but you had to take the forend off to do it.

The Model 11-48 featured a new-designed recoil mechanism called the "self-compensating friction brake" that

Early Model 11-48s had machine-cut checkering, but later models had new impressed checkering.

The Model 11-48's self-adjusting long-recoil system was simplicity itself. A bronze-plated "friction piece" fit inside the barrel extension, and rode atop a large steel cylinder called the "recoil spring ring." As things moved rearward over the magazine tube, the appropriate amount of friction was provided to cycle the action, based on the power of the load.

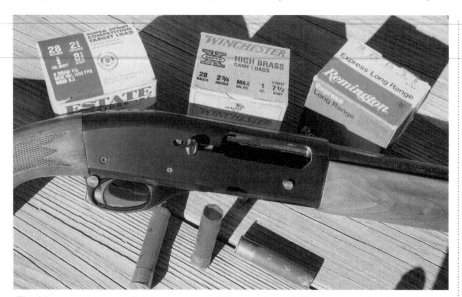

The big ammo companies turn out a terrific selection of 28-gauge fodder, including the popular ¾-ounce target and field loads, Fiocchi's slightly heavier 7/8-ounce hunting load, and Winchester "High Brass" load with one full ounce of shot.

functioned with all loads. A bronze-plated "friction piece" fit inside the barrel extension, and nestled over the end of the "recoil spring ring." The friction piece was split, and as the barrel and these two parts began their rearward journey, the friction piece was compressed around the magazine tube by carefully calibrated bevels inside the barrel extension and on the front end of the recoil spring ring. This compression was proportional to the load's strength, thereby eliminating the need for adjustment when changing loads.

At the time, this was a neat innovation, considering the ever-widening variety of loads becoming available. While the standard load for the 28 gauge is now 3/4 ounce, back then, 5/8 ounce was also popular, so this feature was of some note, even to the diminutive 28. Nowadays, of course, what with the production of 7/8- and 1-ounce 28-gauge loads, this feature would also be useful. The bolt was returned to battery by a stout spring in the buttstock.

All was not wine and roses with the new system, however. Failures to eject were relatively common unless the magazine tube was liberally lubricated. One source bluntly recommended "30-wt. motor oil." Another pesky problem was that on guns with considerable use, the bolt handle would fly off upon firing. The gun would work just fine without the part, it was just there to pull the bolt back. Some folks drilled a hole in the handle, and attached it to the gun with a cord, making it easy to find when it was launched into space. As production neared its end, engineering changes had solved most of these problems, however.

Almost all Model 11-48s in 28 gauge had 25-inch barrels, and both plain and ventilated rib barrels were offered, and field, skeet, special, and tournament grades were available. Chokes were full, modified (the most often encountered), improved cylinder, and skeet.

My neat little Model 11-48 is totally representative of the breed. It has a nicely figured walnut stock, impressed checkering, and a black plastic butt-plate. Its 25-inch plain barrel is marked "MOD." at the left rear, and the date code

Smoke! Every skeet shooter's goal on the low house target from station 8.

The 28 gauge is a fine companion in the field after small game, and the light and lively Model 11-48 is responsive for quail over dogs or cottontails in the brush.

"AP" indicates that it was made in March of 1967, just a year before the model was discontinued.

While the Model 11-48 used new – and cheaper – but totally functional stamped parts and an aluminum trigger guard, the receiver was machined from a solid billet of ordnance steel. The fire-control group could be easily removed for cleaning by drifting out two pins. The magazine holds five rounds, and a plug limiting the capacity to two rounds is provided.

While most gun votaries would be aghast at the thought of firing such a pristine find, I figure guns are made to be shot, so I gathered up a host of ¾-ounce factory loads, and headed to the nearest skeet range. "Nearest" is relative here, since it was 130 miles, one way. But no matter; it needed to be christened. There I learned of the admonition about magazine-tube lubrication. After several failures to eject, I removed the forend and sprayed the magazine tube with a good dose of some kind of spray oil, and everything worked fine after that.

Back home, I ran three 28-gauge factory loads over the chronograph. While they are rated at 1,200 to 1,295 fps, one clocked 1,173 fps, and as expected, failed to cycle the action. Loads at 1,200 fps or faster worked just fine, however. My handloads with modern components also cycled the action – if the speed (and momentum) was up there. The lesson is clear: test your ammo (chronograph it, if possible) before venturing afield or to the clays range, and lube that mag tube!

Today, the fine old 28 gauge seems to be making a comeback. Several firms make lithe little gas-operated semi-autos and pumps, and for the well heeled there are the lovely doubles and stack barrels. Skeet shooting is probably the biggest use for the gauge today, but many aficionados hunt quail, grouse, and doves with their 28, and marvel at its efficiency.

So come next September, I plan to call in sick (again), plant myself at the edge of a cut field, and leisurely await the arrival of a flight of mourning doves. I might even bag a few, but that's not the end, just the means. I'm sure the M-11-48 and I will have fun.

28 Gauge Load Table

Factory Loads

Ammo	Shot Charge (oz.)	Shot Size	Velocity (fps)	SD (fps)	Cycled Action?
Winchester AA Target	3/4	9	1185.4	25.9	yes
Fiocchi Target	3/4	7½	1173.2	19.5	no
Remington Express	3/4	6	1209.1	39.9	yes

Handloads

Powder	Powder Charge (gr.)	Case	Wad	Shot charge (oz.)	Velocity (fps)	SD (fps)	Cycled Action?
Alliant 20/28	13.0	Federal	Rem. PT-28	3/4	1,172.2	44.6	no
Alliant 20/28	13.0	Class Doubles	Rem. PT-28	3/4	1,213.8	20.2	yes
Alliant 20/28	13.0	Win. AA-HS	Win. AA-28	3/4	1,196.0	15.2	yes
Alliant 20/28	13.0	R-P STS	Rem. PT-28	3/4	1,172.0	20.4	no
Alliant 20/28	13.0	Federal	Rem. PT-28	3/4	1,198.1	12.3	yes

Notes: A Remington Model 11-48 with a 25-inch modified choke barrel was used for all testing. Velocities were measured with a PACT chronograph with the front screen at 2 feet. Range temperatures were 50-55°F. No. 8 shot, Federal cases, and Winchester No. 209 primers were used for all handloads.

ONE GOOD GUN:
GRANDPA'S GUNS

There was a time long ago when one shot was enough.

BY **ANDY EWERT**

When the author's grandfather was a boy, money was tight and sometimes one shot had to be enough. His guns' simple, sturdy, single-shot designs were well suited to a youngster needs. (Top to bottom): Iver Johnson Champion .410 shotgun, Stevens Favorite .22 rifle, and Hopkins & Allen .22 pistol.

Slowed somewhat by the Great Recession, the American consumer market continues to be driven by consumption, abetted by an endless array of new products, "good-enough" quality, planned obsolescence, and a throw-away mentality. This mindset defies the lessons in thrift devised by our grandparents during another global economic upheaval: the Great Depression.

People behaved very differently when my grandfather was a boy. Back then, folks used a product until it broke or wore out, then fixed it and used it some more. They didn't spend money until they earned it. And the earning took time – perhaps a year or more of running a paper route or performing household chores to buy a .22 rifle or shotgun. Ammunition was costly too. You bought it as your pocket money permitted, sometimes a few rounds at a time.

I know these things because grandpa told me. Guns were a part of his life as a boy and as a man. He was hard-working, church-going, and dedicated to his family. Bird hunting and trap shooting were among his pleasures. So were bourbon whiskey, risqué humor, and Green Bay Packers football. I was fortunate enough

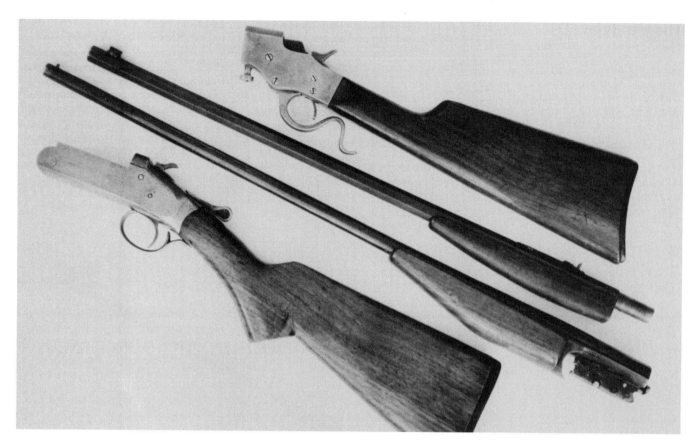

Both the Stevens Favorite .22 rifle (top) and Iver Johnson Champion .410 shotgun break down easily and compactly for travel.

to share some of these with him during his later years. He died while I was in college. Grandma distributed his possessions across our family. Included in my inheritance were a couple dozen well-worn duck decoys, a hunting canoe, a vintage, leather-cased Thermos bottle, and his three boyhood firearms: a rifle, pistol, and shotgun – all single shot.

As I began to learn about these guns, I realized they were a testament to grandpa's times as much as his personal tastes. Each of the the trio, manufactured during thé early 20th century, is simple in design, rugged, economical, and well suited for what it was intended to do. Each has its own story.

The Rifle

Grandpa's rifle is an American classic: the .22 caliber Stevens Favorite. Over a million of them were manufactured from 1890 to 1939, in .22, .25, and .32 rimfire. Grandpa's takedown Model 1915, serial number X399, sports a 24-inch octagon barrel and a patina earned after 90 or so years of existence. Its overall length of 38 inches and 4-1/2 lb. weight are ideal for a boy's physique. Grandpa employed his Favorite to bag rabbits and squirrels

for the pot, terminate troublesome varmints, and perforate tin cans. The rifle's lever-action, falling-block design is strong and reliable. Equipped with adjustable square-notch-and-post sights, it's more than capable of placing .22 long rifle slugs where you want them to go.

Grandpa's .22 is still with us today. Savage Arms offers the Stevens Favorite in takedown and non-take-down models for under $400.

The Shotgun

Like grandpa's rifle, his .410 Iver Johnson Champion shotgun, serial number 31785, is an American stalwart. Introduced during 1909 in 12, 16, and 20 gauges, the single-barrel Champion features a "side-snap" action, operated by unlocking the breech with a lever on the top of the receiver and tilting the barrel downward for loading and unloading. When snapped shut, the action locks. The hammer is then manually cocked to fire. The Iver Johnson's robust design, 42-inch overall length, 5-3/4-lb. heft, light recoil, and moderate price tag made it a suitable first shotgun for young, budget-conscious nimrods.

Grandpa told me he used the 26-inch-barreled .410 during the early 1920s to shoot ducks along Milwaukee's Lake Michigan shoreline and pheasants in the adjoining farm fields. He recounted how, during one outing, a strong lake breeze updraft rendered incoming waterfowl briefly motionless overhead as they set their wings to land. He filled a sack with mallards for the family table that day.

At some point, grandpa had the Champion's 2-1/2-inch chamber reamed out to accept 3-inch magnum shells. When I was a youngster, he hunted waterfowl and upland game with a 12-gauge Winchester Model 50 semi-automatic and later a Beretta 20-gauge magnum over/under. The Champion of his youth rested undisturbed in a display case for at least three decades. During the mid 1970s, my young cousin cut his teeth on it during family duck hunts. (In those pre-steel shot days, you could occasionally find a full-choked .410 in duck blinds.)

While the Iver Johnson Company closed its doors in 1993, Harrington & Richardson still offers a similar single-shot, break-open scattergun, the Topper, in 12, 16, 20, and .410 chamberings, priced in the $150 to $225 range.

The Handgun

Grandpa's handgun, a single-shot Hopkins & Allen .22, reflected his enjoyment of informal target shooting. With its 10-inch barrel, adjustable rear sight, and smart nickel finish, the H&A is a "looker." Other than its brand name, site of manufacture (Norwich, Connecticut), and serial number 840 stamped on the barrel, the pistol bears no indication of model designation. Its break-top action is unlocked by depressing two spring-loaded buttons at the top of the receiver, one on each side, forward of and beneath the rear site. When opened slowly, the extractor partially draws the fired case from the chamber for manual removal. Opening the action briskly ejects the empty into space. After reloading, the action is closed by hand and the hammer retracted to fire.

Spots of finish wear on the barrel and frame indicate holster use. Grandpa told me he and my grandmother enjoyed handgun plinking sessions on her family farm during their courtship. My great-grandmother occasionally joined in on the fun. Her marksmanship was noted.

Attempts over the years to learn more about grandpa's old one-shooter proved frustrating. H&A product literature and production records were nowhere to be found. What information I did glean was sparse and sometimes contradictory. According to one report, the handgun, designated New Model Target, was introduced in 1913, four years before the company's demise. The same account stated that additional specimens were assembled, presumably from leftover

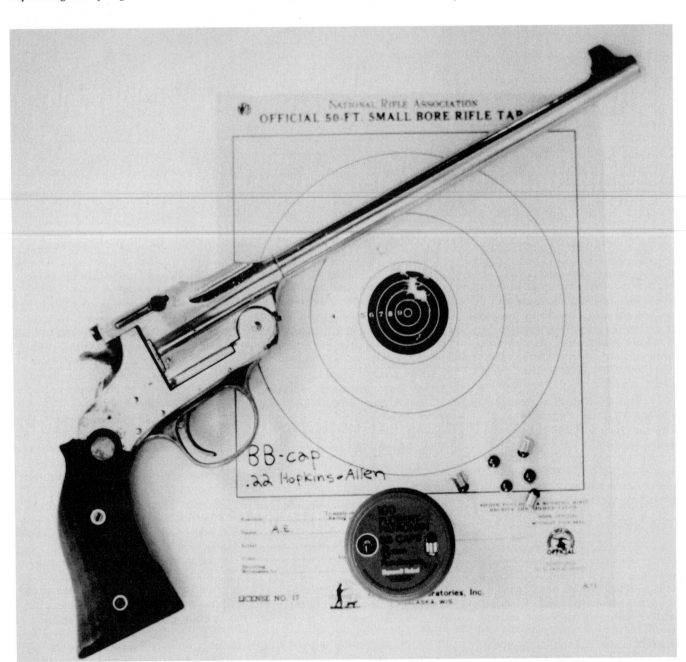

The author's .22 Hopkins & Allen single shot excelled in basement "parlor" shooting. German Dynamit Nobel BB and CB caps, along with CCI .22 Mini Cap CB Rimfire ammunition, proved safe, sufficiently quiet, and accurate during indoor shooting sessions.

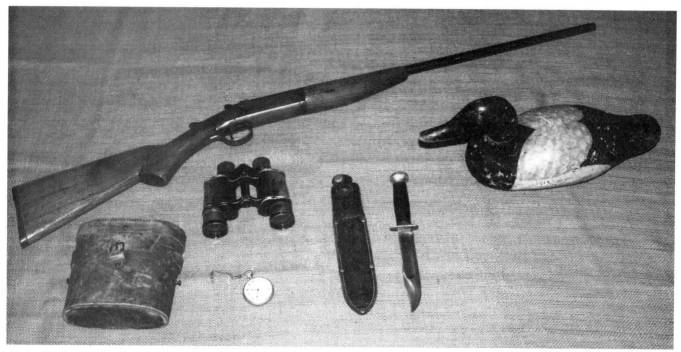

The author's grandfather used this Iver Johnson Champion .410 shotgun for potting ducks and pheasants in Wisconsin around the 1920s. Accompanying him in the field where his Marble Gladstone belt knife, Swiss Cymrex pocket watch, and Du Mor of Paris binoculars.

parts, in 1922 by the Marlin Firearms Corporation.

It appears nothing similar to the H&A single-shot .22 is manufactured today, at least as a mass-produced item. The Thompson/Center Contender probably comes the closest, though it's no more than similar in general concept.

A New Life for Some Old Iron

When I inherited my grandfather's guns, I was the proud owner of a Marlin 39A lever action .22 rifle, a Browning Auto-5 20-gauge magnum and a Smith & Wesson .357 magnum revolver. Other than fond memories of grandpa and our times together, I had little use for these oldtimers. Out of respect, the three were mounted on the basement wall of my parent's home and remained there in obscurity for more than 10 years.

Naturally, the Browning was my go-to gun for a fall grouse and squirrel hunt in northern Wisconsin. Once, on a lark, I also packed the Stevens and a box each of German Dynamit Nobel CB and BB caps. After a day afield, my hunting amigo and I relaxed outside his uncle's cabin before dinner, plinking the empty cans with the powderless, primer-powered *spitzkugel* (pointed

ball) and *rundkugel* (roundball) loads. How that little .22 made the cans dance! On returning home, I cleaned and oiled the rifle and parked it back on the wall, where it languished for another decade or so. Over the years, the price of those Teutonic CB and BB caps rose steadily until, not surprisingly, they disappeared from dealers' shelves.

One day I read a review of CCI .22 Mini Cap CB Rimfire ammunition, a specialized low-power load, in Long and Short versions, developed for use when noise and velocity were concerns. I bought a box of the Longs. Out of curiosity, I pulled one cartridge's 29-grain slug from its case. To my surprise, out spilled 8/10s of a grain of a very fine powder. Listed velocity of the CCI long was 675 fps.

Then the idea hit me: Why not try out the new loading with the Stevens in basement "parlor" shooting? I'm not certain it was legal in my suburb, but I went through a dozen or so boxes of Mini Caps with family and friends. The report was similar to the pop of an air rifle. There was a little smoke but, with the aid of a portable fan, the fumes were tolerable. A thick hardwood board absorbed the slugs without ricochets. My Favorite had a new lease on life as a cellar Schuetzen rifle.

Next was the Hopkins & Allen's turn to shine. Other than one brief range

trial, I never gave Old Longnose a fair shake. The skinny barrel was hard to steady and its hair trigger presented a direct threat to human health. Besides, by that time I acquired a 1933-vintage Colt Woodsman .22 semi-auto that could shoot out X rings almost on demand. But in the basement, with proper caution, eye protection, and a diet of Mini Caps, grandpa's pistola found its niche. I burned off a couple hundred of those squib loads, along with the last of my CB and BB caps, through that single shot.

Sad to say, I never gave the Iver Johnson its due. I still have some of grandpa's old paper 2-1/2-inch shells and more recent 3-inch magnum .410 fodder, but to what purpose? Every trip to the range is spent on more important matters. A single-shot .410 in the game field? I think not. It's a shame to consign the Champion to the display wall but, as we know, life isn't fair.

It's without regret I confess that grandpa's guns are now formally retired. Father and I handle them occasionally and reminisce about the days when they fulfilled a boy's dreams. The world is a very different place today. Perhaps I'll find a youngster worthy of owning them. Until then, they remain family heirlooms, on the basement wall, awaiting a new life.

ONE GOOD GUN:

BOB'S 270

BY STEVE GASH

The red light on the answer machine blinked ominously. "Probably another solicitor," I groused to my wife as I punched the "play" button. A solemn voice intoned: "This is Dan Westervelt. I just wanted to let you know that Dad passed away this morning. We are here at home, and are okay." The voice trailed off, and the line went silent. It was two days before Christmas, 2008.

"Dad" was Robert Earl Westervelt, affectionately know as "Bob" to his legion of friends and hunting buddies. He was born on September 21st, 1933, near Hallowell, Kansas. He worked as a lineman for Kansas Gas & Electric (KG&E), which provided him with the means to live a full and active life. After

Kansas had its first modern deer season in 1966, and Bob Westervelt drew one of the "any deer" tags. Bob took this nice buck that December in Labette County, Kansas with the Model 70 in .270 Winchester. Note the slit on the deer's right jaw. At the mandatory check stations, Kansas F&G officials aged deer to augment harvest data.

The M-70 today, after a careful stock refinishing, and a few embellishments. The metal was in about 95% condition, and was highlighted by the re-done wood. The rifle still wears the 1965-vintage Realist 4x scope that Bob used for his hunts. The Brownells soft case is perfect for pickup-traveling hunters.

The M-70's barrel markings show about all the serious rifleman needed to know in those halcyon days: It was a pre-'64 Winchester, in the caliber of choice of knowledgeable shooters everywhere.

The Winchester trademark stood for quality and dependability, and plenty of history. Note the close inletting of metal to wood; that's the way they made 'em in those days.

In 1966, Bob had several suitable deer rifles, of course, but he counted on the M-70 .270 for that all-important first deer. He purchased it circa 1965, used, and on time, at a local landmark. (Check out the vintage Chevy pickup.)

An older Bob, a newer truck, but the same rifle: the M-70. This buck was taken along Cow Creek, not far from Bob's home in Pittsburg in Crawford County, Kansas.

a promotion, Bob and wife Bethel moved to Pittsburg, Kansas, in 1964, their home for the next 44 years.

In his 75 years, Bob lived hard and played harder. His fondness for Ten High and Kools eventually took their toll on his health, but his love of his family, good dogs, and fine firearms molded him into a unique individual and a loyal friend. If it was in season, Bob hunted it, and I was privileged to accompany him on many forays after pheasants, ducks, quail, and doves – but never deer.

Like most of us, Bob was a gun "accumulator," not a gun collector in the true sense of the word. Nevertheless, over an active career of buying, selling, and horse-trading, he had acquired an eclectic accumulation of firearms suitable for various species. Many were what would be called "shooters" or "working guns," but a few were downright unique and would become highly desirable collector pieces.

On Christmas Eve, we drove to Pittsburg to pay our respects to Bethel

Since Bob bought the M-70 used, it is thought that it came equipped with the Realist 4x scope. This was a step up from the almost universal Weaver K4s found on most centerfires of the day. Realist scopes were introduced 1965, and retailed then for $57.50, almost half as much as the M-70's price of $129.95 in its year of production, 1960. Flip-up Butler Creek scope covers have been added.

Realist scopes were made in a modern factory in Berlin, Wisconsin, with company headquarters in Menomonee. The new line received high marks from gun writers of the day.

The stock screws on the M-70 (all four of them) were horribly "buggered up," and had to go. Fortunately, Galazan makes replacement screw sets for the M-70 (and other guns) that are exact replicas of the originals, and a set was ordered from Brownells, thereby fixing the disfigurement of an unknown earlier shade-tree mechanic.

Another Cow Creek buck, also taken with a .270, but this time a Ruger M-77RL Bob had acquired. This was one of Bob's last deer hunts, as his health problems prevented him from venturing too far afield in later years.

and Bob's family. As we reminisced, it became obvious that Bethel was seriously concerned about something. Bethel was hoping on staying with her daughter Connie and husband Steve in McPherson, Kansas, for a while, and was rightfully afraid that if she left the house unattended for long, the guns would be stolen, as literally everybody in the area knew about his guns. So, Bethel asked if I could help her sell them right away. Of course, I agreed.

The first step was a complete inventory, so into the back room we went, clipboard in hand. Dan and Steve hauled the guns out, one by one. I identified each one for my wife, who dutifully recorded the pertinent data. Luckily she had brought her digital camera, so she took photos of everything.

Bob was especially fond of pursuing deer so he had several centerfire rifles. Two were .270 Winchesters, and one caught my eye. It was a pre-'64 Model 70 Winchester. During the inventory, I gazed longingly at it, and as I relayed

its data to my wife, she was shocked. "A pre-'64 Model 70," she asked? "Isn't that the Holy Grail of rifles? Haven't you wanted one of those since before the Big Bang?" Well, yeah.

But fate was still turning. The next day my wife, bless her, insisted that I call Bethel and offer to buy the M-70. I did, and to my delight, a deal was struck. Later I showed the list of Bob's guns to a local dealer, and he agreed to buy the entire collection, sight unseen, at a very fair price. When I called Bethel with the good news, I could almost feel her release from what she felt was an immense burden.

In 1966, Kansas had its first deer season in many decades, and Bob was first in line to apply for one of the "any deer" permits issued by the Kansas Greenies. And he got one, too. We speculate that he bought the M-70 in the fall of 1966 in anticipation of the upcoming deer season. As a KG&E employee, Bob was allowed to hunt around the company lake in Labette County, where he took

With the safety lever fully retracted, the rifle was "on safe," and the bolt was locked closed. An intermediate position allowed the action to be opened for unloading, but with the firing pin safely blocked, an important safety feature.

An M-70 meant controlled feed, and the robust claw extractor pretty much says it all. Note the cut for the ejector.

a fine, fat buck with the M-70. Bob also hunted deer in subsequent years along Cow Creek near his Pittsburg home with the M-70, and took several. Over the years, he and the M-70 killed deer almost every year. It was one of Bob's hunting rituals.

Thus began my journey back in time. My tenure as custodian of the M-70 began with the usual pursuits. The serial number indicates that it was made in 1960. It is a "Standard Grade," with a 24-inch, four-groove barrel with a 10-inch twist. The rear sight rests on the raised "boss" on the barrel, and the front sight still wears the factory hood, usually the first casualty of serious field use.

The stock has a Monte Carlo comb, but no cheekpiece, and is secured

to the barreled action with the usual three action screws, and a fourth screw at the forend. The rifle was equipped with a Realist 4x scope, which was not introduced until 1965, and which got good reviews in back then. Interestingly, the Realist scope retailed for $57.50, almost half that of the M-70's price in the 1960 ($129.95), so this was a class outfit for the day.

The rifle's metal finish was in very good condition, but the stock showed honest use. The finish was worn off in a few spots, there were a few scratches, and a Pachymar recoil pad had been added. The factory-issue non-detachable sling swivels held a tattered leather sling.

Since this particular model and caliber combination was not particularly

rare, I set out to spruce it up, but carefully. The metal was fine, so I focused on the stock. My intent was not to just refinish the stock, but rather, to the extent possible, "restore" it to as close to original condition as I could. I ordered from Brownells a Galazan refinishing kit to duplicate the original pre-'64 Winchester look. I also ordered a Galazan red recoil pad that was a reproduction of the type Winchester used on the Super Grade M-70s, but which, of course, was non-standard on this model. As time passed, it became obvious that I was never going to have the time to do this job justice, so I took the rifle, pad, and refinish kit to Master Gunsmith Lee Shaver, and let him work his magic. The result is terrific. I told Lee that Winchester never let a

Factory Loads

Ammo	Bullet	Velocity (fps)	SD (fps)	Group (")
Hornady Custom, #8054	130-gr. SST	3,009	13	.83
Hornady Superformance, #80543	130-gr. SST	3,092	22	.94
Hornady Superformance, #80563	140-gr. SST	3,027	9	.90
Federal Premium Trophy Bonded Tip, #P270TT1	130-gr. TBT	3,002	12	.67
Federal Premium, #P270E	150-gr. Nosler Partition	2,729	18	1.16

Handloads					
Powder	Powder Charge (gr.)	Bullet	Velocity (fps)	SD (fps)	Group (")
AA-3100	55.0	Nosler 130-gr. Ballistic Tip	2,856	21	1.28
AA-3100	54.0	Hornady 140-gr. BTSP	2,745	13	.88
AA-3100	54.0	Sierra 140-gr. HPBT	2,843	12	.91
AA-3100	53.0	Speer 150-gr. Hot-Cor	2,708	9	1.18

Notes: A Winchester Model 70 with a 24-inch barrel and a 4x Realist scope was used for all testing. Accuracy is for one, five-shot group at 100 yards. Velocities were measured with an Oehler M-35P with the front screen at 12 feet. Range temperatures were 45° to 58° F. Winchester cases and Federal No. 210 primers were used for all handloads.

rifle escape the factory in 1960 that ever looked this good! Lee also installed QD sling swivels.

In due course, I test-fired Bob's .270 with a factory load and several loads that

The folding-leaf rear sight site sits on a boss in the barrel, and sports a white triangle as an aiming point. It is adjustable for elevation with two tiny screws, and drift-adjustable for windage.

had proven accurate in other .270s. New ammo from Hornady and Federal with 130- and 140-grain bullets shot under an inch, and velocities were over 3,000 fps. Federal ammo with the 150-grain Nosler

The M-70's four-groove barrel is nicely crowned, and very accurate. The minor accretion of jacket fouling whisked away with a dose of Sweet's 7.62 Solvent. The ramp front sight and hood complement the aesthetics, and look right at home – because they are.

Partition clocked 2,729 fps, and shot into 1.16 inches. My mild handloads did not shoot quite as well, but testing has just begun. All in all, an auspicious beginning on the range. So, Bob's .270 still shoots within minute-of-deer.

I am positive that Bob would be delighted with the results of the restoration efforts, and that I will give the M-70 a loving home, just as he did. One of these days, I will put back into service in the deer woods, but it's so darn pretty that I'm afraid I'll scratch it, so for now, I it languishes in the safe.

But I know that if Bob were here, he'd be incredulous. "Hell, take it out and hunt with it," he'd bellow. "That's what it's made for!"

And I will. I promise, Bob.

Special thanks to Bethel and Dan Westervelt and Connie and Steve Swartz for researching family records and for sharing family photographs of Bob's full life.

TESTFIRE:
The Rhino Revolver

BY JIM DICKSON

The Chiappa Rhino is the most innovative revolver to be marketed to the American shooter in more than a hundred years. It fires from the bottom chamber of the cylinder instead of the top for a more straight-line recoil that reduces muzzle jump and perceived recoil. Its innovative lockwork gives a 50 percent shorter trigger pull and a faster reset.

It is a major improvement in revolver design. This extends to the layout of the gun as well; the hand rides much higher on this gun than on conventional revolvers. Cowboy Action shooters will appreciate that, because one of the secrets of shooting the Colt Single Action Army was to hold it as high in the grip as possible; only then did it live up to

The 6-inch Rhino .357 in all its glory.

its reputation as a natural pointer. This also aids in putting the recoil more in line with the arm, instead of having the axis of the recoil above the hand as in a conventional revolver. Thus you don't have the muzzle flipping up like that of a conventional revolver. The layout of the revolver results in its being 1 1/2 inches shorter in overall length than conventional revolvers with the same barrel length. Its imprint under clothes or in a pocket for the 2-inch barrel model is not as easily recognizable as a handgun as a conventional revolver is.

The Rhino is available in both fixed and adjustable sight versions and in barrel lengths of 2, 4, 5 and 6 inches, so there is something for everyone. Rifling is 6 grooves with a 1:18 3/4 inch twist. Working parts are steel and the frame is made of a high strength aluminum alloy called Ergal.

The mechanism is far different from that of conventional revolvers, as you would expect. Pulling the trigger moves an interlink lever by means of a connecting rod. This lever in turn moves both the hammer and the cylinder rotation pin, compressing a spiral spring through two levers. The interlink lever drives these two levers to push on the two spring ends which then propel the hammer and return the trigger and the rest of the mechanism to rest.

The Rhino's double action is operated through a mobile hammer sear that cocks the hammer until it is released upon reaching the preset position, similar to the operation of a traditional revolver. The single action requires a different method due to the low position of the hammer. It was necessary to use an external hammer actuator that uses a lever to push the hammer down until it

engages the counter-hammer, blocking it in the armed position.

When the trigger is pulled, the hammer is released by the interlink lever which pushes up the counter-hammer and allows the action to fire. If you wish to uncock the gun it is necessary to push down the counter-hammer, pulling the trigger to the end and gently releasing the hammer actuator as you would with a standard revolver.

The Rhino's cylinder is released by a lever on the left side of the revolver. When pushed down, this lever engages the locking pin in the center of the rotation shaft. A spring makes the locking pin recoil and at the same time pushes back the pin in the breech shield, thus releasing the cylinder. Once the cylinder is released, it can be pushed to the left to allow the loading and unloading of the weapon. You will encounter a slight

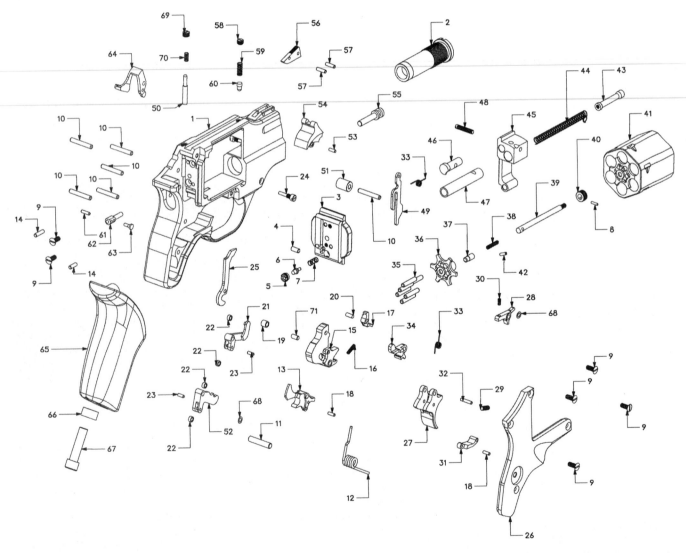

Exploded view of the Rhino.

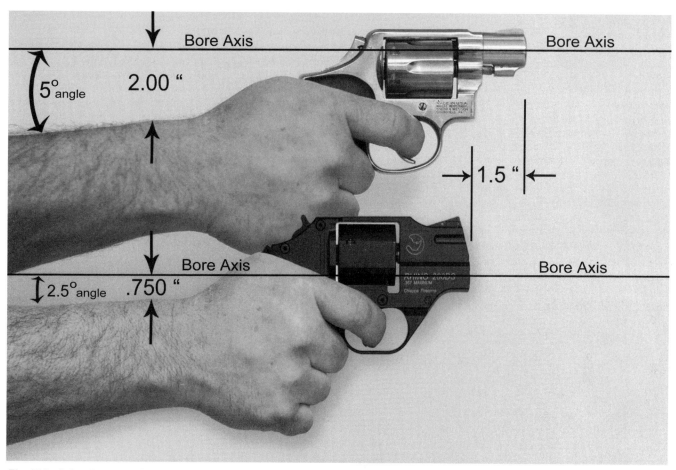

Bore Axis   Bore Axis

5° angle   2.00 "

1.5 "

Bore Axis   Bore Axis

2.5° angle   .750 "

The Rhino's low bore axis (bottom) results in more controllable recoil than that of a conventional revolver (top).

resistance when pushing the cylinder to the left as you have to overcome the spring pressure of the second locking system of the cylinder. This consists of a spring loaded detent pin placed in the frame of the gun on the opposite side of the breech shield, which is wedged into a specific seat in the rotation arm of the cylinder. The arm of the cylinder is wedged in a special joint which allows ample space for opening of the cylinder for quick reloading.

Safety is a big part of this revolver's design. The gun cannot fire without the cylinder being locked in place because if the small piston placed in the center of the rotation shaft of the cylinder is not perfectly seated into its notch in the breech shield, the cylinder opening lever will be in the low position, blocking rotation of the cylinder and stopping the whole mechanism.

The revolver cannot fire if the cylinder chamber in the six o'clock position is not aligned with the barrel. A pin placed on the trigger interferes with the plug blocking the cylinder and prevents the trigger from being fully pulled if the

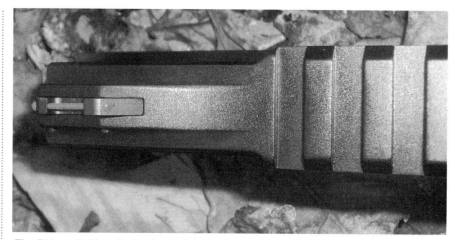

The Rhino's light-gathering front sight.

plug has not gone into its corresponding notch in the cylinder.

The internal hammer makes the Rhino extremely safe from accidental firing caused by falls and shocks. Nevertheless a special safety prevents the accidental release of the hammer when the revolver is cocked in single action. An accidental release of the hammer

could happen only if the gun fell from a great height or as a result of abnormal wear of internal parts. In this case the hammer cannot hit the firing pin as a solid plug on the left side of the frame would interfere with the interlink lever preventing the gun firing. This safety can only be disconnected by pulling the trigger fully through.

A closer look at the Rhino's inner workings.

Advanced design means breaking with tradition and this makes the Rhino a real attention getter. When my 6-inch barrel sample gun arrived at Tucker Guns, it created quite a stir among the employees and customers. There were two standard reactions: "What in the Hell is that?" followed by "That's weird!" Then the comments start to become complimentary: "Nicely machined!" "Points good!" "Has a good trigger pull," etc. Everyone had to see it and play with it and all came away liking it.

I was the first gun writer to get one of the 6-inch barrel guns. Up to then everyone had gotten the 2-inch barrel snubnose. That's fine for it's purpose but I wanted to get all the accuracy and hunting potential out of the .357 Magnum. I am one of a long line of hunters who condemn the use of the .22LR for game shooting because of the high number of wounded animals that escape to die a lingering death after being imperfectly hit with the diminutive .22LR. Like many older hunters, I say the .32-20 is the best small and medium game cartridge, but it's a bit hard to find today. Cost trumps humanity and sportsmanship for many folks so the .22 gets used and a lot of game dies a lingering death. However, the .357 Magnum can be considered a larger-bored .32-20 with a little more killing power – not enough for deer but a far more sure and humane killer of small and medium game than the lowly .22LR. No, the .357 won't spoil a lot of meat or be too powerful, and anyone with enough hunting ethics to want to kill their game cleanly without suffering will feel a lot better about using it than the .22LR.

The Rhino is produced by Chiappa Group in Azzano Mella in Northern Italy from all milled parts made on site. This is a very high-tech, modern facility dedicated to turning out a quality product. Its American subsidiary is Chiappa Firearms Ltd. This group is headed up by Ron Norton and their job is the development and marketing of Chiappa products in North America.

I test fired the Rhino extensively. I had 770 rounds of .38 Special and 500 rounds of .357 Magnum for a total of 1270 rounds. The breakdown was:

.38 Special

100 rounds Georgia Arms 148-grain wadcutter

100 rounds of CorBon 147-grain FMJ

150 rounds of Winchester 130-grain FMJ

100 rounds of BVAC 158-grain lead HP

100 rounds of Remington 158-grain lead RN

100 rounds of Federeal American Eagle 158-grain lead RN

120 rounds Winchester 130-grain JHP Bonded PDXI

150 rounds of NWCP 110-grain Manstopper

.357 Magnum

300 rounds Winchester 125-grain JHP

100 rounds Remington 125-grain JSP

100 rounds of North West Custom Projectile 110-grain Manstopper

I find the FMJ loads very useful. They offer increased penetration on bear or attackers in heavy clothing or behind cover. Sometimes more penetration is better, and not enough can get you killed.

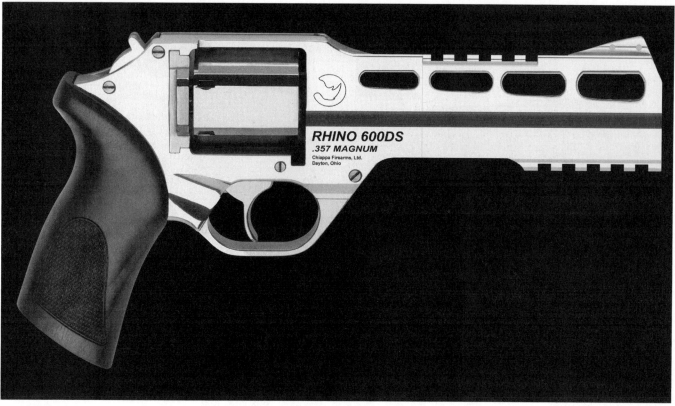

The Rhino stainless is quite an eyeful.

The military doesn't use FMJ ammo for nothing. If the advantages of FMJ over expanding bullets in combat weren't clear, no nation would have signed the treaties banning expanding bullets in combat. Creating a casualty behind cover is more important than stopping power in most military situations.

Anytime you fire a lot of .38 Special and .357 Magnum lead bullets you will have a lot of leading in the bore to clean out, and that is a feature that is no respecter of brand names. It is important to clean the residue at the front of the .357 cylinder out thoroughly if shooting .38 Specials as fouling can quickly build up on any revolver and interfere with chambering the longer .357 Magnum cartridges.

Firing the Rhino was a lot different from firing a conventional revolver. The grip rides much higher in the hand and what appears to be the hammer is a cocking lever that goes back down after the totally hidden internal hammer is cocked. A bright red cocking indicator pops up at the rear of the receiver to let you know it is cocked if the rearward

single action position of the trigger wasn't enough. The cylinder is opened by that strange looking lever on the upper rear left side. Once moved back, this lever permits the flat-sided hexagonal (for concealability) cylinder to swing out for loading or unloading. The rear sight is framed by two green dots and the front sight has a red dot. These are formed by plastic rods with exposed surfaces to catch the light in front of the sight blades, so you always have a bright group of dots even in poor light. Trigger pull was 4 pounds single action and 11 pounds double action as measured by the Lyman trigger pull gauge from Brownell's gunsmithing supplies. This is quite acceptable, although I would prefer both to be lighter.

The Rhino's barrel lies much lower than on other pistols and you can appreciate that and the short trigger travel on double action rapidfire. It is very fast and controllable. I just wish Bill Jordon was alive to see this because I think he would like it. Accuracy is all you need for hunting. At 25 yards I was shooting and hitting 1 1/2- and 2-inch chips easily

and centering a gratifying number of them with all ammo fired. I am not worried about missing any game fired at with this gun. I can think of a lot of rifles I would have less confidence in. The pistol points well for instinct shooting and is easy to hit with.

Aside from hunting, there are those who use the .357 Magnum revolver for police work. These users should try out the Rhino and see if its qualities make it the best choice for them. There is a lot of personal preference involved in choosing a revolver but many of those using the .357 Magnum revolver will be glad that they tried out the Rhino.

There are many factors one considers when selecting a revolver, some real and some imagined. The realities of the advantages the Rhino offers should more than offset its unconventional looks. Remember, the first revolvers looked pretty funny to everyone in 1836 but they sure did displace the single shot pistol.

The moral? Don't be afraid to try something new. You might like it.

TESTFIRE:

Cooper Firearms Model 54

BY **TOM TABOR**

ooper Firearms of Montana certainly isn't a large operation when compared to the many other firearms manufacturers, but they are large in the sense of the quality of rifles that they produce. Once known as Cooper Arms, the company underwent a name change a few years back, but for all practical purposes that involved only a change on the company's letterhead; the company has never deviated from the quality inherent in the Cooper line of products. From the onset the Cooper philosophy seems to have been a simple one: build rifles of superb quality and never compromise on accuracy.

Located in the beautiful Bitter-root Valley of western Montana this company has in the past specialized in producing bolt-action rifles chambered for small cartridges. The choices available included a wide variety of rimfire and centerfire designs in both production cartridges and a host of wildcat calibers. But early in 2010 that philosophy changed a bit when the company introduced their first-ever medium length, clip-fed, bolt-action rifle dedicated to the .243/.308 family of cartridges. Called the Model 54, this rifle has great potential for the sportsmen of the world.

The New Cooper Rifle

Currently the Model 54 is offered in .22-250 Remington, .243 Winchester, .250 Savage, 7mm-08 Remington, .308 Winchester and .260 Remington. In the future, however, more cartridge choices will likely be added, which will include both production cartridges of that same general length and quite possibly some wildcats.

In January 2010 the very first Cooper Firearms of Montana Model 54 was show-cased at the 2010 Las Vegas SHOT Show. This particular rifle was chambered in .308 Winchester and was built in the

The first Cooper Firearms of Montana Model 54 medium action repeater, built in the Custom Classic pattern, made its debut at the 2010 SHOT Show in Las Vegas.

company's Custom Classic design. It was stocked with an absolute gorgeous upgraded piece of French walnut, which combined natural beauty of the wood with a high degree of gunsmithing art. In a word, it was beautiful and as such it turned out to be a real showstopper. I believe that even Cooper's owner, Hugo Vivero, was a bit taken aback by the attention and favorable response that it achieved at the show. Since that first showing, orders have been rolling in and new dealers signed throughout the world.

The Model 54 is currently available in 11 different styles. Within those style variations there are designs that lend themselves more to the competitive shooting crowd and others that are more in line with the characteristics that hunters typically are looking for. The stocks within those variations are diverse, including several high-quality Carlo walnut choices; at least one laminated wood configuration; and even a couple of Bell & Carlson synthetics that are specially designed for the company. Some stocks possess checkering in a couple of different patterns and others have no checkering at all. Some stocks come with checkpieces, while others do not. Some Model 54s come standard with trigger guards machined from lightweight aluminum stock and others are fabricated from steel. There are also variations in the size and style of the barrels; there are a couple of different metal finishes available and other less crucial characteristics.

Some of the features that come standard on all of the Model 54 rifles

The three front locking bolt lug design used on the Model 54 has become a type of trademark for the Cooper rifles. The only exception to this basic bolt face design is found in the Cooper Model 57M, in which the three lugs are at the rear of the bolt.

are: a single-stack three-shot removable magazine (a fourth cartridge can be fed directly into the chamber), a fully adjustable single stage trigger of the Cooper design, plunger style ejectors machined from solid bar stock, Sako-style machined extractors, and a bolt designed with three front locking lugs. The barrels used by Cooper have been made for them for many years by the Connecticut-based Wilson Arms. Coincidentally, both Wilson Arms and Cooper Firearms of Montana now share the same owner, Hugo Vivero. Mr. Vivero purchased the Cooper plant early in 2009 from the founder, Dan Cooper, who

is now completely divorced from the operation and ownership.

In many cases a wide variety of options can be added on a custom basis to further enhance a Cooper rifle. This choice is not available on all Model 54 versions, but in many cases on a special order basis you can specifically tailor a rifle to precisely fit your individual likes and desires. The optical choices are far too many to outline here, but a few of the more popular options include case colored rings, checkered bolt handle, skeleton grip cap and/or butt plate, inlayed sling swivel studs, custom metal engraving and gold inlay work.

Testing of the Model 54

I had anticipated that the new Model 54 would add greatly to Cooper's admirable reputation and for that reason I was eager to get my hands on one of the first to come from the factory for testing. So, even before the first of these rifles had been completed, I made arrangements with the company officials to test one. But rather than having mine built in the SHOT Show model's Custom Classic design, I chose the Varminter pattern chambered for .22-250 Remington. Appropriately named, the Varminter is designed with varmint hunters in mind and comes with such features as a Claro AA walnut stock, broad varmint style forearm, hand-checkered grip, oil finish, Packmayr recoil pad and a premium match-grade barrel. Deviating a bit from the usual, my .22-250, which would normally possess a 1:14 twist barrel, came with a barrel with the faster twist rate of 1:9. Typically a faster twist barrel is expected to stabilize heavier weight bullets a little better. Outside of that change, the test rifle was essentially a typical Model 54 Varminter.

In typical fashion I began my evaluation on the range. In order to provide the most thorough assessment of the rifle's accuracy and functionality, I decided to expose the 54 to a combination of both factory-loaded ammunition as well as some of my own handloads. The factory rounds consisted of two different varieties of Federal Premium V-Shok ammo: one loaded with 55-grain Sierra BlitzKing bullets and the other with Speer's lead-free 43-grain TNT Green bullets. For my own loads I handloaded a fairly diverse selection of bullets including 52-grain Custom Competition HPBT, 55-grain Ballistic Tip, 69-grain Custom Competition HPBT and 77-grain Custom Competition HPBT. With this combination of bullet weights I felt it would provide a type of secondary evaluation on how versatile the 1:9 twist barrel would be. For powders I selected Hodgdon Varget, IMR 3031 and H4350. I have shot and owned many rifles chambered in .22-250 and IMR 3031 and Varget powders have always been good choices when loading the normal bullet weights of 50 to 55 grains. On the other hand, I felt a slower-burning powder would likely be more appropriate for the heavier bullets and

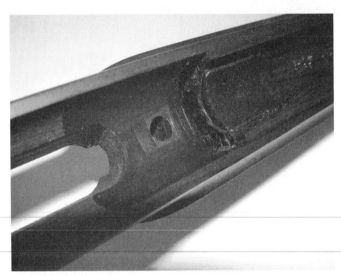

The action lug of the Model 54 came from the Cooper factory fiberglass bedded for improved accuracy.

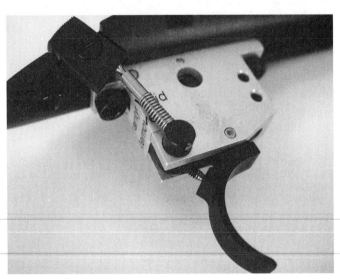

The trigger used on the Model 54 is the typical Cooper design that is fully adjustable, virtually creep-free and very crisp at the letoff.

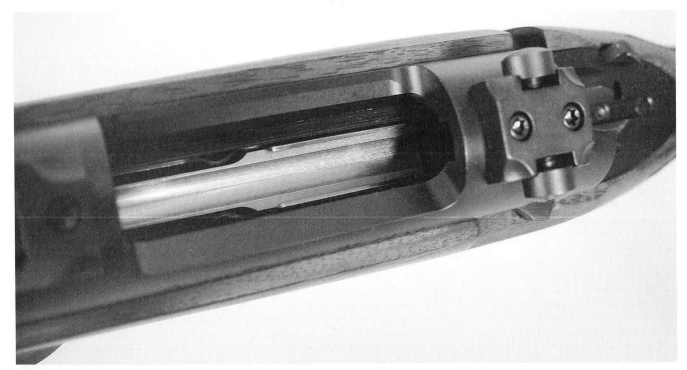

The removable magazine of the Model 54 holds three rounds and is designed as a single-stack feed.

The barrel was free-floated in order to increase the rifle accuracy potential.

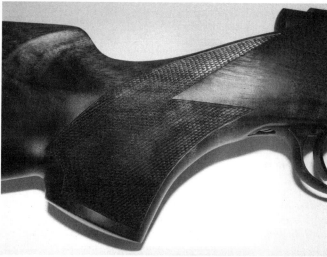

The Cooper rifles are checkered in-house by a staff of highly trained artisans.

in particular the 77-grain. So I selected H4350 for use with the heavier bullet.

Proper barrel break-in is always important with any rifle and even though the test rifle would likely be going back to the factory after my work was completed, I felt it only appropriate to treat it as I would one of my own firearms. So before getting down to the serious evaluation work I followed my normal slow and deliberate barrel conditioning process. Very soon I began to realize

that there seemed to be something special about this rifle. Virtually all of the ammunition shot amazingly well. As I would expect, the carefully crafted handloads seemed to be slightly more accurate than the factory rounds, but those differences were very minute. And also as I had anticipated, the heavier weight bullets seemed to produce slightly tighter groups than did the lighter weight bullets. There were only a few instances when the commonly

recognized standard three-shot/1-inch groups were exceeded and in all cases the average shot groups were well under that performance level.

Overall, I doubt that many shooters would ever find much to complain about with any of the groups I shot and certainly not when it came to this rifle's load versatility. The best three-shot group produced by the Federal ammo loaded with the 43-grain TNT Green bullets measured a mere 3/16 inch, with an

Cooper Firearms of Montana Model 54: 100-yard Accuracy Testing

Federal Premium® Factory V-Shok™ Ammunition

Bullet	Best 3-Shot Group	Worst 3-Shot Group	Average 3-Shot Group
43-grain Speer® TNT Green®	3/16"	1-1/8"	11/16"
55-grain Sierra BlitzKing®	3/8"	1-3/4"	13/16"

Handloads: Varget Powder & Nosler Ballistic Tip 55-grain Bullets

Bullet	Powder	Powder Charge (Gr.)	Best 3-Shot Grp (in.)	Worst 3-Shot Grp (in.)	Avg 3-Shot Grp (in.)
Nosler BT 55-gr.	Varget	33.0	5/8	15/16	3/4
Nosler BT 55-gr.	Varget	34.0	9/16	1-3/16	13/16
Nosler BT 55-gr.	Varget	35.0	1/2	7/8	5/8
Nosler BT 55-gr.	3031	33.0	1/2	1-1/16	3/4
Nosler BT 55-gr.	3031	34.0	1/4	1-1/8	5/8
Nosler BT 55-gr.	3031	35.0	5/16	1-3/8	13/16
Nosler CC 52-gr.	Varget	30.5	9/16	1	3/4
Nosler CC 52-gr.	Varget	31.5	5/16	13/16	11/16
Nosler CC 52-gr.	Varget	32.5	7/16	7/8	11/16
Nosler CC 69-gr.	Varget	30.5	7/16	3/4	9/16
Nosler CC 77-gr.	H4350	35.0	1/4	3/4	1/2

Note: This load data is presented merely as an illustration. It is not intended for use. Neiter the author nor Gun Digest Books assumes any liability or responsibility for such use. Is that clear? For load data, consult the guides published by the component manufacturers and NEVER exceed recommended loads.

average group size of 11/16 inch. And for the Federal ammo loaded with 55-grain Sierra BlitzKing bullets, the best group came in at 3/8 inch with an overall group average of 13/16 inch.

When it came to the handloaded ammunition I was pleased to find that the rifle didn't seem to be too fussy about the powder charge weight. As is always the case, there was some variation between the group sizes when compared to the different charge weights, but overall the groups were very consistent. The best three-shot group loaded with the Nosler 69-grain bullets came in at 7/16 inch and had an overall average group size of 9/16 inch. The Nosler 77-grain bullets produced even better results at a mere 1/4 inch best group and an average of only half an inch. On an overall basis, the lighter-weight bullets didn't fare quite as well, but they certainly weren't bad by anyone's standards.

The best group produced by the 52-grain Nosler Custom Competition bullets and backed by Varget powder generated a 5/16 inch group with an average group size of 11/16 inch. When the 55-grain Nosler Ballistic Tip bullets were backed by the IMR 3031 powder, they produced a best group of only 1/4 inch and an average of 5/8 inch. When those same Ballistic Tips were loaded with Varget powder, the best group came in at 1/2 inch with an average of 5/8 inch.

The Model 54 in the Field

Even though thorough range testing is an important component to most firearm evaluations I personally believe that for a rifle like a Cooper Varminter Model 54 any assessment wouldn't be complete without burning some powder under field conditions. So, after poking a consider amount of holes in paper with the Cooper, I embarked on a three-state tour in an effort to poke holes in some pesky nuisance critters. This involved both sage rats (aka ground squirrels) and a new crop of whistle pigs (known to some as marmots). Unlike the range work, which produces easily comparable results to make judgments and assessments on, any opinions produced in the field are a bit more subjective, but I don't feel they are any less important. I have had rifles that looked great on paper and performed extremely well on the range only to produce disappointing results when I left that sterile environment and took them to the field. In some of these cases I simply was unable to explain the differences in performance. Maybe it is simply a matter of my own mind playing tricks on me, but even then, loss of confidence in a rifle is nothing that should be ignored. In most of these cases those rifles producing what I viewed as disappointments in the field are now under new ownership.

For my fieldwork I decided to restrict the ammo to the same two types of Federal Premium factory rounds that I used on the range. Both of these loads shot to generally the same spot of paper at 100 yards, which made it possible for me to switch back and forth as I saw fit. When it came to the ground squirrels, the shots varied from as close as 30 yards out to well beyond 300 yards. And because of the typically cautious nature of the marmots, I seldom got the opportunity for a shot closer than 100 yards and was frequently challenged by shots out beyond the 400-yard mark. In all cases I found the accuracy of the Model 54 to be superb. The limiting factor, as is frequently the case, was my own somewhat aging abilities. The rifle simply performed and functioned flawlessly.

Overall Evaluation and Conclusion

I believe a major factor to be considered in favor of the Cooper Model 54 is the consistency of its performance. Even with the fast twist rate barrel it seemed to stabilize all of the bullets and loads very well. With the bullets varying from the featherweight, environmentally-friendly, Federal factory-loaded 43-grain Speer TNT to the heavyweight handloaded 77-grain Nosler Custom Competition HPBT - they all produced what I view as very consistent and accu-

After the initial range testing work had been completed, the author took the Model 54 to the field for some ground squirrel shooting.

Ground squirrels pose tremendous problems for farmers and ranchers in the west. They eat huge amounts of crops and choke out much more with the dirt from their dens. The Cooper Model 54 did an excellent job alleviating some of those problems.

A fresh crop of marmots shot at long range using the Federal factory-loaded Premium ammunition put the Model 54 through its paces.

rate performance. The selected powders shot and functioned well and the rifle didn't seem to be sensitive to powder charge weight.

Sometimes I have a tendency to lose track of how many rounds of ammunition I actually fire, particularly when part of that shooting involves trying to reduce the population of nuisance varmints in an area. So, unfortunately, I am unable to provide an exact assessment of how many bullets I sent hurtling down the barrel of the Cooper Model 54. It should, however, be noted that this wasn't the usual writer testing project that sometimes is limited to a couple of boxes of ammo. By the time I was wrapping up my evaluation I found that I was well into my third case of the Federal factory loads and that didn't include all of my own handloaded ammunition. Because a case of centerfire ammo is composed of 10 boxes of 20 rounds each, I would venture to say that my total spent ammo would fall somewhere around 750 to 800 rounds. After that vast amount of bullets sent down the barrel of the Cooper Model 54 I can truthfully report that even under the less than favorable conditions found in the field, the rifle performed exceptionally well. The car-

tridges fed smoothly from the magazine perfectly every time; the magazine fed easily into the rifle, snapping sharply in place, its removal being equally effortless; the trigger pull was without creep or excessive travel; and the metal to wood inlaying was picture perfect. I simply couldn't have been more pleased with the overall performance and quality of this rifle.

The Model 54 is a very fine addition to the Cooper Firearms of Montana's line of quality rifles. It further expands the company's ability to provide what the sportsmen of the world are looking for and moves them into one more aspect of shooting. This new model would be the perfect choice for the east coast whitetail hunter, the westerner looking to harvest a big mule deer, or for the plainsman hunter looking to bag a big pronghorn, as well as the varmint hunter or the competitive shooter.

In the future you should keep your eye on Cooper Firearms of Montana for more innovative new rifle designs. The Model 54 opens the door to the possibility of further additions. No longer are they limiting their production to only small cartridges, but by no means will these little ones be going away.

Resources

Cooper Firearms of Montana
P.O. Box 114
Stevensville, Montana 59870
Telephone: (406) 777-3073
Fax: (406) 777-5228
Email: info@CooperFirearms.com
Website: www.cooperfirearms.com

Federal Cartridge Company
900 Ehlen Drive
Anoka, MN 55303-7503
Telephone: 1-800-322-2342
Fax: (763) 323-2506
Website: http://www.federalpremium.com

Nosler, Inc.
107 SW Columbia Street
Bend, OR 97702
800-285-3701
Telephone: (541) 382-3921
Fax: 541-388-4667
http://www.nosler.com

TESTFIRE:
SPACE GUN!
The New High Standard Olympic Trophy

BY **KEN WALTERS**

Buried in the 2011 *Gun Digest* was a brief mention of the reintroduction of the High Standard Olympic Trophy semi-automatic .22 target pistol, the so-called "space gun." Reintroduced by the reconstituted High Standard Manufacturing Company of Houston, Texas, the futuristic-looking Olympic Trophy earned its "Space Gun" nickname because of its resemblance to something Buck Rogers or Flash Gordon would carry. When I first became interested in firearms I was fascinated by 22-caliber target pistols. No idea why, but I just loved them. I only had the money to buy one, a Smith & Wesson Model 41. It cost an absolute fortune: $90. I still remember feeling extremely guilty about spending such a massive sum on a gun. As Erma Bombeck said, "Guilt is a gift that keeps on giving."

Most of my writing projects are based on experiments. The first really big experiment I did in 1973 for a gun article was on the accuracy of .22 target pistols. I borrowed the guns from friends, all of whom were very generous. As a result, I got a lot of toys to play with, at least for a little while. When the article was finally finished I was REALLY proud of it! It was printed eight years after I wrote it in the 1981 *Gun Digest*. Nobody noticed it, of course, but I loved it. *[Oh, we noticed it. –DMS]*

The author's exhaustive study of .22 target pistol accuracy as it appeared in the 1981 *Gun Digest*.

I keep extensive notes. Decades ago everything was written down in great detail in my notebooks and each notebook page was signed and dated. So recently when I wanted to see what I thought of the High Standard Citation – essentially a less expensive version of the Olympic Trophy and one of the guns I had tested back in 1973 – I just got out the appropriate notebook.

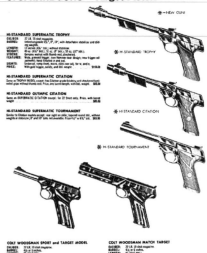

The 1959 *Gun Digest* introduced the original Space Gun, known then as the Supermatic Trophy. The Supermatic Citation below it was a less expensive version.

The research for my article "Accuracy in 22 Target Pistols" in the 1981 *Gun Digest* consumed 250 notebook pages full of calculations. I haven't seen that much algebra in decades. I didn't even remember that I used to be able to do calculations like that. But in the era before Microsoft Excel, if you wanted to compute something you used algebra and a calculator. I've got hundreds of

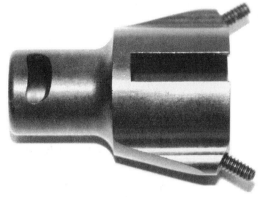

Long and short barrel weights: funky but not particularly effective.

High Standard has always called the Space Gun's muzzle brake a "stabilizer."

pages of calculations all of which were, and had to be, double-checked. To analyze a single target back then took hours. Now my computer does all that in just a couple seconds and I don't have to go back and do everything twice just to make sure I got it right. I had forgotten that in the pre-computer days all those laborious calculations had to be double-checked. (My old article, incidentally, is still available. Gun Digest has digitized all their old editions which you can buy as a three-DVD set from www.gundigest-store.com. Money well spent.)

Nostalgia? I'm beginning to realize how glad I am that it isn't 1970 anymore! I'm glad that I'm not using a slide rule or a calculator to analyze gun results. I'm glad that my work now is in Microsoft Excel spreadsheets and in Microsoft Word documents stored on a flash drive rather than hundreds of pages of notebooks. I also don't miss carbon paper, graph paper or typewriters. And I'm even glad I'm not 30 again because if I were I'd have another 24 years before retirement. And finally I'm glad that today, right at this very moment, a truly beautiful High Standard Olympic Trophy is sitting on my 1970-vintage desk.

Judging from that old *Gun Digest* article, target pistols in the 1970s were very different. For one thing they were made of metal, not plastic. Also they had barrel weights and muzzle brakes. Muzzle brakes still exist, kind of, though now we do not call them that anymore. But barrel weights? As far as I know the only barrel weights still being made are those High Standard is putting on their vintage reproduction semi-automatic 22 target pistols. I wonder if most readers will even know what a barrel weight is? Do a web search on Hammerli-Walther 22 target pistols and you'll see just how complicated these things got.

My High Standard Olympic Trophy has a very thin 10-inch barrel. Other barrel lengths are available and barrels can be changed out easily. Also it has a muzzle brake. And it can use barrel weights. There is a long groove on each side of the barrel and indents on the bottom of the barrel which are used to hold the barrel weights in place. The barrel weights used on this gun are really odd even by 1970 standards. Alas, my new sample gun didn't come with these odd little barrel weights because High Standard has to make new tooling for the slide plates.

My old notes, however, tell how to attach these weights and contain a clue as to why they faded from the scene. These weights came in two sizes, long and short. No idea why there were two sizes, except maybe as a matter of individual preference. The top of each weight is contoured to match the underside of the barrel. Then, for each weight, there are two side plates. The top edge of each side plate goes into one of the grooves in the side of the barrel. The bottom edge of each side plate goes into a groove in the bottom edge of the weight. A setscrew in the bottom of the weight is then tightened up. That is why there are indents in the bottom of the barrel. The end of the setscrew goes into one of those indents.

Sound confusing? Try putting them on the gun. The first time you do that will be interesting.

But it gets worse. According to my old notes, you cannot take these weights off and reattach them exactly as they were. And chances are that if they are attached just a bit differently, accuracy will be affected. If my old notes are to be believed, your group size will not change much but your point of impact might. Still wondering why barrel weights have

disappeared? I wish that my new High Standard Olympic Trophy had come with the weights. Then again, maybe I don't.

Truth to tell, these barrel weights are just silly. A lot of effort went into making them and making the gun capable of using them but, well, the design is just nuts. Clever, cute, silly and nuts. And I love them. I wouldn't buy an Olympic Trophy without them. Why? Because this is the essence of what a High Standard Olympic Trophy pistol is all about.

The High Standard barrel weights, incidentally, were really odd even back when barrel weights were commonplace in expensive target pistols. Back in my 1981 *Gun Digest* article I studied barrel weights in great detail and found that barrel weights that increase barrel rigidity improve accuracy. Barrel weights that did not increase barrel rigidity decrease accuracy. The High Standard barrel weights do not increase barrel rigidity.

Though I didn't remember it, there was another important point in that 1981 article: 1970-vintage .22 target pistols came with two very different barrel styles, flexible and rigid. Well, at least so I thought. I made up those definitions based on the experiments I did. The barrel on the Olympic Trophy is a flexible barrel. The barrel on a S&W Model 41 is a rigid barrel. The rigid barrels are clearly more accurate. There are graphs in that 1981 article showing just how much more accurate a rigid barrel is. I predicted way back then that, because flexible barrel target pistols were less accurate than rigid barrel target pistols, the flexible barrel guns would disappear. They have, at least until High Standard reintroduced the Space Gun.

There is another prediction in that 1981 article that I had forgotten: an explanation of how to alter the High Standard's barrel so as to greatly im-

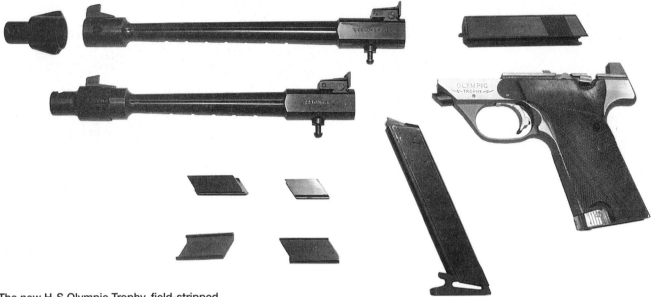

The new H-S Olympic Trophy, field-stripped.

prove its accuracy. There is even a graph showing how much more accurate that modified gun would be.

And there is still more. In my notebooks there is a reference to a phone call from John Amber, the *Gun Digest* editor at the time. He said that he had called High Standard and suggested that they modify a 10-inch barrel to match my suggestion and see if I was right. Never happened. But the gun I was describing is in the current High Standard catalog. Well, not exactly, but close. It is the 10-inch Supermatic Citation. They didn't make that gun because of my old article because I'm sure they didn't know that that article existed. But they eventually came to the same conclusion I did. Interesting.

So is the new Olympic Trophy a highly accurate target pistol? Yes! I've shot it and I've tested it and the answer is yes!

My current shooting studies, incidentally, are almost a match to my 1973 work. According to my old notebooks way back then, I was rushing to finish up. It was late December. The weather was horrible. I didn't go shooting on Christmas day but I went before and after, only stopping when the weather got so horrible it was just impossible to continue. December of 2010 was the same scenario. The first trip to the range was on a beautiful day. Got 10 studies done. Shot 10 20-round targets.

The second day was horrible, really windy. Went anyway. Shot another 10 targets but the results were very disappointing because of the wind. Ever

since, it has been snowing hard. Highly unlikely I'll get to shoot this gun again. But of the 20 targets I got, seven showed exceptional accuracy – truly exceptional accuracy. That's not a statistical fluke. One target could be, but not seven. This gun is capable of exceptional accuracy.

I'm working on an article about how practice affects marksmanship. Been at it for 12 years now. I've fired right at 220,000 rounds (220,002 rounds actually) from almost 90 guns. I've spent over a decade making up Microsoft Excel spreadsheets and graphs of all this data. So if I want to study the accuracy of a pistol I can easily compare a gun's performance to dozens of other guns in my database.

Why does that matter? Because when I tested this new Olympic Trophy I saw something very interesting in its accuracy graph. The plot of its accuracy showed it to be at least as accurate as any handgun I've ever tested.

In all the dozens if not hundreds of graphs that I've developed over the decades showing firearm accuracy one point has stood out that I could never explain. There is an upper limit to the accuracy I can achieve. Not all firearms hit that upper limit. Some don't even come close. But there is an upper limit on accuracy that I cannot cross. And it is the same limit, the same score on a target, across a wide range of handguns. Why would there be such a limit? I never figured that out until now.

Why, you ask, was the Olympic Trophy instrumental in figuring this out?

Because my 1981 article clearly proved that this *is not* the most accurate .22 out there. But my 2010 shooting studied showed that it was as accurate as any gun I've tested. Can both of these observations be true? Yes.

This is really important. What I didn't realize until now is that what ultimately limits accuracy is the shooter. Given a decent gun and adequate ammunition, it is the shooter that limits the upper level of accuracy. It is *not* the gun, *not* the ammunition. It is the shooter. An obvious idea when you finally think of it, if you ever do.

Why did I figure that out here? Because my 1970 vintage tests were done using a Ransom machine rest while my 2010 test were based on off-hand shooting. The Ransom rest does not have a shooter-induced accuracy limit. The Ransom rest is, obviously, capable of far greater accuracy than just off-hand shooting. Far greater. I can, incidentally, compare these two sets of results, those done just a couple of days ago and those done in December of 1973, because of all of those old notebooks. In them are exact mathematical representations of all those decades-old targets. That means that I can re-score them. It is as though they were shot yesterday.

So how can the Olympic Trophy fail to be the most accurate target .22 out there and still yield essentially unbeatable accuracy? *Because even if I had a better gun or better ammunition I would not be physically capable of doing better.* This gun and the inexpensive Federal ammunition

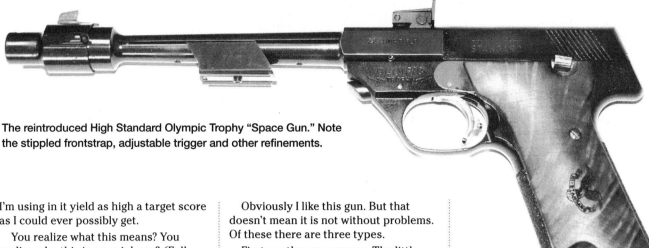

The reintroduced High Standard Olympic Trophy "Space Gun." Note the stippled frontstrap, adjustable trigger and other refinements.

I'm using in it yield as high a target score as I could ever possibly get.

You realize what this means? You realize why this is an epiphany? (Full disclosure: I had to look up "epiphany" in the dictionary to make sure it means what I thought it did. It does.) Among other things, it means that there is no reason to buy really expensive target ammunition. Go to Walmart and buy Federal Value Packs. That's good enough. Pay more and you are just throwing your money away. And it means that you really don't have to buy the very best .22 target pistol out there. Something far less expensive will probably work just fine. No caveats here? There's one. If you are truly a really great shot, then the best possible gun and the best possible ammunition might be worth buying. But for the rest of us, at least for me, those things would just be a waste of money.

So would an inexpensive, plastic S&W Model 22A shoot off-hand as well as the much more expensive S&W Model 41? It just might. The Model 41 is almost certainly the more accurate gun but given the accuracy limitations inherent in most shooters, that difference might not show up.

Wouldn't it be fun to test that theory and see if it was true? It would really be interesting to repeat all those 1970 vintage tests but this time using modern firearms and offhand shooting. I'm going to have to seriously think about doing that!

So the bottom line here is that this High Standard Olympic Trophy with its 10-inch barrel is as accurate as a .22 target pistol gets unless you're are a really exceptional shot. If you are a serious target shooter, skip the counterweights and muzzle brake. If you're not, then use them both because they are just too cute to resist.

Obviously I like this gun. But that doesn't mean it is not without problems. Of these there are three types.

First are the annoyances. The little knob on the side of the magazines used to keep the follower down during loading is a pain. It is just really hard to hold down particularly when the magazine is almost full. But there is a simple solution to this. I went out in the garage and looked for something that had a hole of about the right size that I could use to hold that little devil down. Found a bottlebrush. Worked just fine.

And then there is the problem of getting the magazine out of the gun. In theory you pull out that little plate at the bottom front of the grip. That moves a little plunger that is holding the magazine in place. That is why the bottom of the magazine is so oddly shaped. When you pull that little plate out the magazine should fall out. It is not spring-loaded. Gravity should do the work. But it doesn't always. You can push down on the top of the magazine without damaging the magazine lips, High Standard tells me, but that is only true because those lips on their magazines are heat-treated. Buy someone else's magazines for this gun and all bets are off. Still, I don't like pushing on a magazine's lips. I'd prefer a little boss on the bottom of the magazines so you could just pull the little sucker out.

Second there are some problems that High Standard took pains to point out, to their credit. Though I didn't experience any of these, High Standard indicated that for the gun to work properly it has to be very carefully cleaned and cleaned often. There is a small recess in the bolt face through which the firing pin passes. If that gets clogged with dirt the gun will not fire. A toothpick can clean this out

quickly. And you want to keep the bolt face and back end of the barrel clean or the slide might not close all the way. I saw no sign of these problems but High Standard clearly believes that methodical, frequent cleaning is a must.

Finally there is one problem I did encounter. There were some misfires. Didn't happen often but it did happen. When I examined the cartridge cases I could see why. The firing pin strike was very narrow and light. Not enough of a blow to set the cartridge off. High Standard believes that this problem is due in part to the fact that I'm using inexpensive, relatively dirty ammunition. They also believe that it will go away after the first 500 rounds or so. Certainly could be true. The problem did decrease the more I shot the pistol. Still, I'd really like for the firing pin to be a lot wider and for it to hit with a great deal more force.

As of this writing, the Olympic Trophy Space Gun has an MSRP of $1095 with 6-3/4-, 8- or 10-inch barrel. In comparison, the Ruger Mark III Competition Rimfire Pistol has an MSRP of $625. Still, the Space Gun has an undeniable retro charm, and I wouldn't criticize anyone who thought it was well worth its price tag.

Should you buy this gun? Sure – but be sure to get those silly little barrel weights and that really odd muzzle brake. Both will undoubtedly decrease accuracy but unless you are a champion pistol shot, who cares?

TESTFIRE:
Leupold FX-II
2.5 X 28mm IER Scout Extended Eye-Relief Riflescope

BY TOM TABOR

If you have ever had the rim of your riflescope slam into your face, you will likely appreciate one of the benefits associated with an extended eye-relief scope. I know such a thing is human-caused, but nevertheless it does happen and when it does, personal injury is sure to result.

Probably the most common scenario for this to occur is when a shot is being attempted high overhead from the prone position. In this case the shooter struggles to get low enough in relationship to

the rifle to make the shot. As the trigger is squeezed, the recoil of the rifle causes the rifle butt to slip off the shoulder and under the shooter's armpit, driving the scope directly into the shooter's face.

I have to admit to making this error on a couple of occasions and I can attest to the fact that it really doesn't feel all that good when it happens to you. On one such occasion I was hunting deer with my 12-year old daughter in tow. I was shooting a .300 Winchester Magnum rifle with ammo that was loaded to the

hilt when the butt slipped free from my shoulder, driving the scope back into the bridge of my nose. As is often the case with a head wound, the blood started to gush and soon the snow around me looked as if a massacre had occurred on that very same spot. That occurred a couple of decades ago, but the resulting stigma on my daughter lingers on to this day. Fearing that a similar thing could happen to her, she is still fearful of shooting any rifle more powerful than a .22.

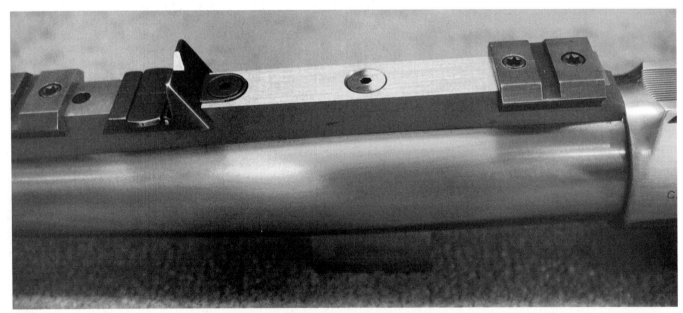

The completed extended eye-relief scope mounting system as fabricated by my gunsmith, Dan Coffin, prior to being blued and going to the engraver. It began with a Dakota Arms quarter rib.

The finished scope mounting system included an N.E.C.G. Classic safari styled folding leaf sight that was mounted between the two Leupold QRW scope bases.

Whether you call this problem scope-bite, Weatherby eye, or any of a number of other terms inappropriate in mixed company, the effects are the same. One way to eliminate the possibility of such an accident occurring involves moving the scope out on the rifle barrel, but to do so it requires the use of a longer than normal eye-relief scope. Some refer to this type of mounting system as a "scout mount." I suppose this method has its roots back in the early days of scopes and Winchester lever action rifles. Because rifles like the Model 1894, as well as a variety of other lever actions, commonly eject out the top of the action, the use of a traditional mounted scope was prohibited, at least until the Angle Eject models were introduced. With an older Winchester lever (except the Model 88), as well as many sporterized military bolt actions and a few commercial models, your choices were to simply be satisfied with using the iron sights, mount your scope along the side of the action, or use an extended eye-relief scope by mounting it in front of the action.

Most traditionally-styled riflescopes come with an optimum eye-relief of somewhere around three inches. In some cases this can be stretched out to around four or even five inches but seldom much farther than that. So if you intend to mount a scope in front of the rifle action it will be necessary for you to use either a riflescope specifically designed as an extended eye-relief model. In some cases you might be able to use a handgun scope. Many scope manufacturers offer these models, but your selection will be considerably limited when compared to the traditional eye-relief models.

A person whom I greatly respect, Carl Laburschagne, now a retired South African professional hunter, first introduced me to the benefits associated with extended eye-relief mounts. Carl and I have been friends for many years and I look at him as being an expert in areas like this. He has guided and hunted throughout southern Africa for virtually every type of game that the continent has to offer and that includes the dangerous Big Five. As such, he is a devout believer that if you shoot a scoped rifle for dangerous game, the scope should be mounted out on the barrel for a host of reasons, including eliminating the possibility of getting punched in the nose with it. Eventually I put his recommendation to use and built a pair of rifles, each with an extended eye-relief scope.

Selecting a Scope

One thing to keep in mind when selecting and mounting any scope is the fact that the lower the magnification, generally the more flexibility you will have when it comes to eye-relief. In other words, a low-powered scope with possibly only 2X magnification will usually be much more tolerant and forgiving when it comes to how far your eye can be from the scope than, say, a 20X scope. All rifles are built a little different and when you start to deviate from a standard scope mount, you can expect to encounter variations in where you can mount the scope. For this reason it is to your advantage to have a little built-in flexibility when it comes to eye-relief distance.

Shooting with both eyes open comes naturally with the Leupold extended eye-relief scope.

Even with the low-magnification 2.5X scope the author's custom-built .500 Jeffery Rimless produced some excellent three-shot groups at 100-yards.

The best way to demonstrate how this flexibility is helpful can be seen in my own rifles. I mounted Leupold FX-II 2.5x28mm IER-Scout scopes on both of the rifles I built. This particular low-magnification scope was designed to have an optimum eye-relief of 9.3 inches, but the design of the rifle prevented me from mounting it that close. Using the mounting system that my gunsmith, Dan Coffin, and I developed, I could not get the scope any closer than 11.5 inches, but the amount of eye-relief variation built into this scope allowed me that extra two-plus inches that I needed, something probably not possible with a higher-magnification scope.

Another Advantage of Extended Eye-Relief

Aside from never having to worry about scope-bite, there are other important advantages inherent in the use of an extended eye-relief scope mounting. One of the things to consider is the increased speed it allows you to get on your target. There are advantages associated with shooting with both eyes open with any scope, but the ability to do so seems to come much more naturally with an extended eye-relief mounting.

Closing your non-shooting eye only reduces your depth perception and narrows your field of view. For quick, close-

quarters shooting it is imperative that the target is acquired quickly. In some cases the speed at which the shooter is able to get on target and squeeze off the shot can mean the difference between a trophy or simply a story to be told around the campfire. In my mind, shooting with both eyes wide open, using a rifle with a low or moderate powered scope that has been mounted out on the barrel, is the best possible scenario for success in this type of situation. And when it comes to encounters at close quarters with dangerous game, the stakes are usually much higher. In this case being able to get on the game and pull off a fatal shot can mean the difference between life and death for the hunter.

How Do You Get There?

If an extended eye-relief scope could be beneficial for your particular type of shooting, you are probably wondering how to go about achieving that objective. Unfortunately, there will be some fairly significant hurdles that must be overcome. In most cases you won't be able to simply jump in your car, head down to your local sporting goods store, and purchase everything you need to do the job. Because rifles and barrel contours are not universal and mounting an extended eye-relief scope isn't what I would call mainstream gunwork, it is likely that you will have to utilize the services of a qualified gunsmith to fabricate, or modify, a mounting system for your rifle.

For the two custom rifles I had built, I started by purchasing a Dakota Arms

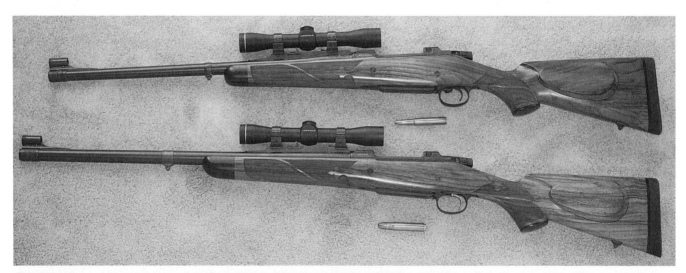

Tom Tabor's two extended eye-relief rifles consist of (top to bottom) .416 Rigby and .500 Jeffrey Rimless. Both rifles were built on CZ 550 actions and were close to identical except for size and weight.

In the Australian outback, the extended eye-relief scope on the .500 Jeffrey provided quick target acquisition.

This was just one of the many Asian buffalo that fell to Tom's extended eye-relief scope mounted .500 Jeffrey during the Australian culling operation.

quarter rib blank and had it fitted to the rifle barrel, then machined to accept the type of scope rings that I wanted to use. Dakota quarter rib blanks can be purchased through the mail-order house of Brownells. Brownells carries ribs that are contoured to match Douglas or Shilen barrels, but in my case it became necessary to custom fit the ribs. Another approach is to start with a set of Leupold gunmaker bases. These are specifically designed for custom firearms work and come equipped to handle the traditional style of scope rings. The bases are considerably oversized with plenty of metal for manipulating into whatever shape is necessary to fit the situation.

My Own Extended Eye-Relief Custom Rifles

I had always dreamed of building a custom big-bore rifle and after years of trying to decide on the perfect cartridge I finally settled on the historical .500 Jeffrey Rimless. Once that decision was out of the way, Dan and I turned our attention to designing the scope base system. For a dangerous game rifle like the .500 I didn't want to be tied solely to the use of a scope, so I purchased a N.E.C.G. Classic Express Sight from Brownells and soon it was dovetailed into the center of the quarter rib. But in order to use the express sights it became necessary to install a set of quick release style scope bases. I have had exceptionally good luck in the past with Leupold's QRW rings and have always found that my bullet point of impact never changes even after repeated removals and remounts of the scope. So that choice was an easy decision to make. The QRW bases took a little modifying in order to get them to fit properly on the quarter rib, but soon they were positioned with the express sight in the center.

By mounting the express sights on the quarter rib, it made the distance between the front and rear sights only 18.5 inches on the Jeffrey and because of the shorter barrel of my second rifle, this span was shortened even further to 16.5 inches. That is not a bad thing. It is the belief of many shooters that a shortened sighting plane actually enables a shooter to get on target more quickly. But no matter where the iron sights are placed on the rifle, an important consideration to be made whenever dual sights are used is the height of the stock comb. In this case it doesn't really matter whether you are modifying a pre-built rifle, or building a custom rifle; you need to make sure that once the rifle is finished that you will be satisfied with how your eye aligns with the sights.

In my case there would be a variation of about 5/8 inch between the center of the scope and the V notch of the express sight and I had to decide which sighting plane would take priority. Did I want my eye perfectly aligned to the iron sights, or the scope, when the rifle was brought up to my shoulder? I decided to give priority to the iron sights, thinking that when I would be using the open sights that it might be under very close quarters and tight time restraints. When using the scope I thought I might have a little more time to precisely align it. I know, no matter what type of sight you are using, they're supposed to be perfectly aligned with the shooter's eye, but in a case like this one you simply can't have it both ways.

At the onset of building the .500 Jeffrey I didn't envision constructing a second rifle having an extended eye-relief scope. I'd always dreamed of building a custom big bore primarily for hunting Cape buffalo, but once I had worked all the kinks out of the design and had the finished rifle in hand I simply couldn't resist building yet another one. This time it would be chambered in a little smaller caliber, but it would still be classed in most circles as a dangerous game rifle. The .416 Rigby seemed to fit perfectly with my wishes. The rifles were built as a matching set and were very close to identical, but the .416 was scaled back a few pounds from the heavy 12.5 pounds of the .500 and rather

Tom's .416 Rigby took this excellent bull elk at a phenomenal 320 yards, helping to demonstrate how a low-power extended eye-relief mounted scope isn't limited to short-range shooting.

Getting used to shooting a rifle with an extended eye-relief scope comes quite naturally, and when the shooter keeps both eyes open it provides both depth of field and a phenomenal wide view.

Leupold gunmaker bases could be the perfect answer to fabricating a custom set of scope bases for an extended eye-relief scope mounting system.

than having a Cape buffalo engraved in the floorplate as the .500 had, the .416 was more appropriately engraved with the head of a lion.

In the Field with the Extended Eye-Relief Rifles

After building my .500 Jeffrey I had intentions of heading to Africa on safari for Cape buffalo. Well, that hasn't yet materialized, but I did manage a trip to Australia where I went after the Cape's cousin, the Asian water buffalo. My Northern Territory outback safari involved hunting two different areas, one for trophy buffs where I took two fine bulls then I was off to help out a game ranger on a buffalo culling operation in the Aborigine Territory. The Jeffrey worked splendidly well and resulted in something around a dozen buffalo succumbing to its charms.

I was amazed by how natural the 2.5X extended eye-relief scope performed. The rifle and scope came up naturally; I shot with both eyes open; and I could pick up my targets amazingly quickly and I was easily able to stay on the buffalo as they weaved their way through the bush. The .416 Rigby hasn't seen quite so much action yet, but this past hunting season in Montana a really great six-point bull elk fell to its report at a whopping 320 yards. This was considerably longer-range shooting than you would normally expect with the big 400-grain .416 Barnes Triple Shock bullet and a 2.5x scope, but the rifle and the scope pulled it off just fine. The extended positioning of the scope didn't hinder the long shot in any way and actually helped me in the placement of my shot as the bull wandered in and out of the 90 or so animals of the herd.

Have I had any regrets to the extended eye-relief mountings? I would answer that question with a resounding "Nope!" For potential dangerous game hunting I don't think there is any better way to go. And, for other types of shooting and hunting where it sometimes involves close quarters action, my answer would be the same. I don't think you could go wrong with a scope mounting like this.

I continue to feel sorry for those hunters shooting extremely heavy-recoiling rifles with their scopes mounted a mere three inches from their face. A rifle like my .500 Jeffrey that sends a huge 570-grain bullet out the muzzle at nearly 2,400 fps would surely do a lot of damage to the face of a shooter if the scope should fly back and make contact. In this instance, the ole cliché that a rifle kills on both ends would certainly apply to a situation like that.

Even when I was faced with the long 320-yard shot on the bull elk, shooting the extended eye-relief scope worked out just fine. So if you believe an extended eye-relief scope mounting would hold some advantage to your particular type of shooting and hunting, my recommendation is, "Go for it!"

Resources

Leupold & Stevens, Inc.
P.O. Box 688
Beaverton, OR 97075-0688
Telephone: 1-800-LEUPOLD or 1-503-646-9171
Website: www.leupold.com

Brownells, Inc.
200 S. Front St.
Montezuma, IA 50171-9989
Telephone: 1-800-741-0015
Website: www.brownells.com

Coffin Gunsmithing LLC
375 Sweathouse Creek Rd.
Victor, Montana 59875
Telephone: 406-642-3058
Email: coffingunsmithing@msn.com

The I.O. Inc. AK-47 and .380 Pocket Pistol

BY **JIM DICKSON**

I.O. Inc. (Short for International Ordnance Inc.) was founded originally as an import firm by two German brothers, Uli and Ollie Wiegand. I have known and liked them since they first came to this country. Even more important, both men impressed me as having the integrity of the old German Officer Corps, a group of men whose word was more physically binding to them than any contract.

Although I.O. Inc. started business as an importer, the quality control problems that they had on some of the guns that they imported led them to begin manufacturing their own guns in Monroe, North Carolina, a pro-gun area with a German-style work ethic and attention to quality. Ollie left the firm to pursue business interests in the Old World while Uli stayed utilizing tradi-

Uli Wiegand firing the Hellhound AK-47.

Left and Right side views of I.O. Inc. basic AK-47.

tional German precision workmanship to build one of the best gunmaking firms in the New World.

The turn from importer to manufacturer began modestly enough when they began importing Romanian AK-47s and converting them to the East German StG 940 configuration which they called the StG-2000C. This East German development of the AK-47 was intended for the international arms market in competition with the Soviet built AK-47, but the collapse of communism and the reunification of Germany brought an end to the project. I.O. Inc. revived the gun and still makes it.

Problems with quality control on the Romanian AKs led to the decision to produce an all American-made AK. These new guns are made to the Polish factory drawings as they made the highest quality AK-47s. All parts are new

and no surplus parts are used. American match grade barrels capable of one minute of angle accuracy combined with Uli's German precision manufacturing result in the most accurate AK-47s in the world. These guns will fire as accurately as the M16 but with far greater reliability. The configuration is improved by the addition of a CNC machined scope mount rail, a 1.5 inch longer straighter stock for less muzzle jump, a Picatinny rail system for add-on accessories, and a sling swivel that allows a tactical sling. Thirty-round polymer ProMags offer an increase in reliability over what was already one of the best combat magazines ever fielded. The guns will also accept any other AK-47 magazine. The receivers are all properly heat treated and the guns are given a nice manganese phosphate Parkerized finish.

Originally designed as a Russian

peasant-proof weapon, the new breed of semi-auto only AK-47s are fast proving the new all-around American rifle. Cheaper than other assault rifles, they boast power comparable to that of the vaunted .30-30 Winchester in a gun with 30 shots as fast as you can pull the trigger and a drastic reduction in recoil from the manually operated gun. Shooters can choose the flatter shooting 123-grain load or they can use the 150-grain CorBon load to exactly duplicate the tried-and-true .30-30 Winchester round.

Anything you can use a .30-30 on you can use an AK-47 on. That makes it far more useful and versatile than guns in 5.56 caliber for the 5.56 will always be a varmint cartridge and not a deer rifle cartridge. Heaven help you if you have to take on a bear with a 5.56. Reliability of the AK-47 has always been much greater than that of the M16, too. That's important when you are depending on a gun in a tight spot. It is from the standpoint of a weapon to defend yourself and your family that the instantly recognizable AK really stands out. As the most widely used modern assault weapon, its effectiveness needs no elaboration here. Whether you are dealing with burglers, rioters, looters in the aftermath of a disaster, or enemy troops in a future war, you will be well armed with a very well proven weapon. It's also extremely easy to field strip and maintain.

For the farmer, I have always said that a modern assault rifle is the best farm rifle for dealing with all the pests that besiege a farm. If you have a pack of wild dogs after your calves you must kill all of them before they make the tree line lest they only come back after dark to prey on your livestock. That means a 30-shot magazine and aimed rapidfire. Note that a German 3-post reticle is needed for proper aimed rapidfire with a scope as crosshairs blur with the recoil. The best one I have found is the Burris Gunsite Scout 2-3/4X scope with the 3-post reticle. Its forward mounting lets you use it with both eyes open for infinitely faster target acquisition and firing.

People up to no good seem to respect an assault rifle more than they do the traditional single barrel shotgun. Avoiding trouble by being too formidable to challenge is always a good thing. For all these reasons the AK-47 has become Americanized, like so many foreign guns before it, to the point we now consider it one of our own. This all American-made AK-47 from I.O. is certainly an American gun.

I.O. AK-47

I had two versions sent to me for testing: the AK47005, a basic AK-47 with the improved stock, scope rail, and Picatinny rail, and two examples of a version Uli calls the "Hellhound" with all the bells and whistles popular today. By the time each of these was sent separately along with two Hellcat .380 pistols, I had worn ruts in the road to Tucker Guns in Tucker, Georgia, as I went to pick them up. Uli was determined that I would get a good sample group to draw my conclusions on instead of just the one gun that gun writers usually get. I had 40 rounds of CorBon 150-grain SP, 40 rounds of CorBon 123-grain DPX, 140 rounds of Winchester 123-grain SP, and 80 rounds of Winchester 123-grain FMJ ammo for test firing. All brands seemed equally accurate and I think any differences in groups can safely be attributed to the shooter.

The basic AK-47 proved exceptionally well fitted and finished. There are no tool marks, gaps, or tight spots. Everything fits and functions perfectly and precisely. It performed flawlessly as you would expect from this design. The trigger was a very good 5.5 pound pull, certainly far better than what you got from the original Russian models. Recoil was slight and accuracy was better than anyone ever thought possible with an AK-47 in 7.62X39 caliber. These American made guns will deliver 1- to 1-1/2-inch groups all day long. (By the way, I strongly recommend the Bulls Bag Shooting Sandbags for this sort of shooting. Their X shaped cross section enables them to grip the gun tightly and improves stability many times over what you get with plain sandbags. They even have a high model to help get an assault rifle's magazine clear of the shooting bench.)

As far as I.O.'s AK-47 is concerned, I would like to see the open patridge sight replaced with an eighth-inch peep aperture on the tangent rear sight. Such a sight could be used with both eyes open more effectively than target peep sights traditionally mounted farther to the rear. This forward-mounted peep sight position has been proven most effective in the Running Jackrabbit Matches where you shoot aimed rapidfire at a clay bird hopping and skipping across the ground at 55 mph 50 yards in front of you. It is far superior to other iron sights for this game. Allowing the shooter to fire with both eyes open puts it ahead of the rear mounted peep sights when speed is needed.

AK-47 in tall Bulls Bag made for long magazine assault rifles showing how the X cross section of the bag grips the gun.

AK-47 in 15-inch long Bulls Bag for conventional rifles. The 30-round magazine must hang behind the bench on this one.

Besides the previously thought impossible feat of making the AK accurate, I.O. Inc. has eliminated the telltale *clack!* of the safety being let off. This loud-loud-loud noise saved many a G.I. in Nam from ambush as they moved down the jungle trails. It was a good thing on the enemy's guns but a very bad thing on your own weapon. Well, it's not on this AK and that's important. The noise of the safety was always one of the big complaints lodged against the AK-47 by combat users. It led to many guns being carried unsafed to the risk of their comrades. You were damned if you did and damned if you didn't with that damned safety but no more. Uli Weigand's AK will let you deer hunt with the safety on and quietly take it off without spooking game. Another triumph of German precision made in America.

Ergonomics are very good, being greatly increased by the new stock design. Because of the synthetic stock the gun comes in a pound lighter than the old-wood stocked AKs. At 7.5 pounds you have a very handy, light, mild-kicking gun that the wife and children can easily handle. Remember that come deer season.

The Hellhound version has all the basic features such as a side mounted scope rail but adds a Picatinny rail on each side of the forend to match the top and bottom Picatinney rails. Instead of the offset Soviet AK-47 shovel compensator it has a birdcage flash hider with lathe turned ribs for disrupting the flash along with a four-pronged front to further disrupt and suppress muzzle flash. This is very important if you are shooting at night. Most defense scenarios play out after dark and a farmer shooting coyotes with a night vision scope is going to find that the flash suppressor can help prevent the muzzle blast from temporarily blinding the night vision scope. Night vision devices vary drastically in their susceptibility to muzzle flash depending on the make and model. Always buy U.S. Govt. issue night vision items from the manufacturer or their distributor as these are the only ones that you can depend on getting parts and service for several years after purchase. Night vision is a rapidly improving technology and the more modern the unit, the better it will work. Mil-spec units frequently can be upgraded a generation forward when required.

The ranges are marked out in white on the tangent rear sight going up to 1000 yards. While the AK-47's effective range is limited like the M16's, the purpose of the long range adjustment is to enable the troops to fire in mass at enemy troop concentrations at long range or simply to plow up a particular area with enough bullets to render it impassable to the enemy. Hey, it's cheaper and quicker than air strikes and it works.

The Hellhound has a number of

Hellhound with vertical foregrip and Singlepoint sight on rear quick detachable mount.

Hellhound with vertical foregrip and Singlepoint sight mounted forward.

Hellhound with Dragunov scope and laser sight.

fascinating options offered with it. There is a very nice 6X42 scope with sniper rangefinding bars complete with clear instructions in their use. The scope is made in China and I could find no fault with it whatsoever. It mounts on the sidebar mount and is quickly detached the way the Germans always prefer their scopes. It can be taken on and off without losing its zero so you don't have to sight it in each time. 6X is all the magnification you should ever need with the 7.62X39 cartridge. Anything more begins to look out of place and a bit ridiculous on this mid-power cartridge. The side mount also accepts the Singlepoint red dot sight system for those who want fast target acquisition at close range. Whether for combat use or fast shots at deer flushing in heavy brush this system is superlative. It is used with both eyes open and can be mounted on the quick detachable scope mount or on the forward Picatinny rail for those who want more eye relief.

There is also a very bright LED flashlight that mounts on the Picatinny rail for those times you want to see the fox in the chicken house at night as well as a red dot laser sight to help you shoot the fox in the dark where your other sights won't work. The red dot offers a powerful psychological threat when aimed at someone and has real crowd control potential for law enforcement. In a gunfight I prefer not to have tracers or lights as that is a two-way street revealing your position. I must caution the reader that threatening someone with a gun when you aren't justified in shooting may result in your arrest if you aren't a law enforcement officer. Pointing that laser sight will be considered threatening by

the law as well as the person targeted.

Finally there is the forward handgrip that mounts on the bottom Picatinny rail. I always shoot better with a vertical foregrip. I find the gun points faster, more accurately, and is steadier with one. I strongly recommend this feature for all uses. For those who say it's not traditional I say then let them hunt with a lever action .30-30. This is an AK-47 and you want the best of the modern features for the modern gun. This is my favorite of all the add-on optional accessories and would be first on my list to acquire.

The second Hellhound Uli sent me had a Dragunov scope on it and

I shot the best group of all with this gun. Thanks to the steadiness of the Bullsbag sandbag system I finally got a 3/4-inch group. I was quite surprised as I didn't think it possible with the AK or its cartridge.

It's always fun to read about different guns but in the end the big question is always why should I buy this assault rifle? Here's why: The AK-47 is a much more rugged and reliable gun than the M16, is chambered for a more versatile hunting cartridge, and costs less. I.O. Inc. makes the highest quality and most accurate AK-47 available. You can't go wrong buying one.

Uli Wiegand firing the Hellcat miniature .380 pistol.

Right and Left side views of the Hellcat miniature .380 pistol.

I.O. Hellcat .380 Pocket Auto

The next gun tested was the new pocket pistol. The I.O. Hellcat .380 Pocket Pistol is certainly one of the best of the new breed of sub-compact .380s, if not the best. Extensive work has resulted in it definitely being the most reliable of its kind. A polymer-framed double action only design, it holds six rounds in the magazine plus one in the chamber. It comes with a stainless steel magazine, a zipper pouch, and a clearly written manual. It weighs only 9.4 ounces and measures 7-3/16 inches long by 3/4-inch thick by four inches high. That doesn't require a very big pocket. It will even fit in the pocket of a T-shirt. It has a 2.75-inch barrel rifled with six grooves with a 1:16 rate of twist. Sights are fixed with good visibility but any sights are superfluous on a close range point-and-shoot weapon like this.

The gun is a locked-breech design with the barrel and slide starting rearward together until the barrel is cammed down, letting the slide complete the cycle by itself. Locked breech operation reduces recoil significantly compared to plain blowback in a flyweight gun like this. In order to simplify the design, there is no bolt hold open device for the last shot. Like most of its contemporary competitors, the hammer must be precocked by operating the slide before starting the double action trigger pull. This allows a smoother, lighter trigger pull than on the older double action designs like the P38. Some folks think that being able to pull the trigger again on a dud primer is an advantage. They have never been in a gunfight at short range. What makes you think it will fire with

the second try? You better be ejecting it and getting a live round in the chamber instead of screwing around with bad primers while someone is shooting at you.

Workmanship is first rate throughout the pistol. There were no flaws or substandard fitting or finishing inside or out. Everything was pure German precision – exactly what you would expect from Uli Wiegand. Ergonomics

were superb for such a tiny pistol, a vital factor on a deep-cover point-and-shoot weapon where a clumsy gun could make you miss. Speed is of the essence at the ranges you use a weapon like this and that has popularized the double-action-only trigger which requires no safety on guns of this type. You just draw, point, and fire in one fast motion.

Firing was done with 100 rounds of CCI/Speer Blazer Brass .380 FMJ 95-grain;

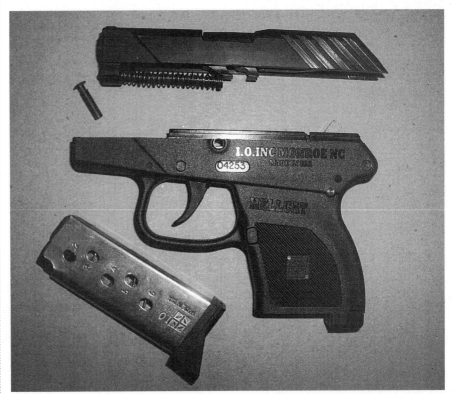

The Hellcat is disassembled by simply prying out the takedown pin with the magazine feed lips. The slide can then be removed and the recoil spring and barrel plucked out. Nothing could be easier.

The Hellcat beside a mint surplus German P1 Pistol imported by I.O. Inc. shows its small size.

50 rounds of Georgia Arms .380 FMJ 95-grain; 250 rounds of Winchester 95-grain FMJ; 120 rounds of Winchester .380 Supreme Elite; 60 rounds of CorBon 80-grain DPX; and 60 rounds of Glaser 70-grain PowRBall. All but the first three types were high velocity loads but the guns didn't seem to care and I could tell no difference in recoil between any of the loads fired. Trigger pull was measured with a Lyman Trigger Pull Gauge from Brownell's Shooting Supplies and measured seven pounds. It was smooth and clean.

As would be expected, the combination of a seven-pound trigger on a 9.4 ounce gun with a 2.75-inch barrel does not make a target or hunting pistol.

Once I got the hang of it I was able to gett two- and three-inch groups at 10 yards with any of the ammo tested firing rapid fire offhand with one hand. That is far more accuracy than you will ever need in a close quarters hideout gun like this. The gun points accurately and is fast and easy to use. Recoil is moderate but obviously present in any super light gun like this. Still it won't be enough to discourage the shooter. A little recoil is the price you pay for a subcompact lightweight masterpiece.

I was particularly impressed with the ease of disassembly of this piece. Just pull out the takedown button, using the magazine lips to pry it out, and pull the slide assembly off the front. Remove the recoil spring assembly of a spring within a spring on a guide rod from the barrel and lift out the barrel. That's all, folks, and it goes together again just as easy with no cussing. I like that in a gun. A weapon that is a beast to strip and reassemble may not get cleaned properly very often and may fail as a result. That is especially true if the gun is actually carried in a pocket. This is the dirtiest carry environment that there is. Some of the subcompact designs have had trouble with the takedown pin coming out in firing but the slide and frame of the Hellcat are designed to make that impossible.

All sub-compact double action only automatics, whatever the caliber, are intended for ease of concealment and close range defense. They are not the all around handguns that a full size M1911A1, Luger, or Colt SAA is. Neither are they as big and bulky or hard to carry and conceal as their bigger brothers. The limited effective range of the micro-guns makes them ineffective as an offensive military and police weapon and they would be almost useless for target and hunting work but that is not their purpose in life. They are there at times and places the bigger gun would not be for the sole purpose of defending your life from close range attack. They do this very well. I.O. Inc.'s little masterpiece is one of the best examples of this category.

Uli Wegand's successful marriage of German precision with "Made in America" has produced some of the best made guns available. This is a firm destined to take its place alongside Winchester, Remington, Colt, and Smith and Wesson as one of America's finest gunmakers. No one will ever regret choosing one of their products.

TESTFIRE:
The CzechPoint vz. 61 Skorpion

BY AL DOYLE

Despite clever ad campaigns and marketing hype, the word "unique" seldom applies to modern firearms. If anything, most 21st century guns fall into the categories of "It's a lot like Model X" or "It's sorta like Model Y." While there is an abundance of dependable and accurate weapons on the market, few are truly odd or revolutionary.

Does that leave any room for a gun that defies being pigeonholed? One such gun immediately comes to mind: the vz. 61 Skorpion made in the Czech Republic and imported by CzechPoint of Knoxville, Tennessee. It's a bundle of intriguing contradictions in a 39-ounce package.

Chambered in .32 ACP, the Skorpion was first produced in the former Czechoslovakia in 1961, which explains the vz. 61 designation. (*Samopal vzor,* abbreviated *vzor,* is Czech for submachinegun). Designed by firearms engineer Miroslav Rybar (1924-1970), the Skorpion was originally a machine pistol with a folding wire shoulder stock designed for use by secondary troops, police, tank crews and others who might need a compact weapon with select fire capability.

Why would a nation that was part of the former Soviet bloc go for the .32 ACP when the Makarov 9mm x 18 and the Czech 7.62 x 25 were already in widespread usage?

"Unlike the rest of eastern Europe under the Soviets, the Czechs kind of went their own way when it came to firearms," explained CzechPoint president Dan Brown. "They have a 700-year history of making guns, and they may have been

CzechPoint's sellsheet for the Skorpion.

looking at the export market with the Skorpion. The .32 was popular in Europe and elsewhere then." The Skorpion's blowback action is ideal for the low-pressure .32 ACP, and Rybar would have had to come up with a significantly different design for more potent calibers.

The Skorpion was used as a niche weapon. It was licensed for production in the former Yugoslavia, where the gun was dubbed the vz. 64 and chambered

for the .380 ACP, known as the 9mm x 17 in Europe. The Skorpion has seen duty in Serbia, Slovenia, Montenegro, Afghanistan. Angola, Egypt, Indonesia, Libya and Mozambique.

A few specimens have turned up in various regional conflicts, as simplicity of design and durability are high priorities in third world conditions. Like Elvis sightings, rumors of a run of made in Yugoslavia 9mm Skorpions refuse to die.

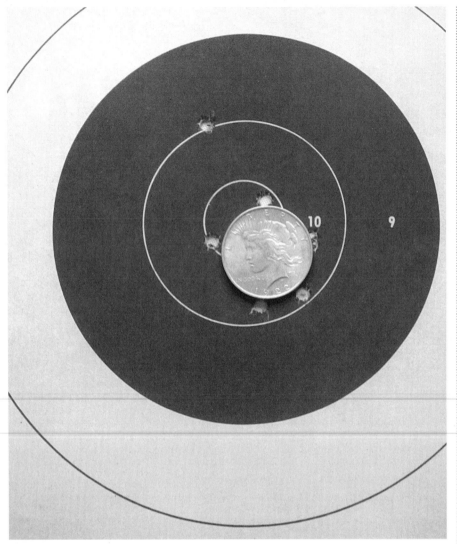

The CzechPoint vz. 61 Skorpion is capable of surprisingly good accuracy.

An assortment of Winchester, Aguila and Sellier and Belliot ammunition – all 71-grain jacketed rounds – was used to get familiar with the weapon. The only jam came in the first few rounds. This wasn't unexpected with a brand-new pistol being shot in below-freezing (25° F) conditions. Feeding and extraction were flawless afterwards.

Speaking of extraction, that is one of the interesting quirks of the Skorpion. Cases are forcefully launched straight upward as high as 15 feet. They sometimes land with a gentle plop on the shoulder after spinning down like an airplane propeller.

The other unexpected feature is the rear sight, which has settings for 75 and 150 meters. That is clearly wishful thinking for the modest ballistics of the .32 ACP, so keep it on the lower end for best results.

From 25 feet, the first five-shot groups were in the 3- to 4-inch range, with the Winchester ammo proving to be the most accurate of the bunch. Once I was more familiar with the gun, groups shrank considerably, and I'm far from an expert pistolero.

On one target, 16 of 20 Winchester rounds from a full magazine could be covered by a silver dollar, with three more rounds just outside the boundaries of the coin. The lone flyer touched the upper border of the 10 ring. Aguila and S&B bullets were of the traditional roundnose design found in mass-market .32 ACP fodder, while Winchester white box was loaded with a semi-wadcutter bullet. Could that have made a difference in accuracy?

Recoil was negligible, which is to be expected in a .32 ACP pistol that is in the same weight class as a Model 1911 .45 ACP or a .357 Magnum revolver with a six-inch barrel. Go ahead and run a few hundred rounds through the Skorpion, as nothing will ache after a long range session. The trigger pull has some slack, but it's amazingly smooth and may be even lighter than the three pounds claimed by CzechPoint.

There is far more chatter, video clips and reviews of the Skorpion on the internet than would normally be expected for an oddball gun that is relatively new to the American market. A trip to YouTube alone can occupy the better part of an hour viewing Skorpion-related programming.

"Gamers are familiar with the Skorpion, since it's in a couple of popular video games," Brown said. Famed actor

Brown says he knows a buyer who is prepared to pay serious money if someone produces this ghost of a weapon.

This 50-year-old concept is currently made in the Czech Republic by D-Technik A.S., a division of Czech Small Arms. Originally sold in the U.S. by CZ, the Skorpion is now available exclusively through CzechPoint. The gun comes in a sturdy plastic case that includes two 20-round and one 10-round magazines (or three 10-rounders to residents of states where the larger magazines are banned) along with a nylon holster and ammo pouch.

So what's it like to shoot the Skorpion minus its wire stock? CzechPoint sells the original version for an extra $100, but buyers will need to pay a $200 tax and pass the BATF's extensive background check to obtain a Class 3 license for a restricted weapon. A vz. 61 with

a silencer-ready barrel is also offered by CzechPoint. Most customers opt for the standard pistol version, so that is what was tested. Blued and nickel-plated frames are offered.

There is more than one way to hold the Skorpion. The strong hand on the grip combined with the weak hand on the magazine tends to be the most popular method, but the traditional two-handed approach also works well for accuracy. A one-handed hold is less comfortable than on other handguns, as the Skorpion is a bit muzzle heavy.

"I liked the accuracy, and it never malfunctioned, but how do you hold it?" said my son, a Marine Corps corporal on active duty. "I felt like there was no right way to hold it without the shoulder stock." Suggestion: Two hands on the grip might not work for those with larger paws.

The vz. 61 comes with all the goodies you need to have some serious fun.

Leonardo DiCaprio also used a Skorpion as an assassination tool in the film *Body of Lies*. The design is from the Kalashnikov school of utter simplicity. Pull the pin at the front of the receiver, and the Skorpion clamshells open from the rear for easy cleaning and inspection.

While a stout .32 ACP pistol with a 4-1/2-inch barrel isn't a practical choice for concealed carry or the top choice for home defense, the Skorpion is more than an interesting eccentricity in the firearms market. Older shooters who suffer from arthritis or have other physical problems that are aggravated by recoil can have 20 rounds of Silvertips on tap for "just in case." Put a fluorescent coat of paint on the black front sight if your Skorpion might be needed at 2 a.m.

Since the current retail price of .32 ACP ammo is right in line with the cost of .45 ACP, the Skorpion may be an ideal project for reloaders. Cast bullets and three grains or less of powder per round means the Skorpion could be a frugal shooter's delight.

There are other niches for the Skorpion. Old-school types who dislike polymer and synthetics can grab a fistful of steel with this retro Czech classic. Its Iron Curtain heritage is another nod to the nostalgia market.

Brown reports his product is very popular among shooting range owners who rent guns. That makes sense, as the Skorpion isn't for everyone – but it screams "Try me out!" Yes, it's clunky for a pocket pistol, but the vz. 61 Skorpion is pure fun and capable of excellent accuracy. If more power is desired, Brown reports that a .380 ACP Skorpion should be available in late 2012.

CzechPoint sells the Skorpion directly for $599, and the price includes a commission to your FFL dealer. View the firm's web site at www. czechpoint-usa.com for more details.

Many manufacturers do not supply suggested retail prices. Others did not get their pricing to us before press time. All pricing can vary dependent on the exact brand and style of ammo selected and/or the retail outlet from which you make your purchase. Pricing has been rounded to the nearest dollar and represents our best estimate of average pricing.
An * after the cartridge means these loads are available with Nosler Partition or Swift A-Frame bullets. Listed pricing may or may not reflect this bullet type.
** = these are packed 50 to box, all others are 20 to box. Wea. Mag.= Weatherby Magnum. Spfd. = Springfield. A-Sq. = A-Square. N.E.=Nitro Express.

Cartridge	Bullet Wgt. Grs.	VELOCITY (fps)					ENERGY (ft. lbs.)					TRAJ. (in.)				Est. Price/box
		Muzzle	100 yds.	200 yds.	300 yds.	400 yds.	Muzzle	100 yds.	200 yds.	300 yds.	400 yds.	100 yds.	200 yds.	300 yds.	400 yds.	
17, 22																
17 Remington Fireball	20	4000	3380	2840	2360	1930	710	507	358	247	165	1.6	1.5	-2.8	-13.5	NA
17 Remington Fireball	25	3850	3280	2780	2330	1925	823	597	429	301	206	0.9	0.0	-5.4	NA	NA
17 Remington	25	4040	3284	2644	2086	1606	906	599	388	242	143	+2.0	+1.7	-4.0	-17.0	$17
204 Ruger (Fed)	32 Green	4030	3320	2710	2170	1710	1155	780	520	335	205	0.9	0.0	-5.7	-19.1	NA
204 Ruger	32	4225	3632	3114	2652	2234	1268	937	689	500	355	.6	0.0	-4.2	-13.4	NA
204 Ruger	40	3900	3451	3046	2677	2336	1351	1058	824	636	485	.7	0.0	-4.5	-13.9	NA
204 Ruger	45	3625	3188	2792	2428	2093	1313	1015	778	589	438	1.0	0.0	-5.5	-16.9	NA
221 Fireball	50	2800	2137	1580	1180	988	870	507	277	155	109	+0.0	-7.0	-28.0	0.0	$14
22 Hornet (Fed)	30 Green	3150	2150	1390	990	830	660	310	130	65	45	0.0	-6.6	-32.7	NA	NA
22 Hornet	34	3050	2132	1415	1017	852	700	343	151	78	55	+0.0	-6.6	-15.5	-29.9	NA
22 Hornet	35	3100	2278	1601	1135	929	747	403	199	100	67	+2.75	0.0	-16.9	-60.4	NA
22 Hornet	45	2690	2042	1502	1128	948	723	417	225	127	90	+0.0	-7.7	-31.0	0.0	$27**
218 Bee	46	2760	2102	1550	1155	961	788	451	245	136	94	+0.0	-7.2	-29.0	0.0	$46**
222 Remington	40	3600	3117	2673	2269	1911	1151	863	634	457	324	+1.07	0.0	-6.13	-18.9	NA
222 Remington	50	3140	2602	2123	1700	1350	1094	752	500	321	202	+2.0	-0.4	-11.0	-33.0	$11
222 Remington	55	3020	2562	2147	1773	1451	1114	801	563	384	257	+2.0	-0.4	-11.0	-33.0	$12
22 PPC	52	3400	2930	2510	2130	NA	1335	990	730	525	NA	+2.0	1.4	-5.0	0.0	NA
223 Remington	40	3650	3010	2450	1950	1530	1185	805	535	340	265	+2.0	+1.0	-6.0	-22.0	$14
223 Remington	40	3800	3305	2845	2424	2044	1282	970	719	522	371	0.84	0.0	-5.34	-16.6	NA
223 Remington (Rem)	45 Green	3550	2911	2355	1865	1451	1259	847	554	347	210	2.5	2.3	-4.3	-21.1	NA
223 Remington	50	3300	2874	2484	2130	1809	1209	917	685	504	363	1.37	0.0	-7.05	-21.8	NA
223 Remington	52/53	3330	2882	2477	2106	1770	1305	978	722	522	369	+2.0	+0.6	-6.5	-21.5	$14
223 Remington (Win)	55 Green	3240	2747	2304	1905	1554	1282	921	648	443	295	1.9	0.0	-8.5	-26.7	NA
223 Remington	55	3240	2748	2305	1906	1556	1282	922	649	444	296	+2.0	-0.2	-9.0	-27.0	$12
223 Remington	60	3100	2712	2355	2026	1726	1280	979	739	547	397	+2.0	+0.2	-8.0	-24.7	$16
223 Remington	64	3020	2621	2256	1920	1619	1296	977	723	524	373	+2.0	-0.2	-9.3	-23.0	$14
223 Remington	69	3000	2720	2460	2210	1980	1380	1135	925	750	600	+2.0	+0.8	-5.7	-17.5	$15
223 Remington	75	2790	2554	2330	2119	1926	1296	1086	904	747	617	2.37	0.0	-8.75	-25.1	NA
223 Rem. Super Match	75	2930	2694	2470	2257	2055	1429	1209	1016	848	703	1.20	0.0	-6.9	-20.7	NA
223 Remington	77	2750	2584	2354	2169	1992	1293	1110	948	804	679	1.93	0.0	-8.2	-23.8	NA
223 WSSM	55	3850	3438	3064	2721	2402	1810	1444	1147	904	704	0.7	0.0	-4.4	-13.6	NA
223 WSSM	64	3600	3144	2732	2356	2011	1841	1404	1061	789	574	1.0	0.0	-5.7	-17.7	NA
222 Rem. Mag.	55	3240	2748	2305	1906	1556	1282	922	649	444	296	+2.0	-0.2	-9.0	-27.0	$14
225 Winchester	55	3570	3066	2616	2208	1838	1556	1148	836	595	412	+2.0	+1.0	-5.0	-20.0	$19
224 Wea. Mag.	55	3650	3192	2780	2403	2057	1627	1244	943	705	516	+2.0	+1.2	-4.0	-17.0	$32
22-250 Rem.	40	4000	3320	2720	2200	1740	1420	980	660	430	265	+2.0	+1.8	-3.0	-16.0	$14
22-250 Rem.	45 Green	4000	3293	2690	2159	1696	1598	1084	723	466	287	1.7	1.7	-3.2	-15.7	NA
22-250 Rem.	50	3725	3264	2641	2455	2103	1540	1183	896	669	491	0.89	0.0	-5.23	-16.3	NA
22-250 Rem.	52/55	3680	3137	2656	2222	1832	1654	1201	861	603	410	+2.0	+1.3	-4.0	-17.0	$13
22-250 Rem.	60	3600	3195	2826	2485	2169	1727	1360	1064	823	627	+2.0	+2.0	-2.4	-12.3	$19
220 Swift	40	4200	3678	3190	2739	2329	1566	1201	904	666	482	+0.51	0.0	-4.0	-12.9	NA
220 Swift	50	3780	3158	2617	2135	1710	1586	1107	760	506	325	+2.0	+1.4	-4.4	-17.9	$20
220 Swift	50	3850	3396	2970	2576	2215	1645	1280	979	736	545	0.74	0.0	-4.84	-15.1	NA
220 Swift	55	3800	3370	2990	2630	2310	1765	1390	1090	850	650	0.8	0.0	-4.7	-14.4	NA
220 Swift	55	3650	3194	2772	2384	2035	1627	1246	939	694	506	+2.0	+2.0	-2.6	-13.4	$19
220 Swift	60	3600	3199	2824	2475	2156	1727	1364	1063	816	619	+2.0	+1.6	-4.1	-13.1	$19
22 Savage H.P.	71	2790	2340	1930	1570	1280	1225	860	585	390	190	+2.0	-1.0	-10.4	-35.7	NA
6mm (24)																
6mm BR Rem.	100	2550	2310	2083	1870	1671	1444	1185	963	776	620	+2.5	-0.6	-11.8	0.0	$22
6mm Norma BR	107	2822	2667	2517	2372	2229	1893	1690	1506	1337	1181	+1.73	0.0	-7.24	-20.6	NA
6mm PPC	70	3140	2750	2400	2070	NA	1535	1175	895	665	NA	+2.0	+1.4	-5.0	0.0	NA
243 Winchester	55	4025	3597	3209	2853	2525	1978	1579	1257	994	779	+0.6	0.0	-4.0	-12.2	NA
243 Winchester	60	3600	3110	2660	2260	1890	1725	1285	945	680	475	+2.0	+1.8	-3.3	-15.5	$17
243 Winchester	70	3400	3040	2700	2390	2100	1795	1435	1135	890	685	1.1	0.0	-5.9	-18.0	NA
243 Winchester	75/80	3350	2955	2593	2259	1951	1993	1551	1194	906	676	+2.0	+0.9	-5.0	-19.0	$16
243 W. Superformance	80	3425	3080	2760	2463	2184	2083	1684	1353	1077	847	1.1	0.0	-5.7	-17.1	NA
243 Winchester	85	3320	3070	2830	2600	2380	2080	1770	1510	1280	1070	+2.0	+1.2	-4.0	-14.0	$18
243 Winchester	90	3120	2871	2635	2411	2199	1946	1647	1388	1162	966	1.4	0.0	-6.4	-18.8	NA
243 Winchester*	100	2960	2697	2449	2215	1993	1945	1615	1332	1089	882	+2.5	+1.2	-6.0	-20.0	$16
243 Winchester	105	2920	2689	2470	2261	2062	1988	1686	1422	1192	992	+2.5	+1.6	-5.0	-18.4	$21
243 Light Mag.	100	3100	2839	2592	2358	2138	2133	1790	1491	1235	1014	+1.5	0.0	-6.8	-19.8	NA
243 WSSM	55	4060	3628	3237	2880	2550	2013	1607	1280	1013	794	0.6	0.0	-3.9	-12.0	NA
243 WSSM	95	3250	3000	2763	2538	2325	2258	1898	1610	1359	1140	1.2	0.0	-5.7	-16.9	NA
243 WSSM	100	3110	2838	2583	2341	2112	2147	1789	1481	1217	991	1.4	0.0	-6.6	-19.7	NA
6mm Remington	80	3470	3064	2694	2352	2036	2139	1667	1289	982	736	+2.0	+1.1	-5.0	-17.0	$16
6mm R. Superformance	95	3235	2955	2692	2443	3309	2207	1841	1528	1259	1028	1.2	0.0	-6.1	-18.0	NA
6mm Remington	100	3100	2829	2573	2332	2104	2133	1777	1470	1207	983	+2.5	+1.6	-5.0	-17.0	$16
6mm Remington	105	3060	2822	2596	2381	2177	2105	1788	1512	1270	1059	+2.5	+1.1	-3.3	-15.0	$21
6.17(.243) Spitfire	100	3350	3122	2905	2698	2501	2493	2164	1874	1617	1389	2.4	3.2	0.0	-8.0	NA
240 Wea. Mag.	87	3500	3202	2924	2663	2416	2366	1980	1651	1370	1127	+2.0	+2.0	-2.0	-12.0	$32
240 Wea. Mag.	100	3395	3106	2835	2581	2339	2559	2142	1785	1478	1215	+2.5	+2.8	-2.0	-11.0	$43

Cartridge	Bullet Wgt. Grs.	VELOCITY (fps)					ENERGY (ft. lbs.)					TRAJ. (in.)				Est. Price/box
		Muzzle	100 yds.	200 yds.	300 yds.	400 yds.	Muzzle	100 yds.	200 yds.	300 yds.	400 yds.	100 yds.	200 yds.	300 yds.	400 yds.	
25-20 Win.	86	1460	1194	1030	931	858	407	272	203	165	141	0.0	-23.5	0.0	0.0	$32**
25-35 Win.	117	2230	1866	1545	1282	1097	1292	904	620	427	313	+2.5	-4.2	-26.0	0.0	$24
250 Savage	100	2820	2504	2210	1936	1684	1765	1392	1084	832	630	+2.5	+0.4	-9.0	-28.0	$17
257 Roberts	100	2980	2661	2363	2085	1827	1972	1572	1240	965	741	+2.5	-0.8	-5.2	-21.6	$20
257 Roberts+P	117	2780	2411	2071	1761	1488	2009	1511	1115	806	576	-0.2	-10.2	-32.6		$18
257 R. Superformance	117	2946	2705	2478	2265	2057	2253	1901	1595	1329	1099	1.1	0.0	-5.7	-17.1	NA
257 Roberts+P	120	2780	2560	2360	2160	1970	2060	1750	1480	1240	1030	+2.5	+1.2	-6.4	-23.6	$22
257 Roberts	122	2600	2331	2078	1842	1625	1831	1472	1169	919	715	+2.5	0.0	-10.6	-31.4	$21
25-06 Rem.	87	3440	2995	2591	2222	1884	2286	1733	1297	954	686	+2.0	+1.1	-2.5	-14.4	$17
25-06 Rem.	90	3440	3043	2680	2344	2034	2364	1850	1435	1098	827	+2.0	+1.8	-3.3	-15.6	$17
25-06 Rem.	100	3230	2893	2580	2287	2014	2316	1858	1478	1161	901	+2.0	+0.8	-5.7	-18.9	$17
25-06 Rem.	117	2990	2770	2570	2370	2190	2320	2000	1715	1465	1246	+2.5	+1.0	-7.9	-26.6	$19
25-06 R. Superformance	117	3110	2861	2626	2403	2191	2512	2127	1792	1500	1246	1.4	0.0	-6.4	-18.9	NA
25-06 Rem.*	120	2990	2730	2484	2252	2032	2382	1985	1644	1351	1100	+2.5	+1.2	-5.3	-19.6	$17
25-06 Rem.	122	2930	2706	2492	2289	2095	2325	1983	1683	1419	1189	+2.5	+1.8	-4.5	-17.5	$23
25 WSSM	85	3470	3156	2863	2589	2331	2273	1880	1548	1266	1026	1.0	0.0	-5.2	-15.7	NA
25 WSSM	115	3060	284	2639	2442	2254	2392	2066	1778	1523	1398	1.4	0.0	-6.4	-18.6	NA
25 WSSM	120	2990	2717	2459	2216	1987	2383	1967	1612	1309	1053	1.6	0.0	-7.4	-21.8	NA
257 Wea. Mag.	87	3825	3456	3118	2805	2513	2826	2308	1870	1520	1220	+2.0	+2.7	-0.3	-7.6	$32
257 Wea. Mag.	100	3555	3237	2941	2665	2404	2806	2326	1920	1576	1283	+2.5	+3.2	0.0	-8.0	$32
257 Scramjet	100	3745	3450	3173	2912	2666	3114	2643	2235	1883	1578	+2.1	+2.77	0.0	-6.93	NA
6.5																
6.5x47 Lapua	123	2887	NA	2554	NA	2244	2285	NA	1788	NA	1380	NA	4.53	0.0	-10.7	NA
6.5x50mm Jap.	139	2360	2160	1970	1790	1620	1720	1440	1195	985	810	+2.5	-1.0	-13.5	0.0	NA
6.5x50mm Jap.	156	2070	1830	1610	1430	1260	1475	1155	900	695	550	+2.5	-4.0	-23.8	0.0	NA
6.5x52mm Car.	139	2580	2360	2160	1970	1790	2045	1725	1440	1195	985	+2.5	0.0	-9.9	-29.0	NA
6.5x52mm Car.	156	2430	2170	1930	1700	1500	2045	1630	1285	1005	780	+2.5	-1.0	-13.9	0.0	NA
6.5x52mm Carcano	160	2250	1963	1700	1467	1271	1798	1369	1027	764	574	+3.8	0.0	-15.9	-48.1	NA
6.5x55mm Swe.	93	2625	2350	2090	1850	1630	1425	1140	905	705	550	2.4	0.0	-10.3	-31.1	NA
6.5x55mm Swe.	123	2750	2570	2400	2240	2080	2065	1810	1580	1370	1185	1.9	0.0	-7.9	-22.9	NA
6.5x55mm Swe.	140	2550	NA	NA	NA	NA	2020	NA	NA	NA	NA	0.0	0.0	0.0	0.0	$18
6.5x55mm Swe.*	139/140	2850	2640	2440	2250	2070	2525	2170	1855	1575	1330	+2.5	+1.6	-5.4	-18.9	$18
6.5x55mm Swe.	156	2650	2370	2110	1870	1650	2425	1950	1550	1215	945	+2.5	0.0	-10.3	-30.6	NA
260 Remington	125	2875	2669	2473	2285	2105	2294	1977	1697	1449	1230	1.71	0.0	-7.4	-21.4	NA
260 Remington	140	2750	2544	2347	2158	1979	2351	2011	1712	1448	1217	+2.2	0.0	-8.6	-24.6	NA
6.5 Creedmoor	120	3020	2815	2619	2430	2251	2430	2111	1827	1574	1350	1.4	0.0	-6.5	-18.9	NA
6.5 C. Superformance	129	2950	2756	2570	2392	2221	2492	2175	1892	1639	1417	1.5	0.0	-6.8	-19.7	NA
6.5 Creedmoor	140	2820	2654	2494	2339	2190	2472	2179	1915	1679	1467	1.7	0.0	-7.2	-20.6	NA
6.5-284 Norma	142	3025	2890	2758	2631	2507	2886	2634	2400	2183	1982	1.13	0.0	-5.7	-16.4	NA
6.71 (264) Phantom	120	3150	2929	2718	2517	2325	2645	2286	1969	1698	1440	+1.3	0.0	-6.0	-17.5	NA
6.5 Rem. Mag.	120	3210	2905	2621	2353	2102	2745	2248	1830	1475	1177	+2.5	+1.7	-4.1	-16.3	Disc.
264 Win. Mag.	140	3030	2782	2548	2326	2114	2854	2406	2018	1682	1389	+2.5	+1.4	-5.1	-18.0	$24
6.71 (264) Blackbird	140	3480	3261	3053	2855	2665	3766	3307	2899	2534	2208	+2.4	+3.1	0.0	-7.4	NA
6.8mm Rem.	115	2775	2472	2190	1926	1683	1966	1561	1224	947	723	+2.1	0.0	-3.7	-9.4	NA
27																
270 Winchester	100	3430	3021	2649	2305	1988	2612	2027	1557	1179	877	+2.0	+1.0	-4.9	-17.5	$17
270 Win. (Rem.)	115	2710	2482	2265	2059	NA	1875	1485	1161	896	NA	0.0	4.8	-17.3	0.0	NA
270 Winchester	130	3060	2776	2510	2259	2022	2702	2225	1818	1472	1180	+2.5	+1.4	-5.3	-18.2	$17
270 Win. Supreme	130	3150	2881	2628	2388	2161	2865	2396	1993	1646	1348	1.3	0.0	-6.4	-18.9	NA
270 W. Superformance	130	3200	2984	2788	2582	2393	2955	2570	2228	1924	1653	1.2	0.0	-5.7	-16.7	NA
270 Winchester	135	3000	2780	2570	2369	2178	2697	2315	1979	1682	1421	+2.5	+1.4	-6.0	-17.6	$23
270 Winchester*	140	2940	2700	2480	2260	2060	2685	2270	1905	1590	1315	+2.5	+1.8	-4.6	-17.9	$20
270 Winchester*	150	2850	2585	2336	2100	1879	2705	2226	1817	1468	1175	+2.5	+1.2	-6.5	-22.0	$17
270 Win. Supreme	150	2930	2693	2468	2254	2051	2860	2416	2030	1693	1402	1.7	0.0	-7.4	-21.6	NA
270 WSM	130	3275	3041	2820	2609	2408	3096	2669	2295	1564	1673	1.1	0.0	-5.5	-16.1	NA
270 WSM	140	3125	2865	2619	2386	2165	3035	2559	2132	1769	1457	1.4	0.0	-6.5	-19.0	NA
270 WSM	150	3120	2923	2734	2554	2380	3242	2845	2490	2172	1886	1.3	0.0	-5.9	-17.2	NA
270 Wea. Mag.	100	3760	3380	3033	2712	2412	3139	2537	2042	1633	1292	+2.0	+2.4	-1.2	-10.1	$32
270 Wea. Mag.	130	3375	3119	2878	2649	2432	3287	2808	2390	2026	1707	+2.5	-2.9	-0.9	-9.9	$32
270 Wea. Mag.*	150	3245	3036	2837	2647	2465	3507	3070	2681	2334	2023	+2.5	+2.6	-1.8	-11.4	$47
7mm																
7mm BR	140	2216	2012	1821	1643	1481	1525	1259	1031	839	681	+2.0	-3.7	-20.0	0.0	$23
7mm Mauser*	139/140	2660	2435	2221	2018	1827	2199	1843	1533	1266	1037	+2.5	0.0	-9.6	-27.7	$17
7mm Mauser	145	2690	2442	2206	1985	1777	2334	1920	1568	1268	1017	+2.5	+0.1	-9.6	-28.3	$18
7mm Mauser	154	2690	2490	2300	2120	1940	2475	2120	1810	1530	1285	+2.5	+0.8	-7.5	-23.5	$17
7mm Mauser	175	2440	2137	1857	1603	1382	2313	1774	1340	998	742	+2.5	-1.7	-16.1	0.0	$17

Cartridge	Bullet Wgt. Grs.	VELOCITY (fps)					ENERGY (ft. lbs.)					TRAJ. (in.)				Est. Price/box
		Muzzle	100 yds.	200 yds.	300 yds.	400 yds.	Muzzle	100 yds.	200 yds.	300 yds.	400 yds.	100 yds.	200 yds.	300 yds.	400 yds.	
7x30 Waters	120	2700	2300	1930	1600	1330	1940	1405	990	685	470	+2.5	-0.2	-12.3	0.0	$18
7mm-08 Rem.	120	3000	2725	2467	2223	1992	2398	1979	1621	1316	1058	+2.0	0.0	-7.6	-22.3	$18
7mm-08 Rem.*	140	2860	2625	2402	2189	1988	2542	2142	1793	1490	1228	+2.5	+0.8	-6.9	-21.9	$18
7mm-08 Rem.	154	2715	2510	2315	2128	1950	2520	2155	1832	1548	1300	+2.5	+1.0	-7.0	-22.7	$23
7-08 R. Superformance	139	2950	2857	2571	2393	2222	2686	2345	2040	1768	1524	1.5	0.0	-6.8	-19.7	NA
7x64mm Bren.	140								Not Yet Announced							$17
7x64mm Bren.	154	2820	2610	2420	2230	2050	2720	2335	1995	1695	1430	+2.5	+1.4	-5.7	-19.9	NA
7x64mm Bren.*	160	2850	2669	2495	2327	2166	2885	2530	2211	1924	1667	+2.5	+1.6	-4.8	-17.8	$24
7x64mm Bren.	175								Not Yet Announced							$17
284 Winchester	150	2860	2595	2344	2108	1886	2724	2243	1830	1480	1185	+2.5	+0.8	-7.3	-23.2	$24
280 R. Superformance	139	3090	2890	2699	2516	2341	2946	2578	2249	1954	1691	1.3	0.0	-6.1	-17.7	NA
280 Remington	140	3000	2758	2528	2309	2102	2797	2363	1986	1657	1373	+2.5	+1.4	-5.2	-18.3	$17
280 Remington*	150	2890	2624	2373	2135	1912	2781	2293	1875	1518	1217	+2.5	+0.8	-7.1	-22.6	$17
280 Remington	160	2840	2637	2442	2556	2078	2866	2471	2120	1809	1535	+2.5	+0.8	-6.7	-21.0	$20
280 Remington	165	2820	2510	2220	1950	1701	2913	2308	1805	1393	1060	+2.5	+0.4	-8.8	-26.5	$17
7x61mm S&H Sup.	154	3060	2720	2400	2100	1820	3200	2520	1965	1505	1135	+2.5	+1.8	-5.0	-19.8	NA
7mm Dakota	160	3200	3001	2811	2630	2455	3637	3200	2808	2456	2140	+2.1	+1.9	-2.8	-12.5	NA
7mm Rem. Mag. (Rem.)	140	2710	2482	2265	2059	NA	2283	1915	1595	1318	NA	0.0	-4.5	-1.57	0.0	NA
7mm Rem. Mag.*	139/140	3150	2930	2710	2510	2320	3085	2660	2290	1960	1670	+2.5	+2.4	-2.4	-12.7	$21
7 R.M. Superformance	139	3240	3033	2836	2648	2467	3239	2839	2482	2163	1877	1.1	0.0	-5.5	-15.9	NA
7mm Rem. Mag.	150/154	3110	2830	2568	2320	2085	3221	2667	2196	1792	1448	+2.5	+1.6	-4.6	-16.5	$21
7mm Rem. Mag.*	160/162	2950	2730	2520	2320	2120	3090	2650	2250	1910	1600	+2.5	+1.8	-4.4	-17.8	$34
7 R.M. Superformance	154	3100	2914	2736	2565	2401	3286	2904	2560	2250	1970	1.3	0.0	-5.9	-17.2	NA
7mm Rem. Mag.	165	2900	2699	2507	2324	2147	3081	2669	2303	1978	1689	+2.5	+1.2	-5.9	-19.0	$28
7mm Rem Mag.	175	2860	2645	2440	2244	2057	3178	2718	2313	1956	1644	+2.5	+1.0	-6.5	-20.7	$21
7mm Rem. SA ULTRA MAG	140	3175	2934	2707	2490	2283	3033	2676	2277	1927	1620	1.3	0.0	-6	-17.7	NA
7mm Rem. SA ULTRA MAG	150	3110	2828	2563	2313	2077	3221	2663	2188	1782	1437	2.5	2.1	-3.6	-15.8	NA
7mm Rem. SA ULTRA MAG	160	2960	2762	2572	2390	2215	3112	2709	2350	2029	1743	2.6	2.2	-3.6	-15.4	NA
7mm Rem. WSM	140	3225	3008	2801	2603	2414	3233	2812	2438	2106	1812	1.2	0.0	-5.6	-16.4	NA
7mm Rem. WSM	160	2990	2744	2512	2081	1883	3176	2675	2241	1864	1538	1.6	0.0	-7.1	-20.8	NA
7mm Wea. Mag.	140	3225	2970	2729	2501	2283	3233	2741	2315	1943	1621	+2.5	+2.0	-3.2	-14.0	$35
7mm Wea. Mag.	154	3260	3023	2799	2586	2382	3539	3044	2609	2227	1890	+2.5	+2.8	-1.5	-10.8	$32
7mm Wea. Mag.*	160	3200	3004	2816	2637	2464	3637	3205	2817	2469	2156	+2.5	+2.7	-1.5	-10.6	$47
7mm Wea. Mag.	165	2950	2747	2553	2367	2189	3188	2765	2388	2053	1756	+2.5	+1.8	-4.2	-16.4	$43
7mm Wea. Mag.	175	2910	2693	2486	2288	2098	3293	2818	2401	2033	1711	+2.5	+1.2	-5.9	-19.4	$35
7.21(.284) Tomahawk	140	3300	3118	2943	2774	2612	3386	3022	2693	2393	2122	2.3	3.2	0.0	-7.7	NA
7mm STW	140	3325	3064	2818	2585	2364	3436	2918	2468	2077	1737	+2.3	+1.8	-3.0	-13.1	NA
7mm STW Supreme	160	3150	2894	2652	2422	2204	3526	2976	2499	2085	1727	1.3	0.0	-6.3	-18.5	NA
7mm Rem. Ultra Mag.	140	3425	3184	2956	2740	2534	3646	3151	2715	2333	1995	1.7	1.6	-2.6	-11.4	NA
7mm Firehawk	140	3625	3373	3135	2909	2695	4084	3536	3054	2631	2258	+2.2	+2.9	0.0	-7.03	NA
7.21 (.284) Firebird	140	3750	3522	3306	3101	2905	4372	3857	3399	2990	2625	1.6	2.4	0.0	-6.0	NA

30

Cartridge	Bullet Wgt. Grs.	Muzzle	100 yds.	200 yds.	300 yds.	400 yds.	Muzzle	100 yds.	200 yds.	300 yds.	400 yds.	100 yds.	200 yds.	300 yds.	400 yds.	Est. Price/box
30 Carbine	110	1990	1567	1236	1035	923	977	600	373	262	208	0.0	-13.5	0.0	0.0	$28**
303 Savage	190	1890	1612	1327	1183	1055	1507	1096	794	591	469	+2.5	-7.6	0.0	0.0	$24
30 Remington	170	2120	1822	1555	1328	1153	1696	1253	913	666	502	+2.5	-4.7	-26.3	0.0	$20
7.62x39mm Rus.	123/125	2300	2030	1780	1550	1350	1445	1125	860	655	500	+2.5	-2.0	-17.5	0.0	$13
30-30 Win.	55	3400	2693	2085	1570	1187	1412	886	521	301	172	+2.0	0.0	-10.2	-35.0	$18
30-30 Win.	125	2570	2090	1660	1320	1080	1830	1210	770	480	320	-2.0	-2.6	-19.9	0.0	$13
30-30 Win.	150	2390	2040	1723	1447	1225	1902	1386	989	697	499	0.0	-7.5	-27.0	-63.0	NA
30-30 Win. Supreme	150	2480	2095	1747	1446	1209	2049	1462	1017	697	487	0.0	-6.5	-24.5	0.0	NA
30-30 Win.	160	2300	1997	1719	1473	1268	1879	1416	1050	771	571	+2.5	-2.9	-20.2	0.0	$18
30-30 Win. Lever Evolution	160	2400	2150	1916	1699	NA	2046	1643	1304	1025	NA	3.0	0.2	-12.1	NA	NA
30-30 PMC Cowboy	170	1300	1198	1121			638	474				0.0	-27.0	0.0	0.0	NA
30-30 Win.*	170	2200	1895	1619	1381	1191	1827	1355	989	720	535	+2.5	-5.8	-23.6	0.0	$13
300 Savage	150	2630	2354	2094	1853	1631	2303	1845	1462	1143	886	+2.5	-0.4	-10.1	-30.7	$17
300 Savage	180	2350	2137	1935	1754	1570	2207	1825	1496	1217	985	+2.5	-1.6	-15.2	0.0	$17
30-40 Krag	180	2430	2213	2007	1813	1632	2360	1957	1610	1314	1064	+2.5	-1.4	-13.8	0.0	$18
7.65x53mm Arg.	180	2590	2390	2200	2010	1830	2685	2280	1925	1615	1345	+2.5	0.0	-27.6	0.0	NA
7.5x53mm Argentine	150	2785	2519	2269	2032	1814	2583	2113	1714	1376	1096	+2.0	0.0	-8.8	-25.5	NA
308 Marlin Express	160	2660	2430	2226	2026	1836	2513	2111	1761	1457	1197	3.0	1.7	-6.7	-23.5	NA
307 Winchester	150	2760	2321	1924	1575	1289	2530	1795	1233	826	554	+2.5	-1.5	-13.6	0.0	Disc.
307 Winchester	180	2510	2179	1874	1599	1362	2519	1898	1404	1022	742	+2.5	-1.6	-15.6	0.0	$20
7.5x55 Swiss	180	2650	2450	2250	2060	1880	2805	2390	2020	1700	1415	+2.5	+0.6	-8.1	-24.9	NA
7.5x55mm Swiss	165	2720	2515	2319	2132	1954	2710	2317	1970	1665	1398	+2.0	0.0	-8.5	-24.6	NA
30 Remington AR	123/125	2800	2465	2154	1867	1606	2176	1686	1288	967	716	2.1	0.0	-9.7	-29.4	NA

Cartridge	Bullet Wgt. Grs.	VELOCITY (fps)					ENERGY (ft. lbs.)					TRAJ. (in.)				Est. Price/box
		Muzzle	100 yds.	200 yds.	300 yds.	400 yds.	Muzzle	100 yds.	200 yds.	300 yds.	400 yds.	100 yds.	200 yds.	300 yds.	400 yds.	
308 Winchester	55	3770	3215	2726	2286	1888	1735	1262	907	638	435	-2.0	+1.4	-3.8	-15.8	$22
308 Winchester	150	2820	2533	2263	2009	1774	2648	2137	1705	1344	1048	+2.5	+0.4	-8.5	-26.1	$17
308 W. Superformance	150	3000	2772	2555	2348	1962	2997	2558	2173	1836	1540	1.5	0.0	-6.9	-20.0	NA
308 Winchester	165	2700	2440	2194	1963	1748	2670	2180	1763	1411	1199	+2.5	0.0	-9.7	-28.5	$20
308 Winchester	168	2680	2493	2314	2143	1979	2678	2318	1998	1713	1460	+2.5	0.0	-8.9	-25.3	$18
308 Win. Super Match	168	2870	2647	2462	2284	2114	3008	2613	2261	1946	1667	1.7	0.0	-7.5	-21.6	NA
308 Win. (Fed.)	170	2000	1740	1510	NA	NA	1510	1145	860	NA	NA	0.0	0.0	0.0	0.0	NA
308 Winchester	178	2620	2415	2220	2034	1857	2713	2306	1948	1635	1363	+2.5	0.0	-9.6	-27.6	$23
308 Win. Super Match	178	2780	2609	2444	2285	2132	3054	2690	2361	2064	1797	1.8	0.0	-7.6	-21.9	NA
308 Winchester*	180	2620	2393	2178	1974	1782	2743	2288	1896	1557	1269	+2.5	-0.2	-10.2	-28.5	$17
30-06 Spfd.	55	4080	3485	2965	2502	2083	2033	1483	1074	764	530	+2.0	+1.9	-2.1	-11.7	$22
30-06 Spfd. (Rem.)	125	2660	2335	2034	1757	NA	1964	1513	1148	856	NA	0.0	-5.2	-18.9	0.0	NA
30-06 Spfd.	125	3140	2780	2447	2138	1853	2736	2145	1662	1279	953	+2.0	+1.0	-6.2	-21.0	$17
30-06 Spfd.	150	2910	2617	2342	2083	1853	2820	2281	1827	1445	1135	+2.5	+0.8	-7.2	-23.4	$17
30-06 Superformance	150	3080	2848	2617	2417	2216	3159	2700	2298	1945	1636	1.4	0.0	-6.4	-18.9	NA
30-06 Spfd.	152	2910	2654	2413	2184	1968	2858	2378	1965	1610	1307	+2.5	+1.0	-6.6	-21.3	$23
30-06 Spfd.*	165	2800	2534	2283	2047	1825	2872	2352	1909	1534	1220	+2.5	+0.4	-8.4	-25.5	$17
30-06 Spfd.	168	2710	2522	2346	2169	2003	2739	2372	2045	1754	1497	+2.5	+0.4	-8.0	-23.5	$18
30-06 Spfd. (Fed.)	170	2000	1740	1510	NA	NA	1510	1145	860	NA	NA	0.0	0.0	0.0	0.0	NA
30-06 Spfd.	178	2720	2511	2311	2121	1939	2924	2491	2111	1777	1486	+2.5	+0.4	-8.2	-24.6	$23
30-06 Spfd.*	180	2700	2469	2250	2042	1846	2913	2436	2023	1666	1362	-2.5	0.0	-9.3	-27.0	$17
30-06 Superformance	180	2820	2630	2447	2272	2104	3178	2764	2393	2063	1769	1.8	0.0	-7.6	-21.9	NA
30-06 Spfd.	220	2410	2130	1870	1632	1422	2837	2216	1708	1301	988	+2.5	-1.7	-18.0	0.0	$17
30-06 High Energy	180	2880	2690	2500	2320	2150	3315	2880	2495	2150	1845	+1.7	0.0	-7.2	-21.0	NA
30 T/C Superformance	150	3000	2772	2555	2348	2151	2997	2558	2173	1836	1540	1.5	0.0	-6.9	-20.0	NA
30 T/C Superformance	165	2850	2644	2447	2258	2078	2975	2560	2193	1868	1582	1.7	0.0	-7.6	-22.0	NA
300 Rem SA Ultra Mag	150	3200	2901	2622	2359	2112	3410	2803	2290	1854	1485	1.3	0.0	-6.4	-19.1	NA
300 Rem SA Ultra Mag	165	3075	2792	2527	2276	2040	3464	2856	2339	1898	1525	1.5	0.0	-7	-20.7	NA
300 Rem SA Ultra Mag	180	2960	2761	2571	2389	2214	3501	3047	2642	2280	1959	2.6	2.2	-3.6	-15.4	NA
7.82 (308) Patriot	150	3250	2999	2762	2537	2323	3519	2997	2542	2145	1798	+1.2	0.0	-5.8	-16.9	NA
300 RCM Superformance	150	3310	3065	2833	2613	2404	3648	3128	2673	2274	1924	1.1	0.0	-5.4	-16.0	NA
300 RCM Superformance	165	3185	2964	2753	2552	2360	3716	3217	2776	2386	2040	1.2	0.0	-5.8	-17.0	NA
300 RCM Superformance	180	3040	2840	2649	2466	2290	3693	3223	2804	2430	2096	1.4	0.0	-6.4	-18.5	NA
300 WSM	150	3300	3061	2834	2619	2414	3628	3121	2676	2285	1941	1.1	0.0	-5.4	-15.9	NA
300 WSM	180	2970	2741	2524	2317	2120	3526	3005	2547	2147	1797	1.6	0.0	-7.0	-20.5	NA
300 WSM	180	3010	2923	2734	2554	2380	3242	2845	2490	2172	1886	1.3	0	-5.9	-17.2	NA
308 Norma Mag.	180	3020	2820	2630	2440	2270	3645	3175	2755	2385	2050	+2.5	+2.0	-3.5	-14.8	NA
300 Dakota	200	3000	2824	2656	2493	2336	3996	3542	3131	2760	2423	+2.2	+1.5	-4.0	-15.2	NA
300 H&H Magnum*	180	2880	2640	2412	2196	1990	3315	2785	2325	1927	1583	+2.5	+0.8	-6.8	-21.7	$24
300 H&H Magnum	220	2550	2267	2002	1757	NA	3167	2510	1958	1508	NA	-2.5	-0.4	-12.0	0.0	NA
300 Win. Mag.	150	3290	2951	2636	2342	2068	3605	2900	2314	1827	1424	+2.5	+1.9	-3.8	-15.8	$22
300 WM Superformance	150	3400	3150	2914	2690	2477	3850	3304	2817	2409	2043	1.0	0.0	-5.1	-15.0	NA
300 Win. Mag.	165	3100	2877	2665	2462	2269	3522	3033	2603	2221	1897	+2.5	+2.4	-3.0	-16.9	$24
300 Win. Mag.	178	2900	2760	2568	2375	2191	3509	3030	2606	2230	1897	+2.5	+1.4	-5.0	-17.6	$29
300 WM Super Match	178	2960	2770	2587	2412	2243	3462	3031	2645	2298	1988	1.5	0.0	-6.7	-19.4	NA
300 Win. Mag.*	180	2960	2745	2540	2344	2157	3501	3011	2578	2196	1859	+2.5	+1.2	-5.5	-18.5	$22
300 WM Superformance	180	3130	2927	2732	2546	2366	3917	3424	2983	2589	2238	1.3	0.0	-5.9	-17.3	NA
300 Win. Mag.	190	2885	1691	2506	2327	2156	3511	3055	2648	2285	1961	+2.5	+1.2	-5.7	-19.0	$26
300 Win. Mag.*	200	2825	2595	2376	2167	1970	3545	2991	2508	2086	1742	-2.5	+1.6	-4.7	-17.2	$36
300 Win. Mag.	220	2680	2448	2228	2020	1823	3508	2927	2424	1993	1623	+2.5	0.0	-9.5	-27.5	$23
300 Rem. Ultra Mag.	150	3450	3208	2980	2762	2556	3964	3427	2956	2541	2175	1.7	1.5	-2.6	-11.2	NA
300 Rem. Ultra Mag.	150	2910	2686	2473	2279	2077	2820	2403	2037	1716	1436	1.7	0.0	-7.4	-21.5	NA
300 Rem. Ultra Mag.	180	3250	3037	2834	2640	2454	4221	3686	3201	2786	2407	2.4	0.0	-3.0	-12.7	NA
300 Rem. Ultra Mag.	180	2960	2774	2505	2294	2093	3501	2971	2508	2103	1751	2.7	2.2	-3.8	-16.4	NA
300 Rem. Ultra Mag.	200	3032	2791	2562	2345	2138	4083	3459	2916	2442	2030	1.5	0.0	-6.8	-19.9	NA
300 Wea. Mag.	100	3900	3441	3038	2652	2305	3714	2891	2239	1717	1297	+2.0	+2.6	-0.6	-8.7	$32
300 Wea. Mag.	150	3600	3307	3033	2776	2533	4316	3642	3064	2566	2137	+2.5	+3.2	0.0	-8.1	$32
300 Wea. Mag.	165	3450	3210	3000	2792	2593	4360	3796	3297	2855	2464	+2.5	+3.2	0.0	-7.8	NA
300 Wea. Mag.	178	3120	2902	2695	2497	2308	3847	3329	2870	2464	2104	+2.5	-1.7	-3.6	-14.7	$43
300 Wea. Mag.	180	3330	3110	2910	2710	2520	4430	3875	3375	2935	2540	+1.0	0.0	-5.2	-15.1	NA
300 Wea. Mag.	190	3030	2830	2638	2455	2279	3873	3378	2936	2542	2190	+2.5	+1.6	-4.3	-16.0	$38
300 Wea. Mag.	220	2850	2541	2283	1964	1736	3967	3155	2480	1922	1471	+2.5	+0.4	-8.5	-26.4	$35
300 Warbird	180	3400	3180	2971	2772	2582	4620	4042	3528	3071	2664	+2.59	+3.25	0.0	-7.95	NA
300 Pegasus	180	3500	3319	3145	2978	2817	4896	4401	3953	3544	3172	+2.28	+2.89	0.0	-6.79	NA
31																
32-20 Win.	100	1210	1021	913	834	769	325	231	185	154	131	0.0	-32.3	0.0	0.0	$23**

Cartridge	Bullet Wgt. Grs.	VELOCITY (fps)					ENERGY (ft. lbs.)					TRAJ. (in.)				Est. Price/box
		Muzzle	100 yds.	200 yds.	300 yds.	400 yds.	Muzzle	100 yds.	200 yds.	300 yds.	400 yds.	100 yds.	200 yds.	300 yds.	400 yds.	
303 British	180	2460	2124	1817	1542	1311	2418	1803	1319	950	687	+2.5	-1.8	-16.8	0.0	$18
303 Light Mag.	150	2830	2570	2325	2094	1884	2667	2199	1800	1461	1185	+2.0	0.0	-8.4	-24.6	NA
7.62x54mm Rus.	146	2950	2730	2520	2320	NA	2820	2415	2055	1740	NA	+2.5	+2.0	-4.4	-17.7	NA
7.62x54mm Rus.	180	2580	2370	2180	2000	1820	2650	2250	1900	1590	1100	+2.5	0.0	-9.8	-28.5	NA
7.7x58mm Jap.	150	2640	2399	2170	1954	1752	2321	1916	1568	1271	1022	+2.3	0.0	-9.7	-28.5	NA
7.7x58mm Jap.	180	2500	2300	2100	1920	1750	2490	2105	1770	1475	1225	+2.5	0.0	-10.4	-30.2	NA
8mm																
8x56 R	205	2400	2188	1987	1797	1621	2621	2178	1796	1470	1196	+2.9	0.0	-11.7	-34.3	NA
8x57mm JS Mau.	165	2850	2520	2210	1930	1670	2965	2330	1795	1360	1015	+2.5	+1.0	-7.7	0.0	NA
32 Win. Special	165	2410	2145	1897	1669	NA	2128	1685	1318	1020	NA	2.0	0.0	-13.0	-19.9	NA
32 Win. Special	170	2250	1921	1626	1372	1175	1911	1393	998	710	521	+2.5	-3.5	-22.9	0.0	$14
8mm Mauser	170	2360	1969	1622	1333	1123	2102	1464	993	671	476	+2.5	-3.1	-22.2	0.0	$18
325 WSM	180	3060	2841	2632	2432	2242	3743	3226	2769	2365	2009	+1.4	0.0	-6.4	-18.7	NA
325 WSM	200	2950	2753	2565	2384	2210	3866	3367	2922	2524	2170	+1.5	0.0	-6.8	-19.8	NA
325 WSM	220	2840	2605	2382	2169	1968	3941	3316	2772	2300	1893	+1.8	0.0	-8.0	-23.3	NA
8mm Rem. Mag.	185	3080	2761	2464	2186	1927	3896	3131	2494	1963	1525	+2.5	+1.4	-5.5	-19.7	$30
8mm Rem. Mag.	220	2830	2581	2346	2123	1913	3912	3254	2688	2201	1787	+2.5	+0.6	-7.6	-23.5	Disc.
33																
338 Federal	180	2830	2590	2350	2130	1930	3200	2670	2215	1820	1480	1.8	0.0	-8.2	-23.9	NA
338 Marlin Express	200	2565	2365	2174	1992	1820	2922	2484	2099	1762	1471	3.0	1.2	-7.9	-25.9	NA
338 Federal	185	2750	2550	2350	2160	1980	3105	2660	2265	1920	1615	1.9	0.0	-8.3	-24.1	NA
338 Federal	210	2630	2410	2200	2010	1820	3225	2710	2265	1880	1545	2.3	0.0	-9.4	-27.3	NA
338-06	200	2750	2553	2364	2184	2011	3358	2894	2482	2118	1796	+1.9	0.0	-8.22	-23.6	NA
330 Dakota	250	2900	2719	2545	2378	2217	4668	4103	3595	3138	2727	+2.3	+1.3	-5.0	-17.5	NA
338 Lapua	250	2963	2795	2640	2493	NA	4842	4341	3881	3458	NA	+1.9	0.0	-7.9	0.0	NA
338 RCM Superformance	185	2980	2755	2542	2338	2143	3647	3118	2653	2242	1887	1.5	0.0	-6.9	-20.3	NA
338 RCM Superformance	200	2950	2744	2547	2358	2177	3846	3342	2879	2468	2104	1.6	0.0	-6.9	-20.1	NA
338 RCM Superformance	225	2750	2575	2407	2245	2089	3778	3313	2894	2518	2180	1.9	0.0	-7.9	-22.7	NA
338 WM Superformance	185	3080	2850	2632	2424	2226	3896	3337	2845	2413	2034	1.4	0.0	-6.4	-18.8	NA
338 Win. Mag.*	210	2830	2590	2370	2150	1940	3735	3130	2610	2155	1760	+2.5	+1.4	-6.0	-20.9	$33
338 Win. Mag.*	225	2785	2517	2266	2029	1808	3871	3165	2565	2057	1633	+2.5	+0.4	-8.5	-25.9	$27
338 WM Superformance	225	2840	2758	2582	2414	2252	4318	3798	3331	2911	2533	1.5	0.0	-6.8	-19.5	NA
338 Win. Mag.	230	2780	2573	2375	2186	2005	3948	3382	2881	2441	2054	+2.5	+1.2	-6.3	-21.0	$40
338 Win. Mag.*	250	2660	2456	2261	2075	1898	3927	3348	2837	2389	1999	+2.5	+0.2	-9.0	-26.2	$27
338 Ultra Mag.	250	2860	2645	2440	2244	2057	4540	3882	3303	2794	2347	1.7	0.0	-7.6	-22.1	NA
338 Lapua Match	250	2900	2760	2625	2494	2366	4668	4229	3825	3452	3108	1.5	0.0	-6.6	-18.8	NA
338 Lapua Match	285	2745	2623	2504	2388	2275	4768	4352	3966	3608	3275	1.8	0.0	-7.3	-20.8	NA
8.59.(.338) Galaxy	200	3100	2899	2707	2524	2347	4269	3734	3256	2829	2446	3	3.8	0.0	-9.3	NA
340 Wea. Mag.*	210	3250	2991	2746	2515	2295	4924	4170	3516	2948	2455	+2.5	+1.9	-1.8	-11.8	$56
340 Wea. Mag.*	250	3000	2806	2621	2443	2272	4995	4371	3812	3311	2864	+2.5	+2.0	-3.5	-14.8	$56
338 A-Square	250	3120	2799	2500	2220	1958	5403	4348	3469	2736	2128	+2.5	+2.7	-1.5	-10.5	NA
338-378 Wea. Mag.	225	3180	2974	2778	2591	2410	5052	4420	3856	3353	2902	3.1	3.8	0.0	-8.9	NA
338 Titan	225	3230	3010	2800	2600	2409	5211	4524	3916	3377	2898	+3.07	+3.8	0.0	-8.95	NA
338 Excalibur	200	3600	3361	3134	2920	2715	5755	5015	4363	3785	3274	+2.23	+2.87	0.0	-6.99	NA
338 Excalibur	250	3250	2922	2618	2333	2066	5863	4740	3804	3021	2370	+1.3	0.0	-6.35	-19.2	NA
34, 35																
348 Winchester	200	2520	2215	1931	1672	1443	2820	2178	1656	1241	925	+2.5	-1.4	-14.7	0.0	$42
357 Magnum	158	1830	1427	1138	980	883	1175	715	454	337	274	0.0	-16.2	-33.1	0.0	$25**
35 Remington	150	2300	1874	1506	1218	1039	1762	1169	755	494	359	+2.5	-4.1	-26.3	0.0	$16
35 Remington	200	2080	1698	1376	1140	1001	1921	1280	841	577	445	+2.5	-6.3	-17.1	-33.6	$16
35 Rem. Lever Evolution	200	2225	1963	1721	1503	NA	2198	1711	1315	1003	NA	3.0	-1.3	-17.5	NA	NA
356 Winchester	200	2460	2114	1797	1517	1284	2688	1985	1434	1022	732	+2.5	-1.8	-15.1	0.0	$31
356 Winchester	250	2160	1911	1682	1476	1299	2591	2028	1571	1210	937	+2.5	-3.7	-22.2	0.0	$31
358 Winchester	200	2490	2171	1876	1619	1379	2753	2093	1563	1151	844	+2.5	-1.6	-15.6	0.0	$31
358 STA	275	2850	2562	2292	2039	NA	4958	4009	3208	2539	NA	+1.9	0.0	-8.6	0.0	NA
350 Rem. Mag.	200	2710	2410	2130	1870	1631	3261	2579	2014	1553	1181	+2.5	-0.2	-10.0	-30.1	$33
35 Whelen	200	2675	2378	2100	1842	1606	3177	2510	1958	1506	1145	+2.5	-0.2	-10.3	-31.1	$20
35 Whelen	225	2500	2300	2110	1930	1770	3120	2650	2235	1870	1560	+2.6	0.0	-10.2	-29.9	NA
35 Whelen	250	2400	2197	2005	1823	1652	3197	2680	2230	1844	1515	+2.5	-1.2	-13.7	0.0	$20
358 Norma Mag.	250	2800	2510	2230	1970	1730	4350	3480	2750	2145	1655	+2.5	+1.0	-7.6	-25.2	NA
358 STA	275	2850	2562	229*2	2039	1764	4959	4009	3208	2539	1899	+1.9	0.0	-8.58	-26.1	NA
9.3mm																
9.3x57mm Mau.	286	2070	1810	1590	1390	1110	2710	2090	1600	1220	955	+2.5	-2.6	-22.5	0.0	NA
9.3x62mm Mau.	286	2360	2089	1844	1623	NA	3538	2771	2157	1670	1260	+2.5	-1.6	-21.0	0.0	NA
370 Sako Mag.	286	3550	2370	2200	2040	2880	4130	3570	3075	2630	2240	2.4	0.0	-9.5	-27.2	NA
9.3x64mm	286	2700	2505	2318	2139	1968	4629	3984	3411	2906	2460	+2.5	+2.7	-4.5	-19.2	NA

Cartridge	Bullet Wgt. Grs.	VELOCITY (fps) Muzzle	100 yds.	200 yds.	300 yds.	400 yds.	ENERGY (ft. lbs.) Muzzle	100 yds.	200 yds.	300 yds.	400 yds.	TRAJ. (in.) 100 yds.	200 yds.	300 yds.	400 yds.	Est. Price/box
9.3x74Rmm	286	2360	2136	1924	1727	1545	3536	2896	2351	1893	1516	0.0	-6.1	-21.7	-49.0	NA
375																
375 Winchester	200	2200	1841	1526	1268	1089	2150	1506	1034	714	527	+2.5	-4.0	-26.2	0.0	$27
375 Winchester	250	1900	1647	1424	1239	1103	2005	1506	1126	852	676	+2.5	-6.9	-33.3	0.0	$27
376 Steyr	225	2600	2331	2078	1842	1625	3377	2714	2157	1694	1319	2.5	0.0	-10.6	-31.4	NA
376 Steyr	270	2600	2372	2156	1951	1759	4052	3373	2787	2283	1855	2.3	0.0	-9.9	-28.9	NA
375 Dakota	300	2600	2316	2051	1804	1579	4502	3573	2800	2167	1661	+2.4	0.0	-11.0	-32.7	NA
375 N.E. 2-1/2"	270	2000	1740	1507	1310	NA	2398	1815	1362	1026	NA	+2.5	-6.0	-30.0	0.0	NA
375 Flanged	300	2450	2150	1886	1640	NA	3998	3102	2369	1790	NA	+2.5	-2.4	-17.0	0.0	NA
375 Ruger	270	2840	2600	2372	2156	1951	4835	4052	3373	2786	2283	1.8	0.0	-8.0	-23.6	NA
375 Ruger	300	2660	2344	2050	1780	1536	4713	3660	2800	2110	1572	2.4	0.0	-10.8	-32.6	NA
375 H&H Magnum	250	2670	2450	2240	2040	1850	3955	3335	2790	2315	1905	+2.5	-0.4	-10.2	-28.4	NA
375 H&H Magnum	270	2690	2420	2166	1928	1707	4337	3510	2812	2228	1747	+2.5	0.0	-10.0	-29.4	$28
375 H&H Magnum*	300	2530	2245	1979	1733	1512	4263	3357	2608	2001	1523	+2.5	-1.0	-10.5	-33.6	$28
375 H&H Hvy. Mag.	270	2870	2628	2399	2182	1976	4937	4141	3451	2150	1845	+1.7	0.0	-7.2	-21.0	NA
375 H&H Hvy. Mag.	300	2705	2386	2090	1816	1568	4873	3793	2908	2195	1637	+2.3	0.0	-10.4	-31.4	NA
375 Rem. Ultra Mag.	270	2900	2558	2241	1947	1678	5041	3922	3010	2272	1689	1.9	2.7	-8.9	-27.0	NA
375 Rem. Ultra Mag.	300	2760	2505	2263	2035	1822	5073	4178	3412	2759	2210	2.0	0.0	-8.8	-26.1	NA
375 Wea. Mag.	300	2700	2420	2157	1911	1685	4856	3901	3100	2432	1891	+2.5	-.04	-10.7	0.0	NA
378 Wea. Mag.	270	3180	2976	2781	2594	2415	6062	5308	4635	4034	3495	+2.5	+2.6	-1.8	-11.3	$71
378 Wea. Mag.	300	2929	2576	2252	1952	1680	5698	4419	3379	2538	1881	+2.5	+1.2	-7.0	-24.5	$77
375 A-Square	300	2920	2626	2351	2093	1850	5679	4594	3681	2917	2281	+2.5	+1.4	-6.0	-21.0	NA
38-40 Win.	180	1160	999	901	827	764	538	399	324	273	233	0.0	-33.9	0.0	0.0	$42**
40, 41																
400 A-Square DPM	400	2400	2146	1909	1689	NA	5116	2092	3236	2533	NA	2.98	0.0	-10.0	NA	NA
400 A-Square DPM	170	2980	2463	2001	1598	NA	3352	2289	1512	964	NA	2.16	0.0	-11.1	NA	NA
408 CheyTac	419	2850	2752	2657	2562	2470	7551	7048	6565	6108	5675	-1.02	0.0	1.9	4.2	NA
405 Win.	300	2200	1851	1545	1296		3224	2282	1589	1119		4.6	0.0	-19.5	0.0	NA
450/400-3"	400	2050	1815	1595	1402	NA	3732	2924	2259	1746	NA	0.0	NA	-33.4	NA	NA
416 Ruger	400	2400	2151	1917	1700	NA	5116	4109	3264	2568	NA	0.0	-6.0	-21.6	0.0	NA
416 Dakota	400	2450	2294	2143	1998	1859	5330	4671	4077	3544	3068	+2.5	-0.2	-10.5	-29.4	NA
416 Taylor	400	2350	2117	1896	1693	NA	4905	3980	3194	2547	NA	+2.5	-1.2	15.0	0.0	NA
416 Hoffman	400	2380	2145	1923	1718	1529	5031	4087	3285	2620	2077	+2.5	-1.0	-14.1	0.0	NA
416 Rigby	350	2600	2449	2303	2162	2026	5253	4661	4122	3632	3189	+2.5	-1.8	-10.2	-26.0	NA
416 Rigby	400	2370	2210	2050	1900	NA	4990	4315	3720	3185	NA	+2.5	-0.7	-12.1	0.0	NA
416 Rigby	410	2370	2110	1870	1640	NA	5115	4050	3165	2455	NA	+2.5	-2.4	-17.3	0.0	$110
416 Rem. Mag.*	350	2520	2270	2034	1814	1611	4935	4004	3216	2557	2017	+2.5	-0.8	-12.6	-35.0	$82
416 Wea. Mag.*	400	2700	2397	2115	1852	1613	6474	5104	3971	3047	2310	+2.5	0.0	-10.1	-30.4	$96
10.57 (416) Meteor	400	2730	2532	2342	2161	1987	6621	5695	4874	4147	3508	+1.9	0.0	-8.3	-24.0	NA
404 Jeffrey	400	2150	1924	1716	1525	NA	4105	3289	2614	2064	NA	+2.5	-4.0	-22.1	0.0	NA
425, 44																
425 Express	400	2400	2160	1934	1725	NA	5115	4145	3322	2641	NA	+2.5	-1.0	-14.0	0.0	NA
44-40 Win.	200	1190	1006	900	822	756	629	449	360	300	254	0.0	-33.3	0.0	0.0	$36**
44 Rem. Mag.	210	1920	1477	1155	982	880	1719	1017	622	450	361	0.0	-17.6	0.0	0.0	$14
44 Rem. Mag.	240	1760	1380	1114	970	878	1650	1015	661	501	411	0.0	-17.6	0.0	0.0	$13
444 Marlin	240	2350	1815	1377	1087	941	2942	1753	1001	630	472	+2.5	-15.1	-31.0	0.0	$22
444 Marlin	265	2120	1733	1405	1160	1012	2644	1768	1162	791	603	+2.5	-6.0	-32.2	0.0	Disc.
444 Mar. Lever Evolution	265	2325	1971	1652	1380	NA	3180	2285	1606	1120	NA	3.0	-1.4	-18.6	NA	NA
444 Mar. Superformance	265	2400	1976	1603	1298	NA	3389	2298	1512	991	NA	4.1	0.0	-17.8	NA	NA
45																
45-70 Govt.	300	1810	1497	1244	1073	969	2182	1492	1031	767	625	0.0	-14.8	0.0	0.0	$21
45-70 Govt. Supreme	300	1880	1558	1292	1103	988	2355	1616	1112	811	651	0.0	-12.9	-46.0	-105.0	NA
45-70 Lever Evolution	325	2050	1729	1450	1225	NA	3032	2158	1516	1083	NA	3.0	-4.1	-27.8	NA	NA
45-70 Govt. CorBon	350	1800	1526	1296			2519	1810	1307			0.0	-14.6	0.0	0.0	NA
45-70 Govt.	405	1330	1168	1055	977	918	1590	1227	1001	858	758	0.0	-24.6	0.0	0.0	$21
45-70 Govt. PMC Cowboy	405	1550	1193				1639	1280				0.0	-23.9	0.0	0.0	NA
45-70 Govt. Garrett	415	1850					3150					3.0	-7.0	0.0	0.0	NA
45-70 Govt. Garrett	530	1550	1343	1178	1062	982	2828	2123	1633	1327	1135	0.0	-17.8	0.0	0.0	NA
450 Bushmaster	250	2200	1831	1508	1480	1073	2686	1860	1262	864	639	0.0	-9.0	-33.5	0.0	NA
450 Marlin	350	2100	1774	1488	1254	1089	3427	2446	1720	1222	922	0.0	-9.7	-35.2	0.0	NA
450 Mar. Lever Evolution	325	2225	1887	1585	1331	NA	3572	2569	1813	1278	NA	3.0	-2.2	-21.3	NA	NA
458 Win. Magnum	350	2470	1990	1570	1250	1060	4740	3065	1915	1205	870	+2.5	-2.5	-21.6	0.0	$43
458 Win. Magnum	400	2380	2170	1960	1770	NA	5030	4165	3415	2785	NA	+2.5	-0.4	-13.4	0.0	$73
458 Win. Magnum	465	2220	1999	1791	1601	NA	5088	4127	3312	2646	NA	+2.5	-2.0	-17.7	0.0	NA

Cartridge	Bullet Wgt. Grs.	VELOCITY (fps)					ENERGY (ft. lbs.)					TRAJ. (in.)				Est. Price/box
		Muzzle	100 yds.	200 yds.	300 yds.	400 yds.	Muzzle	100 yds.	200 yds.	300 yds.	400 yds.	100 yds.	200 yds.	300 yds.	400 yds.	
458 Win. Magnum	500	2040	1823	1623	1442	1237	4620	3689	2924	2308	1839	+2.5	-3.5	-22.0	0.0	$61
458 Win. Magnum	510	2040	1770	1527	1319	1157	4712	3547	2640	1970	1516	+2.5	-4.1	-25.0	0.0	$41
450 N.E. 3-1/4"	465	2190	1970	1765	1577	NA	4952	4009	3216	2567	NA	+2.5	-3.0	-20.0	0.0	NA
450 N.E. 3-1/4"	500	2150	1920	1708	1514	NA	5132	4093	3238	2544	NA	+2.5	-4.0	-22.9	0.0	NA
450 No. 2	465	2190	1970	1765	1577	NA	4952	4009	3216	2567	NA	+2.5	-3.0	-20.0	0.0	NA
450 No. 2	500	2150	1920	1708	1514	NA	5132	4093	3238	2544	NA	+2.5	-4.0	-22.9	0.0	NA
458 Lott	465	2380	2150	1932	1730	NA	5848	4773	3855	3091	NA	+2.5	-1.0	-14.0	0.0	NA
458 Lott	500	2300	2062	1838	1633	NA	5873	4719	3748	2960	NA	+2.5	-1.6	-16.4	0.0	NA
450 Ackley Mag.	465	2400	2169	1950	1747	NA	5947	4857	3927	3150	NA	+2.5	-1.0	-13.7	0.0	NA
450 Ackley Mag.	500	2320	2081	1855	1649	NA	5975	4085	3820	3018	NA	+2.5	-1.2	-15.0	0.0	NA
460 Short A-Sq.	500	2420	2175	1943	1729	NA	6501	5250	4193	3319	NA	+2.5	-0.8	-12.8	0.0	NA
460 Wea. Mag.	500	2700	2404	2128	1869	1635	8092	6416	5026	3878	2969	+2.5	+0.6	-8.9	-28.0	$72
475																
500/465 N.E.	480	2150	1917	1703	1507	NA	4926	3917	3089	2419	NA	+2.5	-4.0	-22.2	0.0	NA
470 Rigby	500	2150	1940	1740	1560	NA	5130	4170	3360	2695	NA	+2.5	-2.8	-19.4	0.0	NA
470 Nitro Ex.	480	2190	1954	1735	1536	NA	5111	4070	3210	2515	NA	+2.5	-3.5	-20.8	0.0	NA
470 Nitro Ex.	500	2150	1890	1650	1440	1270	5130	3965	3040	2310	1790	+2.5	-4.3	-24.0	0.0	$177
475 No. 2	500	2200	1955	1728	1522	NA	5375	4243	3316	2573	NA	+2.5	-3.2	-20.9	0.0	NA
50, 58																
505 Gibbs	525	2300	2063	1840	1637	NA	6166	4922	3948	3122	NA	+2.5	-3.0	-18.0	0.0	NA
500 N.E.-3"	570	2150	1928	1722	1533	NA	5850	4703	3752	2975	NA	+2.5	-3.7	-22.0	0.0	NA
500 N.E.-3"	600	2150	1927	1721	1531	NA	6158	4947	3944	3124	NA	+2.5	-4.0	-22.0	0.0	NA
495 A-Square	570	2350	2117	1896	1693	NA	5850	4703	3752	2975	NA	+2.5	-1.0	-14.5	0.0	NA
495 A-Square	600	2280	2050	1833	1635	NA	6925	5598	4478	3562	NA	+2.5	-2.0	-17.0	0.0	NA
500 A-Square	600	2380	2144	1922	1766	NA	7546	6126	4920	3922	NA	+2.5	-3.0	-17.0	0.0	NA
500 A-Square	707	2250	2040	1841	1567	NA	7947	6530	5318	4311	NA	+2.5	-2.0	-17.0	0.0	NA
500 BMG PMC	660	3080	2854	2639	2444	2248	13688	500 yd. zero				+3.1	+3.9	+4.7	+2.8	NA
577 Nitro Ex.	750	2050	1793	1562	1360	NA	6990	5356	4065	3079	NA	+2.5	-5.0	-26.0	0.0	NA
577 Tyrannosaur	750	2400	2141	1898	1675	NA	9591	7633	5996	4671	NA	+3.0	0.0	-12.9	0.0	NA
600, 700																
600 N.E.	900	1950	1680	1452	NA	NA	7596	5634	4212	NA	NA	+5.6	0.0	0.0	0.0	NA
700 N.E.	1200	1900	1676	1472	NA	NA	9618	7480	5774	NA	NA	+5.7	0.0	0.0	0.0	NA
50 BMG																
50 BMG Match	750	2820	2728	2637	2549	2462	13241	12388	11580	10815	10090	1.5	0.0	-6.5	-18.3	NA

Notes: Blanks are available in 32 S&W, 38 S&W and 38 Special. "V" after barrel length indicates test barrel was vented to produce ballistics similar to a revolver with a normal barrel-to-cylinder gap. Ammo prices are per 50 rounds except when marked with an ** which signifies a 20 round box; *** signifies a 25-round box. Not all loads are available from all ammo manufacturers. Listed loads are those made by Remington, Winchester, Federal, and others. DISC. is a discontinued load. Prices are rounded to the nearest whole dollar and will vary with brand and retail outlet. † = new bullet weight this year; "c" indicates a change in data.

Cartridge	Bullet Wgt. Grs.	VELOCITY (fps)			ENERGY (ft. lbs.)			Mid-Range Traj. (in.)		Bbl. Lgth. (in).	Est. Price/ box
		Muzzle	50 yds.	100 yds.	Muzzle	50 yds.	100 yds.	50 yds.	100 yds.		
22, 25											
221 Rem. Fireball	50	2650	2380	2130	780	630	505	0.2	0.8	10.5"	$15
25 Automatic	35	900	813	742	63	51	43	NA	NA	2"	$18
25 Automatic	45	815	730	655	65	55	40	1.8	7.7	2"	$21
25 Automatic	50	760	705	660	65	55	50	2.0	8.7	2"	$17
30											
7.5mm Swiss	107	1010	NA	NA	240	NA	NA	NA	NA	NA	NEW
7.62mm Tokarev	87	1390	NA	NA	365	NA	NA	0.6	NA	4.5"	NA
7.62 Nagant	97	790	NA	NA	134	NA	NA	NA	NA	NA	NEW
7.63 Mauser	88	1440	NA	NA	405	NA	NA	NA	NA	NA	NEW
30 Luger	93†	1220	1110	1040	305	255	225	0.9	3.5	4.5"	$34
30 Carbine	110	1790	1600	1430	785	625	500	0.4	1.7	10"	$28
30-357 AeT	123	1992	NA	NA	1084	NA	NA	NA	NA	10"	NA
32											
32 S&W	88	680	645	610	90	80	75	2.5	10.5	3"	$17
32 S&W Long	98	705	670	635	115	100	90	2.3	10.5	4"	$17
32 Short Colt	80	745	665	590	100	80	60	2.2	9.9	4"	$19
32 H&R Magnum	85	1100	1020	930	230	195	165	1.0	4.3	4.5"	$21
32 H&R Magnum	95	1030	940	900	225	190	170	1.1	4.7	4.5"	$19
327 Federal Magnum	85	1400	1220	1090	370	280	225	NA	NA	4-V	NA
327 Federal Magnum	100	1500	1320	1180	500	390	310	-0.2	-4.50	4-V	NA
32 Automatic	60	970	895	835	125	105	95	1.3	5.4	4"	$22
32 Automatic	60	1000	917	849	133	112	96			4"	NA
32 Automatic	65	950	890	830	130	115	100	1.3	5.6	NA	NA
32 Automatic	71	905	855	810	130	115	95	1.4	5.8	4"	$19
8mm Lebel Pistol	111	850	NA	NA	180	NA	NA	NA	NA	NA	NEW
8mm Steyr	112	1080	NA	NA	290	NA	NA	NA	NA	NA	NEW
8mm Gasser	126	850	NA	NA	200	NA	NA	NA	NA	NA	NEW
9mm, 38											
380 Automatic	60	1130	960	NA	170	120	NA	1.0	NA	NA	NA
380 Automatic	85/88	990	920	870	190	165	145	1.2	5.1	4"	$20
380 Automatic	90	1000	890	800	200	160	130	1.2	5.5	3.75"	$10
380 Automatic	95/100	955	865	785	190	160	130	1.4	5.9	4"	$20
38 Super Auto +P	115	1300	1145	1040	430	335	275	0.7	3.3	5"	$26
38 Super Auto +P	125/130	1215	1100	1015	425	350	300	0.8	3.6	5"	$26
38 Super Auto +P	147	1100	1050	1000	395	355	325	0.9	4.0	5"	NA
9x18mm Makarov	95	1000	930	874	211	182	161	NA	NA	4"	NEW
9x18mm Ultra	100	1050	NA	NA	240	NA	NA	NA	NA	NA	NEW
9x21	124	1150	1050	980	365	305	265	NA	NA	4"	NA
9x23mm Largo	124	1190	1055	966	390	306	257	0.7	3.7	4"	NA
9x23mm Win.	125	1450	1249	1103	583	433	338	0.6	2.8	NA	NA
9mm Steyr	115	1180	NA	NA	350	NA	NA	NA	NA	NA	NEW
9mm Luger	88	1500	1190	1010	440	275	200	0.6	3.1	4"	$24
9mm Luger	90	1360	1112	978	370	247	191	NA	NA	4"	$26
9mm Luger	95	1300	1140	1010	350	275	215	0.8	3.4	4"	NA
9mm Luger	100	1180	1080	NA	305	255	NA	0.9	NA	4"	NA
9mm Luger Guard Dog	105	1230	1070	970	355	265	220	NA	NA	4"	NA
9mm Luger	115	1155	1045	970	340	280	240	0.9	3.9	4"	$21
9mm Luger	123/125	1110	1030	970	340	290	260	1.0	4.0	4"	$23
9mm Luger	140	935	890	850	270	245	225	1.3	4.5	4"	$23
9mm Luger	147	990	940	900	320	290	265	1.1	4.9	4"	$26
9mm Luger +P	90	1475	NA	NA	437	NA	NA	NA	NA	NA	NA
9mm Luger +P	115	1250	1113	1019	399	316	265	0.8	3.5	4"	$27
9mm Federal	115	1280	1130	1040	420	330	280	0.7	3.3	4"V	$24
9mm Luger Vector	115	1155	1047	971	341	280	241	NA	NA	4"	NA
9mm Luger +P	124	1180	1089	1021	384	327	287	0.8	3.8	4"	NA
38											
38 S&W	146	685	650	620	150	135	125	2.4	10.0	4"	$19
38 Short Colt	125	730	685	645	150	130	115	2.2	9.4	6"	$19
39 Special	100	950	900	NA	200	180	NA	1.3	NA	4"V	NA
38 Special	110	945	895	850	220	195	175	1.3	5.4	4"V	$23
38 Special	110	945	895	850	220	195	175	1.3	5.4	4"V	$23

Notes: Blanks are available in 32 S&W, 38 S&W and 38 Special. "V" after barrel length indicates test barrel was vented to produce ballistics similar to a revolver with a normal barrel-to-cylinder gap. Ammo prices are per 50 rounds except when marked with an ** which signifies a 20 round box; *** signifies a 25-round box. Not all loads are available from all ammo manufacturers. Listed loads are those made by Remington, Winchester, Federal, and others. DISC. is a discontinued load.
Prices are rounded to the nearest whole dollar and will vary with brand and retail outlet. † = new bullet weight this year; "c" indicates a change in data.

Cartridge	Bullet Wgt. Grs.	VELOCITY (fps)			ENERGY (ft. lbs.)			Mid-Range Traj. (in.)		Bbl. Lgth. (in).	Est. Price/ box
		Muzzle	50 yds.	100 yds.	Muzzle	50 yds.	100 yds.	50 yds.	100 yds.		
38 Special	130	775	745	710	175	160	120	1.9	7.9	4"V	$22
38 Special Cowboy	140	800	767	735	199	183	168			7.5" V	NA
38 (Multi-Ball)	140	830	730	505	215	130	80	2.0	10.6	4"V	$10**
38 Special	148	710	635	565	165	130	105	2.4	10.6	4"V	$17
38 Special	158	755	725	690	200	185	170	2.0	8.3	4"V	$18
38 Special +P	95	1175	1045	960	290	230	195	0.9	3.9	4"V	$23
38 Special +P	110	995	925	870	240	210	185	1.2	5.1	4"V	$23
38 Special +P	125	975	929	885	264	238	218	1	5.2	4"	NA
38 Special +P	125	945	900	860	250	225	205	1.3	5.4	4"V	#23
38 Special +P	129	945	910	870	255	235	215	1.3	5.3	4"V	$11
38 Special +P	130	925	887	852	247	227	210	1.3	5.50	4"V	NA
38 Special +P	147/150(c)	884	NA	NA	264	NA	NA	NA	NA	4"V	$27
38 Special +P	158	890	855	825	280	255	240	1.4	6.0	4"V	$20
357											
357 SIG	115	1520	NA	NA	593	NA	NA	NA	NA	NA	NA
357 SIG	124	1450	NA	NA	578	NA	NA	NA	NA	NA	NA
357 SIG	125	1350	1190	1080	510	395	325	0.7	3.1	4"	NA
357 SIG	150	1130	1030	970	420	355	310	0.9	4.0	NA	NA
356 TSW	115	1520	NA	NA	593	NA	NA	NA	NA	NA	NA
356 TSW	124	1450	NA	NA	578	NA	NA	NA	NA	NA	NA
356 TSW	135	1280	1120	1010	490	375	310	0.8	3.5	NA	NA
356 TSW	147	1220	1120	1040	485	410	355	0.8	3.5	5"	NA
357 Mag., Super Clean	105	1650									NA
357 Magnum	110	1295	1095	975	410	290	230	0.8	3.5	4"V	$25
357 (Med.Vel.)	125	1220	1075	985	415	315	270	0.8	3.7	4"V	$25
357 Magnum	125	1450	1240	1090	585	425	330	0.6	2.8	4"V	$25
357 (Multi-Ball)	140	1155	830	665	420	215	135	1.2	6.4	4"V	$11**
357 Magnum	140	1360	1195	1075	575	445	360	0.7	3.0	4"V	$25
357 Magnum FlexTip	140	1440	1274	1143	644	504	406	NA	NA	NA	NA
357 Magnum	145	1290	1155	1060	535	430	360	0.8	3.5	4"V	$26
357 Magnum	150/158	1235	1105	1015	535	430	360	0.8	3.5	4"V	$25
357 Mag. Cowboy	158	800	761	725	225	203	185				NA
357 Magnum	165	1290	1189	1108	610	518	450	0.7	3.1	8-3/8"	NA
357 Magnum	180	1145	1055	985	525	445	390	0.9	3.9	4"V	$25
357 Magnum	180	1180	1088	1020	557	473	416	0.8	3.6	8"V	NA
357 Mag. CorBon F.A.	180	1650	1512	1386	1088	913	767	1.66	0.0		NA
357 Mag. CorBon	200	1200	1123	1061	640	560	500	3.19	0.0		NA
357 Rem. Maximum	158	1825	1590	1380	1170	885	670	0.4	1.7	10.5"	$14**
40, 10mm											
40 S&W	135	1140	1070	NA	390	345	NA	0.9	NA	4"	NA
40 S&W Guard Dog	135	1200	1040	940	430	325	265	NA	NA	4"	NA
40 S&W	155	1140	1026	958	447	362	309	0.9	4.1	4"	$14***
40 S&W	165	1150	NA	NA	485	NA	NA	NA	NA	4"	$18***
40 S&W	180	985	936	893	388	350	319	1.4	5.0	4"	$14***
40 S&W	180	1015	960	914	412	368	334	1.3	4.5	4"	NA
400 Cor-Bon	135	1450	NA	NA	630	NA	NA	NA	NA	5"	NA
10mm Automatic	155	1125	1046	986	436	377	335	0.9	3.9	5"	$26
10mm Automatic	170	1340	1165	1145	680	510	415	0.7	3.2	5"	$31
10mm Automatic	175	1290	1140	1035	650	505	420	0.7	3.3	5.5"	$11**
10mm Auto. (FBI)	180	950	905	865	361	327	299	1.5	5.4	4"	$16**
10mm Automatic	180	1030	970	920	425	375	340	1.1	4.7	5"	$16**
10mm Auto H.V.	180†	1240	1124	1037	618	504	430	0.8	3.4	5"	$27
10mm Automatic	200	1160	1070	1010	495	510	430	0.9	3.8	5"	$14**
10.4mm Italian	177	950	NA	NA	360	NA	NA	NA	NA	NA	NEW
41 Action Exp.	180	1000	947	903	400	359	326	0.5	4.2	5"	$13**
41 Rem. Magnum	170	1420	1165	1015	760	515	390	0.7	3.2	4"V	$33
41 Rem. Magnum	175	1250	1120	1030	605	490	410	0.8	3.4	4"V	$14**
41 (Med. Vel.)	210	965	900	840	435	375	330	1.3	5.4	4"V	$30
41 Rem. Magnum	210	1300	1160	1060	790	630	535	0.7	3.2	4"V	$33
41 Rem. Magnum	240	1250	1151	1075	833	706	616	0.8	3.3	6.5V	NA
44											
44 S&W Russian	247	780	NA	NA	335	NA	NA	NA	NA	NA	NA
44 S&W Special	180	980	NA	NA	383	NA	NA	NA	NA	6.5"	NA
44 S&W Special	180	1000	935	882	400	350	311	NA	NA	7.5"V	NA

Notes: Blanks are available in 32 S&W, 38 S&W and 38 Special. "V" after barrel length indicates test barrel was vented to produce ballistics similar to a revolver with a normal barrel-to-cylinder gap. Ammo prices are per 50 rounds except when marked with an ** which signifies a 20 round box; *** signifies a 25-round box. Not all loads are available from all ammo manufacturers. Listed loads are those made by Remington, Winchester, Federal, and others. DISC. is a discontinued load.
Prices are rounded to the nearest whole dollar and will vary with brand and retail outlet. † = new bullet weight this year; "c" indicates a change in data.

Cartridge	Bullet Wgt. Grs.	VELOCITY (fps)			ENERGY (ft. lbs.)			Mid-Range Traj. (in.)		Bbl. Lgth. (in).	Est. Price/ box
		Muzzle	50 yds.	100 yds.	Muzzle	50 yds.	100 yds.	50 yds.	100 yds.		
44 S&W Special	200†	875	825	780	340	302	270	1.2	6.0	6"	$13**
44 S&W Special	200	1035	940	865	475	390	335	1.1	4.9	6.5"	$13**
44 S&W Special	240/246	755	725	695	310	285	265	2.0	8.3	6.5"	$26
44-40 Win. Cowboy	225	750	723	695	281	261	242				NA
44 Rem. Magnum	180	1610	1365	1175	1035	745	550	0.5	2.3	4"V	$18**
44 Rem. Magnum	200	1400	1192	1053	870	630	492	0.6	NA	6.5"	$20
44 Rem. Magnum	210	1495	1310	1165	1040	805	635	0.6	2.5	6.5"	$18**
44 Rem. Mag. FlexTip	225	1410	1240	1111	993	768	617	NA	NA	NA	NA
44 (Med. Vel.)	240	1000	945	900	535	475	435	1.1	4.8	6.5"	$17
44 R.M. (Jacketed)	240	1180	1080	1010	740	625	545	0.9	3.7	4"V	$18**
44 R.M. (Lead)	240	1350	1185	1070	970	750	610	0.7	3.1	4"V	$29
44 Rem. Magnum	250	1180	1100	1040	775	670	600	0.8	3.6	6.5"V	$21
44 Rem. Magnum	250	1250	1148	1070	867	732	635	0.8	3.3	6.5"V	NA
44 Rem. Magnum	275	1235	1142	1070	931	797	699	0.8	3.3	6.5"	NA
44 Rem. Magnum	300	1200	1100	1026	959	806	702	NA	NA	7.5"	$17
44 Rem. Magnum	330	1385	1297	1220	1406	1234	1090	1.83	0.00	NA	NA
440 CorBon	260	1700	1544	1403	1669	1377	1136	1.58	NA	10"	NA

45, 50

Cartridge	Bullet Wgt. Grs.	Muzzle	50 yds.	100 yds.	Muzzle	50 yds.	100 yds.	50 yds.	100 yds.	Bbl. Lgth.	Est. Price/box
450 Short Colt/450 Revolver	226	830	NA	NA	350	NA	NA	NA	NA	NA	NEW
45 S&W Schofield	180	730	NA	NA	213	NA	NA	NA	NA	NA	NA
45 S&W Schofield	230	730	NA	NA	272	NA	NA	NA	NA	NA	NA
45 G.A.P.	185	1090	970	890	490	385	320	1.0	4.7	5"	NA
45 G.A.P.	230	880	842	NA	396	363	NA	NA	NA	5"	NA
45 Automatic	165	1030	930	NA	385	315	NA	1.2	NA	5"	NA
45 Automatic Guard Dog	165	1140	1030	950	475	390	335	NA	NA	5"	NA
45 Automatic	185	1000	940	890	410	360	325	1.1	4.9	5"	$28
45 Auto. (Match)	185	770	705	650	245	204	175	2.0	8.7	5"	$28
45 Auto. (Match)	200	940	890	840	392	352	312	2.0	8.6	5"	$20
45 Automatic	200	975	917	860	421	372	328	1.4	5.0	5"	$18
45 Automatic	230	830	800	675	355	325	300	1.6	6.8	5"	$27
45 Automatic	230	880	846	816	396	366	340	1.5	6.1	5"	NA
45 Automatic +P	165	1250	NA	NA	573	NA	NA	NA	NA	NA	NA
45 Automatic +P	185	1140	1040	970	535	445	385	0.9	4.0	5"	$31
45 Automatic +P	200	1055	982	925	494	428	380	NA	NA	5"	NA
45 Super	185	1300	1190	1108	694	582	504	NA	NA	5"	NA
45 Win. Magnum	230	1400	1230	1105	1000	775	635	0.6	2.8	5"	$14**
45 Win. Magnum	260	1250	1137	1053	902	746	640	0.8	3.3	5"	$16**
45 Win. Mag. CorBon	320	1150	1080	1025	940	830	747	3.47			NA
455 Webley MKII	262	850	NA	NA	420	NA	NA	NA	NA	NA	NA
45 Colt	200	1000	938	889	444	391	351	1.3	4.8	5.5"	$21
45 Colt	225	960	890	830	460	395	345	1.3	5.5	5.5"	$22
45 Colt + P CorBon	265	1350	1225	1126	1073	884	746	2.65	0.0		NA
45 Colt + P CorBon	300	1300	1197	1114	1126	956	827	2.78	0.0		NA
45 Colt	250/255	860	820	780	410	375	340	1.6	6.6	5.5"	$27
454 Casull	250	1300	1151	1047	938	735	608	0.7	3.2	7.5"V	NA
454 Casull	260	1800	1577	1381	1871	1436	1101	0.4	1.8	7.5"V	NA
454 Casull	300	1625	1451	1308	1759	1413	1141	0.5	2.0	7.5"V	NA
454 Casull CorBon	360	1500	1387	1286	1800	1640	1323	2.01	0.0		NA
460 S&W	200	2300	2042	1801	2350	1851	1441	0	-1.60	NA	NA
460 S&W	260	2000	1788	1592	2309	1845	1464	NA	NA	7.5"	NA
460 S&W	250	1450	1267	1127	1167	891	705	NA	NA	8.375-V	NA
460 S&W	250	1900	1640	1412	2004	1494	1106	0	-2.75	NA	NA
460 S&W	300	1750	1510	1300	2040	1510	1125	NA	NA	8.4-V	NA
460 S&W	395	1550	1389	1249	2108	1691	1369	0	-4.00	NA	NA
475 Linebaugh	400	1350	1217	1119	1618	1315	1112	NA	NA	NA	NA
480 Ruger	325	1350	1191	1076	1315	1023	835	2.6	0.0	7.5"	NA
50 Action Exp.	325	1400	1209	1075	1414	1055	835	0.2	2.3	6"	$24**
500 S&W	275	1665	1392	1183	1693	1184	854	1.5	NA	8.375	NA
500 S&W	325	1800	1560	1350	2340	1755	1315	NA	NA	8.4-V	NA
500 S&W	350	1400	1231	1106	1523	1178	951	NA	NA	10"	NA
500 S&W	400	1675	1472	1299	2493	1926	1499	1.3	NA	8.375	NA
500 S&W	440	1625	1367	1169	2581	1825	1337	1.6	NA	8.375	NA
500 S&W	500	1425	1281	1164	2254	1823	1505	NA	NA	10"	NA

Note: The actual ballistics obtained with your firearm can vary considerably from the advertised ballistics.
Also, ballistics can vary from lot to lot with the same brand and type load.

Cartridge	Bullet Wt. Grs.	Velocity (fps) 22-1/2" Bbl.		Energy (ft. lbs.) 22-1/2" Bbl.		Mid-Range Traj. (in.)	Muzzle Velocity
		Muzzle	100 yds.	Muzzle	100 yds.	100 yds.	6" Bbl.
17 Aguila	20	1850	1267	NA	NA	NA	NA
17 Hornady Mach 2	17	2100	1530	166	88	0.7	NA
17 HMR Lead Free	15.5	2550	1901	NA	NA	.90	NA
17 HMR TNT Green	16	2500	1642	222	96	NA	NA
17 HMR	17	2550	1902	245	136	NA	NA
17 HMR	20	2375	1776	250	140	NA	NA
5mm Rem. Rimfire Mag.	30	2300	1669	352	188	NA	24
22 Short Blank	—	—	—	—	—	—	—
22 Short CB	29	727	610	33	24	NA	706
22 Short Target	29	830	695	44	31	6.8	786
22 Short HP	27	1164	920	81	50	4.3	1077
22 Colibri	20	375	183	6	1	NA	NA
22 Super Colibri	20	500	441	11	9	NA	NA
22 Long CB	29	727	610	33	24	NA	706
22 Long HV	29	1180	946	90	57	4.1	1031
22 LR Pistol Match	40	1070	890	100	70	4.6	940
22 LR Shrt. Range Green	21	1650	912	127	NA	NA	NA
22 LR Sub Sonic HP	38	1050	901	93	69	4.7	NA
22 LR Segmented HP	40	1050	897	98	72	NA	NA
22 LR Standard Velocity	40	1070	890	100	70	4.6	940
22 LR AutoMatch	40	1200	990	130	85	NA	NA
22 LR HV	40	1255	1016	140	92	3.6	1060
22 LR Silhoutte	42	1220	1003	139	94	3.6	1025
22 SSS	60	950	802	120	86	NA	NA
22 LR HV HP	40	1280	1001	146	89	3.5	1085
22 Velocitor GDHP	40	1435	0	0	0	NA	NA
22 LR Segmented HP	37	1435	1080	169	96	2.9	NA
22 LR Hyper HP	32/33/34	1500	1075	165	85	2.8	NA
22 LR Expediter	32	1640	NA	191	NA	NA	NA
22 LR Stinger HP	32	1640	1132	191	91	2.6	1395
22 LR Lead Free	30	1650	NA	181	NA	NA	NA
22 LR Hyper Vel	30	1750	1191	204	93	NA	NA
22 LR Shot #12	31	950	NA	NA	NA	NA	NA
22 WRF LFN	45	1300	1015	169	103	3	NA
22 Win. Mag. Lead Free	28	2200	NA	301	NA	NA	NA
22 Win. Mag.	30	2200	1373	322	127	1.4	1610
22 Win. Mag. V-Max BT	33	2000	1495	293	164	0.60	NA
22 Win. Mag. JHP	34	2120	1435	338	155	1.4	NA
22 Win. Mag. JHP	40	1910	1326	324	156	1.7	1480
22 Win. Mag. FMJ	40	1910	1326	324	156	1.7	1480
22 Win. Mag. Dyna Point	45	1550	1147	240	131	2.60	NA
22 Win. Mag. JHP	50	1650	1280	300	180	1.3	NA
22 Win. Mag. Shot #11	52	1000	—	NA	—		NA

NOTES: * = 10 rounds per box. ** = 5 rounds per box. Pricing variations and number of rounds per box can occur with type and brand of ammunition. Listed pricing is the average nominal cost for load style and box quantity shown. Not every brand is available in all shot size variations. Some manufacturers do not provide suggested list prices. All prices rounded to nearest whole dollar. The price you pay will vary dependent upon outlet of purchase. # = new load spec this year; "C" indicates a change in data.

10 Gauge 3-1/2" Magnum

Dram Equiv.	Shot Ozs.	Load Style	Shot Sizes	Brands	Avg. Price/box	Velocity (fps)
4-1/2	2-1/4	premium	BB, 2, 4, 5, 6	Win., Fed., Rem.	$33	1205
Max	2	premium	4, 5, 6	Fed., Win.	NA	1300
4-1/4	2	high velocity	BB, 2, 4	Rem.	$22	1210
Max	18 pellets	premium	00 buck	Fed., Win.	$7**	1100
Max	1-7/8	Bismuth	BB, 2, 4	Bis.	NA	1225
Max	1-3/4	high density	BB, 2	Rem.	NA	1300
4-1/4	1-3/4	steel	TT, T, BBB, BB, 1, 2, 3	Win., Rem.	$27	1260
Mag	1-5/8	steel	T, BBB, BB, 2	Win.	$27	1285
Max	1-5/8	Bismuth	BB, 2, 4	Bismuth	NA	1375
Max	1-1/2	steel	T, BBB, BB, 1, 2, 3	Fed.	NA	1450
Max	1-3/8	steel	T, BBB, BB, 1, 2, 3	Fed., Rem.	NA	1500
Max	1-3/8	steel	T, BBB, BB, 2	Fed., Win.	NA	1450
Max	1-3/4	slug, rifled	slug	Fed.	NA	1280
Max	24 pellets	Buckshot	1 Buck	Fed.	NA	1100
Max	54 pellets	Super-X	4 Buck	Win.	NA	1150

12 Gauge 3-1/2" Magnum

Dram Equiv.	Shot Ozs.	Load Style	Shot Sizes	Brands	Avg. Price/box	Velocity (fps)
Max	2-1/4	premium	4, 5, 6	Fed., Rem., Win.	$13*	1150
Max	2	Lead	4, 5, 6	Fed.	NA	1300
Max	2	Copper plated turkey	4, 5	Rem.	NA	1300
Max	18 pellets	premium	00 buck	Fed., Win., Rem.	$7**	1100
Max	1-7/8	Wingmaster HD	4, 6	Rem.	NA	1225
Max	1-7/8	heavyweight	5, 6	Fed.	NA	1300
Max	1-3/4	high density	BB, 2, 4, 6	Rem.		1300
Max	1-7/8	Bismuth	BB, 2, 4	Bis.	NA	1225
Max	1-5/8	Hevi-shot	T	Hevi-shot	NA	1350
Max	1-5/8	Wingmaster HD	T	Rem.	NA	1350
Max	1-5/8	high density	BB, 2	Fed.	NA	1450
Max	1-5/8	Blind side	Hex, BB, 2	Win.	NA	1400
Max	1-3/8	Heavyweight	2, 4, 6	Fed.	NA	1450
Max	1-3/8	steel	T, BBB, BB, 2, 4	Fed., Win., Rem.	NA	1450
Max	1-1/2	FS steel	BBB, BB, 2	Fed.	NA	1500
Max	1-1/2	Supreme H-V	BBB, BB, 2, 3	Win.	NA	1475
Max	1-3/8	H-speed steel	BB, 2	Rem.	NA	1550
Max	1-1/4	Steel	BB, 2	Win.	NA	1625
Max	24 pellets	Premium	1 Buck	Fed.	NA	1100
Max	54 pellets	Super-X	4 Buck	Win.	NA	1050

12 Gauge 3" Magnum

Dram Equiv.	Shot Ozs.	Load Style	Shot Sizes	Brands	Avg. Price/box	Velocity (fps)
4	2	premium	BB, 2, 4, 5, 6	Win., Fed., Rem.	$9*	1175
4	1-7/8	premium	BB, 2, 4, 6	Win., Fed., Rem.	$19	1210
4	1-7/8	duplex	4x6	Rem.	$9*	1210
Max	1-3/4	turkey	4, 5, 6	Fed., Fio., Win., Rem.	NA	1300
Max	1-3/4	high density	BB, 2, 4	Rem.	NA	1450
Max	1-5/8	high density	BB, 2	Fed.	NA	1450

12 Gauge 3" Magnum (cont.)

Dram Equiv.	Shot Ozs.	Load Style	Shot Sizes	Brands	Avg. Price/box	Velocity (fps)
Max	1-5/8	Wingmaster HD	4, 6	Rem.	NA	1227
Max	1-5/8	high velocity	4, 5, 6	Fed.	NA	1350
4	1-5/8	premium	2, 4, 5, 6	Win., Fed., Rem.	$18	1290
Max	1-1/2	Wingmaster HD	T	Rem.	NA	1300
Max	1-1/2	Hevi-shot	T	Hevi-shot	NA	1300
Max	1-1/2	high density	BB, 2, 4	Rem.	NA	1300
Max	1-5/8	Bismuth	BB, 2, 4, 5, 6	Bis.	NA	1250
4	24 pellets	buffered	1 buck	Win., Fed., Rem.	$5**	1040
4	15 pellets	buffered	00 buck	Win., Fed., Rem.	$6**	1210
4	10 pellets	buffered	000 buck	Win., Fed., Rem.	$6**	1225
4	41 pellets	buffered	4 buck	Win., Fed., Rem.	$6**	1210
Max	1-3/8	heavyweight	5, 6	Fed.	NA	1300
Max	1-3/8	high density	B, 2, 4, 6	Rem. Win.	NA	1450
Max	1-3/8	slug	slug	Bren.	NA	1476
Max	1-1/4	slug, rifled	slug	Fed.	NA	1600
Max	1-3/16	saboted slug	copper slug	Rem.	NA	1500
Max	7/8	slug, rifled	slug	Rem.	NA	1875
Max	1-1/8	low recoil	BB	Fed.	NA	850
Max	1-1/8	steel	BB, 2, 3, 4	Fed., Win., Rem.	NA	1550
Max	1-1/16	high density	2, 4	Win.	NA	1400
Max	1	steel	4, 6	Fed.	NA	1330
Max	1-3/8	buckhammer	slug	Rem.	NA	1500
Max	1	slug, rifled	slug, magnum	Win., Rem.	$5**	1760
Max	1	saboted slug	slug	Rem., Win., Fed.	$10**	1550
Max	385 grs.	partition gold	slug	Win.	NA	2000
Max	1-1/8	Rackmaster	slug	Win.	NA	1700
Max	300 grs.	XP3	slug	Win.	NA	2100
3-5/8	1-3/8	steel	BBB, BB, 1, 2, 3, 4	Win., Fed., Rem.	$19	1275
Max	1-1/8	snow goose FS	BB, 2, 3, 4	Fed.	NA	1635
Max	1-1/8	steel	BB, 2, 4	Rem.	NA	1500
Max	1-1/8	steel	T, BBB, BB, 2, 4, 5, 6	Fed., Win.	NA	1450
Max	1-1/8	steel	BB, 2	Fed.	NA	1400
Max	1-1/8	FS lead	3, 4	Fed.	NA	1600
Max	1-3/8	Blind side	Hex, BB, 2	Win.	NA	1400
4	1-1/4	steel	T, BBB, BB, 1, 2, 3, 4, 6	Win., Fed., Rem.	$18	1400
Max	1-1/4	FS steel	BBB, BB, 2	Fed.	NA	1450

12 Gauge 2-3/4"

Dram Equiv.	Shot Ozs.	Load Style	Shot Sizes	Brands	Avg. Price/box	Velocity (fps)
Max	1-5/8	magnum	4, 5, 6	Win., Fed.	$8*	1250
Max	1-3/8	lead	4, 5, 6	Fiocchi	NA	1485
Max	1-3/8	turkey	4, 5, 6	Fio.	NA	1250
Max	1-3/8	steel	4, 5, 6	Fed.	NA	1400
Max	1-3/8	Bismuth	BB, 2, 4, 5, 6	Bis.	NA	1300

NOTES: * = 10 rounds per box. ** = 5 rounds per box. Pricing variations and number of rounds per box can occur with type and brand of ammunition. Listed pricing is the average nominal cost for load style and box quantity shown. Not every brand is available in all shot size variations. Some manufacturers do not provide suggested list prices. All prices rounded to nearest whole dollar. The price you pay will vary dependent upon outlet of purchase. # = new load spec this year; "C" indicates a change in data.

12 Gauge 2-3/4" (cont.)

Dram Equiv.	Shot Ozs.	Load Style	Shot Sizes	Brands	Avg. Price/box	Velocity (fps)
3-3/4	1-1/2	magnum	BB, 2, 4, 5, 6	Win., Fed., Rem.	$16	1260
Max	1-1/4	Supreme H-V	4, 5, 6, 7-1/2	Win. Rem.	NA	1400
3-3/4	1-1/4	high velocity	BB, 2, 4, 5, 6, 7-1/2, 8, 9	Win., Fed., Rem., Fio.	$13	1330
Max	1-1/4	high density	B, 2, 4	Win.	NA	1450
Max	1-1/4	high density	4, 6	Rem.	NA	1325
3-1/4	1-1/4	standard velocity	6, 7-1/2, 8, 9	Win., Fed., Rem., Fio.	$11	1220
Max	1-1/8	Hevi-shot	5	Hevi-shot	NA	1350
3-1/4	1-1/8	standard velocity	4, 6, 7-1/2, 8, 9	Win., Fed., Rem., Fio.	$9	1255
Max	1-1/8	steel	2, 4	Rem.	NA	1390
Max	1	steel	BB, 2	Fed.	NA	1450
3-1/4	1	standard velocity	6, 7-1/2, 8	Rem., Fed., Fio., Win.	$6	1290
3-1/4	1-1/4	target	7-1/2, 8, 9	Win., Fed., Rem.	$10	1220
3	1-1/8	spreader	7-1/2, 8, 8-1/2, 9	Fio.	NA	1200
3	1-1/8	target	7-1/2, 8, 9, 7-1/2x8	Win., Fed., Rem., Fio.	$7	1200
2-3/4	1-1/8	target	7-1/2, 8, 8-1/2, 9, 7-1/2x8	Win., Fed., Rem., Fio.	$7	1145
2-3/4	1-1/8	low recoil	7-1/2, 8	Rem.	NA	1145
2-1/2	26 grams	low recoil	8	Win.	NA	980
2-1/4	1-1/8	target	7-1/2, 8, 8-1/2, 9	Rem., Fed.	$7	1080
Max	1	spreader	7-1/2, 8, 8-1/2, 9	Fio.	NA	1300
3-1/4	28 grams (1 oz)	target	7-1/2, 8, 9	Win., Fed., Rem., Fio.	$8	1290
3	1	target	7-1/2, 8, 8-1/2, 9	Win., Fio.	NA	1235
2-3/4	1	target	7-1/2, 8, 8-1/2, 9	Fed., Rem., Fio.	NA	1180
3-1/4	24 grams	target	7-1/2, 8, 9	Fed., Win., Fio.	NA	1325
3	7/8	light	8	Fio.	NA	1200
3-3/4	8 pellets	buffered	000 buck	Win., Fed., Rem.	$4**	1325
4	12 pellets	premium	00 buck	Win., Fed., Rem.	$5**	1290
3-3/4	9 pellets	buffered	00 buck	Win., Fed., Rem., Fio.	$19	1325
3-3/4	12 pellets	buffered	0 buck	Win., Fed., Rem.	$4**	1275
4	20 pellets	buffered	1 buck	Win., Fed., Rem.	$4**	1075
3-3/4	16 pellets	buffered	1 buck	Win., Fed., Rem.	$4**	1250
4	34 pellets	premium	4 buck	Fed., Rem.	$5**	1250
3-3/4	27 pellets	buffered	4 buck	Win., Fed., Rem., Fio.	$4**	1325
		PDX1	1 oz. slug, 3-00 buck	Win.	NA	1150
Max	1	saboted slug	slug	Win., Fed., Rem.	$10**	1450
Max	1-1/4	slug, rifled	slug	Fed.	NA	1520
Max	1-1/4	slug	slug	Lightfield		1440

12 Gauge 2-3/4" (cont.)

Dram Equiv.	Shot Ozs.	Load Style	Shot Sizes	Brands	Avg. Price/box	Velocity (fps)
Max	1-1/4	saboted slug	attached sabot	Rem.	NA	1550
Max	1	slug, rifled	slug, magnum	Rem., Fio.	$5**	1680
Max	1	slug, rifled	slug	Win., Fed., Rem.	$4**	1610
Max	1	sabot slug	slug	Sauvestre		1640
Max	7/8	slug, rifled	slug	Rem.	NA	1800
Max	400	plat. tip	sabot slug	Win.	NA	1700
Max	385 grains	Partition Gold Slug	slug	Win.	NA	1900
Max	385 grains	Core-Lokt bonded	sabot slug	Rem.	NA	1900
Max	325 grains	Barnes Sabot	slug	Fed.	NA	1900
Max	300 grains	SST Slug	sabot slug	Hornady	NA	2050
Max	3/4	Tracer	#8 + tracer	Fio.	NA	1150
Max	130 grains	Less Lethal	.73 rubber slug	Lightfield	NA	600
Max	3/4	non-toxic	zinc slug	Win.	NA	NA
3	1-1/8	steel target	6-1/2, 7	Rem.	NA	1200
2-3/4	1-1/8	steel target	7	Rem.	NA	1145
3	1#	steel	7	Win.	$11	1235
3-1/2	1-1/4	steel	T, BBB, BB, 1, 2, 3, 4, 5, 6	Win., Fed., Rem.	$18	1275
3-3/4	1-1/8	steel	BB, 1, 2, 3, 4, 5, 6	Win., Fed., Rem., Fio.	$16	1365
3-3/4	1	steel	2, 3, 4, 5, 6, 7	Win., Fed., Rem., Fio.	$13	1390
Max	7/8	steel	7	Fio.	NA	1440

16 Gauge 2-3/4"

Dram Equiv.	Shot Ozs.	Load Style	Shot Sizes	Brands	Avg. Price/box	Velocity (fps)
3-1/4	1-1/4	magnum	2, 4, 6	Fed., Rem.	$16	1260
3-1/4	1-1/8	high velocity	4, 6, 7-1/2	Win., Fed., Rem., Fio.	$12	1295
Max	1-1/8	Bismuth	4, 5	Bis.	NA	1200
2-3/4	1-1/8	standard velocity	6, 7-1/2, 8	Fed., Rem., Fio.	$9	1185
2-1/2	1	dove	6, 7-1/2, 8, 9	Fio., Win.	NA	1165
2-3/4	1		6, 7-1/2, 8	Fio.	NA	1200
Max	15/16	steel	2, 4	Fed., Rem.	NA	1300
Max	7/8	steel	2, 4	Win.	$16	1300
3	12 pellets	buffered	1 buck	Win., Fed., Rem.	$4**	1225
Max	4/5	slug, rifled	slug	Win., Fed., Rem.	$4**	1570
Max	.92	sabot slug	slug	Sauvestre	NA	1560

20 Gauge 3" Magnum

Dram Equiv.	Shot Ozs.	Load Style	Shot Sizes	Brands	Avg. Price/box	Velocity (fps)
3	1-1/4	premium	2, 4, 5, 6, 7-1/2	Win., Fed., Rem.	$15	1185
Max	1-1/4	Wingmaster HD	4, 6	Rem.	NA	1185
3	1-1/4	turkey	4, 6	Fio.	NA	1200
Max	1-1/4	Hevi-shot	2, 4, 6	Hevi-shot	NA	1250
Max	1-1/8	high density	4, 6	Rem.	NA	1300
Max	18 pellets	buck shot	2 buck	Fed.	NA	1200

NOTES: * = 10 rounds per box. ** = 5 rounds per box. Pricing variations and number of rounds per box can occur with type and brand of ammunition. Listed pricing is the average nominal cost for load style and box quantity shown. Not every brand is available in all shot size variations. Some manufacturers do not provide suggested list prices. All prices rounded to nearest whole dollar. The price you pay will vary dependent upon outlet of purchase. # = new load spec this year; "C" indicates a change in data.

20 Gauge 3" Magnum (cont.)

Dram Equiv.	Shot Ozs.	Load Style	Shot Sizes	Brands	Avg. Price/box	Velocity (fps)
Max	24 pellets	buffered	3 buck	Win.	$5**	1150
2-3/4	20 pellets	buck	3 buck	Rem.	$4**	1200
3-1/4	1	steel	1, 2, 3, 4, 5, 6	Win., Fed., Rem.	$15	1330
Max	7/8	steel	2, 4	Win.	NA	1300
Max	7/8	FS lead	3, 4	Fed.	NA	1500
Max	1-1/16	high density	2, 4	Win.	NA	1400
Max	1-1/16	Bismuth	2, 4, 5, 6	Bismuth	NA	1250
Mag	5/8	saboted slug	275 gr.	Fed.	NA	1900

20 Gauge 2-3/4"

Dram Equiv.	Shot Ozs.	Load Style	Shot Sizes	Brands	Avg. Price/box	Velocity (fps)
2-3/4	1-1/8	magnum	4, 6, 7-1/2	Win., Fed., Rem.	$14	1175
2-3/4	1	high velocity	4, 5, 6, 7-1/2, 8, 9	Win., Fed., Rem., Fio.	$12	1220
Max	1	Bismuth	4, 6	Bis.	NA	1200
Max	1	Hevi-shot	5	Hevi-shot	NA	1250
Max	1	Supreme H-V	4, 6, 7-1/2	Win. Rem.	NA	1300
Max	1	FS lead	4, 5, 6	Fed.	NA	1350
Max	7/8	Steel	2, 3, 4	Fio.	NA	1500
2-1/2	1	standard velocity	6, 7-1/2, 8	Win., Rem., Fed., Fio.	$6	1165
2-1/2	7/8	clays	8	Rem.	NA	1200
2-1/2	7/8	promotional	6, 7-1/2, 8	Win., Rem., Fio.	$6	1210
2-1/2	1	target	8, 9	Win., Rem.	$8	1165
Max	7/8	clays	7-1/2, 8	Win.	NA	1275
2-1/2	7/8	target	8, 9	Win., Fed., Rem.	$8	1200
Max	3/4	steel	2, 4	Rem.	NA	1425
2-1/2	7/8	steel - target	7	Rem.	NA	1200
Max	1	buckhammer	slug	Rem.	NA	1500
Max	5/8	Saboted Slug	Copper Slug	Rem.	NA	1500
Max	20 pellets	buffered	3 buck	Win., Fed.	$4	1200
Max	5/8	slug, saboted	slug	Win.,	$9**	1400
2-3/4	5/8	slug, rifled	slug	Rem.	$4**	1580
Max	3/4	saboted slug	copper slug	Fed., Rem.	NA	1450
Max	3/4	slug, rifled	slug	Win., Fed., Rem., Fio.	$4**	1570
Max	.9	sabot slug	slug	Sauvestre		1480
Max	260 grains	Partition Gold Slug	slug	Win.	NA	1900
Max	260 grains	Core-Lokt Ultra	slug	Rem.	NA	1900

20 Gauge 2-3/4" (cont.)

Dram Equiv.	Shot Ozs.	Load Style	Shot Sizes	Brands	Avg. Price/box	Velocity (fps)
Max	260 grains	saboted slug	platinum tip	Win.	NA	1700
Max	3/4	steel	2, 3, 4, 6	Win., Fed., Rem.	$14	1425
Max	250 grains	SST slug	slug	Hornady	NA	1800
Max	1/2	rifled, slug	slug	Rem.	NA	1800
Max	67 grains	Less lethal	2/.60 rubber balls	Lightfield	NA	900

28 Gauge 3"

Dram Equiv.	Shot Ozs.	Load Style	Shot Sizes	Brands	Avg. Price/box	Velocity (fps)
Max	7/8	tundra tungsten	4, 5, 6	Fiocchi	NA	TBD

28 Gauge 2-3/4"

Dram Equiv.	Shot Ozs.	Load Style	Shot Sizes	Brands	Avg. Price/box	Velocity (fps)
2	1	high velocity	6, 7-1/2, 8	Win.	$12	1125
2-1/4	3/4	high velocity	6, 7-1/2, 8, 9	Win., Fed., Rem., Fio.	$11	1295
2	3/4	target	8, 9	Win., Fed., Rem.	$9	1200
Max	3/4	sporting clays	7-1/2, 8-1/2	Win.	NA	1300
Max	5/8	Bismuth	4, 6	Bis.	NA	1250
Max	5/8	steel	6, 7	NA	NA	1300
Max	5/8	slug		Bren.	NA	1450

410 Bore 3"

Dram Equiv.	Shot Ozs.	Load Style	Shot Sizes	Brands	Avg. Price/box	Velocity (fps)
Max	11/16	high velocity	4, 5, 6, 7-1/2, 8, 9	Win., Fed., Rem., Fio.	$10	1135
Max	9/16	Bismuth	4	Bis.	NA	1175
Max	3/8	steel	6	NA	NA	1400
		judge	5 pellets 000 Buck	Fed.	NA	960
		judge	9 pellets #4 Buck	Fed.	NA	1100

410 Bore 2-1/2"

Dram Equiv.	Shot Ozs.	Load Style	Shot Sizes	Brands	Avg. Price/box	Velocity (fps)
Max	1/2	high velocity	4, 6, 7-1/2	Win., Fed., Rem.	$9	1245
Max	1/5	slug, rifled	slug	Win., Fed., Rem.	$4**	1815
1-1/2	1/2	target	8, 8-1/2, 9	Win., Fed., Rem., Fio.	$8	1200
Max	1/2	sporting clays	7-1/2, 8, 8-1/2	Win.	NA	1300
Max		Buckshot	5-000 Buck	Win.	NA	1135
		judge	12-bb's, 3 disks	Win.	NA	TBD
Max	42 grains	Less lethal	4/.41 rubber balls	Lightfield	NA	1150

ACCU-TEK AT-380 II 380 ACP PISTOL

Caliber: 380 ACP, 6-shot magazine. **Barrel:** 2.8". **Weight:** 23.5 oz. **Length:** 6.125" overall. **Grips:** Textured black composition. **Sights:** Blade front, rear adjustable for windage. **Features:** Made from 17-4 stainless steel, has an exposed hammer, manual firing-pin safety block and trigger disconnect. Magazine release located on the bottom of the grip. American made, lifetime warranty. Comes with two 6-round stainless steel magazines and a California-approved cable lock. Introduced 2006. Made in U.S.A. by Excel Industries.
Price: Satin stainless **$262.00**

AKDAL GHOST TR-01

Caliber: 9x19mm 15-round double stacked magazine. **Barrel:** 4.45". **Weight:** 29.10 oz. **Length:** 7.5" overall. **Grips:** Polymer black polycoat. **Sights:** Fixed, open type with notched rear sight dovetailed into the slide. Adjustable sight also available. **Features:** Compact single action pre-cocked, semiautomatic pistol with short recoil operation and locking breech. It uses modified Browning-type locking, in which barrel engages the slide with single lug, entering the ejection window. Pistol also has no manual safeties; instead, it has automatic trigger and firing pin safeties. The polymer frame features removable backstraps (of different sizes), and an integral accessory Picatinny rail below the barrel.
Price: **$499.00**

AKDAL GHOST TR-02

Caliber: 9x19mm 15-round double stacked magazine. **Barrel:** 4.45". **Weight:** 29.10 oz. **Length:** 7.5" overall. **Grips:** Polymer black polycoat. **Sights:** Fixed, open type with notched rear sight dovetailed into the slide. Adjustable sight also available. **Features:** Compact single action pre-cocked, semiautomatic pistol with short recoil operation and locking breech. It uses modified Browning-type locking, in which barrel engages the slide with single lug, entering the ejection window. Pistol also has no manual safeties; instead, it has automatic trigger and firing pin safeties. The polymer frame features removable backstraps (of different sizes), and an integral accessory Picatinny rail below the barrel.
Price: **$499.00**

AMERICAN CLASSIC 1911-A1

1911-style semiauto pistol chambered in .45 ACP. Features include Series 90 lockwork, 7+1 capacity, walnut grips, 5-inch barrel, blued or hard-chromed steel frame, checkered wood grips, drift adjustable sights.
Price: . . . . **N/A**

AMERICAN CLASSIC COMMANDER

1911-style semiauto pistol chambered in .45 ACP. Features include 7+1 capacity, checkered mahogany grips, 4.25-inch barrel, blued or hard-chromed steel frame, drift adjustable sights.
Price: . . . . **N/A**

ARMALITE AR-24 PISTOL

Caliber: 9mm Para., 10- or 15-shot magazine. **Barrel:** 4.671", 6 groove, right-hand cut rifling. **Weight:** 34.9 oz. **Length:** 8.27" overall. **Grips:** Black polymer. **Sights:** Dovetail front, fixed rear, 3-dot luminous design. **Features:** Machined slide, frame and barrel. Serrations on forestrap and backstrap, external thumb safety and internal firing pin box, half cock. Two 15-round magazines, pistol case, pistol lock, manual and cleaning brushes. Manganese phosphate finish. Compact comes with two 13-round magazines, 3.89" barrel, weighs 33.4 oz. Made in U.S.A. by ArmaLite.
Price: AR-24 Full Size **$550.00**
Price: AR-24K Compact **$550.00**

ARMSCOR/ROCK ISLAND ARMORY 1911A1-45 FS GI

1911-style semiauto pistol chambered in .45 ACP (8 rounds), 9mm Parabellum, .38 Super (9 rounds). Features include checkered plastic or hardwood grips, 5-inch barrel, parkerized steel frame and slide, drift adjustable sights.
Price: . . . . **N/A**

ARMSCOR/ROCK ISLAND ARMORY 1911A1-45 CS GI

1911-style Officer's-size semiauto pistol chambered in .45 ACP. Features plain hardwood grips, 3.5-inch barrel, parkerized steel frame and slide, drift adjustable sights.
Price: . . . . **N/A**

ARMSCOR/ROCK ISLAND ARMORY MAP1 & MAPP1 PISTOLS

Caliber: 9mm, 16-round magazine. Browning short recoil action style pistols with: integrated front sight; Snag-free rear sight (police standard); Tanfoglio barrel; Single & double-action trigger; automatic safety on firing pin & manual on rear lever; standard hammer; side extractor; standard or Ambidextrous rear safety; combat slide stop; parkerized finish for nickel steel parts; polymer frame with accessory rail.
Price: . . . . **N/A**

ARMSCOR/ROCK ISLAND ARMORY XT22 PISTOL

Caliber: .22 LR, 15-round magazine std. **Barrel:** 5" **Weight:** 38 oz. The XT-22 is a combat 1911 .22 pistol. Unlike most .22 1911 conversions, this pistol is built as a complete gun. Designed for durability, it is the only .22 1911 with a forged 4140 steel slide and the only .22 1911 with a one piece 4140 chrome moly barrel. Available soon.
Price: . . . . **(pre-order) $473.99**

AUTO-ORDNANCE TA5 SEMI-AUTO PISTOL

Caliber: 45 ACP, 30-round stick magazine (standard), 50- or 100-round drum magazine optional. **Barrel:** 10.5", finned. **Weight:** 6.5 lbs. **Length:** 25" overall. **Features:** Semi-auto pistol patterned after Thompson Model 1927 semi-auto carbine. Horizontal vertical foregrip, aluminum receiver, top cocking knob, grooved walnut pistolgrip.
Price: **$1,143.00**

AUTO-ORDNANCE 1911A1 AUTOMATIC PISTOL

Caliber: 45 ACP, 7-shot magazine. **Barrel:** 5". **Weight:** 39 oz. **Length:** 8.5" overall. **Grips:** Brown checkered plastic with medallion. **Sights:** Blade front, rear drift-adjustable for windage.

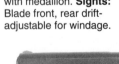

Features: Same specs as 1911A1 military guns-parts interchangeable. Frame and slide blued; each radius has non-glare finish. Introduced 2002. Made in U.S.A. by Kahr Arms.

Prices given are believed to be accurate at time of publication however, many factors affect retail pricing so exact prices are not possible.

Price: 1911PKZSE Parkerized, plastic grips $627.00
Price: 1911PKZSEW Parkerized $662.00
Price: 1911PKZMA Parkerized, Mass. Compliant (2008). $627.00

BAER H.C. 40 AUTO PISTOL
Caliber: 40 S&W, 18-shot magazine. **Barrel:** 5". **Weight:** 37 oz. **Length:** 8.5" overall. **Grips:** Wood. **Sights:** Low-mount adjustable rear sight with hidden rear leaf, dovetail front sight. **Features:** Double-stack Caspian frame, beavertail grip safety, ambidextrous thumb safety, 40 S&W match barrel with supported chamber, match stainless steel barrel bushing, lowered and flared ejection port, extended ejector, match trigger fitted, integral mag well, bead blast blue finish on lower, polished sides on slide. Introduced 2008. Made in U.S.A. by Les Baer Custom, Inc.
Price: $2,960.00

BAER 1911 CUSTOM CARRY AUTO PISTOL
Caliber: 45 ACP, 7- or 10-shot magazine. **Barrel:** 5". **Weight:** 37 oz. **Length:** 8.5" overall. **Grips:** Checkered walnut. **Sights:** Baer improved ramp-style dovetailed front, Novak low-mount rear. **Features:** Baer forged NM frame, slide and barrel with stainless bushing. Baer speed trigger with 4-lb. pull. Partial listing shown. Made in U.S.A. by Les Baer Custom, Inc.
Price: Custom Carry 5", blued $1,995.00
Price: Custom Carry 5", stainless $2,120.00
Price: Custom Carry 4" Commanche length, blued $1,995.00
Price: Custom Carry 4" Commanche length, stainless $2,120.00

BAER 1911 ULTIMATE RECON PISTOL
Caliber: 45 ACP, 7- or 10-shot magazine. **Barrel:** 5". **Weight:** 37 oz. **Length:** 8.5" overall. **Grips:** Checkered cocobolo. **Sights:** Baer improved ramp-style dovetailed front, Novak low-mount rear. **Features:** NM Caspian frame, slide and barrel with stainless bushing. Baer speed trigger with 4-lb. pull. Includes integral Picatinny rail and Sure-Fire X-200 light. Made in U.S.A. by Les Baer Custom, Inc. Introduced 2006.
Price: Bead blast blued $3,070.00
Price: Bead blast chrome $3,390.00

BAER 1911 PREMIER II AUTO PISTOL
Caliber: 38 Super, 400 Cor-Bon, 45 ACP, 7- or 10-shot magazine. **Barrel:** 5". **Weight:** 37 oz. **Length:** 8.5" overall. **Grips:** Checkered rosewood, double diamond pattern. **Sights:** Baer dovetailed front, low-mount Bo-Mar rear with hidden leaf. **Features:** Baer NM forged steel frame and barrel with stainless bushing, deluxe Commander hammer and sear, beavertail grip safety with pad, extended ambidextrous safety; flat mainspring housing; 30 lpi checkered front strap. Made in U.S.A. by Les Baer Custom, Inc.
Price: 5" 45 ACP $1,790.00
Price: 5" 400 Cor-Bon $1,890.00
Price: 5" 38 Super $2,070.00
Price: 6" 45 ACP, 400 Cor-Bon, 38 Super, from. $1,990.00
Price: Super-Tac, 45 ACP, 400 Cor-Bon, 38 Super, from . . $2,280.00

BAER 1911 S.R.P. PISTOL
Caliber: 45 ACP. **Barrel:** 5". **Weight:** 37 oz. **Length:** 8.5" overall. **Grips:** Checkered walnut. **Sights:** Trijicon night sights. **Features:** Similar to the F.B.I. contract gun except uses Baer forged steel frame. Has Baer match barrel with supported chamber, complete tactical action. Has Baer Ultra Coat finish. Introduced 1996. Made in U.S.A. by Les Baer Custom, Inc.
Price: Government or Commanche length $2,590.00

BAER 1911 STINGER PISTOL
Caliber: 45 ACP, 7-round magazine. **Barrel:** 5". **Weight:** 34 oz. **Length:** 8.5" overall. **Grips:** Checkered cocobolo. **Sights:** Baer dovetailed front, low-mount Bo-Mar rear with hidden leaf. **Features:**

Baer NM frame. Baer Commanche slide, Officer's style grip frame, beveled mag well. Made in U.S.A. by Les Baer Custom, Inc.
Price: Blued $1,890.00
Price: Stainless $1,970.00

BAER 1911 PROWLER III PISTOL
Caliber: 45 ACP, 8-round magazine. **Barrel:** 5". **Weight:** 34 oz. **Length:** 8.5" overall. **Grips:** Checkered cocobolo. **Sights:** Baer dovetailed front, low-mount Bo-Mar rear with hidden leaf. **Features:** Similar to Premier II with tapered cone stub weight, rounded corners. Made in U.S.A. by Les Baer Custom, Inc.
Price: Blued $2,580.00

BERETTA 85FS CHEETAH
Caliber: 9x19 15-round double stack magazine. **Barrel:** 4.45". **Weight:** 29.10 oz. **Length:** 7.5" overall. **Grips:** Plastic and Wood. **Sights:** Standard 3-dot system. Notched rear sight is dovetailed to slide. Blade front sight is integral with slide. **Features:** An open slide design that increases the reliability of the firearm. The frame is made from an aluminum alloy that delivers the strength and durability of steel – but with 65% less weight. The automatic firing pin block (FS models) prevents the gun from firing in case of inadvertent drops or strikes against hard surfaces. Available in nickel finish.
Price: Standard (black) finish. $770.00
Price: Nickel finish $830.00

BERETTA MODEL 92FS PISTOL
Caliber: 9mm Para., 10-shot magazine. **Barrel:** 4.9". **Weight:** 34 oz. **Length:** 8.5" overall. **Grips:** Checkered black plastic. **Sights:** Blade front, rear adjustable for windage. Tritium night sights available. **Features:** Double action. Extractor acts as chamber loaded indicator, squared trigger guard, grooved front and backstraps, inertia firing pin. Matte or blued finish. Introduced 1977. Made in U.S.A.
Price: With plastic grips $650.00

BERETTA MODEL 80 CHEETAH SERIES DA PISTOLS
Caliber: 380 ACP, 10-shot magazine (M84); 8-shot (M85); 22 LR, 7-shot (M87). **Barrel:** 3.82". **Weight:** About 23 oz. (M84/85); 20.8 oz. (M87). **Length:** 6.8" overall. **Grips:** Glossy black plastic (wood optional at extra cost). **Sights:** Fixed front, drift-adjustable rear. **Features:** Double action, quick takedown, convenient magazine release. Introduced 1977. Made in U.S.A.
Price: Model 84 Cheetah, plastic grips $650.00

BERETTA MODEL 21 BOBCAT PISTOL
Caliber: 22 LR or 25 ACP. Both double action. **Barrel:** 2.4". **Weight:** 11.5 oz.; 11.8 oz. **Length:** 4.9" overall. **Grips:** Plastic. **Features:** Available in nickel, matte, engraved or blue finish. Introduced in 1985.

Price: Bobcat, 22 or 25, blue . . $335.00
Price: Bobcat, 22, Inox $420.00
Price: Bobcat, 22 or 25, matte $335.00

BERETTA MODEL 3032 TOMCAT PISTOL
Caliber: 32 ACP, 7-shot magazine. **Barrel:** 2.45". **Weight:** 14.5 oz. **Length:** 5" overall. **Grips:** Checkered

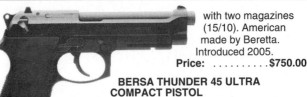

black plastic. **Sights:** Blade front, drift-adjustable rear. **Features:** Double action with exposed hammer; tip-up barrel for direct loading/unloading; thumb safety; polished or matte blue finish. Made in U.S.A. Introduced 1996.

Price: Matte **$435.00**
Price: Inox **$555.00**

BERETTA MODEL U22 NEOS

Caliber: 22 LR, 10-shot magazine. **Barrel:** 4.5"; 6".
Weight: 32 oz.; 36 oz. **Length:** 8.8"; 10.3". **Sights:** Target.

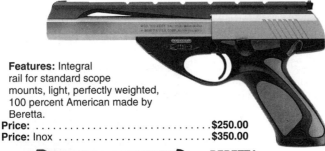

Features: Integral rail for standard scope mounts, light, perfectly weighted, 100 percent American made by Beretta.
Price: **$250.00**
Price: Inox **$350.00**

BERETTA MODEL PX4 STORM

Caliber: 9mm Para., 40 S&W. Capacity: 17 (9mm Para.); 14 (40 S&W). **Barrel:** 4". **Weight:** 27.5 oz. **Grips:** Black checkered w/3 interchangeable backstraps. **Sights:** 3-dot system coated in Superluminova; removable front and rear sights. **Features:** DA/SA, manual safety/hammer decocking lever (ambi) and automatic firing pin block safety. Picatinny rail. Comes with two magazines (17/10 in 9mm Para. and 14/10 in 40 S&W). Removable hammer unit. American made by Beretta. Introduced 2005.
Price: **$600.00**
Price: 45 ACP **$650.00**

BERETTA MODEL PX4 STORM SUB-COMPACT

Caliber: 9mm, 40 S&W. Capacity: 13 (9mm); 10 (40 S&W). **Barrel:** 3". **Weight:** 26.1 oz. **Length:** 6.2" overall. **Grips:** NA. **Sights:** NA. **Features:** Ambidextrous manual safety lever, interchangeable backstraps included, lock breech and tilt barrel system, stainless steel barrel, Picatinny rail.
Price: **$600.00**

BERETTA MODEL M9

Caliber: 9mm Para. Capacity: 15. **Barrel:** 4.9". **Weight:** 32.2-35.3 oz. **Grips:** Plastic. **Sights:** Dot and post, low profile, windage adjustable rear. **Features:** DA/SA, forged aluminum alloy frame, delayed locking-bolt system, manual safety doubles as decocking lever, combat-style trigger guard, loaded chamber indicator. Comes with two magazines (15/10). American made by Beretta. Introduced 2005.
Price: **$650.00**

BERETTA MODEL M9A1

Caliber: 9mm Para. Capacity: 15. **Barrel:** 4.9". **Weight:** 32.2-35.3 oz. **Grips:** Plastic. **Sights:** Dot and post, low profile, windage adjustable rear. **Features:** Same as M9, but also includes integral Mil-Std-1913 Picatinny rail, has checkered frontstrap and backstrap. Comes

with two magazines (15/10). American made by Beretta. Introduced 2005.
Price: **$750.00**

BERSA THUNDER 45 ULTRA COMPACT PISTOL

Caliber: 45 ACP. **Barrel:** 3.6". **Weight:** 27 oz. **Length:** 6.7" overall. **Grips:** Anatomically designed polymer. **Sights:** White outline rear. **Features:** Double action; firing pin safeties, integral locking system. Available in matte, satin nickel, gold, or duo-tone. Introduced 2003. Imported from Argentina by Eagle Imports, Inc.

Price: Thunder 45, matte blue **$402.00**
Price: Thunder 45, stainless **$480.00**
Price: Thunder 45, satin nickel **$445.00**

BERSA THUNDER 380 SERIES PISTOLS

Caliber: 380 ACP, 7 rounds
Barrel: 3.5". **Weight:** 23 oz.
Length: 6.6" overall. **Features:** Otherwise similar to Thunder 45 Ultra Compact. 380 DLX has 9-round capacity. 380 Concealed Carry has 8 round capacity. Imported from Argentina by Eagle Imports, Inc.

Price: Thunder 380 Matte **$310.00**
Price: Thunder 380 Satin Nickel **$336.00**
Price: Thunder 380 Blue DLX **$332.00**
Price: Thunder 380 Matte CC (2006) **$315.00**

BERSA THUNDER 9 ULTRA COMPACT/40 SERIES PISTOLS

Caliber: 9mm Para., 40 S&W. **Barrel:** 3.5". **Weight:** 24.5 oz. **Length:** 6.6" overall. **Features:** Otherwise similar to Thunder 45 Ultra Compact. 9mm Para. High Capacity model has 17-round capacity. 40 High Capacity model has 13-round capacity. Imported from Argentina by Eagle Imports, Inc.

Price: Thunder 9mm Para. Matte **$402.00**
Price: Thunder 40 High Capacity Satin Nickel . . **$419.00**

BROWNING 1911-22 COMPACT

Caliber: .22 L.R.,10-round magazine. **Barrel:** 3.625". **Weight:** 15 oz. **Length:** 6.5" overall. **Grips:** Brown composite. **Sights:** Fixed. **Features:** Slide is machined aluminum with alloy frame and matte blue finish. Blowback action and single action trigger with manual thumb and grip safetys. Works, feels and functions just like a full size 1911. It is simply scaled down and chambered in the best of all practice rounds: 22 LR. for focus on the fundamentals.
Price: **$600.00**

BROWNING 1911-22 A1

Caliber: .22 L.R.,10-round magazine. **Barrel:** 4.25". **Weight:** 16 oz. **Length:** 7.0625" overall. **Grips:** Brown composite. **Sights:** Fixed. **Features:** Slide is machined aluminum with alloy frame and matte blue finish. Blowback action and single action trigger with manual thumb and grip safetys. Works, feels and functions just like a full size 1911. It is simply scaled down and chambered in the best of all practice rounds: 22 LR. for focus on the fundamentals
Price: **$600.00**

BROWNING HI POWER 9MM AUTOMATIC PISTOL

Caliber: 9mm Para., 13-round magazine; 40 S&W, 10-round magazine. **Barrel:** 4-5/8". **Weight:** 32 to 39 oz. **Length:** 7.75" overall. **Metal Finishes:** Blued (Standard); black-epoxy/silver-chrome (Practical); black-epoxy (Mark III). **Grips:** Molded (Mark III); wraparound Pachmayr (Practical); or walnut grips (Standard).

Sights: Fixed (Practical, Mark III, Standard); low-mount adjustable rear (Standard). Cable lock supplied. **Features:** External hammer with half-cock and thumb safeties. Fixed rear sight model available. Commander-style (Practical) or spur-type hammer, single action. Includes gun lock. Imported from Belgium by Browning.

Price: Mark III **$979.00**
Price: Standard, fixed sights, from **$999.00**
Price: SMark III, Digital green (2009) **$985.00**

BROWNING BUCK MARK PISTOLS

Common Features: Caliber: 22 LR, 10-shot magazine. **Action:** Blowback semi-auto. **Trigger:** Wide grooved style. **Sights:** Ramp front, Browning Pro-Target rear adjustable for windage and elevation. **Grips:** Cocobolo, target-style (Hunter, 5.5 Target, 5.5 Field); polymer (Camper, Camper Stainless, Micro Nickel, Standard, STD Stainless); checkered walnut (Challenge); laminated (Plus and Plus Nickel); laminated rosewood (Bullseye Target, FLD Plus); rubber (Bullseye Standard). **Metal finishes:** Matte blue (Hunter, Camper, Challenge, Plus, Bullseye Target, Bullseye Standard, 5.5 Target, 5.5 Field, FLD Plus); matte stainless (Camper Stainless, STD Stainless, Micro Standard); nickel-plated (Micro Nickel, Plus Nickel, and Nickel). **Features:** Machined aluminum frame. Includes gun lock. Introduced 1985. Hunter, Camper Stainless, STD Stainless, 5.5 Target, 5.5 Field all introduced 2005. Multiple variations, as noted below. Made in U.S.A. From Browning.

Price: Hunter, 7.25" heavy barrel, 38 oz., Truglo sight **$429.00**
Price: Camper, 5.5" heavy barrel, 34 oz. **$329.00**
Price: FLD Camper Stainless URX, 5.5" tapered bull barrel, 34 oz. **$359.00**
Price: Standard URX, 5.5" flat-side bull barrel, 34 oz. **$399.00**
Price: Standard Stainless URX, 5.5" flat-side bull barrel, 34 oz. **$439.00**
Price: Micro Standard URX, 4" flat-side bull barrel, 32 oz. . . . **$399.00**
Price: Micro Standard Stainless URX, 4" flat-side bull barrel, 32 oz. **$439.00**

Price: Challenge, 5.5" lightweight taper barrel, 25 oz. **$399.00**
Price: Contour 5.5 URX, 5.5" barrel, 36 oz. **$469.00**
Price: Contour 7.25 URX, 7.25", 39 oz. **$479.00**
Price: Contour Lite 5.5 URX, 5.5" barrel, 28 oz., adj. sights . **$519.00**
Price: Contour Lite 7.25 URX, 7.25" barrel, 30 oz., adj. sights **$529.00**
Price: Bullseye URX, 7.25" fluted bull barrel, 36 oz. **$549.00**
Price: Bullseye Target Stainless, 7.25" fluted bull barrel, 36 oz. **$719.00**
Price: 5.5 Target, 5.5" round bull barrel, target sights, 35.5 oz. **$579.00**
Price: 5.5 Field, 5.5" round bull barrel, 35 oz. **$579.00**
Price: Plus Stainless UDX (2007) **$509.00**
Price: Plus UDX (2007) **$469.00**
Price: FLD Plus Rosewood UDX (2007) **$469.00**
Price: Stainless Camper, 5.5" tapered bull barrel (2008) **$379.00**
Price: Practical URX Fiber-Optic, 5.5" barrel (2009) **$379.00**
Price: Lite Splash 5.5 URX **$489.00**
Price: Lite Splash 7.25 URX **$509.00**

BUSHMASTER CARBON 15 .223 PISTOL

Caliber: 5.56/223, 30-round. **Barrel:** 7.25" stainless steel. **Weight:** 2.88 lbs. **Length:** 20" overall. **Grips:** Pistol grip, Hogue overmolded unit for ergonomic comfort. **Sights:** A2-type front with dual-aperture slip-up rear. **Features:** AR-style semi-auto pistol with carbon composite receiver, shortenend handguard, full-length optics rail.

Price: . . . . **N/A**
Price: Type 97 pistol, without handguard **$1,055.00**

CHARLES DALY ENHANCED 1911 PISTOLS

Caliber: 45 ACP. **Barrel:** 5". **Weight:** 38 oz. **Length:** 8.75" overall. **Grips:** Checkered double diamond hardwood. **Sights:** Dovetailed front and dovetailed snag-free low profile rear sights, 3-dot system. **Features:** Extended high-rise beavertail grip safety, combat trigger, combat hammer, beveled magazine well, flared and lowered ejection port. Field Grade models are satin-finished blued steel. EMS series includes an ambidextrous safety, 4" barrel, 8-shot magazine. ECS series has a contoured left hand safety, 3.5" barrel, 6-shot magazine. Two magazines, lockable carrying case. Introduced 1998. Empire series are stainless versions. Imported from the Philippines by K.B.I., Inc.

Price: EFS, blued, 39.5 oz., 5" barrel **$649.00**
Price: EMS, blued, 37 oz., 4" barrel **$649.00**
Price: ECS, blued, 34.5 oz., 3.5" barrel **$649.00**

CHARLES DALY M-5 POLYMER-FRAMED HI-CAP 1911 PISTOL

Caliber: 9mm Para., 12-round magazine; 40 S&W 17-round magazine; 45 ACP, 13-round magazine. **Barrel:** 5". **Weight:** 33.5 oz. **Length:** 8.5" overall. **Grips:** Checkered polymer. **Sights:** Blade front, adjustable low-profile rear. **Features:** Stainless steel beavertail grip safety, rounded trigger-guard, tapered bull barrel, full-length guide rod, matte blue finish on frame and slide. 40 S&W models in M-5 Govt. 1911, M-5 Commander, and M-5 IPSC introduced 2006; M-5 Ultra X Compact in 9mm Para. and 45 ACP introduced 2006; M-5 IPSC .45 ACP introduced 2006. Made in Israel by BUL, imported by K.B.I., Inc.

Price: M-5 Govt. 1911, 40 S&W/45 ACP, matte blue **$749.00**
Price: M-5 Commander, 40 S&W/45 ACP, matte blue **$749.00**
Price: M-5 Ultra X Compact, 9mm Para., 3.1" barrel, 7" OAL, 28 oz. **$749.00**
Price: M-5 Ultra X Compact, 45 ACP, 3.1" barrel, 7" OAL, 28 oz. **$749.00**

CHIAPPA 1911-22

1911-style semiauto pistol chambered in .22 LR. Features include

alloy frame; steel barrel; matte blue-black or bright nickel finish, walnut-like grips, two 10-round magazines, fixed sights. Straight blowback action.
Price: $295.00

CHIAPPA AR-15 .22 M-FOUR TACTICAL HANDGUN

Caliber: .22 LR., 28-shot magazine capacity **Barrel:** 6" **Weight:** 4.1 lbs. **Length:** 14.5". **Grips:** Black polymer. **Finish:** Black. **Sights:** Adjustable sites. **Features:** Mfour-22 pistol is a scaled down, hand-held replica of the M4 Carbine. It is small enough to fit in your hand, yet unique enough in appearance to draw a crowd. It sports many of the features of the full size M4 Carbine. Interchangeable MIL-SPEC features include fire control group, grip, functioning dust cover, and adjustable sights. Comes standard with: two 28-round magazines, black polymer grips, adjustable sights, pseudo flash hider, forward assist, and steel trigger & hammer assembly.
Price: ....(available soon) $469.00
Price: .... w/red-dot scope $550.00

CHIAPPA M9-22 STANDARD

Caliber: .22 LR. **Barrel:** 5" **Weight:** 2.3 lbs. **Length:** 8.5". **Grips:** Black molded plastic or walnut. **Sights:** Fixed front sight and windage adjustable rear sight. **Features:** The M9-9mm has been a U.S. standard-issue service pistol since 1990. Chiappa's M9-22 is a replica of this pistol in 22 LR. The M9-22 has the same weight and feel as its 9mm counterpart but has an affordable 10 shot magazine for the 22 long rifle cartridge which makes it a true rimfire reproduction. Comes standard with steel trigger, hammer assembly and a 1/2-28 threaded barrel.
Price: ....(available soon) $369.00

CHIAPPA M9-22 TACTICAL

Caliber: .22 LR. **Barrel:** 5" **Weight:** 2.3 lbs. **Length:** 8.5". **Grips:** Black molded plastic. **Sights:** Fixed front sight and Novak style rear sites. **Features:** The M9-22 Tactical model has Novak style rear sites and comes with a fake suppressor (this ups the "cool factor" on the range and extends the barrel to make it even more accurate). It also has a 1/2 x 28 thread adaptor which can be used by those with a legal suppressor.
Price: ....(available soon) $419.00

COBRA ENTERPRISES FS32, FS380 AUTO PISTOL

Caliber: 32 ACP, 380 ACP, 7-shot magazine. **Barrel:** 3.5". **Weight:** 2.1 lbs. **Length:** 6-3/8". **Grips:** Black composition. **Sights:** Fixed. **Features:** Choice of bright chrome, satin nickel or black finish. Introduced 2002. Made in U.S.A. by Cobra Enterprises of Utah, Inc.
Price: $165.00

COBRA ENTERPRISES PATRIOT 45 PISTOL

Caliber: 45 ACP, 6, 7, or 10-shot magazine. **Barrel:** 3.3". **Weight:** 20 oz. **Length:** 6" overall. **Grips:** Black polymer. **Sights:** Rear adjustable. **Features:** Stainless steel or black melonite slide with

load indicator; Semi-auto locked breech, DAO. Made in U.S.A. by Cobra Enterprises of Utah, Inc.
Price: $380.00

COBRA ENTERPRISES CA32, CA380 PISTOL

Caliber: 32 ACP, 380 ACP. **Barrel:** 2.8". **Weight:** 22 oz. **Length:** 5.4". **Grips:** Black molded synthetic. **Sights:** Fixed. **Features:** Choice of black, satin nickel, or chrome finish. Made in U.S.A. by Cobra Enterprises of Utah, Inc.
Price: $157.00

COLT MODEL 1991 MODEL O AUTO PISTOL

Caliber: 45 ACP, 7-shot magazine. **Barrel:** 5". **Weight:** 38 oz. **Length:** 8.5" overall. **Grips:** Checkered black composition. **Sights:** Ramped blade front, fixed square notch rear, high profile. **Features:** Matte finish. Continuation of serial number range used on original G.I. 1911A1 guns. Comes with one magazine and molded carrying case. Introduced 1991.
Price: Blue $786.00
Price: Stainless $839.00

COLT XSE SERIES MODEL O AUTO PISTOLS

Caliber: 45 ACP, 8-shot magazine. **Barrel:** 4.25", 5". **Grips:** Checkered, double diamond rosewood. **Sights:** Drift-adjustable 3-dot combat. **Features:** Brushed stainless finish; adjustable, two-cut aluminum trigger; extended ambidextrous thumb safety; upswept beavertail with palm swell; elongated slot hammer. Introduced 1999. From Colt's Mfg. Co., Inc.
Price: XSE Government (5" bbl.) $944.00
Price: XSE Government (4.25" bbl.) $944.00

COLT XSE LIGHTWEIGHT COMMANDER AUTO PISTOL

Caliber: 45 ACP, 8-shot. **Barrel:** 4.25". **Weight:** 26 oz. **Length:** 7.75" overall. **Grips:** Double diamond checkered rosewood. **Sights:** Fixed, glare-proofed blade front, square notch rear; 3-dot system. **Features:** Brushed stainless slide, nickeled aluminum frame; McCormick elongated slot enhanced hammer, McCormick two-cut adjustable aluminum hammer. Made in U.S.A. by Colt's Mfg. Co., Inc.
Price: Stainless $944.00

COLT DEFENDER

Caliber: 45 ACP, 7-shot magazine. **Barrel:** 3". **Weight:** 22-1/2 oz. **Length:** 6.75" overall. **Grips:** Pebble-finish rubber wraparound with finger grooves. **Sights:** White dot front, snag-free Colt competition rear. **Features:** Stainless finish; aluminum frame; combat-style hammer; Hi Ride grip safety, extended manual safety, disconnect safety. Introduced 1998. Made in U.S.A. by Colt's Mfg. Co., Inc.
Price: 07000D, stainless.......................... $885.00

COLT SERIES 70

Caliber: 45 ACP. **Barrel:** 5". **Weight:** NA. **Length:** NA. **Grips:** Rosewood with double diamond checkering pattern. **Sights:** Fixed. **Features:** Custom replica of the Original Series 70 pistol with a Series 70 firing system, original rollmarks. Introduced 2002. Made in U.S.A. by Colt's Mfg. Co., Inc.
Price: Blued $919.00
Price: Stainless $950.00

Prices given are believed to be accurate at time of publication however, many factors affect retail pricing so exact prices are not possible.

COLT 38 SUPER
Caliber: 38 Super. **Barrel:** 5". **Weight:** NA. **Length:** 8.5" **Grips:** Checkered rubber (stainless and blue models); wood with double diamond checkering pattern (bright stainless model). **Sights:** 3-dot. **Features:** Beveled magazine well, standard thumb safety and service-style grip safety. Introduced 2003. Made in U.S.A. by Colt's Mfg. Co., Inc.
Price: Blued **$837.00**
Price: Stainless **$866.00**
Price: Bright Stainless **$1,090.00**

COLT 1918 WWI REPLICA
Caliber: 45 ACP, 2 7-round magazines. **Barrel:** 5". **Weight:** 38 oz. **Length:** 8.5". **Grips:** Checkered walnut with double diamond checkering pattern. **Sights:** Tapered blade front sight, U-shaped rear notch. **Features:** Reproduction based on original 1911 blueprints. Original rollmarks and inspector marks. Smooth mainspring housing with lanyard loop, WWI-style manual thumb and grip safety, black oxide finish. Introduced 2007. Made in U.S.A. by Colt's Mfg. Co., Inc.
Price: Blued **$990.00**

COLT RAIL GUN
Caliber: 45 ACP (8+1). **Barrel:** NA. **Weight:** NA. **Length:** NA. **Grips:** Rosewood double diamond. **Sights:** White dot front and Novak rear. **Features:** 1911-style semi-auto. Stainless steel frame and slide, front and rear slide serrations, skeletonized trigger, integral; accessory rail, Smith & Alexander upswept beavertail grip palm swell safety, tactical thumb safety, National Match barrel.
Price: . . . . **TO BE ANNOUNCED**

COLT NEW AGENT
Caliber: 45 ACP (7+1). **Barrel:** 3". **Weight:** 25 oz. **Length:** 6.75" overall. **Grips:** Double diamond slim fit. **Sights:** Snag free trench style. **Features:** Semi-auto pistol with blued finish and enhanced black anodized aluminum receiver. Skeletonized aluminum trigger, series 80 firing system, front strap serrations, beveled magazine well.
Price: **$885.00**

COLT DEFENDER PISTOL
1911-style semiauto pistol chambered in .45 ACP and 9mm Parabellum. Features include Series 90 lockwork, 7+1 (.45) or 8+1 (9mm) capacity, wraparound rubber grips, 3-inch barrel, beveled magazine well, aluminum alloy frame with stainless steel slide, white dot carry sights.
Price: **$939.00**

COLT NEW AGENT PISTOL
Similar to Colt Defender but with steel frame and fixed sights.
Price: **$939.00**

COLT SPECIAL COMBAT GOVERNMENT CARRY MODEL
Caliber: 45 ACP (8+1), 38 Super (9+1). **Barrel:** 5". **Weight:** NA. **Length:** NA. **Grips:** Black/silver synthetic. **Sights:** Novak front and rear night. **Features:** 1911-style semi-auto. Skeletonized three-hole trigger, slotted hammer, Smith & Alexander upswept beavertail grip palm swell safety and extended magazine well, Wilson tactical ambidextrous safety. Available in blued, hard chrome, or blue/satin nickel finish, depending on chambering.
Price: **$1,676.00**

CZ 75 B AUTO PISTOL
Caliber: 9mm Para., 40 S&W, 10-shot magazine. **Barrel:** 4.7". **Weight:** 34.3 oz. **Length:** 8.1" overall. **Grips:** High impact checkered plastic. **Sights:** Square post front, rear adjustable for windage; 3-dot system. **Features:** Single action/double action design; firing pin block safety; choice of black polymer, matte or high-polish blue finishes. All-steel frame. B-SA is a single action with a drop-free magazine. Imported from the Czech Republic by CZ-USA.
Price: 75 B, black polymer, 16-shot magazine **$597.00**
Price: 75 B, dual-tone or satin nickel **$617.00**
Price: 40 S&W, black polymer, 12-shot magazine **$615.00**
Price: 40 S&W, glossy blue, dual-tone, satin nickel **$669.00**
Price: 75 B-SA, 9mm Para./40 S&W, single action **$609.00**

CZ 75 BD Decocker
Similar to the CZ 75B except has a decocking lever in place of the safety lever. All other specifications are the same. Introduced 1999. Imported from the Czech Republic by CZ-USA.
Price: 9mm Para., black polymer **$609.00**

CZ 75 B Compact Auto Pistol
Similar to the CZ 75 B except has 14-shot magazine in 9mm Para., 3.9" barrel and weighs 32 oz. Has removable front sight, non-glare ribbed slide top. Trigger guard is squared and serrated; combat hammer. Introduced 1993. Imported from the Czech Republic by CZ-USA.
Price: 9mm Para., black polymer **$631.00**
Price: 9mm Para., dual tone or satin nickel **$651.00**
Price: 9mm Para. D PCR Compact, alloy frame **$651.00**

CZ 75 Champion Pistol
Similar to the CZ 75 B except has a longer frame and slide, rubber grip to accommodate new heavy-duty magazine. Ambidextrous thumb safety, extended magazine release; three-port compensator. Blued slide and stain nickel frame finish. Introduced 2005. Imported from the Czech Republic by CZ-USA.
Price: 40 S&W, 12-shot mag. **$1,739.00**

CZ 75 P-07 DUTY
Caliber: 40 S&W, 9mm Luger (16+1). **Barrel:** 3.8". **Weight:** 27.2 oz. **Length:** 7.3" overall. **Grips:** Polymer black polycoat. **Sights:** Blade front, fixed groove rear. **Features:** The ergonomics and accuracy of the CZ 75 with a totally new trigger system. The new Omega trigger system simplifies the CZ 75 trigger system, uses fewer parts and improves the trigger pull. In addition, it allows users to choose between using the handgun with a decocking lever (installed) or a manual safety (included) by a simple parts change. The polymer frame design of the Duty and a new sleek slide profile (fully machined from bar stock) reduce weight, making the P-07 Duty a great choice for concealed carry.
Price: **$487.00**

CZ 75 Tactical Sport
Similar to the CZ 75 B except the CZ 75 TS is a competition ready pistol designed for IPSC standard division (USPSA limited division). Fixed target sights, tuned single-action operation, lightweight polymer match trigger with adjustments for take-up and overtravel, competition hammer, extended magazine catch, ambidextrous manual safety, checkered walnut grips, polymer magazine well, two tone finish. Introduced 2005. Imported from the Czech Republic by CZ-USA.
Price: 9mm Para., 20-shot mag. **$1,338.00**
Price: 40 S&W, 16-shot mag. **$1,338.00**

CZ 75 SP-01 Pistol
Similar to NATO-approved CZ 75 Compact P-01 model. Features an integral 1913 accessory rail on the dust cover, rubber grip panels, black polycoat finish, extended beavertail, new grip geometry with checkering on front and back straps, and double or single action

operation. Introduced 2005. The Shadow variant designed as an IPSC "production" division competition firearm. Includes competition hammer, competition rear sight and fiber-optic front sight, modified slide release, lighter recoil and main spring for use with "minor power factor" competition ammunition. Includes polycoat finish and slim walnut grips. Finished by CZ Custom Shop. Imported from the Czech Republic by CZ-USA.
Price: SP-01 9mm Para., black polymer, 19+1 . . . . **$850.00**

CZ 75 SP-01 Phantom
Similar to the CZ 75 B. 9mm Luger, 19-round magazine, weighs 26 oz. and features a polymer frame with accessory rail, and a forged steel slide with a weight-saving scalloped profile. Two interchangeable grip inserts are included to accommodate users with different-sized hands.
Price: **$695.00**

CZ 85 B/85 Combat Auto Pistol
Same gun as the CZ 75 except has ambidextrous slide release and safety levers; non-glare, ribbed slide top; squared, serrated trigger guard; trigger stop to prevent overtravel. Introduced 1986. The CZ 85 Combat features a fully adjustable rear sight, extended magazine release, ambidextrous slide stop and safety catch, drop free magazine and overtravel adjustment. Imported from the Czech Republic by CZ-USA.
Price: 9mm Para., black polymer **$628.00**
Price: Combat, black polymer **$702.00**
Price: Combat, dual-tone, satin nickel **$732.00**

CZ 75 KADET AUTO PISTOL
Caliber: 22 LR, 10-shot magazine. **Barrel:** 4.88". **Weight:** 36 oz. **Grips:** High impact checkered plastic. **Sights:** Blade front, fully adjustable rear. **Features:** Single action/double action mechanism; all-steel construction. Introduced 1999. Kadet conversion kit consists of barrel, slide, adjustable sights, and magazine to convert the centerfire 75 to rimfire. Imported from the Czech Republic by CZ-USA.
Price: Black polymer **$689.00**
Price: Kadet conversion kit **$412.00**

CZ 83 DOUBLE-ACTION PISTOL
Caliber: 32 ACP, 380 ACP, 12-shot magazine. **Barrel:** 3.8". **Weight:** 26.2 oz. **Length:** 6.8" overall. **Grips:** High impact checkered plastic. **Sights:** Removable square post front, rear adjustable for windage; 3-dot system. **Features:** Single action/double action; ambidextrous magazine release and safety. Blue finish; non-glare ribbed slide top. Imported from the Czech Republic by CZ-USA.
Price: Glossy blue, 32 ACP or 380 ACP **$495.00**
Price: Satin Nickel **$522.00**

CZ 97 B AUTO PISTOL
Caliber: 45 ACP, 10-shot magazine. **Barrel:** 4.85". **Weight:** 40 oz. **Length:** 8.34" overall. **Grips:** Checkered walnut. **Sights:** Fixed. **Features:** Single action/double action; full-length slide rails; screw-in barrel bushing; linkless barrel; all-steel construction; chamber loaded indicator; dual transfer bars. Introduced 1999. Imported from the Czech Republic by CZ-USA.
Price: Black polymer $779.00
Price: Glossy blue $799.00

CZ 97 BD Decocker
Similar to the CZ 97 B except has a decocking lever in place of the safety lever. Tritium night sights. Rubber grips. All other specifica-

tions are the same. Introduced 1999. Imported from the Czech Republic by CZ-USA.
Price: 9mm Para., black polymer **$874.00**

CZ 2075 RAMI/RAMI P AUTO PISTOL
Caliber: 9mm Para., 40 S&W. **Barrel:** 3". **Weight:** 25 oz. **Length:** 6.5" overall. **Grips:** Rubber. **Sights:** Blade front with dot, white outline rear drift adjustable for windage. **Features:** Single-action/double-action; alloy or polymer frame, steel slide; has laser sight mount. Imported from the Czech Republic by CZ-USA.
Price: 9mm Para., alloy frame, 10 and 14-shot magazines . . . **$671.00**
Price: 40 S&W, alloy frame, 8-shot magazine **$671.00**
Price: RAMI P, polymer frame, 9mm Para., 40 S&W **$612.00**

CZ P-01 AUTO PISTOL
Caliber: 9mm Para., 14-shot magazine. **Barrel:** 3.85". **Weight:** 27 oz. **Length:** 7.2" overall. **Grips:** Checkered rubber. **Sights:** Blade front with dot, white outline rear drift adjustable for windage. **Features:** Based on the CZ 75, except with forged aircraft-grade aluminum alloy frame. Hammer forged barrel, decocker, firing-pin block, M3 rail, dual slide serrations, squared trigger guard, re-contoured trigger, lanyard loop on butt. Serrated front and back strap. Introduced 2006. Imported from the Czech Republic by CZ-USA.
Price: CZ P-01 . . . .**$672.00**

DAN WESSON FIREARMS POINTMAN SEVEN AUTO PISTOL
Caliber: 10mm, 40 S&W, 45 ACP. **Barrel:** 5". **Grips:** Diamond checkered cocobolo. **Sights:** Bo-Mar style adjustable target sight. **Weight:** 38 oz. **Features:** Stainless-steel frame and serrated slide. Series 70-style 1911, stainless-steel frame, forged stainless-steel slide. One-piece match-grade barrel and bushing. 20-LPI checkered mainspring housing, front and rear slide cocking serrations, beveled magwell, dehorned by hand. Lowered and flared ejection port, Ed Brown slide stop and memory groove grip safety, tactical extended thumb safety. Commander-style match hammer, match grade sear, aluminum trigger with stainless bow, Wolff springs. Introduced 2000. Made in U.S.A. by Dan Wesson Firearms, distributed by CZ-USA.
Price: 45 ACP, 7+1 . . . . **$1,158.00**
Price: 10mm, 8+1 . . . . **$1,191.00**
Price: 40 S&W, stainless **$1,189.00**
Price: 45 ACP, Desert Tan **$1,269.00**

Dan Wesson Commander Classic Bobtail Auto Pistols
Similar to Pointman Seven, a Commander-sized frame with 4.25" barrel. Available with stainless finish, fixed night sights. Introduced 2005. Made in U.S.A. by Dan Wesson Firearms, distributed by CZ-USA.
Price: 45 ACP, 7+1, 33 oz. **$1,191.00**
Price: 10mm, 8+1, 33 oz., stainless **$1,224.00**
Price: 10mm, 33 oz. two-tone **$1,530.00**

DAN WESSON DW RZ-10 AUTO PISTOL
Caliber: 10mm, 9-shot. **Barrel:** 5". **Grips:** Diamond checkered cocobolo. **Sights:** Bo-Mar style adjustable target sight. **Weight:** 38.3 oz. **Length:** 8.8" overall. **Features:** Stainless-steel frame and serrated slide. Series 70-style 1911, stainless-steel frame, forged stainless-steel slide. Commander-style match hammer. Reintroduced 2005. Made in U.S.A. by Dan Wesson Firearms, distributed by CZ-USA.
Price: 10mm, 8+1 . . . . **$1,191.00**

Dan Wesson DW RZ-10 Sportsman
Similar to the RZ-10 Auto except with 8-shot magazine. Weighs 36 oz., length is 8.8" overall.
Price: **$1,448.00**

Dan Wesson DW RZ-45 Heritage
Similar to the RZ-10 Auto except in 45 ACP with 7-shot magazine. Weighs 36 oz., length is 8.8" overall.
Price: 10mm, 8+1 . . . . **$1,141.00**

DAN WESSON VALOR 1911 PISTOL
Caliber: .45 ACP, 8-shot. **Barrel:** 5". **Grips:** Slim Line G10. **Sights:** Heinie ledge straight eight adjustable night sights. **Weight:** 2.4 lbs. **Length:** 8.8" overall. **Features:** The defensive style Valor, is a base stainless 1911 with our matte black "Duty" finish. This finish is a ceramic base coating that has set the standard for all coating tests. Other features include forged stainless frame and match barrel with 25 LPI checkering and undercut trigger guard, adjustable defensive night sites, and Slim line VZ grips. Made in U.S.A. by Dan Wesson Firearms, distributed by CZ-USA.
Price: Stainless. **$1,594.00**
Price: Black. **$1,977.00**

DESERT EAGLE MARK XIX PISTOL
Caliber: 357 Mag., 9-shot; 44 Mag., 8-shot; 50 AE, 7-shot. **Barrel:** 6", 10", interchangeable. **Weight:** 357 Mag.-62 oz.; 44 Mag.-69 oz.; 50 AE-72 oz. **Length:** 10.25" overall (6" bbl.). **Grips:** Polymer; rubber available. **Sights:** Blade on ramp front, combat-style rear. Adjustable available. **Features:** Interchangeable barrels; rotating three-lug bolt; ambidextrous safety; adjustable trigger. Military epoxy finish. Satin, bright nickel, chrome, brushed, matte or black-oxide finishes available. 10" barrel extra. Imported from Israel by Magnum Research, Inc.
Price: Black-6, 6" barrel **$1,475.00**
Price: Black-10, 10" barrel **$1,575.00**
Price: Component System Package, 3 barrels, carrying case, from **$2,801.00**

DESERT BABY MICRO DESERT EAGLE PISTOL
Caliber: 380 ACP, 6-rounds. **Barrel:** 2.22". **Weight:** 14 oz. **Length:** 4.52" overall. **Grips:** NA. **Sights:** Fixed low-profile. **Features:** Small-frame DAO pocket pistol. Steel slide, aluminum alloy frame, nickel-teflon finish.
Price: **$535.00**

DESERT BABY EAGLE PISTOLS
Caliber: 9mm Para., 40 S&W, 45 ACP, 10- or 15-round magazines. **Barrel:** 3.64", 3.93", 4.52". **Weight:** 26.8 to 39.8 oz. **Length:** 7.25" to 8.25" overall. **Grips:** Polymer. **Sights:** Drift-adjustable rear, blade front. **Features:** Steel frame and slide; slide safety; decocker. Reintroduced in 1999. Imported from Israel by Magnum Research, Inc.
Price: **$619.00**

DIAMONDBACK DB380 PISTOL
Caliber: .380, 6+1-shot capacity. **Barrel:** 2.8". **Weight:** 8.8 oz. **Features:** A micro-compact .380 automatic pistol made entirely in the USA. Designed with safety in mind, the DB380 features a "ZERO-Energy" striker firing system (patent pending) with a mechanical firing pin block, a steel magazine catch to secure a sheet metal magaine and real windage-adjustable sights, all in a lightweight pistol. A steel trigger with dual connecting bars allows for a crisp smooth, five-pound DAO trigger pull. The DB380 features a FEA (Finite Element Analysis) designed slide and barrel that is

stronger than any comparable firearm, resulting in durability with less felt recoil, and the absence of removable pins or tools makes field stripping easier than ever. The slide, barrel, and internal parts are coated to resist corrosion.
Price: 290.00

DIAMONDBACK DB9 PISTOL
Caliber: 9mm, 6+1-shot capacity. **Barrel:** 3". **Weight:** 11 oz. **Length:** 5.60". **Features:** A micro-compact 9mm automatic pistol made entirely in the USA. Designed with safety in mind, the DB9 features a "ZERO-Energy" striker firing system (patent pending) with a mechanical firing pin block, a steel magazine catch to secure a sheet metal magazine and real windage-adjustable sights, all in a lightweight pistol. A steel trigger with dual connecting bars allows for a crisp smooth, five-pound DAO trigger pull. The DB9 features a FEA (Finite Element Analysis) designed slide and barrel that is stronger than any comparable firearm, resulting in durability with less felt recoil, and the absence of removable pins or tools makes field stripping easier than ever. The slide, barrel, and internal parts are coated to resist corrosion.
Price: **$365.00**

EAA WITNESS FULL SIZE AUTO PISTOL
Caliber: 9mm Para., 38 Super, 18-shot magazine; 40 S&W, 10mm, 15-shot magazine; 45 ACP, 10-shot magazine. **Barrel:** 4.50". **Weight:** 35.33 oz. **Length:** 8.10" overall. **Grips:** Checkered rubber. **Sights:** Undercut blade front, open rear adjustable for windage. **Features:** Double-action/single-action trigger system; round trigger guard; frame-mounted safety. Introduced 1991. Polymer frame introduced 2005. Imported from Italy by European American Armory.
Price: 9mm Para., 38 Super, 10mm, 40 S&W, 45 ACP, full-size steel frame, Wonder finish **$514.00**
Price: 45/22 22 LR, full-size steel frame, blued **$472.00**
Price: 9mm Para., 40 S&W, 45 ACP, full-size polymer frame . **$472.00**

EAA WITNESS COMPACT AUTO PISTOL
Caliber: 9mm Para., 40 S&W, 10mm, 12-shot magazine; 45 ACP, 8-shot magazine. **Barrel:** 3.6". **Weight:** 30 oz. **Length:** 7.3" overall. Otherwise similar to Full Size Witness. Polymer frame introduced 2005. Imported from Italy by European American Armory.
Price: 9mm Para., 10mm, 40 S&W, 45 ACP, steel frame, Wonder finish **$514.00**
Price: 9mm Para., 40 S&W, 45 ACP, polymer frame **$472.00**

EAA WITNESS-P CARRY AUTO PISTOL
Caliber: 10mm, 15-shot magazine; 45 ACP, 10-shot magazine. **Barrel:** 3.6". **Weight:** 27 oz. **Length:** 7.5" overall. Otherwise similar to Full Size Witness. Polymer frame introduced 2005. Imported from Italy by European American Armory.
Price: 10mm, 45 ACP, polymer frame, from **$598.00**

EAA ZASTAVA EZ PISTOL
Caliber: 9mm Para., 15-shot magazine; 40 S&W, 11-shot magazine; 45 ACP, 10-shot magazine. **Barrel:** 3.5" or 4." **Weight:** 30-33 oz. **Length:** 7.25" to 7.5" overall. **Features:** Ambidextrous decocker, slide release and magazine release; three dot sight system, aluminum frame, steel slide, accessory rail, full-length claw extractor, loaded chamber indicator. M88 compact has 3.6" barrel, weighs 28 oz. Introduced 2008. Imported by European American Armory.
Price: 9mm Para. or 40 S&W, blued **$547.00**
Price: 9mm Para. or 40 S&W, chromed **$587.00**
Price: 45 ACP, chromed **$587.00**
Price: M88, from **$292.00**

ED BROWN CLASSIC CUSTOM

Caliber: 45 ACP, 7 shot. **Barrel:** 5". **Weight:** 40 oz. **Grips:** Cocobolo wood. **Sights:** Bo-Mar adjustable rear, dovetail front. **Features:** Single-action, M1911 style, custom made to order, stainless frame and slide available. Special mirror-finished slide.
Price: Model CC-BB, blued **$3,155.00**
Price: Model CC-SB, blued and stainless **$3,155.00**
Price: Model CC-SS, stainless **$3,155.00**

ED BROWN KOBRA AND KOBRA CARRY

Caliber: 45 ACP, 7-shot magazine. **Barrel:** 5" (Kobra); 4.25" (Kobra Carry). **Weight:** 39 oz. (Kobra); 34 oz. (Kobra Carry). **Grips:** Hogue exotic wood. **Sights:** Ramp, front; fixed Novak low-mount night sights, rear. **Features:** Has snakeskin pattern serrations on forestrap and mainspring housing, dehorned edges, beavertail grip safety.
Price: Kobra K-BB, blued **$2,195.00**
Price: Kobra K-SB, stainless and blued **$2,195.00**
Price: Kobra K-SS, stainless **$2,195.00**
Price: Kobra Carry blued, blued/stainless, or stainless from **$2,445.00**

ED BROWN KOBRA CARRY LIGHTWEIGHT

Caliber: 45 ACP, 7-shot magazine. **Barrel:** 4.25" (Commander model slide). **Weight:** 27 oz. **Grips:** Hogue exotic wood. **Sights:** 10-8 Performance U-notch plain black rear sight with .156 notch, for fast aquisition of close targets. Fixed dovetail front night sight with high visibility white outlines. **Features:** Aluminium frame and Bobtail™ housing. Matte finished Gen III coated slide for low glare, with snakeskin on rear of slide only. Snakeskin pattern serrations on forestrap and mainspring housing, dehorned edges, beavertail grip safety. "LW" insignia on slide, which stands for "Lightweight".
Price: Kobra KC-LW-G3 . . . . **$2,920.00**
Price: Kobra KC-LW-G3-A **$2,995.00**

Ed Brown Executive Pistols

Similar to other Ed Brown products, but with 25-lpi checkered frame and mainspring housing.
Price: Elite blued, blued/stainless, or stainless, from **$2,395.00**
Price: Carry blued, blued/stainless, or stainless, from **$2,645.00**
Price: Target blued, blued/stainless, or stainless (2006) from **$2,595.00**

Ed Brown Special Forces Pistol

Similar to other Ed Brown products, but with ChainLink treatment on forestrap and mainspring housing. Entire gun coated with Gen III

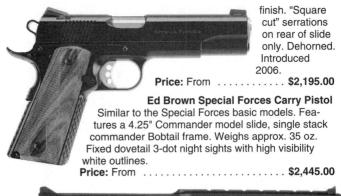

finish. "Square cut" serrations on rear of slide only. Dehorned. Introduced 2006.
Price: From **$2,195.00**

Ed Brown Special Forces Carry Pistol

Similar to the Special Forces basic models. Features a 4.25" Commander model slide, single stack commander Bobtail frame. Weighs approx. 35 oz. Fixed dovetail 3-dot night sights with high visibility white outlines.
Price: From **$2,445.00**

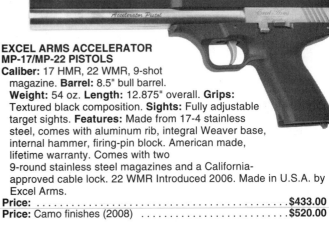

EXCEL ARMS ACCELERATOR MP-17/MP-22 PISTOLS

Caliber: 17 HMR, 22 WMR, 9-shot magazine. **Barrel:** 8.5" bull barrel. **Weight:** 54 oz. **Length:** 12.875" overall. **Grips:** Textured black composition. **Sights:** Fully adjustable target sights. **Features:** Made from 17-4 stainless steel, comes with aluminum rib, integral Weaver base, internal hammer, firing-pin block. American made, lifetime warranty. Comes with two 9-round stainless steel magazines and a California-approved cable lock. 22 WMR Introduced 2006. Made in U.S.A. by Excel Arms.
Price: **$433.00**
Price: Camo finishes (2008) **$520.00**

FIRESTORM AUTO PISTOLS

Caliber: 22 LR, 32 ACP, 10-shot magazine; 380 ACP, 7-shot magazine; 9mm Para., 40 S&W, 10-shot magazine; 45 ACP, 7-shot magazine. **Barrel:** 3.5". **Weight:** From 23 oz. **Length:** From 6.6" overall. **Grips:** Rubber. **Sights:** 3-dot. **Features:** Double action. Distributed by SGS Importers International.
Price: 22 LR, matte or duotone, from **$309.95**
Price: 380, matte or duotone, from **$311.95**
Price: Mini Firestorm 9mm Para., matte, duotone, nickel, from **$395.00**
Price: Mini Firestorm 40 S&W, matte, duotone, nickel, from . . **$395.00**
Price: Mini Firestorm 45 ACP, matte, duotone, chrome, from **$402.00**

GIRSAN MC27E PISTOL

Caliber: 9x19mm Parabellum. 15-shot magazine. **Barrel:** 98.5mm. **Weight:** 650 gr. (without magazine). **Length:** 184.5 mm overall. **Grips:** Black polymer. **Sights:** Fixed. **Features:** Cold forged barrel,polymer frame, short recoil operating system and locked breech. Semi-automatic, double action with a right and left safety sytem latch.
Price: . . . .**NA**

GLOCK 17/17C AUTO PISTOL

Caliber: 9mm Para., 17/19/33-shot magazines. **Barrel:** 4.49". **Weight:** 22.04 oz. (without magazine). **Length:** 7.32" overall. **Grips:** Black polymer. **Sights:** Dot on front blade, white outline rear adjustable for windage. **Features:** Polymer frame, steel slide; double-action trigger with "Safe Action" system; mechanical firing pin safety, drop safety; simple takedown without tools; locked breech, recoil operated action. ILS designation refers to Internal Locking System. Adopted by Austrian armed forces 1983. NATO approved 1984. Imported from Austria by Glock, Inc.
Price: Fixed sight **$690.00**

GLOCK 17 GEN4

Similar to Model G17 but with multiple backstrap system allowing three options: a short frame version, medium frame or large frame; reversible, enlarged magazine release catch; dual recoil spring assembly; new Rough Textured Frame (RTF) surface designed to enhance grip traction.
Price: . . . . **N/A**

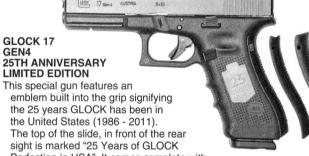

GLOCK 17 GEN4 25TH ANNIVERSARY LIMITED EDITION

This special gun features an emblem built into the grip signifying the 25 years GLOCK has been in the United States (1986 - 2011). The top of the slide, in front of the rear sight is marked "25 Years of GLOCK Perfection in USA". It comes complete with two magazines, a speed loader, cable lock, cleaning rod and brush, two interchangeable backstraps, a limited edition silver GLOCK case, and a letter of authenticity! Each gun is identified by the special prefix of 25YUSA. Similar to Model G17 but with multiple backstrap system allowing three options: a short frame version, medium frame or large frame; reversible, enlarged magazine release catch; dual recoil spring assembly; new Rough Textured Frame (RTF) surface designed to enhance grip traction.
Price: **$850.00**

GLOCK 19/19C AUTO PISTOL

Caliber: 9mm Para., 15/17/19/33-shot magazines. **Barrel:** 4.02". **Weight:** 20.99 oz. (without magazine). **Length:** 6.85" overall. Compact version of Glock 17. Pricing the same as Model 17. Imported from Austria by Glock, Inc.
Price: Fixed sight **$699.00**
Price: 19C Compensated (fixed sight) **$675.00**

GLOCK 20/20C 10MM AUTO PISTOL

Caliber: 10mm, 15-shot magazines. **Barrel:** 4.6". **Weight:** 27.68 oz. (without magazine). **Length:** 7.59" overall. **Features:** Otherwise similar to Model 17. Imported from Austria by Glock, Inc. Introduced 1990.
Price: Fixed sight, from **$700.00**

GLOCK MODEL 20 SF SHORT FRAME PISTOL

Caliber: 10mm. **Barrel:** 4.61" with hexagonal rifling. **Weight:** 27.51 oz. **Length:** 8.07" overall. **Sights:** Fixed. **Features:** Otherwise similar to Model 20 but with short-frame design, extended sight radius.
Price: **$664.00**

GLOCK 21/21C AUTO PISTOL

Caliber: 45 ACP, 13-shot magazines. **Barrel:** 4.6". **Weight:** 26.28 oz. (without magazine). **Length:** 7.59" overall. **Features:** Otherwise similar to Model 17. Imported from Austria by Glock, Inc. Introduced 1991. SF version has tactical rail, smaller diameter grip, 10-round magazine capacity. Introduced 2007.
Price: Fixed sight, from **$700.00**

GLOCK 22/22C AUTO PISTOL

Caliber: 40 S&W, 15/17-shot magazines. **Barrel:** 4.49". **Weight:** 22.92 oz. (without magazine). **Length:** 7.32" overall. **Features:** Otherwise similar to Model 17, including pricing. Imported from Austria by Glock, Inc. Introduced 1990.
Price: Fixed sight, from **$641.00**

GLOCK 22 GEN4

Similar to Model G22 but with multiple backstrap system allowing three options: a short frame version, medium frame or large frame; reversible, enlarged magazine release catch; dual recoil spring assembly; new Rough Textured Frame (RTF) surface designed to enhance grip traction.
Price: . . . .**N/A**

GLOCK 23/23C AUTO PISTOL

Caliber: 40 S&W, 13/15/17-shot magazines. **Barrel:** 4.02". **Weight:** 21.16 oz. (without magazine). **Length:** 6.85" overall. **Features:** Otherwise similar to Model 22, including pricing. Compact version of Glock 22. Imported from Austria by Glock, Inc. Introduced 1990.
Price: Fixed sight **$641.00**
Price: 23C Compensated (fixed sight) **$694.00**

GLOCK 26 AUTO PISTOL

Caliber: 9mm Para. 10/12/15/17/19/33-shot magazines. **Barrel:** 3.46". **Weight:** 19.75 oz. **Length:** 6.29" overall. Subcompact version of Glock 17. Pricing the same as Model 17. Imported from Austria by Glock, Inc.
Price: Fixed sight **$690.00**

GLOCK 27 AUTO PISTOL

Caliber: 40 S&W, 9/11/13/15/17-shot magazines. **Barrel:** 3.46". **Weight:** 19.75 oz. (without magazine). **Length:** 6.29" overall. **Features:** Otherwise similar to Model 22, including pricing. Subcompact version of Glock 22. Imported from Austria by Glock, Inc. Introduced 1996.
Price: Fixed sight **$750.00**

GLOCK 29 AUTO PISTOL

Caliber: 10mm, 10/15-shot magazines. **Barrel:** 3.78". **Weight:** 24.69 oz. (without magazine). **Length:** 6.77" overall. **Features:** Otherwise similar to Model 20, including pricing. Subcompact version of Glock 20. Imported from Austria by Glock, Inc. Introduced 1997.
Price: Fixed sight **$672.00**

GLOCK MODEL 29 SF SHORT FRAME PISTOL

Caliber: 10mm. **Barrel:** 3.78" with hexagonal rifling. **Weight:** 24.52 oz. **Length:** 6.97" overall. **Sights:** Fixed. **Features:** Otherwise similar to Model 29 but with short-frame design, extended sight radius.
Price: **$660.00**

GLOCK 30 AUTO PISTOL

Caliber: 45 ACP, 9/10/13-shot magazines. **Barrel:** 3.78". **Weight:** 23.99 oz. (without magazine). **Length:** 6.77" overall. **Features:** Otherwise similar to Model 21, including pricing. Subcompact version of Glock 21. Imported from Austria by Glock, Inc. Introduced 1997. SF version has tactical rail, octagonal rifled barrel with a 1:15.75 rate of twist, smaller diameter grip, 10-round magazine capacity. Introduced 2008
Price: Fixed sight **$700.00**

GLOCK 31/31C AUTO PISTOL
Caliber: 357 Auto, 15/17-shot magazines. **Barrel:** 4.49". **Weight:** 23.28 oz. (without magazine). **Length:** 7.32" overall. **Features:** Otherwise similar to Model 17. Imported from Austria by Glock, Inc.
Price: Fixed sight, from $641.00

GLOCK 32/32C AUTO PISTOL
Caliber: 357 Auto, 13/15/17-shot magazines. **Barrel:** 4.02". **Weight:** 21.52 oz. (without magazine). **Length:** 6.85" overall. **Features:** Otherwise similar to Model 31. Compact. Imported from Austria by Glock, Inc.
Price: Fixed sight $669.00

GLOCK 33 AUTO PISTOL
Caliber: 357 Auto, 9/11/13/15/17-shot magazines. **Barrel:** 3.46". **Weight:** 19.75 oz. (without magazine). **Length:** 6.29" overall. **Features:** Otherwise similar to Model 31. Subcompact. Imported from Austria by Glock, Inc.
Price: Fixed sight, from $641.00

GLOCK 34 AUTO PISTOL
Caliber: 9mm Para. 17/19/33-shot magazines. **Barrel:** 5.32". **Weight:** 22.9 oz. **Length:** 8.15" overall. Competition version of Glock 17 with extended barrel, slide, and sight radius dimensions. Imported from Austria by Glock, Inc.
Price: Adjustable sight, from $648.00

GLOCK 35 AUTO PISTOL
Caliber: 40 S&W, 15/17-shot magazines. **Barrel:** 5.32". **Weight:** 24.52 oz. (without magazine). **Length:** 8.15" overall. **Features:** Otherwise similar to Model 22. Competition version of Glock 22 with extended barrel, slide, and sight radius dimensions. Imported from Austria by Glock, Inc. Introduced 1996.
Price: Adjustable sight $648.00

GLOCK 36 AUTO PISTOL
Caliber: 45 ACP, 6-shot magazines. **Barrel:** 3.78". **Weight:** 20.11 oz. (without magazine). **Length:** 6.77" overall. **Features:** Single-stack magazine, slimmer grip than Glock 21/30. Subcompact. Imported from Austria by Glock, Inc. Introduced 1997.
Price: Adjustable sight $616.00

GLOCK 37 AUTO PISTOL
Caliber: 45 GAP, 10-shot magazines. **Barrel:** 4.49". **Weight:** 25.95 oz. (without magazine). **Length:** 7.32" overall. **Features:** Otherwise similar to Model 17. Imported from Austria by Glock, Inc. Introduced 2005.
Price: Fixed sight, from $562.00

GLOCK 38 AUTO PISTOL
Caliber: 45 GAP, 8/10-shot magazines. **Barrel:** 4.02". **Weight:** 24.16 oz. (without magazine). **Length:** 6.85" overall. **Features:** Otherwise similar to Model 37. Compact. Imported from Austria by Glock, Inc.
Price: Fixed sight $614.00

GLOCK 39 AUTO PISTOL
Caliber: 45 GAP, 6/8/10-shot magazines. **Barrel:** 3.46". **Weight:** 19.33 oz. (without magazine). **Length:** 6.3" overall. **Features:** Otherwise similar to Model 37. Subcompact. Imported from Austria by Glock, Inc.
Price: Fixed sight $614.00

GLOCK MODEL G17/G22/G19/G23 RTF
Similar to Models G17, G22, G19 and G23 but with rough textured frame.
Price: .... N/A

HECKLER & KOCH USP AUTO PISTOL
Caliber: 9mm Para., 15-shot magazine; 40 S&W, 13-shot magazine; 45 ACP, 12-shot magazine. **Barrel:** 4.25-4.41". **Weight:** 1.65 lbs. **Length:** 7.64-7.87" overall. **Grips:** Non-slip stippled black polymer. **Sights:** Blade front, rear adjustable for windage. **Features:** New HK design with polymer frame, modified Browning action with recoil reduction system, single control lever. Special "hostile environment" finish on all metal parts. Available in SA/DA, DAO, left- and right-hand versions. Introduced 1993. 45 ACP Introduced 1995. Imported from Germany by Heckler & Koch, Inc.
Price: USP 45 ....$919.00
Price: USP 40 and USP 9mm $859.00

HECKLER & KOCH USP COMPACT AUTO PISTOL
Caliber: 9mm Para., 13-shot magazine; 40 S&W and .357 SIG, 12-shot magazine; 45 ACP, 8-shot magazine. Similar to the USP except the 9mm Para., 357 SIG, and 40 S&W have 3.58" barrels, measure 6.81" overall, and weigh 1.47 lbs. (9mm Para.). Introduced 1996. 45 ACP measures 7.09" overall. Introduced 1998. Imported from Germany by Heckler & Koch, Inc.
Price: USP Compact 45 .... $959.00
Price: USP Compact 9mm Para., 40 S&W $879.00

HECKLER & KOCH USP45 TACTICAL PISTOL
Caliber: 40 S&W, 13-shot magazine; 45 ACP, 12-shot magazine. **Barrel:** 4.90-5.09". **Weight:** 1.9 lbs. **Length:** 8.64" overall. **Grips:** Non-slip stippled polymer. **Sights:** Blade front, fully adjustable target rear. **Features:** Has extended threaded barrel with rubber O-ring; adjustable trigger; extended magazine floorplate; adjustable trigger stop; polymer frame. Introduced 1998. Imported from Germany by Heckler & Koch, Inc.
Price: USP Tactical 45 .... $1,239.00
Price: USP Tactical 40 .... $1,179.00

HECKLER & KOCH USP COMPACT TACTICAL PISTOL
Caliber: 45 ACP, 8-shot magazine. Similar to the USP Tactical except measures 7.72" overall, weighs 1.72 lbs. Introduced 2006. Imported from Germany by Heckler & Koch, Inc.
Price: USP Compact Tactical $1,179.00

HECKLER & KOCH MARK 23 SPECIAL OPERATIONS PISTOL
Caliber: 45 ACP, 12-shot magazine. **Barrel:** 5.87". **Weight:** 2.42 lbs. **Length:** 9.65" overall. **Grips:** Integral with frame; black polymer. **Sights:** Blade front, rear drift adjustable for windage; 3-dot. **Features:** Civilian version of the SOCOM pistol. Polymer frame; double action; exposed hammer; short recoil, modified Browning action. Introduced 1996. Imported from Germany by Heckler & Koch, Inc.
Price: $2,139.00

HECKLER & KOCH P30L AND P30LS AUTO PISTOLS
Caliber: 9mm x 19 and .40 S&W with 15-shot magazines. **Barrel:** 4.45". **Weight:** 27.52 oz. **Length:** 7.56" overall.

Prices given are believed to be accurate at time of publication however, many factors affect retail pricing so exact prices are not possible.

Grips: Interchangeable panels. **Sights:** Open rectangular notch rear sight with contrast points (no radioactive). **Features:** Like the P30, the P30L was designed as a modern police and security pistol and combines optimal function and safety. Ergonomic features include a special grip frame with interchangeable backstraps inserts and lateral plates, allowing the pistol to be individually adapted to any user. Imported from Germany by Heckler & Koch, Inc. Browning type action with modified short recoil operation. Ambidextrous controls include dual slide releases, magazine release levers, and a serrated decocking button located on the rear of the frame (for applicable variants). A Picatinny rail molded into the front of the frame makes mounting lights, laser aimers, or other accessories easy and convenient. The extractor serves as a loaded chamber indicator providing a reminder of a loaded chamber that can be subtly seen and felt. The standard P30L is a 9 mm "Variant 3 (V3)" with a conventional double-action/single action trigger mode with a serrated decocking button on the rear of the slide.

Price: P30L **$826.00**
Price: P30L Variant 2 Law Enforcement Modification
(LEM) enhanced DAO . . . . **NA**
Price: P30L Variant 3 Double Action/Single Action
(DA/SA) with Decocker . . . . **NA**
Price: P30LS **$879.95**

HECKLER & KOCH P2000 AUTO PISTOL

Caliber: 9mm Para., 13-shot magazine; 40 S&W and .357 SIG, 12-shot magazine. **Barrel:** 3.62". **Weight:** 1.5 lbs. **Length:** 7" overall. **Grips:** Interchangeable panels. **Sights:** Fixed Patridge style, drift adjustable for windage, standard 3-dot. **Features:** Incorporates features of HK USP Compact pistol, including Law Enforcement Modification (LEM) trigger, double-action hammer system, ambidextrous magazine release, dual slide-release levers, accessory mounting rails, recurved, hook trigger guard, fiber-reinforced polymer frame, modular grip with exchangeable back straps, nitro-carburized finish, lock-out safety device. Introduced 2003. Imported from Germany by Heckler & Koch, Inc.

Price: **$879.00**
Price: P2000 LEM DAO, 357 SIG, intr. 2006 . . . . **$879.00**
Price: P2000 SA/DA, 357 SIG, intr. 2006 . . . . **$879.00**

HECKLER & KOCH P2000 SK AUTO PISTOL

Caliber: 9mm Para., 10-shot magazine; 40 S&W and .357 SIG, 9-shot magazine. **Barrel:** 3.27". **Weight:** 1.3 lbs. **Length:** 6.42" overall. **Sights:** Fixed Patridge style, drift adjustable. **Features:** Standard accessory rails, ambidextrous slide release, polymer frame, polygonal bore profile. Smaller version of P2000. Introduced 2005. Imported from Germany by Heckler & Koch, Inc.

Price: **$919.00**

HI-POINT FIREARMS MODEL 9MM COMPACT PISTOL

Caliber: 9mm Para., 8-shot magazine. **Barrel:** 3.5". **Weight:** 25 oz. **Length:** 6.75" overall. **Grips:** Textured plastic. **Sights:** Combat-style adjustable 3-dot system; low profile. **Features:** Single-action design; frame-mounted magazine release; polymer frame. Scratch-resistant matte finish. Introduced 1993. Comps are similar except they have a 4" barrel with muzzle brake/compensator. Compensator is slotted for laser or flashlight mounting. Introduced 1998. Made in U.S.A. by MKS Supply, Inc.

Price: C-9 9mm **$155.00**

Hi-Point Firearms Model 380 Polymer Pistol

Similar to the 9mm Compact model except chambered for 380 ACP, 8-shot magazine, adjustable 3-dot sights. Weighs 25 oz. Polymer

frame. Action locks open after last shot. Includes 10-shot and 8-shot magazine; trigger lock. Introduced 1998. Comps are similar except they have a 4" barrel with muzzle compensator. Introduced 2001. Made in U.S.A. by MKS Supply, Inc.

Price: CF-380 . . . . **$135.00**

HI-POINT FIREARMS 40SW/POLY AND 45 AUTO PISTOLS

Caliber: 40 S&W, 8-shot magazine; 45 ACP (9-shot). **Barrel:** 4.5". **Weight:** 32 oz. **Length:** 7.72" overall. **Sights:** Adjustable 3-dot. **Features:** Polymer frames, last round lock-open, grip mounted magazine release, magazine disconnect safety, integrated accessory rail, trigger lock. Introduced 2002. Made in U.S.A. by MKS Supply, Inc.

Price: 40SW-B **$186.00**
Price: 45 ACP **$186.00**

HIGH STANDARD VICTOR 22 PISTOL

Caliber: 22 Long Rifle (10 rounds) or .22 Short (5 rounds). **Barrel:** 4.5"-5.5". **Weight:** 45 oz.-46 oz. **Length:** 8.5"-9.5" overall. **Grips:** Freestyle wood. **Sights:** Frame mounted, adjustable. **Features:** Semi-auto with drilled and tapped barrel, tu-tone or blued finish.

Price: **$845.00**

High Standard 10X Custom 22 Pistol

Similar to the Victor model but with precision fitting, black wood grips, 5.5" barrel only. High Standard Universal Mount, 10-shot magazine, barrel drilled and tapped, certificate of authenticity. Overall length is 9.5". Weighs 44 oz. to 46 oz. From High Standard Custom Shop.

Price: **$1,095.00**

HIGH STANDARD SUPERMATIC TROPHY 22 PISTOL

Caliber: 22 Long Rifle (10 rounds) or .22 Short (5 rounds/Citation version), not interchangable. **Barrel:** 5.5", 7.25". **Weight:** 44 oz., 46 oz. **Length:** 9.5", 11.25" overall. **Grips:** Wood. **Sights:** Adjustable. **Features:** Semi-auto with drilled and tapped barrel, tu-tone or blued finish with gold accents.

Price: 5.5" **$845.00**

High Standard Olympic Military 22 Pistol

Similar to the Supermatic Trophy model but in 22 Short only with 5.5" bull barrel, five-round magazine, aluminum alloy frame, adjustable sights. Overall length is 9.5", weighs 42 oz.

Price: **$875.00**

High Standard Supermatic Citation Series 22 Pistol

Similar to the Supermatic Trophy model but with heavier trigger pull, 10" barrel, and nickel accents. 22 Short conversion unit available. Overall length 14.5", weighs 52 oz.

Price: **$895.00**

HIGH STANDARD SUPERMATIC TOURNAMENT 22 PISTOL

Caliber: 22 LR. **Barrel:** 5.5" bull barrel. **Weight:** 44 oz. **Length:** 9.5" overall. **Features:** Limited edition; similar to High Standard Victor model but with rear sight mounted directly to slide.

Price: **$835.00**

HIGH STANDARD SPORT KING 22 PISTOL

Caliber: 22 LR. **Barrel:** 4.5" or 6.75" tapered barrel. **Weight:** 40 oz. to 42 oz. **Length:** 8.5" to 10.75". **Features:** Sport version of High Standard Supermatic. Two-tone finish, fixed sights.

Price: **$725.00**

HI-STANDARD SPACE GUN

Semiauto pistol chambered in .22 LR. Recreation of famed competition "Space Gun" from 1960s. Features include 6.75- 8- or 10-inch barrel; 10-round magazine; adjustable sights; barrel weight; adjustable muzzle brake; blue-black finish with gold highlights.

Price: $1095.00

KAHR CM SERIES

Caliber: 9mm (6+1). **Barrel:** 3". **Weight:** 15.9 oz. **Length:** 5.42" overall. **Grips:** Textured polymer with integral steel rails molded into frame. **Sights:** CM9093 - Pinned in polymer sight; PM9093 - Drift adjustable, white bar-dot combat. **Features:** A conventional rifled barrel instead of the match grade polygonal barrel on Kahr's PM series; the CM slide stop lever is MIM (metal-injection-molded) instead of machined; the CM series slide has fewer machining operations and uses simple engraved markings instead of roll marking and finally the CM series are shipped with one magazine instead of two magazines.

The CM9 slide is only .90 inch wide and machined from solid 416 stainless slide with a matte finish, each gun is shipped with one 6 rd stainless steel magazine with a flush baseplate. Magazines are USA made, plasma welded, tumbled to remove burrs and feature Wolff Gunsprings. The magazine catch in the polymer frame is all metal and will not wear out on the stainless steel magazine after extended use.

Price: CM9093. . . . . $565.00
Price: PM9093 Match Grade $786.00

KAHR K SERIES AUTO PISTOLS

Caliber: K9: 9mm Para., 7-shot; K40: 40 S&W, 6-shot magazine. **Barrel:** 3.5". **Weight:** 25 oz. **Length:** 6" overall. **Grips:** Wraparound textured soft polymer. **Sights:** Blade front, rear drift adjustable for windage; bar-dot combat style. **Features:** Trigger-cocking double-action mechanism with passive firing pin block. Made of 4140 ordnance steel with matte black finish. Contact maker for complete price list. Introduced 1994. Made in U.S.A. by Kahr Arms.

Price: K9093C K9, matte stainless steel $855.00
Price: K9093NC K9, matte stainless steel w/tritium
night sights $985.00
Price: K9094C K9 matte blackened stainless steel $891.00
Price: K9098 K9 Elite 2003, stainless steel $932.00
Price: K4043 K40, matte stainless steel $855.00
Price: K4043N K40, matte stainless steel w/tritium
night sights $985.00
Price: K4044 K40, matte blackened stainless steel $891.00
Price: K4048 K40 Elite 2003, stainless steel . . . .
$932.00

Kahr MK Series Micro Pistols

Similar to the K9/K40 except is 5.35" overall, 4" high, with a 3.08" barrel. Weighs 23.1 oz. Has snag-free bar-dot sights, polished feed ramp, dual recoil spring system, DA-only trigger. Comes with 5-round flush baseplate and 6-shot grip extension magazine. Introduced 1998. Made in U.S.A. by Kahr Arms.
Price: M9093 MK9, matte stainless steel $855.00

Price: M9093N MK9, matte stainless steel, tritium
night sights $958.00
Price: M9098 MK9 Elite 2003, stainless steel $932.00
Price: M4043 MK40, matte stainless steel $855.00
Price: M4043N MK40, matte stainless steel, tritium
night sights $958.00
Price: M4048 MK40 Elite 2003, stainless steel $932.00

KAHR P SERIES PISTOLS

Caliber: 380 ACP, 9x19, 40 S&W, 45 ACP. Similar to K9/K40 steel frame pistol except has polymer frame, matte stainless steel slide. Barrel length 3.5"; overall length 5.8"; weighs 17 oz. Includes two 7-shot magazines, hard polymer case, trigger lock. Introduced 2000. Made in U.S.A. by Kahr Arms.
Price: KP9093 9mm Para. $739.00
Price: KP4043 40 S&W $739.00
Price: KP4543 45 ACP $805.00
Price: KP3833 380 ACP (2008) $649.00

KAHR PM SERIES PISTOLS

Caliber: 9x19, 40 S&W, 45 ACP. Similar to P-Series pistols except has smaller polymer frame (Polymer Micro). Barrel length 3.08"; overall length 5.35"; weighs 17 oz. Includes two 7-shot magazines, hard polymer case, trigger lock. Introduced 2000. Made in U.S.A. by Kahr Arms.
Price: PM9093 PM9 . . . . $786.00
Price: PM4043 PM40 . . . . $786.00
Price: PM4543 (2007) $855.00

KAHR T SERIES PISTOLS

Caliber: T9: 9mm Para., 8-shot magazine; T40: 40 S&W, 7-shot magazine. **Barrel:** 4". **Weight:** 28.1-29.1 oz. **Length:** 6.5" overall. **Grips:** Checkered Hogue Pau Ferro wood grips. **Sights:** Rear: Novak low profile 2-dot tritium night sight, front tritium night sight. **Features:** Similar to other Kahr makes, but with longer slide and barrel upper, longer butt. Trigger cocking DAO; lock breech; "Browning-type" recoil lug; passive striker block; no magazine disconnect. Comes with two magazines. Introduced 2004. Made in U.S.A. by Kahr Arms.
Price: KT9093 T9 matte stainless steel $831.00
Price: KT9093-NOVAK T9, "Tactical 9," Novak night sight . . . $968.00
Price: KT4043 40 S&W. $831.00

KAHR TP SERIES PISTOLS

Caliber: TP9: 9mm Para., 7-shot magazine; TP40: 40 S&W, 6-shot magazine. **Barrel:** 4". **Weight:** 19.1-20.1 oz. **Length:** 6.5-6.7" overall. **Grips:** Textured polymer. Similar to T-series guns, but with polymer frame, matte stainless slide. Comes with two magazines. TP40s introduced 2006. Made in U.S.A. by Kahr Arms.
Price: TP9093 TP9 . . . . $697.00
Price: TP9093-Novak TP9
(Novak night sights) $838.00
Price: TP4043 TP40 . . . . $697.00
Price: TP4043-Novak
(Novak night sights) $838.00
Price: TP4543 (2007) $697.00
Price: TP4543-Novak
(4.04 barrel, Novak night sights) $838.00

Prices given are believed to be accurate at time of publication however, many factors affect retail pricing so exact prices are not possible.

KAHR CW SERIES PISTOL

Caliber: 9mm Para., 7-shot magazine; 40 S&W and 45 ACP, 6-shot magazine. **Barrel:** 3.5-3.64". **Weight:** 17.7-18.7 oz. **Length:** 5.9-6.36" overall. **Grips:** Textured polymer. Similar to P-Series, but CW Series have conventional rifling, metal-injection-molded slide stop lever, no front dovetail cut, one magazine. CW40 introduced 2006. Made in U.S.A. by Kahr Arms.
Price: CW9093 CW9 . . . . **$549.00**
Price: CW4043 CW40 . . . . **$549.00**
Price: CW4543 45 ACP (2008) **$606.00**

KAHR P380

Very small double action only semiauto pistol chambered in .380 ACP. Features include 2.5-inch Lothar Walther barrel; black polymer frame with stainless steel slide; drift adjustable white bar/dot combat/sights; optional tritium sights; two 6+1 magazines. Overall length 4.9 inches, weight 10 oz. without magazine.
Price: Standard sights **$649.00**

KEL-TEC P-11 AUTO PISTOL

Caliber: 9mm Para., 10-shot magazine. **Barrel:** 3.1". **Weight:** 14 oz. **Length:** 5.6" overall. **Grips:** Checkered black polymer. **Sights:** Blade front, rear adjustable for windage. **Features:** Ordnance steel slide, aluminum frame. Double-action-only trigger mechanism. Introduced 1995. Made in U.S.A. by Kel-Tec CNC Industries, Inc.
Price: From **$333.00**

KEL-TEC PF-9 PISTOL

Caliber: 9mm Para.; 7 rounds. **Weight:** 12.7 oz. **Sights:** Rear sight adjustable for windage and elevation. **Barrel Length:** 3.1". **Length:** 5.85". **Features:** Barrel, locking system, slide stop, assembly pin, front sight, recoil springs and guide rod adapted from P-11. Trigger system with integral hammer block and the extraction system adapted from P-3AT. MIL-STD-1913 Picatinny rail. Made in U.S.A. by Kel-Tec CNC Industries, Inc.
Price: From **$333.00**

KEL-TEC P-32 AUTO PISTOL

Caliber: 32 ACP, 7-shot magazine. **Barrel:** 2.68". **Weight:** 6.6 oz. **Length:** 5.07" overall. **Grips:** Checkered composite. **Sights:** Fixed. **Features:** Double-action-only mechanism with 6-lb. pull; internal slide stop. Textured composite grip/frame. Now available in 380 ACP. Made in U.S.A. by Kel-Tec CNC Industries, Inc.
Price: From **$318.00**

KEL-TEC P-3AT PISTOL

Caliber: 380 ACP; 7-rounds. **Weight:** 7.2 oz. **Length:** 5.2". **Features:** Lightest 380 ACP made; aluminum frame, steel barrel.
Price: From **$324.00**

KEL-TEC PLR-16 PISTOL

Caliber: 5.56mm NATO; 10-round magazine. **Weight:** 51 oz. **Sights:** Rear sight adjustable for windage, front sight is M-16 blade. **Barrel Length:** 9.2". **Length:** 18.5". **Features:** Muzzle is threaded 1/2"-28 to accept standard attachments such as a muzzle brake. Except for the barrel, bolt, sights, and mechanism, the PLR-16 pistol is made of high-impact glass fiber reinforced polymer. Gas-operated semi-auto. Conventional gas-piston operation with M-16 breech locking system. MIL-STD-1913 Picatinny rail. Made in U.S.A. by Kel-Tec CNC Industries, Inc.
Price: Blued **$665.00**

Kel-Tec PLR-22 Pistol

Semi-auto pistol chambered in 22 LR; based on centerfire PLR-16 by same maker. Blowback action, 26-round magazine. Open sights and picatinny rail for mounting accessories; threaded muzzle. Overall length is 18.5", weighs 40 oz.
Price: **$390.00**

KEL-TEC PMR-30

Caliber: .22 Magnum (.22WMR) 30-rounds. **Barrel:** 4.3". **Weight:** 13.6 oz. **Length:** 7.9" overall. **Grips:** Glass reinforced Nylon (Zytel). **Sights:** Dovetailed aluminum with front & rear fiber optics. **Features:** Operates on a unique hybrid blowback/locked-breech system. It uses a double stack magazine of a new design that holds 30 rounds and fits completely in the grip of the pistol. Dual opposing extractors for reliability, heel magazine release to aid in magazine retention, Picatinny accessory rail under the barrel, Urethane recoil buffer, captive coaxial recoil springs. The barrel is fluted for light weight and effective heat dissipation. PMR30 disassembles for cleaning by removal of a single pin.

Price: **$415.00**

KIMBER CUSTOM II AUTO PISTOL

Caliber: 45 ACP. **Barrel:** 5". **Weight:** 38 oz. **Length:** 8.7" overall. **Grips:** Checkered black rubber, walnut, rosewood. **Sights:** Dovetailed front and rear, Kimber low profile adj. or fixed sights. **Features:** Slide, frame and barrel machined from steel or stainless steel. Match grade barrel, chamber and trigger group. Extended thumb safety, beveled magazine well, beveled front and rear slide serrations, high ride beavertail grip safety, checkered flat mainspring housing, kidney cut under trigger guard, high cut grip, match grade stainless steel barrel bushing, polished breech face, Commander-style hammer, lowered and flared ejection port, Wolff springs, bead blasted black oxide or matte stainless finish. Introduced in 1996. Made in U.S.A. by Kimber Mfg., Inc.
Price: Custom II **$828.00**
Price: Custom II Walnut (double-diamond walnut grips) **$872.00**

Kimber Stainless II Auto Pistols

Similar to Custom II except has stainless steel frame. 9mm Para. chambering and 45 ACP with night sights introduced 2008. Also chambered in 38 Super. Target version also chambered in 10mm.
Price: Stainless II 45 ACP **$964.00**
Price: Stainless II 9mm Para. (2008) **$983.00**
Price: Stainless II 45 ACP w/night sights (2008) **$1,092.00**
Price: Stainless II Target 45 ACP (stainless, adj. sight) **$942.00**

Kimber Pro Carry II Auto Pistol

Similar to Custom II, has aluminum frame, 4" bull barrel fitted directly to the slide without bushing. Introduced 1998. Made in U.S.A. by Kimber Mfg., Inc.
Price: Pro Carry II, 45 ACP **$888.00**
Price: Pro Carry II, 9mm **$929.00**
Price: Pro Carry II w/night sights **$997.00**

KIMBER SOLO CARRY

Caliber: 9mm, 6-shot magazine. **Barrel:** 2.7". **Weight:** 17 oz. **Length:** 5.5" overall. **Grips:** Black synthetic, Checkered/smooth. **Sights:** Fixed low-profile dovetail-mounted 3-dot system. **Features:** Single action striker-fired trigger that sets a new standard for small pistols. A premium finish that is self-lubricating and resistant to salt and moisture. Ergonomics that ensure comfortable shooting. Ambidextrous thumb safety, slide release lever and magazine release button are pure 1911 – positive, intuitive and fast. The thumb safety provides additional security not found on most small pistols. Also available in stainless.

Price: $747.00

Kimber Compact Stainless II Auto Pistol

Similar to Pro Carry II except has stainless steel frame, 4-inch bbl., grip is .400" shorter than standard, no front serrations. Weighs 34 oz. 45 ACP only. Introduced in 1998. Made in U.S.A. by Kimber Mfg., Inc.
Price: $1,009.00

Kimber Ultra Carry II Auto Pistol

Lightweight aluminum frame, 3" match grade bull barrel fitted to slide without bushing. Grips .4" shorter. Low effort recoil. Weighs 25 oz. Introduced in 1999. Made in U.S.A. by Kimber Mfg., Inc.
Price: Stainless Ultra Carry II 45 ACP ... **$980.00**
Price: Stainless Ultra Carry II 9mm Para. (2008) **$1,021.00**
Price: Stainless Ultra Carry II 45 ACP with night sights (2008) **$1,089.00**

Kimber Gold Match II Auto Pistol

Similar to Custom II models. Includes stainless steel barrel with match grade chamber and barrel bushing, ambidextrous thumb safety, adjustable sight, premium aluminum trigger, hand-checkered double diamond rosewood grips. Barrel hand-fitted for target accuracy. Made in U.S.A. by Kimber Mfg., Inc.
Price: Gold Match II **$1,345.00**
Price: Gold Match Stainless II 45 ACP ... **$1,519.00**
Price: Gold Match Stainless II 9mm Para. (2008) **$1,563.00**

Kimber Team Match II Auto Pistol

Similar to Gold Match II. Identical to pistol used by U.S.A. Shooting Rapid Fire Pistol Team, available in 45 ACP and 38 Super. Standard features include 30 lines-per-inch front strap extended and beveled magazine well, red, white and blue Team logo grips. Introduced 2008.
Price: 45 ACP **$1,539.00**
Price: 9mm **$1,546.00**

Kimber CDP II Series Auto Pistol

Similar to Custom II, but designed for concealed carry. Aluminum frame. Standard features include stainless steel slide, fixed Meprolight tritium 3-dot (green) dovetail-mounted night sights, match grade barrel and chamber, 30 LPI front strap checkering, two-tone finish, ambidextrous thumb safety, hand-checkered double diamond rosewood grips. Introduced in 2000. Made in U.S.A. by Kimber Mfg., Inc.
Price: Ultra CDP II 9mm Para. (2008) **$1,359.00**

Price: Ultra CDP II 45 ACP $1,318.00
Price: Compact CDP II 45 ACP $1,318.00
Price: Pro CDP II 45 ACP $1,318.00
Price: Custom CDP II (5" barrel, full length grip) $1,318.00

Kimber Eclipse II Series Auto Pistol

Similar to Custom II and other stainless Kimber pistols. Stainless slide and frame, black oxide, two-tone finish. Gray/black laminated grips. 30 lpi front strap checkering. All models have night sights; Target versions have Meprolight adjustable Bar/Dot version. Made in U.S.A. by Kimber Mfg., Inc.
Price: Eclipse Ultra II (3" barrel, short grip) $1,236.00
Price: Eclipse Pro II (4" barrel, full length grip) $1,236.00
Price: Eclipse Pro Target II (4" barrel, full length grip, adjustable sight) $1,236.00
Price: Eclipse Custom II 10mm $1,291.00
Price: Eclipse Target II (5" barrel, full length grip, adjustable sight) $1,345.00

KIMBER TACTICAL ENTRY II PISTOL

Caliber: 45 ACP, 7-round magazine. **Barrel:** 5". **Weight:** 40 oz. **Length:** 8.7" overall. **Features:** 1911-style semi auto with checkered frontstrap, extended magazine well, night sights, heavy steel frame, tactical rail.
Price: $1,428.00

KIMBER TACTICAL CUSTOM HD II PISTOL

Caliber: 45 ACP, 7-round magazine. **Barrel:** 5" match-grade. **Weight:** 39 oz. **Length:** 8.7" overall. **Features:** 1911-style semi auto with night sights, heavy steel frame.
Price: $1,333.00

KIMBER SIS AUTO PISTOL

Caliber: 45 ACP, 7-round magazine. **Barrel:** 3", ramped match grade. **Weight:** 31 oz. **Grips:** Stippled black laminate logo grips. **Sights:** SIS fixed tritium Night Sight with cocking shoulder. **Features:** Named for LAPD Special Investigation Section. Stainless-steel slides, frames and serrated mainspring housings. Flat top slide, solid trigger, SIS-pattern slide serrations, gray KimPro II finish, black small parts. Bumped and grooved beavertail grip safety, Kimber Service Melt on slide and frame edges, ambidextrous thumb safety, stainless steel KimPro Tac-Mag magazine. Rounded mainspring housing and frame on Ultra version. Introduced 2007. Made in U.S.A. by Kimber Mfg., Inc.
Price: SIS Ultra (2008) $1,427.00
Price: SIS Pro (2008) $1,427.00
Price: SIS Custom $1,427.00
Price: Custom/RL $1,522.00

KIMBER SUPER CARRY PRO

1911-syle semiauto pistol chambered in .45 ACP. Features include 8-round magazine; ambidextrous thumb safety; carry melt profiling; full length guide rod; aluminum frame with stainless slide; satin silver finish; super carry serrations; 4-inch barrel; micarta laminated grips; tritium night sights.
Price: $1,530.00

KIMBER SUPER CARRY HD SERIES

Designated as HD (Heavy Duty), each is chambered in .45 ACP and features a stainless steel slide and frame, premium KimPro II™ finish and night sights with cocking shoulder for one-hand operation. Like the original Super Carry pistols, HD models have directional serrations on slide, front strap and mainspring housing for unequaled control under recoil. A round heel frame and Carry Melt treatment make them comfortable to carry and easy to conceal.

SUPER CARRY ULTRA HD™
Caliber: .45 ACP, 7-shot magazine.
Barrel: 3". **Weight:** 32 oz. **Length:** 6.8" overall. **Grips:** G-10, Checkered with border.
Sights: Night sights with cocking shoulder radius (inches): 4.8.
Features: Rugged stainless steel slide and frame with KimPro II finish. Aluminum match grade trigger with a factory setting of approximately 4-5 pounds.
Price: . . . .

$1,625.00

SUPER CARRY PRO HD™
Caliber: .45 ACP, 8-shot magazine. **Barrel:** 4". **Weight:** 35 oz. **Length:** 7.7" overall. **Grips:** G-10, Checkered with border. **Sights:** Night sights with cocking shoulder radius (inches): 5.7. **Features:** Rugged stainless steel slide and frame with KimPro II finish. Aluminum match grade trigger with a factory setting of approximately 4-5 pounds.

Price: **$1,625.00**

SUPER CARRY CUSTOM HD™
Caliber: .45 ACP, 8-shot magazine. **Barrel:** 5". **Weight:** 38 oz. **Length:** 8.7" overall. **Grips:** G-10, Checkered with border. **Sights:** Night sights with cocking shoulder radius (inches): 4.8.
Features: Rugged stainless steel slide and frame with KimPro II finish. Aluminum match grade trigger with a factory setting of approximately 4-5 pounds.

Price: **$1,625.00**

KIMBER CENTENNIAL EDITION 1911
Highly artistic 1911-style semiauto pistol chambered in .45 ACP. Features include color case-hardened steel frame; extended thumb safety; charcoal-blue finished steel slide; 5-inch match grade barrel; special serial number; solid smooth ivory grips; nitre blue pins; adjustable sights; presentation case. Edition limited to 250 units. Finished by Doug Turnbull Restoration.
Price: **$4,352.00**

KIMBER ULTRA CDP II
Compact 1911-syle semiauto pistol chambered in .45 ACP. Features include 7-round magazine; ambidextrous thumb safety; carry melt profiling; full length guide rod; aluminum frame with stainless slide; satin silver finish; checkered frontstrap; 3-inch barrel; rosewood double diamond Crimson Trace lasergrips grips; tritium 3-dot night sights.
Price: **$1,603.00**

KIMBER STAINLESS ULTRA TLE II
1911-syle semiauto pistol chambered in .45 ACP. Features include 7-round magazine; full length guide rod; aluminum frame with stainless slide; satin silver finish; checkered frontstrap; 3-inch barrel; tactical gray double diamond grips; tritium 3-dot night sights.
Price: **$1,210.00**

KIMBER ROYAL II
Caliber: .45 ACP, 7-shot magazine.
Barrel: 5". **Weight:** 38 oz. **Length:** 8.7" overall. **Grips:** Solid bone-smooth. **Sights:** Fixed low profile radius (inches): 6.8.
Features: A classic full-size pistol wearing a stunning charcoal blue finish complimented with solid bone grip panels. Frint and rear serations. Aluminum match grade trigger with a factory setting of approximately 4-5 pounds.
Price: **$1,938.00**

KORTH USA PISTOL SEMI-AUTO
Caliber: 9mm Para., 9x21. **Barrel:** 4", 4.5". **Weight:** 39.9 oz. **Grips:** Walnut, Palisander, Amboinia, Ivory. **Sights:** Fully adjustable. **Features:** DA/SA, 2 models available with either rounded or combat-style trigger guard, recoil-operated, locking block system, forged steel. Available finishes: High polish blue plasma, high polish or matted silver plasma, gray pickled finish, or high polish blue. "Schalldampfer Modell" has special threaded 4.5" barrel and thread protector for a suppressor, many deluxe options available, 10-shot mag. From Korth USA.
Price: From **$15,000.00**

LES BAER 1911 BOSS .45
Caliber: .45 ACP, 8+1 capacity. **Barrel:** 5". **Weight:** 37 oz. **Length:** 8.5" overall.
Grips: Premium Checkered Cocobolo Grips.
Sights: Low-Mount LBC Adj Sight, Red Fiber Optic Front. **Features:** Speed Trgr, Beveled Mag Well, Rounded for Tactical. Rear cocking serrations on the slide, Baer fiber optic front sight (red), flat mainspring housing, checkered at 20 lpi, extended combat safety, Special tactical package, chromed complete lower, blued slide, (2) 8-round premium magazines.

Price: **$2,109.00**

MAGNUM RESEARCH MICRO DESERT EAGLE PISTOL
Double action only semiauto pistol chambered in .380. Features include steel slide, aluminum allow frame, black polymer grips, nickel silver or blue anodized frame, 6-round capacity, fixed sights, 2.2-inch barrel. Weight less than 14 oz.
Price: **$535.00**

MAGNUM RESEARCH DESERT EAGLE MAGNUM PISTOL

Enormous gas-operated semiauto pistol chambered in .50 AE, .44 Magnum, .357 Magnum. Features include 6- or 10-inch barrel, adjustable sights, variety of finishes. Now made in the USA. **Price:** . . . . $1,650.00 to $2,156.00.

MOSSBERG INTERNATIONAL MODELS 702 AND 802 PLINKSTER PISTOLS

Semiauto (702) or bolt action (802) pistols chambered in .22 LR. Features include black synthetic or laminated wood stock, 10-inch blued barrel, ergonomic grips, 10-shot detachable box magazine. **Price:** . . . . **N/A**

MPA380P PROTECTOR

Caliber: .380 ACP, 5+1 magazine capacity. **Barrel:** 2". **Weight:** 29 oz. **Length:** 6.7" overall. **Grips:** machined aluminum grips with a bead blasted finish. **Sights:** Fixed low-profile dovetail-mounted 3-dot system. **Features:** Dubbed the MPA380P (the "P" stands for "Premium"), the new model features bead blasted finish protected by a clear anodize coat, and an extended magazine pad for added shooting comfort. The Protector is a subcompact double-action-only semiauto. It features a fully machined 4140 steel upper slide, a fully machined 4140 steel lower receiver and advanced handle and grip designs. The pistol is American made and comes with a lifetime guarantee. **Price:** $345.90

NORTH AMERICAN ARMS GUARDIAN DAO PISTOL

Caliber: 25 NAA, 32 ACP, 380 ACP, 32 NAA, 6-shot magazine. **Barrel:** 2.49". **Weight:** 20.8 oz. **Length:** 4.75" overall. **Grips:** Black polymer. **Sights:** Low profile fixed. **Features:** Double-action only mechanism. All stainless steel construction. Introduced 1998. Made in U.S.A. by North American Arms. **Price:** From $402.00

OLYMPIC ARMS MATCHMASTER 5 1911 PISTOL

Caliber: 45 ACP, 7-shot magazine. **Barrel:** 5" stainless steel. **Weight:** 40 oz. **Length:** 8.75" overall. **Grips:** Smooth walnut with laser-etched scorpion icon. **Sights:** Ramped blade, LPA adjustable rear. **Features:** Matched frame and slide, fitted and head-spaced barrel, complete ramp and throat jobs, lowered and widened ejection port, beveled mag well, hand-stoned-to-match hammer and sear, lightweight long-shoe over-travel adjusted trigger, shaped and tensioned extractor, extended thumb safety, wide beavertail grip safety and full-length guide rod. Made in U.S.A. by Olympic Arms, Inc. **Price:** $903.00

OLYMPIC ARMS MATCHMASTER 6 1911 PISTOL

Caliber: 45 ACP, 7-shot magazine. **Barrel:** 6" stainless steel. **Weight:** 44 oz. **Length:** 9.75" overall. **Grips:** Smooth walnut with laser-etched scorpion icon. **Sights:** Ramped blade, LPA adjustable rear. **Features:** Matched frame and slide, fitted and head-spaced barrel, complete ramp and throat jobs, lowered and widened ejection port,

beveled mag well, hand-stoned-to-match hammer and sear, lightweight long-shoe over-travel adjusted trigger, shaped and tensioned extractor, extended thumb safety, wide beavertail grip safety and full length guide rod. Made in U.S.A. by Olympic Arms, Inc. **Price:** $973.00

OLYMPIC ARMS ENFORCER 1911 PISTOL

Caliber: 45 ACP, 6-shot magazine. **Barrel:** 4" bull stainless steel. **Weight:** 35 oz. **Length:** 7.75" overall. **Grips:** Smooth walnut with etched black widow spider icon. **Sights:** Ramped blade front, LPA adjustable rear. **Features:** Compact Enforcer frame. Bushingless bull barrel with triplex counter-wound self-contained recoil system. Matched frame and slide, fitted and head-spaced barrel, complete ramp and throat jobs, lowered and widened ejection port, beveled mag well, hand-stoned-to-match hammer and sear, lightweight longshoe over-travel adjusted trigger, shaped and tensioned extractor, extended thumb safety, wide beavertail grip safety and full length guide rod. Made in U.S.A. by Olympic Arms. **Price:** $1,033.50

OLYMPIC ARMS COHORT PISTOL

Caliber: 45 ACP, 7-shot magazine. **Barrel:** 4" bull stainless steel. **Weight:** 36 oz. **Length:** 7.75" overall. **Grips:** Fully checkered walnut. **Sights:** Ramped blade front, LPA adjustable rear. **Features:** Full size 1911 frame. Bushingless bull barrel with triplex counter-wound self-contained recoil system. Matched frame and slide, fitted and head-spaced barrel, complete ramp and throat jobs, lowered and widened ejection port, beveled mag well, hand-stoned-to-match hammer and sear, lightweight long-shoe over-travel adjusted trigger, shaped and tensioned extractor, extended thumb safety, wide beavertail grip safety and full length guide rod. Made in U.S.A. by Olympic Arms. **Price:** $973.70

OLYMPIC ARMS BIG DEUCE PISTOL

Caliber: 45 ACP, 7-shot magazine. **Barrel:** 6" stainless steel. **Weight:** 44 oz. **Length:** 9.75" overall. **Grips:** Double diamond checkered exotic cocobolo wood. **Sights:** Ramped blade front, LPA adjustable rear. **Features:** Carbon steel parkerized slide with satin bead blast finish full size frame. Matched frame and slide, fitted and head-spaced barrel, complete ramp and throat jobs, lowered and widened ejection port, beveled mag well, hand-stoned-to-match hammer and sear, lightweight long-shoe over-travel adjusted trigger, shaped and tensioned extractor, extended thumb safety, wide beavertail grip safety and full length guide rod. Made in U.S.A. by Olympic Arms. **Price:** $1,033.50

HANDGUNS—Autoloaders, Service & Sport

OLYMPIC ARMS WESTERNER SERIES 1911 PISTOLS
Caliber: 45 ACP, 7-shot magazine. **Barrel:** 4", 5", 6" stainless steel. **Weight:** 35-43 oz. **Length:** 7.75-9.75" overall. **Grips:** Smooth ivory laser-etched Westerner icon. **Sights:** Ramped blade, LPA adjustable rear.
Features: Matched frame and slide, fitted and head-spaced barrel, complete ramp and throat jobs, lowered and widened ejection port, beveled mag well, hand-stoned-to-match hammer and sear, lightweight long-shoe over-travel adjusted trigger, shaped and tensioned extractor, extended thumb safety, wide beavertail grip safety and full length guide rod. Entire pistol is fitted and assembled, then disassembled and subjected to the color case hardening process. Made in U.S.A. by Olympic Arms, Inc.
Price: Constable, 4" barrel, 35 oz. $1,163.50
Price: Westerner, 5" barrel, 39 oz. $1,033.50
Price: Trail Boss, 6" barrel, 43 oz. $1,103.70

OLYMPIC ARMS SCHUETZEN PISTOL WORKS 1911 PISTOLS
Caliber: 45 ACP, 7-shot magazine. **Barrel:** 4", 5.2", bull stainless steel. **Weight:** 35-38 oz. **Length:** 7.75-8.75" overall. **Grips:** Double diamond checkered exotic cocobolo wood. **Sights:** Ramped blade, LPA adjustable rear. **Features:** Carbon steel parkerized slide with satin bead blast finish full size frame. Matched frame and slide, fitted and head-spaced barrel, complete ramp and throat jobs, lowered and widened ejection port, beveled mag well, hand-stoned-to-match hammer and sear, lightweight long-shoe over-travel adjusted trigger, shaped and tensioned extractor, extended thumb safety, wide beavertail grip safety and full length guide rod. Custom made by Olympic Arms Schuetzen Pistol Works. Parts are hand selected and fitted by expert pistolsmiths. Several no-cost options to choose from. Made in U.S.A. by Olympic Arms Schuetzen Pistol Works.
Price: Journeyman, 4" bull barrel, 35 oz. $1,293.50
Price: Street Deuce, 5.2" bull barrel, 38 oz. $1,293.50

OLYMPIC ARMS OA-93 AR PISTOL
Caliber: 5.56 NATO. **Barrel:** 6.5" button-rifled stainless steel. **Weight:** 4.46 lbs. **Length:** 17" overall. **Sights:** None.
Features: Olympic Arms integrated recoil system on the upper receiver eliminates the buttstock, flat top upper, free floating tubular match handguard, threaded muzzle with flash suppressor. Made in U.S.A. by Olympic Arms, Inc.
Price: $1,202.50

OLYMPIC ARMS K23P AR PISTOL
Caliber: 5.56 NATO. **Barrel:** 6.5" button-rifled chrome-moly steel. **Length:** 22.25" overall. **Weight:** 5.12 lbs. **Sights:** Adjustable A2 rear, elevation adjustable front post. **Features:** A2 upper with rear sight, free floating tubular match handguard, threaded muzzle with flash suppressor, receiver extension tube with foam cover, no bayonet lug. Made in U.S.A. by Olympic Arms, Inc. Introduced 2007.
Price: $973.70

OLYMPIC ARMS K23P-A3-TC AR PISTOL
Caliber: 5.56 NATO. **Barrel:** 6.5" button-rifled chrome-moly steel. **Length:** 22.25" overall. **Weight:** 5.12 lbs. **Sights:** Adjustable A2 rear, elevation adjustable front post. **Features:** Flat-top upper with detachable carry handle, free floating FIRSH rail handguard, threaded muzzle with flash suppressor, receiver extension tube with foam cover, no bayonet lug. Made in U.S.A. by Olympic Arms, Inc. Introduced 2007.
Price: $1,118.20

OLYMPIC ARMS WHITNEY WOLVERINE PISTOL
Caliber: 22 LR, 10-shot magazine. **Barrel:** 4.625" stainless steel. **Weight:** 19.2 oz. **Length:** 9" overall. **Grips:** Black checkered with fire/safe markings. **Sights:** Ramped blade front, dovetail rear. **Features:** Polymer frame with natural ergonomics and ventilated rib. Barrel with 6-groove 1x16 twist rate. All metal magazine shell. Made in U.S.A. by Olympic Arms.
Price: $291.00

PARA USA GI EXPERT PISTOLS
Caliber: .45 ACP, 7+1-round capacity. **Barrel:** 5" stainless. **Weight:** 39 oz. **Length:** 8.5" overall. **Grips:** Checkered Polymer. **Sights:** Dovetail Fixed, 3-White Dot. **Features:** The Para "GI Expert" is an entry level 1911 pistol that will allow new marksmen to own a pistol with features such as, Lowered and flared ejection port, beveled magazine well, flat mainspring housing, grip safety contoured for spur hammer.
Price: 1911 Wild Bunch (official SASS) . . . $789.00
Price: 1911 LTC Single Action Single Stack Model (8+1) $849.00
Price: 1911 100th Anniversary w/cocobolo grips $1079.00

PARA USA PXT 1911 SINGLE-ACTION SINGLE-STACK AUTO PISTOLS
Caliber: 38 Super, 9mm Para., 45 ACP. **Barrel:** 3.5", 4.25", 5".
Weight: 28-40 oz. **Length:** 7.1-8.5" overall. **Grips:** Checkered cocobolo, textured composition, Mother of Pearl synthetic. **Sights:** Blade front, low-profile Novak Extreme Duty adjustable rear. High visibility 3-dot system. **Features:** Available with alloy, steel or stainless steel frames. Skeletonized trigger, spurred hammer. Manual thumb, grip and firing pin lock safeties. Full-length guide rod. PXT designates new Para Power Extractor throughout the line. Introduced 2004. Made in U.S.A. by Para USA.
Price: 1911 SSP 9mm Para. (2008) $959.00
Price: 1911 SSP 45 ACP (2008) $959.00

PARA USA PXT 1911 SINGLE-ACTION HIGH-CAPACITY AUTO PISTOLS
Caliber: 9mm Para., 45 ACP, 10/14/18-shot magazines. **Barrel:** 3", 5". **Weight:** 34-40 oz. **Length:** 7.1-8.5" overall. **Grips:** Textured composition. **Sights:** Blade front, low-profile Novak Extreme Duty adjustable rear or fixed sights. High visibility 3-dot system. **Features:** Available with alloy, steel or stainless steel frames. Skeletonized match trigger, spurred hammer, flared ejection port. Manual thumb, grip and firing pin lock safeties. Full-length guide rod. Introduced 2004. Made in U.S.A. by Para USA.
Price: PXT P14-45 Gun Rights (2008), 14+1, 5" barrel **$1,149.00**
Price: P14-45 (2008), 14+1, 5" barrel $919.00

Para USA PXT Limited Pistols
Similar to the PXT-Series pistols except with full-length recoil guide system; fully adjustable rear sight; tuned trigger with over-travel stop; beavertail grip safety; competition hammer; front and rear slide serrations; ambidextrous safety; lowered ejection port; ramped match-grade barrel; dove-tailed front sight. Introduced 2004. Made in U.S.A. by Para USA.
Price: Todd Jarrett 40 S&W, 16+1, stainless $1,729.00

Para USA LDA Single-Stack Auto Pistols
Similar to LDA-series with double-action trigger mechanism. Cocobolo and polymer grips. Available in 45 ACP. Introduced 1999. Made in U.S.A. by Para USA.
Price: SSP, 8+1, 5" barrel **$899.00**

Para USA LDA Hi-Capacity Auto Pistols
Similar to LDA-series with double-action trigger mechanism. Polymer grips. Available in 9mm Para., 40 S&W, 45 ACP. Introduced 1999. Made in U.S.A. by Para USA.
Price: High-Cap 45, 14+1 . . . . $1,279.00

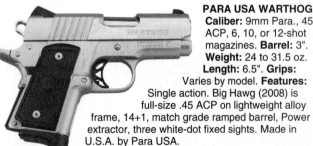

PARA USA WARTHOG
Caliber: 9mm Para., 45 ACP, 6, 10, or 12-shot magazines. **Barrel:** 3". **Weight:** 24 to 31.5 oz. **Length:** 6.5". **Grips:** Varies by model. **Features:** Single action. Big Hawg (2008) is full-size .45 ACP on lightweight alloy frame, 14+1, match grade ramped barrel, Power extractor, three white-dot fixed sights. Made in U.S.A. by Para USA.
Price: Slim Hawg (2006) single stack .45 ACP, stainless, 6+1 . . . . $1,099.00
Price: Nite Hawg .45 ACP, black finish, 10+1 . . . . $1,099.00
Price: Warthog .45 ACP, Regal finish, 10+1 . . . .$959.00
Price: Warthog Stainless $1,069.00

Price: Big Hawg (2008) . **$959.00**
Price: PXT Hawg w/fiber optic sight,regal finish, 10+1 . . . . **$999.00**
Price: PXT Hawg 7 3.5" barrel, covert black finish, 7+1. . . . .$919.00

PARA USA PXT TACTICAL PISTOLS
Caliber: .45 ACP, 8+1 round capacity. **Barrel:** 4.25". **Weight:** 36 oz. **Length:** 8.5" overall. **Grips:** Checkered Polymer. **Sights:** Fiber-Optic Front/ Adj. Rear. **Features:** A compact tactical pistol equipped with a super strong integral light rail built into the dust shield. The front strap of the frame is checkered 30 lpi for improved gripping surface with or without gloves. The Match grade integral ramp 4.25-inch barrel is locked up at the muzzle with an Ed Brown National Match bushing. ylinder and Slide provides its Tactical II hammer, sear and disconnector for a clean crisp trigger. PARA's Power Extractor insures reliable extraction. A flat, checkered mainspring housing mates to the Ed Brown magazine well to funnel the 8-round PXT magazines with alloy base pads into the pistol.
Price: LTC Model $1,599.00
Price: 14•45 Model 14+1 high-capacity . . $1,599.00

PHOENIX ARMS HP22, HP25 AUTO PISTOLS
Caliber: 22 LR, 10-shot (HP22), 25 ACP, 10-shot (HP25). **Barrel:** 3". **Weight:** 20 oz. **Length:** 5.5" overall. **Grips:** Checkered composition. **Sights:** Blade front, adjustable rear. **Features:** Single action, exposed hammer; manual hold-open; button magazine release. Available in satin nickel, matte blue finish. Introduced 1993. Made in U.S.A. by Phoenix Arms.

Prices given are believed to be accurate at time of publication however, many factors affect retail pricing so exact prices are not possible.

Price: With gun lock **$130.00**
Price: HP Range kit with 5" bbl., locking case and accessories
(1 Mag) **$171.00**
Price: HP Deluxe Range kit with 3" and 5" bbls.,
2 mags, case **$210.00**

PICUDA .17 MACH-2 GRAPHITE PISTOL
Caliber: 17 HM2, 22 LR, 10-shot magazine. **Barrel:** 10" graphite barrel, "French grey" anodizing. **Weight:** 3.2 pounds. **Length:** 20.5" overall. **Grips:** Barracuda nutmeg laminated pistol stock. **Sights:** None, integral scope base. **Features:** MLP-1722 receiver, target trigger, match bolt kit. Introduced 2008. Made in U.S.A. by Magnum Research, Inc.
Price: **$699.00**

ROCK RIVER ARMS BASIC CARRY AUTO PISTOL
Caliber: 45 ACP. **Barrel:** NA. **Weight:** NA. **Length:** NA. **Grips:** Rosewood, checkered. **Sights:** dovetail front sight, Heinie rear sight. **Features:** NM frame with 20-, 25- or 30-LPI checkered front strap, 5-inch slide with double serrations, lowered and flared ejection port, throated NM Kart barrel with NM bushing, match Commander hammer and match sear, aluminum speed trigger, dehorned, Parkerized finish, one magazine, accuracy guarantee. 3.5 lb. Trigger pull. Introduced 2006. RRA Service Auto 9mm has forged NM frame with beveled mag well, fixed target rear sight and dovetail front sight, KKM match 1:32 twist 9mm Para. barrel with supported ramp. Guaranteed to shoot 1-inch groups at 25 yards with quality 9mm Para. 115-124 grain match ammunition. Intr. 2008. Made in U.S.A. From Rock River Arms.
Price: Basic Carry PS2700 . . . . **$1,600.00**
Price: Limited Match PS2400 . . . . **$2,185.00**
Price: RRA Service Auto 9mm Para. PS2715 . . . . **$1,790.00**

ROCK RIVER ARMS LAR-15/LAR-9 PISTOLS
Caliber: .223/5.56mm NATO chamber 4-shot magazine. **Barrel:** 7", 10.5" Wilson chrome moly, 1:9 twist, A2 flash hider, 1/2-28 thread. **Weight:** 5.1 lbs. (7" barrel), 5.5 lbs. (10.5" barrel). **Length:** 23" overall. Stock: Hogue rubber grip. **Sights:** A2 front. **Features:** Forged A2 or A4 upper, single stage trigger, aluminum free-float tube, one magazine. Similar 9mm Para. LAR-9 also available. From Rock River Arms, Inc.
Price: LAR-15 7" A2 AR2115 . . . . **$955.00**
Price: LAR-15 10.5" A4 AR2120 . . . . **$945.00**
Price: LAR-9 7" A2 9MM2115 . . . . **$1,125.00**

ROHRBAUGH R9 SEMI-AUTO PISTOL
Caliber: 9mm Parabellum, 380 ACP. **Barrel:** 2.9". **Weight:** 12.8 oz. **Length:** 5.2" overall. **Features:** Very small double-action-only semi-auto pocket pistol. Stainless steel slide with matte black aluminum frame. Available with or without sights. Available with all-black (Stealth) and partial Diamond Black (Stealth Elite) finish.
Price: **$1,149.00**

RUGER SR9 AUTOLOADING PISTOL
Caliber: 9mm Para. **Barrel:** 4.14". **Weight:** 26.25, 26.5 oz. **Grips:** Glass-filled nylon in two color options—black or OD Green, w/flat or arched reversible backstrap. **Sights:** Adjustable 3-dot, built-in Picatinny-style rail. **Features:** Semi-DA, 6 configurations, striker-fired, through-hardened stainless steel slide, brushed or blackened stainless slide with black grip frame or blackened stainless slide with OD Green grip frame, ambi manual 1911-style safety, ambi mag release, mag disconnect, loaded chamber indicator, Ruger camblock design to absorb recoil, two 10 or 17-shot mags. Intr. 2008. Made in U.S.A. by Sturm, Ruger & Co.
Price: SR9 (17-Round), SR9-10 (SS) **$525.00**
Price: KBSR9 (17-Round), KBSR9-10 (Blackened SS) **$565.00**
Price: KODBSR9 (17-Round), KODBSR9-10
(OD Green Grip) **$565.00**

RUGER SR9C COMPACT PISTOL
Compact double action only semiauto pistol chambered in 9mm Parabellum. Features include 1911-style ambidextrous manual safety; internal trigger bar interlock and striker blocker; trigger safety; magazine disconnector; loaded chamber indicator; two magazines, one 10-round and the other 17-round; 3.5-inch barrel; 3-dot sights; accessory rail; brushed stainless or blackened allow finish. Weight 23.40 oz.
Price: **$525.00**

RUGER LC9
Caliber: 9mm luger, 7+1 capacity. **Barrel:** 3.12" **Weight:** 17.10 oz. **Grips:** Glass-filled nylon. **Sights:** Adjustable 3-dot. **Features:** double-action-only, hammer-fired, locked-breech pistol with a smooth trigger pull. Control and confident handling of the Ruger LC9 are accomplished through reduced recoil and aggressive frame checkering for a positive grip in all conditions. The Ruger LC9 features smooth "melted" edges for ease of holstering, carrying and drawing. Made in U.S.A. by Sturm, Ruger & Co.
Price: **$443.00**

RUGER LCP
Caliber: .380 ACP. **Barrel:** 2.75" **Weight:** 9.4 oz. **Grips:** Glass-filled nylon. **Sights:** Fixed. **Features:** SA, one configuration, ultra-light compact carry pistol in Ruger's smallest pistol frame, through-hardened stainless steel slide, blued finish, lock breach design, 6-shot mag. Intr. 2008. Made in U.S.A. by Sturm, Ruger & Co.
Price: LCP **$347.00**

RUGER P90 MANUAL SAFETY MODEL AUTOLOADING PISTOL
Caliber: 45 ACP, 8-shot magazine. **Barrel:** 4.50". **Weight:** 33.5 oz. **Length:** 7.75" overall. **Grips:** Grooved black synthetic composition. **Sights:** Square post front, square notch rear adjustable for windage, both with white dot. **Features:** Double action; ambidextrous slide-mounted safety-levers. Stainless steel only. Introduced 1991.
Price: KP90 with extra mag, loader, case and gunlock **$617.00**
Price: P90 (blue) **$574.00**

Ruger KP944 Autoloading Pistol
Sized midway between full-size P-Series and compact KP94. 4.2" barrel, 7.5" overall length, weighs about 34 oz. KP94 manual safety model. Slide gripping grooves roll over top of slide. KP94 has ambidextrous safety-levers; Stainless slide, barrel, alloy frame. Also blue. Includes hard case and lock, spare magazine. Introduced 1994. Made in U.S.A. by Sturm, Ruger & Co.
Price: P944, blue, manual safety, .40 cal. . . . **$541.00**
Price: KP944 (40-caliber)
(manual safety-stainless) **$628.00**

RUGER P95 AUTOLOADING PISTOL

Caliber: 9mm, 15-shot magazine. **Barrel:** 3.9". **Weight:** 30 oz. **Length:** 7.25" overall. **Grips:** Grooved; integral with frame. **Sights:** Blade front, rear drift adjustable for windage; 3-dot system. **Features:** Molded polymer grip frame, stainless steel or chrome-moly slide. Suitable for +P+ ammunition. Safety model, decocker. Introduced 1996. Made in U.S.A. by Sturm, Ruger & Co. Comes with lockable plastic case, spare magazine, loader and lock, Picatinny rails.

Price: KP95PR15 safety model, stainless steel.............$424.00
Price: P95PR15 safety model, blued finish...................$395.00
Price: P95PR 10-round model, blued finish..................$393.00
Price: KP95PR 10-round model, stainless steel..............$424.00

RUGER 22 CHARGER PISTOL

Caliber: .22 LR. **Barrel:** 10". **Weight:** 3.5 lbs (w/out bi-pod). Stock: Black Laminate. **Sights:** None. **Features:** Rimfire Autoloading, one configuration, 10/22 action, adjustable bi-pod, new mag release for easier removal, precision-rifled barrel, black matte finish, combination Weaver-style and tip-off scope mount, 10-shot mag. Intr. 2008. Made in U.S.A. by Sturm, Ruger & Co.

Price: CHR22-10.................................$380.00

RUGER MARK III STANDARD AUTOLOADING PISTOL

Caliber: 22 LR, 10-shot magazine. **Barrel:** 4.5", 4.75", 5.5", 6", or 6-7/8". **Weight:** 33 oz. (4.75" bbl.). **Length:** 9" (4.75" bbl.). **Grips:** Checkered composition grip panels. **Sights:** Fixed, fiber-optic front, fixed rear. **Features:** Updated design of original Standard Auto and Mark II series. Hunter models have lighter barrels. Target models have cocobolo grips; bull, target, competition, and hunter barrels; and adjustable sights. Introduced 2005.

Price: MKIII4, MKIII6 (blued) $352.00
Price: MKIII512 (blued bull barrel) $417.00
Price: KMKIII512 (stainless bull barrel) $527.00
Price: MKIII678 (blued) $417.00
Price: KMKIII678GC (stainless slabside barrel) $606.00
Price: KMKIII678H (stainless fluted barrel) $620.00
Price: KMKIII45HCL (Crimson Trace Laser Grips, intr. 2008) $787.00
Price: KMKIII454 (2009) $620.00

Ruger 22/45 Mark III Pistol

Similar to other 22 Mark III autos except has Zytel grip frame that matches angle and magazine latch of Model 1911 45 ACP pistol. Available in 4" standard, 4.5", 5.5", 6-7/8" bull barrels. Comes with extra magazine, plastic case, lock. Introduced 1992. Hunter introduced 2006.

Price: P4MKIII, 4" bull barrel, adjustable sights $380.00
Price: P45GCMKIII, 4.5" bull barrel, fixed sights $380.00
Price: P512MKIII (5.5" bull blued barrel, adj. sights) $380.00
Price: KP512MKIII (5.5" stainless bull barrel, adj. sights $475.00
Price: Hunter KP45HMKIII 4.5" barrel (2007), KP678HMKIII, 6-7/8" stainless fluted bull barrel, adj. sights $562.00

SABRE DEFENCE SPHINX PISTOLS

Caliber: 9mm Para., 45 ACP., 10-shot magazine. **Barrel:** 4.43". **Weight:** 39.15 oz. **Length:** 8.27" overall. **Grips:** Textured polymer. **Sights:** Fixed Trijicon Night Sights. **Features:** CNC engineered from stainless steel billet; grip frame in stainless steel, titanium or high-strength aluminum. Integrated accessory rail, high-cut beavertail, decocking lever. Made in Switzerland. Imported by Sabre Defence Industries.

Price: 45 ACP (2007) $2,990.00
Price: 9mm Para. Standard, titanium w/decocker $2,700.00

SEECAMP LWS 32/380 STAINLESS DA AUTO

Caliber: 32 ACP, 380 ACP Win. Silvertip, 6-shot magazine. **Barrel:** 2", integral with frame. **Weight:** 10.5 oz. **Length:** 4-1/8" overall. **Grips:** Glass-filled nylon. **Sights:** Smooth, no-snag, contoured slide and barrel top. **Features:** Aircraft quality 17-4 PH stainless steel. Inertia-operated firing pin. Hammer fired double-action-only. Hammer automatically follows slide down to safety rest position after each shot, no manual safety needed. Magazine safety disconnector. Polished stainless. Introduced 1985. From L.W. Seecamp.

Price: 32 ....$446.25
Price: 380 ....$795.00

SIG SAUER 250 COMPACT AUTO PISTOL

Caliber: 9mm Para. (16-round magazine), 357 SIG, 40 S&W and 45 ACP. **Barrel:** NA. **Weight:** 24.6 oz. **Length:** 7.2" overall. **Grips:** Interchangeable polymer. **Sights:** Siglite night sights. **Features:** Modular design allows for immediate change in caliber and size; subcompact, compact and full. Six different grip combinations for each size. Introduced 2008. From Sig Sauer, Inc.

Price: P250 ....$750.00

SIG SAUER 1911 PISTOLS

Caliber: 45 ACP, 8-10 shot magazine. **Barrel:** 5". **Weight:** 40.3 oz. **Length:** 8.65" overall. **Grips:** Checkered wood grips. **Sights:** Novak night sights. Blade front, drift adjustable rear for windage. **Features:** Single-action 1911. Hand-fitted dehorned stainless-steel frame and slide; match-grade barrel, hammer/sear set and trigger; 25-lpi front strap checkering, 20-lpi mainspring housing checkering. Beavertail grip safety with speed bump, extended thumb safety, firing pin safety and hammer intercept

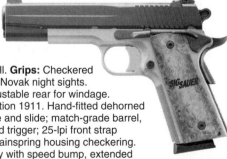

Prices given are believed to be accurate at time of publication however, many factors affect retail pricing so exact prices are not possible.

notch. Introduced 2005. XO series has contrast sights, Ergo Grip XT textured polymer grips. Target line features adjustable target night sights, match barrel, custom wood grips, non-railed frame in stainless or Nitron finishes. TTT series is two-tone 1911 with Nitron slide and black controls on stainless frame. Includes burled maple grips, adjustable combat night sights. STX line available from Sig Sauer Custom Shop; two-tone 1911, non-railed, Nitron slide, stainless frame, burled maple grips. Polished cocking serrations, flat-top slide, magwell. Carry line has Novak night sights, lanyard attachment point, gray diamondwood or rosewood grips, 8+1 capacity. Compact series has 6+1 capacity, 7.7" OAL, 4.25" barrel, slim-profile wood grips, weighs 30.3 oz. RCS line (Compact SAS) is Customs Shop version with anti-snag dehorning. Stainless or Nitron finish, Novak night sights, slim-profile gray diamondwood or rosewood grips. 6+1 capacity. 1911 C3 (2008) is a 6+1 compact .45 ACP, rosewood custom wood grips, two-tone and Nitron finishes. Weighs about 30 ounces unloaded, lightweight alloy frame. Length is 7.7". From SIG SAUER, Inc.

Price: Model 1911-22-B .22 LR
w/custom wood grips $399.99
Price: Nitron $1,200.00
Price: Stainless $1,170.00
Price: XO Black $1,005.00
Price: Target Nitron (2006) $1,230.00
Price: TTT (2006) $1,290.00
Price: STX (2006) $1,455.00
Price: Carry Nitron (2006) $1,200.00
Price: Compact Nitron $1,200.00
Price: RCS Nitron $1,305.00
Price: C3 (2008) $1,200.00
Price: Platinum Elite $1,275.00
Price: Blackwater (2009) $1,290.00
Price: Scorpion $1,128.00

SIG SAUER P210 AUTO PISTOLS

Caliber: 9mm, 8-shot magazine. **Barrel:** 4.7". **Weight:** 37.4 oz. **Length:** 8.5" overall. **Grips:** Custom wood. **Sights:** Post and notch and adjustable target sights. **Features:** The carbon steel slide, machined from solid billet steel, now features a durable Nitron® coating, and the improved beavertail adorns the Nitron coated, heavy-style, carbon steel frame. The P210 Legend also offers an improved manual safety, internal drop safety, side magazine release, and custom wood grips.
Price: P210-9-LEGEND $2,199.00
Price: P210-9-LEGEND-TGT w/adjustable target sights . . . $2,399.00

SIG SAUER P220 AUTO PISTOLS

Caliber: 45 ACP, (7- or 8-shot magazine). **Barrel:** 4.4". **Weight:** 27.8 oz. **Length:** 7.8" overall. **Grips:** Checkered black plastic. **Sights:** Blade front, drift adjustable rear for windage. Optional Siglite night sights. **Features:** Double action. Stainless-steel slide, Nitron finish, alloy frame, M1913 Picatinny rail; safety system of decocking lever, automatic firing pin safety block, safety intercept notch, and trigger bar disconnector. Squared combat-type trigger guard. Slide stays open after last shot. Introduced 1976. P220 SAS Anti-Snag has dehorned stainless steel slide, front Siglite Night Sight, rounded trigger guard, dust cover, Custom Shop wood grips. Equinox line is Custom Shop product with Nitron stainless-steel slide with a black hard-anodized alloy frame, brush-polished flats and nickel accents. Truglo tritium fiber-optic front sight, rear Siglite night sight, gray laminated wood grips with checkering and stippling. From SIG SAUER, Inc.

Price: P220 Two-Tone, matte-stainless slide,
black alloy frame $1,110.00
Price: P220 Elite Stainless (2008) $1,350.00
Price: P220 Two-Tone SAO, single action (2006), from . . . $1,086.00
Price: P220 DAK (2006) $853.00
Price: P220 Equinox (2006) $1,200.00
Price: P220 Elite Dark (2009) $1,200.00
Price: P220 Elite Dark, threaded barrel (2009) $1,305.00

SIG SAUER P220 CARRY AUTO PISTOLS

Caliber: 45 ACP, 8-shot magazine. **Barrel:** 3.9". **Weight:** NA. **Length:** 7.1" overall. **Grips:** Checkered black plastic. **Sights:** Blade front, drift adjustable rear for windage. Optional Siglite night sights. **Features:** Similar to full-size P220, except is "Commander" size. Single stack, DA/SA operation, Nitron finish, Picatinny rail, and either post and dot contrast or 3-dot Siglite night sights. Introduced 2005. Many variations availble. From SIG SAUER, Inc.
Price: P220 Carry, from . . . . $975.00; w/night sights $1,050.00
Price: P220 Carry Elite Stainless (2008) $1,350.00

SIG SAUER P229 DA Auto Pistol

Similar to the P220 except chambered for 9mm Para. (10- or 15-round magazines), 40 S&W, 357 SIG (10- or 12-round magazines). Has 3.86" barrel, 7.1" overall length and 3.35" height. Weight is 32.4 oz. Introduced 1991. Snap-on modular grips. Frame made in Germany, stainless steel slide assembly made in U.S.; pistol as-sembled in U.S. Many variations available. From SIG SAUER, Inc.
Price: P229, from . . . . $975.00; w/night sights $1,050.00
Price: P229 Platinum Elite (2008) $1,275.00
Price: P229 Enhanced Elite $1,175.00

SIG SAUER P226 Pistols

Similar to the P220 pistol except has 4.4" barrel, measures 7.7" overall, weighs 34 oz. Chambered in 9mm, 357 SIG, or 40 S&W. X-Five series has factory tuned single-action trigger, 5" slide and barrel, ergonomic wood grips with beavertail, ambidextrous thumb safety and stainless slide and frame with magwell, low-profile adjustable target sights, front cocking serrations and a 25-meter factory test target. Many variations available. Snap-on modular grips. From SIG SAUER, Inc.

Price: P226, from **$975.00**
Price: P226 Blackwater Tactical
(2009) **$1,300.00**
Price: P226 Extreme **$1,146.00**
Price: P226 Enhanced Elite **$1,175.00**
Price: P226 Diamond Plate
w/diamond plate detailed slide . . **$1,100.00**

SIG SAUER SP2022 PISTOLS

Caliber: 9mm Para., 357 SIG, 40 S&W, 10-, 12-, or 15-shot magazines. **Barrel:** 3.9". **Weight:** 30.2 oz. **Length:** 7.4" overall. **Grips:** Composite and rubberized one-piece. **Sights:** Blade front, rear adjustable for windage. Optional Siglite night sights. **Features:** Polymer frame, stainless steel slide; integral frame accessory rail; replaceable steel frame rails; left- or right-handed magazine release, two interchangeable grips. From SIG SAUER, Inc.
Price: SP2009, Nitron finish **$613.00**

SIG SAUER P232 PERSONAL SIZE PISTOL

Caliber: 380 ACP, 7-shot. **Barrel:** 3.6". **Weight:** 17.6-22.4 oz. **Length:** 6.6" overall. **Grips:** Checkered black composite. **Sights:** Blade front, rear adjustable for windage. **Features:** Double action/single action or DAO. Blowback operation, stationary barrel. Introduced 1997. From SIG SAUER, Inc.
Price: P232, from **$660.00**

SIG SAUER P238 PISTOLS

Caliber: .380 ACP (9mm short), 6-7-shot magazine. **Barrel:** 2.7". **Weight:** 15.4 oz. **Length:** 5.5" overall. **Grips:** Hogue® G-10 and Rosewood grips. **Sights:** Contrast / SIGLITE night sights. **Features:** the P238 has redefined the role of a .380 ACP caliber pistol for concealed personal protection, ultimate firepower in an all metal beavertail-style frame.
Price: **$643.00**
Price: P238 Lady
w/rosewood grips **$752.00**
Price: P238 Gambler
w/rosewood grip. **$752.00**

Price: P238 Extreme
w/X-Grip extended
magazine **$752.00**
Price: P238 Diamond Plate
w/diamond plate
detailed slide **$752.00**

SIG SAUER P290 PISTOLS

Caliber: 9mm, 6/8-shot magazine. **Barrel:** 2.9". **Weight:** 20.5 oz. **Length:** 5.5" overall. **Grips:** Polymer. **Sights:** Contrast / SIGLITE night sights.
Features: Unlike many small pistols, the P290 features drift adjustable sights in the standard SIG SAUER dovetails. This gives shooters the option of either standard contrast sights or SIGLITE® night sights. The slide is machined from a solid billet of stainless steel and is available in a natural stainless or a durable Nitron® coating. A reversible magazine catch is left-hand adjustable. Interchangeable grip panels allow for personalization as well as a custom fit. In addition to the standard polymer inserts, optional panels will be available in aluminum, G10 and wood.
Price: Model 290-9-BSS **$758.00**
Price: Model 290-9-TSS **$786.00**
Price: Model 290-9-BSS-L
with laser sights **$828.00**
Price: Model 290-9-TSS
with laser sights **$856.00**

SIG SAUER P239 PISTOL

Caliber: 9mm Para., 8-shot, 357 SIG 40 S&W, 7-shot magazine. **Barrel:** 3.6". **Weight:** 25.2 oz. **Length:** 6.6" overall. **Grips:** Checkered black composite. **Sights:** Blade front, rear adjustable for windage. Optional Siglite night sights. **Features:** SA/DA or DAO; blackened stainless steel slide, aluminum alloy frame. Introduced 1996. Made in U.S.A. by SIG SAUER, Inc.
Price: P239, from **$840.00**

SIG SAUER MOSQUITO PISTOL

Caliber: 22 LR, 10-shot magazine. **Barrel:** 3.9". **Weight:** 24.6 oz. **Length:** 7.2" overall. **Grips:** Checkered black composite. **Sights:** Blade front, rear adjustable for windage. **Features:** Blowback operated, fixed barrel, polymer frame, slide-mounted ambidextrous safety. Introduced 2005. Made in U.S.A. by SIG SAUER, Inc.
Price: Mosquito, from **$375.00**

SIG SAUER P522 PISTOL

Semiauto blowback pistol chambered in .22 LR. Pistol version of SIG522 rifle. Features include a 10-inch barrel; lightweight polymer lower receiver with pistol grip; ambi mag catch; aluminum upper; faux gas valve; birdcage; 25-round magazine; quad rail or "clean" handguard; optics rail.
Price: . . . .**$572.00 to $643.00**

Prices given are believed to be accurate at time of publication however, many factors affect retail pricing so exact prices are not possible.

SMITH & WESSON M&P AUTO PISTOLS

Caliber: .22 LR, 9mm Para., 40 S&W, 357 Auto. **Barrel:** 4.25". **Weight:** 24.25 oz. **Length:** 7.5" overall. **Grips:** One-piece Xenoy, wraparound with straight backstrap. **Sights:** Ramp dovetail mount front; tritium sights optional; Novak Lo-mount Carry rear. **Features:** Zytel polymer frame, embedded stainless steel chassis; stainless steel slide and barrel, stainless steel structural components, black Melonite finish, reversible magazine catch, 3 interchangeable palmswell grip sizes, universal rail, sear deactivation lever, internal lock system, magazine disconnect. Ships with 2 magazines. Internal lock models available. Overall height: 5.5"; width: 1.2"; sight radius: 6.4". Introduced November 2005. 45 ACP version introduced 2007, 10+1 or 14+1 capacity. **Barrel:** 4.5". **Length:** 8.05". **Weight:** 29.6 ounces. **Features:** Picatinny-style equipment rail; black or bi-tone, dark-earth-brown frame. Bi-tone M&P45 includes ambidextrous, frame-mounted thumb safety, take down tool with lanyard attachment. Compact 9mm Para./357 SIG/40 S&W versions introduced 2007. Compacts have 3.5" barrel, OAL 6.7". 10+1 or 12+1 capacity. **Weight:** 21.7 ounces. **Features:** Picatinny-style equipment rail. Made in U.S.A. by Smith & Wesson.

Price: M&P22 .22 LR model $419.00
Price: Full Size, from $719.00
Price: Compacts, from $719.00
Price: Midsize, from $758.00
Price: Crimson Trace Lasergrip models, from . . $988.00
Price: Thumb-safety M&P models, from $719.00

SMITH & WESSON PRO SERIES MODEL M&P40

Striker-fired DAO semiauto pistol chambered in .40 S&W. Features include 4.25- or 5-inch barrel, matte black polymer frame and stainless steel slide, tactical rail, Novak front and rear sights or two-dot night sights, polymer grips, 15+1 capacity.

Price: $830.00
Price: VTAC® Viking Tactics $779.00

SMITH & WESSON PRO SERIES MODEL M&P9

Similar to M&P40 but chambered in 9mm Parabellum. Capacity 17+1, 4.25-inch barrel, two-dot night sights.
Price: $830.00

SMITH & WESSON MODEL 908 AUTO PISTOL

Caliber: 9mm Para., 8-shot magazine. **Barrel:** 3.5". **Weight:** 24 oz. **Length:** 6-13/16". **Grips:** One-piece Xenoy, wraparound with straight backstrap. **Sights:** Post front, fixed rear, 3-dot system. **Features:** Aluminum alloy frame, matte blue carbon steel slide; bobbed hammer; smooth trigger. Introduced 1996. Made in U.S.A. by Smith & Wesson.

Price: Model 908, black matte finish $679.00
Price: Model 908S, stainless matte finish $679.00
Price: Model 908S Carry Combo, with holster $703.00

SMITH & WESSON MODEL 4013TSW AUTO

Caliber: 40 S&W, 9-shot magazine. **Barrel:** 3.5". **Weight:** 26.8 oz. **Length:** 6 3/4" overall. **Grips:** Xenoy one-piece wraparound. **Sights:** Novak 3-dot system. **Features:** Traditional double-action system; stainless slide, alloy frame; fixed barrel bushing; ambidextrous decocker; reversible magazine catch, equipment rail. Introduced 1997. Made in U.S.A. by Smith & Wesson.
Price: Model 4013TSW $1,027.00

SMITH & WESSON MODEL 910 DA AUTO PISTOL

Caliber: 9mm Para., 10-shot magazine. **Barrel:** 4". **Weight:** 28 oz. **Length:** 7-3/8" overall. **Grips:** One-piece Xenoy, wraparound with straight backstrap. **Sights:** Post front with white dot, fixed 2-dot rear. **Features:** Alloy frame, blue carbon steel slide. Slide-mounted decocking lever. Introduced 1995.
Price: $648.00

SMITH & WESSON MODEL 3913 TRADITIONAL DOUBLE ACTIONS

Caliber: 9mm Para., 8-shot magazine. **Barrel:** 3.5". **Weight:** 24.8 oz. **Length:** 6.75" overall. **Grips:** One-piece Delrin wraparound, textured surface. **Sights:** Post front with white dot, Novak LoMount Carry with two dots. **Features:** TSW has aluminum alloy frame, stainless slide. Bobbed hammer with no half-cock notch; smooth .304" trigger with rounded edges. Straight backstrap. Equipment rail. Extra magazine included. Introduced 1989. The 3913-LS Ladysmith has frame that is upswept at the front, rounded trigger guard. Comes in frosted stainless steel with matching gray grips. Grips are ergonomically correct for a woman's hand. Novak LoMount Carry rear sight adjustable for windage. Extra magazine included. Introduced 1990.
Price: 3913TSW $924.00
Price: 3913-LS $909.00

SMITH & WESSON MODEL SD9 PISTOLS

Caliber: .40 S&W and 9mm, 10+1, 14+1 and 16+1 round capacities. **Barrel:** 4". **Weight:** 39 oz. **Length:** 8.7". **Grips:** Wood or rubber. **Sights:** Front: Tritium Night Sight, Rear: Steel Fixed 2-Dot. **Features:** SDT™ - Self Defense Trigger for optimal, consistent pull first round to Last, standard picatinny-style rail, slim ergonomic textured grip, textured finger locator and aggressive front and back strap texturing with front and rear slide serrations.

Price: 9mm Std. Capacity $459.00
Price: 9mm Low Capacity $459.00
Price: .40 S&W Std. Capacity. $459.00
Price: .40 S&W Low Capacity. $459.00

SMITH & WESSON MODEL SW1911 PISTOLS

Caliber: 45 ACP, 8 rounds; 9mm, 11 rounds. **Barrel:** 5". **Weight:** 39 oz. **Length:** 8.7". **Grips:** Wood or rubber. **Sights:** Novak Lo-Mount Carry, white dot front. **Features:** Large stainless frame and slide with matte finish, single-side external safety. No. 108284 has adjustable target rear sight, ambidextrous safety levers, 20-lpi checkered front strap, comes with two 8-round magazines. DK model (Doug Koenig) also has oversized magazine well, Doug Koenig speed hammer, flat competition speed trigger with overtravel stop, rosewood grips with Smith & Wesson silver medallions, oversized magazine well, special serial number run. No. 108295 has olive drab Crimson Trace lasergrips. No. 108299 has carbon-steel frame and slide with polished flats on slide, standard GI recoil guide, laminated double-diamond walnut grips with silver Smith & Wesson medallions, adjustable target sights. Tactical Rail No. 108293 has a Picatinny rail, black Melonite finish, Novak Lo-Mount Carry Sights, scandium alloy frame. Tactical Rail Stainless introduced 2006. SW1911PD gun is Commander size, scandium-alloy frame, 4.25" barrel, 8" OAL, 28.0 oz., non-reflective black matte finish. Gunsite edition has scandium alloy frame, beveled edges, solid match aluminum trigger, Herrett's logoed tactical oval walnut stocks, special serial number run, brass bead Novak front sight. SC model has 4.25" barrel, scandium alloy frame, stainless-steel slide, non-reflective matte finish.

Price: From **$1,130.00**
Price: Crimson Trace Laser Grips **$1,493.00**
Price: SW1911 E Series .45 ACP **$919.00**
Price: SW1911 E Series Tactical Accessory Rail **$1,319.00**
Price: SW1911 E Series Round Butt, Scandium Frame **$1,369.00**
Price: SW1911 E Series Crimson Trace® Lasergrips **$1,089.00**

SMITH & WESSON MODEL 1911 SUB-COMPACT PRO SERIES

Caliber: 45 ACP, 7 + 1-shot magazine. **Barrel:** 3". **Weight:** 24 oz. **Length:** 6-7/8". **Grips:** Fully stippled synthetic. **Sights:** Dovetail white dot front, fixed white 2-dot rear. **Features:** Scandium frame with stainless steel slide, matte black finish throughout. Oversized external extractor, 3-hole curved trigger with overtravel stop, full-length guide rod, and cable lock. Introduced 2009.
Price: **$1,304.00**

SMITH & WESSON ENHANCED SIGMA SERIES DAO PISTOLS

Caliber: 9mm Para., 40 S&W; 10-, 16-shot magazine. **Barrel:** 4". **Weight:** 24.7 oz. **Length:** 7.25" overall. **Grips:** Integral. **Sights:** White dot front, fixed rear; 3-dot system. Tritium night sights available. **Features:** Ergonomic polymer frame; low barrel centerline; internal striker firing system; corrosion-resistant slide; Teflon-filled, electroless-nickel coated magazine, equipment rail. Introduced 1994. Made in U.S.A. by Smith & Wesson.
Price: From **$482.00**

SMITH & WESSON BODYGUARD® 380

Caliber: .380 Auto, 6+1 round capacity. **Barrel:** 2.75". **Weight:** 11.85 oz. **Length:** 5.25". **Grips:** Polymer. **Sights:** Integrated laser sights with front: stainless steel, rear: drift adjustable. **Features:** The frame of the Bodyguard is made of reinforced polymer, as is the magazine base plate and follower, magazine catch, and the trigger. The slide, sights, and guide rod are made of stainless steel, with the slide and sights having a Melonite hard coating.
Price: **$399.00**

SMITH & WESSON MODEL CS9 CHIEF'S SPECIAL AUTO

Caliber: 9mm Para., 7-shot magazine. **Barrel:** 3". **Weight:** 20.8 oz. **Length:** 6.25" overall. **Grips:** Hogue wraparound rubber. **Sights:** White dot front, fixed 2-dot rear. **Features:** Traditional double-action trigger mechanism. Alloy frame, stainless slide. Ambidextrous safety. Introduced 1999. Made in U.S.A. by Smith & Wesson.
Price: Stainless **$782.00**

SMITH & WESSON MODEL CS45 CHIEF'S SPECIAL AUTO

Caliber: 45 ACP, 6-shot magazine. **Weight:** 23.9 oz. **Features:** Introduced 1999. Made in U.S.A. by Smith & Wesson.
Price: From **$787.00**

SPRINGFIELD ARMORY EMP ENHANCED MICRO PISTOL

Caliber: 9mm Para., 40 S&W; 9-round magazine. **Barrel:** 3" stainless steel match grade, fully supported ramp, bull. **Weight:** 26 oz. **Length:** 6.5" overall. **Grips:** Thinline cocobolo hardwood. **Sights:** Fixed low profile combat rear, dovetail front, 3-dot tritium. **Features:** Two 9-round stainless steel magazines with slam pads, long aluminum match-grade trigger adjusted to 5 to 6 lbs., forged aluminum alloy frame, black hardcoat anodized; dual spring full-length guide rod, forged satin-finish stainless steel slide. Introduced 2007. From Springfield Armory.
Price: 9mm Para. Compact Bi-Tone **$1,329.00**
Price: 40 S&W Compact Bi-Tone (2008) **$1,329.00**

SPRINGFIELD ARMORY XD POLYMER AUTO PISTOLS

Caliber: 9mm Para., 40 S&W, 45 ACP. **Barrel:** 3", 4", 5". **Weight:** 20.5-31 oz. **Length:** 6.26-8" overall. **Grips:** Textured polymer. **Sights:** Varies by model; Fixed sights are dovetail front and rear steel 3-dot units. **Features:** Three sizes in X-Treme Duty (XD) line: Sub-Compact (3" barrel), Service (4" barrel), Tactical (5" barrel). Three ported models available. Ergonomic polymer frame, hammer-forged barrel, no-tool disassembly, ambidextrous magazine release, visual/tactile loaded chamber indicator, visual/tactile striker status indicator, grip safety, XD gear system included. Introduced 2004. XD 45 introduced 2006. Compact line introduced 2007. Compacts ship with one extended magazine (13) and one compact magazine (10). From Springfield Armory.
Price: Sub-Compact OD Green 9mm Para./40 S&W, fixed sights **$543.00**
Price: Compact 45 ACP, 4" barrel, Bi-Tone finish (2008) **$589.00**
Price: Compact 45 ACP, 4" barrel, OD green frame, stainless slide (2008) **$653.00**
Price: Service Black 9mm Para./40 S&W, fixed sights **$543.00**
Price: Service Dark Earth 45 ACP, fixed sights **$571.00**
Price: Service Black 45 ACP, external thumb safety (2008) **$571.00**
Price: V-10 Ported Black 9mm Para./40 S&W **$573.00**

Prices given are believed to be accurate at time of publication however, many factors affect retail pricing so exact prices are not possible.

Price: Tactical Black 45 ACP, fixed sights **$616.00**
Price: Service Bi-Tone 40 S&W, Trijicon night sights (2008) . . **$695.00**

SPRINGFIELD ARMORY GI 45 1911A1 AUTO PISTOLS
Caliber: 45 ACP; 6-, 7-, 13-shot magazines. **Barrel:** 3", 4", 5". **Weight:** 28-36 oz. **Length:** 5.5-8.5" overall. **Grips:** Checkered double-diamond walnut, "U.S" logo. **Sights:** Fixed GI style. **Features:** Similar to WWII GI-issue 45s at hammer, beavertail, mainspring housing. From Springfield Armory.
Price: GI .45 4" Champion Lightweight, 7+1, 28 oz. **$619.00**
Price: GI .45 5" High Capacity, 13+1, 36 oz. **$676.00**
Price: GI .45 5" OD Green, 7+1, 36 oz. **$619.00**
Price: GI .45 3" Micro Compact, 6+1, 32 oz. **$667.00**

SPRINGFIELD ARMORY MIL-SPEC 1911A1 AUTO PISTOLS
Caliber: 38 Super, 9-shot magazines; 45 ACP, 7-shot magazines. **Barrel:** 5". **Weight:** 35.6-39 oz. **Length:** 8.5-8.625" overall. **Features:** Similar to GI 45s. From Springfield Armory.
Price: Mil-Spec Parkerized, 7+1, 35.6 oz. **$715.00**
Price: Mil-Spec Stainless Steel, 7+1, 36 oz. **$784.00**
Price: Mil-Spec 38 Super, 9+1, 39 oz. **$775.00**

Springfield Armory Custom Loaded Champion 1911A1 Pistol
Similar to standard 1911A1, slide and barrel are 4". 7.5" OAL. Available in 45 ACP only. Novak Night Sights. Delta hammer and cocobolo grips. Parkerized or stainless. Introduced 1989.
Price: Stainless, 34 oz. **$1,031.00**
Price: Lightweight, 28 oz. **$989.00**

Springfield Armory Custom Loaded Ultra Compact Pistol
Similar to 1911A1 Compact, shorter slide, 3.5" barrel, 6+1, 7" OAL. Beavertail grip safety, beveled magazine well, fixed sights. Videki speed trigger, flared ejection port, stainless steel frame, blued slide, match grade barrel, rubber grips. Introduced 1996. From Springfield Armory.
Price: Stainless Steel **$1,031.00**

SPRINGFIELD ARMORY CUSTOM LOADED MICRO-COMPACT 1911A1 PISTOL
Caliber: 45 ACP, 6+1 capacity. **Barrel:** 3" 1:16 LH. **Weight:** 24-32 oz. **Length:** 4.7". **Grips:** Slimline cocobolo. **Sights:** Novak LoMount tritium. Dovetail front. **Features:** Aluminum hard-coat anodized alloy frame, forged steel slide, forged barrel, ambi-thumb safety, Extreme Carry Bevel dehorning. Lockable plastic case, 2 magazines.
Price: Lightweight Bi-Tone **$992.00**

SPRINGFIELD ARMORY CUSTOM LOADED LONG SLIDE 1911A1 PISTOL
Caliber: 45 ACP, 7+1 capacity. **Barrel:** 6" 1:16 LH. **Weight:** 41 oz. **Length:** 9.5". **Grips:** Slimline cocobolo. **Sights:** Dovetail front; fully adjustable target rear. **Features:** Longer sight radius, 7.9".
Price: Bi-Tone Operator w/light rail **$1,189.00**

Springfield Armory Tactical Response Loaded Pistols
Similar to 1911A1 except 45 ACP only, checkered front strap and main-spring housing, Novak Night Sight combat rear sight and matching dove-tailed front sight, tuned, polished extractor, oversize barrel link; lightweight speed trigger and combat action job, match barrel and bushing, extended ambidextrous thumb safety and fitted beavertail grip safety. Checkered cocobolo wood grips, comes with two Wilson 7-shot magazines. Frame is engraved "Tactical" both sides of frame with "TRP." Introduced 1998. TRP-Pro Model meets FBI specifications for SWAT Hostage Rescue Team. From Springfield Armory.
Price: 45 TRP Service Model, black Armory Kote finish, fixed Trijicon night sights **$1,741.00**

SPRINGFIELD ARMORY XDM-3.8
Double action only semiauto pistol chambered in 9mm Parabellum (19+1) and .40 S&W (16+1). Features include 3.8-inch steel full-ramp barrel; dovetail front and rear 3-dot sights (tritium and fiber-optics sights available); polymer frame; stainless steel slide with slip-resistant slide serrations; loaded chamber indicator; grip safety. Black, bi-tone or stainless steel finish. Overall length 7 inches, weight 27.5 oz. (9mm). Also available with 4.5-inch barrel as Model XDM-4.5.
Price: . . . . **N/A**

STOEGER COMPACT COUGAR PISTOL
Caliber: 9mm, 13+1 round capacity. **Barrel:** 3.6". **Weight:** 32 oz. **Length:** 7". **Grips:** Wood or rubber. **Sights:** Quick read 3-dot. **Features:** Double/single action with a Bruniton® Matte black finish. The ambidextrous safety and decocking lever is easily accessible to the thumb of a right-handed or left-handed shooter.
Price: **$449.00**

STI LIMITED EDITION STI 20TH ANNIVERSARY PISTOL
1911-style semiauto pistol chambered in 9x19, .38 Super, .40 S&W, and .45 ACP to commemorate STI's 20th anniversary. Features include ambidextrous thumb safeties and knuckle relief high-rise beavertail grip safety; gold TiN (or Titanium Nitride) coating; full length steel bar stock slide with custom serrations specific to this model; 5-inch fully ramped and supported bull barrel; STI adjustable rear sight and a Dawson fiber optic front sight. STI will only build 200 of these pistols and the serial numbers reflect this (1 of 200, 2 of 200, etc.).
Price: . . . . **N/A**

STI DUTY ONE PISTOL

1911-style semiauto pistol chambered in .45 ACP. Features include government size frame with integral tactical rail and 30 lpi checkered frontstrap; milled tactical rail on the dust cover of the frame; ambidextrous thumb safeties; high rise beavertail grip safety; lowered and flared ejection port; fixed rear sight; front and rear cocking serrations; 5-inch fully supported STI International ramped bull barrel.

Price: . . . . **N/A**

STI APEIRO PISTOL

1911-style semiauto pistol chambered in 9x19, .40 S&W, and .45 ACP. Features include Schuemann "Island" barrel; patented modular steel frame with polymer grip; high capacity double-stack magazine; stainless steel ambidextrous thumb safeties and knuckle relief high-rise beavertail grip safety; unique sabertooth rear cocking serrations; 5-inch fully ramped, fully supported "island" bull barrel, with the sight milled in to allow faster recovery to point of aim; custom engraving on the polished sides of the (blued) stainless steel slide; stainless steel magwell; STI adjustable rear sight and Dawson fiber optic front sight; blued frame.

Price: . . . . **N/A**

STI EAGLE PISTOL

1911-style semiauto pistol chambered in .45 ACP, 9mm, .40 S&W. Features include modular steel frame with polymer grip; high capacity doule-stack magazines; scalloped slide with front and rear cocking serrations; dovetail front sight and STI adjustable rear sight; stainless steel STI hi-ride grip safety and stainless steel STI ambi-thumb safety; 5- or 6-inch STI stainless steel fully supported, ramped bull barrel or the traditional bushing barrel; blued or stainless finish.

Price: . . . . **N/A**

STI ECLIPSE PISTOL

Compact 1911-tyle semiauto pistol chambered in 9x19, .40 S&W, and .45 ACP. Features include 3-inch slide with rear cocking serrations, oversized ejection port; 2-dot tritium night sights recessed into the slide; high-capacity polymer grip; single sided blued thumb safety; bobbed, high-rise, blued, knuckle relief beavertail grip safety; 3-inch barrel.

Price: . . . . **N/A**

STI ESCORT PISTOL

Similar to STI Eclipse but with aluminum allow frame and chambered in .45 ACP only.

Price: . . . . **N/A**

TAURUS MODEL 800 SERIES

Caliber: 9mm Para., 40 S&W, 45 ACP. **Barrel:** 4". **Weight:** 32 oz. **Length:** 8.25". **Grips:** Checkered. **Sights:** Novak. **Features:** DA/SA. Blue and Stainless Steel finish. Introduced in 2007. Imported from Brazil by Taurus International.
Price: 809B, 9mm Para., Blue, 17+1 . . . . **$623.00**

TAURUS MODEL 1911

Caliber: 45 ACP, 8+1 capacity. **Barrel:** 5". **Weight:** 33 oz. **Length:** 8.5". **Grips:** Checkered black. **Sights:** Heinie straight 8. **Features:** SA. Blue, stainless steel, duotone blue, and blue/gray finish. Standard/picatinny rail, standard frame, alloy frame, and alloy/picatinny rail. Introduced in 2007. Imported from Brazil by Taurus International.
Price: 1911B, Blue **$719.00**
Price: 1911SS, Stainless Steel **$816.00**
Price: 1911SS-1, Stainless Steel **$847.00**
Price: 1911 DT, Duotone Blue **$795.00**

TAURUS MODEL 917

Caliber: 9mm Para., 19+1 capacity. **Barrel:** 4.3". **Weight:** 32.2 oz. **Length:** 8.5". **Grips:** Checkered rubber. **Sights:** Fixed. **Features:** SA/DA. Blue and stainless steel finish. Medium frame. Introduced in 2007. Imported from Brazil by Taurus International.
Price: 917B-20, Blue **$542.00**
Price: 917SS-20, Stainless Steel **$559.00**

TAURUS MODEL PT-22/PT-25 AUTO PISTOLS

Caliber: 22 LR, 8-shot (PT-22); 25 ACP, 9-shot (PT-25). **Barrel:** 2.75". **Weight:** 12.3 oz. **Length:** 5.25" overall. **Grips:** Smooth rosewood or mother-of-pearl. **Sights:** Fixed. **Features:** Double action. Tip-up barrel for loading, cleaning. Blue, nickel, duo-tone or blue with gold accents. Introduced 1992. Made in U.S.A. by Taurus International.
Price: PT-22B or PT-25B, checkered wood grips **$248.00**

TAURUS MODEL 22PLY SMALL POLYMER FRAME PISTOLS

Similar to Taurus Models PT-22 and PT-25 but with lightweight polymer frame. Features include 22 LR (9+1) or 25 ACP (8+1) chambering. 2.33" tip-up barrel, matte black finish, extended magazine with finger lip, manual safety. Overall length is 4.8". Weighs 10.8 oz.
Price: . . . . **TO BE ANNOUNCED**

TAURUS MODEL 24/7

Caliber: 9mm Para., 40 S&W, 45 ACP. **Barrel:** 4". **Weight:** 27.2 oz. **Length:** 7-1/8". **Grips:** "Ribber" rubber-finned overlay on polymer. **Sights:** Adjustable. **Features:** SA/DA; accessory rail, four safeties, blue or stainless finish. One-piece guide rod, flush-fit magazine, flared bushingless barrel, Picatinny accessory rail, manual safety, user changeable sights, loaded chamber indicator, tuned ejector and lowered port, one piece guide rod and flat wound captive spring. Introduced 2003. Long Slide models have 5" barrels, measure 8-1/8" overall, weigh 27.2 oz. Imported from Brazil by Taurus International.
Price: 40BP, 40 S&W, blued, 10+1 or 15+1 . . . . **$452.00**
Price: 24/7-PRO Standard Series: 4" barrel; stainless, duotone or blued finish **$452.00**
Price: 24/7-PRO Compact Series; 3.2" barrel; stainless, titanium or blued finish **$467.00**
Price: 24/7-PRO Long Slide Series: 5.2" barrel; matte stainless, blued or stainless finish **$506.00**
Price: 24/7PLS, 5" barrel, chambered in 9mm Parabellum, 38 Super and 40 S&W **$506.00**

Prices given are believed to be accurate at time of publication however, many factors affect retail pricing so exact prices are not possible.

TAURUS 24/7 G2

Double/single action semiauto pistol chambered in 9mm Parabellum (15+1), .40 S&W (13+1), and .45 ACP (10+1). Features include blued or stainless finish; "Strike Two" capability; new trigger safety; low-profile adjustable rear sights for windage and elevation; ambidextrous magazine release; 4.2-inch barrel; Picatinny rail; polymer frame; polymer grip with metallic inserts and three interchangeable backstraps. Also offered in compact model with shorter grip frame and 3.5-inch barrel.
Price: . . . . **N/A**

TAURUS MODEL 2045 LARGE FRAME PISTOL

Similar to Taurus Model 24/7 but chambered in 45 ACP only. Features include polymer frame, blued or matte stainless steel slide, 4.2" barrel, ambidextrous "memory pads" to promote safe finger position during loading, ambi three-position safety/decocker. Picatinny rail system, fixed sights. Overall length is 7.34". Weighs 31.5 oz.
Price: **$577.00**

TAURUS MODEL 58 PISTOL

Caliber: 380 ACP (19+1). **Barrel:** 3.25. **Weight:** 18.7 oz. **Length:** 6.125" overall. **Grips:** Polymer. **Sights:** Fixed. **Features:** SA/DA semi-auto. Scaled-down version of the full-size Model 92; steel slide, alloy frame, frame-mounted ambi safety, blued or stainless finish, and extended magazine.
Price: 58HCB **$602.00**
Price: 58HCSS **$617.00**

TAURUS MODEL 92 AUTO PISTOL

Caliber: 9mm Para., 10- or 17-shot mags. **Barrel:** 5". **Weight:** 34 oz. **Length:** 8.5" overall. **Grips:** Checkered rubber, rosewood, mother-of-pearl. **Sights:** Fixed notch rear. 3-dot sight system. Also offered with micrometer-click adjustable night sights. **Features:** Double action, ambidextrous 3-way hammer drop safety, allows cocked & locked carry. Blue, stainless steel, blue with gold highlights, stainless steel with gold highlights, forged aluminum frame, integral key-lock. .22 LR conversion kit available. Imported from Brazil by Taurus International.
Price: 92B **$542.00**
Price: 92SS **$559.00**

TAURUS MODEL 99 AUTO PISTOL

Similar to Model 92, fully adjustable rear sight.
Price: 99B **$559.00**

TAURUS MODEL 90-TWO SEMI-AUTO PISTOL

Similar to Model 92 but with one-piece wraparound grips, automatic disassembly latch, internal recoil buffer, addition slide serrations, picatinny rail with removable cover, 10- and 17-round magazine (9mm) or 10- and 12-round magazines (40 S&W). Overall length is 8.5". Weight is 32.5 oz.
Price: **$725.00**

TAURUS MODEL 100/101 AUTO PISTOL

Caliber: 40 S&W, 10- or 11-shot mags. **Barrel:** 5". **Weight:** 34 oz. **Length:** 8.5". **Grips:** Checkered rubber, rosewood, mother-of-pearl. **Sights:** 3-dot fixed or adjustable; night sights available. **Features:** Single/double action with three-position safety/decocker. Reintroduced in 2001. Imported by Taurus International.
Price: 100B **$542.00**

TAURUS MODEL 111 MILLENNIUM PRO AUTO PISTOL

Caliber: 9mm Para., 10- or 12-shot mags. **Barrel:** 3.25". **Weight:** 18.7 oz. **Length:** 6-1/8" overall. **Grips:** Checkered polymer. **Sights:** 3-dot fixed; night sights available. Low profile, 3-dot combat. **Features:** Double action only, polymer frame, matte stainless or blue steel slide, manual safety, integral key-lock. Deluxe models with wood grip inserts.
Price: 111BP, 111BP-12. . . . .**$419.00**
Price: 111PTi titanium slide **$592.00**

TAURUS 132 MILLENNIUM PRO AUTO PISTOL

Caliber: 32 ACP, 10-shot mag. **Barrel:** 3.25". **Weight:** 18.7 oz. **Grips:** Polymer. **Sights:** 3-dot fixed; night sights available. **Features:** Double-action-only, polymer frame, matte stainless or blue steel slide, manual safety, integral key-lock action. Introduced 2001.
Price: 132BP. **$419.00**

TAURUS 138 MILLENNIUM PRO SERIES

Caliber: 380 ACP, 10- or 12-shot mags. **Barrel:** 3.25". **Weight:** 18.7 oz. **Grips:** Polymer. **Sights:** Fixed 3-dot fixed. **Features:** Double-action-only, polymer frame, matte stainless or blue steel slide, manual safety, integral key-lock.
Price: 138BP. **$419.00**

TAURUS 140 MILLENNIUM PRO AUTO PISTOL

Caliber: 40 S&W, 10-shot mag. **Barrel:** 3.25". **Weight:** 18.7 oz. **Grips:** Checkered polymer. **Sights:** 3-dot fixed; night sights available. **Features:** Double action only; matte stainless or blue steel slide, black polymer frame, manual safety, integral key-lock action. From Taurus International.
Price: 140BP **$436.00**

TAURUS 145 MILLENNIUM PRO AUTO PISTOL

Caliber: 45 ACP, 10-shot mag. **Barrel:** 3.27". **Weight:** 23 oz. **Stock:** Checkered polymer. **Sights:** 3-dot fixed; night sights available. **Features:** Double-action only, matte stainless or blue steel slide, black polymer frame, manual safety, integral key-lock. Compact model is 6+1 with a 3.25" barrel, weighs 20.8 oz. From Taurus International.
Price: 145BP, blued **$436.00**
Price: 145SSP, stainless, ...**$453.00**

Taurus Model 609Ti-Pro

Similar to other Millennium Pro models but with titanium slide. Chambered in 9mm Parabellum. Weighs 19.7 oz. Overall length is 6.125". Features include 13+1 capacity, 3.25" barrel, checkered polymer grips, and Heinie Straight-8 sights.
Price: **$608.00**

TAURUS SLIM 700 SERIES

Compact double/single action semiauto pistol chambered in 9mm Parabellum (7+1), .40 S&W (6+1), and .380 ACP (7+1). Features include polymer frame; blue or stainless slide; single action/double action trigger pull; low-profile fixed sights. Weight 19 oz., length 6.24 inches, width less than an inch.
Price: . . . . **N/A**

TAURUS MODEL 709 G2 SLIM PISTOL

Caliber: 9mm., 9+1-shot magazine. **Barrel:** 3". **Weight:** 19 oz. **Length:** 6.24" overall. **Grips:** Black. **Sights:** Low profile. **Features:** The most heralded concealed carry semi-auto in company history is getting even better with the G2 Slim. Even under the lightest clothing the Slim design reveals nothing. Now with the best in features and performance from the elite G2 series.

HANDGUNS—Autoloaders, Service & Sport

Also, with the G2 Slim, there are extra rounds with an extended magazine for added confidence.

Price: **$376.00**

TAURUS MODEL 738 TCP COMPACT PISTOL
Caliber: 380 ACP, 6+1 (standard magazine) or 8+1 (extended magazine). **Barrel:** 3.3". **Weight:** 9 oz. (titanium slide) to 10.2 oz. **Length:** 5.19". **Sights:** Low-profile fixed. **Features:** Lightweight DAO semi-auto with polymer frame; blued (738B), stainless (738SS) or titanium (738Ti) slide; concealed hammer; ambi safety; loaded chamber indicator.
Price: . . . . **$623.00 to $686.00**

TAURUS SLIM 740 PISTOL
Caliber: .380 ACP and .40 cal., 6+1/8+1-shot magazines. **Barrel:** 4". **Weight:** 19 oz. **Length:** 6.24" overall. **Grips:** Polymer Grips. **Features:** Double action with stainless steel finish. Remarkably lean, lightweight design, but it still steps up with big firepower.
Price: **$483.00**

TAURUS 800 SERIES COMPACT
Compact double/single action semiauto pistol chambered in 9mm (12+1), .357 SIG (10+1) and .40 cal (10+1). Features include 3.5-inch barrel; external hammer; loaded chamber indicator; polymer frame; blued or stainless slide.
Price: . . . . **N/A**

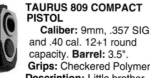

TAURUS 809 COMPACT PISTOL
Caliber: 9mm, .357 SIG and .40 cal. 12+1 round capacity. **Barrel:** 3.5". **Grips:** Checkered Polymer. **Description:** Little brother of the 800 Series, these new pistols were born to perform. They give everything you could want in a 3.5" barrel semi-auto—the best in features, handling, speed and reliability.
Price: **$555.00**

TAURUS 822
Compact double/single action semiauto pistol chambered in .22 LR (10+1). Features include ambidextrous magazine release; external hammer; checkered grip; adjustable sights; 4.5-inch or 6-inch barrel; loaded chamber indicator; and Picatinny rail. Centerfire-to-rimfire conversion kit also available.
Price: . . . . **N/A**

TAURUS MODEL 911B AUTO PISTOL
Caliber: 9mm Para., 10-shot mag. **Barrel:** 4". **Weight:** 28.2 oz. **Length:** 7" overall. **Grips:** Checkered rubber, rosewood, mother-of-pearl. **Sights:** Fixed, 3-dot blue or stainless; night sights optional. **Features:** Double action, semi-auto ambidextrous 3-way hammer drop safety, allows cocked & locked carry. Blue, stainless steel, blue with gold highlights, or stainless steel with gold highlights, forged aluminum frame, integral key-lock.
Price: From **$584.00**

TAURUS MODEL 940B AUTO PISTOL
Caliber: 40 S&W, 10-shot mag. **Barrel:** 3-5/8". **Weight:** 28.2 oz. **Length:** 7" overall. **Grips:** Checkered rubber, rosewood or mother-of-pearl. **Sights:** Fixed, 3-dot blue or stainless; night sights optional. **Features:** Double action, semi-auto ambidextrous 3-way hammer drop safety, allows cocked & locked carry. Blue, stainless steel, blue

with gold highlights, or stainless steel with gold highlights, forged aluminum frame, integral key-lock.
Price: From **$584.00**

TAURUS MODEL 945B/38S SERIES
Caliber: 45 ACP, 8-shot mag. **Barrel:** 4.25". **Weight:** 28.2/29.5 oz. **Length:** 7.48" overall. **Grips:** Checkered rubber, rosewood or mother-of-pearl. **Sights:** Fixed, 3-dot; night sights optional. **Features:** Double-action with ambidextrous 3-way hammer drop safety allows cocked & locked carry. Forged aluminum frame, 945C has ported barrel/slide. Blue, stainless, blue with gold highlights, stainless with gold highlights, integral key-lock. Introduced 1995. 38 Super line based on 945 frame introduced 2005. 38S series is 10+1, 30 oz., 7.5" overall. Imported by Taurus International.
Price: From **$625.00**

THOMPSON CUSTOM 1911A1 AUTOMATIC PISTOL
Caliber: 45 ACP, 7-shot magazine. **Barrel:** 4.3". **Weight:** 34 oz. **Length:** 8" overall. **Grips:** Checkered laminate grips with a Thompson bullet logo inlay. **Sights:** Front and rear sights are black with serrations and are dovetailed into the slide. **Features:** Machined from 420 stainless steel, matte finish. Thompson bullet logo on slide. Flared ejection port, angled front and rear serrations on slide, 20-lpi checkered mainspring housing and frontstrap. Adjustable trigger, combat hammer, stainless steel full-length recoil guide rod, extended beavertail grip safety; extended magazine release; checkered slide-stop lever. Made in U.S.A. by Kahr Arms.
Price: 1911TC, 5", 39 oz., 8.5" overall, stainless frame **$813.00**

THOMPSON TA5 1927A-1 LIGHTWEIGHT DELUXE PISTOL
Caliber: 45 ACP, 50-round drum magazine. **Barrel:** 10.5" 1:16 right-hand twist. **Weight:** 94.5 oz. **Length:** 23.3" overall. **Grips:** Walnut, horizontal foregrip **Sights:** Blade front, open rear adjustable. **Features:** Based on Thompson machine gun design. Introduced 2008. Made in U.S.A. by Kahr Arms.
Price: TA5 (2008) **$1,237.00**

TURNBULL MFG. CO. 1911 CENTENIAL PISTOL
Features: Forged slide with appropriate shape and style. Proper size and shape of sights. Barrel of correct external contour. Safety lock is the thin style, with a knurled undercut thumb-piece. Short, wide spur hammer with standard checkering. Early style slide stop. Lanyard loop, punch and saw cut magazine, finished in two tone. Pistol is hand-polished in the same manner as an original early production vintage pistol. Period-correct Carbonia Charcoal Blueing on all parts. Stamped United States Property as original. Circled Turning Bull trademark on left of slide behind serrations. Early 1913 patent markings and Turnbull Mfg. Co. Bloomfield, NY slide address. Model(s) of 1911 U.S. Army, U.S. Navy and U.S. Marine Corps variations are all available. Inspector's marks are available from Doug Turnbull (TMC Owner, founder) and Keith VanOrman (TMC President).
Price: **$3895.00**

U.S. FIRE ARMS 1910 COMMERCIAL MODEL AUTOMATIC PISTOL
Caliber: 45 ACP, 7-shot magazine. **Barrel:** 5". **Weight:** NA. **Length:** NA. **Grips:** Browning original wide design, full checkered diamond walnut grips. **Sights:** Fixed. **Features:** High polish Armory Blue, fire blue appointments, 1905 patent dates, grip safety, small contoured checkered thumb safety and round 1905 fire

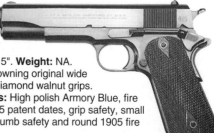

Prices given are believed to be accurate at time of publication however, many factors affect retail pricing so exact prices are not possible.

blue hammer with hand cut checkering. Introduced 2006. Made in U.S.A. by United States Fire Arms Mfg. Co.
Price: $1,895.00

U.S. FIRE ARMS 1911 MILITARY MODEL AUTOMATIC PISTOL
Caliber: 45 ACP, 7-shot magazine. **Barrel:** 5". **Weight:** NA. **Length:** NA. **Grips:** Browning original wide design, full checkered diamond walnut grips. **Sights:** Fixed. **Features:** Military polish Armory Blue, fire blue appointments, 1905 patent dates, grip safety, small contoured checkered thumb safety and round 1905 fire blue hammer with hand cut checkering. Introduced 2006. Made in U.S.A. by United States Fire Arms Mfg. Co.
Price: $1,895.00

U.S. FIRE ARMS SUPER 38 AUTOMATIC PISTOL
Caliber: 38 Auto, 9-shot magazine. **Barrel:** 5". **Weight:** NA. **Length:** NA. **Grips:** Browning original wide design, full checkered diamond walnut grips. **Sights:** Fixed. **Features:** Armory blue, fire blue appointments, 1913 patent date, grip safety, small contoured checkered thumb safety and spur 1911 hammer with hand cut checkering. Supplied with two Super 38 Auto. mags. Super .38 roll mark on base. Introduced 2006. Made in U.S.A. by United States Fire Arms Mfg. Co.
Price: $1,895.00

U.S. FIRE ARMS ACE .22 LONG RIFLE AUTOMATIC PISTOL
Caliber: 22 LR, 10-shot magazine. **Barrel:** 5". **Weight:** NA. **Length:** NA. **Grips:** Browning original wide design, full checkered diamond walnut grips. **Sights:** Fixed. **Features:** Armory blue commercial finish, fire blue appointments, 1913 patent date, grip safety, small contoured checkered thumb safety and spur 1911 hammer with hand cut checkering. Supplied with two magazines. Ace roll mark on base. Introduced 2006. Made in U.S.A. by United States Fire Arms Mfg. Co.
Price: $1,995.00

WALTHER PPS PISTOL
Caliber: 9mm Para., 40 S&W. 6-, 7-, 8-shot magazines for 9mm Para.; 5-, 6-, 7-shot magazines for 40 S&W. **Barrel:** 3.2". **Weight:** 19.4 oz. **Length:** 6.3" overall. **Stocks:** Stippled black polymer. **Sights:** Picatinny-style accessory rail, 3-dot low-profile contoured sight. **Features:** PPS-"Polizeipistole Schmal," or Police Pistol Slim. Measures 1.04 inches wide. Ships with 6- and 7-round magazines. Striker-fired action, flat slide stop lever, alternate backstrap sizes. QuickSafe feature decocks striker assembly when backstrap is removed. Loaded chamber indicator. First Edition model, limited to 1,000 units, has anthracite grey finish, aluminum gun case. Introduced 2008. Made in U.S.A. by Smith & Wesson.
Price: $713.00
Price: First Edition. $665.00

WALTHER PPK/S AMERICAN AUTO PISTOL
Caliber: 32 ACP, 380 ACP, 7-shot magazine. **Barrel:** 3.27". **Weight:** 23-1/2 oz. **Length:** 6.1" overall. **Stocks:** Checkered plastic. **Sights:** Fixed, white markings. **Features:** Double action; manual safety blocks firing pin and drops hammer; chamber loaded indicator on 32 and 380; extra finger rest magazine provided. Made in the United States. Introduced 1980. Made in U.S.A. by Smith & Wesson.
Price: $605.00

WALTHER MODEL PPK/S MACHINE ENGRAVED
Caliber: .380 ACP, 7 & 8-round capacity. **Barrel:** 3.3". **Weight:** 22.4 oz. **Length:** 6.1". **Grips:** Engraved wood. **Sights:** Fixed. **Features:** Traditional Double Action with Stainless frame, slide and barrel. Mahogany Presentation Case Included.
Price: $799.00

WALTHER P99 AUTO PISTOL
Caliber: 9mm Para., 9x21, 40 S&W, 10-shot magazine. **Barrel:** 4". **Weight:** 25 oz. **Length:** 7" overall. **Grips:** Textured polymer. **Sights:** Blade front (comes with three interchangeable blades for elevation adjustment), micrometer rear adjustable for windage. **Features:** Double-action mechanism with trigger safety, decock safety, internal striker safety; chamber loaded indicator; ambidextrous magazine release levers; polymer frame with interchangeable backstrap inserts. Comes with two magazines. Introduced 1997. Made in U.S.A. by Smith & Wesson.
Price: From $799.00

WALTHER P99AS NIGHT SIGHT DEFENSE KIT
Striker-fired DAO semiauto pistol similar to Walther P99AS but with front and rear tritium sights. Chambered in .40 S&W (12 rounds) or 9mm Parabellum (15 rounds). Features include polymer frame and grip, decocker button, 4-inch (9mm) or 4.17-inch (.40) stainless steel barrel, integral weaver-style accessory rail, black Tenifer finish overall.
Price: . . . . N/A

WALTHER PPS NIGHT SIGHT DEFENSE KIT
Striker-fired compact DAO semiauto pistol similar to Walther PPS but with front and rear tritium sights. Chambered in .40 S&W (6 rounds) or 9mm Parabellum (7 rounds). Features include polymer frame and grip, decocker button, loaded chamber indicator, 3.2-inch stainless steel barrel, integral weaver-style accessory rail, black Tenifer finish overall.
Price: . . . . N/A

WALTHER P22 PISTOL
Caliber: 22 LR. **Barrel:** 3.4", 5". **Weight:** 19.6 oz. (3.4"), 20.3 oz. (5"). **Length:** 6.26", 7.83". **Grips:** NA. **Sights:** Interchangeable white dot, front, 2-dot adjustable, rear. **Features:** A rimfire version of the Walther P99 pistol, available in nickel slide with black frame, or green frame with black slide versions. Made in U.S.A. by Smith & Wesson.
Price: From $362.00

WILSON COMBAT ELITE PROFESSIONAL
Caliber: 9mm Para., 38 Super, 40 S&W; 45 ACP, 8-shot magazine. **Barrel:** Compensated 4.1" hand-fit, heavy flanged cone match grade. **Weight:** 36.2 oz. **Length:** 7.7" overall. **Grips:** Cocobolo. **Sights:** Combat Tactical yellow rear tritium inserts, brighter green tritium front insert. **Features:** High-cut front strap, 30-lpi checkering on front strap and flat mainspring housing, High-Ride Beavertail grip safety. Dehorned, ambidextrous thumb safety, extended ejector, skeletonized ultralight hammer, ultralight trigger, Armor-Tuff finish on frame and slide. Introduced 1997. Made in U.S.A. by Wilson Combat.
Price: From $2,600.00

BAER 1911 ULTIMATE MASTER COMBAT PISTOL

Caliber: 38 Super, 400 Cor-Bon 45 ACP (others available), 10-shot magazine. **Barrel:** 5", 6"; Baer NM. **Weight:** 37 oz. **Length:** 8.5" overall. **Grips:** Checkered cocobolo. **Sights:** Baer dovetail front, low-mount Bo-Mar rear with hidden leaf. **Features:** Full-house competition gun. Baer forged NM blued steel frame and double serrated slide; Baer triple port, tapered cone compensator; fitted slide to frame; lowered, flared ejection port; Baer reverse recoil plug; full-length guide rod; recoil buff; beveled magazine well; Baer Commander hammer, sear; Baer extended ambidextrous safety, extended ejector, checkered slide stop, beavertail grip safety with pad, extended magazine release button; Baer speed trigger. Made in U.S.A. by Les Baer Custom, Inc.
Price: 45 ACP Compensated $2,790.00
Price: 38 Super Compensated $2,940.00

BAER 1911 NATIONAL MATCH HARDBALL PISTOL

Caliber: 45 ACP, 7-shot magazine. **Barrel:** 5". **Weight:** 37 oz. **Length:** 8.5" overall. **Grips:** Checkered walnut. **Sights:** Baer dovetail front with under-cut post, low-mount Bo-Mar rear with hidden leaf. **Features:** Baer NM forged steel frame, double serrated slide and barrel with stainless bushing; slide fitted to frame; Baer match trigger with 4-lb. pull; polished feed ramp, throated barrel; checkered front strap, arched mainspring housing; Baer beveled magazine well; lowered, flared ejection port; tuned extractor; Baer extended ejector, checkered slide stop; recoil buff. Made in U.S.A. by Les Baer Custom, Inc.
Price: $1,890.00

BAER 1911 BULLSEYE WADCUTTER PISTOL

Similar to National Match Hardball except designed for wadcutter loads only. Polished feed ramp and barrel throat; Bo-Mar rib on slide; full length recoil rod; Baer speed trigger with 3-1/2-lb. pull; Baer deluxe hammer and sear; Baer beavertail grip safety with pad; flat mainspring housing checkered 20 lpi. Blue finish; checkered walnut grips. Made in U.S.A. by Les Baer Custom, Inc.
Price: From $1,890.00

BF CLASSIC PISTOL

Caliber: Customer orders chamberings. **Barrel:** 8-15" Heavy Match Grade with 11-degree target crown. **Weight:** Approx 3.9 lbs. **Length:** From 16" overall. **Grips:** Thumbrest target style. **Sights:** Bo-Mar/Bond ScopeRib I Combo with hooded post front adjustable for height and width, rear notch available in .032", .062", .080" and .100" widths; 1/2-MOA clicks. **Features:** Hand fitted and headspaced, drilled and tapped for scope mount. Etched receiver; gold-colored trigger. Introduced 1988. Made in U.S.A. by E. Arthur Brown Co. Inc.
Price: $699.00

COLT GOLD CUP TROPHY PISTOL

Caliber: 45 ACP, 8-shot + 1 magazine. **Barrel:** 5". **Weight:** NA. **Length:** 8.5". **Grips:** Checkered rubber composite with silver-plated medallion. **Sights:** (O5070X) Dovetail front, Champion rear; (O5870CS) Patridge Target Style front, Champion rear. **Features:** Adjustable aluminum trigger, Beavertail grip safety, full length recoil spring and target recoil spring, available in blued finish and stainless steel.
Price: O5070X $1,022.00
Price: O5870CS $1,071.00

COLT SPECIAL COMBAT GOVERNMENT

Caliber: 45 ACP, 38 Super. **Barrel:** 5". **Weight:** 39 oz. **Length:** 8.5". **Grips:** Rosewood w/double diamond checkering pattern. **Sights:** Clark dovetail, front; Bo-Mar adjustable, rear. **Features:** A competition-ready pistol with enhancements such as skeletonized trigger, upswept grip safety, custom tuned action, polished feed ramp. Blue or satin nickel finish. Introduced 2003. Made in U.S.A. by Colt's Mfg. Co.
Price: $1,676.00

COMPETITOR SINGLE-SHOT PISTOL

Caliber: 22 LR through 50 Action Express, including belted magnums. **Barrel:** 14" standard; 10.5" silhouette; 16" optional. **Weight:** About 59 oz. (14" bbl.). **Length:** 15.12" overall. **Grips:** Ambidextrous; synthetic (standard) or laminated or natural wood. **Sights:** Ramp front, adjustable rear. **Features:** Rotary cannon-type action cocks on opening; cammed ejector; interchangeable barrels, ejectors. Adjustable single stage trigger, sliding thumb safety and trigger safety. Matte blue finish. Introduced 1988. From Competitor Corp., Inc.
Price: 14", standard calibers, synthetic grip $660.00

CZ 75 CHAMPION COMPETITION PISTOL

Caliber: 9mm Para., 40 S&W, 16-shot mag. **Barrel:** 4.4". **Weight:** 2.5 lbs. **Length:** 9.4" overall. **Grips:** Black rubber. **Sights:** Blade front, fully adjustable rear. **Features:** Single-action trigger mechanism; three-port compensator (40 S&W, 9mm Para. have two port) full-length guide rod; extended magazine release; ambidextrous safety; flared magazine well; fully adjustable match trigger. Introduced 1999. Imported from the Czech Republic by CZ-USA.
Price: Dual-tone finish $1,691.00

CZ 75 TS CZECHMATE

Caliber: 9mm Luger, 20-shot magazine. **Barrel:** 130mm. **Weight:** 1360 g **Length:** 266 mm overall. **Features:** The handgun is custom-built, therefore the quality of workmanship is fully comparable with race pistols built directly to IPSC shooters wishes. Individual parts and components are excellently match fitted, broke-in and tested. Every handgun is outfitted with a four-port compensator, nut for shooting without a compensator, the slide stop with an extended finger piece, the slide stop without a finger piece, ergonomic grip panels from aluminium with a new type pitting and side mounting provision with the C-More red dot sight. For the shooting without a red dot sight there is included a standard target rear sight of Tactical Sports type, package contains also the front sight.
Price: $2,864.00

Prices given are believed to be accurate at time of publication however, many factors affect retail pricing so exact prices are not possible.

CZ 75 TACTICAL SPORTS
Caliber: 9mm Luger and .40 S&W, 17-20-shot magazine capacity.
Barrel: 114mm. Weight: 1270 g Length: 225 mm overall.
Features: semi-automatic handgun with a locked breech. This pistol model is designed for competition shooting in accordance with world IPSC (International Practical Shooting Confederation) rules and regulations. The pistol allow rapid and accurate shooting within a very short time frame.The CZ 75 TS pistol model design stems from the standard CZ 75 model. However, this model feature number of special modifications, which are usually required for competitive handguns: - single-action trigger mechanism (SA) - match trigger made of plastic featuring option for trigger travel adjustments before discharge (using upper screw), and for overtravel (using bottom screw). The adjusting screws are set by the manufacturer - sporting hammer specially adapted for a reduced trigger pull weight - an extended magazine catch - grip panels made of walnut wood - guiding funnel made of plastic for quick inserting of the magazine into pistol's frame. Glossy blue slide, silver polycoat frame. Packaging includes 3 pcs of magazines.
Price: $1,093.00

CZ 85 COMBAT
Caliber: 9mm Luger, 16-shot magazine. Barrel: 114mm. Weight: 1000 g Length: 206 mm overall. Features: The CZ 85 Combat modification was created as an extension to the CZ 85 model in its standard configuration with some additional special elements. The rear sight is adjustable for elevation and windage, and the trigger for overtravel regulation. An extended magazine catch, elimination of the magazine brake and ambidextrous controlling elements directly predispose this model for sport shooting competitions. Characteristic features of all versions A universal handgun for both left-handers and right-handers,. The selective SA/DA firing mechanism, a large capacity double-column magazine, a comfortable grip and balance in either hand lead to good results at instinctive shooting (without aiming). Low trigger pull weight and high accuracy of fire. A long service life and outstanding reliability - even when using various types of cartridges. The slide stays open after the last cartridge has been fired, suitable for COMBAT shooting. The sights are fitted with a three-dot illuminating system for better aiming in poor visibility conditions. The COMBAT version features an adjustable rear sight by means of micrometer screws.
Price: $563.00

CZ DAN WESSON "ELITE SERIES" HAVOC
Caliber: 9mm Luger & .38 Super, 21-shot magazine capacity. Barrel: 4.25". Weight: 2.20 lbs. Length: 8" overall. Features: The HAVOC is based on an "All Steel" Hi-capacity version of the 1911 frame. It comes ready to dominate Open IPSC/USPSA division. The C-more mounting system offers the lowest possible mounting configuration possible, enabling extremely fast target acquisition. The barrel and compensator arrangement pairs the highest level of accuracy with the most effective compensator available. The combination of the all steel frame with industry leading parts delivers the most well balanced, softest shooting Open gun on the market.
Price: $4,299.00

CZ DAN WESSON "ELITE SERIES" MAYHEM
Caliber: .40 S&W, 18-shot magazine capacity. Barrel: 6". Weight: 2.42 lbs. Length: 8.75" overall. Features: The MAYHEM is based on an "All Steel" Hi-capacity version of the 1911 frame. It comes ready to dominate Limited IPSC/USPSA division or fulfill the needs of anyone looking for a superbly accurate target grade 1911. Taking weight away from where you don't want it and adding it to where you do want it was the first priority in designing this handgun. The 6" bull barrel and the tactical rail add to the static weight "good weight". We wanted a 6" long slide for the added sight radius and the enhanced pointability, but that would add to the "bad weight" so the 6" slide has been lightened to equal the weight of a 5". The result is a 6" long slide that balances and feels like a 5" but shoots like a 6". The combination of the all steel frame with industry leading parts delivers the most well balanced, softest shooting 6" limited gun on the market.
Price: $3,899.00

CZ DAN WESSON "ELITE SERIES" TITAN
Caliber: 10mm, 21-shot magazine capacity. Barrel: 4.25". Weight: 1.62 lbs. Length: 8" overall. Features: The TITAN is based on an "All Steel" Hi-capacity version of the 1911 frame. Turning the most well known defensive pistol "1911" into a true combat handgun was no easy task. The rugged HD night sights are moved forward and recessed deep in the slide yielding target accuracy and extreme durability. The Snake Scale serrations' aggressive 25 lpi checkering, and the custom competition G-10 grips ensure controllability even in the harshest of conditions. The combination of the all steel frame, bull barrel, and tactical rail enhance the balance and durability of the most formidable target grade Combat handgun on the market.
Price: $4,118.99

EAA WITNESS ELITE GOLD TEAM AUTO
Caliber: 9mm Para., 9x21, 38 Super, 40 S&W, 45 ACP. Barrel: 5.1". Weight: 44 oz. Length: 10.5" overall. Grips: Checkered walnut, competition-style. Sights: Square post front, fully adjustable rear. Features: Triple-chamber cone compensator; competition SA trigger; extended safety and magazine release; competition hammer; beveled magazine well; beavertail grip. Hand-fitted major components. Hard chrome finish. Match-grade barrel. From E.A.A. Custom Shop. Introduced 1992. Limited designed for IPSC Limited Class competition. Features include full-length dust-cover frame, funneled magazine well, interchangeable front sights. Stock (2005) designed for IPSC Production Class competition. Match introduced 2006. Made in Italy, imported by European American Armory.
Price: Gold Team $1,902.00
Price: Limited, 4.5" barrel, 18+1 capacity $1,219.00
Price: Stock, 4.5" barrel, hard-chrome finish $930.00
Price: Match, 4.75" barrel, two-tone finish $632.00

FN

FNP-45 COMPETITION
Caliber: .45 ACP caliber, 15-shot magazine. Barrel: 4.5". Weight: 33.3 ounces Length: 7-7/8" overall. Features: Ambidextrous magazine release button and slide release lever, ambidextrous frame-mounted decocking lever, single/double-action, loaded chamber indicator on external extractor, textured and checkered frame surfaces, 2 interchangeable arched and flat backstrap inserts with lanyard holes, melonite matte black stainless metal finish, integrated accessory rail, full length guide rod and flat-coil recoil spring, fiber optic front and rear sights.
Price: $962.00

FREEDOM ARMS MODEL 83 22 FIELD GRADE SILHOUETTE CLASS
Caliber: 22 LR, 5-shot cylinder. Barrel: 10". Weight: 63 oz. Length: 15.5" overall. Grips: Black micarta. Sights: Removable Patridge front blade; Iron Sight Gun Works silhouette rear, click adjustable for windage and elevation (optional adj. front sight and

hood). **Features:** Stainless steel, matte finish, manual sliding-bar safety system; dual firing pins, lightened hammer for fast lock time, pre-set trigger stop. Introduced 1991. Made in U.S.A. by Freedom Arms.
Price: Silhouette Class $1,860.00

FREEDOM ARMS MODEL 83 CENTERFIRE SILHOUETTE MODELS
Caliber: 357 Mag., 41 Mag., 44 Mag.; 5-shot cylinder. **Barrel:** 10", 9" (357 Mag. only). **Weight:** 63 oz. (41 Mag.). **Length:** 15.5", 14.5" (357 only). **Grips:** Pachmayr Presentation. **Sights:** Iron Sight Gun Works silhouette rear sight, replaceable adjustable front sight blade with hood. **Features:** Stainless steel, matte finish, manual sliding-bar safety system. Made in U.S.A. by Freedom Arms.
Price: Silhouette Models, from $1,741.65

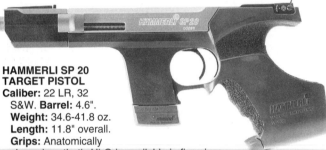

HAMMERLI SP 20 TARGET PISTOL
Caliber: 22 LR, 32 S&W. **Barrel:** 4.6". **Weight:** 34.6-41.8 oz. **Length:** 11.8" overall. **Grips:** Anatomically shaped synthetic Hi-Grip available in five sizes. **Sights:** Integral front in three widths, adjustable rear with changeable notch widths. **Features:** Extremely low-level sight line; anatomically shaped trigger; adjustable JPS buffer system for different recoil characteristics. Receiver available in red, blue, gold, violet or black. Introduced 1998. Imported from Switzerland by Larry's Guns of Maine.
Price: Hammerli 22 LR $1,539.00

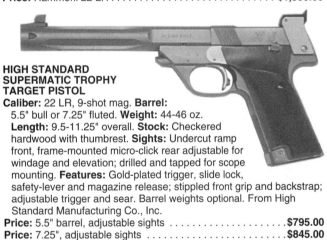

HIGH STANDARD SUPERMATIC TROPHY TARGET PISTOL
Caliber: 22 LR, 9-shot mag. **Barrel:** 5.5" bull or 7.25" fluted. **Weight:** 44-46 oz. **Length:** 9.5-11.25" overall. **Stock:** Checkered hardwood with thumbrest. **Sights:** Undercut ramp front, frame-mounted micro-click rear adjustable for windage and elevation; drilled and tapped for scope mounting. **Features:** Gold-plated trigger, slide lock, safety-lever and magazine release; stippled front grip and backstrap; adjustable trigger and sear. Barrel weights optional. From High Standard Manufacturing Co., Inc.
Price: 5.5" barrel, adjustable sights $795.00
Price: 7.25", adjustable sights $845.00

HIGH STANDARD VICTOR TARGET PISTOL
Caliber: 22 LR, 10-shot magazine. **Barrel:** 4.5" or 5.5" polished blue; push-button takedown. **Weight:** 46 oz. **Length:** 9.5" overall. **Stock:** Checkered walnut with thumbrest. **Sights:** Undercut ramp front, micro-click rear adjustable for windage and elevation. Also available with scope mount, rings, no sights.

Features: Stainless steel frame. Full-length vent rib. Gold-plated trigger, slide lock, safety-lever and magazine release; stippled front grip and backstrap; polished blue slide; adjustable trigger and sear. Comes with barrel weight. From High Standard Manufacturing Co., Inc.
Price: 4.5" or 5.5" barrel, vented sight rib, universal scope base $795.00

KIMBER SUPER MATCH II
Caliber: 45 ACP, 8-shot magazine. **Barrel:** 5". **Weight:** 38 oz. **Length:** 8.7" overall. **Grips:** Rosewood double diamond. **Sights:** Blade front, Kimber fully adjustable rear. **Features:** Guaranteed shoot 1" group at 25 yards. Stainless steel frame, black KimPro slide; two-piece magazine well; premium aluminum match-grade trigger; 30 lpi front strap checkering; stainless match-grade barrel; ambidextrous safety; special Custom Shop markings. Introduced 1999. Made in U.S.A. by Kimber Mfg., Inc.
Price: $2,225.00

KIMBER RIMFIRE TARGET
Caliber: 22 LR, 10-shot magazine. **Barrel:** 5". **Weight:** 23 oz. **Length:** 8.7" overall. **Grips:** Rosewood, Kimber logo, double diamond checkering, or black synthetic double diamond. **Sights:** Blade front, Kimber fully adjustable rear. **Features:** Bumped beavertail grip safety, extended thumb safety, extended magazine release button. Serrated flat top slide with flutes, machined aluminum slide and frame, matte black or satin silver finishes, 30 lines-per-inch checkering on frontstrap and under trigger guard; aluminum trigger, test target, accuracy guarantee. No slide lock-open after firing the last round in the magazine. Introduced 1999. Made in U.S.A. by Kimber Mfg., Inc.
Price: $833.00

RUGER MARK III TARGET MODEL AUTOLOADING PISTOL
Caliber: 22 LR, 10-shot magazine. **Barrel:** 5.5" to 6-7/8". **Weight:** 41 to 45 oz. **Length:** 9.75" to 11-1/8" overall. **Grips:** Checkered cocobolo/laminate. **Sights:** .125" blade front, micro-click rear, adjustable for windage and elevation, loaded chamber indicator; integral lock, magazine disconnect. Plastic case with lock included. Mark II series introduced 1982, discontinued 2004. Mark III introduced 2005.
Price: MKIII512 (bull barrel, blued) $417.00
Price: KMKIII512 (bull barrel, stainless) $527.00
Price: MKIII678 (blued Target barrel, 6-7/8") $417.00
Price: KMKIII678GC (stainless slabside barrel) $606.00
Price: KMKIII678H (stainless fluted barrel) $620.00
Price: KMKIII45HCL (Crimson Trace Laser Grips, intr. 2008) .$787.00
Price: KMKIII45H (2009) $620.00

SMITH & WESSON MODEL 41 TARGET
Caliber: 22 LR, 10-shot clip. **Barrel:** 5.5", 7". **Weight:** 41 oz. (5.5" barrel). **Length:** 10.5" overall (5.5" barrel). **Grips:** Checkered walnut with modified thumbrest, usable with either hand. **Sights:** 1/8" Patridge on ramp base; micro-click rear adjustable for windage and elevation. **Features:** 3/8" wide, grooved trigger; adjustable trigger stop drilled and tapped.
Price: S&W Bright Blue, either barrel $1,288.00

SMITH & WESSON MODEL 22A PISTOLS
Caliber: 22 LR, 10-shot magazine. **Barrel:** 4", 5.5" bull. **Weight:** 28-39 oz. **Length:** 9.5" overall. **Grips:** Dymondwood with ambidextrous thumbrests and flared bottom or rubber soft touch with thumbrest. **Sights:** Patridge front, fully adjustable rear. **Features:** Sight bridge

Prices given are believed to be accurate at time of publication however, many factors affect retail pricing so exact prices are not possible.

with Weaver-style integral optics mount; alloy frame, stainless barrel and slide; blue/black finish. Introduced 1997. The 22S is similar to the Model 22A except has stainless steel frame. Introduced 1997. Made in U.S.A. by Smith & Wesson.

Price: from **$308.00**
Price: Realtree APG camo finish (2008). **$356.00**

SPRINGFIELD ARMORY LEATHAM LEGEND TGO SERIES PISTOLS

Three models of 5" barrel, 45 ACP 1911 pistols built for serious competition. TGO 1 has deluxe low mount Bo-Mar rear sight, Dawson fiber optics front sight, 3.5 lb. trigger pull.
Price: TGO 1 . . . . $3,095.00

SPRINGFIELD ARMORY TROPHY MATCH PISTOL

Similar to Springfield Armory's Full Size model, but designed for bullseye and action shooting competition. Available with a Service Model 5" frame with matching slide and barrel in 5" and 6" lengths. Fully adjustable sights, checkered frame front strap, match barrel and bushing. In 45 ACP only. From Springfield Inc.
Price: **$1,573.00**

STI EAGLE 5.0, 6.0 PISTOL

Caliber: 9mm Para., 9x21, 38 & 40 Super, 40 S&W, 10mm, 45 ACP, 10-shot magazine. **Barrel:** 5", 6" bull. **Weight:** 34.5 oz. **Length:** 8.62" overall. **Grips:** Checkered polymer. **Sights:** STI front, Novak or Heinie rear. **Features:** Standard frames plus 7 others; adjustable match trigger; skeletonized hammer; extended grip safety with locator pad. Introduced 1994. Made in U.S.A. by STI International.
Price: (5.0 Eagle) **$1,940.12**
Price: (6.0 Eagle) **$1,049.98**

STI EXECUTIVE PISTOL

Caliber: 40 S&W.
Barrel: 5" bull.
Weight: 39 oz.
Length: 8-5/8".
Grips: Gray polymer. **Sights:** Dawson fiber optic, front; STI adjustable rear. **Features:** Stainless mag. well, front and rear serrations on slide. Made in U.S.A. by STI.
Price: **$2,464.00**

STI STEELMASTER

Caliber: 9mm minor, comes with one 126mm magazine. **Barrel:** 4.15". **Weight:** 38.9 oz. **Length:** 9.5" overall. **Features:** Based on the renowned STI race pistol design, the SteelMaster is a shorter and lighter pistol that allows for faster target acquisition with reduced muzzle flip and dip. Designed to shoot factory 9mm

(minor) ammo, this gun delivers all the advantages of a full size race pistol in a smaller, lighter, faster reacting, and less violent package. The Steelmaster is built on the patented modular steel frame with polymer grip. It has a 4.15" classic slide which has been flat topped. Slide lightening cuts on the front and rear further reduce weight while "Sabertooth" serrations further enhance the aesthtics of this superior pistol. It also uses the innovative Trubor compensated barrel which has been designed to eliminate misalignment of the barrel and compensator bore or movement of the compensator on the barrel. The shorter Trubor barrel system in the SteelMaster gives an even greater reduction in muzzle flip, and the shorter slide decreases overall slide cycle time allowing the shooter to achieve faster follow up shots. The SteelMaster is mounted with a C-More, 6-minute, red-dot scope with blast shield and thumb rest. Additional enhancements include aluminum magwell, stainless steel ambidextrous safeties, stainless steel high rise grip safety, STI's "Spur" hammer, STI's RecoilMaster guide rod system, and checkered front strap and mainspring housing.
Price: **$2,864.00**

STI TROJAN

Caliber: 9mm Para., 38 Super, 40 S&W, 45 ACP. **Barrel:** 5", 6". **Weight:** 36 oz. **Length:** 8.5". **Grips:** Rosewood. **Sights:** STI front with STI adjustable rear.
Features: Stippled front strap, flat top slide, one-piece steel guide rod.
Price: (Trojan 5") **$1,110.00**
Price: (Trojan 6", not available in 38 Super) **$1,419.60**

STI TRUBOR

Caliber: 9mm 'Major', 9x23, .38 Super - USPSA, IPSC. **Barrel:** 5" with integrated compensator. **Weight:** 41.3 oz. (including scope and mount) **Length:** 10.5" overall. **Features:** Built on the patented modular steel frame with polymer grip, the STI Trubor utilizes the Trubor compensated barrel which is machined from ONE PIECE of 416, Rifle Grade, Stainless Steel. The Trubor is designed to eliminate misalignment of the barrel and compensator bore or movement of the compensator along the barrel threads, giving the shooter a more consistent performance and reduced muzzle flip. True to 1911 tradition, the Trubor has a classic scalloped slide with front and rear cocking serrations on a forged steel slide (blued) with polished sides, aluminum magwell, stainless steel ambidextrous safeties, stainless steel high rise grip safety, full length guide rod, checkered front strap, and checkered mainspring housing. With mountedC-More Railway sight included with the pistol.
Price: **$2,864.00**

AWA MATEBA AUTO REVOLVER

Caliber: .357, .44 Remington Magnum, .44 S&W Special, and .454 Casull - 6-round cylinder. **Barrel:** 4", 5", 6" and 8 3/8" (In addition, their barrels can be changed with interchangeable 3", 6", 7" and 8" inch barrels). **Weight:** 2.96 lb. **Length:** 10.83" overall. **Grips:** Wood. **Sights:** Iron sights, fixed two-dot night sight **Features:** The Mateba Mo. 6 uses the recoil from firing to rotate the cylinder and cock the hammer, unlike conventional revolvers, which depend on the user physically pulling the trigger and/or cocking the hammer to actuate the weapon's mechanism of operation. The Mateba Autorevolver's barrel alignment is different from most other revolvers. The barrel is aligned with the bottom of the cylinder instead of the top. This lowers the bore sight (line of the barrel) which directs the recoil in line with the shooter's hand thereby reducing the twisting motion or "muzzle flip" of normal revolvers. The gun's entire upper assembly (barrel, cylinder and frame) are mounted on rails on the lower frame, which houses the trigger, hammer, and grip, and recoils approximately 7/8 of an inch / 22mm on firing. The rearward motion of the upper assembly cocks the hammer, and the cylinder is rotated on the forward stroke. Mateba Autorevolvers chambered in .357 Magnum can be loaded with .38 Special ammunition but typical .38 Special loads do not have enough power to fully cycle the recoil mechanism although the weapon will still function with a double action trigger pull. There are two optional recoil springs designed specifically for .38 Special cartridges that can be installed by the operator to overcome this problem (.38 Special and .38 Wadcutter). Replacing the spring requires the removal of the slide assembly, which is blocked by a retaining pin held in place by a small set screw in the triggerguard. The barrel shroud acts as the spring keeper and guide rod bushing. Finishes vary: .357 & .44 Mag. blue MSRP $1,800.00, .454 Casull blue MSRP $1,900.00 and for matte-nickel add $170.00.

Price: Defense, 4" barrel. . . . . **N/A**
Price: Home Protection, 5" barrel . . . . **N/A**
Price: Dynamic Sportiva, 5" or 6" barrel . . . . **N/A**
Price: Hunter, 8 3/8" barrel . . . . **N/A**

CHARTER ARMS BULLDOG REVOLVER

Caliber: 44 Special. **Barrel:** 2.5". **Weight:** NA. **Sights:** Blade front, notch rear. **Features:** 6-round cylinder, soft-rubber pancake-style grips, shrouded ejector rod, wide trigger and hammer spur. American made by Charter Arms, distributed by MKS Supply.
Price: Blued **$455.00**
Price: Stainless **$465.00**
Price: Target Bulldog, 4" barrel, 23 oz. **$459.00**
Price: Heller Commemortaive stainless 2.5" **$1595.00**

CHARTER ARMS CHIC LADY & CHIC LADY DAO REVOLVERS

Caliber: .38 special - 5-round cylinder. **Barrel:** 2". **Weight:** 12 oz. **Grip:** Combat. **Sights:** Fixed. **Features:** 2-tone pink & stainless with aluminum frame. American made by Charter Arms, distributed by MKS Supply.
Price: Chic Lady **$481.00**
Price: Chic Lady DAO **$492.00**

CHARTER COUGAR UNDERCOVER LITE REVOLVER

Caliber: .38 special +P - 5-round cylinder. **Barrel:** 2". **Weight:** 12 oz. **Grip:** Full. **Sights:** Fixed. **Features:** 2-tone pink & stainless with aluminum frame. Constructed of tough aircraft-grade aluminum and steel, the Undercover Lite offers rugged reliability and comfort. This ultra-lightweight 5-shot .38 Special features a 2" barrel, fixed sights and traditional spurred hammer. American made by Charter Arms, distributed by MKS Supply.
Price: **$443.00**

CHARTER ARMS CRIMSON UNDERCOVER REVOLVER

Caliber: .38 special +P - 5-round cylinder. **Barrel:** 2". **Weight:** 16 oz. **Grip:** Crimson Trace™. **Sights:** Fixed. **Features:** Stainless finish & frame. American made by Charter Arms, distributed by MKS Supply.
Price: **$636.00**

CHARTER ARMS OFF DUTY REVOLVER

Caliber: 38 Spec. **Barrel:** 2". **Weight:** 12.5 oz. **Sights:** Blade front, notch rear. **Features:** 5-round cylinder, aluminum casting, DAO. American made by Charter Arms, distributed by MKS Supply.
Price: Aluminum **$438.00**

CHARTER ARMS MAG PUG REVOLVER

Caliber: 357 Mag. **Barrel:** 2.2". **Weight:** 23 oz. **Sights:** Blade front, notch rear. **Features:** Five-round cylinder. American made by Charter Arms, distributed by MKS Supply.
Price: Blued or stainless **$409.00**

CHARTER PANTHER BRONZE & BLACK CAMO STANDARD REVOLVER

Caliber: .22 Mag.- 5-round cylinder. **Barrel:** 1-1/8". **Weight:** 6 oz. **Grip:** Compact. **Sights:** Fixed. **Features:** 2-tone bronze & black with aluminum frame. Constructed of tough aircraft-grade aluminum and steel, the Undercover Lite offers rugged reliability and comfort. This ultra-lightweight 5-shot .38 Special features a 2" barrel, fixed sights and traditional spurred hammer. American made by Charter Arms, distributed by MKS Supply.
Price: **$443.00**

CHARTER ARMS PINK LADY REVOLVER

Caliber: 32 H&R Magnum, 38 Special +P. **Barrel:** 2". **Weight:** 12 oz. **Grips:** Rubber Pachmayr-style. **Sights:** Fixed. **Features:** Snubnose, five-round cylinder. Pink anodized aluminum alloy frame.
Price: **$438.00**
Price: Lavender Lady, lavender frame **$438.00**
Price: Goldfinger, gold anodized frame, matte black barrel and cylinder assembly **$438.00**

CHARTER ARMS SOUTHPAW REVOLVER

Caliber: 38 Special +P. **Barrel:** 2". **Weight:** 12 oz. **Grips:** Rubber Pachmayr-style. **Sights:** NA. **Features:** Snubnose, five-round cylinder, matte black aluminum alloy frame with stainless steel cylinder. Cylinder latch and crane assembly are on right side of frame for convenience to left-hand shooters.
Price: **$469.00**

CHARTER ARMS TARGET PATHFINDER COMBO REVOLVER

Caliber: .22 LR / .22 Mag. - 6-round cylinder. **Barrel:** 4". **Weight:** 20 oz. **Grip:** Full. **Sights:** Fixed. **Features:** Stainless finish & frame. Charter's Target Pathfinder is a great introductory revolver for the novice shooter. It has the look, feel and weight of a higher-caliber revolver, allowing you to gain proficiency while using relatively inexpensive .22 ammo. Part of the fun of shooting is doing it well, and proficiency requires practice. That's why Charter makes target configurations, with 4" barrels and precision sights. American made by Charter Arms, distributed by MKS Supply.
Price: **$548.00**

CHARTER ARMS UNDERCOVER REVOLVER

Caliber: **Barrel:** 2". **Weight:** 12 oz. **Sights:** Blade front, notch rear. **Features:** 6-round cylinder. American made by Charter Arms, distributed by MKS Supply.
Price: Blued **$438.00**

     Prices given are believed to be accurate at time of publication however, many factors affect retail pricing so exact prices are not possible.

CHARTER ARMS UNDERCOVER SOUTHPAW REVOLVER
Caliber: 38 Spec. +P. **Barrel:** 2". **Weight:** 12 oz. **Sights:** NA.
Features: Cylinder release is on the right side and the cylinder opens to the right side. Exposed hammer for both single and double-action firing. 5-round cylinder. American made by Charter Arms, distributed by MKS Supply.
Price: Blued $469.00

CHARTER ARMS UNDERCOVER LITE, RED & BLACK STANDARD REVOLVER
Caliber: .38 special +P - 5-round cylinder. **Barrel:** 2". **Weight:** 12 oz.
Grip: Standard. **Sights:** Fixed. **Features:** 2-tone red & black with aluminum frame. American made by Charter Arms, distributed by MKS Supply.
Price: $422.00

CHIAPPA RHINO
Ugly-as-hell revolver chambered in .357 Magnum. Features include 2-, 4-, 5- or 6-inch barrel; fixed or adjustable sights; visible hammer or hammerless design. Weight 24 to 33 oz. Walnut or synthetic grips with black frame; hexagonal-shaped cylinder. Unique design fires from bottom chamber of cylinder.
Price: . . . . **N/A**

COMANCHE I, II, III DA REVOLVERS
Caliber: 22 LR, 9 shot. 38 Spec., 6 shot. 357 Mag, 6 shot. **Barrel:** 6", 22 LR; 2" and 4", 38 Spec.; 2" and 3", 357 Mag.
Weight: 39 oz. **Length:** 10.8" overall.
Grips: Rubber. **Sights:** Adjustable rear.
Features: Blued or stainless. Distributed by SGS Importers.
Price: I Blue $236.95
Price: I Alloy $258.95
Price: II 38 Spec., 3" bbl., 6-shot, stainless, intr. 2006 . . . .$236.95
Price: II 38 Spec., 4" bbl., 6-shot, stainless $219.95
Price: III 357 Mag, 3" bbl., 6-shot, blue $253.95
Price: III 357 Mag, 4" bbl., 6-shot, blue $274.95

EAA WINDICATOR REVOLVERS
Caliber: 38 Spec., 6-shot; 357 Mag., 6-shot. **Barrel:** 2", 4".
Weight: 30 oz. (4"). **Length:** 8.5" overall (4" bbl.). **Grips:** Rubber with finger grooves. **Sights:** Blade front, fixed or adjustable on rimfires; fixed only on 32, 38. **Features:** Swing-out cylinder; hammer block safety; blue finish. Introduced 1991. Imported from Germany by European American Armory.
Price: 38 Spec. 2" barrel, alloy frame $277.00
Price: 38 Spec. 4" barrel, alloy frame $292.00
Price: 357 Mag, 2" barrel, steel frame $292.00
Price: 357 Mag, 4" barrel, steel frame $311.00

KORTH USA REVOLVERS
Caliber: 22 LR, 22 WMR, 32 S&W Long, 38 Spec., 357 Mag., 9mm Para. **Barrel:** 3", 4", 5.25", 6". **Weight:** 36-52 oz. Grips, Combat, Sport: Walnut, Palisander, Amboinia, Ivory. Grips, Target: German Walnut, matte with oil finish, adjustable ergonomic competition style. **Sights:** Adjustable Patridge (Sport) or Baughman (Combat), interchangeable and adjustable rear w/Patridge front (Target) in blue and matte. **Features:** DA/SA, 3 models, over 50 configurations, externally adjustable trigger stop and weight, interchangeable cylinder, removable wide-milled trigger shoe on Target model. Deluxe models are highly engraved editions. Available finishes include high polish blue finish, plasma coated in high polish or matted silver, gold, blue, or charcoal. Many deluxe options available.

6-shot. From Korth USA.
Price: From $8,000.00
Price: Deluxe Editions, from $12,000.00

ROSSI R461/R462
Caliber: .357 Mag. **Barrel:** 2". **Weight:** 26-35 oz. **Grips:** Rubber.
Sights: Fixed. **Features:** DA/SA, +P rated frame, blue carbon or high polish stainless steel, patented Taurus Security System, 6-shot.
Price: From $352.00

ROSSI MODEL R351/R352/R851 REVOLVERS
Caliber: .38 Spec. **Barrel:** 2" (R35), 4" (R851).
Weight: 24-32 oz. **Grips:** Rubber.
Sights: Fixed (R35), Fully Adjustable (R851). **Features:** DA/SA, 3 models available, +P rated frame, blue carbon or high polish stainless steel, patented Taurus Security System, 5-shot (R35) 6-shot (R851).
Price: From **$352.00**

ROSSI MODEL R971/R972 REVOLVERS
Caliber: 357 Mag. +P, 6-shot. **Barrel:** 4", 6". **Weight:** 32 oz. **Length:** 8.5" or 10.5" overall. **Grips:** Rubber.
Sights: Blade front, adjustable rear. **Features:** Single/double action. Patented key-lock Taurus Security System; forged steel frame. Introduced 2001. Made in Brazil by Amadeo Rossi. Imported by BrazTech/Taurus.
Price: Model R971 (blued finish, 4" bbl.) $406.00
Price: Model R972 (stainless steel finish, 6" bbl.) $460.00

ROSSI MODEL 851
Similar to Model R971/R972, chambered for 38 Spec. +P. Blued finish, 4" barrel. Introduced 2001. Made in Brazil by Amadeo Rossi. From BrazTech/Taurus.
Price: $352.00

RUGER GP-100 REVOLVERS
Caliber: 327 Federal, 38 Spec. +P, 357 Mag., 6-shot.
Barrel: 3" full shroud, 4" full shroud, 6" full shroud.

Weight: 3" full shroud-36 oz., 4" full shroud-38 oz. **Sights:** Fixed; adjustable on 4" full shroud, all 6" barrels. **Grips:** Ruger Santoprene Cushioned Grip with Goncalo Alves inserts. **Features:** Uses action, frame features of both the Security-Six and Redhawk revolvers. Full length, short ejector shroud. Satin blue and stainless steel.

Price: GP-141 (357, 4" full shroud, adj. sights, blue) **$616.00**
Price: GP-161 (357, 6" full shroud, adj. sights, blue), 46 oz. . . **$616.00**
Price: KGP-141 (357, 4" full shroud, adj. sights, stainless) . . . **$680.00**
Price: KGP-161 (357, 6" full shroud, adj. sights, stainless)
46 oz. **$680.00**
Price: KGPF-331 (357, 3" full   shroud, stainless) **$659.00**

RUGER LCR REVOLVER

Caliber: .38 Special and .357 Mag., 5-shot cylinder. **Barrel:** 1-7/8". **Weight:** 13.5 oz. –17.10 oz. **Length:** 6-1/2" overall. **Grips:** Hogue® Tamer™ or Crimson Trace® Lasergrips® . **Sights:** Pinned ramp front, U-notch integral rear. **Features:** The Ruger Lightweight Compact Revolver (LCR), a 13.5 ounce, small frame revolver with a smooth, easy-to-control trigger and highly manageable recoil. Packed with the latest technological advances and features required by today's most demanding shooters.

Price: .38 Special, XS® Standard Dot Tritium **$575.00**
Price: .357 Mag., Replaceable, Pinned Ramp **$575.00**
Price: .38 Special, Pinned Ramp **$525.00**
Price: .38 Special, Replaceable, Pinned Ramp **$792.00**

RUGER SP-101 REVOLVERS

Caliber: 327 Federal, 6-shot; 38 Spec. +P, 357 Mag., 5-shot. **Barrel:** 2.25", 3-1/16". **Weight:** (38 & 357 mag models) 2.25"-25 oz.; 3-1/16"-27 oz. **Sights:** Adjustable on 327, fixed on others. **Grips:** Ruger Cushioned Grip with inserts. **Features:** Compact, small frame, double-action revolver. Full-length ejector shroud. Stainless steel only. Introduced 1988.

Price: KSP-321X (2.25", 357 Mag.) **$589.00**
Price: KSP-331X (3-1/16", 357 Mag.) **$589.00**
Price: KSP-821X (2.25", 38 Spec.) **$589.00**
Price: KSP-32731X (3-1/16", 327 Federal, intr. 2008) **$589.00**
Price: KSP-321X-LG (Crimson Trace Laser Grips, intr. 2008) . **$839.00**

RUGER SP-101 DOUBLE-ACTION-ONLY REVOLVER

Similar to standard SP-101 except double-action-only with no single-action sear notch. Spurless hammer, floating firing pin and transfer bar safety system. Available with 2.25" barrel in 357 Mag. Weighs 25 oz., overall length 7". Natural brushed satin, high-polish stainless steel. Introduced 1993.
Price: KSP321XL (357 Mag.) **$589.00**
Price: KSP321XL-LG (357 Mag., Crimson Trace Laser Grips,
intr. 2008) **$839.00**

RUGER REDHAWK

Caliber: 44 Rem. Mag., 45 Colt, 6-shot. **Barrel:** 4", 5.5", 7.5". **Weight:** About 54 oz. (7.5" bbl.). **Length:** 13" overall (7.5" barrel). **Grips:** Square butt cushioned grip panels. **Sights:** Interchangeable Patridge-type front, rear adjustable for windage and elevation. **Features:** Stainless steel, brushed satin finish, blued ordnance

steel. 9.5" sight radius. Introduced 1979.
Price: KRH-44, stainless, 7.5" barrel **$861.00**
Price: KRH-44R, stainless 7.5" barrel w/scope mount **$915.00**
Price: KRH-445, stainless 5.5" barrel **$861.00**
Price: KRH-444, stainless 4" barrel (2007) **$861.00**
Price: KRH-45-4, Hogue Monogrip, 45 Colt (2008) **$861.00**

RUGER SUPER REDHAWK REVOLVER

Caliber: 44 Rem. Mag., 45 Colt, 454 Casull, 480 Ruger, 5 or 6-shot. **Barrel:** 2.5", 5.5", 7.5", 9.5". **Weight:** About 54 oz. (7.5" bbl.). **Length:** 13" overall (7.5" barrel). **Grips:** Hogue Tamer Monogrip. **Features:** Similar to standard Redhawk except has heavy extended frame with Ruger Integral Scope Mounting System on wide topstrap. Wide hammer spur lowered for better scope clearance. Incorporates mechanical design features and improvements of GP-100. Ramp front sight base has Redhawk-style Interchangeable Insert sight blades, adjustable rear sight. Satin stainless steel and low-glare stainless finishes. Introduced 1987.

Price: KSRH-2454, 2.5" 454 Casull/45 Colt, Hogue Tamer
Monogrip, Alaskan Model **$992.00**
Price: KSRH-7, 7.5" 44 Mag, Ruger grip **$915.00**
Price: KSRH-7454, 7.5" 45 Colt/454 Casull **$992.00**
Price: KSRH-9, 9" 44 Mag, Ruger grip **$915.00**
Price: KSRH-9480-5, 9.5", 480 Ruger, intr. 2008 . . . . **$963.00**
Price: KSRH-2, 2.5" 44 Mag, Alaskan Model,   intr. 2008. **$992.00**

SMITH & WESSON MODEL GOVENOR™ REVOLVER

Caliber: .410 2 1/2", .45 ACP, .45 Colt; 6 rounds. **Barrel:** 2.75". **Weight:** 35 oz. (2.5" barrel). **Length:** 7.5", (2.5" barrel). **Sights:** Front: Tritium Night Sight (Dovetailed), Rear: fixed. **Grips:** Synthetic. **Finish:** Matte Black. **Weight:** 29.6 oz. **Features:** Capable of chambering a mixture of .45 Colt, .45 ACP and .410 gauge 2 ½-inch shotshells, the Governor is suited for both close and distant encounters, allowing users to customize the load to their preference. The shooter's choice of ammunition is housed in the revolver's six-shot stainless PVD-coated cylinder, which adds an extra level of protection to this already rugged platform. On top of the revolver's compact 2-3/4" barrel, Smith & Wesson has added a dovetailed Tritium front night sight for enhanced accuracy in low-light conditions, while the Governor's fixed rear sight is aptly suited for this self-defense handgun. The Governor measures 8-1/2" inches in overall length along with a width of 1-3/4". Carry ability of this revolver has been further enhanced with the Governor's unloaded weight of 29.6 ounces and standard matte black finish designed to reduce unwanted glare while adding an all-business like demeanor to this self-defense handgun. On the lower portion of the frame, the revolver will be packaged with either shock absorbing synthetic grips or with factory-installed laser grips from Crimson Trace®. Accurate, rugged and reliable, the Governor is further enhanced by Smith & Wesson's renowned smooth double-action and crisp single-action trigger pull. The new revolver will also come standard with 2-round and 6-round moon clips. Made in U.S.A. by Smith & Wesson.
Price: **$679.00**
Price: with Crimson Trace® Laser Grip **$899.00**

SMITH & WESSON MODEL 14 CLASSIC

Caliber: 38 Spec. +P, 6-shot. **Barrel:** 6". **Weight:** 35 oz. **Length:** 11.5". **Grips:** Wood. **Sights:** Pinned Patridge front, micro adjustable rear. **Features:** Recreation of the vintage Model 14 revolver. Carbon steel frame and cylinder with blued finish.
Price: **$995.00**
Price: Model 14 150253, nickel finish **$1,074.00**

SMITH & WESSON M&P REVOLVERS

Caliber: 38 Spec., 357 Mag., 5 rounds (Centennial), 8 rounds (large frame). **Barrel:** 1.87" (Centennial), 5" (large frame). **Weight:** 13.3 oz. (Centennial), 36.3 oz. (large frame). **Length:** 6.31" overall (small frame), 10.5" (large frame). **Grips:** Synthetic. **Sights:** Integral U-Notch rear, XS Sights 24/7 Tritium Night. **Features:** Scandium alloy frame, stainless steel cylinder, matte black finish. Made in U.S.A. by Smith & Wesson.
Price: M&P 340, double action **$869.00**
Price: M&P 340CT, Crimson Trace Lasergrips. **$1,122.00**
Price: M&P R8 large frame.......................... **$1,311.00**

SMITH & WESSON NIGHT GUARD REVOLVERS

Caliber: 357 Mag., 38 Spec. +P, 5-, 6-, 7-, 8-shot. **Barrel:** 2.5 or 2.75" (45 ACP). **Weight:** 24.2 oz. (2.5" barrel). **Length:** 7.325" overall (2.5" barrel). **Grips:** Pachmayr Compac Custom. **Sights:** XS Sight 24/7 Standard Dot Tritium front, Cylinder & Slide Extreme Duty fixed rear. **Features:** Scandium alloy frame, stainless PVD cylinder, matte black finish. Introduced 2008. Made in U.S.A. by Smith & Wesson.
Price: Model 310, 10mm/40 S&W (interchangeable), 2.75" barrel, large-frame snubnose **$1,153.00**
Price: Model 315, 38 Special +P, 2.5" barrel, medium-frame snubnose **$995.00**
Price: Model 325, 45 ACP, 2.75" barrel, large-frame snubnose **$1,153.00**
Price: Model 327, 38/357, 2.5" barrel, large-frame snubnose **$1,153.00**
Price: Model 329, 44 Magnum/38 Special (interchangeable), 2.5" barrel, large-frame snubnose **$1,153.00**
Price: Model 357, 41 Magnum, 2.75" barrel, large-frame snubnose **$1,153.00**
Price: Model 386, 357 Magnum/44 Special +P (interchangeable), 2.5" barrel, medium-frame snubnose. **$1,074.00**
Price: Model 396, 44 Special, 2.5" barrel, medium-frame snubnose **$1,074.00**

SMITH & WESSON J-FRAME REVOLVERS

The smallest S&W wheelguns come in a variety of chamberings, barrel lengths, and materials, as noted in the individual model listings.

SMITH & WESSON 60LS/642LS LADYSMITH REVOLVERS

Caliber: .38 Spec. +P, 357 Mag., 5-shot. **Barrel:** 1-7/8" (642LS); 2-1/8" (60LS) **Weight:** 14.5 oz. (642LS); 21.5 oz. (60LS); **Length:** 6.6" overall (60LS); . **Grips:** Wood. **Sights:** Black blade, serrated ramp front, fixed notch rear. **Features:** 60LS model has a Chiefs Special-style frame. 642LS has Centennial-style frame, frosted matte finish, smooth combat wood grips. Introduced 1996. Comes in a fitted carry/storage case. Introduced 1989. Made in U.S.A. by Smith & Wesson.
Price: From **$782.00**

SMITH & WESSON MODEL 63

Caliber: 22 LR, 8-shot. **Barrel:** 5". **Weight:** 28.8 oz. **Length:** 9.5" overall. **Grips:** Black rubber. **Sights:** Black ramp front sight, adjustable black blade rear sight. **Features:** Stainless steel construction throughout. Made in U.S.A. by Smith & Wesson.
Price: **$845.00**

SMITH & WESSON MODEL 442/637/638/642 AIRWEIGHT REVOLVERS

Caliber: 38 Spec. +P, 5-shot. **Barrel:** 1-7/8", 2-1/2". **Weight:** 15 oz. (37, 442); 20 oz. (3); 21.5 oz.; **Length:** 6-3/8" overall. **Grips:** Soft rubber. **Sights:** Fixed, serrated ramp front, square notch rear. **Features:** Aluminum-alloy

frames. Models 37, 637; Chiefs Special-style frame with exposed hammer. Introduced 1996. Models 442, 642; Centennial-style frame, enclosed hammer. Model 638, Bodyguard style, shrouded hammer. Comes in a fitted carry/storage case. Introduced 1989. Made in U.S.A. by Smith & Wesson.
Price: From **$600.00**

SMITH & WESSON MODELS 637 CT/638 CT/642 CT

Similar to Models 637, 638 and 642 but with Crimson Trace Laser Grips.
Price: **$920.00**

SMITH & WESSON MODEL 60 CHIEF'S SPECIAL

Caliber: 357 Mag., 38 Spec. +P, 5-shot.
Barrel: 2-1/8", 3" or 5". **Weight:** 22.5 oz. (2-1/8" barrel). **Length:** 6-5/8" overall (2-1/8" barrel). **Grips:** Rounded butt synthetic grips. **Sights:** Fixed, serrated ramp front, square notch rear. **Features:** Stainless steel construction, satin finish, internal lock. Introduced 1965. The 5"-barrel model has target semi-lug barrel, rosewood grip, red ramp front sight, adjustable rear sight. Made in U.S.A. by Smith & Wesson.
Price: 2-1/8" barrel, intr. 2005 .... **$798.00**
Price: 3" barrel, 7.5" OAL, 24 oz. **$830.00**

SMITH & WESSON MODEL 317 AIRLITE REVOLVERS

Caliber: 22 LR, 8-shot. **Barrel:** 1-7/8", 3". **Weight:** 10.5 oz. **Length:** 6.25" overall (1-7/8" barrel). **Grips:** Rubber. **Sights:** Serrated ramp front, fixed notch rear. **Features:** Aluminum alloy, carbon and stainless steels, Chiefs Special-style frame with exposed hammer. Smooth combat trigger. Clear Cote finish. Introduced 1997. Made in U.S.A. by Smith & Wesson.
Price: Model 317, 1-7/8" barrel **$766.00**
Price: Model 317 w/HiViz front sight, 3" barrel, 7.25 OAL **$830.00**

SMITH & WESSON MODEL 340/340PD AIRLITE SC CENTENNIAL

Caliber: 357 Mag., 38 Spec. +P, 5-shot. **Barrel:** 1-7/8". **Weight:** 12 oz. **Length:** 6-3/8" overall (1-7/8" barrel). **Grips:** Rounded butt rubber. **Sights:** Black blade front, rear notch **Features:** Centennial-style frame, enclosed hammer. Internal lock. Matte silver finish. Scandium alloy frame, titanium cylinder, stainless steel barrel liner. Made in U.S.A. by Smith & Wesson.
Price: Model 340 .... **$1,051.00**
Price: Model 340PD **$1,122.00**

SMITH & WESSON MODEL 351PD REVOLVER

Caliber: 22 Mag., 7-shot. **Barrel:** 1-7/8". **Weight:** 10.6 oz. **Length:** 6.25" overall (1-7/8" barrel). **Sights:** HiViz front sight, rear notch. **Grips:** Wood. **Features:** Seven-shot, aluminum-alloy frame. Chiefs Special-style frame with exposed hammer. Nonreflective matte-black finish. Internal lock. Made in U.S.A. by Smith & Wesson.
Price: **$830.00**

SMITH & WESSON MODEL 360/360PD AIRLITE CHIEF'S SPECIAL

Caliber: 357 Mag., 38 Spec. +P, 5-shot. **Barrel:** 1-7/8". **Weight:** 12 oz. **Length:** 6-3/8" overall (1-7/8" barrel). **Grips:** Rounded butt rubber. **Sights:** Black blade front, fixed rear notch. **Features:** Chief's Special-style frame with exposed hammer. Internal

lock. Scandium alloy frame, titanium cylinder, stainless steel barrel. Made in U.S.A. by Smith & Wesson.
Price: 360PD **$988.00**

SMITH & WESSON MODEL M&P360
Single/double-action J-frame revolver chambered in .357 Magnum. Features include 3-inch barrel, 5-round cylinder, fixed XS tritium sights, scandium frame, stainless steel cylinder, matte black finish, synthetic grips.
Price: **$980.00**

SMITH & WESSON BODYGUARD® 38 REVOLVER
Caliber: .38 S&W Special +P; 5 rounds. **Barrel:** 1.9". **Weight:** 14.3 oz. **Length:** 6.6". **Grip:** Synthetic. **Sights:** Front: Black ramp, Rear: integral. **Grips:** Synthetic. **Finish:** Matte Black. **Features:** The Smith & Wesson BODYGUARD® series is the first in personal protection with integrated lasers. The BODYGUARD® 38 and BODYGUARD® 380 are uniquely engineered as the most state-of-the-art, concealable and accurate personal protection possible. Lightweight, simple to use and featuring integrated laser sights – nothing protects like a BODYGUARD.
Price: **$509.00**

SMITH & WESSON MODEL 438
Caliber: 38 Spec. +P, 5-shot. **Barrel:** 1-7/8". **Weight:** 15.1 oz. **Length:** 6.31" overall. **Grips:** Synthetic. **Sights:** Fixed front and rear. **Features:** Aluminum alloy frame, stainless steel cylinder. Matte black finish throughout. Made in U.S.A. by Smith & Wesson.
Price: **$624.00**

SMITH & WESSON MODEL 632 POWERPORT PRO SERIES
Caliber: 327 Mag., 6-shot. **Barrel:** 3". **Weight:** 24.5 oz. **Length:** 7.5". **Grips:** Synthetic. **Sights:** Pinned serrated ramp front, adjustable rear. **Features:** Full-lug ported barrel with full-length extractor. Stainless steel frame and cylinder. Introduced 2009.
Price: $980.00

SMITH & WESSON MODEL 640 CENTENNIAL DA ONLY
Caliber: 357 Mag., 38 Spec. +P, 5-shot. **Barrel:** 2-1/8". **Weight:** 23 oz. **Length:** 6.75" overall. **Grips:** Uncle Mike's Boot grip. **Sights:** Serrated ramp front, fixed notch rear. **Features:** Stainless steel. Fully concealed hammer, snag-proof smooth edges. Internal lock. Introduced 1995 in 357 Mag.
Price: $798.00

SMITH & WESSON MODEL 649 BODYGUARD REVOLVER
Caliber: 357 Mag., 38 Spec. +P, 5-shot. **Barrel:** 2-1/8". **Weight:** 23 oz. **Length:** 6-5/8" overall. **Grips:** Uncle Mike's Combat. **Sights:** Black pinned ramp front, fixed notch rear. **Features:** Stainless steel construction, satin finish. Internal lock. Bodyguard style, shrouded hammer. Made in U.S.A. by Smith & Wesson.
Price: $798.00

SMITH & WESSON MODEL 442/642/640/632 PRO SERIES REVOLVERS
Double action only J-frame with concealed hammers chambered in .38 Special +P (442 & 642), .357 Magnum (640) or .327 Federal (632). Features include 5-round cylinder, matte stainless steel frame, fixed sights or dovetail night sights (632, 640), synthetic grips, cylinder cut for moon clips (442, 642, 640).
Price: . . . **$640.00 (standard) to $916.00 (night sights)**

SMITH & WESSON K-FRAME/L-FRAME REVOLVERS
These mid-size S&W wheelguns come in a variety of chamberings, barrel lengths, and materials, as noted in individual model listings.

SMITH & WESSON MODEL 10 CLASSIC
Single/double action K frame revolver chambered in .38 Special. Features include bright blue steel frame and cylinder, checkered wood grips, 4-inch barrel, adjustable patridge-style sights.
Price: **$814.00**

SMITH & WESSON MODEL 48 CLASSIC
Single/double action K frame revolver chambered in .22 Magnum Rimfire (.22 WMR). Features include bright blue steel frame and cylinder, checkered wood grips, 4- or 6-inch barrel, adjustable patridge-style sights.
Price: . . . .**$1,043.00 to $1,082.00**

SMITH & WESSON MODEL 10 REVOLVER
Caliber: 38 Spec. +P, 6-shot. **Barrel:** 4". **Weight:** 36 oz. **Length:** 8-7/8" overall. **Grips:** Soft rubber; square butt. **Sights:** Fixed; black blade front, square notch rear. Blued carbon steel frame.
Price: Blue **$758.00**

SMITH & WESSON MODEL 64/67 REVOLVERS
Caliber: 38 Spec. +P, 6-shot. **Barrel:** 3". **Weight:** 33 oz. **Length:** 8-7/8" overall. **Grips:** Soft rubber. **Sights:** Fixed, 1/8" serrated ramp front, square notch rear. Model 67 (**Weight:** 36 oz. **Length:** 8-7/8") similar to Model 64 except for adjustable sights. **Features:** Satin finished stainless steel, square butt.
Price: From **$758.00**

SMITH & WESSON MODEL 617 REVOLVERS
Caliber: 22 LR, 6- or 10-shot. **Barrel:** 4". **Weight:** 41 oz. (4" barrel). **Length:** 9-1/8" (4" barrel). **Grips:** Soft rubber. **Sights:** Patridge front, adjustable rear. Drilled and tapped for scope mount. **Features:** Stainless steel with satin finish; 4" has .312" smooth trigger, .375" semi-target hammer; 6" has either .312" combat or .400" serrated trigger; .375" semi-target or .500" target hammer; 8-3/8" with .400" serrated trigger, .500" target hammer. Introduced 1990.
Price: From **$916.00**

Prices given are believed to be accurate at time of publication however, many factors affect retail pricing so exact prices are not possible.

SMITH & WESSON MODELS 620 REVOLVERS
Caliber: 38 Spec. +P; 357 Mag., 7 rounds. **Barrel:** 4". **Weight:** 37.5 oz. **Length:** 9.5". **Grips:** Rubber. **Sights:** Integral front blade, fixed rear notch on the 619; adjustable white-outline target style rear, red ramp front on 620. **Features:** Replaces Models 65 and 66. Two-piece semi-lug barrel. Satin stainless frame and cylinder. Made in U.S.A. by Smith & Wesson.
Price: $893.00

SMITH & WESSON MODEL 386 XL HUNTER
Single/double action L-frame revolver chambered in .357 Magnum. Features include 6-inch full-lug barrel, 7-round cylinder, Hi-Viz fiber optic front sight, adjustable rear sight, scandium frame, stainless steel cylinder, black matte finish, synthetic grips.
Price: $1,019.00

SMITH & WESSON MODEL 686/686 PLUS REVOLVERS
Caliber: 357 Mag., 38 S&W Special; 6 rounds. **Barrel:** 2.5", 4", 6". **Weight:** 35 oz. (2.5" barrel). **Length:** 7.5", (2.5" barrel). **Grips:** Rubber. **Sights:** White outline adjustable rear, red ramp front. **Features:** Satin stainless frame and cylinder. Plus series guns have 7-shot cylinders. Introduced 1996. Powerport (PP) has Patridge front, adjustable rear sight. Introduced early 1980s. Stock Service Revolver (SSR) intr. 2007. **Capacity:** 6. **Barrel:** 4". **Sights:** Interchangeable front, adjustable rear. **Grips:** Wood. **Finish:** Satin stainless frame and cylinder. **Weight:** 38.3 oz. **Features:** Chamfered charge holes, custom barrel w/recessed crown, bossed mainspring. High-hold ergonomic grip. Made in U.S.A. by Smith & Wesson.
Price: 686 ....$909.00
Price: Plus, 7 rounds $932.00
Price: PP, 6" barrel, 6 rounds, 11-3/8" OAL $877.00
Price: SSR $1,059.00

SMITH & WESSON MODEL 686 PLUS PRO SERIES
Single/double-action L-frame revolver chambered in .357 Magnum. Features include 5-inch barrel with tapered underiug, 7-round cylinder, satin stainless steel frame and cylinder, synthetic grips, interchangeable and adjustable sights.
Price: $1,059.00

SMITH & WESSON N-FRAME REVOLVERS
These large-frame S&W wheelguns come in a variety of chamberings, barrel lengths, and materials, as noted in the individual model listings.

SMITH & WESSON MODEL 21
Caliber: 44 Special, 6-round. **Barrel:** 4" tapered. **Weight:** NA. **Length:** NA. **Grips:** Smooth wood. **Sights:** Pinned half-moon service front; service rear. **Features:** Carbon steel frame, blued finish.
Price: $924.00

SMITH & WESSON MODEL 29 CLASSIC
Caliber: 44 Mag, 6-round. **Barrel:** 6.5". **Weight:** 48.5 oz. **Length:** 12". **Grips:** Altamont service walnut. **Sights:** Adjustable white-outline rear, red ramp front. **Features:** Carbon steel frame, polished-blued or nickel finish. Has integral key lock safety feature to prevent accidental discharges. Alo available with 3" barrel. Original

Model 29 made famous by "Dirty Harry" character created in 1971 by Clint Eastwood.
Price: $1240.00

SMITH & WESSON MODEL 329PD AIRLITE REVOLVERS
Caliber: 44 Spec., 44 Mag., 6-round. **Barrel:** 4". **Weight:** 26 oz. **Length:** 9.5". **Grips:** Wood. **Sights:** Adj. rear, HiViz orange-dot front. **Features:** Scandium alloy frame, blue/black finish.
Price: From $1,264.00

SMITH & WESSON MODEL 625/625JM REVOLVERS
Caliber: 45 ACP, 6-shot. **Barrel:** 4", 5". **Weight:** 43 oz. (4" barrel). **Length:** 9-3/8" overall (4" barrel). **Grips:** Soft rubber; wood optional. **Sights:** Patridge front on ramp, S&W micrometer click rear adjustable for windage and elevation. **Features:** Stainless steel construction with .400" semi-target hammer, .312" smooth combat trigger; full lug barrel. Glass beaded finish. Introduced 1989. "Jerry Miculek" Professional (JM) Series has .265"-wide grooved trigger, special wooden Miculek Grip, five full moon clips, gold bead Patridge front sight on interchangeable front sight base, bead blast finish. Unique serial number run. Mountain Gun has 4" tapered barrel, drilled and tapped, Hogue Rubber Monogrip, pinned black ramp front sight, micrometer click-adjustable rear sight, satin stainless frame and barrel, weighs 39.5 oz.
Price: 625JM $1,074.00

SMITH & WESSON MODEL 629 REVOLVERS
Caliber: 44 Magnum, 44 S&W Special, 6-shot. **Barrel:** 4", 5", 6.5". **Weight:** 41.5 oz. (4" bbl.). **Length:** 9-5/8" overall (4" bbl.). **Grips:** Soft rubber; wood optional. **Sights:** 1/8" red ramp front, white outline rear, internal lock, adjustable for windage and elevation. Classic similar to standard Model 629, except Classic has full-lug 5" barrel, chamfered front of cylinder, interchangeable red ramp front sight with adjustable white outline rear, Hogue grips with S&W monogram, drilled and tapped for scope mounting. Factory accurizing and endurance packages. Introduced 1990. Classic Power Port has Patridge front sight and adjustable rear sight. Model 629CT has 5" barrel, Crimson Trace Hoghunter Lasergrips, 10.5" OAL, 45.5 oz. weight. Introduced 2006.
Price: From $1,035.00

SMITH & WESSON MODEL 329 XL HUNTER
Similar to Model 386 XL Hunter but built on large N-frame and chambered in .44 Magnum. Other features include 6-round cylinder and 6.5-barrel.
Price: $1,138.00

SMITH & WESSON X-FRAME REVOLVERS
These extra-large X-frame S&W wheelguns come in a variety of chamberings, barrel lengths, and materials, as noted in individual model listings.

SMITH & WESSON MODEL 500 REVOLVERS
Caliber: 500 S&W Mag., 5 rounds. **Barrel:** 4", 8-3/8". **Weight:** 72.5 oz. **Length:** 15" (8-3/8" barrel). **Grips:** Hogue Sorbothane Rubber. **Sights:** Interchangeable blade, front, adjustable rear. **Features:** Recoil compensator, ball detent cylinder

latch, internal lock. 6.5"-barrel model has orange-ramp dovetail Millett front sight, adjustable black rear sight, Hogue Dual Density Monogrip, .312" chrome trigger with over-travel stop, chrome teardrop hammer, glassbead finish. 10.5"-barrel model has red ramp front sight, adjustable rear sight, .312 chrome trigger with overtravel stop, chrome tear drop hammer with pinned sear, hunting sling. Compensated Hunter has .400 orange ramp dovetail front sight, adjustable black blade rear sight, Hogue Dual Density Monogrip, glassbead finish w/black clear coat. Made in U.S.A. by Smith & Wesson.

Price: From $1,375.00

SMITH & WESSON MODEL 460V REVOLVERS

Caliber: 460 S&W Mag., 5-shot. Also chambers 454 Casull, 45 Colt. **Barrel:** 8-3/8" gain-twist rifling. **Weight:** 62.5 oz. **Length:** 11.25". **Grips:** Rubber. **Sights:** Adj. rear, red ramp front. **Features:** Satin stainless steel frame and cylinder, interchangeable compensator. 460XVR (X-treme Velocity Revolver) has black blade front sight with interchangeable green Hi-Viz tubes, adjustable rear sight. 7.5"-barrel version has Lothar-Walther barrel, 360-degree recoil compensator, tuned Performance Center action, pinned sear, integral Weaver base, non-glare surfaces, scope mount accessory kit for mounting full-size scopes, flashed-chromed hammer and trigger, Performance Center gun rug and shoulder sling. Interchangeable Hi-Viz green dot front sight, adjustable black rear sight, Hogue Dual Density Monogrip, matte-black frame and shroud finish with glass-bead cylinder finish, 72 oz. Compensated Hunter has tear drop chrome hammer, .312 chrome trigger, Hogue Dual Density Monogrip, satin/matte stainless finish, HiViz interchangeable front sight, adjustable black rear sight. XVR introduced 2006.

Price: 460V $1,446.00
Price: 460XVR, from $1,446.00

SUPER SIX CLASSIC BISON BULL

Caliber: 45-80 Government, 6-shot. **Barrel:** 10" octagonal with 1:14 twist. **Weight:** 6 lbs. **Length:** 17.5"overall. **Grips:** NA. **Sights:** Ramp front sight with dovetailed blade, click-adjustable rear. **Features:** Manganese bronze frame. Integral scope mount, manual crossbolt safety.

Price: .... Appx. $1,100.00

TAURUS MODEL 17 "TRACKER"

Caliber: 17 HMR, 7-shot. **Barrel:** 6.5". **Weight:** 45.8 oz. **Grips:** Rubber. **Sights:** Adjustable. **Features:** Double action, matte stainless, integral key-lock.

Price: From $453.00

TAURUS MODEL 44 REVOLVER

Caliber: 44 Mag., 6-shot. **Barrel:** 4", 6.5", 8-3/8". **Weight:** 44-3/4 oz. **Grips:** Rubber. **Sights:** Adjustable. **Features:** Double-action. Integral key-lock. Introduced 1994. New Model 44S12 has 12" vent rib barrel. Imported from Brazil by Taurus International Manufacturing, Inc.

Price: From..............................$633.00

TAURUS MODEL 65 REVOLVER

Caliber: 357 Mag., 6-shot. **Barrel:** 4". **Weight:** 38 oz. **Length:** 10.5" overall. **Grips:** Soft rubber. **Sights:** Fixed. **Features:** Double action, integral key-lock. Seven models for 2006 Imported by Taurus International.

Price: From $419.00

TAURUS MODEL 66 REVOLVER

Similar to Model 65, 4" or 6" barrel, 7-shot cylinder, adjustable rear sight. Integral key-lock action. Imported by Taurus International.

Price: From $469.00

TAURUS MODEL 82 HEAVY BARREL REVOLVER

Caliber: 38 Spec., 6-shot. **Barrel:** 4", heavy. **Weight:** 36.5 oz. **Length:** 9-1/4" overall (4" bbl.). **Grips:** Soft black rubber. **Sights:** Serrated ramp front, square notch rear. **Features:** Double action, solid rib, integral key-lock. Imported by Taurus International.

Price: From $403.00

TAURUS MODEL 85 REVOLVER

Caliber: 38 Spec., 5-shot. **Barrel:** 2". **Weight:** 17-24.5 oz., titanium 13.5-15.4 oz. **Grips:** Rubber, rosewood or mother-of-pearl. **Sights:** Ramp front, square notch rear. **Features:** Blue, matte stainless, blue with gold accents, stainless with gold accents; rated for +P ammo. Integral keylock. Some models have titantium frame. Introduced 1980. Imported by Taurus International.

Price: From $403.00

TAURUS PROTECTOR POLYMER

Single/double action revolver chambered in .38 Special +P. Features include 5-round cylinder; polymer frame; faux wood rubber-feel grips; fixed sights; shrouded hammer with cocking spur; blued finish; 2.5-inch barrel. Weight 18.2 oz.

Price: .... N/A

TAURUS 851 & 651 REVOLVERS

Small frame SA/DA revolvers similar to Taurus Model 85 but with Centennial-style concealed-hammer frame. Chambered in 38 Special +P (Model 851) or 357 Magnum (Model 651). Features include five-shot cylinder; 2" barrel; fixed sights; blue, matte blue, titanium or stainless finish; Taurus security lock. Overall length is 6.5". Weighs 15.5 oz. (titanium) to 25 oz. (blued and stainless).

Price: From $411.00

TAURUS MODEL 94 REVOLVER

Caliber: 22 LR, 9-shot cylinder; 22 Mag, 8-shot cylinder **Barrel:** 2", 4", 5". **Weight:** 18.5-27.5 oz. **Grips:** Soft black rubber. **Sights:** Serrated ramp front, click-adjustable rear. **Features:** Double action, integral key-lock. Introduced 1989. Imported by Taurus International.

Price: From $369.00

TAURUS MODEL 4510 JUDGE

Caliber: 3" .410/45 LC, 2.5" .410/45 LC. **Barrel:** 3", 6.5" (blued finish). **Weight:** 35.2 oz., 22.4 oz. **Length:** 7.5". **Grips:** Ribber. **Sights:** Fiber Optic. **Features:** DA/SA. Matte Stainless and Ultra-Lite Stainless finish. Introduced in 2007. Imported from Brazil by Taurus International.

Price: 4510T TrackerSS Matte Stainless $569.00
Price: 4510TKR-3B Judge $558.00
Price: 4510TKR-SSR, ported barrel, tactical rail $608.00

TAURUS JUDGE PUBLIC DEFENDER POLYMER

Single/double action revolver chambered in .45 Colt/.410 (2-1/2). Features include 5-round cylinder; polymer frame; Ribber rubber-feel grips; fiber-optic front sight; adjustable rear sight; blued or stainless cylinder; shrouded hammer with cocking spur; blued finish; 2.5-inch barrel. Weight 27 oz.

Price: .... N/A

TAURUS JUDGE PUBLIC DEFENDER ULTRA-LITE

Single/double action revolver chambered in .45 Colt/.410 (2-1/2).

Prices given are believed to be accurate at time of publication however, many factors affect retail pricing so exact prices are not possible.

Features include 5-round cylinder; lightweight aluminum frame; Ribber rubber-feel grips; fiber-optic front sight; adjustable rear sight; blued or stainless cylinder; shrouded hammer with cocking spur; blued finish; 2.5-inch barrel. Weight 20.7 oz.
Price: . . . . **N/A**

TAURUS RAGING JUDGE MAGNUM
Single/double action revolver chambered for .454 Casull, .45 Colt, 2.5-inch and 3-inch .410. Features include 3- or 6-inch barrel; fixed sights with fiber-optic front; blued or stainless steel finish; vent rib for scope mounting (6-inch only); cushioned Raging Bull grips.
Price: . . . . **N/A**

TAURUS RAGING JUDGE MAGNUM ULTRA-LITE
Single/double action revolver chambered for .454 Casull, .45 Colt, 2.5-inch and 3-inch .410. Features include 3- or 6-inch barrel; aluminum alloy frame; fixed sights with fiber-optic front; blued or stainless steel finish; cushioned Raging Bull grips. Weight: 41.4 oz. (3-inch barrel).
Price: . . . . **N/A**

TAURUS RAGING BULL MODEL 416
Caliber: 41 Magnum, 6-shot. **Barrel:** 6.5". **Weight:** 61.9 oz. **Grips:** Rubber. **Sights:** Adjustable. **Features:** Double-action, ported, ventilated rib, matte stainless, integral key-lock.
Price: **$706.00**

TAURUS MODEL 425 TRACKER REVOLVERS
Caliber: 357 Mag., 7-shot; 41 Mag., 5-shot. **Barrel:** 4" and 6". **Weight:** 28.8-40 oz. (titanium) 24.3-28. (6"). **Grips:** Rubber. **Sights:** Fixed front, adjustable rear. **Features:** Double-action stainless steel, Shadow Gray or Total Titanium; vent rib (steel models only); integral key-lock action. Imported by Taurus International.
Price: From **$569.00**

TAURUS MODEL 444 ULTRA-LIGHT
Caliber: 44 Mag, 5-shot. **Barrel:** 4". **Weight:** 28.3 oz. **Length:** 9.8"overall. **Grips:** Cushioned inset rubber. **Sights:** Fixed red-fiber optic front, adjustable rear. **Features:** UltraLite titanium blue finish, titanium/alloy frame built on Raging Bull design. Smooth trigger shoe, 1.760" wide, 6.280" tall. Barrel rate of twist 1:16", 6 grooves. Introduced 2005. Imported by Taurus International.
Price: **$666.00**

TAURUS MODEL 416/444/454 RAGING BULL REVOLVERS
Caliber: 41 Mag., 44 Mag., 454 Casull. **Barrel:** 2.25" (454 Casull only), 5", 6.5", 8-3/8". **Weight:** 53-63 oz. **Length:** 12" overall (6.5" barrel). **Grips:** Soft black rubber. **Sights:** Patridge front, adjustable rear. **Features:** Double-action, ventilated rib, ported, integral key-lock. Introduced 1997. Imported by Taurus International.
Price: From **$641.00**

TAURUS MODEL 605 REVOLVER
Caliber: 357 Mag., 5-shot. **Barrel:** 2". **Weight:** 24 oz. **Grips:** Rubber. **Sights:** Fixed. **Features:** Double-action, blue or stainless or titanium, concealed hammer models DAO, porting optional, integral key-lock. Introduced 1995. Imported by Taurus International.
Price: From **$403.00**

TAURUS MODEL 608 REVOLVER
Caliber: 357 Mag. 38 Spec., 8-shot. **Barrel:** 4", 6.5", 8-3/8". **Weight:** 44-57 oz. **Length:** 9-3/8" overall. **Grips:** Soft black rubber. **Sights:** Adjustable. **Features:** Double-action, integral key-lock action. Available in blue or stainless. Introduced 1995. Imported by Taurus International.
Price: From **$584.00**

TAURUS MODEL 617 REVOLVER
Caliber: 357 Mag., 7-shot. **Barrel:** 2". **Weight:** 28.3 oz. **Length:** 6.75" overall. **Grips:** Soft black rubber. **Sights:** Fixed. **Features:** Double-action, blue, Shadow Gray, bright spectrum blue or matte stainless steel, integral key-lock. Available with porting, concealed hammer. Introduced 1998. Imported by Taurus International.
Price: **$436.00**

TAURUS MODEL 650 CIA REVOLVER
Caliber: 357 Mag., 5-shot. **Barrel:** 2". **Weight:** 24.5 oz. **Grips:** Rubber. **Sights:** Ramp front, square notch rear. **Features:** Double-action only, blue or matte stainless steel, integral key-lock, internal hammer. Introduced 2001. From Taurus International.
Price: From **$411.00**

TAURUS MODEL 651 PROTECTOR REVOLVER
Caliber: 357 Mag., 5-shot. **Barrel:** 2". **Weight:** 17-24.5 oz. **Grips:** Rubber. **Sights:** Fixed. **Features:** Concealed single-action/double-action design. Shrouded cockable hammer, blue, matte stainless, Shadow Gray, Total Titanium, integral key-lock. Made in Brazil. Imported by Taurus International Manufacturing, Inc.
Price: From **$411.00**

TAURUS MODEL 731 REVOLVER
Similar to the Taurus Model 605, except in .32 Magnum.
Price: **$469.00**

TAURUS MODEL 817 ULTRA-LITE REVOLVER
Caliber: 38 Spec., 7-shot. **Barrel:** 2". **Weight:** 21 oz. **Length:** 6.5" overall. **Grips:** Soft rubber. **Sights:** Fixed. **Features:** Double-action, integral key-lock. Rated for +P ammo. Introduced 1999. Imported from Brazil by Taurus International.
Price: From **$436.00**

TAURUS MODEL 850 CIA REVOLVER
Caliber: 38 Spec., 5-shot. **Barrel:** 2". **Weight:** 17-24.5 oz. **Grips:** Rubber, mother-of-pearl. **Sights:** Ramp front, square notch rear. **Features:** Double-action only, blue or matte stainless steel, rated for +P ammo, integral key-lock, internal hammer. Introduced 2001. From Taurus International.
Price: From **$411.00**

TAURUS MODEL 941 REVOLVER
Caliber: 22 LR (Mod. 94), 22 WMR (Mod. 941), 8-shot. **Barrel:** 2", 4", 5". **Weight:** 27.5 oz. (4" barrel). **Grips:** Soft black rubber. **Sights:** Serrated ramp front, rear adjustable. **Features:** Double-action, integral key-lock. Introduced 1992. Imported by Taurus International.
Price: From **$386.00**

TAURUS MODEL 970/971 TRACKER REVOLVERS
Caliber: 22 LR (Model 970), 22 Magnum (Model 971); 7-shot. **Barrel:** 6". **Weight:** 53.6 oz. **Grips:** Rubber. **Sights:** Adjustable. **Features:** Double barrel, heavy barrel with ventilated rib; matte stainless finish, integral key-lock. Introduced 2001. From Taurus International.
Price: **$453.00**
Price: Model 17SS6, chambered in 17 HMR **$453.00**

BERETTA STAMPEDE SINGLE-ACTION REVOLVER

Caliber: 357 Mag, 45 Colt, 6-shot. **Barrel:** 4.75", 5.5", 7.5", blued. **Weight:** 36.8 oz. (4.75" barrel). **Length:** 9.5" overall (4.75" barrel). **Grips:** Wood, walnut, black polymer. **Sights:** Blade front, notch rear. **Features:** Transfer-bar safety. Introduced 2003. Stampede Inox (2004) is stainless steel with black polymer grips. Compact Stampede Marshall (2004) has birdshead-style walnut grips, 3.5" barrel, color-case-hardened frame, blued barrel and cylinder. Manufactured for Beretta by Uberti.

Price: Nickel, 45 Colt	$630.00
Price: Blued, 45 Colt, 357 Mag, 4.75", 5-1/2"	$575.00
Price: Deluxe, 45 Colt, 357 Mag. 4.75", 5-1/2"	$675.00
Price: Marshall, 45 Colt, 357 Mag. 3.5"	$575.00
Price: Bisley nickel, 4.75", 5.5"	$775.00
Price: Bisley, 4.75", 5.5"	$675.00
Price: Stampede Deluxe, 45 Colt 7.5"	$775.00
Price: Stampede Blued, 45 Colt 7.5"	$575.00
Price: Marshall Old West, 45 Colt 3.5"	$650.00

CHARTER DIXIE DERRINGER COMBO REVOLVER

Caliber: .38 special +P - 5-round cylinder. **Barrel:** 2". **Weight:** 12 oz. **Grip:** Compact. **Sights:** Fixed. **Features:** Stainless finish & frame. Chambered in .22 LR., .22 Magnum, or in Combo, the single action Dixie Derringer is a fun little pocket gun. It is also a lightweight revolver ideal for moderate-risk concealed carry applications. This quick-drawing pocket revolver is accurate at close range and features Charter's patent-pending hammer block safety. American made by Charter Arms, distributed by MKS Supply.

Price: $264.00

CHARTER DIXIE DERRINGER REVOLVER

Caliber: .38 special +P - 5-round cylinder. **Barrel:** 2". **Weight:** 12 oz. **Grip:** Compact. **Sights:** Fixed. **Features:** Black & stainless finish & stainless frame. Chambered in .22 Magnum, the single action Dixie Derringer is a fun little pocket gun. It is also a lightweight revolver ideal for moderate-risk concealed carry applications. This quick-drawing pocket revolver is accurate at close range and features Charter's patent-pending hammer block safety. American made by Charter Arms, distributed by MKS Supply.

Price: $221.00

CIMARRON 1872 OPEN TOP REVOLVER

Caliber: 38, 44 Special, 44 Colt, 44 Russian, 45 LC, 45 S&W Schofield. **Barrel:** 5.5" and 7.5". **Grips:** Walnut. **Sights:** Blade front, fixed rear. **Features:** Replica of first cartridge-firing revolver. Blue, charcoal blue, nickel or Original finish; Navy-style brass or steel Army-style frame. Introduced 2001 by Cimarron F.A. Co.

Price: $467.31

CIMARRON 1875 OUTLAW REVOLVER

Caliber: .357, .38 special, .44 W.C.F., .45 Colt, .45 ACP. **Barrel:** 5-1/2" and 7-1/2". **Weight:** 2.5-2.6 lbs. **Grip:** 1 piece walnut. **Features:** Standard blue finish with color case hardened frame.

Price: $559.94
Price: CA150 Dual Cyl. $665.40

CIMARRON MODEL 1890 REVOLVER

Caliber: .357, .38 special, .44 W.C.F., .45 Colt, .45 ACP. **Barrel:** 5-1/2". **Weight:** 2.4-2.5 lbs. **Grip:** 1 piece walnut. **Features:** Standard blue finish with standard blue frame.

Price: $576.28
Price: CA159 Dual Cyl. $681.73

CIMARRON BISLEY MODEL SINGLE-ACTION REVOLVERS

Similar to 1873 Model P, special grip frame and trigger guard, knurled wide-spur hammer, curved trigger. Available in 357 Mag., 44 WCF, 44 Spl., 45 Colt. Introduced 1999. Imported by Cimarron F.A. Co.

Price: From $574.43

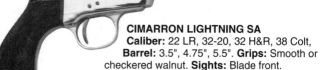

CIMARRON LIGHTNING SA

Caliber: 22 LR, 32-20, 32 H&R, 38 Colt, **Barrel:** 3.5", 4.75", 5.5". **Grips:** Smooth or checkered walnut. **Sights:** Blade front. **Features:** Replica of the Colt 1877 Lightning DA. Similar to Cimarron Thunderer, except smaller grip frame to fit smaller hands. Standard blue, charcoal blue or nickel finish with forged, old model, or color case hardened frame. Introduced 2001. From Cimarron F.A. Co.

Price: From $480.70

CIMARRON MAN WITH NO NAME REVOLVER

Caliber: .45 LC. **Barrel:** 4-3/4" and 5-1/2". **Weight:** 2.66-2.76 lbs. **Grip:** 1 piece walnut with silver rattle snake inlay in both sides. **Features:** Standard blue finish with case hardened pre-war frame. An accurate copy of the gun used by our nameless hero in the classic Western movies "Fist Full Of Dollars" & "For A Few Dollars More".

Price: $889.71

CIMARRON MODEL P

Caliber: 32 WCF, 38 WCF, 357 Mag., 44 WCF, 44 Spec., 45 Colt, 45 LC and 45 ACP. **Barrel:** 4.75", 5.5", 7.5". **Weight:** 39 oz. **Length:** 10" overall (4" barrel). **Grips:** Walnut. **Sights:** Blade front, fixed or adjustable rear. **Features:** Uses "old model" black powder frame with "Bullseye" ejector or New Model frame. Imported by Cimarron F.A. Co.

Price: From $494.09
Price: Laser Engraved, from $879.00
Price: New Sheriff, from $494.09

CIMARRON MODEL "P" JR.

Caliber: 32-20, 32 H&R, **Barrel:** 3.5", 4.75", 5.5". **Grips:** Checkered walnut. **Sights:** Blade front. **Features:** Styled after 1873 Colt Peacemaker, except 20 percent smaller. Blue finish with color case-hardened frame; Cowboy action. Introduced 2001. From Cimarron F.A. Co.

Price: $400.36

CIMARRON ROOSTER SHOOTER REVOLVER

Caliber: .357, .38 special, .45 Colt, and .44 W.C.F. **Barrel:** 4-3/4". **Weight:** 2.49-2.53 lbs. **Grip:** 1 piece orange finger grooved. **Features:** A replica of John Wayne's Colt® Single Action, used in many of his great Westerns, including his Oscar winning performance in "True Grit", where he brings thecolorful character Rooster Cogburn to life.

Price: $845.11

CIMARRON THUNDERER REVOLVER

Caliber: 357 Mag, 44 WCF, 45 Colt, 6-shot. **Barrel:** 3.5", 4.75", with ejector. **Weight:** 38 oz. (3.5" barrel). **Grips:** Smooth or checkered walnut. **Sights:** Blade front, notch rear. **Features:** Thunderer grip. Introduced 1993. Imported by Cimarron F.A. Co.

Price: Stainless $534.26

Prices given are believed to be accurate at time of publication however, many factors affect retail pricing so exact prices are not possible.

HANDGUNS—Single-Action Revolvers

CIMARRON U.S.V. ARTILLERY MODEL SINGLE-ACTION
Caliber: 45 Colt. **Barrel:** 5.5". **Weight:** 39 oz. **Length:** 11.5" overall. **Grips:** Walnut. **Sights:** Fixed. **Features:** U.S. markings and cartouche, case-hardened frame and hammer; 45 Colt only. Imported by Cimarron F.A. Co.
Price: **$547.65**

COBRA SHADOW REVOLVER
Caliber: .38 special +P- 5-round cylinder. **Barrel:** 1-7/8". **Weight:** 15 oz. **Grip:** Rosewood, black rubber, and Crimson Trace™ Laser. **Features:** The Shadow is ultra lightweight and designed for maximum protection and quick response. It features a small J-frame with a sold stainless steel cylinder and barrel. The fully enclosed hammer makes it streamlined and easy to conceal. Both men and women enjoy the ease and power of this beautiful 5 shot revolver. Custom anodied finshes include: titanium, black, red, pink, gold, and blue. Made in U.S.A. by Cobra Enterprises of Utah, Inc.
Price: .... **N/A**

COLT 175TH ANNIVERSARY SINGLE ACTION ARMY REVOLVER
Caliber: .45 Colt. **Barrel:** 4-3/4", 5-1/2",and 7-1/2". **Features:** No gun in the company's history better exemplifies the celebration of Colt's 175th Anniversary than the Single Action Army® revolver. From its innovative beginnings as the first breech-loaded revolver using self-contained metallic cartridges, the gun that became world-famous as the The Peacemaker® is honored on this momentous occasion. The Limited Edition 175th Anniversary Single Action Army® revolver, exclusively from the Colt Custom Shop, comes with a black powder style frame with all metal surfaces polished and finished in Colt Royal Blue. The guns are embellished with Selective Gold Plating and limited to the production of 175 units.
Price: **$1,495.00**

COLT NEW FRONTIER REVOLVER
Caliber: .357 Magnum, .44 Special and .45 Colt. **Barrel:** 4-3/4", 5-1/2",and 7-1/2". **Grip:** Walnut. **Features:** The legend of Colt continues in the New Frontier®, Single Action Army for 2011. From 1890 to 1898, Colt manufactured a variation of the venerable Single Action Army with a uniquely different profile. The "Flattop Target Model" was fitted with an adjustable leaf rear sight and blade front sights. Colt has taken this concept several steps further to bring shooters a reintroduction of a Colt classic. The New Frontier has that sleek flattop design with an adjustable rear sight for windage and elevation and a target ready ramp style front sight. The guns are meticulously finished in Colt Royal Blue on both the barrel and cylinder, with a case colored frame.
Price: **$1455.00**

COLT SINGLE-ACTION ARMY REVOLVER
Caliber: 357 Mag., 38 Spec., .32/20, 44-40, 45 Colt, 6-shot. **Barrel:** 4.75", 5.5", 7.5". **Weight:** 40 oz. (4.75" barrel). **Length:** 10.25" overall (4.75" barrel). **Grips:** Black Eagle composite. **Sights:** Blade front, notch rear. **Features:** Available in full nickel finish with nickel grip medallions, or Royal Blue with color case-hardened frame. Reintroduced 1992. Sheriff's Model and Frontier Six introduced 2008, available in nickel in 2010.
Price: P1540, 32-20, 4.75" barrel, color case-hardened/blued finish **$1,290.00**

Price: P1656, 357 Mag., 5.5" barrel, nickel finish **$1,490.00**
Price: P1876, 45 LC, 7.5" barrel, nickel finish **$1,490.00**
Price: P2830S SAA Sheriff's, 3" barrel, 45 LC (2008) **$1,290.00**
Price: P2950FSS Frontier Six Shooter, 5.5" barrel, 44-40 (2008) **$1,350.00**

EAA BOUNTY HUNTER SA REVOLVERS
Caliber: 22 LR/22 WMR, 357 Mag., 44 Mag., 45 Colt, 6-shot. **Barrel:** 4.5", 7.5". **Weight:** 2.5 lbs. **Length:** 11" overall (4-5/8" barrel). **Grips:** Smooth walnut. **Sights:** Blade front, grooved topstrap rear. **Features:** Transfer bar safety; 3-position hammer; hammer forged barrel. Introduced 1992. Imported by European American Armory.
Price: Blue or case-hardened, from **$392.00**
Price: Nickel **$432.00**
Price: 22 LR/22 WMR, blue **$292.00**
Price: As above, nickel **$325.00**

EMF MODEL 1873 FRONTIER MARSHAL
Caliber: 357 Mag., 45 Colt. **Barrel:** 4.75", 5-1/2", 7.5". **Weight:** 39 oz. **Length:** 10.5" overall. **Grips:** One-piece walnut. **Sights:** Blade front, notch rear. **Features:** Bright brass trigger guard and backstrap, color case-hardened frame, blued barrel and cylinder. Introduced 1998. Imported from Italy.
Price: **$485.00**

EMF HARTFORD SINGLE-ACTION REVOLVERS
Caliber: 357 Mag., 32-20, 38-40, 44-40, 44 Spec., 45 Colt. **Barrel:** 4.75", 5.5", 7.5". **Weight:** 45 oz. **Length:** 13" overall (7.5" barrel). **Grips:** Smooth walnut. **Sights:** Blade front, fixed rear. **Features:** Identical to the original Colts. All major parts serial numbered using original Colt-style lettering, numbering. Bullseye ejector head and color case-hardening on old model frame and hammer. Introduced 1990. Imported by E.M.F. Co.
Price: Old Model **$489.90**
Price: Case-hardened New Model frame **$489.90**

EMF GREAT WESTERN II EXPRESS SINGLE-ACTION REVOLVER
Same as the regular model except uses grip of the Colt Lightning revolver. Barrel lengths of 4.75". Introduced 2006. Imported by E.M.F. Co.
Price: Stainless, Ultra Ivory grips **$715.00**
Price: Walnut grips **$690.00**

EMF 1875 OUTLAW REVOLVER
Caliber: 357 Mag., 44-40, 45 Colt. **Barrel:** 7.5", 9.5". **Weight:** 46 oz. **Length:** 13.5" overall. **Grips:** Smooth walnut. **Sights:** Blade front, fixed groove rear. **Features:** Authentic copy of 1875 Remington with firing pin in hammer; color case-hardened frame, blue cylinder, barrel, steel backstrap and trigger guard. Also available in nickel, factory engraved. Imported by E.M.F. Co.
Price: All calibers **$479.90**
Price: Laser Engraved **$684.90**

EMF 1890 POLICE REVOLVER
Similar to the 1875 Outlaw except has 5.5" barrel, weighs 40 oz., with 12.5" overall length. Has lanyard ring in butt. No web under barrel. Calibers: 45 Colt. Imported by E.M.F. Co.
Price: **$489.90**

EMF 1873 GREAT WESTERN II
Caliber: .357, 45 LC, 44/40. **Barrel:** 4 3/4", 5.5", 7.5". **Weight:** 36 oz. **Length:** 11" (5.5"). **Grips:** Walnut. **Sights:** Blade front, notch rear. **Features:** Authentic reproduction of the original 2nd generation

HANDGUNS—Single-Action Revolvers

Colt single-action revolver. Standard and bone case hardening. Coil hammer spring. Hammer-forged barrel.
Price: 1873 Californian **$520.00**
Price: 1873 Custom series, bone or nickel, ivory-like grips . . **$689.90**
Price: 1873 Stainless steel, ivory-like grips **$589.90**

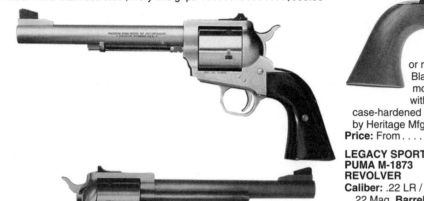

44-40, 45 LC, 22 LR, 22 LR/22 WMR combo, 6-shot. **Barrel:** 2.75", 3.5", 4.75", 5.5", 6.5", 7.5", 9". **Weight:** 31 to 38 oz. **Length:** NA. **Grips:** Exotic cocobolo laminated wood or mother-of-pearl; bird's-head models offered. **Sights:** Blade front, fixed rear. Adjustable sight on 4", 6" and 9" models. **Features:** Hammer block safety. Transfer bar with Big Bores. High polish blue, black satin, silver satin, case-hardened and stainless finish. Introduced 1993. Made in U.S.A. by Heritage Mfg., Inc.
Price: From **$169.95**

FREEDOM ARMS MODEL 83 PREMIER GRADE REVOLVER

Caliber: 357 Mag., 41 Mag., 44 Mag., 454 Casull, 475 Linebaugh, 500 Wyo. Exp., 5-shot. **Barrel:** 4.75", 6", 7.5", 9" (357 Mag. only), 10" (except 357 Mag. and 500 Wyo. Exp. **Weight:** 53 oz. (7.5" bbl. In 454 Casull). **Length:** 13" (7.5" bbl.). **Grips:** Impregnated hardwood. **Sights:** Adjustable rear with replaceable front sight. Fixed rear notch and front blade. **Features:** Stainless steel construction with brushed finish; manual sliding safety bar. Micarta grips optional. 500 Wyo. Exp. Introduced 2006. Lifetime warranty. Made in U.S.A. by Freedom Arms, Inc.
Price: From **$2,099.00**

LEGACY SPORTS PUMA M-1873 REVOLVER

Caliber: .22 LR / .22 Mag. **Barrel:** 4.75", 5.5", and 7.5". **Weight:** 2.2 lbs. - 2.4 lbs. **Grips:** Wood or plastic. **Features:** With the frame size and weight of a Single Action Army revolver, the M-1873 makes a great practice gun for Cowboy Action or an ideal carry gun for camping, hiking or fishing. The M-1873 loads from a side gate and at the half cock position just like a centerfire "Peacemaker", but is chambered for .22 LR or .22 magnum rounds. The hammer is made to traditional SAA appearance and feel. A key-operated, hammer block safety is standard on the left side of the recoil shield. The M-1873 is offered in matte black or antiqued finish. Construction is of alloy and steel.
Price: Antique/Synthetic TGT Extra Cylinder, 5.5" **$333.00**
Price: Black/Walnut TGT Extra Cylinder, 5.5". **$333.00**
Price: Antique/Synthetic TGT Extra Cylinder, 7.5" **$333.00**
Price: Black/Walnut TGT Extra Cylinder, 7.5". **$333.00**
Price: 22LR Antique/Synthetic, 4.75" **$224.00**
Price: 22LR Black/Walnut, 4.75" **$224.00**

FREEDOM ARMS MODEL 83 FIELD GRADE REVOLVER

Caliber: 22 LR, 357 Mag., 41 Mag., 44 Mag., 454 Casull, 475 Linebaugh, 500 Wyo. Exp., 5-shot. **Barrel:** 4.75", 6", 7.5", 9" (357 Mag. only), 10" (except 357 Mag. and 500 Wyo. Exp.) **Weight:** 56 oz. (7.5" bbl. In 454 Casull). **Length:** 13.1" (7.5" bbl.). **Grips:** Pachmayr standard, impregnated hardwood or Micarta optional. **Sights:** Adjustable rear with replaceable front sight. Model 83 frame. All stainless steel. Introduced 1988. Made in U.S.A. by Freedom Arms Inc.
Price: From **$1,623.00**

MAGNUM RESEARCH BFR SINGLE ACTION REVOLVER

Caliber: .45/70, .480 Ruger/.475 Linebaugh, .450 Marlin, .500 S&W, .50AE, .444 Marlin, .30/30 Winchester, .45 Long Colt/.410 (not for sale in CA), and the new .460 S&W Magnum - as well as .454 Casull. **Barrel:** 6.5", 7.5", and 10". **Weight:** 3.6 lbs. - 5.3 lbs. **Grips:** Black rubber. **Sights:** Rear sights are the same configuration as the Ruger revolvers. Many after-market rear sights will fit the BFR. Front sights are machined by Magnum in four heights and anodized flat black. The four heights accommodate all shooting styles, barrel lengths and calibers. All sights are interchangeable with each BFR's. **Features:** Crafted in the U.S.A., the BFR single action 5-shot stainless steel revolver frames are CNC machined inside and out from a "pre-heat treated" investment casting. This is done to prevent warping and dimensional changes or shifting that occurs during the heat treat process. The result is a dimensionally perfect-machined frame. Magnum Research designed the frame with large calibers and large recoil in mind, built to close tolerances to handle the pressure of true big-bore calibers. The BFR is equiped with Transfer Bar. This is a safety feature that allows the gun to be carried safely with all five chambers loaded. The transfer bar allows the revolver to fire ONLY after the hammer has been fully cocked and trigger pulled. If the revolver is dropped or the hammer slips while in the process of cocking it the gun will not accidentally discharge.
Price: **$1050.00**

FREEDOM ARMS MODEL 97 PREMIER GRADE REVOLVER

Caliber: 17 HMR, 22 LR, 32 H&R, 357 Mag., 6-shot; 41 Mag., 44 Special, 45 Colt, 5-shot. **Barrel:** 4.25", 5.5", 7.5", 10" (17 HMR, 22 LR & 32 H&R). **Weight:** 40 oz. (5.5" 357 Mag.). **Length:** 10.75" (5.5" bbl.). **Grips:** Impregnated hardwood; Micarta optional. **Sights:** Adjustable rear, replaceable blade front. Fixed rear notch and front blade. **Features:** Stainless steel construction, brushed finish, automatic transfer bar safety system. Introduced 1997. Lifetime warranty. Made in U.S.A. by Freedom Arms.
Price: From **$1,772.00**

HERITAGE ROUGH RIDER REVOLVER

Caliber: 17 HMR, 17 LR, 32 H&R, 32 S&W, 32 S&W Long, 357 Mag,

Prices given are believed to be accurate at time of publication however, many factors affect retail pricing so exact prices are not possible.

NAVY ARMS BISLEY MODEL SINGLE-ACTION REVOLVER

Caliber: 44-40 or 45 Colt, 6-shot cylinder. **Barrel:** 4.75", 5.5", 7.5". **Weight:** 40 oz. **Length:** 12.5" overall (7.5" barrel). **Grips:** Smooth walnut. **Sights:** Blade front, notch rear. **Features:** Replica of Colt's Bisley Model. Polished blue finish, color case-hardened frame. Introduced 1997. Imported by Navy Arms.
Price: **$503.00**

NAVY ARMS 1873 GUNFIGHTER SINGLE-ACTION REVOLVER

Caliber: 357 Mag., 44-40, 45 Colt, 6-shot cylinder. **Barrel:** 4.75", 5.5", 7.5". **Weight:** 37 oz. **Length:** 10.25" overall (4.75" barrel). **Grips:** Checkered black polymer. **Sights:** Blade front, notch rear.
Features: Blued with color case-hardened receiver, trigger and hammer; German Silver backstrap and triggerguard. American made Wolff trigger and mainsprings installed. Introduced 2005. Imported by Navy Arms.
Price: **$545.00**

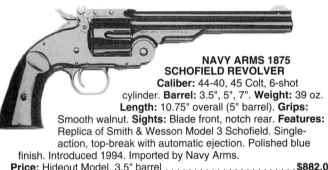

NAVY ARMS 1875 SCHOFIELD REVOLVER

Caliber: 44-40, 45 Colt, 6-shot cylinder. **Barrel:** 3.5", 5", 7". **Weight:** 39 oz. **Length:** 10.75" overall (5" barrel). **Grips:** Smooth walnut. **Sights:** Blade front, notch rear. **Features:** Replica of Smith & Wesson Model 3 Schofield. Single-action, top-break with automatic ejection. Polished blue finish. Introduced 1994. Imported by Navy Arms.
Price: Hideout Model, 3.5" barrel **$882.00**
Price: Wells Fargo, 5" barrel **$882.00**
Price: U.S. Cavalry model, 7" barrel, military markings **$882.00**

NAVY ARMS FOUNDER'S MODEL SCHOFIELD REVOLVER

Caliber: 45 Colt, 38 Spl., 6-shot cylinder. **Barrel:** 7.5". **Weight:** 41 oz. **Length:** 13.75". **Grips:** Deluxe hand-rubbed walnut with cartouching. **Sights:** Blade front, notch rear. **Features:** Charcoal blued with bone color case-hardened receiver, trigger, hammer and backstrap. Limited production "VF" serial number prefix. Introduced 2005. Imported by Navy Arms.
Price: **$924.00**

NAVY ARMS NEW MODEL RUSSIAN REVOLVER

Caliber: 44 Russian, 6-shot cylinder. **Barrel:** 6.5". **Weight:** 40 oz. **Length:** 12" overall. **Grips:** Smooth walnut. **Sights:** Blade front, notch rear. **Features:** Replica of the S&W Model 3 Russian Third Model revolver. Spur trigger guard, polished blue finish. Introduced 1999. Imported by Navy Arms.
Price: **$924.00**

NAVY ARMS SCOUT SMALL FRAME SINGLE-ACTION REVOLVER

Caliber: 38 Spec., 6-shot cylinder. **Barrel:** 4.75", 5.5". **Weight:** 37 oz. **Length:** 10.75" overall (5.5" barrel). **Grips:** Checkered black polymer. **Sights:** Blade front, notch rear. **Features:** Blued with color case-hardened receiver, trigger and hammer; German silver backstrap and triggerguard. Introduced 2005. Imported by Navy Arms.
Price: **$545.00**

NORTH AMERICAN ARMS MINI REVOLVERS

Caliber: 22 Short, 22 LR, 22 WMR, 5-shot. **Barrel:** 1-1/8", 1-5/8". **Weight:** 4 to 6.6 oz. **Length:** 3-5/8" to 6-1/8" overall. **Grips:** Laminated wood. **Sights:** Blade front, notch fixed rear. **Features:** All stainless steel construction. Polished satin and matte finish. Engraved models available. From North American Arms.
Price: 22 Short, 22 LR **$229.00**

NORTH AMERICAN ARMS MINI-MASTER

Caliber: 22 LR, 22 WMR, 5-shot cylinder. **Barrel:** 4". **Weight:** 10.7 oz. **Length:** 7.75" overall. **Grips:** Checkered hard black rubber. **Sights:** Blade front, white outline rear adjustable for elevation, or fixed. **Features:** Heavy vented barrel; full-size grips. Non-fluted cylinder. Introduced 1989.
Price: Fixed sight **$284.00**
Price: Adjustable sight **$314.00**

NORTH AMERICAN ARMS BLACK WIDOW REVOLVER

Similar to Mini-Master, 2" heavy vent barrel. Built on 22 WMR frame. Non-fluted cylinder, black rubber grips. Available with Millett Low Profile fixed sights or Millett sight adjustable for elevation only. Overall length 5-7/8", weighs 8.8 oz. From North American Arms.
Price: Adjustable sight, 22 LR or 22 WMR **$299.00**
Price: Fixed sight, 22 LR or 22 WMR **$269.00**

NORTH AMERICAN ARMS "THE EARL" SINGLE-ACTION REVOLVER

Caliber: 22 Magnum with 22 LR accessory cylinder, 5-shot cylinder. **Barrel:** 4" octagonal. **Weight:** 6.8 oz. **Length:** 7-3/4" overall. **Grips:** Wood. **Sights:** Barleycorn front and fixed notch rear. **Features:** Single-action mini-revolver patterned after 1858-style Remington percussion revolver. Includes a spur trigger and a faux loading lever that serves as cylinder pin release.
Price: . . . .**$289.00** (22 Magnum only); **$324.00** (convertible)

RUGER NEW MODEL SINGLE SIX & NEW MODEL .32 H&R SINGLE SIX REVOLVERS

Caliber: 17 HMR, 22 LR, 22 Mag. **Barrel:** 4-5/8", 5.5", 6.5", 7.5", 9.5". 6-shot. **Grips:** Rosewood, black laminate. **Sights:** Adjustable or fixed. **Features:** Blued or stainless metalwork, short grips available, convertible models available. Introduced 2003 in 17 HMR.
Price: 17 HMR (blued) **$519.00**
Price: 22 LR/22 Mag., from **$506.00**

RUGER NEW MODEL BLACKHAWK/BLACKHAWK CONVERTIBLE

Caliber: 30 Carbine, 327 Federal, 357 Mag./38 Spec., 41 Mag., 44 Special, 45 Colt, 6-shot. **Barrel:** 4-5/8", 5.5", 6.5", 7.5" (30 carbine and 45 Colt). **Weight:** 36 to 45 oz. **Lengths:** 10-3/8" to 13.5". **Grips:** Rosewood or black checkered. **Sights:** 1/8" ramp front, micro-click rear adjustable for windage and elevation. **Features:** Rosewood grips, Ruger transfer bar safety system, independent firing pin, hardened chrome-moly steel frame, music wire springs through-out. Case and

HANDGUNS—Single-Action Revolvers

lock included. Convertibles come with extra cylinder.

Price: 30 Carbine, 7.5" (BN31, blued) **$541.00**
Price: 357 Mag. (blued or satin stainless), from...............**$541.00**
Price: 41 Mag. (blued) **$541.00**
Price: 45 Colt (blued or satin stainless), from ..**$541.00**
Price: 357 Mag./9mm Para. Convertible (BN34XL, BN36XL) **$617.00**
Price: 45 Colt/45 ACP Convertible (BN44X, BN455XL) **$617.00**

RUGER BISLEY SINGLE-ACTION REVOLVER
Similar to standard Blackhawk, hammer is lower with smoothly curved, deeply checkered wide spur. The trigger is strongly curved with wide smooth surface. Longer grip frame. Adjustable rear sight, ramp-style front. Unfluted cylinder and roll engraving, adjustable sights. Chambered for 44 Mag. and 45 Colt; 7.5" barrel; overall length 13.5"; weighs 48-51 oz. Plastic lockable case. Orig. fluted cylinder introduced 1985; discontinued 1991. Unfluted cylinder introduced 1986.
Price: RB-44W (44 Mag), RB45W (45 Colt) **$683.00**

RUGER NEW MODEL SUPER BLACKHAWK
Caliber: 44 Mag., 6-shot. Also fires 44 Spec. **Barrel:** 4-5/8", 5.5", 7.5", 10.5" bull. **Weight:** 45-55 oz. **Length:** 10.5" to 16.5" overall. **Grips:** Rosewood. **Sights:** 1/8" ramp front, micro-click rear adjustable for windage and elevation. **Features:** Ruger transfer bar safety system, fluted or unfluted cylinder, steel grip and cylinder frame, round or square back trigger guard, wide serrated trigger, wide spur hammer. With case and lock.
Price: Blue, 4-5/8", 5.5", 7.5" (S-458N, S-45N, S-47N) **$650.00**
Price: Blue, 10.5" bull barrel (S-411N) **$667.00**
Price: Stainless, 4-5/8", 5.5", 7.5" (KS-458N, KS-45N, KS-47N) **$667.00**
Price: Stainless, 10.5" bull barrel (KS-411N) **$694.00**
Price: Super Blackhawk 50th Anniversary: Gold highlights, ornamentation; commemorates 50-year anniversary of Super Blackhawk **$729.00**

RUGER NEW MODEL SUPER BLACKHAWK HUNTER
Caliber: 44 Mag., 6-shot. **Barrel:** 7.5", full-length solid rib, unfluted cylinder. **Weight:** 52 oz. **Length:** 13-5/8". **Grips:** Black laminated wood. **Sights:** Adjustable rear, replaceable front blade. **Features:** Reintroduced Ultimate SA revolver. Includes instruction manual, high-impact case, set 1" medium scope rings, gun

---

lock, ejector rod as standard.
Price: Hunter model, satin stainless, 7.5" (KS-47NHNN) **$781.00**
Price: Hunter model, Bisley frame, satin stainless 7.5" (KS-47NHB) **$781.00**

RUGER NEW VAQUERO SINGLE-ACTION REVOLVER
Caliber: 357 Mag., 45 Colt, 6-shot. **Barrel:** 4-5/8", 5.5", 7.5". **Weight:** 39-45 oz. **Length:** 10.5" overall (4-5/8" barrel). **Grips:** Rubber with Ruger medallion. **Sights:** Fixed blade front, fixed notch rear. **Features:** Transfer bar safety system and loading gate interlock. Blued model color case-hardened finish on frame, rest polished and blued. Engraved model available. Gloss stainless. Introduced 2005.
Price: 357 Mag., blued or stainless **$659.00**
Price: 45 Colt, blued or stainless **$659.00**
Price: 357 Mag., 45 Colt, ivory grips, 45 oz. (2009) **$729.00**

RUGER NEW MODEL BISLEY VAQUERO
Similar to New Vaquero but with Bisley-style hammer and grip frame. Chambered in 357 and 45 Colt. Features include a 5.5" barrel, simulated ivory grips, fixed sights, six-shot cylinder. Overall length is 11.12", weighs 45 oz.
Price: **$729.00**

RUGER NEW BEARCAT SINGLE-ACTION
Caliber: 22 LR, 6-shot. **Barrel:** 4". **Weight:** 24 oz. **Length:** 9" overall. **Grips:** Smooth rosewood with Ruger medallion. **Sights:** Blade front, fixed notch rear. **Features:** Reintroduction of the Ruger Bearcat with slightly lengthened frame, Ruger transfer bar safety system. Available in blue only. Rosewood grips. Introduced 1996 (blued), 2003 (stainless). With case and lock.
Price: SBC-4, blued **$501.00**
Price: KSBC-4, satin stainless **$540.00**

STI TEXICAN SINGLE-ACTION REVOLVER
Caliber: 45 Colt, 6-shot. **Barrel:** 5.5", 4140 chrome-moly steel by Green Mountain Barrels. 1:16 twist, air gauged to .0002". Chamber to bore alignment less than .001". Forcing cone angle, 3 degrees. **Weight:** 36 oz. **Length:** 11". **Grips:** "No crack" polymer. **Sights:** Blade front, fixed notch rear. **Features:** Parts made by ultra-high speed or electron discharge machined processes from chrome-moly steel forgings or bar stock. Competition sights, springs, triggers and hammers. Frames, loading gates, and hammers are color case hardened by Turnbull Restoration. Frame, back strap, loading gate, trigger guard, cylinders made of 4140 re-sulphurized Maxell 3.5 steel. Hammer firing pin (no transfer bar). S.A.S.S. approved. Introduced 2008. Made in U.S.A. by STI International.
Price: 5.5" barrel **$1,299.99**

TAURUS SINGLE-ACTION GAUCHO REVOLVERS
Caliber: 38 Spl, 357 Mag, 44-40, 45 Colt, 6-shot. **Barrel:** 4.75", 5.5", 7.5", 12". **Weight:** 36.7-37.7 oz. **Length:** 13". **Grips:** Checkered black polymer. **Sights:** Blade front, fixed notch rear. **Features:** Integral transfer bar; blue, blue with case hardened frame, matte stainless and the hand polished "Sundance" stainless finish. Removable

428 GUN DIGEST® Prices given are believed to be accurate at time of publication however, many factors affect retail pricing so exact prices are not possible.

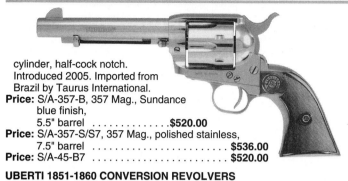

cylinder, half-cock notch.
Introduced 2005. Imported from
Brazil by Taurus International.
Price: S/A-357-B, 357 Mag., Sundance
blue finish,
5.5" barrel **$520.00**
Price: S/A-357-S/S7, 357 Mag., polished stainless,
7.5" barrel $536.00
Price: S/A-45-B7 . . . .**$520.00**

UBERTI 1851-1860 CONVERSION REVOLVERS
Caliber: 38 Spec., 45 Colt, 6-shot engraved cylinder. **Barrel:** 4.75",
5.5", 7.5", 8" **Weight:** 2.6 lbs. (5.5" bbl.). **Length:** 13" overall (5.5"
bbl.). **Grips:** Walnut. **Features:** Brass backstrap, trigger guard;
color case-hardened frame, blued barrel, cylinder. Introduced 2007.
Imported from Italy by Stoeger Industries.
Price: 1851 Navy **$519.00**
Price: 1860 Army **$549.00**

UBERTI 1871-1872 OPEN TOP REVOLVERS
Caliber: 38 Spec., 45 Colt, 6-shot engraved cylinder. **Barrel:** 4.75",
5.5", 7.5". **Weight:** 2.6 lbs. (5.5" bbl.). **Length:** 13" overall (5.5" bbl.).
Grips: Walnut. **Features:** Blued backstrap, trigger guard; color case-
hardened frame, blued barrel, cylinder. Introduced 2007. Imported
from Italy by Stoeger Industries.
Price: **$499.00**

UBERTI 1873 CATTLEMAN SINGLE-ACTION
Caliber: 45 Colt; 6-shot fluted cylinder.
Barrel: 4.75", 5.5", 7.5". **Weight:** 2.3 lbs.
(5.5" bbl.). **Length:** 11" overall (5.5" bbl.).
Grips: Styles: Frisco (pearl styled); Desperado (buffalo
horn styled); Chisholm (checkered walnut); Gunfighter
(black checkered), Cody (ivory styled), one-piece walnut.
Sights: Blade front, groove rear. **Features:** Steel or
brass backstrap, trigger guard; color case-hardened frame, blued
barrel, cylinder. NM designates New Model plunger style frame; OM
designates Old Model screw cylinder pin retainer. Imported from Italy
by Stoeger Industries.
Price: 1873 Cattleman Frisco **$789.00**
Price: 1873 Cattleman Desperado (2006) **$789.00**
Price: 1873 Cattleman Chisholm (2006) **$539.00**
Price: 1873 Cattleman NM, blued 4.75" barrel **$479.00**
Price: 1873 Cattleman NM, Nickel finish, 7.5" barrel **$609.00**
Price: 1873 Cattleman Cody. **$789.00**

UBERTI 1873 CATTLEMAN BIRD'S HEAD SINGLE ACTION
Caliber: 357 Mag., 45 Colt; 6-shot fluted cylinder **Barrel:** 3.5", 4",
4.75", 5.5". **Weight:** 2.3 lbs. (5.5" bbl.). **Length:** 10.9" overall (5.5"
bbl.). **Grips:** One-piece walnut. **Sights:** Blade front, groove rear.
Features: Steel or brass backstrap, trigger guard; color case-
hardened frame, blued barrel, cylinder. Imported from Italy by
Stoeger Industries.
Price: 1873 Cattleman Bird's Head OM 3.5" barrel **$539.00**

UBERTI 1873 BISLEY SINGLE-ACTION REVOLVER
Caliber: 357 Mag., 45 Colt (Bisley); 22 LR and 38 Spec. (Stallion),
both with 6-shot fluted cylinder. **Barrel:** 4.75", 5.5", 7.5". **Weight:** 2 to
2.5 lbs. **Length:** 12.7" overall (7.5" barrel). **Grips:** Two-piece walnut.
Sights: Blade front, notch rear. **Features:** Replica of Colt's Bisley
Model. Polished blue finish, color case-hardened frame. Introduced
1997. Imported by Stoeger Industries.
Price: 1873 Bisley, 7.5" barrel **$569.00**

UBERTI 1873 BUNTLINE AND REVOLVER CARBINE SINGLE-ACTION
Caliber: 357 Mag., 44-40, 45 Colt; 6-shot fluted cylinder **Barrel:** 18".
Length: 22.9" to 34". **Grips:** Walnut pistol grip or rifle stock. **Sights:**

Fixed or adjustable. **Features:** Imported from Italy by Stoeger
Industries.
Price: 1873 Revolver Carbine, 18" barrel, 34" OAL **$729.00**
Price: 1873 Catttleman Buntline Target, 18" barrel, 22.9" OAL **$639.00**

UBERTI OUTLAW, FRONTIER, AND POLICE REVOLVERS
Caliber: 45 Colt, 6-shot fluted cylinder. **Barrel:** 5.5", 7.5". **Weight:** 2.5
to 2.8 lbs. **Length:** 10.8" to 13.6" overall. **Grips:** Two-piece smooth
walnut. **Sights:** Blade front, notch rear. **Features:** Cartridge version
of 1858 Remington percussion revolver. Nickel and blued finishes.
Imported by Stoeger Industries.
Price: 1875 Outlaw nickel finish **$629.00**
Price: 1875 Frontier, blued finish **$539.00**
Price: 1890 Police, blued finish **$549.00**

UBERTI 1870 SCHOFIELD-STYLE TOP BREAK REVOLVER
Caliber: 38, 44 Russian, 44-40, 45 Colt, 6-shot cylinder. **Barrel:** 3.5",
5", 7". **Weight:** 2.4 lbs. (5" barrel) **Length:** 10.8" overall (5" barrel).
Grips: Two-piece smooth walnut or pearl. **Sights:** Blade front, notch
rear. **Features:** Replica of Smith & Wesson Model 3 Schofield.
Single-action, top break with automatic ejection. Polished blue finish
(first model). Introduced 1994. Imported by Stoeger Industries.
Price: No. 3-2nd Model, nickel finish **$1,369.00**

U.S. FIRE ARMS SINGLE-ACTION REVOLVER
Caliber: 45 Colt (standard); 32 WCF,
38 WCF, 38 Spec., 44 WCF, 44 Special,
6-shot cylinder. **Barrel:** 4.75", 5.5", 7.5".
Weight: 37 oz. **Length:** NA. **Grips:** Hard
rubber. **Sights:** Blade front, notch rear. **Features:**
Recreation of original guns; 3" and 4" have no
ejector. Available with all-blue, blue with color case-
hardening, or full nickel-plate finish. Other models include Custer
Battlefield Gun ($1,625, 7.5" barrel), Flattop Target ($1,625), Sheriff's
Model ($875, with barrel lengths starting at 2"), Snubnose ($1,475,
barrel lengths 2", 3", 4"), Omni-Potent Six-Shooter and Omni-Target
Six-Shooter (from $1,625), Bisley ($1,350, introduced 2006). Made in
U.S.A. by United States Fire Arms Mfg. Co.
Price: Blue/cased-colors **$875.00**
Price: Nickel **$1,220.00**

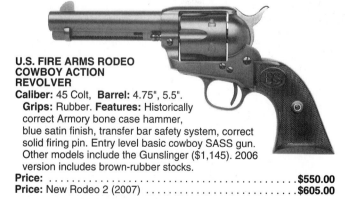

U.S. FIRE ARMS RODEO COWBOY ACTION REVOLVER
Caliber: 45 Colt, **Barrel:** 4.75", 5.5".
Grips: Rubber. **Features:** Historically
correct Armory bone case hammer,
blue satin finish, transfer bar safety system, correct
solid firing pin. Entry level basic cowboy SASS gun.
Other models include the Gunslinger ($1,145). 2006
version includes brown-rubber stocks.
Price: **$550.00**
Price: New Rodeo 2 (2007) **$605.00**

U.S. FIRE ARMS U.S. PRE-WAR
Caliber: 45 Colt (standard); 32 WCF, 38 WCF, 38 Spec., 44 WCF,
44 Special. **Barrel:** 4.75", 5.5", 7.5". **Grips:** Hard rubber. **Features:**
Armory bone case/Armory blue finish standard, cross-pin or black
powder frame. Introduced 2002. Made in U.S.A. by United States
Firearms Mfg. Co.
Price: **$1,270.00**

BOND ARMS TEXAS DEFENDER DERRINGER

Caliber: From 22 LR to 45 LC/410 shotshells. **Barrel:** 3". **Weight:** 20 oz. **Length:** 5". **Grips:** Rosewood. **Sights:** Blade front, fixed rear. **Features:** Interchangeable barrels, stainless steel firing pins, cross-bolt safety, automatic extractor for rimmed calibers. Stainless steel construction, brushed finish. Right or left hand.
Price: **$399.00**
Price: Interchangeable barrels, 22 LR thru 45 LC, 3" **$139.00**
Price: Interchangeable barrels, 45 LC, 3.5" . .**$159.00 to $189.00**

BOND ARMS RANGER

Caliber: 45 LC/.410 shotshells. **Barrel:** 4.25". **Weight:** 23.5 oz. **Length:** 6.25". **Features:** Similar to Snake Slayer except no trigger guard. Intr. 2008. From Bond Arms.
Price: **$649.00**

BOND ARMS CENTURY 2000 DEFENDER

Caliber: 45 LC/.410 shotshells. **Barrel:** 3.5". **Weight:** 21 oz. **Length:** 5.5". **Features:** Similar to Defender series.
Price: **$420.00**

BOND ARMS COWBOY DEFENDER

Caliber: From 22 LR to 45 LC/.410 shotshells. **Barrel:** 3". **Weight:** 19 oz. **Length:** 5.5". **Features:** Similar to Defender series. No trigger guard.
Price: **$399.00**

BOND ARMS SNAKE SLAYER

Caliber: 45 LC/.410 shotshell (2.5" or 3"). **Barrel:** 3.5". **Weight:** 21 oz. **Length:** 5.5". **Grips:** Extended rosewood. **Sights:** Blade front, fixed rear. **Features:** Single-action; interchangeable barrels; stainless steel firing pin. Introduced 2005.
Price: **$469.00**

BOND ARMS SNAKE SLAYER IV

Caliber: 45 LC/410 shotshell (2.5" or 3"). **Barrel:** 4.25". **Weight:** 22 oz. **Length:** 6.25". **Grips:** Extended rosewood. **Sights:** Blade front, fixed rear. **Features:** Single-action; interchangeable barrels; stainless steel firing pin. Introduced 2006.
Price: **$499.00**

CHARTER ARMS DIXIE DERRINGERS

Caliber: 22 LR, 22 WMR. **Barrel:** 1.125". **Weight:** 6 oz. **Length:** 4" overall. **Grips:** Black polymer **Sights:** Blade front, fixed notch rear. **Features:** Stainless finish. Introduced 2006. Made in U.S.A. by Charter Arms, distributed by MKS Supply.
Price: **$215.00**

COBRA BIG BORE DERRINGERS

Caliber: 22 WMR, 32 H&R Mag., 38 Spec., 9mm Para., 380 ACP. **Barrel:** 2.75". **Weight:** 14 oz. **Length:** 4.65" overall. **Grips:**

Textured black or white synthetic or laminated rosewood. **Sights:** Blade front, fixed notch rear. **Features:** Alloy frame, steel-lined barrels, steel breech block. Plunger-type safety with integral hammer block. Black, chrome or satin finish. Introduced 2002. Made in U.S.A. by Cobra Enterprises of Utah, Inc.
Price: **$165.00**

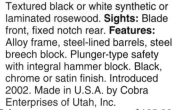

COBRA STANDARD SERIES DERRINGERS

Caliber: 22 LR, 22 WMR, 25 ACP, 32 ACP. **Barrel:** 2.4". **Weight:** 9.5 oz. **Length:** 4" overall. **Grips:** Laminated wood or pearl. **Sights:** Blade front, fixed notch rear. **Features:** Choice of black powder coat, satin nickel or chrome finish. Introduced 2002. Made in U.S.A. by Cobra Enterprises of Utah, Inc.
Price: **$145.00**

COBRA LONG-BORE DERRINGERS

Caliber: 22 WMR, 38 Spec., 9mm Para. **Barrel:** 3.5". **Weight:** 16 oz. **Length:** 5.4" overall. **Grips:** Black or white synthetic or rosewood. **Sights:** Fixed. **Features:** Chrome, satin nickel, or black Teflon finish. Introduced 2002. Made in U.S.A. by Cobra Enterprises of Utah, Inc.
Price: **$165.00**

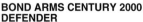

COBRA TITAN .45 LC/.410 DERRINGER

Caliber: .45 LC, .410 or 9mm, 2 round capacity. **Barrel:** 3-1/2". **Weight:** 16.4 oz. **Grip:** Rosewood. **Features:** The Titan is a powerhouse derringer designed to shoot a .45 Long Colt or the wide range of personal protection .410 shells with additional calibers to follow soon. Standard finshes include: satin stainless, black stainless, and brushed stainless. Made in U.S.A. by Cobra Enterprises of Utah, Inc.
Price: **$419.00**

COMANCHE SUPER SINGLE-SHOT PISTOL

Caliber: 45 LC, .410 **Barrel:** 10". **Sights:** Adjustable. **Features:** Blue finish, not available for sale in CA, MA. Distributed by SGS Importers International, Inc.
Price: **$200.00**

MAXIMUM SINGLE-SHOT PISTOL

Caliber: 22 LR, 22 Hornet, 22 BR, 22 PPC, 223 Rem., 22-250, 6mm BR, 6mm PPC, 243, 250 Savage, 6.5mm-35M, 270 MAX, 270 Win., 7mm TCU, 7mm BR, 7mm-35, 7mm INT-R, 7mm-08, 7mm Rocket, 7mm Super-Mag., 30 Herrett, 30 Carbine, 30-30, 308 Win., 30x39, 32-20, 350 Rem. Mag., 357 Mag., 357 Maximum, 358 Win., 375 H&H, 44 Mag., 454 Casull. **Barrel:** 8.75", 10.5", 14". **Weight:** 61 oz. (10.5" bbl.); 78 oz. (14" bbl.). **Length:** 15", 18.5" overall (with 10.5" and 14" bbl.,

Prices given are believed to be accurate at time of publication however, many factors affect retail pricing so exact prices are not possible.

respectively). **Grips:** Smooth walnut stocks and forend. Also available with 17" finger groove grip. **Sights:** Ramp front, fully adjustable open rear. **Features:** Falling block action; drilled and tapped for M.O.A. scope mounts; integral grip frame/receiver; adjustable trigger; Douglas barrel (interchangeable). Introduced 1983. Made in U.S.A. by M.O.A. Corp.

Price: Stainless receiver, blue barrel **$839.00**
Price: Stainless receiver, stainless barrel **$937.00**

PUMA BOUNTY HUNTER RIFLE

Caliber: .44/40, .44 Mag. and .45 Colt, 6-shot magazine capacity. **Barrel:** 12". **Weight:** 4.5 lbs. **Length:** 24". **Stock:** Walnut. **Sights:** Fixed sights. **Features:** A piece of 1950's TV nostalgia, the Bounty Hunter is a reproduction of the gun carried by Western character Josh Randall in the series "Wanted: Dead or Alive". The Bounty Hunter is based on a Model 92 rifle, but is considered by Federal Law as a pistol, because it is built from the ground up as a handgun. Manufactured in the U.S.A. by Chiappa Firearms of Dayton, OH, the Bounty Hunter features a 12" barrel and 6 round tubular magazine. At just 24" OAL, the Bounty Hunter makes an ideal pack gun or camp defense pistol. The Bounty Hunter has a teardrop shaped loop lever and is built with the same fit, finish and high grade Italian walnut stocks as our Puma M-92 and M-86 rifles.

Price: .45LC, Case Hardened/Blued. **$1,372.00**
Price: .44/40, Case Hardened/Blued **$1,372.00**
Price: .44MAG, Case Hardened/Blued. **$1,372.00**

ROSSI MATCHED PAIR PISTOL, "DUAL THREAT PERFORMER"

Caliber: .22LR, .45 Colt and .410 GA. 2.5" shotshells, single shot. **Sights:** Fiber optic front sights, adjustable rear. **Features:** Two-in-one pistol system with sinle-shot simplicity. Removable choke and cushioned grip with a Taurus Security System.

Price: **$336.00**

ROSSI RANCH HAND PISTOL

Caliber: .38/.357, .45 Colt or .44 magnum, 6-shot. **eight:** 4 lbs. **Length:** 24" overall. **Stock:** Brazilian hardwood. **Sights:** Adjustable buckhorn. **Features:** Matte blue or case hardened finish with

oversized lever loop to accomodate gloved hands. Equipped with classic buckhorn sights for fast target aquisition and a Taurus Security Sytem.

Price: **$615.00**

ROSSI WIZARD PISTOL

Caliber: .243 Win. or .22-.250 Rem with other calibers coming soon, single shot. **Barrel:** 11" **Length:** 20.4" **Features:** Offered in blue finish, additional features include pistol grip with custom grooves for fast handling and comfort, manual safety with "S" mark for visual confirmation, hammer extension, scope rail and the unique onboard Taurus Security System. Pistol offers outstanding and reliable performance in a versatile package. Its ingenious break-open barrel system changes quickly by unscrewing the front swivel with no tools needed.

Price: . . . . **N/A**

THOMPSON/CENTER ENCORE PISTOL

Caliber: 22-250, 223, 204 Ruger, 6.8 Rem., 260 Rem., 7mm-08, 243, 308, 270, 30-06, 375 JDJ, 204 Ruger, 44 Mag., 454 Casull, 480 Ruger, 444 Marlin single shot, 450 Marlin with muzzle tamer, no sights. **Barrel:** 12", 15", tapered round. **Weight:** NA. **Length:** 21" overall with 12" barrel. **Grips:** American walnut with finger grooves, walnut forend. **Sights:** Blade on ramp front, adjustable rear, or none. **Features:** Interchangeable barrels; action opens by squeezing the trigger guard; drilled and tapped for scope mounting; blue finish. Announced 1996. Made in U.S.A. by Thompson/Center Arms.

Price: **$615.00**

THOMPSON/CENTER G2 CONTENDER PISTOL

A second generation Contender pistol maintaining the same barrel interchangeability with older Contender barrels and their corresponding forends (except Herrett forend). The G2 frame will not accept old-style grips due to the change in grip angle. Incorporates an automatic hammer block safety with built-in interlock. Features include trigger adjustable for overtravel, adjustable rear sight; ramp front sight blade, blued steel finish.

Price: **$600.00**

ARMALITE M15A2 CARBINE

Caliber: 223 Rem., 30-round magazine. **Barrel:** 16" heavy chrome lined; 1:9" twist. **Weight:** 7 lbs. **Length:** 35-11/16" overall. **Stock:** Green or black composition. **Sights:** Standard A2. **Features:** Upper and lower receivers have push-type pivot pin; hard coat anodized; A2-style forward assist; M16A2-type raised fence around magazine release button. Made in U.S.A. by ArmaLite, Inc.

Price: Green **$1,150.00**
Price: Black. **$1,150.00**

ARMALITE AR-10A4 SPECIAL PURPOSE RIFLE

Caliber: 308 Win., 10- and 20-round magazine. **Barrel:** 20" chrome-lined, 1:11.25" twist. **Weight:** 9.6 lbs. **Length:** 41" overall. **Stock:** Green or black composition. **Sights:** Detachable handle, front sight, or scope mount available; comes with international style flattop receiver with Picatinny rail. **Features:** Forged upper receiver with case deflector. Receivers are hard-coat anodized. Introduced 1995. Made in U.S.A. by ArmaLite, Inc.

Price: Green **$1,557.00**
Price: Black. **$1,557.00**

ARMALITE AR-10A2

Utilizing the same 20" double-lapped, heavy barrel as the ArmaLite AR10A4 Special Purpose Rifle. Offered in 308 Win. only. Made in U.S.A. by ArmaLite, Inc.

Price: AR-10A2 rifle or carbine **$1,561.00**

ARMALITE AR-10B RIFLE

Caliber: 308 Win. **Barrel:** 20" chrome lined. **Weight:** 9.5 lbs. **Length:** 41". **Stock:** Synthetic. **Sights:** Rear sight adjustable for windage, small and large apertures. **Features:** Early-style AR-10. Lower and upper receivers made of forged aircraft alloy. Brown Sudanese-style furniture, elevation scale window. Charging handle in carry handle. Made in U.S.A. by Armalite.

Price: **$1,699.00**

ARSENAL, INC. SLR-107F

Caliber: 7.62x39mm. **Barrel:** 16.25". **Weight:** 7.3 lbs. **Stock:** Left-side folding polymer stock. **Sights:** Adjustable rear. **Features:** Stamped receiver, 24mm flash hider, bayonet lug, accessory lug, stainless steel heat shield, two-stage trigger. Introduced 2008. Made in U.S.A. by Arsenal, Inc.

Price: SLR-107FR, includes scope rail. **$1,035.00**

ARSENAL, INC. SLR-107CR

Caliber: 7.62x39mm. **Barrel:** 16.25". **Weight:** 6.9 lbs. **Stock:** Left-side folding polymer stock. **Sights:** Adjustable rear. **Features:** Stamped receiver, front sight block/gas block combination, 500-meter rear sight, cleaning rod, stainless steel heat shield, scope rail, and removable muzzle attachment. Introduced 2007. Made in U.S.A. by Arsenal, Inc.

Price: SLR-107CR **$1,200.00**

ARSENAL, INC. SLR-106CR

Caliber: 5.56 NATO. **Barrel:** 16.25", Steyr chrome-lined barrel, 1:7 twist rate. **Weight:** 6.9 lbs. **Stock:** Black polymer folding stock with cutout for scope rail. Stainless-steel heatshield handguard. **Sights:** 500-meter rear sight and rear sight block calibrated for 5.56 NATO.

Warsaw Pact scope rail. **Features:** Uses Arsenal, Bulgaria, Mil-Spec receiver, two-stage trigger, hammer and disconnector. Polymer magazines in 5- and 10-round capacity in black and green, with Arsenal logo. Others are 30-round black waffles, 20- and 30-round versions in clear/smoke waffle, featuring the "10" in a double-circle logo of Arsenal, Bulgaria. Ships with 5-round magazine, sling, cleaning kit in a tube, 16" cleaning rod, oil bottle. Introduced 2007. Made in U.S.A. by Arsenal, Inc.

Price: SLR-106CR **$1,200.00**

AUTO-ORDNANCE 1927A-1 THOMPSON

Caliber: 45 ACP. **Barrel:** 16.5". **Weight:** 13 lbs. **Length:** About 41" overall (Deluxe). **Stock:** Walnut stock and vertical forend. **Sights:** Blade front, open rear adjustable for windage. **Features:** Recreation of Thompson Model 1927. Semi-auto only. Deluxe model has finned barrel, adjustable rear sight and compensator; Standard model has plain barrel and military sight. From Auto-Ordnance Corp.

Price: Deluxe **$1,420.00**
Price: Lightweight model (9.5 lbs.) **$1,145.00**

AUTO-ORDNANCE THOMPSON M1/M1-C

Similar to the 1927 A-1 except is in the M-1 configuration with side cocking knob, horizontal forend, smooth unfinned barrel, sling swivels on butt and forend. Matte-black finish. Introduced 1985.

Price: M1 semi-auto carbine. **$1,334.00**
Price: M1-C lightweight semi-auto **$1,065.00**

AUTO-ORDNANCE 1927 A-1 COMMANDO

Similar to the 1927 A-1 except has Parkerized finish, black-finish wood butt, pistol grip, horizontal forend. Comes with black nylon sling. Introduced 1998. Made in U.S.A. by Auto-Ordnance Corp.

Price: T1-C **$1,393.00**

BARRETT MODEL 82A-1 SEMI-AUTOMATIC RIFLE

Caliber: 50 BMG, 10-shot detachable box magazine. **Barrel:** 29". **Weight:** 28.5 lbs. **Length:** 57" overall. **Stock:** Composition with energy-absorbing recoil pad. **Sights:** Scope optional. **Features:** Semi-automatic, recoil operated with recoiling barrel. Three-lug locking bolt; muzzle brake. Adjustable bipod. Introduced 1985. Made in U.S.A. by Barrett Firearms.

Price: From. **$8,900.00**

BENELLI R1 RIFLE

Caliber: 300 Win. Mag., 300 WSM, 270 WSM (24" barrel); 30-06 Spfl., 308 Win. (22" barrel); 300 Win. Mag., 30-06 Spfl., (20" barrel). **Weight:** 7.1 lbs. **Length:** 43.75" to 45.75". **Stock:** Select satin walnut or synthetic. **Sights:** None. **Features:** Auto-regulating gas-operated system, three-lug rotary bolt, interchangeable barrels, optional recoil pads. Introduced 2003. Imported from Italy by Benelli USA.

Price: Synthetic with ComforTech gel recoil pad **$1,549.00**
Price: Satin walnut **$1,379.00**
Price: APG HD camo, 30-06 (2008) **$1,689.00**

Prices given are believed to be accurate at time of publication however, many factors affect retail pricing so exact prices are not possible.

BENELLI MR1 RIFLE

Gas-operated semiauto rifle chambered in 5.56 NATO. Features include 16-inch 1:9 hard chrome-lined barrel, synthetic stock with pistol grip, rotating bolt, military-style aperture sights with picatinny rail. Comes equipped with 5-round detachable magazine but accepts M16 magazines.
Price: **$1299.00**

BERETTA CX4/PX4 STORM CARBINE

Caliber: 9mm Para., 40 S&W, 45 ACP. **Weight:** 5.75 lbs. **Barrel Length:** 16.6", chrome lined, rate of twist 1:16 (40 S&W) or 1:10 (9mm Para.). **Length:** NA. **Stock:** Black synthetic. **Sights:** NA. **Features:** Introduced 2005. Imported from Italy by Beretta USA.
Price: **$900.00**

BROWNING BAR SAFARI AND SAFARI W/BOSS SEMI-AUTO RIFLES

Caliber: Safari: 243 Win., 25-06 Rem., 270 Win., 7mm Rem. Mag., 30-06 Spfl., 308 Win., 300 Win. Mag., 338 Win. Mag. Safari w/BOSS: 270 Win., 7mm Rem. Mag., 30-06 Spfl., 300 Win. Mag., 338 Win. Mag., plus 270 WSM, 7mm WSM, 300 WSM. **Barrel:** 22-24" round tapered. **Weight:** 7.4-8.2 lbs. **Length:** 43-45" overall. **Stock:** French walnut pistol grip stock and forend, hand checkered. **Sights:** No sights. **Features:** Has new bolt release lever; removable trigger assembly with larger trigger guard; redesigned gas and buffer systems. Detachable 4-round box magazine. Scroll-engraved receiver is tapped for scope mounting. BOSS barrel vibration modulator and muzzle brake system available. Mark II Safari introduced 1993. Imported from Belgium by Browning.
Price: BAR MK II Safari, from **$1,109.00**
Price: BAR Safari w/BOSS, from **$1,229.00**

BROWNING BAR SHORTTRAC/LONGTRAC AUTO RIFLES

Caliber: (ShortTrac models) 270 WSM, 7mm WSM, 300 WSM, 243 Win., 308 Win., 325 WSM; (LongTrac models) 270 Win., 30-06 Spfl., 7mm Rem. Mag., 300 Win. Mag. **Barrel:** 23". **Weight:** 6 lbs. 10 oz. to 7 lbs. 4 oz. **Length:** 41.5" to 44". **Stock:** Satin-finish walnut, pistol-grip, fluted forend. **Sights:** Adj. rear, bead front standard, no sights on BOSS models (optional). **Features:** Designed to handle new WSM chamberings. Gas-operated, blued finish, rotary bolt design (LongTrac models).
Price: BAR ShortTrac, 243 Win., 308 Win. from **$1,079.00**
Price: BAR ShortTrac Left-Hand, intr. 2007, from **$1,129.00**
Price: BAR ShortTrac Mossy Oak New Break-up
. . . . **$1,249.00 to $1,349.00**
Price: BAR LongTrac Left Hand, 270 Win., 30-06 Spfl.,
from **$1,129.00**
Price: BAR LongTrac, from **$1,079.00**
Price: BAR LongTrac Mossy Oak Break Up, intr. 2007,
from **$1,249.00**
Price: Bar LongTrac, Digital Green camo (2009)
. . . . **$1,247.00 to $1,347.00**

BROWNING BAR STALKER AUTO RIFLES

Caliber: 243 Win., 308 Win., 270 Win., 30-06 Spfl., 270 WSM, 7mm WSM, 300 WSM, 300 Win. Mag., 338 Win. Mag. **Barrel:** 20-24". **Weight:** 7.1-7.75 LBS. **Length:** 41-45" overall. **Stock:** Black composite stock and forearm. **Sights:** Hooded front and adjustable rear. **Features:** Gas-operated action with seven-lug rotary bolt; dual action bars; 2-, 3- or 4-shot magazine (depending on cartridge). Introduced 2001. Imported by Browning.
Price: BAR ShortTrac or LongTrac Stalker, from **$1,119.00**
Price: BAR Lightweight Stalker, from **$1,099.00**

BUSHMASTER 308 HUNTER RIFLES

Caliber: .308 Win / 7.62 NATO., 5-round magazine. **Barrel:** 20". **Weight:** 8-1/2 lbs. **Length:** 38-1/4" overall. **Stock:** Standard A2 stock with Hogue® rubberized pistol grip. **Sights:** Two ¾" mini-risers for optics mounting. **Features:** These top quality Bushmaster .308 Rifles were developed for the Hunter who intends to immediately add optics (scope, red dot or holographic sight) to the rifle. The premium 20" heavy fluted profile barrel is chrome lined in both bore and chamber to provide Bushmaster accuracy, durability and maintenance ease.
Price: 308 Hunter. **$1518.00**
Price: 308 Vista Hunter. **$1,618.00**

BUSHMASTER ACR RIFLES

Caliber: 5.56mm, 6.5mm, 6.8mm., 30-round polymer magazine. **Barrel:** All three calibers are availaible with 10-1/2", 14-1/2", 16-1/2" and 18" barrels. **Weight:** 14-1/2 bbl 7 lbs.. **Length:** 14-1/5" bbl with stock folded: 25-3/4", with stock deployed (mid) 32-5/8", 10.5" bbl with stock folded: 21-5/16", with stock deployed (mid): 27-7/8", with stock deployed and extended: 31-3/4". Folding Stock Length of Pull - 3". **Stock:** Fixed high-impact composite A-frame stock with rubber butt pad and sling mounts (ORC & A-TACS®) **Features:** Cold hammer-forged barrels with melonite coating for extreme long life. A2 birdcage-type hider to control muzzle flash and adjustable, two-position, gas piston-driven system for firing suppressed or unsuppressed, supported by hardened internal bearing rails. Tool-less, quick-change barrel system available in 10.5", 14.5" and 16.5" and in multiple calibers. Multi-caliber bolt carrier assembly quickly and easily changes from 223/5.56mm NATO to 6.8mm Rem SPC (spec II chamber) Free-floating MIL-STD 1913 monolithic top rail for optic mounting. Fully ambidextrous controls including magazine release, bolt catch and release, fire selector and non reciprocating charging handle. High-impact composite hand guard with heat shield – accepts rail inserts. High-impact composite lower receiver with textured magazine well and modular grip storage. Fire Control – Semi and Full Auto two-stage standard AR capable of accepting drop-in upgrade. Magazine – Optimized for MagPul PMAG Accepts standard NATO/M-16 magazines.
Price: Basic ORC Configuration **$2,343.00**
Price: A-TACS Basic Configuration **$2,540.00**
Price: Basic Folder Configuration **$2,490.00**
Price: Basic State Compliant Configuration **$2,343.00**

BUSHMASTER SUPERLIGHT CARBINES

Caliber: 223 Rem., 30-shot magazine. **Barrel:** 16", heavy; 1:9 twist. **Weight:** 6.25 lbs. **Length:** 31.25-34.5" overall. **Stock:** 6-position telestock or Stubby (7.25" length). **Sights:** Fully adjustable M16A2 sight system. **Features:** Adapted from original G.I. pencil-barrel profile. Chrome-lined barrel with manganese phosphate finish. "Shorty" handguards. Has forged aluminum receivers with pushpin.

CENTERFIRE RIFLES—Autoloaders

Made in U.S.A. by Bushmaster Firearms, Inc.
Price: From $1,250.00

BUSHMASTER XM15 E2S DISSIPATOR CARBINE
Similar to the XM15 E2S Shorty carbine except has full-length "Dissipator" handguards. Weighs 7.6 lbs.; 34.75" overall; forged aluminum receivers with push-pin style takedown. Made in U.S.A. by Bushmaster Firearms, Inc.
Price: From $1,240.00

BUSHMASTER XM15 E25 AK SHORTY CARBINE
Similar to the XM15 E2S Shorty except has 14.5" barrel with an AK muzzle brake permanently attached giving 16" barrel length. Weighs 7.3 lbs. Introduced 1999. Made in U.S.A. by Bushmaster Firearms, Inc.
Price: From $1,215.00

BUSHMASTER M4 POST-BAN CARBINE
Similar to the XM15 E2S except has 14.5" barrel with Mini Y compensator, and fixed telestock. MR configuration has fixed carry handle.
Price: $1,190.00

BUSHMASTER VARMINTER RIFLE
Caliber: 223 Rem., 5-shot. **Barrel:** 24", 1:9" twist, fluted, heavy, stainless. **Weight:** 8.75 lbs. **Length:** 42.25". **Stock:** Rubberized pistol grip. **Sights:** 1/2" scope risers. **Features:** Gas-operated, semi-auto, two-stage trigger, slotted free floater forend, lockable hard case.
Price: $1,360.00
Price: Bushmaster Predator: 20" 1:8 barrel, 223 Rem. $1,245.00
Price: Bushmaster Stainless Varmint Special: Same as Varminter but with 24" stainless barrel $1,277.00

BUSHMASTER 6.8 SPC CARBINE
Caliber: 6.8 SPC, 26-shot mag. **Barrel:** 16" M4 profile. **Weight:** 6.57 lbs. **Length:** 32.75" overall. **Features:** Semi-auto AR-style with Izzy muzzle brake, six-position telestock. Available in A2 (fixed carry handle) or A3 (removable carry handle) configuration.
Price: $1,500.00

BUSHMASTER ORC CARBINE
Caliber: 5.56/223. **Barrel:** 16" M4 profile. **Weight:** 6 lbs. **Length:** 32.5" overall. **Features:** AR-style carbine with chrome-lined barrel, fixed carry handle, receiver-length picatinny optics rail, heavy oval M4-style handguards.
Price: $1,085.00

BUSHMASTER 11.5" BARREL CARBINE
Caliber: 5.56/223, 30-shot mag. **Barrel:** 11.5". **Weight:** 6.46 lbs. or 6.81 lbs. **Length:** 31.625" overall. **Features:** AR-style carbine with chrome-lined barrel with permanently attached BATF-approved 5.5" flash suppressor, fixed or removable carry handle, optional optics rail.
Price: $1,215.00

BUSHMASTER HEAVY-BARRELED CARBINE
Caliber: 5.56/223. **Barrel:** 16". **Weight:** 6.93 lbs. to 7.28 lbs. **Length:** 32.5" overall. **Features:** AR-style carbine with chrome-lined heavy profile vanadium steel barrel, fixed or removable carry handle, six-position telestock.
Price: $1,215.00

BUSHMASTER MODULAR CARBINE
Caliber: 5.56/223, 30-shot mag. **Barrel:** 16". **Weight:** 7.3 lbs. **Length:** 36.25" overall. **Features:** AR-style carbine with chrome-lined chrome-moly vanadium steel barrel, skeleton stock or six-position telestock, clamp-on front sight and detachable flip-up dual aperature rear.
Price: $1,745.00

BUSHMASTER CARBON 15 TOP LOADER RIFLE
Caliber: 5.56/223, internal 10-shot mag. **Barrel:** 16" chrome-lined M4 profile. **Weight:** 5.8 lbs. **Length:** 32.75" overall. **Features:** AR-style carbine with standard A2 front sight, dual aperture rear sight, receiver-length optics rail, lightweight carbon fiber receiver, six-position telestock. Will not accept detachable box magazines.
Price: $1,070.00

BUSHMASTER CARBON 15 FLAT-TOP CARBINE
Caliber: 5.56/223, 30-shot mag. **Barrel:** 16" M4 profile. **Weight:** 5.77 lbs. **Length:** 32.75" overall. **Features:** AR-style carbine Izzy flash suppressor, AR-type front sight, dual aperture flip, lightweight carbon composite receiver with receiver-length optics rail.
Price: $1,155.00
Price: Carbon 15 9mm, chambered in 9mm Parabellum . . . $1,025.00

BUSHMASTER 450 RIFLE AND CARBINE
Caliber: 450 Bushmaster. **Barrel:** 20" (rifle), 16" (carbine), five-round mag. **Weight:** 8.3 lbs. (rifle), 8.1 lbs. (carbine). **Length:** 39.5" overall (rifle), 35.25" overall (carbine). **Features:** AR-style with chrome-lined chrome-moly barrel, synthetic stock, Izzy muzzle brake.
Price: $1,350.00

BUSHMASTER GAS PISTON RIFLE
Caliber: 223, 30-shot mag. **Barrel:** 16". **Weight:** 7.46 lbs. **Length:** 32.5" overall. **Features:** Semi-auto AR-style with telescoping stock, carry handle, piston assembly rather than direct gas impingement.
Price: $1,795.00

BUSHMASTER TARGET RIFLE
Caliber: 5.56/223, 30-shot mag. **Barrel:** 20" or 24" heavy or standard. **Weight:** 8.43 lbs. to 9.29 lbs. **Length:** 39.5" or 43.5" overall. **Features:** Semi-auto AR-style with chrome-lined or stainless steel 1:9 barrel, fixed or removable carry handle, manganese phosphate finish.
Price: $1,195.00

BUSHMASTER M4A3 TYPE CARBINE
Caliber: 5.56/223, 30-shot mag. **Barrel:** 16". **Weight:** 6.22 to 6.7 lbs. **Length:** 31" to 32.5" overall. **Features:** AR-style carbine with chrome-moly vanadium steel barrel, Izzy-type flash-hider, six-position telestock, various sight options, standard or multi-rail handguard, fixed or removable carry handle.
Price: $1,270.00
Price: Patrolman's Carbine: Standard mil-style sights $1,270.00
Price: State Compliance Carbine: Compliant with various state regulations $1,270.00

CENTURY INTERNATIONAL AES-10 HI-CAP RIFLE
Caliber: 7.62x39mm. 30-shot magazine. **Barrel:** 23.2". **Weight:** NA. **Length:** 41.5" overall. **Stock:** Wood grip, forend. **Sights:** Fixed-notch rear, windage-adjustable post front. **Features:** RPK-style, accepts standard double-stack AK-type mags. Side-mounted scope mount, integral carry handle, bipod. Imported by Century Arms Int'l.
Price: AES-10, from $450.00

CENTURY INTERNATIONAL GP WASR-10 HI-CAP RIFLE
Caliber: 7.62x39mm. 30-shot magazine. **Barrel:** 16.25", 1:10 right-hand twist. **Weight:** 7.2 lbs. **Length:** 34.25" overall. **Stock:** Wood laminate or composite, grip, forend. **Sights:** Fixed-notch rear, windage-adjustable post front. **Features:** Two 30-rd. detachable box magazines, cleaning kit, bayonet. Version of AKM rifle; U.S.-parts added for BATFE compliance. Threaded muzzle, folding stock, bayonet lug, compensator, Dragunov stock available. Made in Romania by Cugir Arsenal. Imported by Century Arms Int'l.
Price: GP WASR-10, from $350.00

CENTURY INTERNATIONAL WASR-2 HI-CAP RIFLE
Caliber: 5.45x39mm. 30-shot magazine. **Barrel:** 16.25". **Weight:** 7.5

lbs. **Length:** 34.25" overall. Stocks: Wood laminate. **Sights:** Fixed-notch rear, windage-adjustable post front. **Features:** 1 30-rd. detachable box magazine, cleaning kit, sling. WASR-3 HI-CAP chambered in 223 Rem. Imported by Century Arms Int'l.
Price: GP WASR-2/3, from $250.00

CENTURY INTERNATIONAL M70AB2 SPORTER RIFLE
Caliber: 7.62x39mm. 30-shot magazine. **Barrel:** 16.25". **Weight:** 7.5 lbs. **Length:** 34.25" overall. Stocks: Metal grip, wood forend. **Sights:** Fixed-notch rear, windage-adjustable post front. **Features:** 2 30-rd. double-stack magazine, cleaning kit, compensator, bayonet lug and bayonet. Paratrooper-style Kalashnikov with under-folding stock. Imported by Century Arms Int'l.
Price: M70AB2, from $480.00

COLT MATCH TARGET MODEL RIFLE
Caliber: 223 Rem., 5-shot magazine. **Barrel:** 16.1" or 20". **Weight:** 7.1 to 8.5 lbs. **Length:** 34.5" to 39" overall. **Stock:** Composition stock, grip, forend. **Sights:** Post front, rear adjustable for windage and elevation. **Features:** 5-round detachable box magazine, flash suppressor, sling swivels. Forward bolt assist included. Introduced 1991. Made in U.S.A. by Colt's Mfg. Co., Inc.
Price: Match Target HBAR MT6601 . . . . $1,182.00

COLT MATCH TARGET M4
Similar to above but with carbine-length barrel.
Price: . . . . **NA**

DPMS PANTHER ARMS AR-15 RIFLES
Caliber: 223 Rem., 7.62x39. **Barrel:** 16" to 24". **Weight:** 7.75 to 11.75 lbs. **Length:** 34.5" to 42.25" overall. **Stock:** Black Zytel composite. **Sights:** Square front post, adjustable A2 rear. **Features:** Steel or stainless steel heavy or bull barrel; hardcoat anodized receiver; aluminum free-float tube handguard; many options. From DPMS Panther Arms.
Price: Panther Bull Twenty (20" stainless bull bbl.) $920.00
Price: Arctic Panther. $1,099.00
Price: Panther Classic $799.00
Price: Panther Bull Sweet Sixteen (16" stainless bull bbl.) . . .$885.00
Price: DCM Panther (20" stainless heavy bbl., n.m. sights) $1,099.00
Price: Panther 7.62x39 (20" steel heavy bbl.) $859.00

DPMS PANTHER ARMS CLASSIC AUTO RIFLE
Caliber: 5.56x45mm. **Barrel:** Heavy 16" to 20" w/flash hider. **Weight:** 7 to 9 lbs. **Length:** 34-11/16" to 38-7/16". **Sights:** Adj. rear and front. **Stock:** Black Zytel w/trap door assembly. **Features:** Gas operated rotating bolt, mil spec or Teflon black finish.
Price: Panther A2 Tactical 16" $814.00
Price: Panther Lite 16 . . . .$725.00
Price: Panther Carbine $799.00
Price: Panther The Agency Rifle. $1,999.00

DPMS PANTHER ARMS 5.56 PANTHER ORACLE
Semiauto AR-style rifle chambered in 5.56 NATO. Features include 16-inch 4140 chrome-moly 1:9 barrel; phosphated steel bolt; oval GlacierGuard handguard; flattop upper with Picatinny rail; aluminum lower; two 30-round magazines; Pardus 6-position telescoping stock. Also available on larger platform in .308 Winchester/7.62 NATO.
Price: $759.00

DPMS PANTHER ARMS PANTHER 3G1
Semiauto AR-style rifle chambered in 5.56 NATO. Features include 18-inch 416 stainless 1:9 barrel; phosphated steel bolt; VTAC modular handguard; flattop upper with Picatinny rail; aluminum lower; two 30-round magazines; Magpul CTR adjustable stock.
Price: $1,499.00

DPMS PANTHER ARMS PRAIRIE PANTHER
Semiauto AR-style rifle chambered in 5.56 NATO. Features include 20-inch 416 stainless fluted heavy 1:8 barrel; phosphated steel bolt; free-floated carbon fiber handguard; flattop upper with Picatinny rail; aluminum lower; two 30-round magazines; skeletonized Zytel stock; finished in King's Desert Shadow camo overall.
Price: $1,249.00

DPMS PANTHER ARMS PANTHER RAPTR
Semiauto AR-style rifle chambered in 5.56 NATO. Features include 16-inch 4140 chrome-moly 1:9 barrel; phosphated steel bolt; ERGO Z-Rail 4-rail handguard; front vertical grip; standard A2 sights; aluminum lower; four 30-round magazines.
Price: $1,649.00

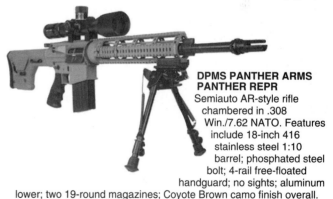

DPMS PANTHER ARMS PANTHER REPR
Semiauto AR-style rifle chambered in .308 Win./7.62 NATO. Features include 18-inch 416 stainless steel 1:10 barrel; phosphated steel bolt; 4-rail free-floated handguard; no sights; aluminum lower; two 19-round magazines; Coyote Brown camo finish overall.
Price: $2,549.00

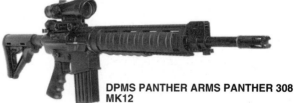

DPMS PANTHER ARMS PANTHER 308 MK12
Semiauto AR-style rifle chambered in .308 Win./7.62 NATO. Features include 16-inch 4140 chrome-moly heavy 1:10 barrel; phosphated steel bolt; 4-rail free-floated handguard; flip-

up front and rear sights; aluminum lower; two 19-round magazines; matte black finish overall; Magpul CTR adjustable stock.
Price: **$2,549.00**

DSA Z4 GTC CARBINE WITH C.R.O.S.
Caliber: 5.56 NATO **Barrel:** 16" 1:9 twist M4 profile fluted chrome lined heavy barrel with threaded Vortec flash hider. **Weight:** 7.6 lbs. **Stock:** 6 position collapsible M4 stock, Predator P4X free float tactical rail. **Sights:** Chrome lined Picatinny gas block w/removable front sight. **Features:** The Corrosion Resistant Operating System incorporates the new P.O.F. Gas Trap System with removable gas plug eliminates problematic features of standard AR gas system, Forged 7075T6 DSA lower receiver. Introduced 2006. Made in U.S.A. by DSA, Inc.
Price: **$1,800.00**

DSA CQB MRP, STANDARD MRP
Caliber: 5.56 NATO **Barrel:** 16" or 18" 1:7 twist chrome-lined or stainless steel barrel with A2 flash hider **Stock:** 6 position collapsible M4 stock. **Features:** LMT 1/2" MRP upper receiver with 20.5" Standard quad rail or 16.5" CQB quad rail, LMT-enhanced bolt with dual extractor springs, free float barrel, quick change barrel system, forged 7075T6 DSA lower receiver. EOTech and vertical grip additional. Introduced 2006. Made in U.S.A. by DSA, Inc.
Price: CQB MRP w/16" chrome-lined barrel **$2,420.00**
Price: CQB MRP w/16" stainless steel barrel. **$2,540.00**
Price: Standard MRP w/16" chrome-lined barrel **$2,620.00**
Price: Standard MRP w/16" or 18" stainless steel barrel . . . **$2,740.00**

DSA STD CARBINE
Caliber: 5.56 NATO. **Barrel:** 16" 1:9 twist D4 w/A2 flash hider. **Weight:** 6.25 lbs. **Length:** 31". **Stock:** A2 buttstock, D4 handguard w/heatshield. **Sights:** Forged A2 front sight with lug. **Features:** Forged 7075T6 DSA lower receiver, forged A2 or flattop upper receiver. Introduced 2006. Made in U.S.A. by DSA, Inc.
Price: A2 or Flattop STD Carbine. **$1,025.00**
Price: With LMT SOPMOD stock **$1,267.00**

DSA 1R CARBINE
Caliber: 5.56 NATO. **Barrel:** 16" 1:9 twist D4 w/A2 flash hider. **Weight:** 6.25 lbs. **Length:** Variable. **Stock:** 6 position collapsible M4 stock, D4 handguard w/heatshield. **Sights:** Forged A2 front sight with lug. **Features:** Forged 7075T6 DSA lower receiver, forged A2 or flattop upper receiver. Introduced 2006. Made in U.S.A. by DSA, Inc.
Price: A2 or Flattop 1R Carbine **$1,055.00**
Price: With VLTOR ModStock **$1,175.00**

DSA XM CARBINE
Caliber: 5.56 NATO. **Barrel:** 11.5" 1:9 twist D4 with 5.5" permanently attached flash hider. **Weight:** 6.25 lbs. **Length:** Variable. **Stock:** Collapsible, Handguard w/heatshield. **Sights:** Forged A2 front sight with lug. **Features:** Forged 7075T6 DSA lower receiver, forged A2 upper receiver. Introduced 2006. Made in U.S.A. by DSA, Inc.
Price: **$1,055.00**

DSA STANDARD
Caliber: 5.56 NATO. **Barrel:** 20" 1:9 twist heavy barrel w/A2 flash hider. **Weight:** 6.25 lbs. **Length:** 38-7/16". **Stock:** A2 buttstock, A2 handguard w/heatshield. **Sights:** Forged A2 front sight with lug. **Features:** Forged 7075T6 DSA lower receiver, forged A2 or flattop upper receiver. Introduced 2006. Made in U.S.A. by DSA, Inc.
Price: A2 or Flattop Standard **$1,025.00**

DSA DCM RIFLE
Caliber: 223 Wylde Chamber. **Barrel:** 20" 1:8 twist chrome moly match grade Badger Barrel. **Weight:** 10 lbs. **Length:** 39.5". **Stock:** DCM freefloat handguard system, A2 buttstock. **Sights:** Forged A2 front sight with lug. **Features:** NM two stage trigger, NM rear sight, forged 7075T6 DSA lower receiver, forged A2 upper receiver. Introduced 2006. Made in U.S.A. by DSA, Inc.
Price: **$1,520.00**

DSA S1
Caliber: 223 Rem. Match Chamber. **Barrel:** 16", 20" or 24" 1:8 twist stainless steel bull barrel. **Weight:** 8.0, 9.5 and 10 lbs. **Length:** 34.25", 38.25" and 42.25". **Stock:** A2 buttstock with free float aluminum handguard. **Sights:** Picatinny gas block sight base. **Features:** Forged 7075T6 DSA lower receiver, Match two stage trigger, forged flattop upper receiver, fluted barrel optional. Introduced 2006. Made in U.S.A. by DSA, Inc.
Price: **$1,155.00**

DSA SA58 CONGO, PARA CONGO
Caliber: 308 Win. **Barrel:** 18" w/short Belgian short flash hider. **Weight:** 8.6 lbs. (Congo); 9.85 lbs. (Para Congo). **Length:** 39.75" **Stock:** Synthetic w/military grade furniture (Congo); Synthetic with non-folding steel para stock (Para Congo). **Sights:** Elevation adjustable protected post front sight, windage adjustable rear peep (Congo); Belgian type Para Flip Rear (Para Congo). **Features:** Fully-adjustable gas system, high-grade steel upper receiver with carry handle. Made in U.S.A. by DSA, Inc.
Price: Congo. **$1,850.00**
Price: Para Congo **$2,095.00**

DSA SA58 GRAY WOLF
Caliber: 308 Win. **Barrel:** 21" match-grade bull w/target crown. **Weight:** 13 lbs. **Length:** 41.75". **Stock:** Synthetic. **Sights:** Elevation-adjustable post front sight, windage-adjustable match rear peep. **Features:** Fully-adjustable gas system, high-grade steel upper receiver, Picatinny scope mount, DuraCoat finish. Made in U.S.A. by DSA, Inc.
Price: **$2,120.00**

DSA SA58 PREDATOR
Caliber: 243 Win., 260 Rem., 308 Win. **Barrel:** 16" and 19" w/target crown. **Weight:** 9 to 9.3 lbs. **Length:** 36.25" to 39.25". **Stock:** Green synthetic. **Sights:** Elevation-adjustable post front; windage-adjustable match rear peep. **Features:** Fully-adjustable gas system, high-grade steel upper receiver, Picatinny scope mount, DuraCoat solid and camo finishes. Made in U.S.A. by DSA, Inc.
Price: 243 Win., 260 Rem. **$1,695.00**
Price: 308 Win. **$1,640.00**

DSA SA58 T48
Caliber: 308 Win. **Barrel:** 21" with Browning long flash hider. **Weight:** 9.3 lbs. **Length:** 44.5". **Stock:** European walnut. **Sights:** Elevation-adjustable post front, windage adjustable rear peep. **Features:** Gas-operated semi-auto with fully adjustable gas system, high grade steel upper receiver with carry handle. DuraCoat finishes. Made in U.S.A. by DSA, Inc.
Price: **$1,995.00**

DSA SA58 G1
Caliber: 308 Win. **Barrel:** 21" with quick-detach flash hider. **Weight:** 10.65 lbs. **Length:** 44". **Stock:** Steel bipod cut handguard with hardwood stock and synthetic pistol grip.

CENTERFIRE RIFLES—Autoloaders

Sights: Elevation-adjustable post front, windage adjustable rear peep. **Features:** Gas-operated semi-auto with fully adjustable gas system, high grade steel upper receiver with carry handle, original GI steel lower receiver with GI bipod. DuraCoat finishes. Made in U.S.A. by DSA, Inc.
Price: $1,850.00

DSA SA58 STANDARD
Caliber: 308 Win. **Barrel:** 21" bipod cut w/threaded flash hider. **Weight:** 8.75 lbs. **Length:** 43". **Stock:** Synthetic, X-Series or optional folding para stock. **Sights:** Elevation-adjustable post front, windage-adjustable rear peep. **Features:** Fully adjustable short gas system, high grade steel or 416 stainless upper receiver. Made in U.S.A. by DSA, Inc.
Price: High-grade steel $1,595.00
Price: Folding para stock $1,845.00

DSA SA58 CARBINE
Caliber: 308 Win. **Barrel:** 16.25" bipod cut w/threaded flash hider. **Weight:** 8.35 lbs. **Length:** 37.5". **Stock:** Synthetic, X-Series or optional folding para stock. **Sights:** Elevation-adjustable post front, windage-adjustable rear peep. **Features:** Fully adjustable short gas system, high grade steel or 416 stainless upper receiver. Made in U.S.A. by DSA, Inc.
Price: High-grade steel $1,595.00
Price: Stainless steel $1,850.00

DSA SA58 TACTICAL CARBINE
Caliber: 308 Win. **Barrel:** 16.25" fluted with A2 flash hider. **Weight:** 8.25 lbs. **Length:** 36.5". **Stock:** Synthetic, X-Series or optional folding para stock. **Sights:** Elevation-adjustable post front, windage-adjustable match rear peep. **Features:** Shortened fully adjustable short gas system, high grade steel or 416 stainless upper receiver. Made in U.S.A. by DSA, Inc.
Price: High-grade steel $1,595.00
Price: Stainless steel $1,850.00

DSA SA58 MEDIUM CONTOUR
Caliber: 308 Win. **Barrel:** 21" w/threaded flash hider. **Weight:** 9.75 lbs. **Length:** 43". **Stock:** Synthetic military grade. **Sights:** Elevation-adjustable post front, windage-adjustable match rear peep. **Features:** Gas-operated semi-auto with fully adjustable gas system, high grade steel receiver. Made in U.S.A. by DSA, Inc.
Price: $1,595.00

DSA SA58 BULL BARREL RIFLE
Caliber: 308 Win. **Barrel:** 21". **Weight:** 11.1 lbs. **Length:** 41.5". **Stock:** Synthetic, free floating handguard. **Sights:** Elevation-adjustable windage-adjustable post front, match rear peep. **Features:** Gas-operated semi-auto with fully adjustable gas system, high grade steel or stainless upper receiver. Made in U.S.A. by DSA, Inc.
Price: $1,745.00
Price: Stainless steel $1,995.00

DSA SA58 MINI OSW
Caliber: 308 Win. **Barrel:** 11" or 13" w/A2 flash hider. **Weight:** 9 to 9.35 lbs. **Length:** 32.75" to 35". **Stock:** Fiberglass reinforced short synthetic handguard, para folding stock and synthetic pistol grip. **Sights:** Adjustable post front, para rear sight. **Features:** Semi-auto or select fire with fully adjustable short gas system, optional FAL rail handguard, SureFire Vertical Foregrip System, EOTech HOLOgraphic Sight and ITC cheekrest. Made in U.S.A. by DSA, Inc.
Price: $1,845.00

EXCEL ARMS ACCELERATOR RIFLES
Caliber: 17 HMR, 22 WMR, 17M2, 22 LR, 9-shot magazine. **Barrel:** 18" fluted stainless steel bull barrel. **Weight:** 8 lbs. **Length:** 32.5" overall. **Grips:** Textured black polymer. **Sights:** Fully adjustable target sights. **Features:** Made from 17-4 stainless steel, aluminum shroud w/Weaver rail, manual safety, firing-pin block, last-round bolt-hold-open feature. Four packages with various equipment available. American made, lifetime warranty. Comes with one 9-round stainless steel magazine and a California-approved cable lock. Introduced 2006. Made in U.S.A. by Excel Arms.
Price: MR-17 17 HMR. $488.00
Price: MR-22 22 WMR $523.00

HECKLER & KOCH MODEL MR556A1 RIFLE
Caliber: .223 Remington/5.56 NATO, 10+1 capacity. **Barrel:** 16.5". **Weight:** 8.9 lbs. **Length:** 33.9"-37.68". **Stock:** Black Synthetic Adjustable. **Features:** A direct descendent of the HK416, the MR556A1 is a semi-automatic rifle developed by Heckler & Koch as a premium level commercial/civilian firearm. Like the HK416, the MR556A1 is a major product improvement of conventional AR-type carbines and rifles. Using the HK- proprietary gas piston system found on the HK416 and G36, the MR556A1 does not introduce propellant gases and carbon fouling back into the rifle's interior, making it the most reliable of any AR-type firearm. The MR556A1 uses many of the same assemblies and accessories originally developed for the HK416 including the HK free-floating four-quadrant rail system. This handguard system allows all current accessories, sights, lights, and aimers used on M4/M16-type weapons to be fitted to the MR rifles. The HK rail system can be installed and removed without tools and returns to zero when reinstalled. The MR566A1 will be produced in the USA from both American and German-made components. Additionally, subassemblies like the MR556A1's upper receiver will be fully interchangeable with other high quality AR-style firearms. Like the famous HK416, the MR556A1 uses a barrel produced by Heckler & Koch's famous cold hammer forging process. The highest quality steel is used in this manufacturing process, producing a long life barrel that provides superior performance with minimal degradation of accuracy and muzzle velocity after prolonged use.
Price: $2,995.00

HECKLER & KOCH USC CARBINE
Caliber: 45 ACP, 10-shot magazine. **Barrel:** 16". **Weight:** 8.6 lb.

Length: 35.4" overall. **Stock:** Skeletonized polymer thumbhole. **Sights:** Blade front with integral hood, fully adjustable diopter. **Features:** Based on German UMP submachine gun. Blowback operation; almost entirely constructed of carbon fiber-reinforced polymer. Free-floating heavy target barrel. Introduced 2000. From H&K.
Price: $1,249.00

HI-POINT 9MM CARBINE
Caliber: 9mm Para., 40 S&W, 10-shot magazine. **Barrel:** 16.5" (17.5" for 40 S&W). **Weight:** 4.5 lbs. **Length:** 31.5" overall. **Stock:** Black polymer, camouflage. **Sights:** Protected post front, aperture rear. Integral scope mount. **Features:** Grip-mounted magazine release. Black or chrome finish. Sling swivels. Available with laser or red dot sights. Introduced 1996. Made in U.S.A. by MKS Supply, Inc.
Price: 995-B (black) $220.00
Price: 995-CMO (camo) $235.00

LES BAER CUSTOM ULTIMATE AR 223 RIFLES
Caliber: 223. **Barrel:** 18", 20", 22", 24". **Weight:** 7.75 to 9.75 lb. **Length:** NA. **Stock:** Black synthetic. **Sights:** None furnished; Picatinny-style flattop rail for scope mounting. **Features:** Forged receiver; Ultra single-stage trigger (Jewell two-stage trigger optional); titanium firing pin; Versa-Pod bipod; chromed National Match carrier; stainless steel, hand-lapped and cryo-treated barrel; guaranteed to shoot 1/2 or 3/4 MOA, depending on model. Made in U.S.A. by Les Baer Custom Inc.
Price: Super Varmint Model $2,390.00
Price: Super Match Model (introduced 2006) $2,490.00
Price: M4 Flattop model $2,360.00
Price: Police Special 16" (2008) $1,690.00
Price: IPSC Action Model $2,640.00

LR 300 RIFLES
Caliber: 5.56 NATO, 30-shot magazine. **Barrel:** 16.5"; 1:9" twist. **Weight:** 7.4-7.8 lbs. **Length:** NA. **Stock:** Folding. **Sights:** YHM flip front and rear. **Features:** Flattop receive, full length top picatinny rail. Phantom flash hider, multi sling mount points, field strips with no tools. Made in U.S.A. from Z-M Weapons.
Price: AXL, AXLT $2,139.00
Price: NXL $2,208.00

MERKEL MODEL SR1 SEMI-AUTOMATIC RIFLE
Caliber: 308 Win., 300 Win Mag. **Features:** Streamlined profile, checkered walnut stock and forend, 19.7- (308) or 20-8" (300 SM)

barrel, two- or five-shot detachable box magazine. Adjustable front and rear iron sights with Weaver-style optics rail included. Imported from Germany by Merkel USA.
Price: $1,595.00

OLYMPIC ARMS K9, K10, K40, K45 PISTOL-CALIBER AR15 CARBINES
Caliber: 9mm Para., 10mm, 40 S&W, 45 ACP; 32/10-shot modified magazines. **Barrel:** 16" button rifled stainless steel, 1x16 twist rate. **Weight:** 6.73 lbs. **Length:** 31.625" overall. **Stock:** A2 grip, M4 6-point collapsible stock. **Features:** A2 upper with adjustable rear sight, elevation adjustable front post, bayonet lug, sling swivel, threaded muzzle, flash suppressor, carbine length handguards. Made in U.S.A. by Olympic Arms, Inc.
Price: K9GL, 9mm Para., Glock lower $1,092.00
Price: K10, 10mm, modified 10-round Uzi magazine $1,006.20
Price: K40, 40 S&W, modified 10-round Uzi magazine $1,006.20
Price: K45, 45 ACP, modified 10-round Uzi magazine $1,006.20

OLYMPIC ARMS K3B SERIES AR15 CARBINES
Caliber: 5.56 NATO, 30-shot magazines. **Barrel:** 16" button rifled chrome-moly steel, 1x9 twist rate. **Weight:** 5-7 lbs. **Length:** 31.75" overall. **Stock:** A2 grip, M4 6-point collapsible buttstock. **Features:** A2 upper with adjustable rear sight, elevation adjustable front post, bayonet lug, sling swivel, threaded muzzle, flash suppressor, carbine length handguards. Made in U.S.A. by Olympic Arms, Inc.
Price: K3B base model, A2 upper. $815.00
Price: K3B-M4 M4 contoured barrel & handguards $1,038.70
Price: K3B-M4-A3-TC A3 upper, M4 barrel, FIRSH rail handguard. $1,246.70
Price: K3B-CAR 11.5" barrel with 5.5" permanent flash suppressor $968.50
Price: K3B-FAR 16" featherweight contoured barrel $1,006.20

OLYMPIC ARMS PLINKER PLUS AR15 MODELS
Caliber: 5.56 NATO, 30-shot magazine. Barrel 16" or 20" button-rifled chrome-moly steel, 1x9 twist. **Weight:** 7.5-8.5 lbs. **Length:** 35.5"-39.5" overall. **Stock:** A2 grip, A2 buttstock with trapdoor. **Sights:** A1 windage rear, elevation-adjustable front post. **Features:** A1 upper, fiberlite handguards, bayonet lug, threaded muzzle and flash suppressor. Made in U.S.A. by Olympic Arms, Inc.

Prices given are believed to be accurate at time of publication however, many factors affect retail pricing so exact prices are not possible.

Price: Plinker Plus. **$713.70**
Price: Plinker Plus 20 . . . .**$843.70**

OLYMPIC ARMS GAMESTALKER

Sporting AR-style rifle chambered in .223, .243 and .25 WSSM and .300 OSSM. Features include forged aluminum upper and lower; flat top receiver with Picatinny rail; gas block front sight; 22-inch stainless steel fluted barrel; free-floating slotted tube handguard; camo finish overall; ACE FX skeleton stock.
Price: **$1,359.00**

REMINGTON MODEL R-15 MODULAR REPEATING RIFLE

Caliber: 223, 450 Bushmaster
and 30 Rem. AR, five-shot magazine. Barrel: 18" (carbine), 22", 24".
Weight: 6.75 to 7.75 lbs. **Length:** 36.25" to 42.25". **Stock:** Camo.
Features: AR-style with optics rail, aluminum alloy upper and lower.
Price: R-15 Hunter: 30 Rem. AR, 22" barrel, Realtree AP HD
camo **$1,225.00**
Price: R-15 VTR Byron South Edition: 223, 18" barrel,
Advantage MAX-1 HD camo **$1,772.00**
Price: R-15 VTR SS Varmint: Same as Byron South Edition
but with 24" stainless steel barrel **$1,412.00**
Price: R-15 VTR Thumbhole: Similar to R-15 Hunter but with
thumbhole stock **$1,412.00**
Price: R-15 VYR Predator: 204 Ruger or .223, 22" barrel . . **$1,225.00**
Price: R-15 Predator Carbine: Similar to above but with
18" barrel **$1,225.00**

REMINGTON MODEL R-25 MODULAR REPEATING RIFLE

Caliber: 243, 7mm-08, 308 Win., four-shot magazine. **Barrel:** 20"
chrome-moly. **Weight:** 7.75 lbs. **Length:** 38.25" overall. **Features:**
AR-style semi-auto with single-stage trigger, aluminum alloy upper and lower, Mossy Oak Treestand camo finish overall.
Price: **$1,567.00**

REMINGTON MODEL 750 WOODSMASTER

Caliber: 243 Win., 270 Win., 308 Win., 30-06 Spfl., 35 Whelen.
4-shot magazine. **Barrel:** 22" round tapered. **Weight:** 7.5 lbs.
Length: 42.6" overall. **Stock:** Restyled American walnut forend and stock with machine-cut checkering. Satin finish. **Sights:** Gold bead front sight on ramp; step rear sight with windage adjustable.
Features: Replaced wood-stocked Model 7400 line introduced 1981. Gas action, SuperCell recoil pad. Positive cross-bolt safety. Carbine chambered in 308 Win., 30-06 Spfl., 35 Whelen. Receiver tapped for scope mount. Introduced 2006. Made in U.S.A. by Remington Arms Co.
Price: 750 Woodsmaster **$879.00**
Price: 750 Woodsmaster Carbine (18.5" bbl.) **$879.00**
Price: 750 Synthetic stock (2007). **$773.00**

ROCK RIVER ARMS STANDARD A2 RIFLE

Caliber: 45 ACP. **Barrel:** NA. **Weight:** 8.2 lbs. **Length:** NA. **Stock:**
Thermoplastic. **Sights:** Standard AR-15 style sights. **Features:**
Two-stage, national match trigger; optional muzzle brake. Pro-Series Government package includes side-mount sling swivel, chrome-lined 1:9 twist barrel, mil-spec forged lower receiver, Hogue rubber grip, NM two-stage trigger, 6-position tactical CAR stock, Surefire M73 quad rail handguard, other features. Made in U.S.A. From Rock River Arms.
Price: Standard A2 AR1280 . . . .**$945.00**
Price: Pro-Series Government Package
GOVT1001 (2008) **$2,290.00**
Price: Elite Comp AR1270 (2008). **$1,145.00**

RUGER SR-556

AR-style semiauto rifle chambered in 5.56 NATO.
Feature include two-stage piston;
quad rail handguard; Troy Industries sights; black synthetic fixed or telescoping buttstock; 16.12-inch 1:9 steel barrel with birdcage; 10- or 30-round detachable box magazine; black matte finish overall.
Price: **$1,995.00**

RUGER MINI-14 RANCH RIFLE AUTOLOADING RIFLE

Caliber: 223 Rem., 5-shot
detachable box magazine. **Barrel:** 18.5". Rifling twist 1:9". **Weight:**
6.75 to 7 lbs. **Length:** 37.25" overall. **Stock:** American hardwood, steel reinforced, or synthetic. **Sights:** Protected blade front, fully adjustable Ghost Ring rear. **Features:** Fixed piston gas-operated, positive primary extraction. New buffer system, redesigned ejector system. Ruger S100RM scope rings included on Ranch Rifle. Heavier barrels added in 2008, 20-round magazine added in 1009.
Price: Mini-14/5, Ranch Rifle, blued, scope rings **$855.00**
Price: K-Mini-14/5, Ranch Rifle, stainless, scope rings **$921.00**
Price: K-Mini-6.8/5P, All-Weather Ranch Rifle, stainless,
synthetic stock (2008) **$921.00**
Price: Mini-14 Target Rifle: laminated thumbhole stock,
heavy crowned 22" stainless steel barrel, other
refinements **$1,066.00**
Price: Mini-14 ATI Stock: Tactical version of Mini-14 but with
six-position collapsible stock or folding stock, grooved
pistol grip. multiple picatinny optics/accessory rails . . . **$872.00**
Price: Mini-14 Tactical Rifle: Similar to Mini-14 but with 16-21"
barrel with flash hider, black synthetic stock, adjustable
sights **$894.00**

RUGER NRA MINI-14 RIFLE

Similar to the Mini-14 Ranch Rifle except comes with two 20-round magazines and special Black Hogue OverMolded stock with NRA gold-tone medallion in grip cap. Special serial number sequence (NRA8XXXXX). For 2008 only.
Price: M-14/20C-NRA **$1,035.00**
Price: M-14/5C-NRA (5-round magazines). **$1,035.00**

RUGER MINI THIRTY RIFLE

Similar to the Mini-14 Ranch Rifle except modified to chamber the 7.62x39 Russian service round. **Weight:** 6.75 lbs. Has 6-groove barrel with 1:10" twist, Ruger Integral Scope Mount bases and protected blade front, fully adjustable Ghost Ring rear. Detachable 5-shot staggered box magazine. Available 2010 with two 30-round magazines. Stainless w/synthetic stock. Introduced 1987.
Price: Stainless, scope rings **$921.00**

SABRE DEFENCE SABRE RIFLES

Caliber: 5.56 NATO, 6.5 Grendel, 30-shot magazines. **Barrel:** 20"
410 stainless steel, 1x8 twist rate; or 18" vanadium alloy, chrome-lined barrel with Sabre Gill-Brake. **Weight:** 6.77 lbs. **Length:** 31.75" overall. **Stock:** SOCOM 3-position stock with Samson M-EX handguards. **Sights:** Flip-up front and rear sights. **Features:** Fluted barrel, Harris bipod, two-stage match trigger, Ergo Grips; upper and matched lower CNC machined from 7075-T6 forgings. SOCOM adjustable stock, Samson tactical handguards, M4 contour barrels

available in 14.5" and 16" are made of MIL-B-11595 vanadium alloy and chrome lined. Introduced 2002. From Sabre Defence Industries.

Price: 6.5 Grendel, from **$1,409.00**
Price: Competition Extreme, 20" barrel, from **$2,189.00**
Price: Competition Deluxe, from **$2,299.00**
Price: Competition Special, 5.56mm, 18" barrel, from **$1,899.00**
Price: SPR Carbine, from **$2,499.00**
Price: M4 Tactical, from **$1,969.00**
Price: M4 Carbine, 14.5" barrel, from **$1,399.00**
Price: M4 Flat-top Carbine, 16" barrel, from **$1,349.00**
Price: M5 Flat-top, 16" barrel, from **$1,399.00**
Price: M5 Tactical, 14.5" barrel, from **$2,099.00**
Price: M5 Carbine, from **$1,309.00**
Price: Precision Marksman, 20" barrel, from **$2,499.00**
Price: A4 Rifle, 20" barrel, from **$1,349.00**
Price: A3 National Match, 20" barrel **$1,699.00**
Price: Heavy Bench Target, 24" barrel, from **$1,889.00**
Price: Varmint, 20" barrel **$1,709.00**

SIG 556 AUTOLOADING RIFLE

Caliber: 223 Rem., 30-shot detachable box magazine. **Barrel:** 16". Rifling twist 1:9". **Weight:** 6.8 lbs. **Length:** 36.5" overall. **Stock:** Polymer, folding style. **Sights:** Flip-up front combat sight, adjustable for windage and elevation. **Features:** Based on SG 550 series rifle. Two-position adjustable gas piston operating rod system, accepts standard AR magazines. Polymer forearm, three integrated Picatinny rails, forward mount for right- or left-side sling attachment. Aircraft-grade aluminum alloy trigger housing, hard-coat anodized finish; two-stage trigger, ambidextrous safety, 30-round polymer magazine, battery compartments, pistol-grip rubber-padded watertight adjustable butt stock with sling-attachment points. SIG 556 SWAT model has flat-top Picatinny railed receiver, tactical quad rail. SIG 556 HOLO sight options include front combat sight, flip-up rear sight, and red-dot style

holographic sighting system with four illuminated reticle patterns. DMR features a 24" military grade cold hammer-forged heavy contour barrel, 5.56mm NATO, target crown. Imported by Sig Sauer, Inc.

Price: SIG 556 . . . . **$2,099.00**
Price: SIG 556 HOLO (2008) **$1,832.00**
Price: SIG 556 DMR (2008) **$2,400.00**
Price: SIG 556 SWAT **$2,000.00**
Price: SIG 556 SCM **$1,838.00**

SIG-SAUER SIG516 GAS PISTON RIFLE

AR-style rifle chambered in 5.56 NATO. Features include 14.5-, 16-, 18- or 20-inch chrome-lined barrel; free-floating, aluminum quad rail fore-end with four M1913 Picatinny rails; threaded muzzle with a standard (0.5x28TPI) pattern; aluminum upper and lower receiver is machined; black anodized finish; 30-round magazine; flattop upper; various configurations available.

Price: . . . . **N/A**

SIG-SAUER SIG716 TACTICAL PATROL RIFLE

AR-10 type rifle chambered in 7.62 NATO/.308 Winchester. Features include gas-piston operation with 3 round-position (4-position optional) gas valve; 16-, 18- or 20-inch chrome-lined barrel with threaded muzzle and nitride finish; free-floating aluminum quad rail fore-end with four M1913 Picatinny rails; telescroping buttstock; lower receiver is machined from a 7075-T6 Aircraft grade aluminum forging; upper receiver, machined from 7075-T6 aircraft grade aluminum with integral M1913 Picatinny rail.

Price: . . . . **N/A**

SMITH & WESSON M&P15 RIFLES

Caliber: 5.56mm NATO/223, 30-shot steel magazine. **Barrel:** 16", 1:9 **Weight:** 6.74 lbs., w/o magazine. **Length:** 32-35" overall. **Stock:** Black synthetic. **Sights:** Adjustable post front sight, adjustable dual aperture rear sight. **Features:** 6-position telescopic stock, thermo-set M4 handguard. 14.75" sight radius. 7-lbs. (approx.) trigger pull. 7075 T6 aluminum upper, 4140 steel barrel. Chromed barrel bore, gas key, bolt carrier. Hard-coat black-anodized receiver and barrel finish. Introduced 2006. Made in U.S.A. by Smith & Wesson.

Price: M&P15 No. 811000 . . . . **$1,406.00**
Price: M&P15T No. 811001, free float modular rail forend . **$1,888.00**
Price: M&P15A No. 811002, folding battle rear sight **$1,422.00**
Price: M&P15A No. 811013, optics ready compliant (2008). **$1,169.00**

SMITH & WESSON MODEL M&P15VTAC VIKING TACTICS MODEL

Caliber: 223 Remington/5.56 NATO, 30-round magazine. **Barrel:** 16". **Weight:** 6.5 lbs. **Length:** 35" extended, 32" collapsed, overall. **Features:** Six-position CAR stock. Surefire flash-hider and G2 light with VTAC light mount; VTAC/JP handguard; JP single-stage match trigger and speed hammer; three adjustable picatinny rails; VTAC padded two-point adjustable sling.

Price: **$2,196.00**

SMITH & WESSON M&P15PC CAMO

Caliber: 223 Rem/5.56 NATO, A2 configuration, 10-round mag. **Barrel:** 20" stainless with 1:8 twist. **Weight:** 8.2 lbs. **Length:** 38.5" overall. **Features:** AR-style, no sights but integral front and rear optics rails.

Prices given are believed to be accurate at time of publication however, many factors affect retail pricing so exact prices are not possible.

Two-stage trigger, aluminum lower. Finished in Realtree Advantage Max-1 camo.
Price: **$2,046.00**

SMITH & WESSON M&P15 PISTON RIFLE

Similar to AR-derived M&P15 but with gas piston. Chambered in 5.56 NATO. Features include adjustable gas port, optional Troy quad mount handguard, chromed bore/gas key/bolt carrier/chamber, 6-position telescoping or MagPul MOE stock, flattop or folding MBUS sights, aluminum receiver, alloy upper and lower, black anodized finish, 30-round magazine, 16-inch barrel with birdcage.
Price Standard handguard. **$1,531.00**
Price: Troy quad mount handguard **$1,692.00**

SPRINGFIELD ARMORY M1A RIFLE

Caliber: 7.62mm NATO (308), 5- or 10-shot box magazine. **Barrel:** 25-1/16" with flash suppressor, 22" without suppressor. **Weight:** 9.75 lbs. **Length:** 44.25" overall. **Stock:** American walnut with walnut-colored heat-resistant fiberglass handguard. Matching walnut handguard available. Also available with fiberglass stock. **Sights:** Military, square blade front, full click-adjustable aperture rear. **Features:** Commercial equivalent of the U.S. M-14 service rifle with no provision for automatic firing. From Springfield Armory
Price: SOCOM 16. . . . . **$1,855.00**
Price: SOCOM II, from **$2,090.00**
Price: Scout Squad, from **$1,726.00**
Price: Standard M1A, from **$1,608.00**
Price: Loaded Standard, from **$1,759.00**
Price: National Match, from **$2,249.00**
Price: Super Match
(heavy premium barrel) about **$2,818.00**
Price: Tactical, from **$3,780.00**

STAG ARMS MODEL 3 RIFLE

Caliber: 5.56 NATO., 30-shot magazine capacity. **Barrel:** 16". **Stock:** Six position collapsible stock. **Sights:** N/A. **Features:** A short barrel with a chrome lined bore and a 6 position collapsible stock. It uses a gas-operated firing system, so the recoil is delayed until the round exits the barrel. Although it doesn't have any sights, it does have a Diamondhead Versa Rail System, which allows users to add Picatinny rails to the top, bottom and sides. The Picatinny rail allows for easy mounting of optics and accessories. Features the Diamondhead Versa Rail System; and right and left handed models are available. Perfect for modification, the Stag Arms Model 3 AR 15 is made to mil-spec requirements to give you the most authentic experience possible.
Price: **$895.00**

STONER SR-15 M-5 RIFLE

Caliber: 223. **Barrel:** 20".
Weight: 7.6 lbs. **Length:** 38" overall. **Stock:** Black synthetic. **Sights:** Post front, fully adjustable rear (300-meter sight). **Features:** Modular weapon system; two-stage trigger. Black finish. Introduced 1998. Made in U.S.A. by Knight's Mfg.
Price: **$1,695.00**

STONER SR-25 CARBINE

Caliber: 7.62 NATO, 10-shot steel magazine. **Barrel:** 16" free-floating **Weight:** 7.75 lbs. **Length:** 35.75" overall. **Stock:** Black synthetic.

Sights: Integral Weaver-style rail. Scope rings, iron sights optional.
Features: Shortened, non-slip handguard; removable carrying handle. Matte black finish. Introduced 1995. Made in U.S.A. by Knight's Mfg. Co.
Price: **$3,345.00**

TAURUS CT G2 CARBINE

Caliber: .40 S&W, 9 mm and .45 ACP, Capacity is 34+1 for 9mm, 15+1 for .40 S&W and 10+1 for .45 ACP. **Barrel:** 16". **Weight:** 134-148 ozs. **Length:** 35.75" overall. **Stock:** Aluminum & Polymer. **Sights:** Adjustable rear sight and fixed front sight. **Features:** Full length Picatinny rail, ambidextrous slide catch, two-position safety/fire selector (semi-auto only…) Made in U.S.A. by Knight's Mfg. Co.
Price: **$639.00**

WILSON COMBAT TACTICAL RIFLES

Caliber: 5.56mm NATO, accepts all M-16/AR-15 Style Magazines, includes one 20-round magazine. **Barrel:** 16.25", 1:9 twist, match-grade fluted. **Weight:** 6.9 lbs. **Length:** 36.25" overall. **Stock:** Fixed or collapsible. **Features:** Free-float ventilated aluminum quad-rail handguard, Mil-Spec parkerized barrel and steel components, anodized receiver, precision CNC-machined upper and lower receivers, 7075 T6 aluminum forgings. Single stage JP Trigger/Hammer Group, Wilson Combat Tactical Muzzle Brake, nylon tactical rifle case. M-4T version has flat-top receiver for mounting optics, OD green furniture, 16.25" match-grade M-4 style barrel. SS-15 Super Sniper Tactical Rifle has 1-in-8 twist, heavy 20" match-grade fluted stainless steel barrel. Made in U.S.A by Wilson Combat.
Price: UT-15 Tactical Carbine. **$1,785.00**
Price: M4-TP Tactical Carbine **$1,575.00**
Price: SS-15P Super Sniper **$1,795.00**

WINCHESTER SUPER X RIFLE

Caliber: 270 WSM, 30-06 Spfl., 300 Win. Mag., 300 WSM, 4-shot steel magazine. **Barrel:** 22", 24", 1:10, blued. **Weight:** 7.25 lbs. **Length:** up to 41-3/8". **Stock:** Walnut, 14-1/8"x 7/8"x 1.25". **Sights:** None. **Features:** Gas operated, removable trigger assembly, detachable box magazine, drilled and tapped, alloy receiver, enlarged trigger guard, crossbolt safety. Reintroduced 2008. Made in U.S.A. by Winchester Repeating Arms.
Price: Super X Rifle, from **$949.00**

BERETTA 1873 RENEGADE SHORT LEVER-ACTION RIFLE
Caliber: 45 Colt, 357 Magnum. **Barrel:** 20" round or 24-1/2" octagonal. **Features:** Blued finish, checkered walnut buttstock and forend, adjustable rear sight and fixed blade front, ten-round tubular magazine.
Price: **$1,350.00**

BERETTA GOLD RUSH SLIDE-ACTION RIFLE AND CARBINE
Caliber: 357 Magnum, 45 Colt. **Barrel:** 20" round or 24-1/2"octagonal. **Features:** External replica of old Colt Lightning Magazine Rifle. Case-hardened receiver, walnut buttstock and forend, crescent buttplate, 13-round (rifle) or 10-round (carbine) magazine. Available as Standard Carbine, Standard Rifle, or Deluxe Rifle.
Price: Standard Carbine **$1,375.00**
Price: Standard Rifle **$1,425.00**
Price: Deluxe Rifle **$11,950.00**

BIG HORN ARMORY MODEL 89 RIFLE AND CARBINE
Lever action rifle or carbine chambered for .500 S&W Magnum. Features include 22- or 18-inch barrel; walnut or maple stocks with pistol grip; aperture rear and blade front sights; recoil pad; sling swivels; enlarged lever loop; magazine capacity 5 (rifle) or 7 (carbine) rounds.
Price: **$1,889.00**

BROWNING BLR RIFLES
Action: Lever action with rotating bolt head, multiple-lug breech bolt with recessed bolt face, side ejection. Rack-and-pinion lever. Flush-mounted detachable magazines, with 4+1 capacity for magnum cartridges, 5+1 for standard rounds. **Barrel:** Button-rifled chrome-moly steel with crowned muzzle. **Stock:** Buttstocks and forends are American walnut with grip and forend checkering. Recoil pad installed. Trigger: Wide-groove design, trigger travels with lever. Half-cock hammer safety; fold-down hammer. **Sights:** Gold bead on ramp front; low-profile square-notch adjustable rear. **Features:** Blued barrel and receiver, high-gloss wood finish. Receivers are drilled and tapped for scope mounts, swivel studs included. Action lock provided. Introduced 1996. Imported from Japan by Browning.

BROWNING BLR LIGHTWEIGHT W/PISTOL GRIP, SHORT AND LONG ACTION; LIGHTWEIGHT '81, SHORT AND LONG ACTION
Calibers: Short Action, 20" Barrel: 22-250 Rem., 243 Win., 7mm-08 Rem., 308 Win., 358, 450 Marlin. Calibers: Short Action, 22" Barrel: 270 WSM, 7mm WSM, 300 WSM, 325 WSM. Calibers: Long Action 22" Barrel: 270 Win., 30-06. Calibers: Long Action 24" Barrel: 7mm Rem. Mag., 300 Win. Mag. **Weight:** 6.5-7.75 lbs. **Length:** 40-45" overall. **Stock:** New checkered pistol grip and Schnabel forearm. Lightweight '81 differs from Pistol Grip models with a Western-style straight grip stock and banded forearm. Lightweight w/Pistol Grip Short Action and Long Action introduced 2005. Model '81 Lightning Long Action introduced 1996.
Price: Lightweight w/Pistol Grip Short Action, from **$879.00**
Price: Lightweight w/Pistol Grip Long Action **$929.00**
Price: Lightweight '81 Short Action **$839.00**
Price: Lightweight '81 Long Action **$889.00**
Price: Lightweight '81 Takedown Short Action, intr. 2007, from **$949.00**
Price: Lightweight '81 Takedown Long Action, intr. 2007, from **$999.00**

CHARLES DALY MODEL 1892 LEVER-ACTION RIFLES
Caliber: 45 Colt; 5-shot magazine with removable plug. **Barrel:** 24.25" octagonal. **Weight:** 6.8 lbs. **Length:** 42" overall. **Stock:** Two-piece American walnut, oil finish. **Sights:** Post front, adjustable open rear. **Features:** Color case-hardened receiver, lever, buttplate, forend cap. Introduced 2007. Imported from Italy by K.B.I., Inc.
Price: 1892 Rifle **$1,094.00**
Price: Take Down Rifle **$1,249.00**

CIMARRON 1860 HENRY RIFLE CIVIL WAR MODEL
Caliber: 44 WCF, 45 LC; 12-shot magazine. **Barrel:** 24" (rifle). **Weight:** 9.5 lbs. **Length:** 43" overall (rifle). **Stock:** European walnut.

Sights: Bead front, open adjustable rear. **Features:** Brass receiver and buttplate. Uses original Henry loading system. Copy of the original rifle. Charcoal blue finish optional. Introduced 1991. Imported by Cimarron F.A. Co.
Price: From **$1,444.78**

CIMARRON 1866 WINCHESTER REPLICAS
Caliber: 38 Spec., 357, 45 LC, 32 WCF, 38 WCF, 44 WCF. **Barrel:** 24" (rifle), 20" (short rifle), 19" (carbine), 16" (trapper). **Weight:** 9 lbs. **Length:** 43" overall (rifle). **Stock:** European walnut. **Sights:** Bead front, open adjustable rear. **Features:** Solid brass receiver, buttplate, forend cap. Octagonal barrel. Copy of the original Winchester '66 rifle. Introduced 1991. Imported by Cimarron F.A. Co.
Price: 1866 Sporting Rifle, 24" barrel, from **$1,096.64**
Price: 1866 Short Rifle, 20" barrel, from **$1,096.64**
Price: 1866 Carbine, 19" barrel, from **$1,123.42**
Price: 1866 Trapper, 16" barrel, from **$1,069.86**

CIMARRON 1873 SHORT RIFLE
Caliber: 357 Mag., 38 Spec., 32 WCF, 38 WCF, 44 Spec., 44 WCF, 45 Colt. **Barrel:** 20" tapered octagon. **Weight:** 7.5 lbs. **Length:** 39" overall. **Stock:** Walnut. **Sights:** Bead front, adjustable semi-buckhorn rear. **Features:** Has half "button" magazine. Original-type markings, including caliber, on barrel and elevator and "Kings" patent. From Cimarron F.A. Co.
Price: **$1,203.76**

CIMARRON 1873 DELUXE SPORTING RIFLE
Similar to the 1873 Short Rifle except has 24" barrel with half-magazine.
Price: **$1,324.70**

CIMARRON 1873 LONG RANGE RIFLE
Caliber: 44 WCF, 45 Colt. **Barrel:** 30", octagonal. **Weight:** 8.5 lbs. **Length:** 48" overall. **Stock:** Walnut. **Sights:** Blade front, semi-buckhorn ramp rear. Tang sight optional. **Features:** Color case-hardened frame; choice of modern blue-black or charcoal blue for other parts. Barrel marked "Kings Improvement." From Cimarron F.A. Co.
Price: **$1,284.10**

DIXIE ENGRAVED 1873 SPORTING RIFLE
Caliber: 44-40, 13-shot magazine. **Barrel:** 24.25", tapered octagon. **Weight:** 8.25 lbs. **Length:** 43.25" overall. **Stock:** Walnut. **Sights:** Blade front, adjustable rear. **Features:** Engraved frame polished bright (casehardened on plain). Replica of Winchester 1873. Made in Italy. From Dixie Gun Works.
Price: Plain, blued rifle in .44/40, .45 LC, .32/20, .38/40. . . . **$ 1,050.00**

DIXIE 1873 DELUXE SPORTING RIFLE
Caliber: .44-40, .45 LC, .32-20 and .38-40, 13-shot magazine. **Barrel:** 24.25", tapered octagon. **Weight:** 8.25 lbs. **Length:** 43.25" overall. **Stock:** Walnut. Checkered pistol grip buttstock and forearm. **Sights:** Blade front, adjustable rear. **Features:** Color casehardened frame. Engraved frame polished bright. Replica of Winchester 1873. Made in Italy. From Dixie Gun Works.
Price: . . . . **$ 1,050.00 to $ 1,100.00**

DIXIE LIGHTNING RIFLE AND CARBINE
Caliber: .44-40 or .45 LC, 10-shot magazine. **Barrel:** 26" round or octagon, 1:16" or 1:36" twist. **Weight:** 7.25 lbs. **Length:** 43" overall. **Stock:** Walnut. **Sights:** Blade front, open adjustable rear. **Features:** Checkered forearm, blued steel furniture. Made by Pedersoli in Italy. Imported by Dixie Gun Works.
Price: **$1,095.00**
Price: Carbine **$1,225.00**

Prices given are believed to be accurate at time of publication however, many factors affect retail pricing so exact prices are not possible.

EMF 1860 HENRY RIFLE
Caliber: 44-40 or 45 Colt. **Barrel:** 24". **Weight:** About 9 lbs. **Length:** About 43.75" overall. **Stock:** Oil-stained American walnut. **Sights:** Blade front, rear adjustable for elevation. **Features:** Reproduction of the original Henry rifle with brass frame and buttplate, rest blued. Imported by EMF.
Price: Brass frame **$1,149.90**
Price: Casehardened frame **$1,229.90**

EMF 1866 YELLOWBOY LEVER ACTIONS
Caliber: 38 Spec., 44-40, 45 LC. **Barrel:** 19" (carbine), 24" (rifle). **Weight:** 9 lbs. **Length:** 43" overall (rifle). **Stock:** European walnut. **Sights:** Bead front, open adjustable rear. **Features:** Solid brass frame, blued barrel, lever, hammer, buttplate. Imported from Italy by EMF.
Price: Rifle **$1,044.90**
Price: Border Rifle, Short **$969.90**

EMF MODEL 1873 LEVER-ACTION RIFLE
Caliber: 32/20, 357 Mag., 38/40, 44-40, 45 Colt. **Barrel:** 18", 20", 24", 30". **Weight:** 8 lbs. **Length:** 43.25" overall. **Stock:** European walnut. **Sights:** Bead front, rear adjustable for windage and elevation. **Features:** Color case-hardened frame (blue on carbine). Imported by EMF.
Price: **$1,099.90**

EMF MODEL 1873 REVOLVER CARBINE
Caliber: 357 Mag., 45 Colt. **Barrel:** 18". **Weight:** 4 lbs., 8 oz. **Length:** 43-3/4" overall. **Stock:** One-piece walnut. **Sights:** Blade front, notch rear. **Features:** Color case-hardened frame, blue barrel, backstrap and trigger guard. Introduced 1998. Imported from Italy by EMF.
Price: Standard . . . . **$979.90 to $1,040.00**

HENRY BIG BOY LEVER-ACTION CARBINE
Caliber: 357 Magnum, 44 Magnum, 45 Colt, 10-shot tubular magazine. **Barrel:** 20" octagonal, 1:38 right-hand twist. **Weight:** 8.68 lbs. **Length:** 38.5" overall. **Stock:** Straight-grip American walnut, brass buttplate. **Sights:** Marbles full adjustable semi-buckhorn rear, brass bead front. **Features:** Brasslite receiver not tapped for scope mount. Made in U.S.A. by Henry Repeating Arms.
Price: H006 44 Magnum, walnut, blued barrel **$899.95**
Price: H006DD Deluxe 44 Magnum, engraved receiver. . . . **$1,995.95**

HENRY .30/30 LEVER-ACTION CARBINE
Same as the Big Boy except has straight grip American walnut, 30-30 only, 6-shot. Receivers are drilled and tapped for scope mount. Made in U.S.A. by Henry Repeating Arms.
Price: H009 Blued receiver, round barrel **$749.95**
Price: H009B Brass receiver, octagonal barrel. **$969.95**

MARLIN MODEL 336C LEVER-ACTION CARBINE
Caliber: 30-30 or 35 Rem., 6-shot tubular magazine. **Barrel:** 20" Micro-Groove. **Weight:** 7 lbs. **Length:** 38.5" overall. **Stock:** Checkered American black walnut, capped pistol grip. Mar-Shield finish; rubber buttpad; swivel studs. **Sights:** Ramp front with Wide-Scan hood, semi-buckhorn folding rear adjustable for windage and elevation. **Features:** Hammer-block safety. Receiver tapped for scope mount, offset hammer spur; top of receiver sandblasted to prevent glare. Includes safety lock.
Price: **$530.00**

MARLIN MODEL 336SS LEVER-ACTION CARBINE
Same as the 336C except receiver, barrel and other major parts are machined from stainless steel. 30-30 only, 6-shot; receiver tapped for scope. Includes safety lock.
Price: **$650.00**

MARLIN MODEL 336W LEVER-ACTION RIFLE
Similar to the Model 336C except has walnut-finished, cut-checkered Maine birch stock; blued steel barrel band has integral sling swivel; no front sight hood; comes with padded nylon sling; hard rubber buttplate. Introduced 1998. Includes safety lock. Made in U.S.A. by Marlin.

Price: **$452.00**
Price: With 4x scope and mount **$495.00**

MARLIN 336BL
Lever action rifle chambered for .30-30. Features include 6-shot full length tubular magazine; 18-inch blued barrel with Micro-Groove rifling (12 grooves); big-loop finger lever; side ejection; blued steel receiver; hammer block safety; brown laminated hardwood pistol-grip stock with fluted comb; cut checkering; deluxe recoil pad; blued swivel studs.
Price: . . . . **N/A**

MARLIN 336 DELUXE
Lever action rifle chambered in .30-30.
Features include 6-shot tubular magazine; side ejection; solid top receiver; highly polished deep blue finish; hammer block safety; #1 grade full fancy American black walnut stock and forend; 20-inch barrel with Micro-Groove rifling (12 grooves); adjustable semi-buckhorn folding rear, ramp front sight with brass bead and Wide-Scan™ hood. Solid top receiver tapped for scope mount; offset hammer spur (right or left hand) for scope use.
Price: . . . . **N/A**

MARLIN MODEL XLR LEVER-ACTION RIFLES
Similar to Model 336C except has an 24" stainless barrel with Ballard-type cut rifling, stainless steel receiver and other parts, laminated hardwood stock with pistol grip, nickel-plated swivel studs. Chambered for 30-30 Win. with Hornady spire-pointed Flex-Tip cartridges. Includes safety lock. Introduced 2006. Similar models chambered for 308 Marlin Express introduced in 2007
Price: Model 336XLR **$816.00**

MARLIN MODEL 338MXLR
Caliber: 338 Marlin Express. **Barrel:** 24" stainless steel. **Weight:** 7.5 lbs. **Length:** 42.5" overall. **Features:** Stainless steel receiver, lever and magazine tube. Black/gray laminated checkered stock and forend. Hooded ramp front sight and adjustable semi-buckhorn rear; drilled and tapped for scope mounts. Receiver-mounted crossbolt safety.
Price: Model 338MXLR **$806.00**
Price: Model 308MXLR: 308 Marlin Express **$806.00**
Price: Model 338MX: Similar to Model 338MXLR but with blued metal and walnut stock and forend **$611.00**
Price: Model 308MX: 308 Marlin Express **$611.00**

MARLIN MODEL 444 LEVER-ACTION SPORTER
Caliber: 444 Marlin, 5-shot tubular magazine. **Barrel:** 22" deep cut Ballard rifling. **Weight:** 7.5 lbs. **Length:** 40.5" overall. **Stock:** Checkered American black walnut, capped pistol grip, rubber rifle buttpad. Mar-Shield finish; swivel studs. **Sights:** Hooded ramp front, folding semi-buckhorn rear adjustable for windage and elevation. **Features:** Hammer-block safety. Receiver tapped for scope mount; offset hammer spur. Includes safety lock.
Price: **$619.00**

MARLIN MODEL 444XLR LEVER-ACTION RIFLE
Similar to Model 444 except has an 24" stainless barrel with Ballard-type cut rifling, stainless steel receiver and other parts, laminated hardwood stock with pistol grip, nickel-plated swivel studs. Chambered for 444 Marlin with Hornady Evolution spire-pointed Flex-Tip cartridges. Includes safety lock. Introduced 2006.
Price: (Model 444XLR) **$816.00**

CENTERFIRE RIFLES—Lever & Slide

MARLIN MODEL 1894 LEVER-ACTION CARBINE
Caliber: 44 Spec./44 Mag., 10-shot tubular magazine. **Barrel:** 20"
Ballard-type rifling. **Weight:** 6 lbs. **Length:** 37.5" overall. **Stock:**
Checkered American black walnut, straight grip and forend. Mar-
Shield finish. Rubber rifle buttpad; swivel studs. **Sights:** Wide-
Scan hooded ramp front, semi-buckhorn folding rear adjustable for
windage and elevation. **Features:** Hammer-block safety. Receiver
tapped for scope mount, offset hammer spur, solid top receiver sand
blasted to prevent glare. Includes safety lock.
Price: **$576.00**

MARLIN MODEL 1894C CARBINE
Similar to the standard Model 1894 except chambered for 38
Spec./357 Mag. with full-length 9-shot magazine, 18.5" barrel,
hammer-block safety, hooded front sight. Introduced 1983. Includes
safety lock.
Price: **$576.00**

MARLIN MODEL 1894 COWBOY
Caliber: 357 Mag., 44 Mag., 45 Colt, 10-
shot magazine. **Barrel:** 20" tapered octagon, deep cut
rifling. **Weight:** 7.5 lbs. **Length:** 41.5" overall. **Stock:** Straight grip
American black walnut, hard rubber buttplate, Mar-Shield finish.
Sights: Marble carbine front, adjustable Marble semi-buckhorn
rear. **Features:** Squared finger lever; straight grip stock; blued steel
forend tip. Designed for Cowboy Shooting events. Introduced 1996.
Includes safety lock. Made in U.S.A. by Marlin.
Price: **$822.00**

MARLIN MODEL 1894SS
Similar to Model 1894 except has stainless steel barrel, receiver,
lever, guard plate, magazine tube and loading plate. Nickel-plated
swivel studs.
Price: **$704.00**

MARLIN 1894 DELUXE
Lever action rifle chambered in .44
Magnum/.44 Special. Features include 10-shot tubular
magazine; squared finger lever; side ejection; richly polished
deep blued metal surfaces; solid top receiver; hammer block safety;
#1 grade fancy American black walnut straight-grip stock and forend;
cut checkering; rubber rifle butt pad; Mar-Shield finish; blued steel
fore-end cap; swivel studs; deep-cut Ballard-type rifling (6 grooves).
Price: . . . . **N/A**

MARLIN 1894CSS
Lever action rifle chambered in .357
Magnum/.38 Special. Features include 9-shot tubular
magazine; stainless steel receiver, barrel, lever, trigger and
hammer; squared finger lever; side ejection; solid top receiver;
hammer block safety; American black walnut straight-grip stock and
forend; cut checkering; rubber rifle butt pad; Mar-Shield finish.
Price: . . . . **N/A**

MARLIN MODEL 1895 LEVER-ACTION RIFLE
Caliber: 45-70 Govt., 4-shot tubular magazine. **Barrel:** 22"
round. **Weight:** 7.5 lbs. **Length:** 40.5" overall. **Stock:** Checkered
American black walnut, full pistol grip. Mar-Shield finish; rubber
buttpad; quick detachable swivel studs. **Sights:** Bead front with Wide-
Scan hood, semi-buckhorn folding rear adjustable for windage and
elevation. **Features:** Hammer-block safety. Solid receiver tapped for
scope mounts or receiver sights; offset hammer spur. Includes safety
lock.
Price: **$619.00**

MARLIN MODEL 1895G GUIDE GUN LEVER-ACTION RIFLE
Similar to Model 1895 with deep-cut Ballard-type rifling; straight-grip
walnut stock. Overall length is 37", weighs 7 lbs. Introduced 1998.
Includes safety lock. Made in U.S.A. by Marlin.
Price: **$630.00**

MARLIN MODEL 1895GS GUIDE GUN
Similar to Model 1895G except receiver, barrel and most metal parts
are machined from stainless steel. Chambered for 45-70 Govt.,
4-shot, 18.5" barrel. Overall length is 37", weighs 7 lbs. Introduced
2001. Includes safety lock. Made in U.S.A. by Marlin.
Price: **$752.00**

MARLIN MODEL 1895 SBLR
Similar to Model 1895GS Guide Gun but with stainless steel barrel
(18.5"), receiver, large loop lever and magazine tube. Black/gray
laminated buttstock and forend, XS ghost ring rear sight, hooded
ramp front sight, receiver/barrel-mounted top rail for mounting
accessory optics. Chambered in 45-70 Government. Overall length is
42.5", weighs 7.5 lbs.
Price: **$979.00**

MARLIN MODEL 1895 COWBOY LEVER-ACTION RIFLE
Similar to Model 1895 except has 26" tapered octagon barrel with
Ballard-type rifling, Marble carbine front sight and Marble adjustable
semi-buckhorn rear sight. Receiver tapped for scope or receiver
sight. Overall length is 44.5", weighs about 8 lbs. Introduced 2001.
Includes safety lock. Made in U.S.A. by Marlin.
Price: **$785.00**

MARLIN MODEL 1895XLR LEVER-ACTION RIFLE
Similar to Model 1895 except has an 24" stainless barrel with Ballard-type cut rifling, stainless steel receiver and other parts, laminated
hardwood stock with pistol grip, nickel-plated swivel studs. Chambered
for 45-70 Govt. Government with Hornady Evolution spire-pointed
Flex-Tip cartridges. Includes safety lock. Introduced 2006.
Price: (Model 1895MXLR) **$816.00**

MARLIN MODEL 1895M LEVER-
ACTION RIFLE
Similar to Model 1895G except has an 18.5" barrel with
Ballard-type cut rifling. Chambered for 450 Marlin. Includes
safety lock.
Price: (Model 1895M) **$678.00**

MARLIN MODEL 1895MXLR LEVER-ACTION RIFLE
Similar to Model 1895M except has an 24" stainless barrel with
Ballard-type cut rifling, stainless steel receiver and other parts,
laminated hardwood stock with pistol grip, nickel-plated swivel studs.
Chambered for 450 Marlin with Hornady Evolution spire-pointed
Flex-Tip cartridges. Includes safety lock. Introduced 2006.
Price: (Model 1895MXLR) **$874.00**

MARLIN 1895GBL
Lever action rifle chambered in .45-70
Government. Features include 6-shot, full-
length tubular magazine; 18-1/2-inch barrel with deep-cut
Ballard-type rifling (6 grooves); big-loop finger lever; side ejection;
solid-top receiver; deeply blued metal surfaces; hammer block
safety; pistol-grip two tone brown laminate stock with cut checkering;
ventilated recoil pad; Mar-Shield finish, swivel studs.

Price: . . . . **N/A**

MOSSBERG 464 LEVER ACTION RIFLE
Caliber: 30-30 Win., 6-shot tubular magazine. **Barrel:** 20" round.
Weight: 6.7 lbs. **Length:** 38.5" overall. **Stock:** Hardwood with
straight or pistol grip, quick detachable swivel studs. **Sights:** Folding
rear sight, adjustable for windage and elevation. **Features:** Blued
receiver and barrel, receiver drilled and tapped, two-position top-tang
safety. Available with straight grip or semi-pistol grip. Introduced
2008. From O.F. Mossberg & Sons, Inc.
Price: **$497.00**

Prices given are believed to be accurate at time of publication however, many factors affect retail pricing so exact prices are not possible.

NAVY ARMS 1874 SHARPS #2 CREEDMORE RIFLE
Caliber: .45-70 Govt. **Barrel:** 30" octagon. **Weight:** 10 lbs. **Length:** 48" overall. **Sights:** Soule target grade rear tang sight, front globe with 12 inserts. **Features:** Highly polished nickel receiver and action, double-set triggers. From Navy Arms.
Price: Model SCR072 (2008) $1,816.00

NAVY ARMS MILITARY HENRY RIFLE
Caliber: 44-40 or 45 Colt, 12-shot magazine. **Barrel:** 24.25". **Weight:** 9 lbs., 4 oz. **Stock:** European walnut. **Sights:** Blade front, adjustable ladder-type rear. **Features:** Brass frame, buttplate, rest blued. Replica of the model used by cavalry units in the Civil War. Has full-length magazine tube, sling swivels; no forend. Imported from Italy by Navy Arms.
Price: $1,199.00

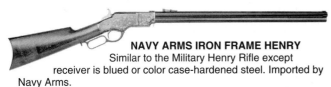

NAVY ARMS IRON FRAME HENRY
Similar to the Military Henry Rifle except receiver is blued or color case-hardened steel. Imported by Navy Arms.
Price: Blued $1,247.00

NAVY ARMS 1866 YELLOW BOY RIFLE
Caliber: 38 Spec., 44-40, 45 Colt, 12-shot magazine. **Barrel:** 20" or 24", full octagon. **Weight:** 8.5 lbs. **Length:** 42.5" overall. **Stock:** Walnut. **Sights:** Blade front, adjustable ladder-type rear. **Features:** Brass frame, forend tip, buttplate, blued barrel, lever, hammer. Introduced 1991. Imported from Italy by Navy Arms.
Price: Yellow Boy Rifle, 24.25" barrel $915.00
Price: Yellow Boy Carbine, 19" barrel $882.00

NAVY ARMS 1873 WINCHESTER-STYLE RIFLE
Caliber: 357 Mag., 44-40, 45 Colt, 12-shot magazine. **Barrel:** 24.25". **Weight:** 8.25 lbs. **Length:** 43" overall. **Stock:** European walnut. **Sights:** Blade front, buckhorn rear. **Features:** Color case-hardened frame, rest blued. Full-octagon barrel. Imported by Navy Arms.
Price: $1,047.00
Price: 1873 Carbine, 19" barrel $1,024.00
Price: 1873 Sporting Rifle (octagonal bbl., checkered walnut stock and forend) $1,183.00
Price: 1873 Border Model, 20" octagon barrel $1,047.00
Price: 1873 Deluxe Border Model $1,183.00

PUMA BOUNTY HUNTER RIFLE
Caliber: .44/40, .44 Mag. and .45 Colt, 6-shot magazine capacity. **Barrel:** 12". **Weight:** 4.5 lbs. **Length:** 24". **Stock:** Walnut. **Sights:** Fixed sights. **Features:** A piece of 1950's TV nostalgia, the Bounty Hunter is a reproduction of the gun carried by Western character Josh Randall in the series "Wanted: Dead or Alive". The Bounty Hunter is based on a Model 92 rifle, but is considered by Federal Law as a pistol, because it is built from the ground up as a handgun. Manufactured in the U.S.A. by Chiappa Firearms of Dayton, OH, the Bounty Hunter features a 12" barrel and 6 round tubular magazine. At just 24" OAL, the Bounty Hunter makes an ideal pack gun or camp defense pistol. The Bounty Hunter has a teardrop shaped loop lever and is built with the same fit, finish and high grade Italian walnut stocks as our Puma M-92 and M-86 rifles.
Price: .45LC, Case Hardened/Blued $1,372.00
Price: .44/40, Case Hardened/Blued $1,372.00
Price: .44MAG, Case Hardened/Blued $1,372.00

PUMA MODEL 92 RIFLES AND CARBINES
Caliber: 17 HMR (XP and Scout models, only; intr. 2008), 38 Spec./357 Mag., 44 Mag., 45 Colt, 454 Casull, 480 Ruger (.44-40 in 20" octagonal barrel). **Barrel:** 16" and 20" round; 20" and 24" octagonal. 1:30" rate of twist (exc. 17 HMR is 1:9"). **Weight:** 7.7 lbs. **Stock:** Walnut stained hardwood. **Sights:** Blade front, V rear, buckhorn sights sold separately. **Features:** Finishes available in blue/blue, blue/case colored and stainless/stainless with matching crescent butt plates. .454 and .480 calibers have rubber recoil pads.

Full-length magazines, thumb safety. Large lever loop or HiViz sights available on select models. Magazine capacity is 12 rounds with 24" bbl.; 10 rounds with 20" barrel; 8 rounds in 16" barrel. Introduced in 2002. Scout includes long-eye-relief scope, rail, elevated cheekpiece, intr. 2008. XP chambered in 17 HMR, 38 Spec./357 Mag. and 44 Mag., loads through magazine tube or loading gate, intr. 2008. Imported from Brazil by Legacy Sports International.
Price: From $959.00
Price: Scout Model, w/2.5x32 Nikko-Stirling Nighteater scope, intr. 2008, from $739.00
Price: XP Model, tube feed magazine, intr. 2008, from $613.00

REMINGTON MODEL 7600/7615 PUMP ACTION
Caliber: 243 Win., 270 Win., 30-06 Spfl., 308; 223 Rem. (7615 only). **Barrel:** 22" round tapered. **Weight:** 7.5 lbs. **Length:** 42.6" overall. **Stock:** Cut-checkered walnut pistol grip and forend, Monte Carlo with full cheekpiece. Satin or high-gloss finish. Also, black synthetic. **Sights:** Gold bead front sight on matted ramp, open step adjustable sporting rear. **Features:** Redesigned and improved version of the Model 760. Detachable 4-shot clip. Cross-bolt safety. Receiver tapped for scope mount. Introduced 1981. Model 7615 Tactical chambered in 223 Rem. **Features:** Knoxx SpecOps NRS (Non Recoil Suppressing) adjustable stock, parkerized finish, 10-round detachable magazine box, sling swivel studs. Introduced 2007.
Price: 7600 Wood $792.00
Price: 7600 Synthetic. $665.00
Price: 7615 Ranch Carbine $955.00
Price: 7615 Camo Hunter $1,009.00
Price: 7615 Tactical 223 Rem., 16.5" barrel, 10-rd. magazine (2008). $932.00

ROSSI R92 LEVER-ACTION CARBINE
Caliber: 38 Special/357 Mag, 44 Mag., 44-40 Win., 45 Colt, 454 Casull. **Barrel:** 16" or 20" with round barrel, 20" or 24" with octagon barrel. **Weight:** 4.8 lbs. to 7 lbs. **Length:** 34" to 41.5". **Features:** Blued or stainless finish. Various options available in selected chamberings (large lever loop, fiber optic sights, cheekpiece, etc.).
Price: From $499.00

TAURUS THUNDERBOLT PUMP ACTION
Caliber: 38/.357, 45 Long Colt, 12 or 14 rounds. **Barrel:** 26" blue or polished stainless. **Weight:** 8.1 lbs. **Length:** 43" overall. **Stock:** Hardwood stock and forend. Gloss finish. **Sights:** Longhorn adjustable rear. Introduced 2004. Imported from Brazil by Taurus International.
Price: C45BR (blued) $705.00
Price: C45SSR (stainless) $813.00

TRISTAR SHARPS 1874 SPORTING RIFLE
Caliber: 45-70 Govt. **Barrel:** 28", 32", 34" octagonal. **Weight:** 9.75 lbs. **Length:** 44.5" overall. **Stock:** Walnut. **Sights:** Dovetail front, adjustable rear. **Features:** Cut checkering, case colored frame finish.
Price: $1,099.00

UBERTI 1873 SPORTING RIFLE
Caliber: 357 Mag., 44-40, 45 Colt. **Barrel:** 19" to 24.25". **Weight:** Up to 8.2 lbs. **Length:** Up to 43.3" overall. **Stock:** Walnut, straight grip and pistol grip. **Sights:** Blade front adjustable for windage, open rear adjustable for elevation. **Features:** Color case-hardened frame, blued barrel, hammer, lever, buttplate, brass elevator. Imported by Stoeger Industries.
Price: 1873 Carbine, 19" round barrel $1,199.00

Price: 1873 Short Rifle, 20" octagonal barrel **$1,249.00**
Price: 1873 Special Sporting Rifle, 24.25" octagonal barrel   **$1,379.00**

UBERTI 1866 YELLOWBOY CARBINE, SHORT RIFLE, RIFLE

Caliber: 38 Spec., 44-40, 45 Colt. **Barrel:** 24.25", octagonal. **Weight:** 8.2 lbs. **Length:** 43.25" overall. **Stock:** Walnut. **Sights:** Blade front adjustable for windage, rear adjustable for elevation. **Features:** Frame, buttplate, forend cap of polished brass, balance charcoal blued. Imported by Stoeger Industries.
Price: 1866 Yellowboy Carbine, 19" round barrel **$1,079.00**
Price: 1866 Yellowboy Short Rifle, 20" octagonal barrel . . . **$1,129.00**
Price: 1866 Yellowboy Rifle, 24.25" octagonal barrel **$1,129.00**

UBERTI 1860 HENRY RIFLE

Caliber: 44-40, 45 Colt. **Barrel:** 24.25", half-octagon. **Weight:** 9.2 lbs. **Length:** 43.75" overall. **Stock:** American walnut. **Sights:** Blade front, rear adjustable for elevation. Imported by Stoeger Industries.
Price: 1860 Henry Trapper, 18.5" barrel, brass frame **$1,329.00**
Price: 1860 Henry Rifle Iron Frame, 24.25" barrel **$1,419.00**

UBERTI LIGHTNING RIFLE

Caliber: 357 Mag., 45 Colt, 10+1. **Barrel:** 20" to 24.25". **Stock:** Walnut. **Finish:** Blue or case-hardened. Introduced 2006. Imported by Stoeger Industries.
Price: 1875 Lightning Rifle, 24.25" barrel **$1,259.00**
Price: 1875 Lightning Short Rifle, 20" barrel **$1,259.00**
Price: 1875 Lightning Carbine, 20" barrel **$1,179.00**

UBERTI SPRINGFIELD TRAPDOOR RIFLE

Caliber: 4-70, single shot. **Barrel:** 22" or 32.5". **Stock:** Walnut. **Finish:** Blue and case-hardened. Introduced 2006. Imported by Stoeger Industries.
Price: Springfield Trapdoor Carbine, 22" barrel **$1,429.00**
Price: Springfield Trapdoor Army, 32.5" barrel **$1,669.00**

U.S. FIRE ARMS STANDARD LIGHTNING MAGAZINE RIFLE

Caliber: 45 Colt, 44 WCF, 44 Spec., 38 WCF, 15-shot. **Barrel:** 26". **Stock:** Oiled walnut. **Finish:** High polish blue. Nickel finish also available. Introduced 2002. Made in U.S.A. by United States Fire-Arms Manufacturing Co.
Price: Round barrel. **$1,480.00**
Price: Octagonal barrel, checkered forend **$1,750.00**
Price: Half-round barrel, checkered forend **$1,995.00**
Price: Premium Carbine, 20" round barrel **$1,480.00**
Price: Baby Carbine, 20" special taper barrel **$1,995.00**
Price: Deluxe Lightning **$2,559.00**

WINCHESTER MODEL 1895 SAFARI CENTENNIAL HIGH GRADE

Caliber: 405 Win. **Barrel:** 24" blued round, four-round box mag. **Weight:** 8 lbs. **Length:** NA. **Features:** Patterned after original Winchester Model 1895. Commemorates Theodore Roosevelt's

---

1909 African safari. Checkered walnut forend and buttstock with inlaid "TR" medallion, engraved and silvered receiver.
Price: **$1,749.00**
Price: Custom Grade: Jeweled hammer, fancier wood and angraving, gold-filled highlights and numerous accessories. Production limited to 100 sets **$3,649.00**

WINCHESTER MODEL 1894 CUSTOM GRADE

Lever-action rifle chambered in .30-30. Features include 24-inch half-round, half octagon deeply blued barrel; buckhorn rear sight with Marble's gold bead front sight; Grade IV/V walnut stock and forend with a rich, high gloss finish; deep scroll engraving on both sides of the blued receiver. Commemorates the 200th anniversary of Oliver F. Winchester's birth. An early Winchester Repeating Arms crest graces the left side of the receiver, with the right side bearing the words, "Two Hundred Years, Oliver F. Winchester," and the dates, "1810 — 2010," in gold. The barrel is deeply polished, with the signature of Oliver F. Winchester in gold on the top of the bolt. Sold individually in limited quantities and in 500 sets with the High Grade.
Price (single rifle): **$1,959.00**

WINCHESTER MODEL 1894 HIGH GRADE

Lever-action rifle chambered in .30-30. Features include 24-inch half-round, half octagon deeply blued barrel; buckhorn rear sight with Marble's gold bead front sight; silver nitride receiver; Grade II/III high gloss walnut stock and forend with a rich, high gloss finish; delicate scroll work, with Oliver F. Winchester's signature in gold on top of the bolt. The left side of receiver bears an early Winchester Repeating Arms crest; on right side are the words, "Two Hundred Years, Oliver F. Winchester," and the dates, "1810 — 2010." Sold individually in limited quantities and in 500 sets with the Custom Grade.
Price (single rifle): **$1,469.00**

Prices given are believed to be accurate at time of publication however, many factors affect retail pricing so exact prices are not possible.

BARRETT MODEL 95 BOLT-ACTION RIFLE

Caliber: 50 BMG, 5-shot magazine. **Barrel:** 29". **Weight:** 23.5 lbs. **Length:** 45" overall. **Stock:** Energy-absorbing recoil pad. **Sights:** Scope optional. **Features:** Bolt-action, bullpup design. Disassembles without tools; extendable bipod legs; match-grade barrel; muzzle brake. Introduced 1995. Made in U.S.A. by Barrett Firearms Mfg., Inc.
Price: From **$6,500.00**

BLASER R93 BOLT-ACTION RIFLE

Caliber: 22-250 Rem., 243 Win., 6.5x55, 270 Win., 7x57, 7mm-08 Rem., 308 Win., 30-06 Spfl., 257 Wby. Mag., 7mm Rem. Mag., 300 Win. Mag., 300 Wby. Mag., 338 Win. Mag., 375 H&H, 416 Rem. Mag. **Barrel:** 22" (standard calibers), 26" (magnum). **Weight:** 7 lbs. **Length:** 40" overall (22" barrel). **Stock:** Two-piece European walnut. **Sights:** None furnished; drilled and tapped for scope mounting. **Features:** Straight pull-back bolt action with thumb-activated safety slide/cocking mechanism; interchangeable barrels and bolt heads. Introduced 1994. Imported from Germany by Blaser USA.
Price: R93 Prestige, wood grade 3 . . . . **$3,275.00**
Price: R93 Luxus **$4,460.00**
Price: R93 Professional **$2,950.00**
Price: R93 Grand Luxe **$8,163.00**
Price: R93 Attache **$6,175.00**

BROWNING A-BOLT RIFLES

Common Features: Short-throw (60") fluted bolt, three locking lugs, plunger-type ejector; adjustable trigger is grooved. Chrome-plated trigger sear. Hinged floorplate, detachable box magazine. Slide tang safety. Receivers are drilled and tapped for scope mounts, swivel studs included. Barrel is free-floating and glass-bedded, recessed muzzle. Safety is top-tang sliding button. Engraving available for bolt sleeve or rifle body. Introduced 1985. Imported from Japan by Browning.

BROWNING A-BOLT HUNTER

Calibers: 22" Barrel: 223 Rem., 22-250 Rem., 243 Win., 270 Win., 30-06 Spfl., 7mm-08 Win. **Barrel:** 270 WSM, 7mm WSM, 300 WSM, 325 WSM (intr. 2005). **Calibers:** 24" Barrel: 25-06 Rem. **Calibers:** 26" Barrel: 7mm Rem. Mag., 300 Win. Mag., 338 Win. Mag. **Weight:** 6.25-7.2 lbs. **Length:** 41.25-46.5" overall. **Stock:** Sporter-style walnut; checkered grip and forend. **Metal Finish:** Low-luster blueing.
Price: Hunter, left-hand, from **$819.00**

BROWNING A-BOLT HUNTER FLD

Caliber: 23" Barrel: 270 WSM, 7mm WSM, 300 WSM, 325 WSM (intr. 2005). **Weight:** 6.6 lbs. **Length:** 42.75" overall. **Features:** FLD has low-luster blueing and select Monte Carlo stock with right-hand palm swell, double-border checkering. Otherwise similar to A-Bolt Hunter.
Price: FLD **$899.00**

BROWNING A-BOLT TARGET

Similar to A-Bolt Hunter but with 28" heavy bull blued barrel, blued receiver, satin finish gray laminated stock

with adjustable comb and semi-beavertail forend. Chambered in 223, 308 Winchester and 300 WSM. Available also with stainless receiver and barrel.
Price: From **$1,269.00**
Price: Stainless, from **$1,489.00**

BROWNING A-BOLT MOUNTAIN TI

Caliber: 223 WSSM, 243 WSSM, 25 WSSM (all added 2005); 270 WSM, 7mm WSM, 300 WSM. **Barrel:** 22" or 23". **Weight:** 5.25-5.5 lbs. **Length:** 41.25-42.75" overall. **Stock:** Lightweight fiberglass Bell & Carlson model in Mossy-Oak New Break Up camo. **Metal Finish:** Stainless barrel, titanium receiver. **Features:** Pachmayr Decelerator recoil pad. Introduced 1999.
Price: From **$1,819.00**

BROWNING A-BOLT MICRO HUNTER AND MICRO HUNTER LEFT-HAND

Calibers: 20" Barrel: 22-250 Rem., 243 Win., 308 Win., 7mm-08. 22" Barrel: 22 Hornet, 270 WSM, 7mm WSM, 300 WSM, 325 WSM (2005). **Weight:** 6.25-6.4 lbs. **Length:** 39.5-41.5" overall. **Features:** Classic walnut stock with 13.3" LOP. Otherwise similar to A-Bolt Hunter.
Price: Micro Hunter, from **$759.00**
Price: Micro Hunter left-hand, from **$799.00**

BROWNING A-BOLT MEDALLION

Calibers: 22" Barrel: 223 Rem., 22-250 Rem., 243 Win., 308 Win., 270 Win., 280 Rem., 30-06; 23" Barrel: 270 WSM, 7mm WSM, 300 WSM, 325 WSM (intr. 2005); 24" Barrel: 25-06 Rem.; 26" Barrel: 7mm Rem. Mag., 300 Win. Mag., 338 Win. Mag., 375 H&H. **Weight:** 6.25-7.1 lbs. **Length:** 41.25-46.5" overall. **Stock:** Select walnut stock, glossy finish, rosewood grip and forend caps, checkered grip and forend. **Metal Finish:** Engraved high-polish blued receiver.
Price: Medallion, from **$909.00**
Price: Medallion WSM **$959.00**
Price: Medallion w/BOSS, intr. 1987, from **$1,009.00**

BROWNING A-BOLT WHITE GOLD MEDALLION, RMEF WHITE GOLD, WHITE GOLD MEDALLION W/BOSS

Calibers: 22" Barrel: 270 Win., 30-06. Calibers: 23" Barrel: 270 WSM, 7mm WSM, 300 WSM, 325 WSM (intr. 2005). Calibers: 26" Barrel: 7mm Rem. Mag., 300 Win. Mag. **Weight:** 6.4-7.7 lbs. **Length:** 42.75-46.5" overall. **Stock:** select walnut stock with brass spacers between rubber recoil pad and between the rosewood gripcap and forend tip; gold-filled barrel inscription; palm-swell pistol grip, Monte Carlo comb, 22 lpi checkering with double borders. **Metal Finish:** Engraved high-polish stainless receiver and barrel. BOSS version chambered in 270 Win. and 30-06 (22" barrel) and 7mm Rem. Mag. and 300 Win. Mag. (26" barrel). Introduced 1988. RMEF version has engraved gripcap, continental cheekpiece; gold engraved, stainless receiver and bbl. Introduced 2004.
Price: White Gold Medallion, from **$1,309.00**
Price: Rocky Mt. Elk Foundation White Gold, 325 WSM, intr. 2007 . . . . **$1,399.00**

BROWNING A-BOLT STAINLESS STALKER, STAINLESS STALKER LEFT-HAND

Calibers: 22" Barrel: 223 Rem., 243 Win., 270 Win., 280 Rem., 7mm-08 Rem., 30-06 Spfl., 308 Win. Calibers: 23" Barrel: 270 WSM, 7mm WSM, 300 WSM, 325 WSM (intr. 2005). Calibers: 24" Barrel: 25-06 Rem. Calibers: 26" Barrel: 7mm Rem. Mag., 300 Win. Mag., 338 Win. Mag., 375 H&H. **Weight:** 6.1-7.2 lbs. **Length:** 40.9-46.5" overall. **Features:** Similar to the A-Bolt Hunter model except receiver and barrel are made of stainless steel; other exposed metal surfaces

are finished silver-gray matte. Graphite-fiberglass composite textured stock. No sights are furnished, except on 375 H&H, which comes with open sights. Introduced 1987.
Price: Stainless Stalker left-hand, from **$1,029.00**
Price: Stainless Stalker w/Boss, from. **$1,119.00**

BROWNING A-BOLT COMPOSITE STALKER
Calibers: 22 Barrel: 270 Win., 30-06 Sprg.; 23" Barrel: 270 WSM, 7mm WSM, 300 WSM, 325 WSM; 24" Barrel: 25-06 Rem.; 26" Barrel: 7mm Rem. Mag., 300 Win. Mag., 338 Win. Mag. **Weight:** 6.6-7.3 lbs. **Length:** 42.5-46.5" overall. **Features:** Similar to the A-Bolt Stainless Stalker except has black composite stock with textured finish and matte-blued finish on all exposed metal surfaces except bolt sleeve. No sights are furnished.
Price: Composite Stalker w/BOSS, from **$869.00**
Price: Stainless Stalker **$1,009.00**
Price: Stainless Stalker w/Boss, from. **$1,079.00**

BROWNING A-BOLT ECLIPSE HUNTER W/ BOSS, M-1000 ECLIPSE W/BOSS, M-1000 ECLIPSE WSM, STAINLESS M-1000 ECLIPSE WSM
Calibers: 22" Barrel: 270 Win., 30-06. Calibers: 26" Barrel: 7mm Rem. Mag., 300 Win. Mag., 270 WSM, 7mm WSM, 300 WSM. **Weight:** 7.5-9.9 lbs. **Length:** 42.75-46.5" overall. **Features:** All models have gray/black laminated thumbhole stock. Introduced 1996. Two versions have BOSS barrel vibration modulator and muzzle brake. Hunter has sporter-weight barrel. M-1000 Eclipses have long actions and heavy target barrels, adjustable triggers, bench-style forends, 3-shot magazines. Introduced 1997.
Price: Eclipse Hunter w/BOSS, from **$1,259.00**
Price: M-1000 Eclipse, from **$1,169.00**
Price: M-1000 Eclipse w/BOSS, from **$1,259.00**
Price: Stainless M-1000 Eclipse WSM, from **$1,399.00**
Price: Stainless M-1000 Eclipse w/BOSS, from **$1,489.00**

BROWNING X-BOLT HUNTER
Calibers: 223, 22-250, 243 Win., 25-06 Rem., 270 Win., 270 WSM, 280 Rem., 30-06 Spfl., 300 Win. Mag., 300 WSM, 308 Win., 325 WSM, 338 Win. Mag., 375 H&H Mag., 7mm Rem. Mag., 7mm WSM, 7mm-08 Rem. **Barrels:** 22", 23", 24", 26", varies by model. Matte blued or stainless free-floated barrel, recessed muzzle crown. **Weight:** 6.3-7 lbs. **Stock:** Hunter and Medallion models have wood stocks; Composite Stalker and Stainless Stalker models have composite stocks. Inflex Technology recoil pad. **Sights:** None, drilled and tapped receiver, X-Lock scope mounts. **Features:** Adjustable three-lever Feather Trigger system, polished hard-chromed steel components, factory pre-set at 3.5 lbs., alloy trigger housing. Bolt unlock button, detachable rotary magazine, 60-degree bolt lift, three locking lugs, top-tang safety, sling swivel studs. Medallion has metal engraving, gloss finish walnut stock, rosewood fore-end grip and pistol grip cap. Introduced 2008. From Browning.

BROWNING X-BOLT MICRO HUNTER
Similar to Browning X-Bolt Hunter but with compact dimensions (13-15/16 length of pull, 41-1/4 overall length).

Price: Standard chamberings . . **$839.00**
Price: Magnum **$869.00**

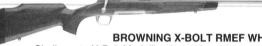

BROWNING X-BOLT MICRO MIDAS RIFLES
Caliber: 243 Win., 7mm-08 Rem., 308 Win., 22-250 Rem. **Barrel:** 20". **Weight:** 6 lbs.1 oz. **Length:** 37-5/8" to 38-1/8" overall. **Stock:** Satin finish checkered walnut stock. **Sights:** Hooded front and adjustable rear. **Features:** Steel receiver with low-luster blued finish. Glass bedded, drilled and tapped for scope mounts. Barrel is free-floating and hand chambered with target crown. Bolt-action with adjustable Feather Trigger™ and detachable rotary magazine. Compact 12-1/2" length of pull for smaller shooters, designed to fit smaller-framed shooters like youth and women. This model has all the same features as the full-size model with sling swivel studs installed and Inflex Technology recoil pad. (Scope and mounts not included).
Price: 243 Win. **$800**
Price: 7mm-08 Rem. **$800**
Price: 308 Win. **$800**
Price: 22-250 Rem. **$800**

BROWNING X-BOLT VARMINT STALKER
Similar to Browning X-Bolt Stalker but with medium-heavy free-floated barrel, target crown, composite stock. Chamberings available: 223, 22-250, 243 Winchester and 308 Winchester only.
Price: **$1,019.00**

BROWNING X-BOLT RMEF WHITE GOLD
Similar to X-Bolt Medallion but with gold-engraved matte stainless finish and Rocky Mountain Elk Foundation grip cap. Chambered in 325 WSM only.
Price: **$1,399.00**

BROWNING X-BOLT RMEF SPECIAL HUNTER
Similar to above but with matte blued finish without gold highlights.
Price: **$919.00**

BUSHMASTER BA50 BOLT-ACTION RIFLE
Caliber: 50 Browning BMG. **Barrel:** 30" (rifle), 22" (carbine), 10-round mag. **Weight:** 30 lbs. (rifle), 27 lbs. (carbine). **Length:** 58" overall (rifle), 50" overall (carbine). **Features:** Free-floated Lother Walther barrel with muzzle brake, Magpul PRS adjustable stock.
Price: **$4,895.00**

CARBON ONE BOLT-ACTION RIFLE
Caliber: 22-250 to 375 H&H. **Barrel:** Up to 28". **Weight:** 5.5 to 7.25 lbs. **Length:** Varies. **Stock:** Synthetic or wood. **Sights:** None furnished. **Features:** Choice of Remington, Browning or Winchester action with free-floated Christensen graphite/epoxy/steel barrel, trigger pull tuned to 3 to 3.5 lbs. Made in U.S.A. by Christensen Arms.
Price: Carbon One Hunter Rifle, 6.5 to 7 lbs. **$1,775.00**
Price: Carbon One Custom, 5.5 to 6.5 lbs., Shilen trigger . . **$3,900.00**
Price: Carbon Extreme **$2,450.00**

CENTERFIRE RIFLES— Bolt-Action

CENTURY INTERNATIONAL M70 SPORTER DOUBLE-TRIGGER BOLT ACTION RIFLE

Caliber: 22-250 Rem., 270 Win., 300 Win. Mag, 308 Win., 24" barrel. **Weight:** 7.95 lbs. **Length:** 44.5". **Sights:** Flip-up U-notch rear sight, hooded blade front sight. **Features:** Mauser M98-type action; 5-rd fixed box magazine. 22-250 has hinged floorplate. Monte Carlo stock, oil finish. Adjustable trigger on double-trigger models. 300 Win. Mag. Has 3-rd. fixed box magazine. 308 Win. holds 5 rounds. 300 and 308 have buttpads. Manufactured by Zastava in Yugoslavia, imported by Century International.

Price: M70 Sporter Double-Trigger $500.00
Price: M70 Sporter Double-Trigger 22-250 . . . .$475.00
Price: M70 Sporter Single-Trigger .300 Win. Mag. $475.00
Price: M70 Sporter Single/Double Trigger 308 Win. $500.00

CHEYTAC M-200

Caliber: 408 CheyTac, 7-round magazine. **Barrel:** 30". **Length:** 55", stock extended. **Weight:** 27 lbs. (steel barrel); 24 lbs. (carbon fiber barrel). **Stock:** Retractable. **Sights:** None, scope rail provided. **Features:** CNC-machined receiver, attachable Picatinny rail M-1913, detachable barrel, integral bipod, 3.5-lb. trigger pull, muzzle brake. Made in U.S. by CheyTac, LLC.

Price: $13,795.00

COOPER MODEL 21 BOLT-ACTION RIFLE

Caliber: 17 Rem., 19-223, Tactical 20, .204 Ruger, 222 Rem, 222 Rem. Mag., 223 Rem, 223 Rem A.I., 6x45, 6x47. **Barrel:** 22" or 24" in Classic configurations, 24"-26" in Varminter configurations. **Weight:** 6.5-8.0 lbs., depending on type. **Stock:** AA-AAA select claro walnut, 20 lpi checkering. **Sights:** None furnished. **Features:** Three front locking-lug bolt-action single shot. Action: 7.75" long, Sako extractor. Button ejector. Fully adjustable single-stage trigger. Options include wood upgrades, case-color metalwork, barrel fluting, custom LOP, and many others.

Price: From $1,395.00

COOPER MODEL 22 BOLT-ACTION RIFLE

Caliber: 22-250 Rem., 22-250 Rem. AI, 25-06 Rem., 25-06 Rem. AI, 243 Win., 243 Win. AI, 220 Swift, 250/3000 AI, 257 Roberts, 257 Roberts AI, 7mm-08 Rem., 6mm Rem., 260 Rem., 6 x 284, 6.5 x 284, 22 BR, 6mm BR, 308 Win. **Barrel:** 24" or 26" stainless match in Classic configurations. 24" or 26" in Varminter configurations. **Weight:** 7.5 to 8.0 lbs. depending on type. **Stock:** AA-AAA select claro walnut, 20 lpi checkering. **Sights:** None furnished. **Features:** Three front locking-lug bolt-action single shot. Action: 8.25" long, Sako style extractor. Button ejector. Fully adjustable single-stage trigger. Options include wood upgrades, case-color metalwork, barrel fluting, custom LOP, and many others.

Price: From $1,495.00

COOPER MODEL 38 BOLT-ACTION RIFLE

Caliber: 17 Squirrel, 17 He Bee, 17 Ackley Hornet, 17 Mach IV, 19 Calhoon, 20 VarTarg, 221 Fireball, 22 Hornet, 22 K-Hornet, 22 Squirrel, 218 Bee, 218 Mashburn Bee. **Barrel:** 22" or 24" in Classic configurations, 24" or 26" in Varminter configurations. **Weight:** 6.5-8.0 lbs. depending on type. **Stock:** AA-AAA select claro walnut, 20 lpi checkering. **Sights:** None furnished. **Features:** Three front locking-lug bolt-action single shot. Action: 7" long, Sako style extractor. Button ejector. Fully adjustable single-stage trigger. Options include wood upgrades, case-color metalwork, barrel fluting, custom LOP, and many others.

Price: From $1,395.00

COOPER MODEL 56 BOLT-ACTION RIFLE

Caliber: .257 Weatherby Mag., .264 Win. Mag., .270 Weatherby Mag., 7mm Remington Mag., 7mm Weatherby Mag., 7mm Shooting Times Westerner, .300 Holland & Holland, .300 Winchester Mag., .300 Weatherby Mag., .308 Norma Mag., 8mm Rem. Mag., .338 Win. Mag., .340 Weatherby V. **Barrel:** 22" or 24" in Classic configurations, 24" or 26" in Varminter configurations. **Weight:** 7.75 - 8 lbs. depending on type. **Stock:** AA-AAA select claro walnut, 20 lpi checkering. **Sights:** None furnished. **Features:** Three front locking-lug bolt-action single shot. Action: 7" long, Sako style extractor.

Button ejector. Fully adjustable single-stage trigger. Options include wood upgrades, case-color metalwork, barrel fluting, custom LOP, and many others.

Price: Classic. $1518.00
Price: Custom Classic $1,618.00
Price: Western Classic.. . . . . $1518.00
Price: Jackson Game.. . . . . $1,618.00
Price: Jackson Hunter. $1518.00
Price: Excalibur. $1,618.00

CZ 527 LUX BOLT-ACTION RIFLE

Caliber: 204 Ruger, 22 Hornet, 222 Rem., 223 Rem., detachable 5-shot magazine. **Barrel:** 23.5"; standard or heavy barrel. **Weight:** 6 lbs., 1 oz. **Length:** 42.5" overall. **Stock:** European walnut with Monte Carlo. **Sights:** Hooded front, open adjustable rear. **Features:** Improved mini-Mauser action with non-rotating claw extractor; single set trigger; grooved receiver. Imported from the Czech Republic by CZ-USA.

Price: Brown laminate stock $718.00
Price: Model FS, full-length stock, cheekpiece $827.00

CZ 527 AMERICAN BOLT-ACTION RIFLE

Similar to the CZ 527 Lux except has classic-style stock with 18 lpi checkering; free-floating barrel; recessed target crown on barrel. No sights furnished. Introduced 1999. Imported from the Czech Republic by CZUSA.

Price: From $751.00

CZ 550 AMERICAN CLASSIC BOLT-ACTION RIFLE

Caliber: 22-250 Rem., 243 Win., 6.5x55, 7x57, 7x64, 308 Win., 9.3x62, 270 Win., 30-06. **Barrel:** free-floating barrel; recessed target crown. **Weight:** 7.48 lbs. **Length:** 44.68" overall. **Stock:** American classic-style stock with 18 lpi checkering or FS (Mannlicher). **Sights:** No sights furnished. **Features:** Improved Mauser-style action with claw extractor, fixed ejector, square bridge dovetailed receiver; single set trigger. Introduced 1999. Imported from the Czech Republic by CZ-USA.

Price: FS (full stock) $894.00
Price: American, from $827.00

CZ 550 SAFARI MAGNUM/AMERICAN SAFARI MAGNUM BOLT-ACTION RIFLES

Similar to CZ 550 American Classic. Chambered for 375 H&H Mag., 416 Rigby, 458 Win. Mag., 458 Lott. Overall length is 46.5"; barrel length 25"; weighs 9.4 lbs., 9.9 lbs (American). Hooded front sight, express rear with one standing, two folding leaves. Imported from the Czech Republic by CZ-USA.

Price: $1,179.00
Price: American $1,261.00
Price: American Kevlar $1,714.00

CZ 550 VARMINT BOLT-ACTION RIFLE

Similar to CZ 550 American Classic. Chambered for 308 Win. and 22-250. Kevlar, laminated stocks. Overall length is 46.7"; barrel length 25.6"; weighs 9.1 lbs. Imported from the Czech Republic by CZ-USA.
Price: $841.00
Price: Kevlar $1,037.00
Price: Laminated $966.00

CZ 550 MAGNUM H.E.T. BOLT-ACTION RIFLE

Similar to CZ 550 American Classic. Chambered for 338 Lapua, 300 Win. Mag., 300 RUM. Overall length is 52"; barrel length 28"; weighs 14 lbs. Adjustable sights, satin blued barrel. Imported from the Czech Republic by CZ-USA.
Price: $3,673.00

CENTERFIRE RIFLES—Bolt Action

CZ 550 ULTIMATE HUNTING BOLT-ACTION RIFLE
Similar to CZ 550 American Classic. Chambered for 300 Win Mag. Overall length is 44.7"; barrel length 23.6"; weighs 7.7 lbs. Imported from the Czech Republic by CZ-USA.
Price: **$4,242.00**

CZ 750 SNIPER RIFLE
Caliber: 308 Winchester, 10-shot magazine. **Barrel:** 26". **Weight:** 11.9 lbs. **Length:** 48" overall. **Stock:** Polymer thumbhole. **Sights:** None furnished; permanently attached Weaver rail for scope mounting. **Features:** 60-degree bolt throw; oversized trigger guard and bolt handle for use with gloves; full-length equipment rail on forend; fully adjustable trigger. Introduced 2001. Imported from the Czech Republic by CZ-USA.
Price: **$2,404.00**

DAKOTA 76 TRAVELER TAKEDOWN RIFLE
Caliber: 257 Roberts, 25-06 Rem., 7x57, 270 Win., 280 Rem., 30-06 Spfl., 338-06, 35 Whelen (standard length); 7mm Rem. Mag., 300 Win. Mag., 338 Win. Mag., 416 Taylor, 458 Win. Mag. (short magnums); 7mm, 300, 330, 375 Dakota Magnums. **Barrel:** 23". **Weight:** 7.5 lbs. **Length:** 43.5" overall. **Stock:** Medium fancy-grade walnut in classic style. Checkered grip and forend; solid buttpad. **Sights:** None furnished; drilled and tapped for scope mounts. **Features:** Threadless disassembly. Uses modified Model 76 design with many features of the Model 70 Winchester. Left-hand model also available. Introduced 1989. African chambered for 338 Lapua Mag., 404 Jeffery, 416 Rigby, 416 Dakota, 450 Dakota, 4-round magazine, select wood, two stock cross-bolts. 24" barrel, weighs 9-10 lbs. Ramp front sight, standing leaf rear. Introduced 1989.Made in U.S.A. by Dakota Arms, Inc.
Price: Classic **$6,095.00**
Price: Safari **$7,895.00**
Price: African **$9,495.00**

DAKOTA 76 CLASSIC BOLT-ACTION RIFLE
Caliber: 257 Roberts, 270 Win., 280 Rem., 30-06 Spfl., 7mm Rem. Mag., 338 Win. Mag., 300 Win. Mag., 375 H&H, 458 Win. Mag. **Barrel:** 23". **Weight:** 7.5 lbs. **Length:** 43.5" overall. **Stock:** Medium fancy grade walnut in classic style. Checkered pistol grip and forend; solid buttpad. **Sights:** None furnished; drilled and tapped for scope mounts. **Features:** Has many features of the original Winchester Model 70. One-piece rail trigger guard assembly; steel gripcap. Model 70-style trigger. Many options available. Left-hand rifle available at same price. Introduced 1988. From Dakota Arms, Inc.
Price: From **$4,595.00**

DAKOTA LONGBOW T-76 TACTICAL RIFLE
Caliber: 300 Dakota Magnum, 330 Dakota Magnum, 338 Lapua Magnum. **Barrel:** 28", .950" at muzzle **Weight:** 13.7 lbs. **Length:** 50" to 52" overall. **Stock:** Ambidextrous McMillan A-2 fiberglass, black or olive green color; adjustable cheekpiece and buttplate. **Sights:** None furnished. Comes with Picatinny one-piece optical rail. **Features:** Uses the Dakota 76 action with controlled-round feed; three-position firing pin block safety, claw extractor; Model 70-style trigger. Comes with bipod, case tool kit. Introduced 1997. Made in U.S.A. by Dakota Arms, Inc.
Price: **$4,795.00**

DAKOTA MODEL 97 BOLT-ACTION RIFLE
Caliber: 22-250 to 330. **Barrel:** 22" to 24". **Weight:** 6.1 to 6.5 lbs. **Length:** 43" overall. **Stock:** Fiberglass. **Sights:** Optional. **Features:** Matte blue finish, black stock. Right-hand action only. Introduced 1998. Made in U.S.A. by Dakota Arms, Inc.
Price: From **$3,395.00**

DAKOTA PREDATOR RIFLE
Caliber: 17 VarTarg, 17 Rem., 17 Tactical, 20 VarTarg, 20 Tactical, .20 PPC, 204 Ruger, 221 Rem Fireball, 222 Remington, 22 PPC, 223 Rem., 6mm PPC, 6.5 Grendel. **Barrel:** 22" match grade stainless;. **Weight:** NA. **Length:** NA. **Stock:** Special select walnut, sporter-style stock, 23 lpi checkering on forend and grip. **Sights:** None furnished. Drilled and tapped for scope mounting. **Features:** 13-5/8" LOP, 1/2" black presentation pad, 11" recessed target crown. Serious Predator includes XXX walnut varmint style stock w/semi-beavertail forend, stainless receiver. All-Weather Predator includes varmint style composite stock w/semi-beavertail forend, stainless receiver. Introduced 2007. Made in U.S.A. by Dakota Arms, Inc.
Price: Classic **$4,295.00**
Price: Serious **$3,295.00**
Price: All-Weather. **$1,995.00**

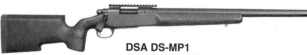

DSA DS-MP1
Caliber: 308 Win. match chamber. **Barrel:** 22", 1:10 twist, hand-lapped stainless-steel match-grade Badger Barrel with recessed target crown. **Weight:** 11.5 lbs. **Length:** 41.75". **Stock:** Black McMillan A5 pillar bedded in Marine-Tex with 13.5" length of pull. **Sights:** Tactical Picatinny rail. **Features:** Action, action threads and action bolt locking shoulder completely trued, Badger Ordnance precision ground heavy recoil lug, machined steel Picatinny rail sight mount, trued action threads, action bolt locking shoulder, bolt face and lugs, 2.5-lb. trigger pull, barrel and action finished in Black DuraCoat, guaranteed to shoot 1/2 MOA at 100 yards with match-grade ammo. Introduced 2006. Made in U.S.A. by DSA, Inc.
Price: **$2,800.00**

EAA/ZASTAVA M-93 BLACK ARROW RIFLE
Caliber: 50 BMG. **Barrel:** 36". **Weight:** 7 to 8.5 lbs. **Length:** 60". **Stock:** Synthetic. **Sights:** Scope rail and iron sights. **Features:** Features: Mauser action, developed in early 1990s by Zastava Arms Factory. Fluted heavy barrel with recoil reducing muzzle brake, self-leveling and adjustable folding integral bipod, back up iron sights, heavy duty carry handle, detachable 5 round box magazine, and quick detachable scope mount. Imported by EAA. Imported from Russia by EAA Corp.
Price: **$6,986.25**

ED BROWN HUNTING SERIES RIFLES
Caliber: Many calibers available. **Barrel:** 24" (Savanna, Express, Varmint); 23-24" (Damara); 22" (Compact Varmint). **Weight:** 8 to 8.5 lbs. (Savanna); 6.2 to 6.9 lbs. (Damara); 9 lbs. (Express); 10 lbs. (Varmint), 8.75 lbs. (Compact Varmint). **Stock:** Fully glass-bedded McMillan fiberglass sporter. **Sights:** None furnished. Talley scope mounts utilizing heavy-duty 8-40 screws. **Features:** Custom action with machined steel trigger guard and hinged floor plate.
Price: Savanna **$3,895.00**
Price: Damara . . . . **$3,995.00 to $4,095.00**
Price: Express **$4,995.00**
Price: Varmint & Compact Varmint. **$3,895.00**

ED BROWN MODEL 704 BUSHVELD
Caliber: 338 Win. Mag., 375 H&H, 416 Rem. Mag., 458 Win. Mag., 458 Lott and all Ed Brown Savanna long action calibers. **Barrel:** 24" medium or heavy weight. **Weight:** 8.25 lbs. **Stock:** Fully bedded McMillan fiberglass with Monte Carlo style cheekpiece, Pachmayr Decelerator recoil pad. **Sights:** None furnished. Talley scope mounts utilizing heavy-duty 8-40 screws. **Features:** Stainless steel barrel,

Prices given are believed to be accurate at time of publication however, many factors affect retail pricing so exact prices are not possible.

CENTERFIRE RIFLES—Bolt Action

additional calibers: iron sights.
Price: From $2,995.00

ED BROWN MODEL 704 EXPRESS
Caliber: 375 H&H, 416 Rem, 458 Lott, other calibers available. **Barrel:** 24" #4 Stainless barrel with black Gen III coating for superior rust protection. **Weight:** 9 lbs. Stocks: Hand-bedded McMillan fiberglass stock. Monte Carlo style with cheek piece and full 1" thick Pachmayr Decel recoil pad. **Sights:** Adjustable iron sights. **Features:** Ed Brown controlled feed action. A special dropped box magazine ensures feeding and allows a full four-round capacity in the magazine, plus one in the chamber. Barrel band is standard for lower profile when carrying the rifle through heavy brush.
Price: From $3,695.00

HOWA M-1500 RANCHLAND COMPACT
Caliber: 223 Rem., 22-250 Rem., 243 Win., 308 Win. and 7mm-08. **Barrel:** 20" #1 contour, blued finish. **Weight:** 7 lbs. **Stock:** Hogue Overmolded in black, OD green, Coyote Sand colors. 13.87" LOP. **Sights:** None furnished; drilled and tapped for scope mounting. **Features:** Three-position safety, hinged floor plate, adjustable trigger, forged one-piece bolt, M-16 style extractor, forged flat-bottom receiver. Also available with Nikko-Stirling Nighteater 3-9x42 riflescope. Introduced in 2008. Imported from Japan by Legacy Sports International.
Price: Rifle Only, (2008) $479.00
Price: Rifle with 3-9x42 Nighteater scope (2008) $599.00

HOWA M-1500 THUMBHOLE SPORTER
Caliber: 204, 223 Rem., 22-250 Rem., 243 Win., 6.5x55 (2008) 25-06 Rem., 270 Win., 7mm Rem. Mag., 308 Win., 30-06 Spfl., 300 Win. Mag., 338 Win. Mag., 375 Ruger. Similar to Camo Lightning except stock. **Weight:** 7.6 to 7.7 lbs. **Stock:** S&K laminated wood in nutmeg (brown/black) or pepper (grey/black) colors, raised comb with forward taper, flared pistol grip and scalloped thumbhole. **Sights:** None furnished; drilled and tapped for scope mounting. **Features:** Three-position safety, hinged floor plate, adjustable trigger, forged one-piece bolt, M-16 style extractor, forged flat-bottom receiver. Introduced in 2001. Imported from Japan by Legacy Sports International.
Price: Blue/Nutmeg, standard calibers . . . . $649.00 to $669.00
Price: Stainless/Pepper, standard calibers . . . . . . $749.00 to $769.00

HOWA M-1500 VARMINTER SUPREME AND THUMBHOLE VARMINTER SUPREME
Caliber: 204, 223 Rem., 22-250 Rem., 243 Win., 308 Win. **Stock:** Varminter Supreme: Laminated wood in nutmeg (brown), pepper (grey) colors, raised comb and rollover cheekpiece, full pistol grip with palm-filling swell and broad beavertail forend with six vents for barrel cooling. Thumbhole Varminter Supreme similar, adds a high, straight comb, more vertical pistol grip. **Sights:** None furnished; drilled and tapped for scope mounting. **Features:** Three-position safety, hinged floor plate, adjustable trigger, forged one-piece bolt, M-16 style extractor, forged flat-bottom receiver, hammer forged bull barrel and recessed muzzle crown; overall length, 43.75", 9.7 lbs. Introduced 2001. Barreled actions imported by Legacy Sports International; stocks by S&K Gunstocks.
Price: Varminter Supreme, Blue/Nutmeg $679.00
Price: Varminter Supreme, Stainless/Pepper $779.00
Price: Thumbhole Varminter Supreme, Blue/Nutmeg $679.00
Price: Thumbhole Varminter Supreme, Stainless/Pepper $779.00

HOWA CAMO LIGHTNING M-1500
Caliber: 204, 223 Rem., 22-250 Rem., 243 Win., 25-06 Rem., 270 Win., 308 Win., 30-06 Spfl., 300 Win. Mag., 338 Win. Mag., 7mm Rem. Mag. **Barrel:** 22" standard calibers; 24" magnum calibers; #2 and #6 contour; blue and stainless. **Weight:** 7.6 to 9.3 lbs. **Length:** 42" to 44.5" overall. **Stock:** Synthetic with molded cheek piece, checkered grip and forend. **Sights:** None furnished; drilled and tapped for scope mounting. **Features:** Three-position safety, hinged floor plate, adjustable trigger, forged one-piece bolt, M-16 style extractor, forged flat bottom receiver. Introduced in 1993. Barreled

actions imported by Legacy Sports International.
Price: Blue, #2 barrel, standard calibers $377.00
Price: Stainless, #2 barrel, standard calibers $479.00
Price: Blue, #2 barrel, magnum calibers $390.00
Price: Stainless, #2 barrel, magnum calibers $498.00
Price: Blue, #6 barrel, standard calibers $425.00
Price: Stainless, #6 barrel, standard calibers $498.00

HOWA/HOGUE M-1500
Caliber: 204, 223 Rem., 22-250 Rem., 243 Win., 6.5x5 (2008), 25-06 Rem., 270 Win., 308 Win., 30-06 Spfl., 300 Win. Mag., 338 Win. Mag., 7mm Rem. Mag., 375 Ruger (2008). **Barrel:** Howa barreled action; stainless or blued; 22" #2 contour. **Weight:** 7.4 to 7.6 lbs. **Stock:** Hogue Overmolded, black, or OD green; ambidextrous palm swells. **Sights:** None furnished; drilled and tapped for scope mounting. **Length:** 42" to 44.5" overall. **Features:** Three-position safety, hinged floor plate, adjustable trigger, forged one-piece bolt, M-16 style extractor, forged flat bottom receiver, aluminum pillar bedding and free-floated barrels. Introduced in 2006. Available w/3-10x42 Nikko-Stirling Nighteater scope, rings, bases (2008). from Imported from Japan by Legacy Sports International.
Price: Blued, rifle only . . . . $479.00 to $499.00
Price: Blue, rifle with scope package (2008) . . . . . $599.00 to $619.00
Price: Stainless, rifle only . . . . $625.00 to $675.00

HOWA/HOGUE M-1500 COMPACT HEAVY BARREL VARMINTER
Chambered in 223 Rem., 308 Win., has 20" #6 contour heavy barrel, recessed muzzle crown. **Stock:** Hogue Overmolded, black, or OD green; ambidextrous palm swells. **Sights:** None furnished; drilled and tapped for scope mounting. **Length:** 44.0" overall. **Features:** Three-position safety, hinged floor plate, adjustable trigger, forged one-piece bolt, M-16 style extractor, forged flat bottom receiver, aluminum pillar bedding and free-floated barrels. **Weight:** 9.3 lbs. Introduced 2008. Imported from Japan by Legacy Sports International.
Price: From $559.00

HOWA/AXIOM M-1500
Caliber: 204, 223 Rem., 22-250 Rem., 243 Win., 6.5x55 (2008), 25-06 Rem. (2008), 270 Win., 308 Win., 30-06 Spfl., 7mm Rem, 300 Win. Mag., 338 Win. Mag., 375 Ruger standard barrel; 204, 223 Rem., 243 Win. and 308 Win. heavy barrel. **Barrel:** Howa barreled action, 22" contour standard barrel, 20" #6 contour heavy barrel, and 24" #6 contour heavy barrel. **Weight:** 8.6-10 lbs. **Stock:** Knoxx Industries Axiom V/S synthetic, black or camo. Adjustable length of pull from 11.5" to 15.5". **Sights:** None furnished; drilled and tapped for scope mounting. **Features:** Three-position safety, adjustable trigger, hinged floor plate, forged receiver with large recoil lug, forged one-piece bolt with dual locking lugs Introduced in 2007. Standard-barrel scope packages come with 3-10x42 Nikko-Stirling Nighteater scope, rings, bases (2008). Heavy barrels come with 4-16x44 Nikko-Stirling scope. Imported from Japan by Legacy Sports International.
Price: Axiom Standard Barrel, black stock, from $699.00
Price: Axiom 20" and 24" Varminter, black or camo stock, from $799.00
Price: Axiom 20" and 24" Varminter, camo stock w/scope (2008), from $819.00

HOWA M-1500 ULTRALIGHT 2-N-1 YOUTH
Caliber: 223 Rem., 22-250 Rem., 243 Win., 308 Win., 7mm-08. **Barrel:** 20" #1 contour, blued. **Weight:** 6.8 lbs. **Length:** 39.25" overall. **Stock:** Hogue Overmolded in black, 12.5" LOP. Also includes adult-size Hogue Overmolded in OD green. **Sights:** None furnished; drilled and tapped for scope mounting. **Features:** Bolt and receiver milled to reduce weight, three-position safety, hinged floor plate, adjustable trigger, forged one-piece bolt, M-16 style extractor, forged flat-bottom receiver. Scope package includes 3-9x42 Nikko-Stirling riflescope with bases and rings. Imported from Japan by Legacy Sports International.
Price: Blue, Youth Rifle $539.00
Price: w/Scope package (2008) $589.00

H-S PRECISION PRO-SERIES BOLT-ACTION RIFLES
Caliber: 30 chamberings, 3- or 4-round magazine. **Barrel:** 20", 22", 24" or 26", sporter contour Pro-Series 10X match-grade stainless steel barrel. Optional muzzle brake on 30 cal. or smaller. **Weight:** 7.5 lbs. **Length:** NA. **Stock:** Pro-Series synthetic stock with full-

length bedding block chassis system, sporter style. **Sights:** None; drilled and tapped for bases. **Features:** Accuracy guarantee: up to 30 caliber, 1/2 minute of angle (3 shots at 100 yards), test target supplied. Stainless steel action, stainless steel floorplate with detachable magazine, matte black Teflon finish. Made in U.S.A. by H-S Precision, Inc.

Price: SPR **$2,680.00**
Price: SPL Lightweight (2008) **$2,825.00**

KEL-TEC RFB

Caliber: 7.62 NATO (308 Win.). **Barrels:** 18" to 32". **Weight:** 11.3 lbs. (unloaded). **Length:** 40" overall. **Features:** Gas-operated semi-auto bullpup-style, forward-ejecting. Fully ambidextrous controls, adjustable trigger mechanism, no open sights, four-sided picatinny forend. Accepts standard FAL-type magazines. Production of the RFB has been delayed due to redesign but was expected to begin first quarter 2009.

Price: **$1,800.00**

KENNY JARRETT BOLT-ACTION RIFLE

Caliber: 223 Rem., 243 Improved, 243 Catbird, 7mm-08 Improved, 280 Remington, .280 Ackley Improved, 7mm Rem. Mag., 284 Jarrett, 30-06 Springfield, 300 Win. Mag., .300 Jarrett, 323 Jarrett, 338 Jarrett, 375 H&H, 416 Rem., 450 Rigby., other modern cartridges. **Barrel:** NA. **Weight:** NA. **Length:** NA. **Stock:** NA. **Features:** Tri-Lock receiver. Talley rings and bases. Accuracy guarantees and custom loaded ammunition.

Price: Signature Series. **$7,640.00**
Price: Wind Walker **$7,380.00**
Price: Original Beanfield (customer's receiver) **$5,380.00**
Price: Professional Hunter **$10,400.00**
Price: SA/Custom **$6,630.00**

KIMBER MODEL 8400 BOLT-ACTION RIFLE

Caliber: 25-06 Rem., 270 Win., 7mm, 30-06 Spfl., 300 Win. Mag., 338 Win. Mag., or 325 WSM, 4 shot. **Barrel:** 24". **Weight:** 6 lbs. 3 oz. to 6 lbs 10 oz. **Length:** 43.25". **Stock:** Claro walnut or Kevlar-reinforced fiberglass. **Sights:** None; drilled and tapped for bases. **Features:** Mauser claw extractor, two-position wing safety, action bedded on aluminum pillars and fiberglass, free-floated barrel, match grade adjustable trigger set at 4 lbs., matte or polished blue or matte stainless finish. Introduced 2003. Sonora model (2008) has brown laminated stock, hand-rubbed oil finish, chambered in 25-06 Rem., 30-06 Spfl., and 300 Win. Mag. Weighs 8.5 lbs., measures 44.50" overall length. Front swivel stud only for bipod. Stainless steel bull barrel, 24" satin stainless finish. Made in U.S.A. by Kimber Mfg. Inc.

Price: Classic **$1,172.00**
Price: Classic Select Grade, French walnut stock (2008). . . **$1,359.00**
Price: SuperAmerica, AAA walnut stock. **$2,240.00**
Price: Sonora **$1,359.00**
Price: Police Tactical, synthetic stock, fluted barrel
(300 Win. Mag only) **$2,575.00**

KIMBER MODEL 8400 CAPRIVI BOLT-ACTION RIFLE

Similar to 8400 bolt rifle, but chambered for .375 H&H and 458 Lott, 4-shot magazine. Stock is Claro walnut or Kevlar-reinforced fiberglass. Features twin steel crossbolts in stock, AA French walnut, pancake cheekpiece, 24 lines-per-inch wrap-around checkering, ebony forend tip, hand-rubbed oil finish, barrel-mounted sling swivel stud, 3-leaf express sights, Howell-type rear sling swivel stud and a Pachmayr Decelerator recoil pad in traditional orange color. Introduced 2008. Made in U.S.A. by Kimber Mfg. Inc.

Price: **$3,196.00**

KIMBER MODEL 8400 TALKEETNA BOLT-ACTION RIFLE

Similar to 8400 bolt rifle, but chambered for .375 H&H, 4-shot magazine. Weighs 8 lbs, overall length is 44.5". Stock is synthetic. Features free-floating match grade barrel with tapered match grade chamber and target crown, three-position wing safety acts directly on the cocking piece for greatest security, and Pacmayr Decelerator. Made in U.S.A. by Kimber Mfg. Inc.

Price: **$2,108.00**

KIMBER MODEL 84M BOLT-ACTION RIFLE

Caliber: 22-250 Rem., 204 Ruger, 223 Rem., 243 Win., 260 Rem., 7mm-08 Rem., 308 Win., 5-shot. **Barrel:** 22", 24", 26". **Weight:** 5 lbs., 10 oz. to 10 lbs. **Length:** 41" to 45". **Stock:** Claro walnut, checkered with steel gripcap; synthetic or gray laminate. **Sights:** None; drilled and tapped for bases. **Features:** Mauser claw extractor, three-position wing safety, action bedded on aluminum pillars, free-floated barrel, match-grade trigger set at 4 lbs., matte blue finish. Includes cable lock. Introduced 2001. Montana (2008) has synthetic stock, Pachmayr Decelerator recoil pad, stainless steel 22" sporter barrel. Made in U.S.A. by Kimber Mfg. Inc.

Price: Classic (243 Win., 260, 7mm-08 Rem., 308) **$1,114.00**
Price: Varmint (22-250) **$1,224.00**
Price: Montana **$1,276.00**
Price: Classic Stainless, matte stainless steel receiver
and barrel (243 Win., 7mm-08, 308 Win.) **$1,156.00**

KIMBER MODEL 84L CLASSIC RIFLE

Bolt action rifle chambered in .270 Win. and .30-06. Features include 24-inch sightless matte blue sporter barrel; hand-rubbed A-grade walnut stock with 20 lpi panel checkering; pillar and glass bedding; Mauser claw extractor; 3-position M70-style safety; 5-round magazine; adjustable trigger.

Price: **$1,172.00**

KIMBER MODEL 8400 PATROL RIFLE

Bolt action tactical rifle chambered in .308 Win. Features include 20-inch 1:12 fluted sightless matte blue heavy barrel; black epoxy-coated laminated wood stock with 20 lpi panel checkering; pillar and glass bedding; Mauser claw extractor; 3-position M70-style safety; 5-round magazine; adjustable trigger.

Price: **$1,476.00**

L.A.R. GRIZZLY 50 BIG BOAR RIFLE

Caliber: 50 BMG, single shot. **Barrel:** 36". **Weight:** 30.4 lbs. **Length:** 45.5" overall. **Stock:** Integral. Ventilated rubber recoil pad. **Sights:** None furnished; scope mount. **Features:** Bolt-action bullpup design, thumb and bolt stop safety. All-steel construction. Introduced 1994. Made in U.S.A. by L.A.R. Mfg., Inc.

Price: From **$2,350.00**

MAGNUM RESEARCH MOUNTAIN EAGLE MAGNUMLITE RIFLES

Caliber: .22-250, .223, .224, .243, .257, 7mm Rem. Mag., 7mm WSM, .280, .300 Win. Mag., .300 WSM, .30-06, 3-shot magazine. **Barrel:** 24" sport taper graphite; 26" bull barrel graphite. **Weight:** 7.1-9.2 lbs. **Length:** 44.5-48.25" overall (adjustable on Tactical model). **Stock:** Hogue OverMolded synthetic, H-S Precision Tactical synthetic, H-S Precision Varmint synthetic. **Sights:** None. **Features:** Remington Model 700 receiver. Introduced in 2001. From Magnum Research, Inc.

Price: MLR3006ST24 Hogue stock **$2,295.00**
Price: MLR7MMBST24 Hogue stock **$2,295.00**
Price: MLRT22250 H-S Tactical stock, 26" bull barrel **$2,400.00**
Price: MLRT300WI Tactical **$2,400.00**

Prices given are believed to be accurate at time of publication however, many factors affect retail pricing so exact prices are not possible.

MARLIN XL7 BOLT ACTION RIFLE
Caliber: 25-06 Rem. 270 Win., 30-06 Spfl., 4-shot magazine. **Barrel:** 22" 1:10" right-hand twist, recessed barrel crown. **Weight:** 6.5 lbs. **Length:** 42.5" overall. **Stock:** Black synthetic or Realtree APG-HD camo, Soft-Tech recoil pad, pillar bedded. **Sights:** None. **Features:** Pro-Fire trigger is user adjustable down to 2.5 lbs. Fluted bolt, steel sling swivel studs, high polished blued steel, checkered bolt handle, molded checkering, one-piece scope base. Introduced in 2008. From Marlin Firearms, Inc.
Price: Black Synthetic **$326.00**
Price: Camouflaged **$356.00**

MARLIN XS7 SHORT-ACTION BOLT-ACTION RIFLE
Similar to Model XL7 but chambered in 7mm-08, 243 Winchester and 308 Winchester.
Price: . . . . **NA**
Price: XS7Y Youth **$341.00**
Price: XS7C Camo, Realtree APG HD camo stock **$341.00**
Price: XS7S Stainless. . . . .**NA**

MERKEL KR1 BOLT-ACTION RIFLE
Caliber: 223 Rem., 243 Rem., 6.5x55, 7mm-08, 308 Win., 270 Win., 30-06, 9.3x62, 7mm Rem. Mag., 300 Win. Mag., 270 WSM, 300 WSM, 338 Win. Mag. **Features:** Short lock, short bolt movement, take-down design with interchangeable barrel assemblies, three-position safety, detachable box magazine, fine trigger with set feature, checkered walnut pistol-grip semi-schnable stock. Adjustable iron sights with quick release mounts. Imported from Germany by Merkel USA.
Price: **$1,995.00**
Price: Model KR1 Stutzen Antique: 20.8" barrel, case-colored receiver, Mannlicher-style stock **$3,395.00**

MOSSBERG 100 ATR BOLT-ACTION RIFLE
Caliber: 243 Win. (2006), 270 Win., 308 Win. (2006), 30-06 Spfl., 4-round magazine. **Barrel:** 22", 1:10 twist, free-floating, button-rifled, recessed muzzle crown. **Weight:** 6.7 to 7.75 lbs. **Length:** 42"-42.75" overall. **Stock:** Black synthetic, walnut, Mossy Oak New Break Up camo, Realtree AP camo. **Sights:** Factory-installed Weaver-style scope bases; scoped combos include 3x9 factory-mounted, bore-sighted scopes. **Features:** Marinecote and matte blue metal finishes, free gun lock, side lever safety. Introduced 2005. Night Train (2008)comes with Picatinny rail and factory-mounted 4-16x50mm variable scope. From O.F. Mossberg & Sons, Inc.
Price: Short-Action 243 Win., wood stock, matte blue, from . .**$424.00**
Price: Long-Action 270 Win., Mossy Oak New Break Up camo, matte blue, from **$424.00**
Price: Scoped Combo 30-06 Spfl., Walnut-Dura-Wood stock, Marinecote finish, from **$481.00**
Price: Bantam Short Action 308 Win., 20" barrel **$471.00**
Price: Night Train Short-Action Scoped Combo (2008) **$567.00**

NOSLER MODEL 48 VARMINT RIFLE
Caliber: 204 Ruger, .223 Rem., 22-250 Rem., Heavy barrel, 4-shot capacity. **Barrel:** 24". **Weight:** 7.25 lbs. **Stock:** Coyote tan or Onyx black Kevlar® and carbon fiber. **Sights:** Fixed sights. **Features:** The NoslerCustom® Model 48 is built on the same action as our Custom rifles. Nosler's proprietary push-feed action features a 2-position safety and an adjustable trigger set to a crisp, 3 lb. let-off. The action features a classic one-piece bottom metal and trigger guard. To achieve the highest level of accuracy, the Model 48 integrates the unique MicroSlick™ Coating on interior metal surfaces, including inside the bolt body, and on the firing pin and firing pin spring, for maximum corrosion and wear-resistance, even with extensive dry firing.
Price: 204 Ruger **$2,995.00**
Price: .223 Rem., (Black) **$2,995.00**
Price: 22-250, (Black) **$2,995.00**
Price: 22-250, (Grey) **$2,995.00**

REMINGTON MODEL 700 CDL CLASSIC DELUXE RIFLE
Caliber: 223 Rem., 243 Win., 25-06 Rem., 270 Win., 7mm-08 Rem., 280 Remington, 7mm Rem. Mag., 7mm Rem. Ultra Mag., 30-06 Spfl., 300 Rem. Ultra Mag., 300 Win. Mag., 35 Whelen. **Barrel:** 24" or 26" round tapered. **Weight:** 7.4 to 7.6 lbs. **Length:** 43.6" to 46.5" overall. **Stock:** Straight-comb American walnut stock, satin finish, checkering, right-handed cheek piece, black fore-end tip and grip cap, sling swivel studs. **Sights:** None. **Features:** Satin blued finish, jeweled bolt body, drilled and tapped for scope mounts. Hinged-floorplate magazine capacity: 4, standard calibers; 3, magnum calibers. SuperCell recoil pad, cylindrical receiver, integral extractor. Introduced 2004. CDL SF (stainless fluted) chambered for 260 Rem., 257 Wby. Mag., 270 Win., 270 WSM, 7mm-08 Rem., 7mm Rem. Mag., 30-06 Spfl., 300 WSM. Left-hand versions introduced 2008 in six calibers. Made in U.S. by Remington Arms Co., Inc.
Price: Standard Calibers: 24" barrel **$959.00**
Price: Magnum Calibers: 26" barrel **$987.00**
Price: CDL SF (2007), from **$1,100.00**
Price: CDL LH (2008), from **$987.00**
Price: CDL High Polish Blued (2008), from **$959.00**
Price: CDL SF (2009), 257 Roberts . . . . **NA**
Price: CDL DM **$1,041.00**
Price: CDL SF LE **$1,203.00**

REMINGTON MODEL 700 BDL RIFLE
Caliber: 243 Win., 270 Win., 7mm Rem. Mag. 30-06 Spfl., 300 Rem Ultra Mag. **Barrel:** 22, 24, 26" round tapered. **Weight:** 7.25-7.4 lbs. **Length:** 41.6-46.5" overall. **Stock:** Walnut. Gloss-finish pistol grip stock with skip-line checkering, black forend tip and gripcap with white line spacers. Quick-release floorplate. **Sights:** Gold bead ramp front; hooded ramp, removable step-adjustable rear with windage screw. **Features:** Side safety, receiver tapped for scope mounts, matte receiver top, quick detachable swivels.
Price: 243 Win., 270 Win., 30-06 . . . .**$927.00**
Price: 7mm Rem. Mag. 300 Rem Ultra Mag. **$955.00**

REMINGTON MODEL 700 SPS RIFLES
Caliber: 17 Rem. Fireball, 204 Ruger, 22-250 Rem., 6.8 Rem SPC, 223 Rem., 243 Win., 270 Win. 270 WSM, 7mm-08 Rem., 7mm Rem. Mag., 7mm Rem. Ultra Mag., 30-06 Spfl., 308 Win., 300 WSM, 300 Win. Mag., 300 Rem. Ultra Mag. **Barrel:** 20", 24" or 26" carbon steel. **Weight:** 7 to 7.6 lbs. **Length:** 39.6" to 46.5" overall. **Stock:** Black synthetic, sling swivel studs, SuperCell recoil pad. **Sights:** None. Introduced 2005. SPS Stainless replaces Model 700 BDL Stainless Synthetic. **Barrel:** Bead-blasted 416 stainless steel. **Features:** Plated internal fire control component. SPS DM features detachable box magazine. Buckmaster Edition versions feature Realtree Hardwoods HD camouflage and Buckmasters logo engraved on floorplate. SPS Varmint includes X-Mark Pro trigger, 26" heavy contour barrel, vented beavertail forend, dual front sling swivel studs. Made in U.S. by Remington Arms Co., Inc.
Price: SPS, from **$639.00**
Price: SPS DM (2005) **$672.00**
Price: SPS Youth, 20" barrel (2007) 243 Win., 7mm-08. . . . . .**$604.00**
Price: SPS Varmint (2007) **$665.00**

CENTERFIRE RIFLES—Bolt Action

Price: SPS Stainless, (2005), from **$732.00**
Price: SPS Buckmasters Youth (2008), 243 Win. **$707.00**
Price: SPS Youth LH (2008), 243 Win., 7mm-08 . . . .**$620.00**
Price: SPS Varmint LH (2008) **$692.00**
Price: SPS Synthetic Left-Hand . . . .**NA**
Price: SPS CAMO. **$777.00**
Price: SPS TACTICAL AAC SD **$780.00**

REMINGTON 700 SPS TACTICAL
Bolt action rifle chambered in .223 and .308 Win. Features include 20-inch heavy-contour tactical-style barrel; dual-point pillar bedding; black synthetic stock with Hogue overmoldings; semi-beavertail fore-end; X-Mark Pro adjustable trigger system; satin black oxide metal finish; hinged floorplate magazine; SuperCell recoil pad.
Price **$734.00**

REMINGTON 700 VTR A-TACS CAMO WITH SCOPE
Bolt action rifle chambered in .223 and .308 Win. Features include ATACS camo finish overall; triangular contour 22-inch barrel has an integral muzzle brake; black overmold grips; 1:9 (.223 caliber) 0r 1:12 (.308) twist; factory-mounted scope.
Price: . . . .**NA**

REMINGTON MODEL 700 MOUNTAIN LSS RIFLES
Caliber: 270 Win., 280 Rem., 7mm-08 Rem., 30-06. **Barrel:** 22" satin stainless steel. **Weight:** 6.6 lbs. **Length:** 41.6" to 42.5" overall. **Stock:** Brown laminated, sling swivel studs, SuperCell recoil pad, black forend tip. **Sights:** None. **Barrel:** Bead-blasted 416 stainless steel, lightweight contour. Made in U.S. by Remington Arms Co., Inc.
Price: **$1,052.00**

REMINGTON MODEL 700 ALASKAN TI
Caliber: 25-06 Rem., 270 Win., 270 WSM, 280 Rem., 7mm-08 Rem., 7mm Rem. Mag., 30-06 Spfl., 300 WSM, 300 Win. Mag. **Barrel:** 24" round tapered. **Weight:** 6 lbs. **Length:** 43.6" to 44.5" overall. **Stock:** Bell & Carlson carbon-fiber synthetic, sling swivel studs, SuperCell gel recoil pad. **Sights:** None. **Features:** Formerly Model 700 Titanium, introduced 2001. Titanium receiver, spiral-cut fluted bolt, skeletonized bolt handle, X-Mark Pro trigger, satin stainless finish. Drilled and tapped for scope mounts. Hinged-floorplate magazine capacity: 4, standard calibers; 3, magnum calibers. Introduced 2007. Made in U.S. by Remington Arms Co., Inc.
Price: From **$2,225.00**

REMINGTON MODEL 700 VLS/VLSS TH RIFLES
Caliber: 204 Ruger, 223 Rem., 22-250 Rem., 243 Win., 308 Win. **Barrel:** 26" heavy contour barrel (0.820" muzzle O.D.), concave target-style barrel crown **Weight:** 9.4 lbs. **Length:** 45.75" overall. **Stock:** Brown laminated stock, satin finish, with beavertail forend, gripcap, rubber buttpad. **Sights:** None. **Features:** Introduced 1995. VLSS TH (varmint laminate stock

stainless) thumbhole model introduced 2007. Made in U.S. by Remington Arms Co., Inc.
Price: VLS. **$979.00**
Price: VL SS TH **$1,085.00**

REMINGTON MODEL 700 VSSF-II/SENDERO SF II RIFLES
Caliber: 17 Rem. Fireball, 204 Ruger, 220 Swift, 223 Rem., 22-250 Rem., 308 Win. **Barrel:** satin blued 26" heavy contour (0.820" muzzle O.D.). VSSF has satin-finish stainless barreled action with 26" fluted barrel. **Weight:** 8.5 lbs. **Length:** 45.75" overall. **Stock:** H.S. Precision composite reinforced with aramid fibers, black (VSSF-II) Contoured beavertail fore-end with ambidextrous finger grooves, palm swell, and twin front tactical-style swivel studs. **Sights:** None. **Features:** Aluminum bedding block, drilled and tapped for scope mounts, hinged floorplate magazines. Introduced 1994. Sendero model is similar to VSSF-II except chambered for 264 Win. Mag., 7mm Rem. Mag., 7mm Rem. Ultra Mag., 300 Win. Mag., 300 Rem. Ultra Mag. Polished stainless barrel. Introduced 1996. Made in U.S. by Remington Arms Co., Inc.
Price: VSSF-II. **$1,332.00**
Price: Sendero SF II **$1,359.00**

REMINGTON MODEL 700 XCR RIFLE
Caliber: 25-06 Rem., 270 Win., 270 WSM, 7mm-08 Rem., 7mm Rem. Mag., 7mm Rem Ultra Mag., 30-06 Spfl., 300 WSM, 300 Win. Mag., 300 Rem. Ultra Mag., 338 Rem. Ultra Mag., 338 Win. Mag., 375 H&H Mag., 375 Rem. Ultra Mag. **Barrel:** 24" standard caliber; 26" magnum. **Weight:** 7.4 to 7.6 lbs. **Length:** 43.6" to 46.5" overall. **Stock:** Black synthetic, SuperCell recoil pad, rubber overmolded grip and forend. **Sights:** None. **Features:** XCR (Xtreme Conditions Rifle) includes TriNyte Corrosion Control System; drilled and tapped for scope mounts. 375 H&H Mag., 375 Rem. Ultra Mag. chamberings come with iron sights. Introduced 2005. XCR Tactical model introduced 2007. **Features:** Bell & Carlson OD green tactical stock, beavertail forend, recessed thumbhook behind pistol grip, TriNyte coating over stainless steel barrel, LTR fluting. Chambered in 223 Rem., 300 Win. Mag., 308 Win. 700XCR Left Hand introduced 2008 in 270 Win., 7mm Rem. Mag., 30-06 Spfl., 300 Rem Ultra Mag. Made in U.S. by Remington Arms Co., Inc.
Price: From **$1,065.00**
Price: XCR Tactical (2007) **$1,407.00**
Price: XCR Left Hand (2008) **$1,092.00**
Price: XCR Compact Tactical (2008), 223 Rem., 308 Win. . **$1,434.00**

REMINGTON MODEL 700 XCR CAMO RMEF
Similar to Model 700 XCR but with stainless barrel and receiver, AP HD camo stock, TriNyte coating overall, 7mm Remington Ultra Mag chambering.
Price: **$1,199.00**

REMINGTON 700 XCR II
Bolt action rifle chambered in .25-06 Remington, .270 Win, .280 Remington, 7mm Remington Mag., 7mm Remington Ultra Mag., .300 WSM, .300 Win Mag., .300 Remington Ultra Mag., .338 Win. Mag., .338 Remington Ultra Mag., .375 H&H, .375 Remington Ultra Mag., .30-06 Springfield. Features include black TriNyte corrosion control system coating; coated stainless steel barrel and receiver; olive drab green Hogue overmolded synthetic stock; SuperCell recoil pad; X-Mark Pro Trigger System; 2- or 26-inch barrel, depending on chambering.
Price: XCR II. **$970.00**
Price: XCR II CAMO **$1,063.00**

REMINGTON 700 XCR II - BONE COLLECTOR EDITION
Sim- ilar to Remington 700 XCR II but with Realtree AP HD camo stock.
Price: **$1,101.00**

Prices given are believed to be accurate at time of publication however, many factors affect retail pricing so exact prices are not possible.

CENTERFIRE RIFLES—Bolt Action

REMINGTON 700 XHR EXTREME HUNTING RIFLE

Caliber: 243 Win., 25-06, 270 Win., 7mm-08, 7mm Rem. Mag., 300 Win. Mag, 7mm Rem. Ultra Mag. **Barrel:** 24", 25", or 26" triangular magnum-contour counterbored. **Weight:** 7-1/4 to 7-5/8 lbs. **Length:** 41-5/8 to 46-1/2 overall. **Features:** Adjustable trigger, synthetic stock finished in Realtree AG HD camo, satin black oxide finish on exposed metal surfaces, hinged floorplate, SuperCell recoil pad.
Price: . . . . **$879.00 to $927.00**

REMINGTON MODEL 700 XCR TARGET TACTICAL RIFLE

Caliber: 308 Win. **Barrel:** 26" triangular counterbored, 1:11-1/2 rifling. **Weight:** 11.75 lbs. **Length:** 45-3/4" overall. **Features:** Textured green Bell & Carlson varmint/tactical stock with adjustable comb and length of pull, adjustable trigger, satin black oxide finish on exposed metal surfaces, hinged floorplate, SuperCell recoil pad, matte blue on exposed metal surfaces.
Price: **$1,407.00**

REMINGTON MODEL 700 VTR VARMINT/TACTICAL RIFLE

Caliber: 17 Rem. Fireball, 204 Ruger, 22-250, 223 Rem., 243 Win., 308 Win. **Barrel:** 22" triangular counterbored. **Weight:** 7.5 lbs. **Length:** 41-5/8" overall. **Features:** Olive drab overmolded or Digital Tiger TSP Desert Camo stock with vented semi-beavertail forend, tactical-style dual swivel mounts for bipod, matte blue on exposed metal surfaces.
Price: **$1,972.00**
Price: VTR Desert Recon, Digital Desert Camo stock,
  223 and 308 Win. only **$1,972.00**

REMINGTON MODEL 700 VARMINT SF RIFLE

Caliber: 17 Rem. Fireball, 204 Ruger, 22-250, 223, 220 Swift. **Barrel:** 26" stainless steel fluted. **Weight:** 8.5 lbs. **Length:** 45.75". **Features:** Synthetic stock with ventilated forend, stainless steel/triggerguard/floorplate, dual tactical swivels for bipod attachment.
Price: **$825.00**

REMINGTON MODEL 770 BOLT-ACTION RIFLE

Caliber: 243 Win., 270 Win., 7mm Rem. Mag., 7mm-08 Rem., 308 Win., 30-06 Spfl., 300 Win. Mag. **Barrel:** 22" or 24", button rifled. **Weight:** 8.5 lbs. **Length:** 42.5" to 44.5" overall. **Stock:** Black synthetic. **Sights:** Bushnell Sharpshooter 3-9x scope mounted and bore-sighted. **Features:** Upgrade of Model 710 introduced 2001. Unique action locks bolt directly into barrel; 60-degree bolt throw; 4-shot dual-stack magazine; all-steel receiver. Introduced 2007. Made in U.S.A. by Remington Arms Co.
Price: **$460.00**
Price: Youth, 243 Win. **$460.00**
Price: Stainless Camo (2008), stainless barrel, nickel-plated bolt,
  Realtree camo stock **$540.00**

REMINGTON MODEL SEVEN CDL/CDL MAGNUM

Caliber: 17 Rem. Fireball, 243 Win., 260 Rem., 270 WSM, 7mm-08 Rem., 308 Win., 300 WSM, 350 Rem. Mag. **Barrel:** 20"; 22" magnum. **Weight:** 6.5 to 7.4 lbs. **Length:** 39.25" to 41.25" overall.

Stock: American walnut, SuperCell recoil pad, satin finished. **Sights:** None. **Features:** Satin finished carbon steel barrel and action, 3- or 4-round magazine, hinged magazine floorplate. Furnished with iron sights and sling swivel studs, drilled and tapped for scope mounts. CDL versions introduced 2007. Made in U.S.A. by Remington Arms Co.
Price: CDL **$959.00**
Price: CDL Magnum **$1,01200**
Price: Predator (2008) **$825.00**
Price: 25th Anniversary (2008), 7mm-08 . . . . **$969.00**
Price: CDL Synthetic. . . . . **NA**

REMINGTON MODEL 798/799 BOLT-ACTION RIFLES

Caliber: 243 Win., 270 Win., 7mm Rem. Mag., 308 Win., .30-06 Spfl., .300 Win. Mag., .375 H&H Mag., .458 Win. Mag. **Barrel:** 20" to 26". **Weight:** 7.75 lbs. **Length:** 39.5" to 42.5" overall. **Stock:** Brown or green laminated, 1-inch rubber butt pad. **Sights:** None. Receiver drilled and tapped for standard Mauser 98 (long- and short-action) scope mounts. **Features:** Model 98 Mauser action (square-bridge Mauser 98). Claw extractor, sporter style 2-position safety, solid steel hinged floorplate magazine. Introduced 2006. Made in U.S.A. by Remington Arms Co.
Price: Model 798 SPS, black synthetic stock (2008), from **$527.00**
Price: Model 798 Satin Walnut Stock (2008), from **$648.00**
Price: Model 798 Safari Grade (2008), from **$1,141.00**
Price: Model 799,   from **$648.00**

REMINGTON 40-XB TACTICAL

Bolt action rifle chambered in .308 Winchester. Features include stainless steel bolt with Teflon coating; hinged floorplate; adjustable trigger; 27-1/4-inch tri-fluted 1:14 barrel; H-S precision pro series tactical stock, black color with dark green spiderweb; two front swivel studs; one rear swivel stud; vertical pistol grip.
Price: . . . . **NA**

REMINGTON 40-XS TACTICAL - 338LM SYSTEM

Bolt action rifle chambered in .338 Lapua Magnum. Features include 416 stainless steel Model 40-X 24-inch 1:12 barreled action; black polymer coating; McMillan A3 series stock with adjustable length of pull and adjustable comb; adjustable trigger and Sunny Hill heavy duty, all-steel trigger guard; Harris bi-pod with quick adjust swivel lock Leupold Mark IV 3.5-10x40mm long range M1 scope with Mil Dot reticle; Badger Ordnance all-steel Picatinny scope rail and rings.
Price: . . . . **NA**

RUGER MAGNUM RIFLE

Caliber: 375 H&H, 416 Rigby, 458 Lott. **Barrel:** 23". **Weight:** 9.5 to 10.25 lbs. **Length:** 44". **Stock:** AAA Premium Grade Circassian walnut with live-rubber recoil pad, metal gripcap, and studs for mounting sling swivels. **Sights:** Blade, front; V-notch rear express sights (one stationary, two folding) drift-adjustable for windage. **Features:** Floorplate latch secures the hinged floorplate against accidental dumping of cartridges; one-piece bolt has a non-rotating Mauser-type controlled-feed extractor; fixed-blade ejector.
Price: M77RSM MKII **$2,334.00**

RUGER COMPACT MAGNUMS

Caliber: .338 RCM, .300 RCM; 3-shot magazine. **Barrel:** 20". **Weight:** 6.75 lbs. **Length:** 39.5-40" overall. **Stock:** American walnut and black synthetic; stainless steel and Hawkeye Matte blued finishes. **Sights:** Adjustable Williams "U" notch rear sight and brass bead front sight. **Features:** Based on a shortened .375 Ruger case, the .300 and .338 RCMs match the .300 and .338 Win. Mag. in performance; RCM stock is 1/2 inch shorter than standard M77 Hawkeye stock;

LC6 trigger; steel floor plate engraved with Ruger logo and "Ruger Compact Magnum"; Red Eagle recoil pad; Mauser-type controlled feeding; claw extractor; 3-position safety; hammer-forged steel barrels; Ruger scope rings. Walnut stock includes extensive cut-checkering and rounded profiles. Intr. 2008. Made in U.S.A. by Sturm, Ruger & Co.
Price: HM77RCM (walnut/Hawkeye matte blued) **$995.00**
Price: HKM77PRCM (synthetic/SS) **$995.00**

RUGER GUNSITE SCOUT RIFLE

Caliber: .308 WIN., 10-shot magazine capacity. **Barrel:** 16.5". **Weight:** 7 lbs. **Length:** 38-39.5". **Stock:** Black laminate. **Sights:** Front post sight and rear adjustable. **Features:** Gunsite Scout Rifle is a credible rendition of Col. Jeff Cooper's "fighting carbine" Scout Rifle. The Ruger Gunsite Scout Rifle is a new platform in the Ruger M77 family. While the Scout Rifle has M77 features such as controlled round feed and integral scope mounts (scope rings included), the 10-round detachable box magazine is the first clue this isn't your grandfather's Ruger rifle. The Ruger Gunsite Scout Rifle has a 16.5 medium contour, cold hammer-forged, alloy steel barrel with a Mini-14 protected non-glare post front sight and receiver mounted, adjustable ghost ring rear sight for out-of-the-box usability. A forward mounted Picatinny rail offers options in mounting an assortment of optics – including Scout Scopes available from Burris and Leupold, for "both eyes open" sighting and super-fast target acquisition.
Price: $995.00

RUGER 77/22 BOLT-ACTION RIFLE

Caliber: 22 Hornet, 6-shot rotary magazine. **Barrel:** 20" or 24". **Weight:** About 6.25 to 7.5 lbs. **Length:** 39.5" to 43.5" overall. **Stock:** Checkered American walnut, black rubber buttpad; brown laminate. **Sights:** None. **Features:** Same basic features as rimfire model except slightly lengthened receiver. Uses Ruger rotary magazine. Three-position safety. Comes with 1" Ruger scope rings. Introduced 1994.
Price: 77/22-RH (rings only, no sights). **$754.00**
Price: K77/22-VHZ Varmint, laminated stock, no sights **$836.00**

RUGER M77 HAWKEYE RIFLES

Caliber: 204 Ruger, 223 Rem., 22-250 Rem., 243 Win., 257 Roberts, 25-06 Rem., 270 Win., 280 Rem., 7mm/08, 7mm Rem. Mag., 308 Win., 30-06 Spfl., 300 Win. Mag., 338 Win. Mag., 338 Federal, 358 Win. Mag., 416 Ruger, 375 Ruger, 300 Ruger Compact Magnum, 338 Ruger Compact Magnum; 4-shot magazine, except

3-shot magazine for magnums; 5-shot magazine for 204 Ruger and 223 Rem. **Barrel:** 22", 24". **Weight:** 6.75 to 8.25 lbs. **Length:** 42-44.4" overall. **Stock:** American walnut. **Sights:** None furnished. Receiver has Ruger integral scope mount base, Ruger 1" rings. **Features:** Includes Ruger LC6 trigger, new red rubber recoil pad, Mauser-type controlled feeding, claw extractor, 3-position safety, hammer-forged steel barrels, Ruger scope rings. Walnut stock includes wrap-around cut checkering on the forearm and, more rounded contours on stock and top of pistol grips. Matte stainless version features synthetic stock. Hawkeye Alaskan and African chambered in 375 Ruger. Alaskan features matte-black finish, 20" barrel, Hogue OverMolded synthetic stock. African has 23" blued barrel, checkered walnut stock, left-handed model. 375's have windage-adjustable shallow "V" notch rear sight, white bead front sights. Introduced 2007. Left-hand models available 2008.
Price: Standard, right- and left-hand. **$803.00**
Price: All-Weather. **$803.00**
Price: Laminate, left-hand **$862.00**
Price: Ultra Light **$862.00**
Price: All-Weather Ultra Light **$803.00**
Price: Compact **$803.00**
Price: Laminate Compact **$862.00**
Price: Compact Magnum **$899.00**
Price: African **$1,079.00**
Price: Alaskan **$1,079.00**
Price: Sporter **$862.00**
Price: Tactical **$1,138.00**
Price: Predator **$935.00**
Price: International **$939.00**

RUGER M77VT TARGET RIFLE

Caliber: 22-250 Rem., 223 Rem., 204 Ruger, 243 Win., 25-06 Rem., 308 Win. **Barrel:** 26" heavy stainless steel with target grey finish. **Weight:** 9 to 9.75 lbs. **Length:** Approx. 45.75" to 46.75" overall. **Stock:** Laminated American hardwood with beavertail forend, steel swivel studs; no checkering or gripcap. **Sights:** Integral scope mount bases in receiver. **Features:** Ruger diagonal bedding system. Ruger steel 1" scope rings supplied. Fully adjustable trigger. Steel floorplate and trigger guard. New version introduced 1992.
Price: KM77VT MKII **$935.00**

SAKO A7 AMERICAN BOLT-ACTION RIFLE

Caliber: 22-250, 243 Win., 25-06, 260 Rem., 270 Win., 270 WSM, 300 WSM, 30-06, 300 WM, 308 Win., 338 Federall, 7mm Rem. Mag., 7mm-08. **Barrel:** 22-7/16" standard, 24-3/8" magnum. **Weight:** 6 lbs. 3 oz. to 6 lbs. 13 oz. **Length:** 42-5/16" to 44-5/16" overall. **Features:** Blued or stainless barrel and receiver, black composite stock with sling swivels and recoil pad, two-position safety, adjustable trigger, detachable 3+1 box magazine.
Price: From . . . . **$850.00** (blued); **$950.00** (stainless)

SAKO TRG-22 AND TRG-42 TACTICAL RIFLES

Bolt action rifles chambered in .308 Winchester (TRG-22) or .338 Lapua Magnum (TRG-42). Features include target grade Cr-Mo or stainless barrels with muzzle brake; three locking lugs; 60° bolt throw; adjustable two-stage target trigger; adjustable or folding synthetic stock; receiver-mounted integral 17mm axial optics rails with recoil stop-slots; tactical scope mount for modern three turret tactical scopes (30 and 34 mm tube diameter); optional bipod.
Price: . . . .**$2,850.00 to $4,400.00**

SAKO MODEL 85 BOLT-ACTION RIFLES

Caliber: 22-250 Rem., 243 Win., 25-06 Rem., 260, 6.5x55mm, 270 Win., 270 WSM, 7mm-08 Rem., 308 Win., 30-06; 7mm WSM, 300 WSM, 338 Federal. **Barrel:** 22.4", 22.9", 24.4". **Weight:** 7.75 lbs. **Length:** NA. **Stock:** Polymer, laminated or high-grade walnut, straight comb, shadow-line cheekpiece. **Sights:** None furnished. **Features:** Controlled-round feeding, adjustable trigger,

Prices given are believed to be accurate at time of publication however, many factors affect retail pricing so exact prices are not possible.

matte stainless or nonreflective satin blue. Quad model is polymer/stainless with four interchangeable barrels in 22 LR, 22 WMR 17 HMR and 17 Mach 2; 50-degree bolt-lift, ambidextrous palm-swell, adjustable butt-pad. Introduced 2006. Imported from Finland by Beretta USA.

Price: Sako 85 Hunter, walnut/blued **$1,700.00**
Price: Sako 85 Grey Wolf, laminated/stainless **$1,575.00**
Price: Sako 85 Quad, polymer/stainless **$925.00**
Price: Sako 85 Quad Combo, four barrels **$2,175.00**

SAKO 85 FINNLIGHT

Similar to Model 85 but chambered in 243 Win., 25-06, 260 Rem., 270 Win., 270 WSM, 300 WSM, 30-06, 300 WM, 308 Win., 6.5x55mm, 7mm Rem Mag., 7mm-08. Weighs 6 lbs., 3 oz. to 6 lbs. 13 oz. Stainless steel barrel and receiver, black synthetic stock.
Price: **$1,600.00**

SAKO 75 HUNTER BOLT-ACTION RIFLE

Caliber: 223 Rem., 22-250 Rem., 243 Win., 25-06 Rem., 260, 270 Win., 270 WSM, 280 Rem., 300 Win. Mag., 30-06; 7mm-08 Rem., 308 Win., 270 Wby. Mag., 7mm Rem. Mag., 7mm STW, 7mm Wby. Mag., 300 Wby. Mag., 338 Win. Mag., 340 Wby. Mag., 375 H&H. **Barrel:** 22", standard calibers; 24", 26" magnum calibers. **Weight:** About 6 lbs. **Length:** NA. **Stock:** European walnut with matte lacquer finish. **Sights:** None furnished; dovetail scope mount rails. **Features:** New design with three locking lugs and a mechanical ejector, key locks firing pin and bolt, cold hammer-forged barrel is free-floating, two-position safety, hinged floorplate or detachable magazine that can be loaded from the top, short 70-degree bolt lift. Five action lengths. Introduced 1997. Imported from Finland by Beretta USA.
Price: From **$1,375.00**

SAKO 75 DELUXE RIFLE

Similar to 75 Hunter except select wood rosewood gripcap and forend tip. Available in 17 Rem., 222, 223 Rem., 25-06 Rem., 243 Win., 7mm-08 Rem., 308 Win., 25-06 Rem., 270 Win., 280 Rem., 30-06; 270 Wby. Mag., 7mm Rem. Mag., 7mm STW, 7mm Wby. Mag., 300 Wby. Mag., 338 Win. Mag., 340 Wby. Mag., 375 H&H, 416 Rem. Mag. Introduced 1997. Imported from Finland by Beretta USA.
Price: From **$2,175.00**

SAKO 75 VARMINT RIFLE

Similar to Model 75 Hunter except chambered only for 17 Rem., 222 Rem., 223 Rem., 22-250 Rem., 22 PPC and 6mm PPC, 24" heavy barrel with recessed crown; set trigger; beavertail forend. Introduced 1998. Imported from Finland by Beretta USA.
Price: **$1,850.00**

SAVAGE AXIS (EDGE) SERIES BOLT ACTION RIFLES

Caliber: .243 WIN., 7mm-08 REM., .308 WIN., .25-06 REM., .270 WIN., .30-06 SPFLD., .223 REM., .22-250 REM. **Barrel:** 22". **Weight:** 6.5 lbs. **Length:** 43.875". **Stock:** Black synthetic. **Sights:** Drilled and tapped for scope mounts. **Features:** The AXIS Stainless has a very sleek and modern design plus a silky-smooth operation. It benefits from a very handy detachable box magazine and is available only as a rifle and in a scoped package. It sports a stainless steel barrel with a high luster finish. The stock is synthetic and has a black matte finish. It is one of the most affordable rifles in the 2011 Savage lineup of hunting guns.
Price: Axis **$349.00**

Price: Axis Youth **$349.00**
Price: Axis XP **$389.00**
Price: Axis Camo **$399.00**
Price: Axis XP Youth **$399.00**
Price: Axis Stainless **$414.00**
Price: Axis XP Camo **$449.00**
Price: Axis Stainless XP **$469.00**

SAVAGE MODEL 25 BOLT ACTION RIFLES

Caliber: 204 Ruger, 223 Rem., 4-shot magazine. **Barrel:** 24", medium-contour fluted barrel with recessed target crown, free-floating sleeved barrel, dual pillar bedding. **Weight:** 8.25 lbs. **Length:** 43.75" overall. **Stock:** Brown laminate with beavertail-style forend. **Sights:** Weaver-style bases installed. **Features:** Diameter-specific action built around the 223 Rem. bolthead dimension. Three locking lugs, 60-degree bolt lift, AccuTrigger adjustable from 2.5 to 3.25 lbs. Model 25 Classic Sporter has satin lacquer American walnut with contrasting forend tip, wraparound checkering, 22" blued barrel. **Weight:** 7.15 lbs. **Length:** 41.75". Introduced 2008. Made in U.S.A. by Savage Arms, Inc.
Price: Model 25 Lightweight Varminter **$641.00**
Price: Model 25 Lightweight Varminter Thumbhole **$691.00**
Price: Model 25 Classic Sporter **$672.00**

SAVAGE CLASSIC SERIES MODEL 14/114 RIFLES

Caliber: 204 Ruger, 223 Rem., 22-250 Rem., 243 Win., 7mm-08 Rem., 308 Win., 270 WSM, 300 WSM (short action Model 14), 2- or 4-shot magazine; 270 Win., 7mm Rem. Mag., 30-06 Spfl., 300 Win. Mag. (long action Model 114), 3- or 4-shot magazine. **Barrel:** 22" or 24". **Weight:** 7 to 7.5 lbs. **Length:** 41.75" to 43.75" overall (Model 14); 43.25" to 45.25" overall (Model 114). **Stock:** Satin lacquer American walnut with ebony forend, wraparound checkering, Monte Carlo Comb and cheekpiece. **Sights:** None furnished. Receiver drilled and tapped for scope mounting. **Features:** AccuTrigger, high luster blued barreled action, hinged floorplate. From Savage Arms, Inc.
Price: Model 14 or 114 Classic, from **$826.00**
Price: Model 14 or 114 American Classic, detachable box magazine, from **$779.00**
Price: Model 14 or 114 Euro Classic, oil finish, from **$875.00**
Price: Model 14 Left Hand, 250 Savage and 300 Savage only **$779.00**

SAVAGE MODEL 12 SERIES VARMINT RIFLES

Caliber: 204 Ruger, 223 Rem., 22-250 Rem. 4-shot magazine. **Barrel:** 26" stainless barreled action, heavy fluted, free-floating and button-rifled barrel. **Weight:** 10 lbs. **Length:** 46.25" overall. **Stock:** Dual pillar bedded, low profile, laminated stock with extra-wide beavertail forend. **Sights:** None furnished; drilled and tapped for scope mounting. **Features:** Recessed target-style muzzle. AccuTrigger, oversized bolt handle, detachable box magazine, swivel studs. Model 112BVSS has heavy target-style prone laminated stock with high comb, Wundhammer palm swell, internal box magazine. Model 12FVSS has black synthetic stock, additional chamberings in 308 Win., 270 WSM, 300 WSM. Model 12FV has blued receiver. Model 12BTCSS has brown laminate vented thumbhole stock. Made in U.S.A. by Savage Arms, Inc.
Price: Model 12 Varminter, from **$991.00**
Price: Model 12BVSS **$899.00**
Price: Model 12FVSS, from **$815.00**
Price: Model 12FV **$658.00**
Price: Model 12BTCSS (2008) **$1,041.00**
Price: Model 12 Long Range (2008) **$1,239.00**
Price: Model 12 LRPV, single-shot only with right bolt/left port or left load/right eject receiver **$1,273.00**

SAVAGE MODEL 16/116 WEATHER WARRIORS

Caliber: 204 Ruger, 223 Rem., 22-250 Rem., 243 Win., 7mm-08 Rem., 308 Win., 270 WSM, 7mm WSM, 300 WSM (short action Model 16), 2- or 4-shot magazine; 270 Win., 7mm Rem. Mag., 30-06 Spfl., 300 Win. Mag., 338 Win. Mag. (long action Model 114), 3- or 4-shot magazine. **Barrel:** 22", 24"; stainless steel with matte finish, free-floated barrel. **Weight:** 6.5 to 6.75 lbs. **Length:** 41.75" to 43.75" overall (Model 16);

CENTERFIRE RIFLES—Bolt-Action

42.5" to 44.5" overall (Model 116). **Stock:** Graphite/fiberglass filled composite. **Sights:** None furnished; drilled and tapped for scope mounting. **Features:** Quick-detachable swivel studs; laser-etched bolt. Left-hand models available. Model 116FSS introduced 1991; 116FSAK introduced 1994. Made in U.S.A. by Savage Arms, Inc.

Price: Model 16FHSS or 116FHSS, hinged floorplate magazine, from..**$755.00**
Price: Model 16FLHSS or 116FLHSS, left hand models, from. **$755.00**
Price: Model 16FSS or 116FSS, internal box magazine, from. **$678.00**
Price: Model 16FCSS or 116FCSS, detachable box magazine, from..**$755.00**
Price: Model 16FHSAK or 116FHSAK, adjustable muzzle brake..**$822.00**

SAVAGE MODEL 10GXP3, 110GXP3 PACKAGE GUNS
Caliber: 223 Rem., 22-250 Rem., 243 Win., 7mm-08 Rem., 308 Win., 300 WSM (10GXP3). 25-06 Rem., 270 Win., 30-06 Spfl., 7mm Rem. Mag., 300 Win. Mag., 300 Rem. Ultra Mag. (110GXP3). **Barrel:** 22" 24", 26". **Weight:** 7.5 lbs. average. **Length:** 43" to 47". **Stock:** Walnut Monte Carlo with checkering. **Sights:** 3-9x40mm scope, mounted & bore sighted. **Features:** Blued, free floating and button rifled, internal box magazines, swivel studs, leather sling. Left-hand available.
Price: AccuTrigger, from..............................**$669.00**

SAVAGE MODEL 11FXP3, 111FXP3, 111FCXP3, 11FYXP3 (YOUTH) PACKAGE GUNS
Caliber: 223 Rem., 22-250 Rem., 243 Win., 308 Win., 300 WSM (11FXP3). 270 Win., 30-06 Spfl., 25-06 Rem., 7mm Rem. Mag., 300 Win. Mag., 338 Win. Mag., 300 Rem. Ultra Mag. (11FCXPE & 111FXP3). **Barrel:** 22" to 26". **Weight:** 6.5 lbs. **Length:** 41" to 47". **Stock:** Synthetic checkering, dual pillar bed. **Sights:** 3-9X40mm scope, mounted & bore sighted. **Features:** Blued, free floating and button rifled, Top loading internal box mag (except 111FXCP3 has detachable box magazine). Nylon sling and swivel studs. Some left-hand available.
Price: Model 11FXP3, from.........................**$640.00**
Price: Model 111FCXP3 ....**$519.00**
Price: Model 11FYXP3, 243 Win., 12.5" pull (youth) **$519.00**
Price: Model 11FLYXP3 Youth: Left-handed configuration of Model 11FYXP3 Youth **$640.00**

SAVAGE MODEL 16FXP3, 116FXP3 SS ACTION PACKAGE GUNS
Caliber: 223 Rem., 243 Win., 6.5x.284, 308 Win., 300 WSM, 270 Win., 30-06 Spfl., 7mm Rem. Mag., 300 Win. Mag., 338 Win. Mag., 375 H&H, 7mm S&W, 7mm Rem. Ultra Mag., 300 Rem. Ultra Mag. **Barrel:** 22", 24", 26". **Weight:** 6.75 lbs. average. **Length:** 41" to 46". **Stock:** Synthetic checkering, dual pillar bed. **Sights:** 3-9X40mm scope, mounted & bore sighted. **Features:** Free floating and button rifled. Internal box magazine, nylon sling and swivel studs.
Price: From..**$736.00**

SAVAGE MODEL 11/111 HUNTER SERIES BOLT ACTIONS
Caliber: 223 Rem., 22-250 Rem., 243 Win., 7mm-08 Rem., 308 Win., 270 WSM, 7mm WSM, 300 WSM (short action Model 11), 2- or 4-shot magazine; 25-06 Rem., 270 Win., 7mm Rem. Mag., 30-06 Spfl., 300 Win. Mag., (long action Model 111), 3- or 4-shot magazine. **Barrel:** 22" or 24"; blued free-floated barrel. **Weight:** 6.5 to 6.75 lbs. **Length:** 41.75" to 43.75" overall (Model 11); 42.5" to 44.5" overall (Model 111). **Stock:** Graphite/fiberglass filled composite or hardwood. **Sights:** Ramp front, open fully adjustable rear; drilled and tapped for scope mounting. **Features:** Three-position top tang safety, double front locking lugs. Introduced 1994. Made in U.S.A. by Savage Arms, Inc.
Price: Model 11FL or 111FL **$564.00**
Price: Model 11FL or 111FL, left hand models, from.......**$564.00**
Price: Model 11FCNS or 111FCNS, detachable box magazine, from..**$591.00**

Price: Model 11FLNS or 111FLNS **$564.00**
Price: Model 11G or 111G, hardwood stock, from **$582.00**
Price: Model 11BTH or 111BTH, laminate thumbhole stock (2008)..**$779.00**
Price: Model 11FNS Model FLNS **$591.00**
Price: Model 11FHNS or 111FHNS.......................**$656.00**
Price: Model 11FYCAK Youth **$691.00**
Price: Model 11GNS or 111GNS **$618.00**
Price: Model 11GLNS or 111GLSN **$618.00**
Price: Model 11GCNS or 111GCNS **$659.00**
Price: Model 11/111 Long-Range Hunter ....**$934 .00**

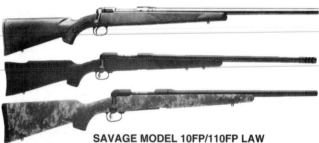

SAVAGE MODEL 10 BAS LAW ENFORCEMENT BOLT-ACTION RIFLE
Caliber: 380 Win. **Barrel:** 24" fluted heavy with muzzle brake. **Weight:** 13.4 lbs. **Length:** NA. **Features:** Bolt-action repeater based on Model 10 action but with M4-style collapsible buttstock, pistolgrip with palm swell, all-aluminum Accustock, picatinny rail for mounting optics.
Price: **$1,852.00**
Price: 10 BAT/S, multi-adjustable buttstock **$1,991.00**

SAVAGE MODEL 10FP/110FP LAW ENFORCEMENT SERIES RIFLES
Caliber: 223 Rem., 308 Win. (Model 10), 4-shot magazine; 25-06 Rem., 300 Win. Mag., (Model 110), 3- or 4-shot magazine. **Barrel:** 24"; matte blued free-floated heavy barrel and action. **Weight:** 6.5 to 6.75 lbs. **Length:** 41.75" to 43.75" overall (Model 10); 42.5" to 44.5" overall (Model 110). **Stock:** Black graphite/fiberglass composition, pillar-bedded, positive checkering. **Sights:** None furnished. Receiver drilled and tapped for scope mounting. **Features:** Black matte finish on all metal parts. Double swivel studs on the forend for sling and/or bipod mount. Right- or left-hand. Model 110FP introduced 1990. Model 10FP introduced 1998. Model 10FCPXP has HS Precision black synthetic tactical stock with molded alloy bedding system, Leupold 3.5-10x40mm black matte scope with Mil Dot reticle, Farrell Picatinny Rail Base, flip-open lens covers, 1.25" sling with QD swivels, Harris bipod, Storm heavy duty case. Made in U.S.A. by Savage Arms, Inc.
Price: Model 10FP, 10FLP (left hand), 110FP **$649.00**
Price: Model 10FP folding Choate stock....................**$896.00**
Price: Model 10FCP McMillan, McMillan fiberglass tactical stock **$1,178.00**
Price: Model 10FCP-HS HS Precision, HS Precision tactical stock **$984.00**
Price: Model 10FPXP-HS Precision **$2,715.00**
Price: Model 10FCP **$866.00**
Price: Model 10FLCP, left-hand model, standard stock or Accu-Stock **$866.00**
Price: Model 110FCP **$866.00**
Price: Model 10 Precision Carbine, 20" medium contour barrel, synthetic camo Accu-Stock, 223/308 ....**$829.00**
Price: Model 10 FCM Scout **$646.00**

SAVAGE MODEL 110-50TH ANNIVERSARY RIFLE
Same action as 110-series rifles, except offered in 300 Savage, limited edition of 1,000 rifles. Has high-luster blued barrel and action,

Prices given are believed to be accurate at time of publication however, many factors affect retail pricing so exact prices are not possible.

unique checkering pattern, high-grade hinged floorplate, scroll pattern on receiver, 24-karat gold-plated double barrel bands, 24-karat gold-plated AccuTrigger, embossed recoil pad. Introduced 2008. Made in U.S.A. from Savage Arms, Inc.
Price: Model 110 50th Anniversary **$1,724.00**

SAVAGE 110 BA LAW ENFORCEMENT RIFLE

Bolt action rifle chambered .300 Win. Mag. And .338 Lapua Mag. Features include aluminum stock that features Savage's innovative three-dimensional bedding system; interchangeable buttstocks and pistol grips; three-sided accessory rail; 5-round detachable magazine; high-efficiency muzzlebrake; Magpul PRS adjustable stock; 26-inch carbon steel barrel.
Price: **$2,267.00**

SAVAGE MODEL 10 PREDATOR SERIES

Caliber: 223, 22-250, 243, 204 Ruger. **Barrel:** 22", medium-contour. **Weight:** 7.25 lbs. **Length:** 43"overall. **Stock:** Synthetic with rounded forend and oversized bolt handle. **Features:** Entirely covered in either Mossy Oak Brush or Realtree Hardwoods Snow pattern camo. Also features AccuTrigger, AccuStock, detachable box magazine.
Price: **$806.00**

SAVAGE MODEL 10XP PREDATOR HUNTING BOLT-ACTION RIFLE PACKAGE

Similar to Model 10 but chambered in 223, 204, 22-250 or 243 Win. Includes 4-12x40 scope, 22" barrel, AccuTrigger, choice of Realtree Snow or Mossy Oak Brush camo overall.
Price: **$839.00**

SAVAGE MODEL 12 PRECISION TARGET SERIES BENCHREST RIFLE

Caliber: 308 Win, 6.5x284 Norman, 6mm Norma BR. **Barrel:** 29" ultra-heavy. **Weight:** 12.75 lbs. **Length:** 50" overall. **Stock:** Gray laminate. **Features:** New Left-Load, Right-Eject target action, Target AccuTrigger adjustable from approx 6 oz to 2.5 lbs, oversized bolt handle, stainless extra-heavy free-floating and button-rifled barrel.
Price: **$1,375.00**

SAVAGE MODEL 12 PRECISION TARGET PALMA RIFLE

Similar to Model 12 Benchrest but in 308 Palma only, 30" barrel, multi-adjustable stock, weighs 13.3 lbs.
Price: **$1,798.00**

SAVAGE MODEL 12 F CLASS TARGET RIFLE

Similar to Model 12 Benchrest but in 6.5x284 Norma, 6 Norma BR, 30" barrel, weighs 11.5 lbs.
Price: **$1,341.00**

SAVAGE MODEL 12 F/TR TARGET RIFLE

Similar to Model 12 Benchrest but in 308 Win. only, 30" barrel, weighs 12.65 lbs.
Price: **$1,265.00**

SMITH & WESSON I-BOLT RIFLES

Caliber: 25-06 Rem., 270 Win., 30-06 Win. (4-round magazine), 7mm Rem. Mag., 300 Win. Mag. (3-round magazine). **Barrel:** 23", 1:10" right-hand twist, 1:9" right-hand twist for 7mm Mag. Thompson/Center barrel. Blued and stainless. **Weight:** 6.75 lbs. **Stock:** Black synthetic, Realtree AP camo, walnut. Length of pull, 13-5/8", drop at comb, 7/8". Monte Carlo cheekpiece. **Sights:** Adjustable post front sight, adjustable dual aperture rear sight. **Features:** Adjustable Tru-Set Trigger. Introduced 2008. Made in U.S.A. by Smith & Wesson.
Price: Black synthetic stock, weather shield finish **$588.00**
Price: Camo stock, weather shield finish **$658.00**

STEVENS MODEL 200 BOLT-ACTION RIFLES

Caliber: 223, 22-250, 243, 7mm-08, 308 Win. (short action) or 25-06, 270 Win., 30-06, 7mm Rem. Mag., 300 Win Mag. Barrel: 22" (short action) or 24" (long action blued). **Weight:** 6.5 lbs. **Length:** 41.75" overall. **Stock:** Black synthetic or camo. **Sights:** None. **Features:** Free-floating and button-rifled barrel, top loading internal box magazine, swivel studs.
Price: . . . . **$399.00** (standard); **$439.00** (camo)
Price: Model 200XP Long or Short Action
   Package Rifle with 4x12 scope. **$449.00**
Price: Model 200XP Camo, camo stock **$499.00**

STEYR MANNLICHER CLASSIC RIFLE

Caliber: 222 Rem., 223 Rem., 243 Win., 25-06 Rem., 308 Win., 6.5x55, 6.5x57, 270 Win., 270 WSM, 7x64 Brenneke, 7mm-08 Rem., 7.5x55, 30-06 Spfl., 9.3x62, 6.5x68, 7mm Rem. Mag., 300 WSM, 300 Win. Mag., 8x68S, 4-shot magazine. **Barrel:** 23.6" standard; 26" magnum; 20" full stock standard calibers. **Weight:** 7 lbs. **Length:** 40.1" overall. **Stock:** Hand-checkered fancy European oiled walnut with standard forend. **Sights:** Ramp front adjustable for elevation, V-notch rear adjustable for windage. **Features:** Single adjustable trigger; 3-position roller safety with "safe-bolt" setting; drilled and tapped for Steyr factory scope mounts. Introduced 1997. Imported from Austria by Steyr Arms, Inc.
Price: Half stock, standard calibers **$3,799.00**
Price: Full stock, standard calibers. **$4,199.00**

STEYR PRO HUNTER RIFLE

Similar to the Classic Rifle except has ABS synthetic stock with adjustable butt spacers, straight comb without cheekpiece, palm swell, Pachmayr 1" swivels. Special 10-round magazine conversion kit available. Introduced 1997. Imported from Austria by Steyr Arms, Inc.
Price: From **$1,500.00**

STEYR SCOUT BOLT-ACTION RIFLE

Caliber: 308 Win., 5-shot magazine. **Barrel:** 19", fluted. **Weight:** NA. **Length:** NA. **Stock:** Gray Zytel. **Sights:** Pop-up front & rear, Leupold M8 2.5x28 IER scope on Picatinny optic rail with Steyr mounts. **Features:** luggage case, scout sling, two stock spacers, two magazines. Introduced 1998. Imported from Austria by Steyr Arms, Inc.
Price: From **$2,199.00**

STEYR SSG08 BOLT-ACTION RIFLE

Caliber: 7.62x51mmNATO (.308Win) or 7.62x63B (.300 Win Mag)., 10-shot magazine capacity. **Barrel:** 508mm or 600mm. **Weight:** 5.5 kg - 5.7 kg. **Length:** 1090mm - 1182mm. **Stock:** Dural aluminium foldingstock black with 280 mm long UIT-rail and various Picatinny-rails. **Sights:** Front post sight and rear adjustable. **Features:** The STEYR SSG 08 features high grade alumnium folding stock, adjustable cheek piece and butt plate with height marking, and an ergonomical exchangeable pistol grip. The STEYR SSG 08 also features a Versa-Pod, a muzzle brake, a Picatinny rail, a UIT rail on stock and various Picatinny rails on fore end, and a 10-round HC-magazine. SBSrotary bolt action with four frontal locking lugs, arranged in pairs.Coldhammer-forged barrels are available in standard or compact lengths.
Price: **$4,915.00**

STEYR SSG 69 PII BOLT-ACTION RIFLE

Caliber: 22-250 Rem., 243 Win., 308 Win., detachable 5-shot rotary magazine. **Barrel:** 26". **Weight:** 8.5 lbs. **Length:** 44.5" overall.

CENTERFIRE RIFLES—Bolt Action

Stock: Black ABS Cycolac with spacers for length of pull adjustment. **Sights:** Hooded ramp front adjustable for elevation, V-notch rear adjustable for windage. **Features:** Sliding safety; NATO rail for bipod; 1" swivels; Parkerized finish; single or double-set triggers. Imported from Austria by Steyr Arms, Inc.
Price: **$1,889.00**

THOMPSON/CENTER ICON BOLT-ACTION RIFLE

Caliber: 22-250 Rem., 243 Win., 308 Win., 30TC, 3-round box magazine. **Barrel:** 24", button rifled. **Weight:** 7.5 lbs. **Length:** 44.5" overall. **Stock:** Walnut, 20-lpi grip and forend cut checkering with ribbon detail. **Sights:** None; integral Weaver style scope mounts. **Features:** Interchangeable bolt handle, 60-degree bolt lift, Interlok Bedding System, 3-lug bolt with T-Slot extractor, cocking indicator, adjustable trigger, preset to 3 to 3.5 lbs of pull. Introduced 2007. From Thompson/Center Arms.
Price: **$1,025.00**

THOMPSON/CENTER ICON PRECISION HUNTER RIFLE

Similar to the basic ICON model. Available in 204 Ruger, 223 Rem., 22-250 Rem., 243 Win. and 308 Win. 22" heavy barrel, blued finish, varminter-style stock. Introduced 2009.
Price: **$1,149.00**

THOMPSON/CENTER VENTURE BOLT-ACTION RIFLE

Caliber: 270 Win., 7mm Rem. Mag., 30-06 Springfield, 300 Win. Mag., 3-round magazine. **Barrel:** 24". **Weight:** NA. **Length:** NA. **Stock:** Composite. **Sights:** NA. **Features:** Nitride fat bolt design, externally adjustable trigger, two-position safety, textured grip. Introduced 2009.
Price: **$489.00**

THOMPSON/CENTER VENTURE MEDIUM ACTION RIFLE

Bolt action rifle chambered in .204, .22-250, .223, .243, 7mm-08, .308 and 30TC. Features include a 24-inch crowned medium weight barrel, classic styled composite stock with inlaid traction grip panels, adjustable 3.5 to 5 pound trigger along with a drilled and tapped receiver (bases included). 3+1 detachable nylon box magazine. **Weight:** 7 lbs. **Length:** 43.5 inches.
Price: **$499.00**

THOMPSON/CENTER VENTURE PREDATOR PDX RIFLE

Bolt action rifle chambered in .204, .22-250, .223, .243, .308. Similar to Venture Medium action but with heavy, deep-fluted 22-inch barrel and Max-1 camo finish overall. **Weight:** 8 lbs. **Length:** 41.5 inches.
Price: .... **$549.00 to $599.00**

TIKKA T3 HUNTER

Caliber: 223 Rem., 22-250 Rem., 243 Win., 308 Win., 25-06 Rem., 270 Win., 30-06 Spfl., 300 Win. Mag., 338 Win. Mag., 270 WSM, 300 WSM, 6.5x55 Swedish Mauser, 7mm Rem. Mag. **Stock:** Walnut. **Sights:** None furnished. **Barrel:** 22-7/16", 24-3/8". **Features:** Detachable magazine, aluminum scope rings. Introduced 2005. Imported from Finland by Beretta USA.
Price: **$675.00**

TIKKA T3 STAINLESS SYNTHETIC

Similar to the T3 Hunter except stainless steel, synthetic stock. Available in 243 Win., 2506, 270 Win., 308 Win., 30-06 Spfl., 270 WSM, 300 WSM, 7mm Rem. Mag., 300 Win. Mag., 338 Win. Mag.

Introduced 2005. Imported from Finland by Beretta USA.
Price: **$700.00**

TIKKA T3 LITE BOLT-ACTION RIFLE

Similar to the T3 Hunter, available in 223 Rem., 22-250 Rem., 308 Win., 243 Win., 25-06 Rem., 270 Win., 270 WSM, 30-06 Sprg., 300 Win Mag., 300 WSM, 338 Federal, 338 Win Mag., 7mm Rem. Mag., 7mm-08 Rem. Barrel lengths vary from 22-7/16" to 24-3/8". Made in Finland by Sako. Imported by Beretta USA.
Price: **$695.00**
Price: Stainless steel synthetic **$600.00**
Price: Stainless steel synthetic, left-hand **$700.00**

TIKKA T3 VARMINT/SUPER VARMINT RIFLE

Similar to the T3 Hunter, available in 223 Rem., 22-250 Rem., 308 Win. Length is 23-3/8" (Super Varmint). Made in Finland by Sako. Imported by Beretta USA.
Price: **$900.00**
Price: Super Varmint **$1,425.00**

ULTRA LIGHT ARMS BOLT-ACTION RIFLES

Caliber: 17 Rem. to 416 Rigby. **Barrel:** Douglas, length to order. **Weight:** 4.75 to 7.5 lbs. **Length:** Varies. **Stock:** Kevlar graphite composite, variety of finishes. **Sights:** None furnished; drilled and tapped for scope mounts. **Features:** Timney trigger, hand-lapped action, button-rifled barrel, hand-bedded action, recoil pad, sling-swivel studs, optional Jewell trigger. Made in U.S.A. by New Ultra Light Arms.
Price: Model 20 (short action)............... **$3,000.00**
Price: Model 24 (long action) **$3,100.00**
Price: Model 28 (magnum action) **$3,400.00**
Price: Model 40 (300 Wby. Mag., 416 Rigby) **$3,400.00**
Price: Left-hand models, add **$100.00**

WEATHERBY MARK V BOLT-ACTION RIFLES

Caliber: Deluxe version comes in all Weatherby calibers plus 243 Win., 270 Win., 7mm-08 Rem., 30-06 Spfl., 308 Win. **Barrel:** 24", 26", 28". **Weight:** 6.75 to 10 lbs. **Length:** 44" to 48.75" overall. **Stock:** Walnut, Monte Carlo with cheekpiece; high luster finish; checkered pistol grip and forend; recoil pad. **Sights:** None furnished. **Features:** 4 models with Mark V action and wood stocks; other common elements include cocking indicator; adjustable trigger; hinged floorplate, thumb safety; quick detachable sling swivels. Ultramark has hand-selected exhibition-grade walnut stock, maplewood/ebony spacers, 20-lpi checkering. Chambered for 257 and 300 Wby Mags. Lazermark same as Mark V Deluxe except stock has extensive oak leaf pattern laser carving on pistol grip and forend; chambered in Wby. Magnums—257, 270 Win., 7mm., 300, 340, with 26" barrel. Introduced 1981. Sporter is same as the Mark V Deluxe without the embellishments. Metal has low-luster blue, stock is Claro walnut with matte finish, Monte Carlo comb, recoil pad. Chambered for these Wby. Mags: 257, 270 Win., 7mm, 300, 340. Other chamberings: 7mm Rem. Mag., 300 Win. Introduced 1993. Six Mark V models come with synthetic stocks. Ultra Lightweight rifles weigh 5.75 to 6.75 lbs.; 24", 26" fluted stainless barrels with recessed target crown; Bell & Carlson stock with CNC-machined aluminum bedding plate and tan "spider web" finish, skeletonized handle and sleeve. Available in 243 Win., Wby. Mag., 25-06 Rem., 270 Win., 7mm-08 Rem., 7mm Rem. Mag., 280 Rem., 308 Win., 30-06 Spfl., 300 Win. Mag. Wby. Mag chamberings: 240, 257, 270 Win., 7mm, 300. Introduced 1998. Accumark uses Mark V action with heavy-contour 26" and 28" stainless barrels with black oxidized flutes, muzzle diameter of .705". No sights, drilled and tapped for scope mounting. Stock is composite with matte gel-coat finish, full length aluminum bedding Hasblock. Weighs 8.5 lbs. Chambered for these Wby. Mags: 240 (2007), 257, 270, 7mm, 300, 340, 338-378, 30-378. Other chamberings: 22-250 (2007), 243 Win. (2007), 25-06 Rem. (2007), 270 Win. (2007), 308 Win.(2007), 7mm Rem. Mag., 300 Win. Mag. Introduced 1996. SVM (Super VarmintMaster) has 26"

Prices given are believed to be accurate at time of publication however, many factors affect retail pricing so exact prices are not possible.

fluted stainless barrel, spiderweb-pattern tan laminated synthetic stock, fully adjustable trigger. Chambered for 223 Rem., 22-250 Rem., 243. Mark V Synthetic has lightweight injection-molded synthetic stock with raised Monte Carlo comb, checkered grip and forend, custom floorplate release. Weighs 6.5-8.5 lbs., 24-28" barrels. Available in 22-250 Rem., 243 Win., 25-06 Rem., 270 Win., 7mm-08 Rem., 7mm Rem., Mag, 280 Rem., 308 Win., 30-06 Spfl., 308 Win., 300 Win. Mag., 375 H&H Mag, and these Wby. Magnums: 240, 257, 270 Win., 7mm, 300, 30-378, 338-378, 340. Introduced 1997. Fibermark composites are similar to other Mark V models except has black Kevlar and fiberglass composite stock and bead-bead-blast blue or stainless finish. Chambered for 9 standard and magnum calibers. Introduced 1983; reintroduced 2001. SVR comes with 22" button-rifled chrome-moly barrel, .739 muzzle diameter. Composite stock w/bedding block, gray spiderweb pattern. Made in U.S.A. From Weatherby.

Price: Mark V Deluxe **$2,199.00**
Price: Mark V Ultramark **$2,979.00**
Price: Mark V Lazermark **$2,479.00**
Price: Mark V Sporter **$1,499.00**
Price: Mark V SVM **$1,959.00**
Price: Mark V Ultra Lightweight **$1,879.00**
Price: Mark V Ultra Lightweight LH **$1,911.00**
Price: Mark V Accumark **$1,879.00**
Price: Mark V Synthetic **$1,209.00**
Price: Mark V Fibermark Composite **$1,449.00**
Price: Mark V SVR Special Varmint Rifle **$1,259.00**

WEATHERBY VANGUARD BOLT-ACTION RIFLES

Caliber: 257, 300 Wby Mags; 223 Rem., 22-250 Rem., 243 Win., 25-06 Rem. (2007), 270 Win., 270 WSM, 7mm Rem. Mag., 308 Win., 30-06 Spfl., 300 Win. Mag., 300 WSM, 338 Win. Mag. **Barrel:** 24" barreled action, matte black. **Weight:** 7.5 to 8.75 lbs. **Length:** 44" to 46-3/4" overall. **Stock:** Raised comb, Monte Carlo, injection-molded composite stock. **Sights:** None furnished. **Features:** One-piece forged, fluted bolt body with three gas ports, forged and machined receiver, adjustable trigger, factory accuracy guarantee. Vanguard Stainless has 410-Series stainless steel barrel and action, bead blasted matte metal finish. Vanguard Deluxe has raised comb, semi-fancy grade Monte Carlo walnut stock with maplewood spacers, rosewood forend and grip cap, polished action with high-gloss-blued metalwork. Vanguard Synthetic Package includes Vanguard Synthetic rifle with Bushnell Banner 3-9x40mm scope mounted and boresighted, Leupold Rifleman rings and bases, Uncle Mikes nylon sling, and Plano PRO-MAX injection-molded case. Sporter has Monte Carlo walnut stock with satin urethane finish, fineline diamond point checkering, contrasting rosewood forend tip, matte-blued metalwork. Sporter SS metalwork is 410 Series bead-blasted stainless steel. Vanguard Youth/Compact has 20" No. 1 contour barrel, short action, scaled-down non-reflective matte black hardwood stock with 12.5" length of pull and full-size, injection-molded composite stock. Chambered for 223 Rem., 22-250 Rem., 243 Win., 7mm-08 Rem., 308 Win. Weighs 6.75 lbs.; OAL 38.9". Sub-MOA Matte and Sub-MOA Stainless models have pillar-bedded Fiberguard composite stock (Aramid, graphite unidirectional fibers and fiberglass) with 24" barreled action; matte black metalwork, Pachmayr Decelerator recoil pad. Sub-MOA Stainless metalwork is 410 Series bead-blasted stainless steel. Sub-MOA Varmint guaranteed to shoot 3-shot group of .99" or less when used with specified Weatherby factory or premium (non-Weatherby calibers) ammunition. Hand-laminated, tan Monte Carlo composite stock with black spiderwebbing; CNC-machined aluminum bedding block, 22" No. 3 contour barrel, recessed target crown. Varmint Special has tan injection-molded Monte Carlo composite stock, pebble grain finish, black spiderwebbing. 22" No. 3 contour barrel (.740 muzzle dia.), bead blasted matte black finish, recessed target crown. Made in U.S.A. From Weatherby.

Price: Vanguard Synthetic **$399.00**
Price: Vanguard Stainless **$709.00**
Price: Vanguard Deluxe, 7mm Rem. Mag., 300 Win. Mag. (2007) **$989.00**
Price: Vanguard Synthetic Package, 25-06 Rem. (2007) **$552.00**
Price: Vanguard Sporter **$689.00**
Price: Vanguard Sporter SS **$869.00**
Price: Vanguard Youth/Compact **$649.00**
Price: Vanguard Sub-MOA Matte, 25-06 Rem. (2007) **$929.00**
Price: Vanguard Sub-MOA Stainless, 270 WSM **$1,079.00**
Price: Vanguard Sub-MOA Varmint, 204 Ruger (2007) **$1,009.00**

WINCHESTER MODEL 70 BOLT-ACTION RIFLES

Caliber: Varies by model. **Barrel:** Blued, or free-floating, fluted stainless hammer-forged barrel, 22", 24", 26". Recessed target crown. **Weight:** 6.75 to 7.25 lbs. **Length:** 41 to 45.75 " overall. **Stock:** Walnut (three models) or Bell and Carlson composite; textured charcoal-grey matte finish, Pachmayr Decelerator recoil pad. **Sights:** None. **Features:** Claw extractor, three-position safety, M.O.A. three-lever trigger system, factory-set at 3.75 lbs. Super Grade features fancy grade walnut stock, contrasting black fore-end tip and pistol grip cap, and sculpted shadowline cheekpiece. Featherweight Deluxe has angled-comb walnut stock, Schnabel fore-end, satin finish, cut checkering. Sporter Deluxe has satin-finished walnut stock, cut checkering, sculpted cheekpiece. Extreme Weather SS has composite stock, drop @ comb, 0.5"; drop @ heel, 0.5". Introduced 2008. Made in U.S.A. from Winchester Repeating Arms.

Price: Extreme Weather SS, 270 Win., 270 WSM, 30-06 Spfl., 300 Win. Mag., 300 WSM, 308 Win., 325 WSM, 243 Winchester, 7mm WSM, from **$1,069.00**
Price: Super Grade, 30-06 Sprg., 300 Win. Mag., 270 WSM, 300 WSM, 270 Winchester, from **$1,139.00**
Price: Featherweight Deluxe, 243 Win., 270 Win., 270 WSM, 30-06 Spfl., 300 Win. Mag., 300 WSM, 308 Win., 325 WSM, 7mm-08 Rem., from **$999.00**
Price: Sporter Deluxe, 270 Win., 270 WSM, 30-06 Spfl., 300 Win. Mag., 300 WSM, 325 WSM, from **$999.00**

WINCHESTER MODEL 70 COYOTE LIGHT

Caliber: 22-250, 243 Winchester, 308 Winchester, 270 WSM, 300 WSM and 325 WSM, five-shot magazine (3-shot in 270 WSM, 300 WSM and 325 WSM). **Barrel:** 22" fluted stainless barrel (24" in 270 WSM, 300 WSM and 325 WSM). **Weight:** 7.5 lbs. **Length:** NA. **Features:** Composite Bell and Carlson stock, Pachmayr Decelerator pad. Controlled round feeding. No sights but drilled and tapped for mounts.

Price: **$1,099.00**

WINCHESTER MODEL 70 FEATHERWEIGHT

Caliber: 22-250, 243, 7mm-08, 308, 270 WSM, 7mm WSM, 300 WSM, 325 WSM, 25-06, 270, 30-06, 7mm Rem. Mag., 300 Win. Mag., 338 Win. Mag. Capacity 5 rounds (short action) or 3 rounds (long action). **Barrel:** 22" blued barrel (24" in magnum chamberings). **Weight:** 6-1/2 to 7-1/4 lbs. **Length:** NA. **Features:** Satin-finished checkered Grade I walnut stock, controlled round feeding. Pachmayr Decelerator pad. No sights but drilled and tapped for scope mounts.

Price: Short action **$799.00**
Price: Long action and magnum) **$839.00**

WINCHESTER MODEL 70 SPORTER

Caliber: 270 WSM, 7mm WSM, 300 WSM, 325 WSM, 25-06, 270, 30-06, 7mm Rem. Mag., 300 Win. Mag., 338 Win. Mag. Capacity 5 rounds (short action) or 3 rounds (long action). **Barrel:** 22", 24" or 26" blued. **Weight:** 6-1/2 to 7-1/4 lbs. **Length:** NA. **Features:** Satin-finished checkered Grade I walnut stock with sculpted cheekpiece, controlled round feeding. Pachmayr Decelerator pad. No sights but drilled and tapped for scope mounts.

Price: Short action **$799.00**
Price: Long action and magnum) **$839.00**

WINCHESTER MODEL 70 ULTIMATE SHADOW

Caliber: 243, 308, 270 WSM, 7mm WSM, 300 WSM, 325 WSM, 270, 30-06, 7mm Rem. Mag., 300 Win. Mag. Capacity 5 rounds (short action) or 3 rounds (long action). **Barrel:** 22" matte stainless (24" or 26" in magnum chamberings). **Weight:** 6-1/2 to 7-1/4 lbs. **Length:** NA. **Features:** Synthetic stock with WinSorb recoil pad, controlled round feeding. Pachmayr Decelerator pad. No sights but drilled and tapped for scope mounts.

Price: Standard **$739.00**
Price: Magnum **$769.00**

ARMALITE AR-50 RIFLE
Caliber: 50 BMG **Barrel:** 31". **Weight:** 33.2 lbs. **Length:** 59.5" **Stock:** Synthetic. **Sights:** None furnished. **Features:** A single-shot bolt-action rifle designed for long-range shooting. Available in left-hand model. Made in U.S.A. by Armalite.
Price: **$3,359.00**

BALLARD 1875 1 1/2 HUNTER RIFLE
Caliber: NA. **Barrel:** 26-30". **Weight:** NA **Length:** NA. **Stock:** Hand-selected classic American walnut. **Sights:** Blade front, Rocky Mountain rear. **Features:** Color case-hardened receiver, breechblock and lever. Many options available. Made in U.S.A. by Ballard Rifle & Cartridge Co.
Price: **$3,250.00**

BALLARD 1875 #3 GALLERY SINGLE SHOT RIFLE
Caliber: NA. **Barrel:** 24-28" octagonal with tulip. **Weight:** NA. **Length:** NA. **Stock:** Hand-selected classic American walnut. **Sights:** Blade front, Rocky Mountain rear. **Features:** Color case-hardened receiver, breechblock and lever. Many options available. Made in U.S.A. by Ballard Rifle & Cartridge Co.
Price: **$3,300.00**

BALLARD 1875 #4 PERFECTION RIFLE
Caliber: 22 LR, 32-40, 38-55, 40-65, 40-70, 45-70 Govt., 45-90, 45-110, 50-70, 50-90. **Barrel:** 30" or 32" octagon, standard or heavyweight. **Weight:** 10.5 lbs. (standard) or 11.75 lbs. (heavyweight bbl.). **Length:** NA. **Stock:** Smooth walnut. **Sights:** Blade front, Rocky Mountain rear. **Features:** Rifle or shotgun-style buttstock, straight grip action, single or double-set trigger, "S" or right lever, hand polished and lapped Badger barrel. Made in U.S.A. by Ballard Rifle & Cartridge Co.
Price: **$3,950.00**

BALLARD 1875 #7 LONG RANGE RIFLE
Caliber: 32-40, 38-55, 40-65, 40-70 SS, 45-70 Govt., 45-90, 45-110. **Barrel:** 32", 34" half-octagon. **Weight:** 11.75 lbs. **Length:** NA. **Stock:** Walnut; checkered pistol grip shotgun butt, ebony forend cap. **Sights:** Globe front. **Features:** Designed for shooting up to 1000 yards. Standard or heavy barrel; single or double-set trigger; hard rubber or steel buttplate. Introduced 1999. Made in U.S.A. by Ballard Rifle & Cartridge Co.
Price: From **$3,600.00**

BALLARD 1875 #8 UNION HILL RIFLE
Caliber: 22 LR, 32-40, 38-55, 40-65 Win., 40-70 SS. **Barrel:** 30" half-octagon. **Weight:** About 10.5 lbs. **Length:** NA. **Stock:** Walnut; pistol grip butt with cheekpiece. **Sights:** Globe front. **Features:** Designed for 200-yard offhand shooting. Standard or heavy barrel; double-set triggers; full loop lever; hook Schuetzen buttplate. Introduced 1999. Made in U.S.A. by Ballard Rifle & Cartridge Co.
Price: From **$4,175.00**

BALLARD MODEL 1885 LOW WALL SINGLE SHOT RIFLE
Caliber: NA. **Barrel:** 24-28". **Weight:** NA. **Length:** NA. **Stock:** Hand-selected classic American walnut. **Sights:** Blade front, sporting rear. **Features:** Color case hardened receiver, breech block and lever. Many options available. Made in U.S.A. by Ballard Rifle & Cartridge Co.
Price: **$3,300.00**

BALLARD MODEL 1885 HIGH WALL STANDARD SPORTING SINGLE SHOT RIFLE
Caliber: 17 Bee, 22 Hornet, 218 Bee, 219 Don Wasp, 219 Zipper, 22 Hi-Power, 225 Win., 25-20 WCF, 25-35 WCF, 25 Krag, 7mmx57R, 30-30, 30-40 Krag, 303 British, 33 WCF, 348 WCF, 35 WCF, 35-30/30, 9.3x74R, 405 WCF, 50-110 WCF, 500 Express, 577 Express. **Barrel:** Lengths to 34". **Weight:** NA. **Stock:** Straight-grain American walnut. **Sights:** Buckhorn or flattop rear, blade front. **Features:** Faithful copy of original Model 1885 High Wall; parts interchange with original rifles; variety of options available. Introduced 2000. Made in U.S.A. by Ballard Rifle & Cartridge Co.
Price: **$3,300.00**

BALLARD MODEL 1885 HIGH WALL SPECIAL SPORTING SINGLE SHOT RIFLE
Caliber: NA. **Barrel:** 28-30" octagonal. **Weight:** NA. **Length:** NA. **Stock:** Hand-selected classic American walnut. **Sights:** Blade front, sporting rear. **Features:** Color case hardened receiver, breech block and lever. Many options available. Made in U.S.A. by Ballard Rifle & Cartridge Co.
Price: **$3,600.00**

BARRETT MODEL 99 SINGLE SHOT RIFLE
Caliber: 50 BMG. **Barrel:** 33". **Weight:** 25 lbs. **Length:** 50.4" overall. **Stock:** Anodized aluminum with energy-absorbing recoil pad. **Sights:** None furnished; integral M1913 scope rail. **Features:** Bolt action; detachable bipod; match-grade barrel with high-efficiency muzzle brake. Introduced 1999. Made in U.S.A. by Barrett Firearms.
Price: From **$4,000.00**

BROWN MODEL 97D SINGLE SHOT RIFLE
Caliber: 17 Ackley Hornet through 45-70 Govt. **Barrel:** Up to 26", air gauged match grade. **Weight:** About 5 lbs., 11 oz. **Stock:** Sporter style with pistol grip, cheekpiece and Schnabel forend. **Sights:** None furnished; drilled and tapped for scope mounting. **Features:** Falling block action gives rigid barrel-receiver matting; polished blue/black finish. Hand-fitted action. Many options. Made in U.S.A. by E. Arthur Brown Co., Inc.
Price: From **$999.00**

BROWNING MODEL 1885 HIGH WALL SINGLE SHOT RIFLE
Caliber: 22-250 Rem., 30-06 Spfl., 270 Win., 7mm Rem. Mag., 454 Casull, 45-70 Govt. **Barrel:** 28". **Weight:** 8 lbs., 12 oz. **Length:** 43.5" overall. **Stock:** Walnut with straight grip, Schnabel forend. **Sights:** None furnished; drilled and tapped for scope mounting. **Features:** Replica of J.M. Browning's high-wall falling block rifle. Octagon barrel with recessed muzzle. Imported from Japan by Browning. Introduced 1985.
Price: **$1,260.00**

C. SHARPS ARMS MODEL 1875 TARGET & SPORTING RIFLE
Caliber: 38-55, 40-65, 40-70 Straight or Bottlenecks, 45-70, 45-90. **Barrel:** 30" heavy taperred round. **Weight:** 11 lbs. **Length:** NA. **Stock:** American walnut. **Sights:** Globe with post front sight. **Features:** Long Range Vernier tang sight with windage adjustments. Pistol grip stock with cheek rest; checkered steel buttplate. Introduced 1991. From C. Sharps Co.
Price: Without sights. **$1,325.00**
Price: With blade front & Buckhorn rear barrel sights. **$1,420.00**
Price: With standard Tang & Globe w/post & ball front
     sights **$1,615.00**
Price: With deluxe vernier Tang & Globe w/spirit level &
     aperture sights **$1,730.00**
Price: With single set trigger, add **$125.00**

C. SHARPS ARMS 1875 CLASSIC SHARPS
Similar to New Model 1875 Sporting Rifle except 26", 28" or 30" full octagon barrel, crescent buttplate with toe plate, Hartford-style forend with cast German silver nose cap. Blade front sight, Rocky Mountain buckhorn rear. Weighs 10 lbs. Introduced 1987. From C. Sharps Arms Co.
Price: **$1,670.00**

C. SHARPS ARMS 1874 BRIDGEPORT SPORTING RIFLE
Caliber: 38-55 TO 50-3.25. **Barrel:** 26", 28", 30" tapered octagon. **Weight:** 10.5 lbs. **Length:** 47". **Stock:** American black walnut; shotgun butt with checkered steel buttplate; straight grip, heavy forend with Schnabel tip. **Sights:** Blade front, buckhorn rear. Drilled and tapped for tang sight. **Features:** Double-set triggers. Made in U.S.A. by C. Sharps Arms.
Price: **$1,895.00**

C. SHARPS ARMS NEW MODEL 1885 HIGHWALL RIFLE
Caliber: 22 LR, 22 Hornet, 219 Zipper, 25-35 WCF, 32-40 WCF, 38-55 WCF, 40-65, 30-40 Krag, 40-50 ST or BN, 40-70 ST or BN, 40-90 ST or BN, 45-70 Govt. 2-1/10" ST, 45-90 2-4/10" ST, 45-100 2-6/10" ST, 45-110 2-7/8" ST, 45-120 3-1/4" ST. **Barrel:** 26", 28", 30", tapered full octagon. **Weight:** About 9 lbs., 4 oz. **Length:** 47" overall. **Stock:** Oil-finished American walnut; Schnabel-style forend. **Sights:** Blade front, buckhorn rear. Drilled and tapped for optional tang sight. **Features:** Single trigger; octagonal receiver top; checkered steel buttplate; color case-hardened receiver and buttplate, blued barrel. Many options available. Made in U.S.A. by C. Sharps Arms Co.
Price: From **$1,750.00**

CENTERFIRE RIFLES—Single Shot

C. SHARPS ARMS CUSTOM NEW MODEL 1877 LONG RANGE TARGET RIFLE
Caliber: 44-90 Sharps/Rem., 45-70 Govt., 45-90, 45-100 Sharps.
Barrel: 32", 34" tapered round with Rigby flat. **Weight:** About 10 lbs.
Stock: Walnut checkered. Pistol grip/forend. **Sights:** Classic long range with windage. **Features:** Custom production only.
Price: From **$7,250.00**

CABELA'S 1874 SHARPS SPORTING RIFLE
Caliber: 45-70. **Barrel:** 32", tapered octabon. **Weight:** 10.5 lbs. **Length:** 49.25" overall. **Stock:** Checkered walnut. **Sights:** Blade front, open adjustable rear. **Features:** Color case-hardened receiver and hammer, rest blued. Introduced 1995. Imported by Cabela's.
Price: 45-70 . . . . **$1,399.99**
Price: Quigley Sharps, 45-70 Govt., 45-120, 45-110 . . . . . . **$1,699.99**

CIMARRON BILLY DIXON 1874 SHARPS SPORTING RIFLE
Caliber: 40-40, 50-90, 50-70, 45-70 Govt. **Barrel:** 32" tapered octagonal. **Weight:** NA. **Length:** NA. **Stock:** European walnut. **Sights:** Blade front, Creedmoor rear. **Features:** Color case-hardened frame, blued barrel. Hand-checkered grip and forend; hand-rubbed oil finish. Introduced 1999. Imported by Cimarron F.A. Co.
Price: From **$1,987.70**

CIMARRON QUIGLEY MODEL 1874 SHARPS SPORTING RIFLE
Caliber: 45-110, 50-70, 50-40, 45-70 Govt., 45-90, 45-120. **Barrel:** 34" octagonal. **Weight:** NA. **Length:** NA. **Stock:** Checkered walnut. **Sights:** Blade front, adjustable rear. **Features:** Blued finish; double-set triggers. From Cimarron F.A. Co.
Price: From **$2,156.70**

CIMARRON SILHOUETTE MODEL 1874 SHARPS SPORTING RIFLE
Caliber: 45-70 Govt. **Barrel:** 32" octagonal. **Weight:** NA. **Length:** NA. **Stock:** Walnut. **Sights:** Blade front, adjustable rear. **Features:** Pistol-grip stock with shotgun-style buttplate; cut-rifled barrel. From Cimarron F.A. Co.
Price: **$1,597.70**

CIMARRON MODEL 1885 HIGH WALL RIFLE
Caliber: 38-55, 40-65, 45-70 Govt., 45-90, 45-120, 30-40 Krag, 348 Winchester. **Barrel:** 30" octagonal. **Weight:** NA. **Length:** NA. **Stock:** European walnut. **Sights:** Bead front, semi-buckhorn rear. **Features:** Replica of the Winchester 1885 High Wall rifle. Color case-hardened receiver and lever, blued barrel. Curved buttplate. Optional double-set triggers. Introduced 1999. Imported by Cimarron F.A. Co.
Price: From **$1,002.91**
Price: With pistol grip, from **$1,136.81**

DAKOTA MODEL 10 SINGLE SHOT RIFLE
Caliber: Most rimmed and rimless commercial calibers. **Barrel:** 23". **Weight:** 6 lbs. **Length:** 39.5" overall. **Stock:** Medium fancy grade walnut in classic style. Checkered grip and forend. **Sights:** None furnished. Drilled and tapped for scope mounting. **Features:** Falling block action with underlever. Top tang safety. Removable

---

trigger plate for conversion to single set trigger. Introduced 1990. Made in U.S.A. by Dakota Arms.
Price: From **$4,695.00**
Price: Action only **$1,875.00**
Price: Magnum action only **$1,875.00**

EMF PREMIER 1874 SHARPS RIFLE
Caliber: 45/70, 45/110, 45/120. **Barrel:** 32", 34". **Weight:** 11-13 lbs. **Length:** 49", 51" overall. **Stock:** Pistol grip, European walnut. **Sights:** Blade front, adjustable rear. **Features:** Superb quality reproductions of the 1874 Sharps Sporting Rifles; casehardened locks; double-set triggers; blue barrels. Imported from Pedersoli by EMF.
Price: Business Rifle **$1,199.90**
Price: "Quigley", Patchbox, heavy barrel **$1,799.90**
Price: Silhouette, pistol-grip **$1,499.90**
Price: Super Deluxe Hand Engraved **$3,500.00**

HARRINGTON & RICHARDSON ULTRA VARMINT/ULTRA HUNTER RIFLES
Caliber: 204 Ruger, 22 WMR, 22-250 Rem., 223 Rem., 243 Win., 25-06 Rem., 30-06. **Barrel:** 22" to 26" heavy taper. **Weight:** About 7.5 lbs. **Stock:** Laminated birch with Monte Carlo comb or skeletonized polymer. **Sights:** None furnished. Drilled and tapped for scope mounting. **Features:** Break-open action with side-lever release, positive ejection. Scope mount. Blued receiver and barrel. Swivel studs. Introduced 1993. Ultra Hunter introduced 1995. From H&R 1871, Inc.
Price: Ultra Varmint Fluted, 24" bull barrel, polymer stock **$406.00**
Price: Ultra Hunter Rifle, 26" bull barrel in 25-06 Rem., laminated stock **$357.00**
Price: Ultra Varmint Rifle, 22" bull barrel in 223 Rem., laminated stock **$357.00**

HARRINGTON & RICHARDSON/NEW ENGLAND FIREARMS STAINLESS ULTRA HUNTER WITH THUMBHOLE STOCK
Caliber: 45-70 Govt. **Barrel:** 24". **Weight:** 8 lbs. **Length:** 40".
Features: Stainless steel barrel and receiver with scope mount rail, hammer extension, cinnamon laminate thumbhole stock.
Price: **$439.00**

HARRINGTON & RICHARDSON/NEW ENGLAND FIREARMS HANDI-RIFLE/SLUG GUN COMBOS
Chamber: 44 Mag./12-ga. rifled slug and 357 Mag./20-ga. rifled slug. **Barrel:** Rifle barrel 22" for both calibers; shotgun barrels 28" (12 ga.) and 40" (20 ga.) fully rifled. **Weight:** 7-8 lbs. **Length:** 38" overall (both rifle chamberings). **Features:** Single-shot break-open rifle/shotgun combos (one rifle barrel, one shotgun barrel per combo). Rifle barrels are not interchangeable; shotgun barrels are interchangeable. Stock is black matte high-density polymer with sling swivel studs, molded checkering and recoil pad. No iron sights; scope rail included.
Price: **$362.00**

HARRINGTON & RICHARDSON CR-45LC
Caliber: 45 Colt. **Barrel:** 20". **Weight:** 6.25 lbs. **Length:** 34"overall. **Features:** Single-shot break-open carbine. Cut-checkered American black walnut with case-colored crescent steel buttplate, open sights, case-colored receiver.
Price: **$407.00**

HARRINGTON & RICHARDSON BUFFALO CLASSIC RIFLE
Caliber: 45-70 Govt. **Barrel:** 32" heavy. **Weight:** 8 lbs. **Length:** 46" overall. **Stock:** Cut-checkered American black walnut. **Sights:**

Williams receiver sight; Lyman target front sight with 8 aperture inserts. **Features:** Color case-hardened Handi-Rifle action with exposed hammer; color case-hardened crescent buttplate; 19th century checkering pattern. Introduced 1995. Made in U.S.A. by H&R 1871, Inc.
Price: Buffalo Classic Rifle **$449.00**

KRIEGHOFF HUBERTUS SINGLE-SHOT RIFLE
Caliber: 222, 243 Win., 270 Win., 308 Win., 30-06 Spfl., 5.6x50R Mag., 5.6x52R, 6x62R Freres, 6.5x57R, 6.5x65R, 7x57R, 7x65R, 8x57JRS, 8x75RS, 9.3x74R, 7mm Rem. Mag., 300 Win. Mag. **Barrel:** 23.5". **Weight:** 6.5 lbs. **Length:** 40.5. **Stock:** High-grade walnut. **Sights:** Blade front, open rear. **Features:** Break-open loading with manual cocking lever on top tang; takedown; extractor; Schnabel forearm; many options. Imported from Germany by Krieghoff International Inc.
Price: Hubertus single shot, from $5,995.00
Price: Hubertus, magnum calibers $6,995.00

MEACHAM HIGHWALL SILHOUETTE OR SCHUETZEN RIFLE
Caliber: any rimmed cartridge. **Barrel:** 26-34". **Weight:** 8-15 lbs. **Sights:** none. Tang drilled for Win. base, 3/8 dovetail slot front. **Stock:** Fancy eastern walnut with cheekpiece; ebony insert in forearm tip. **Features:** Exact copy of 1885 Winchester. With most Winchester factory options available, including double set triggers. Introduced 1994. Made in U.S.A. by Meacham T&H Inc.
Price: From **$4,999.00**

MERKEL K1 MODEL LIGHTWEIGHT STALKING RIFLE
Caliber: 243 Win., 270 Win., 7x57R, 308 Win., 30-06 Spfl., 7mm Rem. Mag., 300 Win. Mag., 9.3x74R. **Barrel:** 23.6". **Weight:** 5.6 lbs. unscoped. **Stock:** Satin-finished walnut, fluted and checkered; sling-swivel studs. **Sights:** None (scope base furnished). **Features:** Franz Jager single-shot break-open action, cocking/uncocking slide-type safety, matte silver receiver, selectable trigger pull weights, integrated, quick detach 1" or 30mm optic mounts (optic not included). Imported from Germany by Merkel USA.
Price: Jagd Stutzen Carbine **$3,795.00**

MERKEL K-2 CUSTOM SINGLE-SHOT "WEIMAR" STALKING RIFLE
Caliber: 308 Win., 30-06 Spfl., 7mm Rem. Mag., 300 Win. Mag. **Features:** Franz Jager single-shot break-open action, cocking. uncocking slide safety, deep relief engraved hunting scenes on silvered receiver, octagin barrel, deluxe walnut stock. Includes front and reare adjustable iron sights, scope rings. Imported from Germany by Merkel USA.
Price: Jagd Stutzen Carbine **$15,595.00**

NAVY ARMS 1874 SHARPS "QUIGLEY" RIFLE
Caliber: .45-70 Govt. **Barrel:** 34" octagon. **Weight:** 10 lbs. **Length:** 50" overall. **Grips:** Walnut checkered at wrist and forend. **Sights:** High blade front, full buckhorn rear. **Features:** Color case-hardened receiver, trigger, military patchbox, hammer and lever. Double-set triggers, German silver gripcap. Reproduction of rifle from "Quigley Down Under" movie.
Price: Model SQR045 (20087) $2,026.00

NAVY ARMS 1874 SHARPS #2 CREEDMOOR RIFLE
Caliber: 45/70. **Barrel:** 30" tapered round. **Stock:** Walnut. **Sights:** Front globe, "soule" tang rear. **Features:** Nickel receiver and action. Lightweight sporting rifle.
Price: **$1,816.00**

NAVY ARMS SHARPS SPORTING RIFLE
Same as the Navy Arms Sharps Plains Rifle except

has pistol grip stock. Introduced 1997. Imported by Navy Arms.
Price: 45-70 Govt. only **$1,711.00**
Price: #2 Sporting with case-hardened receiver **$1,739.00**
Price: #2 Silhouette with full octagonal barrel **$1,739.00**

NAVY ARMS 1885 HIGH WALL RIFLE
Caliber: 45-70 Govt.; others available on special order. **Barrel:** 28" round, 30" octagonal. **Weight:** 9.5 lbs. **Length:** 45.5" overall (30" barrel). **Stock:** Walnut. **Sights:** Blade front, vernier tang-mounted peep rear. **Features:** Replica of Winchester's High Wall designed by Browning. Color case-hardened receiver, blued barrel. Introduced 1998. Imported by Navy Arms.
Price: 28", round barrel, target sights $1,120.00
Price: 30" octagonal barrel, target sights $1,212.00

NAVY ARMS 1873 SPRINGFIELD CAVALRY CARBINE
Caliber: 45-70 Govt. **Barrel:** 22". **Weight:** 7 lbs. **Length:** 40.5" overall. **Stock:** Walnut. **Sights:** Blade front, military ladder rear. **Features:** Blued lockplate and barrel; color case-hardened breechblock; saddle ring with bar. Replica of 7th Cavalry gun. Officer's Model Trapdoor has single-set trigger, bone case-hardened buttplate, trigger guard and breechblock. Deluxe walnut stock hand-checkered at the wrist and forend. German silver forend cap and rod tip. Adjustable rear peep target sight. Authentic flip-up 'Beech' front target sight. Imported by Navy Arms.
Price: Model STC073 . . . . $1,261.00
Price: Officer's Model Trapdoor (2008). $1,648.00

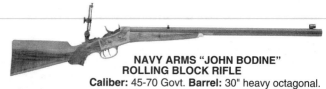

NAVY ARMS "JOHN BODINE" ROLLING BLOCK RIFLE
Caliber: 45-70 Govt. **Barrel:** 30" heavy octagonal. **Stock:** Walnut. **Sights:** Globe front, "soule" tang rear. **Features:** Double-set triggers.
Price: $1,928.00
Price: (#2 with deluxe nickel finished receiver) $1,928.00

NAVY ARMS 1874 SHARPS NO. 3 LONG RANGE RIFLE
Caliber: 45-70 Govt. **Barrel:** 34" octagon. **Weight:** 10 lbs., 14 oz. **Length:** 51.2". **Stock:** Deluxe walnut. **Sights:** Globe target front and match grade rear tang. **Features:** Shotgun buttplate, German silver forend cap, color case hardened receiver. Imported by Navy Arms.
Price: $2,432.00

NEW ENGLAND FIREARMS HANDI-RIFLE
Caliber: 204 Ruger, 22 Hornet, 223 Rem., 243 Win., 30-30, 270 Win., 280 Rem., 7mm-08 Rem., 308 Win., 7.62x39 Russian, 30-06 Spfl., 357 Mag., 35 Whelen, 44 Mag., 45-70 Govt., 500 S&W. **Barrel:** From 20" to 26", blued or stainless. **Weight:** 5.5 to 7 lbs. **Stock:** Walnut-finished hardwood or synthetic. **Sights:** Vary by model, but most have ramp front, folding rear, or are drilled and tapped for scope mount. **Features:** Break-open action with side-lever release. Swivel

Prices given are believed to be accurate at time of publication however, many factors affect retail pricing so exact prices are not possible.

CENTERFIRE RIFLES—Single Shot

studs on all models. Blue finish. Introduced 1989. From H&R 1871, Inc.
Price: Various cartridges **$292.00**
Price: 7.62x39 Russian, 35 Whelen, intr. 2006 . . . .**$292.00**
Price: Youth, 37" OAL, 11.75" LOP, 6.75 lbs. **$292.00**
Price: Handi-Rifle/Pardner combo, 20 ga. synthetic, intr.
2006 . . . .**$325.00**
Price: Handi-Rifle/Pardner Superlight, 20 ga., 5.5 lbs., intr.
2006 . . . .**$325.00**
Price: Synthetic **$302.00**
Price: Stainless **$364.00**
Price: Superlight, 20" barrel, 35.25" OAL, 5.5 lbs. **$302.00**

NEW ENGLAND FIREARMS SURVIVOR RIFLE
Caliber: 223 Rem., 308 Win., .410 shotgun, 45 Colt, single shot. **Barrel:** 20" to 22". **Weight:** 6 lbs. **Length:** 34.5" to 36" overall. **Stock:** Black polymer, thumbhole design. **Sights:** None furnished; scope mount provided. **Features:** Receiver drilled and tapped for scope mounting. Stock and forend have storage compartments for ammo, etc.; comes with integral swivels and black nylon sling. Introduced 1996. Made in U.S.A. by H&R 1871, Inc.
Price: Blue or nickel finish **$304.00**

NEW ENGLAND FIREARMS SPORTSTER/VERSA PACK RIFLE
Caliber: 17M2, 17 HMR, 22 LR, 22 WMR, .410 bore single shot. **Barrel:** 20" to 22". **Weight:** 5.4 to 7 lbs. **Length:** 33" to 38.25" overall. **Stock:** Black polymer. **Sights:** Adjustable rear, ramp front. **Features:** Receiver drilled and tapped for scope mounting. Made in U.S.A. by H&R 1871, Inc.
Price: Sportster 17M2, 17 HMR **$193.00**
Price: Sportster **$161.00**
Price: Sportster Youth **$161.00**

REMINGTON MODEL SPR18 SINGLE SHOT RIFLES
Caliber: 223 Rem., 243 Win., 270 Win., .30-06 Spfl., 308 Win., 7.62x39mm. **Barrel:** 23.5" chrome-lined hammer forged, all steel receiver, spiral-cut fluting. **Weight:** 6.75 lbs. **Stock:** Walnut stock and fore-end, swivel studs. **Sights:** adjustable, with 11mm scope rail. **Length:** 39.75" overall. **Features:** Made in U.S. by Remington Arms Co., Inc.
Price: Blued/walnut (2008) **$277.00**
Price: Nickel/walnut (2008) **$326.00**

REMINGTON NO. 1 ROLLING BLOCK MID-RANGE SPORTER
Caliber: 45-70 Govt. **Barrel:** 30" round. **Weight:** 8.75 lbs. **Length:** 46.5" overall. **Stock:** American walnut with checkered pistol grip and forend. **Sights:** Beaded blade front, adjustable center-notch buckhorn rear. **Features:** Recreation of the original. Polished blue metal finish. Many options available. Introduced 1998. Made in U.S.A. by Remington.
Price: **$2,927.00**
Price: Silhouette model with single-set trigger, heavy barrel **$3,366.00**

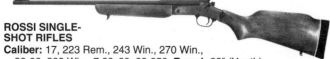

ROSSI SINGLE-SHOT RIFLES
Caliber: 17, 223 Rem., 243 Win., 270 Win., .30-06, 308 Win., 7.62x39, 22-250. **Barrel:** 22" (Youth), 23". **Weight:** 6.25-7 lbs. **Stocks:** Wood, Black Synthetic (Youth). **Sights:** Adjustable sights, drilled and tapped for scope. **Features:** Single-shot break open, 13 models available, positive ejection, internal transfer bar mechanism, manual external safety, trigger

block system, Taurus Security System, Matte blue finish, youth models available.
Price: **$238.00**

ROSSI MATCHED PAIRS
Gauge/Caliber: 12, 20, .410, 22 Mag, 22 LR, 17 HMR, 223 Rem, 243 Win., 270 Win., .30-06, 308Win., .50 (black powder). **Barrel:** 23", 28". **Weight:** 5-6.3 lbs. Stocks: Wood or black synthetic. **Sights:** Bead front on shotgun barrel, fully adjustable front and rear on rifle barrel, drilled and tapped for scope, fully adjustable fiber optic sights (black powder). **Features:** Single-shot break open, 27 models available, internal transfer bar mechanism, manual external safety, blue finish, trigger block system, Taurus Security System, youth models available.
Price: Rimfire/Shotgun, from **$178.00**
Price: Centerfire/Shotgun **$299.00**
Price: Black Powder Matched Pair, from **$262.00**

ROSSI WIZARD
Single shot rifle chambered in 18 different rimfire/centerfire/shotshell/muzzleloading configurations. Featured include drop-barrel action; quick, toolless barrel interchangeability; fiber optic front sight; adjustable rear sight with barrel-mounted optics rail; hardwood or camo Monte Carlo stock.
Price: . . . .**NA**

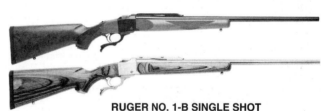

RUGER NO. 1-B SINGLE SHOT
Caliber: 223 Rem., 204 Ruger, 25-06 Rem., 6.5 Creedmore, 270 Win., 30-06 Spfl., 7mm Rem. Mag., 300 Win. Mag., 308 Win. **Barrel:** 26" round tapered with quarter-rib; with Ruger 1" rings. **Weight:** 8.25 lbs. **Length:** 42.25" overall. **Stock:** Walnut, two-piece, checkered pistol grip and semi-beavertail forend. **Sights:** None, 1" scope rings supplied for integral mounts. **Features:** Under-lever, hammerless falling block design has auto ejector, top tang safety.
Price: 1-B **$1,093.00**
Price: K1-B-BBZ stainless steel, laminated stock 25-06 Rem., 7mm Rem. Mag., 270, 300 Win. Mag., 243 Win., 30-06 . . . .**$1,186.00**

RUGER NO. 1-A LIGHT SPORTER
Caliber: 243 Win., 270 Win., 7x57, 30-06, 300 Ruger Compact Magnum. **Weight:** 7.25 lbs. Similar to the No. 1-B Standard Rifle except has lightweight 22" barrel, Alexander Henry-style forend, adjustable folding leaf rear sight on quarter-rib, dovetailed ramp front with gold bead.
Price: No. 1A **$1,147.00**

RUGER NO. 1-V VARMINTER
Similar to the No. 1-B Standard Rifle except has 24" heavy barrel. Semi-beavertail forend, barrel ribbed for target scope block, with 1" Ruger scope rings. Calibers 204 Ruger (26" barrel), 22-250 Rem., 223 Rem., 25-06 Rem. Weight about 9 lbs.
Price: No. 1-V **$1,147.00**

CENTERFIRE RIFLES—Single Shot

RUGER NO. 1 RSI INTERNATIONAL
Similar to the No. 1-B Standard Rifle except has lightweight 20" barrel, full-length International-style forend with loop sling swivel, adjustable folding leaf rear sight on quarter-rib, ramp front with gold bead. Calibers 30-06 Spfl., 270 and 7x57. Weight is about 7.25 lbs.
Price: No. 1 RSI **$1,186.00**

RUGER NO. 1-H TROPICAL RIFLE
Similar to the No. 1-B Standard Rifle except has Alexander Henry forend, adjustable folding leaf rear sight on quarter-rib, ramp front with dovetail gold bead, 24" heavy barrel. Calibers 375 H&H, 416 Rigby, 458 Lott, 405 Win., 450/400 Nitro Express 3" (weighs about 9 lbs.), 416 Ruger.
Price: No. 1H **$1,147.00**

RUGER NO. 1-S MEDIUM SPORTER
Similar to the No. 1-B Standard Rifle except has Alexander Henry-style forend, adjustable folding leaf rear sight on quarter-rib, ramp front sight base and dovetail-type gold bead front sight. Calibers include 9.3x74R, 45-70 Govt. with 22" barrel, 300 H&H Mag, 338 Ruger Compact Magnum, 375 Ruger, 460 S&W Magnum, 480 Ruger/475 Linebaugh. Weighs about 7.25 lbs.
Price: No. 1-S **$1,147.00**
Price: K1-S-BBZ, S/S, 45-70 Govt. **$1,186.00**

SHILOH RIFLE CO. SHARPS 1874 LONG RANGE EXPRESS
Caliber: 40-50 BN, 40-70 BN, 40-90 BN, 45-70 Govt. ST, 45-90 ST, 45-110 ST, 50-70 ST, 50-90 ST, 38-55, 40-70 ST, 40-90 ST. **Barrel:** 34" tapered octagon. **Weight:** 10.5 lbs. **Length:** 51" overall. **Stock:** Oil-finished walnut (upgrades available) with pistol grip, shotgun-style butt, traditional cheek rest, Schnabel forend. **Sights:** Customer's choice. **Features:** Re-creation of the Model 1874 Sharps rifle. Double-set triggers. Made in U.S.A. by Shiloh Rifle Mfg. Co.
Price: **$1,902.00**
Price: Sporter Rifle No. 1 (similar to above except with 30" barrel, blade front, buckhorn rear sight) **$1,902.00**
Price: Sporter Rifle No. 3 (similar to No. 1 except straight-grip stock, standard wood) **$1,800.00**

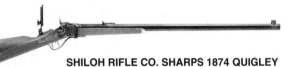

SHILOH RIFLE CO. SHARPS 1874 QUIGLEY
Caliber: 45-70 Govt., 45-110. **Barrel:** 34" heavy octagon. **Stock:** Military-style with patch box, standard grade American walnut. **Sights:** Semi buckhorn, interchangeable front and midrange vernier tang sight with windage. **Features:** Gold inlay initials, pewter tip, Hartford collar, case color or antique finish. Double-set triggers.
Price: **$3,298.00**

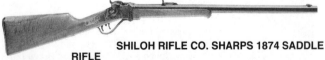

SHILOH RIFLE CO. SHARPS 1874 SADDLE RIFLE
Caliber: 38-55, 40-50 BN, 40-65 Win., 40-70 BN, 40-70 ST, 40-90 BN, 40-90 ST, 44-77 BN, 44-90 BN, 45-70 Govt. ST, 45-90 ST, 45-100 ST, 45-110 ST, 45-120 ST, 50-70 ST, 50-90 ST. **Barrel:** 26" full or half octagon. **Stock:** Semi fancy American walnut. Shotgun style with cheekrest. **Sights:** Buckhorn and blade. **Features:** Double-set trigger, numerous custom features can be added.
Price: **$1,852.00**

SHILOH RIFLE CO. SHARPS 1874 MONTANA ROUGHRIDER
Caliber: 38-55, 40-50 BN, 40-65 Win., 40-70 BN, 40-70 ST, 40-90 BN, 40-90 ST, 44-77 BN, 44-90 BN, 45-70 Govt. ST, 45-90 ST, 45-100 ST, 45-110 ST, 45-120 ST, 50-70 ST, 50-90 ST. **Barrel:** 30" full or half octagon. **Stock:** American walnut in shotgun or military style. **Sights:** Buckhorn and blade. **Features:** Double-set triggers, numerous custom features can be added.
Price: **$1,902.00**

SHILOH RIFLE CO. SHARPS CREEDMOOR TARGET
Caliber: 38-55, 40-50 BN, 40-65 Win., 40-70 BN, 40-70 ST, 40-90 BN, 40-90 ST, 44-77 BN, 44-90 BN, 45-70 Govt. ST, 45-90 ST, 45-100 ST, 45-110 ST, 45-120 ST, 50-70 ST, 50-90 ST. **Barrel:** 32", half round-half octagon. **Stock:** Extra fancy American walnut. Shotgun style with pistol grip. **Sights:** Customer's choice. **Features:** Single trigger, AA finish on stock, polished barrel and screws, pewter tip.
Price: **$2,743.00**

THOMPSON/CENTER ENCORE RIFLE
Caliber: 22-250 Rem., 223 Rem., 243 Win., 204 Ruger, 6.8 Rem. Spec., 25-06 Rem., 270 Win., 7mm-08 Rem., 308 Win., 30-06 Spfl., 7mm Rem. Mag., 300 Win. Mag. **Barrel:** 24", 26". **Weight:** 6 lbs., 12 oz. (24" barrel). **Length:** 38.5" (24" barrel). **Stock:** American walnut. Monte Carlo style; Schnabel forend or black composite. **Sights:** Ramp-style white bead front, fully adjustable leaf-type rear. **Features:** Interchangeable barrels; action opens by squeezing trigger guard; drilled and tapped for T/C scope mounts; polished blue finish. Introduced 1996. Made in U.S.A. by Thompson/Center Arms.
Price: . . . .**$604.00 to $663.00**
Price: Extra barrels **$277.00**

THOMPSON/CENTER STAINLESS ENCORE RIFLE
Similar to blued Encore except stainless steel with blued sights, black composite stock and forend. Available in 22-250 Rem., 223 Rem., 7mm-08 Rem., 30-06 Spfl., 308 Win. Introduced 1999. Made in U.S.A. by Thompson/Center Arms.
Price: . . . .**$680.00 to $738.00**

THOMPSON/CENTER ENCORE "KATAHDIN" CARBINE
Caliber: 45-70 Govt., 450 Marlin. **Barrel:** 18" with muzzle tamer. **Stock:** Composite.
Price: **$619.00**

THOMPSON/CENTER G2 CONTENDER RIFLE
Similar to the G2 Contender pistol, but in a compact rifle format. Weighs 5.5 lbs. Features interchangeable 23" barrels, chambered for 17 HMR, 22 LR, 223 Rem., 30/30 Win. and 45/70 Govt.; plus a 45 cal. muzzleloading barrel. All of the 16.25" and 21" barrels made for

 Prices given are believed to be accurate at time of publication however, many factors affect retail pricing so exact prices are not possible.

the old-style Contender will fit. Introduced 2003. Made in U.S.A. by Thompson/Center Arms.

Price: . . . .$622.00 to $637.00

THOMPSON/CENTER ENCORE PROHUNTER PREDATOR RIFLE

Contender-style break-action single shot rifle chambered in .204 Ruger, .223 Remington, .22-250 and .308 Winchester. Features include 28-inch deep-fluted interchangeable barrel, composite buttstock and forend with non-slip inserts in cheekpiece, pistol grip and forend. Max 1 camo finish overall. Overall length: 42.5 inches. Weight: 7-3/4 lbs.

Price: $799.00

TRADITIONS 1874 SHARPS DELUXE RIFLE

Caliber: 45-70 Govt. **Barrel:** 32" octagonal; 1:18" twist. **Weight:** 11.67 lbs. **Length:** 48.8" overall. **Stock:** Checkered walnut with German silver nose cap and steel buttplate. **Sights:** Globe front, adjustable Creedmore rear with 12 inserts. **Features:** Color case-hardened receiver; double-set triggers. Introduced 2001. Imported from Pedersoli by Traditions.

Price: $1,545.00

TRADITIONS 1874 SHARPS SPORTING DELUXE RIFLE

Similar to Sharps Deluxe but custom silver engraved receiver, European walnut stock and forend, satin finish, set trigger, fully adjustable.

Price: $2,796.00

TRADITIONS 1874 SHARPS STANDARD RIFLE

Similar to 1874 Sharps Deluxe except has blade front and adjustable buckhorn-style rear sight. Weighs 10.67 pounds. Introduced 2001. Imported from Pedersoli by Traditions.

Price: $1,324.00

TRADITIONS ROLLING BLOCK SPORTING RIFLE

Caliber: 45-70 Govt. **Barrel:** 30" octagonal; 1:18" twist. **Weight:** 11.67 lbs. **Length:** 46.7" overall. **Stock:** Walnut. **Sights:** Blade front, adjustable rear. **Features:** Antique silver, color case-hardened receiver, drilled and tapped for tang/globe sights; brass buttplate and trigger guard. Introduced 2001. Imported from Pedersoli by Traditions.

Price: $1,029.00

UBERTI 1874 SHARPS SPORTING RIFLE

Caliber: 45-70 Govt. **Barrel:** 30", 32", 34" octagonal. **Weight:** 10.57 lbs. with 32" barrel. **Length:** 48.9" with 32" barrel. **Stock:** Walnut. **Sights:** Dovetail front, Vernier tang rear. **Features:** Cut checkering, case-colored finish on frame, buttplate, and lever. Imported by

Stoeger Industries.

Price: Standard Sharps (2006), 30" barrel $1,459.00
Price: Special Sharps (2006) 32" barrel $1,729.00
Price: Deluxe Sharps (2006) 34" barrel $2,749.00
Price: Down Under Sharps (2006) 34" barrel $2,249.00
Price: Long Range Sharps (2006) 34" barrel $2,279.00
Price: Buffalo Hunters Sharps, 32" barrel $2,219.00
Price: Calvary Carbine Sharps, 22" barrel $1,569.00
Price: Sharps Extra Deluxe, 32" barrel (2009) $4,199.00
Price: Sharps Hunter, 28" barrel $1,459.00

UBERTI 1885 HIGH-WALL SINGLE-SHOT RIFLES

Caliber: 45-70 Govt., 45-90, 45-120 single shot. **Barrel:** 28" to 23". **Weight:** 9.3 to 9.9 lbs. **Length:** 44.5" to 47" overall. **Stock:** Walnut stock and forend. **Sights:** Blade front, fully adjustable open rear. **Features:** Based on Winchester High-Wall design by John Browning. Color case-hardened frame and lever, blued barrel and buttplate. Imported by Stoeger Industries.

Price: 1885 High-Wall, 28" round barrel $969.00
Price: 1885 High-Wall Sporting, 30" octagonal barrel $1,029.00
Price: 1885 High-Wall Special Sporting, 32" octagonal barrel $1,179.00

BERETTA EXPRESS SSO O/U DOUBLE RIFLES
Caliber: 375 H&H, 458 Win. Mag., 9.3x74R. **Barrel:** 25.5". **Weight:** 11 lbs. **Stock:** European walnut with hand-checkered grip and forend. **Sights:** Blade front on ramp, open V-notch rear. **Features:** Sidelock action with color case-hardened receiver (gold inlays on SSO6 Gold). Ejectors, double triggers, recoil pad. Introduced 1990. Imported from Italy by Beretta U.S.A.
Price: SSO6 . . . . **$21,000.00**
Price: SSO6 Gold **$23,500.00**

BERETTA MODEL 455 SXS EXPRESS RIFLE
Caliber: 375 H&H, 458 Win. Mag., 470 NE, 500 NE 3", 416 Rigby. **Barrel:** 23.5" or 25.5". **Weight:** 11 lbs. **Stock:** European walnut with hand-checkered grip and forend. **Sights:** Blade front, folding leaf V-notch rear. **Features:** Sidelock action with easily removable sideplates; color case-hardened finish (455), custom big game or floral motif engraving (455EELL). Double triggers, recoil pad. Introduced 1990. Imported from Italy by Beretta U.S.A.
Price: Model 455. . . . . **$36,000.00**
Price: Model 455EELL **$47,000.00**

CZ 584 SOLO COMBINATION GUN
Caliber/Gauge: 7x57R; 12, 2-3/4" chamber. **Barrel:** 24.4". **Weight:** 7.37 lbs. **Length:** 45.25" overall. **Stock:** Circassian walnut. **Sights:** Blade front, open rear adjustable for windage. **Features:** Kersten-style double lump locking system; double-trigger Blitz-type mechanism with drop safety and adjustable set trigger for the rifle barrel; auto safety, dual extractors; receiver dovetailed for scope mounting. Imported from the Czech Republic by CZ-USA.
Price: **$851.00**

CZ 589 STOPPER OVER/UNDER GUN
Caliber: 458 Win. Magnum. **Barrels:** 21.7". **Weight:** 9.3 lbs. **Length:** 37.7" overall. **Stock:** Turkish walnut with sling swivels. **Sights:** Blade front, fixed rear. **Features:** Kersten-style action; Blitz-type double trigger; hammer-forged, blued barrels; satin-nickel, engraved receiver. Introduced 2001. Imported from the Czech Republic by CZ USA.
Price: **$2,999.00**
Price: Fully engraved model **$3,999.00**

DAKOTA DOUBLE RIFLE
Caliber: 470 Nitro Express, 500 Nitro Express. **Barrel:** 25". **Stock:** Exhibition-grade walnut. **Sights:** Express-style. **Features:** Round action; selective ejectors; recoil pad; Americase. From Dakota Arms Inc.
Price: **$25,000.00**

GARBI EXPRESS DOUBLE RIFLE
Caliber: 7x65R, 9.3x74R, 375 H&H. **Barrel:** 24.75". **Weight:** 7.75 to 8.5 lbs. **Length:** 41.5" overall. **Stock:** Turkish walnut. **Sights:** Quarter-rib with express sight. **Features:** Side-by-side double; H&H-pattern sidelock ejector with reinforced action, chopper lump barrels of Boehler steel; double triggers; fine scroll and rosette engraving, or full coverage ornamental; coin-finished action. Introduced 1997. Imported from Spain by Wm. Larkin Moore.
Price: **$25,000.00**

HOENIG ROTARY ROUND ACTION DOUBLE RIFLE
Caliber: Most popular calibers from 225 Win. to 9.3x74R. **Barrel:** 22" to 26". **Stock:** English Walnut; to customer specs. **Sights:** Swivel hood front with button release (extra bead stored in trap door gripcap), express-style rear on quarter-rib adjustable for windage and elevation; scope mount. **Features:** Round action opens by rotating barrels, pulling forward. Inertia extractor system, rotary safety blocks strikers. Single lever quick-detachable scope mount. Simple takedown without removing forend. Introduced 1997. Made in U.S.A. by George Hoenig.
Price: **$19,980.00**

HOENIG ROTARY ROUND ACTION COMBINATION
Caliber: 28 ga. **Barrel:** 26". **Weight:** 7 lbs. **Stock:** English Walnut to customer specs. **Sights:** Front ramp with button release blades. Foldable aperture tang sight windage and elevation adjustable. Quarter-rib with scope mount. **Features:** Round action opens by rotating barrels, pulling forward. Inertia extractor; rotary safety blocks strikers. Simple takedown without removing forend. Made in U.S.A. by George Hoenig.
Price: **$25,000.00**

KRIEGHOFF CLASSIC DOUBLE RIFLE
Caliber: 7x57R, 7x65R, 308 Win., 30-06 Spfl., 8x57 JRS, 8x75RS, 9.3x74R, 375NE, 500/416NE, 470NE, 500NE. **Barrel:** 23.5". **Weight:** 7.3 to 8 lbs; 10-11 lbs. Big 5. **Stock:** High grade European walnut. Standard model has conventional rounded cheekpiece, Bavaria model has Bavarian-style cheekpiece. **Sights:** Bead front with removable, adjustable wedge (375 H&H and below), standing leaf rear on quarter-rib. **Features:** Boxlock action; double triggers; short opening angle for fast loading; quiet extractors; sliding, self-adjusting wedge for secure bolting; Purdey-style barrel extension; horizontal firing pin placement. Many options available. Introduced 1997. Imported from Germany by Krieghoff International.
Price: With small Arabesque engraving **$8,950.00**
Price: With engraved sideplates **$12,300.00**
Price: For extra barrels **$5,450.00**
Price: Extra 20-ga., 28" shotshell barrels **$3,950.00**

KRIEGHOFF CLASSIC BIG FIVE DOUBLE RIFLE
Similar to the standard Classic except available in 375 Flanged Mag. N.E., 500/416 NE, 470 NE, 500 NE. Has hinged front trigger, non-removable muzzle wedge (models larger than 375 caliber), Universal Trigger System, Combi Cocking Device, steel trigger guard, specially weighted stock bolt for weight and balance. Many options available. Introduced 1997. Imported from Germany by Krieghoff International. Imperial Model introduced 2006.
Price: **$11,450.00**
Price: With engraved sideplates **$14,800.00**

LEBEAU-COURALLY EXPRESS RIFLE SXS
Caliber: 7x65R, 8x57JRS, 9.3x74R, 375 H&H, 470 N.E. **Barrel:** 24" to 26". **Weight:** 7.75 to 10.5 lbs. **Stock:** Fancy French walnut with cheekpiece. **Sights:** Bead on ramp front, standing left express rear on quarter-rib. **Features:** Holland & Holland-type sidelock with automatic ejectors; double triggers. Built to order only. Imported from Belgium by Wm. Larkin Moore.
Price: **$50,000.00**

MERKEL DRILLINGS
Caliber/Gauge: 12, 20, 3" chambers, 16, 2-3/4" chambers; 22 Hornet, 5.6x50R Mag., 5.6x52R, 222 Rem., 243 Win., 6.5x55, 6.5x57R, 7x57R, 7x65R, 308 Win., 30-06 Spfl., 8x57JRS, 9.3x74R, 375 H&H. **Barrel:** 25.6". **Weight:** 7.9 to 8.4 lbs. depending upon caliber. **Stock:** Oil-finished walnut with pistol grip; cheekpiece on 12-, 16-gauge. **Sights:** Blade front, fixed rear. **Features:** Double barrel locking lug with Greener cross bolt; scroll-engraved, case-hardened receiver; automatic trigger safety; Blitz action; double triggers. Imported from Germany by Merkel USA.
Price: Model 96K
    (manually cocked rifle system), from **$8,495.00**
Price: Model 96K engraved
    (hunting series on receiver) **$9,795.00**

MERKEL BOXLOCK DOUBLE RIFLES
Caliber: 5.6x52R, 243 Winchester, 6.5x55, 6.5x57R, 7x57R, 7x65R, 308 Win., 30-06 Springfield, 8x57 IRS, 9.3x74R. **Barrel:** 23.6". **Weight:** 7.7 oz. **Length:** NA. **Stock:** Walnut, oil finished, pistol grip. **Sights:** Fixed 100 meter. **Features:** Anson & Deely boxlock action with cocking indicators, double triggers, engraved color case-hardened receiver. Introduced 1995. Imported from Germany by Merkel USA.
Price: Model 140-2, from **$11,995.00**
Price: Model 141 Small Frame SXS Rifle; built on smaller
    frame, chambered for 7mm Mauser, 30-06, or
    9.3x74R **$8,195.00**
Price: Model 141 Engraved; fine hand-engraved hunting
    scenes on silvered receiver **$9,495.00**

RIZZINI EXPRESS 90L DOUBLE RIFLE
Caliber: 30-06 Spfl., 7x65R, 9.3x74R. **Barrel:** 24". **Weight:** 7.5 lbs. **Length:** 40" overall. **Stock:** Select European walnut with satin oil finish; English-style cheekpiece. **Sights:** Ramp front, quarter-rib with express sight. **Features:** Color case-hardened boxlock action; automatic ejectors; single selective trigger; polished blue barrels. Extra 20 gauge shotgun barrels available. Imported for Italy by Wm. Larkin Moore.
Price: With case **$3,850.00**

AMERICAN TACTICAL IMPORTS GSG-522
Semiauto tactical rifle chambered in .22 LR. Features include 16.25-inch barrel; black finish overall; polymer forend and buttstock; backup iron sights; receiver-mounted Picaatinny rail; 10-round magazine. Several other rifle and carbine versions available.
Price: **$475.00**

BROWNING BUCK MARK SEM-AUTO RIFLES
Caliber: 22 LR, 10+1. **Action:** A rifle version of the Buck Mark Pistol; straight blowback action; machined aluminum receiver with integral rail scope mount; manual thumb safety. **Barrel:** Recessed crowns. **Stock:** Stock and forearm with full pistol grip. **Features:** Action lock provided. Introduced 2001. Four model name variations for 2006, as noted below. **Sights:** FLD Target, FLD Carbon, and Target models have integrated scope rails. Sporter has Truglo/Marble fiber optic sights. Imported from Japan by Browning.
Price: FLD Target, 5.5 lbs., bull barrel, laminated stock. **$659.00**
Price: Target, 5.4 lbs., blued bull barrel, wood stock **$639.00**
Price: Sporter, 4.4 lbs., blued sporter barrel w/sights **$639.00**

BROWNING SA-22 SEMI-AUTO 22 RIFLES
Caliber: 22 LR, 11+1. **Barrel:** 16.25". **Weight:** 5.2 lbs. **Length:** 37" overall. **Stock:** Checkered select walnut with pistol grip and semi-beavertail forend. **Sights:** Gold bead front, folding leaf rear. **Features:** Engraved receiver with polished blue finish; cross-bolt safety; tubular magazine in buttstock; easy takedown for carrying or storage. The Grade VI is available with either grayed or blued receiver with extensive engraving with gold-plated animals: right side pictures a fox and squirrel in a woodland scene; left side shows a beagle chasing a rabbit. On top is a portrait of the beagle. Stock and forend are of high-grade walnut with a double-bordered cut checkering design. Introduced 1987. Imported from Japan by Browning.
Price: Grade I, scroll-engraved blued receiver **$619.00**
Price: Grade VI BL, gold-plated engraved blued receiver . .**$1,329.00**

CITADEL M-1 CARBINE
Caliber: .22LR., 10-round magazines. **Barrel:** 18". **Weight:** 4.8 lbs. **Length:** 35". **Features:** Straight from the pages of history ... the greatest conflict of modern times, World War II ... comes the new Citadel M-1 carbine. Built to the exacting specifications of the G.I. model used by U.S. infantrymen in both WWII theaters of battle and in Korea, this reproduction rifle comes to you chambered in the fun and economical .22 LR cartridge. Used by officers as well as tankers, drivers, artillery crews, mortar crews, and other personnel in lieu of the larger, heavier M1 Garrand rifle, the M-1 carbine weighed only 4.5 to 4.75 pounds. The Citadel M-1, made by Chiappa in Italy, weighs in at 4.8 lbs. – nearly the exact weight of the original. Barrel length and OAL are also the same as the "United States Carbine, Caliber .30, M1", its official military designation.
Price: **$331.00**

CZ 455 AMERICAN RIFLE
Caliber: .22LR and .17 HMR., 5-round magazines. **Barrel:** 20.8". **Weight:** 6.1 lbs. **Length:** 38.2". **Stock:** Walnut. **Sights:** No sights. Integrated 11mm dovetail scope base. **Features:** The new CZ 455 is the next generation of the CZ bolt action rimfire. The 455 model will eventually consolidate all of the receivers currently used in the 452 line into one common platform. This combined with the new interchangeable barrel system of the CZ 455 will allow the user to easily change the stock configuration as well as the

caliber of their rifle. The 455 retains the accuracy and quality of the adjustable trigger, hammer forged barrel and billet machined receiver from the CZ 452. Improvements that the 455 brings include new manufacturing technology and tighter tolerances for improved accuracy and smoother operation. The CZ 455 American Combo Package is now available from CZ-USA. The package features the new CZ 455 in .22LR and a .17 HMR barrel along with everything you need to make the caliber change.The CZ 455 eliminates the need to spend the extra expense on a second rifle when you want to add another quality shooter to your rimfire battery.
Price: **$417.00**

CZ MODEL 512 RIFLE
Caliber: .22 LR/.22 WMR, 5-round magazines. **Barrel:** 20.6". **Weight:** 5.9 lbs. **Length:** 39.3". **Stock:** Beech. **Sights:** Fixed adjustable. **Features:** The CZ 512 is an entirely new semi-auto rimfire rifle from CZ. The modular design is easily maintained, requiring only a coin as a tool for field stripping. The action of the 512 is composed of an aluminum alloy upper receiver that secures the barrel and bolt assembly and a fiberglass reinforced polymer lower half that houses the trigger mechanism and detachable magazine. The 512 shares the same magazines and scope rings with the CZ 455 making it the perfect companion to your bolt-action rifle.
Price: **$449.00**

CZ 513 RIFLE
Caliber: 22 LR, 5-shot magazine. **Barrel:** 20.9". **Weight:** 5.7 lbs. **Length:** 39" overall. **Stock:** Beechwood. **Sights:** Tangent iron. **Features:** Simplified version of the CZ 452, no checkering on stock, simple non-adjustable trigger. Imported from the Czech Republic by CZ-USA.
Price: **$328.00**

HENRY U.S. SURVIVAL RIFLE AR-7 22

Caliber: 22 LR, 8-shot magazine. **Barrel:** 16" steel lined. **Weight:** 2.25 lbs. **Stock:** ABS plastic. **Sights:** Blade front on ramp, aperture rear. **Features:** Takedown design stores barrel and action in hollow stock. Light enough to float. Silver, black or camo finish. Comes with two magazines. Introduced 1998. From Henry Repeating Arms Co.
Price: H002S Silver finish. **$245.00**
Price: H002B Black finish **$245.00**
Price: H002C Camo finish **$310.00**

KEL-TEC SU-22CA
Caliber: 22 LR. **Features:** Blowback action, cross bolt safety, adjustable front and rear sights with integral picatinny rail. Threaded muzzle, 26-round magazine.
Price: . . . .**Appx. $400.00**

MAGNUM RESEARCH MAGNUMLITE RIFLES

Caliber: 22 WMR, 17 HMR, 22 LR 17M2, 10-shot magazine. **Barrel:** 17" graphite. **Weight:** 4.45 lbs. **Length:** 35.5" overall. **Stock:** Hogue OverMolded synthetic or walnut. **Sights:** Integral scope base. **Features:** Magnum Lite graphite barrel, French grey anodizing, match bolt, target trigger. 22 LR/17M2 rifles use factory Ruger 10/22 magazines. 4-5 lbs. average trigger pull. Graphite carbon-fiber barrel weighs approx. 13.04 ounces in 22 LR, 1:16 twist. Introduced: 2007. From Magnum Research, Inc.
Price: MLR22H 22 LR. **$640.00**

MARLIN MODEL 60 AUTO RIFLE
Caliber: 22 LR, 14-shot tubular magazine. **Barrel:** 19" round tapered. **Weight:** About 5.5 lbs. **Length:** 37.5" overall. **Stock:** Press-

checkered, walnut-finished Maine birch with Monte Carlo, full pistol grip; Mar-Shield finish. **Sights:** Ramp front, open adjustable rear. **Features:** Matted receiver is grooved for scope mount. Manual bolt hold-open; automatic last-shot bolt hold-open. Model 60C is similar except has hardwood Monte Carlo stock with Mossy Oak Break-Up camouflage pattern. From Marlin.

Price: **$179.00**
Price: With 4x scope **$186.00**
Price: Model 60C camo **$211.00**

MARLIN MODEL 60SS SELF-LOADING RIFLE

Same as the Model 60 except breech bolt, barrel and outer magazine tube are made of stainless steel; most other parts are either nickel-plated or coated to match the stainless finish. Monte Carlo stock is of black/gray Maine birch laminate, and has nickel-plated swivel studs, rubber buttpad. Introduced 1993. From Marlin.
Price: **$283.00**

MARLIN 60DLX

Semiauto rifle chambered for .22 LR. Features include 14-shot tubular magazine; side ejection; manual and automatic last-shot bolt hold-opens; receiver top with serrrated, non-glare finish; cross-bolt safety; steel charging handle; Monte Carlo American walnut-finished hardwood; full pistol grip; tough Mar-Shield finish; 19-inch barrel with Micro-Groove® rifling. Limited availability.
Price: . . . . **NA**

MARLIN 70PSS PAPOOSE STAINLESS RIFLE

Caliber: 22 LR, 7-shot magazine. **Barrel:** 16.25" stainless steel, Micro-Groove rifling. **Weight:** 3.25 lbs. **Length:** 35.25" overall. **Stock:** Black fiberglass-filled synthetic with abbreviated forend, nickel-plated swivel studs, molded-in checkering. **Sights:** Ramp front with orange post, cut-away Wide Scan hood; adjustable open rear. Receiver grooved for scope mounting. **Features:** Takedown barrel; cross-bolt safety; manual bolt hold-open; last shot bolt hold-open; comes with padded carrying case. Introduced 1986. Made in U.S.A. by Marlin.
Price: **$284.00**

MARLIN MODEL 795 AUTO RIFLE

Caliber: 22. **Barrel:** 18" with 16-groove Micro-Groove rifling. Ramp front sight, adjustable rear. Receiver grooved for scope mount. **Stock:** Black synthetic, hardwood, synthetic thumbhole, solid pink, pink camo, or Mossy Oak New Break-up camo finish. **Features:** 10-round magazine, last shot hold-open feature. Introduced 1997. SS is similar to Model 795 except stainless steel barrel. Most other parts nickel-plated. Adjustable folding semi-buckhorn rear sights, ramp front high-visibility post and removable cutaway wide scan hood. Made in U.S.A. by Marlin Firearms Co.
Price: 795 . . . . **$157.00**
Price: 795SS **$227.00**

MOSSBERG MODEL 702 PLINKSTER AUTO RIFLE

Caliber: 22 LR, 10-round detachable magazine. **Barrel:** 18" free-floating. **Weight:** 4.1 to 4.6 lbs. **Sights:** Adjustable rifle. Receiver grooved for scope mount. **Stock:** Solid pink or pink marble finish synthetic. **Features:** Ergonomically placed magazine release and safety buttons, crossbolt safety, free gun lock. Made in U.S.A. by O.F. Mossberg & Sons, Inc.
Price: Pink Plinkster (2008) **$199.00**

MOSSBERG MODEL 702 PLINKSTER AUTOLOADING RIFLE WITH MUZZLE BRAKE

Semiauto rifle chambered in .22 LR. Features include a black synthetic stock with Schnabel, 10-round detachable box magazine,

---

21-inch matte blue barrel with muzzle brake, receiver grooved for scope mount.
Price: **$271.00**

REMINGTON MODEL 552 BDL DELUXE SPEEDMASTER RIFLE

Caliber: 22 S (20), L (17) or LR (15) tubular magazine. **Barrel:** 21" round tapered. **Weight:** 5.75 lbs. **Length:** 40" overall. **Stock:** Walnut. Checkered grip and forend. **Sights:** Big game. **Features:** Positive cross-bolt safety, receiver grooved for tip-off mount.
Price: **$593.00**
Price: Smoothbore model (2007) **$633.00**

REMINGTON 597 AUTO RIFLE

Caliber: 22 LR, 10-shot clip; 22 WMR, 8-shot clip. **Barrel:** 20". **Weight:** 5.5 lbs. **Length:** 40" overall. **Stock:** Black synthetic. **Sights:** Big game. **Features:** Matte black finish, nickel-plated bolt. Receiver is grooved and drilled and tapped for scope mounts. Introduced 1997. Made in U.S.A. by Remington.
Price: Synthetic Scope Combo (2007) **$239.00**
Price: Model 597 Magnum **$492.00**
Price: Model 597 w/Mossy Oak Blaze Pink or Orange,
   22 LR (2008) **$260.00**
Price: Model 597 Stainless TVP, 22 LR (2008) **$552.00**
Price: Model 597 TVP: Skeletonized laminated stock with
   undercut forend, optics rail **$552.00**
Price: Model 597 FLX: Similar to Model 597, Blaze/Pink camo
   but with FLX Digital Camo stock **$260.00**
Price: Model 597 AAC-SD **$231.00**

REMINGTON 597 VTR - QUAD RAIL

Semiauto rifle chambered in .22 LR, styled to resemble AR. Features include matte blued finished and black synthetic stock; 16-inch barrel; Pardus A2-style collapsible pistol-grip stock; quad-rail free-floated tube; 10-round magazine.
Price: **$618.00**

REMINGTON 597 VTR A-2 FIXED STOCK

Similar to Remington 597 VTR - Quad Rail but with fixed A2-style stock and standard handguard with quad rail.
Price: **$618.00**

REMINGTON 597 VTR COLLAPSIBLE STOCK

Similar to 597 VTR A-2 Fixed Stock but with Pardus A2-style collapsible pistol-grip stock.
Price: **$618.00**

REMINGTON 597 VTR A-TACS CAMO

Semiauto rifle chambered in .22 LR, styled to resemble AR. Features include ATACS camo finish overall; 16-inch barrel; Pardus A2-style collapsible pistol-grip stock; round handguard without rails; receiver-mounted optics rail; 10-round magazine.
Price: **$618.00**

RUGER 10/22 AUTOLOADING CARBINE

Caliber: 22 LR, 10-shot rotary magazine. **Barrel:** 18.5" round tapered. **Weight:** 5 lbs. **Length:** 37.25" overall. **Stock:** American hardwood with pistol grip and barrel band or synthetic. **Sights:** Brass bead front, folding leaf rear adjustable for elevation. **Features:** Detachable rotary magazine fits flush into stock, cross-bolt safety, receiver tapped and grooved for scope blocks or tip-off mount. Scope base adaptor furnished with each rifle.
Price: Model 10/22-RB (black matte) **$269.00**
Price: Model 10/22-CRR Compact RB (black matte), 2006 . . . **$307.00**

RUGER 10/22 DELUXE SPORTER

Same as 10/22 Carbine except walnut stock with hand checkered pistol grip and forend; straight buttplate, no barrel

---

band, has sling swivels.
Price: Model 10/22-DSP **$355.00**

RUGER 10/22-T TARGET RIFLE
Similar to the 10/22 except has 20" heavy, hammer-forged barrel with tight chamber dimensions, improved trigger pull, laminated hardwood stock dimensioned for optical sights. No iron sights supplied. Introduced 1996. Made in U.S.A. by Sturm, Ruger & Co.
Price: 10/22-T **$485.00**
Price: K10/22-T, stainless steel **$533.00**

RUGER K10/22-RPF ALL-WEATHER RIFLE
Similar to the stainless K10/22/RB except has black composite stock of thermoplastic polyester resin reinforced with fiberglass; checkered grip and forend. Brushed satin, natural metal finish with clear hardcoat finish. Weighs 5 lbs., measures 37" overall. Introduced 1997. From Sturm, Ruger & Co.
Price: **$318.00**

RUGER 10/22VLEH TARGET TACTICAL RIFLE
Semiauto rimfire rifle chambered in .22 LR. Features include precision-rifled, cold hammer-forged, spiral-finished 16-1/8-inch crowned match barrel; Hogue® OverMolded® stock; 10/22T target trigger; precision-adjustable bipod for steady shooting from the bench; 10-round rotary magazine. Weight: 6-7/8 lbs.
Price: **$555.00**

RUGER RUGER SR-22 RIFLE
AR-style semiauto rifle chambered in .22 LR, based on 0/22 action. Features include all-aluminum chassis replicating the AR-platform dimensions between the sighting plane, buttstock height, and grip; Picatinny rail optic mount includes a six-position, telescoping M4-style buttstock (on a Mil-Spec diameter tube); Hogue Monogrip pistol grip; buttstocks and grips interchangeable with any AR-style compatible option; round, mid-length handguard mounted on a standard-thread AR-style barrel nut; precision-rifled, cold hammer forged 16-1/8-inch alloy steel barrel capped with an SR-556/Mini-14 flash suppressor.
Price: . . . . **NA**

SAVAGE MODEL 64G AUTO RIFLE
Caliber: 22 LR, 10-shot magazine. **Barrel:** 20", 21". **Weight:** 5.5 lbs. **Length:** 40", 41". **Stock:** Walnut-finished hardwood with Monte Carlo-type comb, checkered grip and forend. **Sights:** Bead front, open adjustable rear. Receiver grooved for scope mounting. **Features:** Thumb-operated rotating safety. Blue finish. Side ejection, bolt hold-open device. Introduced 1990. Made in Canada, from Savage Arms.
Price: . . . . **From $187.00**

SAVAGE BRJ SERIES SEMIAUTO RIMFIRE RIFLES
Similar to Mark II, Model 93 and Model 93R17 semiauto rifles but feature spiral fluting pattern on a heavy barrel, blued finish and Royal Jacaranda wood laminate stock.
Price: Mark II BRJ – .22 LR) **$456.00**
Price: Model 93 BRJ – .22 Mag. **$464.00**
Price: Model 93 R17 BRJ – .17 HMR $464 . . . . **$464.00**

SAVAGE TACTICAL SEMIAUTO RIMFIRE RIFLES
Similar to Savage Model BRJ series semiauto rifles but feature heavy barrel, matte finish and a tactical-style wood stock.
Price: Mark II TR – .22 LR) **$469.00**
Price: Mark II TRR – .22 LR with three-way accessory rail) . **$539.00**
Price: Model 93R17 TR – .17 HMR **$477.00**
Price: Model 93R17 TRR – .17 HMR
with three-way accessory rail) **$536.00**

SMITH & WESSON M&P15-22
.22 LR rimfire verson of AR-derived M&P tactical autoloader. Features include blowback action, 15.5- or 16-inch barrel, 6-position

telescoping or fixed stock, quad mount picatinny rails, plain barrel or compensator, alloy upper and lower, matte black finish, 10- or 25-round magazine.
Price: **$589.00**

THOMPSON/CENTER 22 LR CLASSIC RIFLE
Caliber: 22 LR, 8-shot magazine. **Barrel:** 22" match-grade. **Weight:** 5.5 pounds. **Length:** 39.5" overall. **Stock:** Satin-finished American walnut with Monte Carlo-type comb and pistol gripcap, swivel studs. **Sights:** Ramp-style front and fully adjustable rear, both with fiber optics. **Features:** All-steel receiver drilled and tapped for scope mounting; barrel threaded to receiver; thumb-operated safety; trigger guard safety lock included. New 22 Classic Benchmark TGT target rifle variant has 18" heavy barrel, brown laminated target stock, blued with matte finish, 10-shot magazine and no sights; drilled and tapped.
Price: T/C 22 LR Classic (blue) **$396.00**
Price: T/C 22 LR Classic Benchmark **$505.00**

UMAREX COLT TACTICAL RIMFIRE M4 OPS CARBINE
Blowback semiauto rife chambered in .22 LR, styled to resemble Colt M16. Features include 16.2.2-inch barrel; front sight adjustable for elevation; adjustable rear sight; alloy lower; adjustable telestock; flattop receiver with removable carry handle; 10- or 30-round detachable magazine.
Price: **$599.00**

UMAREX COLT TACTICAL RIMFIRE M4 CARBINE
Blowback semiauto rifle chambered in .22 LR, styled to resemble Colt M4. Features include 16.2-inch barrel; front sight adjustable for elevation; adjustable rear sight; alloy lower; adjustable telestock; flattop receiver with optics rail; 10- or 30-round detachable magazine.
Price: **$640.00**

UMAREX COLT TACTICAL RIMFIRE M16 RIFLE
Blowback semiauto rifle chambered in .22 LR, styled to resemble Colt M16. Features include 21.2-inch barrel; front sight adjustable for elevation; adjustable rear sight; alloy lower; fixed stock; flattop receiver; removable carry handle; 10- or 30-round detachable magazine.
Price: **$599.00**

UMAREX COLT TACTICAL RIMFIRE M16 SPR RIFLE
Blowback semiauto rifle chambered in .22 LR, styled to resemble Colt M16 SPR. Features include 21.2-inch barrel; front sight adjustable for elevation; adjustable rear sight; alloy lower; fixed stock; flattop receiver with optics rail; removable carry handle; 10- or 30-round detachable magazine.
Price: **$670.00**

UMAREX H&K 416-22
Blowback semiauto rife chambered in .22 LR, styled to resemble H&K 416. Features include metal upper and lower receivers; RIS – rail interface system; retractable stock; pistol grip with storage compartment; on-rail sights; rear sight adjustable for wind and elevation; 16.1-inch barrel; 10- or 20-round magazine. Also available in pistol version with 9-inch barrel.
Price: **$675.00**

UMAREX H&K MP5 A5
Blowback semiauto rifle chambered in .22 LR, styled to resemble H&K MP5. Features include metal receiver; compensator; bolt catch; NAVY pistol grip; on-rail sights; rear sight adjustable for wind and elevation; 16.1-inch barrel; 10- or 25-round magazine. Also available in pistol version with 9-inch barrel. Also available with SD-type forend.
Price: **$525.00**

BROWNING BL-22 RIFLES

Action: Short-throw lever action, side ejection. Rack-and-pinion lever. Tubular magazines, with 15+1 capacity for 22 LR. **Barrel:** Recessed muzzle. **Stock:** Walnut, two-piece straight grip Western style. **Trigger:** Half-cock hammer safety; fold-down hammer. **Sights:** Bead post front, folding-leaf rear. Steel receiver grooved for scope mount. **Weight:** 5-5.4 lbs. **Length:** 36.75-40.75" overall. **Features:** Action lock provided. Introduced 1996. FLD Grade II Octagon has octagonal 24" barrel, silver nitride receiver with scroll engraving, gold-colored trigger. FLD Grade I has satin-nickel receiver, blued trigger, no stock checkering. FLD Grade II has satin-nickel receivers with scroll engraving; gold-colored trigger, cut checkering. Both introduced 2005. Grade I has blued receiver and trigger, no stock checkering. Grade II has gold-colored trigger, cut checkering, blued receiver with scroll engraving. Imported from Japan by Browning.

Price: BL-22 Grade I/II, from. $529.00
Price: BL-22 FLD Grade I/II, from $569.00
Price: BL-22 FLD, Grade II Octagon $839.00

HENRY LEVER-ACTION RIFLES

Caliber: 22 Long Rifle (15 shot), 22 Magnum (11 shots), 17 HMR (11 shots). **Barrel:** 18.25" round. **Weight:** 5.5 to 5.75 lbs. **Length:** 34" overall (22 LR). **Stock:** Walnut. **Sights:** Hooded blade front, open adjustable rear. **Features:** Polished blue finish; full-length tubular magazine; side ejection; receiver grooved for scope mounting. Introduced 1997. Made in U.S.A. by Henry Repeating Arms Co.

Price: H001 Carbine 22 LR. $325.00
Price: H001L Carbine 22 LR, Large Loop Lever. $340.00
Price: H001Y Youth model (33" overall, 11-round 22 LR) $325.00
Price: H001M 22 Magnum, 19.25" octagonal barrel, deluxe
    walnut stock $475.00
Price: H001V 17 HMR, 20" octagonal barrel, Williams Fire
    Sights $549.95

HENRY LEVER OCTAGON FRONTIER MODEL

Same as Lever rifles except chambered in 17 HMR, 22 Short/22 Long/22 LR, 22 Magnum; 20" octagonal barrel **Sights:** Marbles full adjustable semi-buckhorn rear, brass bead front. Weighs 6.25 lbs. Made in U.S.A. by Henry Repeating Arms Co.

Price: H001T Lever Octagon $425.00
Price: H001TM Lever Octagon 22 Magnum. $539.95

HENRY GOLDEN BOY 22 LEVER-ACTION RIFLE

Caliber: 17 HMR, 22 LR (16-shot), 22 Magnum. **Barrel:** 20" octagonal. **Weight:** 6.25 lbs. **Length:** 38" overall. **Stock:** American walnut. **Sights:** Blade front, open rear. **Features:** Brasslite receiver, brass buttplate, blued barrel and lever. Introduced 1998. Made in U.S.A. from Henry Repeating Arms Co.

Price: H004 22 LR $515.00
Price: H004M 22 Magnum $595.00
Price: H004V 17 HMR $615.00
Price: H004DD 22 LR Deluxe, engraved receiver $1,200.00

HENRY PUMP-ACTION 22 PUMP RIFLE

Caliber: 22 LR, 15-shot. **Barrel:** 18.25".
Weight: 5.5 lbs. **Length:** NA. **Stock:** American walnut. **Sights:** Bead on ramp front, open adjustable rear. **Features:** Polished blue finish; receiver grooved for scope mount; grooved slide handle; two barrel

---

bands. Introduced 1998. Made in U.S.A. from Henry Repeating Arms Co.

Price: H003T 22 LR $515.00
Price: H003TM 22 Magnum $595.00

MARLIN MODEL 39A GOLDEN LEVER-ACTION RIFLE

Caliber: 22, S (26), L (21), LR (19), tubular magazine. **Barrel:** 24" Micro-Groove. **Weight:** 6.5 lbs. **Length:** 40" overall. **Stock:** Checkered American black walnut; Mar-Shield finish. Swivel studs; rubber buttpad. **Sights:** Bead ramp front with detachable Wide-Scan hood, folding rear semi-buckhorn adjustable for windage and elevation. **Features:** Hammer block safety; rebounding hammer. Takedown action, receiver tapped for scope mount (supplied), offset hammer spur, gold-colored steel trigger. From Marlin Firearms.

Price: $593.00

MOSSBERG MODEL 464 RIMFIRE LEVER-ACTION RIFLE

Caliber: 22 LR. **Barrel:** 20" round blued. **Weight:** 5.6 lbs. **Length:** 35-3/4" overall. **Features:** Adjustable sights, straight grip stock, 124-shot tubular magazine, plain hardwood straight stock and forend.

Price: . . . . **NA; apparently not yet in production**

REMINGTON 572 BDL DELUXE FIELDMASTER PUMP RIFLE

Caliber: 22 S (20), L (17) or LR (15), tubular magazine. **Barrel:** 21" round tapered. **Weight:** 5.5 lbs. **Length:** 40" overall. **Stock:** Walnut with checkered pistol grip and slide handle. **Sights:** Big game. **Features:** Cross-bolt safety; removing inner magazine tube converts rifle to single shot; receiver grooved for tip-off scope mount.

Price: $607.00

RUGER MODEL 96 LEVER-ACTION RIFLE

Caliber: 22 WMR, 9 rounds; 17 HMR, 9 rounds. **Barrel:** 18.5". **Weight:** 5.25 lbs. **Length:** 37-3/8" overall. **Stock:** Hardwood. **Sights:** Gold bead front, folding leaf rear. **Features:** Sliding cross button safety, visible cocking indicator; short-throw lever action. Introduced 1996. Made in U.S.A. by Sturm, Ruger & Co.

Price: 96/22M, 22 WMR or 17 HMR $451.00

TAURUS MODEL 62 PUMP RIFLE

Caliber: 22 LR, 12- or 13-shot. **Barrel:** 16.5" or 23" round. **Weight:** 72 oz. to 80 oz. **Length:** 39" overall. **Stock:** Premium hardwood. **Sights:** Adjustable rear, bead blade front, optional tang. **Features:** Blue, case hardened or stainless, bolt-mounted safety, pump action, manual firing pin block, integral security lock system. Imported from Brazil by Taurus International.

Price: From $299.00

TAURUS MODEL 72 PUMP RIFLE

Same as Model 62 except chambered in 22 Magnum or 17 HMR; 16.5" barrel holds 10-12 shots, 23" barrel holds 11-13 shots. Weighs 72 oz. to 80 oz. Introduced 2001. Imported from Brazil by Taurus International.

Price: From $329.00

Prices given are believed to be accurate at time of publication however, many factors affect retail pricing so exact prices are not possible.

ANSCHUTZ 1416D/1516D CLASSIC RIFLES
Caliber: 22 LR (1416D888), 22 WMR (1516D), 5-shot clip. **Barrel:** 22.5". **Weight:** 6 lbs. **Length:** 41" overall. **Stock:** European hardwood with walnut finish; classic style with straight comb, checkered pistol grip and forend. **Sights:** Hooded ramp front, folding leaf rear. **Features:** Uses Match 64 action. Adjustable single-stage trigger. Receiver grooved for scope mounting. Imported from Germany by Merkel USA.
Price: 1416D KL, 22 LR $899.00
Price: 1416D KL Classic left-hand $949.00
Price: 1516D KL, 22 WMR $919.00

ANSCHUTZ 1710D CUSTOM RIFLE
Caliber: 22 LR, 5-shot clip. **Barrel:** 24.25". **Weight:** 7-3/8 lbs. **Length:** 42.5" overall. **Stock:** Select European walnut. **Sights:** Hooded ramp front, folding leaf rear; drilled and tapped for scope mounting. **Features:** Match 54 action with adjustable single-stage trigger; roll-over Monte Carlo cheekpiece, slim forend with Schnabel tip, Wundhammer palm swell on pistol grip, rosewood gripcap with white diamond insert; skip-line checkering on grip and forend. Introduced 1988. Imported from Germany by Merkel USA.
Price: $1,649.00

BROWNING T-BOLT RIMFIRE RIFLE
Caliber: 22 LR, 10-round rotary box Double Helix magazine. **Barrel:** 22", free-floating, semi-match chamber, target muzzle crown. **Weight:** 4.8 lbs. **Length:** 40.1" overall. **Stock:** Walnut, satin finish, cut checkering, synthetic buttplate. **Sights:** None. **Features:** Straight-pull bolt-action, three-lever trigger adjustable for pull weight, dual action screws, sling swivel studs. Crossbolt lockup, enlarged bolt handle, one-piece dual extractor with integral spring and red cocking indicator band, gold-tone trigger. Top-tang, thumb-operated two-position safety, drilled and tapped for scope mounts. Varmint model has raised Monte Carlo comb, heavy barrel, wide forearm. Introduced 2006. Imported from Japan by Browning. Left-hand models added in 2009.
Price: Sporter $679.00
Price: Sporter, left-hand, from $689.00
Price: Sporter, 17 HMR, 22 Mag., intr. 2008. . . . .$709.00
Price: Target/Varmint, intr. 2007 . . . .$709.00
Price: Composite Target/Varmint, intr. 2008 . . . .$709.00
Price: Composite Target/Varmint left-hand, from $689.00
Price: Composite Sporter, 17 HMR, 22 Mag., intr. 2008 . . . . .$709.00
Price: Composite Sporter left-hand, from $689.00

BUSHMASTER DCM-XR COMPETITION RIFLE
Caliber: 223 Rem, 10-shot mag. (2). **Barrel:** Heavy 1"-diameter free-floating match. **Weight:** 13.5 lbs. **Length:** 38.5" overall. **Features:** Fitted bolt, aperture rear sight that accepts four different inserts, choice of two front sight blades, two-stage competition trigger, weighted buttstock. Available in pre-and post-ban configurations.
Price: From . . . . NA

BUSHMASTER PIT VIPER 3-GUN COMPETITION RIFLE
Caliber: 5.56/223 Rem, 20-shot mag. (2). **Barrel:** Lapped/crowned 18" A2-profile 1:8. **Weight:** 7.5 lbs. **Length:** 38" overall. **Features:** AR-style semi-auto rifle designed for three-gun competition. Hybrid chambering to accept mil-spec ammunition, titanium nitride-coated bolt, free-floating handguard with two 3" rails and two 4" rails, JR tactical sight.
Price: From . . . . NA

COOPER MODEL 57-M BOLT-ACTION RIFLE
Caliber: 22 LR, 22 WMR, 17 HMR, 17 Mach 2. **Barrel:** 22" or 24" stainless steel or 4140 match grade. **Weight:** 6.5-7.5 lbs. **Stock:**

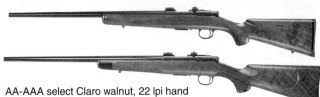

AA-AAA select Claro walnut, 22 lpi hand checkering. **Sights:** None furnished. **Features:** Three rear locking lug, repeating bolt-action with 5-shot magazine. for 22 LR and 17M2; 4-shot magazine for 22 WMR and 17 HMR. Fully adjustable trigger. Left-hand models add $150 to base rifle price. 1/4"-group rimfire accuracy guarantee at 50 yards; 0.5"-group centerfire accuracy guarantee at 100 yards. Options include wood upgrades, case-color metalwork, barrel fluting, custom LOP, and many others.
Price: Classic $1,400.00
Price: LVT $1,595.00
Price: Custom Classic $2,395.00
Price: Western Classic $3,295.00
Price: TRP-3 (22 LR only, benchrest style) $1,395.00
Price: Jackson Squirrel Rifle $1,595.00
Price: Jackson Hunter (synthetic) $1,495.00

CZ 452 LUX BOLT-ACTION RIFLE
Caliber: 22 LR, 22 WMR, 5-shot detachable magazine. **Barrel:** 24.8". **Weight:** 6.6 lbs. **Length:** 42.63" overall. **Stock:** Walnut with checkered pistol grip. **Sights:** Hooded front, fully adjustable tangent rear. **Features:** All-steel construction, adjustable trigger, polished blue finish. Imported from the Czech Republic by CZ-USA.
Price: 22 LR, 22 WMR $427.00

CZ 452 VARMINT RIFLE
Similar to the Lux model except has heavy 20.8" barrel; stock has beavertail forend; weighs 7 lbs.; no sights furnished. Available in 22 LR, 22 WMR, 17HMR, 17M2. Imported from the Czech Republic by CZ-USA.
Price: From $497.00

CZ 452 AMERICAN BOLT-ACTION RIFLE
Similar to the CZ 452 M 2E Lux except has classic-style stock of Circassian walnut; 22.5" free-floating barrel with recessed target crown; receiver dovetail for scope mounting. No open sights furnished. Introduced 1999. Imported from the Czech Republic by CZ-USA.
Price: 22 LR, 22 WMR $463.00

DAVEY CRICKETT SINGLE SHOT RIFLE
Caliber: 22 LR, 22 WMR, single shot. **Barrel:** 16-1/8". **Weight:** About 2.5 lbs. **Length:** 30" overall. **Stock:** American walnut. **Sights:** Post on ramp front, peep rear adjustable for windage and elevation. **Features:** Drilled and tapped for scope mounting using special Chipmunk base ($13.95). Engraved model also available. Made in U.S.A. Introduced 1982. Formerly Chipmunk model. From Keystone Sporting Arms.
Price: From $220.00

HENRY ACU-BOLT RIFLE
Caliber: 22, 22 Mag., 17 HMR; single shot. **Barrel:** 20". **Weight:** 4.15 lbs. **Length:** 36". **Stock:** One-piece fiberglass synthetic. **Sights:** Scope mount and 4x scope included. **Features:** Stainless barrel and receiver, bolt-action.
Price: H007 22 LR $399.95

HENRY "MINI" BOLT ACTION 22 RIFLE

Caliber: 22 LR, single shot youth gun. **Barrel:** 16" stainless, 8-groove rifling. **Weight:** 3.25 lbs. **Length:** 30", LOP 11.5". **Stock:** Synthetic, pistol grip, wraparound checkering and beavertail forearm. **Sights:** William Fire sights. **Features:** One-piece bolt configuration manually operated safety.
Price: H005 22 LR, black fiberglass stock **$249.95**
Price: H005S 22 LR, orange fiberglass stock. **$249.95**

MARLIN MODEL 917 BOLT-ACTION RIFLES

Caliber: 17 HMR, 4- and 7-shot clip. **Barrel:** 22". **Weight:** 6 lbs., stainless 7 lbs. **Length:** 41". **Stock:** Checkered walnut Monte Carlo SS, laminated black/grey. **Sights:** No sights but receiver grooved. **Features:** Swivel studs, positive thumb safety, red cocking indicator, safety lock, SS 1" brushed aluminum scope rings.
Price: 917 . . . .**$240.00**
Price: 917VS Stainless steel barrel **$287.00**
Price: 917VT Laminated thumbhole stock (2008), from **$382.00**
Price: 917VST, stainless-finish metal, gray/black laminated thumbhole stock **$426.00**
Price: 917VSF, fluted barrel **$397.00**
Price: 917VS-CF, carbon fiber-patterned stock **$358.00**

MARLIN MODEL 915YN "LITTLE BUCKAROO"

Caliber: 22 S, L, LR, single shot. **Barrel:** 16.25" Micro-Groove. **Weight:** 4.25 lbs. **Length:** 33.25" overall. **Stock:** One-piece walnut-finished, press-checkered Maine birch with Monte Carlo; Mar-Shield finish. **Sights:** Ramp front, adjustable open rear. **Features:** Beginner's rifle with thumb safety, easy-load feed throat, red cocking indicator. Receiver grooved for scope mounting. Introduced 1989.
Price: **$203.00**
Price: 915YS (stainless steel with fire sights) **$227.00**

MARLIN 981TS

Bolt action rifle chambered in .22 S/L/LR. Features include tubular magazine (holds 25 Short, 19 Long or 17 Long Rifle cartridges; thumb safety; red cocking indicator; black fiberglass-filled synthetic stock with full pistol grip; molded-in checkering and swivel studs; 22-inch stainless steel barrel with Micro-Groove rifling (16 grooves). Adjustable semi-buckhorn folding rear sight, ramp front with high visibility, orange front sight post; cutaway Wide-Scan hood. Receiver grooved for scope mount; drilled and tapped for scope bases.
Price: . . . .**NA**

MARLIN MODEL 982 BOLT-ACTION RIFLE

Caliber: 22 WMR. **Barrel:** 22" Micro-Groove. **Weight:** 6 lbs. **Length:** 41" overall. **Stock:** Walnut Monte Carlo genuine American black walnut with swivel studs; full pistol grip; classic cut checkering; rubber rifle butt pad; tough Mar-Shield finish. **Sights:** Adjustable semi-buckhorn folding rear, ramp front sight with brass bead and Wide-Scan front sight hood. **Features:** 7-shot clip, thumb safety, red cocking indicator, receiver grooved for scope mount. 982S has stainless steel front breech bolt, barrel, receiver and bolt knob. All other parts are either stainless steel or nickel-plated. 982VS has black Monte Carlo stock of fiberglass-filled polycarbonate with molded-in checkering, nickel-plated swivel studs. Introduced 2005. Made in U.S.A. by Marlin Firearms Co.
Price: 982VS (heavy stainless barrel, 7 lbs) **$309.00**
Price: 982VS-CF (carbon fiber stock). **$350.00**

MARLIN MODEL 925M BOLT-ACTION RIFLES

Similar to the Model 982 except chambered for 22 WMR. Has 7-shot clip magazine, 22" Micro-Groove barrel, checkered walnut-finished Maine birch stock. Introduced 1989.
Price: 925M. **$234.00**
Price: 925RM, black fiberglass-filled synthetic stock **$220.95**

MARLIN MODEL 983 BOLT-ACTION RIFLE

Caliber: 22 WMR. **Barrel:** 22"; 1:16" twist. **Weight:** 6 lbs. **Length:** 41" overall. **Stock:** Walnut Monte Carlo with sling swivel studs, rubber buttpad. **Sights:** Ramp front with brass bead, removable hood; adjustable semi-buckhorn folding rear. **Features:** Thumb safety, red cocking indicator, receiver grooved for scope mount. 983S is same as the Model 983 except front breech bolt, striker knob, trigger stud, cartridge lifter stud and outer magazine tube are of stainless steel; other parts are nickel-plated. Introduced 1993. 983T has a black Monte Carlo fiberglass-filled synthetic stock with sling swivel studs. Introduced 2001.Made in U.S.A. by Marlin Firearms Co.
Price: 983 . . . .**$308.00**
Price: 983S (stainless barrel) **$337.00**
Price: 983T (fiberglass stock) **$245.00**

MARLIN MODEL XT-17 SERIES BOLT ACTION RIFLES

Features: The XT Pro-Fire™ Adjustable Trigger produces an extremely consistent trigger pull with an ultra-clean break. Included are 4 and 7-shot clip magazines. The rugged walnut-finished hardwood Monte Carlo stock comes with sling swivel studs. The receiver is drilled, tapped and grooved for your choice of convenient scope mounting options. Also available with a factory-mounted and boresighted 3-9x32mm scope.
Price: . . . .**N/A**

MARLIN MODEL XT-22 SERIES BOLT ACTION RIFLES

Features: This is the new line of 22 caliber rimfire rifles from Marlin. Perfect for target practice and small game, these bolt-action 22s are reliable, accurate and fun to shoot. They come in several different models, with 4 or 7-shot clip magazines or 12-shot tube magazines; synthetic, hardwood or laminated stocks; ramp sights, hood sights or fiber-optic sights. All of them have Marlin innovations such as the Pro-Fire™ Adjustable Trigger and Micro-Groove® rifling. The XT-22 series comes chambered in 22 Short, 22 Long, 22 Long Rifle or 22 Winchester Magnum Rifle (WMR). Made in U.S.A. by Marlin Firearms Co.
Price: . . . .**N/A**

MARLIN MODEL XT-22 YOUTH SERIES BOLT ACTION RIFLES

Features: the first series of rifles designed exclusively for young shooters. It features a shorter stock, shorter trigger reach, smaller grip and a raised comb; making it easier for a youth to acquire and hold the proper sight picture. These guns also feature a reduced bolt release force, for smoother loading and to prevent jams. Our Pro-Fire™ Adjustable Trigger adjusts the trigger pull, too.
Price: . . . .**N/A**

MEACHAM LOW-WALL RIFLE

Caliber: Any rimfire cartridge. **Barrel:** 26-34". **Weight:** 7-15 lbs. **Sights:** none. Tang drilled for Win. base, 3/8" dovetail slot front. **Stock:** Fancy eastern walnut with cheekpiece; ebony insert in forearm tip. **Features;** Exact copy of 1885 Winchester. With most Winchester factory options available including double set triggers. Introduced 1994. Made in U.S.A. by Meacham T&H Inc.
Price: From **$4,999.00**

MOSSBERG MODEL 817 VARMINT BOLT-ACTION RIFLE

Caliber: 17 HMR, 5-round magazine. **Barrel:** 21"; free-floating bull barrel, recessed muzzle crown. **Weight:** 4.9 lbs. (black synthetic), 5.2 lbs. (wood). **Stock:** Black synthetic or wood; length of pull, 14.25". **Sights:** Factory-installed Weaver-style scope bases. **Features:** Blued or brushed chrome metal finishes, crossbolt safety, gun lock. Introduced 2008. Made in U.S.A. by O.F. Mossberg & Sons, Inc.
Price: Black synthetic stock, chrome finish (2008) **$279.00**

MOSSBERG MODEL 801/802 BOLT RIFLES

Caliber: 22 LR, 10-round detachable magazine. **Barrel:** 18" free-floating. **Weight:** 4.1 to 4.6 lbs. **Sights:** Adjustable rifle. Receiver grooved for scope mount. **Stock:** Solid pink or pink marble finish synthetic. **Features:** Ergonomically placed magazine release and safety buttons, crossbolt safety, free gun lock. 801 Half Pint has 12.25" length of pull, 16" barrel, and weighs 4 lbs. Hardwood stock; removable magazine plug. Made in U.S.A. by O.F. Mossberg & Sons, Inc.
Price: Pink Plinkster (2008) **$199.00**
Price: Half Pint (2008). **$199.00**

NEW ENGLAND FIREARMS SPORTSTER SINGLE-SHOT RIFLES

Caliber: 22 LR, 22 WMR, 17 HMR, single-shot. **Barrel:** 20". **Weight:** 5.5 lbs. **Length:** 36.25" overall. **Stock:** Black polymer. **Sights:** None furnished; scope mount included. **Features:** Break open, side-lever release; automatic ejection; recoil pad; sling swivel studs; trigger locking system. Introduced 2001. Made in U.S.A. by New England Firearms.
Price: **$149.00**
Price: Youth model (20" barrel, 33" overall, weighs 5-1/3 lbs.) **$149.00**
Price: Sportster 17 HMR **$180.00**

NEW ULTRA LIGHT ARMS 20RF BOLT-ACTION RIFLE

Caliber: 22 LR, single shot or repeater. **Barrel:** Douglas, length to order. **Weight:** 5.25 lbs. **Length:** Varies. **Stock:** Kevlar/graphite composite, variety of finishes. **Sights:** None furnished; drilled and tapped for scope mount. **Features:** Timney trigger, hand-lapped action, button-rifled barrel, hand-bedded action, recoil pad, sling-swivel studs, optional Jewell trigger. Made in U.S.A. by New Ultra Light Arms.
Price: 20 RF single shot . . . . $**1,300.00**
Price: 20 RF repeater **$1,350.00**

REMINGTON MODEL FIVE SERIES

Caliber: 17 HMR, 22 LR, 22 WMR. **Barrel:** 16.5" (Youth), 22". **Barrel:** Carbon-steel, hammer-forged barrel, 1:16 twist, polished blue finish. **Weight:** 5.5 to 6.75 lbs. **Stock:** Hardwood, laminate, European Walnut. **Length:** 35.25" to 40.75" overall. **Features:** Detachable, steel magazine box with five-round capacity; steel trigger guard; chrome-plated bolt body; single stage trigger with manual two-position safety; buttplate; sling swivel studs (excluding Youth version); adjustable big game-style rifle sights; and dovetail-style receiver. Introduced 2006. Model Five Youth (22 LR) has 12.4-inch length of pull, 16.5-inch barrel, single-shot adapter. Model Five Laminate has weather-resistant brown laminate stock. Model Five European Walnut has classic satin-finish stock. Made in U.S.A. by Remington.
Price: Model Five Youth, 22 LR (2008). **$237.00**
Price: Model Five Laminate, 17 HMR (2008), 22 LR, 22 WMR **$363.00**
Price: Model Five European Walnut, 22 LR (2008) **$279.00**

ROSSI MATCHED PAIR SINGLE-SHOT RIFLE/SHOTGUN

Caliber: 17 HMR, 22 LR, 22 Mag. **Barrel:** 18.5" or 23". **Weight:** 6 lbs. **Stock:** Hardwood (brown or black finish). **Sights:** Fully adjustable front and rear. **Features:** Break-open breech, transfer-bar manual

safety, includes matched 410-, 20 or 12 gauge shotgun barrel with bead front sight. Introduced 2001. Imported by BrazTech/Taurus.
Price: S121280RS **$160.00**
Price: S121780RS **$200.00**
Price: S122280RS **$160.00**
Price: S201780RS **$200.00**

RUGER K77/22 VARMINT RIFLE

Caliber: 22 LR, 10-shot, 22 WMR, 9-shot detachable rotary magazine. **Barrel:** 24", heavy. **Weight:** 7.25 lbs. **Length:** 43.25" overall. **Stock:** Laminated hardwood with rubber buttpad, quick-detachable swivel studs. **Sights:** None furnished. Comes with Ruger 1" scope rings. **Features:** Stainless steel or blued finish. Three-position safety, dual extractors. Stock has wide, flat forend. Introduced 1993.
Price: K77/22VBZ, 22 LR **$836.00**
Price: K77/22VMBZ, 22 WMR **$836.00**

RUGER 77/22 RIMFIRE BOLT-ACTION RIFLE

Caliber: 22 LR, 10-shot rotary magazine; 22 WMR, 9-shot rotary magazine. **Barrel:** 20". **Weight:** About 6 lbs. **Length:** 39.25" overall. **Stock:** Checkered American walnut, laminated hardwood, or synthetic stocks, stainless sling swivels. **Sights:** Plain barrel with 1" Ruger rings. **Features:** Mauser-type action uses Ruger's rotary magazine. Three-position safety, simplified bolt stop, patented bolt locking system. Uses the dual-screw barrel attachment system of the 10/22 rifle. Integral scope mounting system with 1" Ruger rings. Blued model introduced 1983. Stainless steel and blued with synthetic stock introduced 1989.
Price: 77/22R (no sights, rings, walnut stock). **$754.00**
Price: K77/22RP (stainless, no sights, rings, synthetic stock) **$754.00**
Price: 77/22RM (22 WMR, blued, walnut stock) **$754.00**
Price: K77/22RMP (22 WMR, stainless, synthetic stock) **$754.00**

RUGER 77/17 RIMFIRE BOLT-ACTION RIFLE

Caliber: 17 HMR (9-shot rotary magazine. **Barrel:** 22" to 24". **Weight:** 6.5-7.5 lbs. **Length:** 41.25-43.25" overall. **Stock:** Checkered American walnut, laminated hardwood; stainless sling swivels. **Sights:** Plain barrel with 1" Ruger rings. **Features:** Mauser-type action uses Ruger's rotary magazine. Three-position safety, simplified bolt stop, patented bolt locking system. Uses the dual-screw barrel attachment system of the 10/22 rifle. Integral scope mounting system with 1" Ruger rings. Introduced 2002.
Price: 77/17-RM (no sights, rings, walnut stock) **$754.00**
Price: K77/17-VMBBZ (Target grey bbl, black laminate stock) **$836.00**

SAVAGE MARK I-G BOLT-ACTION RIFLE

Caliber: 22 LR, single shot. **Barrel:** 20.75". **Weight:** 5.5 lbs. **Length:** 39.5" overall. **Stock:** Walnut-finished hardwood with Monte Carlo-type comb, checkered grip and forend. **Sights:** Bead front, open adjustable rear. Receiver grooved for scope mounting. **Features:** Thumb-operated rotating safety. Blue finish. Rifled or smooth bore. Introduced 1990. Made in Canada, from Savage Arms Inc.
Price: Mark I-G, rifled or smooth bore, right- or left-handed . . . **$226.00**
Price: Mark I-GY (Youth), 19" barrel, 37" overall, 5 lbs. **$226.00**

SAVAGE MARK II BOLT-ACTION RIFLE

Caliber: 22 LR, 10-shot magazine. **Barrel:** 20.5". **Weight:** 5.5 lbs. **Length:** 39.5" overall. **Stock:** Walnut-finished hardwood with Monte Carlo-type comb, checkered grip and forend. **Sights:** Bead front, open adjustable rear. Receiver grooved for scope mounting. **Features:** Thumb-operated rotating safety. Blue finish. Introduced 1990. Made in Canada, from Savage Arms, Inc.
Price: Mark II-BV. **$342.00**
Price: Mark II-GY (youth), 19" barrel, 37" overall, 5 lbs. **$226.00**
Price: Mark II-GL, left-hand **$226.00**
Price: Mark II-F, 17 HM2 . . . . **$202.00**

RIMFIRE RIFLES—Bolt Actions & Single Shot

Price: Mark II XP Camo Scope Package (2008) **$400.00**
Price: Mark II Classic T, thumbhole walnut stock (2008) **$559.00**
Price: Mark II BTV: laminated thumbhole vent stock,
AccuTrigger, blued receiver and bull barrel **$393.00**
Price: Mark II BVTS: stainless barrel/receiver;
available in right- or left-hand (BTVLS) configuration
. . . . **$393.00** (standard); **$441.00** (left hand)

SAVAGE MARK II-FSS STAINLESS RIFLE
Similar to the Mark II except has stainless steel barreled action and black synthetic stock with positive checkering, swivel studs, and 20.75" free-floating and button-rifled barrel with detachable magazine. Weighs 5.5 lbs. Introduced 1997. Imported from Canada by Savage Arms, Inc.
Price: **$273.00**

SAVAGE MODEL 93G MAGNUM BOLT-ACTION RIFLE
Caliber: 22 WMR, 5-shot magazine. **Barrel:** 20.75". **Weight:** 5.75 lbs. **Length:** 39.5" overall. **Stock:** Walnut-finished hardwood with Monte Carlo-type comb, checkered grip and forend. **Sights:** Bead front, adjustable open rear. Receiver grooved for scope mount. **Features:** Thumb-operated rotary safety. Blue finish. Introduced 1994. Made in Canada, from Savage Arms.
Price: Model 93G **$260.00**
Price: Model 93F (as above with black graphite/fiberglass
stock) **$241.00**
Price: Model 93 Classic, American walnut stock (2008) **$566.00**
Price: Model 93 Classic T, American walnut thumbhole stock
(2008) **$604.00**

SAVAGE MODEL 93FSS MAGNUM RIFLE
Similar to Model 93G except stainless steel barreled action and black synthetic stock with positive checkering. Weighs 5.5 lbs. Introduced 1997. Imported from Canada by Savage Arms, Inc.
Price: **$306.00**

SAVAGE MODEL 93FVSS MAGNUM RIFLE
Similar to Model 93FSS Magnum except 21" heavy barrel with recessed target-style crown, satin-finished stainless barreled action, black graphite/fiberglass stock. Drilled and tapped for scope mounting; comes with Weaver-style bases. Introduced 1998. Imported from Canada by Savage Arms, Inc.
Price: **$347.00**

SAVAGE MODEL 93R17 BOLT-ACTION RIFLES
Similar to Model 93G Magnum but chambered in 17 HMR. Features include standard synthetic, hardwood or walnut stock or thumbhole stock with cheekpiece, 21" or 22" barrel, no sights, detachable box magazine.
Price: Model 93R17BTV: Laminted ventilated thumbhole
stock, blued barrel/receiver **$393.00**
Price: Model 93R17BV: Standard brown laminate stock,
heavy barrel **$342.00**
Price: Model 93R17GV: Checkered hardwood stock **$278.00**
Price: Model 93R17GLV: Left-hand configuration **$278.00**
Price: Model 93R17 Classic T: Checkered walnut thumbhole
stock with unvented forend, blued barrel/receiver **$559.00**
Price: Model 93R17 Classic: Standard walnut stock **$559.00**
Price: Model 93R17BTVS: Laminated thumbhole vent stock,

stainless steel barrel and receiver **$441.00**
Price: Model 93R17BLTVS: Left-hand **$441.00**
Price: Model 93R17BVSS: Similar to Model 93R17BTVS but
with gray laminated non-thumbhole stock **$411.00**
Price: Model 93R17FVS: Black synthetic stock, AccuTrigger,
blued or stainless heavy barrel **$347.00**

SAVAGE MODEL 30G STEVENS "FAVORITE"
Caliber: 22 LR, 22 WMR Model 30GM, 17 HMR Model 30R17. **Barrel:** 21". **Weight:** 4.25 lbs. **Length:** 36.75". **Stock:** Walnut, straight grip, Schnabel forend. **Sights:** Adjustable rear, bead post front. **Features:** Lever action falling block, inertia firing pin system, Model 30G half octagonal barrel, Model 30GM full octagonal barrel.
Price: Model 30G **$344.00**
Price: Model 30 Takedown **$360.00**

SAVAGE CUB T MINI YOUTH
Caliber: 22 S, L, LR; 17 Mach 2. **Barrel:** 16". **Weight:** 3.5 lbs. **Length:** 33". **Stock:** Walnut finished hardwood thumbhole stock. **Sights:** Bead post, front; peep, rear. **Features:** Mini single-shot bolt action, free-floating button-rifled barrel, blued finish. From Savage Arms.
Price: Cub T Thumbhole, walnut stained laminated **$266.00**
Price: Cub T Pink Thumbhole (2008) **$280.00**

THOMPSON/CENTER HOTSHOT YOUTH RIFLE
Single-shot dropping-barrel rifle chambered in .22 Long Rifle. Features include a crowned 19-inch steel barrel, exposed hammer, synthetic forend and buttstock, peep sight (receiver drilled and tapped for optics), three stock pattern options (black, Realtree AP and pink AP). Overall weight 3 lbs., 11.5-inch length of pull.
Price: . . . . $229.00 to $249.00

WINCHESTER WILDCAT BOLT ACTION 22
Caliber: 22 S, L, LR; one 5-round and three 10-round magazines. **Barrel:** 21". **Weight:** 6.5 lbs. **Length:** 38-3/8". **Stock:** Checkered hardwood stock, checkered black synthetic Winchester buttplate, Schnabel fore-end. **Sights:** Bead post, front; buckhorn rear. **Features:** Steel sling swivel studs, blued finish. Wildcat Target/Varmint rifle has .866" diameter bull barrel. Receiver drilled, tapped, and grooved for bases. Adjustable trigger, dual front steel swivel studs. Reintroduced 2008. From Winchester Repeating Arms.
Price: **$259.00**
Price: Wildcat/Varmint **$309.00**

476 ⊕ *GUN DIGEST*®   Prices given are believed to be accurate at time of publication however, many factors affect retail pricing so exact prices are not possible.

ANSCHUTZ 1903 MATCH RIFLE

Caliber: 22 LR, single shot. **Barrel:** 21.25". **Weight:** 8 lbs. **Length:** 43.75" overall. **Stock:** Walnut-finished hardwood with adjustable cheekpiece; stippled grip and forend. **Sights:** None furnished. **Features:** Uses Anschutz Match 64 action. A medium weight rifle for intermediate and advanced Junior Match competition. Available from Champion's Choice.

Price: Right-hand **$965.00**

ANSCHUTZ 64-MP R SILHOUETTE RIFLE

Caliber: 22 LR, 5-shot magazine. **Barrel:** 21.5", medium heavy; 7/8" diameter. **Weight:** 8 lbs. **Length:** 39.5" overall. **Stock:** Walnut-finished hardwood, silhouette-type. **Sights:** None furnished. **Features:** Uses Match 64 action. Designed for metallic silhouette competition. Stock has stippled checkering, contoured thumb groove with Wundhammer swell. Two-stage #5098 trigger. Slide safety locks sear and bolt. Introduced 1980. Available from Champion's Choice.

Price: 64-MP R **$950.00**
Price: 64-S BR Benchrest (2008) **$1,175.00**

ANSCHUTZ 2007 MATCH RIFLE

Uses same action as the Model 2013, but has a lighter barrel. European walnut stock in right-hand, true left-hand or extra-short models. Sights optional. Available with 19.6" barrel with extension tube, or 26", both in stainless or blue. Introduced 1998. Available from Champion's Choice.

Price: Right-hand, blue, no sights. **$2,410.90**

ANSCHUTZ 1827BT FORTNER BIATHLON RIFLE

Caliber: 22 LR, 5-shot magazine. **Barrel:** 21.7". **Weight:** 8.8 lbs. with sights. **Length:** 40.9" overall. **Stock:** European walnut with cheekpiece, stippled pistol grip and forend. **Sights:** Optional globe front specially designed for Biathlon shooting, micrometer rear with hinged snow cap. **Features:** Uses Super Match 54 action and nine-way adjustable trigger; adjustable wooden buttplate, biathlon butthook, adjustable hand-stop rail. Uses Anschutz/Fortner system straight-pull bolt action, blued or stainless steel barrel. Introduced 1982. Available from Champion's Choice.

Price: Nitride finish with sights, about. **$2,895.00**

ANSCHUTZ SUPER MATCH SPECIAL MODEL 2013 RIFLE

Caliber: 22 LR, single shot. **Barrel:** 25.9". **Weight:** 13 lbs. **Length:** 41.7" to 42.9". **Stock:** Adjustable aluminum. **Sights:** None furnished. **Features:** 2313 aluminum-silver/blue stock, 500mm barrel, fast lock time, adjustable cheek piece, heavy action and muzzle tube, w/handstop and standing riser block. Introduced in 1997. Available from Champion's Choice.

Price: Right-hand **$3,195.00**

ANSCHUTZ 1912 SPORT RIFLE

Caliber: 22 LR. **Barrel:** 26" match. **Weight:** 11.4 lbs. **Length:** 41.7" overall. **Stock:** Non-stained thumbhole stock adjustable in length with adjustable butt plate and cheek piece adjustment. Flat forend raiser block 4856 adjustable in height. Hook butt plate. **Sights:** None furnished. **Features:** "Free rifle" for women. Smallbore model 1907 with 1912 **stock:** Match 54 action. Delivered with: Hand stop 6226, forend raiser block 4856, screw driver, instruction leaflet with test target. Available from Champion's Choice.

Price: **$2,595.00**

ANSCHUTZ 1913 SUPER MATCH RIFLE

Same as the Model 1911 except European walnut International-type stock with adjustable cheekpiece, or color laminate, both available with straight or lowered forend, adjustable aluminum hook buttplate, adjustable hand stop, weighs 13 lbs., 46" overall. Stainless or blue barrel. Available from Champion's Choice.

Price: Right-hand, blue, no sights, walnut stock. **$2,695.00**

ANSCHUTZ 1907 STANDARD MATCH RIFLE

Same action as Model 1913 but with 7/8" diameter 26" barrel

(stainless or blue). Length is 44.5" overall, weighs 10.5 lbs. Choice of stock configurations. Vented forend. Designed for prone and position shooting ISU requirements; suitable for NRA matches. Also available with walnut flat-forend stock for benchrest shooting. Available from Champion's Choice.

Price: Right-hand, blue, no sights. **$1,655.00**

ARMALITE AR-10(T) RIFLE

Caliber: 308 Win., 10-shot magazine. **Barrel:** 24" target-weight Rock 5R custom. **Weight:** 10.4 lbs. **Length:** 43.5" overall. **Stock:** Green or black composition; N.M. fiberglass handguard tube. **Sights:** Detachable handle, front sight, or scope mount available. Comes with international-style flattop receiver with Picatinny rail. **Features:** National Match two-stage trigger. Forged upper receiver. Receivers hard-coat anodized. Introduced 1995. Made in U.S.A. by ArmaLite, Inc.

Price: Black **$1,912.00**
Price: AR-10, 338 Federal **$1,912.00**

ARMALITE M15A4(T) EAGLE EYE RIFLE

Caliber: 223 Rem., 10-round magazine. **Barrel:** 24" heavy stainless; 1:8" twist. **Weight:** 9.2 lbs. **Length:** 42-3/8" overall. **Stock:** Green or black butt, N.M. fiberglass handguard tube. **Sights:** One-piece international-style flattop receiver with Weaver-type rail, including case deflector. **Features:** Detachable carry handle, front sight and scope mount (30mm or 1") available. Upper and lower receivers have push-type pivot pin, hard coat anodized. Made in U.S.A. by ArmaLite, Inc.

Price: Green or black furniture **$1,296.00**

ARMALITE M15 A4 CARBINE 6.8 & 7.62X39

Caliber: 6.8 Rem, 7.62x39. **Barrel:** 16" chrome-lined with flash suppressor. **Weight:** 7 lbs. **Length:** 26.6". **Features:** Front and rear picatinny rails for mounting optics, two-stage tactical trigger, anodized aluminum/phosphate finish.

Price: **$1,107.00**

BLASER R93 LONG RANGE SPORTER 2 RIFLE

Caliber: 308 Win., 10-shot detachable box magazine. **Barrel:** 24". **Weight:** 10.4 lbs. **Length:** 44" overall. **Stock:** Aluminum with synthetic lining. **Sights:** None furnished; accepts detachable scope mount. **Features:** Straight-pull bolt action with adjustable trigger; fully adjustable stock; quick takedown; corrosion resistant finish. Introduced 1998. Imported from Germany by Blaser USA.

Price: **$3,848.00**

BUSHMASTER A2/A3 TARGET RIFLE

Caliber: 5.56mm, 223 Rem., 30-round magazine **Barrel:** 20", 24". **Weight:** 8.43 lbs. (A2); 8.78 lbs. (A3). **Length:** 39.5" overall (20" barrel). **Stock:** Black composition;

COMPETITION RIFLES—Centerfire & Rimfire

A2 type. **Sights:** Adjustable post front, adjustable aperture rear. **Features:** Patterned after Colt M-16A2. Chrome-lined barrel with manganese phosphate exterior. Available in stainless barrel. Made in U.S.A. by Bushmaster Firearms Co.
Price: (A3 type) **$1,135.00**

BUSHMASTER DCM-XR COMPETITION RIFLE
Caliber: 5.56mm, 223 Rem., 10-round magazine. **Barrel:** 20" extra-heavy (1" diameter) barrel with 1.8" twist for heavier competition bullets. **Weight:** About 12 lbs. with balance weights. **Length:** 38.5". **Stock:** NA. **Sights:** A2 rear sight. **Features:** Has special competition rear sight with interchangeable apertures, extra-fine 1/2- or 1/4-MOA windage and elevation adjustments; specially ground front sight post in choice of three widths. Full-length handguards over free-floater barrel tube. Introduced 1998. Made in U.S.A. by Bushmaster Firearms, Inc.
Price: A2 . . . . **$1,150.00**
Price: A3 . . . . **$1,250.00**

BUSHMASTER VARMINTER RIFLE
Caliber: 5.56mm. **Barrel:** 24", fluted. **Weight:** 8.4 lbs. **Length:** 42.25" overall. **Stock:** Black composition, A2 type. **Sights:** None furnished; upper receiver has integral scope mount base. **Features:** Chrome-lined .950" extra heavy barrel with counter-bored crown, manganese phosphate finish, free-floating aluminum handguard, forged aluminum receivers with push-pin takedown, hard anodized mil-spec finish. Competition trigger optional. Made in U.S.A. by Bushmaster Firearms, Inc.
Price: **$1,360.00**

COLT MATCH TARGET HBAR & M4 RIFLES
Caliber: 223 Rem. **Barrel:** 20". **Weight:** 8 lbs. **Length:** 39" overall. **Stock:** Synthetic. **Sights:** Front: elevation adj. post; rear: 800-meter, aperture adj. for windage and elevation. **Features:** Heavy barrel, rate of rifling twist 1:7. Introduced 1991. Made in U.S.A. by Colt. M4 variant has 16.1" barrel.
Price: Model MT6601, MT6601C **$1,183.00**
Price: Model 6400C **$1,289.00**

COLT MATCH TARGET COMPETITION HBAR RIFLE
Similar to the Match Target except has removable carry handle for scope mounting, 1:9" rifling twist, 9-round magazine. Weighs 8.5 lbs. Introduced 1991.
Price: Model MT6700C **$1,250.00**

COLT MATCH TARGET COMPETITION HBAR II RIFLE
Similar to the Match Target Competition HBAR except has 16:1" barrel, overall length 34.5", and weighs 7.1 lbs. Introduced 1995.
Price: Model MT6731 . . . . **$1,172.00**

COLT ACCURIZED RIFLE
Similar to the Match Target Model except has 24" barrel. Features flat-top receiver for scope mounting, stainless steel heavy barrel, tubular handguard, and free-floating barrel. Matte black finish. Weighs 9.25 lbs. Made in U.S.A. by Colt's Mfg. Co., Inc.
Price: Model CR6724 . . . . **$1,334.00**

EAA/HW 660 MATCH RIFLE
Caliber: 22 LR. **Barrel:** 26". **Weight:** 10.7 lbs. **Length:** 45.3" overall. **Stock:** Match-type walnut with adjustable cheekpiece and buttplate. **Sights:** Globe front, match aperture rear. **Features:** Adjustable match trigger; stippled pistol grip and forend; forend accessory rail. Introduced 1991. Imported from Germany by European American Armory.
Price: About **$999.00**
Price: With laminate stock **$1,159.00**

ED BROWN MODEL 704, M40A2 MARINE SNIPER
Caliber: 308 Win., 30-06 Springfield. **Barrel:** Match-grade 24". **Weight:** 9.25 lbs. **Stock:** Hand bedded McMillan GP fiberglass tactical stock with recoil pad in special Woodland Camo molded-in colors. **Sights:** None furnished. Leupold Mark 4 30mm scope mounts with heavy-duty screws. **Features:** Steel trigger guard, hinged floor plate, three position safety.
Price: From **$3,695.00**

OLYMPIC ARMS SM SERVICEMATCH AR15 RIFLES
Caliber: 223 Rem. minimum SAAMI spec, 30-shot magazine. **Barrel:** 20" broach-cut Ultramatch stainless steel 1x8 twist rate. **Weight:** 10 lbs. **Length:** 39.5" overall. **Stock:** A2 grip, A2 buttstock with trapdoor. **Sights:** A2 NM rear, elevation adjustable front post. **Features:** DCM-ready AR15, free-floating handguard looks standard, A2 upper, threaded muzzle, flash suppressor. Premium model adds pneumatic recoil buffer, Bob Jones interchangeable sights, two-stage trigger and Turner Saddlery sling. Made in U.S.A. by Olympic Arms, Inc.
Price: SM-1, 20" DCM ready **$1,272.70**
Price: SM-1P, Premium 20" DCM ready **$1,727.70**

OLYMPIC ARMS UM ULTRAMATCH AR15 RIFLES
Caliber: 223 Rem. minimum SAAMI spec, 30-shot magazine. **Barrel:** 20" or 24" bull broach-cut Ultramatch stainless steel 1x10 twist rate. **Weight:** 8-10 lbs. **Length:** 38.25" overall. **Stock:** A2 grip, A2 buttstock with trapdoor. **Sights:** None, flat-top upper and gas block with rails. **Features:** Flat top upper, free floating tubular match handguard, Picatinny gas block, crowned muzzle, factory trigger job and "Ultramatch" pantograph. Premium model adds pneumatic recoil buffer, Harris S-series bipod, hand selected premium receivers and William Set Trigger. Made in U.S.A. by Olympic Arms, Inc.
Price: UM-1, 20" Ultramatch **$1,332.50**
Price: UM-1P **$1,805.70**

OLYMPIC ARMS ML-1/ML-2 MULTIMATCH AR15 CARBINES
Caliber: 223 Rem. minimum SAAMI spec, 30-shot magazine. **Barrel:** 16" broach-cut Ultramatch stainless steel 1x10 twist rate. **Weight:** 7-8 lbs. **Length:** 34-36" overall. **Stock:** A2 grip and varying buttstock. **Sights:** None. **Features:** The ML-1 includes A2 upper with adjustable rear sight, elevation adjustable front post, free floating tubular match handguard, bayonet lug, threaded muzzle, flash suppressor and M4 6-point collapsible buttstock. The ML-2 includes bull diameter barrel, flat top upper, free floating tubular match handguard, Picatinny gas block, crowned muzzle and A2 buttstock with trapdoor. Made in U.S.A. by Olympic Arms, Inc.
Price: ML-1 or ML-2 . . . . **$1,188.20**

478 ✦ *GUN DIGEST®*   Prices given are believed to be accurate at time of publication however, many factors affect retail pricing so exact prices are not possible.

COMPETITION RIFLES—Centerfire & Rimfire

OLYMPIC ARMS K8 TARGETMATCH AR15 RIFLES
Caliber: 5.56 NATO, 223 WSSM, 243 WSSM, .25 WSSM 30/7-shot magazine. **Barrel:** 20", 24" bull button-rifled stainless/chrome-moly steel 1x9/1x10 twist rate. **Weight:** 8-10 lbs. **Length:** 38"-42" overall. **Stock:** A2 grip, A2 buttstock with trapdoor. **Sights:** None. **Features:** Barrel has satin bead-blast finish; flat-top upper, free-floating tubular match handguard, Picatinny gas block, crowned muzzle and "Targetmatch" pantograph on lower receiver. K8-MAG model uses Winchester Super Short Magnum cartridges. Includes 24" bull chrome-moly barrel, flat-top upper, free-floating tubular match handguard, Picatinny gas block, crowned muzzle and 7-shot magazine. Made in U.S.A. by Olympic Arms, Inc.
Price: K8 . . . . **$908.70**
Price: K8-MAG **$1,363.70**

REMINGTON

40-XB RANGEMASTER TARGET CENTERFIRE
Caliber: 15 calibers from 220 Swift to 300 Win. Mag. **Barrel:** 27.25". **Weight:** 11.25 lbs. **Length:** 47" overall. **Stock:** American walnut, laminated thumbhole or Kevlar with high comb and beavertail forend stop. Rubber non-slip buttplate. **Sights:** None. Scope blocks installed. **Features:** Adjustable trigger. Stainless barrel and action. Receiver drilled and tapped for sights. Model 40-XB Tactical (2008) chambered in 308 Win., comes with guarantee of 0.75-inch maximum 5-shot groups at 100 yards. **Weight:** 10.25 lbs. Includes Teflon-coated stainless button-rifled barrel, 1:14 twist, 27.25 inch long, three longitudinal flutes. Bolt-action repeater, adjustable 40-X trigger and precision machined aluminum bedding block. Stock is H-S Precision Pro Series synthetic tactical stock, black with green web finish, vertical pistol grip. From Remington Custom Shop.
Price: 40-XB KS, aramid fiber stock, single shot **$2,780.00**
Price: 40-XB KS, aramid fiber stock, repeater **$2,634.00**
Price: 40-XB Tactical 308 Win. (2008) **$2,927.00**
Price: 40-XB Thumbhole Repeater. **$2,927.00**

REMINGTON 40-XBBR KS
Caliber: Five calibers from 22 BR to 308 Win. **Barrel:** 20" (light varmint class), 24" (heavy varmint class). **Weight:** 7.25 lbs. (light varmint class); 12 lbs. (heavy varmint class). **Length:** 38" (20" bbl.), 42" (24"bbl.). **Stock:** Aramid fiber. **Sights:** None. Supplied with scope blocks. **Features:** Unblued benchrest with stainless steel barrel, trigger adjustable from 1-1/2 lbs. to 3.5 lbs. Special two-oz. trigger extra cost. Scope and mounts extra.
Price: Single shot **$3,806.00**

REMINGTON 40-XC KS TARGET RIFLE
Caliber: 7.62 NATO, 5-shot. **Barrel:** 24", stainless steel. **Weight:** 11 lbs. without sights. **Length:** 43.5" overall. **Stock:** Aramid fiber. **Sights:** None furnished. **Features:** Designed to meet the needs of competitive shooters. Stainless steel barrel and action.
Price: **$3,000.00**

REMINGTON 40-XR CUSTOM SPORTER
Caliber: 22 LR, 22 WM. **Barrel:** 24" stainless steel, no sights. **Weight:** 9.75 lbs. **Length:** 40". **Features:** Model XR-40 Target rifle action. Many options available in stock, decoration or finish.
Price: Single shot **$4,391.00**
Price: 40-XRBR KS, bench rest 22 LR **$2,927.00**

SAKO TRG-22 BOLT-ACTION RIFLE
Caliber: 308 Win., 10-shot magazine. **Barrel:** 26". **Weight:** 10.25 lbs. **Length:** 45.25" overall. **Stock:** Reinforced polyurethane with fully adjustable cheekpiece and buttplate. **Sights:** None furnished. Optional quick-detachable, one-piece scope mount base, 1" or 30mm rings. **Features:** Resistance-free bolt, free-floating heavy stainless barrel, 60-degree bolt lift. Two-stage trigger is adjustable for length, pull, horizontal or vertical pitch. Introduced 2000. Imported from Finland by Beretta USA.
Price: TRG-22 folding stock **$4,560.00**

SPRINGFIELD ARMORY M1A SUPER MATCH
Caliber: 308 Win. **Barrel:** 22", heavy Douglas Premium. **Weight:** About 11 lbs. **Length:** 44.31" overall. **Stock:** Heavy walnut competition stock with longer pistol grip, contoured area behind the rear sight, thicker butt and forend, glass bedded. **Sights:** National Match front and rear. **Features:** Has figure-eight-style operating rod guide. Introduced 1987. From Springfield Armory.
Price: About **$2,479.00**

SPRINGFIELD ARMORY M1A/M-21 TACTICAL MODEL RIFLE
Similar to M1A Super Match except special sniper stock with adjustable cheekpiece and rubber recoil pad. Weighs 11.6 lbs. From Springfield Armory.
Price: **$2,975.00**

SPRINGFIELD ARMORY M-1 GARAND AMERICAN COMBAT RIFLES
Caliber: 30-06 Spfl., 308 Win., 8-shot. **Barrel:** 24". **Weight:** 9.5 lbs. **Length:** 43.6". **Stock:** American walnut. **Sights:** Military square post front, military aperture, MOA adjustable rear. **Features:** Limited production, certificate of authenticity, all new receiver, barrel and stock with remaining parts USGI mil-spec. Two-stage military trigger.
Price: About **$2,479.00**

STI SPORTING COMPETITION RIFLE
AR-style semiauto rifle chambered in 5.56 NATO. Features include 16-inch 410 stainless 1:8 barrel; mid-length gas system; Nordic Tactical Compensator and JP Trigger group; custom STI Valkyrie hand guard and gas block; flat-top design with picatinny rail; anodized finish with black Teflon coating. Also available in Tactical configuration.
Price: **$1328.53**

STONER SR-15 MATCH RIFLE
Caliber: 223. **Barrel:** 20". **Weight:** 7.9 lbs. **Length:** 38" overall. **Stock:** Black synthetic. **Sights:** None furnished; flattop upper receiver for scope mounting. **Features:** Short Picatinny rail, two-stage match trigger. Introduced 1998. Made in U.S.A. by Knight's Mfg. Co.
Price: **$1,650.00**

STONER SR-25 MATCH RIFLE
Caliber: 7.62 NATO, 10-shot steel magazine, 5-shot optional. **Barrel:** 24" heavy match; 1:11.25" twist. **Weight:** 10.75 lbs. **Length:** 44" overall. **Stock:** Black synthetic AR-15A2 design. Full floating forend of mil-spec synthetic attaches to upper receiver at a single point. **Sights:** None furnished. Has integral Weaver-style rail. Rings and iron sights optional. **Features:** Improved AR-15 trigger, AR-15-style seven-lug rotating bolt. Introduced 1993. Made in U.S.A. by Knight's Mfg. Co.
Price: **$3,345.00**
Price: SR-25 Lightweight Match (20" medium match target contour barrel, 9.5 lbs., 40" overall) **$3,345.00**

TIME PRECISION 22 RF BENCH REST RIFLE
Caliber: 22 LR, single shot. **Barrel:** Shilen match-grade stainless. **Weight:** 10 lbs. with scope. **Length:** NA. **Stock:** Fiberglass. Pillar bedded. **Sights:** None furnished. **Features:** Shilen match trigger removable trigger bracket, full-length steel sleeve, aluminum receiver. Introduced 2008. Made in U.S.A. by Time Precision.
Price: **$2,200.00**

BENELLI LEGACY SHOTGUN

Gauge: 12, 20, 2-3/4" and 3" chamber. **Barrel:** 24", 26", 28" (Full, Mod., Imp. Cyl., Imp. Mod., cylinder choke tubes). Mid-bead sight. **Weight:** 5.8 to 7.4 lbs. **Length:** 49-5/8" overall (28" barrel). **Stock:** Select AA European walnut with satin finish. **Features:** Uses the rotating bolt inertia recoil operating system with a two-piece steel/aluminum etched receiver (bright on lower, blue upper). Drop adjustment kit allows the stock to be custom fitted without modifying the stock. Introduced 1998. Ultralight model has gloss-blued finish receiver. Weight is 6.0 lbs., 24" barrel, 45.5" overall length. WeatherCoat walnut stock. Introduced 2006. Imported from Italy by Benelli USA, Corp.

Price: Legacy **$1,689.00**
Price: Sport (2008) **$2,269.00**

BENELLI ULTRA LIGHT SHOTGUN

Gauge: 12, 20, 3" chamber. **Barrel:** 28". Mid-bead sight. **Weight:** 5.2 to 6 lbs. **Features:** Similar to Legacy line. Drop adjustment kit allows the stock to be custom fitted without modifying the stock. WeatherCoat walnut stock. Lightened receiver, shortened magazine tube, carbon-fiber rib and grip cap. Introduced 2008. Imported from Italy by Benelli USA, Corp.

Price: 12 gauge. **$1,539.00**

BENELLI M2 FIELD SHOTGUNS

Gauge: 20 ga., 12 ga., 3" chamber. **Barrel:** 21", 24", 26", 28". **Weight:** 5.4 to 7.2 lbs. **Length:** 42.5 to 49.5" overall. **Stock:** Synthetic, Advantage Max-4 HD, Advantage Timber HD, APG HD. **Sights:** Red bar. **Features:** Uses the Inertia Driven bolt mechanism. Vent rib. Comes with set of five choke tubes. Imported from Italy by Benelli USA.

Price: Synthetic ComforTech gel recoil pad **$1,319.00**
Price: Camo ComforTech gel recoil pad. **$1,335.00**
Price: Satin walnut **$1,229.00**
Price: Rifled slug synthetic **$1,380.00**
Price: Camo turkey model w/SteadyGrip stock **$1,429.00**
Price: Realtree APG HD ComforTech stock (2007) **$1,429.00**
Price: Realtree APG HD ComforTech 20 ga. (2007) **$1,429.00**
Price: Realtree APG HD LH ComforTech (2007) **$1,429.00**
Price: Realtree APG HD ComforTech Slug (2007). **$1,429.00**
Price: Realtree APG HD w/SteadyGrip stock (2007) **$1,429.00**
Price: Black Synthetic Grip Tight 20 ga. (2007) **$1,319.00**

BENELLI MONTEFELTRO SHOTGUNS

Gauge: 12 and 20 ga. Full, Imp. Mod., Mod., Imp. Cyl., Cyl. choke tubes. **Barrel:** 24", 26", 28". **Weight:** 5.3 to 7.1 lbs. **Stock:** Checkered walnut with satin finish. **Length:** 43.6 to 49.5" overall. **Features:** Uses the Inertia Driven rotating bolt system with a simple inertia recoil design. Finish is blue. Introduced 1987.

Price: 24", 26", 28" **$1,219.00**
Price: Left hand. **$1,229.00**
Price: 20 ga. **$1,219.00**
Price: 20 ga. short stock (LOP: 12.5") **$1,120.00**
Price: Silver (AA walnut; nickel-blue receiver) **$1,649.00**
Price: Silver 20 ga. **$1,649.00**

BENELLI SUPER BLACK EAGLE II SHOTGUNS

Gauge: 12, 3-1/2" chamber. **Barrel:** 24", 26", 28" (Cyl. Imp. Cyl., Mod., Imp. Mod., Full choke tubes). **Weight:** 7.1 to 7.3 lbs. **Length:** 45.6 to 49.6" overall. **Stock:** European walnut with satin finish, polymer, or camo. Adjustable for drop. **Sights:** Red bar front. **Features:** Uses Benelli inertia recoil bolt system. Vent rib. Advantage Max-4 HD, Advantage Timber HD camo patterns. Features ComforTech stock. Introduced 1991. Left-hand models available. Imported from

Italy by Benelli USA.

Price: Satin walnut, non-ComforTech. **$1,549.00**
Price: Camo stock, ComforTech gel recoil pad **$1,759.00**
Price: Black Synthetic stock **$1,649.00**
Price: Max-4 HD Camo stock **$1,759.00**
Price: Timber HD turkey model w/SteadyGrip stock. **$1,680.00**
Price: Realtree APG HD w/ComforTech stock (2007) **$1,759.00**
Price: Realtree APG HD LH ComforTech stock (2007) **$1,759.00**
Price: Realtree APG HD Slug Gun (2007) **$1,730.00**

BENELLI CORDOBA SHOTGUN

Gauge: 20; 12; 3" chamber. **Barrel:** 28" and 30", ported, 10mm sporting rib. **Weight:** 7.2 to 7.3 lbs. **Length:** 49.6 to 51.6". **Features:** Designed for high-volume sporting clays and Argentina dove shooting. Inertia-driven action, Extended Sport CrioChokes, 4+1 capacity. Ported. Imported from Italy by Benelli USA.

Price: Black synthetic GripTight ComforTech stock **$1,869.00**
Price: Black synthetic GripTight ComforTech stock, 20 ga., (2007) **$1,869.00**
Price: Max-4 HD ComforTech stock (2007) **$2,039.00**

BENELLI SUPERSPORT & SPORT II SHOTGUNS

Gauge: 20; 12; 3" chamber. **Barrel:** 28" and 30", ported, 10mm sporting rib. **Weight:** 7.2 to 7.3 lbs. **Length:** 49.6 to 51.6". **Stock:** Carbon fiber, ComforTech (Supersport) or walnut (Sport II). **Sights:** Red bar front, metal midbead. Sport II is similar to the Legacy model except has nonengraved dual tone blue/silver receiver, ported wide-rib barrel, adjustable buttstock, and functions with all loads. Walnut stock with satin finish. Introduced 1997. **Features:** Designed for high-volume sporting clays. Inertia-driven action, Extended CrioChokes, 4+1 capacity. Ported. Imported from Italy by Benelli USA.

Price: Carbon fiber ComforTech stock **$1,979.00**
Price: Carbon fiber ComforTech stock, 20 ga. (2007) **$1,979.00**
Price: Sport II 20 ga. (2007) **$1,699.00**

BENELLI VINCI

Gas-operated semiauto shotgun chambered for 2-3/4- and 3-inch 12-gauge. Features include modular disassembly; interchangeable choke tubes; 24- to 28-inch ribbed barrel; black, MAX-4HD or APG HD finish; synthetic contoured stocks; optional Steady-Grip model;. Weight 6.7 to 6.9 lbs.

Price: . . . . **$1379.00 to $1599.00**

BENELLI SUPER VINCI

Gauge: 12 - 2-3/4", 3" and 3-1/2" chamber. **Barrel:** 26" and 28" barrels. **Weight:** 6.9-7 lbs.. **Length:** 48.5"-50.5". **Stock:** Black synthetic, Realtree Max4® and Realtree APG®. **Features:** 3+1 capacity, Crio® Chokes: C,IC,M,IM,F. Length of Pull: 14-3/8". Drop at Heel: 2". Drop at Comb: 1-3/8". Type of Sights: Red bar front sight and metal bead mid-sight. Minimum recommended load: 3-dram, 1-1/8 oz. loads (12-ga.). Receiver drilled and tapped for scope mounting. Imported from Italy by Benelli USA., Corp.

Price: 28" Black synthetic **$1,649.00**
Price: 28" Black synthetic. **$1,649.00**
Price: 28" Realtree Max4® **$1,759.00**
Price: 28" Realtree APG® **$1,759.00**
Price: 28" Realtree Max4® **$1,759.00**

Prices given are believed to be accurate at time of publication however, many factors affect retail pricing so exact prices are not possible.

SHOTGUNS—Autoloaders

BENELLI LEGACY SPORT
Gas-operated semiauto shotgun chambered for 12, 20 (2-3/4- and 3-inch) gauge. Features include Inertia Driven system; sculptured lower receiver with classic game scene etchings; highly polished blued upper receiver; AA-Grade walnut stock; gel recoil pad; ported 24- or 26-inch barrel, Crio chokes. Weight 7.4 to 7.5 lbs.

Price: **$2,369.00**

BERETTA 3901 SHOTGUNS
Gauge: 12, 20 gauge; 3" chamber, semiauto. **Barrel:** 26", 28". **Weight:** 6.55 lbs. (20 ga.), 7.2 lbs. (12 ga.). **Length:** NA. **Stock:** Wood, X-tra wood (special process wood enhancement), and polymer. **Features:** Based on A390 shotgun introduced in 1996. Mobilchokes, removable trigger group. 3901 Target RL uses gas operating system; Sporting style flat rib with steel front bead and mid-bead, walnut stock and forearm, satin matte finish, adjustable LOP from 12P13", adjustable for cast on/off, Beretta's Memory System II to adjust the parallel comb. Weighs 7.2 lbs. 3901 Citizen has polymer stock. 3901 Statesman has basic wood and checkering treatment. 3901 Ambassador has X-tra wood stock and fore end; high-polished receiver with engraving, Gel-Tek recoil pad, optional TruGlo fiber-optic front sight. 3901 Rifled Slug Shotgun has black high-impact synthetic stock and fore end, 24" barrel,1:28 twist, Picatinny cantilever rail. Introduced 2006. Made in U.S. by Beretta USA.

Price: 3901 Target RL. **$900.00**
Price: 3901 Citizen, synthetic or wood, from **$750.00**
Price: 3901 Statesman **$900.00**
Price: 3901 Rifled Slug Shotgun. **$800.00**

BERETTA UGB25 XCEL SEMIAUTO SHOTGUN
Gauge: 12, 2-3/4" chambers. **Barrel:** 28", 30", 32"; competition-style interchangeable vent rib; Optima choke tubes. **Weight:** 7.7-9 lbs. **Stock:** High-grade walnut with oil finish; hand-checkered grip and forend, adjustable. **Features:** Break-open semiautomatic. High-resistance fiberglass-reinforced technopolymer trigger plate, self-lubricating firing mechanism. Rounded alloy receiver, polished sides, external cartridge carrier and feeding port, bottom eject. two technopolymer recoil dampers on breech bolt, double recoil dampers located in the receiver, Beretta Recoil Reduction System, recoil-absorbing Beretta Gel Tek recoil pad. Optima-Bore barrel with a lengthened forcing cone, Optimachoke and Extended Optimachoke tubes. Steel-shot capable, interchangeable aluminum alloy top rib. Introduced 2006. Imported from Italy by Beretta USA.

Price: **$3,875.00**

BERETTA A400 XPLOR UNICO SEMIAUTO SHOTGUN
Self-regulation gas-operated shotgun chambered to shoot all 12-ga. loads from 2-3/4 to 3.5 inches. Features include Kick-Off3 hydraulic damper; 26- or 28-inch "Steelium" barrel with interchangeable choke tubes; anodized aluminum receiver; sculpted, checkered walnut buttstock and forend.

Price: **$1625.00**

BERETTA A400 XPLOR LIGHT SEMIAUTO SHOTGUN
Gauge: 12-gas operated - 2-3/4" & 3" chamber. **Barrel:** 18" barrel. **Weight:** 6.4 lbs.. **Length:** 39.2". **Stock:** Walnut & polymer. **Features:** The A400 Light combines Beretta's exclusive Blink operating system, self compensating exhaust valve and self

cleaning piston, steelium barrel design with 1/4" x 1/4" ventilated rib and Optima-Choke HP, also fitted with the Micro-Core recoil pad. The stock is a wood-oil finish with a mix of walnut and polymer to maximize performance from the forend insert to the trigger guard. Continuing the A400 proprietary family design, the A400 Light is also available with Beretta's improved Kick-Off damper system. Imported from Italy by Benelli USA., Corp.

Price: **$1,400.00**

BERETTA AL391 TEKNYS SHOTGUNS
Gauge: 12, 20 gauge; 3" chamber, semiauto. **Barrel:** 26", 28". **Weight:** 5.9 lbs. (20 ga.), 7.3 lbs. (12 ga.). **Length:** NA. **Stock:** X-tra wood (special process wood enhancement). **Features:** Flat 1/4 rib, TruGlo Tru-Bead sight, recoil reducer, stock spacers, overbored bbls., flush choke tubes. Comes with fitted, lined case.

Price: From **$2,050.00**

BERETTA AL391 URIKA AND URIKA 2 AUTO SHOTGUNS
Gauge: 12, 20 gauge; 3" chamber. **Barrel:** 22", 24", 26", 28", 30"; five Mobilchoke choke tubes. **Weight:** 5.95 to 7.28 lbs. **Length:** Varies by model. **Stock:** Walnut, black or camo synthetic; shims, spacers and interchangeable recoil pads allow custom fit. **Features:** Self-compensating gas operation handles full range of loads; recoil reducer in receiver; enlarged trigger guard; reduced-weight receiver, barrel and forend; hard-chromed bore. Introduced 2000. AL391 Urika 2 (2007) has self-cleaning action, X-Tra Grain stock finish. AL391 Urika 2 Gold has higher-grade select oil-finished wood stock, upgraded engraving (gold-filled gamebirds on field models, gold-filled laurel leaf on competition version). Kick-Off recoil reduction system available in Synthetic, Realtree Advantage Max-4 and AP models. Imported from Italy by Beretta USA.

Price: Urika 2 X-tra Grain, from **$1,400.00**
Price: Urika 2 Gold, from **$1,550.00**
Price: Urika 2 Synthetic **$975.00**
Price: Urika 2 Realtree AP Kick-Off, ... **$1,350.00**

BERETTA A391 XTREMA 2 SEMIAUTO SHOTGUN
Gauge: 12 ga. 3.5" chamber. **Barrel:** 24", 26", 28". **Weight:** 7.8 lbs. **Stock:** Synthetic. **Features:** Gas operation system with exhaust valve and self-cleaning gas cylinder and piston that automatically vents the excess gases of the most powerful cartridges.The result is that the shotgun, without any adjustment, fires everything from the weakest 28g (1 ounce, 3 ¾ dram equivalent) game load to the heaviest 64g (2 ¼ ounce) Super Magnum cartridge. The exhaust valve remains attached to the barrel, ensuring easy and quick assembly and disassembly of the shotgun. Semiauto goes with two-lug rotating bolt, extended tang, cross bolt safety, self-cleaning, with case. Also, all steel par ts are now manufactured from stainless steel or are plated with either: nickel, Bruniton, PVD, Aqua Film (receiver & barrel) or chrome (barrel, bore and bolt), making the Xtrema2 a match for even the most extreme environments.

Price: From . . . .**$1,350.00 - $1,700.00**

BREDA GRIZZLY
Gauge: 12, 3.5" chamber. **Barrel:** 28". **Weight:** 7.2 lbs. **Stock:** Black synthetic or Advantage Timber with matching metal parts. **Features:** Chokes tubes are Mod., IC, Full; inertia-type action, four-round magazine. Imported from Italy by Legacy Sports International.

Price: Blued/black (2008) **$1,826.00**
Price: Advantage Timber Camo (2008) **$2,121.00**

BREDA XANTHOS
Gauge: 12, 3" chamber. **Barrel:** 28". **Weight:** 6.5 lbs. **Stock:** High grade walnut. **Features:** Chokes tubes are Mod., IC, Full; inertia-type action, four-round magazine, spark engraving with hand-engraved

details and hand-gilding figures on receiver. Blued, Grey or Chrome finishes. Imported from Italy by Legacy Sports International.
Price: Blued (2007) **$2,309.00**
Price: Grey (2007) **$2,451.00**
Price: Chrome (2007) **$3,406.00**

BREDA ECHO
Gauge: 12, 20. 3" chamber. **Barrel:** 28". **Weight:** 6.0-6.5 lbs. **Stock:** Walnut. **Features:** Chokes tubes are Mod., IC, Full; inertia-type action, four-round magazine, blue, grey or nickel finishes, modern engraving, fully checkered pistol grip. Imported from Italy by Legacy Sports International.
Price: Blued, 12 ga. (2008) **$1,897.00**
Price: Grey, 12 ga. (2008) **$1,969.00**
Price: Nickel, 12 ga. (2008) **$2,214.00**
Price: Nickel, 20 ga. (2008) **$2,214.00**

BREDA ALTAIR
Gauge: 12, 20. 3" chamber. **Barrel:** 28". **Weight:** 5.7-6.1 lbs. **Stock:** Oil-rubbed walnut. **Features:** Chokes tubes are Mod., IC, Full; gas-actuated action, four-round magazine, blued finish, lightweight frame. Imported from Italy by Legacy Sports International.
Price: Blued, 12 ga. (2008) **$1,320.00**
Price: Grey, 20 ga. (2008) **$1,320.00**

BROWNING GOLD AUTO SHOTGUNS
Gauge: 12, 3" or 3-1/2" chamber; 20, 3" chamber. **Barrel:** 12 ga.-26", 28", 30", Invector Plus choke tubes; 20 ga.-26", 30", Invector choke tubes. **Weight:** 7 lbs., 9 oz. (12 ga.), 6 lbs., 12 oz. (20 ga.). **Length:** 46.25" overall (20 ga., 26" barrel). **Stock:** 14"x1.5"x2-1/3"; select walnut with gloss finish; palm swell grip. **Features:** Self-regulating, self-cleaning gas system shoots all loads; lightweight receiver with special non-glare deep black finish; large reversible safety button; large rounded trigger guard, gold trigger. The 20 gauge has slightly smaller dimensions; 12 gauge have back-bored barrels, Invector Plus tube system. Introduced 1994. Gold Evolve shotguns have new rib design, HiViz sights. Imported by Browning.
Price: Gold Evolve Sporting, 12 ga., 2-3/4" chamber **$1,326.00**
Price: Gold Superlite Hunter, 12 or 20 ga., 26" or 28" barrel, 6.6 lbs............................ **$1,161.00**

BROWNING GOLD NWTF TURKEY SERIES AND MOSSY OAK SHOTGUNS
Gauge: 12, 10, 3-1/2" chamber. Similar to the Gold Hunter except has specialized camouflage patterns, including National Wild Turkey Federation design. Includes extra-full choke tube and HiViz fiber-optic sights on some models and Dura-Touch coating. Camouflage patterns include Mossy Oak New Break-Up (NBU) or Mossy Oak New Shadow Grass (NSG). NWTF models include NWTF logo on stock. Introduced 2001. From Browning.
Price: NWFT Gold Ultimate Turkey, 24" barrel, 12 ga. 3-1/2" chamber **$1,513.00**
Price: NWFT Gold 10 Gauge, 24" barrel, 3-1/2" chamber .. **$1,639.00**

BROWNING GOLD GOLDEN CLAYS AUTO SHOTGUNS
Gauge: 12, 2-3/4" chamber. **Barrel:** 28", 30", Invector Plus choke tubes. **Weight:** about 7.75 lbs. **Length:** From 47.75 to 50.5". **Stock:** Select walnut with gloss finish; palm swell grip, shim adjustable. **Features:** Ported barrels, "Golden Clays" models feature gold inlays and engraving. Imported by Browning.
Price: Gold "Golden Clays" Sporting Clays, intr. 2005 ..... **$1,941.00**

BROWNING GOLD LIGHT 10 GAUGE AUTO SHOTGUN
Similar to the Gold Hunter except has an alloy receiver that is 1 lb. lighter than standard model. Offered in 26" or 28" bbls. With Mossy Oak Break-Up or Shadow Grass coverage; 5-shot magazine. Weighs 9 lbs., 10 oz. (28" bbl.). Introduced 2001. Imported by Browning.
Price: Camo model only **$1,509.00**

BROWNING MAXUS
Gauge: 12; 3" or 3.5" chambers. **Barrel:** 26" or 28". **Weight:** 6-7/8 lbs. **Length:** 47.25" to 49.25". **Stock:** Composite with close radius pistol grip. **Features:** Aluminum receiver, lightweight profile barrel with vent rib, Vector Pro lengthened forcing cone, DuraTouch Armor Coating overall. Handles shorter shells interchangeably.
Price: Stalker, matte black finish overall, 3-1/2" **$1,379.00**
Price: Stalker, matte black finish overall, 3" **$1,199.00**
Price: Mossy Oak Duck Blind overall, 3-1/2" **$1,499.00**
Price: Mossy Oak Duck Blind overall, 3" **$1,339.00**

BROWING MAXUS ALL-PURPOSE, MOSSY OAK BREAK-UP SEMIAUTO SHOTGUN
Gauge: 12 ga., 3-1/2" chamber. **Barrel:** 26" flat ventilated rib with fixed cylinder choke; stainless Steel; Matte finish. **Weight:** 7 lbs. 2 ozs. **Length:** 40.75". **Stock:** Composite stock with close radius pistol grip, speed lock forearm, textured gripping surfaces, shim adjustable for length of pull, cast and drop, Mossy Oak® Break-Up® Infinity™ camo finish, Dura-Touch® Armor Coating. **Features:** Vector Pro™ lengthened forcing cone, four Invector-Plus™ choke tubes (XF Turkey Tube included), HiViz® 4-in-1 fiber-optic sight set with fully adjustable rear sight for windage and elevation, Inflex Technology recoil pad, ivory front bead sight and one 1/4" stock spacer.
Price: **$1,600.00**

BROWING MAXUS HUNTER SEMIAUTO SHOTGUN
Gauge: 12 ga., 3" & 3-1/2" chamber. **Barrel:** 26", 28" & 30" flat ventilated rib with fixed cylinder choke; stainless Steel; Matte finish. **Weight:** 7 lbs. 2 ozs. **Length:** 40.75". **Stock:** Gloss finish walnut stock with close radius pistol grip, sharp 22 lines-per-inch checkering, speed Lock Forearm, shim adjustable for length of pull, cast and drop. **Features:** Vector Pro™ lengthened forcing cone, three Invector-Plus™ choke tubes, Inflex Technology recoil pad, ivory front bead sight, One 1/4" stock spacer. Strong, lightweight aluminum alloy receiver with durable satin nickel finish & laser engraving (pheasant on the right, mallard on the left).
Price: 3-1/2" with 30" barrel **$1,560.00**
Price: 3-1/2" with 28" barrel **$1,560.00**
Price: 3-1/2" with 26" barrel **$1,560.00**
Price: 3" with 30" barrel **$1,420.00**
Price: 3" with 28" barrel **$1,420.00**
Price: 3" with 26" barrel **$1,420.00**

BROWING MAXUS MOSSY OAK BOTTOMLAND SEMIAUTO SHOTGUN
Gauge: 12 ga., 3-1/2" chamber. **Barrel:** 28" flat ventilated rib. **Weight:** 6 lbs. 15 ozs. **Length:** 49.25". **Stock:** Composite stock with close radius pistol grip; Speed Lock forearm; textured gripping surfaces; shim adjustable for length of pull, cast and drop; Mossy Oak® Bottomland™ camo finish; Dura-Touch® Armor Coating. **Features:** Vector Pro™ lengthened forcing cone; three Invector Plus™ choke tubes (F,M,IC); Inflex Technology recoil pad; ivory front bead sight; one 1/4" stock spacer.
Price: **$1,539.00**

BROWING MAXUS MOSSY OAK DUCK BLIND SEMIAUTO SHOTGUN
Gauge: 12 ga., 3" & 3-1/2" chamber. **Barrel:** 26"& 28" flat ventilated rib with fixed cylinder choke; stainless Steel; Matte finish. **Weight:** 6 lbs. 14 ozs.-6 lbs. 15 ozs. **Length:** 47.25"-49.25". **Stock:** Composite stock with close radius pistol grip, Speed Lock forearm, textured gripping surfaces, Mossy Oak® Duck Blind® camo finish, Dura-Touch®

SHOTGUNS—Autoloaders

Armor Coating. **Features:** Vector Pro™ lengthened forcing cone, three Invector-Plus™ choke tubes, Inflex Technology recoil pad, ivory front bead sight, One 1/4" stock spacer. Strong, lightweight aluminum alloy receiver. Gas-operated autoloader, new Power Drive Gas System reduces recoil and cycles a wide range of loads.
Price: 3-1/2" with 28" barrel **$1,540.00**
Price: 3-1/2" with 26" barrel **$1,540.00**
Price: 3" with 28" barrel **$1,340.00**
Price: 3" with 26" barrel **$1,340.00**

BROWING MAXUS SPORTING SEMIAUTO SHOTGUN
Gauge: 12 ga., 3" chamber. **Barrel:** 28" & 30" flat ventilated rib. **Weight:** 7 lbs. 2 ozs. **Length:** 49.25"-51.25". **Stock:** Gloss finish high grade walnut stock with close radius pistol grip , Speed Lock forearm, shim adjustable for length of pull, cast and drop. **Features:** This new model is sure to catch the eye, with its laser engraving of game birds transforming into clay birdson the lightweight alloy receiver. Quail are on the right side, and a mallard duck on the left. The Power Drive Gas System reduces recoil and cycles a wide array of loads. It's available in a 28" or 30" barrel length. The high grade walnut stock and forearm are generously checkered, finished with a deep, high gloss. The stock is adjustable and one 1/4" stock spacer is included. For picking up either clay or live birds quickly, the HiViz Tri-Comp fiber-optic front sight with mid-bead ivory sight does a great job, gathering light on the most overcast days. Vector Pro™ lengthened forcing cone, five Invector-Plus™ choke tubes, Inflex Technology recoil pad ,HiViz® Tri-Comp fiber-optic front sight, ivory mid-bead sight, one ¼" stock spacer.
Price: **$1,630.00**

BROWING MAXUS SPORTING CARBON FIBER SEMIAUTO SHOTGUN
Gauge: 12 ga., 3" chamber. **Barrel:** 28" & 30" flat ventilated rib. **Weight:** 6 lbs. 15 ozs. - 7 lbs. **Length:** 49.25"-51.25". **Stock:** Composite stock with close radius pistol grip, Speed Lock forearm, textured gripping surfaces, shim adjustable for length of pull, cast and drop, carbon fiber finish, Dura-Touch® Armor Coating. **Features:** Strong, lightweight aluminum alloy, carbon fiber finish on top and bottom The stock is finished with Dura-Touch Armor Coating for a secure, non-slip grip when the gun is wet. It has the Browning exclusive Magazine Cut-Off, a patented Turn-Key Magazine Plug and Speed Load Plus. It will be an impossible task to locate an autoloading shotgun for the field with such shooter-friendly features as the Browning Maxus, especially with this deeply finished look of carbon fiber and the Dura-Touch Armor Coating feel. Vector Pro™ lengthened forcing cone, five Invector-Plus™ choke tubes, Inflex Technology recoil pad, HiViz® Tri-Comp fiber-optic front sight, ivory mid-bead sight, one 1/4" stock spacer.
Price: **$1,420.00**

BROWING RIFLED DEER STALKER SEMIAUTO SHOTGUN
Gauge: 12 ga., 3" chamber. **Barrel:** 22" thick-walled, fully rifled for slug ammunition only. **Weight:** 7 lbs. 3 ozs. **Length:** 43.25". **Stock:** Composite stock with close radius pistol grip, Speed Lock forearm, textured gripping surfaces, shim adjustable for length of pull, cast and drop, matte black finish Dura-Touch® Armor Coating. **Features:** Stock is adjustable for length of pull, cast and drop. Cantilever scope mount, one 1/4" stock spacer.
Price: **$1,400.00**

BROWNING SILVER AUTO SHOTGUNS
Gauge: 12, 3" or 3-1/2" chamber; 20, 3" chamber. **Barrel:** 12 ga.-26",

28", 30", Invector Plus choke tubes. Weight: 7 lbs., 9 oz. (12 ga.), 6 lbs., 7 oz. (20 ga.). Stock: Satin finish walnut. Features: Active Valve gas system, semi-humpback receiver. Invector Plus tube system, three choke tubes. Imported by Browning.
Price: Silver Hunter, 12 ga., 3.5" chamber **$1,239.00**
Price: Silver Hunter, 20 ga., 3" chamber, intr. 2008 ...... **$1,079.00**
Price: Silver Micro, 20 ga., 3" chamber, intr. 2008 .... **$1,079.00**
Price: Silver Sporting, 12 ga., 2-3/4" chamber, intr. 2009 .... **$1,199.00**
Price: Silver Sporting Micro, 12 ga., 2-3/4" chamber, intr. 2008 .... **$1,199.00**
Price: Silver Rifled Deer, Mossy Oak New Break-Up, 12 ga., 3" chamber, intr. 2008 .... **$1,319.00**
Price: Silver Rifled Deer Stalker, 12 ga., 3" chamber, intr. 2008 .... **$1,169.00**
Price: Silver Rifled Deer Satin, satin-finished aluminum alloy receiver and satin-finished walnut buttstock and forend **$1,229.00**
Price: Silver Stalker, black composite buttstock and forend **$1,179.00**

CHARLES DALY FIELD SEMIAUTO SHOTGUNS
Gauge: 12, 20, 28. **Barrel:** 22", 24", 26", 28" or 30". **Stock:** Synthetic black, Realtree Hardwoods or Advantage Timber. **Features:** Interchangeable barrels handle all loads including steel shot. Slug model has adjustable sights. Maxi-Mag is 3.5" chamber.
Price: Field Hunter, from............................ **$489.00**

CHARLES DALY SUPERIOR II SEMIAUTO SHOTGUNS
Gauge: 12, 20, 28. **Barrel:** 26", 28" or 30". **Stock:** Select Turkish walnut. **Features:** Factory ported interchangeable barrels; wide vent rib on Trap and Sport models; fluorescent red sights.
Price: Superior II Hunter, from **$649.00**
Price: Superior II Sport............................. **$709.00**
Price: Superior II Trap............................. **$739.00**

CZ921 SEMIAUTO SHOTGUN
Gauge: 12 ga., 3" chamber. **Barrel:** 28" flat ventilated rib. **Weight:** 7.3 lbs. **Length:** 49". **Stock:** Composite stock with close radius pistol grip; Speed Lock forearm; textured gripping surfaces; shim adjustable for length of pull, cast and drop; Mossy Oak® Bottomland™ camo finish; Dura-Touch® Armor Coating. **Features:** Built with a high gloss finish and has a very sleek look with attractive lines both on the alloy receiver and on the walnut stock. The modern style recoil pad provides for not only a significant reduction in perceived recoil, but it is snag free as well. A long recoil spring is located in the butt of the stock that simplifies assembly and allows it to cycle a wide variety of loads across the power spectrum both 2 ¾" and 3". In addition the rearward spring design makes required cleanings less frequent and easier when they are needed. Removal of the installed magazine plug is simple, requiring only the magazine cap to be unscrewed. Without the plug, it gives the upland hunter a 4+1 capacity. fiber optic front bead, 5 interchangeable chokes, chrome lined bbl, gloss black finish.
Price: **$509.00**

ESCORT AVERY WATERFOWL EXTREME SEMIAUTO SHOTGUN
Gauge: 12 & 20 ga., 2-3/4" through 3-1/2" chamber, multi 5+1

capacity. **Barrel:** 28". **Weight:** 7.4 lbs. **Length:** 48". **Stock:** Composite stock with close radius pistol grip; Speed Lock forearm; textured gripping surfaces; shim adjustable for length of pull, cast and drop; Mossy Oak® Bottomland™ camo finish; Dura-Touch® Armor Coating. **Features:** The addition of non-slip grip pads on the forend and pistol grip that give you a superior hold in all weather conditions. These grip panels look great and are strategically placed to give you the wet weather grip you need to control your shot. Escort shotguns also have SMART™ Valve gas pistons that regulate gas blowback to cycle every round – from 2.75 inch range loads through 3.5 inch heavy magnums. Escorts also have FAST™ loading systems that allow one-handed round changes without changing aiming position. Next, we've added Avery Outdoors' KW1™ or Buck Brush™ camo patterns to make these shotguns invisible in the field. We are also offering a HiVis MagniSight™ fiber optic, magnetic sight to enhance sight acquisition in low light conditions. Finally, we went to Hevi•Shot and got their mid-range choke tube for waterfowl to round out the perfect hunting machine.

Price: Black/Synthetic **$623.00**
Price: Avery BuckBrush Camo **$790.00**
Price: Avery KW1 Camo **$790.00**
Price: 3.5" Black/Synthetic **$748.00**
Price: 3.5" Avery KW1 Camo **$873.00**
Price: Left Black/Synthetic **$623.00**
Price: Left Avery KW1 Camo **$790.00**
Price: Left 3.5" Black Synthetic **$748.00**
Price: Left 3.5" Avery KW1 Camo **$873.00**
Price: Black/Synthetic 20 gauge **$623.00**

ESCORT SEMIAUTO SHOTGUNS

Gauge: 12, 20; 3" or 3.5" chambers. **Barrel:** 22" (Youth), 26" and 28". **Weight:** 6.7-7.8 lbs. **Stock:** Polymer in black, Shadow Grass® or Obsession® camo finish, Turkish walnut, select walnut. **Sights:** Optional HiViz Spark front. **Features:** Black-chrome or dipped-camo metal parts, top of receiver dovetailed for sight mounts, gold plated trigger, trigger guard safety, magazine cut-off. Three choke tubes (IC, M, F) except the Waterfowl/Turkey Combo, which adds a .665 turkey choke to the standard three. Waterfowl/Turkey combo is two-barrel set, 24"/26" and 26"/28". Several models have Trio recoil pad. Models are: AS, AS Select, AS Youth, AS Youth Select, PS, PS Spark and Waterfowl/Turkey. Introduced 2002. Camo introduced 2003. Youth, Slug and Obsession camo introduced 2005. Imported from Turkey by Legacy Sports International.
Price: . . . . **$425.00 to $589.00**

FRANCHI INERTIA I-12 SHOTGUN

Gauge: 12, 3" chamber. **Barrel:** 24", 26", 28" (Cyl., IC, Mod., IM, F choke tubes). **Weight:** 7.5 to 7.7. lbs. **Length:** 45" to 49". **Stock:** 14-3.8" LOP, satin walnut with checkered grip and forend, synthetic, Advantage Timber HD or Max-4 camo patterns. **Features:** Inertia-Driven action. AA walnut stock. Red bar front sight, metal mid sight. Imported from Italy by Benelli USA.
Price: Synthetic **$839.00**
Price: Camo **$949.00**
Price: Satin walnut **$949.00**

FRANCHI MODEL 720 SHOTGUNS

Gauge: 20, 3" chamber. **Barrel:** 24", 26", 28" w/(IC, Mod., F choke tubes). **Weight:** 5.9 to 6.1 lbs. **Length:** 43.25" to 49". **Stock:** WeatherCoat finish walnut, Max-4 and Timber HD camo. **Sights:** Front bead. **Features:** Made in Italy and imported by Benelli USA.
Price: **$1,049.00**
Price: Walnut, 12.5" LOP, 43.25" OAL **$999.00**

FRANCHI 48AL FIELD AND DELUXE SHOTGUNS

Gauge: 20 or 28, 2-3/4" chamber. **Barrel:** 24", 26", 28" (Full, Cyl., Mod., choke tubes). **Weight:** 5.4 to 5.7 lbs. **Length:** 42.25" to 48". **Stock:** Walnut with checkered grip and forend. **Features:** Long recoil-operated action. Chrome-lined bore; cross-bolt safety. Imported from Italy by Benelli USA.

Price: AL Field 20 ga. **$839.00**
Price: AL Deluxe 20 ga., A grade walnut **$1,099.00**
Price: AL Field 28 ga. **$999.00**

FRANCHI 720 COMPETITION SHOTGUN

Gauge: 20; 4+1. **Barrel:** 28" ported; tapered target rib and bead front sight. **Weight:** 6.2 lbs. **Stock:** Walnut with WeatherCoat. **Features:** Gas-operated, satin nickel receiver.
Price: **$1,149.00**

HARRINGTON & RICHARDSON EXCELL AUTO 5 SHOTGUNS

Gauge: 12, 3" chamber. **Barrel:** 22", 24", 28", four screw-in choke tubes (IC, M, IM, F). **Weight:** About 7 lbs. **Length:** 42.5" to 48.5" overall, depending on barrel length. **Stock:** American walnut with satin finish; cut checkering; ventilated buttpad. Synthetic stock or camo-finish. **Sights:** Metal bead front or fiber-optic front and rear. **Features:** Ventilated rib on all models except slug gun. Imported by H&R 1871, Inc.
Price: Synthetic, black, 28" barrel, 48.5" OAL **$415.00**
Price: Walnut, checkered grip/forend, 28" barrel, 48.5" OAL . **$461.00**
Price: Waterfowl, camo finish **$521.00**
Price: Turkey, camo finish, 22" barrel, fiber optic sights **$521.00**
Price: Combo, synthetic black stock, with slug barrel **$583.00**

LANBER SEMIAUTOMATIC SHOTGUNS

Gauge: 12, 3". **Barrel:** 26", 28", chrome-moly alloy steel, welded, ventilated top and side ribs. **Weight:** 6.8 lbs. **Length:** 48-3/8". **Stock:** Walnut, oiled finish, laser checkering, rubber buttplate. **Sights:** Fiber-optic front. **Features:** Extractors or automatic ejectors, control and unblocking button. Rated for steel shot. Lanber Polichokes. Imported by Lanber USA.
Price: Model 2533. . . . . **$635.00**

MOSSBERG 930 AUTOLOADER

Gauge: 12, 3" chamber, 4-shot magazine. **Barrel:** 24", 26", 28", over-bored to 10-gauge bore dimensions; factory ported, Accu-Choke tubes. **Weight:** 7.5 lbs. **Length:** 44.5" overall (28" barrel). **Stock:** Walnut or synthetic. Adjustable stock drop and cast spacer system. **Sights:** "Turkey Taker" fiber-optic, adjustable windage and elevation. Front bead fiber-optic front on waterfowl models. **Features:** Self-regulating gas system, dual gas-vent system and piston, EZ-Empty magazine button, cocking indicator. Interchangeable Accu-Choke tube set (IC, Mod, Full) for waterfowl and field models. XX-Full turkey Accu-Choke tube included with turkey models. Ambidextrous thumb-operated safety, Uni-line stock and receiver. Receiver drilled and tapped for scope base attachment, free gun lock. Introduced 2008. From O.F. Mossberg & Sons, Inc.
Price: Turkey, from **$545.00**
Price: Waterfowl, from **$545.00**
Price: Combo, from. **$604.00**
Price: Field, from. **$568.00**
Price: Slugster, from **$539.00**
Price: Turkey Pistolgrip; full pistolgrip stock, matte black or Mossy Oak Obsession camo finish overall **$628.00**
Price: Tactical; 18.5" tactical barrel, black synthetic stock and matte black finish **$653.00**
Price: Road Blocker; includes muzzle brake **$697.00**
Price: SPX; no muzzle brake, M16-style front sight, ghost ring rear sight, full pistolgrip stock, eight-round extended magazine **$667.00**
Price: SPX; conventional synthetic stock **$700.00**
Price: Home Security/Field Combo; 18.5" Cylinder bore barrel and 28" ported Field barrel; black synthetic stock and matte black finish **$604.00**

MOSSBERG MODEL 935 MAGNUM AUTOLOADING SHOTGUNS

Gauge: 12; 3" and 3.5" chamber, interchangeable. **Barrel:** 22", 24", 26", 28". **Weight:** 7.25 to 7.75 lbs. **Length:** 45" to 49" overall. **Stock:** Synthetic. **Features:** Gas-operated semiauto models in blued or camo finish. Fiber optics sights, drilled and tapped receiver, interchangeable Accu-Mag choke tubes.
Price: 935 Magnum Turkey: Realtree Hardwoods, Mossy Oak New Break-up or Mossy Oak Obsession camo overall, 24" barrel **$732.00**
Price: 935 Magnum Turkey Pistolgrip; full pistolgrip stock . . **$831.00**
Price: 935 Magnum Grand Slam: 22" barrel, Realtree Hardwoods or Mossy Oak New Break-up camo overall **$747.00**
Price: 935 Magnum Flyway: 28" barrel and Advantage Max-4 camo overall **$781.00**

SHOTGUNS—Autoloaders

Price: 935 Magnum Waterfowl: 26"or 28" barrel, matte black,
Mossy Oak New Break-up, Advantage Max-4 or Mossy
Oak Duck Blind cam overall . . . . **$613.00 to $725.00**

Price: 935 Magnum Slugster: 24" fully rifled barrel, rifle sights,
Realtree AP camo overall **$747.00**

Price: 935 Magnum Turkey/Deer Combo: interchangeable 24"
Turkey barrel, Mossy Oak New Break-up camo overall **$807.00**

Price: 935 Magnum Waterfowl/Turkey Combo: 24" Turkey
and 28" Waterfowl barrels, Mossy Oak New Break-up
finish overall **$807.00**

coverage; 23-inch barrel with fully adjustable TruGlo rifle sights.
Wingmaster HD Turkey Choke included.

Price: **$972.00**

REMINGTON MODEL 105 CTI SHOTGUN

Gauge: 12, 3" chamber, 4-shot magazine. **Barrel:** 26", 28"
(IC, Mod., Full ProBore chokes). **Weight:** 7 lbs. **Length:** 46.25"
overall (26" barrel). **Stock:** Walnut with satin finish. Checkered grip
and forend. **Sights:** Front bead. **Features:** Aircraft-grade titanium
receiver body, skeletonized receiver with carbon fiber shell. Bottom
feed and eject, target grade trigger, R3 recoil pad, FAA-approved
lockable hard case, .735" overbored barrel with lengthened forcing
cones. TriNyte coating; carbon/aramid barrel rib. Introduced 2006.
Price: **$1,559.00**

REMINGTON MODEL SPR453 SHOTGUN

Gauge: 12; 3.5" chamber, 4+1 capacity. **Barrel:** 24", 26", 28" vent
rib. **Weight:** 8 to 8.25 lbs. **Stock:** Black synthetic. **Features:** Matte
finish, dual extractors, four extended screw-in SPR choke tubes
(improved cylinder, modified, full and super-full turkey. Introduced
2006. From Remington Arms Co.
Price: Black synthetic **$497.00**

REMINGTON MODEL 11-87 SPORTSMAN SHOTGUNS

Gauge: 12, 20, 3" chamber. **Barrel:** 26", 28", RemChoke tubes.
Standard contour, vent rib. **Weight:** About 7.75 to 8.25 lbs. **Length:**
46" to 48" overall. **Stock:** Black synthetic or Mossy Oak Break Up
Mossy Oak Duck Blind, and Realtree Hardwoods HD and AP Green
HD camo finishes. **Sights:** Single bead front. **Features:** Matte-black
metal finish, magazine cap swivel studs. Sportsman Deer gun has
21-inch fully rifled barrel, cantilever scope mount.
Price: Sportsman Camo (2007), 12 or 20 ga. **$879.00**
Price: Sportsman black synthetic, 12 or 20 ga. **$772.00**
Price: Sportsman Deer FR Cantilever, 12 or 20 ga. **$892.00**
Price: Sportsman Youth Synthetic 20 ga., (2008). **$772.00**
Price: Sportsman Youth Camo 20 ga., (2008). **$879.00**
Price: Sportsman Super Magnum 12 ga., 28" barrel (2008). . .**$825.00**
Price: Sportsman Super Magnum Shurshot Turkey
12 ga., (2008) **$972.00**
Price: Sportsman Super Magnum Waterfowl 12 ga., (2008) . .**$959.00**
Price: Sportsman Compact Synthetic; black synthetic but
with reduced overall dimensions **$772.00**

REMINGTON 11-87 SPORTSMAN FIELD

Semiauto shotgun chambered in 12 and 20 ga., 2-3/4- and
3-inch. Features include 26- (20) or 28-inch (12) barrel; vent rib;
RemChokes (one supplied); satin-finished walnut stock and forend
with fleur-de-lis pattern; dual sights; nickel-plated bolt and trigger.
Price: . . . . **Starting at $845.00**

REMINGTON 11-87
SPORTSMAN SUPER MAG SYNTHETIC

Semiauto shotgun chambered in 12-ga. 3-1/2-inch. Features
include black matte synthetic stock and forend; rubber overmolded
grip panels on the stock and forend; black padded sling; HiViz
sights featuring interchangeable light pipe; 28-inch vent rib barrel;
SuperCell recoil pad; RemChoke.
Price: **$859.00**

REMINGTON 11-87 SPORTSMAN SUPER MAG SHURSHOT
TURKEY

Similar to 11-87 Sportsman Super Mag Synthetic but with
ambidextrous ShurShot pistol-grip stock; full Realtree APG HD

REMINGTON MODEL 1100 G3 SHOTGUN

Gauge: 20, 12; 3" chamber. **Barrel:** 26", 28". **Weight:** 6.75-7.6
lbs. **Stock:** Realwood semi-fancy carbon fiber laminate stock, high
gloss finish, machine cut checkering. **Features:** Gas operating
system, pressure compensated barrel, solid carbon-steel engraved
receiver, titanium coating. Action bars, trigger and extended carrier
release, action bar sleeve, action spring, locking block, hammer,
sear and magazine tube have nickel-plated, Teflon coating. R3
recoil pad, overbored (.735" dia.) vent rib barrels, ProBore choke
tubes. 20 gauge have Rem Chokes. Comes with lockable hard case.
Introduced 2006.
Price: G3, 12 or 20 ga. **$1,239.00**
Price: G3 Left Hand, 12 ga. 28" barrel (2008) **$1,329.00**

REMINGTON MODEL 1100 TARGET
SHOTGUNS

Gauge: .410 bore, 28, 20, 12. **Barrel:** 26", 27", 28", 30" light
target contoured vent rib barrel with twin bead target sights. **Stock:**
Semi-fancy American walnut stock and forend, cut checkering, high
gloss finish. **Features:** Gold-plated trigger. Four extended choke
tubes: Skeet, Improved Cylinder, Light Modified and Modified.
1100 Tournament Skeet (20 and 12 gauge) receiver is roll-marked
with "Tournament Skeet." 26" light contour, vent rib barrel has twin
bead sights, Extended Target Choke Tubes (Skeet and Improved
Cylinder). Model 1100 Premier Sporting (2008) has polished nickel
receiver, gold accents, light target contoured vent rib Rem Choke
barrels. Wood is semi-fancy American walnut stock and forend,
high-gloss finish, cut checkering, sporting clays-style recoil pad.
Gold trigger, available in 12, 20, 28 and .410 bore options, Briley
extended choke tubes, Premier Sporting hard case. Competition
model (12 gauge) has overbored (0.735" bore diameter) 30"
barrel. **Weight:** 8 lbs. 10mm target-style rib with twin beads.
Extended ProBore choke tubes in Skeet, Improved Cylinder, Light-
Modified, Modified and Full. Semi-fancy American walnut stock and
forend. Classic Trap model has polished blue receiver with scroll
engraving, gold accents, 30" low-profile, light-target contoured vent
rib barrel with standard .727" dimensions. Comes with specialized
Rem Choke trap tubes: Singles (.027"), Mid Handicap (.034"), and
Long Handicap (.041"). Monte Carlo stock of semi-fancy American
walnut, deep-cut checkering, high-gloss finish.
Price: Sporting 12, 28" barrel, 8 lbs. **$1,105.00**
Price: Sporting 20, 28" barrel, 7 lbs. **$1,105.00**
Price: Sporting 28, 27" barrel, 6.75 lbs. **$1,159.00**
Price: Sporting 410, 27" barrel, 6.75 lbs. **$1,159.00**
Price: Classic Trap, 12 ga. 30" barrel **$1,159.00**
Price: Premier Sporting (2008), from **$1,359.00**
Price: Competition, standard stock, 12 ga. 30" barrel **$1,692.00**
Price: Competition, adjustable comb **$1,692.00**
Price: Competition Synthetic **$1242.00**

REMINGTON MODEL 1100 TAC-4

Similar to Model 1100 but with 18" or 22" barrel with ventilated rib; 12
gauge 2-3/4"only; standard black synthetic stock or Knoxx SpecOps
SpeedFeed IV pistolgrip stock; RemChoke tactical choke tube; matte
black finish overall. Length is 42-1/2" and weighs 7-3/4 lbs.
Price: **$945.00**

REMINGTON MODEL SP-10 MAGNUM SHOTGUN
Gauge: 10, 3-1/2" chamber, 2-shot magazine. **Barrel:** 23", 26", 30" (full and mod. RemChokes). **Weight:** 10.75 to 11 lbs. **Length:** 47.5" overall (26" barrel). **Stock:** Walnut with satin finish (30" barrel) or camo synthetic (26" barrel). Checkered grip and forend. **Sights:** Twin bead. **Features:** Stainless steel gas system with moving cylinder; 3/8" vent rib. Receiver and barrel have matte finish. Brown recoil pad. Comes with padded Cordura nylon sling. Introduced 1989. SP-10 Magnum Camo has buttstock, forend, receiver, barrel and magazine cap covered with Mossy Oak Duck Blind Obsession camo finish; bolt body and trigger guard have matte black finish. RemChoke tube, 26" vent rib barrel with mid-rib bead and Bradley-style front sight, swivel studs and quick-detachable swivels, non-slip Cordura carrying sling. Introduced 1993.
Price: SP-10 Magnum, satin finish walnut stock **$1,772.00**
Price: SP-10 Magnum Full Camo **$1,932.00**
Price: SP-10 Magnum Waterfowl **$1,945.00**

REMINGTON VERSA MAX™ SERIES SEMIAUTO SHOTGUN
Gauge: 12 ga., 2 3/4", 3", 3 1/2" chamber. **Barrel:** 26" and 28" flat ventilated rib. **Weight:** 7.5 lbs.-7.7 lbs. **Length:** 40.25". **Stock:** Synthetic. **Features:** Reliably cycles 12-gauge rounds from 2 3/4" to 3 1/2" magnum. Versaport™ gas system regulates cycling pressure based on shell length. Reduces recoil to that of a 20-gauge. Self-cleaning - Continuously cycled thousands of rounds in torture test. Synthetic stock and fore-end with grey overmolded grips. Drilled and tapped receiver. Enlarged trigger guard opening and larger safety for easier use with gloves. TriNyte® Barrel and Nickel Teflon plated internal components offer extreme corrosion resistance. Includes 5 Flush Mount Pro Bore™ Chokes (Full, Mod, Imp Mod Light Mod, IC)
Price: 26" barrel **$1399.00**
Price: 28" barrel **$1399.00**

SAIGA AUTOLOADING SHOTGUN
Gauge: 12, 20, .410; 3" chamber. **Barrel:** 19", 24". **Weight:** 7.9 lbs. **Length: Stock:** Black synthetic. **Sights:** Fixed or adjustable leaf. **Features:** Magazine fed, 2- or 5-round capacity. Imported from Russia by Russian American Armory Co.
Price: **$347.95**

SMITH & WESSON 1000/1020/1012 SUPER SEMIAUTO SHOTGUNS
Gauge: 12, 20; 3" in 1000; 3-1/2" chamber in Super. **Barrel:** 24", 26", 28", 30". **Stock:** Walnut. Synthetic finishes are satin, black, Realtree MAX-4, Realtree APG. **Sights:** TruGlo fiber-optic. **Features:** 29 configurations. Gas operated, dual-piston action; chrome-lined barrels, five choke tubes, shim kit for adjusting stock. 20-ga. models are Model 1020 or Model 1020SS (short stock). Lifetime warranty. Introduced 2007. Imported from Turkey by Smith & Wesson.
Price: From **$623.00**

STOEGER MODEL 2000 SHOTGUNS
Gauge: 12, 3" chamber, set of five choke tubes (C, IC, M, F, XFT). **Barrel:** 24", 26", 28", 30". **Stock:** Walnut, synthetic, Timber HD, Max-4. **Sights:** Red bar front. **Features:** Inertia-recoil. Minimum recommended load: 3 dram, 1-1/8 oz. Imported by Benelli USA.

Price: Walnut **$499.00**
Price: Synthetic **$499.00**
Price: Max-4 . . . . **$549.00**
Price: Black synthetic pistol grip (2007) **$499.00**
Price: APG HD camo pistol grip (2007), 18.5" barrel **$549.00**

TRISTAR VIPER SEMIAUTOMATIC SHOTGUNS
Gauge: 12, 20; shoots 2-3/4" or 3" interchangeably. **Barrel:** 26", 28" barrels (carbon fiber only offered in 12-ga. 28" and 20-ga. 26"). **Stock:** Wood, black synthetic, Mossy Oak Duck Blind camouflage, faux carbon fiber finish (2008) with the new Comfort Touch technology. **Features:** Magazine cut-off, vent rib with matted sight plane, brass front bead (camo models have fiber-optic front sight), five round magazine-shot plug included, and 3 Beretta-style choke tubes (IC, M, F). Viper synthetic, Viper camo have swivel studs. Five-year warranty. Viper Youth models have shortened length of pull and 24" barrel. Imported by Tristar Sporting Arms Ltd.
Price: From **$469.00**
Price: Camo models (2008), from **$569.00**

TRADITIONS ALS 2100 SERIES SEMIAUTOMATIC SHOTGUNS
Gauge: 12, 3" chamber; 20, 3" chamber. **Barrel:** 24", 26", 28" (Imp. Cyl., Mod. and Full choke tubes). **Weight:** 5 lbs., 10 oz. to 6 lbs., 5 oz. **Length:** 44" to 48" overall. **Stock:** Walnut or black composite. **Features:** Gas-operated; vent rib barrel with Beretta-style threaded muzzle. Introduced 2001 by Traditions.
Price: Field Model (12 or 20 ga., 26" or 28" bbl., walnut stock) **$479.00**
Price: Youth Model (12 or 20 ga., 24" bbl., walnut stock) **$479.00**
Price: (12 or 20 ga., 26" or 28" barrel, composite stock) **$459.00**

TRADITIONS ALS 2100 TURKEY SEMIAUTOMATIC SHOTGUN
Similar to ALS 2100 Field Model except chambered in 12 gauge, 3" only with 26" barrel and Mossy Oak Break Up camo finish. Weighs 6 lbs.; 46" overall.
Price: **$519.00**

TRADITIONS ALS 2100 WATERFOWL SEMIAUTOMATIC SHOTGUN
Similar to ALS 2100 Field Model except chambered in 12 gauge, 3" only with 28" barrel and Advantage Wetlands camo finish. Weighs 6.25 lbs.; 48" overall. Multi chokes.
Price: **$529.00**

TRADITIONS ALS 2100 HUNTER COMBO
Similar to ALS 2100 Field Model except 2 barrels, 28" vent rib and 24" fully rifled deer. Weighs 6 to 6.5 lbs.; 48" overall. Choice TruGlo adj. sights or fixed cantilever mount on rifled barrel. Multi chokes.
Price: Walnut, rifle barrel **$609.00**
Price: Walnut, cantilever **$629.00**
Price: Synthetic **$579.00**

TRADITIONS ALS 2100 SLUG HUNTER SHOTGUN
Similar to ALS 2100 Field Model, 12 ga., 24" barrel, overall length 44"; weighs 6.25 lbs. Designed specifically for the deer hunter. Rifled barrel has 1 in 36" twist. Fully adjustable fiber-optic sights.
Price: Walnut, rifle barrel **$529.00**
Price: Synthetic, rifle barrel **$499.00**
Price: Walnut, cantilever **$549.00**
Price: Synthetic, cantilever **$529.00**

TRADITIONS ALS 2100 HOME SECURITY SHOTGUN
Similar to ALS 2100 Field Model, 12 ga., 20" barrel, overall length 40", weighs 6 lbs. Can be reloaded with one hand while shouldered and ontarget. Swivel studs installed in stock.
Price: **$399.00**

VERONA MODEL 401 SERIES SEMIAUTO SHOTGUNS
Gauge: 12. **Barrel:** 26", 28". **Weight:** 6.5 lbs. **Stock:** Walnut, black composite. **Sights:** Red dot. **Features:** Aluminum receivers, gas-

Prices given are believed to be accurate at time of publication however, many factors affect retail pricing so exact prices are not possible.

operated, 2-3/4" or 3" Magnum shells without adj. or Mod., 4 screw-in chokes and wrench included. Sling swivels, gold trigger. Blued barrel. Imported from Italy by Legacy Sports International.
Price: $1,199.00
Price: 406 Series $1,199.00

WEATHERBY PA-459 TR SERIES SEMIAUTO SHOTGUN
Gauge: 12 ga., 2 3/4" or 3" chamber. **Barrel:** 18 1/2". **Weight:** 7 lbs. **Length:** 20 1/2". **Stock:** Synthetic. **Features:** Ergonomic buttstock with rubber textured grip areas for snag-free shouldering, chrome-lined barrel with removable ported cylinder choke tube, mil-spec, matte black metalwork, 5+1 round capacity (2 3/4") or 4+1 capacity (3"). Made in Turkey.
Price: PA-459 TR $419.00
Price: PA-459 Digital TR $499.00

WEATHERBY SA-08 SERIES SEMIAUTO SHOTGUN
Gauge: 12 ga. & 20 ga., 3" chamber. **Barrel:** 26" and 28" flat ventilated rib. **Weight:** 6.5 lbs. **Stock:** Wood and synthetic.
Features: The SA-08 is a reliable workhorse that lets you move from early season dove loads to late fall's heaviest waterfowl loads in no time. Available with wood and synthetic stock options in 12 and 20 gauge models, including a scaled-down youth model to fit 28 ga. Comes with 3 application-specific choke tubes (SK/IC/M). Made in Turkey.
Price: SA-08 Upland $733.00
Price: SA-08 Synthetic (New 2011) $509.00
Price: SA-08 Waterfowler 3.0 . . . . $710.00
Price: SA-08 Synthetic Youth $565.00
Price: SA-08 Deluxe $754.00
Price: SA-08 Entre Rios $749.00

WINCHESTER SUPER X3 SHOTGUNS
Gauge: 12, 3" and 3.5" chambers. **Barrel:** 26", 28", .742" back-bored; Invector Plus choke tubes. **Weight:** 7 to 7.25 lbs. **Stock:** Composite, 14.25"x1.75"x2". Mossy Oak New Break-Up camo with Dura-Touch Armor Coating. Pachmayr Decelerator buttpad with hard heel insert, customizable length of pull. **Features:** Alloy magazine tube, gunmetal grey Perma-Cote UT finish, self-adjusting Active Valve gas action, lightweight recoil spring system. Electroless nickel-plated bolt, three choke tubes, two length-of-pull stock spacers, drop and cast adjustment spacers, sling swivel studs. Introduced 2006. Made in Belgium, assembled in Portugal by U.S. Repeating Arms Co.
Price: Composite . . . . $1,119.00 to $1.239.00
Price: Cantilever Deer. $1,179.00
Price: Waterfowl w/Mossy Oak Brush camo, intr. 2007 . . . . $1,439.00
Price: Field model, walnut stock, intr. 2007 . . . . $1,439.00
Price: Gray Shadow $1,299.00
Price: All-Purpose Field $1,439.00
Price: Classic Field $1,159.00
Price: NWTF Cantiliever Extreme Turkey $1,499.00

WINCHESTER SUPER X3 FLANIGUN EXHIBITION/SPORTING
Similar to X3 but .742" backbored barrel, red-toned receiver, black Dura-Touch Armor Coated synthetic stock.
Price: $1,459.00

WINCHESTER SUPER X2 AUTO SHOTGUNS
Gauge: 12, 3", 3-1/2" chamber. **Barrel:** Belgian, 24", 26", 28"; Invector Plus choke tubes. **Weight:** 7-1/4 to 7.5 lbs. **Stock:** 14.25"x1.75"x2". Walnut or black synthetic. **Features:** Gas-operated action shoots

all loads without adjustment; vent rib barrels; 4-shot magazine. Introduced 1999. Assembled in Portugal by U.S. Repeating Arms Co.
Price: Universal Hunter T $1,252.00
Price: NWTF Turkey, 3-1/2", Mossy Oak Break-Up camo . . $1,236.00
Price: Universal Hunter Model $1,252.00

WINCHESTER SUPER X2 SPORTING CLAYS AUTO SHOTGUNS
Similar to the Super X2 except has two gas pistons (one for target loads, one for heavy 3" loads), adjustable comb system and high-post rib. Back-bored barrel with Invector Plus choke tubes. Offered in 28" and 30" barrels. Introduced 2001. From U.S. Repeating Arms Co.
Price: Super X2 sporting clays $999.00
Price: Signature red stock. $1,015.00
Price: Practical MK I, composite stock, TruGlo sights $1,116.00

BENELLI SUPERNOVA PUMP SHOTGUNS
Gauge: 12; 3.5" chamber. **Barrel:** 24", 26", 28". **Length:** 45.5-49.5". **Stock:** Synthetic; Max-4 , Timber, APG HD (2007). **Sights:** Red bar front, metal midbead. **Features:** 2-3/4", 3" chamber (3-1/2" 12 ga. only). Montefeltro rotating bolt design with dual action bars, magazine cut-off, synthetic trigger assembly, adjustable combs, shim kit, choice of buttstocks. 4-shot magazine. Introduced 2006. Imported from Italy by Benelli USA.
Price: Synthetic ComforTech **$499.00**
Price: Camo ComforTech **$599.00**
Price: SteadyGrip . . . .**$599.00 to $619.00**
Price: Tactical, Ghost Ring sight. . . . .**$459.00 to $499.00**
Price: Rifled Slug ComforTech, synthetic stock (2007) **$670.00**
Price: Tactical desert camo pistol grip, 18" barrel (2007) **$589.00**

BENELLI NOVA PUMP SHOTGUNS
Gauge: 12, 20. **Barrel:** 24", 26", 28". **Stock:** Black synthetic, Max-4, Timber and APG HD. **Sights:** Red bar. **Features:** 2-3/ 4", 3" chamber (3-1/2" 12 ga. only). Montefeltro rotating bolt design with dual action bars, magazine cut-off, synthetic trigger assembly, 4-shot magazine. Introduced 1999. Field & Slug Combo has 24" barrel and rifled bore; open rifle sights; synthetic stock; weighs 8.1 lbs. Imported from Italy by Benelli USA.
PrPrice: Max-4 HD camo stock **$499.00**
Price: H$_2$0 model, black synthetic, matte nickel finish. **$599.00**
Price: APG HD stock , 20 ga. (2007) **$529.00**
Price: Tactical, 18.5" barrel, Ghost Ring sight **$429.00**
Price: Black synthetic youth stock, 20 ga. **$429.00**
Price: APG HD stock (2007), 20 ga.. . . . .**$529.00**

BROWNING BPS PUMP SHOTGUNS
Gauge: 10, 12, 3-1/2" chamber; 12, 16, or 20, 3" chamber (2-3/4" in target guns), 28, 2-3/4" chamber, 5-shot magazine, .410, 3" chamber. **Barrel:** 10 ga.-24" Buck Special, 28", 30", 32" Invector; 12, 20 ga.-22", 24", 26", 28", 30", 32" (Imp. Cyl., Mod. or Full), .410-26" barrel. (Imp. Cyl., Mod. and Full choke tubes.) Also available with Invector choke tubes, 12 or 20 ga.; Upland Special has 22" barrel with Invector tubes. BPS 3" and 3-1/2" have back-bored barrel. **Weight:** 7 lbs., 8 oz. (28" barrel). **Length:** 48.75" overall (28" barrel). **Stock:** 14.25"x1.5"x2.5". Select walnut, semi-beavertail forend, full pistol grip stock. **Features:** All 12 gauge 3" guns except Buck Special and game guns have back-bored barrels with Invector Plus choke tubes. Bottom feeding and ejection, receiver top safety, high post vent rib. Double action bars eliminate binding. Vent rib barrels only. All 12 and 20 gauge guns with 3" chamber available with fully engraved receiver flats at no extra cost. Each gauge has its own unique game scene. Introduced 1977. Stalker is same gun as the standard BPS except all exposed metal parts have a matte blued finish and the stock has a black finish with a black recoil pad. Available in 10 ga. (3-1/2") and 12 ga. with 3" or 3-1/2" chamber, 22", 28", 30" barrel with Invector choke system. Introduced 1987. Rifled Deer Hunter is similar to the standard BPS except has newly designed receiver/magazine tube/barrel mounting system to eliminate play, heavy 20.5" barrel with rifle-type sights with adjustable rear, solid receiver scope mount, "rifle" stock dimensions for scope or open sights, sling swivel studs. Gloss or matte finished wood with checkering, polished blue metal. Introduced 1992. Imported from Japan by Browning.
Price: Stalker (black syn. stock), 12 ga., from **$549.00**
Price: Rifled Deer Hunter (22" rifled bbl., cantilever mount),
    intr. 2007. . . . .**$699.00**
Price: Trap, intr. 2007. . . . .**$729.00**

Price: Hunter, 16 ga., intr. 2008 . . . .**$569.00**
Price: Upland Special, 16 ga., intr. 2008 . . . .**$569.00**
Price: Mossy Oak New Breakup, 3", 12 ga. only **$679.00**
Price: Mossy Oak New Breakup, 3-1/2", 12 ga. only **$799.00**
Price: Mossy Oak Duck Blind finish overall, 3" **$679.00**
Price: Mossy Oak Duck Blind finish overall, 3-1/2" **$799.00**
Price: Rifled Deer Mossy Oak New Break-Up, 12 ga. **$719.00**
Price: Rifled Deer Mossy Oak New Break-Up, 20 ga. **$839.00**
Price: Micro Trap, similar to BPS Trap but with compact
    dimensions (13-3/4" length of pull, 48-1/4" overall
    length), 12 gauge only **$729.00**

BROWNING BPS 10 GAUGE CAMO PUMP SHOTGUN
Similar to the standard BPS except completely covered with Mossy Oak Shadow Grass camouflage. Available with 26" and 28" barrel. Introduced 1999. Imported by Browning
Price: **$799.00**

BROWNING BPS NWTF TURKEY SERIES PUMP SHOTGUN
Similar to the standard BPS except has full coverage Mossy Oak Break-Up camo finish on synthetic stock, forearm and exposed metal parts. Offered in 12 gauge, 3" or 3-1/2" chamber; 24" bbl. has extra-full choke tube and HiViz fiber-optic sights. Introduced 2001. From Browning.
Price: 12 ga., 3-1/2" chamber **$859.00**
Price: 12 ga., 3" chamber **$709.00**

BROWNING BPS MICRO PUMP SHOTGUN
Similar to the BPS Stalker except 20 ga. only, 22" Invector barrel, stock has pistol grip with recoil pad. Length of pull is 13.25"; weighs 6 lbs., 12 oz. Introduced 1986.
Price: **$569.00**

BROWING BPS ALL WEATHER HIGH CAPACITY PUMP SHOTGUN
Gauge: 12 ga. 3" chamber. **Barrel:** 20" fixed Cylinder choke; stainless Steel; Matte finish. **Weight:** 7 lbs. 2 ozs. **Length:** 40.75". **Stock:** Black composite on All Weather with matte finish. **Features:** Forged and machined steel; satin nickel finish. Bottom ejection; dual steel action bars; top tang safety. HiViz Tactical fiber-optic front sight; stainless internal mechanism; swivel studs installed. 5 total magazine capacity.
Price: From **$689.00**

CHARLES DALY FIELD PUMP SHOTGUNS
Gauge: 12, 20. **Barrel:** Interchangeable 18.5", 24", 26", 28", 30" multi-choked. **Weight:** NA. **Stock:** Synthetic, various finishes, recoil pad. **Receiver:** Machined aluminum. **Features:** Field Tactical and Slug models come with adustable sights; Youth models may be upgraded to full size. Imported from Turkey by K.B.I., Inc.
Price: Field Tactical **$274.00**
Price: Field Hunter **$499.00**
Price: Field Hunter, Realtree Hardwood. **$289.00**
Price: Field Hunter Advantage **$289.00**

CHARLES DALY
MAXI-MAG PUMP SHOTGUNS
Gauge: 12 gauge, 3-1/2". **Barrel:** 24", 26", 28"; multi-choke system. **Weight:** NA. **Stock:** Synthetic black, Realtree Hardwoods, or Advantage Timber receiver, aluminum alloy. **Features:** Handles 2-3/4", 3" and 3-1/2" loads. Interchangeable ported barrels; Turkey

package includes sling, HiViz sights, XX Full choke. Imported from Turkey by K.B.I., Inc.
Price: Field Hunter **$329.00**
Price: Field Hunter Advantage **$319.00**
Price: Field Hunter Hardwoods. **$319.00**
Price: Field Hunter Turkey **$434.00**

EMF OLD WEST PUMP (SLIDE ACTION) SHOTGUN
Gauge: 12. **Barrel:** 20". **Weight:** 7 lbs. **Length:** 39-1/2" overall.
Stock: Smooth walnut with cushioned pad. **Sights:** Front bead.
Features: Authentic reproduction of Winchester 1897 pump shotgun; blue receiver and barrel; standard modified choke. Introduced 2006. Imported from China for EMF by TTN.
Price: **$449.90**

ESCORT PUMP SHOTGUNS
Gauge: 12, 20; 3" chamber. **Barrel:** 18" (AimGuard and MarineGuard), 22" (Youth Pump), 26", and 28" lengths. **Weight:** 6.7-7.0 lbs. **Stock:** Polymer in black, Shadow Grass® camo or Obsession® camo finish. Two adjusting spacers included. Youth model has Trio recoil pad. **Sights:** Bead or Spark front sights, depending on model. AimGuard and MarineGuard models have blade front sights. **Features:** Black-chrome or dipped camo metal parts, top of receiver dovetailed for sight mounts, gold plated trigger, trigger guard safety, magazine cut-off. Three choke tubes (IC, M, F) except AimGuard/MarineGuard which are cylinder bore. Models include: FH, FH Youth, AimGuard and Marine Guard. Introduced in 2003. Imported from Turkey by Legacy Sports International.
Price: . . . .**$389.00 to $469.00**

HARRINGTON & RICHARDSON PARDNER PUMP FIELD GUN FULL-DIP CAMO
Gauge: 12, 20; 3" chamber. **Barrel:** 28" fully rifled. **Weight:** 7.5 lbs. **Length:** 48-1/8" overall. **Stock:** Synthetic or hardwood. **Sights:** NA. **Features:** Steel receiver, double action bars, cross-bolt safety, easy takedown, vent rib, screw-in Modified choke tube. Ventilated recoil pad and grooved forend with Realtree APG-HDTM full camo dip finish.
Price: Full camo version **$278.00**

IAC MODEL 87W-1 LEVER-ACTION SHOTGUN
Gauge: 12; 2-3/4" chamber only. **Barrel:** 20" with fixed Cylinder choke. **Weight:** NA. **Length:** NA. **Stock:** American walnut. **Sights:** Bead front. **Features:** Modern replica of Winchester Model 1887 lever-action shotgun. Includes five-shot tubular magazine, pivoting split-lever design to meet modern safety requirements. Imported by Interstate Arms Corporation.
Price: **$429.95**

ITHACA GUN COMPANY DEERSLAYER III SLUG SHOTGUN
Gauge: 12, 20; 3" chamber. **Barrel:** 26" fully rifled, heavy fluted with 1:28 twist for 12 ga.; 1:24 for 20 ga. **Weight:** 8.14 lbs. to 9.5 lbs. with scope mounted. **Length:** 45.625" overall. **Stock:** Fancy black walnut stock and forend. **Sights:** NA. **Features:** Updated, slug-only version of the classic Model 37. Bottom ejection, blued barrel and receiver.
Price: **$1,189.00**

ITHACA GUN COMPANY MODEL 37 28 GAUGE SHOTGUN
Gauge: 28. **Barrel:** 26" or 28". **Weight:** NA. **Length:** NA. **Stock:** Black walnut stock and forend. **Sights:** NA. **Features:** Scaled down receiver with traditional Model 37 bottom ejection and easy takedown. Available in Fancy "A," Fancy "AA," and Fancy "AAA" grades with increasingly elaborate receiver engraving and decoration. Special order only.
Price: Fancy "A" grade **$999.00**

MOSSBERG MODEL 835 ULTI-MAG PUMP SHOTGUNS
Gauge: 12, 3-1/2" chamber. **Barrel:** Ported 24" rifled bore, 24", 28", Accu-Mag choke tubes for steel or lead shot. **Weight:** 7.75 lbs. **Length:** 48.5" overall. **Stock:** 14"x1.5"x2.5". Dual Comb. Cut-checkered hardwood or camo synthetic; both have recoil pad. **Sights:** White bead front, brass mid-bead; fiber-optic rear. **Features:** Shoots 2-3/4", 3" or 3-1/2" shells. Back-bored and ported barrel to reduce recoil, improve patterns. Ambidextrous thumb safety, twin extractors, dual slide bars. Mossberg Cablelock included. Introduced 1988.
Price: Thumbhole Turkey **$674.00**
Price: Tactical Turkey **$636.00**
Price: Synthetic Thumbhole Turkey, from **$493.00**
Price: Turkey, from **$487.00**
Price: Waterfowl, from **$437.00**
Price: Combo, from. **$559.00**

MOSSBERG 835 ULTI-MAG SPECIAL PURPOSE SERIES PUMP SHOTGUN
Gauge: 12 ga., 2 3/4", 3", 3 1/2" chamber. **Barrel:** 20", 24", 26" and 28" flat ventilated rib. **Weight:** 7.25 lbs. **Length:** 40.25". **Stock:** Large selection of wood, synthetic and camo pattern models available. **Features:** Each and every component of the 835® was designed and tested around the demanding requirements of high-power 3 1/2" 12 gauge magnum ammo. Unlike other new-comers to this specialized market, who just modified their existing 2 3/4" - 3" shotguns, the 835® was designed to stay the course. The robust bolt, receiver, and other components are specifically sized for the longer shells and the downrange punishment they dish out. In addition, all 835® Ulti-Mag® smooth bore barrels are overbored to 10 gauge bore dimensions, reducing recoil and producing exceptionally uniform patterns from both light and heavy shot charges. Working in tandem with the performance-enhancing overbored barrels, strategic placement of eight ports on each side of the 835® barrel direct gasses upward and outward to not only reduce felt recoil, but to minimize muzzle jump for quick second shot recovery.
Price: Turkey THUG Series **$642.00**
Price: Thumbhole Turkey Series **$674.00**
Price: Tactical Turkey™ Series **$674.00**
Price: Synthetic Thumbhole Turkey Series. . . . .**$522.00 - $603.00**

MOSSBERG MODEL 500 JIC II
Takedown pump-action shotgun chambered in 3-inch 12 gauge. Similar to other 500 models but features pistol grip, matte black finish overall and comes packaged in black nylon zippered case.
Price: **$435.00**

MOSSBERG MODEL 500 SPORTING PUMP SHOTGUNS
Gauge: 12, 20, .410, 3" chamber. **Barrel:** 18.5" to 28" with fixed or Accu-Choke, plain or vent rib. **Weight:** 6-1/4 lbs. (.410), 7-1/4

SHOTGUNS—Slide & Lever Actions

lbs. (12). **Length:** 48" overall (28" barrel). **Stock:** 14"x1.5"x2.5". Walnut-stained hardwood, black synthetic, Mossy Oak Advantage camouflage. Cut-checkered grip and forend. **Sights:** White bead front, brass mid-bead; fiber-optic. **Features:** Ambidextrous thumb safety, twin extractors, disconnecting safety, dual action bars. Quiet Carry forend. Many barrels are ported. From Mossberg.

Price: Turkey **$410.00**
Price: Waterfowl, from **$406.00**
Price: Combo, from **$391.00**
Price: Field, from **$354.00**
Price: Slugster, from **$354.00**

MOSSBERG 510 MINI BANTAM PUMP SHOTGUN

Gauge: 20 & .410 ga., 3" chamber. **Barrel:** 18 1/2 " vent-rib. **Weight:** 5 lbs. **Length:** 34 3/4". **Stock:** Synthetic withoption Mossy Oak Break-Up Infinity **Features:** Available in either 20 gauge or .410 bore, the Mini features an 18 1/2 " vent-rib barrel with dual-bead sights. Parents don't have to worry about their young shooter growing out of this gun too quick, the adjustable classic stock can be adjusted from 10 1/2" to 11 1/2" length of pull so the Mini can grow with your child. This adjustability also helps provide a proper fit for young shooters and allowing for a more safe and enjoyable shooting experience. Weighing in at 5 pounds and only 34 3/4" long, the 510 Mini proves that big things do come in small packages.

Price: Standard Stock **$375.00**

MOSSBERG MODEL 500 BANTAM PUMP SHOTGUN

Same as the Model 500 Sporting Pump except 12 or 20 gauge, 22" vent rib Accu-Choke barrel with choke tube set; has 1" shorter stock, reduced length from pistol grip to trigger, reduced forend reach. Introduced 1992.
Price: **$354.00**
Price: Super Bantam (2008), from **$338.00**

NEW ENGLAND PARDNER PUMP SHOTGUN

Gauge: 12 ga., 3". **Barrel:** 28" vent rib, screw-in Modified choke tube. **Weight:** 7.5 lbs. **Length:** 48.5". **Stock:** American walnut, grooved forend, ventilated recoil pad. **Sights:** Bead front. **Features:** Machined steel receiver, double action bars, five-shot magazine.
Price: **$200.00**

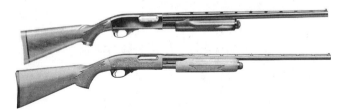

REMINGTON MODEL 870 WINGMASTER SHOTGUNS

Gauge: 12, 20, 28 ga., .410 bore. **Barrel:** 25", 26", 28", 30" (RemChokes). **Weight:** 7-1/4 lbs. **Length:** 46", 48". **Stock:** Walnut, hardwood. **Sights:** Single bead (Twin bead Wingmaster). **Features:** Light contour barrel. Double action bars, cross-bolt safety, blue finish. LW is 28 gauge and .410-bore only, 25" vent rib barrel with RemChoke tubes, high-gloss wood finish. Limited Edition Model 870 Wingmaster 100th Anniversary Commemorative Edition (2008 only) is 12 gauge with gold centennial logo, "100 Years of Remington Pump Shotguns" banner. Gold-plated trigger, American B Grade walnut stock and forend, high-gloss finish, fleur-de-lis checkering.

Price: Wingmaster, walnut, blued **$785.00**
Price: LW .410-bore **$839.00**
Price: 100th Anniversary (2008), 12 ga., 28" barrel **$1,035.00**

REMINGTON MODEL 870 MARINE MAGNUM SHOTGUN

Similar to 870 Wingmaster except all metal plated with electroless nickel, black synthetic stock and forend. Has 18" plain barrel (cyl.), bead front sight, 7-shot magazine. Introduced 1992. XCS version with TriNyte corrosion control introduced 2007.
Price: **$772.00**

REMINGTON MODEL 870 CLASSIC TRAP SHOTGUN

Similar to Model 870 Wingmaster except has 30" vent rib, light contour barrel, singles, mid- and long-handicap choke tubes, semi-fancy American walnut stock, high-polish blued receiver with engraving. Chamber 2.75". From Remington Arms Co.
Price: **$1,039.00**
Price: XCS (2007) **$899.00**

REMINGTON MODEL 870 EXPRESS SHOTGUNS

Similar to Model 870 Wingmaster except laminate, synthetic black, or camo stock with solid, black recoil pad and pressed checkering on grip and forend. Outside metal surfaces have black oxide finish. Comes with 26" or 28" vent rib barrel with mod. RemChoke tube. ShurShot Turkey (2008) has ShurShot synthetic pistol-grip thumbhole design, extended forend, Mossy Oak Obsession camouflage, matte black metal finish, 21" vent rib barrel, twin beads, Turkey Extra Full Rem Choke tube. Receiver drilled and tapped for mounting optics. ShurShot FR CL (Fully Rifled Cantilever, 2008) includes compact 23" fully-rifled barrel with integrated cantilever scope mount.

Price: 12 and 20 ga., laminate or synthetic right-hand stock . . **$383.00**
Price: 12 or 20 ga., laminate or synthetic left-hand stock **$409.00**
Price: Express Synthetic, 12 ga., 18" barrel (2007) **$383.00**
Price: Express Synthetic, 20 ga., 7 round capacity, from **$385.00**
Price: Express Synthetic Deer FR 12 ga., rifle sights **$425.00**
Price: Express Laminate Deer FR 12 ga., rifle sights **$416.00**
Price: Express Synthetic or Laminate Turkey 12 ga.,
    21" barrel **$388.00**
Price: Express Camo Turkey 12 ga., 21" barrel **$445.00**
Price: Express Combo Turkey/Deer Camo 12 ga. **$612.00**
Price: Express Synthetic Youth Combo 20 ga. **$543.00**
Price: Express Magnum ShurShot Turkey (2008) **$492.00**
Price: Express Magnum ShurShot FR CL (2008) **$500.00**
Price: Express ShurShot Synthetic Cantilever; 12 or 20 ga.
    with ShurShot stock and cantilever scope mount **$532.00**
Price: Express Compact Deer; 20 ga., similar to 870 Express
    Laminate Deer but with smaller dimensions **$395.00**
Price: Express Compact Pink Camo; 20 ga. **$429.00**
Price: Express Compact Synthetic; matte black synthetic
    stock **$383.00**
Price: Express Compact Camo; camo buttstock and forend . **$429.00**
Price: Express Compact Jr.; Shorter barrel and LOP **$383.00**

Prices given are believed to be accurate at time of publication however, many factors affect retail pricing so exact prices are not possible.

REMINGTON MODEL 870 EXPRESS SUPER MAGNUM SHOTGUN

Similar to Model 870 Express except 28" vent rib barrel with 3-1/2" chamber, vented recoil pad. Introduced 1998. Model 870 Express Super Magnum Waterfowl (2008) is fully camouflaged with Mossy Oak Duck Blind pattern, 28-inch vent rib Rem Choke barrel, "Over Decoys" Choke tube (.007") fiber-optic HiViz single bead front sight; front and rear sling swivel studs, padded black sling.

Price: **$431.00**
Price: Super Magnum synthetic, 26" **$431.00**
Price: Super Magnum turkey camo (full-coverage
RealTree Advantage camo), 23" **$564.00**
Price: Super Magnum combo (26" with Mod. RemChoke
and 20" fully rifled deer barrel with 3" chamber
and rifle sights; wood stock) **$577.00**
Price: Super Magnum Waterfowl (2008). **$577.00**

REMINGTON MODEL 870 SPECIAL PURPOSE SHOTGUNS (SPS)

Similar to the Model 870 Express synthetic, chambered for 12 ga. 3" and 3-1/2" shells, has Realtree Hardwoods HD or APG HD camo-synthetic stock and metal treatment, TruGlo fiber-optic sights. Introduced 2001. SPS Max Gobbler introduced 2007. Knoxx SpecOps adjustable stock, Williams Fire Sights fiber-optic sights, R3 recoil pad, Realtree APG HD camo. Drilled and tapped for Weaver-style rail

Price: SPS 12 ga. 3" **$671.00**
Price: SPS Super Mag Max Gobbler (2007). **$819.00**
Price: SPS Super Mag Max Turkey ShurShot 3-1/2" (2008) . .**$644.00**
Price: SPS Synthetic ShurShot FR Cantilever 3" (2008) **$671.00**

REMINGTON MODEL 870 EXPRESS TACTICAL

Similar to Model 870 but in 12 gauge only (2-2/4" and 3" interchangeably) with 18.5" barrel, Tactical RemChoke extended/ported choke tube, black synthetic buttstock and forend, extended magazine tube, gray powdercoat finish overall. 38.5" overall length, weighs 7.5 lbs.

Price: **$372.00**
Price: Model 870 TAC Desert Recon; desert camo stock and
sand-toned metal surfaces **$692.00**
Price: Model 870 Express Tactical with Ghost Ring Sights; Top-
mounted accessories rail and XS ghost ring rear sight **$505.00**

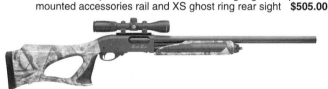

REMINGTON MODEL 870 SPS SHURSHOT SYNTHETIC SUPER SLUG

Gauge: 12; 2-3/4" and 3" chamber, interchangeable. **Barrel:** 25.5" extra-heavy, fully rifled pinned to receiver. **Weight:** 7-7/8 lbs. **Length:** 47" overall. **Features:** Pump-action model based on 870 platform. SuperCell recoil pad. Drilled and tapped for scope mounts with Weaver rail included. Matte black metal surfaces, Mossy Oak Treestand Shurshot buttstock and forend.

Price: . . . . **NA**
Price: 870 SPS ShurShot Synthetic Cantilever; cantilever scope
mount and Realtree Hardwoods camo buttstock and forend . . .
$532.00
Price: 870 SPS ShurShot Synthetic Turkey; adjustable sights and
APG HD camo buttstock and forend **$532.00**

REMINGTON 870 EXPRESS SYNTHETIC SUPER MAG TURKEY-WATERFOWL CAMO

Pump action shotgun chambered in 12-ga., 2-3/4 to 3-1/2 inch.

Features include full Mossy Oak Bottomland camo coverage; 26-inch barrel with HiViz fiber-optics sights; Wingmaster HD Waterfowl and Turkey Extra Full RemChokes; SuperCell recoil pad; drilled and tapped receiver.

Price: **$601.00**

REMINGTON 870 EXPRESS SYNTHETIC TURKEY CAMO

Pump action shotgun chambered for 2-3/4 and 3-inch 12-ga. Features include 21-inch vent rib bead-sighted barrel; standard Express finish on barrel and receiver; Turkey Extra Full RemChoke; synthetic stock with integrated sling swivel attachment.

Price: **$445.00**

REMINGTON 870 SUPER MAG TURKEY-PREDATOR CAMO WITH SCOPE

Pump action shotgun chambered in 12-ga., 2-3/4 to 3-1/2 inch. Features include 20-inch barrel; TruGlo red/green selectable illuminated sight mounted on pre-installed Weaver-style rail; black padded sling; Wingmaster HD™ Turkey/Predator RemChoke; full Mossy Oak Obsession camo coverage; ShurShot pistol grip stock with black overmolded grip panels; TruGlo 30mm Red/Green Dot Scope pre-mounted.

Price: **$679.00**

REMINGTON MODEL 887 NITRO MAG PUMP SHOTGUN

Gauge: 12; 3.5", 3", and 2-3/4" chambers. **Barrel:** 28". **Features:** Pump-action model based on the Model 870. Interchangeable shells, black matte ArmoLokt rustproof coating throughout. SuperCell recoil pad. Solid rib and Hi-Viz front sight with interchangeable light tubes. Black synthetic stock with contoured grip panels.

Price: **$399.00**
Price: Model 887 Nitro Mag Waterfowl, Advantage
Max-4 camo overall **$532.00**

REMINGTON 887 BONECOLLECTOR EDITION

Pump action shotgun chambered in 12-ga., 2-3/4 to 3-1/2 inch. Features include ArmorLokt rustproof coating; synthetic stock and forend; 26-inch barrel; full camo finish; integral swivel studs; SuperCell recoil pad; solid rib and HiViz front sight. Bone Collector logo.

Price: **$623.00**

REMINGTON 887 NITRO MAG CAMO COMBO

Pump action shotgun chambered in 12-ga., 2-3/4 to 3-1/2 inch. Features include 22-inch turkey barrel with HiViz fiber-optic rifle sights and 28-inch waterfowl with a HiViz sight; extended Waterfowl

SHOTGUNS—Slide & Lever Actions

and Super Full Turkey RemChokes are included; SuperCell recoil pad; synthetic stock and forend with specially contoured grip panels; full camo coverage.
Price: **$693.00**

STEVENS MODEL 350 PUMP SHOTGUN
Pump-action shotgun chambered for 2.5- and 3-inch 12-ga. Features include all-steel barrel and receiver; bottom-load and -eject design; black synthetic stock; 5+1 capacity.
Price: Field Model with 28-inch barrel, screw-in choke **$267.00**
Price: Security Model with 18-inch barrel, fixed choke **$241.00**
Price: Combo Model with Field and Security barrels **$307.00**
Price: Security Model with 18.25-inch barrel w/ghost ring rear sight. **$254.00**

STOEGER MODEL P350 SHOTGUNS
Gauge: 12, 3.5" chamber, set of five choke tubes (C, IC, M, IM, XF). **Barrel:** 18.5",24", 26", 28". **Stock:** Black synthetic, Timber HD, Max-4 HD, APG HD camos. **Sights:** Red bar front. **Features:** Inertia-recoil, mercury recoil reducer, pistol grip stocks. Imported by Benelli USA.
Price: Synthetic. **$329.00**
Price: Max-4, Timber HD **$429.00**
Price: Black synthetic pistol grip (2007) **$329.00**
Price: APG HD camo pistol grip (2007) **$429.00**

WEATHERBY PA-08 SERIES PUMP SHOTGUN
Gauge: 12 ga. chamber. **Barrel:** 26" and 28" flat ventilated rib. **Weight:** 6.5 lbs. -7 lbs. **Stock:** Walnut. **Features:** The PA-08 # Walnut stock with gloss finish, all metalwork is gloss black for a distinctive look, vented top rib dissipates heat and aids in target acquisition. Comes with 3 application-specific choke tubes (IC/M/F). Made in Turkey.
Price: PA-08 Upland **$409.00**
Price: PA-08 Synthetic (New 2011) **$329.00**

WINCHESTER SUPER X PUMP SHOTGUNS
Gauge: 12, 3" chambers. **Barrel:** 18"; 26" and 28" barrels are .742" back-bored, chrome plated; Invector Plus choke tubes. **Weight:** 7 lbs. **Stock:** Walnut or composite. **Features:** Rotary bolt, four lugs, dual steel action bars. Walnut Field has gloss-finished walnut stock and forearm, cut checkering. Black Shadow Field has composite stock and forearm, non-glare matte finish barrel and receiver. Speed Pump Defender has composite stock and forearm, chromed plated, 18" cylinder choked barrel, non-glare metal surfaces, five-shot

magazine, grooved forearm. Weight, 6.5 lbs. Reintroduced 2008. Made in U.S.A. from Winchester Repeating Arms Co.
Price: Black Shadow Field **$359.00**
Price: Defender. **$319.00**

WINCHESTER SXP CAMP/FIELD COMBO PUMP SHOTGUN
Gauge: 12 ga., 3" chamber. **Barrel:** 26" or 28" flat ventilated rib. **Weight:** 6 lbs. 12 ozs. - 6 lbs. 14 ozs. **Length:** 46.5"-48.5". **Stock:** Black composite. **Features:** Non-glare matte finish; Chrome plated chamber and bore; Black chrome on exterior surface. Three Invector Plus™ choke tubes (F,M,IC); Inflex Technology recoil pad; Sling swivel studs; Ivory front bead sight; 18" Defender barrel included; 5 +1 magazine capacity with 2 3/4" shells.
Price: **$469.00**

Prices given are believed to be accurate at time of publication however, many factors affect retail pricing so exact prices are not possible.

BERETTA DT10 TRIDENT SHOTGUNS
Gauge: 12, 2-3/4", 3" chambers. **Barrel:** 28", 30", 32", 34"; competition-style vent rib; fixed or Optima choke tubes. **Weight:** 7.9 to 9 lbs. **Stock:** High-grade walnut stock with oil finish; hand-checkered grip and forend, adjustable stocks available. **Features:** Detachable, adjustable trigger group, raised and thickened receiver, forend iron has adjustment nut to guarantee wood-to-metal fit. Introduced 2000. Imported from Italy by Beretta USA.
Price: DT10 Trident Trap, adjustable stock. **$7,400.00**
Price: DT10 Trident Skeet **$7,900.00**
Price: DT10 Trident Sporting, from. **$6,975.00**

BERETTA F3 SUPERSPORT O/U SHOTGUN
Gauge: 12 ga., 3" chamber. **Barrel:** 32". **Weight:** 9 lbs. **Stock:** Adustable semi-custom, turkish walnut wood grade: 4. **Features:** The latest addition to the F3 family is the F3 SuperSport. The perfect blend of overall weight, balance and weight distribution make the F3 SuperSport the ideal competitor. Briley Spectrum-5 chokes, free floating barrels, adjustable barrel hanger system on o/u, chrome plated barrels full length, revolutionary ejector ball system, barrels finished in a powder coated nitride, selectable competition trigger.
Price: From **$6,525.00**

BERETTA SV10 PERENNIA O/U SHOTGUN
Gauge: 12, 3" chambers. **Barrel:** 26", 28", 30". Optima-Bore profile, polished blue. Bore diameter 18.6mm (0.73 in.) Self-adjusting dual conical longitudinal locking lugs, oversized monobloc bearing shoulders, replaceable hinge pins. Ventilated top rib, 6x6mm. Long guided extractors, automatic ejection or mechanical extraction. Optimachoke tubes. **Weight:** 7.3 lbs. **Stock:** Quick take-down stock with pistol grip or English straight stock. Kick-off recoil reduction system available on request on Q-Stock. **Length of pull:** 14.7", drop at comb, 1.5", drop at heel, 2.36" or 1.38"/2.17". Semibeavertail forend with elongated forend lever. New checkering pattern, matte oil finish, rubber pad. **Features:** Floral motifs and game scenes on side panels; nickel-based protective finish, arrowhead-shaped sideplates, solid steel alloy billet. Kick-Off recoil reduction mechanism available on select models. Fixed chokes on request, removable trigger group, titanium single selective trigger. Manual or automatic safety, newly designed safety and selector lever. Gel-Tek recoil pad available on request. Polypropylene case, 5 chokes with spanner, sling swivels, plastic pad, Beretta gun oil. Introduced 2008. Imported from Italy by Beretta USA.
Price: From **$3,250.00**

BERETTA SERIES 682 GOLD E SKEET, TRAP, SPORTING O/U SHOTGUNS
Gauge: 12, 2-3/4" chambers. **Barrel:** skeet-28"; trap-30" and 32", Imp. Mod. & Full and Mobilchoke; trap mono shotguns-32" and 34" Mobilchoke; trap top single guns-32" and 34" Full and Mobilchoke; trap combo sets-from 30" O/U, to 32" O/U, 34" top single. **Stock:** Close-grained walnut, hand checkered. **Sights:** White Bradley bead front sight and center bead. **Features:** Receiver has Greystone gunmetal gray finish with gold accents. Trap Monte Carlo stock has deluxe trap recoil pad. Various grades available. Imported from Italy by Beretta USA.
Price: 682 Gold E Trap with adjustable stock **$4,425.00**
Price: 682 Gold E Trap Unsingle **$4,825.00**
Price: 682 Gold E Sporting **$4,075.00**
Price: 682 Gold E Skeet, adjustable stock **$4,425.00**

BERETTA 686 ONYX O/U SHOTGUNS
Gauge: 12, 20, 28; 3", 3.5" chambers. **Barrel:** 26", 28" (Mobilchoke tubes). **Weight:** 6.8-6.9 lbs. **Stock:** Checkered American walnut. **Features:** Intended for the beginning sporting clays shooter. Has wide, vented target rib, radiused recoil pad. Polished black finish on receiver and barrels. Introduced 1993. Imported from Italy by Beretta U.S.A.
Price: White Onyx **$1,975.00**
PPrice: White Onyx Sporting **$2,175.00**

BERETTA SILVER PIGEON O/U SHOTGUNS
Gauge: 12, 20, 28, 3" chambers (2-3/4" 28 ga.). .410 bore, 3" chamber. **Barrel:** 26", 28". **Weight:** 6.8 lbs. **Stock:** Checkered walnut. **Features:** Interchangeable barrels (20 and 28 ga.), single selective gold-plated trigger, boxlock action, auto safety, Schnabel forend.
Price: Silver Pigeon S **$2,400.00**
Price: Silver Pigeon II **$3,150.00**
Price: Silver Pigeon III **$3,275.00**
Price: Silver Pigeon IV **$3,200.00**
Price: Silver Pigeon V **$3,675.00**

BERETTA ULTRALIGHT O/U SHOTGUNS
Gauge: 12, 2-3/4" chambers. **Barrel:** 26", 28", Mobilchoke tubes. **Weight:** About 5 lbs., 13 oz. **Stock:** Select American walnut with checkered grip and forend. **Features:** Low-profile aluminum alloy receiver with titanium breech face insert. Electroless nickel receiver with game scene engraving. Single selective trigger; automatic safety. Introduced 1992. Ultralight Deluxe except has matte electroless nickel finish receiver with gold game scene engraving; matte oil-finished, select walnut stock and forend. Imported from Italy by Beretta U.S.A.
Price: **$2,075.00**
Price: Ultralight Deluxe **$2,450.00**

BERETTA COMPETITION SHOTGUNS
Gauge: 12, 20, 28, and .410 bore, 2-3/4", 3" and 3-1/2" chambers. **Barrel:** 26" and 28" (Mobilchoke tubes). **Stock:** Close-grained walnut. **Features:** Highly-figured, American walnut stocks and forends, and a unique, weather-resistant finish on barrels. Silver designates standard 686, 687 models with silver receivers; 686 Silver Pigeon has enhanced engraving pattern, Schnabel forend; Gold indicates higher grade 686EL, 687EL models with full sideplates. Imported from Italy by Beretta U.S.A.
Price: S687 EELL Gold Pigeon Sporting (D.R. engraving). . **$7,675.00**

BILL HANUS 16-GAUGE BROWNING CITORI M525 FIELD
Gauge: 16. **Barrel:** 26" and 28". **Weight:** 6-3/4 pounds. **Stock:** 1-1/2" x 2-3/8" x 14-1/4" and cast neutral. Adjusting for cast-on for left-

handed shooters or cast-off for right-handed shooters, $300 extra. Oil finish. **Features:** Full pistol grip with a graceful Schnable forearm and built on a true 16-gauge frame. Factory supplies three Invector choke tubes: IC-M-F and Bill Hanus models come with two Briley-made skeet chokes for close work over dogs and clay-target games.
Price: **$1,795.00**

BROWNING BT-99 TRAP O/U SHOTGUNS
Gauge: 12. **Barrel:** 30", 32", 34". **Stock:** Walnut; standard or adjustable. **Weight:** 7 lbs. 11 oz. to 9 lbs. **Features:** Back-bored single barrel; interchangeable chokes; beavertail forearm; extractor only; high rib.
Price: BT-99 w/conventional comb, 32" or 34" barrels **$1,529.00**
Price: BT-99 w/adjustable comb, 32" or 34" barrels **$1,839.00**
Price: BT-99 Golden Clays w/adjustable comb, 32" or
34" barrels **$3,989.00**
Price: BT-99 Grade III, 32" or 34" barrels, intr. 2008 . . . . . **$2,369.00**

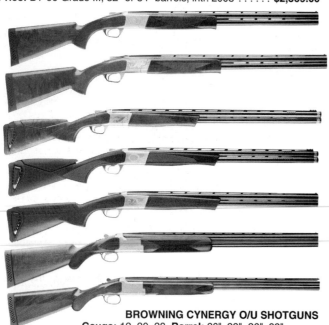

BROWNING CYNERGY O/U SHOTGUNS
Gauge: 12, 20, 28. **Barrel:** 26", 28", 30", 32".
Stock: Walnut or composite. **Sights:** White bead front most models; HiViz Pro-Comp sight on some models; mid bead.
Features: Mono-Lock hinge, recoil-reducing interchangeable Inflex recoil pad, silver nitride receiver; striker-based trigger, ported barrel option. Models include: Cynergy Sporting, Adjustable Comb; Cynergy Sporting Composite CF; Cynergy Field, Composite; Cynergy Classic Sporting; Cynergy Classic Field; Cynergy Camo Mossy Oak New Shadow Grass; Cynergy Camo Mossy Oak New Break-Up; and Cynergy Camo Mossy Oak Brush. Imported from Japan by Browning.
Price: Cynergy Classic Field, 12 ga., from **$2,399.00**
Price: Cynergy Classic Field Grade III, similar to Cynergy
Classic Field but with full coverage high-relief
engraving on reciever and top lever, gloss finish
Grade III/IV walnut, from **$3,499.00**
Price: Cyergy Classic Field Grade VI, similar to Cynergy
Classic Field Grade III but with more extensive,
gold-highlighted engraving, from **$5,229.00**
Price: Cynergy Classic Sporting, from **$3,499.00**
Price: Cynergy Euro Sporting, 12 ga.; 28", 30",
or 32" barrels **$3,719.00**
Price: Cynergy Euro Sporting Composite 12 ga. **$3,499.00**
Price: Cynergy Euro Sporting, adjustable comb, intr. 2006 . **$4,079.00**
Price: Cynergy Feather, 12 ga. intr. 2007 . . . . **$2,579.00**
Price: Cynergy Feather, 20, 28 ga., .410, intr. 2008 . . . . . . **$2,599.00**
Price: Cynergy Euro Sporting, 20 ga., intr. 2008 . . . . **$3,739.00**
Price: Cynergy Euro Field, Invector Plus tubes in 12
and 20 gauge, standard Invector tubes on
28 gauge and 410 . . . . **$2,509.00**

BROWNING CITORI O/U SHOTGUNS
Gauge: 12, 20, 28 and .410. **Barrel:** 26", 28" in 28 and .410. Offered

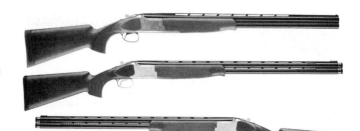

with Invector choke tubes. All 12 and 20 gauge models have back-bored barrels and Invector Plus choke system. **Weight:** 6 lbs, 8 oz. (26" .410) to 7 lbs., 13 oz. (30" 12 ga.). **Length:** 43" overall (26" bbl.). **Stock:** Dense walnut, hand checkered, full pistol grip, beavertail forend. Field-type recoil pad on 12 ga. field guns and trap and skeet models. **Sights:** Medium raised beads, German nickel silver. **Features:** Barrel selector integral with safety, automatic ejectors, three-piece takedown. Citori 625 Field (intr. 2008) includes Vector Pro extended forcing cones, new wood checkering patterns, silver-nitride finish with high-relief engraving, gloss oil finish with Grade II/III walnut with radius pistol grip, Schnabel forearm, 12 gauge, three Invector Plus choke tubes. Citori 625 Sporting (intr. 2008) includes standard and adjustable combs, 32", 30", and 28" barrels, five Diamond Grade extended Invector Plus choke tubes. Triple Trigger System allows adjusting length of pull and choice of wide checkered, narrow smooth, and wide smooth canted trigger shoe. HiViz Pro-Comp fiber-optic front sights. Imported from Japan by Browning.
Price: Lightning, from **$1,763.00**
Price: White Lightning, from **$1,836.00**
Price: Superlight Feather **$2,098.00**
Price: Lightning Feather, combo 20 and 28 ga. **$1,869.00**
Price: 625 Field, 12, 20 or 28 ga. and 410. Weighs
6 lbs. 12 oz. to 7 lbs. 14 oz. **$2,339.00**
Price: 625 Sporting, 12, 20 or 28 ga. and 410,
standard comb, intr. 2008 . . . . **$3,329.00**
Price: 625 Sporting, 12 ga., adj. comb, intr. 2008 . . . . **$3,639.00**

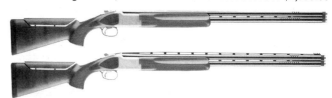

BROWNING CITORI HIGH GRADE SHOTGUNS
Similar to standard Citori except has engraved hunting scenes and gold inlays, high-grade, hand-oiled walnut stock and forearm. Introduced 2000. From Browning.
Price: Grade IV Lightning, engraved gray receiver,
introduced 2005, from. **$2,999.00**
Price: Grade VII Lightning, engraved gray or blue receiver,
introduced 2005, from. **$4,769.00**
Price: GTS High Grade, intr. 2007 . . . . **$4,309.00**

BROWNING CITORI XS SPORTING O/U SHOTGUNS
Similar to the standard Citori except available in 12, 20, 28 or .410 with 28", 30", 32" ported barrels with various screw-in choke combinations: S (Skeet), C (Cylinder), IC (Improved Cylinder), M (Modified), and IM (Improved Modified). Has pistol grip stock, rounded or Schnabel forend. Weighs 7.1 lbs. to 8.75 lbs. Introduced 2004. Ultra XS Prestige (intr. 2008) has silver-nitride finish receiver with gold accented, high-relief Ultra XS Special engraving. Also, single selective trigger, hammer ejectors, gloss oil finish walnut stock with right-hand palm swell, adjustable comb, Schnabel forearm. Comes with five Invector-Plus Midas Grade choke tubes.
Price: XS Special, 12 ga.; 30", 32" barrels **$3,169.00**
Price: XS Skeet, 12 or 20 ga. **$2,829.00**
Price: XS Special High Post Rib, intr. 2007 . . . . **$3,169.00**
Price: Ultra XS Prestige, intr. 2008 . . . . **$4,759.00**

Prices given are believed to be accurate at time of publication however, many factors affect retail pricing so exact prices are not possible.

BROWNING CITORI XT TRAP O/U SHOTGUN

Similar to the Citori XS Special except has engraved silver nitride receiver with gold highlights, vented side barrel rib. Available in 12 gauge with 30" or 32" barrels, Invector-Plus choke tubes, adjustable comb and buttplate. Introduced 1999. Imported by Browning.

Price: XT Trap. **$2,639.00**
Price: XT Trap w/adjustable comb **$2,959.00**
Price: XT Trap Gold w/adjustable comb, introduced 2005 . . **$4,899.00**

CAESAR GUERINI ELLIPSE O/U SHOTGUN

Gauge: 12, 20, 28 gauge, also 20/28 gauge combo. **Barrel:** 28". **Weight:** 6.5 lbs. **Length:** 49.25". **Stock:** High grade walnut. **Features:** Fast as a grouse's wing tip, sleek as a pheasant's tail feather - The new Caesar Guerini Ellipse EVO represents the next generation of upland game gun. With graceful rounded action and streamlined stock it handles, feels and looks like the world's best handmade round body shotguns. We obsessed over every detail from the engraving created to accentuate the curve of the action to something as obscure as the shape of the trigger. This is not a quick makeover of our existing models; the barrels, action and stock are all different. The Ellipse is simply the evolution of the fine over-and-under hunting gun. The Ellipse comes in a fitted case with five choke tube. The EVO is the more expensive of the two Ellipse models and as such boasts more elaborate engraving, a higher grade of walnut in the stock, and a few other aesthetic touches. Otherwise, the two are identical. $205 Additional Charge for Left Hand Stock.

Price: Limited . . . .**$3,995.00 - $5,605.00**
Price: EVO . . . .**$5,495.00 - $7,365.00**

CHARLES DALY MODEL 206 O/U SHOTGUN

Gauge: 12, 3" chambers. **Barrel:** 26", 28", 30", chrome-moly steel. **Weight:** 8 lbs. **Stock:** Checkered select Turkish walnut stocks. **Features:** Single selective trigger, extractors or selective automatic ejectors. Sporting model has 10mm ventilated rib and side ventilated ribs. Trap model comes with 10mm top rib and side ventilated ribs and includes a Monte Carlo Trap buttstock. Both competition ribs have mid-brass bead and front fluorescent sights. Five Multi-Choke tubes. Introduced 2008. Imported from Turkey by K.B.I., Inc.

Price: Field, 26" or 28", extractors **$759.00**
Price: Field, 26" or 28", auto-eject **$884.00**
Price: Sporting, 28" or 30" ported **$999.00**
Price: Trap, 28" or 30" ported, ... **$1,064.00**

CZ SPORTING OVER/UNDER

Gauge: 12, 3" chambers. **Barrel:** 30", 32" chrome-lined, back-bored with extended forcing cones. **Weight:** 9 lbs. **Length:** NA. **Stock:** Neutral cast stock with an adjustable comb, trap style forend, pistol grip and ambidextrous palm swells. #3 grade Circassian walnut. At lowest position, drop at comb: 1-5/8"; drop at heel: 2-3/8"; length of pull: 14-1/2". **Features:** Designed for Sporting Clays and FITASC competition. Hand engraving, satin black-finished receiver. Tapered rib with center bead and a red fiber-optic front bead, 10 choke tubes with wrench, single selective trigger, automatic ejectors, thin rubber pad with slick plastic top. Introduced 2008. From CZ-USA.

Price: **$2,509.00**

CZ CANVASBACK

Gauge: 12, 20, 3" chambers. **Barrel:** 26", 28". **Weight:** 7.3 lbs. **Length:** NA. **Stock:** Round-knob pistol grip, Schnabel forend, Turkish walnut. **Features:** Single selective trigger, set of 5 screw-in chokes, black chrome finished receiver. From CZ-USA.

Price: **$819.00**

CZ MALLARD

Gauge: 12, 20, 28, .410, 3" chambers. **Barrel:** 26". **Weight:** 7.7 lbs. **Length:** NA. **Stock:** Round-knob pistol grip, Schnabel forend, Turkish walnut. **Features:** Double triggers and extractors, coin finished receiver, multi chokes. From CZ-USA.

Price: **$562.00**

CZ REDHEAD

Gauge: 12, 20, 3" chambers. **Barrel:** 28". **Weight:** 7.4 lbs. **Length:** NA. **Stock:** Round-knob pistol grip, Schnabel forend, Turkish walnut. **Features:** Single selective triggers and extractors (12 & 20 ga.), screw-in chokes (12, 20, 28 ga.) choked IC and Mod (.410), coin finished receiver, multi chokes. From CZ-USA.

Price: **$965.00**

CZ WINGSHOOTER O/U SHOTGUN

Gauge: 12, 20, 28 & .410 ga., 2-3/4" chamber. **Barrel:** 28" flat ventilated rib. **Weight:** 6.3 lbs. **Length:** 45.5". **Stock:** Turkish walnut. **Features:** This colorful Over and Under shotgun has the same old world craftsmanship as all of our shotguns but with a new stylish look. This elegant hand engraved work of art is available in four gauges and its eye-catching engraving will stand alone in the field or range. 12 and 20 gauge models have auto ejectors, while the 28 gauge and .410 have extractors only. Heavily engraved scroll work with special side plate design, mechanical selective triggers, box Lock frame design, 18 LPI checkering, coil spring operated hammers, chrome lined, 5 interchangeable choke tubes and special engraved skeleton butt plate.

Price: **$1040.00**

CZ WOODCOCK

Gauge: 12, 20, 28, .410, 3" chambers. **Barrel:** 26". **Weight:** 7.7 lbs. **Length:** NA. **Stock:** Round-knob pistol grip, Schnabel forend, Turkish walnut. **Features:** Single selective triggers and extractors (auto ejectors on 12 & 20 ga.), screw-in chokes (12, 20, 28 ga.) choked IC and Mod (.410), coin finished receiver, multi chokes. The sculptured frame incorporates a side plate, resembling a true side lock, embellished with hand engraving and finished with color casehardening. From CZ-USA.

Price: **$1,246.00**

ESCORT OVER/UNDER SHOTGUNS

Gauge: 12, 3" chamber. **Barrel:** 28". **Weight:** 7.4 lbs. **Stock:** Walnut or select walnut with Trio recoil pad; synthetic stock with adjustable comb. Three adjustment spacers. **Sights:** Bronze front bead. **Features:** Blued barrels, blued or nickel receiver. Trio recoil pad. Five interchangeable chokes (SK, IC, M, IM, F); extractors or ejectors (new, 2008), barrel selector. Hard case available. Introduced 2007. Imported from Turkey by Legacy Sports International.

Price: **$599.00**

FRANCHI RENAISSANCE AND RENAISSANCE SPORTING O/U SHOTGUNS

Gauge: 12, 20, 28, 3" chamber. **Barrel:** 26", 28". **Weight:** 5.0 to 6.0 lbs. **Length:** 42-5/8" to 44-5/8". **Stock:** 14.5" LOP, European oil-finished walnut with standard grade A grade, and AA grade choices. Prince of Wales grip. **Features:** TSA recoil pad, interchangeable chokes, hard case. Introduced 2006. *Sporting model:* **Gauge:** 12, 3". **Barrel:** 30" ported. **Weight:** 7.9 lbs. **Length:** 46 5/8". **Stock:** 14.5" LOP, A-grade

European oil-finished walnut. **Features:** TSA recoil pad, adjustable comb, lengthened forcing cones, extended choke tubes (C, IC, M and wrench), hard case. Introduced 2007. Imported from Italy by Benelli USA.
Price: Field **$1,729.00**
Price: Classic **$1,899.00**
Price: Elite. **$2,399.00**
Price: Sporting **$2,249.00**

KIMBER MARIAS O/U SHOTGUN

Gauge: 20, 16; 3". **Barrel:** 26", 28", 30". **Weight:** 6.5 lbs. **Length:** NA. **Stock:** Turkish walnut stocks, 24-lpi checkering, oil finish. **LOP:** 14.75". **Features:** Hand-detachable back-action sidelock, bone-charcoal case coloring. Hand-engraving on receiver and locks, Belgian rust blue barrels, chrome lined. Five thinwall choke tubes, automatic ejectors, ventilated rib. Gold line cocking indicators on locks. Grade I has 28" barrels, Prince of Wales stock in grade three Turkish walnut in either 12 or 20 gauge. Grade II shas grade four Turkish walnut stocks, 12 gauge in Prince of Wales and 20 with either Prince of Wales or English profiles. Introduced 2008. Imported from Italy by Kimber Mfg., Inc.
Price: Grade II. **$5,799.00**

KOLAR SPORTING CLAYS O/U SHOTGUNS
Gauge: 12, 2-3/4" chambers. **Barrel:** 30", 32", 34"; extended choke tubes. **Stock:** 14-5/8"x2.5"x1-7/8"x1-3/8". French walnut. Four stock versions available. **Features:** Single selective trigger, detachable, adjustable for length; overbored barrels with long forcing cones; flat tramline rib; matte blue finish. Made in U.S. by Kolar.
Price: Standard. **$9,595.00**
Price: Prestige **$14,190.00**
Price: Elite Gold **$16,590.00**
Price: Legend **$17,090.00**
Price: Select **$22,590.00**
Price: Custom . . . . **Price on request**

KOLAR AAA COMPETITION TRAP O/U SHOTGUN

Similar to the Sporting Clays gun except has 32" O/U /34" Unsingle or 30" O/U /34" Unsingle barrels as an over/under, unsingle, or combination set. Stock dimensions are 14.5"x2.5"x1.5"; American or French walnut; step parallel rib standard. Contact maker for full listings. Made in U.S.A. by Kolar.
Price: Over/under, choke tubes, standard **$9,595.00**
Price: Combo (30"/34", 32"/34"), standard **$12,595.00**

KOLAR AAA COMPETITION SKEET O/U SHOTGUN

Similar to the Sporting Clays gun except has 28" or 30" barrels with Kolarite AAA sub gauge tubes; stock of American or French walnut with matte finish; flat tramline rib; under barrel adjustable for point of impact. Many options available. Contact maker for complete listing. Made in U.S.A. by Kolar.
Price: Standard, choke tubes **$10,995.00**
Price: Standard, choke tubes, two-barrel set **$12,995.00**

KRIEGHOFF K-80 SPORTING CLAYS O/U SHOTGUN
Gauge: 12. **Barrel:** 28", 30", 32", 34" with choke tubes. **Weight:** About 8 lbs. **Stock:** #3 Sporting stock designed for gun-down shooting. **Features:** Standard receiver with satin nickel finish and classic scroll engraving. Selective mechanical trigger adjustable for position. Choice of tapered flat or 8mm parallel flat barrel rib. Free-floating barrels. Aluminum case. Imported from Germany by Krieghoff International, Inc.
Price: Standard grade with five choke tubes, from **$9,395.00**

KRIEGHOFF K-80 SKEET O/U SHOTGUNS

Gauge: 12, 2-3/4" chambers. **Barrel:** 28", 30", 32", (skeet & skeet), optional choke tubes). **Weight:** About 7.75 lbs. **Stock:** American skeet or straight skeet stocks, with palm-swell grips. Walnut.
Features: Satin gray receiver finish. Selective mechanical trigger adjustable for position. Choice of ventilated 8mm parallel flat rib or ventilated 8-12mm tapered flat rib. Introduced 1980. Imported from

Germany by Krieghoff International, Inc.
Price: Standard, skeet chokes **$8,375.00**
Price: Skeet Special (28", 30", 32" tapered flat rib, skeet & skeet choke tubes). **$9,100.00**

KRIEGHOFF K-80 TRAP O/U SHOTGUNS

Gauge: 12, 2-3/4" chambers. **Barrel:** 30", 32" (Imp. Mod. & Full or choke tubes). **Weight:** About 8.5 lbs. **Stock:** Four stock dimensions or adjustable stock available; all have palm-swell grips. Checkered European walnut. **Features:** Satin nickel receiver. Selective mechanical trigger, adjustable for position. Ventilated step rib. Introduced 1980. Imported from Germany by Krieghoff International, Inc.
Price: K-80 O/U (30", 32", Imp. Mod. & Full), from **$8,850.00**
Price: K-80 Unsingle (32", 34", Full), standard, from **$10,080.00**
Price: K-80 Combo (two-barrel set), standard, from **$13,275.00**

KRIEGHOFF K-20 O/U SHOTGUN

Similar to the K-80 except built on a 20-gauge frame. Designed for skeet, sporting clays and field use. Offered in 20, 28 and .410; 28", 30" and 32" barrels. Imported from Germany by Krieghoff International Inc.
Price: K-20, 20 gauge, from **$9,575.00**
Price: K-20, 28 gauge, from **$9,725.00**
Price: K-20, .410, from **$9,725.00**

LEBEAU-COURALLY BOSS-VEREES O/U SHOTGUN

Gauge: 12, 20, 2-3/4" chambers. **Barrel:** 25" to 32". **Weight:** To customer specifications. **Stock:** Exhibition-quality French walnut. **Features:** Boss-type sidelock with automatic ejectors; single or double triggers; chopper lump barrels. A custom gun built to customer specifications. Imported from Belgium by Wm. Larkin Moore.
Price: From **$96,000.00**

LJUTIC LM-6 SUPER DELUXE O/U SHOTGUNS
Gauge: 12. **Barrel:** 28" to 34", choked to customer specs for live birds, trap, international trap. **Weight:** To customer specs. **Stock:** To customer specs. Oil finish, hand checkered. **Features:** Custom-made gun. Hollow-milled rib, pull or release trigger, push-button opener in front of trigger guard. From Ljutic Industries.
Price: Super Deluxe LM-6 O/U **$19,995.00**
Price: Over/Under combo (interchangeable single barrel, two trigger guards, one for single trigger, one for doubles) **$27,995.00**
Price: Extra over/under barrel sets, 29"-32" **$6,995.00**

MARLIN L. C. SMITH O/U SHOTGUNS
Gauge: 12, 20. **Barrel:** 26", 28". **Stock:** Checkered walnut w/recoil pad. **Length:** 45". **Weight:** 7.25 lbs. **Features:** 3" chambers; 3 choke tubes (IC, Mod., Full), single selective trigger, selective automatic ejectors; vent rib; bead front sight. Imported from Italy by Marlin. Introduced 2005.
Price: LC12-OU (12 ga., 28" barrel) **$1,254.00**
Price: LC20-OU (20 ga., 26" barrel, 6.25 lbs., OAL 43") . . . **$1,254.00**

MERKEL MODEL 2001EL O/U SHOTGUN
Gauge: 12, 20, 3" chambers, 28, 2-3/4" chambers. **Barrel:** 12-28"; 20, 28 ga.-26.75". **Weight:** About 7 lbs. (12 ga.). **Stock:** Oil-finished walnut; English or pistol grip. **Features:** Self-cocking Blitz boxlock action with cocking indicators; Kersten double cross-bolt lock; silver-grayed receiver with engraved hunting scenes; coil spring ejectors; single selective or double triggers. Imported from Germany by Merkel USA.
Price: **$9,995.00**
Price: Model 2001EL Sporter; full pistol grip stock **$9,995.00**

MERKEL MODEL 2000CL O/U SHOTGUN

Similar to Model 2001EL except scroll-engraved case-hardened receiver; 12, 20, 28 gauge. Imported from Germany by Merkel USA.
Price: **$8,495.00**
Price: Model 2016 CL; 16 gauge **$8,495.00**

SHOTGUNS—Over/Unders

PERAZZI MX8/ MX8 SPECIAL TRAP, SKEET O/U SHOTGUNS

Gauge: 12, 2-3/4" chambers. **Barrel:** Trap: 29.5" (Imp. Mod. & Extra Full), 31.5" (Full & Extra Full). Choke tubes optional. Skeet: 27-5/8" (skeet & skeet). **Weight:** About 8.5 lbs. (trap); 7 lbs., 15 oz. (skeet). **Stock:** Interchangeable and custom made to customer specs. **Features:** Has detachable and interchangeable trigger group with flat V springs. Flat 7/16" vent rib. Many options available. Imported from Italy by Perazzi U.S.A., Inc.
Price: MX Trap Single.................... **$10,934.00**

PERAZZI MX8 SPECIAL SKEET O/U SHOTGUN

Similar to the MX8 Skeet except has adjustable four-position trigger, skeet stock dimensions. Imported from Italy by Perazzi U.S.A., Inc.
Price: From **$11,166.00**

PERAZZI MX8 O/U SHOTGUNS

Gauge: 12, 2-3/4" chambers. **Barrel:** 28-3/8" (Imp. Mod. & Extra Full), 29.5" (choke tubes). **Weight:** 7 lbs., 12 oz. **Stock:** Special specifications. **Features:** Has single selective trigger; flat 7/16" x 5/16" vent rib. Many options available. Imported from Italy by Perazzi U.S.A., Inc.
Price: Standard.............................. **$12,532.00**
Price: Sporting **$11,166.00**
Price: Trap Double Trap (removable trigger group) **$15,581.00**
Price: Skeet **$12,756.00**
Price: SC3 grade (variety of engraving patterns) .... **$23,000.00+**
Price: SCO grade (more intricate engraving, gold inlays). **$39,199.00+**

PERAZZI MX8/20 O/U SHOTGUN

Similar to the MX8 except has smaller frame and has a removable trigger mechanism. Available in trap, skeet, sporting or game models with fixed chokes or choke tubes. Stock is made to customer specifications. Introduced 1993. Imported from Italy by Perazzi U.S.A., Inc.
Price: From...................... **$11,731.00**

PERAZZI MX12 HUNTING O/U SHOTGUNS

Gauge: 12, 2-3/4" chambers. **Barrel:** 26.75", 27.5", 28-3/8", 29.5" (Mod. & Full); choke tubes available in 27-5/8", 29.5" only (MX12C). **Weight:** 7 lbs., 4 oz. **Stock:** To customer specs; interchangeable. **Features:** Single selective trigger; coil springs used in action; Schnabel forend tip. Imported from Italy by Perazzi U.S.A., Inc.
Price: From **$11,166.00**
Price: MX12C (with choke tubes). From............... **$11,960.00**

PERAZZI MX20 HUNTING O/U SHOTGUNS

Similar to the MX12 except 20 ga. frame size. Non-removable trigger group. Available in 20, 28, .410 with 2-3/4" or 3" chambers. 26" standard, and choked Mod. & Full. Weight is 6 lbs., 6 oz. Imported from Italy by Perazzi U.S.A., Inc.
Price: From.................... **$11,166.00**
Price: MX20C (as above, 20 ga. only, choke tubes). From **$11,960.00**

PERAZZI MX10 O/U SHOTGUN

Gauge: 12, 2-3/4" chambers. **Barrel:** 29.5", 31.5" (fixed chokes). **Weight:** NA. **Stock:** Walnut; cheekpiece adjustable for elevation and cast. **Features:** Adjustable rib; vent side rib. Externally selective trigger. Available in single barrel, combo, over/under trap, skeet, pigeon and sporting models. Introduced 1993. Imported from Italy by Perazzi U.S.A., Inc.
Price: MX200410 .... **$18,007.00**

PERAZZI MX28, MX410 GAME O/U SHOTGUN

Gauge: 28, 2-3/4" chambers, .410, 3" chambers. **Barrel:** 26" (Imp. Cyl. & Full). **Weight:** NA. **Stock:** To customer specifications. **Features:** Made on scaled-down frames proportioned to the gauge. Introduced 1993. Imported from Italy by Perazzi U.S.A., Inc.
Price: From............................ **$22,332.00**

PIOTTI BOSS O/U SHOTGUN

Gauge: 12, 20. **Barrel:** 26" to 32", chokes as specified. **Weight:** 6.5 to 8 lbs. **Stock:** Dimensions to customer specs. Best quality figured walnut. **Features:** Essentially a custom-made gun with many options. Introduced 1993. Imported from Italy by Wm. Larkin Moore.
Price: From............................ **$69,000.00**

POINTER OVER/UNDER SHOTGUN

Gauge: 12, 20, 28, .410, 3" chambers. **Barrel:** 28", blued. **Weight:** 6.1 to 7.6 lbs. **Stock:** Turkish Walnut. **Sights:** Fiber-optic front, bronze mid-bead. **Choke:** IC/M/F. **Features:** Engraved nickel receiver, automatic ejectors; fitted hard plastic case. Clays model has oversized fiber-optic front sight and palm swell pistol grip. Introduced 2007. Imported from Turkey by Legacy Sports International.
Price: ....**$1,299.00 to $1,499.00**

REMINGTON PREMIER OVER/UNDER SHOTGUNS

Gauge: 12, 20, 28, 3" chambers; 28, 2-3/4" chambers. **Barrel:** 26", 28", 30" in 12 gauge; overbored (.735), polished blue; 7mm vent rib. **Sights:** Ivory front bead, steel mid bead. **Weight:** 6.5 to 7.5 lbs. **Stock:** Walnut, cut checkering, Schnabel forends. Checkered pistol grip, checkered forend, satin finish, rubber butt pad. Right-hand palm swell. **Features:** Single selective mechanical trigger, selective automatic ejectors; serrated free-floating vent rib. Five flush mount ProBore choke tubes for 12s and 20s; 28-gauge equipped with 3 flush mount ProBore choke tubes. Hard case included. Introduced 2006. Made in Italy, imported by Remington Arms Co.
Price: Premier Field, nickel-finish receiver, from **$2,086.00**
Price: Premier Upland, case-colored receiver finish, from .. **$2,226.00**
Price: Premier Competition STS (2007) **$2,540.00**
Price: Premier Competition STS Adj. Comb (2007) **$2,890.00**

REMINGTON SPR310 OVER/UNDER SHOTGUNS

Gauge: 12, 20, 28, .410 bore, 3" chambers; 28, 2-3/4" chambers. **Barrel:** 26", 28", 29.5"; blued chrome-lined. **Weight:** 7.25 to 7.5 lbs. **Stock:** Checkered walnut stock and forend, 14.5" LOP; 1.5" drop at comb; 2.5" drop at heel. **Features:** Nickel finish or blued receiver. Single selective mechanical trigger, selective automatic ejectors; serrated free-floating vent rib. SC-4 choke tube set on most models. Sporting has ported barrels, right-hand palm swell, target forend, wide rib. Introduced 2008. Imported by Remington Arms Co.
Price: SPR310, from **$598.00**
Price: SPR310 Sporting **$770.00**

RIZZINI S790 EMEL O/U SHOTGUN

Gauge: 20, 28, .410. **Barrel:** 26", 27.5" (Imp. Cyl. & Imp. Mod.). **Weight:** About 6 lbs. **Stock:** 14"x1.5"x2-1/8". Extra fancy select walnut. **Features:** Boxlock action with profuse engraving; automatic ejectors; single selective trigger; silvered receiver. Comes with Nizzoli leather case. Introduced 1996. Imported from Italy by Wm. Larkin Moore & Co.
Price: From.................................. **$14,600.00**

RIZZINI S792 EMEL O/U SHOTGUN

Similar to S790 EMEL except dummy sideplates with extensive engraving coverage. Nizzoli leather case. Introduced 1996. Imported from Italy by Wm. Larkin Moore & Co.
Price: From................................. **$15,500.00**

RIZZINI UPLAND EL O/U SHOTGUN

Gauge: 12, 16, 20, 28, .410. **Barrel:** 26", 27.5", Mod. & Full, Imp. Cyl. & Imp. Mod. choke tubes. **Weight:** About 6.6 lbs. **Stock:** 14.5"x1-

1/2"x2.25". **Features:** Boxlock action; single selective trigger; ejectors; profuse engraving on silvered receiver. Comes with fitted case. Introduced 1996. Imported from Italy by Wm. Larkin Moore & Co.
Price: From **$5,200.00**

RIZZINI ARTEMIS O/U SHOTGUN

Same as Upland EL model except dummy sideplates with extensive game scene engraving. Fancy European walnut stock. Fitted case. Introduced 1996. Imported from Italy by Wm. Larkin Moore & Co.
Price: **$3.260.00**

RIZZINI S782 EMEL O/U SHOTGUN

Gauge: 12, 2-3/4" chambers. **Barrel:** 26", 27.5" (Imp. Cyl. & Imp. Mod.). **Weight:** About 6.75 lbs. **Stock:** 14.5"x1.5"x2.25". Extra fancy select walnut. **Features:** Boxlock action with dummy sideplates, extensive engraving with gold inlaid game birds, silvered receiver, automatic ejectors, single selective trigger. Nizzoli leather case. Introduced 1996. Imported from Italy by Wm. Larkin Moore & Co.
Price: From **$18,800.00**

RUGER RED LABEL O/U SHOTGUNS

Gauge: 12, 20, 3" chambers; 28 2-3/4" chambers. **Barrel:** 26", 28", 30" in 12 gauge. **Weight:** About 7 lbs. (20 ga.); 7.5 lbs. (12 ga.). **Length:** 43" overall (26" barrels). **Stock:** 14"x1.5"x2.5". Straight grain American walnut. Checkered pistol grip or straight grip, checkered forend, rubber butt pad. **Features:** Stainless steel receiver. Single selective mechanical trigger, selective automatic ejectors; serrated free-floating vent rib. Comes with two skeet, one Imp. Cyl., one Mod., one Full choke tube and wrench. Made in U.S. by Sturm, Ruger & Co.
Price: Red Label with pistol grip stock **$1,956.00**
Price: English Field with straight-grip stock **$1,956.00**
Price: Sporting clays (30" bbl.) **$1,956.00**

RUGER ENGRAVED RED LABEL O/U SHOTGUN

Similar to Red Label except scroll engraved receiver with 24-carat gold game bird (pheasant in 12 gauge, grouse in 20 gauge, woodcock in 28 gauge). Introduced 2000.
Price: Engraved Red Label, pistol grip only **$2,180.00**

SAVAGE MILANO O/U SHOTGUNS

Gauge: 12, 20, 28, and 410, 2-3/4" (28 ga.) and 3" chambers. **Barrel:** 28"; chrome lined, elongated forcing cones, automatic ejectors. 12, 20, and 28 come with 3 Interchokes (F-M-IC); 410 has fixed chokes (M-IC). **Weight:** 12 ga., 7.5 lbs; 20, 28 gauge, .410, 6.25 lbs. **Length:** NA. **Stock:** Satin finish Turkish walnut stock with laser-engraved checkering, solid rubber recoil pad, Schnabel forend. **Features:** Single selective, mechanical set trigger, fiber-optic front sight with brass mid-rib bead. Introduced 2006. Imported from Italy by Savage Arms, Inc.
Price: **$1,714.00**

SKB MODEL GC7 O/U SHOTGUNS

Gauge: 12 or 20, 3"; 28, 2-3/4"; .410, 3". **Barrel:** 26", 28", Briley internal chokes. **Weight:** NA. **Length:** NA. **Stock:** Grade II and Grade III American black walnut, high-gloss finish, finger-groove forend. **Sights:** Top ventilated rib, sloped with matte surface (Game). **Features:** Low-profile boxlock action; Greener crossbolt locking action, silver-nitride finish; automatic ejectors, single selective trigger. Introduced 2008. Imported from Japan by SKB Shotguns, Inc.
Price: GC7 Game Bird Grade 1, from. **$1,569.00**
Price: GC7 Clays Grade 1, from. **$1,679.00**

SKB MODEL 85TSS O/U SHOTGUNS

Gauge: 12, 20, .410: 3"; 28, 2-3/4". **Barrel:** Chrome lined 26", 28", 30", 32" (w/choke tubes). **Weight:** 7 lbs., 7 oz. to 8 lbs., 14 oz. **Stock:** Hand-checkered American walnut with matte finish, Schnabel or grooved forend. Target stocks available in various styles. **Sights:** HiViz competition sights. **Features:** Low profile boxlock action with Greener-style cross bolt; single selective trigger; manual safety.

Back-bored barrels with lengthened forcing cones. Introduced 2004. Imported from Japan by SKB Shotguns, Inc.
Price: Sporting Clays, Skeet, fixed comb, from **$2,199.00**
Price: Sporting clays, Skeet, adjustable comb, from **$2,429.00**
Price: Trap, standard or Monte Carlo **$2,329.00**
Price: Trap adjustable comb. **$2,529.00**
Price: Trap Unsingle (2007) **$2,799.00**

SKB MODEL 585 O/U SHOTGUNS

Gauge: 12 or 20, 3"; 28, 2-3/4"; .410, 3". **Barrel:** 12 ga.-26", 28", (InterChoke tubes); 20 ga.-26", 28" (InterChoke tubes); 28-26", 28" (InterChoke tubes); .410-26", 28" (InterChoke tubes). **Weight:** 6.6 to 8.5 lbs. **Length:** 43" to 51-3/8" overall. **Stock:** 14-1/8"x1.5"x2-3/16". Hand checkered walnut with matte finish. **Sights:** Metal bead front (field). **Features:** Boxlock action; silver nitride finish; manual safety, automatic ejectors, single selective trigger. All 12-gauge barrels are back-bored, have lengthened forcing cones and longer choke tube system. Introduced 1992. Imported from Japan by SKB Shotguns, Inc.
Price: Field **$1,699.00**
Price: Two-barrel field set, 12 & 20. . . . . **$2,749.00**
Price: Two-barrel field set, 20 & 28 or 28 & .410 . . . . **$2,829.00**

SMITH & WESSON ELITE SILVER SHOTGUNS

Gauge: 12, 3" chambers. **Barrel:** 26", 28", 30", rust-blued chopper-lump. **Weight:** 7.8 lbs. **Length:** 46-48". **Sights:** Ivory front bead, metal mid-bead. **Stock:** AAA (grade III) Turkish walnut stocks, hand-cut checkering, satin finish. **Features:** Smith & Wesson-designed trigger-plate action, hand-engraved receivers, bone-charcoal case hardening, lifetime warranty. Five choke tubes. Introduced 2007. Made in Turkey, imported by Smith & Wesson.
Price: **$2,380.00**

STEVENS MODEL 512 GOLD WING SHOTGUNS

Gauge: 12, 20, 28, .410; 2-3/4" and 3" chambers. **Barrel:** 26", 28". **Weight:** 6 to 8 lbs. **Sights:** NA. **Features:** Five screw-in choke tubes with 12, 20, and 28 gauge; .410 has fixed M/IC chokes. Black chrome, sculpted receiver with a raised gold pheasant, laser engraved trigger guard and forend latch. Turkish walnut stock finished in satin lacquer and beautifully laser engraved with fleur-de-lis checkering on the side panels, wrist and Schnabel forearm.
Price: **$649.00**

STOEGER CONDOR O/U SHOTGUNS

Gauge: 12, 20, 2-3/4" 3" chambers; 16, .410. **Barrel:** 22", 24", 26", 28", 30". **Weight:** 5.5 to 7.8 lbs. **Sights:** Brass bead. **Features:** IC, M, or F screw-in choke tubes with each gun. Oil finished hardwood with pistol grip and forend. Auto safety, single trigger, automatic extractors.
Price: Condor, 12, 20, 16 ga. or .410 . . . . $399.00
Price: Condor Supreme (w/mid bead), 12 or 20 ga. $599.00
Price: Condor Combo, 12 and 20 ga. Barrels, from $549.00
Price: Condor Youth, 20 ga. or .410 . . . . $399.00
Price: Condor Competition, 12 or 20 ga. $599.00
Price: Condor Combo, 12/20 ga., RH or LH (2007) $829.00
Price: Condor Outback, 12 or 20 ga., 20" barrel. $369.00

TRADITIONS CLASSIC SERIES O/U SHOTGUNS

Gauge: 12, 3"; 20, 3"; 16, 2-3/4"; 28, 2-3/4"; .410, 3". **Barrel:** 26" and 28". **Weight:** 6 lbs., 5 oz. to 7 lbs., 6 oz. **Length:** 43" to 45" overall. **Stock:** Walnut. **Features:** Single-selective trigger; chrome-lined barrels with screw-in choke tubes; extractors (Field Hunter and Field

SHOTGUNS—Over/Unders

I models) or automatic ejectors (Field II and Field III models); rubber butt pad; top tang safety. Imported from Fausti of Italy by Traditions.
Price: Field Hunter: Blued receiver; 12 or 20 ga.; 26" bbl. has IC and Mod. tubes, 28" has mod. and full tubes **$669.00**
Price: Field I: Blued receiver; 12, 20, 28 ga. or .410; fixed chokes (26" has I.C. and mod., 28" has mod. and full) . **$619.00**
Price: Field II: Coin-finish receiver; 12, 16, 20, 28 ga. or .410; gold trigger; choke tubes **$789.00**
Price: Field III: Coin-finish receiver; gold engraving and trigger; 12 ga.; 26" or 28" bbl.; choke tubes **$999.00**
Price: Upland II: Blued receiver; 12 or 20 ga.; English-style straight walnut stock; choke tubes **$839.00**
Price: Upland III: Blued receiver, gold engraving; 20 ga.; high-grade pistol grip walnut stock; choke tubes **$1,059.00**
Price: Upland III: Blued, gold engraved receiver, 12 ga. Round pistol grip stock, choke tubes **$1,059.00**
Price: Sporting Clay II: Silver receiver; 12 ga.; ported barrels with skeet, i.c., mod. and full extended tubes **$959.00**
Price: Sporting Clay III: Engraved receivers, 12 and 20 ga., walnut stock, vent rib, extended choke tubes **$1,189.00**

TRADITIONS MAG 350 SERIES O/U SHOTGUNS
Gauge: 12, 3-1/2". **Barrel:** 24", 26" and 28". **Weight:** 7 lbs. to 7 lbs., 4 oz. **Length:** 41" to 45" overall. **Stock:** Walnut or composite with Mossy Oak Break-Up or Advantage Wetlands camouflage. **Features:** Black matte, engraved receiver; vent rib; automatic ejectors; single selective trigger; three screw-in choke tubes; rubber recoil pad; top tang safety. Imported from Fausti of Italy by Traditions.
Price: (Mag Hunter II: 28" black matte barrels, walnut stock, includes I.C., Mod. and Full tubes) **$799.00**
Price: (Turkey II: 24" or 26" camo barrels, Break-Up camo stock, includes Mod., Full and X-Full tubes) **$889.00**
Price: (Waterfowl II: 28" camo barrels, Advantage Wetlands camo stock, includes IC, Mod. and Full tubes) **$899.00**

TRISTAR HUNTER EX O/U SHOTGUN
Gauge: 12, 20, 28, .410. **Barrel:** 26", 28". **Weight:** 5.7 lbs. (.410); 6.0 lbs. (20, 28), 7.2-7.4 lbs. (12). Chrome-lined steel mono-block barrel, five Beretta-style choke tubes (SK, IC, M, IM, F). **Length:** NA. **Stock:** Walnut, cut checkering. 14.25"x1.5"x2-3/8". **Sights:** Brass front sight. **Features:** All have extractors, engraved receiver, sealed actions, self-adjusting locking bolts, single selective trigger, ventilated rib. 28 ga. and .410 built on true frames. Five-year warranty. Imported from Italy by Tristar Sporting Arms Ltd.
Price: From **$619.00**

VERONA 501 SERIES O/U SHOTGUNS
Gauge: 12, 20, 28, .410 (3" chambers). **Barrel:** 28". **Weight:** 6-7 lbs. **Stock:** Enhanced walnut with Scottish net type checkering and oiled finish. **Features:** Select fire single trigger, automatic ejectors, chromed barrels with X-CONE system to reduce felt recoil, and ventilated rubber butt pad. Introduced 1999. Imported from Italy by Legacy Sports International.
Price: Combos 20/28, 28/.410 . . . . **$1,599.00**

VERONA 702 SERIES O/U SHOTGUNS
Same as 501 series model except. with deluxe nickel receiver.
Price: **$1,699.00**

VERONA LX692 GOLD HUNTING O/U SHOTGUNS
Similar to Verona 501 except engraved, silvered receiver with false sideplates showing gold inlaid bird hunting scenes on three sides; Schnabel forend tip; hand-cut checkering; black rubber butt pad. Available in 12 and 20 gauge only, five Interchoke tubes. Introduced 1999. Imported from Italy by B.C. Outdoors.
Price: **$1,295.00**
Price: LX692G Combo 28/.410. . . . . **$2,192.40**

VERONA LX680 SPORTING O/U SHOTGUN
Similar to Verona 501 except engraved, silvered receiver; ventilated middle rib; beavertail forend; hand-cut checkering; available in 12 or 20 gauge only with 2-3/4" chambers. Introduced 1999. Imported from Italy by B.C. Outdoors.
Price: **$1,159.68**

VERONA LX680 SKEET/SPORTING/TRAP O/U SHOTGUN
Similar to Verona 501 except skeet or trap stock dimensions; beavertail forend, palm swell on pistol grip; ventilated center barrel rib. Introduced 1999. Imported from Italy by B.C. Outdoors.
Price: **$1,736.96**

VERONA LX692 GOLD SPORTING O/U SHOTGUN
Similar to Verona LX680 except false sideplates have gold-inlaid bird hunting scenes on three sides; red high-visibility front sight. Introduced 1999. Imported from Italy by B.C. Outdoors.
Price: Skeet/sporting. **$1,765.12**
Price: Trap (32" barrel, 7-7/8 lbs.) **$1,594.80**

VERONA LX680 COMPETITION TRAP O/U SHOTGUNS
Gauge: 12. **Barrel:** 30" O/U, 32" single bbl. **Weight:** 8-3/8 lbs. combo, 7 lbs. single. **Stock:** Walnut. **Sights:** White front, mid-rib bead. **Features:** Interchangeable barrels switch from OU to single configurations. 5 Briley chokes in combo, 4 in single bbl. extended forcing cones, ported barrels 32" with raised rib. By B.C. Outdoors.
Price: Trap Single (LX680TGTSB) **$1,736.96**
Price: Trap Combo (LX680TC). **$2,553.60**

VERONA LX702 GOLD TRAP COMBO O/U SHOTGUNS
Gauge: 20/28, 2-3/4" chamber. **Barrel:** 30". **Weight:** 7 lbs. **Stock:** Turkish walnut with beavertail forearm. **Sights:** White front bead. **Features:** 2-barrel competition gun. Color case-hardened side plates and receiver with gold inlaid pheasant. Vent rib between barrels. 5 Interchokes. Imported from Italy by B.C. Outdoors.
Price: Combo **$2,467.84**
Price: 20 ga. **$1,829.12**

VERONA LX702 SKEET/TRAP O/U SHOTGUNS
Similar to Verona LX702. Both are 12 gauge and 2-3/4" chamber. Skeet has 28" barrel and weighs 7.75 lbs. Trap has 32" barrel and weighs 7-7/8 lbs. By B.C. Outdoors.
Price: Skeet **$1,829.12**
Price: Trap **$1,829.12**

WEATHERBY ATHENA GRADE V AND GRADE III CLASSIC FIELD O/U SHOTGUNS
Gauge: Grade III and Grade IV: 12, 20, 3" chambers; 28, 2-3/4" chambers. Grade V: 12, 20, 3" chambers. **Barrel:** 26", 28" monobloc, IMC multi-choke tubes. Modified Greener crossbolt action. Matte ventilated top rib with brilliant front bead. **Weight:** 12 ga., 7.25 to 8 lbs.; 20 ga. 6.5 to 7.25 lbs. **Length:** 43" to 45". **Stock:** Rounded pistol grip, slender forend, Old English recoil pad. Grade V has oil-finished AAA American Claro walnut with 20-lpi checkering. Grade III has AA Claro walnut with oil finish, fine-line checkering. **Features:** Silver nitride/gray receivers; Grade III has hunting scene engraving. Grade IV has chrome-plated false sideplates featuring single game scene gold plate overlay. Grade V has rose and scroll engraving with gold-overlay upland game scenes. Top levers engraved with

gold Weatherby flying "W". Introduced 1999. Imported from Japan by Weatherby.

Price: Grade III $2,599.00
Price: Grade IV $2,799.00
Price: Grade V $3,999.00

WEATHERBY ORION D'ITALIA O/U SHOTGUNS

Gauge: 12, 20, 3" chambers; 28, 2-3/4" chamber. **Barrel:** 26", 28", IMC multi-choke tubes. Matte ventilated top rib with brilliant bead front sight. **Weight:** 6-1/2 to 8 lbs. **Stock:** 14.25"x1.5"x2.5". American walnut, checkered grip and forend. Old English recoil pad. **Features:** All models have a triggerguard that features Weatherby's "Flying W" engraved with gold fill. D'Italia I available in 12 and 20 gauge, 26" and 28" barrels. Walnut stock with high lustre urethane finish. Metalwork is blued to high lustre finishand has a gold-plated trigger for corrosion protection. D'Italia II available in 12, 20 and 28 gauge with 26" and 28" barrels. Fancy grade walnut stock, hard chrome receiver with sculpted frameheads, elaborate game and floral engraving pattern, and matte vent mid & top rib with brilliant front bead sight. D'Italia III available in 12 and 20 gauge with 26" and 28" barrels. Hand-selected, oil-finished walnut stock wtih 20 LPI checkering, intricate engraving and gold plate game scene overlay, and damascened monobloc barrel and sculpted frameheads. D'Italia SC available in 12 gauge only with barrel lengths of 28", 30", and 32", weighs 8 lbs. Features satin, oil-finished walnut stock that is adjustable for cheek height with target-style pistol grip and Schnaubel forend, shallow receiver aligns hands for improved balance and pointability, ported barrels reduce muzzle jump, and fiber optic front sight for quick targer acquisition. Introduced 1998. Imported from Japan by Weatherby.

Price: D'Italia I $1,699.00
Price: D'Italia II $1,899.00
Price: D'Italia III $2,199.00
Price: D'Italia SC. $2,599.00

WINCHESTER SELECT MODEL 101 O/U SHOTGUNS

Gauge: 12, 2-3/4", 3" chambers. **Barrel:** 28", 30", 32", ported, Invector Plus choke system. **Weight:** 7 lbs. 6 oz. to 7 lbs. 12. oz. **Stock:** Checkered high-gloss grade II/III walnut stock, Pachmayr Decelerator sporting pad. **Features:** Chrome-plated chambers; back-bored barrels; tang barrel selector/safety; Signature extended choke tubes. Model 101 Field comes with solid brass bead front sight, three tubes, engraved receiver. Model 101 Sporting has adjustable trigger, 10mm runway rib, white mid-bead, Tru-Glo front sight, 30" and 32" barrels. Camo version of Model 101 Field comes with full-coverage Mossy Oak Duck Blind pattern. Model 101 Pigeon Grade Trap has 10mm steel runway rib, mid-bead sight, interchangeable fiber-optic front sight, porting and vented side ribs, adjustable trigger shoe, fixed raised comb or adjustable comb, Grade III/IV walnut, 30" or 32" barrels, molded ABS hard case. Reintroduced 2008. From Winchester Repeating Arms. Co.

Price: Model 101 Field $1,739.00
Price: Model 101 Deluxe Field $1,659.00
Price: Model 101 Sporting $2,139.00
Price: Model 101 Pigeon Grade Trap, intr. 2008 . . . . $2,299.00
Price: Model 101 Pigeon Grade Trap w/adj. comb,
      intr. 2008. . . . . $2,429.00
Price: Model 101 Light (2009) $1,999.00
Price: Model 101 Pigeon Sporting (2009) $2,579.00

 Prices given are believed to be accurate at time of publication however, many factors affect retail pricing so exact prices are not possible.

ARRIETA SIDELOCK DOUBLE SHOTGUNS

Gauge: 12, 16, 20, 28, .410. **Barrel:** Length and chokes to customer specs. **Weight:** To customer specs. **Stock:** To customer specs. Straight English with checkered butt (standard), or pistol grip. Select European walnut with oil finish. **Features:** Essentially custom gun with myriad options. H&H pattern hand-detachable sidelocks, selective automatic ejectors, double triggers (hinged front) standard. Some have selfopening action. Finish and engraving to customer specs. Imported from Spain by Quality Arms, Inc.

Price: Model 557	$4,500.00
Price: Model 570	$5,350.00
Price: Model 578	$5,880.00
Price: Model 600 Imperial	$7,995.00
Price: Model 601 Imperial Tiro	$9,160.00
Price: Model 801	$14,275.00
Price: Model 802	$14,275.00
Price: Model 803	$9,550.00
Price: Model 871	$6,670.00
Price: Model 872	$17,850.00
Price: Model 873	$16,275.00
Price: Model 874	$13,125.00
Price: Model 875	$19,850.00
Price: Model 931	$20,895.00

AYA MODEL 4/53 SHOTGUNS

Gauge: 12, 16, 20, 28, 410. **Barrel:** 26", 27", 28", 30". **Weight:** To customer specifications. **Length:** To customer specifications. **Features:** Hammerless boxlock action; double triggers; light scroll engraving; automatic safety; straight grip oil finish walnut stock; checkered butt. Made in Spain. Imported by New England Custom Gun Service, Lt.

Price:	$2,999.00
Price: No. 2	$4,799.00
Price: No. 2 Rounded Action	$5,199.00

BERETTA 471 SIDE-BY-SIDE SHOTGUNS

Gauge: 12, 20; 3" chamber. **Barrel:** 24", 26", 28"; 6mm rib. **Weight:** 6.5 lbs. **Stock:** English or pistol stock, straight butt for various types of recoil pads. Beavertail forend. English stock with recoil pad in red or black rubber, or in walnut and splinter forend. Select European walnut, checkered, oil finish. **Features:** Optima-Choke Extended Choke Tubes. Automatic ejection or mechanical extraction. Firing-pin block safety, manual or automatic, open top-lever safety. Introduced 2007. Imported from Italy by Beretta U.S.A.

Price: Silver Hawk	$3,750.00

BILL HANUS NOBILE III BY FABARM

Gauge: 20. **Barrel:** 28" Tribor® barrels with 3" chambers and extra-long 82mm (3-1/4") internal choke tubes. **Weight:** 5.75 lbs. **Stock:** Upgraded walnut 1-1/2"x2-1/4"x14-3/8", with 1/4" cast-off to a wood butt plate. Altering to 1/4" cast-on for left-handed shooters, $300 extra. **Features:** Tribor® barrels feature extra-long forcing cones along with over-boring, back-boring and extra-long (82mm vs 50mm) choke tubes which put more pellets in the target area. Paradox®-rifled choke tube for wider patterns at short-range targets. Adjustable for automatic ejectors or manual extraction. Adjustable opening tension. Fitted leather case.

Price:	$3,395.00

CONNECTICUT SHOTGUN MANUFACTURING COMPANY RBL SIDE-BY-SIDE SHOTGUN

Gauge: 12, 16, 20, 28. **Barrel:** 26", 28", 30", 32". **Weight:** NA. **Length:** NA. **Stock:** NA. **Features:** Round-action SXS shotguns made in the USA. Scaled frames, five TruLock choke tubes. Deluxe fancy grade walnut buttstock and forend. Quick Change recoil pad in two lengths. Various dimensions and options available depending on gauge.

Price: 12 gauge	$2,950.00
Price: 20 gauge	$2,799.00
Price: 28 gauge	$3,650.00

CZ BOBWHITE AND RINGNECK SHOTGUNS

Gauge: 12, 20, 28, .410. (5 screw-in chokes in 12 and 20 ga. and fixed chokes in IC and Mod in .410). **Barrel:** 20". **Weight:** 6.5 lbs. **Length:** NA. **Stock:** Sculptured Turkish walnut with straight English-style grip and double triggers (Bobwhite) or conventional American pistol grip with a single trigger (Ringneck). Both are hand checkered 20 lpi. **Features:** Both color case-hardened shotguns are hand engraved.

Price: Bobwhite	$789.00
Price: Ringneck	$1,036.00

CZ HAMMER COACH SHOTGUNS

Gauge: 12, 3" chambers. **Barrel:** 20". **Weight:** 6.7 lbs. **Length:** NA. **Stock:** NA. **Features:** Following in the tradition of the guns used by the stagecoach guards of the 1880's, this cowboy gun features double triggers, 19th century color case-hardening and fully functional external hammers.

Price:	$904.00

DAKOTA PREMIER GRADE SHOTGUN

Gauge: 12, 16, 20, 28, .410. **Barrel:** 27". **Weight:** NA. **Length:** NA. **Stock:** Exhibition-grade English walnut, hand-rubbed oil finish with straight grip and splinter forend. **Features:** French grey finish; 50 percent coverage engraving; double triggers; selective ejectors. Finished to customer specifications. Made in U.S. by Dakota Arms.

Price: From	$14,950.00

DAKOTA LEGEND SHOTGUN

Similar to Premier Grade except has special selection English walnut, full-coverage scroll engraving, oak and leather case. Made in U.S. by Dakota Arms.

Price: From	$19,000.00

EMF OLD WEST HAMMER SHOTGUN

Gauge: 12. **Barrel:** 20". **Weight:** 8 lbs. **Length:** 37" overall. **Stock:** Smooth walnut with steel butt place. **Sights:** Large brass bead. **Features:** Colt-style exposed hammers rebounding type; blued receiver and barrels; cylinder bore. Introduced 2006. Imported from China for EMF by TTN.

Price:	$474.90

FOX, A.H., SIDE-BY-SIDE SHOTGUNS

Gauge: 16, 20, 28, .410. **Barrel:** Length and chokes to customer specifications. Rust-blued Chromox or Krupp steel. **Weight:** 5-1/2 to 6.75 lbs. **Stock:** Dimensions to customer specifications. Hand-checkered Turkish Circassian walnut with hand-rubbed oil finish. Straight, semi or full pistol grip; splinter, Schnabel or beavertail forend; traditional pad, hard rubber buttplate or skeleton butt. **Features:** Boxlock action with automatic ejectors; double or Fox single selective trigger. Scalloped, rebated and color case-hardened receiver; hand finished and handengraved. Grades differ in engraving, inlays, grade of wood, amount of hand finishing. Introduced 1993. Made in U.S. by Connecticut Shotgun Mfg.

Price: CE Grade	$14,500.00
Price: XE Grade	$16,000.00
Price: DE Grade	$19,000.00
Price: FE Grade	$24,000.00

SHOTGUNS—Side-by-Side

Price: 28/.410 CE Grade. **$16,500.00**
Price: 28/.410 XE Grade. **$18,000.00**
Price: 28/.410 DE Grade. **$21,000.00**
Price: 28/.410 FE Grade. **$26,000.00**

GARBI MODEL 100 DOUBLE SHOTGUN
Gauge: 12, 16, 20, 28. **Barrel:** 26", 28", choked to customer specs. **Weight:** 5-1/2 to 7.5 lbs. **Stock:** 14.5"x2.25"x1.5". European walnut. Straight grip, checkered butt, classic forend. **Features:** Sidelock action, automatic ejectors, double triggers standard. Color case-hardened action, coin finish optional. Single trigger; beavertail forend, etc. optional. Five additional models available. Imported from Spain by Wm. Larkin Moore.
Price: From. **$4,850.00**

GARBI MODEL 101 SIDE-BY-SIDE SHOTGUN
Similar to the Garbi Model 100 except hand engraved with scroll engraving; select walnut stock; better overall quality than the Model 100. Imported from Spain by Wm. Larkin Moore.
Price: From. **$6,250.00**

GARBI MODEL 103 A & B SIDE-BY-SIDE SHOTGUNS
Similar to the Garbi Model 100 except has Purdey-type fine scroll and rosette engraving. Better overall quality than the Model 101. Model 103B has nickel-chrome steel barrels, H&H-type easy opening mechanism; other mechanical details remain the same. Imported from Spain by Wm. Larkin Moore.
Price: Model 103A. From **$14,100.00**
Price: Model 103B. From **$21,600.00**

GARBI MODEL 200 SIDE-BY-SIDE SHOTGUN
Similar to the Garbi Model 100 except has heavy-duty locks, magnum proofed. Very fine Continental-style floral and scroll engraving, well figured walnut stock. Other mechanical features remain the same. Imported from Spain by Wm. Larkin Moore.
Price: **$17,100.00**

KIMBER VALIER SIDE-BY-SIDE SHOTGUN
Gauge: 20, 16, 3" chambers. Barrels: 26" or 28", IC and M. **Weight:** 6 lbs. 8 oz. **Stock:** Turkish walnut, English style. **Features:** Sidelock design, double triggers, 50-percent engraving; 24 lpi checkering; auto-ejectors (extractors only on Grade I). Color case-hardened sidelocks, rust blue barrels. Imported from Turkey by Kimber Mfg., Inc.
Price: Grade II. **$4,999.00**

LEBEAU-COURALLY BOXLOCK SIDE-BY-SIDE SHOTGUN
Gauge: 12, 16, 20, 28, .410-bore. **Barrel:** 25" to 32". **Weight:** To customer specifications. **Stock:** French walnut. **Features:** Anson & Deeley-type action with automatic ejectors; single or double triggers. Custom gun built to customer specifications. Imported from Belgium by Wm. Larkin Moore.
Price: From. **$25,500.00**

LEBEAU-COURALLY SIDELOCK SIDE-BY-SIDE SHOTGUN
Gauge: 12, 16, 20, 28, .410-bore. **Barrel:** 25" to 32". **Weight:** To customer specifications. **Stock:** Fancy French walnut. **Features:** Holland & Holland-type action with automatic ejectors; single or double triggers. Custom gun built to customer specifications. Imported from Belgium by Wm. Larkin Moore.
Price: From. **$56,000.00**

MARLIN L. C. SMITH SIDE-BY-SIDE SHOTGUN
Gauge: 12, 20, 28, .410. **Stock:** Checkered walnut w/recoil pad. **Features:** 3" chambers, single trigger, selective automatic ejectors; 3 choke tubes (IC, Mod., Full); solid rib, bead front sight. Imported from Italy by Marlin. Introduced 2005.
Price: LC12-DB (28" barrel, 43" OAL, 6.25 lbs) **$1,962.00**
Price: LC28-DB (26" barrel, 41" OAL, 6 lbs). **$1,484.00**

MERKEL MODEL 47E, 147E SIDE-BY-SIDE SHOTGUNS
Gauge: 12, 3" chambers, 16, 2.75" chambers, 20, 3" chambers. **Barrel:** 12, 16 ga.-28"; 20 ga.-26.75" (Imp. Cyl. & Mod., Mod. & Full).

Weight: About 6.75 lbs. (12 ga.). **Stock:** Oil-finished walnut; straight English or pistol grip. **Features:** Anson & Deeley-type boxlock action with single selective or double triggers, automatic safety, cocking indicators. Color case-hardened receiver with standard arabesque engraving. Imported from Germany by Merkel USA.
Price: Model 47E (H&H ejectors) **$4,595.00**
Price: Model 147E (as above with ejectors) **$5,795.00**

MERKEL MODEL 47EL, 147EL SIDE-BY-SIDE SHOTGUNS
Similar to Model 47E except H&H style sidelock action with cocking indicators, ejectors. Silver-grayed receiver and sideplates have arabesque engraving, engraved border and screws (Model 47E), or fine hunting scene engraving (Model 147E). Limited edition. Imported from Germany by Merkel USA.
Price: Model 47EL **$7,195.00**
Price: Model 147EL **$7,695.00**

MERKEL MODEL 280EL, 360EL SHOTGUNS
Similar to Model 47E except smaller frame. Greener cross bolt with double under-barrel locking lugs, fine engraved hunting scenes on silver-grayed receiver, luxury-grade wood, Anson and Deely boxlock action. H&H ejectors, single-selective or double triggers. Introduced 2000. Imported from Germany by Merkel USA.
Price: Model 280EL (28 gauge, 28" barrel, Imp. Cyl. and Mod. chokes) **$7,695.00**
Price: Model 360EL (.410, 28" barrel, Mod. and Full chokes) **$7,695.00**
Price: Model 280EL Combo **$11,195.00**

MERKEL MODEL 280SL AND 360SL SHOTGUNS
Similar to Model 280EL and 360EL except has sidelock action, double triggers, English-style arabesque engraving. Introduced 2000. Imported from Germany by Merkel USA.
Price: Model 280SL (28 gauge, 28" barrel, Imp. Cyl. and Mod. chokes). **$10,995.00**
Price: Model 360SL (.410, 28" barrel, Mod. and Full chokes) **$10,995.00**

MERKEL MODEL 1620 SIDE-BY-SIDE SHOTGUN
Gauge: 16. **Features:** Greener crossbolt with double under-barrel locking lugs, scroll-engraved case-hardened receiver, Anson and Deely boxlock aciton, Holland & Holland ejectors, English-style stock, single selective or double triggers, or pistol grip stock with single selective trgger. Imported from Germany by Merkel USA.
Price: **$4,995.00**
Price: Model 1620E; silvered, engraved receiver **$5,995.00**
Price: Model 1620 Combo; 16- and 20-gauge two-barrel set **$7,695.00**
Price: Model 1620EL; upgraded wood **$7,695.00**
Price: Model 1620EL Combo; 16- and 20-gauge two-barrel set **$11,195.00**

PIOTTI KING NO. 1 SIDE-BY-SIDE SHOTGUN
Gauge: 12, 16, 20, 28, .410. **Barrel:** 25" to 30" (12 ga.), 25" to 28" (16, 20, 28, .410). To customer specs. Chokes as specified. **Weight:** 6.5 lbs. to 8 lbs. (12 ga. to customer specs.). **Stock:** Dimensions to customer specs. Finely figured walnut; straight grip with checkered butt with classic splinter forend and hand-rubbed oil finish standard. Pistol grip, beavertail forend. **Features:** Holland & Holland pattern sidelock action, automatic ejectors. Double trigger; non-selective single trigger optional. Coin finish standard; color case-hardened optional. Top rib; level, file-cut; concave, ventilated optional. Very fine, full coverage scroll engraving with small floral bouquets. Imported from Italy by Wm. Larkin Moore.
Price: From. **$38,300.00**

PIOTTI LUNIK SIDE-BY-SIDE SHOTGUN
Similar to the Piotti King No. 1 in overall quality. Has Renaissance-style large scroll engraving in relief. Best quality Holland & Holland-

pattern sidelock ejector double with chopper lump (demi-bloc) barrels. Other mechanical specifications remain the same. Imported from Italy by Wm. Larkin Moore.
Price: From **$39,900.00**

PIOTTI PIUMA SIDE-BY-SIDE SHOTGUN
Gauge: 12, 16, 20, 28, .410. **Barrel:** 25" to 30" (12 ga.), 25" to 28" (16, 20, 28, .410). **Weight:** 5-1/2 to 6-1/4 lbs. (20 ga.). **Stock:** Dimensions to customer specs. Straight grip stock with walnut checkered butt, classic splinter forend, hand-rubbed oil finish are standard; pistol grip, beavertail forend, satin luster finish optional. **Features:** Anson & Deeley boxlock ejector double with chopper lump barrels. Level, file-cut rib, light scroll and rosette engraving, scalloped frame. Double triggers; single non-selective optional. Coin finish standard, color case-hardened optional. Imported from Italy by Wm. Larkin Moore.
Price: From **$19,200.00**

REMINGTON SPR210 SIDE-BY-SIDE SHOTGUNS
Gauge: 12, 20, 28, .410 bore, 3" chambers; 28, 2-3/4" chambers. **Barrel:** 26", 28", blued chrome-lined. **Weight:** 6.75 to 7 lbs. **Stock:** checkered walnut stock and forend, 14.5" LOP; 1.5" drop at comb; 2.5" drop at heel. **Features:** Nickel or blued receiver. Single selective mechanical trigger, selective automatic ejectors; SC-4 choke tube set on most models. Steel receiver/mono block, auto tang safety, rubber recoil pad. Introduced 2008. Imported by Remington Arms Co.
Price: SPR210, from **$479.00**

REMINGTON SPR220 SIDE-BY-SIDE SHOTGUNS
Gauge: 12, 20, 2-3/4" or 3" chambers. **Barrel:** 20", 26", blued chrome-lined. **Weight:** 6.25 to 7 lbs. Otherwise similar to SPR210 except has double trigger/extractors. Introduced 2008. Imported by Remington Arms Co.
Price: SPR220, from **$342.00**

RIZZINI SIDELOCK SIDE-BY-SIDE SHOTGUN
Gauge: 12, 16, 20, 28, .410. **Barrel:** 25" to 30" (12, 16, 20 ga.), 25" to 28" (28, .410). To customer specs. Chokes as specified. **Weight:** 6.5 lbs. to 8 lbs. (12 ga. to customer specs). **Stock:** Dimensions to customer specs. Finely figured walnut; straight grip with checkered butt with classic splinter forend and hand-rubbed oil finish standard. Pistol grip, beavertail forend. **Features:** Sidelock action, auto ejectors. Double triggers or non-selective single trigger standard. Coin finish standard. Imported from Italy by Wm. Larkin Moore.
Price: 12, 20 ga. From **$106,000.00**
Price: 28, .410 bore. From **$95,000.00**

RUGER GOLD LABEL SIDE-BY-SIDE SHOTGUN
Gauge: 12, 3" chambers. **Barrel:** 28" with skeet tubes. **Weight:** 6.5 lbs. **Length:** 45". **Stock:** American walnut straight grip. **Sights:** Gold bead front, full length rib, serrated top. **Features:** Spring-assisted break-open, SS trigger, auto eject. Five interchangeable screw-in choke tubes, combination safety/barrel selector with auto safety reset.
Price: **$3,226.00**

SMITH & WESSON ELITE GOLD SHOTGUNS
Gauge: 20, 3" chambers. **Barrel:** 26", 28", 30", rust-blued chopper-lump. **Weight:** 6.5 lbs. **Sights:** Ivory front bead, metal mid-bead. **Stock:** AAA (grade III) Turkish walnut stocks, hand-cut checkering, satin finish. English grip or pistol grip. **Features:** Smith & Wesson-designed trigger-plate action, hand-engraved receivers, bone-charcoal case hardening, lifetime warranty. Five choke tubes. Introduced 2007. Made in Turkey, imported by Smith & Wesson.
Price: **$2,380.00**

STOEGER UPLANDER SIDE-BY-SIDE SHOTGUNS
Gauge: 16, 28, 2-3/4 chambers. 12, 20, .410, 3" chambers. **Barrel:** 22", 24", 26", 28". **Weight:** 7.3 lbs. **Sights:** Brass bead. **Features:**
Double trigger, IC & M fixed choke tubes with gun.
Price: With fixed or screw-in chokes **$369.00**
Price: Supreme, screw-in chokes, 12 or 20 ga. **$489.00**
Price: Youth, 20 ga. or .410, 22" barrel, double trigger **$369.00**
Price: Combo, 20/28 ga. or 12/20 ga. **$649.00**

STOEGER COACH GUN SIDE-BY-SIDE SHOTGUNS
Gauge: 12, 20, 2-3/4", 3" chambers. **Barrel:** 20". **Weight:** 6.5 lbs. **Stock:** Brown hardwood, classic beavertail forend. **Sights:** Brass bead. **Features:** IC & M fixed chokes, tang auto safety, auto extractors, black plastic buttplate. Imported by Benelli USA.
Price: Supreme blued finish **$469.00**
Price: Supreme blued barrel, stainless receiver **$469.00**
Price: Silverado Coach Gun with English synthetic stock. **$469.00**

TRADITIONS ELITE SERIES SIDE-BY-SIDE SHOTGUNS
Gauge: 12, 3"; 20, 3"; 28, 2-3/4"; .410, 3". **Barrel:** 26". **Weight:** 5 lbs., 12 oz. to 6.5 lbs. **Length:** 43" overall. **Stock:** Walnut. **Features:** Chrome-lined barrels; fixed chokes (Elite Field III ST, Field I DT and Field I ST) or choke tubes (Elite Hunter ST); extractors (Hunter ST and Field I models) or automatic ejectors (Field III ST); top tang safety. Imported from Fausti of Italy by Traditions.
Price: Elite Field I DT C 12, 20, 28 ga. or .410; IC and Mod. fixed chokes (F and F on .410); double triggers . . **$789.00 to $969.00**
Price: Elite Field I ST C 12, 20, 28 ga. or .410; same as DT but with single trigger . . . . **$969.00 to $1,169.00**
Price: Elite Field III ST C 28 ga. or .410; gold-engraved receiver; high-grade walnut stock **$2,099.00**
Price: Elite Hunter ST C 12 or 20 ga.; blued receiver; IC and Mod. choke tubes **$999.00**

TRADITIONS UPLANDER SERIES SIDE-BY-SIDE SHOTGUNS
Gauge: 12, 3"; 20, 3". **Barrel:** 26", 28". **Weight:** 6-1/4 lbs. to 6.5 lbs. **Length:** 43" to 45" overall. **Stock:** Walnut. **Features:** Barrels threaded for choke tubes (Improved Cylinder, Modified and Full); top tang safety, extended trigger guard. Engraved silver receiver with side plates and lavish gold inlays. Imported from Fausti of Italy by Traditions.
Price: Uplander III Silver 12, 20 ga. **$2,699.00**
Price: Uplander V Silver 12, 20 ga. **$3,199.00**

TRISTAR BRITTANY CLASSIC SIDE-BY-SIDE SHOTGUN
Gauge: 12, 16, 20, 28, .410, 3" chambers. **Barrel:** 27", chrome lined, three Beretta-style choke tubes (IC, M, F). **Weight:** 6.3 to 6.7 lbs. **Stock:** Rounded pistol grip, satin oil finish. **Features:** Engraved case-colored one-piece frame, auto selective ejectors, single selective trigger, solid raised barrel rib, top tang safety. Imported from Spain by Tristar Sporting Arms Ltd.
Price: From **$1,419.00**

WEATHERBY SBS ATHENA D'ITALIA SIDE-BY-SIDE SHOTGUNS
Gauge: D'Italia: 12, 20, 2-3/4" or 3" chambers, 28, 2-3/4" chambers. **Barrel:** 26" on 20 and 28 gauges; 28" on 12 ga. Chrome-lined, lengthened forcing cones, backbored. **Weight:** 6.75 to 7.25 lbs. **Length:** 42.5" to 44.5". **Stock:** Walnut, 20-lpi laser cut checkering, "New Scottish" pattern. **Features:** All come with foam-lined take-down case. Machined steel receiver, hardened and chromed with coin finish, engraved triggerguard with roll-formed border. D'Italia has double triggers, brass front bead. PG is identical to D'Italia, except for rounded pistol grip and semi-beavertail forearm. Deluxe features sculpted frameheads, Bolino-style engraved game scene with floral engraving. AAA Fancy Turkish walnut, straight grip, 24-lpi hand checkering, hand-rubbed oil finish. Single mechanical trigger; right barrel fires first. Imported from Italy by Weatherby.
Price: SBS Athena D'Italia SBS **$3,129.00**
Price: SBS Athena D'Italia PG SBS **$3,799.00**

BERETTA DT10 TRIDENT TRAP TOP SINGLE SHOTGUN

Gauge: 12, 3" chamber. **Barrel:** 34"; five Optima Choke tubes (Full, Full, Imp. Modified, Mod. and Imp. Cyl.). **Weight:** 8.8 lbs. **Stock:** High-grade walnut; adjustable. **Features:** Detachable, adjustable trigger group; Optima Bore for improved shot pattern and reduced recoil; slim Optima Choke tubes; raised and thickened receiver for long life. Introduced 2000. Imported from Italy by Beretta USA.
Price: **$7,400.00**

BROWING A-BOLT SHOTGUN HUNTER BOLT ACTION SHOTGUN

Gauge: 12 ga. 3" chamber. **Barrel:** 22". **Weight:** 7 lbs. 2 ozs. **Length:** 43.75". **Stock:** Satin finish walnut stock and forearm – checkered. **Features:** Drilled and tapped for scope mounts, 60° bolt action lift, detachable two-round magazine, and top-tang safety. Sling swivel studs installed, rrecoil pad, TRUGLO®/Marble's® fiber-optic front sight with rear sight adjustable for windage and elevation.
Price: From **$1.200.00**

BROWING A-BOLT SHOTGUN, MOSSY OAK BREAK-UP INFINITY BOLT ACTION SHOTGUN

Gauge: 12 ga. 3" chamber. **Barrel:** 22". **Weight:** 7 lbs. 2 ozs. **Length:** 43.75". **Stock:** Composite stock and forearm, textured gripping surfaces, Mossy Oak® Break-Up® Infinity™ camo finish • Dura-Touch® Armor Coating. **Features:** Drilled and tapped for scope mounts, 60° bolt action lift, detachable two-round magazine, and top-tang safety. Sling swivel studs installed, rrecoil pad, TRUGLO®/Marble's® fiber-optic front sight with rear sight adjustable for windage and elevation.
Price: From **$1,240.00**

BROWING A-BOLT SHOTGUN STALKER BOLT ACTION SHOTGUN

Gauge: 12 ga. 3" chamber. **Barrel:** 22". **Weight:** 7 lbs. **Length:** 43.75". **Stock:** Composite stock and forearm, textured gripping surfaces, Dura-Touch® Armor Coating. **Features:** Drilled and tapped for scope mounts, 60° bolt action lift, detachable two-round magazine, and top-tang safety. Sling swivel studs installed, rrecoil pad, TRUGLO®/Marble's® fiber-optic front sight with rear sight adjustable for windage and elevation.
Price: From **$1,100.00**

HARRINGTON & RICHARDSON ULTRA SLUG HUNTER/ TAMER SHOTGUNS

Gauge: 12, 20 ga., 3" chamber, .410. **Barrel:** 20" to 24" rifled. **Weight:** 6 to 9 lbs. **Length:** 34.5" to 40". **Stock:** Hardwood, laminate, or polymer with full pistol grip; semi-beavertail forend. **Sights:** Gold bead front. **Features:** Break-open action with side-lever release, automatic ejector. Introduced 1994. From H&R 1871, LLC.
Price: Ultra Slug Hunter, blued, hardwood $273.00
Price: Ultra Slug Hunter Youth, blued, hardwood, 13-1/8" LOP. $273.00
Price: Ultra Slug Hunter Deluxe, blued, laminated $273.00
Price: Tamer .410 bore, stainless barrel, black polymer stock $173.00

HARRINGTON & RICHARDSON ULTRA LITE SLUG HUNTER

Gauge: 12, 20 ga., 3" chamber. **Barrel:** 24" rifled. **Weight:** 5.25 lbs. **Length:** 40". **Stock:** Hardwood with walnut finish, full pistol grip, recoil pad, sling swivel studs. **Sights:** None; base included. **Features:** Youth Model, available in 20 ga. has 20" rifled barrel. Deluxe Model has checkered laminated stock and forend. From H&R 1871, LLC.
Price: $194.00

HARRINGTON & RICHARDSON ULTRA SLUG HUNTER THUMBHOLE STOCK

Similar to the Ultra Lite Slug Hunter but with laminated thumbhole stock and weighs 8.5 lbs.
Price: . . . . NA

HARRINGTON & RICHARDSON TOPPER MODELS

Gauge: 12, 16, 20, .410, up to 3.5" chamber. **Barrel:** 22 to 28". **Weight:** 5-7 lbs. **Stock:** Polymer, hardwood, or black walnut. **Features:** Satin nickel frame, blued barrel. Reintroduced 1992. From H&R 1871, LLC.
Price: Deluxe Classic, 12/20 ga., 28" barrel w/vent rib $225.00
Price: Topper Deluxe 12 ga., 28" barrel, black hardwood $179.00
Price: Topper 12, 16, 20 ga., .410, 26" to 28", black hardwood $153.00
Price: Topper Junior 20 ga., .410, 22" barrel, hardwood $160.00
Price: Topper Junior Classic, 20 ga., .410, checkered hardwood $160.00

HARRINGTON & RICHARDSON TOPPER TRAP GUN

Similar to other Topper Models but with select checkered walnut stock and forend wtih fluted comb and full pistol grip; 30" barrel with two white beads and screw-in chokes (Improved Modified Extended included); deluxe Pachmayr trap recoil pad.
Price: $360.00

KRIEGHOFF K-80 SINGLE BARREL TRAP GUN

Gauge: 12, 2-3/4" chamber. **Barrel:** 32" or 34" Unsingle. Fixed Full or choke tubes. **Weight:** About 8-3/4 lbs. **Stock:** Four stock dimensions or adjustable stock available. All hand-checkered European walnut. **Features:** Satin nickel finish. Selective mechanical trigger adjustable for finger position. Tapered step vent rib. Adjustable point of impact.
Price: Standard grade Full Unsingle, from **$10,080.00**

KRIEGHOFF KX-5 TRAP GUN

Gauge: 12, 2-3/4" chamber. **Barrel:** 32", 34"; choke tubes. **Weight:** About 8.5 lbs. **Stock:** Factory adjustable stock. European walnut. **Features:** Ventilated tapered step rib. Adjustable position trigger, optional release trigger. Fully adjustable rib. Satin gray electroless nickel receiver. Fitted aluminum case. Imported from Germany by Krieghoff International, Inc.
Price: $5,395.00

LJUTIC MONO GUN SINGLE BARREL SHOTGUN

Gauge: 12 only. **Barrel:** 34", choked to customer specs; hollow-milled rib, 35.5" sight plane. **Weight:** Approx. 9 lbs. **Stock:** To customer specs. Oil finish, hand checkered. **Features:** Custom gun. Pull or release trigger; removable trigger guard contains trigger and hammer mechanism; Ljutic pushbutton opener on front of trigger guard. From Ljutic Industries.

Price: Std., med. or Olympic rib, custom bbls., fixed choke.. **$7,495.00**
Price: Stainless steel mono gun **$8,495.00**

LJUTIC LTX PRO 3 DELUXE MONO GUN
Deluxe, lightweight version of the Mono gun with high quality wood, up-grade checkering, special rib height, screw-in chokes, ported and cased.
Price: **$8,995.00**
Price: Stainless steel model **$9,995.00**

NEW ENGLAND FIREARMS PARDNER AND TRACKER II SHOTGUNS
Gauge: 10, 12, 16, 20, 28, .410, up to 3.5" chamber for 10 and 12 ga. 16, 28, 2-3/4" chamber. **Barrel:** 24" to 30". **Weight:** Varies from 5 to 9.5 lbs. **Length:** Varies from 36" to 48". **Stock:** Walnut-finished hardwood with full pistol grip, synthetic, or camo finish. **Sights:** Bead front on most. **Features:** Transfer bar ignition; break-open action with side-lever release. Introduced 1987. From New England Firearms.
Price: Pardner, all gauges, hardwood stock, 26" to 32"
blued barrel, Mod. or Full choke **$140.00**
Price: Pardner Youth, hardwood stock, straight grip,
22" blued barrel **$149.00**
Price: Pardner Screw-In Choke model, intr. 2006 . . . .**$164.00**
Price: Turkey model, 10/12 ga., camo finish
or black. . . . .**$192.00 to $259.00**
Price: Youth Turkey, 20 ga., camo finish or black **$192.00**
Price: Waterfowl, 10 ga., camo finish or hardwood **$227.00**
Price: Tracker II slug gun, 12/20 ga., hardwood. **$196.00**

REMINGTON SPR100 SINGLE-SHOT SHOTGUNS
Gauge: 12, 20, .410 bore, 3" chambers. **Barrel:** 24", 26", 28", 29.5", blued chrome-lined. **Weight:** 6.25 to 6.5 lbs. **Stock:** Walnut stock and forend. **Features:** Nickel or blued receiver. Cross-bolt safety, cocking indicator, titanium-coated trigger, selectable ejector or extractor. Introduced 2008. Imported by Remington Arms Co.
Price: SPR100, from. **$479.00**

ROSSI CIRCUIT JUDGE
Revolving shotgun chambered in .410 (2-1/2- or 3-inch/.45 Colt. Based on Taurus Judge handgun. Features include 18.5-inch barrel; fiber optic front sight; 5-round cylinder; hardwood Monte Carlo stock.
Price: **$475.00**
Price: Tactical Black Synthetic **$633.00**
Price: 44Mag. **$633.00**
Price: 28Ga. **$633.00**
Price: Stainless Bl Hardwood Monte Carlo Stk. **$680.00**

ROSSI SINGLE-SHOT SHOTGUNS
Gauge: 12, 20, .410. **Barrel:** 22" (Youth), 28". **Weight:** 3.75-5.25 lbs. **Stocks:** Wood. **Sights:** Bead front sight, fully adjustable fiber optic sight on Slug and Turkey. **Features:** Single-shot break open, 8 models available, positive ejection, internal transfer bar mechanism, trigger block system, Taurus Security System, blued finish, Rifle Slug has ported barrel.
Price: From **$117.00**

ROSSI TUFFY SHOTGUN
Gauge: .410. **Barrel:** 18-1/2". **Weight:** 3 lbs. **Length:** 29.5" overall.
Features: Single-shot break-open model with black synthetic

thumbhole stock in blued or stainless finish.
Price: . . . .**$164.00-$172.00**

ROSSI MATCHED PAIRS

Gauge/Caliber: 12, 20, .410, .22 Mag, .22LR, .17HMR, .223 Rem, .243 Win, .270 Win, .30-06, .308 Win, .50 (black powder). **Barrel:** 23", 28". **Weight:** 5-6.3 lbs. **Stocks:** Wood or black synthetic. **Sights:** Bead front on shotgun barrel, fully adjustable front and rear on rifle barrel, drilled and tapped for scope, fully adjustable fiber optic sights (black powder). **Features:** Single-shot break open, 27 models available, internal transfer bar mechanism, manual external safety, blue finish, trigger block system, Taurus Security System, youth models available.
Price: Rimfire/Shotgun, from. **$160.00**
Price: Centerfire/Shotgun **$271.95**
Price: Black Powder Matched Pair, from **$262.00**

ROSSI MATCHED SET
Gauge/Caliber: 12, 20, .22 LR, .17 HMR, .243 Win, .270 Win, .50 (black powder). **Barrel:** 33.5". **Weight:** 6.25-6.3 lbs. **Stocks:** Wood. **Sights:** Bead front on shotgun barrel, fully adjustable front and rear on rifle barrel, drilled and tapped for scope, fully adjustable fiber optic sights (black powder). **Features:** Single-shot break open, 4 models available, internal transfer bar mechanism, manual external safety, blue finish, trigger block system, Taurus Security System, youth models available.
Price: From **$374.00**

TAR-HUNT RSG-12 PROFESSIONAL RIFLED SLUG GUN
Gauge: 12, 2-3/4" or 3" chamber, 1-shot magazine. **Barrel:** 23", fully rifled with muzzle brake. **Weight:** 7.75 lbs. **Length:** 41.5" overall. **Stock:** Matte black McMillan fiberglass with Pachmayr Decelerator pad. **Sights:** None furnished; comes with Leupold windage or Weaver bases. **Features:** Uses rifle-style action with two locking lugs; two-position safety; Shaw barrel; single-stage, trigger; muzzle brake. Many options available. All models have area-controlled feed action. Introduced 1991. Made in U.S. by Tar-Hunt Custom Rifles, Inc.
Price: 12 ga. Professional model **$2,585.00**
Price: Left-hand model add. **$110.00**

TAR-HUNT RSG-16 ELITE SHOTGUN
Similar to RSG-12 Professional except 16 gauge; right- or left-hand versions.
Price: **$2,585.00**

TAR-HUNT RSG-20 MOUNTAINEER SLUG GUN
Similar to the RSG-12 Professional except chambered for 20 gauge (2-3/4" and 3" shells); 23" Shaw rifled barrel, with muzzle brake; two-lug bolt; one-shot blind magazine; matte black finish; McMillan fiberglass stock with Pachmayr Decelerator pad; receiver drilled and tapped for Rem. 700 bases. Right- or left-hand versions. Weighs 6.5 lbs. Introduced 1997. Made in U.S. by Tar-Hunt Custom Rifles, Inc.
Price: **$2,585.00**

THOMPSON/CENTER ENCORE RIFLED SLUG GUN
Gauge: 20, 3" chamber. **Barrel:** 26", fully rifled. **Weight:** About 7 lbs.

Length: 40.5" overall. **Stock:** Walnut with walnut forearm. **Sights:** Steel; click-adjustable rear and ramp-style front, both with fiber optics. **Features:** Encore system features a variety of rifle, shotgun and muzzle-loading rifle barrels interchangeable with the same frame. Break-open design operates by pulling up and back on trigger guard spur. Composite stock and forearm available. Introduced 2000.
Price: **$684.00**

THOMPSON/CENTER ENCORE TURKEY GUN
Gauge: 12 ga. **Barrel:** 24". **Features:** All-camo finish, high definition Realtree Hardwoods HD camo.
Price: **$763.00**

THOMPSON/CENTER ENCORE PROHUNTER TURKEY GUN
Contender-style break-action single shot shotgun chambered in 12 or 20 gauge 3-inch shells. Features include 24-inch barrel with interchangeable choke tubes (Extra Full supplied), composite buttstock and forend with non-slip inserts in cheekpiece, pistol grip and forend. Adjustable fiber optic sights, Sims recoil pad, AP camo finish overall. Overall length: 40.5 inches. Weight: 6-1/2 lbs.
Price: **$799.00**

BENELLI M3 CONVERTIBLE SHOTGUN
Gauge: 12, 2-3/4", 3" chambers, 5-shot magazine. **Barrel:** 19.75" (Cyl). **Weight:** 7 lbs., 4oz. **Length:** 41" overall. **Stock:** High-impact polymer with sling loop in side of butt; rubberized pistol grip on stock. **Sights:** Open rifle, fully adjustable. Ghost ring and rifle type. **Features:** Combination pump/auto action. Alloy receiver with inertia recoil rotating locking lug bolt; matte finish; automatic shell release lever. Introduced 1989. Imported by Benelli USA. Price with pistol grip, open rifle sights.
Price: With ghost ring sights, pistol grip stock **$1,489.00**

BENELLI M2 TACTICAL SHOTGUN
Gauge: 12, 2-3/4", 3" chambers, 5-shot magazine. **Barrel:** 18.5" IC, M, F choke tubes. **Weight:** 6.7 lbs. **Length:** 39.75" overall. **Stock:** Black polymer. **Sights:** Rifle type ghost ring system, tritium night sights optional. **Features:** Semiauto intertia recoil action. Cross-bolt safety; bolt release button; matte-finish metal. Introduced 1993. Imported from Italy by Benelli USA.
Price: With rifle sights. **$1,159.00**
Price: With ghost ring sights, standard stock **$1,269.00**
Price: With ghost ring sights, pistol grip stock **$1,269.00**
Price: With rifle sights, pistol grip stock **$1,159.00**
Price: ComforTech stock, rifle sights **$1,269.00**
Price: Comfortech Stock, Ghost Ring. **$1,379.00**

BENELLI M4 TACTICAL SHOTGUN
Gauge: 12 ga., 3" chamber. **Barrel:** 18.5". **Weight:** 7.8 lbs. **Length:** 40" overall. **Stock:** Synthetic. **Sights:** Ghost Ring rear, fixed blade front. **Features:** Auto-regulating gas-operated (ARGO) action, choke tube, Picatinny rail, standard and collapsible stocks available, optional LE tactical gun case. Introduced 2006. Imported from Italy by Benelli USA.
Price: Pistol grip stock, black synthetic. **$1,699.00**
Price: Desert camo pistol grip (2007) **$1,829.00**

BERETTA TX4 STORM SEMIAUTO SHOTGUN
Gauge: 12-gas operated - 3" chamber. **Barrel:** 18" barrel. **Weight:** 6.4 lbs.. **Length:** 39.2". **Stock:** Fixed in synthetic material with black ruber overlays. **Features:** The reduced felt recoil is complemented by the infallible reliability Beretta shotguns are known for. Weighing under 6 ½ pounds, the compact Tx4 with its 18" barrel is very maneuverable, while maintaining a 5+1 round capacity. Like the Cx4, the shotgun's length of pull may be adjusted with ½" spacers (one included), while the soft rubber grip inlays on the stock and fore-end ensure a firm grip in all situations. A metal Picatinny rail is mounted to the receiver to accept your optics or the included rugged and fully adjustable ghost ring sight. Adopting Beretta's new Optimabore HP

choke tube system, the included choke may be replaced with several optional accessories. Imported from Italy by Benelli USA., Corp.
Price: **$1,450.00**

CITADEL LE TACTICAL PUMP SHOTGUN
Gauge: 12 ga., 3" chamber. **Barrel:** 22". **Weight:** 5.8 lbs -7.15 lbs. **Length:** 49". **Stock:** Composite stock with close radius pistol grip; Speed Lock forearm; textured gripping surfaces; shim adjustable for length of pull, cast and drop; Mossy Oak® Bottomland™ camo finish; Dura-Touch® Armor Coating. **Features:** These shotguns are built in the U.S.A., insuring exacting parts match and a superior fit/finish. Using a common receiver and trigger group, the Citadel LE comes in four models: Spec-Ops, Talon, Pistol Grip with Heat Shield and Standard. All models feature a lightweight receiver, 7 +1 magazine capacity, 20 inch barrel, ergonomic forend, quick feed short stroke pump and rifle style sights. The Spec-Ops model features the BLACKHAWK!® Spec-Ops stock, which is adjustable for 4 inches of LOP, and estimated at absorbing up to 70% of felt recoil. The Spec-Ops gets you on target quickly – and keeps you there shot after shot. The Talon model also offers 70% felt recoil reduction with a skeletonized thumbhole stock from BLACKHAWK! that permits free hand movement with even the heaviest of gloves, and a short, 13.5 inch LOP. Finally, the Pistol Grip and Standard models offer a traditional, synthetic stock with a fixed, 13.5 inch LOP.
Price: Standard Stock **$466.00**
Price: Spec-Ops **$632.00**
Price: Talon **$632.00**
Price: Pistol grip with heat shield **$495.00**

KEL-TEC KSG BULL-PUP TWIN-TUBE SHOTGUN
The shotgun bears a stunning resemblance to the South African designed Neostead pump action scattergun. The operator is able to move a switch located near the top of the grip to select the right or left tube, or move the switch to the center to eject a shell without chambering another round. The bull-pup design results in an overall length of only 26" with an 18.5" barrel while the bottom eject design makes the firearm truly ambidextrous. The incredibly short overall length makes it more nimble than a sawed off shotgun, and with a 14+1 capacity with 2 3/4" you don't sacrifice ammunition capacity to get a shotty in a small package. Optional accessories include a factory installed picatinny rail with flip-up sights and a pistol grip.
Price: . . . . **N/A**

MOSSBERG MODEL 500 SPECIAL PURPOSE SHOTGUNS
Gauge: 12, 20, .410, 3" chamber. **Barrel:** 18.5", 20" (Cyl.). **Weight:** 7 lbs. **Stock:** Walnut-finished hardwood or black synthetic. **Sights:** Metal bead front. **Features:** Available in 6- or 8-shot models. Top-

mounted safety, double action slide bars, swivel studs, rubber recoil pad. Blue, Parkerized, Marinecote finishes. Mossberg Cablelock included. From Mossberg. The HS410 Home Security model chambered for .410 with 3" chamber; has pistol grip forend, thick recoil pad, muzzle brake and has special spreader choke on the 18.5" barrel. Overall length is 37.5", weight is 6.25 lbs. Blue finish; synthetic field stock. Mossberg Cablelock and video included. Mariner model has Marinecote metal finish to resist rust and corrosion. Synthetic field stock; pistol grip kit included. 500 Tactical 6-shot has black synthetic tactical stock. Introduced 1990.
Price: Rolling Thunder, 6-shot **$471.00**
Price: Tactical Cruiser, 18.5" barrel **$434.00**
Price: Persuader/Cruiser, 6 shot, from **$394.00**

Prices given are believed to be accurate at time of publication however, many factors affect retail pricing so exact prices are not possible.

Price: Persuader/Cruiser, 8 shot, from **$394.00**
Price: HS410 Home Security **$404.00**
Price: Mariner 6 or 9 shot, from **$538.00**
Price: Tactical 6 shot, from **$509.00**
Price: 500 Blackwater SPX. **$447.00**
Price: 500 Chainsaw pistol grip only; removable top handle . .**$491.00**
Price: 500 Tactical Tri-Rail Adjustable 6-shot. **$553.00-789.00**

MOSSBERG MODEL 590 SPECIAL PURPOSE SHOTGUN
Gauge: 12, 3" chamber, 9 shot magazine. **Barrel:** 20" (Cyl.). **Weight:** 7.25 lbs. **Stock:** Synthetic field or Speedfeed. **Sights:** Metal bead front or Ghost Ring. **Features:** Top-mounted safety, double slide action bars. Comes with heat shield, bayonet lug, swivel studs, rubber recoil pad. Blue, Parkerized or Marinecote finish. Mossberg Cablelock included. From Mossberg.
Price: Synthetic stock, from **$471.00**
Price: Speedfeed stock, from **$552.00**

MOSSBERG 930 TACTICAL AUTOLOADER WITH HEAT SHIELD
Similar to Model 930 Tactical but with ventilated heat shield handguard.
Price: **$626.00**

MOSSBERG 930 SPECIAL PURPOSE SERIES SEMIAUTO SHOTGUN
Gauge: 12 ga., 3" chamber. **Barrel:** 28" flat ventilated rib. **Weight:** 7.3 lbs. **Length:** 49". **Stock:** Composite stock with close radius pistol grip; Speed Lock forearm; textured gripping surfaces; shim adjustable for length of pull, cast and drop; Mossy Oak® Bottomland™ camo finish; Dura-Touch® Armor Coating. **Features:** 930 Special Purpose shotguns feature a self-regulating gas system that vents excess gas to aid in recoil reduction and eliminate stress on critical components. All 930 autoloaders chamber both 2 3/4 inch and 3-inch 12-gauge shotshells with ease—from target loads, to non-toxic magnum loads, to the latest sabot slug ammo. Magazine capacity is 7+1 on models with extended magazine tube, 4+1 on models without. To complete the package, each Mossberg 930 includes a set of specially designed spacers for quick adjustment of the horizontal and vertical angle of the stock, bringing a custom-feel fit to every shooter. All 930 Special Purpose models feature a drilled and tapped receiver, factory-ready for Picatinny rail, scope base or optics installation. 930 SPX models conveniently come with a factory-mounted Picatinny rail and LPA/M16-Style Ghost Ring combination sight right out of the box. Other sighting options include a basic front bead, or white-dot front sights. Mossberg 930 Special Purpose shotguns are available in a variety of configurations; 5-shot tactical barrel, 5-shot with muzzle brake, 8-shot pistol-grip, and even a 5-shot security / field combo.
Price: 930 Blackwater Series **$807.00**
Price: 930 Roadblocker **$650.00**
Price: 930 Spx Pistol Grip. **$824.00**
Price: 930 Home Security. **$572.00**
Price: 930 Special Purpose **$634.00**
Price: 930 Special Purpose Tactical. **$617.00**
Price: 930 Tactical Lpa M-16 . . . .**$734.00**
Price: 930 Tactical Barrel With Heat Shield **$638.00**

REMINGTON MODEL 870 AND MODEL 1100 TACTICAL SHOTGUNS
Gauge: 870: 12, 2-3/4 or 3" chamber; 1100: 2-3/4". **Barrel:** 18", 20", 22" (Cyl or IC). **Weight:** 7.5-7.75 lbs. **Length:** 38.5-42.5" overall. **Stock:**

Black synthetic, synthetic Speedfeed IV full pistol-grip stock, or Knoxx Industries SpecOps stock w/recoil-absorbing spring-loaded cam and adjustable length of pull (12" to 16", 870 only). **Sights:** Front post w/dot only on 870; rib and front dot on 1100. **Features:** R3 recoil pads, LimbSaver technology to reduce felt recoil, 2-, 3- or 4-shot extensions based on barrel length; matte-olive-drab barrels and receivers. Model 1100 Tactical is available with Speedfeed IV pistol grip stock or standard black synthetic stock and forend. Speedfeed IV model has an 18" barrel with two-shot extension. Standard synthetic-stocked version is equipped with 22" barrel and four-shot extension. Introduced 2006. From Remington Arms Co.
Price: 870, Speedfeed IV stock, 3" chamber,
38.5" overall, from **$587.00**
Price: 870, SpecOps stock, 3" chamber, 38.5" overall, from . .**$587.00**
Price: 1100, synthetic stock, 2-3/4" chamber, 42.5" overall . . .**$945.00**
Price: 870 TAC Desert Recon (2008), 18" barrel, 2-shot **$692.00**

REMINGTON 870 EXPRESS TACTICAL A-TACS CAMO
Pump action shotgun chambered for 2-3/4- and 3-inch 12-ga. Features include full A-TACS digitized camo; 18-1/2-inch barrel; extended ported Tactical RemChoke; SpeedFeed IV pistol-grip stock with SuperCell recoil pad; fully adjustable XS® Ghost Ring Sight rail with removable white bead front sight; 7-round capacity with factory-installed 2-shot extension; drilled and tapped receiver; sling swivel stud.
Price: **$665.00**

REMINGTON 887 NITRO MAG TACTICAL
Pump action shotgun chambered in 12-ga., 2-3/4 to 3-1/2 inch. Features include 18-1/2-inch barrel with ported, extended tactical RemChoke; 2-shot magazine extension; barrel clamp with integral Picatinny rails; ArmorLokt coating; synthetic stock and forend with specially contour grip panels.
Price: **$498.00**

TACTICAL RESPONSE TR-870 STANDARD MODEL SHOTGUNS
Gauge: 12, 3" chamber, 7-shot magazine. **Barrel:** 18" (Cyl.). **Weight:** 9 lbs. **Length:** 38" overall. **Stock:** Fiberglass-filled polypropolene with non-snag recoil absorbing butt pad. Nylon tactical forend houses flashlight. **Sights:** Trak-Lock ghost ring sight system. Front sight has Tritium insert. **Features:** Highly modified Remington 870P with Parkerized finish. Comes with nylon three-way adjustable sling, high visibility non-binding follower, high performance magazine spring, Jumbo Head safety, and Side Saddle extended 6-shot shell carrier on left side of receiver. Introduced 1991. From Scattergun Technologies, Inc.
Price: Standard model **$1,050.00**
Price: Border Patrol model, from **$1,050.00**
Price: Professional model, from **$1,070.00**

TRISTAR COBRA PUMP
Gauge: 12, 3". **Barrel:** 28". **Weight:** 6.7 lbs. Three Beretta-style choke tubes (IC, M, F). **Length:** NA. **Stock:** Matte black synthetic stock and forearm. **Sights:** Vent rib with matted sight plane. **Features:** Five-year warranty. Cobra Tactical Pump Shotgun magazine holds 7, return spring in forearm, 20" barrel, Cylinder choke. Introduced 2008. Imported by Tristar Sporting Arms Ltd.
Price: Tactical **$349.00**

FRENCH-STYLE DUELING PISTOL
Caliber: 44. **Barrel:** 10". **Weight:** 35 oz. **Length:** 15.75" overall. **Stocks:** Carved walnut. **Sights:** Fixed. **Features:** Comes with velvet-lined case and accessories. Imported by Mandall Shooting Supplies.
Price: $295.00

HARPER'S FERRY 1805 PISTOL
Caliber: 58 (.570" round ball). **Barrel:** 10". **Weight:** 39 oz. **Length:** 16" overall. **Stocks:** Walnut. **Sights:** Fixed. **Features:** Case-hardened lock, brass-mounted German silver-colored barrel. Replica of the first U.S. gov't.-made flintlock pistol. Imported by Navy Arms, Dixie Gun Works.
Price: Dixie Gun Works RH0225 .... $495.00
Price: Dixie Kit FH0411............................ $395.00

KENTUCKY FLINTLOCK PISTOL
Caliber: 45, 50, 54. **Barrel:** 10.4". **Weight:** 37-40 oz. **Length:** 15.4" overall. **Stocks:** Walnut. **Sights:** Fixed. **Features:** Specifications, including caliber, weight and length may vary with importer. Case-hardened lock, blued barrel; available also as brass barrel flintlock Model 1821. Imported by The Armoury.
Price: Single cased set (Navy Arms) $375.00

KENTUCKY PERCUSSION PISTOL
Similar to Flint version but percussion lock. Imported by The Armoury, Navy Arms, CVA (50-cal.).
Price: .... $129.95 to $225.00
Price: Steel barrel (Armoury) $179.00
Price: Single cased set (Navy Arms) $355.00
Price: Double cased set (Navy Arms) $600.00

LE PAGE PERCUSSION DUELING PISTOL
Caliber: .45. **Barrel:** 10.25" octagon, rifled. **Weight:** 36-41 oz. **Length:** 16.9" overall. **Stocks:** Walnut, fluted butt. **Sights:** Blade front, open style rear. **Features:** Double set trigger. Bright barrel, brass furniture (silver plated). Imported by Dixie Gun Works
Price: PH0310...................$525.00

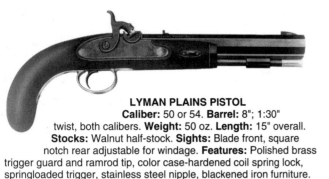

LYMAN PLAINS PISTOL
Caliber: 50 or 54. **Barrel:** 8"; 1:30" twist, both calibers. **Weight:** 50 oz. **Length:** 15" overall. **Stocks:** Walnut half-stock. **Sights:** Blade front, square notch rear adjustable for windage. **Features:** Polished brass trigger guard and ramrod tip, color case-hardened coil spring lock, springloaded trigger, stainless steel nipple, blackened iron furniture. Hooked patent breech, detachable belt hook. Introduced 1981. From Lyman Products.
Price: Finished $349.95
Price: Kit $289.95

PEDERSOLI MANG TARGET PISTOL
Caliber: 38. **Barrel:** 10.5", octagonal; 1:15" twist, **Weight:** 2.5 lbs. **Length:** 17.25" overall. **Stocks:** Walnut with fluted grip. **Sights:** Blade front, open rear adjustable for windage. **Features:** Browned barrel, polished breech plug, remainder color case-

hardened. Imported from Italy by Dixie Gun Works.
Price: PH0503. .... $1,250.00

QUEEN ANNE FLINTLOCK PISTOL
Caliber: 50 (.490" round ball). **Barrel:** 7.5", smoothbore. **Stocks:** Walnut. **Sights:** None. **Features:** German silver-colored steel barrel, fluted brass trigger guard, brass mask on butt. Lockplate left in the white. Made by Pedersoli in Italy. Introduced 1983. Imported by Dixie Gun Works. **Baby Dragoon 1848**
Price: RH0211 .... $375.00
Price: Kit FH0421 .... $295.00

TRADITIONS KENTUCKY PISTOL
Caliber: 50. **Barrel:** 10"; octagon with 7/8" flats; 1:20" twist. **Weight:** 40 oz. **Length:** 15" overall. **Stocks:** Stained beech. **Sights:** Blade front, fixed rear. **Features:** Bird's-head grip; brass thimbles; color case-hardened lock. Percussion only. Introduced 1995. From Traditions.
Price: Finished $209.00
Price: Kit $174.00

TRADITIONS TRAPPER PISTOL
Caliber: 50. **Barrel:** 9.75"; 7/8" flats; 1:20" twist. **Weight:** 2.75 lbs. **Length:** 16" overall. **Stocks:** Beech. **Sights:** Blade front, adjustable rear. **Features:** Double-set triggers; brass buttcap, trigger guard, wedge plate, forend tip, thimble. From Traditions.
Price: Percussion $286.00
Price: Flintlock $312.00
Price: Kit $149.00

TRADITIONS VEST-POCKET DERRINGER
Caliber: 31. **Barrel:** 2.25"; brass. **Weight:** 8 oz. **Length:** 4.75" overall. **Stocks:** Simulated ivory. **Sights:** Bead front. **Features:** Replica of riverboat gamblers' derringer; authentic spur trigger. From Traditions.
Price: $165.00

TRADITIONS WILLIAM PARKER PISTOL
Caliber: 50. **Barrel:** 10-3/8"; 15/16" flats; polished steel. **Weight:** 37 oz. **Length:** 17.5" overall. **Stocks:** Walnut with checkered grip. **Sights:** Brass blade front, fixed rear. **Features:** Replica dueling pistol with 1:20" twist, hooked breech. Brass wedge plate, trigger guard, cap guard; separate ramrod. Double-set triggers. Polished steel barrel, lock. Imported by Traditions.
Price: $381.00

Prices given are believed to be accurate at time of publication however, many factors affect retail pricing so exact prices are not possible.

ARMY 1860 PERCUSSION REVOLVER
Caliber: 44, 6-shot. **Barrel:** 8". **Weight:** 40 oz. **Length:** 13-5/8" overall. **Stocks:** Walnut. **Sights:** Fixed. **Features:** Engraved Navy scene on cylinder; brass trigger guard; case-hardened frame, loading lever and hammer. Some importers supply pistol cut for detachable shoulder stock, have accessory stock available. Imported by Cabela's (1860 Lawman), EMF, Navy Arms, The Armoury, Cimarron, Dixie Gun Works (half-fluted cylinder, not roll engraved), Euroarms of America (brass or steel model), Armsport, Traditions (brass or steel), Uberti U.S.A. Inc., United States Patent Fire-Arms.
Price: Dixie Gun Works RH0125 . . . . **$240.00**
Price: Brass frame (EMF) **$215.00**
Price: Single cased set (Navy Arms) **$300.00**
Price: Double cased set (Navy Arms) **$490.00**
Price: 1861 Navy: Same as Army except 36-cal., 7.5" bbl., weighs 41 oz., cut for shoulder stock; round cylinder (fluted available), from Cabela's, CVA (brass frame, 44 cal.), United States Patent Fire-Arms . . . . **$99.95 to $385.00**
Price: Steel frame kit (EMF) **$240.00**
Price: Colt Army Police, fluted cyl., 5.5", 36-cal. (Cabela's) **$229.99**
Price: With nickeled frame, barrel and backstrap, gold-tone fluted cylinder, trigger and hammer, simulated ivory grips (Traditions) **$199.00**

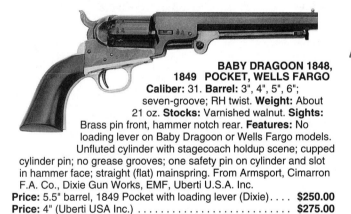

BABY DRAGOON 1848, 1849 POCKET, WELLS FARGO
Caliber: 31. **Barrel:** 3", 4", 5", 6"; seven-groove; RH twist. **Weight:** About 21 oz. **Stocks:** Varnished walnut. **Sights:** Brass pin front, hammer notch rear. **Features:** No loading lever on Baby Dragoon or Wells Fargo models. Unfluted cylinder with stagecoach holdup scene; cupped cylinder pin; no grease grooves; one safety pin on cylinder and slot in hammer face; straight (flat) mainspring. From Armsport, Cimarron F.A. Co., Dixie Gun Works, EMF, Uberti U.S.A. Inc.
Price: 5.5" barrel, 1849 Pocket with loading lever (Dixie). . . . **$250.00**
Price: 4" (Uberti USA Inc.) **$275.00**

DIXIE WYATT EARP REVOLVER
Caliber: 44. **Barrel:** 12", octagon. **Weight:** 46 oz. **Length:** 18" overall. **Stocks:** One-piece hardwood. **Sights:** Fixed. **Features:** Highly polished brass frame, backstrap and trigger guard; blued barrel and cylinder; case-hardened hammer, trigger and loading lever. Navy-size shoulder stock requires minor fitting. From Dixie Gun Works.
Price: RH0130 . . . . **$187.50**

LE MAT REVOLVER
Caliber: 44/20 ga. **Barrel:** 6.75" (revolver); 4-7/8" (single shot). **Weight:** 3 lbs., 7 oz. **Length:** 14" overall. **Stocks:** Hand-checkered walnut. **Sights:** Post front, hammer notch rear. **Features:** Exact reproduction with all-steel construction;

44-cal. 9-shot cylinder, 20-gauge single barrel; color case-hardened hammer with selector; spur trigger guard; ring at butt; lever-type barrel release. From Navy Arms.
Price: Cavalry model (lanyard ring, spur trigger guard) **$750.00**
Price: Army model (round trigger guard, pin-type barrel release) **$750.00**
Price: Naval-style (thumb selector on hammer) **$750.00**

NAVY MODEL 1851 PERCUSSION REVOLVER
Caliber: 36, 44, 6-shot. **Barrel:** 7.5". **Weight:** 44 oz. **Length:** 13" overall. **Stocks:** Walnut finish. **Sights:** Post front, hammer notch rear. **Features:** Brass backstrap and trigger guard; some have 1st Model squareback trigger guard, engraved cylinder with navy battle scene; case-hardened frame, hammer, loading lever. Imported by The Armoury, Cabela's, Cimarron F.A. Co., Navy Arms, EMF, Dixie Gun Works, Euroarms of America, Armsport, CVA (44-cal. only), Traditions (44 only), Uberti U.S.A. Inc., United States Patent Fire-Arms.
Price: Brass frame (Dixie Gun Works RH0100) **$275.00**
Price: Steel frame (Dixie Gun Works RH0210). **$200.00**
Price: Engraved model (Dixie Gun Works RH0110) **$275.00**
Price: Confederate Navy (Cabela's) **$139.99**
Price: Hartford model, steel frame, German silver trim, cartouche (EMF) **$190.00**
Price: Man With No Name Conversion (Cimarron, 2006) . . . **$480.00**

NEW MODEL 1858 ARMY PERCUSSION REVOLVER
Caliber: 36 or 44, 6-shot. **Barrel:** 6.5" or 8". **Weight:** 38 oz. **Length:** 13.5" overall. **Stocks:** Walnut. **Sights:** Blade front, groove-in-frame rear. **Features:** Replica of Remington Model 1858. Also available from some importers as Army Model Belt Revolver in 36-cal., a shortened and lightened version of the 44. Target Model (Uberti U.S.A. Inc., Navy Arms) has fully adjustable target rear sight, target front, 36 or 44. Imported by Cimarron F.A. Co., CVA (as 1858 Army, brass frame, 44 only), Navy Arms, The Armoury, EMF, Euroarms of America (engraved, stainless and plain), Armsport, Traditions (44 only), Uberti U.S.A. Inc.
Price: Steel frame, Dixie RH0220. . . . . **$315.00**
Price: Steel frame kit (Euroarms) . . . . **$115.95 to $150.00**
Price: Stainless steel Model 1858 (Euroarms, Uberti U.S.A. Inc., Navy Arms, Armsport, Traditions) . . . . **$169.95 to $380.00**
Price: Target Model, adjustable rear sight (Cabela's, Euroarms, Uberti U.S.A. Inc., Stone Mountain Arms) . . . . **$95.95 to $399.00**
Price: Brass frame (CVA, Cabela's, Traditions, Navy Arms) . . . . **$79.95 to $199.99**
Price: Buffalo model, 44-cal. (Cabela's) **$119.99**
Price: Hartford model, steel frame, cartouche (EMF) **$225.00**
Price: Improved Conversion (Cimarron) **$492.00**

NORTH AMERICAN COMPANION PERCUSSION REVOLVER
Caliber: 22. **Barrel:** 1-1/8". **Weight:** 5.1 oz. **Length:** 4.5" overall. **Stocks:** Laminated wood. **Sights:** Blade front, notch fixed rear. **Features:** All stainless steel construction. Uses standard #11 percussion caps. Comes with bullets, powder measure, bullet seater, leather clip holster, gun rag. Long Rifle or Magnum frame size. Introduced 1996. Made in U.S. by North American Arms.
Price: Long Rifle frame. **$215.00**

North American Super Companion Percussion Revolver
Similar to the Companion except has larger frame. Weighs 7.2 oz., has 1-5/8" barrel, measures 5-7/16" overall. Comes with bullets, pow-

BLACKPOWDER REVOLVERS

der measure, bullet seater, leather clip holster, gun rag. Introduced 1996. Made in U.S. by North American Arms.
Price: **$230.00**

POCKET POLICE 1862 PERCUSSION REVOLVER
Caliber: 36, 5-shot. **Barrel:** 4.5",
5.5", 6.5", 7.5". **Weight:** 26 oz. **Length:**
12" overall (6.5" bbl.). **Stocks:** Walnut. **Sights:**
Fixed. **Features:** Round tapered barrel; half-fluted and rebated cylinder; case-hardened frame, loading lever and hammer; silver or brass trigger guard and backstrap. Imported by Dixie Gun Works, Navy Arms (5.5" only), Uberti U.S.A. Inc. (5.5", 6.5" only), United States Patent Fire-Arms and Cimarron F.A. Co.
Price: Dixie Gun Works RH0422 .... **$315.00**
Price: Hartford model, steel frame, cartouche (EMF) **$300.00**

ROGERS & SPENCER PERCUSSION REVOLVER
Caliber: 44. **Barrel:** 7.5". **Weight:** 47 oz. **Length:** 13.75" overall. **Stocks:** Walnut. **Sights:** Cone front, integral groove in frame for rear. **Features:** Accurate reproduction of a Civil War design. Solid frame; extra large nipple cut-out on rear of cylinder; loading lever and cylinder easily removed for cleaning. From Dixie Gun Works, Euroarms of America (standard blue, engraved, burnished, target models), Navy Arms.
Price: Dixie Gun Works RH1320 .... **$425.00**
Price: Nickel-plated **$215.00**
Price: Engraved (Euroarms) **$430.00**
Price: Target version (Euroarms) .... **$239.00 to $270.00**
Price: Burnished London Gray (Euroarms) ..... **$245.00 to $370.00**

SHERIFF MODEL 1851 PERCUSSION REVOLVER
Caliber: 36, 44, 6-shot. **Barrel:** 5". **Weight:** 40 oz. **Length:** 10.5" overall. **Stocks:** Walnut. **Sights:** Fixed. **Features:** Brass backstrap and trigger guard; engraved navy scene; case-hardened frame, hammer, loading lever. Imported by EMF.
Price: Steel frame **$169.95**
Price: Brass frame **$140.00**

SPILLER & BURR REVOLVER
Caliber: 36 (.375" round ball). **Barrel:** 7", octagon. **Weight:** 2.5 lbs. **Length:** 12.5" overall. **Stocks:** Two-piece walnut. **Sights:** Fixed. **Features:** Reproduction of the C.S.A. revolver. Brass frame and trigger guard. Also available as a kit. From Dixie Gun Works, Navy Arms.
Price: **$232.50**

UBERTI 1847 WALKER REVOLVERS
Caliber: 44 6-shot engraved cylinder. **Barrel:** 9" 7 grooves. **Weight:** 4.5 lbs. **Length:** 15.7" overall. **Stocks:** One-piece hardwood. **Sights:** Fixed. **Features:** Copy of Sam Colt's first commercially-made revolving pistol, loading lever available, no trigger guard. Case-hardened hammer. Blued finish. Made in Italy by Uberti, imported by Benelli USA.
Price: **$429.00**

UBERTI 1848 DRAGOON AND POCKET REVOLVERS
Caliber: 44 6-shot engraved cylinder. **Barrel:** 7.5" 7 grooves. **Weight:** 4.1 lbs. **Stocks:** One-piece walnut. **Sights:** Fixed. **Features:** Copy of Eli Whitney's design for Colt using Walker parts. Blued barrel, backstrap, and trigger guard. Made in Italy by Uberti, imported by Benelli USA.
Price: 1848 Whitneyville Dragoon, 7.5" barrel ... **$429.00**
Price: 1848 Dragoon, 1st-3rd models, 7.5" barrel . **$409.00**
Price: 1848 Baby Dragoon, 4" barrel **$339.00**

UBERTI 1858 NEW ARMY REVOLVERS
Caliber: 44 6-shot engraved cylinder. **Barrel:** 8" 7 grooves. **Weight:** 2.7 lbs. **Length:** 13.6". **Stocks:** Two-piece walnut. **Sights:** Fixed. **Features:** Blued or stainless barrel, backstrap; brass trigger guard. Made in Italy by Uberti, imported by Benelli USA.
Price: 1858 New Army Stainless 8" barrel **$429.00**
Price: 1858 New Army 8" barrel **$349.00**
Price: 1858 Target Carbine 18" barrel **$549.00**
Price: 1862 Pocket Navy 5.5" barrel, 36 caliber **$349.00**
Price: 1862 Police 5.5" barrel, 36 caliber **$349.00**

UBERTI 1861 NAVY PERCUSSION REVOLVER
Caliber: 36, 6-shot. **Barrel:** 7.5", 7-groove, round. **Weight:** 2 lbs., 6 oz. **Length:** 13". **Stocks:** One-piece walnut. **Sights:** German silver blade front sight. **Features:** Rounded trigger guard, "creeping" loading lever, fluted or round cylinder, steel backstrap, trigger guard, cut for stock. Imported by Cimarron F.A. Co., Uberti U.S.A. Inc., Dixie Gun Works.
Price: Dixie RH0420 .... **$295.00**

1862 POCKET NAVY PERCUSSION REVOLVER
Caliber: 36, 5-shot. **Barrel:** 5.5", 6.5", octagonal, 7-groove, LH twist. **Weight:** 27 oz. (5.5" barrel). **Length:** 10.5" overall (5.5" bbl.). **Stocks:** One-piece varnished walnut. **Sights:** Brass pin front, hammer notch rear. **Features:** Rebated cylinder, hinged loading lever, brass or silver-plated backstrap and trigger guard, color-cased frame, hammer, loading lever, plunger and latch, rest blued. Has original-type markings. From Cimarron F.A. Co., Uberti U.S.A. Inc., Dixie Gun Works.
Price: With brass backstrap, trigger guard **$250.00**

WALKER 1847 PERCUSSION REVOLVER
Caliber: 44, 6-shot. **Barrel:** 9". **Weight:** 84 oz. **Length:** 15.5" overall. **Stocks:** Walnut. **Sights:** Fixed. **Features:** Case-hardened frame, loading lever and hammer; iron backstrap; brass trigger guard; engraved cylinder. Imported by Cabela's, Cimarron F.A. Co., Navy Arms, Uberti U.S.A. Inc., EMF, Cimarron, Traditions, United States Patent Fire-Arms.
Price: Dixie RH0200 .... **$385.00**
Price: Dixie Kit RH0400 .... **$300.00**
Price: Hartford model, steel frame, cartouche (EMF) **$350.00**

Prices given are believed to be accurate at time of publication however, many factors affect retail pricing so exact prices are not possible.

BLACKPOWDER MUSKETS & RIFLES

ARMOURY R140 HAWKEN RIFLE
Caliber: 45, 50 or 54. **Barrel:** 29". **Weight:** 8.75 to 9 lbs. **Length:** 45.75" overall. **Stock:** Walnut, with cheekpiece. **Sights:** Dovetailed front, fully adjustable rear. **Features:** Octagon barrel, removable breech plug; double set triggers; blued barrel, brass stock fittings, color case-hardened percussion lock. From Armsport, The Armoury.
Price: . . . . **$225.00 to $245.00**

BOSTONIAN PERCUSSION RIFLE
Caliber: 45. **Barrel:** 30", octagonal. **Weight:** 7.25 lbs. **Length:** 46" overall. **Stock:** Walnut. **Sights:** Blade front, fixed notch rear. **Features:** Color case-hardened lock, brass trigger guard, buttplate, patchbox. Imported from Italy by EMF.
Price: **$285.00**

CABELA'S BLUE RIDGE RIFLE
Caliber: 32, 36, 45, 50, .54. **Barrel:** 39", octagonal. **Weight:** About 7.75 lbs. **Length:** 55" overall. **Stock:** American black walnut. **Sights:** Blade front, rear drift adjustable for windage. **Features:** Color case-hardened lockplate and cock/hammer, brass trigger guard and buttplate, double set, double-phased triggers. From Cabela's.
Price: Percussion **$569.99**
Price: Flintlock **$599.99**

CABELA'S TRADITIONAL HAWKEN
Caliber: 50, 54. **Barrel:** 29". **Weight:** About 9 lbs. **Stock:** Walnut. **Sights:** Blade front, open adjustable rear. **Features:** Flintlock or percussion. Adjustable double-set triggers. Polished brass furniture, color case-hardened lock. Imported by Cabela's.
Price: Percussion, right-hand or left-hand **$339.99**
Price: Flintlock, right-hand **$399.99**

CABELA'S KODIAK EXPRESS DOUBLE RIFLE
Caliber: 50, 54, 58, 72. **Barrel:** Length NA; 1:48" twist. **Weight:** 9.3 lbs. **Length:** 45.25" overall. **Stock:** European walnut, oil finish. **Sights:** Fully adjustable double folding-leaf rear, ramp front. **Features:** Percussion. Barrels regulated to point of aim at 75 yards; polished and engraved lock, top tang and trigger guard. From Cabela's.
Price: 50, 54, 58 calibers **$929.99**
Price: 72 caliber **$959.99**

COOK & BROTHER CONFEDERATE CARBINE
Caliber: 58. **Barrel:** 24". **Weight:** 7.5 lbs. **Length:** 40.5" overall. **Stock:** Select walnut. **Features:** Re-creation of the 1861 New Orleans-made artillery carbine. Color case-hardened lock, browned barrel. Buttplate, trigger guard, barrel bands, sling swivels and nosecap of polished brass. From Euroarms of America.
Price: **$563.00**
Price: Cook & Brother rifle (33" barrel) **$606.00**

CVA OPTIMA ELITE BREAK-ACTION RIFLE
Caliber: 45, 50. **Barrel:** 28" fluted. **Weight:** 8.8 lbs. **Stock:** Ambidextrous solid composite in standard or thumbhole. **Sights:** Adj. fiber-optic. **Features:** Break-action, stainless No. 209 breech plug, aluminum loading rod, cocking spur, lifetime warranty.
Price: CR4002 (50-cal., blued/Realtree HD) **$398.95**
Price: CR4002X (50-cal., stainless/Realtree HD) **$456.95**
Price: CR4003X (45-cal., stainless/Realtree HD) **$456.95**
Price: CR4000T (50-cal), blued/black fiber grip thumbhole) . **$366.95**
Price: CR4000 (50-cal., blued/black fiber grip) **$345.95**
Price: CR4002T (50-cal., blued/Realtree HD thumbhole) . **$432.95**
Price: CR4002S (50-cal., stainless/Realtree HD thumbhole) **$422.95**
Price: CR4000X (50-cal., stainless/black fiber grip thumbhole) **$451.95**
Price: CR4000S (50-cal., stainless steel/black fiber grip) . . . **$400.95**

CVA Optima 209 Magnum Break-Action Rifle
Similar to Optima Elite but with 26" bbl., nickel or blue finish, 50 cal.
Price: PR2008N (nickel/Realtree HD thumbhole) **$345.95**
Price: PR2004N (nickel/Realtree) **$322.95**
Price: PR2000 (blued/black) **$229.95**
Price: PR2006N (nickel/black) **$273.95**

CVA Wolf 209 Magnum Break-Action Rifle
Similar to Optima 209 Mag but with 24 barrel, weighs 7 lbs, and in 50-cal. only.

Price: PR2101N (nickel/camo) **$253.95**
Price: PR2102 (blued/camo). **$231.95**
Price: PR2100 (blued/black) **$180.95**
Price: PR2100N (nickel/black) **$202.95**
Price: PR2100NS (nickel/black scoped package) **$277.95**
Price: PR2100S (blued/black scoped package) **$255.95**

CVA APEX
Caliber: 45, 50. **Barrel:** 27", 1:28 twist. **Weight:** 8 lbs. **Length:** 42". **Stock:** Synthetic. **Features:** Ambi stock with rubber grip panels in black or Realtree APG camo, crush-zone recoil pad, reversible hammer spur, quake claw sling, lifetime warranty.
Price: CR4010S (50-cal., stainless/black) **$576.95**
Price: CR4011S (45-cal., stainless/black) **$576.95**
Price: CR4012S (50-cal., stainless/Realtree HD) **$651.95**
Price: CR4013S (45-cal., stainless/Realtree HD) **$651.95**

CVA ACCURA
Similar to Apex but weighs 7.3 lbs., in stainless steel or matte blue finish, cocking spur.
Price: PR3106S (50-cal, stainless steel/Realtree APG thumbhole) **$495.95**
Price: PR3107S (45-cal., stainless steel/Realtree APG thumbhole) **$495.95**
Price: PR 3104S (50-cal., stainless steel/black fibergrip thumbhole) **$438.95**
Price: PR3100 (50-cal., blued/black fibergrip **$345.95**
Price: PR3100S (50-cal., stainless steel/black fibergrip) **$403.95**
Price: PR3102S (50-cal., stainless steel/Realtree APG) **$460.95**

CVA BUCKHORN 209 MAGNUM
Caliber: 50. **Barrel:** 24". **Weight:** 6.3 lbs. **Sights:** Illuminator fiber-optic. **Features:** Grip-dot stock, thumb-actuated safety; drilled and tapped for scope mounts.
Price: Black stock, blue barrel **$145.00**

CVA KODIAK MAGNUM RIFLE
Caliber: 50. No. 209 primer ignition. **Barrel:** 28"; 1:28" twist. **Stock:** Ambidextrous black or Mossy Oak® camo. **Sights:** Fiber-optic. **Features:** Blue or nickel finish, recoil pad, lifetime warranty. From CVA.
Price: Mossy Oak® camo; nickel barrel **$300.00**
Price: Stainless steel/black fibergrip **$288.95**
Price: Blued/black fibergrip. **$229.95**

DIXIE EARLY AMERICAN JAEGER RIFLE
Caliber: 54. **Barrel:** 27.5" octagonal; 1:24" twist. **Weight:** 8.25 lbs. **Length:** 43.5" overall. **Stock:** American walnut; sliding wooden patchbox on butt. **Sights:** Notch rear, blade front. **Features:** Flintlock or percussion. Browned steel furniture. Imported from Italy by Dixie Gun Works.
Price: Flintlock FR0838. . . . . **$695.00**
Price: Percussion PR0835, case-hardened **$695.00**
Price: Kit **$775.00**

DIXIE DELUXE CUB RIFLE
Caliber: 32, 36, 40, 45. **Barrel:** 28" octagon. **Weight:** 6.25 lbs. **Length:** 44" overall. **Stock:** Walnut. **Sights:** Fixed. **Features:** Short rifle for small game and beginning shooters. Brass patchbox and furniture. Flint or percussion, finished or kit. From Dixie Gun Works
Price: Deluxe Cub (45-cal.) **$525.00**
Price: Deluxe Cub (flint) **$530.00**
Price: Super Cub (50-cal) **$530.00**
Price: Deluxe Cub (32-cal. flint) **$725.00**
Price: Deluxe Cub (36-cal. flint) **$725.00**
Price: Deluxe Cub kit (32-cal. percussion) **$550.00**
Price: Deluxe Cub kit (36-cal. percussion) **$550.00**
Price: Deluxe Cub (45-cal. percussion) **$675.00**
Price: Super Cub (percussion) **$450.00**
Price: Deluxe Cub (32-cal. percussion) **$675.00**
Price: Deluxe Cub (36-cal. percussion) **$675.00**

DIXIE PEDERSOLI 1857 MAUSER RIFLE
Caliber: 54. **Barrel:** 39-3/8". **Weight:** 9.5 lbs. **Length:** 54.75" overall. **Stock:** European walnut with oil finish, sling swivels. **Sights:** Fully adjustable rear, lug front. **Features:** Percussion (musket caps). Armory bright finish with color case-hardened lock and barrel tang, engraved lockplate, steel ramrod. Introduced 2000. Imported from Italy by Dixie Gun Works.
Price: PR1330. . . . . **$995.00**

BLACKPOWDER MUSKETS & RIFLES

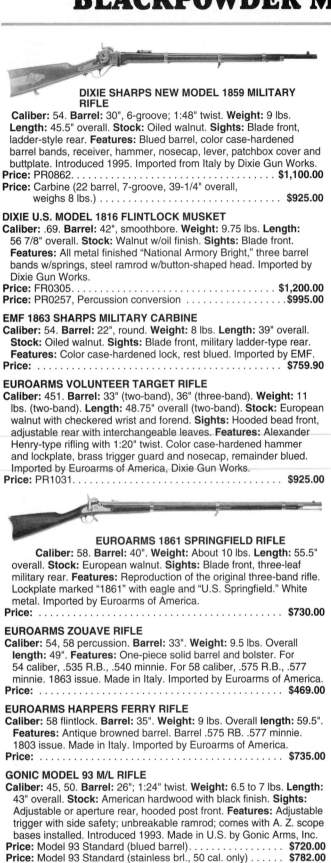

DIXIE SHARPS NEW MODEL 1859 MILITARY RIFLE
Caliber: 54. **Barrel:** 30", 6-groove; 1:48" twist. **Weight:** 9 lbs. **Length:** 45.5" overall. **Stock:** Oiled walnut. **Sights:** Blade front, ladder-style rear. **Features:** Blued barrel, color case-hardened barrel bands, receiver, hammer, nosecap, lever, patchbox cover and buttplate. Introduced 1995. Imported from Italy by Dixie Gun Works.
Price: PR0862 . . . . $1,100.00
Price: Carbine (22 barrel, 7-groove, 39-1/4" overall, weighs 8 lbs.) $925.00

DIXIE U.S. MODEL 1816 FLINTLOCK MUSKET
Caliber: .69. **Barrel:** 42", smoothbore. **Weight:** 9.75 lbs. **Length:** 56 7/8" overall. **Stock:** Walnut w/oil finish. **Sights:** Blade front. **Features:** All metal finished "National Armory Bright," three barrel bands w/springs, steel ramrod w/button-shaped head. Imported by Dixie Gun Works.
Price: FR0305 . . . . $1,200.00
Price: PR0257, Percussion conversion $995.00

EMF 1863 SHARPS MILITARY CARBINE
Caliber: 54. **Barrel:** 22", round. **Weight:** 8 lbs. **Length:** 39" overall. **Stock:** Oiled walnut. **Sights:** Blade front, military ladder-type rear. **Features:** Color case-hardened lock, rest blued. Imported by EMF.
Price: $759.90

EUROARMS VOLUNTEER TARGET RIFLE
Caliber: 451. **Barrel:** 33" (two-band), 36" (three-band). **Weight:** 11 lbs. (two-band). **Length:** 48.75" overall (two-band). **Stock:** European walnut with checkered wrist and forend. **Sights:** Hooded bead front, adjustable rear with interchangeable leaves. **Features:** Alexander Henry-type rifling with 1:20" twist. Color case-hardened hammer and lockplate, brass trigger guard and nosecap, remainder blued. Imported by Euroarms of America, Dixie Gun Works.
Price: PR1031 . . . . $925.00

EUROARMS 1861 SPRINGFIELD RIFLE
Caliber: 58. **Barrel:** 40". **Weight:** About 10 lbs. **Length:** 55.5" overall. **Stock:** European walnut. **Sights:** Blade front, three-leaf military rear. **Features:** Reproduction of the original three-band rifle. Lockplate marked "1861" with eagle and "U.S. Springfield." White metal. Imported by Euroarms of America.
Price: $730.00

EUROARMS ZOUAVE RIFLE
Caliber: 54, 58 percussion. **Barrel:** 33". **Weight:** 9.5 lbs. Overall **length:** 49". **Features:** One-piece solid barrel and bolster. For 54 caliber, .535 R.B., .540 minnie. For 58 caliber, .575 R.B., .577 minnie. 1863 issue. Made in Italy. Imported by Euroarms of America.
Price: $469.00

EUROARMS HARPERS FERRY RIFLE
Caliber: 58 flintlock. **Barrel:** 35". **Weight:** 9 lbs. Overall **length:** 59.5". **Features:** Antique browned barrel. Barrel .575 RB. .577 minnie. 1803 issue. Made in Italy. Imported by Euroarms of America.
Price: $735.00

GONIC MODEL 93 M/L RIFLE
Caliber: 45, 50. **Barrel:** 26"; 1:24" twist. **Weight:** 6.5 to 7 lbs. **Length:** 43" overall. **Stock:** American hardwood with black finish. **Sights:** Adjustable or aperture rear, hooded post front. **Features:** Adjustable trigger with side safety; unbreakable ramrod; comes with A. Z. scope bases installed. Introduced 1993. Made in U.S. by Gonic Arms, Inc.
Price: Model 93 Standard (blued barrel) $720.00
Price: Model 93 Standard (stainless brl., 50 cal. only) $782.00

Gonic Model 93 Deluxe M/L Rifle
Similar to the Model 93 except has classic-style walnut or gray laminated wood stock. Introduced 1998. Made in U.S. by Gonic Arms, Inc.
Price: Blue barrel, sights, scope base, choice of stock . . $902.00
Price: Stainless barrel, sights, scope base, choice of stock (50 cal. only) $964.00

Gonic Model 93 Mountain Thumbhole M/L Rifles
Similar to the Model 93 except has high-grade walnut or gray laminate stock with extensive hand-checkered panels, Monte Carlo cheekpiece and beavertail forend; integral muzzle brake. Introduced 1998. Made in U.S. by Gonic Arms, Inc.
Price: Blued or stainless $2,700.00

HARPER'S FERRY 1803 FLINTLOCK RIFLE
Caliber: 54 or 58. **Barrel:** 35". **Weight:** 9 lbs. **Length:** 59.5" overall. **Stock:** Walnut with cheekpiece. **Sights:** Brass blade front, fixed steel rear. **Features:** Brass trigger guard, sideplate, buttplate; steel patchbox. Imported by Euroarms of America, Navy Arms (54-cal. only), and Dixie Gun Works.
Price: 54-cal. (Navy Arms) $625.00
Price: 54-cal. (Dixie Gun Works), FR0171 . . . . $995.00
Price: 54-cal. (Euroarms) $809.00

HAWKEN RIFLE
Caliber: 45, 50, 54 or 58. **Barrel:** 28", blued, 6-groove rifling. **Weight:** 8.75 lbs. **Length:** 44" overall. **Stock:** Walnut with cheekpiece. **Sights:** Blade front, fully adjustable rear. **Features:** Coil mainspring, double-set triggers, polished brass furniture. From Armsport and EMF.
Price: . . . . $220.00 to $345.00

J.P. HENRY TRADE RIFLE
Caliber: 54. **Barrel:** 34"; 1" flats. **Weight:** 8.5 lbs. **Length:** 45" overall. **Stock:** Premium curly maple. **Sights:** Silver blade front, fixed buckhorn rear. **Features:** Brass buttplate, side plate, trigger guard and nosecap; browned barrel and lock; L&R Large English percussion lock; single trigger. Made in U.S. by J.P. Gunstocks, Inc.
Price: $965.50

J.P. MURRAY 1862-1864 CAVALRY CARBINE
Caliber: 58 (.577" Minie). **Barrel:** 23". **Weight:** 7 lbs., 9 oz. **Length:** 39" overall. **Stock:** Walnut. **Sights:** Blade front, rear drift adjustable for windage. **Features:** Blued barrel, color case-hardened lock, blued swivel and band springs, polished brass buttplate, trigger guard, barrel bands. From Dixie Gun Works.
Price: Dixie Gun Works PR0173 . . . . $750.00

KENTUCKY FLINTLOCK RIFLE
Caliber: 44, 45, or 50. **Barrel:** 35". **Weight:** 7 lbs. **Length:** 50" overall. **Stock:** Walnut stained, brass fittings. **Sights:** Fixed. **Features:** Available in carbine model also, 28" bbl. Some variations in detail, finish. Kits also available from some importers. Imported by The Armoury.
Price: About . . . . $217.95 to $345.00

Kentucky Percussion Rifle
Similar to Flintlock except percussion lock. Finish and features vary with importer. Imported by The Armoury and CVA.
Price: About $259.95
Price: 45 or 50 cal. (Navy Arms) $425.00
Price: Kit, 50 cal. (CVA) $189.95

KNIGHT SHADOW RIFLE
Caliber: 50. **Barrel:** 26". **Weight:** 7 lbs., 12 oz. **Length:** 42" overall. **Stock:** Checkered with recoil pad, swivel studs, Realtree APG HD. or black composite. **Sights:** Fully adjustable, metallic fiber-optic. **Features:** Bolt-action in-line system uses #209 shotshell primer for ignition; primer is held in plastic drop-in Primer Disc. Available in blued or stainless steel. Made in U.S. by Knight Rifles (Modern Muzzleloading).
Price: Blued/black $289.99
Price: Stainless/black $329.99
Price: Realtree APG HD camo (2009) $329.99

Prices given are believed to be accurate at time of publication however, many factors affect retail pricing so exact prices are not possible.

BLACKPOWDER MUSKETS & RIFLES

KNIGHT ROLLING BLOCK RIFLE
Caliber: 50, 52. **Barrel:** 27"; 1:28" twist. **Weight:** 8 lbs. **Length:** 43.5" overall. **Stock:** Brown Sandstone laminate, checkered, recoil pad, sling swivel studs. **Sights:** Fully adjustable, metallic fiber-optic. **Features:** Uses #209 shotshell primer, comes in stainless steel or blued, with walnut or black composite stock. Made in U.S. by Knight Rifles (Modern Muzzleloading).
Price: 50 Stainless/black. **$419.99**
Price: 50 Blued/black **$329.99**
Price: 50 Stainless/Realtree (2009) **$459.99**
Price: 50 Stainless/Brown Sandstone (2009) **$438.88**
Price: 52 Stainless/Next G-1 . . . . **$459.99**

KNIGHT LONG RANGE HUNTER
Caliber: 50. **Barrel:** 27" custom fluted; 1:28" twist. **Weight:** 8 lbs. 6 oz. **Length:** 45.5" overall. **Stock:** Cast-off design thumbhole, checkered, recoil pad, sling swivel studs, in Forest Green or Sandstone. **Sights:** Fully-adjustable, metallic fiber-optic. **Features:** Full plastic jacket ignition system. Made in U.S. by Knight Rifles (Modern Muzzleloading).
Price: SS Forest Green. **$769.99**
Price: SS Forest Green Thumbhole **$799.99**

KNIGHT EXTREME
Caliber: 50, 52. **Barrel:** 26", fluted stainess, 1:28" twist. **Weight:** 7 lbs. 14 oz to 8 lbs. **Length:** 45" overall. **Stock:** Stainless steel laminate, blued walnut, black composite thumbhole with blued or SS, Realtree Hardwoods Green HD with thumbhole. **Sights:** Fully adjustable metallic fiber-optics. **Features:** Full plastic jacket ignition system. Made in U.S. by Knight Rifles (Modern Muzzleloading).
Price: 50 SS/Realtree (2009) **$529.99**
Price: 52 SS/black (2009) **$229.94**
Price: 50 SS/black **$459.99**
Price: 50 SS/black w/thumbhole **$489.99**
Price: 50 SS/brown **$569.99**

KNIGHT BIGHORN
Caliber: 50. **Barrel:** 26"; 1:28" twist. **Weight:** 7 lbs. 3 oz. **Length:** 44.5" overall. **Stock:** Realtree Advantage MAX-1 HD or black composite thumbhole, checkered with recoil pad, sling swivel studs. **Sights:** Fully adjustable metallic fiber-optic. **Features:** Uses 4 different ignition systems (included): #11 nipple, musket nipple, bare 208 shotgun primer and 209 Extreme shotgun primer system (Extreme weatherproof full plastic jacket system); one-piece removable hammer assembly. Made in U.S. by Knight Rifles (Modern Muzzleloading).
Price: Stainless/Realtree w/thumbhole (2009) **$459.99**
Price: Stainless/black **$419.99**
Price: Stainless/black w/thumbhole **$439.99**

KNIGHT 52 MODELS
Caliber: 52. **Barrel:** 26";1:26" twist (composite), 27" 1:28" twist (G-1 camo). **Weight:** 8 lbs. **Length:** 43.5" (G-1 camo); 45" (composite) overall. **Stock:** Standard black composite or Next G-1, checkered with recoil pad, sling swivel studs. **Sights:** Fully adjustable metallic fiber-optic. **Features:** PowerStem breech plug. Made in U.S. by Knight Rifles (Modern Muzzleloading).
Price: Stainless/black (2009) **$299.94**
Price: Stainless/Next G-1 . . . . **$459.99**

LONDON ARMORY 1861 ENFIELD MUSKETOON
Caliber: 58, Minie ball. **Barrel:** 24", round. **Weight:** 7 to 7.5 lbs. **Length:** 40.5" overall. **Stock:** Walnut, with sling swivels. **Sights:** Blade front, graduated military-leaf rear. **Features:** Brass trigger guard, nosecap, buttplate; blued barrel, bands, lockplate, swivels. Imported by Euroarms of America, Navy Arms.
Price: . . . . **$300.00 to $521.00**
Price: Kit . . . . **$365.00 to $402.00**

LONDON ARMORY 2-BAND 1858 ENFIELD
Caliber: .577" Minie, .575" round ball. **Barrel:** 33". **Weight:** 10 lbs. **Length:** 49" overall. **Stock:** Walnut. **Sights:** Folding leaf rear adjustable for elevation. **Features:** Blued barrel, color case-

hardened lock and hammer, polished brass buttplate, trigger guard, nosecap. From Navy Arms, Euroarms of America, Dixie Gun Works.
Price: PR0330 . . . . **$650.00**

LONDON ARMORY 3-BAND 1853 ENFIELD
Caliber: 58 (.577" Minie, .575" round ball, .580" maxi ball). **Barrel:** 39". **Weight:** 9.5 lbs. **Length:** 54" overall. **Stock:** European walnut. **Sights:** Inverted "V" front, traditional Enfield folding ladder rear. **Features:** Re-creation of the famed London Armory Company Pattern 1853 Enfield Musket. One-piece walnut stock, brass buttplate, trigger guard and nosecap. Lockplate marked "London Armoury Co." and with a British crown. Blued Baddeley barrel bands. From Euroarms of America, Navy Arms.
Price: About . . . . $350.00 to $606.00

LYMAN TRADE RIFLE
Caliber: 50, 54. **Barrel:** 28" octagon;1:48" twist. **Weight:** 10.8 lbs. **Length:** 45" overall. **Stock:** European walnut. **Sights:** Blade front, open rear adjustable for windage or optional fixed sights. **Features:** Fast twist rifling for conical bullets. Polished brass furniture with blue steel parts, stainless steel nipple. Hook breech, single trigger, coil spring percussion lock. Steel barrel rib and ramrod ferrules. Introduced 1980. From Lyman.
Price: 50-cal. percussion **$474.95**
Price: 50-cal. flintlock **$499.95**
Price: 54-cal. percussion **$474.95**
Price: 54-cal. flintlock **$499.95**

LYMAN DEERSTALKER RIFLE
Caliber: 50, 54. **Barrel:** 24", octagonal; 1:48" rifling. **Weight:** 10.4 lbs. **Stock:** Walnut with black rubber buttpad. **Sights:** Lyman #37MA beaded front, fully adjustable fold-down Lyman #16A rear. **Features:** Stock has less drop for quick sighting. All metal parts are blackened, with color case-hardened lock; single trigger. Comes with sling and swivels. Available in flint or percussion. Introduced 1990. From Lyman.
Price: 50-cal. flintlock **$529.95**
Price: 50-, 54-cal., flintlock, left-hand **$569.95**
Price: 54 cal. flintlock **$529.95**
Price: 50-, 54 cal. percussion **$487.95**
Price: 50-, 54-cal. stainless steel **$609.95**

LYMAN GREAT PLAINS RIFLE
Caliber: 50, 54. **Barrel:** 32"; 1:60" twist. **Weight:** 11.6 lbs. **Stock:** Walnut. **Sights:** Steel blade front, buckhorn rear adjustable for windage and elevation and fixed notch primitive sight included. **Features:** Blued steel furniture. Stainless steel nipple. Coil spring lock, Hawken-style trigger guard and double-set triggers. Round thimbles recessed and sweated into rib. Steel wedge plates and toe plate. Introduced 1979. From Lyman.
Price: Percussion **$654.95**
Price: Flintlock **$699.95**
Price: Percussion kit **$519.95**
Price: Flintlock kit **$574.95**
Price: Left-hand percussion **$669.95**
Price: Left-hand flintlock **$709.95**

Lyman Great Plains Hunter Model
Similar to Great Plains model except 1:32" twist shallow-groove barrel and comes drilled and tapped for Lyman 57GPR peep sight.
Price: Percussion **$654.95**
Price: Flintlock **$699.95**
Price: Left-hand percussion **$669.95**

MARKESBERY KM BLACK BEAR M/L RIFLE
Caliber: 36, 45, 50, 54. **Barrel:** 24"; 1:26" twist. **Weight:** 6.5 lbs. **Length:** 38.5" overall. **Stock:** Two-piece American hardwood,

walnut, black laminate, green laminate, black composition, X-Tra or Mossy Oak® Break-up™ camouflage. **Sights:** Bead front, open fully adjustable rear. **Features:** Interchangeable barrels; exposed hammer; Outer-Line Magnum ignition system uses small rifle primer or standard No. 11 cap and nipple. Blue, black matte, or stainless. Made in U.S. by Markesbery Muzzle Loaders.

Price: American hardwood walnut, blue finish	$536.63
Price: American hardwood walnut, stainless	$553.09
Price: Black laminate, blue finish	$539.67
Price: Black laminate, stainless	$556.27
Price: Black composite, blue finish	$532.65
Price: Black composite, stainless	$549.93
Price: Green laminate, blue finish	$539.00
Price: Green laminate, stainless	$556.27

Markesbery KM Brown Bear Rifle

Similar to KM Black Bear except one-piece thumbhole stock with Monte Carlo comb. Stock in Crotch Walnut composite, green or black laminate, black composite or X-Tra or Mossy Oak® Break-Up™ camouflage. Made in U.S. by Markesbery Muzzle Loaders, Inc.

Price: Black composite, blue finish	$658.83
Price: Crotch Walnut, blue finish	$658.83
Price: Walnut wood	$662.81
Price: Black wood	$662.81
Price: Black laminated wood	$662.81
Price: Green laminated wood	$662.81
Price: Black composite, stainless	$676.11
Price: Crotch Walnut composite, stainless	$676.11
Price: Walnut wood, stainless	$680.07
Price: Black wood, stainless	$680.07
Price: Black laminated wood, stainless	$680.07
Price: Green laminate, stainless	$680.07

Markesbery KM Grizzly Bear Rifle

Similar to KM Black Bear except thumbhole buttstock with Monte Carlo comb. Stock in Crotch Walnut composite, green or black laminate, black composite or X-Tra or Mossy Oak® Break-Up camouflage. Made in U.S. by Markesbery Muzzle Loaders, Inc.

Price: Black composite, blue finish	$642.96
Price: Crotch Walnut, blue finish	$642.96
Price: Walnut wood	$646.93
Price: Black wood	$646.93
Price: Black laminate wood	$646.93
Price: Green laminate wood	$646.93
Price: Black composite, stainless	$660.98
Price: Crotch Walnut composite, stainless	$660.98
Price: Black laminate wood, stainless	$664.20
Price: Green laminate, stainless	$664.20
Price: Walnut wood, stainless	$664.20
Price: Black wood, stainless	$664.20

Markesbery KM Polar Bear Rifle

Similar to KM Black Bear except one-piece stock with Monte Carlo comb. Stock in American Hard-wood walnut, green or black laminate, black composite, or X-Tra or Mossy Oak® Break-Up™ camouflage. Interchangeable barrel system, Outer-Line ignition system, cross-bolt double safety. Available in 36, 45, 50, 54 caliber. Made in U.S. by Markesbery Muzzle Loaders, Inc.

Price: American Hardwood walnut, blue finish	$539.01
Price: Black composite, blue finish	$536.63
Price: Black laminate, blue finish	$541.17
Price: Green laminate, blue finish	$541.17
Price: American Hardwood walnut, stainless	$556.27
Price: Black composite, stainless	$556.04
Price: Black laminate, stainless	$570.56
Price: Green laminate, stainless	$570.56

MARKESBERY KM COLORADO ROCKY MOUNTAIN RIFLE

Caliber: 36, 45, 50, 54. **Barrel:** 24"; 1:26" twist. **Weight:** 6.5 lbs. **Length:** 38.5" overall. **Stock:** American hardwood walnut, green or black laminate. **Sights:** Firesight bead on ramp front, fully adjustable open rear. **Features:** Replicates Reed/Watson rifle of 1851. Straight grip stock with or without two barrel bands, rubber recoil pad, large-spur hammer. Made in U.S. by Markesbery Muzzle Loaders, Inc.

Price: American hardwood walnut, blue finish	$545.92

Price: Black or green laminate, blue finish	$548.30
Price: American hardwood walnut, stainless	$563.17
Price: Black or green laminate, stainless	$566.34

MDM BUCKWACKA IN-LINE RIFLES

Caliber: 45 Nitro Mag., 50. **Barrel:** 23", 25". **Weight:** 7 to 7.75 lbs. **Stock:** Black, walnut, laminated and camouflage finishes. **Sights:** Williams Fire Sight blade front, Williams fully adjustable rear with ghost-ring peep aperture. **Features:** Break-open action; Incinerating Ignition System incorporates 209 shotshell primer directly into breech plug; 50-caliber models handle up to 150 grains of Pyrodex; synthetic ramrod; transfer bar safety; stainless or blued finish. Made in U.S. by Millennium Designed Muzzleloaders Ltd.

Price: 45 Nitro, stainless steel, walnut stock	$399.95
Price: 45 Nitro, stainless steel, Mossy Oak Break-up stock	$465.95
Price: 45 Nitro, blued action, walnut stock	$369.95
Price: 45 Nitro, blued action, Mossy Oak Break-up stock	$425.95
Price: 50-cal., stainless steel, walnut stock	$399.95
Price: 50-cal., stainless steel, Mossy Oak Break-up stock	$465.95
Price: 50-cal., blued action, walnut stock	$369.95
Price: 50-cal., blued action, Mossy Oak Break-up stock	$435.95
Price: 50-cal., Youth-Ladies, blued action, walnut stock	$369.95
Price: 50-cal., Youth-Ladies, stainless steel, walnut stock	$399.95

MDM M2K In-Line Rifle

Similar to Buckwacka except adjustable trigger and double-safety mechanism designed to prevent misfires. Made in U.S. by Millennium Designed Muzzleloaders Ltd.

Price:	$529.00 to $549.00

MISSISSIPPI 1841 PERCUSSION RIFLE

Caliber: 54, 58. **Barrel:** 33". **Weight:** 9.5 lbs. **Length:** 48-5/8" overall. **Stock:** One-piece European walnut full stock with satin finish. **Sights:** Brass blade front, fixed steel rear. **Features:** Case-hardened lockplate marked "U.S." surmounted by American eagle. Two barrel bands, sling swivels. Steel ramrod with brass end, browned barrel. From Navy Arms, Dixie Gun Works, Euroarms of America.

Price: Dixie Gun Works PR0870.	$825.00

NAVY ARMS 1861 MUSKETOON

Caliber: 58. **Barrel:** 39". **Weight:** NA. **Length:** NA. **Stock:** NA. **Sights:** Front is blued steel base and blade, blued steel lip-up rear adjustable for elevation. **Features:** Brass nosecap, triggerguard, buttplate, blued steel barrel bands, color case-hardened lock with engraved lockplate marked "1861 Enfield" ahead of hammer & crown over "PH" on tail. Barrel is marked "Parker Hale LTD Birmingham England." Imported by Navy Arms.

Price:	$900.00

NAVY ARMS PARKER-HALE 1853 THREE-BAND ENFIELD

Caliber: 58. **Barrel:** 39", tapered, round, blued. **Weight:** NA. **Length:** 55-1/4" overall. **Stock:** Walnut. **Sights:** Front is blued steel base and blade, blued steel lip-up rear adjustable for elevation. **Features:** Meticulously reproduced based on original gauges and patterns. Features brass nosecap, triggerguard, buttplate, blued steel barrel bands, color case-hardened lock with engraved lockplate marked "Parker-Hale" ahead of hammer & crown over "PH" on tail. Barrel is marked "Parker Hale LTD Birmingham England." From Navy Arms.

Price: Finished rifle	$1,050.00

Navy Arms Parker-Hale 1858 Two-Band Enfield

Similar to the Three-band Enfield with 33" barrel, 49" overall length. Engraved lockplate marked "1858 Enfield" ahead of hammer & crown over "PH" on tail. Barrel is marked "Parker Hale LTD Birmingham England."

Price:	$1,050.00

NAVY ARMS PARKER-HALE VOLUNTEER RIFLE

Caliber: 451. **Barrel:** 32", 1:20" twist. **Weight:** 9.5 lbs. **Length:** 49" overall. **Stock:** Walnut, checkered wrist and forend. **Sights:** Globe front, adjustable ladder-type rear. **Features:** Recreation of the type of gun issued to volunteer regiments during the 1860s. Rigby-pattern rifling, patent breech, detented lock. Stock is glass beaded for accuracy. Engfaved lockplate marked "Alex Henry" & crown on tail, barrel marked "Parker Hale LTD Birmingham England" and "Alexander Henry Rifling .451" Imported by Navy Arms.

Price:	$1,400.00

Prices given are believed to be accurate at time of publication however, many factors affect retail pricing so exact prices are not possible.

NAVY ARMS PARKER-HALE WHITWORTH MILITARY TARGET RIFLE

Caliber: 45. **Barrel:** 36". **Weight:** 9.25 lbs. **Length:** 52.5" overall. **Stock:** Walnut. Checkered at wrist and forend. **Sights:** Hooded post front, open step-adjustable rear. **Features:** Faithful reproduction of Whitworth rifle. Trigger has detented lock, capable of fine adjustments without risk of the sear nose catching on the half-cock notch and damaging both parts. Engraved lockplate marked "Whitworth" ahead of hammer & crown on tail. Barrel marked "Parker Hale LTD Birmingham England" in one line on front of sight and "Sir Joseph Whitworth's Rifling .451" on left side. Introduced 1978. Imported by Navy Arms.
Price: **$1,550.00**

NAVY ARMS BROWN BESS MUSKET

Caliber: 75, smoothbore. **Barrel:** 41.8". **Weight:** 9 lbs., 5 oz. **Length:** 41.8" overall. **Features:** Brightly polished steel and brass, one-piece walnut stock. Signature of gunsmith William Grice and the date 1762, the crown and alphabetical letters GR (Georgius Rex). Barrel is made of steel, satin finish; the walnut stock is oil finished. From Navy Arms.
Price: **$1,100.00**

NAVY ARMS COUNTRY HUNTER

Caliber: 50. **Barrel:** 28.4", 6-groove, 1:34 twist. **Weight:** 6 lbs. **Length:** 44" overall. **Features:** Matte finished barrel. From Navy Arms.
Price: **$450.00**

NAVY ARMS PENNSYLVANIA RIFLE

Caliber: 32, 45. **Barrel:** 41.6". **Weight:** 7 lbs. 12 oz. to 8 lbs. 6 oz. **Length:** 56.1" overall. **Features:** Extra long rifle finished wtih rust brown color barrel and one-piece oil finished walnut stock. Adjustable double-set trigger. Vertically adjustable steel front and rear sights. From Navy Arms.
Price: **$675.00**

NEW ENGLAND FIREARMS SIDEKICK

Caliber: 50, 209 primer ignition. **Barrel:** 26" (magnum). **Weight:** 6.5 lbs. **Length:** 41.25". **Stock:** Black matte polymer or hardwood. **Sights:** Adjustable fiber-optic open, tapped for scope mounts. **Features:** Single-shot based on H&R break-open action. Uses No. 209 shotgun primer held in place by special primer carrier. Telescoping brass ramrod. Introduced 2004.
Price: Wood stock, blued frame, black-oxide barrel) **$216.00**
Price: Stainless barrel and frame, synthetic stock) **$310.00**

NEW ENGLAND FIREARMS HUNTSMAN

Caliber: 50, 209 primer ignition. **Barrel:** 22" to 26". **Weight:** 5.25 to 6.5 lbs. **Length:** 40" to 43". **Stock:** Black matte polymer or hardwood. **Sights:** Fiber-optic open sights, tapped for scope mounts. **Features:** Break-open action, transfer-bar safety system, breech plug removable for cleaning. Introduced 2004.
Price: Stainless Huntsman **$306.00**
Price: Huntsman **$212.00**
Price: Pardner Combo 12 ga./50 cal muzzleloader **$259.00**
Price: Tracker II Combo 12 ga. rifled slug barrel /50 cal. **$288.00**
Price: Handi-Rifle Combo 243/50 cal. **$405.00**

New England Firearms Stainless Huntsman

Similar to Huntsman, but with matte nickel finish receiver and stainless bbl. Introduced 2003. From New England Firearms.
Price: **$381.00**

PACIFIC RIFLE MODEL 1837 ZEPHYR

Caliber: 62. **Barrel:** 30", tapered octagon. **Weight:** 7.75 lbs. **Length:** NA. **Stock:** Oil-finished fancy walnut. **Sights:** German silver blade front, semi-buckhorn rear. Options available. **Features:** Improved

underhammer action. First production rifle to offer Forsyth rifle, with narrow lands and shallow rifling with 1:14" pitch for high-velocity round balls. Metal finish is slow rust brown with nitre blue accents. Optional sights, finishes and integral muzzle brake available. Introduced 1995. Made in U.S. by Pacific Rifle Co.
Price: From **$995.00**

Pacific Rifle Big Bore African Rifles

Similar to the 1837 Zephyr except in 72-caliber and 8-bore. The 72-caliber is available in 72-caliber and 8-bore. The 72-caliber is available in standard form with 28" barrel, or as the African with flat buttplate, checkered upgraded wood; weight is 9 lbs. The 8-bore African has dual-cap ignition, 24" barrel, weighs 12 lbs., checkered English walnut, engraving, gold inlays. Introduced 1998. Made in U.S. by Pacific Rifle Co.
Price: 72-caliber, from **$1,150.00**
Price: 8-bore, from **$2,500.00**

PEIFER MODEL TS-93 RIFLE

Caliber: 45, 50. **Barrel:** 24" Douglas premium; 1:20" twist in 45; 1:28" in 50. **Weight:** 7 lbs. **Length:** 43.25" overall. **Stock:** Bell & Carlson solid composite, with recoil pad, swivel studs. **Sights:** Williams bead front on ramp, fully adjustable open rear. Drilled and tapped for Weaver scope mounts with dovetail for rear peep. **Features:** In-line ignition uses #209 shotshell primer; fast lock time; fully enclosed breech; adjustable trigger; automatic safety; removable primer holder. Blue or stainless. Made in U.S. by Peifer Rifle Co. Introduced 1996.
Price: Blue, black stock. **$730.00**
Price: Blue, wood or camouflage composite stock, or
stainless with black composite stock **$803.00**
Price: Stainless, wood or camouflage composite stock **$876.00**

PRAIRIE RIVER ARMS PRA BULLPUP RIFLE

Caliber: 50. **Barrel:** 28"; 1:28" twist. **Weight:** 7.5 lbs. **Length:** 31.5" overall. **Stock:** Hardwood or black all-weather. **Sights:** Blade front, open adjustable rear. **Features:** Bullpup design thumbhole stock. Patented internal percussion ignition system. Left-hand model available. Dovetailed for scope mount. Introduced 1995. Made in U.S. by Prairie River Arms, Ltd.
Price: 4140 alloy barrel, hardwood stock **$199.00**
Price: All Weather stock, alloy barrel **$205.00**

REMINGTON GENESIS MUZZLELOADER

Caliber: 50. **Barrel:** 28", 1-in-28" twist, blued, camo, or stainless fluted. **Weight:** 7.75 lbs. **Length:** NA. **Stock:** Black synthetic, Mossy Oak New Break-Up, Realtree Hardwoods HD. **Sights:** Williams fiber-optic sights, drilled and tapped for scope mounts. **Features:** TorchCam action, 209 primer, up to 150-grain charges. Over-travel hammer, crossbolt safety with ambidextrous HammerSpur (right- and left-handed operation). Buckmasters version has stainless fluted barrel with a Realtree Hardwoods HD camo stock, laser-engraved Buckmasters logo. Aluminum anodized ramrod with jag, front and rear swivel studs, removable 7/16" breech plug; optimized for use with Remington Kleanbore 209 Muzzleloading Primers. Introduced 2006. Made in U.S. by Remington Arms Co.
Price: Genesis ML, black synthetic, carbon matte blued **$237.00**
Price: Genesis MLS Overmold synthetic, stainless satin **$307.00**
Price: Genesis ML Camo Mossy Oak Break-Up full camo . . . **$349.00**
Price: Genesis ML Camo Mossy Oak Break-Up matte blue . **$293.00**
Price: Genesis MLS Camo, Mossy Oak Break-up,
stainless satin **$342.00**
Price: Genesis ML SF Synthetic Thumbhole **$349.00**
Price: Genesis ML SF Synthetic Thumbhole, stainless satin . **$405.00**

BLACKPOWDER MUSKETS & RIFLES

Price: Genesis ML SF Buckmasters (2007) **$363.00**
Price: Genesis ML SF laminate thumbhole, stainless satin . . **$538.00**

RICHMOND, C.S., 1863 MUSKET
Caliber: 58. **Barrel:** 40". **Weight:** 11 lbs. **Length:** 56.25" overall. **Stock:** European walnut with oil finish. **Sights:** Blade front, adjustable folding leaf rear. **Features:** Reproduction of the three-band Civil War musket. Sling swivels attached to trigger guard and middle barrel band. Lockplate marked "1863" and "C.S. Richmond." All white metal. Brass buttplate and forend cap. Imported by Euroarms of America, Navy Arms, and Dixie Gun Works.
Price: Euroarms $730.00
Price: Dixie Gun Works PR0846 . . . . **$1,050.00**
Price: Navy Arms **$1,005.00**

ROCKY MOUNTAIN HAWKEN
Caliber: NA. **Barrel:** 34-11/16". **Weight:** 10 lbs. **Length:** 52" overall. **Stock:** Walnut or maple. **Sights:** Blade front, drift adjustable rear. Fea-tures: Percussion, double set trigger, casehard-ened furniture, hook breech, brown barrel. Made by Pedersoli in Italy. Imported by Dixie Gun Works.
Price: Maple Stock PR3430 . . . .**$925.00**
Price: Walnut Stock PR3435 . . . .**$875.00**

ROSSI MUZZLELOADERS
Caliber: .50. **Barrel:** 20", 23". **Weight:** 5-6.3 lbs. **Stocks:** Wood. **Sights:** Fully adjustable fiber optic sights. **Features:** Black powder break open, 2 models available, manual external safety, Taurus Security System, blue or stainless finish, youth models available. From Rossi USA.
Price: $209.00
Price: Youth Size (2008) $269.00
Price: S50MB $179.95
Price: S50SM $229.95
Price: S45YBM (2009) $195.95
Price: S45YSM (2009) $242.95
Price: S50YBN (2009) $195.95
Price: S50YSM (2009) $242.95

SAVAGE MODEL 10ML MUZZLELOADER RIFLE SERIES
Caliber: 50. **Barrel:** 24", 1:24 twist, blue or stainless. **Weight:** 7.75 lbs. **Stock:** Black synthetic, Realtree Hardwood JD Camo, brown laminate. **Sights:** Green adjustable rear, Red FiberOptic front. **Features:** XP Models scoped, no sights, designed for smokeless powder, #209 primer ignition. Removeable breech plug and vent liner.
Price: Model 10ML-II $531.00
Price: Model 10ML-II Camo $569.00
Price: Model 10MLSS-II Camo $628.00
Price: Model 10MLBSS-II $667.00
Price: Model 10ML-IIXP $569.00
Price: Model 10MLSS-IIXP $628.00

SECOND MODEL BROWN BESS MUSKET
Caliber: 75, uses .735" round ball. **Barrel:** 42", smoothbore. **Weight:** 9.5 lbs. **Length:** 59" overall. **Stock:** Walnut (Navy); walnut-stained hardwood (Dixie). **Sights:** Fixed. **Features:** Polished barrel and lock with brass trigger guard and buttplate. Bayonet and scabbard available. From Navy Arms, Dixie Gun Works.
Price: Finished . . . . **$475.00 to $950.00**
Price: Kit, Dixie Gun Works, FR0825 . . . .$875.00
Price: Carbine (Navy Arms) $835.00
Price: Dixie Gun Works FR0810 . . . . $995.00

THOMPSON/CENTER TRIUMPH MAGNUM MUZZLELOADER
Caliber: 50. **Barrel:** 28" Weather Shield coated. **Weight:** NA. **Length:** NA. **Stock:** Black composite or Realtree AP HD Camo. **Sights:** NA.

Features: QLA 209 shotshell primer ignition. Introduced 2007. Made in U.S. by Thompson/Center Arms.
Price: $457.00

Thompson/Center Bone Collector
Similar to the Triumph Magnum but with added Flex Tech technology and Energy Burners to a shorter stock. Also added is Thompson/Center's premium fluted barrel with Weather Shield and their patented Power Rod.
Price: $708.00

THOMPSON/CENTER ENCORE 209X50 MAGNUM
Caliber: 50. **Barrel:** 26"; interchangeable with centerfire calibers. **Weight:** 7 lbs. **Length:** 40.5" overall. **Stock:** American walnut butt and forend, or black composite. **Sights:** TruGlo fiber-optic front and rear. **Features:** Blue or stainless steel. Uses the stock, frame and forend of the Encore centerfire pistol; break-open design using trigger guard spur; stainless steel universal breech plug; uses #209 shotshell primers. Introduced 1998. Made in U.S. by Thompson/Center Arms.
Price: Stainless with camo stock $772.00
Price: Blue, walnut stock and forend $678.00
Price: Blue, composite stock and forend $637.00
Price: Stainless, composite stock and forend $713.00
Price: All camo Realtree Hardwoods $729.00

THOMPSON/CENTER FIRE STORM RIFLE
Caliber: 50. **Barrel:** 26"; 1:28 twist. **Weight:** 7 lbs. **Length:** 41.75" overall. **Stock:** Black synthetic with rubber recoil pad, swivel studs. **Sights:** Click-adjustable steel rear and ramp-style front, both with fiber-optic inserts. **Features:** Side hammer lock is the first designed for up to three 50-grain Pyrodex pellets; patented Pyrodex Pyramid breech directs ignition fire 360 degrees around base of pellet. Quick Load Accurizor Muzzle System; aluminum ramrod. Flintlock only. Introduced 2000. Made in U.S. by Thompson/Center Arms.
Price: Blue finish, flintlock model with 1:48" twist for round balls, conicals $436.00
Price: SST, flintlock $488.00

THOMPSON/CENTER HAWKEN RIFLE
Caliber: 50. **Barrel:** 28" octagon, hooked breech. **Stock:** American walnut. **Sights:** Blade front, rear adjustable for windage and elevation. **Features:** Solid brass furniture, double-set triggers, button rifled barrel, coil-type mainspring. From Thompson/Center Arms.
Price: Percussion model $590.00
Price: Flintlock model $615.00

THOMPSON/CENTER OMEGA
Caliber: 50". **Barrel:** 28", fluted. **Weight:** 7 lbs. **Length:** 42" overall. **Stock:** Composite or laminated. **Sights:** Adjustable metal rear sight with fiber-optics; metal ramp front sight with fiber-optics. **Features:** Drilled and tapped for scope mounts. Thumbhole stock, sling swivel studs. From T/C..
Price: $777.00

THOMPSON/CENTER IMPACT MUZZLELOADING RIFLE
50-caliber single shot rifle. Features include 209 primer ignition, sliding hood to expose removable breechplug, synthetic stock adjustable from 12.5 to 13.5 inches, 26-inch blued 1:28 rifled barrel, adjustable fiber optic sights, aluminum ramrod, camo composite stock, QLA muzzle system. Weight 6.5 lbs.

Prices given are believed to be accurate at time of publication however, many factors affect retail pricing so exact prices are not possible.

BLACKPOWDER MUSKETS & RIFLES

Price: Impact Camo, Impact Camo / WS Camo, Impact Composite, Impact Weather Shield Black, Impact Weather Shield Camo . . . . **$249.00 to $269.00**

THOMPSON/CENTER NORTHWEST EXPLORER MUZZLELOADING RIFLE
50-caliber single shot rifle. Features include dropping block action, #11 percussion cap ignition, 28-inch blued or Weathershield 1:48 rifled barrel, adjustable fiber optic sights, aluminum ramrod, black or camo composite stock with recoil pad, QLA muzzle system. Weight 7 lbs.
Price: . . . . **$329.00 to $399.00**

TRADITIONS BUCKSKINNER CARBINE
Caliber: 50. **Barrel:** 21"; 15/16" flats, half octagon, half round; 1:20" or 1:66" twist. **Weight:** 6 lbs. **Length:** 37" overall. **Stock:** Beech or black laminated. **Sights:** Beaded blade front, fiber-optic open rear click adjustable for windage and elevation or fiber-optics. **Features:** Uses V-type mainspring, single trigger. Non-glare hardware; sling swivels. From Traditions.
Price: Flintlock **$249.00**
Price: Flintlock, laminated stock **$303.00**

TRADITIONS DEERHUNTER RIFLE SERIES
Caliber: 32, 50 or 54. **Barrel:** 24", octagonal; 15/16" flats; 1:48" or 1:66" twist. **Weight:** 6 lbs. **Length:** 40" overall. **Stock:** Stained hardwood or All-Weather composite with rubber buttpad, sling swivels. **Sights:** Lite Optic blade front, adjustable rear fiber-optics. **Features:** Flint or percussion with color case-hardened lock. Hooked breech, oversized trigger guard, blackened furniture, PVC ramrod. All-Weather has composite stock and C-nickel barrel. Drilled and tapped for scope mounting. Imported by Traditions, Inc.
Price: Percussion, 50-cal.; blued barrel; 1:48" twist **$228.00**
Price: Flintlock, 50 caliber only; 1:48" twist **$278.00**
Price: 50-cal., synthetic/blued **$224.00**
Price: Flintlock, 50-cal., synthetic/blued **$256.00**
Price: Redi-Pak, 50 cal. flintlock **$308.00**
Price: Flintlock, left-handed hardwood, 50 cal. **$337.00**
Price: 50-cal., hardwood/blued **$264.00**

TRADITIONS PURSUIT ULTRALIGHT MUZZLELOADER
Caliber: .50. **Barrel:** 26", Chromoly Tapered, Fluted Barrel with Premium CeraKote Finish. **Weight:** 5.5 lbs. **Length:** 44" overall. **Stock:** Soft Touch camouflage stocks with thumbhole stocks available. **Sights:** 3-9x40 scope with medium rings and bases mounted and bore sighted by a factory trained technician. **Features:** Williams™ fiber optic metal sights provide a clear sight picture even in low light conditions. The Pursuit™ Ultralight comes equipped with our Accelerator Breech Plug™. This patented and award winning breech plug removes in three full rotations and requires no tools! This full featured gun is rounded out with a corrosion resistant lightweight frame that improves overall handling.
Price: **$435.00**

TRADITIONS PURSUIT BREAK-OPEN MUZZLELOADER
Caliber: 45, 54 and 12 gauge. **Barrel:** 28", tapered, fluted; blued, stainless or Hardwoods Green camo. **Weight:** 8.25 lbs. **Length:** 44" overall. **Stock:** Synthetic black or Hardwoods Green. **Sights:** Steel fiber-optic rear, bead front. Introduced 2004 by Traditions, Inc.
Price: Steel, blued, 45 or 50 cal., synthetic stock **$279.00**
Price: Steel, nickel, 45 or 50 cal., synthetic stock **$309.00**
Price: Steel, nickel w/Hardwoods Green stock **$359.00**

Price: Matte blued; 12 ga., synthetic stock **$369.00**
Price: Matte blued; 12 ga. w/Hardwoods Green stock **$439.00**
Price: Lightweight model, blued, synthetic stock **$199.00**
Price: Lightweight model, blued, Mossy Oak® Break-Up™ Camo stock **$239.00**
Price: Lightweight model, nickel, Mossy Oak® Break-Up™ Camo stock **$279.00**

TRADITIONS EVOLUTION LONG DISTANCE BOLT-ACTION BLACKPOWDER RIFLE
Caliber: 45, 50 percussion. **Barrel:** 26", fluted with porting. **Sights:** Steel fiber-optic. **Weight:** 7 to 7.25 lbs. **Length:** 45" overall. **Features:** Bolt-action, cocking indicator, thumb safety, aluminum ramrod, sling studs. Wide variety of stocks and metal finishes. Introduced 2004 by Traditions, Inc.
Price: 50-cal. synthetic stock **$314.00**
Price: 45-cal, synthetic stock **$259.00**
Price: 50-cal. AW/Adv. Timber HD **$370.00**
Price: 50-cal. synthetic black/blued **$293.00**

TRADITIONS PA PELLET FLINTLOCK
Caliber: 50. **Barrel:** 26", blued, nickel. **Weight:** 7 lbs. **Stock:** Hardwood, synthetic and synthetic break-up. **Sights:** Fiber-optic. **Features:** Removeable breech plug, left-hand model with hardwood stock. 1:48" twist.
Price: Hardwood, blued **$343.00**
Price: Hardwood left, blued **$378.00**

TRADITIONS HAWKEN WOODSMAN RIFLE
Caliber: 50. **Barrel:** 28"; 15/16" flats. **Weight:** 7 lbs., 11 oz. **Length:** 44.5" overall. **Stock:** Walnut-stained hardwood. **Sights:** Beaded blade front, hunting-style open rear adjustable for windage and elevation. **Features:** Percussion only. Brass patchbox and furniture. Double triggers. From Traditions.
Price: 50-cal. nickel/black laminate **$299.95**
Price: 50-cal Percussion **$396.00**
Price: 50-cal., left-hand **$415.00**
Price: 50-cal., flintlock **$434.00**

TRADITIONS KENTUCKY RIFLE
Caliber: 50. **Barrel:** 33.5"; 7/8" flats; 1:66" twist. **Weight:** 7 lbs. **Length:** 49" overall. **Stock:** Beech; inletted toe plate. **Sights:** Blade front, fixed rear. **Features:** Full-length, two-piece stock; brass furniture; color case-hardened lock. From Traditions.
Price: **$364.00**

TRADITIONS PENNSYLVANIA RIFLE
Caliber: 50. **Barrel:** 40.25"; 7/8" flats; 1:66" twist, octagon. **Weight:** 9 lbs. **Length:** 57.5" overall. **Stock:** Walnut. **Sights:** Blade front, adjustable rear. **Features:** Brass patchbox and ornamentation. Double-set triggers. From Traditions.
Price: Flintlock **$720.00**
Price: Percussion **$664.00**

TRADITIONS SHENANDOAH RIFLE
Caliber: 36, 50. **Barrel:** 33.5" octagon; 1:66" twist. **Weight:** 7 lbs., 3 oz. **Length:** 49.5" overall. **Stock:** Walnut. **Sights:** Blade front, buckhorn rear. **Features:** V-type mainspring; double-set trigger; solid brass buttplate, patchbox, nosecap, thimbles, trigger guard. Introduced 1996. From Traditions.
Price: Flintlock **$588.00**
Price: Percussion **$551.00**
Price: 36 cal. flintlock, 1:48" twist **$618.00**
Price: 36 cal. percussion, 1:48" twist **$558.00**

TRADITIONS TENNESSEE RIFLE
Caliber: 50. **Barrel:** 24", octagon; 15/16" flats; 1:66" twist. **Weight:**

BLACKPOWDER MUSKETS & RIFLES

6 lbs. **Length:** 40.5" overall. **Stock:** Stained beech. **Sights:** Blade front, fixed rear. **Features:** One-piece stock has inletted brass furniture, cheekpiece; double-set trigger; V-type mainspring. Flint or percussion. From Traditions.
Price: Flintlock **$484.00**
Price: Percussion **$439.00**

TRADITIONS TRACKER 209 IN-LINE RIFLES
Caliber: 45, 50. **Barrel:** 22" blued or C-nickel finish; 1:28" twist, 50 cal. 1:20" 45 cal. **Weight:** 6 lbs., 4 oz. **Length:** 41" overall. **Stock:** Black, Advantage Timber® composite, synthetic. **Sights:** Lite Optic blade front, adjustable rear. **Features:** Thumb safety; adjustable trigger; rubber butt pad and sling swivel studs; takes 150 grains of Pyrodex pellets; one-piece breech system takes 209 shotshell primers. Drilled and tapped for scope. From Traditions.
Price: (Black composite or synthetic stock, 22" blued barrel) . **$161.00**
Price: (Black composite or synthetic stock, 22" C-nickel
    barrel) **$184.00**
Price: (Advantage Timber® stock, 22" C-nickel barrel) **$249.00**
Price: (Redi-Pak, black stock and blued barrel, powder flask,
    capper, ball starter, other accessories) **$219.00**
Price: (Redi-Pak, synthetic stock and blued barrel, with
    scope) **$265.00**

ULTRA LIGHT ARMS MODEL 209 MUZZLELOADER
Caliber: 45 or 50. **Barrel:** 24" button rifled; 1:32 twist. **Weight:** Under 5 lbs. **Stock:** Kevlar/Graphite. **Features:** Recoil pad, sling swivels included. Some color options available. Adj. Timney trigger, positive primer extraction.
Price: **$1,300.00**

WHITE MODEL 97 WHITETAIL HUNTER RIFLE
Caliber: 45, 50. **Barrel:** 22", 1:20" twist (45 cal.); 1:24" twist (50 cal.). **Weight:** 7.7 lbs. **Length:** 40" overall. **Stock:** Black laminated or black composite. **Sights:** Marble TruGlo fully adjustable, steel rear with white diamond, red bead front with high-visibility inserts. **Features:** In-line ignition with FlashFire one-piece nipple and breech plug that uses standard or magnum No. 11 caps, fully adjustable trigger, double safety system, aluminum ramrod; drilled and tapped for scope. Hard case. Made in U.S.A. by Split Fire Sporting Goods.
Price: Whitetail w/laminated or composite stock. **$499.95**
Price: Adventurer w/26" stainless barrel & thumbhole stock) **$699.95**
Price: Odyssey w/24" carbon fiber wrapped barrel
    & thumbhole stock **$1,299.95**

WHITE MODEL 98 ELITE HUNTER RIFLE
Caliber: 45, 50. **Barrel:** 24", 1:24" twist (50 cal). **Weight:** 8.6 lbs. **Length:** 43.5" overall. **Stock:** Black laminate wtih swivel studs. **Sights:** TruGlo fully adjustable, steel rear with white diamond, red bead front with high-visibility inserts. **Features:** In-line ignition with FlashFire one-piece nipple and breech plug that uses standard or magnum No. 11 caps, fully adjustable trigger, double safety system, aluminum ramrod, drilled and tapped for scope, hard gun case. Made in U.S.A. by Split Fire Sporting Goods.
Price: Composite or laminate wood stock. **$499.95**

White Thunderbolt Rifle
Similar to the Elite Hunter but is designed to handle 209 shotgun primers only. Has 26" stainless steel barrel, weighs 9.3 lbs. and is 45.5" long. Composite or laminate stock. Made in U.S.A. by Split Fire Sporting Goods.
Price: **$599.95**

WHITE MODEL 2000 BLACKTAIL HUNTER RIFLE
Caliber: 50. **Barrel:** 22", 1:24" twist (50 cal.). **Weight:** 7.6 lbs. **Length:** 39-7/8" overall. **Stock:** Black laminated with swivel studs with laser engraved deer or elk scene. **Sights:** TruGlo fully adjustable, steel rear with white diamond, red bead front with high-visibility inserts. **Features:** Teflon finished barrel, in-line ignition with FlashFire one-piece nipple and breech plug that uses standard or magnum No. 11 caps, fully adjustable trigger, double safety system, aluminum

ramrod, drilled and tapped for scope. Hard gun case. Made in U.S.A. by Split Fire Sporting Goods.
Price: Laminate wood stock, w/laser engraved game scene . **$599.95**

WHITE LIGHTNING II RIFLE
Caliber: 45 and 50 percussion. **Barrel:** 24", 1:32 twist. **Sights:** Adj. rear. **Stock:** Black polymer. **Weight:** 6 lbs. **Features:** In-line, 209 primer ignition system, blued or nickel-plated bbl., adj. trigger, Delrin ramrod, sling studs, recoil pad. Made in U.S.A. by Split Fire Sporting Goods.
Price: **$299.95**

WHITE ALPHA RIFLE
Caliber: 45, 50 percussion. **Barrel:** 27" tapered, stainless. **Sights:** Marble TruGlo rear, fiber-optic front. **Stock:** Laminated. **Features:** Lever action rotating block, hammerless; adj. trigger, positive safety. All stainless metal, including trigger. Made in U.S.A. by Split Fire Sporting Goods.
Price: **$449.95**

WINCHESTER APEX SWING-ACTION MAGNUM RIFLE
Caliber: 45, 50. **Barrel:** 28". **Stock:** Mossy Oak® Camo, Black Fleck. **Sights:** Adj. fiber-optic. **Weight:** 7 lbs., 12 oz. **Overall length:** 42". **Features:** Monte Carlo cheekpiece, swing-action design, external hammer.
Price: Mossy Oak®/stainless **$489.95**
Price: Black Fleck/stainless **$449.95**
Price: Full Mossy Oak® **$469.95**
Price: Black Fleck/blued **$364.95**

WINCHESTER X-150 BOLT-ACTION MAGNUM RIFLE
Caliber: 45, 50. **Barrel:** 26". **Stock:** Hardwoods or Timber HD, Black Fleck, Break-Up™. **Weight:** 8 lbs., 3 oz. **Sights:** Adj. fiber-optic. **Features:** No. 209 shotgun primer ignition, stainless steel bolt, stainless fluted bbl.
Price: Mossy Oak®, Timber, Hardwoods/stainless. **$349.95**
Price: Black Fleck/stainless **$299.95**
Price: Mossy Oak®, Timber, Hardwoods/blued **$279.95**
Price: Black Fleck/blued **$229.95**

ZOUAVE PERCUSSION RIFLE
Caliber: 58, 59. **Barrel:** 32.5". **Weight:** 9.5 lbs. **Length:** 48.5" overall. **Stock:** Walnut finish, brass patchbox and buttplate. **Sights:** Fixed front, rear adjustable for elevation. **Features:** Color case-hardened lockplate, blued barrel. From Navy Arms, Dixie Gun Works, EMF, Euroarms of America.
Price: Dixie Gun Works PR0853 (58) **$525.00**

BLACKPOWDER SHOTGUNS

CABELA'S BLACKPOWDER SHOTGUNS
Gauge: 10, 12, 20. **Barrel:** 10-ga., 30"; 12-ga., 28.5" (Extra-Full, Mod., Imp. Cyl. choke tubes); 20-ga., 27.5" (Imp. Cyl. & Mod. fixed chokes). **Weight:** 6.5 to 7 lbs. **Length:** 45" overall (28.5" barrel). **Stock:** American walnut with checkered grip; 12- and 20-gauge have straight stock, 10-gauge has pistol grip. **Features:** Blued barrels, engraved, color case-hardened locks and hammers, brass ramrod tip. From Cabela's.
Price: 10-gauge **$849.99**
Price: 12-gauge **$719.99**
Price: 20-gauge **$659.99**

DIXIE MAGNUM PERCUSSION SHOTGUN
Gauge: 10, 12, 20. **Barrel:** 30" (Imp. Cyl. & Mod.) in 10-gauge; 28" in 12-gauge. **Weight:** 6.25 lbs. **Length:** 45" overall. **Stock:** Hand-checkered walnut, 14" pull. **Features:** Double triggers; light hand engraving; case-hardened locks in 12-gauge, polished steel in 10-gauge; sling swivels. From Dixie Gun Works.
Price: 12 ga. PS0930 .... **$825.00**
Price: 12-ga. Kit PS0940 .... **$725.00**
Price: 20-ga. PS0334 .... **$825.00**
Price: 10-ga. PS1030 .... **$900.00**
Price: 10-ga. kit PS1040 .... **$725.00**
Price: Coach Gun, 12 ga. 20" bbl PS0914 .... **$800.00**

KNIGHT TK2000 NEXT G-1 CAMO MUZZLELOADING SHOTGUN
Gauge: 12. **Barrel:** 26", extra-full choke tube. **Weight:** 7 lbs., 7 oz. **Length:** 45" overall. **Stock:** Synthetic black or Realtree Hardwoods; recoil pad; swivel studs. **Sights:** Fully adjustable rear, blade front with fiber-optics. **Features:** Receiver drilled and tapped for scope mount; in-line ignition; adjustable trigger; removable breech plug; double safety system; Imp. Cyl. choke tube available. Made in U.S. by Knight Rifles (Modern Muzzleloading)
Price: **$379.99**

NAVY ARMS SIDE-BY-SIDE SHOTGUN
Caliber: 12 smoothbore. **Barrel:** 28.5". **Weight:** 7 lbs. **Length:** 44.3" overall. **Features:** English model reproduction has checkered walnut stock, slightly choked and inside choked blued barrels, engraved locks. From Navy Arms.
Price: **$910.00**

WHITE TOMINATOR SHOTGUN
Caliber: 12. **Barrel:** 25" blue, straight, tapered stainless steel. **Weight:** NA. **Length:** NA. **Stock:** Black laminated or black wood. **Sights:** Drilled and tapped for easy scope mounting. **Features:** Internchangeable choke tubes. Custom vent rib with high visibility front bead. Double safeties. Fully adjustable custom trigger. Recoil pad and sling swivel studs. Made in U.S.A. by Split Fire Sporting Goods.
Price: **$349.95**

SMOKELESS MUZZLELOADERS

BAD BULL X-SERIES MUZZLELOADER RIFLES
Caliber: 45. **Barrel:** 28". **Stock:** Laminated thumbhole stock. **Weight:** 9 lbs., 10 oz. **Length:** 50" overall. **Features:** Remington bolt action, Shilen select stainless steel barrel, Harrell's custom muzzle brake, laminated thumbhole stock, adjustable trigger, pillar bedded, glass bedded, free floated barrel, 1" decelerator pad, Warne rings/weaver, mag-prime 2 stage breech plug.
Price: **$3950.00**

BAD BULL FB SERIES MUZZLELOADER RIFLES
Caliber: 45. **Barrel:** 26". **Stock:** Laminated thumbhole stock. **Weight:** 8 lbs., 1 oz. **Length:** 44" overall. **Features:** Ruger falling block action, Shilen select stainless steel barrel, Harrell's custom muzzle brake, black and gray laminated stock and forearm, mag-prime 2 stage breech plug, 1" decelerator pad, Warne rings, open sights (optional).
Price: **$3950.00**

BAD BULL G SERIES MUZZLELOADER RIFLES
Caliber: 45. **Barrel:** 26". **Stock:** Laminated thumbhole stock. **Weight:** 7 lbs., 14 oz. **Length:** 46.75" overall. **Features:** Remington bolt action, Shilen stainless steel barrel, Harrell's custom muzzle brake, classic laminated stock, trigger adjusted to 2 ½ lbs., Double pillar bedded, 1" recoil pad, mag prime 2 stage breech plug, Warne rings & grand slam bases. The Bad Bull G Series has the short length and lightweight of the FB Series and the extreme accuracy of the X Series. It is a great hunting muzzleloader. The 275 grain Parker/BB Bullet is used with IMR 4350 Powder. With this combination, we are producing MOA or less. If you are a hunter who likes a shorter, lighter muzzleloader with great accuracy capability all the way to 500 yards, this is your muzzleloader.
Price: **$3950.00**

ARS HUNTING MASTER AR6 AIR PISTOL
Caliber: .22 (.177 + 20 special order). **Barrel:** 12" rifled. **Weight:** 3 lbs. **Length:** 18.25 overall. **Power:** NA. **Grips:** Indonesian walnut with checkered grip. **Sights:** Adjustable rear, blade front. **Features:** 6 shot repeater with rotary magazine, single or double action, receiver grooved for scope, hammer block and trigger block safeties.
Price: **$659.00**

BEEMAN P1 MAGNUM AIR PISTOL
Caliber: .177, 20. **Barrel:** 8.4". **Weight:** 2.5 lbs. **Length:** 11" overall. **Power:** Top lever cocking; spring-piston. **Grips:** Checkered walnut. **Sights:** Blade front, square notch rear with click micrometer adjustments for windage and elevation. Grooved for scope mounting. **Features:** Dual power for .177 and 20 cal.; low setting gives 350-400 fps; high setting 500-600 fps. All Colt 45 auto grips fit gun. Dry-firing feature for practice. Optional wood shoulder stock. Imported by Beeman.
Price: .... **$499.95 to $525.95**

BEEMAN P3 PNEUMATIC AIR PISTOL
Caliber: .177. **Barrel:** NA. **Weight:** 1.7 lbs. **Length:** 9.6" overall. **Power:** Single-stroke pneumatic; overlever barrel cocking. **Grips:** Reinforced polymer. **Sights:** Front and rear fiber-optic sights. **Features:** Velocity 410 fps. Polymer frame; automatic safety; two-stage trigger; built-in muzzle brake.
Price: **$245.95**
Price: With scope **$335.95**

BEEMAN/FEINWERKBAU P44
Caliber: .177, single shot. **Barrel:** 9.17". **Weight:** 2.10 lbs. **Length:** 16.54" overall. **Power:** Pre-charged pneumatic. **Grips:** Walnut grip. **Sights:** front and rear sights. **Features:** 500 fps, sighting line adjustable from 360 to 395mm, adjustable 3-d grip in 3 sizes, adjustable match trigger, delivered in special transport case.
Price: **$2,575.95**
Price: Left-hand model **$2,655.95**

BEEMAN/FEINWERKBAU P56
Caliber: .177, 5-shot magazine. **Barrel:** 8.81". **Weight:** 2.43 lbs. **Length:** 16.54" overall. **Power:** Pre-charged pneumatic. **Grips:** Walnut Morini grip. **Sights:** front and rear sights. **Features:** 500 fps, match-adjustable trigger, adjustable rear sight, front sight accepts interchangeable inserts, delivered in special transport case.
Price: **$2,654.00**

BEEMAN/FWB 103 AIR PISTOL
Caliber: .177. **Barrel:** 10.1", 12-groove rifling. **Weight:** 2.5 lbs. **Length:** 16.5" overall. **Power:** Single-stroke pneumatic, underlever cocking. **Grips:** Stippled walnut with adjustable palm shelf. **Sights:** Blade front, open rear adjustable for windage and elevation. Notch size adjustable for width. Interchangeable front blades. **Features:** Velocity 510 fps. Fully adjustable trigger. Cocking effort 2 lbs. Imported by Beeman.
Price: Right-hand **$2,110.00**
Price: Left-hand **$2,350.00**

BEEMAN HW70A AIR PISTOL
Caliber: .177. **Barrel:** 6-1/4", rifled. **Weight:** 38 oz. **Length:** 12-3/4" overall. **Power:** Spring, barrel cocking. **Grips:** Plastic, with thumbrest. **Sights:** Hooded post front, square notch rear adjustable for windage and elevation. Comes with scope base. **Features:** Adjustable trigger, 31-lb. cocking effort, 440 fps MV; automatic barrel safety. Imported by Beeman.
Price: **$289.95**

BENJAMIN & SHERIDAN CO2 PISTOLS
Caliber: .22, single shot. **Barrel:** 6-3/8", brass. **Weight:** 1 lb. 12 oz. **Length:** 9" overall. **Power:** 12-gram CO2 cylinder. **Grips:** American Hardwood. **Sights:** High ramp front, fully adjustable notched rear. **Features:** Velocity to 500 fps. Turnbolt action with cross-bolt safety. Gives about 40 shots per CO2 cylinder. Black or nickel finish. Made in U.S. by Crosman Corp.
Price: EB22 (.22) **$118.59**

BENJAMIN & SHERIDAN PNEUMATIC PELLET PISTOLS
Caliber: .177, .22, single shot. **Barrel:** 9-3/8", rifled brass. **Weight:** 2 lbs., 8 oz. **Length:** 12.25" overall. **Power:** Underlever pnuematic, hand pumped. **Grips:** American Hardwood. **Sights:** High ramp front, fully adjustable notch rear. **Features:** Velocity to 525 fps (variable). Bolt action with cross-bolt safety. Choice of black or nickel finish. Made in U.S. by Crosman Corp.
Price: Black finish, HB17 (.177), HB22 (.22) **$133.59**

CROSMAN C11
Caliber: .177, 18-shot BB or pellet. **Weight:** 1.4 lbs. **Length:** 8.5". **Power:** 12g CO2. **Sights:** Fixed. **Features:** Compact semi-automatic BB pistol. Velocity up to 480 fps. Under barrel weaver style rail.
Price: **$52.99**

CROSMAN 2240
Caliber: .22. **Barrel:** Rifled steel. **Weight:** 1 lb. 13 oz. **Length:** 11.125". **Power:** CO2. **Grips:** NA. **Sights:** Blade front, rear adjustable. **Features:** Ergonomically designed ambidextrous grip fits the hand for perfect balance and comfort with checkering and a thumbrest on both grip panels. From Crosman.
Price: **$57.83**

CROSMAN 3576 REVOLVER
Caliber: .177, pellets. **Barrel:** Rifled steel. **Weight:** 2 lbs. **Length:** 11.38". **Power:** CO2. **Grips:** NA. **Sights:** Blade front, rear adjustable. **Features:** Semi-auto 10-shot with revolver styling and finger-molded grip design, 6" barrel for increased accuracy. From Crosman.
Price: **$52.59**

CROSMAN MODEL 1088 REPEAT AIR PISTOL
Caliber: .177, 8-shot pellet clip. **Barrel:** Rifled steel. **Weight:** 17 oz. **Length:** 7.75" overall. **Power:** CO2 Powerlet. **Grips:** Checkered black plastic. **Sights:** Fixed blade front, adjustable rear. **Features:** Velocity about 430 fps. Single or double semi-automatic action. From Crosman.
Price: **$60.99**

CROSMAN PRO77
Caliber: .177, 17-shot BB. **Weight:** 1.31 lbs. **Length:** 6.75". **Power:** 12g CO2. **Sights:** Fixed. **Features:** Compact pistol with realistic recoil. Under the barrel weaver style rail. Velocity up to 325 fps.
Price: Pro77CS **$114.00**

CROSMAN T4
Caliber: .177, 8-shot BB or pellet. **Weight:** 1.32 lbs. **Length:** 8.63". **Power:** 12g CO2. **Sights:** Fixed front, windage adjustable rear. **Features:** Shoots BBs or pellets. Easy patent-pending CO2 piercing mechanism. Under the barrel weaver style rail.
Price: T4CS **$89.59**
Price: T4OPS, includes adjustable Red Dot sight, barrel compensator, and pressure operated tactical flashlight. Comes in foam padeed, hard sided protective case **$167.99**

DAISY POWERLINE® MODEL 15XT AIR PISTOL
Caliber: .177 BB, 15-shot built-in magazine. **Barrel:** NA. **Weight:** NA. **Length:** 7.21". **Power:** CO2. **Grips:** NA. **Sights:** NA. **Features:** Velocity 425 fps. Made in the U.S.A. by Daisy Mfg. Co.
Price: **$50.99**
Price: With electronic point sight **$64.99**

DAISY MODEL 717 AIR PISTOL
Caliber: .177, single shot. **Weight:** 2.25 lbs. **Length:** 13-1/2" overall. **Grips:** Molded checkered woodgrain with contoured thumbrest. **Sights:** Blade and ramp front, open rear with windage and elevation adjustments. **Features:** Single pump pneumatic pistol. Rifled steel barrel. Crossbolt trigger block. Muzzle velocity 360 fps. From Daisy Mfg. Co.
Price: **$220.94**

DAISY MODEL 747 TRIUMPH AIR PISTOL
Caliber: .177, single shot. **Weight:** 2.35 lbs. **Length:** 13-1/2" overall.

Grips: Molded checkered woodgrain with contoured thumbrest. **Sights:** Blade and ramp front, open rear with windage and elevation adjustments. **Features:** Single pump pneumatic pistol. Lothar Walther rifled high-grade steel barrel; crowned 12 lands and grooves, right-hand twist. Precision bore sized for match pellets. Muzzle velocity 360 fps. From Daisy Mfg. Co.
Price: **$264.99**

DAISY POWERLINE® 201
Caliber: .177 BB or pellet. **Weight:** 1 lb. **Length:** 9.25" overall. **Sights:** Blade and ramp front, fixed open rear. **Features:** Spring-air action, trigger-block safety and smooth-bore steel barrel. Muzzle velocity 230 fps. From Daisy Mfg. Co.
Price: **$29.99**

DAISY POWERLINE® 693 AIR PISTOL
Caliber: .177, single shot. **Weight:** 1.10 lbs. **Length:** 7.9" overall. **Grips:** Molded checkered. **Sights:** Blade and ramp front, fixed open rear. **Features:** Semi-automoatic BB pistol with a nickel finish and smooth bore steel barrel. Muzzle veocity 400 fps. From Daisy Mfg. Co.
Price: **$76.99**

DAISY POWERLINE® 5170 CO2 PISTOL
Caliber: .177 BB. **Weight:** 1 lb. **Length:** 9.5" overall. **Sights:** Blade and ramp front, open rear. **Features:** CO2 semi-automatic action, manual trigger-block safety, upper and lower rails for mounting sights and other accessories and a smooth-bore steel barrel. Muzzle velocity 520 fps. From Daisy Mfg. Co.
Price: **$59.99**

DAISY POWERLINE® 5501 CO2 BLOWBACK PISTOL
Caliber: .177 BB. **Weight:** 1 lb. **Length:** 9.5" overall. **Sights:** Blade and ramp front, open rear. **Features:** CO2 semi-automatic blow-back action, manual trigger-block safety, and a smooth-bore steel barrel. Muzzle velocity 430 fps. From Daisy Mfg. Co.
Price: **$99.99**

EAA/BAIKAL IZH-M46 TARGET AIR PISTOL
Caliber: .177, single shot. **Barrel:** 10". **Weight:** 2.4 lbs. **Length:** 16.8" overall. **Power:** Underlever single-stroke pneumatic. **Grips:** Adjustable wooden target. **Sights:** Micrometer fully adjustable rear, blade front. **Features:** Velocity about 440 fps. Hammer-forged, rifled barrel. Imported from Russia by European American Armory.
Price: **$430.00**

GAMO P-23, P-23 LASER PISTOL
Caliber: .177, 12-shot. **Barrel:** 4.25". **Weight:** 1 lb. **Length:** 7.5". **Power:** CO2 cartridge, semi-automatic, 410 fps. **Grips:** Plastic. **Sights:** NA. **Features:** Walther PPK cartridge pistol copy, optional laser sight. Imported from Spain by Gamo.
Price: . . . . **$89.95**, (with laser) **$139.95**

GAMO PT-80, PT-80 LASER PISTOL
Caliber: .177, 8-shot. **Barrel:** 4.25". **Weight:** 1.2 lbs. **Length:** 7.2". **Power:** CO2 cartridge, semi-automatic, 410 fps. **Grips:** Plastic. **Sights:** 3-dot. **Features:** Optional laser sight and walnut grips available. Imported from Spain by Gamo.
Price: . . . . **$108.95**, (with laser) **$159.95**
Price: (with walnut grip) **$119.95**

HAMMERLI AP-40 AIR PISTOL
Caliber: .177. **Barrel:** 10". **Weight:** 2.2 lbs. **Length:** 15.5". **Power:** NA. **Grips:** Adjustable orthopedic. **Sights:** Fully adjustable micrometer. **Features:** Sleek, light, well balanced and accurate.
Price: **$1,400.00**

MAGNUM RESEARCH DESERT EAGLE
Caliber: .177, 8-shot pellet. 5.7" rifled. **Weight:** 2.5 lbs. 11" overall. **Power:** 12g CO2. **Sights:** Fixed front, adjustable rear. Velocity of 425 fps. 8-shot rotary clip. Double or single action. The first .177 caliber air pistol with BLOWBACK action. Big and weighty, designed in the likeness of the real Desert Eagle.
Price: **$172.31**

MAGNUM BABY DESERT
Caliber: .177, 15-shot BB. 4" **Weight:** 1.0 lbs. 8-1/4" overall. **Power:** 12g CO2. **Sights:** Fixed front and rear. Velocity of 420 fps. Double action BB repeater. Comes with bonus Picatinny top rail and built-in bottom rail.
Price: **$41.54**

MORINI CM 162 EL MATCH AIR PISTOLS
Caliber: .177, single shot. **Barrel:** 9.4". **Weight:** 32 oz. **Length:** 16.1" overall. **Power:** Scuba air. **Grips:** Adjustable match type. **Sights:** Interchangeable blade front, fully adjustable match-type rear. **Features:** Power mechanism shuts down when pressure drops to a preset level. Adjustable electronic trigger.
Price: **$1,075.00**

PARDINI K58 MATCH AIR PISTOLS
Caliber: .177, single shot. **Barrel:** 9". **Weight:** 37.7 oz. **Length:** 15.5" overall. **Power:** Precharged compressed air; single-stroke cocking. **Grips:** Adjustable match type; stippled walnut. **Sights:** Interchangeable post front, fully adjustable match rear. **Features:** Fully adjustable trigger. Short version K-2 available. Imported from Italy by Larry's Guns.
Price: **$819.00**

RWS 9B/9N AIR PISTOLS
Caliber: .177, single shot. **Barrel:** 8". **Weight:** 2.38 lbs. **Length:** 10.4". **Power:** 550 fps. **Grips:** Right hand with thumbrest. **Sights:** Adjustable. **Features:** Spring-piston powered. Black or nickel finish.
Price: 9B/9N **$150.00**

SMITH & WESSON 586
Caliber: .177, 10-shot pellet. Rifled. **Power:** 12g CO2. **Sights:** Fixed front, adjustable rear. 10-shot rotary clip. Double or single action. Replica revolvers that duplicate both weight and handling.
Price: 4" barrel, 2.5 lbs, 400 fps **$215.34**
Price: 6" barrel, 2.8 lbs, 425 fps **$231.49**
Price: 8" barrel, 3.0 lbs, 460 fps **$247.65**
Price: S&W 686 Nickel, 6" barrel, 2.8 lbs, 425 fps **$253.03**

STEYR LP10P MATCH AIR PISTOL
Caliber: .177, single shot. **Barrel:** 9". **Weight:** 38.7 oz. **Length:** 15.3" overall. **Power:** Scuba air. **Grips:** Adjustable Morini match, palm shelf, stippled walnut. **Sights:** Interchangeable blade in 4mm, 4.5mm or 5mm widths, adjustable open rear, interchangeable 3.5mm or 4mm leaves. **Features:** Velocity about 500 fps. Adjustable trigger, adjustable sight radius from 12.4" to 13.2". With compensator. Recoil elimination.
Price: **$1,400.00**

TECH FORCE SS2 OLYMPIC COMPETITION AIR PISTOL
Caliber: .177 pellet, single shot. **Barrel:** 7.4". **Weight:** 2.8 lbs. **Length:** 16.5" overall. **Power:** Spring piston, sidelever. **Grips:** Hardwood. **Sights:** Extended adjustable rear, blade front accepts inserts. **Features:** Velocity 520 fps. Recoilless design; adjustments allow duplication of a firearm's feel. Match-grade, adjustable trigger; includes carrying case. Imported from China by Compasseco, Inc.
Price: **$295.00**

TECH FORCE 35 AIR PISTOL
Caliber: .177 pellet, single shot. **Weight:** 2.86 lbs. **Length:** 14.9" overall. **Power:** Spring-piston, underlever. **Grips:** Hardwood. **Sights:** Micrometer adjustable rear, blade front. **Features:** Velocity 400 fps. Grooved for scope mount; trigger safety. Imported from China by Compasseco, Inc.
Price: **$39.95**

Tech Force S2-1 Air Pistol
Similar to Tech Force 8 except basic grips and sights for plinking.
Price: **$29.95**

WALTHER LP300 MATCH PISTOL
Caliber: .177. **Barrel:** 236mm. **Weight:** 1.018g. **Length:** NA. **Power:** NA. **Grips:** NA. **Sights:** Integrated front with three different widths, adjustable rear. **Features:** Adjustable grip and trigger.
Price: **$1,800.00**

WALTHER PPK/S
Caliber: .177, 15-shot steel BB. 3-1/2". **Weight:** 1.2 lbs. 6-1/4" overall. **Power:** 12g CO2. **Sights:** Fixed front and rear. Velocity of 295 fps. Lookalike of one of the world's most famous pistols. Realistic recoil. Heavyweight steel construction.
Price: **$71.92**
Price: With laser sight **$94.23**
Price: With BiColor pistol, targets, shooting glasses, BBs **$84.62**

WALTHER CP99 COMPACT
Caliber: .177, 17-shot steel BB semi-auto. 3". **Weight:** 1.7 lbs. 6-1/2" overall. **Power:** 12g CO2. **Sights:** Fixed front and rear. Velocity of 345 fps. Realistic recoil, blowback action. Heavyweight steel construction. Built-in Picatinny mount.
Price: **$83.08**

AIRFORCE CONDOR RIFLE
Caliber: .177, .22 single shot. **Barrel:** 24" rifled. **Weight:** 6.5 lbs. **Length:** 38.75" overall. **Power:** Pre-charged pneumatic. **Stock:** NA. **Sights:** Intended for scope use, fiber-optic open sights optional. **Features:** Lothar Walther match barrel, adjustable power levels from 600-1,300 fps. 3,000 psi fill pressure. Automatic safety. Air tank volume: 490cc. An integral extended scope rail allows easy mounting of the largest air-gun scopes. Operates on high-pressure air from scuba tank or hand pump. Manufactured in the U.S.A by AirForce Airguns.

Price: Gun only (.22 or .177) **$631.00**

AIRFORCE TALON AIR RIFLE
Caliber: .177, .22, single shot. **Barrel:** 18" rifled. **Weight:** 5.5 lbs. **Length:** 32.6". **Power:** Pre-charged pneumatic. **Stock:** NA. **Sights:** Intended for scope use, fiber-optic open sights optional. **Features:** Lothar Walther match barrel, adjustable power levels from 400-1,000 fps, 3,000 psi fill pressure. Automatic safety. Air tank volume: 490cc. Operates on high-pressure air from scuba tank or hand pump. Manufactured in the U.S.A. by AirForce Airguns.

Price: Gun only (.22 or .177). **$514.25**

AIRFORCE TALON SS AIR RIFLE
Caliber: .177, .22, single shot. **Barrel:** 12" rifled. **Weight:** 5.25 lbs. **Length:** 32.75". **Power:** Pre-charged pneumatic. **Stock:** NA. **Sights:** Intended for scope use, fiber-optic open sights optional. **Features:** Lothar Walther match barrel, adjustable power levels from 400-1,000 fps. 3,000 psi fill pressure. Automatic safety. Chamber in front of barrel strips away air turbulence, protects muzzle and reduces firing report. Air tank volume: 490cc. Operates on high-pressure air from scuba tank or hand pump. Manufactured in the U.S.A. by AirForce Airguns.

Price: Gun only (.22 or .177). **$535.50**

AIRROW MODEL A-8SRB STEALTH AIR RIFLE
Caliber: .177, .22, .25, 9-shot. **Barrel:** 20"; rifled. **Weight:** 6 lbs. **Length:** 34" overall. **Power:** CO2 or compressed air; variable power. **Stock:** Telescoping CAR-15-type. **Sights:** Variable 3.5-10x scope. **Features:** Velocity 1100 fps in all calibers. Pneumatic air trigger. All aircraft aluminum and stainless steel construction. Mil-spec materials and finishes. From Swivel Machine Works, Inc.

Price: About **$2,299.00**

AIRROW MODEL A-8S1P STEALTH AIR RIFLE
Caliber: #2512 16" arrow. **Barrel:** 16". **Weight:** 4.4 lbs. **Length:** 30.1" overall. **Power:** CO2 or compressed air; variable power. **Stock:** Telescoping CAR-15-type. **Sights:** Scope rings only. 7 oz. rechargeable cylinder and valve. **Features:** Velocity to 650 fps with 260-grain arrow. Pneumatic air trigger. Broadhead guard. All aircraft aluminum and stainless steel construction. Mil-spec materials and finishes. A-8S Models perform to 2,000 PSIG above or below water levels. Waterproof case. From Swivel Machine Works, Inc.

Price: **$1,699.00**

ARS HUNTING MASTER AR6 AIR RIFLE
Caliber: .22, 6-shot repeater. **Barrel:** 25-1/2". **Weight:** 7 lbs. **Length:** 41-1/4" overall. **Power:** Precompressed air from 3000 psi diving tank. **Stock:** Indonesian walnut with checkered grip; rubber buttpad. **Sights:** Blade front, adjustable peep rear. **Features:** Velocity over 1000 fps with 32-grain pellet. Receiver grooved for scope mounting. Has 6-shot rotary magazine. Imported by Air Rifle Specialists.

Price: **$580.00**

BEEMAN HW100
Caliber: .177 or .22, 14-shot magazine. **Barrel:** 21-1/2". **Weight:** 9 lbs. **Length:** 42.13" overall. **Power:** Pre-charged. **Stock:** Walnut Sporter checkering on the pistol grip & forend; walnut thumbhole with lateral finger grooves on the forend & stippling on the pistol grip. **Sights:** None. Grooved for scope mounting. **Features:** 1140 fps .177 caliber; 945 fps .22 caliber. 14-shot magazine, quick-fill cylinder. Two-stage adjustable match trigger and manual safety.

Price: .177 or .22 caliber Sport Stock **$1,649.95**
Price: .177 or .22 caliber Thumbhole Stock **$1,649.95**

BEEMAN R1 AIR RIFLE
Caliber: .177, .20 or .22, single shot. **Barrel:** 19.6", 12-groove rifling. **Weight:** 8.5 lbs. **Length:** 45.2" overall. **Power:** Spring-piston, barrel cocking. **Stock:** Walnut-stained beech; cut-checkered pistol grip;

Monte Carlo comb and cheekpiece; rubber buttpad. **Sights:** Tunnel front with interchangeable inserts, open rear click-adjustable for windage and elevation. Grooved for scope mounting. **Features:** Velocity 940-1000 fps (.177), 860 fps (20), 800 fps (.22). Non-drying nylon piston and breech seals. Adjustable metal trigger. Milled steel safety. Right- or left-hand stock. Adjustable cheekpiece and buttplate at extra cost. Custom and Super Laser versions available. Imported by Beeman.

Price: Right-hand **$729.95**
Price: Left-hand **$789.95**

BEEMAN R7 AIR RIFLE
Caliber: .177, .20, single shot. **Barrel:** 17". **Weight:** 6.1 lbs. **Length:** 40.2" overall. **Power:** Spring-piston. **Stock:** Stained beech. **Sights:** Hooded front, fully adjustable micrometer click open rear. **Features:** Velocity to 700 fps (.177), 620 fps (20). Receiver grooved for scope mounting; double-jointed cocking lever; fully adjustable trigger; checkered grip. Imported by Beeman.

Price: .177. . . . . **$409.95**
Price: .20 . . . . **$429.95**

BEEMAN R9 AIR RIFLE
Caliber: .177, .20, single shot. **Barrel:** NA. **Weight:** 7.3 lbs. **Length:** 43" overall. **Power:** Spring-piston, barrel cocking. **Stock:** Stained hardwood. **Sights:** Tunnel post front, fully adjustable open rear. **Features:** Velocity to 1000 fps (.177), 800 fps (20). Adjustable Rekord trigger; automatic safety; receiver dovetailed for scope mounting. Imported from Germany by Beeman Precision Airguns.

Price: .177 . . . . **$499.95**
Price: .20 . . . . **$524.95**

BEEMAN R11 MKII AIR RIFLE
Caliber: .177, single shot. **Barrel:** 19.6". **Weight:** 8.6 lbs. **Length:** 43.5" overall. **Power:** Spring-piston, barrel cocking. **Stock:** Walnut-stained beech; adjustable buttplate and cheekpiece. **Sights:** None furnished. Has dovetail for scope mounting. **Features:** Velocity 910-940 fps. All-steel barrel sleeve. Imported by Beeman.

Price: **$679.95**

BEEMAN RX-2 GAS-SPRING MAGNUM AIR RIFLE
Caliber: .177, .20, .22, .25, single shot. **Barrel:** 19.6", 12-groove rifling. **Weight:** 8.8 lbs. **Power:** Gas-spring piston air; single stroke barrel cocking. **Stock:** Laminated wood stock. **Sights:** Tunnel front, click-adjustable rear. **Features:** Velocity adjustable to about 1200 fps. Imported by Beeman.

Price: .177, right-hand **$889.95**
Price: .20, right-hand **$909.95**
Price: .22, right-hand **$889.95**
Price: .25, right-hand **$909.95**

BEEMAN R1 CARBINE
Caliber: .177,. 20, .22 single shot. **Barrel:** 16.1". **Weight:** 8.6 lbs. **Length:** 41.7" overall. **Power:** Spring-piston, barrel cocking. **Stock:** Stained beech; Monte Carlo comb and checkpiece; cut checkered pistol grip; rubber buttpad. **Sights:** Tunnel front with interchangeable inserts, open adjustable rear; receiver grooved for scope mounting. **Features:** Velocity up to 1000 fps (.177). Non-drying nylon piston and breech seals. Adjustable metal trigger. Machined steel receiver end cap and safety. Right- or left-hand stock. Imported by Beeman.

Price: .177, 20, .22, right-hand **$749.95**

BEEMAN/FEINWERKBAU 700 P ALUMINUM OR WOOD STOCK
Caliber: .177, single shot. **Barrel:** 16.6". **Weight:** 10.8 lbs. Aluminum; 9.9 lbs. Wood. **Length:** 43.3-46.25" Aluminum; 43.7" Wood. **Power:** Pre-charged pneumatic. **Stock:** Aluminum stock P laminated hardwood. **Sights:** Tunnel front sight with interchangeable inserts, click micrometer match aperture rear sight. **Features:** Velocity 570 fps. Recoilless action. Anatomical grips can be tilted and pivoted to the barrel axis. Adjustable buttplate and cheekpiece.

Price: Aluminum 700, right, blue or silver **$3,934.95**
Price: Aluminum 700, universal **$3,069.95**

BEEMAN/FEINWERKBAU P70 FIELD TARGET
Caliber: .177, single shot. **Barrel:** 24.6". **Weight:** 10.6 lbs. **Length:** 43.3" overall. **Power:** Pre-charged pneumatic. **Stock:** Aluminum stock (red or blue) anatomical grips, buttplate & cheekpiece. **Sights:**

Prices given are believed to be accurate at time of publication however, many factors affect retail pricing so exact prices are not possible.

None, receiver grooved for scope mounting. **Features:** 870 fps velocity. At 50 yards, this air rifle is capable of achieving 1/2-inch groups. Match adjustable trigger. 2001 US Field Target National Champion.
Price: P70FT, precharged, right (red or blue) $3,819.95
Price: P70FT, precharged, left (red or blue) $3,964.95

BEEMAN/HW 97 AIR RIFLE
Caliber: .177, .20, .22, single shot. **Barrel:** 17.75". **Weight:** 9.2 lbs. **Length:** 44.1" overall. **Power:** Spring-piston, underlever cocking. **Stock:** Walnut-stained beech; rubber buttpad. **Sights:** None. Receiver grooved for scope mounting. **Features:** Velocity 830 fps (.177). Fixed barrel with fully opening, direct loading breech. Adjustable trigger. Imported by Beeman Precision Airguns.
Price: .177 . . . . $779.95
Price: .20, .22 . . . . $799.95

BENJAMIN & SHERIDAN PNEUMATIC (PUMP-UP) AIR RIFLE
Caliber: .177 or .22, single shot. **Barrel:** 19-3/8", rifled brass. **Weight:** 5-1/2 lbs. **Length:** 36-1/4" overall. **Power:** Underlever pneumatic, hand pumped. **Stock:** American walnut stock and forend. **Sights:** High ramp front, fully adjustable notched rear. **Features:** Variable velocity to 800 fps. Bolt action with ambidextrous push-pull safety. Black or nickel finish. Made in the U.S. by Benjamin Sheridan Co.
Price: 392 or 397 . . . . $249.40

BENJAMIN ROGUE .357 CALIBER MULTI-SHOT AIR RIFLE
Caliber: .357, 6-shot mag (optional single-shot tray). **Features:** Electronic precharged pneumatic (ePCP), Bolt-action, 2-stage adjustable electronic trigger with dual electronic switches, Ambidextrous synthetic stock w/adjustable buttstock & sling swivel studs, 11mm, Adjustable power, Up to 900 fps (250 ft-lbs. max), 3000 psi (206 bar) max fill pressure (delivers full-power shots with as little as 1000 psi), Shrouded for stealthy hunting, Up to 20 shots at 100 ft-lbs. when filled to 3000 psi, Built-in manometer (air pressure gauge), Weaver bipod rail, LCD screen for EPiC controls on left side of gun, includes fill adapter. Made in the U.S. by Benjamin Sheridan Co.
Price: . . . . N/A

BERETTA CX4 STORM
Caliber: .177, 30-shot semi-auto. 17-1/2", rifled. **Weight:** 5.25 lbs. **Length:** 30.75" overall. **Power:** 88g CO2. **Stock:** Replica style. **Sights:** Adjustable front and rear. Blowback action. Velocity of 600 fps. Accessory rails.
Price: $276.92

BSA SUPERTEN MK3 AIR RIFLE
Caliber: .177, .22 10-shot repeater. **Barrel:** 17-1/2". **Weight:** 7 lbs., 8 oz. **Length:** 37" overall. **Power:** Precharged pneumatic via buddy bottle. **Stock:** Oil-finished hardwood; Monte Carlo with cheekpiece, cut checkered grip; adjustable recoil pad. **Sights:** No sights; intended for scope use. **Features:** Velocity 1000+ fps (.177), 1000+ fps (.22). Patented 10-shot indexing magazine, bolt-action loading. Left-hand version also available. Imported from U.K.
Price: $599.95

BSA SUPERTEN MK3 BULLBARREL
Caliber: .177, .22, .25, single shot. **Barrel:** 18-1/2". **Weight:** 8 lbs., 8 oz. **Length:** 43" overall. **Power:** Spring-air, underlever cocking. **Stock:** Oil-finished hardwood; Monte Carlo with cheekpiece, checkered at grip; recoil pad. **Sights:** Ramp front, micrometer

adjustable rear. Maxi-Grip scope rail. **Features:** Velocity 950 fps (.177), 750 fps (.22), 600 fps (25). Patented rotating breech design. Maxi-Grip scope rail protects optics from recoil; automatic anti-beartrap plus manual safety. Imported from U.K.
Price: Rifle, MKII Carbine (14" barrel, 39-1/2" overall) $349.95

BSA MAGNUM SUPERSPORT AIR RIFLE, CARBINE
Caliber: .177, .22, .25, single shot. **Barrel:** 18-1/2". **Weight:** 6 lbs., 8 oz. **Length:** 41" overall. **Power:** Spring-air, barrel cocking. **Stock:** Oil-finished hardwood; Monte Carlo with cheekpiece, recoil pad. **Sights:** Ramp front, micrometer adjustable rear. Maxi-Grip scope rail. **Features:** Velocity 950 fps (.177), 750 fps (.22), 600 fps (25). Patented Maxi-Grip scope rail protects optics from recoil; automatic anti-beartrap plus manual tang safety. Muzzle brake standard. Imported for U.K.
Price: $194.95
Price: Carbine, 14" barrel, muzzle brake $214.95

BSA METEOR AIR RIFLE
Caliber: .177, .22, single shot. **Barrel:** 18-1/2". **Weight:** 6 lbs. **Length:** 41" overall. **Power:** Spring-air, barrel cocking. **Stock:** Oil-finished hardwood. **Sights:** Ramp front, micrometer adjustable rear. **Features:** Velocity 650 fps (.177), 500 fps (.22). Automatic anti-beartrap; manual tang safety. Receiver grooved for scope mounting. Imported from U.K.
Price: Rifle $144.95
Price: Carbine $164.95

CROSMAN MODEL POWERMASTER 664SB AIR RIFLES
Caliber: .177 (single shot pellet) or BB, 200-shot reservoir. **Barrel:** 20", rifled steel. **Weight:** 2 lbs. 15 oz. **Length:** 38-1/2" overall. **Power:** Pneumatic; hand-pumped. **Stock:** Wood-grained ABS plastic; checkered pistol grip and forend. **Sights:** Fiber-optic front, fully adjustable open rear. **Features:** Velocity about 645 fps. Bolt action, cross-bolt safety. From Crosman.
Price: $105.50

CROSMAN MODEL PUMPMASTER 760 AIR RIFLES
Caliber: .177 pellets (single shot) or BB (200-shot reservoir). **Barrel:** 19-1/2", rifled steel. **Weight:** 2 lbs., 12 oz. **Length:** 33.5" overall. **Power:** Pneumatic, hand-pump. **Stock:** Walnut-finished ABS plastic stock and forend. **Features:** Velocity to 590 fps (BBs, 10 pumps). Short stroke, power determined by number of strokes. Fiber-optic front sight and adjustable rear sight. Cross-bolt safety. From Crosman.
Price: Model 760 . . . . $40.59

CROSMAN MODEL REPEATAIR 1077 RIFLES
Caliber: .177 pellets, 12-shot clip. **Barrel:** 20.3", rifled steel. **Weight:** 3 lbs., 11 oz. **Length:** 38.8" overall. **Power:** CO2 Powerlet. **Stock:** Textured synthetic or hardwood. **Sights:** Blade front, fully adjustable rear. **Features:** Velocity 590 fps. Removable 12-shot clip. True semi-automatic action. From Crosman.
Price: $73.99

CROSMAN MODEL .2260 AIR RIFLE
Caliber: .22, single shot. **Barrel:** 24". **Weight:** 4 lbs., 12 oz. **Length:** 39.75" overall. **Power:** CO2 Powerlet. **Stock:** Hardwood. **Sights:** Blade front, adjustable rear open or peep. **Features:** Variable pump power; three pumps give 395 fps, six pumps 530 fps, 10 pumps 600 fps (average). Full-size adult air rifle. From Crosman.
Price: $83.84

CROSMAN MODEL CLASSIC 2100 AIR RIFLE
Caliber: .177 pellets (single shot), or BB (200-shot BB reservoir). **Barrel:** 21", rifled. **Weight:** 4 lbs., 13 oz. **Length:** 39-3/4" overall. **Power:** Pump-up, pneumatic. **Stock:** Wood-grained checkered ABS plastic. **Features:** Three pumps give about 450 fps, 10 pumps about 755 fps (BBs). Cross-bolt safety; concealed reservoir holds over 200 BBs. From Crosman.
Price: Model 2100B $62.99

CROSMAN MODEL NITRO VENOM AIR RIFLE
Caliber: .177 & .22. **Features:** Nitro Venom air rifle feature precision, rifled barrel with fluted muzzle brake and sculpted rubber recoil pad. The rifle is equipped with a CenterPoint 3-9x32mm precision scope and a quick-lock mounting system for quick and easy optic mounting. The ambidextrous hardwood stock with raised cheek piece and modified, beavertail forearm. Crosman Nitro Venom air rifle delivers serious hunting power with muzzle energy up to 21 fpe and up to

1200 fps. Take one on a hunt to experience the power, stability and stealth of Nitro Piston® technology.

Price: .177 . . . . **$209.99**
Price: .22 . . . . **N/A**

CROSMAN MODEL NITRO VENOM DUSK AIR RIFLE

Caliber: .177 & .22. **Features:** Nitro Venom air rifle feature precision, rifled barrel with fluted muzzle brake and sculpted rubber recoil pad. The rifle is equipped with a CenterPoint 3-9x32mm precision scope and a quick-lock mounting system for quick and easy optic mounting. The ambidextrous hardwood stock with raised cheek piece and modified, beavertail forearm. Crosman Nitro Venom air rifle delivers serious hunting power with muzzle energy up to 21 fpe and up to 1200 fps. Take one on a hunt to experience the power, stability and stealth of Nitro Piston® technology.

Price: .177 . . . . **$209.99**
Price: .22 . . . . **N/A**

CROSMAN MODEL TRAIL NP ALL WEATHER & LAMINATED HARDWOOD AIR RIFLES

Caliber: .177, .22 & .25, up to 1200 fps (.177), 950 fps (.22) & 900 fps (.25). **Weight:** 6.65 lbs. - 8 lbs. **Length:** 43" overall. **Features:** The Nitro Venom Dusk air rifle features a precision, rifled barrel with fluted muzzle break and sculpted rubber recoil pad. The rifle is equipped with a CenterPoint 3-9x32mm precision scope and a quick-lock mounting system for quick and easy optic mounting. The ambidextrous synthetic stock has a raised cheek piece and modified, beavertail forearm. Crosman Nitro Venom air rifles delivers serious hunting power with muzzle energy up to 18 fpe and up to 1200 fps.. Take one on a hunt to experience the power, stability and stealth of Nitro Piston® technology. The .22 caliber series is equiped with various harwood and laminated thumbhole and standard stocks and also models with bull barrels, imposing 23 ft-lbs of muzzle energy provides 16% more downrange energy than .177 cal. The new XL725 provides 24% more downrange energy than a .177 caliber offers. This is the most powerful Nitro Piston® break barrel available.

Price: .177 Trail NP. **$247.00**
Price: .177 Trail NP XL 1500 . . . . **$247.00**
Price: .22 Trail NP All Weather. **$247.00**
Price: .22 Trail NP Hardwood. **$299.00**
Price: .22 Trail NP All Weather with Realtree APG **$279.95**
Price: .22 Trail NP All Weather 495fps. **$299.00**
Price: .22 Trail NP Laminated Hardwood . . . . **N/A**
Price: .22 Trail NP XL 1100 . . . . **$359.00**
Price: .25 Trail NP XL 725 . . . . **$329.00**

DAISY 1938 RED RYDER AIR RIFLE

Caliber: BB, 650-shot repeating action. **Barrel:** Smoothbore steel with shroud. **Weight:** 2.2 lbs. **Length:** 35.4" overall. **Stock:** Wood stock burned with Red Ryder lariat signature. **Sights:** Post front, adjustable open rear. **Features:** Walnut forend. Saddle ring with leather thong. Lever cocking. Gravity feed. Controlled velocity. From Daisy Mfg. Co.

Price: **$55.99**

DAISY MODEL 840B GRIZZLY AIR RIFLE

Caliber: .177 pellet single shot; or BB 350-shot. **Barrel:** 19", smoothbore, steel. **Weight:** 2.25 lbs. **Length:** 36.8" overall. **Power:** Single pump pneumatic. **Stock:** Molded wood-grain stock and forend. **Sights:** Ramp front, open, adjustable rear. **Features:** Muzzle velocity 320 fps (BB), 300 fps (pellet). Steel buttplate; straight pull bolt action; cross-bolt safety. Forend forms pump lever. From Daisy Mfg. Co.

Price: **$60.99**
Price: (840C in Mossy Oak Breakup Camo) **$64.99**

DAISY MODEL 4841 GRIZZLY

Caliber: .177 pellet single shot. **Barrel:** NA. **Weight:** NA. **Length:** 36.8" overall. **Power:** Single pump pneumatic. **Stock:** Composite camo. **Sights:** Blade and ramp front. **Features:** Muzzle velocity 350 fps. Fixed Daisy Model 808 scope. From Daisy Mfg. Co.

Price: **$69.99**

DAISY MODEL 105 BUCK AIR RIFLE

Caliber: .177 or BB. **Barrel:** Smoothbore steel. **Weight:** 1.6 lbs. **Length:** 29.8" overall. **Power:** Lever cocking, spring air. **Stock:** Stained solid wood. **Sights:** TruGlo fiber-optic, open fixed rear. **Features:** Velocity to 275. Crossbolt trigger block safety. From Daisy Mfg. Co.

Price: **$39.99**

DAISY AVANTI MODEL 888 MEDALIST

Caliber: .177, pellet. **Barrel:** Lothar Walther rifled high-grade steel, crowned, 12 lands and grooves, right-hand twist. Precision bore sized for match pellets. **Weight:** 6.9 lbs. **Length:** 38.5" overall. **Power:** CO_2 single shot bolt. **Stock:** Sporter-style multicolored laminated hardwood. **Sights:** Hooded front with interchangeable aperture inserts; micrometer adjustable rear peep sight. **Features:** Velocity to 500. Crossbolt trigger block safety. From Daisy Mfg. Co.

Price: **$525.99**

DAISY AVANTI MODEL 887 GOLD MEDALIST

Caliber: 177, pellet. **Barrel:** Lothar Walther rifled high-grade steel, crowned, 12 lands and grooves, right hand twist. Precision bore sized for match pellets. **Weight:** 7.3 lbs. **Length:** 39.5" overall. **Power:** CO_2 power single shot bolt. **Stock:** Laminated hardwood. **Sights:** Front globe sight with changeable aperture inserts: rear diopter sight with micrometer click adjustment for windage and elevation. **Features:** Velocity to 500. Crossbolt trigger block safety. Includes rail adapter. From Daisy Mfg. Co.

Price: **$599.99**

DAISY MODEL 853 LEGEND

Caliber: .177, pellet. **Barrel:** Lothar Walther rifled high-grade steel barrel, crowned, 12 lands and grooves, right-hand twist. Precision bore sized for match pellets. **Weight:** 5.5 lbs. **Length:** 38.5" overall. **Power:** Single-pump pneumatic, straight pull-bolt. **Stock:** Full-length, sporter-style hardwood with adjustable length. **Sights:** Hooded front with interchangeable aperture inserts; micrometer adjustable rear. **Features:** Velocity to 510. Crossbolt trigger block safety with red indicator. From Daisy Mfg. Co.

Price: **$432.00**
Price: Model 835 Legend EX; velocity to 490 . . . . **$432.00**

DAISY MODEL 753 ELITE

Caliber: .177, pellet. **Barrel:** Lothar Walther rifled high-grade steel barrel, crowned, 12 lands and grooves, right-hand twist. Precision bore sized for match pellets. **Weight:** 6.4 lbs. **Length:** 39.75" overall. **Power:** Recoilless single pump pneumatic, straight pull bolt. **Stock:** Full length match-style hardwood stock with raised cheek piece and adjustable length. **Sights:** Front globe sight with changeable aperture inserts, diopter rear sight with micrometer adjustable rear. **Features:** Velocity to 510. Crossbolt trigger block safety with red indicator. From Daisy Mfg. Co.

Price: **$558.99**

DAISY MODEL 105 BUCK AIR RIFLE

Caliber: .177 or BB. **Barrel:** Smoothbore steel. **Weight:** 1.6 lbs. **Length:** 29.8" overall. **Power:** Lever cocking, spring air. **Stock:** Stained solid wood. **Sights:** TruGlo fiber-optic, open fixed rear. **Features:** Velocity to 275. Cross-bolt trigger block safety. From Daisy Mfg. Co.

Price: **$39.99**

DAISY POWERLINE® TARGETPRO 953 AIR RIFLE

Caliber: .177 pellets, single shot. **Weight:** 6.40 lbs. **Length:** 39.75"

Prices given are believed to be accurate at time of publication however, many factors affect retail pricing so exact prices are not possible.

overall. **Power:** Pneumatic single-pump cocking lever; straight-pull bolt. **Stock:** Full-length, match-style black composite. **Sights:** Front and rear fiber optic. **Features:** Rifled high-grade steel barrel with 1:15 twist. Max. Muzzle Velocity of 560 fps. From Daisy Mfg. Co.
Price: **$29.99**

DAISY POWERLINE® 500 BREAK BARREL
Caliber: .177 pellet, single shot. **Barrel:** Rifled steel. **Weight:** 6.6 lbs. **Length:** 45.7" overall. **Stock:** Stained solid wood. **Sights:** Truglo® fiber-optic front, micro-adjustable open rear, adjustable 4x32 riflescope. **Features:** Auto rear-button safety. Velocity to 490 fps. Made in U.S.A. by Daisy Mfg. Co.
Price: **$120.99**

DAISY POWERLINE® 800 BREAK BARREL
Caliber: .177 pellet, single shot. **Barrel:** Rifled steel. **Weight:** 6.6 lbs. **Length:** 46.7" overall. **Stock:** Black composite. **Sights:** Truglo fiber-optic front, micro-adjustable open rear, adjustable 4x32 riflescope. **Features:** Auto rear-button safety. Velocity to 800 fps. Made in U.S.A. by Daisy Mfg. Co.
Price: **$120.99**

DAISY POWERLINE® 880 AIR RIFLE
Caliber: .177 pellet or BB, 50-shot BB magazine, single shot for pellets. **Barrel:** Rifled steel. **Weight:** 3.7 lbs. **Length:** 37.6" overall. **Power:** Multi-pump pneumatic. **Stock:** Molded wood grain; Monte Carlo comb. **Sights:** Hooded front, adjustable rear. **Features:** Velocity to 685 fps. (BB). Variable power (velocity, range) increase with pump strokes; resin receiver with dovetailed scope mount. Made in U.S.A. by Daisy Mfg. Co.
Price: **$71.99**

DAISY POWERLINE® 901 AIR RIFLE
Caliber: .177. **Barrel:** Rifled steel. **Weight:** 3.7 lbs. **Length:** 37.5" overall. **Power:** Multi-pump pneumatic. **Stock:** Advanced composite. **Sights:** Fiber-optic front, adjustable rear. **Features:** Velocity to 750 fps. (BB); advanced composite receiver with dovetailed mounts for optics. Made in U.S.A. by Daisy Mfg. Co.
Price: **$83.99**

DAISY POWERLINE® 1000 BREAK BARREL
Caliber: .177 pellet, single shot. **Barrel:** Rifled steel. **Weight:** 6.6 lbs. **Length:** 46.7" overall. **Stock:** Black composite. **Sights:** Truglo® fiber-optic front, micro-adjustable open rear, adjustable 4x32 riflescope. **Features:** Auto rear-button safety. Velocity to 750 fps (BB). Made in U.S.A. by Daisy Mfg. Co.
Price: **$231.99**

EAA/BAIKAL IZH61 AIR RIFLE
Caliber: .177 pellet, 5-shot magazine. **Barrel:** 17.8". **Weight:** 6.4 lbs. **Length:** 31" overall. **Power:** Spring-piston, side-cocking lever. **Stock:** Black plastic. **Sights:** Adjustable rear, fully hooded front. **Features:** Velocity 490 fps. Futuristic design with adjustable stock. Imported from Russia by European American Armory.
Price: **$122.65**

GAMO VIPER AIR RIFLE
Caliber: .177. **Barrel:** NA. **Weight:** 7.25 lbs. **Length:** 43.5". **Power:** Single-stroke pneumatic, 1200 fps. **Stock:** Synthetic. **Sights:** 3-9x40IR scope. **Features:** 30-pound cocking effort. Imported from Spain by Gamo.
Price: **319.95**

GAMO SHADOW AIR RIFLES
Caliber: .177. **Barrel:** 18", fluted polymer bull. **Weight:** 6.1 to 7.15 lbs. **Length:** 43" to 43.3". **Power:** Single-stroke pneumatic, 850-1,000 fps. **Stock:** Tough all-weather molded synthetic. **Sights:** NA.

Features: Single shot, manual safety,
Price: Sport. **$219.95**
Price: Hunter **$219.95**
Price: Big Cat 1200. . . . . **$169.95**
Price: Fox **$279.95**

GAMO HUNTER AIR RIFLES
Caliber: .177. **Barrel:** NA. **Weight:** 6.5 to 10.5 lbs. **Length:** 43.5-48.5". **Power:** Single-stroke pneumatic, 850-1,000 fps. **Stock:** Wood. **Sights:** Varies by model **Features:** Adjustable two-stage trigger, rifled barrel, raised scope ramp on receiver. Realtree camo model available.
Price: Sport. **$219.95**
Price: Pro **$279.95**
Price: Extreme (.177), Extreme .22 . . . . **$529.95**

GAMO WHISPER AIR RIFLES
Caliber: .177, .22. **Barrel:** 18", fluted polymer bull. **Weight:** 5.28 to 7.4 lbs. **Length:** 45.7" to 46". **Stock:** Tough all-weather molded synthetic. **Sights:** Fiber-optic front with sight guard, adjustable rear. **Features:** Single shot, manual trigger safety. Non-removable noise dampener (with up to 52 percent reduction).
Price: Whisper **$279.95**
Price: Whisper Deluxe **$319.95**
Price: Whisper VH (Varmint Hunter/Whisper in one rifle). . . . **$329.95**
Price: Whisper .22 . . . . **$299.95**
Price: CSI Camo (.177) **$329.95**
Price: CSI Camo (.22) **$329.95**

HAMMERLI AR 50 AIR RIFLE
Caliber: .177. **Barrel:** 19.8". **Weight:** 10 lbs. **Length:** 43.2" overall. **Power:** Compressed-air. **Stock:** Anatomically-shaped universal and right-hand; match style; multi-colored laminated wood. **Sights:** Interchangeable element tunnel front, adjustable Hammerli peep rear. **Features:** Vibration-free firing release; adjustable match trigger and trigger stop; stainless air tank, built-in pressure gauge. Gives 270 shots per filling. Imported from Switzerland by SIG SAUER, Inc.
Price: **$1,653.00**

HAMMERLI MODEL 450 MATCH AIR RIFLE
Caliber: .177, single shot. **Barrel:** 19.5". **Weight:** 9.8 lbs. **Length:** 43.3" overall. **Power:** Pneumatic. **Stock:** Match style with stippled grip, rubber buttpad. Beech or walnut. **Sights:** Match tunnel front, Hammerli diopter rear. **Features:** Velocity about 560 fps. Removable sights; forend sling rail; adjustable trigger; adjustable comb. Imported from Switzerland by SIG SAUER, Inc.
Price: Beech stock **$1,355.00**
Price: Walnut stock. **$1,395.00**

HAMMERLI 850 AIR MAGNUM
Caliber: .177, .22, 8-shot repeater. 23-1/2", rifled. **Weight:** 5.8 lbs. 41" overall. **Power:** 88g CO2. **Stock:** All-weather polymer, Monte Carlo, textured grip and forearm. **Sights:** Hooded fiber optic front, fiber optic adjustable rear. Velocity of 760 fps (.177), 655 (22). Blue finish. Rubber buttpad. Bolt-action. Scope compatible.
Price: .177, .22 . . . . **$235.99**

HAMMERLI STORM ELITE
Caliber: .177, single shot. 19-1/2", rifled. **Weight:** 6.8 lbs. 45-1/2" overall. **Power:** Spring-air, break-barrel cocking. **Stock:** Synthetic, burled wood look, checkered grip and forearm, cheekpiece. **Sights:** Hooded fiber optic front, fiber optic adjustable rear. Velocity of 1000 fps. 24 lbs. cocking effort. Nickel finish. Rubber buttpad. Scope compatible.
Price: **$165.90**

HAMMERLI RAZOR
Caliber: .177, .22, single shot. **Barrel:** 19", rifled. **Weight:** 17.5 lbs.

Length: 45-1/2" overall. **Power:** Spring-air, break-barrel cocking. **Stock:** Vaporized beech wood, checkered grip and forearm, cheekpiece. Sleek curves. **Sights:** Hooded fiber optic front, fiber optic adjustable rear. **Features:** Velocity of 1000 fps (.177), 820 (.22). 35 lbs. cocking effort. Blued finish. Rubber buttpad. Scope compatible.
Price: **$219.99**

HAMMERLI NOVA
Caliber: .177, single shot. 18", rifled. **Weight:** 7.8 lbs. 45-1/2" overall. **Power:** Spring-air, under-lever cocking. **Stock:** Vaporized beech wood competition, checkered grip and forearm, cheekpiece. **Sights:** Hooded fiber optic front, fiber optic adjustable rear. **Features:** Velocity of 1000 fps. 36 lbs. cocking effort. Blued finish. Rubber buttpad. Scope compatible.
Price: **$342.00**

HAMMERLI QUICK
Caliber: .177, single shot. 18-1/4", rifled. **Weight:** 5.5 lbs. 41" overall. **Power:** Spring-air, break-barrel cocking. **Stock:** Synthetic impact proof, checkered grip and forearm, cheekpiece. **Sights:** Hooded fiber optic front, fiber optic adjustable rear. Compact, lightweight. Velocity of 620 fps. 18 lbs. cocking effort. Blued finish. Rubber buttpad. Scope compatible. Automatic safety.
Price: **$120.00**

RWS 460 MAGNUM
Caliber: .177, .22, single shot. 18-7/16", rifled. **Weight:** 8.3 lbs. 45" overall. **Power:** Spring-air, underlever cocking. **Stock:** American Sporter, checkered grip and forearm. **Sights:** Ramp front, adjustable rear. Velocity of 1350 fps (.177), 1150 (.22). 36 lbs. cocking effort. Blue finish. Rubber buttpad. Top-side loading port. Scope compatible.
Price: .177, .22 . . . . **$630.99**

RWS MODEL 34
Caliber: .177, .22, single shot. **Barrel:** 19-1/2", rifled. **Weight:** 7.3 lbs. **Length:** 45" overall. **Power:** Spring-air, break-barrel cocking. **Stock:** Wood. **Sights:** Hooded front, adjustable rear. **Features:** Velocity of 1000 fps (.177), 800 (.22). 33 lbs. cocking effort. Blued finish. Scope compatible.
Price: .177, .22 . . . . **$202.00**

RWS 34 PANTHER
Caliber: .177, .22, single shot. 19-3/4", rifled. **Weight:** 7.7 lbs. 46" overall. **Power:** Spring-air, break-barrel cocking. **Stock:** Synthetic black. **Sights:** Ramp fiber optic front, adjustable fiber optic rear. Velocity of 1000 fps (.177), 800 (.22). 33 lbs. cocking effort. Blued finish. Scope compatible. Automatic safety.
Price: .177, .22 . . . . **$192.00**

RWS 48
Caliber: .177, .22, single shot. 17", rifled, fixed. **Weight:** 9.0 lbs. 42-1/2" overall. **Power:** Spring-air, side-lever cocking. **Stock:** Wood stock. **Sights:** Adjustable front, adjustable rear. Velocity of 1100 fps (.177), 900 (.22). 39 lbs. cocking effort. Blued finish. Scope compatible. Automatic safety.
Price: .177, .22 . . . . **$330.00**

TECH FORCE 6 AIR RIFLE
Caliber: .177 pellet, single shot. **Barrel:** 14". **Weight:** 6 lbs. **Length:** 35.5" overall. **Power:** Spring-piston, sidelever action. **Stock:** Paratrooper-style folding, full pistol grip. **Sights:** Adjustable rear, hooded front. **Features:** Velocity 800 fps. All-metal construction; grooved for scope mounting. Imported from China by Compasseco, Inc.
Price: **$69.95**

TECH FORCE 99 AIR RIFLE
Caliber: .177, .22, single shot. **Barrel:** 18", rifled. **Weight:** 8 lbs. **Length:** 44.5" overall. **Power:** Spring piston. **Stock:** Beech wood; raised cheek piece and checkering on pistol grip and forearm, plus soft rubber recoil pad. **Sights:** Insert type front. **Features:** Velocity 1,100 fps (.177; 900 fps: .22); fixed barrel design has an underlever cocking mechanism with an anti-beartrap lock and automatic safety. Imported from China by Compasseco, Inc.
Price: 177 or .22 caliber **$152.96**

WALTHER LEVER ACTION
Caliber: .177, 8-shot lever action. **Barrel:** 19", rifled. **Weight:** 7.5 lbs. **Length:** 38" overall. **Power:** Two 12g CO2. **Stock:** Wood. **Sights:** Fixed front, adjustable rear. **Features:** Classic design. Velocity of 630 fps. Scope compatible.
Price: **$475.50**

WINCHESTER MODEL 1000SB
Caliber: .177, pellet, break-barrel spring air. **Barrel:** Rifled steel. **Weight:** 6.6 lbs. **Length:** 44.5" overall. **Stock:** Sporter style black composite. **Sights:** TRUGLO fiber optic with hooded front and micro adjustable rear. **Features:** Velocity of 1000 fps. 4 X 32 adjustable objective, fog proof/shockproof scope with crosshair reticle. From Daisy Mfg. Co.
Price: **$231.99**

WINCHESTER MODEL 1000B
Caliber: .177, pellet, break-barrel spring air. **Barrel:** Rifled steel, solid steel shroud. **Weight:** 6.6 lbs. **Length:** 44.5" overall. **Stock:** Black composite. **Sights:** TRUGLO fiber optic with hooded front and micro adjustable rear. **Features:** Velocity of 1000 fps. From Daisy Mfg. Co.
Price: **$184.99**

WINCHESTER MODEL 1000XS
Caliber: .177, pellet, break-barrel spring air. **Barrel:** Rifled steel, solid steel shroud. **Weight:** 6.6 lbs. **Length:** 46.7" overall. **Stock:** Walnut. **Sights:** Hooded front with blade and ramp, micro-adjustable rear. **Features:** Velocity of 1000 fps, uniquely designed 4 X 32 scope with adjustable objective. From Daisy Mfg. Co.
Price: **$269.99**

WINCHESTER MODEL 1000X
Caliber: .177, pellet, break-barrel spring air. **Barrel:** Rifled steel, solid steel shroud. **Weight:** 6.6 lbs. **Length:** 46.7" overall. **Stock:** Walnut. **Sights:** Hooded front with blade and ramp, micro-adjustable rear. **Features:** Velocity of 1000 fps. From Daisy Mfg. Co.
Price: **$228.99**

WINCHESTER MODEL 800XS
Caliber: .177, pellet, break-barrel spring air. **Barrel:** Rifled steel, solid steel shroud. **Weight:** 6.6 lbs. **Length:** 46.7" overall. **Stock:** Walnut. **Sights:** Hooded front with blade and ramp, micro-adjustable rear. **Features:** Velocity of 800 fps. Scope is fogproof and shockproof with fully adjustable windage and elevation and cross hair reticle. Also includes mounting rings. From Daisy Mfg. Co.
Price: **$201.99**

WINCHESTER MODEL 800X
Caliber: .177, pellet, break-barrel spring air. **Barrel:** Rifled steel, solid steel shroud. **Weight:** 6.6 lbs. **Length:** 46.7" overall. **Stock:** Walnut. **Sights:** Hooded front with blade and ramp, micro-adjustable rear. **Features:** Velocity of 800 fps. From Daisy Mfg. Co.
Price: **$164.99**

Prices given are believed to be accurate at time of publication however, many factors affect retail pricing so exact prices are not possible.

THE 2012 GUN DIGEST
web directory

BY HOLT BODINSON

The *GUN DIGEST* Web Directory is now in its thirteenth year of publication and grows with every edition. The firearms industry is doing a remarkably good job of adapting to e-commerce.

The Internet is a dynamic environment. One of the most interesting developments since our last edition is widespread adoption of mobile data applications, or "apps". Two years ago, there wasn't an "apps" culture. Now, it is estimated that 35% of Americans have cell phones with software applications loaded on them, and the development of software applications for iPhones and other mobile computing devices has become a major industry.

The cell phone can now be used to access the internet, send or receive e-mail, text or instant messages, take photographs, record videos, play games or play music. The latest studies indicate that 59% of adults now access the internet wirelessly using a cell phone or laptop while 2/3's of American homes have high-speed broadband connections.

We are a mobile, internet culture, and that's why web directories like our own have become such essential references.

The following index of web addresses is offered to our readers as a convenient jumping-off point. Half the fun is just exploring what's out there. Considering that most of the web pages have hot links to other firearm-related web pages, the Internet trail just goes on-and-on once you've taken the initial step to go online.

Here are a few pointers:

If the web site you desire is not listed, try using the full name of the company or product, typed without spaces, between: www.-and-.com, for example,: www.krause.com. Probably 95% of current Web sites are based on this simple, self-explanatory format.

Try a variety of search engines like Google, Bing, Yahoo, Ask.com, Dogpile.com, Metacrawler, GoTo.com, HotBot, AltaVista, Lycos, Excite, InfoSeek, Looksmart, and WebCrawler while using key words such as gun, firearm, rifle, pistol, blackpowder, shooting, hunting— frankly, any word that relates to the sport. Each search engine combs through their indices in a different fashion and produces different results. Google is currently the dominant, general search engine. Accessing the various search engines is simple. Just type: www.google.com for example, and you're on your way.

Welcome to the digital world of firearms. "A journey of a thousand sites begins with a single click."

AMMUNITION AND COMPONENTS

A-Square Co.: www.asquarecompany.com
3-D Ammunition: www.3dammo.com
Accurate Arms Co. Inc,: www.accuratepowder.com
ADCO/Nobel Sport Powder: www.adcosales.com
Advanced Armament Corp.: www.300aacblackout.com
Aguila Ammunition: www.aguilaammo.com
Alexander Arms:: www.alexanderarms.com
Alliant Powder: www.alliantpowder.com
American Ammunition: www.a-merc.com
American Derringer Co.: www.amderringer.com
American Pioneer Powder:
    www.americanpioneerpowder.com
Ammo Depot: www.ammodepot.com
Arizona Ammunition, Inc.:
    www.arizonaammunition.com
Ballistic Products,Inc.: www.ballisticproducts.com
Barnaul Cartridge Plant: www.ab.ru/~stanok
Barnes Bullets: www.barnesbullets.com
Baschieri & Pellagri: www.baschieri-pellagri.com
Beartooth Bullets: www.beartoothbullets.com
Bell Brass: www.bellbrass.com
Berger Bullets, Ltd.: www.bergerbullets.com
Berry's Mfg., Inc.: www.berrysmfg.com
Big Bore Bullets of Alaska:
    www.awloo.com/bbb/index.htm
Big Bore Express: www.powerbeltbullets.com
Bismuth Cartridge Co.: www.bismuth-notox.com
Black Dawge Cartridge:
    www.blackdawgecartridge.com
Black Hills Ammunition, Inc.: www.black-hills.com

Black Hills Shooters Supply: www.bhshooters.com
BlackHorn209: www.blackhorn209.com
Brenneke of America Ltd.: www.brennekeusa.com
Buffalo Arms: www.buffaloarms.com
Calhoon, James, Bullets: www.jamescalhoon.com
Cartuchos Saga: www.saga.es
Cast Performance Bullet: www.castperformance.com
CBC: www.cbc.com.br
CCI: www.cci-ammunition.com
Centurion Ordnance: www.aguilaammo.com
Century International Arms: www.centuryarms.com
Cheaper Than Dirt: www.cheaperthandirt.com
Cheddite France: www.cheddite.com
Claybuster Wads: www.claybusterwads.com
Clean Shot Powder: www.cleanshot.com
Cole Distributing: www.cole-distributing.com
Combined Tactical Systems: www.less-lethal.com
Cor-Bon/Glaser : www.cor-bon.com
Cowboy Bullets: www.cowboybullets.com
D.Dupleks, Ltd.: www.ddupleks.lv
Defense Technology Corp.:
    www.defense-technology.com
Denver Bullet Co. denbullets@aol.com
Dillon Precision: www.dillonprecision.com
Dionisi Cartridge: www.dionisi.com
DKT, Inc.: www.dktinc.com
Down Range Mfg.: www.downrangemfg.com
Dynamic Research Technologies: www.drtammo.com
Dynamit Nobel RWS Inc.: www.dnrws.com
Elephant/Swiss Black Powder:
    www.elephantblackpowder.com
Eley Ammunition: www.eleyusa.com

Eley Hawk Ltd.: www.eleyhawk.com
Environ-Metal: www.hevishot.com
Estate Cartridge: www.estatecartridge.com
Extreme Shock Munitions: www.extremeshockusa.com
Federal Cartridge Co.: www.federalpremium.com
Fiocchi of America: www.fiocchiusa.com
Fowler Bullets: www.benchrest.com/fowler
Gamebore Cartridge: www.gamebore.com
Garrett Cartridges: www.garrettcartridges.com
Gentner Bullets: www.benchrest.com/gentner/
Glaser Safety Slug, Inc.: www.corbon.com
GOEX Inc.: www.goexpowder.com
GPA: www.cartouchegpa.com
Graf & Sons: www.grafs.com
Haendler & Natermann: www.hn-sport.de
Hawk Bullets: www.hawkbullets.com
Hevi.Shot: www.hevishot.com
Hi-Tech Ammunition: www.iidbs.com/hitech
Hodgdon Powder: www.hodgdon.com
Hornady: www.hornady.com
Hull Cartridge: www.hullcartridge.com
Huntington Reloading Products: www.huntingtons.com
Impact Bullets: www.impactbullets.com
IMR Smokeless Powders: www.imrpowder.com
International Cartridge Corp: www.iccammo.com
Israel Military Industries: www.imisammo.co.il
ITD Enterprise: www.itdenterpriseinc.com
Kent Cartridge America: www.kentgamebore.com
Knight Bullets: www.benchrest.com/knight/
Kynoch Ammunition: www.kynochammunition.com
Lapua: www.lapua.com
Lawrence Brand Shot: www.metalico.com

Lazzeroni Arms Co.: www.lazzeroni.com
Leadheads Bullets: www.proshootpro.com
Lightfield Ammunition Corp: www.lightfieldslugs.com
Lomont Precision Bullets: www.klomont.com/kent
Lost River Ballistic Technologies,Inc.:
    www.lostriverballistic.com
Lyman : www.lymanproducts.com
Magkor Industries.: www.magkor.com
Magnum Muzzleloading Products:
    www.mmpsabots.com
Magnus Bullets: www.magnusbullets.com
MagSafe Ammunition:
    www.realpages.com/magsafeammo
Magtech: www.magtechammunition.com
Masterclass Bullet Co.: www.mastercast.com
Meister Bullets: www.meisterbullets.com
MEN: www.men-defencetec.de
Midway USA: www.midwayusa.com
Miltex,Inc.: www.miltexusa.com
Mitchell Mfg. Co.: www.mitchellsales.com
MK Ballistic Systems: www.mkballistics.com
Mullins Ammunition: www.mullinsammunition.com
National Bullet Co.: www.nationalbullet.com
Navy Arms: www.navyarms.com
Nobel Sport: www.nobelsportammo.com
Norma: www.norma.cc
North Fork Technologies: www.northforkbullets.com
Nosler Bullets,Inc.: www.nosler.com
Old Western Scrounger: www.ows-ammunition.com
One Shot, Inc.: www.oneshotmunitions.com
Oregon Trail/Trueshot Bullets: www.trueshotbullets.com
Pattern Control: www.patterncontrol.com
PMC: www.pmcammo.com
Polywad: www.polywad.com
PowerBelt Bullets: www.powerbeltbullets.com
PR Bullets: www.prbullet.com
Precision Ammunition: www.precisionammo.com
Precision Reloading: www.precisionreloading.com
Pro Load Ammunition: www.proload.com
Quality Cartridge: www.qual-cart.com
Rainier Ballistics: www.rainierballistics.com
Ram Shot Powder: www.ramshot.com
Reloading Specialties Inc.:
    www.reloadingspecialties.com
Remington: www.remington.com
Rio Ammunition: www.rioammo.com
Rocky Mountain Cartridge:
    www.rockymountaincartridge.com
RUAG Ammotec: www.ruag.com
RWS: www.ruag-usa.com
Samco Global Arms: www.samcoglobal.com
Scharch Mfg.: www.scharch.com
Schuetzen Powder: www.schuetzenpowder.com
Sellier & Bellot: www.sellier-bellot.cz
Shilen: www.shilen.com
Sierra: www.sierrabullets.com
Silver State Armory: www.ssarmory.com
Simunition.: www.simunition.com
SinterFire, Inc.: www.sinterfire.com
Speer Ammunition: www.speer-ammo.com
Speer Bullets: www.speer-bullets.com
Sporting Supplies Int'l Inc.: www.ssiintl.com
Starline: www.starlinebrass.com
Swift Bullets Co.: www.swiftbullet.com
Ten-X Ammunition: www.tenxammo.com
Top Brass: www.top-brass.com
Triton Cartridge: www.a-merc.com
Trueshot Bullets: www.trueshotbullets.com
Tru-Tracer: www.trutracer.com
Ultramax Ammunition: www.ultramaxammunition.com
Vihtavuori Lapua: www.vihtavuori-lapua.com
Weatherby: www.weatherby.com
West Coast Bullets: www.westcoastbullet.com

Western Powders Inc.: www.westernpowders.com
Widener's Reloading & Shooters Supply:
    www.wideners.com
Winchester Ammunition: www.winchester.com
Windjammer Tournament Wads.:
    www.windjammer-wads.com
Wolf Ammunition: www.wolfammo.com
Woodleigh Bullets: www.woodleighbullets.com.au
Zanders Sporting Goods: www.gzanders.com

CASES, SAFES, GUN LOCKS, AND CABINETS

Ace Case Co.: www.acecase.com
AG English Sales Co.: www.agenglish.com
All Americas' Outdoors: www.innernet.net/gunsafe
Alpine Cases: www.alpinecases.com
Aluma Sport by Dee Zee: www.deezee.com
American Security Products: www.amsecusa.com
Americase: www.americase.com
Assault Systems: www.elitesurvival.com
Avery Outdoors, Inc.: www.averyoutdoors.com
Bear Track Cases: www.beartrackcases.com
Boyt Harness Co.: www.boytharness.com
Bulldog Gun Safe Co.: www.gardall.com
Cannon Safe Co.: www.cannonsafe.com
CCL Security Products: www.cclsecurity.com
Concept Development Corp.: www.saf-t-blok.com
Doskocil Mfg. Co.: www.doskocilmfg.com
Fort Knox Safes: www.ftknox.com
Franzen Security Products: www.securecase.com
Frontier Safe Co.: www.frontiersafe.com
Goldenrod Dehumidifiers:
    www.goldenroddehumidifiers.com
Granite Security Products: www.granitesafe.com
Gunlocker Phoenix USA Inc.: www.gunlocker.com
Gun Storage Solutions: www.storemoreguns.com
GunVault: www.gunvault.com
Hakuba USA Inc.: www.hakubausa.com
Heritage Safe Co.: www.heritagesafecompany.com
Hide-A-Gun: www.hide-a-gun.com
Homak Safes: www.homak.com
Hunter Company: www.huntercompany.com
Kalispel Case Line: www.kalispelcaseline.com
Knouff & Knouff, Inc.: www.kkair.com
Knoxx Industries: www.knoxx.com
Kolpin Mfg. Co.: www.kolpin.com
Liberty Safe & Security: www.libertysafe.com
Morton Enterprises: www.uniquecases.com
New Innovative Products: www.starlightcases
Noble Security Systems Inc.: www.noble.co.ll
Phoenix USA Inc.: www.gunlocker.com
Plano Molding Co.: www.planomolding.com
Plasticase, Inc.: www.nanuk.com
Rhino Gun Cases: www.rhinoguns.com
Rhino Safe: www.rhinosafe.com
Rotary Gun Racks: www.gun-racks.com
Sack-Ups: www.sackups.com
Safe Tech, Inc.: www.safrgun.com
Saf-T-Hammer: www.saf-t-hammer.com
Saf-T-Lok Corp.: www.saf-t-lok.com
San Angelo All-Aluminum Products Inc.:
    www.sasptuld@x.netcom.com
Secure Firearm Products:
    www.securefirearmproducts.com
Securecase: www.securecase.com
Shot Lock Corp.: www.shotlock.com
SKB Cases: www.skbcases.com
Smart Lock Technology Inc.: www.smartlock.com
Sportsmans Steel Safe Co.:
    www.sportsmansteelsafes.com
Stack-On Products Co.: www.stack-on.com

Starlight Cases: www.starlightcases.com
Sun Welding: www.sunwelding.com
Technoframes: www.technoframes.com
T.Z. Case Int'l : www.tzcase.com
U.S. Explosive Storage: www.usexplosivestorage.com
Versatile Rack Co.: www.versatilegunrack.com
V-Line Industries: www.vlineind.com
Winchester Safes: www.winchestersafes.com
Ziegel Engineering: www.ziegeleng.com
Zonetti Armor: www.zonettiarmor.com

CHOKE DEVICES, RECOIL REDUCERS, SUPPRESSORS AND ACCURACY DEVICES

Advanced Armament Corp.:
    www.advanced-armament.com
100 Straight Products: www.100straight.com
Answer Products Co.: www.answerrifles.com
AWC Systems Technology: www.awcsystech.com
Briley Mfg: www.briley.com
Carlson's: www.choketube.com
Colonial Arms: www.colonialarms.com
Comp-N-Choke: www.comp-n-choke.com
Elite Iron: www.eliteiron.net
Gemtech: www.gem-tech.com
Kick's Industries: www.kicks-ind.com
LimbSaver: www.limbsaver.com
Mag-Na-Port Int'l Inc.: www.magnaport.com
Metro Gun: www.metrogun.com
Patternmaster Chokes: www.patternmaster.com
Poly-Choke: www.poly-choke.com
SilencerCo: www.silencerco.com
Sims Vibration Laboratory: www.limbsaver.com
SRT Arms: www.srtarms.com
SureFire: www.surefire.com
SWR Mfg.: www.swrmfg.com
Teague Precision Chokes: www.teague.ca
Truglo: www.truglo.com
Trulock Tool: www.trulockchokes.com

CHRONOGRAPHS AND BALLISTIC SOFTWARE

Barnes Ballistic Program: www.barnesbullets.com
Ballisticard Systems: www.ballisticards.com
Competition Electronics:
    www.competitionelectronics.com
Competitive Edge Dynamics: www.cedhk.com
Hodgdon Shotshell Program: www.hodgdon.com
Lee Shooter Program: www.leeprecision.com
Load From A Disk: www.loadammo.com
Oehler Research Inc.: www.oehler-research.com
PACT: www.pact.com
ProChrony: www.competitionelectronics.com
Quickload: www.neconos.com
RCBS Load: www.rcbs.com
Shooting Chrony Inc: www.shootingchrony.com
Sierra Infinity Ballistics Program:
    www.sierrabullets.com
Winchester Ballistics Calculator:
    www.winchester.com

CLEANING PRODUCTS

Accupro: www.accupro.com
Ballistol USA: www.ballistol.com
Battenfeld Technologies:
    www.battenfeldtechnologies.com
Birchwood Casey: www.birchwoodcasey.com
Blue Wonder: www.bluewonder.com
Bore Tech: www.boretech.com
Break-Free, Inc.: www.break-free.com

Bruno Shooters Supply: www.brunoshooters.com
Butch's Bore Shine: www.lymanproducts.com
C.J. Weapons Accessories: www.cjweapons.com
Clenzoil: www.clenzoil.com
Corrosion Technologies: www.corrosionx.com
Dewey Mfg.: www.deweyrods.com
DuraCoat: www.lauerweaponry.com
Eezox Inc.: www.xmission.com
G 96: www.g96.com
Gun Cleaners: www.guncleaners.com
Gunslick Gun Care: www.gunslick.com
Gunzilla: www.topduckproducts.com
Hollands Shooters Supply: www.hollandgun.com
Hoppes: www.hoppes.com
Hydrosorbent Products: www.dehumidify.com
Inhibitor VCI Products: www.theinhibitor.com
Iosso Products: www.iosso.com
KG Industries: www.kgcoatings.com
Kleen-Bore Inc.: www.kleen-bore.com
L&R Ultrasoncics: www.lrultrasonics.com
Lyman: www.lymanproducts.com
Mil-Comm Products: www.mil-comm.com
Militec-1: www.militec-1.com
MPT Industries: www.mptindustries.com
Mpro7 Gun Care: www.mp7.com
Old West Snake Oil: www.oldwestsnakeoil.com
Otis Technology, Inc.: www.otisgun.com
Outers: www.outers-guncare.com
Ox-Yoke Originals Inc.: www.oxyoke.com
Parker-Hale Ltd.: www.parker-hale.com
Prolix Lubricant: www.prolixlubricant.com
ProShot Products: www.proshotproducts.com
ProTec Lubricants: www.proteclubricants.com
Rusteprufe Labs: www.rusteprufe.com
Sagebrush Products: www.sagebrushproducts.com
Sentry Solutions Ltd.: www.sentrysolutions.com
Shooters Choice Gun Care:
    www.shooters-choice.com
Silencio: www.silencio.com
Slip 2000: www.slip2000.com
Southern Bloomer Mfg.: www.southernbloomer.com
Stony Point Products: www.uncle-mikes.com
Tetra Gun: www.tetraproducts.com
The TM Solution: www.thetmsolution@comsast.net
Top Duck Products: www.topduckproducts.com
Ultra Bore Coat: www.ultracoatingsinc.com
World's Fastest Gun Bore Cleaner:
    www.michaels-oregon.com

FIREARM AUCTION SITES

A&S Auction Co.: www.asauction.com
Alderfer Austion: www.alderferauction.com
Amoskeag Auction Co.: www.amoskeagauction.com
Antique Guns: www.antiqueguns.com
Auction Arms: www.auctionarms.com
Batterman's Auctions: www.battermans.com
Bonhams & Butterfields:
    www.bonhams.com/usarms
Cowan's: www.cowans.com
Fontaine's Auction Gallery:
    www.fontainesauction.net
Greg Martin Auctions: www.gregmartinauctions.com
Guns America: www.gunsamerica.com
Gun Broker: www.gunbroker.com
Guns International: www.gunsinternational.com
Heritage Auction Gallaries: www.ha.com
James D. Julia, Inc.: www.jamesdjulia.com
J.C. Devine, Inc.: www.jcdevine.com
Little John's Auction Service:
    www.littlejohnsauctionservice.com
Morphy Auctions: www.morphyauctions.com
Poulin Auction Co.: www.poulinantiques.com

Rock Island Auction Co.:
    www.rockislandauction.com
Wallis & Wallis: www.wallisandwallis.org

FIREARM MANUFACTURERS AND IMPORTERS

AAR, Inc.: www.iar-arms.com
A-Square: www.asquarecompany.com
Accuracy Int'l North America:
    www.accuracyinternational.com
Accuracy Rifle Systems: www.mini-14.net
Ace Custom 45's: www.acecustom45.com
Advanced Weapons Technology:
    www.AWT-Zastava.com
AIM: www.aimsurplus.com
AirForce Airguns: www.airforceairguns.com
Air Gun, Inc.: www.airrifle-china.com
Airguns of Arizona: www.airgunsofarizona.com
Airgun Express: www.airgunexpress.com
Akkar Sporting Arms: www.akkar-usa.com
Alchemy Arms: www.alchemyltd.com
Alexander Arms: www.alexanderarms.com
American Classic: www.americanclassic1911.com
American Derringer Corp.: www.amderringer.com
American Rifle Co.: www.americanrifleco.com
American Spirit Arms Corp.: www.gunkits.com
American Tactical Imports: www.americantactical.us
American Western Arms: www.awaguns.com
Anics Corp.: www.anics.com
Anschutz: www.anschutz-sporters.com
Answer Products Co.: www.answerrifles.com
AR-7 Industries,LLC: www.ar-7.com
Ares Defense Systems: www.aresdefense.com
Armalite: www.armalite.com
Armi Sport: www.armisport.com
Armory USA: www.globaltraders.com
Armsco: www.armsco.net
Armscorp USA Inc.: www.armscorpusa.com
Arnold Arms: www.arnoldarms.com
Arrieta: www.arrietashotguns.com
Arsenal Inc.: www.arsenalinc.com
Arthur Brown Co.: www.eabco.com
Atlanta Cutlery Corp.: www.atlantacutlery.com
ATA Arms: www.ataarms.com
Auction Arms: www.auctionarms.com
Autauga Arms,Inc.: www.autaugaarms.com
Auto-Ordnance Corp.: www.tommygun.com
AWA Int'l: www.awaguns.com
Axtell Rifle Co.: www.riflesmith.com
Aya: www.aya-fineguns.com
Baikal: www.baikalinc.ru/eng/
Badger Ordnance: www.badgerordnance.com
Ballard Rifles,LLC: www.ballardrifles.com
Barrett Firearms Mfg.: www.barrettrifles.com
Beeman Precision Airguns: www.beeman.com
Benelli USA Corp.: www.benelliusa.com
Benjamin Sheridan: www.crosman.com
Beretta U.S.A. Corp.: www.berettausa.com
Bernardelli: www.bernardelli.com
Bersa: www.bersa.com
Bill Hanus Birdguns: www.billhanusbirdguns.com
Blaser Jagdwaffen Gmbh: www.blaser.de
Bleiker: www.bleiker.ch
Bluegrass Armory: www.bluegrassarmory.com
Bond Arms: www.bondarms.com
Borden's Rifles, Inc.: www.bordensrifles.com
Boss & Co.: www.bossguns.co.uk
Bowen Classic Arms: www.bowenclassicarms.com
Briley Mfg: www.briley.com
BRNO Arms: www.zbrojovka.com
Brown, David McKay: www.mckaybrown.com

Brown, Ed Products: www.brownprecision.com
Browning: www.browning.com
BRP Corp.: www.brpguns.com
BSA Guns: www.bsagunusa.com
BUL Ltd.: www.bultransmark.com
Bushmaster Firearms/Quality Parts:
    www.bushmaster.com
BWE Firearms: www.bwefirearms.com
Caesar Guerini USA: www.gueriniusa.com
Cape Outfitters: www.doublegun.com
Carbon 15: www.professional-ordnance.com
Caspian Arms, Ltd.: www.caspianarmsltd.8m.com
Casull Arms Corp.: www.casullarms.com
Calvary Arms: www.calvaryarms.com
CDNN Investments, Inc.:
    www.cdnninvestments.com
Century Arms: www.centuryarms.com
Chadick's Ltd.: www.chadicks-ltd.com
Champlin Firearms: www.champlinarms.com
Chapuis Arms: www.doubleguns.com/chapuis.htm
Charles Daly: www.charlesdaly.com
Charter Arms: www.charterfirearms.com
CheyTac USA: www.cheytac.com
Chiappa Firearms: www.chiappafirearms.com
Christensen Arms: www.christensenarms.com
Cimarron Firearms Co.:
    www.cimarron-firearms.com
Clark Custom Guns: www.clarkcustomguns.com
Cobra Enterprises: www.cobrapistols.com
Cogswell & Harrison:
    www.cogswell.co.uk/home.htm
Collector's Armory, Ltd.: www.collectorsarmory.com
Colt's Mfg Co.: www.colt.com
Compasseco, Inc.: www.compasseco.com
Connecticut Valley Arms: www.cva.com
Cooper Firearms: www.cooperfirearms.com
Corner Shot: www.cornershot.com
CPA Rifles: www.singleshotrifles.com
Crosman: www.crosman.com
Crossfire, L.L.C.: www.crossfirelle.com
C.Sharp Arms Co.: www.csharparms.com
CVA: www.cva.com
Czechp Int'l: www.czechpoint-usa.com
CZ USA: www.cz-usa.com
Daisy Mfg Co.: www.daisy.com
Dakota Arms Inc.: www.dakotaarms.com
Dan Wesson Firearms:
    www.danwessonfirearms.com
Daniel Defense, Inc.: www.danieldefense.com
Davis Industries: www.davisindguns.com
Detonics USA: www.detonicsusa.com
Diana: www.diana-airguns.de
Dixie Gun Works: www.dixiegunworks.com
Dlask Arms Corp.: www.dlask.com
D.P.M.S., Inc.: www.dpmsinc.com
D.S.Arms,Inc.: www.dsarms.com
Dumoulin: www.dumoulin-herstal.com
Dynamit Noble: www.dnrws.com
EAA Corp.: www.eaacorp.com
Eagle Imports,Inc.: www.bersa-llama.com
Ed Brown Products: www.edbrown.com
EDM Arms: www.edmarms.com
E.M.F. Co.: www.emf-company.com
Enterprise Arms: www.enterprise.com
E R Shaw: www.ershawbarrels.com
European American Armory Corp.:
    www.eaacorp.com
Evans, William: www.williamevans.com
Excel Arms: www.excelarms.com
Fabarm: www.fabarm.com
FAC-Guns-N-Stuff: www.gunsnstuff.com
Falcon Pneumatic Systems:
    www.falcon-airguns.com

Fausti Stefano: **www.faustistefanoarms.com**
Firestorm: **www.firestorm-sgs.com**
Flodman Guns: **www.flodman.com**
FN Herstal: **www.fnherstal.com**
FNH USA: **www.fnhusa.com**
Franchi: **www.franchiusa.com**
Freedom Arms: **www.freedomarms.com**
Freedom Group, Inc.: **www.freedom-group.com**
Galazan: **www.connecticutshotgun.com**
Gambo Renato: **www.renatogamba.it**
Gamo: **www.gamo.com**
Gary Reeder Custom Guns:
www.reeder-customguns.com
Gazelle Arms: **www.gazellearms.com**
German Sport Guns: **www.germansportguns.com**
Gibbs Rifle Company: **www.gibbsrifle.com**
Glock: **www.glock.com**
Griffin & Howe: **www.griffinhowe.com**
Grizzly Big Boar Rifle: **www.largrizzly.com**
GSI Inc.: **www.gsifirearms.com**
Guerini: **www.gueriniusa.com**
Gunbroker.Com: **www.gunbroker.com**
Gun Room Co.: **www.onlylongrange.com**
Hammerli: **www.carl-walther.com**
Hatfield Gun Co.: **www.hatfield-usa.com**
Hatsan Arms Co.: **www.hatsan.com.tr**
Heckler and Koch: **www.hk-usa.com**
Henry Repeating Arms Co.:
www.henryrepeating.com
Heritage Mfg.: **www.heritagemfg.com**
Heym: **www.heym-waffenfabrik.de**
High Standard Mfg.: **www.highstandard.com**
Hi-Point Firearms: **www.hi-pointfirearms.com**
Holland & Holland: **www.hollandandholland.com**
H&R 1871 Firearms: **www.hr1871.com**
H-S Precision: **www.hsprecision.com**
Hunters Lodge Corp.: **www.hunterslodge.com**
IAR Inc.: **www.iar-arms.com**
Imperial Miniature Armory: **www.1800miniature.com**
Interarms: **www.interarms.com**
International Military Antiques, Inc.:
www.ima-usa.com
Inter Ordnance: **www.interordnance.com**
Intrac Arms International LLC: **www.hsarms.com**
Israel Arms: **www.israelarms.com**
ISSC, LLC: **www.issc.austria.com**
Iver Johnson Arms: **www.iverjohnsonarms.com**
Izhevsky Mekhanichesky Zavod: **www.baikalinc.ru**
James River Mfg.: **www.jamesriverarmory.com**
Jarrett Rifles,Inc.: **www.jarrettrifles.com**
J&G Sales, Ltd.: **www.jgsales.com**
Johannsen Express Rifle: **www.johannsen-jagd.de**
Jonathan Arthur Ciener: **www.22lrconversions.com**
JP Enterprises, Inc.: **www.jprifles.com**
Kahr Arms/Auto-Ordnance: **www.kahr.com**
K.B.I.: **www.kbi-inc.com**
KDF, Inc.: **www.kdfguns.com**
Kel-Tec CNC Ind., Inc.: **www.kel-tec.com**
Keystone Sporting Arms:
www.keystonesportingarmsllc.com
Kifaru: **www.kifaru.net**
Kimber: **www.kimberamerica.com**
Knight's Armament Co.: **www.knightsarmco.com**
Knight Rifles: **www.knightrifles.com**
Korth: **www.korthwaffen.de**
Krebs Custom Guns: **www.krebscustom.com**
Kriss: **www.kriss-usa.com**
Krieghoff Int'l: **www.krieghoff.com**
KY Imports, Inc.: **www.kyimports.com**
K-VAR: **www.k-var.com**
Lanber: **www.lanber.net**
L.A.R Mfg: **www.largrizzly.com**
Lazzeroni Arms Co.: **www.lazzeroni.com**

Legacy Sports International: **www.legacysports.com**
Les Baer Custom, Inc.: **www.lesbaer.com**
Lewis Machine & Tool Co.: **www.lewismachine.net**
Linebaugh Custom Sixguns:
www.sixgunner.com/linebaugh
Ljutic: **www.ljuticgun.com**
Llama: **www.bersa-llama.com**
Lone Star Rifle Co.: **www.lonestarrifle.com**
LRB Arms: **www.lrbarms.com**
LWRC Int'l: **www.lwrifles.com**
Magnum Research: **www.magnumresearch.com**
Majestic Arms: **www.majesticarms.com**
Markesbery Muzzleloaders: **www.markesbery.com**
Marksman Products: **www.marksman.com**
Marlin: **www.marlinfirearms.com**
MasterPiece Arms: **www.masterpiecearms.com**
Mauser: **www.mauser.com**
McMillan Bros Rifle Co.: **www.mcfamily.com**
MDM: **www.mdm-muzzleloaders.com**
Meacham Rifles: **www.meachamrifles.com**
Merkel: **www.hk-usa.com**
Miller Arms: **www.millerarms.com**
Miltech: **www.miltecharms.com**
Miltex, Inc.: **www.miltexusa.com**
Mitchell's Mausers: **www.mitchellsales.com**
MK Ballistic Systems: **www.mkballistics.com**
M-Mag: **www.mmag.com**
Montana Rifle Co.: **www.montanarifleman.com**
Mossberg: **www.mossberg.com**
Navy Arms: **www.navyarms.com**
Nesika: **www.nesika.com**
New England Arms Corp.:
www.newenglandarms.com
New England Custom Gun Svc, Ltd.:
www.newenglandcustomgun.com
New England Firearms: **www.hr1871.com**
New Ultra Light Arms: **www.newultralight.com**
Nighthawk Custom: **www.nighthawkcustom.com**
North American Arms:
www.northamericanarms.com
Nosler Bullets,Inc.: **www.nosler.com**
Nowlin Mfg. Inc.: **www.nowlinguns.com**
O.F. Mossberg & Sons: **www.mossberg.com**
Ohio Ordnance Works:
www.ohioordnanceworks.com
Olympic Arms: **www.olyarms.com**
Osprey Defense: **www.gaspiston.com**
Panther Arms: **www.dpmsinc.com**
Para-USA: **www.para-usa.com**
Pedersoli Davide & Co.: **www.davide-pedersoli.com**
Perazzi: **www.perazzi.com**
Pietta: **www.pietta.it**
PKP Knife-Pistol: **www.sanjuanenterprise.com**
Power Custom: **www.powercustom.com**
Precision Small Arm Inc.:
www.precisionsmallarms.com
Professional Arms: **www.professional-arms.com**
PTR 91,Inc.: **www.ptr91.com**
Purdey & Sons: **www.purdey.com**
Pyramid Air: **www.pyramidair.com**
Red Jacket Firearms: **www.redjacketfirearms.com**
Remington: **www.remington.com**
Republic Arms Inc.: **www.republicarmsinc.com**
Rhineland Arms, Inc.: **www.rhinelandarms.com**
Rigby: **www.johnrigbyandco.com**
Rizzini USA: **www.rizziniusa.com**
RM Equipment, Inc.: **www.40mm.com**
Robar Companies, Inc.: **www.robarguns.com**
Robinson Armament Co.: **www.robarm.com**
Rock River Arms, Inc.: **www.rockriverarms.com**
Rogue Rifle Co. Inc.: **www.chipmunkrifle.com**
Rohrbaugh Firearms: **www.rohrbaughfirearms.com**

Rossi Arms: **www.rossiusa.com**
RPM: **www.rpmxlpistols.com**
Russian American Armory: **www.raacfirearms.com**
RUAG Ammotec: **www.ruag.com**
Sabatti SPA: **www.sabatti.com**
Saco Defense: **www.sacoinc.com**
Safari Arms: **www.olyarms.com**
Sako: **www.berettausa.com**
Samco Global Arms Inc.: **www.samcoglobal.com**
Sarco: **www.sarcoinc.com**
Sarsilmaz Silah San: **www.sarsilmaz.com**
Sauer & Sohn: **www.sauer.de**
Savage Arms Inc.: **www.savagearms.com**
Scattergun Technologies Inc.:
www.wilsoncombat.com
Searcy Enterprises: **www.searcyent.com**
Shaw: **www.ershawbarrels.com**
Shiloh Rifle Mfg.: **www.shilohrifle.com**
Sig Sauer, Inc.: **www.sigsauer.com**
Simpson Ltd.: **www.simpsonltd.com**
SKB Shotguns: **www.skbshotguns.com**
Smith & Wesson: **www.smith-wesson.com**
SOG International, Inc.:
www.soginc@go-concepts.com
Sphinx System: **www.sphinxarms.com**
Springfield Armory: **www.springfield-armory.com**
SSK Industries: **www.sskindustries.com**
Stag Arms: **www.stagarms.com**
Steyr Arms, Inc. : **www.steyrarms.com**
STI International: **www.stiguns.com**
Stoeger Industries: **www.stoegerindustries.com**
Strayer-Voigt Inc.: **www.sviguns.com**
Sturm, Ruger & Company: **www.ruger-firearms.com**
Super Six Classic: **www.bisonbull.com**
Surgeon Rifles: **www.surgeonrifles.com**
Tactical Rifles: **www.tacticalrifles.com**
Tactical Solutions: **www.tacticalsol.com**
Tar-Hunt Slug Guns, Inc.: **www.tar-hunt.com**
Taser Int'l: **www.taser.com**
Taurus: **www.taurususa.com**
Taylor's & Co., Inc.: **www.taylorsfirearms.com**
Tempco Mfg. Co.: **www.tempcomfg.com**
Tennessee Guns: **www.tennesseeguns.com**
TG Int'l: **www.tnguns.com**
The 1877 Sharps Co.: **www.1877sharps.com**
Thompson Center Arms: **www.tcarms.com**
Tikka: **www.berettausa.com**
TNW, Inc.: **www.tnwfirearms.com**
Traditions: **www.traditionsfirearms.com**
Tristar Sporting Arms: **www.tristarsportingarms.com**
Uberti: **www.ubertireplicas.com**
Ultralite 50: **www.ultralite50.com**
Ultra Light Arms: **www.newultralight.com**
Umarex: **www.umarex.com**
U.S. Armament Corp.: **www.usarmamentcorp.com**
U.S. Firearms Mfg. Co.: **www.usfirearms.com**
Uselton Arms, Inc.: **www.useltonarmsinc.com**
Valkyrie Arms: **www.valkyriearms.com**
Vektor Arms: **www.vektorarms.com**
Verney-Carron: **www.verney-carron.com**
Volquartsen Custom Ltd.: **www.volquartsen.com**
Vulcan Armament: **www.vulcanarmament.com**
Walther USA: **www.waltheramerica.com**
Weatherby: **www.weatherby.com**
Webley and Scott Ltd.: **www.webley.co.uk**
Westley Richards: **www.westleyrichards.com**
Widley: **www.widleyguns.com**
Wild West Guns: **www.wildwestguns.com**
William Larkin Moore & Co.: **www.doublegun.com**
Wilson Combat: **www.wilsoncombat.com**
Winchester Rifles and Shotguns:
www.winchesterguns.com

GUN PARTS, BARRELS, AFTER-MARKET ACCESSORIES

300 Below: www.300below.com
Accuracy International of North America:
 www.accuracyinternational.org
Accuracy Speaks, Inc.: www.accuracyspeaks.com
Accurary Systems: www.accuracysystemsinc.com
Adam Arms: www.adamarms.net
Advanced Barrel Systems: www.carbonbarrels.com
Advantage Arms: www.advantagearms.com
Aim Surplus: www.aimsurplus.com
AK-USA: www.ak-103.com
American Spirit Arms Corp.: www.gunkits.com
Amhurst-Depot: www.amherst-depot.com
AMT Gun Parts: www.amt-gunparts.com
Armatac Industries: www.armatac.com
Asia Sourcing Corp.: www.asiasourcing.com
Badger Barrels, Inc.: www.badgerbarrels.com
Barnes Precision Machine:
 www.barnesprecision.com
Bar-Sto Precision Machine: www.barsto.com
Battenfeld Technologies:
 www.battenfeldtechnologies.com
Bellm TC's: www.bellmtcs.com
Belt Mountain Enterprises: www.beltmountain.com
Bergara Barrels: www.bergarabarrels.com
Bill Wiseman & Co.: www.wisemanballistics.com
Briley: www.briley.com
Brownells: www.brownells.com
B-Square: www.b-square.com
Buffer Technologies: www.buffertech.com
Bullberry Barrel Works: www.bullberry.com
Bulldog Barrels: www.bulldogbarrels.com
Bushmaster Firearms/Quality Parts:
 www.bushmaster.com
Butler Creek Corp.: www.butler-creek.com
Cape Outfitters Inc.: www.capeoutfitters.com
Caspian Arms Ltd.: www.caspianarms.com
Cheaper Than Dirt: www.cheaperthandirt.com
Chesnut Ridge: www.chestnutridge.com/
Chip McCormick Corp:
 www.chipmccormickcorp.com
Choate Machine & Tool Co.: www.riflestock.com
Christie's Products: www.1022cental.com
Cierner, Jonathan Arthur: www.22lrconversions.com
CJ Weapons Accessories: www.cjweapons.com
Colonial Arms: www.colonialarms.com
Comp-N-Choke: www.comp-n-choke.com
Cylinder & Slide Shop: www.cylinder-slide.com
Daniel Defense: www.danieldefense.com
Dave Manson Precision Reamers.:
 www.mansonreamers.com
Digi-Twist: www.fmtcorp.com
Dixie Gun Works: www.dixiegun.com
Douglas Barrels: www.benchrest.com/douglas/
DPMS: www.dpmsinc.com
D.S.Arms,Inc.: www.dsarms.com
eBay: www.ebay.com
Ed Brown Products: www.edbrown.com
EFK Marketing/Fire Dragon Pistol Accessories:
 www.flmfire.com
E.R. Shaw: www.ershawbarrels.com
Forrest Inc.: www.gunmags.com
Fulton Armory: www.fulton-armory.com
Galazan: www.connecticutshotgun.com
Gemtech: www.gem-tech.com
Gentry, David: www.gentrycustom.com
GG&G: www.gggaz.com
Green Mountain Rifle Barrels:
 www.gmriflebarrel.com
Gun Parts Corp.: www.e-gunparts.com
Harris Engineering: www.harrisbipods.com

Hart Rifle Barrels: www.hartbarrels.com
Hastings Barrels: www.hastingsbarrels.com
Heinie Specialty Products: www.heinie.com
HKS Products, Inc.: wwwhksspeedloaders.com
Holland Shooters Supply: www.hollandgun.com
H-S Precision: www.hsprecision.com
100 Straight Products: www.100straight.com
I.M.A.: www.ima-usa.com
Jack First Gun Shop: www.jackfirstgun.com
Jarvis, Inc.: www.jarvis-custom.com
J&T Distributing: www.jtdistributing.com
John's Guns: www.johnsguns.com
John Masen Co.: www.johnmasen.com
Jonathan Arthur Ciener, Inc.:
 www.22lrconversions.com
JP Enterprises: www.jpar15.com
Keng's Firearms Specialities: www.versapod.com
KG Industries: www.kgcoatings.com
Kick Eez: www.kickeez.com
Kidd Triggers: www.coolguyguns.com
King's Gunworks: www.kingsgunworks.com
Knoxx Industries: www.knoxx.com
Krieger Barrels: www.kriegerbarrels.com
K-VAR Corp.: www.k-var.com
LaRue Tactical: www.laruetactical.com
Les Baer Custom, Inc.: www.lesbaer.com
Lilja Barrels: www.riflebarrels.com
Lone Star Rifle Co.: www.lonestarrifles.com
Lone Wolf Dist.: www.lonewolfdist.com
Lothar Walther Precision Tools Inc.:
 www.lothar-walther.de
M&A Parts, Inc.: www.m-aparts.com
MAB Barrels: www.mab.com.au
Magpul Industries Corp.: www.magpul.com
Majestic Arms: www.majesticarms.com
Marvel Products, Inc.: www.marvelprod.com
MEC-GAR SrL: www.mec-gar.it
Mesa Tactical: www.mesatactical.com
Michaels of Oregon Co.: www.michaels-oregon.com
Midway USA: www.midwayusa.com
NIC Industries: www.nicindustries.com
North Mfg. Co.: www.rifle-barrels.com
Numrich Gun Parts Corp.: www.e-gunparts.com
Pachmayr: www.pachmayr.com
Pac-Nor Barrels: www.pac-nor.com
Power Custom, Inc.: www.powercustom.com
Para Ordinance Pro Shop: www.ltms.com
Point Tech Inc.: www.pointec@ibm.net
Precision Reflex: www.pri-mounts.com
Promag Industries: www.promagindustries.com
RCI-XRAIL: www.xrailbyrci.com
Red Star Arms: www.redstararms.com
Rock Creek Barrels: www.rockcreekbarrels.com
Rocky Mountain Arms:
 www.rockymountainarms.com
Royal Arms Int'l: www.royalarms.com
R.W. Hart: www.rwhart.com
Sage Control Ordnance:
 www.sageinternationalltd.com
Sarco Inc.: www.sarcoinc.com
Scattergun Technologies Inc.:
 www.wilsoncombat.com
Schuemann Barrels: www.schuemann.com
Score High Gunsmithing: www.scorehi.com
Seminole Gunworks Chamber Mates:
 www.chambermates.com
Shaw Barrels: www.ershawbarrels.com
Shilen: www.shilen.com
Sims Vibration Laboratory:
 www.limbsaver.com
Smith & Alexander Inc.:
 www.smithandalexander.com
Speed Shooters Int'l: www.shooternet.com/ssi

Sprinco USA Inc.: www.sprinco@primenet.com
Springfield Sporters, Inc.: www.ssporters.com
STI Int'l: www.stiguns.com
S&S Firearms: www.ssfirearms.com
SSK Industries: www.sskindustries.com
Sun Devil Mfg.: www.sundevilmfg.com
Sunny Hill Enterprises: www.sunny-hill.com
Tac Star: www.lymanproducts.com
Tactical Innovations: www.tacticalinc.com
Tactical Solutions: www.tacticalsol.com
Tactilite: www.tactilite.com
Tapco: www.tapco.com
Trapdoors Galore: www.trapdoors.com
Triple K Manufacturing Co. Inc.: www.triplek.com
U.S.A. Magazines Inc.: www.usa-magazines.com
Verney-Carron SA: www.verney-carron.com
Vintage Ordnance: www.vintageordnance.com
Vltor Weapon Systems: www.vltor.com
Volquartsen Custom Ltd.: www.volquartsen.com
W.C. Wolff Co.: www.gunsprings.com
Waller & Son: www.wallerandson.com
Weigand Combat Handguns:
 www.weigandcombat.com
Western Gun Parts: www.westerngunparts.com
Wilson Arms: www.wilsonarms.com
Wilson Combat: www.wilsoncombat.com
Wisner's Inc.: www.wisnerinc.com
Z-M Weapons: www.zmweapons.com/home.htm

GUNSMITHING SUPPLIES AND INSTRUCTION

American Gunsmithing Institute:
 www.americangunsmith.com
Baron Technology: www.baronengraving.com
Battenfeld Technologies:
 www.battenfeldtechnologies.com
Bellm TC's: www.bellmtcs.com
Blue Ridge Machinery & Tools:
 www.blueridgemachinery.com
Brownells, Inc.: www.brownells.com
B-Square Co.: www.b-square.com
Cerakote Firearm Coatings: www.nciindustries.com
Clymer Mfg. Co.: www.clymertool.com
Craftguard Metal Finishing: www.crftgrd@aol.com
Dem-Bart: www.dembartco.com
Doug Turnbull Restoration: www.
 turnbullrestoration,com
Du-Lite Corp.: www.dulite.com
DuraCoat Firearm Finishes:
 www.lauerweaponry.com
Dvorak Instruments: www.dvorakinstruments.com
Gradiant Lens Corp.: www.gradientlens.com
Grizzly Industrial: www.grizzly.com
Gunline Tools: www.gunline.com
Harbor Freight: www.harborfreight.com
JGS Precision Tool Mfg. LLC: www.jgstools.com
Mag-Na-Port International: www.magnaport.com
Manson Precision Reamers:
 www.mansonreamers.com
Midway USA: www.midwayusa.com
Murray State College: www.mscok.edu
Olympus America Inc.: www.olympus.com
Pacific Tool & Gauge:
 www.pacifictoolandgauge.com
Precision Metalsmiths, Inc.:
 www.precisionmetalsmiths.com
Rail Vise Technologies: www.railvise.com
Trinidad State Junior College: www.trinidadstate.edu

HANDGUN GRIPS

A&G Supply Co.: www.gripextender.com

Ajax Custom Grips, Inc.: www.ajaxgrips.com
Altamont Co.: www.altamontco.com
Aluma Grips: www.alumagrips.com
Badger Grips: www.pistolgrips.com
Barami Corp.: www.hipgrip.com
Blu Magnum Grips: www.blumagnum.com
Buffalo Brothers: www.buffalobrothers.com
Crimson Trace Corp.: www.crimsontrace.com
Eagle Grips: www.eaglegrips.com
Falcon Industries: www.ergogrips.net
Herrett's Stocks: www.herrettstocks.com
Hogue Grips: www.getgrip.com
Kirk Ratajesak: www.kgratajesak.com
Lett Custom Grips: www.lettgrips.com
N.C. Ordnance: www.gungrip.com
Nill-Grips USA: www.nill-grips.com
Pachmayr: www.pachmayr.com
Pearce Grips: www.pearcegrip.com
Trausch Grips Int.Co.: www.trausch.com
Tyler-T Grips: www.t-grips.com
Uncle Mike's: www.uncle-mikes.com

HOLSTERS AND LEATHER PRODUCTS

Akah: www.akah.de
Aker Leather Products: www.akerleather.com
Alessi Distributor R&F Inc.: www.alessiholsters.com
Alfonso's of Hollywood: www.alfonsogunleather.com
Armor Holdings: www.holsters.com
Bagmaster: www.bagmaster.com
Bianchi International: www.bianchi-intl.com
Blackhawk Outdoors: www.blackhawk.com
Blackhills Leather: www.blackhillsleather.com
BodyHugger Holsters: www.nikolais.com
Boyt Harness Co.: www.boytharness.com
Brigade Gun Leather: www.brigadegunleather.com
Chimere: www.chimere.com
Clipdraw: www.clipdraw.com
Conceal It: www.conceal-it.com
Concealment Shop Inc.:
    www.theconcealmentshop.com
Coronado Leather Co.: www.coronadoleather.com
Covert Carry: www.covertcarry.com
Creedmoor Sports, Inc.: www.creedmoorsports.com
Custom Leather Wear:
    www.customleatherwear.com
Defense Security Products: www.thunderwear.com
Dennis Yoder: www.yodercustomleather.com
DeSantis Holster: www.desantisholster.com
Dillon Precision: www.dillonprecision.com
Don Hume Leathergoods, Inc.: www.donhume.com
Ernie Hill International: www.erniehill.com
Fist: www.fist-inc.com
Fobus USA: www.fobusholster.com
Front Line Ltd.: www.frontlin@internet-zahav.net
Galco: www.usgalco.com
Gilmore's Sports Concepts: www.gilmoresports.com
Gould & Goodrich: www.gouldusa.com
Gunmate Products: www.gun-mate.com
Hellweg Ltd.: www.hellwegltd.com
Hide-A-Gun: www.hide-a-gun.com
High Noon Holsters: www.highnoonholsters.com
Holsters.Com: www.holsters.com
Horseshoe Leather Products: www.horseshoe.co.uk
Hunter Co.: www.huntercompany.com
JBP/Master's Holsters: www.jbpholsters.com
Kirkpatrick Leather Company:
    www.kirkpatrickleather.com
KNJ: www.knjmfg.com
Kramer Leather: www.kramerleather.com
Law Concealment Systems:
    www.handgunconcealment.com
Levy's Leathers Ltd.: www.levysleathers.com

Mernickle Holsters: www.mernickleholsters.com
Michaels of Oregon Co.: www.michaels-oregon.com
Milt Sparks Leather: www.miltsparks.com
Mitch Rosen Extraordinary Gunleather:
    www.mitchrosen.com
Old World Leather: www.gun-mate.com
Pacific Canvas & Leather Co.:
    www.paccanadleather@directway.com
Pager Pal: www.pagerpal.com
Phalanx Corp.: www.smartholster.com
PWL: www.pwlusa.com
Rumanya Inc.: www.rumanya.com
S.A. Gunleather: www.elpasoleather.com
Safariland Ltd. Inc.: www.safariland.com
Shooting Systems Group Inc.:
    www.shootingsystems.com
Strictly Anything Inc.: www.strictlyanything.com
Strong Holster Co.: www.strong-holster.com
The Belt Co.: www.conceal-it.com
The Leather Factory Inc.: www.lflandry@flash.net
The Outdoor Connection:
    www.outdoorconnection.com
Top-Line USA inc.: www.toplineusa.com
Triple K Manufacturing Co.: www.triplek.com
Wilson Combat: www.wilsoncombat.com

MISCELLANEOUS SHOOTING PRODUCTS

10X Products Group: www.10Xwear.com
Aero Peltor: www.aearo.com
American Body Armor:
    www.americanbodyarmor.com
American Tactical Imports:
    www.americantactical.com
Ammo-Up: www.ammoupusa.com
Armor Holdings Products: www.armorholdings.com
AutoGun Tracker: www.autoguntracker.com
Battenfeld Technologies:
    www.battenfeldtechnologies.com
Beamhit: www.beamhit.com
Beartooth: www.beartoothproducts.com
Bodyguard by S&W: www.yourbodyguard.com
Burnham Brothers: www.burnhambrothers.com
Collectors Armory: www.collectorsarmory.com
Dalloz Safety: www.cdalloz.com
Deben Group Industries Inc.: www.deben.com
Decot Hy-Wyd Sport Glasses:
    www.sportyglasses.com
Defense Technology:
    www.safariland.com/lesslethal
E.A.R., Inc.: www.earinc.com
First Choice Armor: www.firstchoicearmor.com
Gunstands: www.gunstands.com
Howard Leight Hearing Protectors:
    www.howardleight.com
Hunters Specialities: www.hunterspec.com
Johnny Stewart Wildlife Calls: www.hunterspec.com
Mec-Gar SRL: www.mec-gar.it
Merit Corporation: www.meritcorporation.com
Michaels of Oregon: www.michaels-oregon.com
MPI Outdoors: www.mpioutdoors.com
MT2, LLC: www.mt2.com
MTM Case-Gard: www.mtmcase-gard.com
North Safety Products: www.northsafety-brea.com
Oakley, Inc.: www.usstandardissue.com
Plano Molding: www.planomolding.com
Practical Air Rifle Training Systems:
    www.smallarms.com
Pro-Ears: www.pro-ears.com
Second Chance Body Armor Inc.:
    www.secondchance.com
Silencio: www.silencio.com
Smart Lock Technologies: www.smartlock.com

SportEAR: www.sportear.com
STRAC, Inc.: www.stractech.com
Surefire: www.surefire.com
Taser Int'l: www.taser.com
Vyse-Gelatin Innovations:
    www.gelatininnovations.com
Walker's Game Ear Inc.: www.walkersgameear.com

MUZZLELOADING FIREARMS AND PRODUCTS

American Pioneer Powder:
    www.americanpioneerpowder.com
Armi Sport: www.armisport.com
Barnes Bullets: www.barnesbullets,com
Black Powder Products: www.bpiguns.com
Buckeye Barrels: www.buckeyebarrels.com
Cabin Creek Muzzleloading:
    www.cabincreek.net
CVA: www.cva.com
Caywood Gunmakers: www.caywoodguns.com
Davide Perdsoli & co.: www.davide-pedersoli.com
Dixie Gun Works, Inc.: www.dixiegun.com
Elephant/Swiss Black Powder:
    www.elephantblackpowder.com
Goex Black Powder: www.goexpowder.com
Green Mountain Rifle Barrel Co.:
    www.gmriflebarrel.com
Gunstocks Plus: www.gunstocksplus.com
Harvester Bullets: www.harvesterbullets.com
Hornady: www.hornady.com
Jedediah Starr Trading Co.: www.jedediah-starr.com
Jim Chambers Flintlocks: www.flintlocks.com
Kahnke Gunworks:
    www.powderandbow.com/kahnke/
Knight Rifles: www.knightrifles.com
Knob Mountain Muzzleloading:
    www.knobmountainmuzzleloading.com
The leatherman: www.blackpowderbags.com
Log Cabin Shop: www.logcabinshop.com
L&R Lock Co.: www.lr-rpl.com
Lyman: www.lymanproducts.com
Magkor Industries : www.magkor.com
MDM Muzzleloaders:
    www.mdm-muzzleloaders.com
Middlesex Village Trading:
    www.middlesexvillagetrading.com
Millennium Designed Muzzleloaders:
    www.mdm-muzzleloaders.com
MSM, Inc.: www.msmfg.com
Muzzleloader Builders Supply:
    www.muzzleloadersbuilderssupply.com
Muzzleload Magnum Products:
    www.mmpsabots.com
Muzzleloading Technologies, Inc.:
    www.mtimuzzleloading.com
Navy Arms: www.navyarms.com
Northwest Trade Guns: www.northstarwest.com
Nosler, Inc.: www.nosler.com
October Country Muzzleloading:
    www.oct-country.com
Ox-Yoke Originals Inc.: www.oxyoke.com
Pacific Rifle Co.: www.pacificrifle@aol.com
Palmetto Arms: www.palmetto.it
Pietta: www.pietta.it
Powerbelt Bullets: www.powerbeltbullets.com
PR Bullets: www.prbullets.com
Precision Rifle Dead Center Bullets:
    www.prbullet.com
R.E. Davis CVo.: www.redaviscompany.com
Rightnour Mfg. Co. Inc.: www.rmcsports.com
The Rifle Shop: www.trshoppe@aol.com
Savage Arms, Inc.: www.savagearms.com

Schuetzen Powder: www.schuetzenpowder.com
TDC: www.tdcmfg.com
Tennessee Valley Muzzleloading:
www.avsia.com/tvm
Thompson Center Arms: www.tcarms.com
Tiger Hunt Stocks: www.gunstockwood.com
Track of the Wolf: www.trackofthewolf.com
Traditions Performance Muzzleloading:
www.traditionsfirearms.com
Vernon C. Davis & Co.:
www.stonewallcreekoutfitters.com

PUBLICATIONS, VIDEOS, AND CD'S

Arms and Military Press: www.skennerton.com
A&J Arms Booksellers:
www.ajarmsbooksellers.com
American Cop: www.americancopmagazine.com
American Firearms Industry: www.amfire.com
American Handgunner:
www.americanhandgunner.com
American Hunter: www.nrapublications.org
American Pioneer Video:
www.americanpioneervideo.com
American Rifleman: www.nrapublications.org
American Shooting Magazine:
www.americanshooting.com
Backwoodsman: www.backwoodsmanmag.com
Black Powder Cartridge News:
www.blackpowderspg.com
Blue Book Publications: www.bluebookinc.com
Combat Handguns: www.combathandguns.com
Concealed Carry: www.uscca.us
Cornell Publications: www.cornellpubs.com
Countrywide Press: www.countrysport.com
Krause Publications/F+W Media/ DBI Books:
www.krause.com
Fouling Shot: www.castbulletassoc.org
George Shumway Publisher:
www.shumwaypublisher.com
Gun Digest: www.gundigest.com
Gun Video: www.gunvideo.com
GUNS Magazine: www.gunsmagazine.com
Guns & Ammo: www.gunsandammomag.com
Gun Week: www.gunweek.com
Gun World: www.gunworld.com
Harris Publications: www.harrispublications.com
Hendon Publishing Co.: www.hendonpub.com
Heritage Gun Books: www.gunbooks.com
Krause Publications: www.krause.com
Law and Order: www.hendonpub.com
Man at Arms: www.manatarmsbooks.com
Muzzleloader: www.muzzleloadermag.com
On-Target Productions: www.ontargetdvds.com
Outdoor Channel: www.outdoorchannel.com
Paladin Press: www.paladin-press.com
Police and Security News:
www.policeandsecuritynews.com
Police Magazine: www.policemag.com
Precision Shooting: www.precisionshooting.com
Pursuit Channel: www.pursuitchannel.com
Rifle and Handloader Magazines:
www.riflemagazine.com
Safari Press Inc.: www.safaripress.com
Schiffer Publishing: www.schifferbooks.com
Scurlock Publishing: www.muzzleloadingmag.com
Shoot! Magazine: www.shootmagazine.com
Shooting Illustrated: www.nrapublications.org
Shooting Industry: www.shootingindustry.com
Shooting Sports Retailer:
www.shootingsportsretailer.com
Shooting Sports USA: www.nrapublications.org
Shotgun News: www.shotgunnews.com

Shotgun Report: www.shotgunreport.com
Shotgun Sports Magazine:
www.shotgun-sports.com
Single Shot Rifle Journal: www.assra.com
Small Arms Review: www.smallarmsreview.com
Small Caliber News: www.smallcaliber.com
Sporting Clays Web Edition: www.sportingclays.net
Sports Afield: www.sportsafield.comm
Sportsmen on Film: www.sportsmenonfilm.com
SWAT Magazine: www.swatmag.com
The Single Shot Exchange Magazine:
www.singleshot@earthlink.net
The Sixgunner: www.sskindustries.com
Varmint Hunter: www.varminthunter.org
VSP Publications: www.gunbooks.com

RELOADING TOOLS

Antimony Man: www.theantimonyman.com
Ballisti-Cast Mfg.: www.ballisti-cast.com
Battenfeld Technologies:
www.battenfeldtechnologies.com
Bruno Shooters Supply: www.brunoshooters.com
Buffalo Arms: www.buffaloarms.com
CabineTree: www.castingstuff.com
Camdex, Inc.: www.camdexloader.com
CH/4D Custom Die: www.ch4d.com
Colorado Shooters Supply: www.hochmoulds.com
Corbin Mfg & Supply Co.: www.corbins.com
Dillon Precision: www.dillonprecision.com
Forster Precision Products:
www.forsterproducts.com
GSI International, Inc.: www.gsiinternational.com
Hanned Line: www.hanned.com
Harrell's Precision: www.harrellsprec.com
Holland's Shooting Supplies: www.hollandgun.com
Hornady: www.hornady.com
Huntington Reloading Products:
www.huntingtons.com
J & J Products Co.: www.jandjproducts.com
Lead Bullet Technology: www.lbtmoulds.com
Lee Precision, Inc.: www.leeprecision.com
Littleton Shotmaker: www.leadshotmaker.com
Load Data: www.loaddata.com
Lyman: www.lymanproducts.com
Magma Engineering: www.magmaengr.com
Mayville Engineering Co. (MEC):
www.mecreloaders.com
Midway: www.midwayusa.com
Moly-Bore: www.molybore.com
Montana Bullet Works:
www.montanabulletworks.com
MTM Case-Guard: www.mtmcase-guard.com
NECO: www.neconos.com
NEI : www.neihandtools.com
Neil Jones Custom Products: www.neiljones.com
New Lachaussee SA: www.lachaussee.com
Ponsness/Warren: www.reloaders.com
Quinetics Corp.: www.quineticscorp.com
Ranger Products: www.pages.prodigy.com/ranger-
products.home.htm
Rapine Bullet Mold Mfg Co.: www.bulletmoulds.com
RCBS: www.rcbs.com
Redding Reloading Equipment:
www.redding-reloading.com
Russ Haydon's Shooting Supplies:
www.shooters-supply.com
Sinclair Int'l Inc.: www.sinclairintl.com
Stoney Point Products Inc: www.stoneypoint.com
Thompson Bullet Lube Co.:
www.thompsonbulletlube.com
Vickerman Seating Die: www.castingstuff.com
Wilson (L.E. Wilson): www.lewilson.com

RESTS – BENCH, PORTABLE, ATTACHABLE

Battenfeld Technolgies:
www.battenfeldtechnologies.com
Bench Master: www.bench-master.com
B-Square: www.b-square.com
Bullshooter: www.bullshooterssightingin.com
Center Mass, Inc.: www.centermassinc.com
Desert Mountain Mfg.: www.benchmasterusa.com
Harris Engineering Inc.: www.harrisbipods.com
KFS Industries: www.versapod.com
Kramer Designs: www.snipepod.com
L Thomas Rifle Support: www.ltsupport.com
Level-Lok: www.levellok.com
Midway: www.midwayusa.com
Predator Sniper Styx: www.predatorsniperstyx.com
Ransom International: www.ransom-intl.com
Rotary Gun Racks: www.gun-racks.com
R.W. Hart: www.rwhart.com
Sinclair Intl, Inc.: www.sinclairintl.com
Shooters Ridge: www.shooterridge.com
Stoney Point Products: www.stoneypoint.com
Target Shooting: www.targetshooting.com
Varmint Masters: www.varmintmasters.com
Versa-Pod: www.versa-pod.com

SCOPES, SIGHTS, MOUNTS AND ACCESSORIES

Accumount: www.accumounts.com
Accusight: www.accusight.com
ADCO: www.shooters.com/adco/index/htm
Adirondack Opitcs: www.adkoptics.com
Advantage Tactical Sight:
www.advantagetactical.com
Aimpoint: www.aimpoint.com
Aim Shot, Inc.: www.aimshot.com
Aimtech Mount Systems:
www.aimtech-mounts.com
Alpec Team, Inc.: www.alpec.com
Alpen Outdoor Corp.: www.alpenoutdoor.com
American Technologies Network, Corp.:
www.atncorp.com
AmeriGlo, LLC: www.ameriglo.net
ArmaLaser: www.armalaser.com
Armament Technology, Inc.: www.armament.com
ARMS: www.armsmounts.com
Aro-Tek, Ltd.: www.arotek.com
ATN: www.atncorp.com
Badger Ordnance: www.badgerordnance.com
Barrett: www.barrettrifles.com
Beamshot-Quarton: www.beamshot.com
BKL Technologies, Inc.: www.bkltech.com
BSA Optics: www.bsaoptics.com
B-Square Company, Inc.: www.b-square.com
Burris: www.burrisoptics.com
Bushnell Performance Optics: www.bushnell.com
Carl Zeiss Optical Inc.: www.zeiss.com
Carson Optical: www.carson-optical.com
CenterPoint Precision Optics:
www.centerpointoptics.com
Centurion Arms: www.centurionarms.com
C-More Systems: www.cmore.com
Conetrol Scope Mounts: www.conetrol.com
Crimson Trace Corp.: www.crimsontrace.com
Crossfire L.L.C.: www.amfire.com/hesco/html
Cylinder & Slide, Inc.: www.cylinderslide.com
DCG Supply Inc.: www.dcgsupply.com
D&L Sports: www.dlsports.com
DuraSight Scope Mounting Systems:
www.durasight.com

EasyHit, Inc.: **www.easyhit.com**
EAW: **www.eaw.de**
Elcan Optical Technologies:
    www.armament.com,: www.elcan.com
Electro-Optics Technologies:
    www.eotechmdc.com/holosight
EoTech: **www.eotech-inc.com**
Europtik Ltd.: **www.europtik.com**
Fujinon, Inc.: **www.fujinon.com**
GG&G: **www.w.gggaz.com**
Gilmore Sports: **www.gilmoresports.com**
Gradient Lens Corp.: **www.gradientlens.com**
Hakko Co. Ltd.: **www.hakko-japan.co.jp**
Hahn Precision: **www.hahn-precision.com**
Hesco: **www.hescosights.com**
Hi-Lux Optics: **www.hi-luxoptics.com**
Hitek Industries: **www.nightsight.com**
HIVIZ: **www.hivizsights.com**
Hollands Shooters Supply: **www.hollandguns.com**
Horus Vision: **www.horusvision.com**
Hunter Co.: **www.huntercompany.com**
Innovative Weaponry,Inc.: **www.ptnightsights.com**
Insight: **www.insighttechnology.com**
Ironsighter Co.: **www.ironsighter.com**
ITT Night Vision: **www.ittnightvision.com**
Kahles: **www.kahlesoptik.com**
Knight's Armament: **www.knightarmco.com**
Kowa Optimed Inc.: **www.kowascope.com**
Kwik-Site Co.: **www.kwiksitecorp.com**
L-3 Communications-Eotech: **www.l-3com.com**
LaRue Tactical: **www.laruetactical.com**
Laser Bore Sight: **www.laserboresight.com**
Laser Devices Inc.: **www.laserdevices.com**
Lasergrips: **www.crimsontrace.com**
LaserLyte: **www.laserlytesights.com**
LaserMax Inc.: **www.lasermax.com**
Laser Products: **www.surefire.com**
Leapers, Inc.: **www.leapers.com**
Leatherwood: **www.hi-luxoptics.com**
Legacy Sports: **www.legacysports.com**
Leica Camera Inc.: **www.leica-camera.com/usa**
Leupold: **www.leupold.com**
Lewis Machine & Tool: **www.lewismachine.net**
LightForce/NightForce USA:
    www.nightforcescopes.com
Lyman: **www.lymanproducts.com**
Lynx: **www.b-square.com**
MaTech: **www.adcofirearms.com**
Marble's Outdoors: **www.marblesoutdoors.com**
MDS,Inc.: **www.mdsincorporated.com**
Meopta: **www.meopta.com**
Meprolight: **www.kimberamerica.com**
Micro Sight Co.: **www.microsight.com**
Millett : **www.millettsights.com**
Miniature Machine Corp.: **www.mmcsight.com**
Mini-Scout-Mount: **www.amegaranges.com**
Minox USA: **www.minox.com**
Montana Vintage Arms:
    www.montanavintagearms.com
Moro Vision: **www.morovision.com**
Mounting Solutions Plus: **www.mountsplus.com**
NAIT: **www.nait.com**
Newcon International Ltd.: **www.newcon-optik.com**
Night Force Optics: **www.nightforcescopes.com**
Night Optics USA, Inc.: **www.nightoptics.com**
Night Owl Optics: **www.nightowloptics.com**
Night Vision Systems: **www.nightvisionsystems.com**
Nikon Inc.: **www.nikonhunting.com**
North American Integrated Technologies:
    www.nait.com
O.K. Weber, Inc.: **www.okweber.com**
Optolyth-Optic: **www.optolyth.de**

Osprey Optics: **www.osprey-optics.com**
Pentax Corp.: **www.pentaxlightseeker.com**
Precision Reflex: **www.pri-mounts.com**
Pride Fowler, Inc.: **www.rapidreticle.com**
Premier Reticles: **www.premierreticles.com**
Redfield: **www.redfieldoptics.com**
Rifle Electronics: **www.theriflecam.com**
R&R Int'l Trade: **www.nightoptic.com**
Schmidt & Bender: **www.schmidt-bender.com**
Scopecoat: **www.scopecoat.com**
Scopelevel: **www.scopelevel.com**
Segway Industries: **www.segway-industries.com**
Shepherd Scope Ltd.: **www.shepherdscopes.com**
Sig Sauer: **www.sigsauer.com**
Sightmark: **www.sightmark.com**
Sightron: **www.sightron.com**
Simmons: **www.simmonsoptics.com**
S&K: **www.scopemounts.com**
Springfield Armory: **www.springfield-armory.com**
Sun Optics USA: **www.sunopticsusa.com**
Sure-Fire: **www.surefire.com**
Swarovski/Kahles: **www.swarovskioptik.com**
SWATSCOPE: **www.swatscope.com**
Swift Optics: **www.swiftoptics.com**
Talley Mfg. Co.: **www.talleyrings.com**
Target Scope Blocks-Steve Earl Products:
    www.Steven.m.earle@comcast.net
Tasco: **www.tascosales.com**
Tech Sights: **www.tech-sights.com**
Trijicon Inc.: **www.trijicon.com**
Troy Industries: **www.troyind.com**
Truglo Inc.: **www.truglo.com**
Ultimak: **www.ultimak.com**
UltraDot: **www.ultradotusa.com**
Unertl Optical Co.: **www.unertlopics.com**
US Night Vision: **www.usnightvision.com**
U.S. Optics Technologies Inc.: **www.usoptics.com**
Valdada-IOR Optics: **www.valdada.com**
Viridian Green Laser Sights:
    www.viridiangreenlaser.com
Vortex Optics: **www.vortexoptics.com**
Warne: **www.warnescopemounts.com**
Weaver Mounts: **www.weaver-mounts.com**
Weaver Scopes: **www.weaveroptics.com**
Wilcox Industries Corp.: **www.wilcoxind.com**
Williams Gun Sight Co.: **www.williamsgunsight.com**
Wilson Combat: **www.wilsoncombat.com**
XS Sight Systems: **www.xssights.com**
Zeiss: **www.zeiss.com**

SHOOTING ORGANIZATIONS, SCHOOLS AND RANGES

Amateur Trapshooting Assoc.: **www.shootata.com**
American Custom Gunmakers Guild: **www.acgg.org**
American Gunsmithing Institute:
    www.americangunsmith.com
American Pistolsmiths Guild:
    www.americanpistol.com
American Shooting Sports Council: **www.assc.com**
American Single Shot Rifle Assoc.: **www.assra.com**
American Snipers: **www.americansnipers.org**
Antique Shooting Tool Collector's Assoc.:
    www.oldshootingtools.org
Assoc. of Firearm & Tool Mark Examiners:
    www.afte.org
BATF: **www.atf.ustreas.gov**
Blackwater Lodge and Training Center:
    www.blackwaterlodge.com
Boone and Crockett Club: **www.boone-crockett.org**
Buckmasters, Ltd.: **www.buckmasters.com**
Cast Bullet Assoc.: **www.castbulletassoc.org**

Citizens Committee for the Right to Keep
    & Bear Arms: **www.ccrkba.org**
Civilian Marksmanship Program: **www.odcmp.com**
Colorado School of Trades:
    www.gunsmith-school.com
Cylinder & Slide Pistolsmithing Schools:
    www.cylinder-slide.com
Ducks Unlimited: **www.ducks.org**
4-H Shooting Sports Program:
    www.4-hshootingsports.org
Fifty Caliber Institute: **www.fiftycal.org**
Fifty Caliber Shooters Assoc.: **www.fcsa.org**
Firearms Coalition: **www.nealknox.com**
Front Sight Firearms Training Institute:
    www.frontsight.com
German Gun Collectors Assoc.:
    www.germanguns.com
Gun Clubs: **www.associatedgunclubs.org**
Gun Owners' Action League: **www.goal.org**
Gun Owners of America: **www.gunowners.org**
Gun Trade Asssoc. Ltd.: **www.brucepub.com/gta**
Gunsite Training Center, Inc.: **www.gunsite.com**
Handgun Hunters International:
    www.sskindustries.com
Hunting and Shooting Sports Heritage Fund:
    www.huntandshoot.org
I.C.E. Traing: **www.icetraining.com**
International Defense Pistol Assoc.: **www.idpa.com**
International Handgun Metallic Silhouette Assoc.: **www.
    ihmsa.org**
International Hunter Education Assoc.:
    www.ihea.com
Int'l Law Enforcement Educators and
    Trainers Assoc.: **www.ileeta.com**
International Single Shot Assoc.:
    www.issa-schuetzen.org
Jews for the Preservation of Firearms Ownership: **www.
    jpfo.org**
Mule Deer Foundation: **www.muledeer.org**
Muzzle Loaders Assoc. of Great Britain:
    www.mlagb.com
National 4-H Shooting Sports:
    www.4-hshootingsports.org
National Association of Sporting Goods Wholesalers:
    www.nasgw.org
National Benchrest Shooters Assoc.:
    www.benchrest.com
National Defense Industrial Assoc.: **www.ndia.org**
National Firearms Act Trade & Collectors Assoc.: **www.
    nfatca.org**
National Muzzle Loading Rifle Assoc.: **www.nmlra.org**
National Reloading Manufacturers Assoc:
    www.reload-nrma.com
National Rifle Assoc.: **www.nra.org**
National Rifle Assoc. ILA: **www.nraila.org**
National Shooting Sports Foundation: **www.nssf.org**
National Skeet Shooters Association:
    www.nssa-nsca.com
National Sporting Clays Assoc.: **www.nssa-nsca.com**
National Tactial Officers Assoc.: **www.ntoa.org**
National Wild Turkey Federation: **www.nwtf.com**
NICS/FBI: **www.fbi.gov**
North American Hunting Club: **www.huntingclub.com**
Order of Edwardian Gunners (Vintagers):
    www.vintagers.org
Outdoor Industry Foundation:
    www.outdoorindustryfoundation.org
Pennsylvania Gunsmith School:
    www.pagunsmith.com
Piedmont Community College: **www.piedmontcc.edu**
Quail Unlimited: **www.qu.org**

Remington Society of America:
   www.remingtonsociety.com
Right To Keep and Bear Arms: **www.rkba.org**
Rocky Mountain Elk Foundation: **www.rmef.org**
SAAMI: **www.saami.org**
Safari Club International: **www.scifirstforhunters.org**
Scholastic Clay Target Program: **www.nssf.org/sctp**
Scholastic Shooting Sports Foudnation:
   www.shootsctp.com
Second Amendment Foundation: **www.saf.org**
Second Amendment Sisters: **www.2asisters.org**
Shooting for Women Alliance:
   www.shootingforwomenalliance.com
Shooting Ranges Int'l: **www.shootingranges.com**
Sig Sauer Academy: **www.sigsauer.com**
Single Action Shooting Society: **www.sassnet.com**
Steel Challenge Pistol Tournament:
   www.steelchallenge.com
Students for Second Amendment: **www.sf2a.org**
Sturgis Economic Developemtn Corp.:
   www.sturgisdevelopment.com
Suarez Training: **www.warriortalk.com**
S&W Academy and Nat'l Firearms Trng. Center:
   www.sw-academy.com
Tactical Defense Institute: **www.tdiohio.com**
Tactical Life: **www.tactical-life.com**
Ted Nugent United Sportsmen of America:
   www.tnugent.com
Thunder Ranch: **www.thunderranchinc.com**
Trapshooters Homepage: **www.trapshooters.com**
Trinidad State Junior College: **www.trinidadstate.edu**
United Sportsmen's Youth Foundation: **www.usyf.org**
Universal Shooting Academy:
   www.universalshootingacademy.com
U.S. Concealed Carry Association: **www.uscca.us**
U.S. Int'l Clay Target Assoc.: **www.usicta.com**
U.S. Fish and Wildlife Service: **www.fws.gov**
U.S. Practical Shooting Assoc.: **www.uspsa.org**
U.S. Sportsmen's Alliance: **www.ussportsmen.org**
USA Shooting: **www.usashooting.com**
Varmint Hunter's Assoc.: **www.varminthunter.org**
Winchester Arms Collectors Assoc.:
   www.winchestercollector.com
Women Hunters: **www.womanhunters.com**
Women's Shooting Sports Foundation: **www.wssf.org**

STOCKS, GRIPS, FOREARMS

Ace, Ltd.: **www.aceltdusa.com**
Advanced Technology: **www.atigunstocks.com**
Battenfeld Technologies:
   www.battenfeldtechnologies.com
Bell & Carlson, Inc.: **www.bellandcarlson.com**
Boyd's Gunstock Industries, Inc.:
   www.boydgunstocks.com
Butler Creek Corp: **www.butler-creek.com**
Cadex: **www.vikingtactics.com**
Calico Hardwoods, Inc.: **www.calicohardwoods.com**
Choate Machine: **www.riflestock.com**
Command Arms: **www.commandarms.com**
C-More Systems: **www.cmore.com**
D&L Sports: **www.dlsports.com**
Duo Stock: **www.duostock.com**
Elk Ridge Stocks:
   www.reamerrentals.com/elk_ridge.htm
FAB Tactical: **www.botachtactical.com**
Fajen: **www.battenfeldtechnologies.com**
Falcon Ergo Grip: **www.ergogrips.com**
Great American Gunstocks: **www.gunstocks.com**
Grip Pod: **www.grippod.com**
Gun Stock Blanks: **www.gunstockblanks.com**
Herrett's Stocks: **www.herrettstocks.com**

High Tech Specialties:
   www.bansnersrifle.com/hightech
Hogue Grips: **www.getgrip.com**
Holland's Shooting Supplies: **www.hollandgun.com**
Knight's Mfg. Co.: **wwwknightarmco.com**
Knoxx Industries: **www.blackhawk.com**
KZ Tactical: **www.kleyzion.com**
LaRue Tactical: **www.laruetactical.com**
Laser Stock: **www.laserstock.com**
Lewis Machine & Tool: **www.lewismachine.net**
Lone Wolf: **www.lonewolfriflestocks.com**
Magpul: **www.magpul.com**
Manners Compostie Stocks:
   www.mannerstocks.com
McMillan Fiberglass Stocks: **www.mcmfamily.com**
MPI Stocks: **www.mpistocks.com**
Precision Gun Works: **www.precisiongunstocks.com**
Ram-Line: **www.outers-guncare.com**
Richards Microfit Stocks: **www.rifle-stocks.com**
Rimrock Rifle Stock: **www.rimrockstocks.com**
Royal Arms Gunstocks: **www.imt.net/~royalarms**
S&K Industries: **www.sandkgunstocks.com**
Speedfeed: **www.safariland.com**
TacStar/Pachmayr : **www.tacstar.com**
Tango Down: **www.tangodown.com**
TAPCO: **www.tapco.com**
Surefire: **www.surefire.com**
Tiger-Hunt Curly Maple Gunstocks:
   www.gunstockwood.com
Vltor: **www.vltor.com**
Wenig Custom Gunstocks Inc.: **www.wenig.com**
Wilcox Industries: **www.wilcoxind.com**
Yankee Hill: **www.yhm.net**

TARGETS AND RANGE EQUIPMENT

Action Target Co.: **www.actiontarget.com**
Advanced Interactive Systems: **www.ais-sim.com**
Birchwood Casey: **www.birchwoodcasey.com**
Bullet Proof Electronics: **www.thesnipertarget.com**
Caswell Meggitt Defense Systems:
   www.mds-caswell.com
Champion Traps & Targets:
   www.championtarget.com
Handloader/Victory Targets:
   www.targetshandloader.com
Just Shoot Me Products: **www.ballistictec.com**
Laser Shot: **www.lasershot.com**
Mountain Plains Industries:
   www.targetshandloader.com
MTM Products: **www.mtmcase-gard.com**
Natiional Target Co.: **www.nationaltarget.com**
Newbold Target Systems: **www.newboldtargets.com**
Porta Target,Inc.: **www.portatarget.com**
Range Management Services Inc.:
   www.casewellintl.com
Range Systems: **www.shootingrangeproducts.com**
Reactive Target Systems Inc.:
   www.chrts@primenet.com
ShatterBlast Targets: **www.daisy.com**
Super Trap Bullet Containment Systems:
   www.supertrap.com
Thompson Target Technology:
   www.thompsontarget.com
Tombstone Tactical Targets: **www.tttargets.com**
Visible Impact Targets: **www.crosman.com**
White Flyer: **www.whiteflyer.com**

TRAP AND SKEET SHOOTING EQUIPMENT AND ACCESSORIES

Auto-Sporter Industries: **www.auto-sporter.com**

10X Products Group: **www.10Xwear.com**
Claymaster Traps: **www.claymaster.com**
Do-All Traps, Inc.: **www.doalloutdoors.com**
Laporte USA: **www.laporte-shooting.com**
Outers: **www.blount.com**
Promatic, Inc.: **www.promatic.biz**
Trius Products Inc.: **www.triustraps.com**
White Flyer: **www.whiteflyer.com**

TRIGGERS

American Trigger Corp.: **www.americantrigger.com**
Brownells: **www.brownells.com**
Chip McCormick Corp.:
   www.chipmccormickcorp.com
E-Z Pull Triggers: **www.ezpulltriggerassist.com**
Geissele Automatics, LLC: **www.ar15triggers.com**
Huber Concepts: **www.huberconcepts.com**
Kidd Triggers.: **www.coolguyguns.com**
Shilen: **www.shilen.com**
Timney Triggers: **www.timneytrigger.com**
Williams Trigger Specialties:
   www.williamstriggers.com

MAJOR SHOOTING WEB SITES AND LINKS

24 Hour Campfire: **www.24hourcampfire.com**
Alphabetic Index of Links: **www.gunsgunsguns.com**
Auction Arms: **www.auctionarms.com**
Benchrest Central: **www.benchrest.com**
Big Game Hunt: **www.biggamehunt.net**
Bullseye Pistol: **www.bullseyepistol.com**
Firearms History:
   www.researchpress.co.uk/firearms
Glock Talk: **www.glocktalk.com**
Gun Broker Auctions: **www.gunbroker.com**
Gun Industry: **www.gunindustry.com**
Gun Blast: **www.gunblast.com**
Gun Boards: **www.gunboards.com**
GunsAmerica.com: **www.gunsamerica.com**
Guns Unified Nationally Endorsing Dignity:
   www.guned.com
Gun Shop Finder: **www.gunshopfinder.com**
GUNS and Hunting: **www.gunsandhunting.com**
Hunt and Shoot (NSSF): **www.huntandshoot.org**
Keep and Bear Arms: **www.keepandbeararms.com**
Leverguns: **www.leverguns.com**
Load Swap: **www.loadswap.com**
Outdoor Press Room: **www.outdoorpressroom.com**
Real Guns: **www.realguns.com**
Ruger Forum: **www.rugerforum.com**
SavageShooters: **www.savageshooters.com**
Shooters Forum: **www.shootersforum.com**
Shotgun Sports Resource Guide:
   www.shotgunsports.com
Sixgunner: **www.sixgunner.com**
Sniper's Hide: **www.snipershide.com**
Sportsman's Web: **www.sportsmansweb.com**
Surplus Rifles: **www.surplusrifle.com**
Tactical-Life: **www.tactical-life.com**
Wing Shoooting USA: **www.wingshootingusa.org**

A

A. Uberti S.p.A., Via Artigiana 1, Gardone Val Trompia, Brescia 25063, ITALY, P: 011 390308341800, F: 011 390308341801, www.ubertireplicas.it
Firearms

A.R.M.S., Inc./Atlantic Research Marketing Systems, Inc., 230 W. Center St., West Bridgewater, MA 02379, P: 508-584-7816, F: 508-588-8045, www.armsmounts.com
Scopes, Sights and Accessories

AA & E Leathercraft, 107 W. Gonzales St., Yoakum, TX 77995, P: 800-331-9092, F: 361-293-9127, www.tandybrands.com
Bags & Equipment Cases; Custom Manufacturing; Hunting Accessories; Knives/Knife Cases; Leathergoods; Shooting Range Equipment; Sports Accessories

ACIGI / Fujiiryoki, 4399 Ingot St., Fremong, CA 94538, P: 888-816-0888, F: 510-651-6188, www.fujichair.com
Wholesaler/Distributor

ACR Electronics, Inc., 5757 Ravenswood Rd., Ft. Lauderdale, FL 33312, P: 800-432-0227, F: 954-983-5087, www.acrelectronics.com
Backpacking; Hunting Accessories; Lighting Products; Sports Accessories; Survival Kits/First Aid; Training and Safety Equipment

Accro-Met, Inc., 3406 Westwood Industrial Drive, Monroe, NC 28110, P: 800-543-4755, F: 704-283-2112, www.accromet.com
Gun Barrels; Wholesaler/Distributor

Accu-Fire, Inc., P.O. Box 121990, Arlington, TX 76012, P: 888-MUZZLEMATE, F: 817-303-4505
Firearms Maintenance Equipment

Accu-Shot/B&T Industries, LLC, P.O. Box 771071, Wichita, KS 67277, P: 316-721-3222, F: 316-721-1021, www.accu-shot.com
Gun Grips & Stocks; Hunting Accessories; Law Enforcement; Scopes, Sights & Accessories; Shooting Range Equipment; Sports Accessories; Training and Safety Equipment

Accuracy International North America, Inc., 35100 North State Highway, Mingus, TX 76463-6405, P: 907-440-4024, www.accuracyinternational.org
Firearms; Firearms Maintenance Equipment; Law Enforcement; Magazines, Cartridge; Scopes, Sights & Accessories; Wholesaler/Distributor

AccuSharp Knife Sharpeners/Fortune Products, Inc., 205 Hickory Creek Road, Marble Falls, TX 78654, P: 800-742-7797, F: 800-600-5373, www.accusharp.com
Archery; Camping; Cooking Equipment/Accessories; Cutlery; Hunting Accessories; Knives/Knife Cases; Sharpeners; Sports Accessories

Action Target, P.O. Box 636, Provo, UT 84603-0636, P: 888-377-8033, F: 801-377-8096, www.actiontarget.com
Law Enforcement; Shooting Range Equipment; Targets; Training & Safety Equipment

AcuSport Corp., One Hunter Place, Bellefontaine, OH 43311, P: 800-543-3150, www.acusport.com
Ammunition; Black Powder Accessories; Firearms; Hunting Accessories; Online Services; Retailer Services; Scopes, Sights & Accessories; Wholesaler/Distributor

Adams Arms/Retrofit Piston Systems, 255 Hedden Court, Palm Harbor, FL 34681, P: 727-853-0550, F: 727-353-0551, www.arisfix.com

ADCO Arms Co., Inc., 4 Draper St., Woburn, MA 01801, P: 800-775-3687, F: 781-935-1011, www.adcosales.com
Ammunition; Firearms; Paintball Accessories, Scopes, Sights & Accessories

ADS, Inc., Pinehurst Centre, 477 Viking Dr., Suite 350, Virginia Beach, VA 23452, P: 800-948-9433, F: 757-481-2039, www.adstactical.com

ADSTAR, Inc., 1390 Jerusalem Ave., North Merrick, NY 11566, P: 516-483-1800, F: 516-483-2590
Emblems & Decals; Outdoor Art, Jewelry, Sculpture

Advanced Armament Corp., 1434 Hillcrest Rd., Norcross, GA 30093, P: 770-925-9988, F: 770-925-9989, www.advanced-armament.com
Firearms; Hearing Protection; Law Enforcement

Advanced Engineered Systems, Inc., 14328 Commercial Parkway, South Beloit, IL 61080, P: 815-624-7797, F: 815-624-8198, www.advengsys.com
Ammunition; Custom Manufacturing

Advanced Technology International, 2733 W. Carmen Ave., Milwaukee, WI 53209, P: 800-925-2522, F: 414-664-3112, www.atigunstocks.com
Books/Industry Publications; Gun Grips & Stocks; Gun Parts/Gunsmithing; Hunting Accessories; Law Enforcement; Scopes, Sights & Accessories

Advanced Training Systems, 4524 Highway 61 North, St. Paul, MN 55110, P: 651-429-8091, F: 651-429-8702, www.duelatron.com
Law Enforcement; Shooting Range Equipment; Targets; Training & Safety Equipment

Advantage® Camouflage, P.O. Box 9638, Columbus, GA 31908, P: 800-992-9968, F: 706-569-9346, www.advantagecamo.com
Camouflage

Advantage Tactical Sight/WrenTech Industries, LLC, 7 Avenida Vista Grande B-7, Suite 510, Sante Fe, NM 87508, F: 310-316-6413 or 505-466-1811, F: 505-466-4735, www.advantagetactical.com
Scopes, Sights & Accessories

Adventure Action Gear/+VENTURE Heated Clothing, 5932 Bolsa Ave., Suite 103, Huntington Beach, CA 92649, P: 310-412-1070, F: 610-423-5257, www.ventureheat.com
Men & Women's Clothing; Export/Import Specialists; Footwear; Gloves, Mitts, Hats; Sports Accessories; Vehicles, Utility & Rec.; Wholesaler/Distributor

Adventure Lights, Inc., 444 Beaconsfield Blvd., Suite 201, Beaconsfield, Quebec H9W 4C1, CANADA, P: 514-694-8477, F: 514-694-2353

Adventure Medical Kits, P.O. Box 43309, Oakland, CA 94624, P: 800-324-3517, F: 510-261-7419, www.adventuremedicalkits.com
Backpacking; Books/Industry Publications; Camping; Custom Manufacturing; Hunting Accessories; Sports Accessories; Survival Kits/First Aid; Training & Safety Equipment

AE Light/Div. of Allsman Enterprises, LLC, P.O. Box 1869, Rogue River, OR 97537, P: 541-471-8988, F: 888-252-1473, www.aelight.com
Camping; Custom Manufacturing; Hunting Accessories; Law Enforcement; Lighting Products; Wholesale/Distributor

AES Optics, 201 Corporate Court, Senatobia, MS 38668, P: 800-416-0866, F: 662-301-4739, www.aesoutdoors.com
Eyewear

Aetco, Inc., 2825 Metropolitan Place, Pomona, CA 91767, P: 800-982-5258, F: 800-451-2434, www.aetcoinc.com
Firearms; Hearing Protection; Holsters; Law Enforcement; Leathergoods; Lighting Products; Training & Safety Equipment; Wholesaler/Distributor

Africa Sport Hunting Safaris, 11265 E. Edison St., Tucson, AZ 85749, P: 520-440-5384, F: 520-885-8032, www.africasporthuntingsafaris.com
Archery; Outdoor Art, Jewelry, Sculpture; Outfitter; Tours/Travel

AFTCO Bluewater/Al Agnew, 17351 Murphy Ave., Irvine, CA 92614, P: 949-660-8757, F: 949-660-7067, www.aftcobluewater.com

Aftermath Miami/Stunt Studios, 3911 Southwest 47th Ave., Suite 914, Davie, FL 33314, P: 954-581-5822, F: 954-581-3165, www.aftermathairsoft.com
Airsoft Guns & Accessories

Aguila Ammunition/Centurion Ordnance, Inc., 11614 Rainbow Ridge, Helotes, TX 78023, P: 210-695-4602, F: 210-695-4603, www.aguilaammo.com
Ammunition

Aimpoint, Inc., 14103 Mariah Court, Chantilly, VA 20151, 877-246-7646, F: 703-263-9463, www.aimpoint.com
Scopes, Sights & Accessories

AimShot/Osprey International, Inc., 25 Hawks Farm Rd., White, GA 30184, P: 888-448-3247, F: 770-387-0114, www.aimshot.com, www.miniosprey.com
Archery; Binoculars; Holsters; Hunting Accessories; Law Enforcement; Lighting Products; Scopes, Sights & Accessories; Wholesaler/Distributor

Aimtech Mount Systems, P.O. Box 223, Thomasville, GA 31799-0223, P: 229-226-4313, F: 229-227-0222, www.aimtech-mounts.com
Hunting Accessories; Scopes, Sights & Accessories

Air Gun, Inc., 9320 Harwin Dr., Houston, TX 77036, P: 800-456-0021, F: 713-780-4831, www.airrifle-china.com
Airguns; Ammunition; Hunting Accessories; Scopes, Sights & Accessories; Wholesaler/Distributor

AirForce Airguns, P.O. Box 2478, Fort Worth, TX 76113, P: 877-247-4867, F: 817-451-1613, www.airforceairguns.com
Airguns; Hunting Accessories; Law Enforcement; Scopes, Sights & Accessories

Aitec Co., Ltd., Export Dept., Rm. 817, Crystal Beach ok, Jung Dong Haeundae-Gu Busan, 612 010, SOUTH KOREA, P: 011 82517416497, F: 011 82517462194, www.aitec.co.kr
Lighting Products

Ajax Custom Grips, Inc./Ajax Shooter Supply, 9130 Viscount Row, Dallas, TX 75247, P: 800-527-7537, F: 214-630-4942, www.ajaxgrips.com
Gun Grips & Stocks; Gun Parts/Gunsmithing; Holsters; Law Enforcement; Lighting Products; Magazines, Cartridge; Wholesaler/Distributor

AKDAL/Ucyildiz Arms Ind./Blow & Voltran, Bostanci Cd. Uol Sk. No: 14/A, Y. Dudullu-Umraniye, Istanbul, 34775, TURKEY, P: 011-90 216527671011, F: 011-90 2165276705, www.akdalarms.com, www.voltranarms.com
Airguns; Firearms

Aker International, Inc., 2248 Main St., Suite 6, Chula Vista, CA 91911, P: 800-645-AKER, F: 888-300-AKER, www.akerleather.com
Holsters; Hunting Accessories; Law Enforcement; Leathergoods

Al Mar Knives, P.O. Box 2295, Tualatin, OR 97062, P: 503-670-9080, www.almarknives.com
Custom Manufacturing, Knives/Knife Cases

Alexander Arms, U.S. Army Radford Arsenal, Radford, VA 24141, P: 540-639-8356, F: 540-639-8353, www.alexanderarms.com
Ammunition; Firearms; Magazine, Cartridges; Reloading

All-Star Apparel, 6722 Vista Del Mar Ave., Suite C. La Jolla, CA 92037, P: 858-205-7827, F: 858-225-3544, www.all-star.ws
Camouflage; Men & Women's Clothing; Gloves, Mitts, Hats

All Weather Outerwear, 34 35th St., Brooklyn, NY 11232, P: 800-965-6550, F: 718-788-2205
Camouflage; Men's Clothing

AllClear, LLC dba Auspit Rotisserie BBQ's, 2050 Russett Way, Carson City, NV 89703, P: 775-468-5665, F: 775-546-6091, www.auspitbbq.com

Allen Company, 525 Burbank St., P.O. Box 445, Broomfield, CO 80020, P: 800-876-8600, F: 303-466-7437, www.allencompany.net
Archery; Black Powder Accessories; Eyewear; Gun Cases; Hearing Protection; Hunting Accessories; Scopes, Sights & Accessories; Shooting Range Equipment

Alliant Powder/ATK Commercial Products, Route 114, Building 229, P.O. Box 6, Radford, VA 24143, P: 800-276-9337, F: 540-639-8496, www.alliantpowder.com
Reloading

Alot Enterprise Company, Ltd., 1503 Eastwood Centre, 5 A Kung Ngam Village Rd., Shaukeiwan, HONG KONG, P: 011 85225199728, F: 011 85225190122, www.alothk.com
Binoculars; Compasses; Eyewear; Hunting Accessories; Photographic Equipment; Scopes, Sights, & Accessories; Sports Accessories; Telescopes

Alpen Outdoor Corp., 10329 Dorset St., Rancho Cucamonga, CA 91730, P: 877-987-8379, F: 909-987-8661, www.alpenoutdoor.com
Backpacking; Binoculars; Camping; Hunting Accessories; Scopes, Sights & Accessories; Shooting Range Equipment; Sports Accessories, Wholesaler/Distributor

Alpine Archery, P.O. Box 319, Lewiston, ID 83501, P: 208-746-4717, F: 208-746-1635

ALPS Mountaineering, 1 White Pine, New Haven, MO 63068, P: 800-344-2577, F: 573-459-2044, www.alpsouthdoorz.com
Backpacking; Camouflage; Camping; Hunting Accessories; Sports Accessories

ALS Technologies, Inc., 1103 Central Blvd., P.O. Box 525, Bull Shoals, AR 72619, P: 877-902-4257, F: 870-445-8746, www.alslesslethal.com
Ammunition; Firearms; Gun Parts/Gunsmithing; Law Enforcement; Training & Safety Equipment

Alta Industries, 1460 Cader Lane, Petaluma, CA 94954, P: 707-347-2900, F: 707-347-2950, www.altaindustries.com

Altama Footwear, 1200 Lake Hearn Dr., Suite 475, Atlanta, GA 30319, P: 800-437-9888, F: 404-260-2889, www.altama. com
Footwear; Law Enforcement

Altamont Co., 291 N. Church St., P.O. Box 309, Thomasboro, IL 61878, P: 800-626-5774, F: 217-643-7973, www. altamontco.com
Gun Grips & Stocks

AlumaGrips, 2851 N. 34th Place, Mesa, AZ 85213, P: 602-690-5459, F: 480-807-3955
Firearms Maintenance Equipment; Gun Grips & Stocks; Gun Parts/Gunsmithing; Law Enforcement

AmChar Wholesale, Inc., 100 Airpark Dr., Rochester, NY 14624, P: 585-328-3951, F: 585-328-3749, www.amchar. com

American COP Magazine/FMG Publications, 12345 World Trade Dr., San Diego, CA 92128, P: 800-537-3006, F: 858-605-0247, www.americancopmagazine.com
Books/Industry Publications; Law Enforcement; Videos

American Cord & Webbing Co., Inc., 88 Century Dr., Woonsocket, RI 02895, P: 401-762-5500, F: 401-762-5514, www.acw1.com
Archery; Backpacking; Bags & Equipment Cases; Custom Manufacturing; Law Enforcement; Pet Supplies

American Defense Systems, Inc., 230 Duffy Ave., Hicksville, NY 11801, P: 516-390-5300, F: 516-390-5308, www. adsiarmor.com
Custom Manufacturing; Shooting Range Equipment; Training & Safety Equipment

American Furniture Classics/Div. of Dawson Heritage Furniture, P.O. Box 111, Webb City, MO 64870, P: 888-673-9080, F: 417-673-9081, www. americanfurnitureclassics.com
Gun Cabinets/Racks/Safes; Gun Cases; Home Furnishings

American Gunsmithing Institute (AGI), 1325 Imola Ave. West, P.O. Box 504, Napa, CA 94559, P: 800-797-0867, F: 707-253-7149, www.americangunsmith.com
Books/Industry Publications; Computer Software; Firearms Maintenance Equipment; Gun Parts/ Gunsmithing; Videos

American Pioneer Powder, Inc., 20423 State Road 7, Suite F6-268, Boca Raton, FL 33498, P: 888-756-7693, F: 888-766-7693, www.americanpioneerpowder.com
Black Powder/Smokeless Powder; Reloading

American Plastics/SEWIT, 1225 N. MacArthur Drive, Suite 200, Tracy, CA 95376, P: 209-834-0287, F: 209-834-0924, www.americanplastics.com
Backpacking; Bags & Equipment Cases; Export/ Import Specialists; Gun Cases; Holsters; Hunting Accessories; Survival Kits/First Aid; Wholesaler/ Distributor

American Security Products Co., 11925 Pacific Ave., Fontana, CA 92337, P: 800-421-6142, F: 951-685-9685, www. amsecusa.com
Gun Cabinets/Racks/Safes

American Tactical Imports, 100 Airpark Dr., Rochester, NY 14624, P: 585-328-3951, F: 585-328-3749

American Technologies Network, Corp./ATN, Corp., 1341 San Mateo Ave., South San Francisco, CA 94080, P: 800-910-2862, F: 650-875-0129, www.atncorp.com
Binoculars; Law Enforcement; Lighting Products; Photographic Equipment; Scopes, Sights & Accessories; Telescopes

Americase, Inc., 1610 E. Main St., Waxahachie, TX 75165, P: 800-972-2737, F: 972-937-8373, www.americase.com
Bags & Equipment Cases; Custom Manufacturing; Gun Cases; Hunting Accessories

AmeriGlo, 5579-B Chamblee Dunwoody Rd., Suite 214, Atlanta, GA 30338, P: 770-390-0554, F: 770-390-9781, www.ameriglo.com
Camping; Law Enforcement; Lighting Products; Scopes, Sights & Accessories; Survival Kits/First Aid; Training & Safety Equipment

Ameristep, 901 Tacoma Court, Clio, MI 48420, P: 800-374-7837, F: 810-686-7121, www.ameristep.com
Archery; Blinds; Hunting Accessories; Training & Safety Equipment; Treestands

Ammo-Loan Worldwide, 815 D, Lewiston, ID 83501, P: 208-746-7012, F: 208-746-1703

Ammo-Up, 10601 Theresa Dr., Jacksonville, FL 32246, P: 800-940-2688, F: 904-645-5918, www.ammoupusa.com
Shooting Range Equipment

AMT/Auto Mag Co./C.G., Inc., 5200 Mitchelldale, Suite E17, Houston, TX 77092, P: 713-686-3232, F: 713-681-5665

Anglers Book Supply/Hunters & Shooters Book & DVD Catalog, 1380 W. 2nd Ave., Eugene, OR 97402, P: 800-260-3869, F: 541-342-1785, www.anglersbooksupply.com

Books/Industry Publications; Computer Software; Videos; Wholesaler/Distributor

ANXO-Urban Body Armor Corp., 7359 Northwest 34 St., Miami, FL 33122, P: 866-514-ANXO, F: 305-593-5498, www.urbanbodyarmor.com
Men & Women's Clothing; Custom Manufacturing; Law Enforcement

Apple Creek Whitetails, 14109 Cty. Rd. VV, Gillett, WI 54124, P: 920-598-0154, F: 920-855-1773, www. applecreekwhitetails.com

ARC/ArcticShield, Inc./X-System, 1700 West Albany, Suite A, Broken Arrow, OK 74012, P: 877-974-4353, F: 918-258-8790, www.arcoutdoors.com
Footwear; Hunting Accessories; Scents & Lures; Sports Accessories

Arc'Teryx, 100-2155 Dollarton Hwy., North Vancouver, British Columbia V7H 3B2, CANADA, P: 604-960-3001, F: 604-904-3692, www.arcteryx.com
Backpacking; Camouflage; Men's Clothing; Custom Manufacturing; Gloves, Mitts, Hats; Law Enforcement; Outfitter

Arctic Adventures, 19950 Clark Graham, Baie D'urfe, Quebec H9X 3R8, CANADA, P: 800-465-9474, F: 514-457-9834, www.arcticadventures.ca
Outfitter

Ares Defense Systems, Inc., P.O. Box 10667, Blacksburg, VA 24062, P: 540-639-8633, F: 540-639-8634, www. aresdefense.com
Firearms; Gun Parts/Gunsmithing; Law Enforcement; Lighting Products; Magazines, Cartridge; Scopes, Sights & Accessories; Shooting Range Equipment; Survival Kits/First Aid

Argentina Ducks & Doves LLC, P.O. Box 129, Pittsview, AL 36871, P: 334-855-9474, F: 334-855-9474, www. argentinaducksanddoves.com
Outfitter; Tours/Travel

ArmaLite, Inc., 745 S. Hanford St., Geneseo, IL 61254, P: 309-944-6939, F: 309-944-6949, www.armalite.com
Firearms; Firearms Maintenance Equipment

Armament Technology, Inc./ELCAN Optical Technologies, 3045 Robie St., Suite 113, Halifax, Nova Scotia B3K 4P6, CANADA, P: 902-454-6384, F: 902-454-4641, www. armament.com
International Exhibitors; Law Enforcement; Scopes, Sights & Accessories; Telescopes; Wholesaler/ Distributor

Armatix GmbH, Feringastrabe. 4, Unterfohring, D 85774, GERMANY, P: 011 498999228140, F: 011 498999228228, www.armatix.de

Armi Sport di Chiappa Silvia e C. SNC-Chiappa Firearms, Via Milano, 2, Azzano Mella (Bs), 25020, ITALY, P: 011-39 0309749065, F: 011-39 0309749232, www. chiappafirearms.com
Black Powder Accessories; Firearms; International Exhibitors

Armor Express, 1554 E. Torch Lake Dr., P.O. Box 21, Central Lake, MI 49622, P: 866-357-3845, F: 231-544-6734, www. armorexpress.com
Law Enforcement

Armorshield USA, LLC, 30 ArmorShield Dr., Stearns, KY 42647, P: 800-386-9455, F: 800-392-9455, www. armorshield.net
Law Enforcement

Arms Corp. of the Philippines/Armscor Precision International, Armscorp Ave., Bgy Fortune, Marikina City, 1800, PHILIPPINES, P: 011 6329416243, F: 011 6329420682, www.armscor.com.ph
Airguns; Ammunition; Bags & Equipment Cases; Custom Manufacturing; Firearms; Gun Barrels; Gun Parts/Gunsmithing; International Exhibitors

Arms Tech, Ltd., 5025 North Central Ave., Suite 459, Phoenix, AZ 85012, P: 602-272-9045, F: 602-272-1922, www. armstechltd.com
Firearms; Law Enforcement

Arno Bernard Custom Knives, 19 Duiker St., Bethlehem, 9700, SOUTH AFRICA, P: 011 27583033196, F: 011 27583033196

Arrieta, Morkaiko, 5, Elgoibar, (Guipuzcoa) 20870, SPAIN, P: 011-34 943743150, F: 011-34 943743154, www. arrietashotguns.com
Firearms

Arrow Precision, LLC, 2750 W. Gordon St., Allentown, PA 18104, P: 610-437-7138, F: 610-437-7139, www.arrow-precision.com
Archery; Crossbows & Accessories; Paintballs, Guns & Accessories

ARS Business Solutions, LLC, 940 Industrial Dr., Suite 107, Sauk Rapids, MN 56379, P: 800-547-7120, www.arss.com
Computer Software; Retailer Services

Arsenal, Inc., 3300 S. Decatur Blvd., Suite 10632, Las Vegas, NV 89102, P: 888-539-2220, F: 702-643-8860, www. arsenalinc.com
Firearms

Artistic Plating Co., 405 W. Cherry St., Milwaukee, WI 53212, P: 414-271-8138, F: 414-271-5541, www.artisticplating.net
Airguns; Ammunition; Archery; Cutlery; Firearms; Game Calls; Gun Barrels; Reloading

ARY, Inc., 10301 Hickman Mills Dr., Suite 110, Kansas City, MO 64137, P: 800-821-7849, F: 816-761-0055, www. aryinc.com
Cutlery; Knives/Knife Cases

ASAT Outdoors, LLC, 307 E. Park Ave., Suite 207A, Anaconda, MT 59711, P: 406-563-9336, F: 406-563-7315
Archery; Blinds; Camouflage; Men's Clothing; Gloves, Mitts, Hats; Hunting Accessories; Law Enforcement; Paintball Accessories

Ashbury International Group, Inc., P.O. Box 8024, Charlottesville, VA 22906, P: 434-296-8600, F: 434-296-9260, www.ashburyintlgroup.com
Camouflage; Firearms; Law Enforcement; Scopes, Sights & Accessories; Wholesaler/Distributor

Asociacion Armera, P. I Azitain, 2-J, P.O. Box 277, Eibar, Guipúzcoa 20600, SPAIN, P: 011 34943208493, F: 011 34943700966, www.a-armera.com
Associations/Agencies

ASP, Inc., 2511 E. Capitol Dr., Appleton, WI 54911, P: 800-236-6243, F: 800-236-8601, www.asp-usa.com
Law Enforcement; Lighting Products; Training & Safety Equipment

A-Square Company/A-Square of South Dakota, LLC, 302 Antelope Dr., Chamberlain, SD 57325, P: 605-234-0500, F: 605-234-0510, www.asquareco.com
Ammunition; Books/Industry Publications; Firearms; Reloading

Astra Radio Communications, 2238 N. Glassell St., Suite D., Orange, CA 92865, P: 714-637-2828, F: 714-637-2669, www.arcmics.com
Two-Way Radios

Atak Arms Ind., Co. Ltd., Imes San. Sit. A Blok 107, Sk. No: 70, Y. Dudullu, Umraniye, Istanbul, 34775 TURKEY, P: +902164203996, F: +902164203998, www.atakarms.com
Airguns; Firearms; Training & Safety Equipment

Atascosa Wildlife Supply, 1204 Zanderson Ave., Jourdanton, TX 78026, P: 830-769-9711, F: 830-769-1001

ATK/ATK Commercial Products, 900 Ehlen Dr., Anoka, MN 55303, P: 800-322-2342, F: 763-323-2506, www.atk.com
Ammunition; Binoculars; Clay Targets; Firearms Maintenance Equipment; Reloading; Scopes, Sights & Accessories; Shooting Range Equipment; Targets

ATK /ATK Law Enforcement, 2299 Snake River Ave., Lewiston, ID 83501, P: 800-627-3640, F: 208-798-3392, www.atk. com
Ammunition; Bags & Equipment Cases; Binoculars; Firearms Maintenance Equipment; Reloading; Scopes, Sights & Accessories

Atlanco, 1125 Hayes Industrial Dr., Marietta, GA 30062-2471, P: 800-241-9414, F: 770-427-9011, www.truspec.com
Camouflage; Men's Clothing; Custom Manufacturing; Law Enforcement; Wholesaler/Distributor

Atlanta Cutlery Corp., 2147 Gees Mill Rd., Conyers, GA 30013, P: 800-883-8838, F: 770-760-8993, www. atlantacutlery.com
Custom Manufacturing; Cutlery; Firearms; Holsters; Knives/Knife Cases; Leathergoods; Wholesaler/ Distributor

Atlas Glove Consumer Products/LFS, Inc., 851 Coho Way, Bellingham, WA 98225, P: 800-426-8860, F: 888-571-8175, www.lfsinc.com/atlasoutdoor
Gloves, Mitts, Hats

Atsko, 2664 Russel St., Orangeburg, SC 29115, P: 800-845-2728, F: 803-531-2139, www.atsko.com
Archery; Backpacking; Camouflage; Camping; Custom Manufacturing; Hunting Accessories; Scents & Lures

AuctionArms.com, Inc., 3031 Alhambra Dr., Suite 101, Cameron Park, CA 95682, P: 877-GUN-AUCTION, F: 530-676-2497, www.auctionarms.com
Airguns; Archery; Black Powder Accessories; Black Powder/Smokeless Powder; Camping; Firearms; Online Services

Autumnwood Wool Outfitters, Inc., 828 Upper Pennsylvania Ave., Bangor, PA 18013, P: 610-588-5744, F: 610-588-4868, www.autumnwoodoutfitters.com

Avon Protection Systems, 1369 Brass Mill Rd., Suite A, Belcamp, MD 21017, P: 888-286-6440, F: 410-273-0126, www.avon-protection.com
Law Enforcement; Training & Safety Equipment

A-Way Hunting Products (MI), 3230 Calhoun Rd., P.O. Box 492, Beaverton, MI, 48612, P: 989-435-3879, F: 989-435-8960, www.awayhunting.com

Decoys; Game Calls; Scents & Lures; Videos

AWC Systems Technology, 1515 W. Deer Valley Rd., Suite A-105, Phoenix, AZ 85027, P: 623-780-1050, F: 800-897-5708, www.awcsystech.com

AyA-Aguirre Y Aranzabal, Avda. Otaola, 25-3a Planta, Eibar, (Guipúzcoa) 20600, SPAIN, P: 011-34-943-820437, F: 011-34-943-200133, www.aya-fineguns.com
Firearms

B

B-Square/Div. Armor Holdings, Inc., 8909 Forum Way, Fort Worth, TX 76140, P: 800-433-2909, F: 817-926-7012

BAM Wuxi Bam Co., Ltd., No 37 Zhongnan Rd., Wuxi, JiangSu 214024, CHINA, P: 011-86 51085432361, FL 011-86 51085401258, www.china-bam.com
Airguns; Gun Cases; Scopes, Sights & Accessories

BCS International, 1819 St. George St., Green Bay, WI 54302, P: 888-965-3700, F: 888-965-3701
Bags & Equipment Cases; Camouflage; Men & Women's Clothing; Export/Import Specialists; Leathergoods

B.E. Meyers, 14540 Northeast 91st St., Redmond, WA 98052, P: 800-327-5648, F: 425-867-1759, www.bemeyers.com
Custom Manufacturing; Law Enforcement

B & F System, Inc., The, 3920 S. Walton Walker Blvd., Dallas, TX 75236, P: 214-333-2111, F: 214-333-2137, www.bnfusa.com
Binoculars; Cooking Equipment/Accessories; Cutlery; Gloves, Mitts, Hats; Leathergoods; Scopes, Sights & Accessories; Telescopes; Wholesaler/Distributor

BOGgear, LLC, 111 W. Cedar Lane, Suite A, Payson, AZ 85541, P: 877-264-7637, F: 505-292-9130, www.boggear.com
Binoculars; Firearms; Hunting Accessories; Law Enforcement; Outfitter; Photographic Equipment; Shooting Range Equipment; Training & Safety Equipment

BSA Optics, 3911 S.W. 47th Ave., Suite 914, Ft. Lauderdale, FL 33314, P: 954-581-2144, F: 954-581-3165, www.bsaoptics.com
Binoculars; Scopes, Sights & Accessories; Sports Accessories; Telescopes

B.S.N. Technology Srl, Via Guido Rossa, 46/52, Cellatica (Bs), 25060, ITALY, P: 011 390302522436, F: 011 390302520946, www.bsn.it
Ammunition; Gun Barrels; Reloading

Bad Boy, Inc., 102 Industrial Dr., Batesville, AR 72501, P: 870-698-0090, F: 870-698-2123

Bad Boy Enterprises, LLC/Bad Boy Buggies, 2 River Terminal Rd., P.O. Box 19087, Natchez, MS 39122, P: 866-678-6701, F: 601-442-6707, www.badboybuggies.com
Vehicles, Utility & Rec

Badger Barrels, Inc., 8330 196 Ave., P.O. Box 417, Bristol, WI 53104, P: 262-857-6950, F: 262-857-6988, www.badgerbarrelsinc.com
Gun Barrels

Badger Ordnance, 1141 Swift St., North Kansas City, MO 64116, P: 816-421-4956, F: 816-421-4958, www.badgerordnance.com
Custom Manufacturing; Firearms; Firearms Maintenance Equipment; Gun Parts/Gunsmithing; Law Enforcement; Magazines, Cartridge; Scopes, Sights & Accessories; Telescopes

Badland Beauty, LLC, P.O. Box 151507, Lufkin, TX 75915, P: 936-875-5522, F: 936-875-5525, www.badlandbeauty.com
Women's Clothing

BAE Systems/Mobility & Protection Systems, 13386 International Parkway, Jacksonville, FL 32218, P: 904-741-5600, F: 904-741-9996, www.baesystems.com
Bags & Equipment Cases; Black Powder/Smokeless Powder; Gloves, Mitts, Hats; Holsters; Hunting Accessories; Law Enforcement; Scopes, Sights & Accessories; Training & Safety Equipment

Bandera/Cal-Bind, 1315 Fernbridge Dr., Fortuna, CA 95540, P: 866-226-3378, F: 707-725-1156, www.banderausa.com
Archery; Hunting Accessories; Leathergoods; Sports Accessories; Wholesaler/Distributor

Barbour, Inc., 55 Meadowbrook Dr., Milford, NH 03055-4613, P: 800-338-3474, F: 603-673-6510, www.barbour.com
Bags & Equipment Cases; Men & Women's Clothing; Footwear; Gloves, Mitts, Hats; Leathergoods

Bardin & Marsee Publishing, 1112 N. Shadesview Terrace, Birmingham, AL 35209, P: 205-453-4361, F: 404-474-3086, www.theoutdoorbible.com
Books/Industry Publications

Barnaul Cartridge Plant CJSC, 28 Kulagina St., Barnaul, 656002, RUSSIAN FEDERATION, P: 011 0073852774391, F: 011 0073852771608, www.ab.ru/~stanok
Ammunition

Barnes Bullets, Inc., P.O. Box 620, Mona, UT 84645, P: 801-756-4222, F: 801-756-2465, www.barnesbullets.com
Black Powder Accessories; Computer Software; Custom Manufacturing; Hunting Accessories; Law Enforcement; Recoil Protection Devices & Services; Reloading

Barnett Outdoors, LLC, 13447 Byrd Dr., P.O. Box 934, Odessa, FL 33556, P: 800-237-4507, F: 813-920-5400, www.barnettcrossbows.com
Archery; Crossbows & Accessories; Sports Accessories

Baron Technology, Inc./Baron Engraving, 62 Spring Hill Rd., Trumbull, CT 06611, P: 203-452-0515, F: 203-452-0663, www.baronengraving.com
Custom Manufacturing; Cutlery; Firearms; Gun Parts/Gunsmithing; Knives/Knife Cases; Law Enforcement; Outdoor Art, Jewelry, Sculpture; Sports Accessories

Barrett Firearms Mfg., Inc., P.O. Box 1077, Murfreesboro, TN 37133, P: 615-896-2938, F: 615-896-7313, www.barrettrifles.com
Firearms

Barska Optics, 1721 Wright Ave., La Verne, CA 91750, P: 909-445-8168, F: 909-445-8169, www.barska.com

Bates Footwear/Div. Wolverine World Wide, Inc., 9341 Courtland Dr., Rockford, MI 49351, P: 800-253-2184, F: 616-866-5658, www.batesfootwear.com
Footwear; Law Enforcement

Battenfeld Technologies, Inc., 5885 W. Van Horn Tavern Rd., Columbia, MO 65203, P: 877-509-9160, F: 573-446-6606, www.battenfeldtechnologies.com
Firearms Maintenance Equipment; Gun Grips & Stocks; Gun Parts/Gunsmithing; Hearing Protection; Recoil Protection Devices & Services; Reloading; Shooting Range Equipment; Targets

Battle Lake Outdoors, 203 W. Main, P.O. Box 548, Clarissa, MN 56440, P: 800-243-0465, F: 218-756-2426, www.battlelakeoutdoors.com
Archery; Backpacking; Bags & Equipment Cases; Black Powder Accessories; Camping; Gun Cases; Hunting Accessories; Law Enforcement

Batz Corp., 1524 Highway 291 North, P.O. Box 130, Prattsville, AR 72129, P: 800-637-7627, F: 870-699-4420, www.batzusa.com
Backpacking; Camping; Custom Manufacturing; Hunting Accessories; Knives/Knife Cases; Lighting Products; Pet Supplies; Retail Packaging

Bayco Products, Inc., 640 S. Sanden Blvd., Wylie, TX 75098, P: 800-233-2155, F: 469-326-9401, www.baycoproducts.com

Beamshot-Quarton USA, Inc., 5805 Callaghan Rd., Suite 102, San Antonio, TX 78228, P: 800-520-8435, F: 210-735-1326, www.beamshot.com
Airguns; Archery; Crossbows & Accessories; Hunting Accessories; Law Enforcement; Lighting Products; Paintball Accessories; Scopes, Sights & Accessories

Bear & Son Cutlery, Inc., 1111 Bear Blvd. SW, Jacksonville, AL 36265, P: 800-844-3034, F: 256-435-9348, www.bearandsoncutlery.com
Cutlery; Hunting Accessories; Knives/Knife Cases

Bear Valley Outfitters, P.O. Box 2294, Swan River, Manitoba R0L-1Z0 CANADA, P: 204-238-4342, F: 204-238-4342, www.bearvalleyoutfitters.com

Beeman Precision Airguns, 5454 Argosy Ave., Huntington Beach, CA 92649, P: 714-890-4800, F: 714-890-4808, www.beeman.com
Airguns; Ammunition; Gun Cases; Holsters; Lubricants; Scopes, Sights & Accessories; Targets

Beijing Defense Co., Ltd., 18 B, Unit One, No. 1 Building, Linghangguoji, Guangqumen Nanxiao St., Chongwen District, Beijing, 100061, CHINA, P: 011 861067153626, F: 011 861067152121, www.tacticalgear.com
Backpacking; Bags & Equipment Cases; Gun Cases; Holsters; Training & Safety Equipment

Bell and Carlson, Inc., 101 Allen Rd., Dodge City, KS 67801, P: 620-225-6688, F: 620-225-9095, www.bellandcarlson.com
Camouflage; Custom Manufacturing; Gun Grips & Stocks; Gun Parts/Gunsmithing; Hunting Accessories; Shooting Range Equipment

Bell-Ranger Outdoor Apparel, 1538 Crescent Dr., P.O. Box 14307, Augusta, GA, 30909, P: 800-241-7618, F: 706-738-3608, www.bellranger.com
Camouflage; Men & Women's Clothing; Hunting Accessories

Benchmade Knife Company, Inc., 300 Beavercreek Rd., Oregon City, OR 97045, P: 800-800-7427, F: 503-655-7922, www.benchmade.com
Knives/Knife Cases; Men's Clothing

Benelli Armi S.p.A./Benelli USA, 17603 Indian Head Hwy., Accokeek, MD 20607, P: 301-283-6981, F: 301-283-6986, www.benelli.it, www.benelliusa.com
Firearms

Beretta/Law Enforcement and Defense, 17601 Beretta Dr., Accokeek, MD 20607, P: 800-545-9567, F: 301-283-5111, www.berettale.com
Firearms; Gun Parts/Gunsmithing; Holsters; Law Enforcement; Lighting Products

Beretta U.S.A. Corp., 17601 Beretta Dr., Accokeek, MD 20607, P: 800-636-3420, F: 253-484-3775

Bergan, LLC, 27600 Hwy. 125, Monkey Island, OK 74331, P: 866-217-9606. F: 918-257-8950, www.berganexperience.com
Pet Products

Berger Bullets, 4275 N. Palm St., Fullerton, CA 92835, P: 714-447-5456, F: 714-447-5478, www.bergerbullets.com
Ammunition; Custom Manufacturing; Reloading

Berry's Manufacturing, Inc., 401 N. 3050 East, St. George, UT 84790, P: 800-269-7373, F: 435-634-1683, www.berrysmfg.com
Ammunition; Custom Manufacturing; Export/Import Specialists; Gun Cases; Reloading; Wholesaler/Distributor

Beta Company, The, 2137B Flintstone Dr., Tucker, GA 30084, P: 800-669-2382, F: 770-270-0599, www.betaco.com
Law Enforcement; Magazines, Cartridge

Beyond Clothing/Beyond Tactical, 1025 Conger St., Suite 8, Eugene, OR 97402, P: 800-775-2279, F: 703-997-6581, www.beyondtactical.com
Backpacking; Camouflage; Men & Women's Clothing; Custom Manufacturing; Law Enforcement

BFAST, LLC, 10 Roff Ave., Palasades Park, NJ 07650, P: 973-706-8210, F: 201-943-3546, www.firearmsafetynet.com
Law Enforcement; Shooting Range Equipment; Sports Accessories; Training & Safety Equipment

Bianchi International, 3120 E. Mission Blvd. Ontario, CA 91761, P: 800-347-1200, F: 800-366-1669, www.bianchi-intl.com
Backpacking; Bags & Equipment Cases; Gun Cases; Holsters; Hunting Accessories; Knives/Knife Cases; Leathergoods; Sports Accessories

Big Game Treestands, 1820 N. Redding Ave., P.O. Box 382, Windom, MN 56101, P: 800-268-5077, F: 507-831-4350, www.biggametreestands.com
Blinds; Hunting Accessories; Shooting Range Equipment; Treestands

Big Sky Carvers/Montana Silversmiths, 308 E. Main St., P.O. Box 507, Manhattan, MT 59741, P: 406-284-3193, F: 406-284-4028, www.bigskycarvers.com
Decoys; Home Furnishings; Lighting Products; Outdoor Art, Jewelry, Sculpture; Watches; Wholesaler/Distributor

Big Sky Racks, Inc., 25A Shawnee Way, Bozeman, MT 58715, P: 800-805-8716, F: 406-585-7378, www.bigskyracks.com
Gun Cabinets, Racks, Safes; Gun Locks; Hunting Accessories

BigFoot Bag/PortaQuip, 1215 S. Grant Ave., Loveland, CO 80537, P: 877-883-0200, F: 970-663-5415, www.bigfootbag.com
Bags & Equipment Cases; Camping; Hunting Accessories; Law Enforcement; Paintball Accessories; Sports Accessories; Tours & Travel

Bill's Sewing Machine Co., 301 Main Avenue East, Hildebran, NC 28637, P: 828-397-6941, F: 828-397-6193, www.billsewing.com

Bill Wiseman & Co., Inc., 18456 Hwy. 6 South, College Station, TX 77845, P: 979-690-3456, F: 979-690-0156, www.billwisemanandco.com
Firearms; Gun Barrels; Gun Parts/Gunsmithing

BioPlastics Co., 34655 Mills Rd., North Ridgeville, OH 44039, P: 440-327-0485, F: 440-327-3666, www.bioplastics.us

Birchwood Casey, 7900 Fuller Rd., Eden Prairie, MN 55344, P: 800-328-6156, F: 952-937-7979, www.birchwoodcasey.com
Black Powder Accessories; Camping; Firearms Maintenance Equipment; Gun Cases; Gun Parts/Gunsmithing; Hunting Accessories; Lubricants; Targets

Bison Designs, 735 S. Lincoln St., Longmont, CO 80501, P: 800-558-2476, F: 303-678-9988, www.bisondesigns.com
Backpacking; Men & Women's Clothing; Pet Supplies; Survival Kits/First Aid; Training & Safety Equipment; Wholesaler/Distributor

Black Hills Ammunition, P.O. Box 3090, Rapid City, SD 57709, P: 605-348-5150, F: 605-348-9827, www.black-hills.com
Ammunition

Black Hills Shooters Supply, Inc., 2875 Creek Dr., Rapid City, SD 57703, P: 800-289-2506, F: 800-289-4570, www.bhshooters.com
Reloading; Wholesaler/Distributor

Black Powder Products Group, 5988 Peachtree Corners East, Norcross, GA 30071, P: 800-320-8767, F: 770-242-8546, www.bpiguns.com

Black Powder Accessories; Firearms; Firearms Maintenance Equipment; Hunting Accessories; Scopes, Sights & Accessories

BlackHawk Products Group, 6160 Commander Pkwy., Norfolk, VA 23502, P: 800-694-5263, F: 757-436-3088, www.blackhawk.com
Bags & Equipment Cases; Men's Clothing; Gloves, Mitts, Hats; Holsters; Hunting Accessories; Knives/Knife Cases; Law Enforcement; Recoil Protection Devices & Services

Blackheart International, LLC, RR3, Box 115, Philippi, WV 26416, P: 877-244-8166, F: 304-457-1281, www.bhigear.com
Ammunition; Gun Parts/Gunsmithing; Holsters; Law Enforcement; Magazines, Cartridge; Scopes, Sights & Accessories; Survival Kits/First Aid; Training & Safety Equipment

Blackwater, P.O. Box 1029, Moyock, NC 27958, P: 252-435-2488, F: 252-435-6388, www.blackwaterusa.com
Bags & Equipment Cases; Men's Clothing; Custom Manufacturing; Gun Cases; Holsters; Law Enforcement; Targets; Training & Safety Equipment

Blade-Tech Industries, 2506 104th St. Court S, Suite A, Lakewood, WA 98499, P: 253-581-4347, F: 253-589-0282, www.blade-tech.com
Bags & Equipment Cases; Custom Manufacturing; Cutlery; Holsters; Hunting Accessories; Knives/Knife Cases; Law Enforcement; Sports Accessories

Blaser Jagdwaffen GmbH, Ziegelstadel 1, Isny, 88316, GERMANY, P: 011 4907562702348, F: 011 4907562702343, www.blaser.de
Firearms; Gun Barrels; Gun Cases; Gun Grips & Stocks; Hunting Accessories

Blauer Manufacturing Co. 20 Aberdeen St., Boston, MA 02215, P: 800-225-6715, www.blauer.com
Law Enforcement; Men & Women's Clothing

Blue Book Publications, Inc., 8009 34th Ave. S, Suite 175, Minneapolis, MN 55425, P: 800-877-4867, F: 952-853-1486, www.bluebookinc.com
Books/Industry Publications; Computer Software

Blue Force Gear, Inc., P.O. Box 853, Pooler, GA 31322, P: 877-430-2583, F: 912-964-7701, www.blueforcegear.com
Bags & Equipment Cases; Hunting Accessories; Law Enforcement; Scopes, Sights & Accessories; Sports Accessories

Blue Ridge Knives, 166 Adwolfe Rd., Marion, VA 24354, P: 276-783-6143, F: 276-783-9298, www.blueridgeknives.com
Binoculars; Cutlery; Export/Import Specialists; Knives/Knife Cases; Lighting Products; Scopes, Sights & Accessories; Sharpeners; Wholesaler/Distributor

Blue Stone Safety Products Co., Inc., 2950 W. 63rd St., Chicago, IL 60629, P: 773-776-9472, F: 773-776-9472, www.wolverineholsters.com
Holsters; Law Enforcement

Bluegrass Armory, 145 Orchard St., Richmond, KY 40475, P: 859-625-0874, F: 859-625-0874, www.bluegrassarmory.com
Firearms

Bluestar USA, Inc., 111 Commerce Center Drive, Suite 303, P.O. Box 2903, Huntersville, NC 28078, P: 877-948-7827, F: 704-875-6714, www.bluestar-hunting.com
Archery; Crossbows & Accessories; Hunting Accessories; Law Enforcement; Training & Safety Equipment; Wholesaler/Distributor

BlueWater Ropes/Yates Gear, Inc., 2608 Hartnell Ave., Suite 6, Redding, CA 96002, P: 800-YATES-16, F: 530-222-4640, www.yatesgear.com
Law Enforcement; Training & Safety Equipment; Wholesaler/Distributor

Bobster Eyewear, 12220 Parkway Centre Dr., Suite B, Poway, CA 92064, P: 800-603-2662, F: 858-715-0066, www.bobster.com
Eyewear; Hunting Accessories; Law Enforcement; Shooting Range Equipment; Sports Accessories; Training & Safety Equipment

Body Specs Sunglasses & Goggles, 22846 Industrial Place, Grass Valley, CA 95949, P: 800-824-5907, F: 530-268-1751, www.bodyspecs.com
Eyewear; Law Enforcement; Shooting Range Equipment; Training & Safety Equipment

Bogs Footwear/The Combs Co., 16 Oakway Center, Eugene, OR 97401, P: 800-485-2070, F: 541-484-1345, www.bogsfootwear.com or www.raftersfootwear.com
Footwear

Boker USA, Inc., 1550 Balsam St., Lakewood, CO 80214, P: 800-992-6537, F: 303-462-0668, www.bokerusa.com
Cutlery; Knives/Knife Cases

Border Crossing Scents, 8399 Bristol Rd., Davison, MI 48423, P: 888-653-2759, F: 810-653-2809, www.bordercrossingscents.com
Scents & Lures

Boss Buck, Inc., 210 S. Hwy. 175, Seagoville, TX 75159, P: 972-287-1216, F: 972-287-1892, www.bossbuck.com
Blinds; Feeder Equipment; Hunting Accessories; Scents & Lures; Treestands

Boston Leather, Inc., 1801 Eastwood Dr., P.O. Box 1213, Sterling, IL 61081, P: 800-733-1492, F: 800-856-1650, www.bostonleather.com
Bags & Equipment Cases; Custom Manufacturing; Gun Cases; Holsters; Knives/Knife Cases; Law Enforcement; Leathergoods; Pet Supplies

Boyds' Gunstock Industries, Inc., 25376 403rd Ave., Mitchell, SD 57301, P: 605-996-5011, F: 605-996-9878, www.boydsgunstocks.com
Custom Manufacturing; Firearms Maintenance Equipment; Gun Grips & Stocks; Gun Parts/Gunsmithing; Hunting Accessories; Shooting Range Equipment

Boyt Harness/Bob Allen Sportswear, 1 Boyt Dr., Osceola, IA 50213, P: 800-685-7020, www.boytharness.com
Gun Cases; Hunting Accessories; Law Enforcement; Men & Women's Clothing; Pet Supplies; Shooting Accessories

BraeVal, 23 E. Main St., Torrington, CT 06790, P: 860-482-7260, F: 860-482-7247, www.braeval.net
Men's Clothing

Brass Magnet, 5910 S. University Blvd., Suite C 18-330, Greenwood Village, CO 80121, P: 303-347-2636, F: 360-364-2636

Brazos Walking Sticks, 6408 Gholson Rd., Waco, TX 76705, P: 800-880-7119, F: 254-799-7199, www.brazos-walking-sticks.com
Canes; Walking Sticks

Breaching Technologies, Inc., P.O. Box 701468, San Antonio, TX 78270, P: 866-552-7427, F: 210-590-5193, www.breachingtechnologies.com
Law Enforcement; Training & Safety Equipment

Break-Free, 13386 International Parkway, Jacksonville, FL 32218, P: 800-433-2909, F: 800-588-0339, www.break-free.com
Law Enforcement; Lubricants

Brenneke™ of America, L.P., P.O. Box 1481, Clinton, IA 52733, P: 800-753-9733, F: 563-244-7421, www.brennekeusa.com
Ammunition

Brenzovich Firearms & Training Center/dba BFTC, 22301 Texas 20, Fort Hancock, TX 79839, P: 877-585-3775, F: 915-764-2030, www.brenzovich.com
Airguns; Ammunition; Archery; Black Powder Accessories; Export/Import Specialists; Firearms; Training & Safety Equipment; Wholesaler/Distributor

Brigade Quartermasters, Ltd., 1025 Cobb International Dr., Kennesaw, GA 30152, P: 770-428-1248, F: 720-426-7211

Briley Manufacturing, Inc., 1230 Lumpkin Rd., Houston, TX 77043, P: 800-331-5718, F: 713-932-1043
Chokes, Gun Accessories, Gunsmithing

Brite-Strike Technologies, 26 Wapping Rd., Jones River Industrial Park, Kingston, MA 02364, P: 781-585-5509, F: 781-585-5332, www.brite-strike.com
Law Enforcement; Lighting Products

Broco, Inc., 10868 Bell Ct., Rancho Cucamonga, CA 91730, P: 800-845-7259, F: 800-845-7259, www.brocoinc.com
Law Enforcement

Brookwood/Fine Uniform Co., 1125 E. Broadway, Suite 51, Glendale, CA 91205, P: 626-443-3736, F: 626-444-1551, www.brookwoodbags.com
Archery; Backpacking; Bags & Equipment Cases; Camping; Gun Cases; Hunting Accessories; Knives/Knife Cases; Shooting Range Equipment

Brookwood Companies, Inc., 25 W. 45th St., 11th Floor, New York, NY 10036, P: 800-426-5468, F: 646-472-0294, www.brookwoodcos.com

Brownells/Brownells MIL/LE Supply Group, 200 S. Front St., Montezuma, IA 50171, P: 800-741-0015, F: 800-264-3068, www.brownells.com
Export/Import Specialists; Firearms Maintenance Equipment; Gun Grips & Stocks; Gun Parts/Gunsmithing; Lubricants; Magazines, Cartridge; Scopes, Sights & Accessories; Wholesaler/Distributor

Browning, 1 Browning Place, Morgan, UT 84050, P: 801-876-2711, F: 801-876-3331, www.browning.com

Browning Archery, 2727 N. Fairview Ave., Tucson, AZ 85705, P: 520-838-2000, F: 520-838-2019, www.browning-archery.com
Archery

Browning Footwear, 107 Highland St., Martinsburg, PA 16662, P: 800-441-4319, F: 814-793-9272, www.browningfootwear.com
Footwear

Browning Hosiery/Carolina Hosiery, 2316 Tucker St., Burlington, NC 27215, P: 336-226-5581, F: 336-226-9721, www.browninghosiery.com
Men & Women's Clothing, Footwear

Browning Off Road/Polaris Industries, 2100 Hwy. 55, Medina, MN 55340, P: 763-542-0500, F: 763-542-2317, www.browningoffroad.com
Vehicles, Utility & Rec

Browning Outdoor Health and Safety Products, 1 Pharmacal Way, Jackson, WI 53037, P: 800-558-6614, F: 262-677-9006, www.browningsupplies.com
Survival Kits/First Aid

Browning Signature Automotive/Signature Products Group, 2550 S. Decker Lake Blvd. Suite 1, Salt Lake City, UT 84119, P: 801-237-0184, F: 801-237-0118, www.spgcompany.com
Emblems & Decals

Bruce Foods/Cajun Injector, Inc., P.O. Box 1030, New Iberia, LA 70562, P: 337-365-8101, F: 337-364-3742, www.brucefoods.com
Camping; Cooking Equipment/Accessories; Food; Online Services

Brunton, 2255 Brunton Ct., Riverton, WY 82501, P: 307-857-4700, F: 307-857-4703, www.brunton.com
Backpacking, Binoculars, Camping, Scopes

Buck Gardner Calls, LLC, 2129 Troyer Ave., Building 249, Suite 104, Memphis, TN 38114, P: 901-946-2996, F: 901-946-8747, www.buckgardner.com
Duck Calls & Accessories; Cooking

Buck Knives, Inc., 660 S. Lochsa St., Post Falls, ID 83854, P: 800-326-2825, www.buckknives.com
Backpacking; Camping; Custom Manufacturing; Cutlery; Hunting Accessories; Knives/Knife Cases; Law Enforcement; Sharpeners

Buckaroo-Stoo/BVM Productions, 2253 Kingsland Ave., Bronx, NY 10469, P: 877-286-4599, F: 718-652-3014, www.buckaroostoo.com
Scents & Lures

Buck Stop Lure Company, Inc., 3600 Grow Rd., P.O. Box 636, Stanton, MI 48888, P: 800-477-2368, F: 989-762-5124, www.buckstopscents.com
Archery; Books/Industry Publications; Hunting Accessories; Pet Supplies; Scents & Lures; Videos

Buck Wear, Inc., 2900 Cowan Ave., Baltimore, MD 21223, P: 800-813-7708, F: 410-646-7700, www.buckwear.com
Men & Women's Clothing

Buffalo Tools/Sportsman Series, 1220 N. Price Rd., St. Louis, MO 63132, P: 800-568-6657, F: 636-537-1055, www.buffalotools.com
Cooking Equipment/Accessories; Export/Import Specialists; Wholesaler/Distributor

Buffer Technologies, P.O. Box 105047, Jefferson City, MO 65110, P: 877-628-3337, F: 573-634-8522, www.buffertech.com
Gun Parts/Gunsmithing; Law Enforcement; Magazines, Cartridge; Recoil Protection Devices & Services

Bug Band, 127 Riverside Dr., Cartersville, GA 30120, P: 800-473-9467, F: 678-721-9279, www.bugband.com
Archery; Backpacking; Camping; Hunting Accessories; Law Enforcement; Outfitter; Survival Kits/First Aid; Wholesaler/Distributor

Bul, Ltd., 10 Rival St., Tel Aviv, 67778, ISRAEL, P: 011 97236392911, F: 011 97236874853, www.bultransmark.com
Firearms; Gun Barrels; Gun Parts/Gunsmithing; Law Enforcement

Bulldog Barrels, LLC, 106 Isabella St., 4 North Shore Center, Suite 110, Pittsburgh, PA 15212, P: 866-992-8553, F: 412-322-1912, www.bulldogbarrels.com
Firearms; Gun Barrels; Gun Parts/Gunsmithing

Bulldog Cases, 830 Beauregard Ave., Danville, VA 24541, P: 800-843-3483, F: 434-793-7504
Bags & Equipment Cases; Camouflage; Gun Cases; Holsters

Bulldog Equipment, 3706 SW 30th Ave., Hollywood, FL 33312, P: 954-581-5510 or 954-448-5221, F: 954-581-4221, www.bulldogequipment.us
Backpacking; Bags & Equipment Cases; Custom Manufacturing; Gloves, Mitts, Hats; Gun Cases; Law Enforcement; Outfitter

Bulls and Beavers, LLC, P.O. Box 2870, Sun Valley, ID 83353, P: 208-726-8217, www.bullsandbeavers.com

Burn Machine, LLC, The, 26305 Glendale, Suite 200, Redford, MI 48239, P: 800-380-6527, F: 313-794-4355, www.theburnmachine.com
Sports Accessories; Training & Safety Equipment; Wholesaler/Distributor

Burris Company, Inc., 331 E. 8th St., Greeley, CO 80631, P: 970-356-1670, F: 970-356-8702, www.burrisoptics.com
Binoculars; Scopes, Sights & Accessories; Targets

Bushido Tactical, LLC, P.O. Box 721289, Orlando, FL 32972, P: 407-454-4256, F: 407-286-4416, www.bushidotactical.com
Law Enforcement; Training

Bushnell Law Enforcement/Bushnell Outdoor Products, 9200 Cody St., Overland Park, KS 66214, P: 800-423-3537, F: 800-548-0446, www.unclemikesle.com
Binoculars; Firearms Maintenance Equipment; Gloves, Mitts, Hats; Gun Cases; Holsters; Law Enforcement; Lubricants; Scopes, Sights & Accessories

Business Control Systems Corp., 1173 Green St., Iselin, NJ 08830, P: 800-233-5876, F: 732-283-1192, www.businesscontrol.com
Archery; Computer Software; Firearms; Law Enforcement; Retailer Services; Shooting Range Equipment; Wholesaler/Distributor

Butler Creek Corp./Bushnell Outdoor Accessories, 9200 Cody St., Overland Park, KS 66214, P: 800-423-3537, F: 800-548-0446, www.butlercreek.com
Firearms Maintenance Equipment; Gun Barrels; Gun Grips & Stocks; Hunting Accessories; Leathergoods; Scopes, Sights & Accessories

C

CAM Commerce Solutions, 17075 Newhope St., Fountain Valley, CA 92708, 866-840-4443, F: 702-564-3206, www.camcommerce.com
Computer Software

CASL Industries/Tanglefree/Remington, P.O. Box 1280, Clayton, CA 94517, P: 877-685-5055, F: 925-685-6055, www.tanglefree.com or www.caslinindustries.com
Bags & Equipment Cases; Blinds; Camouflage; Decoys; Gun Cases; Hunting Accessories

CAS Hanwei, 650 Industrial Blvd., Sale Creek, TN 37373-9797, P: 800-635-9366, F: 423-332-7248, www.cashanwei.com
Custom Manufacturing; Cutlery; Knives/Knife Cases; Leathergoods; Wholesaler/Distributor

CCF Race Frames LLC, P.O. Box 29009, Richmond, VA 23242, P: 804-622-4277, F: 804-740-9599, www.ccfraceframes.com
Firearms; Firearms Maintenance Equipment; Gun Parts/Gunsmithing; Law Enforcement

CCI Ammunition/ATK Commercial Products, 2299 Snake River Ave., Lewiston, ID 83501, P: 800-256-8685, F: 208-798-3392, www.cci-ammunition.com
Ammunition

CGTech, 9000 Research Dr., Irvine, CA 92618, P: 949-753-1050, F: 949-753-1053, www.cgtech.com
Computer Software; Custom Manufacturing

CJ Weapons Accessories, 317 Danielle Ct., Jefferson City, MO 65109, P: 800-510-5919, F: 573-634-2355, www.cjweapons.com
Firearms Maintenance Equipment; Gun Parts/Gunsmithing; Hunting Accessories; Law Enforcement; Magazines, Cartridge; Shooting Range Equipment; Sports Accessories; Wholesaler/Distributor

CMMG, Inc., 620 County Rd. 118, P.O. Box 369, Fayette, MO 65248, P: 660-248-2293, F: 660-248-2290, www.cmmginc.com
Firearms; Law Enforcement; Magazines, Cartridge

CTI Industries Corp., 22160 N. Pepper Rd., Barrington, IL 60010, P: 866-382-1707, F: 800-333-1831, www.zipvac.com
Archery; Backpacking; Bags & Equipment Cases; Camping; Cooking Equipment/Accessories; Custom Manufacturing; Food; Hunting Accessories

CVA, 5988 Peachtree Corners East, Norcross, GA 30071, P: 800-320-8767, F: 770-242-8546
Black Powder Accessories; Firearms; Firearms Maintenance Equipment; Gun Barrels

CZ-USA/Dan Wesson, 3327 N. 7th St., Kansas city, KS 66115, P: 800-955-4486, F: 913-321-4901, www.cz-usa.com
Firearms

Cablz, 411 Meadowbrook Lane, Birmingham, AL 35213, P: 205-222-4477, F: 205-870-8847

Caesar Guerini USA, 700 Lake St., Cambridge, MD 21613, P: 866-901-1131, F: 410-901-1137, www.gueriniusa.com
Firearms

CALVI S.p.A., Via Iv Novembre, 2, Merate (LC), 23807, ITALY, P: 011 3903999851, F: 011 390399985240, www.calvi.it
Custom Manufacturing; Firearms; Gun Barrels; Gun Locks; Gun Parts/Gunsmithing

Camdex, Inc., 2330 Alger, Troy, MI 48083, P: 248-528-2300, F: 248-528-0989, www.camdexloader.com
Reloading

Camelbak Products, 2000 S. McDowell Blvd., Petaluma, CA 94954, P: 800-767-8725, F: 707-665-3844, www.camelbak.com
Backpacking; Bags & Equipment Cases; Gloves, Mitts, Hats; Holsters; Law Enforcement

Camerons Products/CM International, Inc., 2547 Durango Dr., P.O. Box 60220, Colorado Springs, CO 80960, P: 888-563-0227, F: 719-390-0946, www.cameronsproducts.com
Backpacking; Camping; Cooking Equipment/Accessories; Hunting Accessories; Retailer Services; Tours/Travel; Wholesaler/Distributor

Camfour, Inc., 65 Westfield Industrial Park Rd., Westfield, MA 01085, P: 800-FIREARM, F: 413-568-9663, www.camfour.com
Ammunition; Black Powder Accessories; Computer Software; Export/Import Specialists; Firearms; Hunting Accessories; Law Enforcement; Wholesaler/Distributor

Cammenga Corp., 100 Aniline Ave. N, Suite 258, Holland, MI 49424, P: 616-392-7999, F: 616-392-9432, www.cammenga.com
Magazines, Cartridge; Reloading; Training & Safety Equipment

Camo Unlimited, 1021 B Industrial Park Dr., Marietta, GA 30062, P: 866-448-CAMO, F: 770-420-2299, www.camounlimited.com
Blinds; Camouflage; Hunting Accessories; Paintball Accessories

C-More Systems, 7553 Gary Rd., P.O. Box 1750, Manassas, VA 20109, P: 888-265-8266, F: 703-361-5881, www.cmore.com
Airguns; Archery; Crossbows & Accessories; Custom Manufacturing; Firearms; Hunting Accessories; Law Enforcement; Scopes, Sights & Accessories; Shooting Range Equipment

CamoSpace.com, P.O. Box 125, Rhodesdale, MD 21659, P: 410-310-0380, F: 410-943-8849

Camouflage Face Paint, 2832 Southeast Loop 820, Fort Worth, TX 76140, P: 877-625-3879, F: 817-615-8670, www.camofacepaint.com
Archery; Camouflage; Custom Manufacturing; Export/Import Specialists; Hunting Accessories; Online Services; Paintball Accessories; Wholesaler/Distributor

Camowraps, 429 South St., Slidell, LA 70460, P: 866-CAMO-MAN, F: 985-661-1447, www.camowraps.com
Camouflage; Custom Manufacturing; Emblems & Decals; Printing Services

Camp Chef, 675 North 600 West, P.O. Box 4057, Logan, UT 84321, P: 800-783-8347, F: 435-752-1592, www.campchef.com
Cooking Equipment/Accessories

Camp Technologies, LLC/Div. DHS Technologies, LLC, 33 Kings Hwy., Orangeburg, NY 10962, P: 866-969-2400, F: 845-365-2114, www.camprtv.com
Backpacking; Camping; Hunting Accessories; Law Enforcement; Outfitter; Sports Accessories; Vehicles, Utility & Rec

CampCo/Smith & Wesson Watches HUMVEE/UZI, 4625 W. Jefferson Blvd., Los Angeles, CA 90016, P: 888-9-CAMPCO, F: 323-766-2424, www.campco.com
Backpacking; Binocular; Camping; Compasses; Knives/Knife Cases; Law Enforcement; Lighting Products; Wholesaler/Distributor

Canal Street Cutlery Co., 30 Canal St., Ellenville, NY 12428, P: 845-647-5900, F: 845-647-1456, www.canalstreetcutlery.com
Cutlery; Knives/Knife Cases

Cannon Safe, Inc., 216 S. 2nd Ave., Building 932, San Bernardino, CA 92408, P: 800-242-1055, F: 909-382-0707, www.cannonsafe.com
Gun Cabinets/Racks/Safes; Gun Locks

Careco Multimedia, Inc., 5717 Northwest Pkwy., Suite 104, San Antonio, TX 78249, P: 800-668-8081, F: 251-948-3011, www.americanaoutdoors.com, www.outdooraction.com, www.fishingandhuntingtexas.com
Online Services; Videos; Wholesaler/Distributor

Carl Zeiss Optronics GmbH, Gloelstr. 3-5, Wetzlar, 35576, GERMANY, P: 011 4964414040, F: 011 496441404510, www.zeiss.com/optronics
Law Enforcement; Scopes, Sights & Accessories; Shooting Range Equipment; Targets; Telescopes

Carl Zeiss Sports Optics/Zeiss, 13005 N. Kingston Ave., Chester, VA 23836, P: 800-441-3005, F: 804-530-8481, www.zeiss.com/sports
Binoculars; Scopes, Sights & Accessories

Carlson's Choke Tubes, 720 S. Second St., P.O. Box 162, Atwood, KS 67730, P: 785-626-3700, F: 785-626-3999, www.choketube.com
Custom Manufacturing; Firearms Maintenance Equipment; Game Calls; Gun Parts/Gunsmithing; Hunting Accessories; Scopes, Sights & Accessories; Shooting Range Equipment

Carson Optical, 35 Gilpin Ave., Hauppauge, NY 11788, P: 800-967-8427, F: 631-427-6749, www.carsonoptical.com
Binoculars; Export/Import Specialists; Scopes, Sights & Accessories; Telescopes

Cartuchos Saga, Pda. Caparrela s/n, Lleida, 25192, SPAIN, P: 011 34973275000, F: 011 34973275008
Ammunition

Case Cutlery (W.R. Case & Sons Cutlery Co.), Owens Way, Bradford, PA 16701, P: 800-523-6350, F: 814-358-1736, www.wrcase.com
Cutlery; Knives/Knife Cases; Sharpeners

Caspian Arms, Ltd., 75 Cal Foster Dr., Wolcott, VT 05680, P: 802-472-6454, F: 802-472-6709, www.caspianarms.com
Firearms; Gun Parts/Gunsmithing; Law Enforcement

Cass Creek International, LLC, 1881 Lyndon Blvd., Falconer, NY 14733, P: 800-778-0389, F: 716-665-6536, www.casscreek.com
Game Calls; Hunting Accessories

Cejay Engineering, LLC/InfraRed Combat Marking Beacons, 2129 Gen Booth Blvd., Suite 103-284, Virginia Beach, VA 23454, P: 603-880-8501, F: 603-880-8502, www.cejayeng.com
Lighting Products

Celestron, 2835 Columbia St., Torrance, CA 90503, P: 310-328-9560, F: 310-212-5835, www.celestron.com
Binoculars; Scopes, Sights & Accessories; Telescopes

Center Mass, Inc., 6845 Woonsocket, Canton, MI 48187, P: 800-794-1216, F: 734-416-0650, www.centermassinc.com
Bags & Equipment Cases; Emblems & Decals; Hunting Accessories; Law Enforcement; Men's Clothing; Shooting Range Equipment; Targets; Training & Safety Equipment

Century International Arms, Inc., 430 S. Congress Dr., Suite 1, DelRay Beach, FL 33445, P: 800-527-1252, F: 561-265-4520, www.centuryarms.com
Ammunition; Firearms; Firearms Maintenance Equipment; Gun Parts/Gunsmithing; Law Enforcement; Magazines, Cartridge; Scopes, Sights & Accessories; Wholesaler/Distributor

Cequre Composite Technologies, 5995 Shier-Rings Rd., Suite A, Dublin, OH 43016, P: 614-526-0095, F: 614-526-0098, www.wearmor.com
Custom Manufacturing; Law Enforcement; Shooting Range Equipment; Targets

Cerakote/NIC Industries, Inc., 7050 Sixth St., White City, OR 97503, P: 866-774-7628, F: 541-830-6518, www.nicindustries.com
Camouflage; Custom Manufacturing; Firearms; Firearms Maintenance Equipment; Knives/Knife Cases; Law Enforcement; Lubricants; Paintball Guns

Champion Traps and Targets/ATK Commercial Products, N5549 Cty. Trunk Z, Onalaska, WI 54650, P: 800-635-7656, F: 763-323-3890, www.championtargetr.com
Clay Targets; Hearing Protection; Shooting Range Equipment; Targets

Chapin International, P.O. Box 549, Batavia, NY 14020, P: 800-444-3140, F: 585-813-0118, www.chapinmfg.com
Feeder Equipment

Chapman Innovations, 343 W. 400 South, Salt Lake City, UT 84101, P: 801-415-0024, F: 801-415-2001, www.carbonx.com
Gloves, Mitts, Hats; Law Enforcement; Men & Women's Clothing

Charter Arms/MKS Supply, Inc., 8611A North Dixie Dr., Dayton, OH 45414, P: 866-769-4867, F: 937-454-0503, www.charterfirearms.com
Firearms

Cheddite France, 99 Route de Lyon, P.O. Box 112, Bourg-les-Valence, 26500, FRANCE, P: 011 33475564545, F: 011 33475563587, www.cheddite.com
Ammunition

Chengdu Lis Business, 4-3-9, 359 Shuhan Rd., Chengdu, SICH 610036, CHINA, P: 0110862887541867, F: 011 862887578686, www.lisoptics.com
Binoculars; Compasses; Cutlery; Lighting Products; Scopes, Sights & Accessories; Telescopes

CheyTac Associates, LLC, 363 Sunset Dr., Arco, ID 83213, P: 256-325-0622, F: 208-527-3328, www.cheytac.com
Ammunition; Computer Software; Custom Manufacturing; Firearms; Law Enforcement; Training & Safety Equipment

Chiappa Firearms-Armi Sport di Chiappa Silvia e C. SNC, Via Milano, 2, Azzano Mella (Bs), 25020, ITALY, P: 011 390309749065, F: 011 390309749232, www.chiappafirearms.com
Black Powder Accessories; Firearms

China Shenzhen Aimbond Enterprises Co., Ltd., 19D, Building No. 1, China Phoenix Building, No. 2008, Shennan Rd., Futian District, Shenzhen, Guangdong 518026, CHINA, P: 011 8675582522730812, F: 011 8675583760022, www.sino-optics.com
Binoculars; Eyewear; Firearms Maintenance Equipment; Hunting Accessories; Lighting Products; Scopes, Sights & Accessories; Telescopes

Chip McCormick Custom, LLC, 105 Sky King Dr., Spicewood, TX 78669, P: 800-328-2447, F: 830-693-4975, www. cmcmags.com
Gun Parts/Gunsmithing; Magazines, Cartridge

Choate Machine & Tool, 116 Lovers Lane, Bald Knob, AR 72010, P: 800-972-6390, F: 501-724-5873, www.riflestock. com
Gun Grips & Stocks; Law Enforcement

Chongqing Dontop Optics Co., Ltd., No. 5 Huangshan Ave. Middle Beibu New District, Chongqing, 401121, CHINA, P: 011 862386815057, F: 011 862386815100, www.dontop. com
Binoculars; Custom Manufacturing; Scopes, Sights & Accessories; Shooting Range Equipment; Telescopes

Chongqing Jizhou Enterprise Co., Ltd., Rm 8-1, Block A3, Jiazhou Garden, Chongqing, Yubei 401147, CHINA, P: 011 862367625115, F: 011 862367625121, www.cqjizhou.com
Binoculars; Compasses; Scopes, Sights & Accessories; Telescopes

Chonwoo Corp./Chonwoo Case & Cover (Tianjin) Co., Ltd., 4-6, SamJun-Dong Songpa-gu, Seoul, 138-837, SOUTH KOREA, P: 011 8224205094, F: 011 8224236154, www. chonwoo.co.kr
Backpacking; Bags & Equipment Cases; Gun Cases; Holsters; Hunting Accessories; Knives/Knife Cases; Leathergoods

Chris Reeve Knives, 2949 S. Victory View Way, Boise, ID 83709, P: 208-375-0367, F: 208-375-0368, www. chrisreeve.com
Backpacking; Camping; Cutlery; Hunting Accessories; Knives/Knife Cases; Law Enforcement; Sports Accessories

Christensen Arms, 192 E. 100 North, Fayette, UT 84630, P: 888-517-8855, F: 435-528-5773, www.christensenarms. com
Custom Manufacturing; Firearms; Gun Barrels

Christie & Christie Enterprises, Inc., 404 Bolivia Blvd., Bradenton, FL 34207, P: 440-413-0031, F: 440-428-5551
Gun Grips & Stocks; Gun Parts/Gunsmithing; Magazines, Cartridge; Scopes, Sights & Accessories; Wholesaler/Distributor

Cimarron Firearms Co., 105 Winding Oaks Rd., P.O. Box 906, Fredericksburg, TX 78624, P: 830-997-9090, F: 830-997-0802, www.cimarron-firearms.com
Black Powder Accessories; Firearms; Gun Cases; Gun Grips & Stocks; Gun Parts/Gunsmithing; Holsters; Leathergoods; Wholesaler/Distributor

Citadel (Cambodia) Pt., Ltd., Nr 5 Str 285 Tuol Kork, Phnom Penh, BP 440, CAMBODIA, P: 011 85512802676, F: 011 85523880015, www.citadel.com.kh
Cutlery

Clark Textile Co./ASF Group, 624 S. Grand Ave., San Pedro, CA 90731, P: 310-831-2334, F: 310-831-2335, www. asfgroup.com
Camouflage; Printing Services

Classic Accessories, 22640 68th Ave. S, Kent, WA 98032, P: 800-854-2315, F: 253-395-3991, www.classicaccessories. com
Bags & Equipment Cases; Camouflage; Gun Cases; Hunting Accessories; Pet Supplies; Wholesaler/Distributor

Classic Old West Styles, 1712 Texas Ave., El Paso, TX 79901, P: 800-595-COWS, F: 915-587-0616, www.cows.com
Custom Manfacturing; Holsters; Hunting Accessories; Leathergoods; Men's Clothing; Outfitter; Sports Accessories; Wholesaler/Distributor

Claude Dozorme Cutlery, Z.A. de Racine-B.P. 19, La Monnerie, 63650, FRANCE, P: 011 33473514106, F: 011 33473514851, www.dozorme-claude.fr
Cutlery

Claybuster Wads/Harvester Muzzleloading, 635 Bob Posey St., Henderson, KY 42420, P: 800-922-6287, F: 270-827-4972, www.claybusterwads.com
Black Powder Accessories; Reloading

Clever SRL, Via A. Da Legnago, 9/A, I-37141 Ponteflorio, Verona, ITALY, P: 011 390458840770, F: 011 390458840380, www.clevervr.com
Ammunition

Cliff Weil, Inc., 8043 Industrial Park Rd., Mechanicsville, VA 23116, P: 800-446-9345, F: 804-746-2595, www.cliffweil. com
Eyewear

Club Red, Inc./Bone Collector by Michael Waddell, 4645 Church Rd., Cumming, GA 30028, P: 888-428-1630, F: 678-947-1445, www.clubredinc.com
Emblems & Decals; Men & Women's Clothing

Clymer Precision, 1605 W. Hamlin Rd., Rochester Hills, MI 48309, P: 877-REAMERS, F: 248-853-1530, www. clymertool.com
Black Powder Accessories; Books/Industry Publications; Custom Manufacturing; Firearms

Maintenance Equipment; Gun Parts/Gunsmithing; Law Enforcement; Reloading

CMere Deer®, 205 Fair Ave., P.O. Box 1336, Winnsboro, LA, 71295, P: 866-644-8600, F: 318-435-3885, www. cmeredeer.com
Scents & Lures

Coastal Boot Co., Inc. 2821 Center Port Circle, Pompano Beach, FL 33064, P: 954-782-3244, F: 954-782-4342, www.coastalboot.com
Footwear

Coast Products/LED Lenser, 8033 NE Holman St., Portland, OR 97218, P: 800-426-5858, F: 503-234-4422, www. coastportland.com
Camping; Compasses; Cutlery; Knives/Knife Cases; Law Enforcement; Lighting Products; Sharpeners

Cobra Enterprises of Utah, Inc., 1960 S. Milestone Dr., Suite F, Salt Lake City, UT 84104, P: 801-908-8300, F: 801-908-8301, www.cobrapistols.net
Firearms

Codet Newport Corp./Big Bill Work Wear, 924 Crawford Rd., Newport, VT 05855, P: 800-992-6338, F: 802-334-8268, www.bigbill.com
Backpacking; Bags & Equipment Cases; Camouflage; Camping; Footwear; Gloves, Mitts, Hats; Men's Clothing

Cold Steel Inc., 3036 Seaborg Ave., Suite A, Ventura, CA 93003, P: 800-255-4716, F: 805-642-9727, www.coldsteel. com
Cutlery; Knives/Knife Cases; Law Enforcement; Sports Accessories; Videos

Collector's Armoury, Ltd., P.O. Box 1050, Lorton, VA 22199, P: 800-336-4572, F: 703-493-9424, www.collectorsarmoury. com
Black Powder Accessories; Books/Industry Publications; Cutlery; Firearms; Holsters; Home Furnishings; Training & Safety Equipment; Wholesaler/Distributor

Colonial Arms, Inc. 1504 Hwy. 31 S, P.O. Box 250, Bay Minette, AL 36507, P: 800-949-8088, F: 251-580-5006, www.colonialarms.com
Firearms; Firearms Maintenance Equipment; Gun Barrels; Gun Parts/Gunsmithing; Hunting Accessories; Lubricants; Recoil Protection Devices & Services; Wholesaler/Distributor

Colt's Manufacturing Co., LLC, P.O. Box 1868, Hartford, CT 06144, P: 800-962-COLT, F: 860-244-1449, www.coltsmfg. com
Custom Manufacturing; Firearms; Gun Parts/ Gunsmithing; Law Enforcement

Columbia River Knife and Tool, 18348 SW 126th Pl., Tualatin, OR 97062, P: 800-891-3100, F: 503-682-9680, www.crkt. com
Knives/Knife Cases; Sharpeners

Columbia Sportswear Co., 14375 NW Science Park Dr., Portland, OR 97229, P: 800-547-8066, F: 503-985-5800, www.columbia.com
Bags & Equipment Cases; Binoculars; Footwear; Gloves, Mitts, Hats; Men & Women's Clothing; Pet Supplies; Scopes, Sights & Accessories

Combined Tactical Systems, 388 Kinsman Rd., P.O. Box 506, Jamestown, PA 16134, P: 724-932-2177, F: 724-932-2166, www.less-lethal.com
Law Enforcement

Compass Industries, Inc., 104 E. 25th St., New York, NW 10010, P: 800-221-9904, F: 212-353-0826, www. compassindustries.com
Binoculars; Camping; Compasses; Cutlery; Export/ Import Specialists; Eyewear; Hunting Accessories; Wholesaler/Distributor

Competition Electronics, 3469 Precision Dr., Rockford, IL 61109, P: 815-874-8001, F: 815-874-8181, www. competitionelectronics.com
Firearms Maintenance Equipment; Reloading; Shooting Range Equipment; Training & Safety Equipment

Condor Outdoor Products, 1866 Business Center Dr., Duarte, CA 93010, P: 800-552-2554, F: 626-303-3383, www. condoroutdoor.com
Backpacking; Bags & Equipment Cases; Camouflage; Footwear; Gun Cases; Holsters; Wholesaler/Distributor

Condor Tool & Knife, Inc., 6309 Marina Dr., Orlando, FL 32819, P: 407-876-0886, F: 407-876-0994, www.condortk.com
Archery; Camping; Custom Manufacturing; Cutlery; Gun Cases; Hunting Accessories; Knives/Knife Cases; Leathergoods

Connecticut Shotgun Mfg. Co., 100 Burritt St., New Britain, CT 06053, P: 800-515-4867, F: 860-832-8707, www. connecticutshotgun.com
Firearms; Firearms Maintenance Equipment; Gun Cabinets/Racks/Safes; Gun Cases; Gun Parts/ Gunsmithing; Hunting Accessories; Knives/Knife Cases; Scopes, Sights & Accessories

Consorzio Armaioli Bresciani, Via Matteotti, 325, Gardone V.T., Brescia 25063, ITALY, P: 011 39030821752, F: 011 39030831425, www.armaiolibresciani.org
Firearms; Gun Parts/Gunsmithing; Videos

Consorzio Cortellinai Maniago SRL, Via Della Repubblica, 21, Maniago, PN 33085, ITALY, P: 011 390427771185, F: 011 390427700440, www.consorziocoltellinai.it
Camping; Cutlery; Hunting Accessories; Knives/Knife Cases; Law Enforcement

Convert-A-Ball Distributing, Inc., 955 Ball St., P.O. Box 199, Sidney, NE 69162, P: 800-543-1732, F: 308-254-7194, www.convert-a-ball.net
Camping; Vehicles, Utility & Rec

Cooper Firearms of MT, Inc./Cooper Arms, 4004 Hwy. 93 North, P.O. Box 114, Stevensville, MT 59870, P: 406-777-0373, F: 406-777-5228, www.cooperfirearms.com
Custom Manufacturing; Firearms

CopShoes.com/MetBoots.com, 6655 Poss Rd., San Antonio, TX 78238, P: 866-280-0400, F: 210-647-1401, www. copshoes.com
Footwear; Hunting Accessories; Law Enforcement

Cor-Bon/Glaser/Div. Dakota Ammo Inc., 1311 Industry Rd., P.O. Box 369, Sturgis, SD 57785, P: 605-347-4544, F: 605-347-5055, www.corbon.com
Ammunition

Cornell Hunting Products, 114 Woodside Dr., Honea Path, SC 29654, P: 864-369-9587, F: 864-369-9587, www. cornellhuntinproducts.com
Backpacking; Game Calls; Hunting Accessories; Wholesaler/Distributor

Corsivia, Poligono El Campillo, Calle Alemania, 59-61, Zuera, (Zaragoza) 50800, SPAIN, P: 011 34976680075, F: 011 34976680124, www.corsivia.com
Clay Targets

Counter Assault Pepper Sprays/Bear Deterrent, Law Enforcement & Personal Defense, 120 Industrial Court, Kalispell, MT 59901, P: 800-695-3394. F: 406-257-6674, www.counterassault.com
Archery; Backpacking; Camping; Hunting Accessories; Law Enforcement; Sports Accessories; Survival Kits/First Aid; Training & Safety Equipment

Crackshot Corp., 2623 E 36th St. N, Tulsa, OK 74110, P: 800-667-1753, F: 918-838-1271, www.crackshotcorp.com
Archery; Backpacking; Camping; Footwear; Hunting Accessories; Men & Women's Clothing; Training & Safety Equipment

Creative Castings/Les Douglas, 12789 Olympic View Rd. NW, Silverdale, WA 98383, P: 800-580-6516, F: 800-580-0495, www.wildlifepins.com
Custom Manufacturing; Emblems & Decals; Outdoor Art, Jewelry, Sculpture; Pet Supplies; Retailer Services; Watches; Wholesaler/Distributor

Creative Pet Products, P.O. Box 39, Spring Valley, WI 54767, P: 888-436-4566, F: 877-269-6911, www.petfirstaidkits. com
Gloves, Mitts, Hats; Pet Supplies; Survival Kits/First Aid; Training & Safety Equipment

Crest Ultrasonics Corp., P.O. Box 7266, Trenton, NJ 08628, P: 800-273-7822, F: 877-254-7939, www.crest-ultrasonics. com
Custom Manufacturing; Firearms Maintenance Equipment; Gun Parts/Gunsmithing; Law Enforcement; Lubricants; Shooting Range Equipment; Wholesaler/Distributor

Crimson Trace Holdings, LLC/Lasergrips, 9780 SW Freeman Dr., Wilsonville, OR 97070, P: 800-442-2406, F: 503-783-5334, www.crimsontrace.com
Firearms; Gun Grips & Stocks; Hunting Accessories; Law Enforcement; Scopes, Sights & Accessories; Training & Safety Equipment

Critter Cribs, P.O. Box 48545, Fort Worth, TX 76148, P: 877-611-2742, F: 866-351-3291, www.crittercribs.com
Camouflage; Hunting Accessories; Law Enforcement; Pet Supplies

Crooked Horn Outfitters, 26315 Trotter Dr., Tehachapi, CA 93561, P: 877-722-5872, F: 661-822-9100, www. crookedhorn.com
Archery; Bags & Equipment Cases; Binoculars; Hunting Accessories

Crosman Corp., Inc., Routes 5 and 20, East Bloomfield, NY 14443, P: 800-724-7486, F: 585-657-5405, www.crosman. com
Airguns; Airsoft; Ammunition; Archery; Crossbows & Accessories; Scopes, Sights & Accessories; Shooting Range Equipment; Targets

Crye Precision, LLC, 63 Flushing Ave., Suite 252, Brooklyn, NY 11205, P: 718-246-3838, F: 718-246-3833, www. cryeprecision.com
Bags & Equipment Cases; Camouflage; Custom Manufacturing; Law Enforcement; Men's Clothing

Cuppa, 3131 Morris St. N, St. Petersburg, FL 33713, P: 800-551-6541, F: 727-820-9212, www.cuppa.net

Custom Manufacturing; Emblems & Decals; Law Enforcement; Outdoor Art, Jewelry, Sculpture; Retailer Services

Custom Leather, 460 Bingemans Centre Dr., Kitchener, Ontario N2B 3X9, CANADA, P: 800-265-4504, F: 519-741-2072, www.customleather.com
Custom Manufacturing; Gun Cases; Hunting Accessories; Leathergoods

Cutting Edge Tactical, 166 Mariners Way, Moyock, NC 27958, P: 800-716-9425, F: 252-435-2284, www.cuttingedgetactical.com
Bags & Equipment Cases; Binoculars; Eyewear; Footwear; Gun Grips & Stocks; Law Enforcement; Lighting Products; Training & Safety Equipment

Cybrics, Ltd., No 68, Xing Yun Rd., Jin San Industrial Area, Yiwu, Zhejiang 322011, CHINA, P: 011 8657985556142, F: 011 8657985556210, www.cybrics.eu
Bags & Equipment Cases; Camouflage; Gloves, Mitts, Hats; Men & Women's Clothing

Cygnus Law Enforcement Group, 1233 Janesville Ave., Fort Atkinson, WI 53538, P: 800-547-7377, F: 303-322-0627, www.officer.com
Law Enforcement

Cylinder & Slide, Inc., 245 E. 4th St., Fremont, NE 68025, P: 800-448-1713, F: 402-721-0263, www.cylinder-slide.com
Firearms; Gun Barrels; Gun Grips & Stocks; Gun Parts/Gunsmithing; Magazines, Cartridge; Scopes, Sights & Accessories; Wholesaler/Distributor

D

DAC Technologies/GunMaster, 12120 Colonel Glenn Rd., Suite 6200, Little Rock, AR 72210, P: 800-920-0098, F: 501-661-9108, www.dactec.com
Black Powder Accessories; Camping; Cooking Equipment/Accessories; Firearms Maintenance Equipment; Gun Cabinets/Racks/Safes; Gun Locks; Hunting Accessories; Wholesaler/Distributor

DMT-Diamond Machine Technology, 84 Hayes Memorial Dr., Marlborough, MA 01752, P: 800-666-4368, F: 508-485-3924, www.dmtsharp.com
Archery; Cooking Equipment/Accessories; Cutlery; Hunting Accessories; Knives/Knife Cases; Sharpeners; Sports Accessories; Taxidermy

D & K Mfg., Co., Inc., 5180 US Hwy. 380, Bridgeport, TX 76426, P: 800-553-1028, F: 940-683-0248, www.d-k.net
Bags & Equipment Cases; Custom Manufacturing; Emblems & Decals; Law Enforcement; Leathergoods

D.S.A., Inc., 27 W. 990 Industrial Ave. (60010), P.O. Box 370, Lake Barrington, IL 60011, P: 847-277-7258, F: 847-277-7263, www.dsarms.com
Ammunition; Books/Industry Publications; Firearms; Gun Grips & Stocks; Gun Parts/Gunsmithing; Law Enforcement; Magazines, Cartridge; Scopes, Sights & Accessories

Daisy Manufacturing Co./Daisy Outdoors Products, 400 W. Stribling Dr., P.O. Box 220, Rogers, AR 72756, P: 800-643-3458, F: 479-636-0573, www.daisy.com
Airguns; Airsoft; Ammunition; Clay Targets; Eyewear; Scopes, Sights & Accessories; Targets; Training & Safety Equipment

Dakota Arms, Inc., 1310 Industry Rd., Sturgis, SD 57785, P: 605-347-4686, F: 605-347-4459, www.dakotaarms.com
Ammunition; Custom Manufacturing; Export/Import Specialists; Firearms; Gun Cases; Gun Grips & Stocks; Gun Parts/Gunsmithing; Reloading

Damascus Protective Gear, P.O. Box 543, Rutland, VT, 05702, P: 800-305-2417, F: 805-639-0610, www.damascusgear.com
Archery; Custom Manufacturing; Gloves, Mitts, Hats; Law Enforcement; Leathergoods

Danalco, Inc., 1020 Hamilton Rd., Suite G, Duarte, CA 91010, P: 800-868-2629, F: 800-216-9938, www.danalco.com
Footwear; Gloves, Mitts, Hats

Dan's Whetstone Co., Inc./Washita Mountain Whetstone Co., 418 Hilltop Rd., Pearcy, AR 71964, P: 501-767-1616, F: 501-767-9598, www.danswhetstone.com
Black Powder Accessories; Camping; Cutlery; Gun Parts/Gunsmithing; Hunting Accessories; Knives/Knife Cases; Sharpeners; Sports Accessories

Daniel Defense, Inc., 6002 Commerce Blvd., Suite 109, Savannah, GA 31408, P: 866-554-4867, F: 912-964-4237, www.danieldefense.com
Firearms

Danner, Inc., 17634 NE Airport Way, Portland, OR 97230, P: 800-345-0430, F: 503-251-1119
Footwear

Darkwoods Blind, LLC, 1209 SE 44th, Suite 2, Oklahoma City, OK 73129, P: 405-520-6754, F: 405-677-2262, www.darkwoodsblind.com
Archery; Blinds; Camouflage; Custom Manufacturing; Firearms; Hunting Accessories; Outfitter; Vehicles, Utility & Rec

Darn Tough Vermont, 364 Whetstone Dr., P.O. Box 307, Northfield, VT 05663, P: 877-DARNTUFF, F: 802-485-6140, www.darntough.com
Backpacking; Camping; Footwear; Hunting Accessories; Men & Women's Clothing

Davidson's, 6100 Wilkinson Dr., Prescott, AZ, 86301, P: 800-367-4867, F: 928-776-0344, www.galleryofguns.com
Ammunition; Firearms; Law Enforcement; Magazines, Cartridge; Online Services; Scopes, Sights & Accessories; Wholesaler/Distributor

Day Six Outdoors, 1150 Brookstone Centre Parkway, Columbus, GA 31904, P: 877-DAY-SIX0, F: 706-323-0178, www.day6outdoors.com
Feeder Equipment; Wildlife Management

Del Norte Outdoors, P.O. Box 5046, Santa Maria, CA 93456, P: 805-474-1793, F: 805-474-1793, www.delnorteoutdoors.com
Archery; Hunting Accessories; Sports Accessories

Del-Ton, Inc., 218B Aviation Pkwy., Elizabethtown, NC 28337, P: 910-645-2172, F: 910-645-2244, www.del-ton.com
Firearms; Gun Barrels; Gun Parts/Gunsmithing; Law Enforcement; Wholesaler/Distributor

DeLorme, Two DeLorme Dr., Yarmouth, ME 04096, P: 800-335-6763, F: 800-575-2244, www.delorme.com
Books/Industry Publications; Computer Software; Hunting Accessories; Sports Accessories; Tours/Travel

Demyan, 10, 2nd Donskoy Ln., Moscow, 119071, RUSSIAN FEDERATION, P: 011 74959847629, F: 011 74959847629, www.demyan.info
Airguns; Firearms

Dengta Sinpraise Weaving & Dressing Co., Ltd., Tai Zihe District, Wangshuitai Pangjiahe, Liao Yang, LiaoNing Province 111000, CHINA, P: 011 964193305888, F: 011 864193990566, www.sinpraise-hunting.com
Camouflage; Camping; Men & Women's Clothing; Sports Accessories

DeSantis Holster and Leather Goods Co., 431 Bayview Ave., Amityville, NY 11701, P: 800-424-1236, F: 631-841-6320, www.desantisholster.com
Bags & Equipment Cases; Gun Cases; Holsters; Hunting Accessories; Law Enforcement; Leathergoods

Desert Tactical Arms, P.O. Box 65816, Salt Lake City, UT 84165, P: 801-975-7272, F: 801-908-6425, www.deserttacticalarms.com
Firearms; Law Enforcement

Desiccare, Inc., 3400 Pomona Blvd., Pomona, CA 91768, P: 800-446-6650, F: 909-444-9045, www.desiccare.com
Food; Footwear; Gun Cabinets/Racks/Safes; Leathergoods; Scents & Lures

Diamondback Tactical, 23040 N. 11th Ave., Bldg. 1, Phoenix, AZ 85027, P: 800-735-7030, F: 623-583-0674, www.diamondbacktactical.com
Law Enforcement

Diana/Mayer & Grammelspacher GmbH & Co. KG, Karlstr, 34, Rastatt, 76437, GERMANY, P: 011 4972227620, F: 011 49722276278, www.diana-airguns.de
Airguns; Scopes, Sights & Accessories

Dillon Precision Products, Inc., 8009 E. Dillon's Way, Scottsdale, AZ 85260, P: 800-223-4570, F: 480-998-2786, www.dillonprecision.com
Bags & Equipment Cases; Feeder Equipment; Hearing Protection; Holsters; Hunting Accessories; Reloading

Dimension 3D Printing, 7655 Commerce Way, Eden Prairie, MN 55344, P: 888-480-3548, F: 952-294-3715, www.dimensionprinting.com
Computer Software; Custom Manufacturing; Gun Parts/Gunsmithing; Hunting Accessories; Scopes, Sights & Accessories

Ding Zing Chemical Products Co., Ltd., No. 8-1 Pei-Lin Rd., Hsiao-Kang Dist., Kaohsiung, 812, TAIWAN, P: 011 88678070166, F: 011 88678071616, www.dingzing.com
Backpacking; Bags & Equipment Cases; Camping; Custom Manufacturing; Footwear; Gloves, Mitts, Hats; Men & Women's Clothing; Sports Accessories

Directex, 304 S. Leighton Ave., Anniston, AL 36207, P: 800-845-3603, F: 256-235-2275, www\directex.net
Archery; Backpacking; Bags & Equipment Cases; Custom Manufacturing; Export/Import Specialists; Gun Cases; Holsters; Hunting Accessories

Dixie Gun Works, Inc., 1412 W. Reelfoot Ave., P.O. Box 130, Union City, TN 38281, P: 800-238-6785, F: 731-885-0440, www.dixiegunworks.com
Black Powder Accessories; Book/Industry Publications; Firearms; Gun Parts/Gunsmithing; Hunting Accessories; Knives/Knife Cases

DNZ Products, LLC/Game Reaper & Freedom Reaper Scope Mounts, 2710 Wilkins Dr., Sanford, NC 27330, P: 919-777-9608, F: 919-777-9609, www.dnzproducts.com

Black Powder Accessories; Custom Manufacturing; Gun Parts/Gunsmithing; Hunting Accessories; Scopes, Sights & Accessories

Do-All Traps, LLC/dba Do-All Outdoors, 216 19th Ave. N, Nashville, TN 37203, P: 800-252-9247, F: 800-633-3172, www.doalloutdoors.com
Clay Targets; Gun Cases; Hunting Accessories; Outdoor Art, Jewelry, Sculpture; Recoil Protection Devices & Services; Shooting Range Equipment; Targets; Taxidermy

Doc's Deer Farm and Scents, 2118 Niles-Cortland Rd., Cortland, OH 44420, P: 330-638-9507, F: 330-638-2772, www.docsdeerscents.com
Archery; Hunting Accessories; Scents & Lures

Docter Optic/Imported by Merkel USA, 7661 Commerce Lane, Trussville, AL 35173, P: 800-821-3021, F: 205-655-7078, www.merkel-usa.com
Binoculars; Scopes, Sights & Accessories

Dogtra Co., 22912 Lockness Ave., Torrance, CA, 90501, P: 888-811-9111, F: 310-534-9111, www.dogtra.com
Hunting Accessories; Pet Supplies; Training & Safety Equipment

Dokken Dog Supply, Inc., 4186 W. 85th St., Northfield, MN 55057, P: 507-744-2616, F: 507-744-5575, www.deadfowltrainer.com
Hunting Accessories; Pet Supplies; Scents & Lures; Training & Safety Equipment

DoubleStar/J&T Distributing, P.O. Box 430, Winchester, KY 40391, P: 888-736-7725, F: 859-745-4638, www.jtdistributing.com
Firearms; Firearms Maintenance Equipment; Gun Barrels; Gun Parts/Gunsmithing; Magazines, Cartridge; Wholesaler/Distributor

Down Range Mfg., LLC, 4170 N. Gun Powder Circle, Hastings, NE 68901, P: 402-463-3415, F: 402-463-3452, www.downrangemfg.com
Ammunition; Clay Targets; Custom Manufacturing; Reloading

Down Wind Scents, LLC, P.O. Box 549, Severna Park, MD 21146, P: 410-647-8451, F: 410-647-7828, www.downwindscents.com
Archery; Firearms Maintenance Equipment; Hunting Accessories; Lubricants; Scents & Lures

DPMS Firearms, LLC, 3312 12th St. SE, St. Cloud, MN 56304, P: 800-578-3767, F: 320-258-4449, www.dpmsinc.com
Firearms; Scopes, Sights & Accessories

Dri Duck Traders, 7007 College Blvd., Suite 700, Overland Park, KS 66221, P: 866-852-8222, F: 913-234-6280, www.driducktraders.com
Camouflage; Men & Women's Clothing

DriFire, LLC, 3151 Williams Rd., Suite E, Columbus, GA 31909, P: 866-266-4035, F: 706-507-7556, www.drifire.com
Camouflage; Men & Women's Clothing; Training & Safety Equipment

DryGuy, LLC, P.O. Box 1102, Mercer Island, WA 98040, P: 888-330-9452, F: 206-232-9830, www.maxxdry.com
Backpacking; Bags & Equipment Cases; Camping; Footwear; Gloves, Mitts, Hats; Hunting Accessories; Sports Accessories; Wholesaler/Distributor

Du-Lite Corp., 171 River Rd., Middletown, CT 06457, P: 860-347-2505, F: 860-344-9404, www.du-lite.com
Gunsmithing; Lubricants

Duck Commander Co., Inc./Buck Commander Co., Inc., 1978 Brownlee Rd., Calhoun, LA 71225, P: 318-396-1126, F: 318-396-1127, www.duckcommander.com
Camping; Emblems & Decals; Food; Game Calls; Gun Cases; Hunting Accessories, Men & Women's Clothing; Videos

Ducks Unlimited, Inc., One Waterfowl Way, Memphis, TN 38120, P: 800-45-DUCKS, F: 901-758-3850, www.ducks.org
Books/Industry Publications; Camouflage; Decoys; Firearms; Hunting Accessories; Outdoor Art, Jewelry, Sculpture; Wildlife Management

Duk-Inn-Blind, 49750 Alpine Dr., Macomb, MI 48044, P: 586-855-7494, F: 603-626-4672
Blinds; Camouflage; Hunting Accessories; Wholesaler/Distributor

Dummies Unlimited, Inc., 2435 Pine St., Pomona, CA 91767, P: 866-4DUMMIES, F: 909-392-7510, F: 909-392-7510, www.dummiesunlimited.com
Law Enforcement; Shooting Range Equipment; Targets; Training & Safety Equipment

Duostock Designs, Inc., P.O. Box 32, Welling, OK 74471, P: 866-386-7865, F: 918-431-3182, www.duostock.com
Firearms; Gun Grips & Stocks; Law Enforcement; Recoil Protection Devices & Services

Durasight Scope Mounting Systems, 5988 Peachtree Corners East, Norcross, GA 30071, P: 800-321-8767, F: 770-242-8546, www.durasight.com
Scopes, Sights & Accessories

Dynamic Research Technologies, LLC, 405 N. Lyon St., Grant City, MO 64456, P: 660-564-2331, F: 660-564-2103, www.drtammo.com
Ammunition; Reloading

E

E-Z Mount Corp., 1706 N. River Dr., San Angelo, TX 76902, P: 800-292-3756, F: 325-658-4951, www.ezmountcorp@zipnet.us
Gun Cabinets/Racks/Safes

E-Z Pull Trigger, 932 W. 5th St., Centralia, IL 62801, P: 618-532-6964, F: 618-532-5154, www.ezpulltriggerassist.com
Firearms; Gun Parts/Gunsmithing; Hunting Accessories

E.A.R., Inc./Insta-Mold Div., P.O. Box 18888, Boulder, CO 80303, P: 800-525-2690, F: 303-447-2637, www.earinc.com
Eyewear; Hearing Protection; Law Enforcement; Shooting Range Equipment; Wholesaler/Distributor

ER Shaw/Small Arms Mfg., 5312 Thoms Run Rd., Bridgeville, PA 15017, P: 412-221-4343, F: 412-221-4303, www.ershawbarrels.com
Custom Manufacturing; Firearms; Gun Barrels

ECS Composites, 3560 Rogue River Hwy., Grants Pass, OR 97527, P: 541-476-8871, F: 541-474-2479, www.transitcases.com
Custom Manufacturing; Gun Cases; Law Enforcement; Sports Accessories

EMCO Supply, Inc./Red Rock Outdoor Gear, 2601 Dutton Ave., Waco, TX 76711, P: 800-342-4654, F: 254-662-0045
Backpacking; Bags & Equipment Cases; Blinds; Camouflage; Compasses; Game Calls; Hunting Accessories; Law Enforcement

E.M.F. Co., Inc./Purveyors of Fine Firearms Since 1956, 1900 E. Warner Ave., Suite 1-D, Santa Ana, CA 92705, P: 800-430-1310, F: 800-508-1824, www.emf-company.com
Black Powder Accessories; Firearms; Gun Parts/Gunsmithing; Holsters; Leathergoods; Wholesaler/Distributor

EOTAC, 1940 Old Dunbar Rd., West Columbia, SC 29172, P: 803-744-9930, F: 803-744-9933, www.eotac.com
Tactical Clothing

ESS Goggles, P.O. Box 1017, Sun Valley, ID 83353, P: 877-726-4072, F: 208-726-4563
Eyewear; Hunting Accessories; Law Enforcement; Shooting Range Equipment; Training & Safety Equipment

ETL/Secure Logic, 2351 Tenaya Dr., Modesto, CA 95354, P: 800-344-3242, F: 209-529-3854, www.securelogiconline.com
Firearms; Gun Cabinets/Racks/Safes; Training & Safety Equipment

EZ 4473/American Firearms Software, 5955 Edmond St., Las Vegas, NV 89118, P: 702-364-9022, F: 702-364-9063, www.ez4473.com
Computer Software; Retailer Services

EZE-LAP® Diamond Products, 3572 Arrowhead Dr., Carson City, NV 89706, P: 800-843-4815, F: 775-888-9555, www.eze-lap.com
Camping; Cooking Equipment/Accessories; Cutlery; Gun Parts/Gunsmithing; Hunting Accessories; Sharpeners; Sports Accessories

Eagle Grips, Inc., 460 Randy Rd., Carol Stream, IL, 60188, P: 800-323-6144, F: 630-260-0486, www.eaglegrips.com
Gun Grips & Stocks

Eagle Imports, Inc., 1750 Brielle Ave., Suite B-1, Wanamassa, NJ 07712, P: 732-493-0333, F: 732-493-0301, www.bersafirearmsusa.com
Export/Import Specialists; Firearms; Holsters; Magazines, Cartridge; Wholesaler/Distributor

Eagle Industries Unlimited, Inc., 1000 Biltmore Dr., Fenton, MO 63026, P: 888-343-7547, F: 636-349-0321, www.eagleindustries.com
Backpacking; Bags & Equipment Cases; Camping; Gun Cases; Holsters; Hunting Accessories; Law Enforcement; Sports Accessories

Eagle Seed Co., 8496 Swan Pond Rd., P.O. Box 308, Weiner, AR 72479, P: 870-684-7377, F: 870-684-2225, www.eagleseed.com
Custom Manufacturing; Retail Packaging; Wholesaler/Distributor; Wildlife Management

Ear Phone Connection, 25139 Avenue Stanford, Valencia, CA 91355, P: 888-372-1888, F: 661-775-5622, www.earphoneconnect.com
Airsoft; Hearing Protection; Law Enforcement; Paintball Accessories; Two-Way Radios

EarHugger Safety Equipment, Inc., 1819 N. Main St., Suite 8, Spanish Fork, UT 84660, P: 800-236-1449, F: 801-371-8901, www.earhuggersafety.com
Law Enforcement

Easy Loop Lock, LLC, 8049 Monetary Dr., Suite D-4, Riviera Beach, FL 33404, P: 561-304-4990, F: 561-337-4655, www.ellock.com
Camping; Gun Locks; Hunting Accessories; Sports Accessories; Wholesaler/Distributor

E-Z Mount Corp., 1706 N. River Dr., San Angelo, TX 76902, P: 800-292-3756, F: 325-658-4951, www.ezmountcorp@zipnet.us
Gun Cabinets/Racks/Safes

E-Z Pull Trigger, 932 W. 5th St., Centralia, IL 62801, P: 618-532-6964, F: 618-532-5154, www.ezpulltriggerassist.com
Firearms; Gun Parts/Gunsmithing; Hunting Accessories

Eberlestock, P.O. Box 862, Boise, ID 83701, P: 877-866-3047, F: 240-526-2632, www.eberlestock.com
Archery; Backpacking; Bags & Equipment Cases; Gun Grips & Stocks; Hunting Accessories; Law Enforcement

Ed Brown Products, Inc., P.O. Box 492, Perry, MO 63462, P: 573-565-3261, F: 573-565-2791, www.edbrown.com
Computer Software; Custom Manufacturing; Firearms; Gun Barrels; Gun Parts/Gunsmithing; Magazines, Cartridge; Scopes, Sights & Accessories

EdgeCraft Corp./Chefs Choice, 825 Southwood Rd., Avondale, PA 19311, P: 800-342-3255, F: 610-268-3545, www.edgecraft.com
Cooking Equipment/Accessories; Custom Manufacturing; Cutlery; Export/Import Specialists; Hunting Accessories; Knives/Knife Cases; Sharpeners

Edgemaker Co., The/(formerly) The Jennex Co., 3902 Funston St., Toledo, OH 43612, P: 800-531-EDGE, F: 419-478-0833, www.edgemaker.com
Camping; Cutlery; Hunting Accessories; Sharpeners; Sports Accessories; Wholesaler/Distributor

El Paso Saddlery, 2025 E. Yandell, El Paso, TX 79903, P: 915-544-2233, F: 915-544-2535, www.epsaddlery.com
Holsters; Leathergoods

Elastic Products/Industrial Opportunities, Inc., 2586 Hwy. 19, P.O. Box 1649, Andrews, NC 28901, P: 800-872-4264, F: 828-321-4784, www.elasticproducts.com
Camouflage; Custom Manufacturing; Hunting Accessories; Men's Clothing

ELCAN Optical Technologies, 1601 N. Plano Rd., Richardson, TX 75081, P: 877-TXELCAN, F: 972-344-8260, www.elcan.com
Binoculars; Custom Manufacturing; Law Enforcement; Scopes, Sights & Accessories

Elder Hosiery Mills, Inc., 139 Homewood Ave., P.O. Box 2377, Burlington, NC 27217, P: 800-745-0267, F: 336-226-5846, www.elderhosiery.com
Footwear

Eley Limited/Eley Hawk Limited, Selco Way, First Ave., Minworth Industrial Estate, Minworth, Sutton Coldfield, West Midlands B76 1BA, UNITED KINGDOM, P: 011 4401213134567, F: 011-4401213134568, www.eleyammunition.com, www.eleyhawkltd.com
Ammunition

Elite First Aid, Inc., 700 E. Club Blvd., Durham, NC 27704, P: 800-556-2537, F: 919-220-6071, www.elite1staid.com
Backpacking; Camping; Cooking Equipment/Accessories; Hunting Accessories; Sports Accessories; Survival Kits/First Aid; Wholesaler/Distributor

Elite Iron, LLC, 1345 Thunders Trail, Bldg. D, Potomac, MT 59823, P: 406-244-0234, F: 406-244-0135, www.eliteiron.net
Law Enforcement; Scopes, Sights & Accessories

Elite Survival Systems, 310 W. 12th St., P.O. Box 245, Washington, MO 63090, P: 866-340-2778, F: 636-390-2977, www.elitesurvival.com
Backpacking; Bags & Equipment Cases; Custom Manufacturing; Footwear; Gun Cases; Holsters; Knives/Knife Cases; Law Enforcement

Ellett Brothers, 267 Columbia Ave., P.O. Box 128, Chapin, SC 29036, P: 800-845-3711, F: 800-323-3006, www.ellettbrothers.com
Ammunition; Archery; Black Powder Accessories; Firearms; Hunting Accessories; Leathergoods; Scopes, Sights & Accessories; Wholesaler/Distributor

Ellington-Rush, Inc./Cough Silencer/SlingStix, 170 Private Dr., Lula, GA 30554, P: 706-677-2394, F: 706-677-3425, www.coughsilencer.com, www.slingstix.com
Archery; Black Powder Accessories; Game Calls; Hunting Accessories; Law Enforcement; Shooting Range Equipment

Elvex Corp., 13 Trowbridge, Bethel, CT 06801, P: 800-888-6582, F: 203-791-2278, www.elvex.com
Eyewear; Hearing Protection; Hunting Accessories; Law Enforcement; Men's Clothing; Paintball Accessories

Emerson Knives, Inc., 2730 Monterey St., Suite 101, Torrance, CA 90503, P: 310-212-7455, F: 310-212-7289, www.emersonknives.com
Camping; Cutlery; Knives/Knife Cases; Men & Women's Clothing; Wholesaler/Distributor

Empire Pewter Manufacturing, P.O. Box 15, Amsterdam, NY 12010, P: 518-843-0048, F: 518-843-7050
Custom Manufacturing; Emblems & Decals; Outdoor Art, Jewelry, Sculpture

Energizer Holdings, 533 Maryville University Dr., St. Louis, MO 63141, P: 314-985-2000, F: 314-985-2207, www.energizer.com
Backpacking; Camping; Hunting Accessories; Law Enforcement; Lighting Products; Sports Accessories; Survival Kits/First Aid; Training & Safety Equipment

Enforcement Technology Group, Inc., 400 N. Broadway, 4th Floor, Milwaukee, WI 53202, P: 800-873-2872, F: 414-276-1533, www.etgi.us
Custom Manufacturing; Law Enforcement; Online Services; Shooting Range Equipment; Training & Safety Equipment; Wholesaler/Distributor

Entreprise Arms, Inc., 5321 Irwindale Ave., Irwindale, CA 91706-2025, P: 626-962-8712, F: 626-962-4692, www.entreprise.com
Firearms; Gun Parts/Gunsmithing

Environ-Metal, Inc./Hevishot®, 1307 Clark Mill Rd., P.O. Box 834, Sweet Home, OR 97386, P: 541-367-3522, F: 541-367-3352, www.hevishot.com
Ammunition; Law Enforcement; Reloading

EOTAC, 1940 Old Dunbar Rd., West Columbia, SC 29172, P: 888-672-0303, F: 803-744-9933, www.eotac.com
Gloves, Mitts, Hats; Men's Clothing

Epilog Laser, 16371 Table Mountain Pkwy., Golden, CO 80403, P: 303-277-1188, F: 303-277-9669, www.epiloglaser.com

Essential Gear, Inc./eGear, 171 Wells St., Greenfield, MA 01301, P: 800-582-3861, F: 413-772-8947, www.essentialgear.com
Backpacking; Camping; Hunting Accessories; Law Enforcement; Lighting Products; Sports Accessories; Survival Kits/First Aid; Training & Safety Equipment

European American Armory Corp., P.O. Box 560746, Rockledge, FL 32956, P: 321-639-4842, F: 321-639-7006, www.eaacorp.com
Airguns; Firearms

Evans Sports, Inc., 801 Industrial Dr., P.O. Box 20, Houston, MO 65483, P: 800-748-8318, F: 417-967-2819, www.evanssports.com
Ammunition; Bags & Equipment Cases; Camping; Custom Manufacturing; Gun Cabinets/Racks/Safes; Hunting Accessories; Retail Packaging; Sports Accessories

Evolved Habitats, 2261 Morganza Hwy., New Roads, LA 70760, P: 225-638-4016, F: 225-638-4009, www.evolved.com
Archery; Export/Import Specialists; Hunting Accessories; Pet Supplies; Scents & Lures; Wildlife Management

Extendo Bed Co., 223 Roedel Ave., Caldwell, ID 83605, P: 800-752-0706, F: 208-286-0925, www.extendobed.com
Law Enforcement; Training & Safety Equipment

Extreme Dimension Wildlife Calls, LLC, 208 Kennebec Rd., Hampden, ME 04444, P: 866-862-2825, F: 207-862-3925, www.phantomcalls.com
Game Calls

Extreme Shock USA, 182 Camp Jacob Rd., Clintwood, VA 24228, P: 877-337-6772, F: 276-926-6092, www.extremeshockusa.net
Ammunition; Law Enforcement; Lubricants; Reloading

ExtremeBeam Tactical, 2275 Huntington Dr., Suite 872, San Marino, CA 91108, P: 626-372-5898, F: 626-609-0640, www.extremebeamtactical.com
Camping; Law Enforcement; Lighting Products; Outfitter

Exxel Outdoors, Inc., 14214 Atlanta Dr., Laredo, TX 78045, P: 956-724-8933, F: 956-725-2516, www.prestigemfg.com
Camping; Export/Import Specialists; Men's Clothing

F

F&W Media/Krause Publications, 700 E. State St., Iola, WI 54990, P: 800-457-2873, F: 715-445-4087, www.krausebooks.com
Books/Industry Publications; Videos

F.A.I.R. Srl, Via Gitti, 41, Marcheno, 25060, ITALY, P: 011 39030861162, F: 011 390308610179, www.fair.it
Firearms; Gun Barrels; Gun Parts/Gunsmithing; Hunting Accessories

F.A.P. F. LLI Pietta SNC, Via Mandolossa, 102, Gussago, Brescia 25064, ITALY, P: 011 390303737098, F: 011 390303737100, www.pietta.it

Black Powder Accessories; Firearms; Gun Cases; Gun Grips & Stocks; Gun Parts/Gunsmithing; Holsters

F.I.A.V. L. Mazzacchera SPA, Via S. Faustino, 62, Milano, 20134, ITALY, P: 011 390221095411, F: 011 390221095530, www.flav.it
Gun Parts/Gunsmithing

FMG Publications/Shooting Industry Magazine, 12345 World Trade Dr., San Diego, CA 92128, P: 800-537-3006, F: 858-605-0247, www.shootingindustry.com
Books/Industry Publications; Videos

FNH USA, P.O. Box 697, McLean, VA 22101, P: 703-288-1292, F: 703-288-1730, www.fnhusa.com
Ammunition; Firearms; Law Enforcement; Training & Safety Equipment

F.T.C. (Friedheim Tool), 1433 Roosevelt Ave., National City, CA 91950, 619-474-3600, F: 619-474-1300, www.ftcsteamers.com
Firearms Maintenance Equipment

Fab Defense, 43 Yakov Olamy St., Moshav Mishmar Hashiva, 50297, ISRAEL, P: 011 972039603399, F: 011 972039603312, www.fab-defense.com
Gun Grips & Stocks; Law Enforcement; Targets

FailZero, 7825 SW Ellipse Way, Stuart, FL 34997, P: 772-223-6699, F: 772-223-9996
Gun Parts/Gunsmithing

Falcon Industries, P.O. Box 1690, Edgewood, NM 87015, P: 877-281-3783, F: 505-281-3991, www.ergogrips.net
Gun Grips & Stocks; Gun Parts/Gunsmithing; Law Enforcement; Scopes, Sights & Accessories; Sports Accessories

Fasnap® Corp., 3500 Reedy Dr., Elkhart, IN 46514, P: 800-624-2058, F: 574-264-0802, www.fasnap.com
Backpacking; Bags & Equipment Cases; Gun Cases; Holsters; Hunting Accessories; Knives/Knife Cases; Leathergoods; Wholesaler/Distributor

Faulk's Game Call Co., Inc., 616 18th St., Lake Charles, LA 70601, P: 337-436-9726, FL 337-494-7205, www.faulkcalls.com
Game Calls

Fausti Stefano s.r.l., Via Martiri dell'Indipendenza 70, Marcheno (BS), 25060, ITALY, P: 011 390308960220, F: 011 390308610155, www.faustistefanoarms.com
Firearms

Feather Flage "Ducks In A Row Camo"/B & D Garments, LLC, P.O. Box 5326, Lafayette, LA 70502, P: 866-DUK-CAMO, F: 337-896-8137, www.featherflage.com
Camouflage; Wholesaler/Distributor

Federal Premium Ammunition/ATK Commercial Products, 900 Ehlen Dr., Anoka, MN 55303, P: 800-322-2342, F: 763-323-2506, www.federalpremium.com
Ammunition

Feijuang International Corp., 4FI-1/7, No. 177 Min-Sheng West Road, Taipei, TAIWAN, P: 011 886225520169, F: 011 886225578359
Blinds; Camping; Compasses; Eyewear; Hearing Protection; Hunting Accessories; Sports Accessories

Fenix Flashlights, LLC/4Sevens, LLC, 4896 N. Royal Atlanta Dr., Suite 305, Tucker, GA 30084, P: 866-471-0749, F: 866-323-9544, www.4sevens.com
Backpacking; Camping; Law Enforcement; Lighting Products

FenixLightUS/Casualhome Worldwide, Inc., 29 William St., Amityville, NY 11701, P: 877-FENIXUS, F: 631-789-2970, www.fenixlightus.com
Camping; Law Enforcement; Lighting Products; Scopes, Sights & Accessories; Shooting Range Equipment; Wholesaler/Distributor

Field & Stream Watches, 12481 NW 44th St., Coral Springs, FL 33065, P: 954-509-1476, F: 954-509-1479, www.tfg24gold.com
Camping; Hunting Accessories; Outfitter; Sports Accessories; Watches; Wholesaler/Distributor

Filson, 1555 4th Ave. S, Seattle, WA 98134, P: 800-297-1897, F: 206-624-4539, www.filson.com
Bags & Equipment Cases; Footwear; Gloves, Mitts, Hats; Gun Cases; Hunting Accessories; Leathergoods; Men & Women's Clothing

Final Approach/Bushnell Outdoor Accessories, 9200 Cody, Overland Park, KS 66214, P: 800-423-3537, F: 913-752-3539, www.kolpin-outdoors.com
Bags & Equipment Cases; Blinds; Decoys; Gun Cases; Hunting Accessories; Videos

Fiocchi of America, Inc., 6930 N. Fremont Rd., Ozark, MO 65721, P: 800-721-AMMO, 417-725-1039, www.fiocciusa.com
Ammunition; Reloading

First Choice Armor & Equipment, Inc., 209 Yelton St., Spindale, NC 28160, P: 800-88-ARMOR, F: 866-481-4929, www.firstchoicearmor.com
Law Enforcement; Training & Safety Equipment

First-Light USA, LLC, 320 Cty. Rd. 1100 North, Seymour, IL 61875, P: 877-454-4450, F: 877-454-4420, www.first-light-usa.com
Backpacking; Camping; Firearms; Law Enforcement; Lighting Products; Survival Kits/First Aid; Training & Safety Equipment

Flambeau, Inc., P.O. Box 97, Middlefield, OH 44062, P: 440-632-1631, F: 440-632-1581, www.flambeauoutdoors.com
Bags & Equipment Cases; Crossbows & Accessories; Custom Manufacturing; Decoys; Game Calls; Gun Cases

Fleming & Clark, Ltd., 3013 Honeysuckle Dr., Spring Hill, TN 37174, P: 800-373-6710, F: 931-487-9972, www.flemingandclark.com
Bags & Equipment Cases; Footwear; Gun Cases; Hunting Accessories; Knives/Knife Cases; Leathergoods; Men's Clothing; Wholesaler/Distributor

Flitz International, Ltd., 821 Mohr Ave., Waterford, WI 53185, P: 800-558-8611, F: 262-534-2991, www.flitz.com
Black Powder Accessories; Firearms Maintenance Equipment; Gun Barrels; Gun Grips & Stocks; Gun Parts/Gunsmithing; Knives/Knife Cases; Lubricants; Scopes, Sights & Accessories

Fobus Holsters/CAA-Command Arms Accessories, 780 Haunted Lane, Bensalem, PA 19020, P: 267-803-1517, F: 267-803-1002, www.fobusholsters.com, www.commandarms.com
Bags & Equipment Cases; Firearms; Gun Cases; Gun Grips & Stocks; Gun Parts/Gunsmithing; Holsters; Law Enforcement; Scopes, Sights & Accessories

Foiles Migrators, Inc., 101 N. Industrial Park Dr., Pittsfield, IL 62363, P: 866-83-GEESE, F: 217-285-5995, www.foilesstraitmeat.com
Game Calls; Hunting Accessories

FoodSaver/Jarden Consumer Solutions, 24 Latour Ln., Little Rock, AR 72223, P: 501-821-0138, F: 501-821-0139, www.foodsaver.com
Backpacking; Camping; Cooking Equipment/Accessories; Food; Hunting Accessories

Force One, LLC, 520 Commercial Dr., Fairfield, OH 45014, P: 800-462-7880, F: 513-939-1166, www.forceonearmor.com
Custom Manufacturing; Law Enforcement

Forster Products, Inc., 310 E. Lanark Ave., Lanark, IL 61046, P: 815-493-6360, F: 815-493-2371, www.forsterproducts.com
Black Powder Accessories; Custom Manufacturing; Firearms Maintenance Equipment; Gun Parts/Gunsmithing; Lubricants; Reloading; Scopes, Sights & Accessories

Fort Knox Security Products, 993 N. Industrial Park Rd., Orem, UT 84057, P: 800-821-5216, F: 801-226-5493, www.ftknox.com
Custom Manufacturing; Gun Cabinets/Racks/Safes; Home Furnishings; Hunting Accessories

Foshan City Nanhai Weihong Mold Products Co., Ltd./Xinwei Photo Electricity Industrial Co., Ltd., Da Wo District, Dan Zhao Town, Nanhai, Foshan City, GuangZhou, 528216, CHINA, P: 011 8675785444666, F: 011 8675785444111, www.weihongmj.net
Binoculars; Scopes, Sights & Accessories

Fox Knives Oreste Frati SNC, Via La Mola, 4, Maniago, Pordenone 33085, ITALY, P: 011 39042771814, F: 011 390427700514, www.foxcutlery.com
Camouflage; Camping; Cutlery; Hunting Accessories; Knives/Knife Cases; Law Enforcement; Wholesaler/Distributor

Fox Outdoor Products, 2040 N. 15th Ave., Melrose Park, IL 60160, P: 800-523-4332, F: 708-338-9210, www.foxoutdoor.com
Bags & Equipment Cases; Camouflage; Eyewear; Gun Cases; Holsters; Law Enforcement; Men's Clothing; Wholesaler/Distributor

FoxFury Personal Lighting Solutions, 2091 Elevado Hill Dr., Vista, CA 92084, P: 760-945-4231, F: 760-758-6283, www.foxfury.com
Backpacking; Camping; Hunting Accessories; Law Enforcement; Lighting Products; Paintball Accessories; Sports Accessories; Training & Safety Equipment

FOXPRO, Inc., 14 Fox Hollow Dr., Lewistown, PA 17044, P: 866-463-6977, F: 717-247-3594, www.gofoxpro.com
Archery; Decoys; Game Calls; Hunting Accessories

Foxy Huntress, 17 Windsor Ridge, Frisco, TX 75034, P: 866-370-1343, F: 972-370-1343, www.foxyhuntress.com
Camouflage; Women's Clothing

Franchi, 17603 Indian Head Hwy., Accokeek, MD 20607, P: 800-264-4962, www.franchiusa.com
Firearms

Franklin Sports, Inc./Uniforce Tactical Division, 17 Campanelli Pkwy., Stoughton, MA 02072, P: 800-225-8647, F: 781-341-3220, www.uniforcetactical.com

Camouflage; Eyewear; Gloves, Mitts, Hats; Law Enforcement; Leathergoods; Men's Clothing; Wholesaler/Distributor

Franzen Security Products, Inc., 680 Flinn Ave., Suite 35, Moorpark, CA 93021, P: 800-922-7656, F: 805-529-0446, www.securecase.com
Bags & Equipment Cases; Custom Manufacturing; Gun Cases; Gun Locks; Hunting Accessories; Law Enforcement; Shooting Range Equipment; Training & Safety Equipment

Fraternal Blue Line, P.O. Box 260199, Boston, MA 02126, P: 617-212-1288, F: 617-249-0857, www.fraternalblueline.org
Custom Manufacturing; Emblems & Decals; Law Enforcement; Men & Women's Clothing; Wholesaler/Distributor

Freedom Arms, Inc., 314 Hwy. 239, Freedom, WY 83120, P: 800-833-4432, F: 800-252-4867, www.freedomarms.com
Firearms; Gun Cases; Holsters; Scopes, Sights & Accessories

Freelinc, 266 W. Center St., Orem, UT 84057, P: 866-467-1199, F: 801-672-3003, www.freelinc.com
Law Enforcement

Frogg Toggs, 131 Sundown Drive NW, P.O. Box 609, Arab, AL 35016, P: 800-349-1835, F: 256-931-1585, www.froggtoggs.com
Backpacking; Camouflage; Footwear; Hunting Accessories; Men & Women's Clothing

Front Line/Army Equipment, Ltd., 6 Platin St., Rishon-Le-Zion, 75653, ISRAEL, P: 011 97239519460, F: 011 97239519463, www.front-line.co.il
Bags & Equipment Cases; Gun Cases; Holsters

Frost Cutlery Co., 6861 Mountain View Rd., Ooltewah, TN 37363, P: 800-251-7768, F: 423-894-9576, www.frostcutlery.com
Camping; Cooking Equipment/Accessories; Cutlery; Hunting Accessories; Knives/Knife Cases; Retail Packaging; Sharpeners; Wholesaler/Distributor

Fujinon, Inc., 10 High Point Dr., Wayne, NJ 07470, P: 973-633-5600, F: 973-694-8299, www.fujinon.jp.com
Binoculars; Scopes, Sights & Accessories

Fusion Tactical, 4200 Chino Hills Pkwy., Suite 820-143, Chino Hills, CA 91709, P: 909-393-9450, F: 909-606-6834
Custom Manufacturing; Retail Packaging; Sports Accessories; Training & Safety Equipment

G

G24 Innovations, Ltd., Solar Power, Westloog Environmental Centre, Cardiff, CF3 2EE, UNITED KINGDON, 011 442920837340, F: 011 443930837341, www.g24i.com
Bags & Equipment Cases; Camping; Custom Manufacturing; Lighting Products

G96 Products Co., Inc., 85-5th Ave., Bldg. 6, P.O. Box 1684, Paterson, NJ 07544, P: 877-332-0035, F: 973-684-3848, www.g96.com
Black Powder Accessories; Firearms Maintenance Equipment; Lubricants

GG&G, 3602 E. 42nd Stravenue, Tucson, AZ 85713, P: 800-380-2540, F: 520-748-7583, www.gggaz.com
Custom Manufacturing; Firearms; Gun Barrels; Gun Grips & Stocks, Gun Parts/Gunsmithing; Law Enforcement; Lighting Products; Scopes, Sights & Accessories

G.A. Precision, 1141 Swift St., N. Kansas City, MO 64116, P: 816-221-1844, F: 816-421-4958, www.gaprecision.net
Firearms

G.G. Telecom, Inc./Spypoint, 555 78 Rd., Suite 353, Swanton, VT 05488, CANADA, P: 888-SPYPOINT, F: 819-604-1644, www.spy-point.com
Hunting Accessories; Photographic Equipment

G-LOX, 520 Sampson St., Houston, TX 77003, P: 713-228-8944, F: 713-228-8947, www.g-lox.com
Archery; Gun Cabinets/Racks/Safes; Gun Locks; Hunting Accessories; Shooting Range Equipment

GSM Products/Walker Game Ear, 3385 Roy Orr Blvd., Grand Prairie, TX 75050, P: 877-269-8490, F: 760-450-1014, www.gsmoutdoors.com
Archery; Feeder Equipment; Hearing Protection; Hunting Accessories; Lighting Products; Scopes, Sights & Accessories; Wildlife Management

GT Industrial Products, 10650 Irma Dr., Suite 1, Northglenn, CO 80233, P: 303-280-5777, F: 303-280-5778, www.gt-ind.com
Camping; Hunting Accessories; Lighting Products; Survival Kits/First Aid

Galati Gear/Galati International, 616 Burley Ridge Rd., P.O. Box 10, Wesco, MO 65586, P: 877-425-2847, F: 573-775-4308, www.galatigear.com, www.galatiinternational.com
Bags & Equipment Cases; Cutlery; Gun Cases; Holsters; Knives/Knife Cases; Law Enforcement; Sports Accessories

Galileo, 13872 SW 119th Ave., Miami, FL 33186, P: 800-548-3537, F: 305-234-8510, www.galileosplace.com
Binoculars; Photographic Equipment; Scopes, Sights & Accessories; Telescopes

Gamebore Cartridge Co., Ltd., Great Union St., Hull, HU9 1AR, UNITED KINGDOM, P: 011 441482223707, F: 011 4414823252225, www.gamebore.com
Ammunition; Cartridges

Gamehide–Core Resources, 12257C Nicollet Ave. S, Burnsville, MN 55337, P: 888-267-3591, F: 952-895-8845, www.gamehide.com
Archery; Camouflage; Custom Manufacturing; Export/Import Specialists; Gloves, Mitts, Hats; Hunting Accessories; Men & Women's Clothing

Gamo USA Corp., 3911 SW 47th Ave., Suite 914, Fort Lauderdale, FL 33314, P: 954-581-5822, F: 954-581-3165, www.gamousa.com
Airguns; Ammunition; Hunting Accessories; Online Services; Scopes, Sights & Accessories; Targets

Garmin International, 1200 E. 151st St., Olathe, KS 66062, P: 913-397-8200, F: 913-397-8282, www.garmin.com
Backpacking; Camping; Compasses; Computer Software; Hunting Accessories; Sports Accessories; Two-Way Radios; Vehicles, Utility & Rec

Garrett Metal Detectors, 1881 W. State St., Garland, TX 75042, P: 972-494-6151, F: 972-494-1881, www.garrett.com
Law Enforcement; Sports Accessories

Geissele Automatics, LLC, 1920 W. Marshall St., Norristown, PA 19403, P: 610-272-2060, F: 610-272-2069, www.ar15trigger.com
Firearms; Gun Parts/Gunsmithing

Gemstar Manufacturing, 1515 N. 5th St., Cannon Falls, MN 55009, P: 800-533-3631, F: 507-263-3129
Bags & Equipment Cases; Crossbows & Accessories; Custom Manufacturing; Gun Cases; Law Enforcement; Paintball Accessories; Sports Accessories; Survival Kits/First Aid

Gemtech, P.O. Box 140618, Boise, ID 83714, P: 208-939-7222, www.gem-tech.com
Firearms; Hearing Protection; Law Enforcement; Training & Safety Equipment; Wildlife Management

General Inspection, LLC, 10585 Enterprise Dr., Davisburg, MI 48350, P: 888-817-6314, F: 248-625-0789, www.geninsp.com
Ammunition; Custom Manufacturing

General Starlight Co., 250 Harding Blvd. W, P.O. Box 32154, Richmond Hill, Ontario L4C 9S3, CANADA, P: 905-850-0990, www.electrooptic.com
Binoculars; Law Enforcement; Photographic Equipment; Scopes, Sights & Accessories; Telescopes; Training & Safety Equipment; Wholesaler/Distributor

Generation Guns–(G2) ICS, No. 6, Lane 205, Dongihou Rd., Shengang Township, Taichung County, 429, TAIWAN, P: 011 886425256461, F: 011 886425256484, www.icsbb.com
Airsoft; Sports Accessories

Gerber Legendary Blades, 14200 SW 72nd Ave., Portland, OR 97224, P: 800-443-4871, F: 307-857-4702, www.gerbergear.com
Knives/Knife Cases; Law Enforcement; Lighting Products

Gerstner & Sons, Inc., 20 Gerstner Way, Dayton, OH 45402, P: 937-228-1662, F: 937-228-8557, www.gerstnerusa.com
Bags & Equipment Cases; Custom Manufacturing; Gun Cabinets/Racks/Safes; Gun Cases; Home Furnishings; Knives/Knife Cases; Shooting Range Equipment

GH Armor Systems, 1 Sentry Dr., Dover, TN 37058, P: 866-920-5940, F: 866-920-5941, www.gharmorsystems.com
Custom Manufacturing; Law Enforcement; Men & Women's Clothing

Giant International/Motorola Consumer Products, 3495 Piedmont Rd., Suite 920, Bldg. Ten, Atlanta, GA 30305, P: 800-638-5119, F: 678-904-6030, www.giantintl.com
Backpacking; Camouflage; Camping; Hunting Accessories; Training & Safety Equipment; Two-Way Radios

Ginsu Outdoors, 118 E. Douglas Rd., Walnut Ridge, AR 72476, P: 800-982-5233, F: 870-886-9142, www.ginsuoutdoors.com
Cutlery; Hunting Accessories; Knives/Knife Cases

Girsan–Yavuz 16, Batlama Deresi Mevkii Sunta Sok. No 19, Giresun, 28200, TURKEY, P: 011 905332160201, F: 011 904542153928, www.yavuz16.com
Firearms; Gun Parts/Gunsmithing

Glacier Glove, 4890 Aircenter Circle, Suite 210, Reno, NV 89502, P: 800-728-8235, F: 775-825-6544, www.glacierglove.com
Gloves, Mitts, Hats; Hunting Accessories; Men's Clothing

Glendo Corp./GRS Tools, 900 Overlander Rd., P.O. Box 1153, Emporia, KS 66801, P: 800-835-3519, F: 620-343-9640, www.glendo.com
Books/Industry Publications; Custom Manufacturing; Lighting Products; Scopes, Sights & Accessories; Videos; Wholesaler/Distributor

Glock, Inc., 6000 Highlands Pkwy., Smyrna, GA 30082, P: 770-432-1202, F: 770-433-8719, www.glock.com, www.teamglock.com, www.glocktraining.com, www.gssfonline.com
Firearms; Gun Parts/Gunsmithing; Holsters; Knives/Knife Cases; Law Enforcement; Men & Women's Clothing; Retailer Services

Goex, Inc., P.O. Box 659, Doyline, LA 71023, P: 318-382-9300, F: 318-382-9303, www.goexpowder.com
Ammunition; Black Powder/Smokeless Powder

Gold House Hardware (China), Ltd., Rm 12/H, 445 Tian He Bei Rd., Guangzhou, 510620, CHINA, P: 011 862038801911, F: 011 862038808485, www.ghhtools.com
Camping; Cutlery; Gun Cases; Hunting Accessories; Knives/Knife Cases; Scopes, Sights & Accessories; Targets

Goldenrod Dehumidifiers, 3600 S. Harbor Blvd., Oxnard, CA 93035, P: 800-451-6797, F: 805-985-1534, www.goldenroddehumidifiers.com
Gun Cabinets/Racks/Safes

Golight, Inc., 37146 Old Hwy. 17, Culbertson, NE 69024, P: 800-557-0098, F: 308-278-2525, www.golight.com
Camping; Hunting Accessories; Law Enforcement; Lighting Products; Vehicles, Utility & Rec

Gore & Associates, Inc., W.L., 295 Blue Ball Rd., Elkton, MD 21921, P: 800-431-GORE, F: 410-392-9057, www.gore-tex.com
Footwear; Gloves, Mitts, Hats; Law Enforcement; Men & Women's Clothing

Gould & Goodrich, Inc., 709 E. McNeil St., Lillington, NC, 27546, P: 800-277-0732, FL 910-893-4742, www.gouldusa.com
Holsters; Law Enforcement; Leathergoods

Grabber/MPI Outdoors, 5760 N. Hawkeye Ct. SW, Grand Rapids, MI 49509, P: 800-423-1233, F: 616-940-7718, www.warmers.com
Archery; Backpacking; Camouflage; Camping; Footwear; Gloves, Mitts, Hats; Hunting Accessories; Survival Kits/First Aid

Gradient Lens Corp., 207 Tremont St., Rochester, NY 14608, P: 800-536-0790, F: 585-235-6645, www.gradientlens.com
Firearms Maintenance Equipment; Gun Barrels; Gun Parts/Gunsmithing; Scopes, Sights & Accessories; Shooting Range Equipment

Grand View Media Group, 200 Croft St., Suite 1, Birmingham, AL 35242, P: 888-431-2877, F: 205-408-3798, www.gvmg.com
Books/Industry Publications

Granite Security Products, Inc., 4801 Esco Dr., Fort Worth, TX 76140, P: 817-561-9095, F: 817-478-3056, www.winchestersafes.com
Gun Cabinets/Racks/Safes

Gransfors Bruks, Inc., P.O. Box 818, Summerville, SC 29484. P: 843-875-0240, F: 843-821-2285
Custom Manufacturing; Law Enforcement; Men's Clothing; Wholesaler/Distributor

Grant Adventures Int'l., 9815 25th St. E, Parrish, FL 34219, P: 941-776-3029, F: 941-776-1092
Archery; Outfitter

Grauer Systems, 38 Forster Ave., Mount Vernon, NY 10552, P: 415-902-4721, www.grauerbarrel.com
Firearms; Gun Barrels; Gun Grips & Stocks; Law Enforcement; Lighting Products; Scopes, Sights & Accessories

Graves Recoil Systems, LLC/Mallardtone, LLC, 9115 Crows Nest Dr., Pine Bluff, AR 71603, P: 870-534-3000, F: 870-534-3000, www.stockabsorber.com
Black Powder Accessories; Firearms; Game Calls; Hunting Accessories; Recoil Protection Devices & Services; Wholesaler/Distributor

Great American Tool Co., Inc./Gatco Sharpeners/Timberline Knives, 665 Hertel Ave., Buffalo, NY 14207, P: 800-548-7427, F: 716-877-2591, www.gatcosharpeners.com
Cutlery; Knives/Knife Cases; Sharpeners

Green Supply, Inc., 3059 Audrain Rd., Suite 581, Vandalia, MO 63382, P: 800-424-4867, F: 573-594-2211, www.greensupply.com
Ammunition; Camping; Computer Software; Firearms; Hunting Accessories; Online Services; Retailer Services; Scopes, Sights & Accessories; Wholesaler/Distributor

Grip On Tools, 4628 Amash Industrial Dr., Wayland, MI 49348, P: 616-877-0000, F: 616-877-4346

Grizzly Industrial, 1821 Valencia St., Bellingham, WA 98229, P: 800-523-4777, F: 800-438-5901, www.grizzly.com

Firearms Maintenance Equipment; Gun Cabinets/Racks/Safes; Gun Parts/Gunsmithing

Grohmann Knives, Ltd., 116 Water St., P.O. Box 40, Pictou, Nova Scotia B0K 1H0, CANADA, P: 888-7-KNIVES, F: 902-485-5872, www.grohmannknives.com
Backpacking; Camping; Cooking Equipment/Accessories; Custom Manufacturing; Cutlery; Hunting Accessories; Knives/Knife Cases; Sharpeners

GrovTec US, Inc., 16071 SE 98t Ave., Clackamas, OR, 97015, P: 503-557-4689, F: 503-557-4936, www.grovtec.com
Custom Manufacturing; Firearms Maintenance Equipment; Gun Parts/Gunsmithing; Holsters

Guay Guay Trading Co., Ltd., 11F-3, No. 27, Lane 169, Kangning St., Shijr City, Taipei County 221, TAIWAN, P: 011 886226922000, F: 011 886226924000, www.guay2.com
Airsoft

Gun Grabber Products, Inc., 3417 E. 54th St., Texarkana, AR 71854, P: 877-486-4722, F: 870-774-2111, www.gungrab.com
Gun Cabinets/Racks/Safes; Hunting Accessories

Gun Video, 4585 Murphy Canyon Rd., San Diego, CA 92123, P: 800-942-8273, F: 858-569-0505, www.gunvideo.com
Books/Industry Publications; Gun Parts/Gunsmithing; Law Enforcement; Training & Safety Equipment; Videos

GunBroker.com, P.O. Box 2511, Kennesaw, GA 30156, P: 720-223-2083, F: 720-223-0164, www.gunbroker.com
Airguns; Computer Software; Firearms; Gun Parts/Gunsmithing; Hunting Accessories; Online Services; Reloading; Retailer Services

GunMate Products/Bushnell Outdoor Accessories, 9200 Cody, Overland Park, KS 66214, P: 800-423-3537, F: 800-548-0446, www.unclemikes.com
Gun Cases; Holsters; Hunting Accessories; Leathergoods

Gunslick Gun Care/ATK Commercial Products, N5549 Cty. Trunk Z, Onalaska, WI 54650, P: 800-635-7656, F: 763-323-3890, www.gunslick.com
Firearms Maintenance Equipment; Lubricants

GunVault, Inc., 216 S. 2nd Ave., Bldg. 932, San Bernardino, CA 92408, P: 800-222-1055, F: 909-382-2042, www.gunvault.com
Gun Cabinets/Racks/Safes; Gun Cases; Gun Locks

H

HKS Products, Inc., 7841 Foundation Dr., Florence, KY 41042, P: 800-354-9814, F: 859-342-5865, www.hksspeedloaders.com
Hunting Accessories; Law Enforcement

H & C Headware/Capco Sportswear, 5945 Shiloh Rd., Alpharetta, GA 30005, P: 800-381-3331, F: 800-525-2613, www.kccaps.com
Camouflage

H & M Metal Processing, 1850 Front St., Cuyanoga Falls, OH 44221, P: 330-928-9021, F: 330-928-5472, www.handmmetal.com
Airguns; Archery; Black Powder Accessories; Custom Manufacturing; Firearms Maintenance Equipment; Gun Barrels; Gun Parts/Gunsmithing

Haas Outdoors, Inc./Mossy Oak, P.O. Box 757, West Point, MS 39773, P: 662-494-8859, F: 662-509-9397

H-S Precision, Inc., 1301 Turbine Dr., Rapid City, SD 57703, P: 605-341-3006, F: 605-342-8964, www.hsprecision.com
Firearms; Gun Barrels; Gun Grips & Stocks; Law Enforcement; Magazines, Cartridge; Shooting Range Equipment

Haix®-Schuhe Produktions-u. Vertriebs GmbH, Aufhofstrasse 10, Mainburg, Bavaria 84048, GERMANY, P: 011 49875186250, F: 011 498751862525, www.haix.com
Footwear; Law Enforcement; Leathergoods

Haix North America, Inc., 157 Venture Ct., Suite 11, Lexington, KY 40511, P: 866-344-4249, F: 859-281-0113, www.haix.com
Footwear; Law Enforcement; Leathergoods

Haley Vines Outdoor Collection Badland Beauty, P.O. Box 150308, Lufkin, TX 75915, P: 936-875-5522, F: 936-875-5525, www.haleyvines.com
Bags & Equipment Cases; Gloves, Mitts, Hats; Wholesaler/Distributor; Women's Clothing

Hallmark Dog Training Supplies, 3054 Beechwood Industrial Ct., P.O. Box 97, Hubertus, WI 53033, P: 800-OK4DOGS, F: 262-628-4434, www.hallmarkdogsupplies.com
Custom Manufacturing; Hunting Accessories; Pet Supplies; Scents & Lures; Videos; Wholesaler/Distributor

Halys, 1205 W. Cumberland, Corbin, KY 40701, P: 606-528-7490, F: 606-528-7497, www.halysgear.com
Custom Manufacturing; Men & Women's Clothing; Wholesaler/Distributor

Hammerhead Ind./Gear Keeper, 1501 Goodyear Ave., Ventura, CA 93003, P: 888-588-9981, F: 805-658-8833, www.gearkeeper.com
Backpacking; Camping; Compasses; Game Calls; Hunting Accessories; Law Enforcement; Lighting Products; Sports Accessories

HangZhou Fujie Outdoor Products, Inc., Qinyuanyashe, Shenghuoguan, Suite 1108, 163# Jichang Rd., Hanzhou, ZHJG 310004, CHINA, P: 011 8657181635196, F: 011 8657187718232, www.hangzhou-outdoor.com
Footwear; Gloves, Mitts, Hats; Gun Cases; Men & Women's Clothing

Hardigg Storm Case, 147 N. Main St., South Deerfield, MA 01373, P: 800-542-7344, F: 413-665-8350
Bags & Equipment Cases; Gun Cases

Harris Engineering, Inc., 999 Broadway, Barlow, KY 42024, P: 270-334-3633, F: 270-334-3000
Hunting Accessories; Shooting Range Equipment; Sports Accessories

Harris Publications, Inc./Harris Tactical Group, 1115 Broadway, 8th Floor, New York, NY 10010, P: 212-807-7100, F: 212-807-1479, www.tactical-life.com
Airguns; Books/Industry Publications; Cutlery; Firearms; Knives/Knife Cases; Law Enforcement; Paintball Guns; Retailer Services

Hastings, 717 4th St., P.O. Box 135, Clay Center, KS 67432, P: 785-632-3169, F: 785-632-6554, www.hastingsammunition.com
Ammunition; Firearms; Gun Barrels

Hatsan Arms Co., Izmir-Ankara Karayolu 26. Km. No. 289, OSB Kemalpasa, Izmir, 35170, TURKEY, P: 011 902328789100, F: 011 902328789723, www.hatsan.com.tr
Airguns; Firearms; Scopes, Sights & Accessories

Havalon Knives/Havels Inc., 3726 Lonsdale St., Cincinnati, OH 45227, P: 800-638-4770, F: 513-271-4714, www.havalon.com
Hunting Accessories; Knives/Knife Cases

Havaser Turizm, Ltd., Nargileci Sokak No. 4, Mercan, Eminonu, 34450, TURKEY, P: 011 90212135452, F: 011 902125128079
Firearms

Hawke Sport Optics, 6015 Highview Dr., Suite G, Fort Wayne, IN 46818, P: 877-429-5347, F: 260-918-3443, www.hawkeoptics.com
Airguns; Binoculars; Computer Software; Crossbows & Accessories; Scopes, Sights & Accessories

Haydel's Game Calls, 5018 Hazel Jones Rd., Bossier City, LA 71111, P: 800-HAYDELS, F: 888-310-3711, www.haydels.com
Archery; Emblems & Decals; Game Calls; Gun Parts/Gunsmithing; Hunting Accessories; Videos

Health Enterprises, 90 George Leven Dr., N. Attleboro, MA 02760, P: 800-633-4243, F: 508-695-3061, www.healthenterprises.com
Hearing Protection

Heat Factory, Inc., 2390 Oak Ridge Way, Vista, CA 92081, P: 800-993-4328, F: 760-727-8721, www.heatfactory.com
Archery; Backpacking; Camping; Footwear; Gloves, Mitts, Hats; Hunting Accessories, Men & Women's Clothing

Heatmax, Inc., 505 Hill Rd., Dalton, GA 30721, P: 800-432-8629, F: 706-226-2195, www.heatmax.com
Archery; Backpacking; Camping; Footwear; Hunting Accessories; Law Enforcement; Pet Supplies; Sports Accessories

Heckler & Koch, Inc., 5675 Transport Blvd., Columbus, GA 31907, P: 706-568-1906, F: 706-568-9151, www.hk-usa.com
Firearms

Helly Hansen Pro (US), Inc., 3703 I St. NW, Auburn, WA 98001, P: 866-435-5902, F: 253-333-8359, www.hellyhansen.com
Men's Clothing

Hen & Rooster Cutlery, 6861 Mountain View Rd., Ooltewah, TN 37363, P: 800-251-7768, F: 423-894-9576, www.henandrooster.com
Camping; Cooking Equipment/Accessories; Cutlery; Hunting Accessories; Retail Packaging; Wholesaler/Distributor

Hendon Publishing Co./Law and Order/Tactical Response Magazines, 130 Waukegan Rd., Suite 202, Deerfield, IL 60015, P: 800-843-9764, F: 847-444-3333, www.hendonpub.com
Books/Industry Publications; Law Enforcement

Heritage Manufacturing, Inc., 4600 NW 135th St., Opa Locka, FL 33054, P: 305-685-5966, F: 305-687-6721, www.heritagemfg.com
Firearms

Heros Pride, P.O. Box 10033, Van Nuys, CA 91410, P: 888-492-9122, F: 888-492-9133, www.herospride.com

Custom Manufacturing; Emblems & Decals; Law Enforcement; Men & Women's Clothing; Wholesaler/Distributor

Hi-Point Firearms/MKS Supply, Inc., 8611-A N. Dixie Dr., Dayton, OH 45414, P: 877-425-4867, F: 937-454-0503, www.hi-pointfirearms.com
Firearms; Holsters; Law Enforcement; Magazines, Cartridge

Hiatt Thompson Corp., 7200 W. 66th St., Bedford Park, IL 60638, P: 708-496-8585, F: 708-496-8618, www.handcuffsusa.com
Law Enforcement

HideAway/Remington Packs/Cerf Bros. Bag Co., 2360 Chaffee Dr., St. Louis, MO 63146, P: 800-237-3224, F: 314-291-5588, www.cerfbag.com
Backpacking; Bags & Equipment Cases; Camouflage; Camping; Gun Cases; Wholesaler/Distributor

High Standard Mfg., Co./F.I., Inc. ATM–AutoMag, 5200 Mitchelldale, Suite E17, Houston, TX 77092, P: 800-272-7816, F: 713-681-5665, www.highstandard.com
Firearms; Gun Barrels; Gun Grips & Stocks; Gun Parts/Gunsmithing; Lubricants; Magazines, Cartridge

Highgear/Highgear USA, Inc., 145 Cane Creek Industrial Park Rd., Suite 200, Fletcher, NC 28732, P: 888-295-4949, F: 828-681-5320, www.highgear.com
Camping; Compasses; Hunting Accessories; Lighting Products; Sports Accessories; Survival Kits/First Aid

Hillman Int., No. 62, Tzar Samuil St., Sofia, Sofia 1000, BULGARIA, P: 011 35929882981, F: 011 35929882981, www.hillman.bg
Backpacking; Camouflage; Footwear; Gloves, Mitts, Hats; Gun Cases; Hunting Accessories; Men & Women's Clothing

HitchSafe Key Vault, 18424 Hwy. 99, Lynnwood, WA 98037, P: 800-654-1786, F: 206-523-9876, www.hitchsafe.com
Gun Cabinets/Racks/Safes; Gun Locks; Hunting Accessories; Outfitter; Sports Accessories; Vehicles, Utility & Rec

HiViz Shooting Systems/North Pass, Ltd., 1941 Heath Pkwy., Suite 1, Fort Collins, CO 80524, P: 800-589-4315, F: 970-416-1208, www.hivizsights.com
Black Powder Accessories; Gun Parts/Gunsmithing; Hunting Accessories; Paintball Accessories; Recoil Protection Devices & Services; Scopes, Sights & Accessories; Sports Accessories

Hobie Cat Co./Hobie Fishing/Hobie Kayaks, 4925 Oceanside Blvd., Oceanside, CA 92056, P: 760-758-9100, F: 760-758-1841, www.hobiecat.com
Bags & Equipment Cases; Camping; Hunting Accessories; Sports Accessories; Tours/Travel

Hodgdon Powder Co., 6231 Robinson, Shawnee Mission, KS 66202, P: 913-362-9455, F: 913-362-1307, www.hodgdon.com
Black Powder/Smokeless Powder; Books/Industry Publications; Reloading

Hog Wild, LLC, 221 SE Main St., Portland, OR 97214, P: 888-231-6465, F: 503-233-0960, www.hogwildtoys.com
Sports Accessories; Watches

Hogue, Inc., 550 Linne Rd., Paso Robles, CA 93447, P: 805-239-1440, F: 805-239-2553, www.hogueinc.com
Gun Grips & Stocks; Holsters

Homak Manufacturing Co., Inc., 1605 Old Rt. 18, Suite 4-36, Wampum, PA 16157, P: 800-874-6625, F: 724-535-1081, www.homak.com
Custom Manufacturing; Gun Cabinets/Racks/Safes; Gun Cases; Gun Locks; Hunting Accessories; Reloading; Retail Packaging

HongKong Meike Digital Technology Co., Ltd., No. 12 Jiaye Rd. Pinghu St., Longgang District, Shenzhen, GNGD 518111, CHINA, P: 011 8613424151607, F: 011 8675528494339, www.mkgrip.com
Scopes, Sights & Accessories

Hope Global, 50 Martin St., Cumberland, RI 02864, P: 401-333-8990, F: 401-334-6442, www.hopeglobal.com
Custom Manufacturing; Footwear; Hunting Accessories; Law Enforcement; Pet Supplies; Scopes, Sights & Accessories; Shooting Range Equipment; Sports Accessories

Hoppe's/Bushnell Outdoor Accessories, 9200 Cody, Overland Park, KS 66214, P: 800-221-9035, F: 800-548-0446, www.hoppes.com
Black Powder Accessories; Firearms Maintenance Equipment; Hearing Protection; Law Enforcement; Lubricants; Shooting Range Equipment

Horizon Manufacturing Ent., Inc./RackEm Racks, P.O. Box 7174, Buffalo Grove, IL 60089, P: 877-722-5369 (877-RACKEM-9), F: 866-782-1550, www.rackems.com
Airguns; Custom Manufacturing; Firearms; Firearms Maintenance Equipment; Footwear; Gloves, Mitts, Hats; Gun Cabinets/Racks/Safes; Holsters; Hunting

Accessories; Law Enforcement; Shooting Range Equipment

Hornady Manufacturing Co., 3625 Old Potash Hwy., P.O. Box 1848, Grand Island, NE 68803, P: 308-382-1390, F: 308-382-5761, www.hornady.com
Ammunition; Black Powder Accessories; Lubricants; Reloading

Horus Vision, LLC, 659 Huntington Ave., San Bruno, CA 94066, P: 650-588-8862, F: 650-588-6264, www.horusvision.com
Computer Software; Law Enforcement; Scopes, Sights & Accessories; Targets; Watches

Howard Leight by Sperian, 900 Douglas Pike, Smithfield, RI 02917, P: 866-786-2353, F: 401-233-7641, www.howardleightshootingsports.com, www.sperianprotection.com
Eyewear; Hearing Protection; Hunting Accessories; Sports Accessories; Training & Safety Equipment

Huanic Corp., No. 67 Jinye Rd., Hi-tech Zone, Xi'an, SHNX 710077, CHINA, P: 011 862981881001, F: 011 862981881011, www.huanic.com
Hunting Accessories; Scopes, Sights & Accessories; Shooting Range Equipment; Targets

Hubertus Solingen Cutlery, 147 Wuppertaler Strasse, Solingen, D-42653, GERMANY, P: 011 49212591994, F: 011 49212591992, www.hubertus-solingen.de
Custom Manufacturing; Cutlery; Knives/Knife Cases; Survival Kits/First Aid

Hunter Co., Inc./Hunter Wicked Optics, 3300 W. 71st Ave., Westminster, CO 80030, P: 800-676-4868, F: 303-428-3980, www.huntercompany.com
Binoculars; Custom Manufacturing; Gun Cases; Holsters; Hunting Accessories; Knives/Knife Cases; Leathergoods; Scopes, Sights & Accessories

Hunter Dan, 64 N. US 231, P.O. Box 103, Greencastle, IN 46135, P: 888-241-4868, F: 765-655-1440, www.hunterdan.com
Archery; Home Furnishings; Hunting Accessories; Outdoor Art, Jewelry, Sculpture; Sports Accessories; Training & Safety Equipment

Hunter's Edge, LLC, 270 Whigham Dairy Rd., Bainbridge, GA 39817, P: 888-455-0970, F: 912-248-6219, www.hunters-edge.com
Archery; Camouflage; Decoys; Game Calls; Gloves, Mitts, Hats; Hunting Accessories; Men's Clothing; Scents & Lures

Hunter's Specialties, 6000 Huntington Ct. NE, Cedar Rapids, IA 52402, P: 800-728-0321, F: 319-395-0326, www.hunterspec.com
Archery; Blinds; Camouflage; Game Calls; Gloves, Mitts, Hats; Hunting Accessories; Scents & Lures; Videos

Hunterbid.com/Chiron, Inc., 38 Crosby Rd., Dover, NH 03820, P: 603-433-8908, F: 603-431-4072, www.hunterbid.com
Gun Grips & Stocks; Gun Parts/Gunsmithing

Hunting's-A-Drag, 42 Maple St., Rifton, NY 12471, P: 845-658-8557, F: 845-658-8569, www.gamesled.com
Hunting Accessories

Huntington Die Specialties, 601 Oro Dam Blvd., P.O. Box 991, Oroville, CA 95965, P: 866-RELOADS, F: 530-534-1212, huntingtons.com
Black Powder Accessories; Books/Industry Publications; Reloading; Wholesaler/Distributor

HyperBeam, 1504 Sheepshead Bay Rd., Suite 300, Brooklyn, NY 11236, P: 888-272-4620, F: 718-272-1797, www.nightdetective.com
Binoculars; Hunting Accessories; Law Enforcement; Lighting Products; Photographic Equipment; Scopes, Sights & Accessories; Shooting Range Equipment; Telescopes

Hyskore/Power Aisle, Inc., 193 West Hills Rd., Huntington Station, NY 11746, P: 631-673-5975, F: 631-673-5976, www.hyskore.com
Custom Manufacturing; Export/Import Specialists; Eyewear; Firearms Maintenance Equipment; Gun Cabinets/Racks/Safes; Hearing Protection; Shooting Range Equipment

I

I.C.E., 68 Route 125, Kingston, NH 03848, P: 603-347-3005, F: 603-642-9291, www.icesigns.com
Retailer Services

ICS, No. 6, Lane 205, Dongzou Rd., Taichung, Shangang 429, TAIWAN, P: 011-88 6425256461, F: 011-88 6425256484, icsbb.com
Airguns; Sports Accessories; Training & Safety Equipment

IHC, Inc., 12400 Burt Rd., Detroit, MI 48228, P: 800-661-4642, F: 313-535-3220, www.ihccorp.com
Archery; Backpacking; Camping; Crossbows & Accessories; Firearms; Lighting Products; Magazines, Cartridge; Scopes, Sights & Accessories

i-SHOT/S.E.R.T. System, 16135 Kennedy St., Woodbridge, VA 22191, P: 703-670-8001, F: 703-940-9148, www.ishot-inc.com
Bags & Equipment Cases; Custom Manufacturing; Firearms; Law Enforcement; Training & Safety Equipment; Wholesaler/Distributor

Icebreaker, Inc., P.O. Box 236, Clarkesville, GA 30523, P: 800-343-BOOT, F: 706-754-0423, www.icebreakerinc.com
Camouflage; Footwear; Gloves, Mitts, Hats; Hunting Accessories

Impact Gel Sports, P.O. Box 128, Melrose, WI 54642, P: 608-488-3630, F: 608-488-3633, www.impactgel.com
Footwear

Import Merchandiser's Inc./MasterVision Cap Lights, N-11254 Industrial Lane, P.O. Box 337, Elcho, WI 54428, P: 715-275-5132, F: 715-275-5176, www.mastervisionlight.com
Camping; Custom Manufacturing; Gloves, Mitts, Hats; Hunting Accessories; Lighting Products; Sports Accessories

IMR Powder Co., 6231 Robinson, Shawnee Mission, KS 66202, P: 913-362-9455, F: 913-362-1307, www.imrpowder.com
Black Powder/Smokeless Powder; Reloading

Indo-US Mim Tec. Pvt., Ltd., 315 Eisenhower Pkwy., Suite 211, Ann Arbor, MI 48108, P: 734-327-9842, F: 734-327-9873, www.mimindia.com
Airguns; Archery; Crossbows & Accessories; Gun Locks; Gun Parts/Gunsmithing; Knives/Knife Cases; Paintball Guns; Scopes, Sights & Accessories

Industrial Revolution/Light My Fire USA, 9225 151st Ave. NE, Redmond, WA 98052, P: 888-297-6062, F: 425-883-0036, www.industrialrev.com
Camping; Cooking Equipment/Accessories; Cutlery; Knives/Knife Cases; Lighting Products; Photographic Equipment; Survival Kits/First Aid; Wholesaler/Distributor

Indusys Techologies Belgium SPRL (UFA–Belgium), 22 Pas Bayard, Tavier, Liege B-4163, BELGIUM, P: 011 3243835234, F: 011 3243835189, www.indusys.be
Ammunition; Reloading; Shooting Range Equipment; Training & Safety Equipment

Innovative Plastech, Inc., 1260 Kingsland Dr., Batavia, IL 60510, P: 630-232-1808, F: 630-232-1978
Custom Manufacturing; Retail Packaging; Sports Accessories

INOVA/Emissive Energy Corp., 135 Circuit Dr., North Kingstown, RI 02852, P: 401-294-2030, F: 401-294-2050, www.inovalight.com
Backpacking; Camping; Hunting Accessories; Law Enforcement; Lighting Products; Sports Accessories; Survival Kits/First Aid; Training & Safety Equipment

Insight Tech-Gear, 23 Industrial Dr., Londonderry, NH 03053, P: 877-744-4802, F: 603-668-1084, www.insighttechgear.com
Hunting Accessories; Law Enforcement; Lighting Products; Paintball Accessories; Scopes, Sights & Accessories; Training & Safety Equipment

Instant Armor, Inc., 350 E. Easy St., Suite 1, Simi Valley, CA 93065, P: 805-526-3046, F: 805-526-9213, www.instantarmor.com
Law Enforcement

Instrument Technology, Inc., P.O. Box 381, Westfield, MA 10186, P: 413-562-3606, F: 413-568-9809, www.scopes.com
Law Enforcement

InterMedia Outdoors, Inc., 512 7th Ave., 11th Floor, New York, NY 10018, P: 212-852-6600, F: 212-302-4472, www.imoutdoorsmedia.com
Books/Industry Publications

International Cartridge Corp., 2273 Route 310, Reynoldsville, PA 15851, P: 877-422-5332, F: 814-938-6821, www.iccammo.com
Ammunition; Law Enforcement; Reloading; Shooting Range Equipment; Training & Safety Equipment

International Supplies/Seahorse Protective Cases, 945 W. Hyde Park, Inglewood, CA 90302, P: 800-999-1984, F: 310-673-5988, www.internationalsupplies.com
Bags & Equipment Cases; Export/Import Specialists; Eyewear; Gun Cases; Lighting Products; Photographic Equipment; Retailer Services; Wholesaler/Distributor

Interstate Arms Corp., 6 Dunham Rd., Billerica, MA 01821, P: 800-243-3006, F: 978-671-0023, www.interstatearms.com
Firearms

Iosso Products, 1485 Lively Blvd., Elk Grove, IL 60007, P: 888-747-4332, F: 847-437-8478, www.iosso.com
Black Powder Accessories; Crossbows & Accessories; Firearms Maintenance Equipment; Gun Parts/Gunsmithing; Hunting Accessories; Law Enforcement; Lubricants; Reloading

Iowa Rotocast Plastics, Inc., 1712 Moellers Dr., P.O. Box 320, Decorah, IA 52101, P: 800-553-0050, F: 563-382-3016, www.irpoutdoors.com
Backpacking; Blinds; Camping; Custom Manufacturing; Emblems & Decals; Printing Services; Sports Accessories; Wholesaler/Distributor

Irish Setter, 314 Main St., Red Wing, MN 55066, P: 888-SETTER-O, www.irishsetterboots.com
Footwear; Men's Clothing

Ironclad Performance Wear, 2201 Park Place, Suite 101, El Segundo, CA 90245, P: 888-314-3197, F: 310-643-0300
Camouflage; Gloves, Mitts, Hats; Hunting Accessories; Leathergoods; Men & Women's Clothing; Sports Accessories

Itasca by C.O. Lynch Enterprises, 2655 Fairview Ave. N, Roseville, MN 55113, P: 800-225-2565, F: 651-633-9095, www.itascacol.com
Footwear

Ithaca Gun Co., LLC, 420 N. Warpole St., Upper Sandusky, OH 43351, P: 877-648-4222, F: 419-294-3230, www.ithacagun.com
Firearms

ITT, 7635 Plantation Rd., Roanoke, VA 24019, P: 800-448-8678, F: 540-366-9015, www.nightvision.com
Binoculars; Scopes, Sights & Accessories

ITW Military Products, 195 E. Algonquin Rd., Des Plaines, IL 60016, P: 203-240-7110, F: 847-390-8727, www.itwmilitaryproducts.com
Backpacking; Bags & Equipment Cases; Camouflage; Cooking Equipment/Accessories; Custom Manufacturing; Law Enforcement

Iver Johnson Arms Inc./Manufacturing Research, 1840 Baldwin St., Suite 10, Rockledge, FL 32955, P: 321-636-3377, F: 321-632-7745, www.iverjohnsonarms.com
Firearms; Gun Parts/Gunsmithing; Training & Safety Equipment

J

J.F. Griffin Publishing, LLC, 430 Main St., Suite 5, Williamstown, MA 01267, P: 413-884-1001, F: 413-884-1039, www.jfgriffin.com
Books/Industry Publications

JBP Holsters/Masters Holsters, 10100 Old Bon Air Pl., Richmond, VA 23235, P: 804-320-5653, F: 804-320-5653, www.jbpholsters.com
Gun Cases; Holsters; Hunting Accessories; Law Enforcement; Leathergoods; Sports Accessories; Training & Safety Equipment; Wholesaler/Distributor

JGS Precision Tool Mfg., LLC, 60819 Selander Rd., Coos Bay, OR 97420, P: 541-267-4331, F: 541-267-5996, www.jgstools.com
Firearms Maintenance Equipment; Gun Parts/Gunsmithing

J & J Armory/Dragon Skin/Pinnacle Armor, 1344 E. Edinger Ave., Santa Ana, CA 92705, P: 866-9-ARMORY, F: 714-558-4817, www.jandjarmory.com
Firearms; Law Enforcement; Training & Safety Equipment

J & J Products Co., 9134 Independence Ave., Chatsworth, CA 91311, P: 626-571-8084, F: 626-571-8704, www.jandjproducts.com
Custom Manufacturing; Hunting Accessories; Recoil Protection Devices & Services; Reloading; Retail Packaging; Sports Accessories

J & K Outdoor Products, Inc., 3864 Cty. Rd. Q, Wisconsin Rapids, WI 54495, P: 715-424-5757, F: 715-424-5757, www.jkoutdoorproducts.com
Archery; Hunting Accessories; Law Enforcement; Paintball Accessories; Scopes, Sights & Accessories

J-Tech (Steady Flying Enterprise Co., Ltd.), 1F, No. 235 Ta You Rd., Sung Shang, Taipei, 105, TAIWAN, P: 011 886227663986, F: 011 886287874836, www.tacticaljtech.com
Backpacking; Custom Manufacturing; Gloves, Mitts, Hats; Gun Cases; Holsters; Law Enforcement; Lighting Products; Wholesaler/Distributor

Jaccard Corp., 3421 N. Benzing Rd., Orchard Park, NY 14127, P: 866-478-7373, F: 716-825-5319, www.jaccard.com
Cooking Equipment/Accessories

Jack Brittingham's World of Hunting Adventure, 609-A E. Clinton Ave., Athens, TX 75751, P: 800-440-4515, F: 903-677-2126, www.jackbrittingham.com
Hunting Accessories; Training & Safety Equipment; Videos; Wildlife Management

Jack Link's Beef Jerky, One Snackfood Ln., P.O. Box 397, Minong, WI 54859, P: 800-346-6896, F: 715-466-5986, www.linksnacks.com
Custom Manufacturing

Jackite, Inc., 2868 W. Landing Rd., Virginia Beach, VA 23456, P: 877-JACKITE, F: 877-JACKFAX, www.jackite.com

Decoys; Hunting Accessories; Outdoor Art, Jewelry, Sculpture; Wholesaler/Distributor*

Jackson Rifles X-Treme Shooting Products, LLC, Glenswinton, Parton, Castle Douglas, SCOTLAND DG7 3NL, P: 011 441644470223, F: 011 441644470227, www.jacksonrifles.com
Firearms; Gun Barrels; Gun Parts/Gunsmithing; Wholesaler/Distributor

Jacob Ash Holdings, Inc., 301 Munson Ave., McKees Rocks, PA 15136, P: 800-245-6111, F: 412-331-6347, www.jacobash.com
Camouflage; Gloves, Mitts, Hats; Hunting Accessories; Law Enforcement; Leathergoods; Men & Women's Clothing; Sports Accessories

James River Manufacturing, Inc./James River Armory, 3601 Commerce Dr., Suite 110, Baltimore, MD 21227, P: 410-242-6991, F: 410-242-6995, www.jamesriverarmory.com
Firearms

Japan Optics, Ltd., 2-11-29, Ukima, Kita-ku, Tokyo, 115-0051, JAPAN, P: 011 81359146680, F: 011 81353722232
Scopes, Sights & Accessories

Jeff's Outfitters, 599 Cty. Rd. 206, Cape Girardeau, MO 63701, P: 573-651-3200, F: 573-651-3207, www.jeffsoutfitters.com
Bags & Equipment Cases; Custom Manufacturing; Gun Cases; Hunting Accessories; Knives/Knife Cases; Leathergoods; Scopes, Sights & Accessories

Jest Textiles, Inc./Bucksuede, 13 Mountainside Ave., Mahwah, NJ 07430, P: 800-778-7918, F: 866-899-4951, www.jesttex.com
Bags & Equipment Cases; Camouflage; Custom Manufacturing; Export/Import Specialists; Gloves, Mitts, Hats; Home Furnishings; Men & Women's Clothing

John Marshall Design, LLC, P.O. Box 46105, Baton Rouge, LA 70895, P: 800-697-2698, F: 225-275-5900
Camouflage; Home Furnishings; Men & Women's Clothing

John's Guns/A Dark Horse Arms Co., 1041 FM 1274, Coleman, TX 76834. P: 325-382-4885, F: 325-382-4887, www.darkhorsearms.com
Custom Manufacturing; Firearms; Hearing Protection; Law Enforcement

Johnston Brothers, 623 Meeting St., Bldg. B, P.O. Box 21810, Charleston, SC 29413, P: 800-257-2595, F: 800-257-2534
Bags & Equipment Cases; Firearms Maintenance Equipment; Gun Cases

Jonathan Arthur Ciener, Inc., 8700 Commerce St., Cap Canaveral, FL 32920, P: 321-868-2200, F: 321-868-2201, www.22lrconversions.com
Firearms; Gun Barrels; Gun Parts/Gunsmithing; Hunting Accessories; Magazines, Cartridge; Recoil Protection Devices & Services; Shooting Range Equipment; Training & Safety Equipment

Jordan Outdoor Enterprises, Ltd., P.O. Box 9638, Columbus, GA 31908, P: 800-992-9968, F: 706-569-9346, www.realtree.com
Camouflage; Videos

Joseph Chiarello & Co., Inc./NSSF Endorsed Insurance Program, 31 Parker Rd., Elizabeth, NJ 07208, P: 800-526-2199, F: 908-352-8512, www.guninsurance.com
Insurance; Retailer Services

Joy Enterprises, 1862 Dr., ML King Jr. Blvd., Port Commerce Center III, Riviera Beach, FL 33404, P: 800-500-FURY, F: 561-863-3277, www.joyenterprises.com
Binoculars; Camping; Compasses; Cutlery; Knives/Knife Cases; Law Enforcement; Sharpeners; Sports Accessories

JP Enterprises, Inc., P.O. Box 378, Hugo, NN 55038, P: 651-426-9196, F: 651-426-2472, www.jprifles.com
Firearms; Gun Parts/Gunsmithing; Recoil Protection Devices & Services; Scopes, Sights & Accessories

JS Products, Inc./Snap-on, 5440 S. Procyon Ave., Las Vegas, NV 89118, P: 702-362-7011, F: 702-362-5084
Lighting Products

K

KA Display Solutions, Inc., P.O. Box 99, 512 Blackman Blvd. W, Wartrace, TN 37183, P: 800-227-9540, F: 931-389-6686, www.kadsi.com
Custom Manufacturing; Gun Cabinets/Racks/Safes; Gun Cases; Home Furnishings; Knives/Knife Cases; Retailer Services; Scopes, Sights & Accessories

K.B.I., Inc./Charles Daly, P.O. Box 6625, Harrisburg, PA 17112, P: 866-325-9486, F: 717-540-8567, www.charlesdaly.com
Ammunition; Export/Import Specialists; Firearms; Hunting Accessories; Law Enforcement; Scopes, Sights & Accessories

Ka-Bar Knives, Inc., 200 Homer St., Olean, NY 14760, P: 800-282-0130, FL 716-790-7188, www.ka-bar.com
Knives/Knife Cases; Law Enforcement

KDF, Inc., 2485 St. Hwy. 46 N, Seguin, TX 78155, P: 800-KDF-GUNS, F: 830-379-8144
Firearms; Gun Grips & Stocks; Recoil Protection Devices & Services; Scopes, Sights & Accessories

KDH Defense Systems, Inc., 401 Broad St., Johnstown, PA 15906, P: 814-536-7701, F: 814-536-7716, www.kdhdefensesystems.com
Law Enforcement

KNJ Manufacturing, LLC, 757 N. Golden Key, Suite D, Gilbert, AZ 85233, P: 800-424-6606, F: 480-497-8480, www.knjmfg.com
Bags & Equipment Cases; Custom Manufacturing; Gun Cases; Holsters; Hunting Accessories; Law Enforcement; Wholesaler/Distributor

KNS Precision, Inc., 112 Marschall Creek Rd., Fredericksburg, TN 78624, P: 830-997-0000, F: 830-997-1443, www.knsprecisioninc.com
Firearms; Gun Grips & Stocks; Gun Parts/Gunsmithing; Law Enforcement; Lighting Products; Scopes, Sights & Accessories; Training & Safety Equipment; Wholesaler/Distributor

KP Industries, Inc., 3038 Industry St., Suite 108, Oceanside, CA 92054, P: 800-956-3377, F: 760-722-9884, www.kpindustries.com
Export/Import Specialists; Law Enforcement; Outfitter; Paintball Accessories; Shooting Range Equipment; Sports Accessories; Training & Safety Equipment

K-VAR Corp., 3300 S. Decatur Blvd., Suite 10601, Las Vegas, NV 89102, P: 702-364-8880, F: 702-307-2303, www.k-var.com
Firearms Maintenance Equipment; Gun Barrels; Gun Grips & Stocks; Magazines, Cartridge; Scopes, Sights & Accessories

Kahr Arms, 130 Goddard Memorial Dr., Worcester, MA 01603, P: 508-795-3919, FL 508-795-7046, www.kahr.com
Firearms; Holsters; Law Enforcement

Kakadu Traders Australia, 12832 NE Airport Way, Portland, OR 97230, P: 800-852-5288, F: 503-255-7819, www.kakaduaustralia.com
Bags & Equipment Cases; Camouflage; Men & Women's Clothing; Wholesaler/Distributor

Kalispel Case Line/Cortona Shotguns, 418641 SR 20, P.O. Box 267, Cusick, WA 99119, P: 509-445-1121, F: 509-445-1082, www.kalispelcaseline.com
Archery; Bags & Equipment Cases; Export/Import Specialists; Firearms; Gun Cases; Law Enforcement; Wholesaler/Distributor

Katz Knives, 10924 Mukilteo Speedway, Suite 287, Mukilteo, WA 98275, P: 800-848-7084, F: 480-786-9338, www.katzknives.com
Backpacking; Camping; Custom Manufacturing; Cutlery; Knives/Knife Cases; Sharpeners; Wholesaler/Distributor

Kel-Tec CNC Ind., Inc., 1475 Cox Rd., Cocoa, FL 32926, P: 321-631-0068, F: 321-631-1169, www.kel-tec-cnc.com
Firearms

Kelbly's, Inc., 7222 Dalton Fox Lk. Rd., North Lawrence, OH 44666, P: 330-683-4674, F: 330-682-7349, www.kelbly.com
Firearms; Scopes, Sights & Accessories

Kenetrek Boots, 237 Quail Run Rd., Suite A, Bozeman, MT, 59718, P: 800-232-6064, F: 406-585-5548, www.kenetrek.com
Footwear; Men's Clothing

Keng's Firearms Specialty, Inc./Versa-Pod/Champion Gun Sights, 875 Wharton Dr. SW, P.O. Box 44405, Atlanta, GA 30336, P: 800-848-4671, F: 404-505-8445, www.versapod.com
Gun Grips & Stocks; Hunting Accessories; Scopes, Sights & Accessories

KenMar Products, 411 Cameron Rd., Mattawa, Ontario P0H 1V0, CANADA, P: 866-456-5959, F: 705-744-6540, www.kenmarproducts.com
Camouflage; Gun Cases; Hunting Accessories; Leathergoods; Men's Clothing; Scents & Lures; Sports Accessories

Kent Cartridge, 727 Hite Rd., P.O. Box 849, Kearneysville, WV, 25430, P: 888-311-5368, F: 304-725-0454, www.kentgamebore.com
Ammunition

Kenyon Consumer Products/KCP Acquisition, LLC, 141 Fairgrounds Rd., West Kingston, RI 02892, P: 800-537-0024, F: 401-782-4870, www.kenyonconsumer.com
Backpacking; Camping; Law Enforcement; Men & Women's Clothing

Kernel Game Call, 13231 Champion Forest Dr., Suite 201, Houston, TX 77069, P: 830-928-2140, F: 830-792-6215
Feeder Equipment; Game Calls

Kershaw Knives, 18600 SW Teton Ave., Tualatin, OR 97062, P: 800-325-2891, F: 503-682-7168, www.kershawknives.com
Cutlery; Knives/Knife Cases

Kestrel Pocket Weather Meters, 21 Creek Circle, Boothwyn, PA 19061, P: 800-784-4221, F: 610-447-1577, www.kestrelweather.com
Backpacking; Camping; Crossbows & Accessories; Hunting Accessories; Law Enforcement; Shooting Range Equipment; Sports Accessories; Training & Safety Equipment

Keyes Hunting Gear, P.O. Box 1047, Pagosa Springs, CO 81147, P: 317-442-8132, F: 317-770-2127, www.keyeshuntinggear.com
Archery; Backpacking; Bags & Equipment Cases; Camouflage; Camping; Hunting Accessories; Men & Women's Clothing

Keystone Sporting Arms, LLC, 155 Sodom Rd., Milton, PA 17847, P: 800-742-0455, F: 570-742-1455, www.crickett.com
Airsoft; Books/Industry Publications; Firearms; Gun Grips & Stocks; Hunting Accessories; Shooting Range Equipment; Targets; Training & Safety Equipment

KG Industries, LLC, 16790 US Hwy. 63 S, Bldg. 2, Hayward, WI 54843, P: 800-348-9558, F: 715-934-3570, www.kgcoatings.com
Camouflage; Custom Manufacturing; Firearms; Firearms Maintenance Equipment; Gun Barrels; Knives/Knife Cases; Law Enforcement; Lubricants

Kick-EEZ Products, 1819 Schurman Way, Suite 106, Woodland, WA 98674, P: 877-KICKEEZ, F: 360-225-9702, www.kickeezproducts.com
Black Powder Accessories; Clay Targets; Gun Grips & Stocks; Gun Parts/Gunsmithing; Hunting Accessories; Recoil Protection Devices & Services; Targets

Kiesler Distributor of Lewis Machine & Tool Co., 2802 Sable Mill Rd., Jeffersonville, IN 47130, P: 800-444-2950, F: 812-284-6651, www.kiesler.com
Firearms

Kilgore Flares Co., LLC, 155 Kilgore Dr., Toone, TN 38381, P; 731-228-5371, F: 731-228-4173, www.kilgoreflares.com
Ammunition

Kimar Srl/Chiappa Firearms, Via Milano, 2, Azzano Mella, 25020, ITALY, P: 011 390309749065, F: 011 390309749232, www.kimar.com
Airguns; Firearms; Pet Supplies; Training & Safety Equipment

Kimber Mfg., Inc./Meprolight, Inc., One Lawton St., Yonkers, NY 10705, P: 888-243-4522, F: 406-758-2223
Firearms; Law Enforcement

Kingman Training/Kingman Group, 14010 Live Oak Ave., Baldwin Park, CA 91706, P: 888-KINGMAN, F: 626-851-8530, www.kingmantraining.com
Bags & Equipment Cases; Eyewear; Gun Cases; Men's Clothing; Paintball Accessories, Guns & Paintballs

Kingport Industries, LLC, 1303 Shermer Rd., Northbrook, IL 60062, P: 866-303-5463, F: 847-446-5663, www.kingportindustries.com
Bags & Equipment Cases; Custom Manufacturing; Export/Import Specialists; Leathergoods; Wholesaler/Distributor

King's Outdoor World, 1450 S. Blackhawk Blvd., P.O. Box 307, Mt. Pleasant, UT 84647, P: 800-447-6897, F: 435-462-7436, www.kingoutdoorworld.com
Camouflage; Custom Manufacturing; Hunting Accessories; Men's Clothing; Wholesaler/Distributor

Kitasho Co., Ltd./Kanetsune, 5-1-11 Sakae-Machi, Seki-City, Gifu-Pref, 501 3253 JAPAN, P: 11 81575241211, FL 011 81575241210, www.kanetsune.com
Knives/Knife Cases

Knight Rifles/Div. Modern Muzzleloading, 715B Summit Dr., Decatur, AL 52544, P: 800-696-1703, F: 256-260-8951, www.knightrifles.com
Firearms

Knight's Manufacturing Co., 701 Columbia Blvd., Titusville, FL 32780, P: 321-607-9900, F: 321-383-2143, www.knightarmco.com
Firearms; Scopes, Sights & Accessories

Kolpin Outdoors/Bushness Outdoor Accessories, 9200 Cody, Overland Park, KS 66214, P: 800-423-3537, F: 800-548-0446, www.kolpin-outdoors.com
Firearms Maintenance Equipment; Gun Cases; Hunting Accessories

Konus USA Corp., 7530 NW 79th St., Miami, FL 33166, P: 305-884-7618, F: 305-884-7620, www.konusa.com
Binoculars; Compasses; Eyewear; Scopes, Sights & Accessories; Sports Accessories; Telescopes; Watches

Kowa Optimed, Inc., 20001 S. Vermont Ave., Torrance CA 90502, P: 800-966-5692, F: 310-327-4177, www.kowa-usa.com
Binoculars; Scopes, Sights & Accessories; Telescopes

Krause Publications/F&W Media, 700 E. State St., Iola, WI 54990, P: 888-457-2873, F: 715-445-4087, www.krausebooks.com
Books/Industry Publications; Videos

Krieger Barrels, Inc., 2024 Mayfield Rd., Richfield, WI 53076, P: 262-628-8558, F: 262-628-8748, www.kriegerbarrels.com
Gun Barrels

Kriss-TDI, 2697 International Dr., Pkwy. 4, 140, Virginia Beach, VA 23452, P: 202-821-1089, F: 202-821-1094, www.kriss-tdi.com
Firearms; Law Enforcement; Magazines, Cartridge

Kroll International, 51360 Danview Tech Ct., Shelby TWP, MI 48315, P: 800-359-6912, F: 800-359-9721, www.krollcorp.com
Bags & Equipment Cases; Footwear; Gloves, Mitts, Hats; Holsters; Hunting Accessories; Knives/Knife Cases; Law Enforcement; Wholesaler/Distributor

Kruger Optical, LLC, 141 E. Cascade Ave., Suite 208, P.O. Box 532, Sisters, OR 97759, P: 541-549-0770, F: 541-549-0769, www.krugeroptical.com
Binoculars; Scopes, Sights & Accessories

Kunming Yuanda Optical Co., Ltd./Norin Optech Co. Ltd., 9/F Huihua Bldg. No. 80 Xianlie, Zhong Rd., Guangzhou, 51007, CHINA, P: 011 862037616375, F: 011 862037619210, www.norin-optech.com
Binoculars; Compasses; Scopes, Sights & Accessories; Sports Accessories; Telescopes

Kutmaster/Div. Utica Cutlery Co., 820 Noyes St., Utica, NY 13503, P: 800-888-4223, F: 315-733-6602, www.kutmaster.com
Backpacking; Camping; Cooking Equipment & Accessories; Cutlery; Hunting Accessories; Knives/Knife Cases; Sports Accessories; Survival Kits/First Aid

Kwik-Site Co./Ironsighter Co., 5555 Treadwell, Wayne, MI 48184, P: 734-326-1500, F: 734-326-4120, www.kwiksitecorp.com
Black Powder Accessories; Firearms Maintenance Equipment; Hunting Accessories; Scopes, Sights & Accessories; Sporting Accessories

L

L.P.A. Srl di Ghilardi, Via Vittorio Alfieri, 26, Gardone V.T., 25063, ITALY, P: 011 390308911481, F: 011 390308910951, www.lpasights.com
Black Powder Accessories; Gun Parts/Gunsmithing; Scopes, Sights & Accessories

L-3 Communications-Eotech, 1201 E. Ellsworth Rd., Ann Arbor, MI 48108, P: 734-741-8868, F: 734-741-8221, www.l-3com.com/eotech
Law Enforcement; Scopes, Sights & Accessories

L-3 Electro-Optical Systems, 3414 Herrmann Dr., Garland, TX 75041, P: 866-483-9972, F: 972-271-2195, www.l3nightvision.com
Law Enforcement; Scopes, Sights & Accessories

L.A. Lighter, Inc./Viclight, 19805 Harrison Ave., City of Industry, CA 91789, P: 800-499-4708, F: 909-468-1859, www.lalighter.com
Camping; Cooking Equipment/Accessories; Lighting Products; Sports Accessories; Training & Safety Equipment; Wholesaler/Distributor

L.A.R. Manufacturing, 4133 W. Farm Rd., West Jordan, UT 84088, P: 801-280-3505, F: 801-280-1972, www.largrizzly.com
Firearms

La Crosse Technology, Ltd., 2809 Losey Blvd. S, La Crosse, WI 54601, P: 800-346-9544, F: 608-796-1020, www.lacrossetechnology.com
Sports Accessories; Wholesaler/Distributor

LEM Products, 109 May Dr., Harrison, OH 45030, P: 513-202-1188, F: 513-202-9494, www.lemproducts.com
Books/Industry Publications; Cooking Equipment/Accessories; Cutlery; Knives/Knife Cases; Sharpeners; Videos; Wholesaler/Distributor

L&R Ultrasonics, 577 Elm St., Kearny, NJ 07032, P: 201-991-5330, F: 201-991-5870, www.lrultrasonics.com
Decoys; Firearms; Firearms Maintenance Equipment; Gun Parts/Gunsmithing; Lubricants; Reloading; Shooting Range Equipment

LRB Arms, 96 Cherry Lane, Floral Park, NY 11001, P: 516-327-9061, F: 516-327-0246, www.lrbarms.com
Firearms; Wholesaler/Distributor

LRI-Photon Micro Light, 20448 Hwy. 36, Blachly, OR 97412, P: 541-925-3741, F: 541-925-3751, www.laughingrabbitinc.com
Backpacking; Camping; Hunting Accessories; Law Enforcement; Lighting Products; Sports Accessories; Survival Kits/First Aid; Training & Safety Equipment

Lachausee/New Lachaussée, UFA Belgium, Rue de Tige, 13, Herstal, Liège B 4040, BELGIUM, P: 011 3242488811, F: 011 3242488800, www.lachausee.com
Ammunition; Firearms Maintenance Equipment; Reloading; Shooting Range Equipment

Lakeside Machine, LLC, 1213 Industrial St., Horseshoe Bend, AR 72512, P: 870-670-4999, F: 870-670-4998, www.lakesideguns.com
Custom Manufacturing; Firearms; Hunting Accessories; Law Enforcement

Lanber, Zubiaurre 3, P.O. Box 3, Zaldibar, (Vizcaya) 48250, SPAIN, P: 011 34946827702, F: 011 34946827999, www.lanber.com
Firearms

Lancer Systems, 7566 Morris Ct., Suite 300, Allentown, PA, 18106, P: 610-973-2614, F: 610-973-2615, www.lancer-systems.com
Custom Manufacturing; Gun Parts/Gunsmithing; Magazines, Cartridge

Landmark Outdoors/Yukon Advanced Optics/Sightmark/Mobile Hunter/Trophy Score/Amacker, 201 Regency Pkwy., Mansfield, TX 76063, P: 877-431-3579, F: 817-453-8770, www.landmarkoutdoors.com
Airsoft; Binoculars; Custom Manufacturing; Feeder Equipment; Hunting Accessories; Law Enforcement; Paintball Accessories; Scopes, Sights & Accessories; Shooting Range Equipment; Treestands; Wholesaler/Distributor

Lanigan Performance Products/KG Industries, 10320 Riverburn Dr., Tampa, FL 33467, P: 813-651-5400, F: 813-991-6156, www.thesacskit.com
Gun Parts/Gunsmithing

Lansky Sharpeners, P.O. Box 50830, Henderson, NV 89016, P: 716-877-7511, F: 716-877-6955, www.lansky.com
Archery; Camping; Cooking Equipment/Accessories; Cutlery; Hunting Accessories; Knives/Knife Cases; Law Enforcement; Sharpeners

Lapua/Vihtavuori, 123 Winchester Dr., Sedalia, MO 65301, P: 660-826-3232, F: 660-826-3232, www.lapua.com
Ammunition; Books/Industry Publications; Reloading; Videos

LaRue Tactical, 850 CR 177, Leander, TX 78641, P: 512-259-1585, F: 512-259-1588, www.laruetactical.com
Custom Manufacturing; Scopes, Sights & Accessories; Targets

Laser Ammo, Ltd., #7 Bar Kochva St., Rishon Lezion, 75353, ISRAEL, P: 682-286-3311, www.laser-ammo.com
Ammunition; Firearms; Law Enforcement; Scopes, Sights & Accessories; Shooting Range Equipment; Training & Safety Equipment

Laser Devices, Inc., 2 Harris Ct., Suite A-4, Monterey, CA 93940, P: 800-235-2162, F: 831-373-0903, www.laserdevices.com
Holsters; Law Enforcement; Lighting Products; Scopes, Sights & Accessories; Shooting Range Equipment; Sports Accessories; Targets; Training & Safety Equipment

Laser Shot, Inc., 4214 Bluebonnet Dr., Stafford, TX 77477, P: 281-240-8241, F: 281-240-8241
Law Enforcement; Training & Safety Equipment

LaserLyte, 101 Airpark Rd., Cottonwood, AZ 86326, P: 928-649-3201, F: 928-649-3970, www.laserlyte.com
Hunting Accessories; Scopes, Sights & Accessories

LaserMax, Inc., 3495 Winton Place Bldg. B, Rochester, NY 14623, P: 800-527-3703, F: 585-272-5427, www.lasermax.com
Airsoft; Crossbows & Accessories; Firearms; Law Enforcement; Paintball Accessories; Scopes, Sights & Accessories; Shooting Range Equipment; Training & Safety Equipment

Lauer Custom Weaponry/Duracoat Products, 3601 129th St., Chippewa Falls, WI 54729, P: 800-830-6677, F: 715-723-2950, www.lauerweaponry.com
Camouflage; Custom Manufacturing; Firearms; Hunting Accessories; Law Enforcement; Lubricants; Magazines, Cartridge; Scopes, Sights & Accessories

Law Enforcement Targets, Inc., 8802 W. 35 W. Service Dr. NE, Blaine, MN 55449, P: 800-779-0182, F: 651-645-5360, www.letargets.com
Eyewear; Gun Cabinets/Racks/Safes; Gun Grips & Stocks; Hearing Protection; Law Enforcement; Targets; Training & Safety Equipment

Law Officer Magazine/Div. Elsevier Public Safety/Elsevier, 525 B St., Suite 1900, San Diego, CA 92101, P: 800-266-5367, F: 619-699-6396, www.lawofficer.com
Books/Industry Publications; Law Enforcement

Lawman Leather Goods, P.O. Box 30115, Las Vegas, NV 89173, P: 877-44LAWMAN, F: 702-227-0036, www.lawmanleathergoods.com
Black Powder Accessories; Books/Industry Publications; Holsters; Law Enforcement; Leathergoods; Wholesaler/Distributor

Lazzeroni Arms Co., 1415 S. Cherry Ave., Tuscon, AZ 85713, P: 888-4-WARBIRD, F: 520-624-6202, www.lazzeroni.com
Ammunition; Firearms

Leapers, Inc., 32700 Capitol St., Livonia, MI 48150, P: 734-542-1500, F: 734-542-7095, www.leapers.com
Airguns; Airsoft; Bags & Equipment Cases; Gun Cases; Holsters; Law Enforcement; Lighting Products; Scopes, Sights & Accessories

Leatherman Tool Group, Inc., 12106 NE Ainsworth Circle, Portland, OR 97220, P: 800-847-8665, F: 503-253-7830, www.leatherman.com
Backpacking; Hunting Accessories; Knives/Knife Cases; Lighting Products; Sports Accessories

Leatherwood/Hi-Lux Optics/Hi-Lux, Inc., 3135 Kashiwa St., Torrance, CA 90505, P: 888-445-8912, F: 310-257-8096, www.hi-luxoptics.com
Binoculars; Scopes, Sights & Accessories; Telescopes

Legacy Sports International, 4750 Longley Lane, Suite 208, Reno, NV 89502, P: 775-828-0555, F: 775-828-0565, www.legacysports.com
Firearms; Gun Cabinets/Racks/Safes; Gun Cases; Scopes, Sights & Accessories

Leica Sport Optics/Leica Camera Inc., 1 Peart Ct., Unit A, Allendale, NJ 07401, P: 800-222-0118, F: 201-955-1686, www.leica-camera.com/usa
Binoculars; Photographic Equipment; Scopes, Sights & Accessories

LensPen–Parkside Optical, 650-375 Water St., Vancouver, British Columbia V6B 5C6, CANADA, P: 877-608-0868, F: 604-681-6194, www.lenspens.com
Binoculars; Hunting Accessories; Law Enforcement; Photographic Equipment; Scopes, Sights & Accessories; Sports Accessories; Telescopes

Les Baer Custom, Inc., 1804 Iowa Dr., Leclaire, IA 52753, P: 563-289-2126, F: 563-289-2132, www.lesbaer.com
Custom Manufacturing; Export/Import Specialists; Firearms; Gun Barrels; Gun Parts/Gunsmithing

Leupold & Stevens, Inc., 14400 NW Greenbriar Pkwy. 9700, P.O. Box 688, Beaverton, OR 97006, P: 503-646-9171, F: 503-526-1478, www.leupold.com
Binoculars; Lighting Products; Scopes, Sights & Accessories

Level Lok Shooting System/Div. Brutis Enterprises Inc., 105 S. 12th St., Pittsburgh, PA 15203, P: 888-461-7468, F: 412-488-5440, www.levellok.com
Binoculars; Firearms; Gun Grips & Stocks; Hunting Accessories; Photographic Equipment; Scopes, Sights & Accessories; Shooting Range Equipment; Sports Accessories

Levy's Leathers Limited, 190 Disraeli Freeway, Winnipeg, Manitoba R3B 2Z4, CANADA, P: 800-565-0203, F: 888-329-5389, www.levysleathers.com
Archery; Bags & Equipment Cases; Hunting Accessories; Knives/Knife Cases; Leathergoods

Lew Horton Distributing Co., Inc., 15 Walkup Dr., P.O. Box 5023, Westboro, MA 01581, P: 800-446-7866, F: 508-366-5332, www.lewhorton.com
Ammunition; Firearms; Hunting Accessories; Knives/Knife Cases; Law Enforcement; Magazines, Cartridge; Scopes, Sights & Accessories; Wholesaler/Distributor

Lewis Machine & Tool, 1305 11th St. W, Milan, IL 61264, P: 309-787-7151, F: 309-787-7193, www.lewismachine.net
Firearms

Liberty Mountain, 4375 W. 1980 S, Suite 100, Salt Lake City, UT 84104, P: 800-366-2666, F: 801-954-0766, www.libertymountain.com
Backpacking; Camping; Cooking Equipment/Accessories; Gloves, Mitts, Hats; Knives/Knife Cases; Lighting Products; Survival Kits/First Aid; Wholesaler/Distributor

Liberty Safe & Security Products, Inc., 1199 W. Utah Ave., Payson, UT 84651, P: 800-247-5625, F: 801-465-5880, www.libertysafe.com
Firearms Maintenance Equipment; Gun Cabinets/Racks/Safes; Gun Locks; Home Furnishings; Hunting Accessories; Law Enforcement; Sports Accessories; Training & Safety Equipment

Light My Fire USA, 9225 151st Ave. NE, Redmond, WA 98052, P: 888-297-6062, F: 425-883-0036
Camping; Cooking Equipment/Accessories; Knives/Knife Cases; Survival Kits/First Aid

Lightfield Ammunition Corp., P.O. Box 162, Adelphia, NJ 07710, P: 732-462-9200, F: 732-780-2437, www.lightfieldslugs.com
Ammunition

LightForce USA, Inc/NightForce Optics, 1040 Hazen Ln., Orofino, ID 83544, P: 800-732-9824, F: 208-476-9817, www.nightforceoptics.com
Law Enforcement; Lighting Products; Scopes, Sights & Accessories; Telescopes

LimbSaver, 50 W. Rose Nye Way, Shelton, WA 98584, P: 877-257-2761, F: 360-427-4025, www.limbsaver.com
Archery; Crossbows & Accessories; Hunting Accessories; Men's Clothing; Paintball Accessories; Recoil Protection Devices & Services; Scopes, Sights & Accessories

Linton Cutlery Co., Ltd., 7F, No. 332, Yongji Rd., Sinyi District, Taipei, 110, TAIWAN, P: 011 886227090905, F: 011 886227003978, www.linton-cutlery.com
Cutlery; Export/Import Specialists; Hunting Accessories; Law Enforcement; Sports Accessories; Wholesaler/Distributor

Linville Knife and Tool Co., P.O. Box 71, Bethania, NC 27010, P: 336-923-2062
Cutlery; Gun Grips & Stocks; Knives/Knife Cases

Lipseys, P.O. Box 83280, Baton Rouge, LA 70884, P: 800-666-1333, FL 225-755-3333, www.lipseys.com
Black Powder Accessories; Firearms; Holsters; Hunting Accessories; Magazines, Cartridge; Online Services; Scopes, Sights & Accessories; Wholesaler/Distributor

Little Giant Ladders, 1198 N. Spring Creek Pl., Springville, UT 84663, P: 800-453-1192, F: 801-489-1130, www.littlegiantladders.com
Law Enforcement; Training & Safety Equipment

Little Sportsman, Inc., 315 N. 400 W, P.O. Box 715, Fillmore, UT 84631, P: 435-743-4400, F: 435-846-2132, www.littlesportsman.com
Books/Industry Publications

LockSAF/VMR Capital Group, 2 Gold St., Suite 903, New York, NY 10038, P: 877-568-5625, F: 877-893-4502, www.locksaf.com
Gun Cabinets/Racks/Safes

Loksak, Inc. (formerly Watchful Eye), P.O. Box 980007, Park City, UT 84098, P: 800-355-1126, F: 435-940-0956, www.loksak.com
Bags & Equipment Cases

Lone Wolf Distributors, Inc., 57 Shepard Rd., P.O. Box 3549, Oldtown, ID 83822, P: 888-279-2077, F: 208-437-1098, www.lonewolfdist.com
Books/Industry Publications; Firearms Maintenance Equipment; Gun Barrels; Gun Parts/Gunsmithing; Holsters; Scopes, Sights & Accessories; Videos; Wholesaler/Distributor

Lone Wolf Knives, 9373 SW Barber St., Suite A, Wilsonville, OR 97070, P: 503-431-6777, F: 503-431-6776, www.lonewolfknives.com
Archery; Backpacking; Camouflage; Camping; Cutlery; Hunting Accessories; Knives/Knife Cases; Law Enforcement

Long Perng Co., Ltd., #16, Hejiang Rd., Chung Li Industrial Zone, Chung Li City, Taoyuan Hsien, 320, TAIWAN, P: 011 88634632468, F: 011 88634631948, www.longperng.com.tw
Binoculars; Scopes, Sights & Accessories; Telescopes

Longleaf Camo, 1505 Airport Rd., Flowood, MS 39232, P: 866-751-2266, F: 601-719-0713, www.longleafcamo.com
Camouflage; Footwear; Gloves, Mitts, Hats; Men & Women's Clothing

Loon Lake Decoy Co., Inc., 170 Industrial Ct., Wabasha, MN 55981, P: 800-555-2696, F: 612-565-4871, www.loonlakedecoycompany.com
Custom Manufacturing; Decoys; Home Furnishings; Hunting Accessories; Lighting Products; Outdoor Art, Jewelry, Sculpture; Wholesaler/Distributor

Lorpen North America, Inc., 100 Ironside Crescent, Suite 8, Toronto, Ontario M1X 1M9, CANADA, P: 888-224-9781, F: 416-335-8201, www.lorpen.com
Footwear

Lothar Walther Precision Tools, Inc., 3425 Hutchinson Rd., Cumming, GA 30040, P: 770-889-9998, F: 770-889-4919, www.lothar-walther.com
Custom Manufacturing; Export/Import Specialists; Gun Barrels

Lou's Police Distributor, 7815 W. 4th Ave., Hialeah, FL 33014, P: 305-822-5362, F: 305-822-9603, www.louspolice.com
Ammunition; Firearms; Gun Grips & Stocks; Hearing Protection; Holsters; Law Enforcement; Scopes, Sights & Accessories; Wholesaler/Distributor

LouderThanWords.US/Heirloom Precision, LLC, 2118 E. 5th St., Tempe, AZ 85281, P: 480-804-1911, www.louderthanwords.us
Firearms; Gun Parts/Gunsmithing; Holsters

Lowa Boots, 86 Viaduct Rd., Stamford, CT 06907, P: 888-335-5692, F: 203-353-0311, www.lowaboots.com
Footwear; Men & Women's Clothing

Lowrance–Navico, Eagle–Navico, 12000 E. Skelly Dr., Tulsa, OK 74128, P: 800-352-1356, F: 918-234-1707, www.lowrance.com

Archery; Backpacking; Camping; Hunting Accessories; Law Enforcement; Sports Accessories; Survival Kits/First Aid; Vehicles, Utility & Rec

Lowy Enterprises, Inc., 1970 E. Gladwick St., Rancho Dominguez, CA 90220, P: 310-763-1111, F: 310-763-1112, www.lowyusa.com
Backpacking; Bags & Equipment Cases; Custom Manufacturing; Law Enforcement; Outfitter; Paintball Accessories; Sports Accessories; Wholesaler/Distributor

Luggage-USA, Inc./L A Luggage, 710 Ducommun St., Los Angeles, CA 90012, P: 888-laluggage, F: 213-626-0800, www.luggage-usa.com
Backpacking; Bags & Equipment Cases; Camouflage; Camping; Export/Import Specialists; Gun Cases; Leathergoods; Wholesaler/Distributor

Lumberjack Tools, 9304 Wolf Pack Terrace, Colorado Springs, CO 80920, P: 719-282-3043, F: 719-282-3046, www.lumberjacktools.com
Camping; Crossbows & Accessories; Firearms; Home Furnishings; Hunting Accessories; Taxidermy; Treestands; Wholesaler/Distributor

Luminox Watch Co., 2301 Kerner Blvd., Suite A, San Rafael, CA 94901, P: 415-455-9500, F: 415-482-8215, www.luminox.com
Backpacking; Camping; Custom Manufacturing; Hunting Accessories; Law Enforcement; Outdoor Art, Jewelry; Sculpture; Sports Accessories; Watches

LWRC International, LLC, 815 Chesapeake Dr., Cambridge, MD 21613, P: 410-901-1348, F: 410-228-1799, www.lwrifles.com
Ammunition; Custom Manufacturing; Firearms; Firearms Maintenance Equipment; Gun Barrels; Gun Parts/Gunsmithing; Law Enforcement; Magazines, Cartridge

Lyalvale Express Limited, Express Estate, Whittington, Lichfield, WS13 8XA, UNITED KINGDOM, P: 011-44 1543434400, F: 011-44 1543434420, www.lyalvaleexpress.com
Ammunition

Lyman-Pachmayr-Trius Products/TacStar-A-Zoom-Butchs-Uni-Dot, 475 Smith St., Middletown, CT 06457, P: 800-225-9626, F: 860-632-1699, www.lymanproducts.com
Black Powder Accessories; Books/Industry Publications; Firearms; Firearms Maintenance Equipment; Gun Parts/Gunsmithing; Reloading; Scopes, Sights & Accessories; Shooting Range Equipment

Lyons Press, 246 Goose Ln., Guilford, CT 06437, P: 800-243-0495, F: 800-820-2329, www.glovepequot.com
Books/Industry Publications; Wholesaler/Distributor

M

MDM/Millennium Designed Muzzleloaders, Ltd., RR 1, Box 405, Maidstone, VT 05905, P: 802-676-331, F: 802-676-3322, www.mdm-muzzleloaders.com
Ammunition; Black Powder Accessories; Black Powder/Smokeless Powder; Custom Manufacturing; Firearms Maintenance Equipment; Gun Barrels; Gun Cases; Scopes, Sights & Accessories

MDS Inc., 3429 Stearns Rd., Valrico, FL 33596, P: 800-435-9352, F: 813-684-5953, www.mdsincorporated.com
Firearms Maintenance Equipment; Gun Parts/Gunsmithing; Law Enforcement

MFI, 563 San Miguel, Liberty, KY 42539, P: 606-787-0022, F: 606-787-0059, www.mfiap.com
Custom Manufacturing; Export/Import Specialists; Firearms; Gun Grips & Stocks; Gun Parts/Gunsmithing; Scopes, Sights & Accessories; Sports Accessories; Wholesaler/Distributor

MGI, 102 Cottage St., Bangor, ME 04401, P: 207-945-5441, F: 207-945-4010, www.mgimilitary.com
Firearms; Gun Barrels; Law Enforcement

MGM–Mike Gibson Manufacturing, 17891 Karcher Rd., Caldwell, ID 83607, P: 888-767-7371, F: 208-454-0666, www.mgmtargets.com
Clay Targets; Custom Manufacturing; Firearms; Gun Cabinets/Racks/Safes; Shooting Range Equipment; Targets; Training & Safety Equipment

MG Arms, Inc., 6030 Treaschwig Rd., Spring, TX 77373, P: 281-821-8282, F: 281-821-6387, www.mgarmsinc.com
Ammunition; Custom Manufacturing; Firearms; Gun Grips & Stocks; Wholesaler/Distributor

MPI Outdoors/Grabber, 5760 N. Hawkeye Ct., Grand Rapids, MI 49509, P: 800-423-1233, F: 616-977-7718, www.warmers.com
Backpacking; Camouflage; Camping; Cooking Equipment/Accessories; Gloves, Mitts, Hats; Hunting Accessories; Lighting Products; Survival Kits/First Aid

MPRI, 10220 Old Columbia Rd., Suites A & B, Columbia, MD 21046, P: 800-232-6448, F: 410-309-1506, www.mpri.com

Ammunition; Gun Barrels; Law Enforcement; Shooting Range Equipment; Targets; Training & Safety Equipment

MPT Industries, 6-B Hamilton Business Park, 85 Franklin Rd., Dover, NJ 07801, P: 973-989-9220, F: 973-989-9234, www.mptindustries.com
Airguns; Camping; Firearms; Firearms Maintenance Equipment; Lubricants; Paintball Guns; Sports Accessories

M-Pro 7 Gun Care/Bushnell Outdoor Accessories, 9200 Cody, Overland Park, KS 66214, P: 800-845-2444, F: 800-548-0446, www.mpro7.com
Black Powder Accessories; Firearms Maintenance Equipment; Gun Parts/Gunsmithing; Hunting Accessories; Law Enforcement; Lubricants

M-Pro 7 Gun Care, 225 W. Deer Valley Rd., Suite 4, Phoenix, AZ 85027, P: 888-YES-4MP7, F: 623-516-0414, www.mpro7.com
Black Powder Accessories; Firearms Maintenance Equipment; Gun Parts/Gunsmithing; Hunting Accessories; Law Enforcement; Lubricants

MSA, 121 Gamma Dr., Pittsburgh, PA 15238, P: 800-672-2222, F: 412-967-3373
Bags & Equipment Cases; Eyewear; Hearing Protection; Law Enforcement; Survival Kits/First Aid; Training & Safety Equipment

MSA Safety Works, 121 Gamma Dr., Pittsburgh, PA 15238, P: 800-969-7562, F: 800-969-7563, www.msasafetyworks.com
Eyewear; Hearing Protection; Shooting Range Equipment; Training & Safety Equipment

MT2, LLC/Metals Treatment Technologies, 14045 W. 66th Ave., Arvada, CO 80004, P: 888-435-6645, F: 303-456-5998, www.mt2.com
Firearms Maintenance Equipment; Shooting Range Equipment

MTM Case-Gard Co., P.O. Box 13117, Dayton, OH 45413, P: 800-543-0548, F: 937-890-1747, www.mtmcase-gard.com
Bags & Equipment Cases; Black Powder Accessories; Camping; Firearms Maintenance Equipment; Gun Cases; Hunting Accessories; Reloading; Targets

Mace Security International, 160 Benmont Ave., Bennington, VT 05201, P: 800-255-2634, F: 802-753-1209, www.mace.com
Archery; Camping; Hunting Accessories; Law Enforcement; Sports Accessories; Training & Safety Equipment

Mag Instrument, Inc./Maglite, 2001 S. Hellman Ave., Ontario, CA 91761, P: 800-289-6241, F: 775-719-4586, www.maglite.com
Backpacking; Camping; Hunting Accessories; Lighting Products; Sports Accessories; Survival Kits/First Aid; Training & Safety Equipment

Magellan Navigation, 471 El Camino Real, Santa Clara, CA 94050, P: 408-615-5100, F: 408-615-5200, www.magellangps.com
Backpacking; Camping; Compasses; Computer Software; Hunting Accessories; Sports Accessories; Vehicles, Utility & Rec

Maglula, Ltd., P.O. Box 302, Rosh Ha'ayin, 48103, ISRAEL, P: 011 97239030902, F: 011 97239030902, www.maglula.com
Firearms Maintenance Equipment; Gun Parts/Gunsmithing; Magazines, Cartridge; Shooting Range Equipment

Magnum USA, 4801 Stoddard Rd., Modesto, CA 95356, P: 800-521-1698, F: 209-545-2079, www.magnumboots.com
Footwear; Law Enforcement; Men's Clothing

Magnum Research, Inc., 7110 University Ave. NE, Minneapolis, MN 55432, P: 800-772-6168, F: 763-574-0109, www.magnumresearch.com
Firearms

Magnum Tents, P.O. Box 18127, Missoula, MT 59808, P: 877-836-8226, F: 877-836-8226, www.magnumtents.com
Camping; Hunting Accessories

Magpul Industries Corp., P.O. Box 17697, Boulder, CO 80308, P: 877-462-4785, F: 303-828-3469, www.magpul.com
Firearms; Gun Grips & Stocks; Gun Parts/Gunsmithing; Law Enforcement; Videos

Magtech Ammunition Co., Inc., 248 Apollo Dr., Suite 180, Lino Lakes, MN 55014, P: 800-466-7191, F: 763-235-4004, www.magtechammunition.com
Ammunition; Export/Import Specialists; Law Enforcement; Reloading; Shooting Range Equipment; Wholesaler/Distributor

Mahco, Inc., 1202 Melissa Dr., Bentonville, AR 72712, P: 479-273-0052, F: 479-271-9248
Bags & Equipment Cases; Binoculars; Camouflage; Camping; Hunting Accessories; Knives/Knife Cases; Scopes, Scopes, Sights & Accessories

Majestic Arms, Ltd., 101-A Ellis St., Staten Island, NY 10307, P: 718-356-6765, F: 718-356-6835, www.majesticarms.com
Firearms; Gun Barrels; Gun Parts/Gunsmithing

Mako Group, 74 Rome St., Farmingdale, NY 11735, P: 631-880-3396, F: 631-880-3397, www.themakogroup.com
Custom Manufacturing; Gun Grips & Stocks; Law Enforcement; Lighting Products; Scopes, Sights & Accessories; Targets; Training & Safety Equipment; Wholesaler/Distributor

Mancom Manufacturing Inc., 1335 Osprey Dr., Ancaster, Ontario L9G 4V5, CANADA, P: 888-762-6266, F: 905-304-6137, www.mancom.ca
Custom Manufacturing; Law Enforcement; Shooting Range Equipment; Training & Safety Equipment

Manners Composite Stocks, 1209 Swift, North Kansas City, MO 64116, P: 816-283-3334, www.mannerstock.com
Custom Manufacturing; Firearms Maintenance Equipment; Gun Grips & Stocks; Law Enforcement; Shooting Range Equipment

Dave Manson Precision Reamers/Div. Loon Lake Precision, Inc., 8200 Embury Rd., Grand Blanc, MI 48439, P: 810-953-0732, F: 810-953-0735, www.mansonreamers.com
Black Powder Accessories; Custom Manufacturing; Firearms Maintenance Equipment; Gun Barrels; Gun Parts/Gunsmithing; Recoil Protection Devices & Services; Reloading

Mantis Knives/Famous Trails, 1580 N. Harmony Circle, Anaheim, CA 92807, P: 877-97-SCOPE, F: 714-701-9672, www.mantisknives.com
Binoculars; Camping; Hunting Accessories; Knives/Knife Cases; Law Enforcement; Photographic Equipment; Scopes, Sights & Accessories; Wholesaler/Distributor

Manzella Productions, 80 Sonwil Dr., Buffalo, NY 14225, P: 716-681-8880, F: 716-681-6888
Hunting Accessories; Law Enforcement

Marbles, 420 Industrial Park, Gladstone, MI 49837, P: 906-428-3710, F: 906-428-3711, www.marblescutlery.com
Compasses; Cutlery; Scopes, Sights & Accessories; Sharpeners

Marlin Firearms/H&R, 100 Kenna Dr., P.O. Box 248, North Haven, CT 06473, P: 888-261-1179, F: 336-548-8736, www.marlinfirearms.com
Firearms

Marvel Precision, LLC, P.O. Box 127, Cortland, NE 68331, P: 800-295-1987, F: 402-791-2246, www.marvelprecision.com
Firearms; Wholesaler/Distributor

Masen Co., Inc., John, 1305 Jelmak St., Grand Prairie, TX 75050, P: 972-970-3691, F: 972-970-3691, www.johnmasen.com
Firearms Maintenance Equipment; Gun Grips & Stocks; Gun Parts/Gunsmithing; Magazines, Cartridge; Online Services; Scopes, Sights & Accessories; Wholesaler/Distributor

Maserin Coltellerie SNC, Via dei Fabbri, 19, Maniago, 33085, ITALY, P: 011 39042771335, F: 011 390427700690, www.maserin.com
Cutlery; Hunting Accessories; Knives/Knife Cases; Law Enforcement; Sports Accessories

Master Cutlery, Inc., 700 Penhorn Ave., Secausus, NJ 07094, P: 888-271-7228, F: 888-271-7228, www.mastercutlery.com
Airsoft; Crossbows & Accessories; Custom Manufacturing; Cutlery

Masterbuilt Manufacturing, Inc., 1 Masterbuilt Ct., Columbus, GA 31907, P: 800-489-1581, F: 706-327-5632, www.masterbuilt.com
Camping; Cooking Equipment/Accessories; Hunting Accessories; Vehicles, Utility & Rec

Matterhorn Footwear/Cove Shoe Co., HH Brown Work & Outdoor Group, 107 Highland St., Martinsburg, PA 16662, P: 800-441-4319, F: 814-793-9272, www.matterhornboot.com
Footwear; Law Enforcement; Training & Safety Equipment

Matz Abrasives/Stagecoach, 1209 W. Chestnut St., Burbank, CA 91506, P: 818-840-8042, F: 818-840-8340, www.matzrubber.com
Black Powder Accessories; Custom Manufacturing; Firearms; Firearms Maintenance Equipment; Gun Grips & Stocks; Gun Parts/Gunsmithing; Hunting Accessories; Recoil Protection Devices & Services

Maurice Sporting Goods, Inc., 1910 Techny Rd., Northbrook, IL 60065, P: 866-477-3474, F: 847-715-1419, www.maurice.net
Archery; Camping; Firearms Maintenance Equipment; Game Calls; Gloves, Mitts, Hats; Hunting Accessories; Sports Accessories; Wholesaler/Distributor

Maxit Designs, Inc., P.O. Box 1052, Carmichael, CA 95609, P: 800-556-2948, F: 916-489-7031, www.maxit-inc.com
Footwear; Gloves, Mitts, Hats; Men & Women's Clothing

Maxpedition Hard-Use Gear/Edgygear, Inc., P.O. Box 5008, Palos Verdes, CA 90274, P: 877-629-5556, F: 310-515-5950, www.maxpedition.com
Backpacking; Bags & Equipment Cases; Gun Cases; Holsters; Hunting Accessories; Knives/Knife Cases; Law Enforcement; Sports Accessories

MaxPro Police & Armor, 4181 W. 5800 N, Mountain Green, UT 84050, P: 801-876-3616, F: 801-876-2746, www.maxpropolice.com
Training & Safety Equipment

Mayville Engineering Co. (MEC), 800 Horicon St., Suite 1, Mayville, WI 53050, P: 800-797-4MEC, F: 920-387-5802, www.mecreloaders.com
Reloading

McConkey, Inc./ATV Backpacker Cart, P.O. Box 1362, Seeley Lake, MT 59868, P: 308-641-1085, F: 866-758-9896, www.atvbackpackercart.com
Ammunition; Backpacking; Camping; Hunting Accessories; Sports Accessories; Vehicles, Utility & Rec; Wholesaler/Distributor

McGowan Manufacturing Co., 4854 N. Shamrock Pl., Suite 100, Tucson, AZ 85705, P: 800-342-4810, F: 520-219-9759, www.mcgowanmfg.com
Archery; Camping; Cooking Equipment/Accessories; Crossbows & Accessories; Cutlery; Hunting Accessories; Knives/Knife Cases; Sharpeners

McKeon Products, Inc./Mack's Hearing Protection, 25460 Guenther, Warren, MI 48091, P: 586-427-7560, F: 586-427-7204, www.macksearplugs.com
Camping; Hearing Protection; Hunting Accessories; Sports Accessories; Training & Safety Equipment

McMillan Fiberglass Stocks, 1638 W. Knudsen Dr., Suite A, Phoenix, AZ 85027, P: 877-365-6148, F: 623-581-3825, www.mcmillanusa.com
Firearms; Gun Grips & Stocks

McNett Corp., 1411 Meador Ave., Bellingham, WA 98229, P: 360-671-2227, F: 360-671-4521, www.mcnett.com
Backpacking; Camouflage; Camping; Hunting Accessories; Knives/Knife Cases; Lubricants; Paintball Accessories; Sports Accessories

Mcusta Knives/Mcusta Knives USA, P.O. Box 22901, Portland, OR 97269, P: 877-714-5487, F: 503-344-4631, www.mcustausa.com
Cooking Equipment/Accessories; Cutlery; Hunting Accessories; Knives/Knife Cases; Law Enforcement; Sports Accessories; Wholesaler/Distributor

Mead Industries, Inc., 411 Walnut St., P.O. Box 402, Wood River, NE 68883, P: 308-583-2875, F: 308-583-2002
Ammunition

MEC-GAR SRL, Via Mandolossa, 102/a, Gussago, Brescia, 25064, ITALY, P: 011 390303735413, F: 011 390303733687, www.mec-gar.it
Gun Parts/Gunsmithing; Law Enforcement; Magazine, Cartridge

Medalist/Performance Sports Apparel, 1047 Macarthur Rd., Reading PA, 19605, P: 800-543-8952, F: 610-373-5400, www.medalist.com
Camouflage; Hunting Accessories; Men & Women's Clothing

Meggitt Training Systems/Caswell, 296 Brogdon Rd., Suwanee, GA 30024, P: 800-813-9046, F: 678-288-1515, www.meggitttrainingsystems.com
Custom Manufacturing; Law Enforcement; Shooting Range Equipment; Targets; Training & Safety Equipment

Meissenberg Designs, 7583 MT Hwy. 35, Bigfork, MT 59911, P: 877-974-7446, F: 866-336-2571, www.oldwoodsigns.com
Home Furnishings; Printing Services

Medota Products, Inc., 120 Bridgepoint Way, Suite B, South St. Paul, MN 55075, P: 800-224-1121, F: 651-457-9085, www.mendotaproducts.com
Custom Manufacturing; Hunting Accessories; Pet Supplies; Training & Safety Equipment

Meopta USA, Inc., 50 Davids Dr., Hauppauge, NY, 11788, P: 800-828-8928, F: 631-436-5920, www.meopta.com
Binoculars; Scopes, Sights & Accessories; Telescopes

Meprolight, 2590 Montana Hwy. 35, Suite B, Kalispell, MT 59901, P: 406-758-2222, F: 406-758-2223
Scopes, Sights & Accessories

Meprolight, Ltd., 58 Hazait St., Or-Akiva Industrial Park, Or-Akiva, 30600, ISRAEL, P: 011 97246244111, F: 011 97246244123, www.meprolight.com
Binoculars; Firearms; Gun Parts/Gunsmithing; Hunting Accessories; Law Enforcement; Lighting Products; Scopes, Sights & Accessories; Telescopes

Mercury Luggage Mfg. Co./Code Alpha Tactical Gear, 4843 Victory St., Jacksonville, FL 32207, P: 800-874-1885, F: 904-733-9671, www.mercuryluggage.com
Bags & Equipment Cases; Camouflage; Custom Manufacturing; Export/Import Specialists; Law Enforcement

Merkel USA, 7661 Commerce Ln., Trussville, AL 35173, P: 800-821-3021, F: 205-655-7078, www.merkel-usa.com
Binoculars; Firearms; Scopes, Sights & Accessories

Mesa Tactical, 1760 Monrovia Ave., Suite A14, Costa Mesa, CA 92627, P: 949-642-3337, F: 949-642-3339, www.mesatactical.com
Gun Grips & Stocks; Law Enforcement; Scopes, Sights & Accessories

Metal Ware Corp./Open Country, 1700 Monroe St., P.O. Box 237, Two Rivers, WI 54241, P: 800-624-2949, F: 920-794-3161, www.opencountrycampware.com
Backpacking; Camping; Cooking Equipment/Accessories; Sports Accessories

Meyerco, 4481 Exchange Service Dr., Dallas, TX 75236, P: 214-467-8949, F: 214-467-9241, www.meyercousa.com
Bags & Equipment Cases; Camping; Cutlery; Gun Cases; Hunting Accessories; Knives/Knife Cases; Law Enforcement; Sharpeners

Mick Lacy Game Calls, 628 W. Main St., Princeville, IL 61559, P: 800-681-1070, F: 309-385-1068, www.micklacygamecalls.com
Game Calls; Hunting Accessories

Microsonic, 2960 Duss Ave., Ambridge, PA 15003, P: 724-266-9480, F: 724-266-9482, www.microsonic-inc.com
Hearing Protection

Microtech Knives, Inc./Microtech Small Arms Research, Inc., 300 Chestnut St., Bradford, PA 16701, P: 814-363-9260, F: 814-363-9284, www.msarinc.com
Custom Manufacturing; Cutlery; Firearms; Knives/Knife Cases; Law Enforcement; Sports Accessories

Midland Radio Corp., 5900 Parretta Dr., Kansas City, MO, 64120, P: 816-241-8500, F: 816-241-5713, www.midlandradio.com
Hunting Accessories; Sports Accessories; Training & Safety Equipment; Two-Way Radios

Midwest Industries, Inc., 828 Philip Dr., Suite 2, Waukesha, WI 53186, P: 262-896-6780, F: 262-896-6756, www.midwestindustriesinc.com
Gun Cases; Gun Parts/Gunsmithing; Law Enforcement; Lubricants; Magazines, Cartridge; Scopes, Sights & Accessories

Midwest Quality Gloves, Inc., 835 Industrial Rd., P.O. Box 260, Chillicothe, MO 64601, P: 800-821-3028, F: 660-646-6933, www.midwestglove.com
Archery; Camouflage; Gloves, Mitts, Hats; Hunting Accessories; Men's Clothing

Mil-Comm Products Co., Inc., 2 Carlton Ave., East Rutherford, NJ 07073, P: 888-947-3273, F: 201-935-6059, www.mil-comm.com
Black Powder Accessories; Firearms Maintenance Equipment; Gun Cabinets/Racks/Safes; Gun Locks; Gun Parts/Gunsmithing; Law Enforcement; Lubricants; Paintball Guns

Mil-Spec Plus/Voodoo Tactical, 435 W. Alondra Blvd., Gardena, CA 90248, P: 310-324-8855, F: 310-324-6909, www.majorsurplus.com
Bags & Equipment Cases; Eyewear; Footwear; Gloves, Mitts, Hats; Gun Cases; Law Enforcement

Mil-Tac Knives & Tools, P.O. Box 642, Wylie, TX 75098, P: 877-MIL-TAC6, F: 972-412-2208, www.mil-tac.com
Cutlery; Eyewear; Gloves, Mitts, Hats; Gun Parts/Gunsmithing; Hunting Accessories; Knives/Knife Cases; Law Enforcement; Survival Kits/First Aid

Militaria, Inc., Rt. 2, P.O. Box 166, Collins, GA 30421, P: 912-693-6411, F: 912-693-2060
Books/Industry Publications; Emblems & Decals; Firearms Maintenance Equipment; Lubricants; Wholesaler/Distributor

Military Outdoor Clothing, Inc., 1917 Stanford St., Greenville, TX 75401, P: 800-662-6430, F: 903-454-2433, www.militaryoutdoorclothing.com
Bags & Equipment Cases; Camouflage; Gloves, Mitts, Hats; Law Enforcement; Men & Women's Clothing

Milkor USA, Inc., 3735 N. Romero Rd., Suite 2M, Tucson, AZ 85705, P: 520-888-0103, F: 520-888-0122, www.milkorusainc.com
Firearms

Millett Sights/Bushnell Outdoor Products, 6200 Cody, Overland Park, KS 66214, P: 888-276-5945, F: 800-548-0446, www.millettsights.com
Black Powder Accessories; Gun Parts/Gunsmithing; Hunting Accessories; Law Enforcement; Scopes, Sights & Accessories

Minox USA, 438 Willow Brook Rd., Merdien, NH 03770, P: 866-469-3080, F: 603-469-3471, www.minox.com
Binoculars

Mocean, 1635 Monrovia Ave., Costa Mesa, CA 92627, P: 949-646-1701, F: 949-646-1590, www.mocean.net
Custom Manufacturing; Law Enforcement; Men & Women's Clothing; Wholesaler/Distributor

MOJO Outdoors, 2984 New Monroe Rd., P.O. Box 8460, Monroe, LA 71211, P: 318-283-7777, F: 318-283-1127, www.mojooutdoors.com
Decoys

Molehill Mt. Equipment, Inc., 416 Laskspur St., Suite A, Ponderay, ID 83852, P: 800-804-0820, F: 208-263-3056, www.molehillmtn.com
Camouflage; Camping; Footwear; Gloves, Mitts, Hats; Men & Women's Clothing

Montana Canvas, 110 Pipkin Way, Belgrade, MT 59714, P: 800-235-6518, F: 406-388-1039, www.montanacanvas.com
Camping; Hunting Accessories

Montana Decoys, P.O. Box 2377, Colstrip, MT 59323, P: 888-332-6998, F: 406-748-3471, www.montanadecoy.com
Decoys

Montana Rifle Co./Montana Rifleman, Inc., 3172 Montana Hwy. 35, Kalispell, MT 59901, P: 406-755-4867, F: 406-755-9449, www.montanarifle.com
Custom Manufacturing; Firearms; Gun Barrels; Gun Parts/Gunsmithing

Moore Texas Hunting, 108 S. Ranch House Rd., Suite 800, Aledo, TX 76008, P: 817-688-1774, F: 817-441-1606, www.mooretexashunting.com
Custom Manufacturing; Hunting Accessories; Sports Accessories; Wholesaler/Distributor

Morovision Night Vision, Inc., P.O. Box 342, Dana Point, CA 92629, P: 800-424-8222, F: 949-488-3361, www.morovision.com
Binoculars; Camping; Hunting Accessories; Law Enforcement; Lighting Products; Photographic Equipment; Scopes, Sights & Accessories; Wholesaler/Distributor

Morton Enterprises, 35 Pilot Ln., Great Cacapon, WV, 25422, P: 877-819-7280, www.uniquecases.com
Bags & Equipment Cases; Custom Manufacturing; Gun Cases; Hunting Accessories; Law Enforcement; Sports Accessories

Mossy Oak, P.O. Box 757, West Point, MS 39773, P: 662-494-8859, F: 662-494-8837, www.mossyoak.com
Books; Camouflage; Home Furnishings; Hunting Accessories; Men & Women's Clothing; Videos

Mostly Signs, 12993 Los Nietos Rd., Sante Fe Springs, CA 90670, P: 888-667-8595, F: 800-906-9855, www.mostlysigns.com
Home Furnishings; Wholesaler/Distributor

Moteng, Inc., 12220 Parkway Centre Dr., Poway, CA 92064, P: 800-367-5900, F: 800-367-5903, www.moteng.com
Camping; Cutlery; Knives/Knife Cases; Law Enforcement; Lighting Products; Online Services; Training & Safety Equipment; Wholesaler/Distributor

Mothwing Camo/Gameday Camo, P.O. Box 2019, Calhoun, GA 30703, P: 800-668-4946, F: 706-625-2484, www.mothwing.com
Camouflage; Men & Women's Clothing; Vehicles, Utility & Rec

Moultrie Products, LLC, 150 Industrial Rd., Alabaster, AL 35007, P: 800-653-3334, F: 205-664-6706, www.moultriefeeders.com
Feeder Equipment; Photographic Equipment; Wildlife Management

Mountain Corp./Mountain Life, 59 Optical Ave., P.O. Box 686, Keene, NH 03431, P: 800-545-9684, F: 603-355-3702, www.themountain.com
Law Enforcement; Men & Women's Clothing; Outfitter; Retail Packaging; Wholesaler/Distributor

Mountain House/Oregon Freeze Dry, 525 25th SW, Albany, OR 97321, P: 800-547-0244, F: 541-812-6601, www.mountainhouse.com
Backpacking; Camping; Hunting Accessories

Mounting Solutions Plus, 10655 SW 185 Terrace, Miami, FL 33157, P: 800-428-9394, F: 305-232-1247, www.mountsplus.com
Scopes, Sights & Accessories; Wholesaler/Distributor

MTM-Multi Time Machine, Inc., 1225 S. Grand Ave., Los Angeles, CA 90015, P: 213-741-0808, F: 213-741-0840, www.specialopswatch.com
Archery; Backpacking; Camouflage; Hunting Accessories; Law Enforcement; Sports Accessories; Watches

Mud River Dog Products, 355 E. Hwy. 264, Suite D, Bethel Heights, AR 72764, P: 479-927-2447, F: 479-927-2667, www.mudriverdogproducts.com
Bags & Equipment Cases; Blinds; Camping; Custom Manufacturing; Hunting Accessories; Men's Clothing; Pet Supplies, Vehicles, Utility & Rec

Muela, Ctra. N-420, KM 165, 500, Argamasilla De Calatrava, (Ciudad Real) 13440, SPAIN, P: 011 34926477093, F: 011 34926477237, www.mmuela.com
Knives/Knife Cases

Muller Prinsloo Knives, P.O. Box 2263, Bethlehem, 9700, SOUTH AFRICA, P: 011 27824663885, F: 011 27583037111
Knives/Knife Cases

Mystery Ranch, 34156 E. Frontage Rd., Bozeman, MT 59715, P: 406-585-1428, F: 406-585-1792, www.mysteryranch.com
Backpacking; Bags & Equipment Cases; Camping; Law Enforcement; Photographic Equipment

N

Nantong Universal Optical Instruments Co., Ltd., No. 1 Pingchao Industrial Garden, Nantong, Jiangsu 226361, CHINA, P: 011 8651386726888, F: 011 8651386718158, www.zoscn.com
Airguns; Binoculars; Gun Cases; Gun Locks; Scopes, Sights & Accessories; Wholesaler/Distributor

National Emblem, Inc., 17036 S. Avalon Blvd., Carson, CA 90746, P: 800-877-6185, F: 310-515-5966, www.nationalemblem.com
Custom Manufacturing; Emblems & Decals; Gloves, Mitts, Hats

National Geographic Maps, P.O. Box 4357, Evergreen, CO 80437, P: 800-962-1643, F: 800-626-8676, www.nationalgeographic.com/map
Archery; Backpacking; Books/Industry Publications; Camping; Compasses; Computer Software; Sports Accessories

National Muzzle Loading Rifle Association, P.O. Box 67, Friendship, IN 47021, P: 812-667-5131, F: 812-667-5137, www.nmlra.com

National Rifle Association, 11250 Waples Mill Rd., Fairfax, VA 22030, P: 800-672-3888, F: 703-267-3810, www.nra.org

National Wild Turkey Federation, 770 Augusta Rd., P.O. Box 530, Edgefield, SC 29824, P: 800-843-6983, F: 803-637-0034, www.nwtf.org

Nation's Best Sports, 4216 Hahn Blvd., Fort Worth, TX 76117, P: 817-788-0034, F: 817-788-8542, www.nationsbestsports.com
Retailer Services

Nature Coast Laser Creations, 9185 Mercedes Terrace N, Crystal River, FL 34428, P: 352-564-0794, www.laserautotags.com
Custom Manufacturing; Emblems & Decals; Hunting Accessories; Outdoor Art, Jewelry, Sculpture; Paintball Accessories; Sports Accessories; Vehicles, Utility & Rec

N-Vision Optics, 220 Reservior St., Suite 26, Neenham, MA 02494, P: 781-505-8360, F: 781-998-5656, www.nvisionoptics.com
Binoculars; Law Enforcement; Scopes, Sights & Accessories

Navy Arms Co./Forgett Militaria, 219 Lawn St., Martinsburg, WV 25405, P: 304-262-1651, F: 304-262-1658, www.navyarms.com
Firearms

Nester Hosiery, Inc., 1400 Carter St., Mount Airy, NC 27030, P: 888-871-1507, F: 336-789-0626, www.nesteroutdoorsocks.com
Backpacking; Camping; Custom Manufacturing; Footwear; Hunting Accessories; Men & Women's Clothing; Sports Accessories

New Century Science & Tech, Inc., 10302 Olney St., El Monte, CA 91731, P: 866-627-8278, F: 626-575-2478, www.ncstar.com
Binoculars; Crossbows & Accessories; Custom Manufacturing; Export/Import Specialists; Firearms Maintenance Equipment; Gun Cases; Lighting Products; Scopes, Sights & Accessories

New Ultra Light Arms, 214 Price St., P.O. Box 340, Granville, WV 26534, P: 304-292-0600, FL 304-292-9662, www.newultralight.com
Firearms

Newcon Optik, 105 Sparks Ave., Toronto M2H 2S5, CANADA, P: 877-368-6666, F: 416-663-9065, www.newcon-optik.com
Binoculars; Hunting Accessories; Law Enforcement; Paintballs; Photographic Equipment; Scopes, Sights & Accessories; Shooting Range Equipment

Nextorch, Inc., 2401 Viewcrest Ave., Everett, WA 98203, P: 425-290-3092, www.nextorch.com
Hunting Accessories; Knives/Knife Cases; Lighting Products

Night Optics USA, Inc., 5122 Bolsa Ave., Suite 101, Huntington Beach, CA 92649, P: 800-30-NIGHT, F: 714-899-4485, www.nightoptics.com

Binoculars; Camping; Hunting Accessories; Law Enforcement; Scopes, Sights & Accessories; Training & Safety Equipment; Wholesaler/Distributor; Wildlife Management

Night Owl Optics/Bounty Hunter/Fisher Research Labs, 1465-H Henry Brennan, El Paso, TX 79936, P: 800-444-5994, F: 915-633-8529, www.nightowloptics.com
Binoculars; Camping; Hunting Accessories; Law Enforcement; Photographic Equipment; Scopes, Sights & Accessories; Sports Accessories; Telescopes

Night Vision Depot, P.O. Box 3415, Allentown, PA 18106, P: 610-395-9743, F: 610-395-9744, www.nvdepot.com
Binoculars; Hunting Accessories; Law Enforcement; Lighting Products; Scopes, Sights & Accessories; Wholesaler/Distributor

Night Vision Systems (NVS), 542 Kemmerer Ln., Allentown, PA 18104, P: 800-797-2849, F: 610-391-9220, www.nighvisionsystems.com
Law Enforcement; Scopes, Sights & Accessories

Nighthawk Custom, 1306 W. Trimble, Berryville, AR 72616, P: 877-268-4867, F: 870-423-4230, www.nighthawkcustom.com
Firearms; Gun Grips & Stocks; Gun Parts/Gunsmithing; Hearing Protection; Holsters

Nikon, Inc., 1300 Walt Whitman Rd., Melville, NY 11747, P: 631-547-4200, FL 631-547-4040, www.nikonhunting.com
Binoculars; Hunting Accessories; Scopes, Sights & Accessories

Ningbo Electric and Consumer Goods I/E. Corp., 17/F, Lingqiao Plaza, 31 Yaohang Street, Ningbo, Zhejiang, 315000 CHINA P: 011 8657487194807; F: 011 8657487296214

Nite Ize, Inc., 5660 Central Ave., Boulder, CO 80301, P: 800-678-6483, F: 303-449-2013, www.niteize.com
Bags & Equipment Cases; Camping; Custom Manufacturing; Holsters; Lighting Products; Pet Supplies

Nite Lite Co., 3801 Woodland Heights Rd., Suite 100, Little Rock, AR 72212, P: 800-648-5483, F: 501-227-4892, www.huntsmart.com
Game Calls; Hunting Accessories; Lighting Products; Men's Clothing; Pet Supplies; Scents & Lures; Scopes, Sights & Accessories; Training & Safety Equipment

Nitrex Optics/ATK Commercial Products, N5549 Cty. Tk. Z, Onalaska, WI 54650, P: 800-635-7656, F: 763-323-3890, www.nitrexoptics.com
Binoculars; Scopes, Sights & Accessories

NiViSys Industries LLC, 400 S. Clark Dr., Suite 105, Tempe, AZ 85281, P: 480-970-3222, F: 480-970-3555, www.nivisys.com
Binoculars; Law Enforcement; Lighting Products; Photographic Equipment; Scopes, Sights & Accessories; Wholesaler/Distributor

Norica Laurona, Avda. Otaola, 16, Eibar, (Guipúzcoa) 20600, P: 011 34943207445, F: 011 34943207449, www.norica.es, www.laurona.es
Airguns; Ammunition; Firearms; Hearing Protection; Hunting Accessories; Knives/Knife Cases; Scopes, Sights & Accessories

Norma Precision AB/RUAG Ammotec, Jagargatan, Amotfors, S-67040, SWEDEN, P: 044-46-571-31500, F: 011-46-571-31540, www.norma.cc
Ammunition; Custom Manufacturing; Reloading

North American Arms, Inc., 2150 S. 950 E, Provo, UT 84606, P: 800-821-5783, F: 801-374-9998, www.northamericanarms.com
Firearms

North American Hunter, 12301 Whitewater Dr., Minnetonka, MN 55343, P: 800-688-7611, F: 952-936-9169, www.huntingclub.com
Books/Industry Publications

Northern Lights Tactical, P.O. 10272, Prescott, AZ 86304, P: 310-376-4266, F: 310-798-9278, www.northernlightstactical.com
Archery; Hunting Accessories; Law Enforcement; Paintball Accessories; Shooting Range Equipment; Targets; Training & Safety Equipment; Vehicles, Utility & Rec

Northridge International, Inc., 23679 Calabasas Rd., Suit 406, Calabasas, CA 91302, P: 661-269-2269, www.northridgeinc.com
Camouflage; Compasses; Cutlery; Firearms; Firearms Maintenance Equipment; Gun Barrels; Gun Cases; Survival Kits/First Aid

Northwest Territorial Mint, P.O. Box 2148, Auburn, WA 98071, P: 800-344-6468, F: 253-735-2210, www.nwtmint.com
Custom Manufacturing; Emblems & Decals; Knives/Knife Cases; Outdoor Art, Jewelry, Sculpture

Northwest Tracker, Inc., 6205 NE 63rd St., Vancouver, WA 98661, P: 360-213-0363, F: 360-693-2212, www.trackeroutpost.com
Gun Cabinets/Racks/Safes; Gun Cases; Hunting Accessories; Treestands

Nosler, Inc., 107 SW Columbia, P.O. Box 671, Bend, OR 97709, P: 800-285-3701, F: 800-766-7537, www.nosler.com
Ammunition; Black Powder Accessories; Books/Industry Publications; Firearms; Reloading

Not Your Daddy's, 7916 High Heath, Knoxville, TN 37919, P: 865-806-8496, F: 865-690-4555
Gun Cases

Nova Silah Sanayi, Ltd., Merkez Mah. Kultur Cad. No: 22/14, Duzce, TURKEY, P: 011-90 2125140279, F: 011-90 2125111999
Firearms

Novatac, Inc., 300 Carlsbad Village Dr., Suite 108A-100, Carlsbad, CA 92008, P: 760-730-7370, FL 760-730-7375, www.novatac.com
Backpacking; Camping; Hunting Accessories; Law Enforcement; Lighting Products; Survival Kits/First Aid; Training & Safety Equipment

NRA FUD, 11250 Waples Mill Rd., Fairfax, VA 22030, P: 703-267-1300, F: 703-267-3800, www.nrafud.com
Decoys; Hunting Accessories; Wholesaler/Distributor

NTA Enterprise, Inc./Huntworth/Thermologic, R J Casey Industrial Park, Columbus Ave., Pittsburgh, PA 15233, P: 877-945-6837, F: 412-325-7865, www.thermologicgear.com
Archery; Backpacking; Camouflage; Gloves, Mitts, Hats; Hunting Accessories; Men & Women's Clothing; Sports Accessories

Numrich Gun Parts Corp./Gun Parts Corp., 226 Williams Ln., P.O. Box 299, West Hurley, NY 12491, P: 866-686-7424, F: 877-GUN-PART, www.e-gunparts.com
Firearms Maintenance Equipment; Gun Barrels; Gun Cases; Gun Grips & Stocks; Gun Parts/Gunsmithing; Hunting Accessories; Magazines, Cartridge; Scopes, Sights & Accessories

Nutri-Vet, LLC, 495 N. Dupont Ave., Boise, ID 83713, P: 877-728-8668, F: 208-377-1941, www.nutri-vet.com
Pet Supplies

Nuwai International Co., Ltd./Nuwai LED Flashlight, 11 FL., 110 Li Gong St., Bei, Tou Taipei, 11261, TAIWAN, P: 011 886228930199, F: 011 886228930198, www.nuwai.com
Camping; Lighting Products; Outfitter

Nylok Corp., 15260 Hallmark Dr., Macomb, MI 48042, P: 586-786-0100, FL 810-780-0598
Custom Manufacturing; Gun Parts/Gunsmithing; Lubricants

O

O'Keeffe's Co., 251 W. Barclay Dr., P.O. Box 338, Sisters, OR 97759, P: 800-275-2718, F: 541-549-1486, www.okeeffescompany.com
Archery; Backpacking; Camping; Footwear; Outfitter; Sports Accessories; Survival Kits/First Aid

O.F. Mossberg & Sons, Inc., 7 Grasso Ave., North Haven, CT 06473, P: 203-230-5300, F: 203-230-5420, www.mossberg.com
Firearms; Gun Barrels; Hunting Accesories; Law Enforcement

Oakley, Inc., One Icon, Foothill Ranch, CA 92610, P: 800-525-4334, F: 858-459-4336, www.usstandardissue.com
Eyewear; Footwear

Odyssey Automotive Specialty, 317 Richard Mine Rd., Wharton, MJ 07885, P: 800-535-9441, F: 973-328-2601, www.odysseyauto.com
Custom Manufacturing; Gun Cabinets/Racks/Safes; Gun Cases; Law Enforcement; Vehicles, Utility & Rec

Oehler Research, Inc., P.O. Box 9135, Austin, TX 78766, P: 800-531-5125, F: 512-327-6903, www.oehler-research.com
Ammunition; Computer Software; Hunting Accessories; Reloading; Shooting Range Equipment; Targets

Oklahoma Leather Products/Don Hume Leathergoods, 500 26th NW, Miami, OK 74354, P: 918-542-6651, F: 918-542-6653, www.oklahomaleatherproducts.com
Black Powder Accessories; Custom Manufacturing; Cutlery; Holsters; Hunting Accessories; Knives/Knife Cases; Law Enforcement; Leathergoods

Old Western Scrounger, Inc., 50 Industrial Pkwy., Carson City, NV 89706, P: 800-UPS-AMMO, F: 775-246-2095, www.ows-ammunition.com
Ammunition; Reloading

Olivon Manufacturing Co., Ltd./Olivon-Worldwide, 600 Tung Pu Rd., Shanghai, China, Shanghai, Jiangsu, CHINA, P: 604-764-7731, F: 604-909-4951, www.olivonmanufacturing.com

Bag & Equipment Cases; Binoculars; Gun Cabinets/ Racks/Safes; Gun Cases; Hunting Accessories; Scopes, Sights & Accessories; Telescopes

Olympic Arms, Inc., 624 Old Pacific Hwy. SE, Olympia, WA 98513, P: 800-228-3471, F: 360-491-3447, www.olyarms. com
Firearms; Gun Barrels; Gun Grips & Stocks; Gun Parts/Gunsmithing; Law Enforcement; Training & Safety Equipment

On-Target Productions, Inc., 6722 River Walk Dr., Valley City, OH 44280, P: 330-483-6183, F: 330-483-6183, www. ontargetdvds.com
Videos

On Time Wildlife Feeders, 110 E. Railroad Ave., Ruston, LA 71270, P:318-225-1834, F: 315-225-1101

One Shot, 6871 Main St., Newtown, OH 45244, P: 513-233-0885, F: 513-233-0887

Ontario Knife Co./Queen Cutlery Co./Ontario Knife Co., 26 Empire St., P.O. Box 145, Franklinville, NY 14737, P: 800-222-5233, F: 800-299-2618, www.ontarioknife.com
Camping; Custom Manufacturing; Cutlery; Hunting Accessories; Knives/Knife Cases; Law Enforcement; Training & Safety Equipment

Op. Electronics Co., Ltd., 53 Shing-Ping Rd. 5/F, Chungli, 320, TAIWAN, P: 011 88634515131, F: 011 88634615130, www. digi-opto.com
Scopes, Sights & Accessories; Training & Safety Equipment

Opti-Logic Corp., 201 Montclair St., P.O. Box 2002, Tullahoma, TN 37388, P: 888-678-4567, F: 931-455-1229, www.opti-logic.com
Archery; Binoculars; Crossbows & Accessories; Hunting Accessories; Law Enforcement; Scopes, Sights & Accessories

Optisan Corp., Taipei World Trade Center 4B06, 5, Hsin Yi Rd., Section 5, Taipei, 110, TAIWAN, P: 011 8675785799936, F: 011 862081117707
Bags & Equipment Cases; Binoculars; Lighting Products; Photographic Equipment; Scopes, Sights & Accessories; Telescopes

Optolyth/Sill Optics GmbH & Co KG, Johann-Höllfritsch-Straße 13, Wendelstein, 90530, GERMANY, P: 011 499129902352, F: 011 499129902323, www.optolyth.de
Binoculars; Scopes, Sights & Accessories

Original Footwear Co., 4213 Technology Dr., Modesto, CA 95356, P: 888-476-7700, F: 209-545-2739, www. originalswat.com
Footwear; Law Enforcement; Wholesaler/Distributor

Original Muck Boot Co., 1136 2nd St., Rock Island, IL 61201, P: 800-790-9296, F: 800-267-6809, www. muckbootcompany.com
Footwear

Osprey International Inc./AimShot, 25 Hawks Farm Rd., White, GA 30184, P: 888-448-3247, F: 770-387-0114, www. osprey-optics.com
Binoculars; Hunting Accessories; Law Enforcement; Lighting Products; Scopes, Sights & Accessories; Wholesaler/Distributor

Otis Technology, Inc., 6987 Laura St., P.O. Box 582, Lyon Falls, NY 13368, P: 800-OTISGUN, F: 315-348-4332, www.otisgun.com
Black Powder Accessories; Firearms Maintenance Equipment; Gun Parts/Gunsmithing; Hunting Accessories; Lubricants; Paintball Accessories; Scopes, Sights & Accessories; Training & Safety Equipment

Otte Gear, 332 Bleecker St., Suite E10, New York, NY 10014, P: 212-604-0304, F: 773-439-5237, www.ottegear.com
Backpacking; Camouflage; Camping; Gloves, Mitts, Hats; Men's Clothing

Otter Outdoors, 411 W. Congress, Maple Lake, MN 55358, P: 877-466-8837, F: 320-963-6192, www.otteroutdoors.com
Blinds; Custom Manufacturing; Hunting Accessories; Sports Accessories; Vehicles, Utility & Rec

Outdoor Cap Co., 1200 Melissa Ln., P.O. Box 210, Bentonville, AR 72712, P: 800-279-3216, F: 800-200-0329, www. outdoorcap.com
Camouflage; Custom Manufacturing; Gloves, Mitts, Hats; Hunting Accessories; Men & Women's Clothing

Outdoor Connection, 424 Neosho, Burlington, NS 66839, P: 888-548-0636, F: 620-364-5563, www.outdoor-connection.com
Outfitter; Tours/Travel

Outdoor Connection, Inc., 7901 Panther Way, Waco, TX 76712, P: 800-533-6076, F: 866-533-6076, www. outdoorconnection.com
Bags & Equipment Cases; Camouflage; Gun Cases; Gun Parts/Gunsmithing; Hunting Accessories; Retail Packaging; Shooting Range Equipment; Sports Accessories

Outdoor Edge Cutlery Corp., 4699 Nautilus Ct. S, Suite 503, Boulder, CO 80301, P: 800-447-3343, F: 303-530-7020, www.outdooredge.com
Cutlery; Hunting Accessories; Sharpeners

Outdoor Kids Club Magazine, P.O. Box 35, Greenville, OH 45341, P: 937-417-0903, www.outdoorkidsclub.com
Books/Industry Publications

Outdoor Research, 2203 First Ave. S, Seattle, WA 98134, P: 888-467-4327, F: 206-467-0374, www.outdoorresearch. com/gov
Gloves, Mitts, Hats; Law Enforcement

OutdoorSportsMarketingCenter.com, 95 Old Stratton Chase, Atlanta, GA 30328, P: 256-653-5087, F: 404-943-1634, www.outdoorsportsmarketingcenter.com
Books/Industry Publications; Computer Software; Emblems & Decals; Online Services; Printing Services; Retail Packaging; Retailer Services

Outers Gun Care/ATK Commercial Products, N5549 Cty. Tk. Z, Onalaska, WI 54650, P: 800-635-7656, F: 763-323-3890, www.outers-guncare.com
Firearms Maintenance Equipment; Lubricants

Over The Hill Outfitters/Adventures Beyond, 4140 Cty. Rd. 234, Durango, CO 81301, P: 970-385-7656, www. overthehilloutfitters.com
Outfitter

Ozonics, 107A This Way, P.O. Box 598, Lake Jackson, TX 77566, P: 979-285-2400, F: 979-297-7744, www. ozonicshunting.com
Scents & Lures

P

PMC/Poongsan, 60-1, Chungmoro - 3ka, Chung-Gu, Seoul 100-705, C.P.O. Box 3537, Seoul, SOUTH KOREA, P: 011 92234065628, F: 011 92234065415, www.pmcammo.com
Ammunition; Law Enforcement

PSC, Pendleton Safe Co., 139 Lee Byrd Rd., Loganville, GA 30052, P: 770-466-6661, F: 678-990-7888
Gun Safes

PSI, LLC, 2 Klarides Village Dr., Suite 336, Seymour, CT 06483, P: 203-262-6484, F: 203-262-6562, www. precisionsalesintl.com
Gun Parts/Gunsmithing; Law Enforcement; Magazines, Cartridge; Scopes, Sights & Accessories

P.S. Products, Inc./Personal Security Products, 414 S. Pulaski St., Suite 1, Little Rock, AR 72201, P: 877-374-7900, F: 501-374-7800, www.psproducts.com
Custom Manufacturing; Export/Import Specialists; Holsters; Law Enforcement; Sports Accessories; Wholesaler/Distributor

Pacific Solution, 14225 Telephone Ave., Suite D, Chino, CA 91710, P: 909-465-9858, F: 909-465-9878
Cutlery; Hunting Accessories; Knives/Knife Cases; Wholesaler/Distributor

Pacific Sun Marketing, 14505 N. 5th St., Bellevue, WA 98007, P: 425-653-3900, F: 425-653-3908
Home Furnishings; Hunting Accessories; Outdoor Art, Jewelry, Sculpture

Pacific Tool & Gauge, Inc., 598 Avenue C, P.O. Box 2549, White City, OR 97503, P: 541-826-5808, F: 541-826-5304, www.pacifictoolandgauge.com
Black Powder Accessories; Books/Industry Publications; Custom Manufacturing; Firearms Maintenance Equipment; Gun Parts/Gunsmithing; Law Enforcement; Reloading

Palco Sports Airsoft, 8575 Monticello Ln. N, Maple Grove, MN 55369-4546, P: 800-882-4656, F: 763-559-2286, www. palcosports.com
Airguns; Airsoft; Crossbows & Accessories; Paintball Guns & Accessories; Sports Accessories

Panthera Outdoors, LLC, 1555 Wedgefield Dr., Rock Hill, SC 29732, P: 276-673-5278

Para USA, Inc., 10620 Southern Loop Blvd., Charlotte, NC 28134-7381, P: 866-661-1911, www.para-usa.com
Firearms

Paragon Luggage, 1111-A Bell Ave., Tustin, CA 92780, P: 714-258-8698, F: 714-258-0018

Paramount Apparel, Inc., 1 Paramount Dr., P.O. Box 98, Bourbon, MO 65441, P: 800-255-4287, F: 800-428-0215, www.paramountoutdoors.com
Camouflage; Custom Manufacturing; Gloves, Mitts, Hats; Hunting Accessories; Men & Women's Clothing; Retailer Services; Sports Accessories

Parker-Hale, Bedford Rd., Petersfield, Hampshire GU32 3XA, UNITED KINGDOM, P: 011-44 1730268011, F: 011-44 1730260074, www.parker-hale.co.uk
Firearms Maintenance Equipment; Law Enforcement; Lubricants

Parmatech Corp., 2221 Pine View Way, Petaluma, CA 94954, P: 800-709-1555, F: 707-778-2262, www.parmatech.com
Custom Manufacturing; Gun Parts/Gunsmithing

Parris Manufacturing, 1825 Pickwick St., P.O. Box 338, Savannah, TN 38372, P: 800-530-7308, F: 731-925-1139, www.parrismfgco.com
Airguns; Archery; Binoculars; Camouflage; Crossbows & Accessories; Wholesaler/Distributor

Passport Sports, Inc., 3545 N. Courtenay Pkwy., P.O. Box 540638, Merritt Island, FL 32953, P: 321-459-0005, F: 321-459-3482, www.passport-holsters.com
Bags & Equipment Cases; Custom Manufacturing; Gun Cases; Holsters; Leathergoods

Patriot3, Inc., P.O. Box 278, Quantico, VA 22134, P: 888-288-0911, F: 540-891-5654, www.patriot3.com
Law Enforcement

Patriot Ordnance Factory, 23623 N. 67th Ave., Glendale, AZ 85310, P: 623-561-9572, F: 623-321-1680, www.pof-usa. com
Custom Manufacturing; Firearms; Gun Barrels; Gun Parts/Gunsmithing; Hunting Accessories; Law Enforcement

PBC, 444 Caribbean Dr., Lakeland, FL 33803, P: 954-304-5948, www.pbcutlery.com
Cutlery; Knives/Knife Cases

Peacekeeper International, 2435 Pine St., Pomona, CA 91767, P: 909-596-6699, F: 909-596-8899, www. peacekeeperproducts.com
Holsters; Law Enforcement; Leathergoods; Targets; Training & Safety Equipment

Peak Beam Systems, Inc., 3938 Miller Rd., P.O. Box 1127, Edgemont, PA 19028, P: 610-353-8505, F: 610-353-8411, www.peakbeam.com
Law Enforcement; Lighting Products

Peca Products, Inc., 471 Burton St., Beloit, WI 53511, P: 608-299-1615, F: 608-229-1827, www.pecaproducts.com
Custom Manufacturing; Firearms Maintenance Equipment; Hunting Accessories; Law Enforcement; Photographic Equipment; Scopes, Sights & Accessories; Sports Accessories; Wholesaler/ Distributor

Pedersoli 2 SRL, Via Artigiani, 13, Gardone V.T., 25063, ITALY, P: 011 390308915000, F: 011 390308911019, www. davide-pedersoli.com
Black Powder Accessories; Firearms; Gun Grips & Stocks

Pedersoli Davide & C. SNC, Via Artigiani, 57, Gardone V.T., Brescia 25063, ITALY, P: 011 39308915000, F: 011 39308911019, www.davide-pedersoli.com
Black Powder Accessories; Cutlery; Firearms; Knives/Knife Cases

Peerless Handcuff Co., 95 State St., Springfield, MA 01103, P: 800-732-3705, F: 413-734-5467, www.peerless.net
Law Enforcement

Peet Shoe Dryer, Inc./Peet Dryer, 919 St. Maries River Rd., P.O. Box 618, St. Maries, ID 83861, 800-222-PEET (7338), F: 800-307-4582, www.peetdryer.com
Footwear; Gloves, Mitts, Hats; Hunting Accessories

Pelican Products, Inc., 23215 Early Ave., Torrance, CA 90505, P: 800-473-5422, F: 310-326-3311
Archery; Backpacking; Bags & Equipment Cases; Camping; Crossbows & Accessories; Gun Cases; Hunting Accessories; Paintball Accessories

Peltor, 5457 W. 79th St., Indianapolis, IN 46268, P: 800-327-3431, F: 800-488-8007, www.aosafety.com
Eyewear; Hearing Protection; Shooting Range Equipment; Two-Way Radios

PentagonLight, 151 Mitchell Ave., San Francisco, CA 94080, P: 800-PENTA-15, F: 650-877-9555, www.pentagonlight. com
Holsters; Hunting Accessories; Law Enforcement; Lighting Products; Sports Accessories; Survival Kits/ First Aid; Wholesaler/Distributor

Pentax Imaging Co., 600 12th St., Suite 300, Golden, CO 80401, P: 800-877-0155, F: 303-460-1628, www. pentaxsportoptics.com
Binoculars; Photographic Equipment; Scopes, Sights & Accessories

Perazzi U.S.A., Inc., 1010 W. Tenth St., Azusa, CA 91702, P: 626-334-1234, F: 626-334-0344
Firearms

Perfect Fit, 39 Stetson Rd., Ruite 222, P.O. Box 439, Corinna, ME 04928, P: 800-634-9208, F: 800-222-0417, www. perfectfitusa.com
Custom Manufacturing; Emblems & Decals; Law Enforcement; Leathergoods; Training & Safety Equipment; Wholesaler/Distibutor

Permalight (Asia) Co., Ltd./Pila Flashlights, 4/F, Waga Commercial Centre, 99 Wellington St., Central HONG KONG, P: 011 85228150616, F: 011 85225423269, www. pilatorch.com
Camping; Firearms; Hunting Accessories; Law Enforcement; Lighting Products; Training & Safety Equipment; Wholesaler/Distributor

Pete Rickard Co., 115 Walsh Rd., Cobleskill, NY 12043, P: 518-234-2731, F: 518-234-2454, www.peterickard.com
Archery; Game Calls; Hunting Accessories; Leathergoods; Lubricants; Pet Supplies; Scents & Lures; Shooting Range Equipment

Petzl America, Freeport Center M-7, P.O. Box 160447, Clearfield, UT 84016, P: 877-807-3805, F: 801-926-1501, www.petzl.com
Gloves, Mitts, Hats; Law Enforcement; Lighting Products; Training & Safety Equipment

Phalanx Corp., 4501 N. Dixie Hwy., Boca Raton, FL 33431, P: 954-360-0000, F: 561-417-0500, www.smartholster.com
Gun Locks; Holsters; Law Enforcement; Training & Safety Equipment

Phillips Plastics, 1201 Hanley Rd., Hudson, WI 54016, P: 877-508-0252, F: 715-381-3291, www.phillipsplastics.com
Custom Manufacturing

Phoebus Tactical Flashlights/Phoebus Manufacturing, 2800 Third St., San Francisco, CA 94107, P: 415-550-0770, F: 415-550-2655, www.phoebus.com
Lighting Products

Photop Suwtech, Inc., 2F, Building 65, 421 Hong Cao Rd., Shanghai, 200233, CHINA, P: 011 862164853978, F: 011 862164850389, www.photoptech.com
Law Enforcement; Lighting Products; Scopes, Sights & Accessories

Pine Harbor Holding Co., Inc., P.O. Box 336, Chippewa Falls, WI 54729, P: 715-726-8714, F: 715-726-8739
Blinds; Camouflage; Decoys; Hunting Accessories

Pinnacle Ammunition Co., 111 W. Port Plaza, Suite 600, St. Louis, MO 63146, P: 888-702-2660, F: 314-293-1943, www.pinnacleammo.com
Ammunition

PistolCam, Inc., 1512 Front St., Keeseville, NY 12944, P: 518-834-7093, F: 518-834-7061, www.pistolcam.com
Firearms; Gun Parts/Gunsmithing; Law Enforcement; Photographic Equipment; Scopes, Sights & Accessories; Videos

Plano Molding Co., 431 E. South St., Plano, IL 60545, P: 800-226-9868, F: 630-552-9737, www.planomolding.com
Archery; Bags & Equipment Cases; Firearms Maintenance Equipment; Gun Cases; Hunting Accessories

Plotmaster Systems, Ltd., 111 Industrial Blvd., P.O. Box 111, Wrightsville, GA 31096, P: 888-629-4263, F: 478-864-9109, www.theplotmaster.com
Feeder Equipment; Wholesaler/Distributor; Wildlife Management

PlotSpike Wildlife Seeds/Ragan and Massey, Inc., 100 Ponchatoula Pkwy., Ponchatoula, LA 70454, P: 800-264-5281, F: 985-386-5565, www.plotspike.com
Scents & Lures; Wildlife Management

Plymouth Engineered Shapes, 201 Commerce Ct., Hopkinsville, KY 42240, P: 800-718-7590, F: 270-886-6662, www.plymouth.com/engshapes.aspx
Crossbows & Accessories; Firearms; Gun Barrels; Gun Parts/Gunsmithing

Point Blank Body Armor/PACA Body Armor, 2102 SW 2 St., Pompano Beach, FL 33069, P: 800-413-5155, F: 954-414-8118, www.pointblankarmor.com, www.pacabodyarmor.com
Law Enforcement

Point Tech, Inc., 160 Gregg St., Suite 1, Lodi, NJ 07644, P: 201-368-0711, F: 201-368-0133
Firearms; Gun Barrels; Gun Parts/Gunsmithing

Polaris USA, Inc./Signal Mobile USA, 4511 N. O'Connor Rd., Suite 1150, Irving, TX 75062, P: 817-719-1086, F: 817-887-0807, www.polarisvision.com, www.ezsignal.com

Police and Security News, 1208 Juniper St., Quakertown, PA 18951, P: 215-538-1240, F: 215-538-1208, www.policeandsecuritynews.com
Books/Industry Publications; Law Enforcement

Police Magazine/Police Recruit Magazine, 3520 Challenger St., Torrance, CA 90503, P: 480-367-1101, F: 480-367-1102, www.policemag.com
Books/Industry Publications; Law Enforcement

PoliceOne.com, 200 Green St., Second Floor, San Francisco, CA 94111, P: 800-717-1199, F: 480-854-7079, www.policeone.com
Law Enforcement

Port-A-Cool, 709 Southview Circle, P.O. Box 2167, Center, TX 75935, P: 800-695-2942, F: 936-598-8901
Camouflage; Custom Manufacturing; Sports Accessories; Training & Safety Equipment

Portman Security Systems Ltd., 330 W. Cummings Park, Woburn, MA 01801, P: 781-935-9288, F: 781-935-9188, www.portmansecurity.com
Custom Manufacturing; Firearms Maintenance Equipment; Gun Parts/Gunsmithing; Law Enforcement; Pet Supplies; Scopes, Sights & Accessories; Vehicles, Utility & Rec

PowerBelt Bullets, 5988 Peachtree Corners E, Norcross, GA 30071, P: 800-320-8767, F: 770-242-8546, www.powerbeltbullets.com
Ammunition; Black Powder Accessories

PowerFlare, 6489 Camden Ave., Suite 108, San Jose, CA 95120, P: 877-256-6907, F: 408-268-5431, www.powerflare.com
Lighting Products; Survival Kits/First Aid; Training & Safety Equipment; Wholesaler/Distributor

PowerTech, Inc./Smith & Wesson Flashlights, 360 E. South St., Collierville, TN 38017, P: 901-850-9393, F: 901-850-9797, www.powertechinc.com
Camping; Hunting Accessories; Law Enforcement; Lighting Products; Sports Accessories

Practical Air Rifle Training Systems, LLC, P.O. Box 174, Pacific, MO 63069, P: 314-271-8465, F: 636-271-8465, www.smallarms.com
Airguns; Custom Manufacturing; Law Enforcement; Shooting Range Equipment; Targets; Training & Safety Equipment

Precision Ammunition, LLC, 5402 E. Diana St., Tampa, FL 33610, P: 888-393-0694, F: 813-626-0078, www.precisionammo.com
Ammunition; Law Enforcement; Reloading

Precision Metalsmiths, Inc., 1081 E. 200th St., Cleveland, OH 44117, P: 216-481-8900, F: 216-481-8903, www.precisionmetalsmiths.com
Archery; Custom Manufacturing; Firearms; Gun Barrels; Gun Locks; Gun Parts/Gunsmithing; Knives/Knife Cases; Scopes, Sights & Accessories

Precision Reflex, Inc., 710 Streine Dr., P.O. Box 95, New Bremen, OH 45869, P: 419-629-2603, F: 419-629-2173, www.pri-mounts.com
Custom Manufacturing; Firearms; Gun Barrels; Law Enforcement; Magazines, Cartridge; Scopes, Sights & Accessories

Predator, Inc., 2605 Coulee Ave., La Crosse, WI 54601, P: 800-430-3305, F: 608-787-0667, www.predatorcamo.com
Archery; Backpacking; Blinds; Camouflage; Men's Clothing

Predator International, 4401 S. Broadway, Suite 201, Englewood, CO 80113, P: 877-480-1636, F: 303-482-2987, www.predatorpellets.com
Airguns; Airsoft; Ammunition

Predator Sniper Products, 102 W. Washington St., P.O. Box 743, St. Francis, KS 67756, P: 785-332-2731, F: 785-332-8943, www.predatorsniperstyx.com
Custom Manufacturing; Game Calls; Hunting Accessories; Shooting Range Equipment; Wholesaler/Distributor

Predator Trailcams LLC, 10609 W. Old Hwy. 10 R.D., Saxon, WI 54559, P: 715-893-5001, F: 715-893-5005, www.predatortrailcams.com
Archery; Firearms; Hunting Accessories; Outfitter; Photographic Equipment; Sports Accessories; Wildlife Management

Premier Reticles, 175 Commonwealth Ct., Winchester, VA 22602, P: 540-868-2044, F: 540-868-2045 www.premierreticles.com
Scopes, Sights & Accessories; Telescopes

Premierlight, 35 Revenge Rd., Unit 9, Lordswood, Kent ME5 8DW, UNITED KINGDOM, P: 011-44-1634-201284, F: 011-44-1634-201286, www.premierlight-uk.com
Backpacking; Camping; Hunting Accessories; Law Enforcement; Lighting Products; Sports Accessories; Training & Safety Equipment; Wholesaler/Distributor

Prestige Apparel Mfg. Co./Exxel Outdoors, 300 American Blvd., Haleyville, AL 35565, P: 800-221-7452, F: 205-486-9882, www.exxel.com
Camouflage; Camping; Custom Manufacturing; Export/Import Specialists; Gloves, Mitts, Hats; Men's Clothing; Wholesaler/Distributor

Primary Weapons Systems, 800 E. Citation Ct., Suite C, Boise, ID 83716, P: 208-344-5217, F: 208-344-5395, www.primaryweapons.com
Firearms; Firearms Maintenance Equipment; Gun Parts/Gunsmithing; Law Enforcement; Recoil Protection Devices & Services

Primax Hunting Gear Ltd., Rm. 309, 3/F Jiali Mansion, 39-5#, Xingning Rd., Ningbo, Zhejiang 315040, CHINA, P: 011 8657487894016, F: 011 8657487894017, www.primax-hunting.com
Backpacking; Bags & Equipment Cases; Blinds; Camping; Compasses; Gun Cases; Hunting Accessories; Scopes, Sights & Accessories

Primos Hunting Calls, 604 First St., Flora, MS 39071, P: 800-523-2395, F: 601-879-9324, www.primos.com
Archery; Blinds; Camouflage; Decoys; Game Calls; Hunting Accessories; Scents & Lures; Videos

Princeton Tec, P.O. Box 8057, Trenton, NJ 08650, P: 800-257-9080, FL 609-298-9601, www.princetontec.com

Backpacking; Camping; Cooking Equipment/Accessories; Lighting Products; Photographic Equipment; Sports Accessories; Training & Safety Equipment

Pro-Iroda Industries, Inc., No. 68, 32nd Rd., Taichung Industrial Park, Taichung, 407, TAIWAN, P: 888-66-IRODA, F: 440-247-4630, www.pro-iroda.com
Archery; Camping; Cooking Equipment/Accessories; Custom Manufacturing

Pro-Shot Products, P.O. Box 763, Taylorville, IL 62568, P: 217-824-9133, F: 217-824-8861, www.proshotproducts.com
Black Powder Accessories; Firearms Maintenance Equipment; Lubricants

Pro-Systems Spa, Via al Corbé 63, ITALY, P: 011 390331576887, F: 011 390331576295, www.pro-systems.it, www.pro-systems.us
Law Enforcement

Pro Ears/Benchmaster, 101 Ridgeline Dr., Westcliffe, CO 81252, P: 800-891-3660, F: 719-783-4162, www.pro-ears.com
Crossbows & Accessories; Custom Manufacturing; Hearing Protection; Hunting Accessories; Law Enforcement; Shooting Range Equipment; Sports Accessories; Training & Safety Equipment

Pro Line Manufacturing Co., 186 Parish Dr., Wayne, NJ 07470, P: 800-334-4612, F: 973-692-0999, www.prolineboots.com
Camouflage; Footwear; Leathergoods; Wholesaler/Distributor

Professionals Choice/G&A Investments, Inc., 2615 Fruitland Ave., Vernon, CA 90058, P: 323-589-2775, F: 323-589-3511, www.theprofessionalschoice.net
Firearms Maintenance Equipment; Gun Parts/Gunsmithing; Lubricants; Wholesaler/Distributor

Proforce Equipment, Inc./Snugpak USA, 2201 NW 102nd Place, Suite 1, Miami, FL 33172, P: 800-259-5962, F: 800-664-5095, www.proforceequipment.com
Backpacking; Camping; Hunting Accessories; Knives/Knife Cases; Law Enforcement; Men's Clothing; Survival Kits/First Aid; Watches

Prois Hunting Apparel for Women, 28000B W. Hwy. 50, Gunnison, CO 81230, P: 970-641-3355, F: 970-641-6602, www.proishunting.com
Camouflage; Hunting Accessories; Women's Clothing

ProMag Industries, Inc./Archangel Manufacturing, LLC, 10654 S. Garfield Ave., South Gate, CA 90280, P: 800-438-2547, F: 562-861-6377, www.promagindustries.com
Gun Grips & Stocks; Gun Parts/Gunsmithing; Law Enforcement; Magazines, Cartridge; Retail Packaging; Scopes, Sights & Accessories

Promatic, Inc., 7803 W. Hwy. 116, Gower, MO 64454, UNITED KINGDOM, P: 888-767-2529, F: 816-539-0257, www.promatic.biz
Airguns; Clay Targets; Shooting Range Equipment; Targets; Training & Safety Equipment

Propper International Sales, 520 Huber Park Ct., St. Charles, MO 63304, P: 800-296-9690, F: 877-296-9690, www.propper.com
Camouflage; Law Enforcement; Men's Clothing

Protective Products International, 1649 NW 136th Ave., Sunrise, FL 33323, P: 800-509-9111, F: 954-846-0555, www.body-armor.com
Custom Manufacturing; Export/Import Specialists; Law Enforcement; Men & Women's Clothing; Training & Safety Equipment; Vehicles, Utility & Rec

Pumo GmbH IP Solingen, An den Eichen 20-22, Solingen, HMBG 42699, GERMANY, P: 011 492851589655, F: 011 492851589660, www.pumaknives.de
Custom Manufacturing; Cutlery; Hunting Accessories; Knives/Knife Cases; Sharpeners

Pyramex Safety Products, 281 Moore Lane, Collierville, TN 38017, P: 800-736-8673, F: 877-797-2639, www.pyramexsafety.com
Eyewear; Hearing Protection; Training & Safety Equipment

Pyramyd Air, 26800 Fargo Ave., Suite L, Bedford, OH 44146, P: 888-262-4867, F: 216-896-0896, www.pyramydair.com
Airguns, Airsoft

Q

Quail Unlimited, 31 Quail Run, Edgefield, SC 29824, P: 803-637-5731, F: 803-637-5303, www.qu.org
Books/Industry Publications; Firearms; Hunting Accessories; Men & Women's Clothing; Outdoor Art, Jewelry, Sculpture; Wildlife Management

Quake Industries, Inc., 732 Cruiser Ln., Belgrade, MT 59714, P: 770-449-4687, F: 406-388-8810, www.quakeinc.com
Archery; Crossbows & Accessories; Custom Manufacturing; Hunting Accessories; Scopes, Sights & Accessories; Sports Accessories; Treestands

Quaker Boy, Inc., 5455 Webster Rd., Orchard Park, NY 14127, P: 716-662-9426, www.quakerboy.com
Camouflage; Game Calls; Gloves, Mitts, Hats; Hunting Accessories; Targets; Videos

Quality Cartridge, P.O. Box 445, Hollywood, MD 20636, P: 301-373-3719, F: 301-373-3719, www.qual-cart.com
Ammunition; Custom Manufacturing; Reloading

Quality Deer Management Assoc., 170 Whitetail Way, P.O. Box 160, Bogart, GA 30622, P: 800-209-3337, F: 706-353-0223, www.qdma.com
Books/Industry Publications; Men & Women's Clothing; Videos; Wholesaler/Distributor; Wildlife Management

Quantico Tactical Supply, 109 N. Main St., Raeford, NC 28376, P: 910-875-1672, F: 910-875-3797, www.quanticotactical. com
Eyewear; Firearms; Footwear; Holsters; Knives/Knife Cases; Law Enforcement; Survival Kits/First Aid

Quayside Publishing Group, 400 1st Ave. N, Suite 300, Minneapolis, MN 55401, P: 800-328-0590, F: 612-344-8691, www.creativepub.com
Books/Industry Publications

Quiqlite, Inc., 6464 Hollister Ave., Suite 4, Goleta, CA 93117, P: 866-496-2606, F: 800-910-5711, www.quiqlite.com
Backpacking; Camping; Hunting Accessories; Law Enforcement; Lighting Products; Reloading; Training & Safety Equipment

R

R & R Racing, Inc., 45823 Oak St., Lyons, OR 97358, P: 503-551-7283, F: 503-859-4711, www.randrracingonline.com
Custom Manufacturing; Hearing Protection; Shooting Range Equipment; Targets; Training & Safety Equipment; Wholesaler/Distributor

R & W Rope Warehouse, 39 Tarkiln Pl., P.O. Box 50420, New Bedford, MA 02745, P: 800-260-8599, F: 508-995-1114, www.rwrope.com
Backpacking; Camouflage; Camping; Custom Manufacturing; Hunting Accessories; Law Enforcement; Pet Supplies; Training & Safety Equipment

Rackulator, Inc., P.O. Box 248, Golden Valley, ND 58541, P: 888-791-4213, F: 701-983-4625, www.rackulator.com
Hunting Accessories

Radians, 7580 Bartlett Corp. Dr., Bartlett, TN 38133, P: 877-723-4267, F: 901-266-2558, www.radiansinc.com
Camouflage; Eyewear; Footwear; Gloves, Mitts, Hats; Hearing Protection; Hunting Accessories; Sports Accessories; Training & Safety Equipment

Raine, Inc., 6401 S. Madison Ave., Anderson, IN 46013, P: 800-826-5354, F: 765-622-7691, www.raineinc.com
Bags & Equipment Cases; Camping; Custom Manufacturing; Holsters; Knives/Knife Cases; Law Enforcement; Two-Way Radios

Rainer Ballistics, 4500 15th St. E, Tacoma, WA 98424, P: 800-638-8722, F: 253-922-7854, www.rainierballistics.com
Ammunition; Reloading; Wholesaler/Distributor

Ram Mounting Systems, 8410 Dallas Ave. S, Seattle, WA 98108, P: 206-763-8361, F: 206-763-9615, www.ram-mount.com
Hunting Accessories; Law Enforcement; Sports Accessories; Vehicles, Utility & Rec

Ramba, Via Giorgio La Pira, 20 Flero (Bs), Brescia 25020, ITALY, P: 011 390302548522, F: 011 390302549749, www.ramba.it
Ammunition; Reloading

Ranch Products, P.O. Box 145, Malinta, OH 43535, P: 419-966-2881, F: 313-565-8536, www.ranchproducts.com
Gun Parts/Gunsmithing; Scopes, Sights & Accessories

Rancho Trinidad, 4803 Fountainhead, Houston, TX 77066, P: 210-487-1640, F: 210-487-1640, www.ranchotrinidad.com
Outfitter; Tours/Travel

Randolph Engineering, Inc., 26 Thomas Patten Dr., Randolph, MA 02368, P: 800-541-1405, F: 781-986-0337, www.randolphusa.com
Eyewear

Range Systems, 5121 Winnetka Ave. N, Suite 150, New Hope, MN 55428, P: 888-999-1217, F: 763-537-6657, www.range-systems.com
Eyewear; Law Enforcement; Shooting Range Equipment; Targets; Training & Safety Equipment

Ranger/Xtratuf/NEOS Footwear, 1136 2nd St., Rock Island, IL 61201, P: 800-790-9296, F: 800-267-6809, www.npsusa.com
Footwear

Rapid Dominance Corp., 2121 S. Wilmington Ave., Compton, CA 90220, P: 800-719-5260, F: 310-608-3648, www.rapiddominance.com
Bags & Equipment Cases; Gloves, Mitts, Hats; Men's Clothing; Wholesaler/Distributor

Rat Cutlery Co., 60 Randall Rd., Gallant, AL 35972, P: 865-933-8436, F: 256-570-0175, www.ratcutlery.com
Backpacking; Camping; Cutlery; Knives/Knife Cases; Law Enforcement; Survival Kits/First Aid; Tours/Travel; Training & Safety Equipment

Rattlers Brand/Boyt Harness Co., One Boyt Dr., Osceola, IA 50213, P: 800-550-2698, F: 641-342-2703, www.rattlersbrand.com
Camouflage; Sports Accessories

Raza Khalid & Co., 14/8, Haji Pura, P.O. Box 1632, Sailkot, Punjab 51310, PAKISTAN, P: 011 92523264232, F: 011 92523254932, www.razakhalid.com
Bags & Equipment Cases; Gloves, Mitts, Hats; Gun Cases; Hunting Accessories; Law Enforcement; Paintball Accessories; Pet Supplies; Shooting Range Equipment

RBR Tactical Armor, Inc., 3113 Aspen Ave., Richmond, VA 23228, P: 800-672-7667, F: 804-726-6027, www.rbrtactical.com
Custom Manufacturing; Law Enforcement

RCBS/ATK Commercial Products, 605 Oro Dam Blvd., Oroville, CA 95965, P: 800-533-5000, F: 530-533-1647, www.rcbs.com
Reloading

Real Geese/Webfoot-LSP, 130 Cherry St., P.O. Box 675, Bradner, OH 43406, P: 419-800-8104, F: 888-642-6369, www.realgeese.com
Bags & Equipment Cases; Custom Manufacturing; Decoys; Emblems & Decals; Home Furnishings; Hunting Accessories; Printing Services; Retail Packaging

Realtree® Camouflage, P.O. Box 9638, Columbus, GA 31908, P: 800-992-9968, F: 706-569-9346, www.realtree.com
Camouflage; Videos

Recknagel, Landwehr 4, Bergrheinfeld, 97493, GERMANY, P: 011 49972184366, F: 011 49972182969, www.recknagel.de
Gun Parts/Gunsmithing; Scopes, Sights & Accessories

Recognition Services, 8577 Zionsville Rd., Indianapolis, IN 46268, P: 877-808-9400, F: 877-808-3565, www.we-belong.com
Custom Manufacturing; Emblems & Decals; Law Enforcement; Outfitter

ReconRobotics, Inc., 770 W. 78th St., Edina, MN 55439, P: 952-935-5515, F: 952-935-5508, www.reconrobotics.com
Law Enforcement

Redding Reloading Equipment, 1089 Starr Rd., Cortland, NY 13045, P: 607-753-3331, F: 607-756-8445, www.redding-reloading.com
Lubricants; Reloading

Redman Training Gear, 10045 102nd Terrace, Sebastian, FL 32958, P: 800-865-7840, F: 800-459-2598, www.redmangear.com
Law Enforcement; Training & Safety Equipment

Redwolf Airsoft Specialist, 7A-C, V GA Building, 532 Castle Peak Rd., Cheung Sha Wan, HONG KONG, P: 011 85228577665, F: 011 85229758305, www.redwolfairsoft.com
Airsoft

Reel Wings Decoy Co., Inc., 1122 Main Ave., Fargo, ND 58103, P: 866-55DECOY, F: 701-293-8234, www.reelwings.com
Camouflage; Decoys; Wholesaler/Distributor

Reflective Art, Inc., 403 Eastern Ave. SE, Grand Rapids, MI 49508, P: 800-332-1075, F: 616-452-2112, www.reflectiveartinc.com
Home Furnishings

Reliable of Milwaukee, P.O. Box 563, Milwaukee, WI 53201, P: 800-336-6876, F: 414-272-6443, www.reliableofmilwaukee.com
Archery; Bags & Equipment Cases; Camouflage; Footwear; Gloves, Mitts, Hats; Hunting Accessories; Men & Women's Clothing

Reminton Apparel/The Brinkmann Corp., 4215 McEwen Rd., Dallas, TX 75244, P: 877-525-9070, F: 800-780-0109, www.brinkmann.net
Camouflage; Gloves, Mitts, Hats; Hunting Accessories; Men's Clothing

Remington Arms Co., Inc., 870 Remington Dr., P.O. Box 700, Madison, NC 27025, P: 800-243-9700
Ammunition; Cutlery; Firearms; Footwear; Gun Parts/Gunsmithing; Hunting Accessories

Repel Products, P.O. Box 348, Marion, IA 52302, P: 866-921-1810, F: 319-447-0967, www.repelproducts.com
Archery; Hunting Accessories; Sports Accessories; Wildlife Management

Rescomp Handgun Technologies/CR Speed, P.O. Box 11786, Queenswood, 0186, SOUTH AFRICA, P: 011 27123234768, F: 011 27123321312, www.crspeed.co.za
Bags & Equipment Cases; Custom Manufacturing; Holsters; Law Enforcement; Scopes, Sights &

Accessories; Sports Accessories; Wholesaler/Distributor

Revision Eyewear, Ltd., 7 Corporate Dr., Essex Junction, VT 05452, CANADA, P: 802-879-7002, F: 802-879-7224, www.revisionready.com
Eyewear; Hunting Accessories; Law Enforcement; Paintball Accessories; Shooting Range Equipment; Sports Accessories; Training & Safety Equipment

Rich-Mar Sports, North 7125 1280 St., River Falls, WI 54022, P: 952-881-6796, F: 952-884-4878, www.richmarsports.com
Cooking Equipment/Accessories; Hunting Accessories; Law Enforcement; Sports Accessories; Training & Safety Equipment

Ridge Outdoors U.S.A., Inc./Ridge Footwear, P.O. Box 389, Eustis, FL 32727-0389, P: 800-508-2668, F: 866-584-2042, www.ridgeoutdoors.com
Footwear; Law Enforcement; Men & Women's Clothing; Sports Accessories

Ring's Manufacturing, 99 East Dr., Melbourne, FL 32904, P: 800-537-7464, F: 321-951-0017, www.blueguns.com
Custom Manufacturing; Law Enforcement; Training & Safety Equipment

Rio Ammunition, Fountainview, Suite 207, Houston, TX 77057, P: 713-266-3091, F: 713-266-3092, www.rioammo.com, www.ueec.es
Ammunition; Black Powder/Smokeless Powder; Law Enforcement

Rio Bonito Ranch, 5309 Rio Bonito Ranch Rd., Junction, TX 76849, P: 800-864-4303, F: 325-446-3859, www.riobonito.com
Outfitter

Rite In The Rain, 2614 Pacific Hwy. E, Tacoma, WA 98424, P: 253-922-5000, F: 253-922-5300, www.riteintherain.com
Archery; Backpacking; Camping; Custom Manufacturing; Law Enforcement; Printing Services; Sports Accessories; Targets

River Oak Outdoors, Inc., 705 E. Market, Warrensburg, MO 64093, P: 660-580-0256, F: 816-222-0427, www.riveroakoutdoors.com
Custom Manufacturing; Game Calls; Gun Cabinets/Racks/Safes; Home Furnishings; Hunting Accessories; Sports Accessories

River Rock Designs, Inc., 900 RR 620 S, Suite C101-223, Austin, TX 78734, P: 512-263-6985, F: 512-263-1277, www.riverrockledlights.com
Backpacking; Camping; Hunting Accessories; Law Enforcement; Lighting Products; Sports Accessories; Training & Safety Equipment

River's Edge Treestands, Inc./Ardisam, Inc./Yukon Tracks, 1690 Elm St., Cumberland, WI 54829, P: 800-450-3343, F: 715-822-2124, www.huntriversedge.com, www.ardisam.com
Archery; Blinds; Camouflage; Gloves, Mitts, Hats; Hunting Accessories; Treestands

Rivers Edge Products, One Rivers Edge Ct., St. Clair, MO 63077, P: 888-326-6200, F: 636-629-7557, www.riversedgeproducts.com
Camouflage; Camping; Home Furnishings; Knives/Knife Cases; Leathergoods; Lighting Products; Pet Supplies; Wholesaler/Distributor

Rivers West/H2P Waterproof System, 2900 4th Ave. S, Seattle, WA 98134, P: 800-683-0887, F: 206-682-8691, www.riverswest.com
Camouflage; Law Enforcement; Men & Women's Clothing

RM Equipment, 6975 NW 43rd St., Miami, FL 33166, P: 305-477-9312, F: 305-477-9620, www.40mm.com
Firearms; Gun Grips & Stocks; Law Enforcement

RNT Calls, Inc./Buckwild Hunting Products and Quackhead Calls, 2315 Hwy. 63 N, P.O. Box 1026, Stuttgart, AR 72160, P: 877-993-4868, F: 601-829-4072, www.rntcalls.com
Custom Manufacturing; Emblems & Decals; Game Calls; Gloves, Mitts, Hats; Hunting Accessories; Scents & Lures; Videos

Robert Louis Company, Inc., 31 Shepard Hill Rd., Newtown, CT 06470, P: 800-979-9156, F: 203-270-3881, www.shotguncombogauge.com
Gun Parts/Gunsmithing; Shooting Range Equipment; Training & Safety Equipment

Rock Creek Barrels, Inc., 101 Ogden Ave., Albany, WI 53502, P: 608-862-2357, F: 608-862-2356, www.rockcreekbarrels.com
Gun Barrels

Rock River Arms, Inc., 1042 Cleveland Rd., Colona, IL 61241, P: 866-980-7625, F: 309-792-5781, www.rockriverarms.com
Custom Manufacturing; Firearms; Gun Barrels; Gun Grips & Stocks; Gun Parts/Gunsmithing; Law Enforcement; Magazines, Cartridge; Scopes, Sights & Accessories

Rockpoint Apparel, 9925 Aldine Westfield Rd., Houston, TX 77093, P: 713-699-9896, F: 713-699-9856, www.rockpoint-apparel.com
Camouflage; Custom Manufacturing; Export/Import Specialists; Gloves, Mitts, Hats; Men & Women's Clothing

Rocky Brands, 39 E. Canal St., Nelsonville, OH 45764, P: 740-753-9100, F: 740-753-7240, www.rockybrands.com
Footwear

Rocky Mountain Elk Foundation, 5705 Grant Creek Rd., P.O. Box 8249, Missoula, MT 59808, P: 800-CALL-ELK, F: 406-523-4550, www.elkfoundation.org
Books/Industry Publications; Wildlife Management

Rohrbaugh Firearms Corp., P.o. Box 785, Bayport, NY 11705, P: 800-803-2233, F: 631-242-3183, www.rohrbaughfirearms.com
Firearms

ROKON, 50 Railroad Ave., Rochester, NH 03839, P: 800-593-2369, F: 603-335-4400, www.rokon.com
Export/Import Specialists; Hunting Accessories; Sports Accessories; Vehicles, Utility & Rec

ROK Straps, 162 Locust Hill Dr., Rochester, NY 14618, P: 585-244-6451, F: 570-694-0773, www.rokstraps.com
Backpacking; Camouflage; Camping; Hunting Accessories; Pet Supplies; Sports Accessories

Rose Garden, The, 1855 Griffin Rd., Suite C370, Dania Beach, FL 33004, P: 954-927-9590, F: 954-927-9591, www.therosegardendb.com
Export/Import Specialists; Home Furnishings; Outdoor Art, Jewelry, Sculpture; Wholesaler/Distributor

Rose Plastic USA, LP, 525 Technology Dr., P.O. Box 698, California, PA 15419, P: 724-938-8530, F: 724-938-8532, www.rose-plastic.us
Bags & Equipment Cases; Custom Manufacturing; Gun Cases; Retail Packaging

Rossi/BrazTech, 16175 NW 49th Ave., Miami, FL 33014, P: 800-948-8029, F: 305-623-7506, www.rossiusa.com
Black Powder Accessories; Firearms

Rothco, 3015 Veterans Memorial Hwy., P.O. Box 1220, Ronkonkoma, NY 11779, P: 800-645-5195, F: 631-585-9447, www.rothco.com
Bags & Equipment Cases; Camouflage; Hunting Accessories; Knives/Knife Cases; Law Enforcement; Men & Women's Clothing; Survival Kits/First Aid; Wholesaler/Distributor

RPM, Inc./Drymate, 6665 W. Hwy. 13, Savage, MN 55378, P: 800-872-8201, F: 952-808-2277, www.drymate.com
Blinds; Camping; Custom Manufacturing; Firearms Maintenance Equipment; Home Furnishings; Hunting Accessories; Pet Supplies; Sports Accessories; Vehicles, Utility & Rec

RSR Group, Inc., 4405 Metric Dr., Winter Park, FL 32792, P: 800-541-4867, F: 407-677-4489, www.rsrgroup.com
Airguns; Ammunition; Cutlery; Firearms; Gun Cases; Holsters; Scopes, Sights & Accessories; Wholesaler/Distributor

RS International Industry/Hong Kong Co., Ltd., Room 1109, 11F, WingHing Industrial Bldg., Chai Wan Kok St., Tsuen Wan N.T., HONG KONG, P: 011 85224021381, F: 011 85224021385, www.realsword.com.hk
Airsoft

RTZ Distribution/HallMark Cutlery, 4436B Middlebrook Pike, Knoxville, TN 37921, P: 866-583-3912, F: 865-588-0425, www.hallmarkcutlery.com
Cutlery; Knifes/Knife Cases; Law Enforcement; Sharpeners

RUAG Ammotec, Uttigenstrasse 67, Thun, 3602, SWITZERLAND, P: 011 41332282879, F: 011 41332282644, www.ruag.com
Ammunition; Law Enforcement

Ruffed Grouse Society, Inc., 451 McCormick Rd., Coraopolis, PA 15108, P: 888-564-6747, F: 412-262-9207, www.ruffedgrousesociety.org
Wildlife Management

Ruger Firearms, 1 Lacey Pl., Southport, CT 06890, P: 203-259-7843, F: 203-256-3367, www.ruger.com
Firearms

Ruko, LLC, P.O. Box 38, Buffalo, NY 14207, P: 716-874-2707, F: 905-826-1353, www.rukoproducts.com
Camping; Compasses; Custom Manufacturing; Cutlery; Export/Import Specialists; Hunting Accessories; Knives/Knife Cases; Sharpeners

Russ Fields Safaris, Gameston, Alicedale Rd., P.O. Box 100, Grahamstown, East Cape, 6140, SOUTH AFRICA, P: 011 27834449753, F: 011 27466225837, www.southafricanhunting.com
Outfitter

Russian American Armory Co., 677 S. Cardinal Ln., Suite A, Scottsburg, IN 47170, P: 877-752-2894, F: 812-752-7683, www.raacfirearms.com
Firearms; Knives/Knife Cases; Magazines, Cartridge

RVJ International/Happy Feet, 6130 W. Flamingo Rd., PMB 460, Las Vegas, NV 89103, P: 702-871-6377, F: 702-222-1212, www.happyfeet.com
Books/Industry Publications; Footwear; Hunting Accessories; Men & Women's Clothing; Sports Accessories

S

S&K Industries, Inc., S. Hwy. 13, Lexington, MO 64067, P: 660-259-4691, F: 660-259-2081, www.sandkgunstocks.com
Custom Manufacturing; Gun Grips & Stocks

Saab Barracuda, LLC, 608 McNeill St., Lillington, NC 27546, P: 910-893-2094, F: 910-893-8807, www.saabgroup.com
Camouflage; Law Enforcement

Sabre Defence Industries, LLC, 450 Allied Dr., Nashville, TN 37211, P: 615-333-0077, F: 615-333-6229, www.sabredefence.com
Firearms; Gun Barrels

Sack-Ups, 1611 Jamestown Rd., Morganton, NC 28655, P: 877-213-6333, F: 828-584-6326, www.sackups.com
Archery; Black Powder Accessories; Firearms Maintenance Equipment; Gun Cases; Hunting Accessories; Knives/Knife Cases; Sports Accessories

Safari Club International, 4800 W. Gates Pass Rd., Tucson, AZ 85745, P: 520-620-1220, F: 520-618-3528, www.safariclub.org
Books/Industry Publications

Safari Nordik, 639 Labelle Blvd., Blainville, Quebec J7C 1V8, CANADA, P: 800-361-3748, F: 450-971-1771, www.safarinordik.com
Outfitter; Tours/Travel

Safari Press, 15621 Chemical Ln., Huntington Beach, CA 92649, P: 714-894-9080, F: 714-894-4949, www.safaripress.com
Books/Industry Publications

Safari Sunsets, 9735 Slater Ln., Overland Park, KS 66212, P: 877-894-1671, F: 913-894-1686, www.safarisunsets.com
Men's Clothing

Safe Guy/Gun Storage Solutions, 18317 N. 2600 East Rd., Cooksville, IL 61730, P: 309-275-1220, www.storemoreguns.com
Gun Cabinets/Racks/Safes

Safety Bullet, Inc., P.O. Box 007, Panama City, FL 32444, P: 850-866-0190, www.safetybullet.com
Gun Locks

Safety Harbor Firearms, Inc., 915 Harbor Lake Dr., Suite D, Safety Harbor, FL 34695, P: 727-725-4700, F: 727-724-1872, www.safetyharborfirearms.com
Firearms

Sage Control Ordnance, Inc./Sage International, Ltd., 3391 E. Eberhardt St., Oscoda, MI 48750, P: 989-739-7000, F: 989-739-7098, www.sageinternationalltd.com
Ammunition; Firearms; Gun Grips & Stocks; Gun Locks; Law Enforcement; Reloading

Salt River Tactical, LLC/Ost-Kraft, LLC, P.O. Box 20397, Mesa, AZ 85277, P: 480-656-2683, www.saltrivertactical.com
Bags & Equipment Cases; Firearms Maintenance Equipment; Hunting Accessories; Law Enforcement; Scopes, Sights & Accessories; Shooting Range Equipment; Wholesaler/Distributor

SAM Medical Products, P.O. Box 3270, Tualatin, OR 97062, P: 800-818-4726, F: 503-639-5425, www.sammedical.com
Backpacking; Camping; Law Enforcement; Outfitter; Shooting Range Equipment; Survival Kits/First Aid; Training & Safety Equipment

Samco Global Arms, Inc., 6995 NW 43rd St., Miami, FL 33166, P: 800-554-1618, F: 305-593-1014, www.samcoglobal.com
Ammunition; Firearms; Sports Accessories

Samson Mfg. Corp., 110 Christian Ln., Whately, MA 01373, P: 888-665-4370, F: 413-665-1163, www.samson-mfg.com
Firearms; Gun Parts/Gunsmithing; Law Enforcement; Scopes, Sights & Accessories

San Angelo/Rio Brands, 10981 Decatur Rd., Philadelphia, PA 19154, P: 800-531-7230, F: 830-393-7621, www.riobrands.com
Backpacking; Blinds; Camping; Cooking Equipment/Accessories; Gun Cabinets/Racks/Safes; Hunting Accessories; Taxidermy

Sandhurst Safaris, P.O. Box 57, Tosca, 8618, SOUTH AFRICA, P: 011 27824535683, F: 011 27539331002, www.sandhurstsafaris.com
Tours/Travel

Sandpiper of California, 687 Anita St., Suite A, Chula Vista, CA 91911, P: 866-424-6622, F: 619-423-9599, www.pipergear.com
Backpacking; Bags & Equipment Cases; Camouflage; Custom Manufacturing; Law Enforcement

Sandviper, 1611 Jamestown Rd., Morganton, NC 28655, P: 800-873-7225, F: 828-584-6326
Law Enforcement

Sante Fe Stone Works, Inc., 3790 Cerillos Rd., Sante Fe, NM 87507, P: 800-257-7625, F: 505-471-0036, www.santefestoneworks.com
Cutlery

Sargent & Greenleaf, Inc., One Security Dr., Nicholasville, KY 40356, P: 800-826-7652, F: 859-887-2057, www.sargentandgreenleaf.com
Gun Cabinets/Racks/Safes

Sarsilmaz Silah San. A.S, Nargileci Sokak, No. 4, Sarsilmaz Is Merkezi, Mercan, Eminonu, Istanbul, 34116, TURKEY, P: 011 902125133507, F: 011 902125111999, www.sarsilmaz.com
Firearms

Savage Arms, Inc., 118 Mountain Rd., Suffield, CT 06078, P: 866-233-4776, F: 860-668-2168, www.savagearms.com
Black Powder/Smokeless Powder; Firearms; Knives/Knife Cases; Law Enforcement; Shooting Range Equipment

Savannah Luggage Works, 3428 Hwy. 297 N, Vidalia, GA 30474, P: 800-673-6341, F: 912-537-4492, www.savannahluggage.com
Backpacking; Bags & Equipment Cases; Custom Manufacturing; Holsters; Law Enforcement; Training & Safety Equipment

SBR Ammunition, 1118 Glynn Park Rd., Suite E, Brunswick, GA 31525, P: 912-264-5822, F: 912-264-5888, www.sbrammunition.com
Ammunition; Firearms; Law Enforcement

Sceery Outdoors, LLC, P.O. Box 6520, Sante Fe, NM 87502; P: 800-327-4322 or 505-471-9110; F: 505-471-3476; www.sceeryoutdoors.net
Decoys; Game Calls; Hunting Accessories

Scent-Lok Technologies, 1731 Wierengo Dr., Muskegon, MI 49442, P: 800-315-5799, F: 231-767-2824, www.scentlok.com
Bags & Equipment Cases; Camouflage; Gloves, Mitts, Hats; Men & Women's Clothing; Videos

SCENTite Blinds, P.O. Box 36635, Birmingham, AL 35236, P: 800-828-1554, F: 205-424-4799, www.fargasonoutdoors.com
Archery; Backpacking; Blinds; Crossbows & Accessories; Hunting Accessories; Photographic Equipment; Scents & Lures; Treestands

Scentote, 1221 Keating, Grand Rapids, MI 49503, P: 616-742-0946, F: 616-742-0978, www.scentote.com
Archery; Hunting Accessories; Men's Clothing; Scents & Lures

Scharch Mfg., Inc/Top Brass, 10325 Cty. Rd. 120, Salida, CO 81201, P: 800-836-4683, F: 719-539-3021, www.scharch.com
Ammunition; Magazines, Cartridge; Reloading; Retail Packaging; Shooting Range Equipment

Scherer Supplies, Inc., 205 Four Mile Creek Rd., Tazewell, TN 37879, P: 423-733-2615, F: 423-733-2073
Custom Manufacturing; Magazines, Cartridge; Wholesaler/Distributor

Schmidt & Bender GmbH, Am Grossacker 42, Biebertal, Hessen 35444, GERMANY, P: 011 49640981570, US: 800-468-3450, F: ++49-6409811511, www.schmidt-bender.de, www.schmidtbender.com
Hunting Accessories; Law Enforcement; Scopes, Sights & Accessories; Sports Accessories; Telescopes

Schott Performance Fabrics, Inc., 2850 Gilchrist Rd., Akron, OH 44305, P: 800-321-2178, F: 330-734-0665, www.schottfabrics.com
Camouflage; Export/Import Specialists; Hunting Accessories; Men's Clothing

Scopecoat by Devtron Diversified, 3001 E. Cholla St., Phoenix, AZ 85028, P: 877-726-7328, F: 602-224-9351, www.scopecoat.com
Scopes, Sights & Accessories

SDG Seber Design Group, Inc. 2438 Cades Way, Vista, CA 92081, P: 760-727-5555, F: 760-727-5551, www.severdesigngroup.com
Camping; Cutlery; Knives/Knife Cases; Law Enforcement

Seasonal Marketing, Inc., P.O. Box 1410, La Pine, OR 97739, P: 972-540-1656, www.caddiswadingsyssytems.net
Footwear; Hunting Accessories

Second Amendment Foundation, 12500 NE Tenth Pl., Bellevue, WA 98005, P: 425-454-7012, F: 425-451-3959, www.saf.org
Books/Industry Publications

SecuRam Systems, Inc., 350 N. Lantana St., Suite 211, Camarillo, CA 93010, P: 805-388-2058, F: 805-383-1728, www.securamsys.com
Gun Cabinets/Racks/Safes

Secure Firearm Products, 213 S. Main, P.O. Box 177, Carl Junction, MO 64834, P: 800-257-8744, F: 417-649-7278, www.securefirearmproducts.com
Bags & Equipment Cases; Custom Manufacturing; Gun Cases; Shooting Range Equipment; Targets

Secure Vault/Boyt Harness Co., One Boyt Dr., Osceola, IA 50213, P: 800-550-2698, F: 641-342-2703
Gun Cabinets/Racks/Safes

Security Equipment Corp., 747 Sun Park Dr., Fenton, MO 63026, P: 800-325-9568, F: 636-343-1318, www.sabrered.com
Backpacking; Camping; Custom Manufacturing; Law Enforcement; Training & Safety Equipment

Seldon Technologies, Inc., P.O. Box 710, Windsor, VT 05089, P: 802-674-2444, F: 802-674-2544, www.seldontech.com
Backpacking; Camping; Hunting Accessories

Self Defense Supply, Inc., 1819 Firman Dr., Suite 101, Richardson, TX 75081, P: 800-211-4186, F: 942-644-6980, www.selfdefensesupply.com
Airguns; Airsoft; Binoculars; Camping; Crossbows & Accessories; Cutlery; Lighting Products; Wholesaler/ Distributor

Sellier & Bellot, USA, Inc., P.O. Box 7307, Shawnee Mission, KS 66207, P: 913-664-5933, F: 913-664-5938, www.sb-usa.com
Ammunition; Law Enforcement

Sentry Group, 900 Linden Ave., Rochester, NY 14625, P: 800-828-1438, F: 585-381-8559, www.sentrysafe.com
Gun Cabinets/Racks/Safes; Home Furnishings; Hunting Accessories; Law Enforcement

Sentry Solutions, Ltd., 5 Souhegan St., P.O. Box 214, Wilton, NH 03086, P: 800-546-8049, F: 603-654-3003, www.sentrysolutions.com
Firearms Maintenance Equipment; Gun Parts/ Gunsmithing; Hunting Accessories; Lubricants; Sharpeners; Sports Accessories

Serbu Firearms, Inc., 6001 Johns Rd., Suite 144, Tampa, FL 33634, P: 813-243-8899, F: 813-243-8899, www.serbu.com
Firearms; Law Enforcement

Sharp Shoot R Precision, Inc., P.O. Box 171, Paola, KS 66071, P: 785-883-4444, F: 785-883-2525, www.sharpshootr.com
Black Powder Accessories; Custom Manufacturing; Firearms Maintenance Equipment; Lubricants; Reloading; Sports Accessories

Shasta Wear, 4320 Mountain Lakes Blvd., Redding, CAR 96003, P: 800-553-2466, F: 530-243-3274, www.shastawear.com
Emblems & Decals; Export/Import Specialists; Gloves, Mitts, Hats; Men & Women's Clothing; Outdoor Art, Jewelry, Sculpture; Retailer Services; Wholesaler/Distributor

SHE Safari, LLC, 15535 W. Hardy, Suite 102, Houston, TX 77060, P: 281-448-4860, F: 281-448-4118, www.shesafari.com
Camouflage; Women's Clothing

Sheffield Cutting Equipment, 4569 Mission Gorge Pl., San Diego, CA 92120, P: 619-280-0278, F: 619-280-0011, www.sheffieldcuttingequip.com
Bags & Equipment Cases; Camouflage; Custom Manufacturing; Holsters; Leathergoods; Men & Women's Clothing

Sheffield Tools/GreatLITE Flashlights, 165 E. 2nd St., P.O. Box 3, Mineola, NY 11501, P: 800-457-0600, F: 516-746-5366, www.sheffield-tools.com
Backpacking; Camping; Cutlery; Hunting Accessories; Knives/Knife Cases; Lighting Products

Shelterlogic, 150 Callender Rd., Watertown, CT 06795, P: 800-932-9344, F: 860-274-9306, www.shelterlogic.com
Camouflage; Camping; Custom Manufacturing; Hunting Accessories; Law Enforcement; Pet Supplies; Sports Accessories

Shenzhen Champion Industry Co., Ltd., Longqin Rd. No. 13, Shahu, Pingshan, Longgang Shenzhen City, GNGD 518118, CHINA, P: 011 8675589785877, F: 011 8675589785875, www.championcase.com
Bags & Equipment Cases; Cutlery; Gun Cabinets/ Racks/Safes; Gun Cases; Gun Locks; Gun Parts/ Gunsmithing; Home Furnishings; Knives/Knife Cases

Shepherd Enterprises, Inc., P.O. Box 189, Waterloo, NE 68069, P: 402-779-2424, F: 402-779-4010, www.shepherdscopes.com
Scopes, Sights & Accessories

Sherluk Marketing, Law Enforcement & Military, P.O. Box 156, Delta, OH 43615, P: 419-923-8011, F: 419-923-8120, www.sherluk.com
Firearms; Firearms Maintenance Equipment; Gun Grips & Stocks; Gun Parts/Gunsmithing; Law Enforcement; Wholesaler/Distributor

Shiloh Rifle Manufacturing, 201 Centennial Dr., P.O. Box 279, Big Timber, MT 59011, P: 406-932-4454, F: 406-932-5627, www.shilohrifle.com
Black Powder Accessories; Firearms

Shirstone Optics/Shinei Group, Inc., Komagome-Spancrete Bldg. 8F, Honkomagome 5-4-7, Bunkyo-Ku, Toyko, 113-0021, JAPAN, P: 011 81339439550, F: 011 81339430695, www.shirstone.com
Binoculars; Firearms; Scopes, Sights & Accessories

Shocknife, Inc., 20 Railway St., Winnipeg, Manitoba R2X 2P9, CANADA, P: 866-353-5055, F: 204-586-2049, www.shocknife.com
Knives/Knife Cases; Law Enforcement; Training & Safety Equipment

Shooter's Choice Gun Care/Ventco, Inc., 15050 Berkshire Industrial Pkwy., Middlefield, OH 44062, P: 440-834-8888, F: 440-834-3388, www.shooters-choice.com
Firearms Maintenance Equipment; Gun Parts/ Gunsmithing; Law Enforcement; Lubricants

Shooters Depot, 5526 Leopard St., Corpus Christi, TX 78408, P: 361-299-1299, F: 361-289-9906, www.shootersdepot.com
Firearms; Gun Barrels

Shooters Ridge/ATK Commercial Products, N5549 Cty. Tk. Z, Onalaska, WI 54650, P: 800-635-7656, F: 763-323-3890, www.shootersridge.com
Bags & Equipment Cases; Gun Cabinets/Racks/ Safes; Hunting Accessories; Magazines, Cartridge; Sports Accessories

Shooting Chrony, Inc., 2446 Cawthra Rd., Bldg. 1, Suite 10, Mississauga, Ontario L5A 3K6, CANADA, P: 800-385-3161, F: 905-276-6295, www.shootingchrony.com
Archery; Black Powder Accessories; Computer Software; Hunting Accessories; Lighting Products; Reloading; Shooting Range Equipment; Sports Accessories

Shooting Ranges International, Inc./Advanced Interactive Systems, 3885 Rockbottom St., North Las Vegas, NV 89030, P: 702-362-3623, F: 702-310-6978, www.shootingrangeintl.com
Firearms; Law Enforcement; Shooting Range Equipment

Shooting Sports Retailer, 255 W. 36th St., Suite 1202, New York, NY 10018, P: 212-840-0660, F: 212-944-1884, www.shootingsportsretailer.com
Books/Industry Publications

Sierra Bullets, 1400 W. Henry St., Sedalia, MO 65301, P: 888-223-3006, F: 660-827-4999, www.sierrabullets.com
Books/Industry Publications; Computer Software; Reloading; Videos

SIG SAUER, 18 Industrial Dr., Exeter, NH 03833, P: 603-772-2302, F: 603-772-9082, www.sigsauer.com
Bags & Equipment Cases; Firearms; Holsters; Knives/Knife Cases; Law Enforcement; Training & Safety Equipment

Sightron, Inc., 100 Jeffrey Way, Suite A, Youngville, NC 27596, P: 800-867-7512, F: 919-556-0157, www.sightron.com
Binoculars; Scopes, Sights & Accessories

Silencio/Jackson Safety, 1859 Bowles Ave., Suite 200, Fenton, MO 63026, P: 800-237-4192, F: 636-717-6820, www.jacksonsafety.com
Eyewear; Hearing Protection; Law Enforcement

Silma SRL, Via I Maggio, 74, Zanano Di Sarezzo, Brescia 25068, ITALY, P: 011 390308900505, F: 011 390308900712, www.silma.net
Firearms

Silver Stag, 328 Martin St., Blaine, WA 98230, P: 888-233-7824, F: 360-332-4390, www.silverstag.com
Black Powder Accessories; Camping; Crossbows & Accessories; Custom Manufacturing; Cutlery; Hunting Accessories; Knives/Knife Cases; Outdoor Art, Jewelry, Sculpture

Silver State Armory, LLC, P.O. Box 2902, Pahrump, NV 89041, P: 775-537-1118, F: 775-537-1119
Ammunition; Firearms

Simmons, 9200 Cody St., Overland Park, KS 66214, P: 913-782-3131, F: 913-782-4189
Binoculars; Hunting Accessories; Law Enforcement; Scopes, Sights & Accessories

Simunition Operations, General Dynamics Ordnance & Tactical Systems, 5 Montée des Arsenaux, Le Gardeur, Quebec J5Z 2P4, CANADA, P: 800-465-8255, F: 450-581-0231, www.simunition.com
Ammunition; Gun Barrels; Law Enforcement; Magazines, Cartridge, Training & Safety Equipment

Sinclair International, 2330 Wayne Haven St., Fort Wayne, IN 46803, P: 800-717-8211, F: 260-493-2530, www.sinclairintl.com
Ammunition; Bags & Equipment Cases; Books; Cleaning Products; Reloading; Scopes, Sights & Accessories; Software; Targets, Videos

SISCO, 2835 Ana St., Rancho Dominguez, CA 90221, P: 800-832-5834, F: 310-638-6489, www.honeywellsafes.com
Gun Cabinets/Racks/Safes; Hunting Accessories

Sitka, Inc., 870 Napa Valley Corporate Way, Suite N, Napa, CA 94558, P: 877-SITKA MG, F: 707-253-1121, www.sitkagear.com
Men's Clothing

SKB Corp., 1607 N. O'Donnell Way, Orange, CA 92867, P: 800-654-5992, F: 714-283-0425, www.skbcases.com
Archery; Bags & Equipment Cases; Gun Cases; Hunting Accessories; Knives/Knife Cases; Law Enforcement; Sports Accessories

SKB Shotguns, 4441 S. 134th St., Omaha, NE 68137, P: 800-752-2767, F: 402-330-8040, www.skbshotguns.com
Firearms

Smith & Warren, 127 Oakley Ave., White Plains, NY 10601, P: 800-53-BADGE, F: 914-948-1627, www.smithwarren.com
Custom Manufacturing; Law Enforcement

Smith & Wesson, 2100 Roosevelt Ave., Springfield, MA 01104, P: 800-331-0852, F: 413-747-3317, www.smith-wesson.com
Firearms; Law Enforcement

Smith Optics Elite Division, 280 Northwood Way, P.O. Box 2999, Ketchum, ID 83340, P: 208-726-4477, F: 208-727-6598, www.elite.smithoptics.com
Eyewear; Law Enforcement; Shooting Range Equipment; Training & Safety Equipment

Smith's, 1700 Sleepy Valley Rd., Hot Springs, AR 71901, P: 800-221-4156, F: 501-321-9232, www.smithsedge.com
Backpacking; Camping; Cutlery; Hunting Accessories; Sharpeners

Smith Security Safes, Inc., P.O. Box 185, Tontogany, OH 43565, P: 800-521-0335, F: 419-823-1505, www.smithsecuritysafes.com
Gun Cabinets/Racks/Safes

Sniper's Hide.com/Snipers Hide, LLC, 3205 Fenton St., Wheat Ridge, CO 80212, P: 203-530-3301, F: 203-622-7331, www.snipershide.com
Books/Industry Publications; Firearms; Law Enforcement; Online Services; Training & Safety Equipment

Snow Peak USA, Inc., P.O. Box 2002, Clackamas, OR 97015, P: 503-697-3330, F: 503-699-1396, www.snowpeak.com
Backpacking; Camping; Cooking Equipment/ Accessories; Cutlery

Soft Air USA Inc./Cybergun, 1452 Hughes Rd., Suite 100, Grapevine, TX 76051, P: 480-330-3358, F: 925-906-1360, www.softairusa.com
Airguns; Airsoft; Paintball Guns & Accessories

Sog Armory, Inc., 11707 S. Sam Houston Pkwy. W, Suite R, Houston, TX 77031, P: 281-568-5685, F: 285-568-9191, www.sogarmory.com
Firearms; Firearms Maintenance Equipment; Gun Barrels; Gun Grips & Stocks; Law Enforcement; Scopes, Sights & Accessories; Wholesaler/Distributor

SOG Specialty Knives, 6521 212th St. SW, Lynnwood, WA 98036, P: 888-405-6433, F: 425-771-7689, www.sogknives.com
Cutlery; Hunting Accessories; Knives/Knife Cases; Law Enforcement

Sohn Mfg., Inc., 544 Sohn Dr., Elkhart Lake, WI 53020, P: 920-876-3361, F: 920-876-2952, www.sohnmanufacturing.com
Emblems & Decals; Printing Services

Solkoa, Inc., 3107 W. Colorado Ave., Suite 256, Colorado Springs, CO 80904, P: 719-685-1072, F: 719-623-0067, www.solkoa.com
Bags & Equipment Cases; Compasses; Hunting Accessories; Law Enforcement; Survival Kits/First Aid; Training & Safety Equipment; Wholesaler/ Distributor

Sona Enterprises, 7825 Somerset Blvd., Suite D, Paramount, CA 90723, P: 562-633-3002, F: 562-633-3583
Binoculars; Camouflage; Camping; Compasses; Lighting Products; Survival Kits/First Aid; Wholesaler/ Distributor

SOTech/Special Operations Technologies, 206 Star of India Ln., Carson, CA 90746, P: 800-615-9007, F: 310-202-0880, www.specopstech.com
Backpacking; Bags & Equipment Cases; Custom Manufacturing; Gun Cases; Holsters; Law Enforcement; Shooting Range Equipment; Survival Kits/First Aid

Source One Distributors, 3125 Fortune Way, Suite 1, Wellington, FL 33414, P: 866-768-4327, F: 561-514-1021, www.buysourceone.com
Bags & Equipment Cases; Binoculars; Eyewear; Firearms; Knives/Knife Cases; Men's Clothing; Scopes, Sights & Accessories; Wholesaler/Distributor

Southern Belle Brass, P.O. Box 36, Memphis, TN 38101, P: 800-478-3016, F: 901-947-1924, www.southernbellebrass.com
Firearms Maintenance Equipment; Holsters; Law Enforcement; Men's Clothing; Paintball Guns; Targets; Training & Safety Equipment; Wholesaler/ Distributor

Southern Bloomer Mfg. Co. & Muzzleloader Originals, 1215 Fifth St., P.O. Box 1621, Bristol, TN 37621, P: 800-655-0342, F: 423-878-8761, www.southernbloomer.com
Ammunition; Black Powder Accessories; Firearms Maintenance Equipment; Gun Parts/Gunsmithing; Hunting Accessories; Law Enforcement; Reloading; Shooting Range Equipment

SPA Defense, 3409 NW 9th Ave., Suite 1104, Ft. Lauderdale, FL 33309, P: 954-568-7690, F: 954-630-4159, www.spa-defense.com
Firearms; Law Enforcement; Scopes, Sights & Accessories; Tactical Equipment

Spartan Imports, 213 Lawrence Ave., San Francisco, CA 94080, P: 650-589-5501, F: 650-589-5552, www.spartanimports.com
Airguns; Firearms; Law Enforcement; Paintball Guns; Scopes, Sights & Accessories; Training & Safety Equipment; Wholesaler/Distributor

Spec.-Ops. Brands, 1601 W. 15th St., Monahans, TX 79756, P: 866-773-2677, F: 432-943-5565, www.specopsbrand.com
Bags & Equipment Cases; Custom Manufacturing; Holsters; Knives/Knife Cases; Law Enforcement; Shooting Range Equipment; Sports Accessories; Training & Safety Equipment

Specialty Bar Products Co., 4 N. Shore Center, Suite 110, 106 Isabella St., Pittsburgh, PA 15212, P: 412-322-2747, F: 412-322-1912, www.specialty-bar.com
Firearms; Gun Barrels; Gun Parts/Gunsmithing

Specter Gear, Inc., 1107 E. Douglas Ave., Visalia, CA 93292, P: 800-987-3605, F: 559-553-8835, www.spectergear.com
Bags & Equipment Cases; Gun Cases; Holsters; Law Enforcement

Speer Ammunition/ATK Commercial Products, 2299 Snake River Ave., Lewiston, ID 83501, P: 800-256-8685, F: 208-746-3904, www.speer-bullets.com
Ammunition; Reloading

Spiewak/Timberland Pro Valor, 463 Seventh Ave., 11th Floor, New York, NY 10018, P: 800-223-6850, F: 212-629-4803, www.spiewak.com
Footwear; Law Enforcement

Spitfire, Ltd., 8868 Research Blvd., Suite 203, Austin, TX 78758, P: 800-774-8347, F: 512-453-7504, www.spitfire.us
Backpacking; Camping; Sporting Range Equipment; Sports Accessories; Training & Safety Equipment

SportDOG Brand, 10427 Electric Ave., Knoxville, TN 37932, P: 800-732-0144, F: 865-777-4815, www.sportdog.com
Hunting Accessories; Pet Supplies; Training & Safety Equipment; Videos

SportEAR/HarrisQuest Outdoor Products, 528 E. 800 N, Orem, UT 84097, P: 800-530-0090, F: 801-224-5660, www.harrisquest.com
Clay Targets; Hearing Protection; Hunting Accessories; Law Enforcement; Scopes, Sights & Accessories; Shooting Range Equipment; Sports Accessories; Training & Safety Equipment

SportHill, 725 McKinley St., Eugene, OR 97402, P: 541-345-9623, F: 541-343-7261, www.sporthillhunting.com
Archery; Camouflage; Gloves, Mitts, Hats; Men & Women's Clothing; Sports Accessories

Sporting Clays Magazine, 317 S. Washington Ave., Suite 201, Titusville, FL 32796, P: 321-268-5010, F: 321-267-7216, www.sportingclays.net
Books/Industry Publications

Sporting Supplies International, Inc.®, P.O. Box 757, Placentia, CA 92871, P: 888-757-WOLF (9653), F: 714-632-9232, www.wolfammo.com
Ammunition

Sports Afield Magazine, 15621 Chemical Ln., Huntington Beach, CA 92649, P: 714-894-9080, F: 714-894-4949, www.sportsafield.com
Books/Industry Publications

Sports South, LLC, 1039 Kay Ln., P.O. Box 51367, Shreveport, LA 71115, 800-388-3845, www.internetguncatalog.com
Ammunition; Binoculars; Black Powder Accessories; Firearms; Hunting Accessories; Reloading; Scopes, Sights & Accessories; Wholesaler/Distributor

Spot, Inc., 461 S. Milpitas Blvd., Milpitas, CA 95035, F: 408-933-4543, F: 408-933-4954, www.findmespot.com
Backpacking; Camping; Outfitter; Sports Accessories; Survival Kits/First Aid; Training & Safety Equipment

Springboard Engineering, 6520 Platt Ave., Suite 818, West Hills, CA 91307, P: 818-346-4647, F: 818-346-4647
Backpacking; Law Enforcement; Lighting Products; Sports Accessories; Survival Kits/First Aid; Training & Safety Equipment; Wholesaler/Distributor

Springfield Armory, 420 W. Main St., Geneseo, IL 61254, P: 800-680-6866, F: 309-944-3676, www.springfield-armory.com
Firearms

Spyder Paintball/Kingman Group, 14010 Live Oak Ave., Baldwin Park, CA 91706, P: 888-KINGMAN, F: 626-851-8530, www.spyder.tv
Bags & Equipment Cases; Eyewear; Gun Cases; Men's Clothing; Paintball Guns & Accessories

Spyderco, Inc., 820 Spyderco Way, Golden, CO 80403, P: 800-525-7770, F: 303-278-2229, www.spyderco.com
Knives/Knife Cases

SRT Supply, 4450 60th Ave. N, St. Petersburg, FL 33714, P: 727-526-5451, F: 727-527-6893, www.srtsupply.com
Ammunition; Export/Import Specialists; Firearms; Law Enforcement; Wholesaler/Distributor

Stack-On Products Co., 1360 N. Old Rand Rd., P.O. Box 489, Wauconda, IL 60084, P: 800-323-9601, F: 847-526-6599, www.stack-on.com
Bags & Equipment Cases; Gun Cabinets/Racks/Safes; Gun Cases; Hunting Accessories; Shooting Range Equipment; Sports Accessories; Training & Safety Equipment

Stackpole Books, Inc., 5067 Ritter Rd., Mechanicsburg, PA 17055, P: 800-732-3669, F: 717-796-0412, www.stackpolebooks.com
Books/Industry Publications

Stag Arms, 515 John Downey Dr., New Britain, CT 06051, P: 860-229-9994, F: 860-229-3738, www.stagarms.com
Firearms; Law Enforcement

Stallion Leather/Helios Systems, 1104 Carroll Ave., South Milwaukee, WI 53172, P: 414-764-7126, F: 414-764-2878, www.helios-sys.com
Bags & Equipment Cases; Holsters; Knives/Knife Cases; Law Enforcement; Leathergoods; Sports Accessories

Stansport, 2801 E. 12th St., Los Angeles, CA 90023, P: 800-421-6131, F: 323-269-2761, www.stansport.com
Backpacking; Bags & Equipment Cases; Camping; Compasses; Cooking Equipment/Accessories; Hunting Accessories; Lighting Products; Survival Kits/First Aid

Stark Equipment Corp., 55 S. Commercial St., 4th Floor, Manchester, NH 03101, P: 603-556-7772, F: 603-556-7344, www.starkequipment.com
Gun Grips & Stocks; Hunting Accessories; Law Enforcement

Starlight Cases™, 2180 Hwy. 70-A E, Pine Level, NC 27568, P: 877-782-7544, F: 919-965-9177, www.starlightcases.com
Bags & Equipment Cases; Custom Manufacturing; Gun Cabinets/Racks/Safes; Gun Cases; Hunting Accessories; Law Enforcement; Scopes, Sights & Accessories; Shooting Range Equipment

Steiner Binoculars, 97 Foster Rd., Suite 5, Moorestown, NJ 08057, P: 800-257-7742, F: 856-866-8615, www.steiner-binoculars.com
Binoculars

SteriPEN/Hydro-Photon, Inc., 262 Ellsworth Rd., Blue Hill, ME 04614, P: 888-783-7473, F: 207-374-5100, www.steripen.com
Backpacking; Camping; Cooking Equipment/Accessories; Law Enforcement; Sports Accessories; Survival Kits/First Aid; Training & Safety Equipment

Sterling Sharpener, P.O. Box 620547, Woodside, CA 94062, P: 800-297-4277, F: 650-851-1434, www.sterlingsharpener.com
Backpacking; Camping; Cooking Equipment/Accessories; Hunting Accessories; Knives/Knife Cases; Law Enforcement; Sharpeners; Survival Kits/First Aid

Stewart EFI, LLC, 45 Old Waterbury Rd., Thomaston, CT 06787, P: 800-228-2509, F: 860-283-3174, www.stewartefi.com
Ammunition; Backpacking; Custom Manufacturing; Firearms Hearing Protection; Law Enforcement; Lighting Products; Magazines, Cartridge

Steyr Arms, Inc., P.O. Box 840, Trussville, GA 35173, P: 205-467-6544, F: 205-467-3015, www.steyrarms.com
Firearms; Law Enforcement

STI International, 114 Halmar Cove, Georgetown, TX 78628, P: 512-819-0656, F: 512-819-0465, www.stiguns.com
Firearms; Gun Barrels; Gun Parts/Gunsmithing

Stil Crin SNC, Via Per Gottolengo, 12A, Pavone Mella, Brescia 25020, ITALY, P: 011-390309599496, F: 011-390309959544, www.stilcrin.it
Firearms Maintenance Equipment; Gun Cases; Gun Locks; Lubricants

Stoeger Industries, 17603 Indian Head Hwy., Accokeek, MD 20607, P: 800-264-4962, F: 301-283-6988, www.stoegerindustries.com
Airguns; Firearms

Stoney-Wolf Productions, 130 Columbia Court W, Chaska, MN 55318, P: 800-237-7583, F: 952-361-4217, www.stoneywolf.com

Books/Industry Publications; Computer Software; Food; Videos

Stoney Point Products, Inc., 9200 Cody, Overland Park, KS 66214, P: 800-221-9035, F: 800-548-0446, www.stoneypoint.com
Backpacking; Hearing Protection; Hunting Accessories; Shooting Range Equipment; Sports Accessories

Stormy Kromer Mercantile, 1238 Wall St., Ironwood, MI 49938, P: 888-455-2253, F: 906-932-1579, www.stormykromer.com
Camouflage; Gloves, Mitts, Hats; Men's Clothing

Strangler Chokes, Inc., 7958 US Hwy. 167 S, Winnfield, LA 71483, P: 318-201-3474, F: 318-473-0982
Custom Manufacturing; Firearms; Gun Barrels; Gun Parts/Gunsmithing; Hunting Accessories; Scopes, Sights & Accessories

Streamlight, Inc., 30 Eagleville Rd., Eagleville, PA 19403, P: 800-523-7488, F: 800-220-7007, www.streamlight.com
Hunting Accessories; Law Enforcement; Lighting Products; Training & Safety Equipment

Streamworks, Inc., 3233 Lance Dr., Suite B, Stockton, CA 92505, P: 209-337-3307, F: 209-337-3342, www.hattail.com
Hearing Protection

Streetwise Security Products/Cutting Edge Products, Inc., 235-F Forlines Rd., Winterville, NC 28590, P: 800-497-0539, F: 252-830-5542, www.streetwisesecurity.net
Law Enforcement

Strider Knives, Inc., 120 N. Pacific St., Suite L7, San Marcos, CA 92069, P: 760-471-8275, F: 503-218-7069, www.striderknives.com
Backpacking; Custom Manufacturing; Cutlery; Hunting Accessories; Knives/Knife Cases; Law Enforcement; Training & Safety Equipment

Strike-Hold/MPH System Specialties, Inc., P.O. Box 1923, Dawsonville, GA 30534, P: 866-331-0572, F: 325-204-2550, www.strikehold.com
Black Powder Accessories; Export/Import Specialists; Firearms Maintenance Equipment; Hunting Accessories; Law Enforcement; Lubricants; Paintball Accessories; Wholesaler/Distributor

Strong Leather Co., 39 Grove St., P.O. Box 1195, Gloucester, MA 01930, P: 800-225-0724, F: 866-316-3666, www.strongbadgecase.com
Bags & Equipment Cases; Holsters; Law Enforcement; Leathergoods

Sturm, 430 S. Erwin St., Cartersville, GA 30120, P: 800-441-7367, F: 770-386-6654, www.sturm-miltec.com
Camouflage; Camping; Firearms; Gun Grips & Stocks; Magazines, Cartridge; Men's Clothing; Scopes, Sights & Accessories

Sun Optics USA, 1312 S. Briar Oaks Rd., Cleburne, TX 76031, P: 817-447-9047, F: 817-717-8461
Binoculars; Custom Manufacturer; Gun Parts/Gunsmithing; Hunting Accessories; Scopes, Sights & Accessories

Sunbuster/Gustbuster, 1966-B Broadhollow Rd., Farmingdale, NY 11735, P: 888-487-8287, F: 631-777-4320, www.sunbuster.info
Clay Targets; Custom Manufacturing; Eyewear; Hunting Accessories; Law Enforcement; Shooting Range Equipment; Sports Accessories; Wholesaler/Distributor

Sunlite Science & Technology, Inc., 345 N. Iowa St., Lawrence, KS 66044, P: 785-832-8818, F: 913-273-1888, www.powerledlighting.com
Camping; Hunting Accessories; Law Enforcement; Lighting Products; Sports Accessories; Survival Kits/First Aid; Tours/Travel; Training & Safety Equipment

Sunny Hill Enterprises, Inc., W. 1015 Cty. HHH, Chilton, WI 53014, P: 920-898-4707, F: 920-898-4749, www.sunny-hill.com
Custom Manufacturing; Firearms; Gun Barrels; Gun Parts/Gunsmithing; Law Enforcement; Magazines, Cartridge

Super Seer Corp., P.O. Box 700, Evergreen, CO 80437, P: 800-645-1285, F: 303-674-8540, www.superseer.com
Law Enforcement

Super Six Classic, LLC, 635 Hilltop Trail W, Fort Atkinson, WI 53538, P: 920-568-8299, F: 920-568-8259
Firearms

Superior Arms, 836 Weaver Blvd., Wapello, IA 52653, P: 319-523-2016, F: 319-527-0188, www.superiorarms.com
Firearms

Superior Concepts, Inc., 10791 Oak St., P.O. Box 465, Donald, OR 97020, P: 503-922-0488, F: 503-922-2236, www.laserstock.com
Gun Grips & Stocks; Gun Parts/Gunsmithing; Hunting Accessories; Magazines, Cartridge; Scopes, Sights & Accessories

Sure Site, Inc., 351 Dion St., P.O. Box 335, Emmett, ID 83617, P: 800-627-1576, F: 208-365-6944, www.suresiteinc.com
Shooting Range Equipment; Targets

SureFire, LLC, 18300 Mount Baldy Circle, Fountain Valley, CA 92708, P: 800-828-8809, F: 714-545-9537, www.surefire.com
Knives/Knife Cases; Lighting Products; Scopes, Sights & Accessories

Surgeon Rifles, 48955 Moccasin Trail Rd., Prague, OK 74864, P: 405-567-0183, F: 405-567-0250, www.surgeonrifles.com
Firearms; Gun Parts/Gunsmithing; Law Enforcement

Survival Armor, Inc., 13881 Plantation Rd., International Center I, Suite 8, Ft. Myers, FL 33912, P: 866-868-5001, F: 239-210-0898, www.survivalarmor.com
Law Enforcement; Training & Safety Equipment

Survival Corps, Ltd., Ostashkovskoe Shosse, house 48a, Borodino, Moscow Obl, Mitishinski Region, 141031, RUSSIAN FEDERATION, P: 011 74952257985, F: 011 74952257986, www.survivalcorps.ru
Bags & Equipment Cases; Camouflage; Holsters; Law Enforcement; Outfitter

Swany America Corp., 115 Corporate Dr., Johnstown, NY 12095, P: 518-725-3333, F: 518-725-2026, www.swanyhunting.com
Gloves, Mitts, Hats

Swarovski Optik North America, 2 Slater Rd., Cranston, RI 02920, P: 800-426-3089, F: 401-734-5888, www.swarovskioptik.com
Bags & Equipment Cases; Binoculars; Knives/Knife Cases; Scopes, Sights & Accessories; Telescopes; Wholesaler/Distributor

SWAT Magazine, 5011 N. Ocean Blvd., Suite 5, Ocean Ridge, FL 33435, P: 800-665-7928, F: 561-276-0895, www.swatmag.com
Books/Industry Publications; Law Enforcement; Online Services; Retailer Services; Training & Safety Equipment

Swift Bullet Co., 201 Main St., P.O. Box 27, Quinter, KS 67752, P: 785-754-3959, F: 785-754-2359, www.swiftbullets.com
Ammunition

Switch Pack, LLC, 302 NW 4th St., Grants Pass, OR 97526, P: 541-479-3919, F: 541-474-4573
Backpacking; Blinds; Hunting Accessories; Retailer Services; Sports Accessories; Wholesaler/Distributor

SWR Manufacturing, LLC, P.O. Box 841, Pickens, SC 29671, P: 864-850-3579, F: 864-751-2823, www.swrmfg.com
Firearms; Hearing Protection; Law Enforcement; Recoil Protection Devices & Services; Training & Safety Equipment

Sylvansport, 10771 Greenville Hwy., Cedar Mountain, NC 28718, P: 828-883-4292, F: 828-883-4817, www.sylvansport.com
Backpacking; Camping; Hunting Accessories; Sports Accessories; Tours/Travel; Vehicles, Utility & Rec

Systema Co., 5542 S. Integrity Ln., Fort Mohave, AZ 86426, P: 877-884-0909, F: 267-222-4787, www.systema-engineering.com
Airguns; Airsoft; Law Enforcement; Training & Safety Equipment

Szco Supplies, Inc., 2713 Merchant Dr., P.O. Box 6353, Baltimore, MD 21230, P: 800-232-6998, F: 410-368-9366, www.szco.com
Camping; Custom Manufacturing; Cutlery; Hunting Accessories; Knives/Knife Cases; Pet Supplies; Sharpeners; Wholesaler/Distributor

T

T.Z. Case, 1786 Curtiss Ct., La Verne, CA 91750, P: 888-892-2737, F: 909-392-8406, www.tzcase.com
Airguns; Archery; Custom Manufacturing; Firearms; Gun Cases; Hunting Accessories

Tac Force, 8653 Garvey Ave., Suite 202, Rosemead, CA 91733, P: 626-453-8377, F: 626-453-8378, www.tac-force.com
Backpacking; Bags & Equipment Cases; Gloves, Mitts, Hats; Gun Cases; Holsters; Law Enforcement; Paintball Accessories

Tac Wear, Inc., 700 Progress Ave., Suite 7, Toronto, Ontario M1H 2Z7, CANADA, P: 866-TAC-WEAR, F: 416-289-1522, www.tacwear.com
Gloves, Mitts, Hats; Hunting Accessories; Law Enforcement; Men & Women's Clothing; Sports Accessories; Training & Safety Equipment

Tactical & Survival Specialties, Inc. (TSSI), 3900 Early Rd., P.O. Box 1890, Harrisonburg, VA 22801, P: 877-535-8774, F: 540-434-7796, www.tacsurv.com
Bags & Equipment Cases; Custom Manufacturing; Knives/Knife Cases; Law Enforcement; Men & Women's Clothing; Survival Kits/First Aid; Training & Safety Equipment; Wholesaler/Distributor

Tactical Assault Gear (TAG), 1330 30th St., Suite A, San Diego, CA 92154, P: 888-899-1199, F: 619-628-0126, www.tacticalassaultgear.com
Bags & Equipment Cases; Holsters; Men's Clothing

Tactical Command Industries, Inc., 2101 W. Tenth St., Suite G, Antioch, CA 94509, P: 888-990-1600, F: 925-756-7977, www.tacticalcommand.com
Custom Manufacturing; Hearing Protection; Law Enforcement; Training & Safety Equipment; Two-Way Radios

Tactical Electronics/SPA Defense, P.O. Box 152, Broken Arrow, OK 74013, P: 866-541-7996, F: 918-249-8328, www.tacticalelectronics.com
Photographic Equipment

Tactical Innovations, Inc., 345 Sunrise Rd., Bonners Ferry, ID 83805, P: 208-267-1585, F: 208-267-1597, www.tacticalinc.com
Firearms; Gun Barrels; Gun Grips & Stocks; Holsters; Law Enforcement; Magazines, Cartridge; Wholesaler/Distributor

Tactical Medical Solutions, Inc., 614 Pinehollow Dr., Anderson, SC 29621, P: 888-TACMED1, F: 864-224-0064
Law Enforcement; Survival Kits/First Aid; Training & Safety Equipment

Tactical Operations Products, 20972 SW Meadow Way, Tualatin, OR 97062, P: 503-638-9873, F: 503-638-0524, www.tacoproducts.com
Airsoft; Backpacking; Bags & Equipment Cases; Camping; Law Enforcement; Lighting Products; Paintball Accessories

Tactical Products Group, Inc., 755 NW 17th Ave., Suite 108, Delray Beach, FL 33445, P: 866-9-TACPRO, F: 561-265-4061, www.tacprogroup.com
Export/Import Specialists; Footwear; Gun Cases; Holsters; Knives/Knife Cases; Law Enforcement; Men's Clothing; Wholesaler/Distributor

Tactical Rifles, 19250 Hwy. 301, Dade City, FL 33523, P: 352-999-0599, F: 352-567-9825, www.tacticalrifles.net
Firearms

Tactical Solutions, 2181 Commerce Ave., Boise, ID 83705, P: 866-333-9901, F: 208-333-9909, www.tacticalsol.com
Firearms; Gun Barrels; Gun Grips & Stocks; Gun Parts/Gunsmithing; Scopes, Sights & Accessories; Wholesaler/Distributor

TacticalTECH1, 251 Beulah Church Rd., Carrollton, GA 30117, P: 800-334-3368, F: 770-832-1676
Bags & Equipment Cases; Eyewear; Law Enforcement; Lighting Products; Training & Safety Equipment

TAG Safari Clothes, 1022 Wirt Rd., Suite 302, Houston, TX 77055, P: 800-TAG-2703, F: 713-688-6806, www.tagsafari.com
Camping; Footwear; Gun Cases; Leathergoods; Men & Women's Clothing; Online Services; Wholesaler/Distributor

Tagua Gun Leather, 3750 NW 28th St., Miami, FL 33142, P: 866-678-2482, F: 866-678-2482, www.taguagunleather.com
Firearms; Holsters; Hunting Accessories; Law Enforcement; Leathergoods; Wholesaler/Distributor

Talley Manufacturing, Inc., 9183 Old Number Six Hwy., P.O. Box 369, Santee, SC 29142, P: 803-854-5700, F: 803-854-9315, www.talleyrings.com
Black Powder Accessories; Custom Manufacturing; Gun Parts/Gunsmithing; Hunting Accessories; Scopes, Sights & Accessories; Sports Accessories

Tandy Brands Outdoors, 107 W. Gonzales St., Yoakum, TX 77995, P: 800-331-9092, F: 361-293-9127, www.tandybrands.com
Bags & Equipment Cases; Custom Manufacturing; Hunting Accessories; Knives/Knife Cases; Leathergoods; Shooting Range Equipment; Sports Accessories

TangoDown, Inc., 1588 Arrow Hwy., Unit F, La Verne, CA 91750-5334, P: 909-392-4757, F: 909-392-4802, www.tangodown.com
Gun Grips & Stocks; Law Enforcement; Lighting Products; Magazines, Cartridge; Scopes, Sights & Accessories; Targets

TAPCO, Inc.,3615 Kennesaw N. Industrial Pkwy., P.O. Box 2408, Kennesaw, GA 30156-9138, P: 800-554-1445, F: 800-226-1662, www.tapco.com
Custom Manufacturing; Firearms Maintenance Equipment; Gun Grips & Stocks; Gun Parts/Gunsmithing; Law Enforcement; Magazines, Cartridge; Recoil Protection Devices & Services; Wholesaler/Distributor

Target Shooting, Inc., 1110 First Ave. SE, Watertown, SD 57201, P: 800-611-2164, F: 605-882-8840, www.targetshooting.com
Scopes, Sights & Accessories; Shooting Range Equipment

Tasco/Bushnell Outdoor Products, 9400 Cody, Overland Park, KS 66214, P: 800-221-9035, F: 800-548-0446, www.tasco.com
Binoculars; Scopes, Sights & Accessories; Telescopes

Taser International, 1700 N. 85th St., Scottsdale, AZ 85255, P: 800-978-2737, F: 480-991-0791, www.taser.com
Law Enforcement

Task Holsters, 2520 SW 22nd St., Suite 2-186, Miami, FL 33145, P: 305-335-8647, F: 305-858-9618, www.taskholsters.com
Bags & Equipment Cases; Export/Import Specialists; Gun Cases; Holsters; Hunting Accessories; Law Enforcement; Leathergoods; Wholesaler/Distributor

Taurus International Manufacturing, Inc., 16175 NW 49th Ave., Miami, FL 33014, P: 800-327-3776, F: 305-623-7506, www.taurususa.com
Firearms

Taylor Brands, LLC/Imperial Schrade & Smith & Wesson Cutting Tools, 1043 Fordtown Rd., Kingsport, TN 37663, P: 800-251-0254, F: 423-247-5371, www.taylorbrandsllc.com
Backpacking; Camping; Cutlery; Hunting Accessories; Knives/Knife Cases; Law Enforcement

Taylor's & Co., Inc., 304 Lenoir Dr., Winchester, VA 22603, P: 800-655-5814, F: 540-722-2018, www.taylorsfirearms.com
Black Powder Accessories; Firearms; Firearms Maintenance Equipment; Gun Parts/Gunsmithing; Wholesaler/Distributor

Team Realtree®, P.O. Box 9638, Columbus, GA 31908, P: 800-992-9968, F: 706-569-9346, www.realtree.com
Camouflage; Men & Women's Clothing

Team SD/TSD Sports, 901 S. Fremont Ave., Suite 218, Alhambra, CA 91803, P: 626-281-0979, F: 626-281-0323, www.airsofttsd.com
Airguns; Airsoft; Paintball Guns & Accessories; Scopes, Sights & Accessories; Sports Accessories; Training & Safety Equipment; Wholesaler/Distributor

Team Wendy, 17000 St. Clair Ave., Bldg. 1, Cleveland, OH 44110, P: 877-700-5544, F: 216-738-2510, www.teamwendy.com
Custom Manufacturing; Hunting Accessories; Law Enforcement; Sports Accessories; Training & Safety Equipment

TEARepair, Inc., 2200 Knight Rd., Bldg. 2, P.O. Box 1879, Land O'Lakes, FL 34639, P: 800-937-3716, F: 813-996-4523, www.tear-aid.com
Camping; Hunting Accessories; Retail Packaging; Sports Accessories; Survival Kits/First Aid; Wholesaler/Distributor

Tech Mix, Inc., 740 Bowman St., Stewart, MN 55385, P: 877-466-6455, F: 320-562-2125, www.techmixinc.com
Pet Supplies

Technoframes, Via Aldo Moro 6, Scanzorosciate Bergamo, 24020, ITALY, P: 866-246-1095, F: 011 39035668328, www.technoframes.com
Ammunition; Bags & Equipment Cases; Gun Cases; Hunting Accessories; Magazines, Cartridge; Reloading; Shooting Range Equipment

Tecomate Seed, 33477 Hwy. 99E, Tangent, OR 97389, P: 800-547-4101, F: 541-926-9435, www.tecomateseed.com
Wildlife Management

Teijin Aramid USA, Inc., 801-F Blacklawn Rd., Conyers, GA 30012, P: 800-451-6586, F: 770-929-8138, www.teijinaramid.com
Law Enforcement

Television Equipment Associates, Inc., 16 Mount Ebo Rd. S, P.O. Box 404, Brewster, NY 10509, P: 310-457-7401, F: 310-457-0023, www.swatheadsets.com
Law Enforcement

Temco Communications, Inc., 13 Chipping Campden Dr., South Barrington, IL 60010, P: 847-359-3277, F: 847-359-3743, www.temcom.net
Hearing Protection; Law Enforcement; Two-Way Radios

Ten-X Ammunition, Inc., 5650 Arrow Hwy., Montclair, CA 91763, P: 909-605-1617, F: 909-605-2844, www.tenxammo.com
Ammunition; Custom Manufacturing; Law Enforcement; Reloading; Training & Safety Equipment; Wholesaler/Distributor

TenPoint Crossbow Technologies, 1325 Waterloo Rd., Suffield, OH 44260, P: 800-548-6837, F: 330-628-0999, www.tenpointcrossbows.com
Archery; Crossbows & Accessories

Teton Grill Co., 865 Xenium Lane N, Plymouth, MN 55441, P: 877-838-6643, F: 763-249-6385, www.tetongrills.com
Cooking Equipment/Accessories; Custom Manufacturing; Cutlery; Knives/Knife Cases

Tetra® Gun Care, 8 Vreeland Rd., Florham Park, NJ 07932, P: 973-443-0004, F: 973-443-0263, www.tetraguncare.com
Firearms Maintenance Equipment; Gun Parts/Gunsmithing; Lubricants

Texas Hunt Co., P.O. Box 10, Monahans, TX 79756, P: 888-894-8682, F: 432-943-5565, www.texashuntco.com
Bags & Equipment Cases; Hunting Accessories; Knives/Knife Cases; Vehicles, Utility & Rec; Wholesaler/Distributor

Texsport, P.O. Box 55326, Houston, TX 77255, P: 800-231-1402, F: 713-468-1535, www.texsport.com
Backpacking; Bags & Equipment Cases; Camouflage; Camping; Compasses; Cooking Equipment/Accessories; Lighting Products; Wholesaler/Distributor

Thermacell/The Schawbel Corp., 100 Crosby Dr., Suite 102, Bedford, MA 01730, P: 866-753-3837, F: 781-541-6007, www.thermacell.com
Archery; Backpacking; Camouflage; Camping; Crossbows & Accessories; Holsters; Hunting Accessories; Scents & Lures

Thermore, 6124 Shady Lane SE, Olympia, WA 98503, P: 800-871-6563, www.thermore.com
Gloves, Mitts, Hats; Men & Women's Clothing; Pet Supplies

Thompson/Center Arms, A Smith & Wesson Co., P.O. Box 5002, Rochester, NH 01104, P: 603-332-2333, F: 603-332-5133, www.tcarms.com
Black Powder Accessories; Black Powder/Smokeless Powder; Firearms; Gun Barrels; Hunting Accessories

Thorogood Shoes, 108 S. Polk St., Merrill, WI 54452, P: 800-826-0002, F: 800-569-6817, www.weinbrennerusa.com
Footwear; Law Enforcement; Leathergoods; Men & Women's Clothing

Thunderbolt Customs, Inc., 7296 S. Section Line Rd., Delaware, OH 43015, P: 740-917-9135, www.thunderboltcustoms.com
Backpacking; Black Powder Accessories; Camping; Firearms; Hunting Accessories; Pet Supplies; Scopes, Sights & Accessories; Shooting Range Accessories

Tiberius Arms, 2717 W. Ferguson Rd., Fort Wayne, IN 46809, P: 888-982-2842, F: 260-572-2210, www.tiberiusarms.com
Airguns; Law Enforcement; Paintball Guns & Accessories; Training & Safety Equipment

Tiger-Vac, Inc., 73 SW 12 Ave., Bldg. 1, Suite 7, Dania, FL 33004, P: 800-668-4437, F: 954-925-3626, www.tiger-vac.com
Shooting Range Equipment; Training & Safety Equipment

Timney Manufacturing, Inc., 3940 W. Clarendon Ave., Phoenix, AZ 85019, P: 866-4TIMNEY, F: 602-241-0361, www.timneytriggers.com
Firearms Maintenance Equipment; Gun Locks; Gun Parts/Gunsmithing

Tinks, 10157 Industrial Dr., Covington, GA 30014, P: 800-624-5988, F: 678-342-9973, www.tinks69.com
Archery; Hunting Accessories; Scents & Lures; Videos

Tisas-Trabzon Gun Industry Corp., Degol Cad. No: 13-1 Tandogan Ankara, 06580, TURKEY, P: 011 903122137509, F: 011 903122138570, www.trabzonsilah.com
Firearms; Gun Barrels

TMB Designs, Unit 11, Highgrove Farm Ind Est Pinvin, Pershore, Worchestershire WR10 2LF, UNITED KINGDOM, P: 011 441905840022, F: 011 441905850022, www.cartridgedisplays.com
Ammunition; Custom Manufacturing; Emblems & Decals; Hunting Accessories; Outdoor Art, Jewelry, Sculpture; Sports Accessories

Toadbak, Inc., P.O. Box 18097, Knoxville, TN 37928-8097, P: 865-548-1283
Camouflage; Men's Clothing

Tony's Custom Uppers & Parts, P.O. Box 252, Delta, OH 43515, P: 419-822-9578, F: 419-822-9578
Custom Manufacturing; Gun Barrels; Gun Parts/Gunsmithing; Wholesaler/Distributor

Tool Logic, Inc., 2290 Eastman Ave., Suite 109, Ventura, CA 93003, P: 800-483-8422, F: 805-339-9712, www.toollogic.com
Backpacking; Compasses; Cutlery; Knives/Knife Cases; Lighting Products; Sports Accessories; Survival Kits/First Aid

Top Brass Tackle/dba Cypress Knees Publishing, P.O. Box 209, Starkville, MS 39760, P: 662-323-1559, F: 662-323-7466, www.outdooryouthadventures.com
Books/Industry Publications

TOPS Knives, P.O. Box 2544, Idaho Falls, ID 82403, P: 208-542-0113, F: 208-552-2945, www.topsknives.com
Backpacking; Custom Manufacturing; Hunting Accessories; Knives/Knife Cases; Law Enforcement; Leathergoods; Men's Clothing; Survival Kits/First Aid

Torel, 107 W. Gonzales St., Yoakum, TX 77995, P: 800-331-9092, F: 361-293-9127, www.tandybrands.com
Bags & Equipment Cases; Custom Manufacturing; Hunting Accessories; Knives/Knife Cases;

Leathergoods; Shooting Range Equipment; Sports Accessories

Torrey Pines Logic, Inc., 12651 High Bluff Dr., Suite 100, San Diego, CA 92130, P: 858-755-4549, F: 858-350-0007, www.tplogic.com
Binoculars; Law Enforcement; Scopes, Sights & Accessories; Telescopes

Traditions Performance Firearms, 1375 Boston Post Rd., P.O. Box 776, Old Saybrook, CT 06475-0776, P: 800-526-9556, F: 860-388-4657, www.traditionsfirearms.com
Black Powder Accessories; Firearms; Hunting Accessories; Scopes, Sights & Accessories

Transarms Handels GmbH & Co. KG, 6 Im Winkel, Worms, Rheinland Pfalz 67547, GERMANY, P: 011 490624197770, F: 011 4906241977777
Ammunition; Export/Import Specialists; Firearms; Firearms Maintenance Equipment; Gun Barrels; Gun Parts/Gunsmithing; Law Enforcement; Magazines, Cartridge

Traser H3 Watches, 2930 Domingo Ave., Suite 159, Berkeley, CA 94705, P: 510-479-7523, F: 510-479-7532, www.traserusa.com
Custom Manufacturing; Export/Import Specialists; Law Enforcement; Lighting Products; Men's Clothing; Training & Safety Equipment; Wholesaler/Distributor

Tree Talon, 148 Main St., P.O. Box 1370, Bucksport, ME 04416, P: 207-469-1900, F: 207-469-6121, www.treetalon.com
Hunting Accessories

Tri-Tronics, Inc., 1705 S. Research Loop, Tucson, AZ 85710, P: 800-765-2275, F: 800-320-3538, www.tritronics.com
Hunting Accessories; Pet Supplies; Sports Accessories

Trijicon, Inc., 49385 Shafer Ave., P.O. Box 930059, Wixom, MI 48393, P: 800-338-0563, F: 248-960-7725, www.trijicon.com
Scopes, Sights & Accessories

Triple K Manufacturing Co., Inc., 2222 Commercial St., San Diego, CA 92113, P: 800-521-5062, F: 877-486-6247, www.triplek.com
Black Powder Accessories; Gun Parts/Gunsmithing; Holsters; Hunting Accessories; Law Enforcement; Leathergoods; Magazines, Cartridge; Pet Supplies

Tristar Sporting Arms, Ltd., 1816 Linn St., North Kansas City, MO 64116, P: 816-421-1400, F: 816-421-4182, www.tristarsporting.com
Export/Import Specialists; Firearms

Trophy Animal Health Care, 1217 W. 12th St., Kansas City, MO 64101, P: 800-821-7925, F: 816-474-0462, www.trophyanimalcare.com
Pet Supplies

Troy Industries, Inc., 128 Myron St., West Springfield, MA 01089, P: 866-788-6412, F: 413-383-0339, www.troyind.com
Firearms; Gun Grips & Stocks; Gun Parts/Gunsmithing; Law Enforcement; Scopes, Sights & Accessories

Tru Hone Corp., 1721 NE 19th Ave., Ocala, FL 34470, P: 800-237-4663, F: 352-622-9180, www.truhone.com
Sharpeners

TruckVault, Inc., 211 Township St., P.O. Box 734, Sedro Woolley, WA 98284, P: 800-967-8107, F: 800-621-4287, www.truckvault.com
Custom Manufacturing; Gun Cabinets/Racks/Safes; Hunting Accessories; Law Enforcement; Pet Supplies; Sports Accessories; Training & Safety Equipment

True North Tactical, 500 N. Birdneck Rd., Suite 200, Virginia Beach, VA 23451, P: 800-TNT-1478, F: 757-491-9652, www.truenorthtactical.com
Backpacking; Bags & Equipment Cases; Gun Cases; Holsters; Law Enforcement; Wholesaler/Distributor

TrueTimber Outdoors, 150 Accurate Way, Inman, SC 29349, P: 864-472-1720, F: 864-472-1834, www.truetimber.com
Bags & Equipment Cases; Blinds; Camouflage; Footwear; Gloves, Mitts, Hats; Hunting Accessories; Men & Women's Clothing

Truglo, Inc., 710 Presidential Dr., Richardson, TX 75081, P: 888-8-TRUGLO, F: 972-774-0323, www.truglo.com
Archery; Binoculars; Black Powder Accessories; Crossbows & Accessories; Hunting Accessories; Law Enforcement; Scopes, Sights & Accessories; Watches

Trulock Tool, 113 Drayton St. NW, P.O. Box 530, Whigham, GA 39897, P: 800-293-9402, F: 229-762-4050, www.trulockchokes.com
Ammunition; Custom Manufacturing; Firearms Maintenance Equipment; Gun Parts/Gunsmithing; Hunting Accessories; Recoil Protection Devices & Services; Sports Accessories; Wholesaler/Distributor

Trumark Mfg. Co., Inc., 1835 38th St., Boulder, CO 80301, P: 800-878-6272, F: 303-442-1380, www.slingshots.com
Archery; Backpacking; Crossbows & Accessories; Hunting Accessories; Sports Accessories

Tuff-N-Lite, 325 Spencer Rd., Conover, NC 28613, P: 877-883-3654, F: 828-322-7881, www.tuffnlite.com
Gloves, Mitts, Hats; Men & Women's Clothing

TufForce, 1734 Ranier Blvd., Canton, MI 48187, P: 800-382-7989, F: 888-686-0373, www.tufforce.com
Bags & Equipment Cases; Gun Cases; Gun Grips & Stocks; Holsters; Hunting Accessories; Law Enforcement; Scopes, Sights & Accessories; Wholesaler/Distributor

Tunilik Adventure, 11600 Philippe Panneton, Montreal, Quebec H1E 4G4, CANADA, P: 866-648-1595, F: 514-648-1431, www.adventuretunilik.com
Outfitter

TurtleSkin Protective Products, 301 Turnpike Rd., New Ipswich, NH 03071, P: 888-477-4675, F: 603-291-1119, www.turtleskin.com
Gloves, Mitts, Hats; Hunting Accessories; Law Enforcement; Men & Women's Clothing; Sports Accessories

U

U.S. Armament Corp., 121 Valley View Dr., Ephrata, PA 17522, P: 717-721-4570, F: 717-738-4890, www.usarmamentcorp.com
Firearms

U.S. Armor Corp., 16433 Valley View Ave., Cerritos, CA 90703, P: 800-443-9798, F: 562-207-4238, www.usarmor.com
Law Enforcement; Training & Safety Equipment

U.S. Explosive Storage, LLC, 355 Industrial Park Dr., Boone, NC 28607, P: 877-233-1481, F: 800-295-1653, www.usexplosive.com
Custom Manufacturing; Firearms Maintenance Equipment; Gun Cabinets/Racks/Safes; Law Enforcement; Magazines, Cartridge; Training & Safety Equipment

U.S. Fire-Arms Mfg. Co., Inc., P.O. Box 1901, Hartford, CT 06144-1901, P: 860-296-7441, F: 860-296-7688, www.usfirearms.com
Firearms; Gun Parts/Gunsmithing

U.S. Optics, Inc., 150 Arovista Circle, Brea, CA 92821, P: 714-582-1956, F: 714-582-1959, www.usoptics.com
Custom Manufacturing; Law Enforcement; Scopes, Sights & Accessories

U.S. Tactical Supply, Inc., 939 Pacific Blvd. SE, Albany, OR 97321, P: 877-928-8645, F: 541-791-2965, www.ustacticalsupply.com
Bags & Equipment Cases; Gun Parts/Gunsmithing; Holsters; Hunting Accessories; Knives/Knife Cases; Law Enforcement; Scopes, Sights & Accessories; Wholesaler/Distributor

Uberti, A., 17603 Indian Head Hwy., Accokeek, MD 20607-2501, P: 800-264-4962, F: 301-283-6988, www.uberti.com
Firearms

Ultimate Hunter, Inc., 610 Prather, P.O. Box 542, Maryville, MO 64468, P: 660-562-3838, F: 660-582-4377, www.ambushlures.com
Decoys

Ultimate Survival Technologies, LLC, 14428 167th Ave. SE, Monroe, WA 98272, P: 866-479-7994, F: 206-965-9659, www.ultimatesurvival.com
Backpacking; Bags & Equipment Cases; Camping; Hunting Accessories; Law Enforcement; Men's Clothing; Sports Accessories; Survival Kits/First Aid

Ultra Dot Distribution, 6304 Riverside Dr., P.O. Box 362, Yankeetown, FL, 34498, P: 352-447-2255, F: 352-447-2266, www.ultradotusa.com
Scopes, Sights & Accessories

Ultra Lift Corp., 475 Stockton Ave., Unit E, San Jose, CA 95126, P: 800-346-3057, F: 408-297-1199, www.ultralift.com/safes.html
Custom Manufacturing; Gun Cabinets/Racks/Safes; Gun Cases; Retailer Services; Sports Accessories; Training & Safety Equipment

Ultra Paws, 12324 Little Pine Rd. SW, Brainerd, MN 56401, P: 800-355-5575, F: 218-855-6977, www.ultrapaws.com
Backpacking; Hunting Accessories; Law Enforcement; Outfitter; Pet Supplies; Survival Kits/First Aid; Training & Safety Equipment; Wholesaler/Distributor

Ultramax Ammunition/Wideview Scope Mount, 2112 Elk Vale Rd., Rapid City, SD 57701, P: 800-345-5852, F: 605-342-8727, www.ultramaxammunition.com
Ammunition

Ultrec Engineered Products, LLC, 860 Maple Ridge Ln., Brookfield, WI 53045, P: 262-821-2023, F: 262-821-1156, www.ultrec.com

Backpacking; Binoculars; Firearms; Hunting Accessories; Law Enforcement; Photographic Equipment; Shooting Range Equipment; Training & Safety Equipment

Umarex/Umarex, USA/RAM–Real Action Marker, 6007 S. 29th St., Fort Smith, AR 72908, P: 479-646-4210, F: 479-646-4206, www.umarexusa.com, www.trainingumarexusa.com
Airguns; Airsoft; Ammunition; Firearms; Law Enforcement; Paintball Guns; Scopes, Sights & Accessories; Training & Safety Equipment

Uncle Mike's/Bushnell Outdoor Accessories, 9200 Cody St., Overland Park, KS 66214, P: 800-423-3537, F: 800-548-0446, www.unclemikes.com
Bags & Equipment Cases; Gloves, Mitts, Hats; Gun Cases; Holsters; Hunting Accessories

Under Armour Performance, 1020 Hull St., Third Floor, Baltimore, MD 21230, P: 888-427-6687, F: 410-234-1027, www.underarmour.com
Bags & Equipment Cases; Camouflage; Gloves, Mitts, Hats; Law Enforcement; Men & Women's Clothing; Outfitter; Sports Accessories

United Cutlery Corp., 201 Plantation Oak Dr., Thomasville, GA 31792, P: 800-548-0835, F: 229-551-0182, www.unitedcutlery.com
Camping; Compasses; Custom Manufacturing; Cutlery; Knives/Knife Cases; Law Enforcement; Sharpeners; Wholesaler/Distributor

United Shield International, 1606 Barlow St., Suite 1, Traverse City, MI 49686, P: 800-705-9153, F: 231-933-5368, www.unitedshield.net
Law Enforcement

United Weavers of America, Inc., 3562 Dug Gap Rd. SW, Dalton, GA 30721, P: 800-241-5754, F: 706-226-8844, www.unitedweavers.net
Home Furnishings

Universal Power Group, 1720 Hayden, Carrollton, TX 75006, P: 866-892-1122, F: 469-892-1123, www.upgi.com, www.deerfeeder.com
Blinds; Camping; Decoys; Export/Import Specialists; Feeder Equipment; Hunting Accessories; Lighting Products; Wholesaler/Distributor

Urban–E.R.T. Slings, LLC, P.O. Box 429, Clayton, IN 46118, P: 317-223-6509, F: 317-539-2710, www.urbanertslings.com
Firearms; Hunting Accessories; Law Enforcement; Paintball Accessories

US Night Vision Corp., 3845 Atherton Rd., Suite 9, Rocklin, CA 95765, P: 800-500-4020, F: 916-663-5986, www.usnightvision.com
Binoculars; Hunting Accessories; Law Enforcement; Paintball Accessories; Scopes, Sights & Accessories; Sports Accessories; Training & Safety Equipment; Wholesaler/Distributor

US Peacekeeper Products, Inc., W245, N5570 Corporate Circle, Sussex, WI 53089, P: 800-428-0800, F: 262-246-4845, uspeacekeeper.com
Bags & Equipment Cases; Gloves, Mitts, Hats; Hunting Accessories; Men & Women's Clothing

Uselton Arms, 390 Southwinds Dr., Franklin, TN 37064, P: 615-595-2255, F: 615-595-2254, www.useltonarms.com
Custom Manufacturing; Firearms; Gun Barrels; Gun Grips & Stocks; Gun Parts/Gunsmithing; Law Enforcement

V

V.H. Blackinton & Co., Inc., 221 John Dietsch Blvd., P.O. Box 1300, Attleboro Falls, MA 02763, P: 800-699-4436, F: 508-695-5349, www.blackinton.com
Custom Manufacturing; Emblems & Decals; Law Enforcement

V-Line Industries, 370 Easy St., Simi Valley, CA 93065, P: 805-520-4987, F: 805-520-6470, www.vlineind.com
Gun Cabinets; Racks/Safes; Gun Cases

Valdada Optics, P.O. Box 270095, Littleton, CO 80127, P: 303-979-4578, F: 303-979-0256, www.valdada.com
Binoculars; Compasses; Custom Manufacturing; Law Enforcement; Photographic Equipment; Scopes, Sights & Accessories; Telescopes; Wholesaler/Distributor

Valiant Armoury, 3000 Grapevine Mills Pkwy., Suite 101, Grapevine, TX 76051, P: 877-796-7374, F: 972-539-9351, www.valliantarmourysswords.com
Wholesaler/Distributor

Valley Operational Wear, LLC/OP Wear Armor, P.O. Box 9415, Knoxville, TN 37940, P: 865-259-6248, F: 865-259-6255
Law Enforcement

Valley Outdoors, P.O. Box 108, Fort Valley, GA 31030, P: 478-397-0531, F: 478-825-3398, www.valleyoutdoors.us
Outfitter

Valor Corp., 1001 Sawgrass Corporate Pkwy., Sunrise, FL 33323, P: 800-899-VALOR, F: 866-248-9594, www.valorcorp.com

Airguns; Ammunition; Cutlery; Firearms; Knives/Knife Cases; Law Enforcement; Magazines, Cartridge; Wholesaler/Distributor

Vang Comp Systems, 400 W. Butterfield Rd., Chino Valley, AZ 86323, P: 928-636-8455, F: 928-636-1538, www.vangcomp.com
Firearms; Gun Barrels; Gun Parts/Gunsmithing

Vanguard USA, Inc., 9157 E. M-36, Whitmore Lake, MI 48189, P: 800-875-3322, F: 888-426-7008, www.vanguardworld.com
Archery; Bags & Equipment Cases; Binoculars; Gun Cases; Hunting Accessories; Photographic Equipment; Scopes, Sights & Accessories; Shooting Range Equipment

Vector Optics, 3964 Callan Blvd., South San Francisco, CA 94080, P: 415-632-7089, CHINA, P: 011 862154040649, www.vectoroptics.com
Scopes, Sights & Accessories; Sports Accessories; Wholesaler/Distributor

Vega Holster srl, Via Di Mezzo 31 Z.I., Calcinaia (PI), 56031, ITALY, P: 011 390587489190, F: 011 390587489901, www.vegaholster.com
Bags & Equipment Cases; Gun Cases; Holsters; Hunting Accessories; Law Enforcement; Leathergoods; Shooting Range Equipment

Vega Silah Sanayi, Ltd., Tigcilar Sokak No. 1 Mercan, Eminonu, Istanbul, 34450, TURKEY, P: 011 902125200103, F: 011 902125120879
Firearms

Verney-Carron SA, 54 Blvd. Thiers, Boite Postale 72, St. Etienne Cedex 1, 42002, FRANCE, P: 011 33477791500, F: 011 33477790702, www.verney-carron.com
Custom Manufacturing; Firearms; Gun Barrels; Law Enforcement; Wholesaler/Distibutor

Versatile Rack Co., 5232 Alcoa Ave., Vernon, CA 90058, P: 323-588-0137, F: 323-588-5067, www.versatilegunrack.com
Firearms Maintenance Equipment; Gun Cabinets/Racks/Safes; Gun Cases; Gun Locks; Hunting Accessories; Reloading; Shooting Range Equipment; Sports Accessories

VibraShine, Inc./Leaf River Outdoor Products, 113 Fellowship Rd., P.O. Box 557, Taylorsville, MS 39168, P: 601-785-9854, F: 601-785-9874, www.myleafriver.com
Firearms Maintenance Equipment; Hunting Accessories; Photographic Equipment; Reloading

Victorinox Swiss Army, 7 Victoria Dr., Monroe, CT 06468, P: 800-243-4032, F: 800-243-4006, www.swissarmy.com
Camping; Cutlery; Hunting Accessories; Knives/Knife Cases; Lighting Products; Sports Accessories

Vintage Editions, Inc., 88 Buff Ln., Taylorsville, NC 28681, P: 800-662-8965, F: 828-632-4187, www.vintageeditions.com
Custom Manufacturing; Home Furnishings; Hunting Accessories; Pet Supplies; Sports Accessories

Virginia Blade, 5177 Boonsboro Rd., Lynchburg, VA 24503, P: 434-384-1282, F: 434-384-4541

Viridian Green Laser Sights/Laser Aiming Systems Corp., 12637 Sable Dr., Burnsville, MN 55337, P: 800-990-9390, F: 952-882-6227, www.viridiangreenlaser.com
Holsters; Law Enforcement; Lighting Products; Scopes, Sights & Accessories

Vixen Optics, 1010 Calle Cordillera, Suite 106, San Clemente, CA 92673, P: 949-429-6363, F: 949-429-6826, www.vixenoptics.com
Binoculars; Scopes, Sights & Accessories; Telescopes; Wholesaler/Distributor

Vltor Weapon Systems, 3735 N. Romero Rd., Tucson, AZ 85705, P: 866-468-5867, F: 520-293-8807, www.vltor.com
Firearms; Gun Grips & Stocks; Gun Parts/Gunsmithing; Law Enforcement; Recoil Protection Devices & Services

Volquartsen Custom, 24276 240th St., P.O. Box 397, Carroll, IA 51401, P: 712-792-4238, F: 712-792-2542, www.volquartsen.com
Custom Manufacturing; Firearms; Gun Barrels; Gun Grips/Stocks; Gun Parts/Gunsmithing

Vortex Optics, 2120 W. Greenview Dr., Middleton, WI 53562, P: 800-426-0048, F: 608-662-7454
Binoculars; Scopes, Sights & Accessories

Vyse-Gelatin Innovations, 5024 N. Rose St., Schiller Park, IL 60176, P: 800-533-2152, F: 800-533-2152, www.vyse.com
Airguns; Ammunition; Firearms; Law Enforcement; Magazines, Cartridge; Paintball Guns & Accessories; Shooting Range Equipment

Vytek, 195 Industrial Rd., Fitchburg, MA 01420, P: 978-342-9800, F: 978-342-0606, www.vy-tek.com
Custom Manufacturing; Emblems & Decals; Retailer Services; Sports Accessories

W

W.R. Case & Sons Cutlery Co., Owens Way, Bradford, PA 16701, P: 800-523-6350, F: 814-368-1736, www.wrcase.com
Cutlery; Knives/Knife Cases; Sharpeners

Walls Industries, Inc., 1905 N. Main, Cleburne, TX 76033, P: 800-433-1765, F: 817-645-8544, www.wallsoutdoors.com
Camouflage; Gloves, Mitts, Hats; Men's Clothing

Walther USA, 2100 Roosevelt Ave., Springfield, MA 01104, P: 800-372-6454, F: 413-747-3317, www.waltheramerica.com
Bags & Equipment Cases; Firearms; Knives/Knife Cases; Law Enforcement; Lighting Products

Warson Group, Inc., 121 Hunter Ave., Suite 204, St. Louis, MO 63124, P: 877-753-2426, F: 314-721-0569, www.warsongroup.com
Footwear

Watershed Drybags, 2000 Riverside Dr., Asheville, NC 28804, P: 828-252-7111, F: 828-252-7107, www.drybags.com
Backpacking; Bags & Equipment Cases; Camping; Gun Cases; Hunting Accessories; Law Enforcement; Survival Kits/First Aid; Training & Safety Equipment

WD-40 Co., 1061 Cudahy Pl., San Diego, CA 92110, P: 800-448-9340, F: 619-275-5823, www.wd40.com
Lubricants

Weatherby, Inc., 1605 Commerce Way, Paso Robles, CA 93446, P: 800-227-2016, F: 805-237-0427, www.weatherby.com
Ammunition; Custom Manufacturing; Firearms

Weaver Optics/ATK Commercial Products, N5549 Cty. Tk. Z, Onalaska, WI 54650, P: 800-635-7656, F: 763-323-3890, www.weaveroptics.com
Binoculars; Scopes, Sights & Accessories

Weber's Camo Leather Goods/Wilderness Dreams Lingerie & Swimwear, 615 Nokomis St., Suite 400, Alexandria, MN 56308, P: 320-762-2816, F: 320-763-9762, www.webersleather.com
Bags & Equipment Cases; Camouflage; Footwear; Home Furnishings; Hunting Accessories; Leathergoods; Men & Women's Clothing

Wellco Enterprises, 150 Westwood Circle, P.O. Box 188, Waynesville, NC 28786, P: 800-840-3155, F: 828-456-3547, www.wellco.com
Footwear; Law Enforcement

Wells Creek Outfitters, 803-12 SW 12th St., Bentonville, AR, 72712, P: 479-273-1174, F: 479-273-0137
Camouflage; Hunting Accessories; Men's Clothing

Wenger N.A./Wenger, Maker of the Genuine Swiss Army Knife, 15 Corporate Dr., Orangeburg, NY 10962, P: 800-431-2996, F: 845-425-4700, www.wengerna.com
Backpacking; Camping; Cutlery; Footwear; Hunting Accessories; Knives/Knife Cases; Watches

Western Powders, Inc., P.O. Box 158, Miles City, MT 59301, P: 800-497-1007, F: 406-234-0430, www.blackhorn209.com
Black Powder/Smokeless Powder; Firearms Maintenance Equipment; Lubricants; Reloading; Wholesaler/Distributor

Western Rivers, Inc., 1582 N. Broad St., Lexington, TN 38351, P: 800-967-0998, F: 731-967-1243, www.western-rivers.com
Decoys; Game Calls; Hunting Accessories; Lighting Products; Pet Supplies; Scents & Lures; Scopes, Sights & Accessories

Westfield Outdoor, Inc., 1593 Esprit Dr., Westfield, IN 46074, P: 317-569-0679, F: 317-580-1834, www.westfieldoutdoor.com
Backpacking; Camping

White Flyer Targets/Div. Reagent Chemical & Research, Inc., 115 Route 202/31 S, Ringoes, NJ 08851, P: 800-322-7855, F: 908-284-2113, www.whiteflyer.com
Clay Targets; Firearms; Shooting Range Equipment; Targets

Whites Boots, E. 4002 Ferry Ave., Spokane, WA 99202, P: 509-535-2422, F: 509-535-2423, www.whitesboots.com
Footwear

Whitetails Unlimited, 2100 Michigan St., Sturgeon Bay, WI 54235, P: 920-743-6777, F: 920-743-4658, www.whitetailsunlimited.com
Online Services; Outdoor Art, Jewelry, Sculpture; Videos; Wildlife Management

Wilcox Industries Corp., 25 Piscataque Dr., Newington, NH 03801, P: 603-431-1331, F: 603-431-1221, www.wilcoxind.com
Law Enforcement; Scopes, Sights & Accessories

Wild West Guns, LLC, 7100 Homer Dr., Anchorage, AK 99518-3229, P: 800-992-4570, F: 907-344-4005, www.wildwestguns.com
Custom Manufacturing; Firearms; Gun Parts/Gunsmithing; Outfitter; Recoil Protection Devices & Services; Scopes, Sights & Accessories; Wholesaler/Distributor

Wild Wings, LLC, 2101 S. Hwy. 61, P.O. Box 451, Lake City, MN 55041, P: 800-445-6413, F: 651-345-2981, www.wildwings.com
Decoys; Home Furnishings; Outdoor Art, Jewelry, Sculpture; Wholesaler/Distributor

Wilderness Calls, 12118 Capur St., Orlando, FL 38837, P: 407-620-8833, F: 407-620-8853

Wilderness Mint, P.O. Box 1866, Orting, WA 98360, P: 800-294-9600, F: 360-893-4400, www.wildernessmint.com
Emblems & Decals; Hunting Accessories; Outdoor Art, Jewelry, Sculpture; Watches

Wildfowler Outfitter/Tundra Quest, LLC, 5047 Walnut Grove, San Gabriel, CA 91776, P: 877-436-7177, F: 626-286-9918
Archery; Blinds, Custom Manufacturing; Export/ Import Specialists; Feeder Equipment; Men's Clothing; Outfitter; Treestands

Wildlife Research Center, Inc., 14485 Azurite St. NW, Ramsey, MN 55303, P: 800-873-5873, F: 763-427-8354, www.wildlife.com
Scents & Lures

Wildsteer, 9 Avenue Eugene Brisson, Bourges, F-18000, FRANCE, P: 011 33248211380, F: 011 33248211380, www.wildsteer.com
Archery; Knives/Knife Cases; Leathergoods

Wiley X, Inc., 7491 Longard Rd., Livermore, CA 94551, P: 800-776-7842, F: 925-455-8860, www.wileyx.com
Eye Protection

William Henry Studio, 3200 NE Rivergate St., McMinnville, OR 97128, P: 888-563-4500, F: 503-434-9704, www.williamhenrystudio.com
Cutlery; Knives/Knife Cases

Williams Gun Sight Co., 7389 Lapeer Rd., Davison, MI 48423, P: 800-530-9028, F: 810-658-2140, www.williamsgunsight.com
Black Powder Accessories; Books/Industry Publications; Compasses; Gun Parts/Gunsmithing; Hunting Accessories; Scopes, Sights & Accessories

Wilson Arms Co., 97 Leetes Island Rd., Branford, CT 06405, P: 203-488-7297, F: 203-488-0135, www.wilsonarms.com
Custom Manufacturing; Firearms; Gun Barrels

Winchester Ammunition/Div. Olin Corp., 427 N. Shamrock St., East Alton, IL 62024, P: 618-258-2365, F: 618-258-3609, www.winchester.com
Ammunition

Winchester Repeating Arms, 275 Winchester Ave., Morgan, UT 84050, P: 801-876-3440, F: 801-876-3737, www.winchesterguns.com
Firearms

Winchester Safes/Granite Security Products, Inc., 4801 Esco Dr., Fort Worth, TX 76140, P: 817-561-9095, F: 817-478-3056, www.winchestersafes.com
Gun Cabinets/Racks/Safes

Winchester Smokeless Propellant, 6231 Robinson, Shawnee Mission, KS 66202, P: 913-362-9455, F: 913-362-1307
Black Powder/Smokeless Powder; Reloading

Winfield Galleries, LLC, 2 Ladue Acres, Ladue, MO 63124, P: 314-645-7636, F: 314-781-0224, www.winfieldgalleries.com
Computer Software; Outdoor Art, Jewelry, Sculpture

Wing-Sun Trading, Inc., 15501 Heron Ave., La Mirada, CA 90638, P: 866-944-1068, F: 714-522-6417
Backpacking; Binoculars; Camping; Compasses; Lighting Products; Photographic Equipment; Scopes, Sights & Accessories; Wholesaler/Distributor

Witz Sport Cases, 11282 Pyrites Way, Gold River, CA 95670, P: 800-499-1568, F: 916-638-1250, www.witzprod.com
Bags & Equipment Cases

Wolf Peak International, 1221 Marshall Way, Layton, UT 84041, P: 866-953-7325, F: 801-444-9353, www.wolfpeak.net
Airguns; Airsoft; Backpacking; Camouflage; Eyewear; Hunting Accessories; Law Enforcement; Shooting Range Equipment

Wolfe Publishing Co., 2625 Stearman Rd., Suite A, Prescott, AZ 86301, P: 800-899-7810, F: 928-778-5124, www.riflemagazine.com
Books/Industry Publications; Footwear; Gun Cabinets/Racks/Safes; Online Services; Outdoor Art, Jewelry, Sculpture

Wolverine, 9341 Courtland Dr., Rockford, MI 49351, P: 800-253-2184, F: 616-866-5666, www.wolverine.com
Footwear; Gloves, Mitts, Hats; Men's Clothing

Woods Outfitting, P.O. Box 3037, Palmer, AK 99645, P: 907-746-2534, F: 907-745-6283, www.woods-outfitting.com
Outfitter

Woods Wise Products, P.O. Box 681552, Franklin, TN 37068, P: 800-735-8182, F: 931-364-7925, www.woodswise.com
Blinds; Custom Manufacturing; Decoys; Game Calls; Hunting Accessories; Scents & Lures; Videos

Woolrich, Inc./Elite Series Tactical, 1 Mill St., Woolrich, PA 17779, P: 800-996-2299, F: 570-769-7662, www.woolrich.com, www.woolricheliteseriestactical.com
Footwear; Gloves, Mitts, Hats; Home Furnishings; Law Enforcement; Men & Women's Clothing; Wholesaler/Distributor

World Famous Sports, 3625 Dalbergia St., Suite A, San Diego, CA 92113, P: 800-848-9848, F: 619-231-1717, www.worldfamoussports.com
Bags & Equipment Cases; Camouflage; Camping; Gloves, Mitts, Hats; Hunting Accessories; Men & Women's Clothing

Wrangler Rugged Wear/Wrangler ProGear, 400 N. Elm St., Greensboro, NC 27401, P: 336-332-3977, F: 336-332-3518, www.wrangler.com
Men's Clothing

Wycon Safari Inc. (WY)/Wynn Condict, P.O. Box 1126, Saratoga, MY 82331, P: 307-327-5502, F: 307-327-5332, www.wyconsafariinc.com
Outfitter

X

X-Caliber Accuracy Systems, 1837 First St., Bay City, MI 48708, P: 989-893-3961, F: 989-893-0241, www.xcaliberaccuracy.com
Hunting Accessories

X-Caliber Tactical, 1111 Winding Creek Pl., Round Rock, TX 78664, P: 512-524-2621, www.xcalibertactical.com
Airguns; Airsoft; Custom Manufacturing; Export/ Import Specialists; Law Enforcement; Wholesaler/ Distributor

Xenonics Holdings, Inc., 2236 Rutherford Rd., Suite 123, Carlsbad, CA 92008, P: 760-448-9700, FL 760-929-7571, www.xenonics.com
Law Enforcement; Lighting Products

XGO/Polarmax, 5417 N.C. 211, P.O. Box 968, West End, NC 27376, P: 800-552-8585, F: 910-673-3875, www.xgotech.com
Men & Women's Clothing

Xisico USA, Inc./Rex Optics USA, Inc., 16802 Barker Springs, Suite 550, Houston, TX 77084, P: 281-647-9130, F: 208-979-2848, www.xisicousa.com
Airguns; Ammunition; Binoculars; Scopes, Sights & Accessories

XS Sight Systems, 2401 Ludella St., Fort Worth, TX 76105, P: 888-744-4880, F: 800-734-7939, www.xssights.com
Gun Parts/Gunsmithing; Law Enforcement; Scopes, Sights & Accessories

Y

Yaktrax, 9221 Globe Center Dr., Morrisville, NC 27560, P: 800-446-7587, F: 919-544-0975, www.yaktrax.com
Backpacking; Camping; Footwear; Sports Accessories

Yamaha Motor Corp., U.S.A., 6555 Katella Ave., Cypress, CA 90630, P: 714-761-7300, F: 714-503-7184
Vehicles, Utility & Rec

Yankee Hill Machine Co., Inc., 20 Ladd Ave., Suite 1, Florence, MA 01062, P: 877-892-6533, F: 413-586-1326, www.yhm.net
Firearms; Gun Barrels; Gun Cases; Gun Parts/ Gunsmithing; Law Enforcement; Scopes, Sights & Accessories

Yukon Advanced Optics, 201 Regency Pkwy., Mansfield, TX 76063, P: 817-453-9966, F: 817-453-8770
Archery; Backpacking; Binoculars; Camping; Custom Manufacturing; Hunting Accessories; Scopes, Sights & Accessories; Wholesaler/Distributor

Z

Z-Blade, Inc., 28280 Alta Vista Ave., Valencia, CA 91355, P: 800-734-5424, F: 661-295-2615, www.pfimold.com
Custom Manufacturing; Hunting Accessories; Knives/Knife Cases

Zak Tool, 319 San Luis Rey Rd., Arcadia, CA 91007, P: 615-504-4456, F: 931-381-2568, www.zaktool.com
Law Enforcement; Training & Safety Equipment

Zanotti USA, 7907 High Knoll Ln., Houston, TX 77095, P: 281-414-2184, www.zanottiusa.com
Custom Manufacturing; Firearms

Zarc International, Inc., P.O. Box 108, Minonk, IL 61760, P: 800-882-7011, F: 309-432-3490, www.zarc.com
Law Enforcement; Retail Packaging

Zephyr Graf-x, 5443 Earhart Rd., Loveland, CO 80538, P: 970-663-3242, F: 970-663-7695, www.zhats.com
Camouflage; Custom Manufacturing; Gloves, Mitts, Hats; Men & Women's Clothing; Retailer Services

Zero Tolerance Knives, 18600 SW Tetaon Ave., Tualatin, OR 97062, P: 800-325-2891, F: 503-682-7168, www.ztknives.com
Knives/Knife Cases; Law Enforcement

Ziegel Engineering Working Designs, Jackass Field Carts, 2108 Lomina Ave., Long Beach, CA 90815, P: 562-596-9481, F: 562-598-4734, www.ziegeleng.com
Archery; Bags & Equipment Cases; Black Powder Accessories; Custom Manufacturing; Gun Cabinets/ Racks/Safes; Gun Cases; Law Enforcement; Shooting Range Equipment

Zippo Manufacturing Co., 33 Barbour St., Bradford, PA 16701, P: 814-368-2700, F: 814-362-1350, www.zippo.com
Camping; Knives/Knife Cases; Lighting Products; Sports Accessories

Zistos Corp., 1736 Church St., Holbrook, NY 11741, P: 631-434-1370, F: 631-434-9104, www.zistos.com
Law Enforcement

Zodi Outback Gear, P.O. Box 4687, Park City, UT 84060, P: 800-589-2849, F: 800-861-8228
Archery; Backpacking; Camping; Cooking Equipment/Accessories; Hunting Accessories; Pet Supplies; Sports Accessories; Training & Safety Equipment

ZOLL Medical Corp., 269 Mill Rd., Chelmsford, MA 01824, P: 800-348-9011, F: 978-421-0025, www.zoll.com
Law Enforcement; Survival Kits/First Aid; Training & Safety Equipment

NUMBERS

10 Minute Deer Skinner, P.O. Box 158, Stillwater, OK 74076; P: 405-377-2222, F: 405-624-6060, www.tenminutedeerskinner.com
Cooking Equipment/Accessories; Hunting Accessories; Outfitter, Videos

32north Corp - STABILicers, 6 Arctic Circle, Buddeford, ME 04005, P: 800-782-2423, F: 207-284-5015, www.32north.com
Backpacking; Footwear; Hunting Accessories; Law Enforcement; Sports Accessories

3M Thinsulate™ Insulation / 3M Scotchgard™ Protector, 3M Center Building 235-2F-06, St. Paul, MN 55144-1000, P: 800-364-3577, F: 651-737-7659, www.thinsulate.com
Men & Women's Clothing; Footwear; Gloves, Mitts, Hats

3Point5.com, 224 South 200 West, Suite 230, Salt Lake City, UT 84101, P: 801-456-6900/2007, F: 801-485-5039, www.3point5.com

5.11 Tactical Series, 4300 Spyres Way, Modesto, CA 95356, P: 866-451-1726/348, F: 209-548-5348, www.511tactical.com
Bags & Equipment Cases; Men & Women's Clothing; Eyewear; Footwear; Gloves, Mitts, Hats; Law Enforcement; Watches

5-Hour Energy, 46570 Humboldt Drive, Novi, MI 48377, P: 248-960-1700/209, F: 248-960-1980, www.fivehour.com
Food; Hunting Accessories; Law Enforcement; Outfitter; Sports Accessories; Wholesaler/Distributor

More Great Titles From Gun Digest® Books

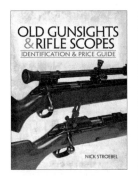

Old Gunsights and Rifle Scopes
Product Code: Z2346
ISBN-13: 978-0-89689-698-7

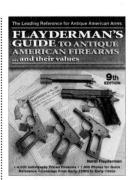

Flayderman's Guide to Antique American Firearms and Their Values
Product Code: Z0620
ISBN-13: 978-0-89689-455-6

The Gun Digest® Book of Modern Gun Values
Product Code: W1804
ISBN-13: 978-1-4402-1831-6

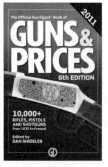

Gun Digest® Book of Guns & Prices 2011
Product Code: Y0049
ISBN-13: 978-1-4402-1435-6

2012 Standard Catalog of Firearms, 22nd Edition
Product Code: X4714
ISBN-13: 978-1-4402-1688-6

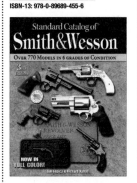

Customize the Ruger 10/22
Product Code: NGRTT
ISBN-13: 978-0-89689-323-8

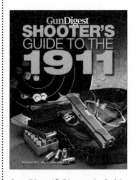

Standard Catalog of® Smith & Wesson
Product Code: FSW03
ISBN-13: 978-0-89689-293-4

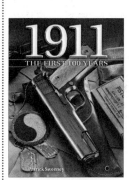

Gun Digest® Shooter's Guide to the 1911
Product Code: Y0048
ISBN-13: 978-1-4402-1434-9

1911: The First 100 Years
Product Code: Z7019
ISBN-13: 978-1-4402-1115-7

Gun Digest® Book of the Revolver
Product Code: W1576
ISBN-13: 978-1-4402-1812-5

Standard Catalog of® Browning Firearms
Product Code: Z2782
ISBN-13: 978-0-89689-731-1

Standard Catalog of® Winchester Firearms
Product Code: Z0932
ISBN-13: 978-0-89689-535-5

Standard Catalog of® Remington Firearms
Product Code: Z1828
ISBN-13: 978-0-89689-625-3

Standard Catalog of® Colt Firearms
Product Code: Z0931
ISBN-13: 978-0-89689-534-8

Winchester Model 94
Product Code: Z5058
ISBN 13: 978-1-4402-0391-6

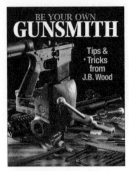

Be Your Own Gunsmith
Product Code: W0931
ISBN-13: 978-1-4402-1769-2

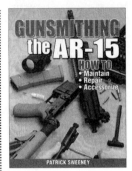

Gunsmithing the AR-15
Product Code: Z6613
ISBN-13: 978-1-4402-0899-7

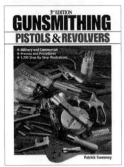

Gunsmithing: Pistols & Revolvers
Product Code: Z5056
ISBN-13: 978 1 4402-0389-3

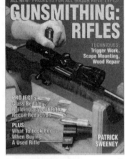

Gunsmithing: Rifles
Product Code: GRIF
ISBN-13: 978-0-8734-1665-8

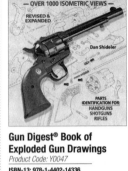

Gun Digest® Book of Exploded Gun Drawings
Product Code: Y0047
ISBN-13: 978-1-4402-14336

Gun Digest® Book of Revolvers Assembly/Disassembly
Product Code: Y0773
ISBN-13: 978-1-4402-1452-3

Gun Digest® Book of Rimfire Rifles Assembly/Disassembly
Product Code: W1577
ISBN-13: 978-1-4402-1813-7

Automatic Pistols Assembly/Disassembly
Product Code: Z0737
ISBN-13: 978-0-89689-473-0

The Gun Digest® Book of Tactical Weapons Assembly/Disassembly
Product Code: Z2297
ISBN-13: 978-0-89689-692-5

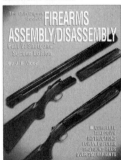

The Gun Digest® Book of Firearms Assembly/Disassembly Part V: Shotguns
Product Code: AS5R2
978-0-87349-400-7

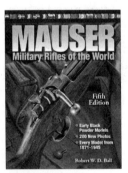

Mauser Military Rifles of the World
Product Code: Y1287
ISBN-13: 978-1-4402-1544-5

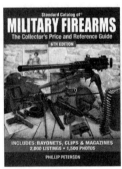

Standard Catalog of Military Firearms
Product Code: Y0772
ISBN-13: 978-1-4402-1451-6

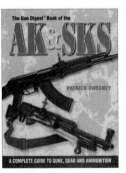

The Gun Digest® Book of the AK & SKS
Product Code: Z2207
ISBN-13: 978-0-89689-678-9

The Gun Digest® Book of Assault Weapons
Product Code: Z0769
ISBN-13: 978-0-89689-498-3

The Gun Digest® Book of Firearms Assembly/Disassembly Part IV: Centerfire Rifles
Product Code: AS4R2
ISBN-13: 978-0-87349-631-5

Military Small Arms of the 20th Century
Product Code: MSA7
ISBN-13: 978-0-87341-824-9

Standard Catalog of® Civil War Firearms
Product Code: Z1784
ISBN-13: 978-0-89689-613-0

The Complete Gun Owner
Product Code: Z2614
ISBN-13: 978-0-89689-715-1

The Gun Digest® Buyer's Guide to Guns
Product Code: Z3048
ISBN-13: 978-0-89689-844-8

The Gun Digest® Book of Firearms Fakes & Reproductions
Product Code: Z2208
ISBN-13: 978-0-89689-679-6

**Gun Digest® Book of
Long-Range Shooting**
Product Code: Z0735
ISBN 13: 978-0-89689-471-6

**The Gun Digest® Book of
Combat Handgunnery**
Product Code: Z0880
ISBN-13: 978-0-89689-525-6

Personal Defense for Women
Product Code: Z5057
ISBN 13: 978-1-4402-0390-9

**The Gun Digest®
Book of Concealed Carry**
Product Code: Z1782
ISBN-13: 978-0-89689-611-6

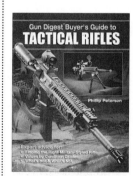

**Combat Shooting with
Massad Ayoob**
Product Code: W1983
ISBN-13: 978-1-4402-1857-6

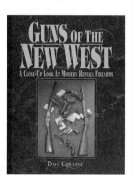

Guns of the New West
Product Code: GNW
ISBN-13: 978-0-87349-768-8

Effective Handgun Defense
Product Code: CCFH
ISBN-13: 978-0-87349-899-9

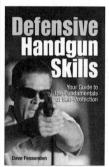

Own the Night
Selection & Use of Tactical Lights
& Laser Sights
Product Code: Z5015
ISBN 13: 978-1-4402-0371-8

Defensive Handgun Skills
Product Code: Z8888
ISBN-13: 978-1-4402-1381-6

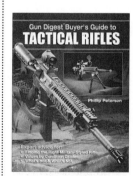

Armed for Personal Defense
Product Code: Z9404
ISBN-13: 978-1-4402-1408-0

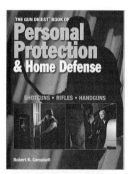

**The Gun Digest® Book of
Personal Protection & Home
Defense**
Product Code: Z3653
ISBN-13: 978-0-89689-938-4

**Gun Digest® Buyer's
Guide to Assault Weapons**
Product Code: Z2209
ISBN-13: 978-0-89689-680-2

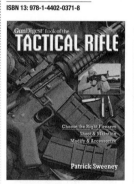

**Gun Digest® Book of the
Tactical Rifle**
Product Code: Y0046
978-1-4402-1432--5

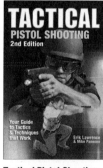

Tactical Pistol Shooting
Product Code: Z5954
ISBN 13: 978-1-4402-0436-4

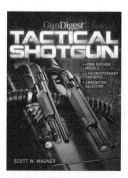

**Gun Digest® Buyer's
Guide to Tactical Rifles**
Product Code: Y0625
ISBN-13: 978-1-4402-1446-2

**The Gun Digest® Book of
Tactical Gear**
Product Code: Z2251
ISBN-13: 978-0-89689-684-0

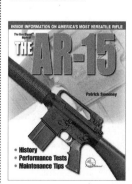

**The Gun Digest® Book of the
AR-15**
Product Code: GDAR
ISBN-13: 978-0-87349-947-7

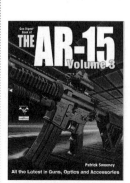

**Gun Digest® Book of the
AR-15 Volume II**
Product Code: Z0738
ISBN-13: 978-0-89689-474--7

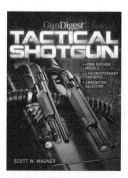

**Gun Digest® Book of the
AR-15, Volume 3**
Product Code: Z8816
ISBN-13: 978-1-4402-137-6-2

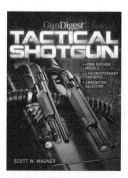

**Gun Digest® Book of the
Tactical Shotgun**
Product Code: Y1448
ISBN-13: 978-1-4402-1553-7

Gun Digest® Book of Classic Combat Handguns
Product Code: W4464

ISBN-13: 978-1-4402-2384-6

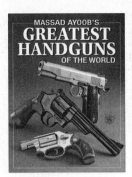

Massad Ayoob's Greatest Handguns of the World
Product Code: Z6495

ISBN-13: 978-1-4402-0825-6

Gun Digest® Buyer's Guide to Concealed Carry Handguns
Product Code: Z8905

ISBN-13: 978-1-4402-0825-6

The Gun Digest® Book of the Glock
Product Code: Z1926

ISBN-13: 978-0-89689-642-0

The Gun Digest® Book of the 1911
Product Code: PITO

ISBN-13: 978-0-87349-281-2

The Gun Digest® Book of the 1911, Volume 2
Product Code: VIIPT

ISBN-13: 978-0-89689-269-9

Reloading for Handgunners
Product Code: W0932

ISBN-13: 978-1-4402-1770-8

ABCs of Reloading
Product Code: Z9165

ISBN-13: 978-1-4402-1396-0

Reloading for Shotgunners
Product Code: Z7241

ISBN-13: 978-0-87349-813-5

The Complete Blackpowder Handbook
Product Code: Z7241

ISBN-13: 978-0-89689-390-0

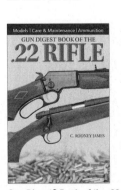

Gun Digest® Book of the .22 Rifle
Product Code: Z8581

ISBN-13: 978-1-4402-1372-4

Gun Digest® Book of Green Shootings
Product Code: Z8039

ISBN-13: 978-1-4402-1362-5

Gun Digest® Big Fat Book of the .45 ACP
Product Code: Z4204

ISBN 13: 978-1-4402-0219-3

Cartridges of the World
Product Code: Z3651

ISBN 13: 978-0-89689-936-0

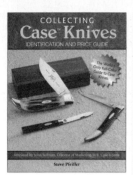

Collecting Case Knives
Product Code: Z4387
ISBN-13: 978-1-4402-0238-4

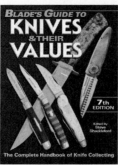

**Blade's Guide to Knives &
Their Values**
Product Code: Z5054
ISBN-13: 978-1-4402-0387-9

The Wonder of Knifemaking
Product Code: Z7241
ISBN-13: 978-1-4402-1156-0

**Bladesmithing with
Murray Carter**
Product Code: W1852
ISBN-13: 978-1-4402-1838-5

**Knifemaking with
Bob Loveless**
Product Code: Z7240
ISBN-13: 978-1-4402-1155-3

**American Premium Guide to
Knives & Razors**
Product Code: Z2189
ISBN-13: 978-0-89689-672-7

**Wayne Goddard's $50 Knife
Shop, Revised**
Product Code: WGBW2
ISBN-13: 978-0-89689-295-8

The Tactical Knife
Product Code: Z6614
ISBN-13: 978-1-4402-0900-0

The Wonder of Knifemaking
Product Code: X3269
ISBN-13: 978-1-4402-1684-8

Knives 2012
Product Code: Z4713
ISBN-13: 978-1-4402-1687-9

How to Knifes
Product Code: KHM01
ISBN-13: 978-0-87341-389-3

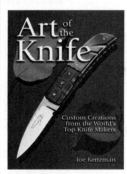

**BLADE's Guide to Making
Knives**
Product Code: BGKFM
ISBN-13: 978-0-89689-240-8

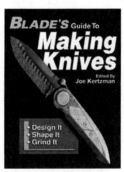

Art of the Knife
Product Code: Z0733
ISBN-13: 978-0-89689-470-9

Calendars

Whitetails 2012 Daily Calendar
Product Code: W4539
ISBN-13: 978-1-4402-2388-4

***Gun Digest®* Great Guns 2012
Daily Calendar**
Product Code: W4556
ISBN-13: 978-1-4402-2395-5

www.gundigeststore.com

FREE

1911 eMAGAZINE

www.gundigest.com/1911emag

As a thank you for your purchase, log on and download **Gun Digest Presents The 1911** - a FREE digital e-magazine celebrating 100 years of the 1911. Visit gundigest.com/1911emag to see the hottest 1911s on the market today!

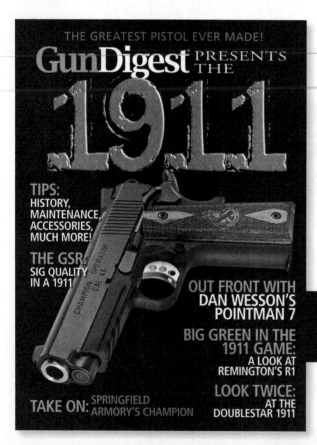

This **FREE** e-magazine — a $9.95 value — is packed with articles on the "greatest pistol of all time!"

LOG ON TODAY FOR YOUR YOUR FREE 1911 eMAG!
www.gundigest.com/1911emag

GunDigest®

www.gundigest.com/1911emag